THE CULTURAL HERITAGE OF INDIA

VOLUME IV

THE RELIGIONS

EDITOR

HARIDAS BHATTACHARYYA, M.A., B.L., P.R.S., DARŚANASĀGARA
Formerly Head of the Department of Philosophy, Dacca University, and Honorary University Professor of Indian Philosophy and Religion, Banaras Hindu University

INTRODUCTION BY

BHAGAVAN DAS, M.A., D.LITT.

THE RAMAKRISHNA MISSION
INSTITUTE OF CULTURE
CALCUTTA

Published by
Swami Akunthananda, Secretary
The Ramakrishna Mission Institute of Culture
Gol Park, Calcutta

First Edition (3 vols) 1937
© *Second Edition : Revised and Enlarged (independent volumes),*
Vol. IV 1956
Reprint 1969

The Ramakrishna Mission Institute of Culture
Calcutta

PRINTED IN INDIA
BY PHOTO-OFFSET AT S. ANTOOL & CO. PRIVATE LTD.
91 ACHARYA PRAFULLA CHANDRA ROAD, CALCUTTA 9

PUBLISHER'S NOTE

THE Ramakrishna Mission established this Institute of Culture in 1938 in fulfilment of one of the projects to commemorate the Birth Centenary of Sri Ramakrishna (1936). At the same time the Institute was vested with the entire rights of *The Cultural Heritage of India.* This publication is thus one of the major responsibilities of the Institute; it also serves to fulfil a prim ry aim of the Institute, which is to promote the study, interpretation, and dissemination of the cultural heritage of India.

The first edition of *The Cultural Heritage of India,* in three volumes and about 2,000 pages in all, the work of one hundred distinguished Indian scholars, was published in 1937 by the Sri Ramakrishna Birth Centenary Publication Committee as a Birth Centenary memorial. This work presented for the first time a panorama of the cultural history of India, and it was immediately acclaimed as a remarkable contribution to the cultural literature of the world. This edition was sold out within a few years, and the work had long been out of print. When considering the question of a second edition, it was felt that, instead of reprinting the work in its original form, advantage should be taken of the opportunity to enlarge the scope of the work, making it more comprehensive, more authoritative, and adequately representative of different aspects of Indian thought, and, at the same time, thoroughly to revise the old articles to bring them up to date.

According to a new scheme drawn up on this basis, the number of volumes has been increased. The plan of arrangement has been improved by grouping the topics in such a way that each volume may be fairly complete and fulfil the requirements of those interested in any particular branch of learning. Each volume will be self-contained, with separate pagination, bibliography, and index, and will be introduced by an outstanding authority. Since due regard will be paid to historicity and critical treatment, it is hoped that this work will provide a useful guide to the study of the complex pattern of India's cultural history.

In keeping with the ancient Indian tradition of imparting instruction to students without remuneration, the distinguished band of scholars, who have co-operated so ably in this task, have done their work as a labour of love in a spirit of service to scholarship and world understanding. Equally essential to the success of the undertaking was the assistance of the Government of India who ma le a generous grant towards the cost of publication.

Without this dual co-operation, it would have been impossible to set out on a venture of this magnitude; and to the contributors as well as to the Government of India the Institute therefore expresses its deepest gratitude.

In presenting this fourth volume of the second edition of *The Cultural Heritage of India,* following the publication of Volume III in 1953, it is perhaps necessary to explain how it happened that these two volumes were the first to be published. In the first edition of this work, there were a fairly large number of representative articles on philosophy and religion, the two subjects which, under the new scheme, have been assigned to Volumes III and IV. Thus these two volumes acquired an advantage over the others, which required a much greater proportion of fresh material, and it was therefore thought expedient to publish them first.

The onerous task of editing these two volumes was assigned to the capable hands of the late Professor Haridas Bhattacharyya, M.A., B.L., P.R.S., Darśanasāgara, who was formerly Head of the Department of Philosophy at the Dacca University, and later Honorary University Professor of Indian Philosophy and Religion at the College of Indology, Banaras Hindu University. When he passed away in January this year, he had completed his editing of the present volume. The Institute is deeply indebted to him for the way in which he gave unsparingly of his time and energy in tackling the many difficulties inherent in a work of this nature. Over many years he stood as a true friend to the Institute, always willing to serve its cause. He is now greatly missed, and the fact that he did not live to see this volume in print tinges with sadness the Institute's pleasure in sending it out into the world. The Institute also records its sense of deep sorrow at the passing away of Dr. P. C. Bagchi, one of the new contributors to this volume.

This volume contains forty-five articles, twenty-two of which appeared in the first edition of this work. Most of these have been revised by the authors themselves for the present edition.

Help has been received from many sources in the preparation of this volume. To Dr. Bhagavan Das, that great savant who has been honoured by the President of India with the highest Indian Order of Bhārataratna as a token of respect in which he is widely held for his high ideals, special thanks are due for finding time, in spite of failing health, to write the Introduction to this volume. Thanks are also due to Dr. Suniti Kumar Chatterji, M.A., D.LIT., for kindly writing the Preface. Professor Jnanendra Chandra Datta, M.A., undertook the arduous task of preparing the Index, as he had done for Volume III. Mr. J. A. O'Brien, Regional Representative of the British Council, Calcutta, carefully went through most of the articles from the point of view of language. A few articles were seen by Mr. R. Y. Copland, M.A., and Miss A. G. Stock,

Professor of English at the University of Calcutta. To all these friends the Institute offers sincere thanks for their generous assistance.

Religion has been the basis of India's thought and life and the guiding principle of her civilization through the ages. She has steadfastly held on to this principle against the varied vicissitudes of her history. The freedom of the soul has been for her the *summum bonum* of life ; and the divinity of man and oneness of existence, her eternal message. May India's spiritual wisdom help the world in discovering the spirit which will unite men in building a Kingdom of God upon earth!

October 1956

CONTENTS

PART II

THE SAINTS AND THEIR TEACHINGS

PAGE

PART III

RELIGION IN PRACTICE

PART IV

RELIGIONS FROM BEYOND THE BORDERS

CONTENTS

ILLUSTRATIONS

ABBREVIATIONS

A. V.	*Atharva-Veda*
Ai. U.	*Aitareya Upaniṣad*
B. G.	*Bhagavad-Gītā*
B. S.	*Brahma-Sūtra*
Bhā.	*Bhāgavata*
Bṛ. U.	*Bṛhadāraṇyaka Upaniṣad*
Chā. U.	*Chāndogya Upaniṣad*
Ī. U.	*Īśa Upaniṣad*
Ka. U.	*Kaṭha Upaniṣad*
Ke. U.	*Kena Upaniṣad*
Mā. U.	*Māṇḍūkya Upaniṣad*
Mbh.	*Mahābhārata*
Mm.	Mahāmahopādhyāya
Mu. U.	*Muṇḍaka Upaniṣad*
Pra. U.	*Praśna Upaniṣad*
Rām.	*Rāmāyaṇa*
Ṛ. V.	*Ṛg-Veda*
S. V.	*Sāma-Veda*
Śve. U.	*Śvetāśvatara Upaniṣad*
Tai. U.	*Taittirīya Upaniṣad*
U.	*Upaniṣad*
Y. V.	*Yajur-Veda*

PREFACE

JUST as water falling from the sky goes to the sea, so the salutations offered to the various gods reach God alone (*Ākāśāt patitaṁ toyaṁ yathā gacchati sāgaram ; sarva-deva-namaskāraḥ Keśavaṁ pratigacchati*).

This Sanskrit saying is echoed in most languages in India which still carry on the traditions of Hindu culture. It conveys a sentiment that is understood and immediately subscribed to by most people in India, and certainly by all Hindus ; and it indicates one of the fundamental attitudes in Hindu culture—its great sense of understanding and hospitality. This basic mentality is very old in India—as old as the Vedas. One of the commonplaces in the Indian mental make-up is the sentiment expressed in that great passage from the *Ṛg-Veda*, '*Ekaṁ sad, viprā bahudhā vadanti*'—That which is, is One ; sages describe It in manifold ways.

After the passage of centuries, the same sentiment was made incarnate, so to say, in the person of Sri Ramakrishna, who made this great statement, '*Jata mat, tata path*'—There are as many ways as there are points of view.

The present volume of *The Cultural Heritage of India*, planned by the Ramakrishna Mission Institute of Culture, is a testimony to this ancient sentiment, and the forty-five articles it contains, each by an eminent scholar and specialist, bear ample testimony to the great hospitality of the Indian mind in encouraging and inviting different points of view and different lines of approach to the great quest for the Unknown—in 'the flight of the alone to the Alone'.

Men are equal on the basis of their common humanity, though no two individuals are the same in their intellectual and spiritual framework, as much as in their physical complexion. There are some people who are intellectually strong, and there are others who are easy to move emotionally. And there is a larger group which reacts to impulses and instincts more than to anything else. To people of these three main types of outlook, and those of other types also, religion, both as an individual experience and practice and as a social vehicle carrying the individual members of a particular society in their progress in life, must *ipso facto* present a bewildering series of diversities. The scriptural religions like Islam and Christianity theoretically insist on dogmas and a uniform and unalterable creed. Yet we have in Christianity so many different sects, sometimes with notions and ideologies which go counter to one another. And Islam, too, recognizes the seventy-two *firqahs* or sectarian organizations. Christ is quoted to have said, 'In my Father's house are many mansions'. Could we not legitimately take it to mean that a great latitude was allowed by him in the sum total of the faith and behaviour of the elect, all together forming the entire body of the faithful who believed in Christ? Similarly, in spite of the preachings in Islam of the path of orthodoxy as embodied in a literal interpretation of the Word of God, *Kalām Ilāhi,* which is the *Qur'ān,* one of the *Hadith* or traditional sayings as ascribed to the Prophet runs like this: *'Turuqu-llāhi ka-'adadi 'anfāsi-l-makhlūqāti'*—The ways of God are like unto the breathings of all created beings. There are many people who therefore consider that it would be nothing less than blasphemy to assert that the ultimate Reality can be approached only by one path—and that path presumably is the one which the person making such an assertion believes in.

Those who realize the miserably insignificant character of the human individual in face of the great Infinity, and, at the same time, are conscious of the majesty of man as a reflection of the Divinity that is behind life, can only have a great and joyful sympathy with the idea that all creatures should be permitted to follow their own lines of approach in this matter, provided they do not transgress the rights of others. They would be able to accept the position as the most natural that, like a diamond of great price, the ultimate Truth presents itself to us through various facets, and the human being cannot ordinarily conceive of more than the facet that is presented to him. That facet alone is, for a particular individual, the only true experience, the only thing that matters for him. There, he and his God are alone. As the great Indian musical composer and singer of the sixteenth century, Tānasena, the court-musician of Emperor Akbar, expressed in one of his devotional songs, *'Bahu-ballaha, Tānasena-kau eka-ballaha'*—Thou art beloved of many ; but so far as Tānasena is concerned, Thou art the beloved one of only one (i.e. himself alone). That is the Hindu attitude towards the various facets through which Truth presents itself to the human mind in all climes and ages.

To the Hindu mind, Truth presents itself in diverse ways, the validity of each of which is always admitted ; and similarly Truth presents itself also to the Christian mind and the Islamic mind, the Confucian and the Taoist mind, and the mind of the Buddhist, through their various sects and schools. And these facets, so to say, have been stated and formulated in philosophical systems and forms of practical religion.

The philosophical aspects of the theories and practices, which the Hindu mind created for itself, have been discussed in another volume (Volume III). And the sects and cults that originated in India and are actually present (including also certain other ones from foreign lands which found a hospitable reception on the soil of India), and to which the people of India have, according to their temperaments, hereditary environment, or developed predilections, dedicated themselves, form the characteristic expression of religion in India. The heritage of India for the average man basically or largely finds a fulfilment in these sects and cults. As such, a study of these cannot be neglected: they are of vital importance, as being a crystallized expression of the Indian spirit working through the centuries. Perhaps the word 'crystallized' should not be used, for crystallization takes place only when there is absence of dynamic life, when a system becomes dead. No Hindu or Indian cult or sect is absolutely dead and at a stand-still, as if it had no life. Newer and newer developments are taking place every day. In this development, we have to note, foreign influences and inspirations have also been playing a part. But that is a different matter.

The present volume gives a sketch of the more important sects which one finds as living religions, or which are the diverse expressions of a living Religion in India. The paths with their connected ideologies and practices are sometimes very simple, and sometimes very complicated. But that is of no consequence. In the sphere of taste and mental structure, there is no dispute, *'Rucīnāṁ vaicitryād ṛju-kuṭila-nānā-patha-juṣām ; nṛṇām eko gamyas tvam asi payasām arṇava iva'*—Owing to their diversity in taste, people prefer different ways, straight or crooked ; but Thou art the only goal for man, just as the sea is the goal of all waters.

This basic tendency of India towards understanding and accommodation is the result of a great synthesis in the evolution of the Indian man. The Indian man of the present day (excepting for some extreme types which have remained on the fringes, like the Kashmiri Brāhmaṇas and Kol or Munda or Mongoloid tribesmen) represents a racial mixture of at least four types of humanity. Each of these four types had its own physical form or forms, its own language, and its own culture and mentality associated with that language. But from very early times, there has taken place a miscegenation on the soil of India on a scale which seems to be unparalleled anywhere else in the world. The white Aryans, the brown or copper-coloured Dravidians, the dark-skinned Niṣādas or Austrics, and the yellow Kirātas or Mongoloids—all these races mixed with each other through what are known in Sanskrit literature as *anuloma* (high-caste man, low-caste wife) and *pratiloma* (low-caste man, high-caste wife) marriages, and as a result, as the late Dr. F. W. Thomas had observed, a common type of Indian man was evolved towards the end of the Vedic period. These originally diverse racial and linguistic worlds also approached and met one another—including cults and ideas about life and death and being.

Indian tradition acknowledges two main strands in Indian religion—the Vedic or the Nigama and the Tāntric-Paurāṇic or the Āgama. There has been interaction between these two. The Vedic tradition is mainly the Aryan tradition, and the Āgama tradition is basically the pre-Aryan tradition. But there has been a final blend of these two sets of ideologies, which differed in their original forms, in some very deep or fundamental points. We are not, however, concerned with that, as it was pre-historic. What is remarkable is the attitude of the Hindu thinkers through the centuries, after the Vedic period, in trying to fit in these two systems together. And the result has been something which is unique in the world, and it fills us with admiration for the comprehensive spirit which was displayed in making a new fabric out of the warp and weft of the diverse sects and ideas. The fabric is the fabric of Hinduism, in all its wonderful variety.

An account of the various sects and cults as they are still living in India, and as they have been described in this volume, will show the remarkable variety of the religious quest in India, each of them following its own line of argument, and its own special view-point. It is not necessary to recapitulate them. A glance through the list of contents of the present volume would be quite enough. These sects or religions, of course, form the path *par excellence* for those who believe in them or follow them.

India has not disdained to enrich herself with the ideologies of other cults and sects from outside. Old Iranians and Greeks and Scythian and other peoples of Central Asia came to India in the past. The relationship between India and China through the centuries did not mean a one-way traffic only. India gave many things to China, but we are now becoming more and more conscious of the fact that India also took a number of things from the great civilization of China. So, too, the world of the rude or primitive Hūṇas and Turks had something to give to India. India welcomed to her shores the early Christians who came from Syria. It would not be a matter of surprise if the early Christians—and also the Jews, who came equally early—were enabled to give certain new things to the religious thought of India. The Zoroastrian Iranians, after the conquest of their country by the Muslim Arabs, also came to India and became a part of the Indian body politic. So, too, in the case of Islam, which has influenced India profoundly during the long centuries of its contact with the country, from the beginning of the eighth century A.D., and, may be, even earlier. The more we would study the matter closely, the greater would appear to be the points of contact between Indian religion and Sufistic Islam. Sufism was deeply influenced by the Vedānta in its formative period, but, as a system, with its philosophy, its monastic organization, and its devotional exercises through singing and dancing, it also impressed Indian religious life in late mediaeval times. It must be said, however, that whatever India took from other outside faiths, it completely assimilated it to itself. So all these different melodies have brought in a great harmony in India, and that harmony can be felt only by men and women who have a corresponding harmony in their own souls. Otherwise, with a narrow outlook within, what really is a symphony would appear to be a disordered jangle or discordant noises.

The variety of the religious cults within Hinduism, each of which offers its allegiance to the Vedas and the Upaniṣads as the *fons et origo* of Indian religion and religious experience, is quite bewildering. And yet, through these, we find a most wonderful display of the oneness of the human spirit.

It was an Indian scholar, Mādhavācārya, who many centuries ago wrote his very valuable treatise in Sanskrit, *Sarva-darśana-saṅgraha,* on the various systems of philosophy he found in India. In the middle of the nineteenth century, Horace Hayman Wilson wrote his valuable monograph on the various religious cults of India, a work which still has its unique value. On the basis of this work, but with some additions of his own, Akshay Kumar Dutta, during the third quarter of the nineteenth century, compiled in Bengali an equally valuable work on the same subject, the *Bhāratavarṣīya Upāsaka-sampradāya.* And in the present volume, we have now a formal and authoritative presentation of the subject. This volume particularly displays before us, as it were, the various petals that go to make the lotus as a single flower. Hinduism in its various ramifications derived from a common stock is an exceedingly interesting and instructive subject to pursue. It is not at all a single religion with a creed to which everybody must subscribe. It is rather a federation of different kinds of approach to the Reality that is behind life. That is the unique character of Hinduism, and that character is unfolded in the pages that follow.

The preface to this volume was to have been written, in the usual course, by its able editor, Professor Haridas Bhattacharyya. But it is a matter for great sorrow that he passed away before the completion of the volume, and the task of writing this preface has devolved upon me, which I have tried to fulfil in my own humble way.

SUNITI KUMAR CHATTERJI

Calcutta
October 1956

INTRODUCTION

TRIMŪRTI (SADĀŚIVA)

1

INTRODUCTION

I

RELIGION, THE PIVOT OF INDIAN LIFE

'INDIA is not only the Italy of Asia ; it is not only the land of romance, of art and beauty. It is in religion earth's central shrine. India is religion.'

The above remarks of Cramb are amply borne out if we take into consideration the religious history of this vast sub-continent. The discovery of the Indus valley civilization pushed back the cultural history of India beyond the Vedic age, and this culture included not only material civilization, but also spiritual achievements. Since then more light has been thrown on what is called the prehistoric civilization of this ancient land. This testifies not only to the antiquity of Indian culture, but also to the continuity of its spiritual progress. Nowhere else in the world has religion been made the object of such vast experimentation as in India. This great land has grappled at all times with ultimate problems, and this search after truth has been undertaken not by one race or one area, but by the whole population spread over the entire land. Looking geographically at India, we find that every where from Kashmir to Kanyā-Kumārī (Cape Comorin), and from Gandhāra to Kāmarūpa (Assam), there have been strenuous endeavours to discover truth. One significant feature of this phenomenon is that at no stage was theology dissociated from philosophy. If the Vedic seers sent up hymns and laudations to their gods, they speculated at the same time upon their ultimate nature and came to the conclusion that, at bottom, they were all manifestations of one primal Being.

The religious urge was materially affected by the rise of Jainism and Buddhism ; but even these were obliged, in the course of their philosophical speculation, to raise theological issues and, later on, establish some form of religious cult. In the protest against the Vedic cult of sacrifice, which involved ceremonial cruelty, they were joined not only by Brāhmaṇical thinkers who put allegorical interpretations on Vedic rituals, but also by those of a more metaphysical bent of mind to whom the world owes the magnificent mystic monism of the Upaniṣads. The gods remained, but only in a subordinate and colourless form, and, towering above them all, came Brahman, mostly regarded as the impersonal Absolute, though sometimes viewed with personal attributes. Although thereafter there came a counter-reformation, it nevertheless became obvious that the Vedic age had irrevocably passed away and that there was a definite shift towards monotheism in intimate association with the theory of Brahman. Strict monotheism was yet to come ; there was, however, ushered in a monolatry which amounted almost to monotheism. We need not enter into the disputes of the philosophical schools or the conflicts of the religious sects, but we are interested in the epics and the Purāṇas as valuable human documents testifying to the groping of the human mind for a stable foundation of religious faith and social morality. When, at a later time, acquaintance and clash with foreign monotheistic creeds necessitated a reformation of her religious beliefs and practices, India was able to find within her rich spiritual heritage all the materials she needed for reorienting her religious life and establishing a more equitable social order.

CONTRIBUTION OF DIFFERENT PARTS OF INDIA TO ITS RELIGIOUS LIFE

We have already mentioned that no particular part of the country can claim monopoly in spiritual speculation. Where theologians turn metaphysicians and, conversely, metaphysics culminates in theology, doctrines propounded tend to have both a metaphysical and a theological bearing. Thus to Kashmir we owe the Trika philosophy in association with Śaivism. The Punjab (including the outermost north-western areas, of which Afghanistan once formed a part) gave us the hymns of the Vedas, as also the magnificent Gandhāra school of sculpture in Buddhism. The heart of Āryāvarta gave us the ritualistic literature, the earlier Upaniṣads, the epics, and some of the older Purāṇas. Mithilā is famous for the spiritual fellowship of Janaka and Yājñavalkya. To Magadha, we owe the inspiring messages of Mahāvīra and Buddha. Bengal has given us the Caitanya movement as also the later Tantras. Assam has similarly given us the pure Vaiṣṇavism of Śaṅkara Deva and, in earlier times, the magico-religious cults of the Tāntrikas. The mediaeval Siddhas, whose cult-descendants are the Kānphaṭa Yogīs or the followers of Matsyendra Nātha and Gorakṣa Nātha, probably came from eastern regions. To Nepal, we owe the synthesis of Brāhmaṇical and Buddhist religions, and the schools of painters and braziers, who, with the Tibetans, have given form and shape to the multitudinous gods and goddesses of the Mahāyāna pantheon. Orissa is justly celebrated for its magnificent Bauddha, Śākta, Vaiṣṇava, and Saura monuments, as also for its philosophical works supporting the theism of the Caitanya school, and for the continuance of the Buddhist tradition in a veiled manner in religious and social practices. Orissa may also probably claim the distinction of having provided the *Sāmba Purāṇa* in honour of Sūrya.

When we reach the Dravidian area, we enter a region that has given India not only the foremost commentaries on the *Brahma-Sūtra*, which provide a philosophical basis of religious belief, but also the most lyrical of religious singers, both Vaiṣṇava and Śaiva, whose devotional outpourings have been justly praised. The Vaiṣṇava Āḷvārs and the Śaiva Nāyanārs and the numerous writers of Saṁhitās and Āgamas brought religion to the heart of all, and, ultimately, orthodoxy itself was forced to recognize the vernacular hymns also as acceptable offerings to the deity. Mostly free from fear of iconoclasm and far away from the seat of alien political authority, the religious South turned the whole country into a vast cathedral-city with gorgeous temples and spectacular rites, and the year into a round of festivals and pilgrimages. The Smārtas toned down the sectarian bitterness which Pāñcarātra and Āgamic conflict tended to produce. In the Karṇāṭaka country was evolved the Liṅgāyata cult which, in alliance with the Jainism of the South, attacked many items of the orthodox Brāhmaṇic creed and custom. The saints of Karṇāṭaka vie with the Tamil Śaiva and Vaiṣṇava lyricists in their rapturous devotion to God. Mahārāṣṭra has given us the galaxy of saints, Tukārāma, Nāmadeva, and others, whose *abhaṅgas* (devotional verses) have illuminated innumerable souls with their mystic light. Like the mediaeval mystics of North India—Kabīr, Dādū, Ravidāsa, Nānak, Mīrābāī, Tulasīdāsa, and others—and the Tamil saints of Vaiṣṇavism and Śaivism, they have proved that when the barrier of the sacred Sanskrit language is removed, religion overflows all boundaries of caste and convention, and establishes a new hierarchy in the spiritual field enriched by the waters of living faith. Gujarat and Kathiawad may claim the distinction of having given us the early Bhāgavatism, the redaction of the Śvetāmbara Jaina canon, and the consolidation of the solar cult, while to the south, in the Karṇāṭaka and other areas, the Digambara Jaina literature was consolidated and extended. Who can forget the kingly patronage that was so lavishly bestowed by different dynasties and individual rulers to further the cause of this or that religion, all through the centuries, in different parts of the country, especially beyond the Vindhyas? Nor must we forget that Dayananda Saraswati, the founder of the Ārya Samāj, hailed from Gujarat, though his greatest following was in the Punjab, where, like the Sikhs, the Ārya Samājists so liberalized Hinduism that the challenge of Islam was effectively met in that area. Sind has given us the great Sufi thinkers of India.

It is only in recent years that we are coming to realize the value, from the cultural standpoint, of regions like Rajasthan, Vindhya Pradesh, Madhya Pradesh, Hyderabad, the tribal areas of Assam, and the southern part of Bihar. Here we have remnants not only of archaic religious beliefs among the Kolarians, who predated the Dravidians, but also of the prehistoric peoples of the different Stone ages, whose religious life we are painfully reconstructing with fragments of cult-objects. The Austric culture, that extends up to Nasik in the west and covers a wide area, including Nepal and the hills of Assam, is of a piece with the Pacific culture ; but it is now changing almost beyond recognition with elements drawn from Aryan and Dravidian civilizations. In Rajasthan we are now discovering sites belonging to the Mohenjo-daro and Harappā civilization. Thus, even these dark areas were at one time illuminated by religious traditions with hoary antiquities of their own. We can therefore justifiably repeat the assertion that 'India is religion'. We do not exclude from this description Ceylon which has given us the Pali Tripiṭaka and other Buddhist religious literature and also imperishable Buddhist religious monuments.

COMMINGLING OF DIFFERENT CULTURES

In the evolution of this nation-wide and country-wide religious life, the contributions of different racial elements have so commingled that today it is difficult to separate them. The Indus valley, the Aryan, the Dravidian, the Austric, the Scythian, the Greek, the Hūṇa, the Iranian, the Mongolian, and even the Semitic (Islamic and Christian) races have all joined their currents of religious thought to build up this mighty stream of Indian culture. Nowhere else in the world have so many races and cultures met and coalesced, in the course of time, as in India. Her toleration prompted her to give shelter to all faiths, and her catholicity of olden days enabled her to absorb foreign elements with ease and export her own culture to the countries round about. Latterly, she kept the foreigners out by stiffening the caste rules, and shut herself in by discontinuing religious missions to foreign lands. The first restriction is being slowly removed now, but the second task of re-establishing cultural contacts abroad has yet to assume greater vigour.

The bulk of the now very small but highly intellectual, wealthy, enterprising, charitable Parsi population of the world, following Zoroaster, has had its home in the western part of this country for over ten centuries. There is an ancient colony of Jews in Cochin. Tradition says that St. Thomas, one of Christ's twelve Apostles, came and planted the seed of Christianity in South India shortly after the passing away of Jesus. Hindus, Jains, and Sikhs, barring a comparatively small number of emigrants scattered in British possessions, have no other home than India, which is the motherland of some hundred million Muslims also (including those of Pakistan). And it is well known that it is the birth-place of Buddhism and contains all the first and earliest sacred places of that religion, to which pilgrims have been coming year after year from all the Asian countries where Buddhism has spread. Lao-tzism, Confucianism, and Shinto practically all merged into an amalgam with Buddhism in China and Japan.

Thus we see that all living religions are gathered in and around India. Her geographical position has enabled her to establish contact of various kinds with both eastern and western Asia, to receive from, as well as to send to, other countries spiritual gifts, and thereby, to deepen and widen her own culture.

UNITY OF INDIA THROUGH PLACES OF PILGRIMAGE

There can be little wonder that India became religious not only in the composition and compilation of sacred texts and the rise of sects all over the country, but also in being equipped with visible symbols of religious value. From Kashmir to Kanyā-Kumārī, the whole country became studded with sacred streams, famous places of pilgrimage, magnificent temples, and centres of big seasonal religious gatherings. Some like Prayāga (Allahabad), Kāśī (Banaras), and Kāñcī (Kancheepuram) are still sacred to both orthodox and heterodox sects ; some like Haridvāra (Hardwar) and Rājagṛha (Rajgir) are patronized by more than one sect ; there are others like Purī, Ayodhyā, Mathurā (with Vṛndāvana), Ujjayinī (Ujjain), Śrīraṅga, Tirupati, Paṇḍharapura, Dvārakā, Nāsika, Kāmākhyā (near Gauhati), Buddha Gayā, Sāranātha, Pāvāpurī, and Navadvīpa that are patronized generally by a single religious community. At the four cardinal points stand the four *dhāmans*—Badarikāśrama, Purī, Rāmeśvara, and Dvārakā, and in or near them the four seats of Śaṅkarācārya, which every pious Hindu aspires to visit once in his life. The religious unity of India was achieved by eliminating all geographical distinctions and distributing places of pilgrimage all over the country.

Thus a Śākta has his fifty-one places of pilgrimage strewn all over from Hinglaj (in Baluchistan) to Kāmākhyā and from Kashmir to Ceylon. Similarly, a Śaiva has his Mount Kailāsa and temple of Paśupatinātha beyond Indian boundaries, and, within them, those of Amaranātha and Kedāranātha in the north, Rāmeśvara in the south, Somanātha in the west, and Bhuvaneśvara and Candranātha in the east. The Vaiṣṇava, too, can point to the seats of Badarinātha in the north, Padmanābhasvāmin at Trivandrum in the south, Purī in the east, and Dvārakā in the west.

ROYAL PATRONAGE TO RELIGION AND TEMPLES

India was fortunate in that her kings were also the patrons of religion in more senses than one, though the religious headship really belonged to the Brāhmaṇas. Kings not only encouraged scholars and religious writers to compose noble literature, but also summoned councils to settle religious disputes and fix the canon, and sometimes took part in religious discussions themselves. In the Upaniṣads, they even appear as teachers of the highest wisdom, *Brahmavidyā*, and Brāhmaṇas, too, approached them for spiritual enlightenment. They settled scholars on lands donated by themselves. The many copperplate grants bearing the royal insignia, often a religious symbol, found all over the country, testify to their religious zeal and charitable disposition. Religious brotherhoods received liberal gifts from their hands. They struck coins with divine effigies and took pride in calling themselves the followers of this or that mighty god, or of this or that founder of faith. They built magnificent temples to house divine images, and endowed them with suitable land grants for the maintenance and provision of scriptural instruction. In ancient times, the toleration of some kings showed itself in active charity to faiths other than their own. Kings like Aśoka and Harṣa even went beyond this ; they had sincere faith in, and respect for, other religious creeds.

Buddhism spread far and wide under the patronage of Aśoka ; Brāhmaṇism throve under the Imperial Guptas, the Cālukyas of the Deccan, and the Colas of South India ; and Jainism had the powerful princely support of the Cālukyas of Gujarat and the Rāṣṭrakūṭas of Malkhed. Ruling dynasties like the Pālas of Bengal and the Karas of Orissa, who supported Buddhism ; the Western Gaṅgas of Mysore, who patronized Jainism ; the Senas of Bengal, the Eastern Gaṅgas of Orissa, and the Hoysaḷas in South India, who patronized the Brāhmaṇical faith ; and rulers like Śaśāṅka of Bengal, who upheld Śaivism ; Harṣa, who promoted Buddhism ; and Bijjaḷa Kalacurya of Kalyāṇa and Kumārapāla Cālukya of Anhilvāḍa, who supported Jainism—these can be instanced at random as powerful patrons of different religions. The fortunes of faiths often swayed with the faith of the ruling prince, as for example, under the Kuṣāṇas, and evidence can be adduced to show that in South India places of religious worship changed hands between the Śaivas and the Jains more than once, according to the religion of the reigning monarch.

Religion as a culture survives in the hearts of men ; but religion as a temple cult depends upon patronage. The rise and fall of many religions have depended in India, as elsewhere, to a great extent on princely patronage. In the heart of the country, both in North and South India, every sect can point with pride to the numerous caves and temples, images and statues, of unsurpassed splendour in religious architecture and sculpture, that bear testimony to the popular devotion to the gods, and to social and State support of religious institutions. There are huge and rich temples in

South India, wonderful specimens of titanic architecture, each one of which can house and run a whole university of thousands of students. When this royal patronage was lacking or withdrawn, the temples fell into disrepair, and were often abandoned, and the stream of visitors and pilgrims flowed in other channels. Further complications arose when Islamic iconoclasm smashed images and desecrated temples, for then these ceased to be objects of religious worship altogether.

In the heyday of their glory, the income of temples went mainly to the benefit of the people at large by way of the promotion of education and help to the needy. Later, such ideals gradually receded into the background, particularly where the right of worship descended by the law of lineal succession, and it became a private property of certain specified families, not always composed of religious men or moral exemplars.

It is only in the South that, in recent times, the first successful attempt has been made to tackle the problem of properly utilizing temple funds and to bring the temples under some sort of State control. Under the auspices of one such religious centre a university has now been started. But the experiment is bound to be repeated on a wide scale, owing to a general intellectual awakening among the masses, caused as much by the spread of literacy as by the growth of political and social consciousness.

DIFFICULTIES OF THE SANSKRIT LANGUAGE

In reviewing this phenomenon of religious growth in India, we are not passing any judgement on the spiritual value of each and every one of the religious movements, institutions, and practices. Everything is not ideal or idyllic in this picture. For one thing, the lesson was lost that language is the spontaneous expression of thought and emotion, and that therefore *mantras* in an archaic tongue may acquire a mystic value, but are unintelligible to most of those who utter them. A belief in the magical efficacy of Vedic *mantras,* which became an article of faith with the Brāhmaṇa literature and the Pūrva-Mīmāṁsā philosophy, was inevitable under such circumstances. In this the Aryan of India erred indeed in the goodly company of the Zoroastrian, the Roman Catholic, and the Mohammedan, all of whom repeat prayers in Zend, Latin, and Arabic, respectively, without often understanding their meaning. The one purpose that this retention of old language really served was the saving of the Vedas from oblivion at a time when the human mind was the only tablet on which the Śruti was written.

Classical Sanskrit replaced the Vedic language for all purposes in later times, even in the composition of books on law and religion ; and the Paurāṇika *pūjās,* which supplemented the Vedic invocations (*sandhyāvan-*

dana) and sacrifices (*yajña*), were conducted in classical Sanskrit. But when this Sanskrit itself became unintelligible to the masses (if it ever was completely understood by them), a similar indulgence was not shown to the provincial languages as vehicles of religious expression except in heterodox systems like Jainism and Buddhism in earlier times (and they too latterly developed a tendency to lapse back into Sanskrit) and in popular religious movements of later times like Vaiṣṇavism, Śaivism, Sikhism, etc. The mystic syllables and formulae of the esoteric Tantras, when divorced from their philosophical and religious setting, are a logical corollary of the faith in the force of the unintelligible spoken word, to which not only Brāhmaṇism, but also Jainism and Buddhism succumbed.

DRAWBACKS OF THE CASTE SYSTEM

The rise of a sacerdotal caste, specializing in the performance of religious rights, has not been an unmixed blessing either. Among the Jews and the Zoroastrians also there was a priestly class, but in India the system attained a rigidity unknown elsewhere. Though originally all the three higher castes, Brāhmaṇa, Kṣatriya, and Vaiśya, were regarded as twice-born (*dvija*) and had the right of access to the Vedas, in the course of time, the Brāhmaṇas monopolized this function in such a way that not only were the other two castes ousted from the performance of Vedic rites, but their attempt to regain their lost position, e.g. by Viśvāmitra, was resented by the Brāhmaṇas. On the other hand, caste not only assumed a rigid form, but conferred spiritual dignity on some unworthy shoulders. One born of Brāhmaṇa parents could claim privileges and pre-eminence irrespective of his possessing the necessary spiritual qualification for Brāhmaṇahood. The Śūdras were excluded altogether not only from the religious field as ministrants, except for some insignificant functions, but also from the study of some philosophical disciplines which required, as a preliminary qualification, the study of the Vedas, which they were not entitled to undertake. Mixing of blood, however, could not be prevented altogether; but the caste of children born of miscegenation or inter-caste union was higher or lower according as the mother belonged to a lower or higher caste than that of the father, all marriages of men above their caste being disfavoured and discouraged and heavily laden with disabilities. Under this ban fell the Caṇḍālas, born of Śūdra father and Brāhmaṇa mother, who became an untouchable class.

The mediaeval mystics of India, who inveighed against caste and religious custom alike, had ample justification for their bitter attack on the religious practices of the day; and their contribution towards a purer conception of the deity and a better social organization cannot be over-estimated. A living faith was brought to the door of the meanest by preachers who often came from the submerged classes of Hindu society, and that in the very citadel of orthodoxy, namely, Āryāvarta, so highly extolled in the *Manu Saṁhitā*. Islam brought not only a levelling, but also a leavening influence to India, with its uncompromising monotheism and social equality of all adherents of the faith. Brāhmaṇism had to put its house in order against the danger of Islam, and some sects like Sikhism owe their inspiration as much to Islamic as to Hindu sources.

Orthodoxy, however, reacted characteristically to this new menace by tightening social control in its various later Smṛtis (as, for example, of Raghunandana in Bengal). But it began to multiply new religious vows (*vratas*), so much so that the whole year was turned into a round of rites and festivals. This served to make the common people more superstitious and yet, at the same time, more religious in a way. The one solid good that was achieved, however, was that popular methods of religious instruction were evolved, the contents of the learned books brought to the knowledge of the masses at large, and certain high ideals of virtue which constitute the priceless heritage of India, like the dutifulness of Rāma, the chastity of Sītā and Sāvitrī, the brotherly love of the *Rāmāyaṇa* and the *Mahābhārata* heroes, the religious devotion of Dhruva and Prahlāda, the truthfulness of Yudhiṣṭhira, the charity of Śibi, Karṇa, and Hariścandra, and the achievement of Viśvāmitra in re-establishing the principle of social eminence according to personal qualification, were held up before the public for admiration and emulation. No wonder that the *Mahābhārata* should come to be regarded as the fifth Veda, open to all alike, the Purāṇas to be religiously recited, and in the South the popular devotional literature should come to be known as the Tamil Veda.

SOME RELIEVING BASIC FEATURES

In tracing the evolution of religion in India, we are constantly reminded of certain basic features of surpassing interest. In this land of religion, a prophet never lacked an appreciative audience, nor freedom to express his views. The *parivrājakas* (itinerant religious teachers) in Buddha's time often belonged to non-Brāhmaṇic castes, and in mediaeval times the reformers who followed Rāmānanda came from some of the lowest classes of society and even from outside the fold of Hinduism; nevertheless, neither the one nor the other class of teachers failed to get a respectful hearing, though the message preached was often radically opposed to the accepted code of orthodoxy and cut at the root of Brāhmaṇical supremacy. Again, being an ethnological rather than a prophetic faith, the religion of the masses was never stereotyped, and this gave to the adherents of the faith a latitude in picking and choosing materials suited to individual temperaments. The man of faith, the man of action, and the man of knowledge and meditation could each find in the capacious religion of his forefathers something to justify his own method of spiritual practice.

When even the Vedas were regarded as *apauruṣeya* (superhuman), conformity to religious prescription did not imply blind obedience to the command of a personal deity, but connoted the aligning of conduct to the rules of order (*ṛta*) and truth (*satya*), which, in a magnificent hymn (*Ṛ. V.*, X. 190) of Ṛṣi Aghamarṣaṇa (lit. sin-destroying), are called the first products of divine fervour (*tapas*). It was on the supremacy of the moral order that the later concept of Karma could be easily superimposed by Jainism and Buddhism. Not having to subscribe to what Dr. Radhakrishnan has described as a statutory method of salvation, it was open to religious men to speculate freely upon the problems of faith and conduct, and to propound diverse theories of faith versus works, devotion versus intellection, absolutism versus theism, and activity versus passivity, which are still the wonder of other creeds. But difference did not breed rancour, and hence religious animosity very seldom reached the stage of persecuting intolerance. It is orthodoxy, and not reformation, that was mostly on the defensive all through the centuries, as the evolution of the legal literature (Dharma-śāstra) shows. Conciliation, concession, and compromise are the weapons with which orthodoxy fought daring innovations in thought. When in the sub-Vedic era there was a large absorption of non-Aryan elements, the system of imageless worship (*yajña*) was supplemented by the system of *pūjā* (worship) to a concrete religious symbol ; Vedic Sanskrit did not remain the sole medium of communion or communication with the deity ; and the claims of non-Brāhmaṇas to the possession of supreme knowledge were admitted.

It is a matter of question whether all such developments were ultimately to the best interest of communal spirituality. The painfully achieved gain of the Upaniṣadic height of spirituality was lost to the popular demand for crude faith and comfortable virtue, and was replaced by the resurgence of rank polytheism, or else by bickerings over the name of the one supreme God. For over a dozen centuries, popular ideas about religion were widely held, and the eternal, universal, rational religion was deflected from the worshipful contemplation of the supreme universal Self, embracing and including all individual selves, to the worship of innumerable trees, animals, and idols ; and that wonderful scheme of a universal society, based on the four *varṇas* (vocational classes) and four *āśramas* (stages of life), was shifted from its true, scientific, and psychological basis in the congenital vocational temperament and aptitude to the dubious but socially convenient one of rigid heredity.

II

THE VARṆĀŚRAMA-DHARMA

The wonderful scheme of *varṇāśrama-dharma* is propounded in *Manu Smṛti,* the oldest Indian law-book, whose injunctions are still followed by the Hindus, though in a very distorted form. The first glimpses of the *varṇa* scheme we already get in Ṛg-Vedic *Puruṣa-sūkta,* where the whole of society is regarded as a universal or social Man, of whom society is a reflex, and the various vocational groups, his different limbs. The mouth, or rather the head, of this collective social Man or human race, according to the *Puruṣa-sūkta* (*Ṛ. V.*, X. 90), was the Brāhmaṇa, his arms constituted the Kṣatriya, his trunk was the Vaiśya, his legs were represented by the Śūdra. Such is the thousand-headed, thousand-eyed, thousand-legged social Man, who spread over all the earth and ruled over all other living creatures.

The *Manu Smṛti* organizes the whole human race, in accordance with the conception in the *Puruṣa-sūkta,* through the scheme of *varṇāśrama-dharma,* into four natural psycho-physical types (*varṇas*) of human beings, and four natural stages (*āśramas*) in each individual life. In other words, the basic social components are (1) the man of knowledge, of science, literature, thought, learning—Brāhmaṇa, (2) the man of action, of valour —Kṣatriya, (3) the man of desire, of acquisitive business enterprise—Vaiśya, and (4) the man of little intelligence, uneducable beyond certain low limits, incapable of dealing with abstract ideas, fit for only manual labour—Śūdra. And the four stages are those of a student (*brahmacārin*), a householder (*gṛhastha*), a hermit (*vānaprastha*), and a monk (*sannyāsin*).

Nietzsche, the famous philosopher and *litterateur,* has declared of *Manu Smṛti* as follows in his *The Twilight of the Idols*:

'Such a law-book as that of Manu sums up the experience, sagacity, and experimental morals of long centuries; it comes to a final decision, it does not devise expedients any longer.... At a certain point in the development of a nation, the book with the most penetrative insight pronounces that the experience according to which people are to live, i.e. according to which they can live, has, at last, been decided upon.... To draw up a law-book like that of Manu means to permit a nation henceforth to get the upper hand, to become perfect, to be ambitious of the highest art of living.... The arrangement of castes, the highest cardinal law, is only the sanction of a *natural order*, natural legality of the highest rank, over which no arbitrariness, no "modern idea", holds sway. In every healthy society, three mutually conditioning types, differently gravitating physiologically, separate themselves, each type having its own hygiene, its own domain of labour, own special sentiment of perfection, own special superiority. Nature, and not Manu, separates those mainly intellectual, those mainly endowed with muscular and temperamental strength, and those distinguished neither for the one nor the other, the mediocre third class, one from the other; the latter being the great number, the former the select individuals.'

THE FOUR PURUṢĀRTHAS

The goal of life, according to the Sanātana Dharma (Hinduism), is two-fold—*abhyudaya* and *niḥśreyasa*—consisting of the four values (*puruṣārtha*) of *dharma, artha, kāma,* and *mokṣa. Abhyudaya* consists of *dharma, artha,* and *kāma,* or, to put them in the reverse order, sense-joy, refined by wealth, and regulated by law. This group of triple values is, broadly speaking, to be pursued in the first half of life, the first two *āśramas*—those of a *brahmacārin* (student) and a *gṛhastha* (householder). The second half of life, made up of the next two *āśramas*—those of a *vānaprastha* (hermit) and a *sannyāsin* (monk), is to be devoted to the achievement of *niḥśreyasa* (*summum bonum*), which consists in attaining *mokṣa* (salvation), deliverance form all sorrow, doubt, and fear.

From all this, it will be apparent that Sanātana Dharma was a very practical religion. India was religious not only in an other-worldly sense, but also very much in this-worldly sense. It set before human beings not only heaven in the hereafter, but also heaven here, a welfare State (*sarvodaya samāja*), in which all would be pleasantly and profitably occupied. To quote Manu: 'That which secures *abhyudaya* (prosperity) here, and *niḥśreyasa* (highest bliss) or *mokṣa* (deliverance from all fear) hereafter, is *dharma.*' 'Some say *dharma* and *artha,* (law-religion and wealth) are best; others, *kāma* (joy of the senses) and *artha*; others, *dharma* only; yet others, *artha* only. But the final truth is that *abhyudaya* consists in, and is achievable by, all three together.' Supreme happiness, termed differently as *niḥśreyasa, nirvāṇa, mokṣa, mukti,* etc., results from a realization of the identity of the individual self with the supreme universal Self, of Jīvātman with Paramātman, and therefore with all the countless individual selves.

The neglect of such an integrated scheme of life is the mother of all ills in individual and social lives. Veda-Vyāsa cried out in the agony of his heart: 'I cry with arms uplifted, but none heareth! *Artha* and *kāma* result from *dharma.* Why then is it not followed?' (*Mbh.,* XVIII. 5. 62).

But none listened, and the Kauravas, the Pāṇḍavas, and the Yādavas all came to destruction. Two world wars, each far more destructive than the Mahābhārata war, within the first half of the twentieth century, have illustrated the same law: grab, greed, hate, and lust are followed by vast butcheries.

But even those who feel no need to believe in a God or gods, an after-life, and the like agree that some laws, some rules of conduct, are indispensable for social life. Laws and rules of conduct may differ from time to time and place to place, but without some curb on human vagaries and evil propensities, no decent and secure social life is possible. Hence the necessity of balancing social interests on the foundation of the spiritual kinship of men, howsoever conceived. Hindu India strained the rules of true *dharma* when it advocated in theory the equality of all in relation to Brahman, but in practice negated it by an atrocious multiplication of mutually repellent castes and sub-castes, thereby weakening the integrity of the social system and falling an easy prey to foreign aggression, first Muslim, then European, which not only seized its body, but also made an assault upon its spiritual citadel by capturing the imagination of the socially neglected, degraded, and oppressed classes by an offer of social equality.

III

LAW OF KARMA AND MAINTENANCE OF SOCIAL ORDER

We now turn to a fundamental belief among the religious faiths in India, namely, the law of Karma. The immanent working of the divine spirit in the universe, especially in the maintenance of the social order, is a cardinal tenet of Hinduism. As in Confucian belief, an intimate relation is supposed to exist between cosmic happenings and social phenomena, particularly the ordering in the State. If the king ruled justly and proper social relations were maintained, rains fell in season, and no premature death could take place in the kingdom. Any calamity to individual or social life indicated the presence of some social disorder and prompted search for the offending event. A king who failed to punish the criminal incurred the guilt of sin by his lapse, as the authors of disciplinary literature (Nīti-śāstra) point out. As the upholder of the moral order, he is the representative of the Divine in whose universe good is destined for reward and evil for punishment. The law of Karma acts as an invisible and impersonal law of recompense and retribution, but really it is the hand of God that operates in restoring moral equilibrium.

So also, the impersonal laws of the land draw their authority and validity from the king. Good rulers are embodiments of the law of Karma.

'As ye sow, even so must ye reap.' 'As ye do unto others, so shall it be done unto ye.' The good ruler punishes or rewards evil or good acts quickly, in this very life, whereas the law of Karma would do it, slowly, in a subsequent life. As Manu says, 'If the ruler fails to punish criminals according to law, then the strong would devour the weak, as fish do in water' (VII. 20). 'If the ruler wields the rod of punishment justly, he and his people prosper and increase in all the three desiderata of life, namely, *dharma, artha,* and *kāma.* But if he is lustful, dissipated, unjust, mean-minded, then he should be slain by that same rod of punishment' (VII. 27). The *Mahābhārata* echoes the same thought: 'He who, having sworn by solemn oath at his coronation to protect the people from wrongful oppression, fails to do so, should be combined against by the people and slain, even as a mad dog' (*Anuśāsanaparvan,* LXI. 33)

The sanctity of contracts, oaths, and vows rests upon the same belief in the pervasive operation of the divine power in all human dealings. The name of the Lord must not be taken in vain, nor must engagements and promises be lightly made and broken. An ascetic cannot abjure his religious vows and enter upon matrimony, nor can even laymen perjure themselves without grave spiritual consequences. The hounds of heaven never go to sleep, and they can never be hoodwinked. The hearts of men are ever open to the gaze of the divine ; conscience will dog the footsteps of the moral delinquent, when alive, and doom will overtake him, when dead, if not also here below.

THE WHEEL OF LIFE

The recognition of an ultimate and eternal substratum of the world does not obviate the necessity of recognizing the fact of phenomenal existence. Birth and death, day and night, creation and destruction, evolution and involution, descent of spirit-mind into matter and re-ascent therefrom, the will to live and the will to die—such are the form, method, and manner of the world-process (*saṁsāra* or *bhava-cakra*). Out of this arises the important problem of rebirth or reincarnation (*punarjanma*) and transmigration or metempsychosis of the soul.

Once metaphysics accepts the position that the soul (Jīva) is subject to ignorance and the moral law, it follows that one brief life of a few years on this earth cannot exhaust the whole life-activity of the Jīva, or suffice for the realization of its oneness with the Eternal. It must have repeated incarnations strictly determined according to moral worth. Sanātana Dharma, Buddhism, and Jainism all believe in the law of Karma. Jātaka tales describe some five hundred previous births of the Buddha.

Sanātana Dharma makes it plain, however, that the consequences of sin as well as of merit become exhausted, sooner or later, according to the nature of that sin or merit, and then souls return to earth, with sub- and supra-conscious memories, to profit by lessons of past birth, and advance or recede in varying degrees on the path of evolution. The ultimate objective is always liberation or cessation of embodiment, through a spiritual illumination about the independence of the soul and its freedom from the bondage of matter at all times.

OTHER WORLDS

To the fact of rebirth necessarily attaches the third great truth that, as there is this physical world corresponding to our five senses and waking state, there are other worlds corresponding to subtle senses and other states of consciousness. Through these our souls pass between death and rebirth in this world, even as we pass through dreams between night and day; and as these dreams are painful or pleasant according to the impressions stored up in our mind, even so our souls spend periods in hells or heavens of various grades according to the quality of our sinful and meritorious acts; and also there are sub-human, co-human, and super-human kingdoms of beings which inhabit them, and man, by special training, can develop inner subtle senses and latent psychical powers which would open these worlds to him.

Svargas, narakas, and *lokas* or *bhuvanas,* i.e. paradises, hells and purgatories of higher and lower levels, and worlds or subtle and gross planes of matter—are affirmed by all religions. *Devas* and *upa-devas* (gods and demigods), angels and devils, and good and evil spirits of earth, water, fire, air, woods, hills, etc. are common to all religions and peoples, at least as items of popular belief. Many such popular conceptions were simply carried over into Brāhmaṇical religion from primitive beliefs, and some have travelled down from Vedic times. Personification and deification have both played their part, with the effect that not only were the powers of nature personified into divine and semi-divine beings, but also the ancestors (*pitṛs*) and sages of the race were given divine status. Even abstract qualities, like *śraddhā* (faith), *manyu* (anger), *nirṛti* (death), *dhī* (intellect), *hrī* (modesty), *puṣṭi* (nutrition), *medhā* (intelligence), *dhṛti* (patience), etc., were personified as worshipful beings. With the rise of sectarianism, the different heavenly abodes (*lokas*) of the various gods were more sharply distinguished, and each god was provided with a retinue of semi-divine beings in keeping with his function and status. Even Buddhism and Jainism, which worshipped no gods proper in their philosophy, admitted in their religious developments a multitude of heavens and hells and popular semi-divine beings, like *yakṣas* and *gandharvas,* as also the denizens of various grades of the nether region or hell. Also the prophets of their respective faiths received an adoration bordering on religious devotion.

THE LAW OF CYCLES

A corollary of the law of action and reaction is the law of cycles. Involution and evolution (*saṅkoca-vikāsa*) and vice versa characterize the world-process. Orbs of heaven are always rotating as well as revolving round greater orbs in ever larger circles and cycles of space and time. The Purāṇas speak of vast periods of time, such as *yugas, mahāyugas, manvantaras, kalpas,* and *mahākalpas,* governing our earth and the solar system. In the *sthūla* (gross) world, we have birth, growth, decay, and death of the body. In the *sūkṣma* (subtle) world, we have increase and decrease of mental powers, the will to live and the will to die. The Purāṇas tell us that the same Jīvas may become *devas* or *suras* (gods) in one *kalpa* (aeon), and *daityas* or *asuras* (demons) in the next, and come back again as men. Spirit descending into matter and ascending out of it again, attaching itself to it and detaching itself therefrom, on all possible scales—is the universal law of world-process.

THREE EXPLANATIONS OF THE WORLD-PROCESS

When the soul comes to the human stage, the possibility of inquiry as to the how and why of all we see around us, as to the meaning and purpose of life, arises. But it is only after a soul has turned from descent to ascent, from extrovertness (*parāk-cetana*) to introvertness (*pratyak-cetana*), that the urge for inquiry becomes stronger and stronger, until it becomes verily a matter of life and death to it to understand the how and why of all existence. In its anxious search, the soul passes through two stages and finds a solution of its harassing problems, and then attains rest and peace in the third and last stage. In terms of knowledge, these stages of inquiry constitute the three chief *darśanas* (views), the Dvaita, Viśiṣṭādvaita, and Advaita.

These three views correspond, in western phraseology, to deism, personalistic theism or concrete monism, and absolutistic monism ; in rationalistic terms, to the popular view of causation, namely, that an extra-cosmic personal God has created the cosmos, the scientific view of causation, namely, that thought and extension are inseparable aspects of one and the same ultimate Reality and are undergoing transformation perpetually, and the metaphysical view of causation, namely, that the cosmos is a dream-illusion of the one Spirit or universal supreme Self or Principle of consciousness. Broadly speaking, these correspond to Ārambhavāda of Nyāya-Vaiśeṣika, Pariṇāmavāda of Sāṁkhya-Yoga, and Vivartavāda or Ābhāsavāda or

Adhyāsavāda of Vedānta. These three views correspond generally to temperaments of active energism, devotional pietism and mysticism, and enlightened mysticism, and in spiritual life to paths of salvation by works, faith, and knowledge.

Advaita Vedānta is indeed the culmination of the Sanātana Dharma, and religion, philosophy, science, and art all meet in it and merge into one. Monism obviously means belief in One. But the world-process is not, and cannot be, explained in terms of One only. It is patently made up of countless many. The duality of the One and the many is reconciled by Advaita by showing that they are both penultimates and lose their separate identity in the non-dual Absolute or Parabrahman.

THE GOAL OF LIFE

A corollary of the explanation of the how and why of the world-process is the great question, What is the goal, the end and aim of life?

The final aim, cherished by every human heart, is the return to that original state of perfection from which we have strayed; it is to gain the realization that all world-process is but play, *līlā*, of oneself. Some time, sooner or later, this realization comes to every soul, after the experience of all sorts of joys and sorrows, sins and good deeds, and depths and heights of life, because all souls are identical in essence with the one supreme Self. The outcome of this realization is freedom from all bondage, and from all fear and sorrow, for there is no other entity apart from and other than the Self.

IV

METAPHYSICAL AND THEOLOGICAL SPECULATIONS

The concept of a spiritual universe has been a hard-won victory for the human mind. A western poet has well written of this mystery that has created and runs this world-process: 'Some call It Chance and some call It God, some call It Fate . . .' The *Śvetāśvatara Upaniṣad* gives a similar list of primal principles. But the best, dearest, and nearest name for this supreme mystery came to be known as 'I', Self, Ātman, and Paramātman in Hindu religious thought. All else may be doubted, but the fact of 'I' can never be doubted by any one. And this 'I am', this universal principle of consciousness, is eternal and infinite. Its beginning and end have never been witnessed by any one. As the *Devī-Bhāgavata* says, 'The cessation of this principle of consciousness has never been, nor can ever be, witnessed by anyone. For if it is seen, then that witness himself remains as embodiment of that continuous consciousness'.

But there may be, and are, innumerable doubts as to the exact nature of the Self or ultimate Being. The different philosophical views of the nature of God bear eloquent testimony to the ineffectual attempts of man to know God unto perfection. The relations between the infinite and the finite, spirit and matter, eternity and time, are all unsolved problems of philosophy not only in India, but elsewhere also. But in India, philosophy was put to religious, and even sectarian, use, and that is how philosophical speculations supplied the basis of sectarian beliefs and practices.

In India, theological speculation may be said to have described a complete circle. The Vedic hymns started with the gods as facts. The *ṛṣis* (Vedic seers) may have had their preferences for this or that deity as supreme ; but the concept of the totality of gods (*viśvedevāḥ*) was gradually evolved, and within this totality new gods must have been included from time to time. The hieratic religion deified even the accessories of worship and the qualities of mind that are favourable for religious devotion. But at a very early stage some thinkers began to speculate philosophically and to search for a primal unitary principle behind all diversity of divine manifestations. Being, non-being, supreme Puruṣa—all came, in turn, to supply the unitary basis. But by the time of the greater Upaniṣads, the discovery was made that Brahman, whose reflex and image the soul is, is the true explanatory principle of all existence. The devotionally inclined, who were nearer the ritualists in respect of admitting divine personality, continued to think of God in anthropomorphic terms, and were the forerunners of the theists of epic and Paurāṇic times, who instituted creeds like Vaiṣṇavism and Śaivism. On the other hand, the intellectually inclined, who were nearer Buddhism, Jainism, and Sāṁkhya and were against importing emotional elements into spiritual contemplation, thought of Brahman in impersonal terms, and considered even the divine personality to be a lower form of the Absolute.

It is still an unsolved problem which of these two views was put in the *sūtra* form by Bādarāyaṇa in his *Brahma-Sūtra*. One thing, however, is certain, namely, that religion has here passed into philosophy, and discussion, not devotion, was expected to decide the religious issue. Later on, the devotionalists also composed their *Bhakti-Sūtra* ; but even there, the relation between faith and knowledge, and the superiority of the one over the other, had to be established by argument. When we come to a book like the *Nyāya-kusumāñjali* of Udayana, the need of devotion as a basis of religious belief is relegated to the background, and regular logical arguments, like the theistic proofs of western theology, are advanced to establish the reality, nature, and attributes of God. The sceptic, the scoffer, the agnostic, the materialist, the fatalist, and even the polytheist would still find the arguments of the old Indian philosophers stimulating. In the process, the gods disappeared, but God remained; and the non-sectarian designation of Bhagavat or Īśvara or Īśa was chosen to obviate sectarian quarrel over the name of the supreme Deity. Man did not assist in the *nāmakaraṇa* (christening or naming) ceremony of God, and yet religious communities and sects have fought relentlessly with one another over the question of naming God as Yahveh or Lord or Allah, Viṣṇu or Śiva or Śakti. Is it not far better to be devoted to the Lord who calls Himself 'I am' than to worship the Lord whose name is 'Jealous' in the Mosaic inspiration?

The ascent of the soul from Vedic deities to Vedāntic Brahman was followed, however, by a descent from Brahman or Paramātman to sectarian gods in the commentaries on the *Brahma-Sūtra.* If Śaṅkara, in spite of his probable devotional leanings, had made the religious position rather insecure by relegating Īśvara to a secondary stage and extolling a non-differentiated Brahman, Bhāskara, Rāmānuja, Madhva, Nimbārka, Śrī-kaṇṭha or Nīlakaṇṭha, Vallabha, and Baladeva, in their interpretations of the *Brahma-Sūtra,* went back to a personal God and denied the illusory character of the Jīvas and the world. The assimilation of Śākta ideas was responsible for the personification of the power (*śakti*) of God into a female principle, almost coeval with, and only slightly lower in status and duration than, God Himself. The flood-gates of emotion were opened by this conjugal relationship of God, and a sanctification of human passions and sentiments overlaid the calm resignation, absolute trust, and perfect self-surrender, which characterize a life of austere spiritual devotion.

Small wonder that erotic mysticism, as in some Sufi sects, should have crept in, and left-hand (*vāmācāra*) Tāntrika practices, mixed with esoteric teaching in enigmatical language, should follow in its train. True, un-mitigated polytheism did not return, but in some of the Vedāntic schools sanction for the multiplicity of divine manifestations and even for image-worship was exegetically established. With the rise of the Smārta school of religious thought, a kind of modified polytheism, now limited to five major gods, Viṣṇu, Śiva, Śakti, Sūrya, and Gaṇeśa (or Skanda, Kārttikeya or Subrahmaṇya, or, occasionally, Brahmā), or indulgent monolatry grew up, which may be due either to a counter-reformation or to social tolera-tion, or simply to religious *laissez faire,* or spiritual inanity.

NAMES OF GOD

The theistic commentators of the Vedānta reared on the same *Brahma-Sūtra* of Bādarāyaṇa their respective theories and dogmas, calling God and His *śakti* by different names. But they dwelt on the essence of Godhood, and not on its concrete manifestations and functions. This was reserved for the mythologists, hymnologists, and rhapsodists, who multiplied the names of God *ad libitum*, and virtually found themselves in functional polytheism. From the Vedic times onwards, the same God has been given a string of names, the process starting in real earnest with the *Śatarudrīya* (the hundred names of Rudra), though smaller groupings of the Ādityas, Vasus, etc. are not unknown in the Vedas. It is the Paurānika fables about the exploits of different gods that provided the abundance of names to sectarian deities, some lists running not to hundreds, but to thousands, of names. These often serve as mnemonics of divine exploits and functions, and are daily counted on beads of different materials held sacred by different religious associations, or recited on special occasions to avert injury, or to promote prosperity, or simply to acquire religious merit. A popular philosophy extolled the name of God even above God or, at least, equated the two, and thus justified the verbal remembrance of the deity. The theory of devotion made inroads upon the inexorability of fate, and men in distress turned to God as a sure shield against misfortune. An old Sanskrit hymn to Devī says, 'Children immersed in play never think of their mother. But when they become hungry and thirsty, they forthwith run to her'.

SYMBOLS AND SHRINES OF GOD

A vexed problem of every religion is the place to be assigned to visible symbols that emerge everywhere in connection with the contemplation of the spiritual. Man clings to form. He himself is God incarnate in a form. Therefore he finds it difficult to turn, at once, to the formless. Hence wise, loving teachers of all faiths endeavour to take their adherents, step by step, from outer worship to inner worship. The *Agni Purāṇa* says:

> The child's toy-gods are made of clay and wood;
> Of the average man, gods live in holy streams;
> Of the intelligent, in heavenly orbs;
> The wise man's God is his inner Self.

Śrī Kṛṣṇa counsels in the *Gītā*: 'Those who know all should not violently shake the faith of those who know little' (III. 29).

Image-worship, kept within rightful limits, can serve the very useful purpose of stimulating devotion, prompting religious art, and creating mythological literature. But teachers should miss no opportunity of explaining that images are only symbols of spiritual ideals; otherwise worship would degenerate into a soulless social practice.

SCRIPTURES

All religions call their scriptures by names having the same significance, viz. the 'word of God'. All have evolved a science of theology and exegesis. All interpret them in various ways, literal, allegorical, mystical, moral, philosophical, and the like. All also indicate that they have two aspects, one for the masses, another for the select. The orthodox Hindus claim for their main scripture, the Vedas, a non-personal origin, though those theistically inclined, e.g. the Bhāgavatas, the Śaivas, and the Śāktas, naturally base revelation on divine saying. Truth as embodied in the Vedas is eternal, and is revealed in successive cycles or world-systems in an unmodified form, not being dependent on any divine fiat. Buddhism and Jainism partially accept this view, for they, too, hold that the truths of spiritual life revealed by successive Buddhas and Tīrthaṅkaras are identical in essence, and are retold to humanity that has forgotten them in the course of time.

V

ESSENTIALS OF UNIVERSAL RELIGION

Let us turn now to the essentials of universal religion. The *Mahābhārata* propounds the golden rule thus: 'Do not to others what ye do not wish done to yourself; and wish for others too what ye desire and long for yourself. This is the whole of *dharma,* heed it well.' Jesus Christ enjoins upon his followers the same rule in the positive form: 'Whatsoever ye would that men should do unto you, do ye even so to them', and this he characterizes as 'the whole of the law and the prophets'. Some six hundred years later, Mohammed instructed his followers thus:

> Noblest religion this—that thou shouldst like
> For others what thou likest for thyself;
> And what thou feelest painful for thyself,
> Hold that as painful for all others too.
>
> —*Hadis*

Similar teaching is given by Buddha, Mahāvīra, and Confucius (Kung-fu-tsu). There are verses to the same effect in *Manu Saṁhitā,* the *Gītā,* the *Bhāgavata,* and other Sanskrit scriptures. To quote the *Gītā* (VI. 32):

> By self-analogy who feels for all
> In gladness or in sorrow, everywhere,
> Highest of *yogins* is he to be deemed.

But why should a person act in accord with this golden rule? As Deussen points out, the answer to this question is not clearly and expressly given in the extant scriptures of any other religion than the Vedānta which proclaims: 'Because all other selves are your own self.' As you do unto others, so shall it be done unto you. Here we have the rationale of the law of Karma.

Sādi, the renowned poet of Iran, has uttered the same thought as that enshrined in the *Puruṣa-sūkta*:

> The progeny of Adam are all limbs
> Of but one body, since in origin
> And essence they are all identical.
> If one limb of the body suffer pain,
> Can the others ever rest in painless ease?
> If thou art careless of thy brother's pain,
> The name of 'man' thou oughtest not to gain!

Real happiness belongs only to the universal supreme Spirit or Self. When the individualized self realizes its identity with the supreme Self, then, and then only, does it attain *mokṣa,* and become free from the sense of clash of interest with other selves.

THE THREEFOLD PATH: JÑĀNA, BHAKTI, AND KARMA

The ascent of the soul to this position is mediated by different stages in strict consonance with the level of illumination attained. In life, cognition, desire, and action (*jñāna, icchā,* and *kriyā*) are always rotating. We perceive something; we feel a desire for or against it according as it is pleasant or painful; we act to secure it or to remove it from us. New activity brings new knowledge that engenders new desire; that, again, causes new movement. These three life-functions are always circling round and round; they are inseparable, though distinguishable. The same three factors are the distinguishable but inseparable components of religion. In a new-born infant, probably desire (undefined, instinctive) for breath and nourishment comes first; in any case, it is predominant. Yet, inasmuch as it is a desire for something, however indefinite, it is simultaneous with some vague inchoate knowledge. In religion, the first stage is desire (more or less inchoate) for 'nourishment for the soul', for something more than what this life offers. This desire leads to activity, the 'way of works', Karma-mārga, comprising rites and ceremonies for propitiating all sorts of things believed to have divinity and the power to help. The next stage is characterized by a somewhat clearer notion of other worlds and of God, leading to a more earnest desire for God, the 'way of devotion', Bhakti-mārga, expressing itself in yearnings, worship, internal prayers, etc. Then comes the stage of intense study and reflection on the ultimate Reality, the 'way of knowledge', Jñāna-mārga, which leads one to illumination, or realization of the Absolute. When this has been achieved, one's heart spontaneously overflows for the good of the many (*bahujanahitāya*), for the happiness of the many (*bahujanasukhāya*).

The Sanātana Dharma has delineated the three paths of *bhakti, jñāna,* and *karma* corresponding to *icchā, jñāna,* and *kriyā,* i.e. the affective, cognitive, and conative aspects of our psychological make-up. Here we do not stand alone, for similar triads are known in other religions also: the way of works, of knowledge, and of devotion in Christianity; *sharīat, tarīqat,* and *haqīqat* in Islam; *śīla, prajñā,* and *samādhi* in Buddhism; and *saṁyak-cāritra, saṁyak-jñāna,* and *saṁyak-darśana* in Jainism.

RULES OF SPIRITUAL AND ETHICAL DISCIPLINE

Spiritual discipline involves the pursuit of the path of rectitude. Five primary virtues (*yamas*) have been extolled in Brāhmaṇism (and more or less in Buddhism and Jainism) and have moulded Indian thought and conduct. They are: non-violence (*ahiṁsā*); truthfulness in thought, speech, and action (*satya*); non-stealing or non-taking of things lawfully not belonging to oneself (*asteya*); sexual purity (*brahmacarya*); and non-acceptance of unnecessary gifts (*aparigraha*). These five virtues are the whole of *dharma* in brief, and are binding equally on all the four *varṇas* or castes. The *Yoga-Sūtra* enjoins these on every one, and the last two, particularly, on complete renunciants.

Buddha's five principal virtues are thus stated in Edwin Arnold's *The Light of Asia* (Book VIII):

> Kill not—for Pity's sake—and lest ye stay
> The meanest thing upon its upward way.
> Give freely and receive, but take from none
> By greed, or force, or fraud, what is his own.
> Bear not false witness, slander not, nor lie;
> Truth is the speech of inward purity.
> Shun drugs and drinks which work the wit abuse;
> Clear minds, clean bodies, need no Soma juice.
> Touch not thy neighbour's wife, neither commit
> Sins of the flesh unlawful and unfit.

Next in importance are the other five observances and abstinences called *niyamas*. They are: cleanliness (*śauca*); contentment (*santoṣa*); asceticism, fast, and vigil (*tapas*); study of the scriptures and *darśanas* which help the understanding of the nature of Paramātman (*svādhyāya*); and surrender of the lower self to the higher Self, to God (*īśvara-praṇidhāna*).

Another important ethical injunction of all religions is: Honour the father, mother, teacher, and elders. In India, where teachers and ancestors are actually worshipped, there is definite direction, as in the *Taittirīya Upaniṣad* (I. 11. 2), to treat the parents and the preceptor as gods (*pitṛdeva, mātṛdeva, ācāryadeva*). Says Manu: 'The *ācārya* (teacher of the Vedas and all subsidiary sciences) is ten times more deserving of reverence than the *upādhyāya* (teacher of some few subsidiaries); the father, a hundred times more than the *ācārya*; but the mother exceeds the father a thousand times' (II. 145). Elsewhere, Manu declares that the spiritual preceptor, who imparts knowledge of the Self, is greater than the father, and even the mother, for, while parents give a physical body, he gives the spiritual, eternal body, whence a person who had become thus regenerate is known as *dvija*, twice-born.

Hindu ethics declares that the six internal enemies, against which we should always be on our guard, are *kāma*, lust; *krodha*, anger; *lobha*, greed; *moha*, infatuation; *mada*, pride; and *mātsarya*, envy. It may be noted that the six ennobling virtues are: *śama*, tranquillity; *dama*, self-control; *uparati*, detachment (from worldly things); *titikṣā*, fortitude; *śraddhā*, faith; and *samādhāna*, collected single-mindedness.

But we may say that the two root-sins, whence all others spring, are *rāga* (attachment) and *dveṣa* (aversion), or *kāma* and *krodha*, and the root of these, again, is *ahaṅkāra* (egoism).

Even as egoism is the ultimate source of all sins, so is altruism the fountain of all virtues, because it sees the one Self in all and acts accordingly.

Besides these spiritual and ethical disciplines, all religions emphasize the necessity of prayer, charity, pilgrimage, and service of fellow-beings as accessories of a religious life.

VI

THE BASIC IDENTITY OF HUMAN RELIGIOUS URGE

What do all these religious thoughts and expressions indicate? These similarities of belief and conduct serve to bring out into relief the basic identity of human equipment when at its best, the sameness of the religious urge all over the world, and the inherent desire to be at peace with one's surroundings and live up to the highest ideals. Ignorance, infatuation, and greed may blind us to the realities of a higher life, but they are removable by discipline; they are only temporary fetters which keep the potentially infinite human soul in bondage and untruth. Even the most primitive religion is designed to ennoble life, and it is only the mistaken notion of what constitutes true nobility that drags the primitives down. Enlightenment of the soul, darkened by passion, ill-will, and false view, is therefore a paramount necessity in spiritual redemption.

DISTINCTIVE FEATURES OF INDIAN RELIGIOUS THOUGHT

Perhaps, in India, the colour has been laid a little too thick on the self-negating side of life, the Nivṛtti-mārga ; but that is because plenty could be obtained by merely scratching the soil, and life was not so hard as it was, for instance, in Iran or Arabia or Palestine, where men had to earn their bread by the sweat of their brow. Where nature is all attraction, there is an obvious danger in yielding to her seductive influence ; hence the constant warning to be alert and mindful of spiritual obligations. The Semitic mind is preoccupied with the power aspect of God and, hence, the constant dread of offending His majesty and the need of intercession through prophets to make peace with God play such a large part in the Semitic religious consciousness. The Indian mind was latterly turned more inward and was, so to say, afraid of the blandishments of nature ; it felt the greater need of self-discipline and indifference to the attractions of sense for realizing the inner Self. It is these that have given the distinctive twist to the Indian religious mind resulting in the abnegation of the lower self and reliance on the higher Self. Each man has been called upon to fight his lonely battle with the solicitations of the flesh and to conquer his lower self almost unaided. Buddhism, Jainism, Sāṁkhya, Yoga—all exhort the individual to be self-reliant in his spiritual struggles, to avoid the bondage caused by evil action, and to resist the temptation of even a pleasurable heavenly existence, where the senses are regaled by agreeable enjoyments. There is no spiritual advancement in heaven as held by many types of theism.

The boldness of this creed of self-help has proved baffling to those who have been brought up in the belief that at every step the helping hand of God is indispensable for the attainment of spiritual heights. For when the Indian mind swung over to the opposite side, it went beyond the personal aspect of the Divine, and posited the impersonal Brahman that could be contemplated and realized, but not loved or reverenced in the ordinary sense of these terms. This concept is equally enigmatic to western minds brought up in the tradition of an intensely personal God who demands obedience, worship, and love from His devotees. From this absolutistic position the Indian mind has drawn the logical conclusion that everywhere the universal Consciousness is present, images not excepted, and that therefore all the earth is equally sacred, and all souls are identical in essence through their common identity with Brahman. It is a moot question whether life and logic have ever completely coincided in any system of religious belief, and it is not impossible to find contradictions in every institutional religion. But the fact remains that India has succeeded in developing a degree of spirituality that is a marvel, judging by its long history, its penetrating influence upon the masses, and its beneficent contributions to the spiritual uplift of the surrounding world. To a study of this romantic history of the Indian religious life, which is unfolded in the pages of this volume, one can always turn with profit.

We may conclude by quoting one who was speaking with the conviction that only profound knowledge could give. Says Max Müller: 'If one would ask me under what sky the human mind has most fully developed its precious gifts, has scrutinized most profoundly the greatest problems of life, and has, at least for some, provided solutions which deserve to be admired even by those who have studied Plato and Kant, I would indicate India.

'And if one would ask me which literature would give us back (us Europeans, who have been exclusively fed on Greek and Roman thought, and on that of a Semitic race) the necessary equilibrium in order to make our inner life more perfect, more comprehensive, more universal, in short, more human, a life not only for this life, but for a transformed and eternal life, once again I would indicate India.'

PART I

RELIGIOUS SECTS AND CULTS

2

EVOLUTION OF RELIGIO-PHILOSOPHIC CULTURE IN INDIA

THIS chapter is intended to be a brief treatment of the history of the religio-philosophic culture in India, from its rude beginnings in the lower Indus valley down to the age of Sri Ramakrishna. It is limited to a rapid survey of the whole field, assigning proper places to the individual topics of this volume. Even this comparatively humble task is beset with difficulties. Sufficient data are lacking to enable us to follow, even with a tolerable degree of certainty, the rise and development of the various religious movements and philosophical schools in India. Opinions differ widely, and the differences are accentuated, and not unoften embittered, by sectarian jealousy and fanaticism. The Indians are particularly sensitive in any matter concerning their religion. Amid the passions and prejudices that have slowly gathered force, it is not easy to get a detached view of things, which is essential to the writing of a historical survey of religious growth.

Religion, in its essence, is based largely on intuition and emotion and not on a purely rational attitude of mind, and it is inspired and fed by faith and belief rather than reason and argument. While this offers no great difficulty in appreciating the essence of any particular religious belief, it is a standing obstacle to the historical interpretation of a religion and its critical appraisal, which can only proceed on the basis of reason and reason alone. In writing this outline, mainly the views of modern secular writers, trained in the western method of scholarship, have been followed, rather than those of the accredited exponents of the various religious movements, whose names are justly held in the highest veneration by all of us. If we seek to dive deep into the religious mysteries, we can do no better than try to appreciate and emulate the intuitive experience of the latter. But if we propose to follow the more matter-of-fact course of tracing the origin and development of the different religious systems, they cannot be our unfailing guides. For a proper appreciation of the beauty of the Taj Mahal we can do no better than turn to the poets and artists, but for an idea of its nature and origin and a proper estimate of its worth we have to adopt the modern historians as our guide.

For the sake of convenience of treatment we may divide this review of the religio-philosophic culture of India into six well-defined chronological periods.

I. THE PRE-ARYAN PERIOD (C. 3000-2000 B.C.)

The beginnings of religion in Indian society have been pushed back by two thousand years or even more by the discoveries at Mohenjo-daro. Mohenjo-daro, 'mounds of the dead', is the local name of a high mound situated in a narrow strip of land between the main bed of the Indus river and the western Nara canal in the plains of Larkana District in Sind. Here a city was built about five thousand years ago, and was destroyed and rebuilt no less than seven times. The ruins of these successive cities afford us a glimpse of a civilization which was indeed of a very high order, at least from the materialistic point of view. The people who lived in these cities cannot be definitely affiliated to any known race of men in India. It is certain, however, that they had long emerged from primitive barbarism and developed an urban life with all its amenities. Of their religious culture some traces are left in their icons which include the Mother Goddess, the phallus, and a male god, seated in yogic posture, who has been regarded as Śiva. In the absence of any written document, our knowledge of this religion must necessarily remain vague, but there are enough indications that the worship of Śiva in the form of phallus, which is a prominent feature in later Hinduism but is condemned in the Vedas, is possibly to be traced to this source. Once this is conceded, it is easy to assume that many traits of later Hinduism, specially those which cannot be directly traced to the Vedas, might have been a legacy of these unknown people. Their cult of the Mother Goddess may not be exactly the same as Śakti-worship of later days, but both seem to be inspired by the same fundamental belief in a female energy as the source of all creation. The worship of tree, fire, and water seems to have been in vogue. The seal-amulets, containing figures of a variety of animals, have been taken as evidence for the worship of animals, but they might be symbols or carriers of deities who were the real objects of worship. These are, no doubt, matters of dispute, but the cumulative effect of the discoveries at Mohenjo-daro and the neighbouring regions may be summed up in the form of the following general conclusions:

(1) That some fundamental ideas of Hinduism as well as some primitive beliefs and observances, still current in India, may be traced as far back as the third millennium B.C.

(2) That the worship of Śiva and Śakti may be regarded as the oldest form of Indian theistic religion.

This old religion and culture was widely spread in Sind, Baluchistan, and parts of the Punjab. How and when it receded to the background is not definitely known to us. It is generally held that the influx of the Aryan race into India is the cause of the downfall of this older culture and civilization of the Indus valley. In spite of some uncertainties, this must be regarded as the only satisfactory hypothesis at the present state of our knowledge.

II. THE VEDIC PERIOD (C. 2000-600 B.C.)

The civilization of the Aryans and particularly their philosophical thought and religious practices during the first thousand years are known to us from sacred books collectively known as the Vedas. This term denotes not any particular book, but the whole mass of literature produced by the Aryans during the first thousand years or more of their settlement in India. Although definite dates cannot be assigned to the different texts, it is possible to give a general idea of their chronological sequence. The Saṁhitās, Brāhmaṇas, Āraṇyakas, and Upaniṣads represent the four successive stages in the development of Vedic literature. The *Ṛg-Veda Saṁhitā*, the earliest text, may be referred to a date between 2000 and 1500 B.C., while the principal Upaniṣads were composed by 600 B.C. Between these two extreme dates we have to put the other Saṁhitās, Brāhmaṇas, Āraṇyakas, and the principal Upaniṣads.

In the *Ṛg-Veda Saṁhitā*, we first come across the ideas of definite gods, as a normal evolution from the striking phenomena of nature. The same Saṁhitā shows that the development of the Aryan religion and philosophy proceeded along two well-marked directions. On the one hand, we find the idea of propitiating the different gods by means of worship, which led to the religious sacraments known as *yajña* or sacrifice. On the other hand, there was developed a more philosophic conception about the nature of these gods, which culminated in the idea that all these gods are but the manifestations of a higher Spirit. The later Vedic literature saw a further development in these directions. The Brāhmaṇas developed the ritualistic side by elaborating the mechanical details of the *yajña*, while the philosophical ideas were developed in the Upaniṣads.

The Upaniṣads are works of various authors living in different ages. They do not present a coherent or consistent system of philosophy. They are the utterances of spiritually minded people who obtained glimpses of the highest truths by earnest meditation. Their process is intuitive rather than logical, and their object is to satisfy the natural yearnings of the human mind for an ultimate knowledge of the reality about God, man, and the world around us. The answers given to these questions are many, and it is not always easy to say definitely what the teachings of the Upaniṣads as a whole are. The hints, suggestions, guesses, and implications contained in them are so many and so diverse that in subsequent ages they have been quoted as authority by the founders of almost all the religious and philosophical systems in India, even though they differed on essential points.

But in spite of the mystic character of the Upaniṣads, certain fundamental conceptions clearly emerge out of the mass of spiritual and metaphysical thoughts. The first and foremost is the idea of one all-powerful, all-pervading, self-existent, eternal, and incomprehensible Absolute (Brahman), in whom all creatures find their origin and dissolution.

Secondly, the Upaniṣads lay stress on the miseries of life, which are perpetuated by transmigration or rebirth due to our *karma* or actions. But they pin their faith on the ultimate hope of deliverance (*mukti*), which means cessation of miseries and enjoyment of eternal bliss. This can only be obtained by a true knowledge of the universal Spirit or Soul (Brahman). Such knowledge can only be derived by purity of life and intense meditation (*nididhyāsana*). By implication, if not by express mention, they deny that the ritualistic sacrifices (*yajña*) can achieve the same result. Lastly, the Upaniṣads elaborate the idea of the eternal human soul, as distinct from the body, and, by a bold flight of imagination, regard the individual human soul as identical with the universal Soul or God. When true knowledge comes by meditation, the individual souls merge in the universal Soul, as rivers merge in the ocean. A solution was thus offered of the problems of life and death and of God and man, which are at the root of all philosophy and religion.

In spite of the profundity and brilliance of Upaniṣadic ideas, they cannot be regarded as sufficient for the moral or religious needs of the masses. In the first place, they could make their appeal only to the intelligentzia, but fell flat on the average man to whom the attainment of such a profound knowledge appeared as a Utopian ideal. Secondly, while the *Ṛg-Veda Saṁhitā* showed an analytic process in discovering one great God behind the visible phenomena of nature, the Upaniṣads follow from the beginning an intuitive method. Their conclusions were not based on an intelligible chain of reasoning and arguments, but held out merely as the experience or realization of great minds. They were therefore to be accepted on faith. Thirdly, although by implication they denied the efficacy of ritualistic *yajña* for the purpose of salvation, they prescribed no substitute for it, which an average man could normally pursue for developing his religious life.

Thus while the Upanisadic philosophers soared to a dizzy height and indicated the line on which Indian thoughts were to be developed, in later years, they failed to satisfy all the normal religious cravings of the human heart and the legitimate spiritual needs of the human mind.

III. THE AGE OF REVOLT (C. 600 B.C. TO A.D. 300)

The age that followed the early Upaniṣads saw new developments in religious thoughts with a view to removing these deficiencies. They started with the Upaniṣadic teachings as their background, but proceeded in different directions to build up different systems of religious belief. The chief characteristics which distinguished them may be summed up as follows:

(1) Belief in a personal God to be worshipped with devotion (*bhakti*) rather than an impersonal Absolute (Brahman) to be realized through meditation and knowledge (*jñāna*).

(2) Broad practical view of everyday life, laying stress on morality and discounting the metaphysical discussions about God and soul. Emphasis is laid on the control of will and emotions, and the right actions of a man are regarded as the only means to his salvation.

(3) A rational interpretation of all the problems of human life and an attempt to solve them by a co-ordinated system based on analytical reasoning.

(4) Aversion to mechanical sacrificial performances as detailed in the Brāhmaṇas, and regard for the sanctity of animal life.

EARLY DEVELOPMENTS IN THE UPANIṢADS

The germs of these developments no doubt lay in the Upaniṣads themselves. This is best seen in the rise of the theistic Śaiva system, to the history of which we may now devote our attention.

The god Rudra is mentioned as early as the *Ṛg-Veda* as a terrific god whose wrath had to be appeased by offerings. The idea is further developed in the *Śatarudrīya* (*Taittirīya Saṁhitā*), where he is represented both as a malevolent and as a benevolent god. In the latter aspect he was known as Śiva.

In the age of the Upaniṣads, when the conception of an impersonal God was the prevailing idea, we find the first beginnings of a theistic system in the *Śvetāśvatara Upaniṣad.* This Upaniṣad is earlier than the *Bhagavad-Gītā* which in XIII. 13, 14 quotes a verse and a half from it (III. 16, 17). It expounds the characteristic Upaniṣadic doctrines but occasionally identifies Brahman with the god Rudra-Śiva.

There is only one Rudra, so says this Upaniṣad, and they do not recognize another. This God—the great Soul whose work is the universe —always dwells in the hearts of men.

Śiva is knowable by faith, love, or the pure heart. Having known Śiva one attains eternal peace.[1]

[1] *Śvetāśvatara Upaniṣad,* III. 2; IV. 14, 16, 17; V. 14.

Here we find the beginnings of the theistic system which was further developed in the Bhāgavata school. From the conception of an absolute Brahman to that of a personal God, whom an average man can love and comprehend, the transition is no doubt easy and natural, and almost inevitable. But why the particular god Rudra-Śiva should be chosen for this purpose is not so easy to understand. Long ago, R. G. Bhandarkar, after a painstaking analysis of the attributes of Rudra-Śiva, came to the conclusion that this god had a close connection with non-Aryan tribes, and that the element of phallic worship associated with his cult was entirely borrowed from them. The discoveries of Mohenjo-daro, to which reference has already been made above, corroborate this view, and we may now assume, with a tolerable degree of certainty, that Rudra-Śiva was, or was assumed to be, identical with the great God of the pre-Aryan settlers of the Indus valley, and that, with the large absorption of these people into the Aryan society, he came to occupy a pre-eminent position. The Upaniṣadic doctrine of an impersonal God was fused with the devotional worship of a personal God, and a beginning was thus made which led to almost revolutionary changes.

JAINISM, BUDDHISM, AND BHĀGAVATISM

These changes were brought about by the Bhāgavatas, Buddhists, and Jains, who all first come into notice about the sixth century B.C. In spite of early opinions to the contrary, it is now admitted by all scholars that all these religious doctrines grew independently in or about this period and their founders were real historical persons. Gautama Buddha is no longer a solar myth, but is recognized as an historical personage, born in the republican Śākya clan. The traditional date of his death, viz. 543 B.C., is not accepted by modern scholars. They regard 487 B.C. as a close approximation to the real date of his death. As by all accounts he lived for 80 years and became the Buddha at the age of 35, the years 532-487 B.C. may be regarded as the period when the fundamental principles of Buddhism were enunciated by him.

Vardhamāna Mahāvīra, usually regarded as the founder of the Jaina religion, was born in a suburb of Vaiśālī, the capital of the famous republican clan of the Licchavis. The traditional date of his birth, viz. 599 B.C., has not been accepted by modern scholars who place it about 539 B.C. He attained supreme knowledge at the age of 42 and died thirty years later. So the effective period of his religious life may be put between 497 and 467 B.C.

But Jainism seems to be much older than this period. The Jains claim that there were twenty-three prophets (Tīrthaṅkaras) before Mahāvīra, and have woven absurdly fantastic tales around them. It is said, for example, that the first prophet lived several millions of years and his stature was about a mile high. Somewhat similar claims are made by the Buddhists, but their stories about the six Buddhas who preceded the historical Gautama are not of an absurdly exaggerated character. The germs of all religion may be traced back to inchoate thoughts or speculations of an earlier period, and to this extent we can accept the claims of a higher antiquity advanced by many religious sects. We have no grounds to believe that as a system of religion, with definite dogmas and an established organization, Buddhism existed before Gautama Buddha. As regards Jainism, however, there are clear indications that Pārśvanātha, the twenty-third Tīrthaṅkara, who is reputed to have died 250 years before Mahāvīra, was really an historical person and he founded a religious sect known as Nirgrantha. Mahāvīra belonged to this sect, but gave a decided stamp to it by his own personality. As an historical religion of recognized status, with a definite system and organization, we can hardly trace Jainism long before the time of Vardhamāna Mahāvīra.

Although the historical character of Gautama Buddha and Vardhamāna Mahāvīra is now freely admitted, that of Kṛṣṇa-Vāsudeva, the founder of the Bhāgavata religion, is still doubted by many. Eminent scholars have held that Kṛṣṇa-Vāsudeva was not a human being, but a popular deity—a solar deity according to some, a vegetation deity according to others, and a tribal deity according to still others. But recent researches leave no doubt that Kṛṣṇa-Vāsudeva of Mathurā was a human teacher, belonging to the republican Kṣatriya clan known as Sātvataṣ or Vṛṣṇis, a branch of the Yādava tribe which was famous in the age of the Brāhmaṇas. The earliest account of this great teacher is found in the *Chāndogya Upaniṣad* (III. 17. 6), where he is represented as the son of Devakī and a pupil of the *ṛṣi* Ghora Āṅgirasa. Incidentally the Upaniṣad has preserved some of the doctrines which Kṛṣṇa learnt from his preceptor. It is a noteworthy fact that these fundamental doctrines reappear in the *Bhagavad-Gītā,* which contains the most authoritative exposition of the principles held by the Bhāgavatas.

The reference in the *Chāndogya Upaniṣad* shows that Vāsudeva-Kṛṣṇa flourished before the sixth century B.C. As to the incidents of his life we know little beyond what has already been stated above.

The popular tales about Kṛṣṇa, particularly his amorous relations with the *gopīs,* are found only in the *Harivaṁśa* and the Purāṇas. His association with Rādhā first occurs in still later literature. To derive the life-story of Kṛṣṇa from books which were written five hundred to thousand years later is against the elementary principles of historical study. No importance therefore attaches to these books, as a source of information for the true life of Kṛṣṇa, although they constitute important landmarks for the development of the Kṛṣṇa cult and the evolution of the Vaiṣṇava religion.

THE NATURE AND SIGNIFICANCE OF THE THREE MOVEMENTS

Having briefly surveyed the historical origin of the three great religious movements, we may next proceed to explain their nature and great significance in the evolution of religio-philosophical culture of India.

At the very start we must remember that all these three constitute a revolt against, or at least a decided break from, the accepted religious creeds of the day. And it is not perhaps a mere accident that all of them originated in the free atmosphere of independent republican clans, the Śākyas, the Licchavis, and the Sātvatas. The history of the world has again and again demonstrated that nurseries of political freedom often tend to develop freedom in the domains of thoughts and beliefs. Besides, all the three clans lived in regions which may be described as the outer fringe of the stronghold of Vedic culture and therefore comparatively free from its rigid control.

Further, we should remember that these three religious movements were not isolated events, but there were similar other movements, and all these were merely the products of the age. The bold Upaniṣadic speculations were the outcome of a creative intellect and critical spirit which revolted against the mechanical, and sometimes cruel, ceremonials of the Brāhmaṇa age. But freedom of thought and a spirit of inquiry once aroused are not likely to observe any limit, and it is no wonder that the sixth and fifth centuries B.C. saw a great outburst of intellectual activity which defied established traditions and was out to seek truth by new experiments. The result was almost a wild growth of new views and ideas leading to the foundation of numerous sects and religious systems. Some of these, no doubt, displayed a high degree of intellectual, spiritual, and moral fervour, but others proved a victim to unbridled passions and lack of all moral or intellectual discipline. Thus, while the tide of free speculations led on the one hand to the rise of the important sects like Buddhism, Jainism, Śaivism, and Bhāgavatism, it culminated on the other in different types of heretical systems like that of Cārvāka in which immoral practices masqueraded in the name of religion.

The revolution was started on a moderate scale by the Bhāgavata religion. It substituted a personal God called Hari in place of the abstract idea of a universal Soul. Hari, the God of gods, was not, however, visible to one who followed the traditional mode of worship, viz. *yajñas* and austerities. He could only be seen by one who worshipped Him with devotion. By an open denial of the efficacy of sacrifices and austerities, denunciation of the slaughter of animals, and stressing the element of *bhakti* (devotion) in place of abstract knowledge, it constituted a fundamental break from the accepted creeds and beliefs.

Buddhism, which represents the other extreme of reaction, agreed with the Bhāgavatas in the first two of these important principles, but went still further, both in its disregard for sacrifices and austerities and in its upholding the sanctity of animal life. Moreover, it differed from the Bhāgavatas in several important points. It did not acknowledge any personal God, or, for the matter of that, any supreme God at all. Consequently, neither *bhakti* nor metaphysical and abstract knowledge of God had any place in it, and a highly developed ethical life was offered as the solo means of attaining salvation. Further, it denied the Vedic literature as a divine revelation and refused to accept the social order of the day, particularly the system of caste. This completed the revolution which was began by the Bhā avatas.

The Jains accepted most of these points, but regarded austerity as the essential means of salvation. Besides, their philosophic conception was different. They believed in eternal individual souls which were denied by the Buddhists. But, unlike the Upaniṣadic doctrine, they regarded each individual soul as eternal, and they had no conception of one eternal soul in which the individual souls are to be ultimately merged.

The rise of these revolutionary religious sects reacted on the orthodox system and led to the formulation of its doctrines in a more co-ordinated and logical form. The complacent dogmatism of old was rudely shattered by Buddhism and Jainism, which raised anew the fundamental problems of religion and approached them with a new and critical outlook. The orthodox leaders, in order to meet their bold challenge, tried to set their house in order by two distinct methods. First, they codified and systematized their philosophical and religious doctrines and tried to put them on the unassailable basis of logic and reason. Secondly, they tried to outflank the heterodox systems by accepting those elements which seemed to be the basis of their universal appeal and widespread popularity.

FRESH DEVELOPMENTS

The religio-philosophic culture of the period 400-200 B.C. is the result of this interaction between these contending forces ; and we may note the following developments as the chief landmarks of the period:

(1) The formulation of the six systems of philosophy, viz. Nyāya, Vaiśeṣika, Sāṁkhya, Yoga, Pūrva-Mīmāṁsā, and Vedānta.

Among these the Pūrva-Mīmāṁsā is an attempt to give a rational and philosophic interpretation of the Vedic teachings, specially the sacrificial system.

(2) Development of Śaivism into a complete theistic system within the orthodox fold.

(3) Winning over of the Bhāgavata sect for the orthodox faith by the identification of Kṛṣṇa with the Vedic god Viṣṇu.

(4) Popularization of the remodelled religion and philosophy by means of epics like the *Rāmāyaṇa* and the *Mahābhārata.*

(5) Buddhism and Jainism were alone left outside the pale of orthodox culture to continue the struggle. They gradually gained in power and popularity and for a time almost completely overshadowed their rivals. Buddhism spread far beyond the frontiers of India, and ultimately became a world-religion.

These characteristic features, originating during the period from 400 to 200 B.C., continued to mark the religio-philosophic culture for the next five hundred years (200 B.C. to A.D. 300). A brief outline indicating their lines of development is given below.

(1) All the philosophical systems have grown from insignificant beginnings through several stages. The philosophical views formulated by a great man in the dim past were gradually defined and systematized by a succession of followers in the shape of philosophical Sūtras or Kārikās. The authors of the Sūtras should therefore be regarded more as formulators than as founders or authors of the systems. The date of the Sūtras is a matter of dispute. Generally they are regarded as posterior to Buddhism and anterior to the Christian era, and the dates suggested for them range from 400 to 200 B.C. This view is not perhaps very far from truth.

The later development of the six systems also proceeded along the older traditional method. Each system, as it grew, had to elaborate its own doctrines, meet criticisms of its opponents, and offer solutions of new problems. This was done by successive texts each of which professed to be merely a commentary on the preceding. The later philosophers in India were thus content to write merely commentaries or commentaries on commentaries (*bhāṣya, ṭīkā,* etc.), and never claimed to formulate, far less to found, any original system. Even Śaṅkarācārya, the greatest philosopher that India has produced so far, wrote merely commentaries on the *Brahma-Sūtra,* the *Bhagavad-Gītā,* and the Upaniṣads. It is in this way that Indian philosophy has grown from age to age, becoming a more and more perfect system with each succeeding century. It has been aptly compared to the gradual growth of a baby to a fully developed human form.

Commentaries on the six systems continued to be written till recent times, Rāmānanda Sarasvatī's commentary on the *Yoga-Sūtra,* called *Maṇi-prabhā,* being written as late as about A.D. 1600. The high position always occupied by these philosophical systems in the Hindu mind appears from the fact that the leaders of all religious sects attempted to derive their basic principles from one or other of them. No sectarian religion had a chance of securing prestige so long as it could not at least reconcile its fundamental doctrines with one or other of the philosophical systems.

(2) The theistic ideas of Śaivism, which we first meet with in the *Śvetāśvatara Upaniṣad,* are further developed in the *Atharvaśiras Upaniṣad.* The first reference to a definite religious sect of the Śaivas occurs in Patañjali (second century B.C.). The members of the sect were known as Śiva-bhāgavatas. The more well-known Pāśupata sect is mentioned in the Nārāyaṇīya section of the *Mahābhārata.* Śiva, the consort of Umā, is said to have himself revealed the texts of this school. This implies that the founder of the sect was a human being who was afterwards regarded as an *avatāra* of Śiva. The implication is rendered explicit in later literature like the *Vāyu Purāṇa* (XXIII) and the *Liṅga Purāṇa* (XXIV). According to these, at the time when Vāsudeva was born in the Yadu family, Śiva entered a dead body and incarnated himself as a *brahmacārin* by the name Nakulīśa (or Lakulīśa) at a place called Kāyāvatāra or Kāyā-varohaṇa, identified with Karvan in Baroda. He had four disciples, namely, Kuśika, Garga, Mitra, and Kauruṣya (or Ruṣṭa). Two stone inscriptions corroborate this story, and one of them names the four disciples as founders of the four branches amongst the Pāśupatas.

The discovery of an inscription of the Gupta emperor Candragupta II at Mathurā, dated the year 61 (A.D. 380), enables us to fix with tolerable certainty the date of Kuśika. The inscription tells us that Ārya Uditācārya, its author, was tenth (in succession) from Bhāgavata Kuśika. Assigning a century for three generations, Kuśika may be placed about the middle of the first century A.D. The date, of course, would be later by a century if we assign four generations to a century.

Now if we take Kuśika as disciple of Nakulīśa, the latter must be placed some time between A.D. 75 and 125. But although this view is supported by later tradition recorded in literary and epigraphic evidences, we must give due weight to the popular tendency to regard the founders of branches as immediate disciples of the original founder of the sect. The autnors of the Purāṇas regard Nakulīśa as a contemporary of Vāsudeva-Kṛṣṇa, which, of course, is impossible if we accept the date given above. R. G. Bhandarkar interpreted this statement of the Purāṇas to mean that traditionally the Pāśupata system was intended to take the same place in the Rudra-Śiva cult as the Pāñcarātra did in the Vāsudeva-Kṛṣṇa cult.

Accordingly, he referred the rise of the Pāśupata school to about the second century B.C. It must be admitted that there is some force in his argument, and we cannot definitely reject his view on the strength of the newly discovered inscription.

The human figure of Śiva on the coins of Wema Kadphises (middle of the first century A.D.) may be regarded as a figure of Nakulīśa.

(3) The worship of Vāsudeva as an object of devotion (*bhakti*) goes back to the time of Pāṇini (fifth century B.C.) and is also proved by a statement of Megasthenes (end of fourth century B.C.) The religious ideas formulated by Vāsudeva-Kṛṣṇa developed into the Bhāgavata system. As in the case of Śaivism, we find a very early account of the system in the Nārāyaṇīya section of the *Mahābhārata*. There it is called Ekāntika Dharma and is said to have been revealed by Nārāyaṇa himself. The same text tells us that this Ekāntika Dharma was communicated to Arjuna at the beginning of the war. The allusion is, no doubt, to the *Bhagavad-Gītā* which contains the earliest philosophical exposition of this system. The composition of this work may be referred to the period 400-200 B.C. It is not only the most popular religious work, but is generally regarded as forming the basis of popular Hinduism. But that it truly represents the moderate revolution heralded by the Bhāgavatas, as noted above, will be apparent to anybody who carefully considers its deprecatory, if not hostile, attitude towards the Vedas as an infallible authority, and its liberal views about the caste system and sacrificial performances. At the same time, it is equally clear that it was more conservative in character than either Buddhism or Jainism, and its protest against the accepted views and beliefs is less thoroughgoing. As regards ideas of life and ethical principles, there is a striking resemblance between Buddhism and the *Gītā*, but by discountenancing the ascetic life and the negative attitude of the Buddhists towards metaphysical doctrines, the *Gītā* showed its greater adherence to the old orthodox creed.

It was thus a comparatively easy task to win over this school to the orthodox side. This was effected first by regarding Vāsudeva as an *avatāra* or incarnation of the Vedic god Viṣṇu, and secondly by the identification of Vāsudeva with Nārāyaṇa who came to be regarded as the supreme Being in the later Brāhmaṇical period. It is worthy of note that the first point was not generally conceded, and the second had not taken place at all, when the *Bhagavad-Gītā* was composed. Viṣṇu grew to be the supreme God in the epic age, and the identification of Vāsudeva with Nārāyaṇa and Viṣṇu completed the transformation of the Bhāgavata religion as the great religion of the orthodox Hindus.

Two developments of the Bhāgavata religion, as promulgated in the *Bhagavad-Gītā*, require special notice. The first is the Pāñcarātra system which consists of the worship of Vāsudeva in his fourfold *vyūha* or form. According to this doctrine, Vāsudeva created from himself Saṅkarṣaṇa, Pradyumna, and Aniruddha. Evidently all these Yādava heroes (to which list Sāmba was added later) were deified along with Vāsudeva. This is not mentioned in the *Gītā,* but forms a characteristic element of the Bhāgavata school. It appears to have been evolved shortly after the *Bhagavad-Gītā* was composed, and probably not much later than second century B.C.

The second development is the story of Kṛṣṇa as a cowherd boy, which was perhaps added in the early centuries of the Christian era. There are reasons to believe that the idea was originally based upon the Viṣṇu legends in the Vedic literature and subsequently developed by tribes like the Ābhīras. It must be noted, however, that one important element, that of Rādhā, the chief beloved of the cowherd Kṛṣṇa, was not added till a considerably later date.

(4) The date and nature of the two epics, the *Rāmāyaṇa* and the *Mahābhārata,* are uncertain, and different views have been expressed on this subject. But it is unnecessary to dwell upon them here. It will suffice to state that the *Mahābhārata* was not the product of any one age or any one author, and from a small nucleus it grew by gradual additions to a voluminous cyclopaedia of knowledge. The nucleus of the epic must be placed about the fifth century B.C., if not even earlier, and the composition of the present text may be placed in the fourth century A.D. The epic, which covers a wide period from *c.* 400 B.C. to A.D. 400, faithfully reflects the religio-philosophic spirit of the age. The development of this popular epic followed closely the lines of the development of religious thoughts, and an originally heroic poem was, on account of its popularity, converted into a Brāhmaṇical work and used as a highly valuable means of religious and moral propaganda among the masses.

The *Rāmāyaṇa,* like the *Mahābhārata,* must have been originally a heroic ballad with a tribal hero Rāma as its centre. It must have attained its present form long before the last additions were made in the *Mahābhārata,* for not only the complete Rāma story, but even the epic *Rāmāyaṇa* is known to the latter. The beginnings of the *Rāmāyaṇa* may be placed about the same time as those of the *Mahābhārata.* The two epics show a striking resemblance in style, metre, and general views of religion and society.

The first and the last Book of the *Rāmāyaṇa* are later additions. The bulk, consisting of Books II-VI, represents Rāma as an ideal hero. In Books I and VII, however, Rāma is made an *avatāra* or incarnation of Viṣṇu, and the epic poem is transformed into a Vaiṣṇava text. The reference to the Greeks, Parthians, and Śakas shows that these Books cannot be earlier than the second century B.C.

It is impossible to exaggerate the value of the two epics in popularizing the new theistic religions of Śaivism and Vaiṣṇavism and giving a new turn altogether to the popular forms of Hinduism.

(5) Buddhism and Jainism remained outside the pale of orthodoxy, not so much on account of their religious and philosophical views, as of their steady refusal to recognize the sanctity of the Vedas as an infallible authority and their disregard of the system of caste.

As in the case of the Bhāgavata and Śaiva sects, perhaps some time elapsed after the death of Gautama Buddha and Mahāvīra before their followers organized themselves into regular sects with a systematic philosophy and a body of codified doctrines. Certain it is that none of them wielded considerable power and influence before the end of the fourth or the beginning of the third century B.C.

The patronage of the Nanda kings and the emperor Candragupta Maurya gave an impetus to the Jaina religion. During the reign of the latter (*c.* 321-296 B.C.), it spread nearly over the whole of India ; but the period of this greatest expansion was also marked by the beginning of that schism which ultimately (first century A.D.) divided the Jains into two rival sects known as the Digambaras and the Śvetāmbaras. The existing canonical literature of the Jains, called Siddhāntas, was drawn up in a council at Pāṭaliputra in the beginning of the third century B.C. and subsequently revised in another council at Valabhī in the fifth or the beginning of the sixth century A.D. The canon is, however, accepted only by the Śvetāmbaras. The Digambaras, who took no part in the council at Pāṭaliputra, deny their authenticity and believe that the real canon is lost.

Buddhism first obtained a dominant position in India under the patronage of the great emperor Aśoka (*c.* 273-236 B.C.), the grandson of Candragupta. It is now a matter of common knowledge that by his missionary propaganda Buddhism not only spread all over India, but even far outside its boundaries, and ultimately became a world-religion, a position which it even now occupies, as its votaries number about one-third of the entire human race.

With the dominance of Buddhism, Jainism lost its stronghold in eastern India, but found a secure shelter in the south and west, with powerful centres at Mathurā and Ujjayinī in the north. Buddhism rapidly spread in all corners of India and planted its outposts in Tibet, Ceylon, and Burma, as well as in Western, Central, and South-East Asia. By the first century A.D., it had reached China ; and from China it ultimately penetrated into Korea and Japan. The foreign races like the Greeks and the Scythians who invaded India during 200 B.C. to A.D. 100 largely adopted this faith.

The adoption of Buddhism by diverse races with varying types and grades of civilization could not but exert a great influence upon its subsequent history. New tendencies are noticeable since the time of Aśoka, which ultimately took a definite shape in the time of Kaniṣka (*c.* first century A.D.). The old and new doctrines are known respectively as Hīnayāna and Mahāyāna. The transition was so gradual that one almost imperceptibly led to the other. Yet some fundamental differences can be easily discerned between the early doctrines of Buddhism, as formulated in the Pali canon (fourth and third century B.C.), and the principles of Mahāyāna in its fully developed form, as expounded in its Sanskrit texts. The Hīnayānist had no concern for God, and regarded Buddha as a perfect man whose precepts and examples were to be followed by each individual for reaching *nirvāṇa* or freedom from bondage, and cessation of existence, practically annihilation. Mahāyānism regarded Buddha as a god, and evolved an elaborate metaphysics involving a pantheon of gods and goddesses. Devotion to Buddha and worship of his images formed a more essential part than the pursuit of an arduous life of morality. The ideal is not the state of an Arhat, who reaches the perfect state through his own powers, but that of a Bodhisattva, who stops short of Arhatship in order to help struggling humanity on the path to salvation. The Hīnayāna ideal is more or less egoistic, whereas the Mahāyānists are inspired by love for fellow-beings, and their goal is not annihilation, but positive bliss. Consciously or unconsciously the Mahāyāna was making a near approach to theistic systems.

There is little doubt that the transformation of Buddhism is partially due to the impact of the rude uncivilized races that adopted Buddhism. The need of presenting the religion in a form which could easily appeal to their heart and mind could not but alter its character, nor could these races embrace Buddhism without introducing into it many of their superstitious rites and practices. The Mahāyāna had to tolerate them and developed a flexible adaptability which characterized it throughout its history. This attitude brought it great popularity and enabled it to stride in triumph across the whole continent of Asia.

We have some means of testing the relative strength of the different religious sects in India during the period 300 B.C. to A.D. 300. More than fifteen hundred inscriptions belonging to this period have been discovered so far. Of these, not even fifty belong to the religious sects other than Buddhism and Jainism. The proportion should not be taken as an exact measure of the relative strength and popularity of the orthodox and heterodox doctrines, because accident must have played a great part in the preservation and destruction of records, and some of the disparity may be due to the habit of engraving numerous records on religious structures, which was more marked in one sect than in another. But even making due allowance for all these factors, no doubt can remain of the preponderating influence of the two heterodox religious sects during the period 300 B.C. to A.D. 300. This view is further strengthened by the fact that if we take the epigraphic records for the five centuries following A.D. 300, we find that the position had almost entirely been reversed, and the orthodox sects like Vaiṣṇavism and Śaivism now occupy the position of dominance which had hitherto been enjoyed by their heterodox rivals.

In conclusion, the fact must be emphasized that in addition to the main religious sects mentioned above, there were a large number of minor ones such as the Ājīvikas, and reference is made to worshippers of not only divine or semi-divine beings like Pūrṇabhadra, Maṇibhadra, Candra, Sūrya, *gandharvas*, etc., but also of animals like elephant, horse, cow, dog, and crow.

IV. THE PAURĀṆIC AGE (C. A.D. 300-1200)

The fourth century A.D. may be regarded as a turning-point in the religious history of India. Since that date we find the gradual dominance of Brāhmaṇical religion and the steady decline of Buddhism and Jainism. By the twelfth century A.D., Buddhism, as an independent sect, had well-nigh vanished from India, while Jainism was almost reduced to the position of a local sect in western India.

The most important characteristic features of the religio-philosophic culture of the period may be studied under the following heads:

(1) Downfall of Buddhism in India.
(2) Decline of Jainism.
(3) Reconciliation of Vedic faith with sectarianism, and the evolution of synthetic Hinduism.
(4) History of Śaivism, Śāktism, Vaiṣṇavism, and minor religious sects and popular beliefs.
(5) Introduction of new religions.

Before we proceed to discuss these in detail, a few general observations may be made regarding the religious development of the period.

In the first place, it appears from a study of the history of the period that the fortunes of religions depend to no small extent upon the patronage of royal families. At the beginning of the period, the Guptas were the leading power, and for two centuries they dominated over nearly the whole of northern India. They were powerful adherents of the Bhāgavata sect, and this undoubtedly was the main factor in the history of its rapid progress and development at the cost of Buddhism. Of the dynasties that succeeded the Guptas in various parts of northern India, the later Guptas, the Pratīhāras, the Candellas, the Maukharis, the Kalacuris, the Valabhīs, and the Varman kings of Kāmarūpa were either Vaiṣṇavas or Śaivas. The Pālas of Bengal were patrons of Buddhism, but their successors, the Senas, were Śaivas and Vaiṣṇavas. It must be mentioned, however, that the line of difference between Śaivism and Vaiṣṇavism was not very marked, and the official records of the same dynasty bear invocation to either Śiva or Viṣṇu. We have also examples of individual kings like Harṣavardhana, who, although officially professing Śaivism, was strongly inclined towards Buddhism as Hiuen-Tsang informs us. Again, in the same family, different kings belonged to different sects, the most typical example being that of Harṣavardhana, the kings of which were devotees of the Sun-god, Buddha, and Śiva.

In the Deccan, the early Cālukya kings were patrons of Jainism, but the Brāhmaṇical religions, both orthodox and sectarian, flourished under the later kings. The Rāṣṭrakūṭa dynasty also professed Brāhmaṇical religion, though some of the kings patronized Jainism.

In the extreme south, Jainism was patronized by the early Pallavas and Hoysaḷas, but the later Pallavas were Śaivas and the later Hoysaḷas most ardent devotees of Vaiṣṇavism.

This brief, though very incomplete, historical survey would show the gradual loss of royal patronage suffered by both the Jains and the Buddhists.

Secondly, we must note the rise of a debased element in the religions of the day which is generally, though not perhaps very accurately, referred to as Tāntricism. Though more closely associated with the Śākta sect, to be noted later, some of its characteristics such as mystic magical beliefs, degraded erotic practices, and extreme veneration for the *guru*—sometimes leading to gross indecency and lax morality—are common features to be observed in greater or lesser degree in all the principal religions of the time, except Jainism.

Thirdly, we may note that the worship of images of gods, with elaborate rituals and erection of large temples for them, becomes a characteristic feature of the religions of the period.

We may now proceed to discuss in detail the five characteristic features of the period noted above.

DOWNFALL OF BUDDHISM

The most potent cause of the decline of Buddhism in India was the loss of royal patronage. In northern India, the patronage of Harṣavardhana and the Pāla emperors gave a long lease of life to Buddhism, but with those notable exceptions the other royal families were staunch adherents of the Brāhmaṇical sects. The passing away of the Pālas in the twelfth century A.D. and the destruction of the Buddhist monasteries by the Islamic invaders dealt the final death-blow to Buddhism. The monasteries were the chief strongholds of Buddhism, while the strength of the Jains lay rather in the mass of lay followers. Hence Jainism survived the downfall of its monasteries, while Buddhism perished in its ruins.

The decline of royal patronage was perhaps as much a cause, as the result, of the growing unpopularity of Buddhism. The chief cause of this unpopularity was the development of the Tāntric beliefs and rituals which we have noted above. Whatever might have been the original ideal behind it, some of the debased forms which are met with from the seventh century onwards can only be regarded as a travesty of Buddhism. Even gross sensuality and carnal passions of man found a religious sanction in some tenets of these schools, and the result was a looseness of sexual morality masquerading in the name of religion. It would be, of course, untrue to say that purer forms of Buddhism did not flourish at the period. But the masses naturally followed what was more suited to their tastes, and their unbridled licentiousness brought odium upon the whole religion and hastened its decline and downfall.

In addition to these causes, another powerful factor was working to the same end. The Mahāyāna form of Buddhism, as we have seen before, made a very near approach to the theistic system. Adaptability was always a great characteristic of Buddhism, and its close *rapprochement* to Brāhmaṇical religion was dangerous to its separate existence. The leaders of the Brāhmaṇical religion were not yet too rigid and conservative to let slip any opportunity of capturing the great stronghold of a powerful rival. As in old days Vaiṣṇavism was won over by the acceptance of Kṛṣṇa as an *avatāra* of Viṣṇu, so about a thousand years later Buddha was regarded as another *avatāra* of the same God. This well-conceived and bold stroke of olicy cut the ground from under the feet of Buddhism which was already stetdily losing ground, and the ultimate result was the complete effacement of Buddhism from India as a separate sect.

DECLINE OF JAINISM

Jainism, alone of all religions, was free from the Tāntric development. The rigid conservatism, to which it owed this fortune, however, paved the way for its decline, as it failed to keep abreast with the changing spirit of the times. The new rituals and practices of Vaiṣṇavism, Śaivism, and other sects proved too alluring, and gradually Jainism lost its importance in Mysore and Mahārāṣṭra, where it had exercised a dominant influence for nearly a thousand years. Jainism has steadily maintained its old character and has chosen to die rather than surrender its essentials. Fortunately it still maintains its hold among a very influential section of the community in western India. This may partly be due to the fact that it preserved some essential Hindu practices like caste and winked at the worship of some popular deities like Gaṇeśa.

EVOLUTION OF SYNTHETIC HINDUISM

With the decline of Buddhism and Jainism, the Brāhmaṇical religion gradually rose into importance. But there was no homogeneity in it. It included orthodox Brāhmaṇism, i.e. the remnant of the old Vedic cult, and the different sectarian religions, notably Śaivism, Śāktism, and Vaiṣṇavism. Although these were admitted within the orthodox fold, they still retained their essential characteristics and formed distinct entities.

At the very beginning of the period, we notice a systematization of their faiths and beliefs in a number of texts, known as Purāṇas and Smṛtis. The Smṛtis preserve a link with the old Gṛhya-Sūtras, describing the Vedic rituals and sacrifices. The Purāṇas present the theology of the new sects with the old philosophical and cosmogonical beliefs in the background.

The orthodox Vedic religion was patronized by the Pallavas, Vākāṭakas, the Bhagadatta dynasty of Kāmarūpa (Assam), and other royal dynasties, and the inscriptions of the period contain frequent references to Vedic cults and sacrifices. These are, however, not unoften combined with pure sectarian worship.

Indeed, one of the most important traits of the Brāhmaṇical religion of this period is this spirit of reconciliation and harmony between orthodox and sectarian forms. Its most notable expression is to be found in the theological conception of the Trimūrti, i.e. the manifestation of the supreme God in three forms of Brahmā, Viṣṇu, and Śiva—Brahmā, the creator, being undoubtedly a pale reflex of the Upaniṣadic Brahman. But the attempt cannot be regarded as a great success, for Brahmā never gained an ascendancy comparable to that of Śiva or Viṣṇu, and the different sects often conceived the Trimūrti as really the three manifestations of their own sectarian god, whom they regarded as Brahman or Absolute. Still the spirit of reconciliation bore significant results. Henceforth the Hindus may be divided broadly into two classes, viz. (1) extreme sectarians who confined their devotion and worship almost exclusively to their sectarian deity like Viṣṇu, Śiva, Śakti, etc.; and (2) general followers of the Brāhmaṇical religion who revered and worshipped all these and other gods, even though they might have been specially attached to one sectarian deity, and also followed some of the important Vedic rituals and practices. Thus the Smārtas prescribed the regular worship of the five gods Viṣṇu, Śiva, Durgā, Sūrya, and Gaṇeśa, while the rest of the Hindu pantheon was also freely worshipped by many. The *samuccaya* doctrine lays down that a Hindu, even when seeking Brahman, must perform his ordinary duties, and should have a knowledge of the Karma-Mīmāṁsā as well as the Vedānta. The use of the sacred thread and performance of the *gāyatrī* and other rituals by the sectarians may be ascribed to this spirit.

A further step towards the reconciliation of the different sects may be traced in the attempt to establish the identity of Viṣṇu and Śiva, such as we find in the *Skanda Upaniṣad*. The image of Hari-Hara, like that of Ardhanārīśvara (Śiva-Pārvatī), is a visible symbol of this doctrine. There is hardly any doubt that, in spite of the existence of the extreme sectarians who would not tolerate any god other than their own, the general mass of Hindus, even today, while professing one sect or other, have a general reverence for all the Hindu gods. The epigraphical records prove that this has been the case throughout the period under review.

Lastly, there was an attempt to prove that the six systems of Hindu philosophy are not really opposed to each other, but they all proclaim the same eternal Truth. This view is first met with in *Prabodha-candrodaya*, an allegorical Sanskrit drama written in the court of the Candella king Kīrtivarman in the latter half of the eleventh century A.D. In a famous scene in this drama, there is a dispute between the Buddhists, Jains, and followers of other heterodox sects on the one side, and the Vaiṣṇavas, Śaivas, and Sauras, aided by the six schools of philosophy, on the other. The basic unity of orthodox Hinduism as against the heterodox sects, which is so vividly brought into prominence in this scene, forms a feature of Hinduism up to the present. Vijñāna Bhikṣu, a Sāṁkhya philosopher of the sixteenth century, also proclaims the essential unity of the six systems of philosophy.

HISTORY OF THE DIFFERENT RELIGIOUS SECTS

It now remains for us to trace the fortunes of the two great sectarian theistic systems, Śaivism and Vaiṣṇavism, together with Śāktism and other minor religious sects and popular beliefs from the fourth century A.D. onwards. At the very beginning of the period, we notice a systematization of their faiths and beliefs in the Purāṇas. These texts are many in number, and while some like *Vāyu, Viṣṇu, Matsya, Mārkaṇḍeya, Bhāgavata,* and *Brahmāṇḍa Purāṇas* are really old, others were added in much later times. These Purāṇas present the two theistic (and also other sectarian) beliefs in a complete form, a form which they have retained till today.

ŚAIVISM

The Pāśupata sect continued to flourish during this period. Hiuen-Tsang and Bāṇa Bhaṭṭa, both belonging to the seventh century A.D., refer to it as one of the prominent religious sects of the time.

In addition to the Purāṇas such as *Vāyu, Liṅga, Kūrma,* etc., the Śaiva theism was expounded in the Āgamas. There are twenty-eight of these manuals, each of which has got a number of Upāgamas, the total number of texts reaching to about 200. The Āgamas were composed before the seventh century A.D., and their dualistic teaching formed the foundation of a new Śaiva school which is usually referred to as Āgamic Śaivism. The Advaita philosophy of Śaṅkara gave a new turn to Śaivism. A distinct school flourished in Kashmir, about the middle of the ninth century A.D., mainly under the influence of Śaṅkara's philosophy, and substituted the Advaita philosophy for the dualistic teachings of the Āgamas.

There was a great upsurge of Śaivism in South India, which was mainly due to the devotional poems of Nāyanmārs (Śaiva saints), written in Tamil. These are divided into eleven collections which, together with the Tamil Purāṇa called *Periya Purāṇam,* constitute the sacred literature of the saints and form the foundation of Tamil Śaivism. The first seven collections, known as *Devāram,* composed by the saints Sambandar, his older contemporary Appar, and Sundarar, all of whom flourished in the seventh century A.D. or shortly thereafter, are regarded as equivalent to the Vedas and are sung along with Vedic hymns in certain religious processions. The eighth collection, *Tiruvācakam* of Māṇikkavācagar, occupies the foremost place in Śaiva literature. This, together with the tenth collection *Tirumandiram* of Tirumūlar, reflects the theology of the Āgamas, and both are masterpieces of poetic composition. The patronage of the later Pallava kings (from sixth century A.D.) and the mighty Coḷa emperors (tenth century A.D.) gave a great impetus to Śaivism in the Draviḍa country.

A further development of Tamil Śaivism took place in the thirteenth and fourteenth centuries A.D., perhaps even a little earlier. This was the rise of Śaiva Siddhānta. The Āgamas were now replaced by the fourteen Siddhānta-śāstras, which laid the foundation of this new system.

An influential and very powerful Śaiva sect, known as the Vīraśaivas or Liṅgāyatas rose in the Karṇāṭaka and Mahārāṣṭra countries. The early history of the sect is obscure, but it was most probably founded, or at least brought into prominence, by Basava, the Brāhmaṇa prime minister of Bijjaḷa who had usurped the Cālukya throne about A.D. 1160. This new sect flourished at the cost of Jainism and Buddhism and was the main cause of their decay in the Deccan and Kannada districts, which constitute now its main stronghold.

The Vīraśaivas have several peculiar characteristics. They give great prominence to the monasteries. 'In every Liṅgāyata village there is a monastery, and every Liṅgāyata must belong to a monastery and have a *guru* ; he need not visit a temple at all.' 'The members of the sect worship Śiva in his phallic form, reject the authority of the Vedas, disbelieve in the doctrine of rebirth, object to child-marriage, approve of the remarriage of widows, and cherish an intense aversion to the Brāhmaṇas.'

ŚĀKTISM

The cult of Śakti, consort of Śiva, attained a great predominance during this period. It is based upon the Sāṁkhya philosophy, according to which Spirit or Puruṣa (here identified with Śiva) is inactive, while Prakṛti (identified with Śakti) is productive and the universal material cause. Hence Śakti is in a sense superior to Śiva.

The system lays stress on the inherent power of sounds and the presence, in the human body, of a large number of minute channels or threads of occult force (*nāḍī*) and six great centres of that force (*cakra*), described as so many lotuses, one above the other. Hence arise the supernatural powers of *mantras* or mystic syllables such as *hrīṁ, huṁ, phaṭ*, etc., and the working of miracles by mystic forms of *yoga*. Besides, the Śāktas also believe in the magic power of diagrams (*yantra*) and ritualistic gestures made with fingers (*mudrā*).

The worship of the goddess Śakti was accompanied with sacrifices of animals and occasionally also human beings. But the most characteristic feature of the cult was the *cakra-pūjā*, i.e. circle worship in which an equal number of men and women sit round a circle and, uttering mystic *mantras*, partake of the *pañcatattva* consisting of five elements, viz. wine, meat, fish, parched grain, and sex. Many sorcerous practices formed a part of the cult, and a picture of this is given in the Sanskrit drama *Mālatī-Mādhava*. Detailed instructions of these practices are given in the texts known as Tantras. Hence Tāntricism is used as a general name for similar rituals which are found in many religious sects. The Śaiva Kāpālikas and Kālāmukhas, for example, followed similar rituals and practices, and they are found associated with the worship of many other goddesses.

Taken at its best, the Tāntric doctrine, both in Brāhmaṇical religions and Buddhism, is a philosophy, according to which the absolute is associated with a dynamic principle for the origination of the universe and the different deities can be located in the different parts of the human body (*nyāsa*) by means of a form of *yoga*. By worshipping Śakti, Prajñā (Mahāyānist goddess), or other goddesses, in the manner indicated above, it seeks to attain, in a supernatural manner, and in an incredibly short time, objects of either material nature (wealth, longevity, invulnerability, etc.) or spiritual character (power of evoking Buddha or union with some divinity even in this life). Some Tantras, however, at their worst, uphold theories and practices which are revolting and horrible.

VAIṢṆAVISM

We have noted above the three basic elements of Vaiṣṇavism, viz. the original Bhāgavata doctrine, the Pāñcarātra system, and the Gopāla (cowherd) -kṛṣṇa saga, culminating in the Rādhā-Kṛṣṇa cult. During the period under review the Pāñcarātra first comes into prominent notice and is later superseded by the third element.

The most important development of the system is the growth of Pāñcarātra Saṁhitās which give a complete exposition of the faiths, beliefs, and practices of the Vaiṣṇavas. The traditional number of these Saṁhitās is 108, but nearly double that number of texts are named. Their dates are uncertain, but may be placed between A.D. 600 and 800. They show a considerable influence of the Tāntric element and lay stress on the Śakti of Viṣṇu. Otherwise, they show a normal development of the teaching formulated in the Nārāyaṇīya section of the *Mahābhārata,* noted above.

But the Pāñcarātra system shows from the beginning the influence of the third element. The *Viṣṇu Purāṇa,* which is an important text of the system, contains the detailed story of cowherd Kṛṣṇa and his youthful sports. The *Bhāgavata Purāṇa* heralds a new departure. It concentrates its attention almost solely on the cowherd-life of Kṛṣṇa and dwells specially on his amorous sports with the *gopīs* which are described here in all their details, while in the life of Kṛṣṇa such as we find in the *Harivaṁśa* and *Viṣṇu Purāṇa* they are hardly noticed at all. But the most distinguishing feature of the *Bhāgavata Purāṇa* is the exalted tone of *bhakti* or devotion which is displayed throughout the work. The fervent emotionalism which characterizes mediaeval Vaiṣṇavism has its origin in this really great work.

The date of the *Bhāgavata Purāṇa* is uncertain, but it is generally regarded as a late work. The various dates suggested range from the seventh to the ninth century A.D. It must be noted, however, that even the *Bhāgavata Purāṇa* does not mention Rādhā, though it undoubtedly contained elements which might easily give rise to this cult. For, according to it, among the *gopīs* there was one who was the special favourite of Kṛṣṇa. But it is difficult to say when this Rādhā cult actually came into being. It was a well-known thing in Bengal by the time of Jayadeva, the Bengali poet, who composed his immortal *Gīta-Govinda* in the court of Lakṣmaṇa Sena during the last quarter of the twelfth century A.D. Rādhā is mentioned in a verse quoted in the *Dhvanyāloka* (*c.* A.D. 850) and in the *Gopālatāpanī Upaniṣad* and *Brahmavaivarta Purāṇa*. But the dates of the last two works are not known, and they may not be earlier than the eleventh century A.D. A ruined temple, discovered at Paharpur in Bengal, contains sculptured representations of Kṛṣṇa's life, and in one of these, Kṛṣṇa is accompanied by a female. This has been taken to be a representation of Kṛṣṇa and Rādhā, but there is no positive evidence in support of it. The date of the temple is also uncertain, but it may belong to the sixth or seventh century A.D. The name of Rādhā occurs in Hāla's *Saptaśatī*, and if the verse is really as old as the time of Hāla, it furnishes the solitary evidence of the prevalence of the cult in the early centuries of the Christian era.

It is generally believed that the *Bhāgavata Purāṇa* was written in South India. Whether this is true or not, there is no doubt that the pure devotional element of Vaiṣṇavism flourished in the Tamil country. The most remarkable specimen of this is contained in the songs of the famous Āḷvārs, the Vaiṣṇava counterpart of the Śaiva Nāyanmārs, mentioned above. Their number is usually reckoned as twelve, and although their dates are uncertain, they may be all placed between the fifth and ninth centuries A.D. Their devotional songs, called *Prabandham*, written mostly in Tamil, are known as the Vaiṣṇava Veda, and their images are worshipped along with those of Viṣṇu.

The next great landmark in the history of Tamil Vaiṣṇavism is the rise of a school of philosophers known as Ācāryas. Nāthamuni, the first of these, flourished about the end of the tenth or the beginning of the eleventh century A.D. He organized the Śrī-Vaiṣṇavas, and popularized the cult among the masses by collecting the songs of the Āḷvārs, setting them to Dravidian music, and having them regularly sung in the temples. But he was also a great theologian, and his school took up the task of giving a philosophical background to the Vaiṣṇava theories and creeds. Nāthamuni was followed by three Ācāryas, of whom the last, his grandson Yāmunācārya, was a great scholar.

Yāmunācārya was succeeded by the famous Rāmānuja (eleventh century A.D.). His great task was to put the religion on a secure philosophical basis. The great Śaṅkarācārya's doctrine of monism (Advaitavāda) was a direct challenge to the cult of *bhakti*. If there is only one absolute Spirit, and all else is unreal, there is no scope for devotion to the supreme God by the individual, for the two are really one and the same. Rāmānuja set up against it a full and critical exposition of the Viśiṣṭādvaitavāda or qualified monism, first propounded by Yāmunācārya. It was based upon the Upaniṣads and the *Brahma-Sūtra*, and construed the individual soul as an attribute of the supreme Soul, but distinct from it. The latter dwells in the individual heart and can therefore be an object of devotion. Rāmānuja follows closely the tenets of the *Bhagavad-Gītā* in describing the mode of salvation, but his *bhakti* is not so much an unbounded love as a continuous meditation or *upāsanā* prescribed in the Upaniṣads. Both in his philosophy and general practices, Rāmānuja follows the orthodox Brāhmaṇism. But his sect, known as the Śrī-Vaiṣṇavas or Śrī-sampradāya, has nothing to do with Gopāla-kṛṣṇa, i.e. Kṛṣṇa as a cowherd boy. On the other hand, he recognizes Śrī (Lakṣmī), Bhū (Earth), and Līlā (Sport) as the consorts of Viṣṇu.

The philosophy of Rāmānuja was further developed by Madhva or Ānanda Tīrtha (thirteenth century A.D.), the founder of another sect. He conceived God as altogether distinct from the individual spirit. He travelled all over India, fighting the philosophical doctrines of Śaṅkara and establishing the Vaiṣṇava creed on a definite dualistic basis.

Rāmānuja lived his early life in Kāñcī, while Madhva's activities were chiefly confined to the western or Malabar coast. But in his old age Rāmānuja was forced by the persecution of the Śaiva Coḷa king to take shelter with the Hoysaḷa king Viṣṇuvardhana of Dorasamudra (Mysore). The latter adopted Vaiṣṇavism, and his patronage counted a great deal for the success of the faith.

Rāmānuja had followed more or less Vāsudevism of the old Pāñcarātra system, recognizing Vāsudeva with his four *vyūhas*, and his identity with Viṣṇu and Nārāyaṇa. But Madhva ignored Vāsudeva and his *vyūhas* and referred to the supreme Spirit mostly as Viṣṇu. Thus a general Vaiṣṇavism took the place of the old Bhāgavata school.

The southern Vaiṣṇavism laid little stress on the cowherd element of Kṛṣṇa and altogether ignored Rādhā. Far different, however, was the case with Vaiṣṇavism in northern India, which was first put on a philosophic basis by Nimbārka who flourished after Rāmānuja, probably in the twelfth century A.D. His philosophy is a compromise between those of Rāmānuja and Madhva, as he believes God to be both identical with, and distinct from, the individual spirit. But his chief difference from his predecessor Rāmānuja lies in substituting the old and pure *bhakti* (devotion) for *upāsanā* (meditation), and giving prominence to the elements of Kṛṣṇa and Rādhā. Born in the family of a Tailaṅga Brāhmaṇa in the South (perhaps Bellary District), Nimbārka lived in Vṛndāvana (near Mathurā) and his sect, known as Sanaka-sampradāya, flourishes in northern India.

According to Nimbārka, Rādhā was the eternal consort of Viṣṇu and was incarnated like him in Vṛndāvana. There is also a suggestion, though not a clear statement, that she became the wife of her lord. A further progress of the Rādhā cult is found in Jayadeva's *Gīta-Govinda,* where Rādhā is the mistress and not the wife of Kṛṣṇa.

Among other sects stressing the worship of Rādhā may be mentioned the followers of Viṣṇusvāmin, about whom, however, very little is known. He closely follows the system of Madhva, but introduces the Rādhā element. He may have preceded Nimbārka.

It may be noted that Nimbārka worshipped only Kṛṣṇa and his consort to the exclusion of other gods. He thus discarded the *samuccaya* doctrine followed by the Śrī-Vaiṣṇavas, Mādhvas, Viṣṇusvāmins, and generally by all the Bhāgavatas, and became a purely sectarian Vaiṣṇava.

MINOR RELIGIOUS SECTS AND POPULAR BELIEFS

In addition to the main sects hitherto described, there were during the period under review minor sects worshipping various other deities. Most of these are associated with either Śiva or Viṣṇu. Thus Durgā, Gaṇapati, and Skanda (Kārttika), the consort and sons of Śiva, were regularly worshipped under various names, and each had an organized following and a sectarian literature. Similarly there were sects worshipping the Narasiṁha and Rāma incarnations of Viṣṇu.

The worship of Dharma was very much prevalent in Bengal and had an important literature. It is traced to a Buddhist origin, the second member of the Buddhist *triratna* (Buddha, Dharma, and Saṅgha) being converted to a Hindu god.

Far greater importance attaches to the sects connected with the worship of Brahmā and Sūrya. Brahmā, though less important than Viṣṇu or Śiva, was the god of a sect which is referred to in the *Mārkaṇḍeya Purāṇa* and the *Padma Purāṇa.* There is a famous temple of Brahmā in Puṣkara, near Ajmer.

Of the vast Vedic pantheon, Sūrya alone formed the god of a particular sect, and many temples were erected for his worship. This seems to be due to three reasons. In the first place the *gāyatrī-mantra,* daily repeated by the Brāhmaṇas, kept alive the memory of the Sun-god. Secondly, the orb of the sun being daily visible, the idea of his worship could not be dropped altogether. Further, the Magis of Persia brought a cult of the sun into India about the third century of the Christian era. The two streams mingled and saved the Sun-god from the fate of the other Vedic deities. Many inscriptions dating from the Gupta period refer to the worship of the Sun-god, and big temples were erected in his honour.

Outside the circle of sectarian gods mentioned above, there were quite a large number of popular deities who claimed devotion and worship from a clientele which, though not numerically insignificant, are not known to have been organized into sects. Among these may be mentioned Śrī and Lakṣmī (originally regarded as separate personalities), Gaṅgā, Yamunā, Sarasvatī, Ṣaṣṭhī, Śītalā, the *dikpālas* (especially Yama, Varuṇa, Kubera, and Agni), and *navagrahas* (Rāhu, Ketu, and seven others whose names correspond to the week days).

Reference may also be made to semi-divine beings like *yakṣas, nāgas, gandharvas, vidyādharas,* and *apsarasas,* who had their iconic forms like the popular deities mentioned above.

It is a notable thing that the worship of, and veneration for, such multiplicity of deities may be traced to a very early period and have persisted throughout the ages. Along with these, many popular beliefs, such as the sanctity of certain localities, efficacy of pilgrimage, recitation of sacred texts, and many religious or semi-religious vows, fairs, and festivals, have formed a substantial part of the total content of religion in the minds of the masses.

INTRODUCTION OF NEW RELIGIONS

Two new religious faiths, Christianity and Zoroastrianism, were established in India during the period under review. There are some grounds for believing that there were small Christian communities in India as early as second century A.D. But the evidence in favour of it is not quite satisfactory and, in any case, our knowledge about them is very vague and scanty. It appears from the account of Cosmas, surnamed Indicopleustes (the Indian voyager), that small Christian communities were settled in India by the sixth century A.D. These were confined to its western coast and were probably Nestorians under the jurisdiction of the Church in Persia. Christianity soon spread to the Coromandel coast, but it never came to be an important element before the establishment of political authority in India by the Christian powers of Europe.

The small Parsi community in India represents the last waves of migration of the followers of Zarathushtra from their homeland in Persia after its conquest by the Muslim Arabs. Successive batches of them, forced to leave their country, found, after some wanderings, a safe refuge in India. The first of these ultimately settled at Sanjan, about 90 miles north of Bombay, probably in the tenth century A.D. Although numerically very small, the Parsis in India are almost the only surviving members of a great religious faith, and have distinguished themselves in many fields of activity, particularly politics, trade, industry, and commerce.

The Jews of Cochin, who form a small community, can be traced back to the end of the seventh century A.D., when they fled from persecutions in Arabia and Persia and migrated to the tolerant religious climate of India,

V. THE MUSLIM PERIOD (C. A.D. 1200-1757)

The most outstanding feature of the religious development during the period under review was the establishment of a powerful Muslim community on a permanent footing all over India.

For the first time in Indian history Hinduism was confronted with an alien faith which kept severely aloof and derived its strength not only from its political dominance, but also from the gradually increasing number of its followers. It was not only alien, but militant in character, and radically differed in some of its fundamental aspects from Hinduism. The most important of these were the inherent fanatical hatred of Islam towards Hindu temples and images, and of Hinduism towards the social usages and customs of the Muslims, particularly the absence of caste and the eating of beef. The fury and iconoclastic zeal with which the Muslims demolished the temples, images, and other religious symbols of the Hindus created a gulf between the two which could never be bridged, and the rigid social customs and usages of the Hindus raised an impassable barrier between the two. The result has been that they have not, unlike other foreign invaders who preceded them, merged with the Hindus, and though the two have lived together for seven hundred years, even today they exist as two separate and distinct communities.

It would, however, be a mistake to suppose that these two communities lived in two water-tight compartments. For while Islam was a proselytizing religion and kept its doors wide open for converts, Hinduism had a hundred doors for exit and none for entrance. The consequence was that the Hindu rank was considerably thinned by conversion on a large scale, which added to a handful of foreign Muslims hundreds of times their number.

Although differing in fundamental religious and social ideas, it was inevitable that two powerful communities living side by side would exercise some amount of influence over each other, both in respect of higher ideals which would concern only a few, as well as of popular beliefs, observances, and practices which would affect the common people at large. Instances are not wanting to show that such influence was exercised. But before considering the question, we must take note of the progress of Hinduism during the period under review.

NEW PHASES OF THE BHAKTI CULT

Most of the features of Hinduism noted above continued, but though no noticeable difference marks the Śaiva, Śākta, and other minor religious sects, the Vaiṣṇava cult of Kṛṣṇa and Rādhā showed new and remarkable tendencies, no doubt influenced by the *Padma* and the *Brahmavaivarta Purāṇas* in which Rādhā plays an important part in the life of Kṛṣṇa.

The cult was carried to its extreme form by a Tailaṅga Brāhmaṇa named Vallabha whose activity falls in the first half of the sixteenth century A.D. His Vaiṣṇavism centres round Kṛṣṇa, the beloved of the *gopīs,* and his eternal consort Rādhā. Elaborate rituals for the worship of Kṛṣṇa and religious feasts and festivals were fully developed—all marked by a spirit of sportive enjoyment. This, coupled with a less exacting demand on spiritual fervour and high tone of morality in the sect, seems to be the secret of its great hold on the masses whose ordinary inclinations find in it a comfortable religious sanction. One of the distinguishing characteristics of this sect is the exalted position of the *guru,* or the spiritual guide, called the *mahārāja.* God can only be worshipped in the house or temple of the *guru,* to whom the devotees are enjoined to surrender all their belongings. The highest spiritual object is to join in the eternal sport of Kṛṣṇa and Rādhā. The worldly life offers no bar to this salvation. True to this doctrine, the *gurus* were married men and led worldly lives. In its degraded form, this sect countenanced antinomian practices, and made Vaiṣṇavism a byword of reproach. The doctrine flourished mostly among the mercantile communities of Gujarat and Rajasthan, though its baneful effects spread far beyond these limits.

Bengal Vaiṣṇavism was saved from this degradation by the famous Caitanya or Śrī Gaurāṅga (A.D. 1485-1533), a contemporary of Vallabha. The elements of Rādhā and Kṛṣṇa had taken deep root in its soil, as the songs of Jayadeva (twelfth century A.D.) clearly show. But the merit of Caitanya lies in the fact that he elevated the passions of the couple to a high spiritual plane and stressed the emotional at the cost of the ceremonial side of religion. His piety, devotion, and fervour introduced a pure and spiritual element in Vaiṣṇavism which offers a bright and refreshing contrast to that promulgated by Vallabha. But with the lapse of time, Rādhā gained more and more prominence, and many degrading elements crept into Bengal Vaiṣṇavism also. An extreme form is represented by the Sakhībhāvas, the ideal of the male members of which is to obtain the womanhood of Rādhā even in the physical sense.

The history of religions teaches us an important lesson. It is that any exaggerated importance attached to the female element in religion, or the association of religion with amorous elements, even though inspired or prompted by the highest spiritual motive and backed by metaphysical or mystic interpretations, is sure to lead to the degradation of its followers. This is best illustrated by the fate of the Śākta and Rādhā-Kṛṣṇa cults.

It is refreshing therefore to turn to some sects of Vaiṣṇavism which realized this truth and gave a new tone to the religion by avoiding the fatal process. This was done by twofold means. In Mahārāṣṭra, Rādhā was replaced by Rukmiṇī, the lawful wife of Kṛṣṇa, who plays all along a subordinate rôle to her husband. The great preachers of this sect were Nāmadeva (end of the fourteenth century A.D.) and Tukārāma (seventeenth century), the founders of the popular form of Vaiṣṇavism in Mahārāṣṭra. Another mode, propounded by Rāmānanda (fourteenth century), was to replace Kṛṣṇa and Rādhā by Rāma and Sītā. This was further developed by his famous disciples, the chief among whom were Kabīr and Ravidāsa, (fifteenth century A.D.), Dādū and Malūkdāsa (*c.* A.D. 1600), and Tulasīdāsa (A.D. 1532-1623).

The religion propounded by them was chaste and pure. The simple, beautiful verses of Nāmadeva, Tukārāma, and the disciples of Rāmānanda are full of piety and devotion, and they have acquired wide celebrity far beyond sectarian limits.

THE SYNTHETIC AND REFORMIST MOVEMENTS

In addition to the purification of the Bhakti cult and its elevation to a high spiritual level based on secure foundations of morality, these Vaiṣṇava teachers, together with Caitanya, have made other notable contributions to the culture of the mediaeval age. These may be summed up as (1) preaching in vernacular which thereby got a great impetus ; (2) ignoring the caste distinctions and admitting even the lowest castes to their fold ; and (3) definitely rejecting rites and ceremonials as useless and laying stress on morality and purity of the heart. Excepting Rāmānanda and Caitanya, the others carried this last feature to an extreme form by discarding altogether the worship of images.

These characteristics need not be treated in detail. The debt which Bengali, Hindi, and Marathi literatures owe to these Vaiṣṇava preachers is too well known. As to the second, it is interesting to recall that, of the chief disciples of Rāmānanda, who founded different schools, Kabīr was a Mohammedan weaver, Dādū a cotton-cleaner, and Ravidāsa a leather-worker. People of all classes and castes, including Mohammedans, were taken into these sects, and thus began a levelling process which, unfortunately, did not make much progress and touched only a fringe of the society. In fact, for all practical purposes, the two great communities—Hindu and Muslim—were hardly affected by it, and maintained, as before, their severely exclusive character.

The socio-religious revolution sketched above followed closely the lines which marked that of the fifth century B.C. culminating in Buddhism. The only difference is that emotionalism replaced rationalism, and a pious devotion to God took the place of the austere morality of the agnostic Buddhists.

In a similar way, we may notice the revival of the pure monotheistic doctrine of the Upaniṣads in the Sikh religion founded by Nānak (1469-1539). He invoked the one true God, without any name, and without the intermediacy of any prophet or incarnation. 'Numerous Mohammeds have there been', says he, 'and multitudes of Brahmās, Viṣṇus, and Śivas, but the chief of gods is the one Lord, the true Name of God.' He discarded the Vedas, Kṛṣṇa, saints, and pilgrimages, and put faith in one self-existent Creator and Destroyer who cannot be conceived in any other form, and whose true nature cannot be expressed in words. So far it has a wonderful agreement with the Upaniṣadic doctrine. But then Nānak denied that God can be comprehended by knowledge or wisdom, and instead of meditation he relied on faith and grace. Here we find the influence of the Bhakti cult which moulded all religious thoughts of the age. Although Nānak deliberately placed himself outside the pale of Hinduism, his doctrine, like that of Rāmānanda and Caitanya, may be looked upon as an attempt to purify the Bhakti cult on a line different from, but equally rooted in, the Hindu religion and philosophy of the past. He did away altogether with caste distinctions and ceremonials, and preached in vernacular. He also decried the worship of images. He was a more courageous reformer and went much further than the other two. The result was that his doctrines had never any great effect upon the masses, and were confined to the province of the Punjab where he lived and preached.

Although, as noted above, there is nothing new in the special characteristic features of these religions, including even the rejection of the worship of images—and all of them may be traced to ancient Indian religious systems—, still it is possible that the monotheism and democratic spirit of Islam served as a potent factor in leading to these developments. It is not perhaps a mere accident that from the fourteenth century A.D., the two characteristic features of Islam, viz. the absence of social distinctions among its followers and the total rejection of the worship of images, began to influence the Vaiṣṇava reformers and mediaeval saints. A more direct and thorough influence of Islam may be traced in the severe monotheistic doctrines of Nānak. It is also to be noted that these principles are almost absent in South India, precisely that part of the country where the influence of Islam was the least. We cannot thus altogether ignore the influence of Islam in shaping the religious doctrines of North India and Mahārāṣṭra from the fourteenth century down to the end of the seventeenth, though it is difficult to form an estimate of its nature and extent.

VI. THE MODERN AGE (A.D. 1757-1947)

The eighteenth century is similarly marked by the impact with western thought which led to the religious reforms of the nineteenth century. It brought back the rationalism of the fifth century B.C., and Raja Rammohun Roy was its great exponent. The new spirit led to the foundation of the Brāhmo Samāj (including Prārthanā Samāj), the Ārya Samāj, and the Theosophical Society on the one hand, and all-round reform in the orthodox Hindu religion and society on the other. The spirit of reform also inspired the Muslim community. It led to the Wahhābī movement, early in the nineteenth century, which originally aimed at internal reform, but was gradually deflected into a political move against the British. Its failure led to the Aligarh movement initiated by Sir Syed Ahmed, which is still a living force in the Muslim community.

Towards the close of the century flourished Sri Ramakrishna who sought to reconcile not only the rationalist doctrine with the emotionalism and ritualistic orthodoxy of the earlier ages, but also the different seemingly conflicting religions on the basis of experience gained through spiritual culture. His disciple Swami Vivekananda gave a definite shape to his catholic views and broadbased the doctrine of the Vedānta philosophy. He formulated the teachings of his Master as a definite creed and founded the great Ramakrishna Mission which is now a potent force not only in India, but far beyond its boundaries. It is powerfully moulding the Hinduism of the present day and giving it a wide catholic character. But its sphere of activity far transcends the narrow circle of Hinduism. By carrying to its logical conclusion the Vedāntic doctrine of the identity of man with God, it has established the fundamental equality of man on a secure basis. Coupled with its other doctrine, that all religions, if truly followed, are but different ways to salvation, and there is no inherent conflict between one religion and another, it has offered a solution of the most complicated problem of the day. To an historian, its significance lies in the wonderful synthesis of the varied cultures of India—the philosophy of the Upaniṣads and Śaṅkara is combined with the theistic beliefs, and the pursuit of the highest knowledge of abstract principles is accompanied by meditation and devotion. The rituals of the Paurāṇic religion are performed with meticulous care, but it knows no distinctions of caste and creed and equally honours not only Buddha and Caitanya, but Christ, Mohammed, Zoroaster, and other founders of great religious systems of the world. A great future lies before it, but it is as yet too early to foresee or forecast its ultimate destiny.

3

AN HISTORICAL SKETCH OF ŚAIVISM

THE ORIGINS OF ŚAIVISM

THE origins of Śaivism are lost in obscurity, but it is clear that the Śaivism of history is a blend of two lines of development, the Aryan or Vedic and the pre-Aryan. Much more than the urbane cult of Viṣṇu, it has exhibited a close alliance with *yoga* and thaumaturgy, and a constant tendency to run into the extremes of ascetic fervour. It is not a single cult, but a federation of allied cults, whose practices range from the serenest form of personal life in the faith to the most repulsive excesses that alienate one's sympathy for the cult. The hold of Śaivism extends not only over the whole of India, from the Indus valley to Bengal, but stretches out across the sea to Greater India and the Archipelago, and beyond the northern mountains to Central Asia. We shall endeavour to indicate the genesis of this powerful creed and the chief stages of its growth, and briefly survey the evidence from literature and epigraphy of the range and extent of its influence.

The characteristics of Śaivism are the exaltation of Śiva above all other gods, the highly concrete conception of the deity, and the intensely personal nature of the relation between him and his devotees. These traits are most clearly seen in the *Śvetāśvatara Upaniṣad,* a treatise which resembles the *Bhagavad-Gītā* in many ways, but seems to have been the work of an earlier age. Just as the *Gītā* voices the intense theism of Vaiṣṇavism in very general terms, and in close relation to broad philosophical principles, so does the *Śvetāśvatara* expound the supremacy of Śiva as the result of the theistic strain of thought developed in the Upaniṣads. On the one hand, Śiva is here identified with the eternal Absolute. 'There is no form for Him whose name is supreme celebrity' (IV. 19). On the other hand, he is the God of all gods, potent for good and evil. He is Giriśa ; he holds the arrow in his hand ready to shoot ; he is the great Master (Īśāna), the giver of boons, the origin of the gods, Rudra, the great seer, the supreme Lord (Maheśvara), and so on, and his nature is clearly revealed in the repetition of the Ṛg-Vedic prayer to Rudra imploring him to accept the *haviḥ* (oblation), and spare the lives and property of the worshipper and his kindred. He is attained by true *tapas* (austerity), and then comes the removal of all bondage. There is nothing else to be known, and there is no other way. The end of this Upaniṣad differs from the rest of it in its style, and is most probably a later addition. But it is not without interest.

We read here that 'men would sooner be able to roll up the ether like a skin than reach the end of sorrow without knowledge of the Lord' (VI. 20). Intense devotion to the Lord and equal devotion to the *guru* (teacher) are the essential preliminaries to a realization of the true path (VI. 23).

We have here all the elements of Śaivism, and the further growth of the creed meant only the elaboration of the details of the doctrine and the rise of local variations in the practice of the cult, leading to the formation of different schools or sub-sects.

The name Śiva hardly occurs in the *Ṛg-Veda* as a proper noun. It is often applied to many gods of the pantheon in the sense of 'propitious', and once indeed to Rudra himself (X. 92. 9). The name came to be applied euphemistically to the god of terrors, for Rudra, the prototype of Śiva in the *Ṛg-Veda,* is really a terrible god, and much supplication was needed to humour him into a good temper.[1] And there is none more powerful than Rudra. The Ṛg-Vedic Rudra exhibits more of the traits of the Rudra-Śiva of later times than have generally been allowed. In one hymn (II. 33), for instance, the term '*vṛṣabha*' is applied to him five times, and he is called the doctor of doctors, Īśāna, Yuvan, Ugra, and so on. He carries the bow and arrows and wears necklaces of all sorts, and is followed by his hosts; and curiously enough, in one of the stanzas in this hymn also occurs the term '*kumāra*'. Thus most of the stuff from which Śaiva legends take their rise is apparently as old as the oldest part of the *Ṛg-Veda*.

There are, of course, striking differences, and it would be indeed strange if it were not so. And these differences persist in the later Saṁhitās as well. Thus Rudra is the father or chief of the Maruts; he is identical with Agni (Fire).[2] Ambikā is his sister, not his wife.[3] Bhava, Śarva, Kāla, and others figure as independent deities, who have not yet merged in the great God, Mahādeva.

In the *Yajur-Veda,* however, we meet with stories concerning Rudra's exploits, such as killing the *asuras* and destroying their *tripura* (three cities),[4] breaking into the midst of a sacrifice and taking violent possession of offerings meant for other gods. But it is the *Śatarudrīya* which draws together all the floating conceptions regarding Rudra-Śiva of the early Vedic

[1] Macdonell, *Vedic Mythology,* p. 77. Eliot, *Hinduism and Buddhism,* II. p. 141. Muir, *Original Sanskrit Texts,* IV is an invaluable collection of the sources. The derivation of 'Śiva' from Tamil *Śivappu,* which is sometimes suggested, appears to be far-fetched. Rudra is generally understood to mean 'roarer'. Sāyaṇa suggests no fewer than six derivations (Muir, *op. cit.*, p. 303, f.n. 9), and a seventh is suggested in the *Atharvaśiras Upaniṣad*—a clear proof of the obscurity of its origin. The text in *Taittirīya Saṁhitā,* VI. 1. 7. 7-8 is the criticism of a later age on the Rudra of the *Ṛg-Veda*.

[2] Cf. *Mahābhārata,* cited by Muir, *op. cit.*, pp. 198-99.

[3] One of the early references to Umā Haimavatī is in the *Kena Upaniṣad* where her relation to Śiva is not made explicit.

[4] *Taittirīya Saṁhitā,* VI. 2. 3.

times and provides a fresh starting point for new developments which culminate in the theistic Vedānta of the *Śvetāśvatara,* while, at the same time, the biography of Śiva is developed, from the stray hints of an earlier time, into the elaborate legends narrated in the later Upaniṣads and the Śaiva Purāṇas. The *Śatarudrīya* came to occupy a large place in later Śaivism. Its *japa* (repetition) was a sure road to immortality (*Jābālopaniṣad,* 3), the expiation for all sin, and the means of attaining release. The importance of the *Śatarudrīya* has also been emphasized in the *Periya Purāṇam.*

WAS ŚAIVISM PRE-VEDIC ?

Was Śaivism pre-Vedic and non-Aryan in its origin? An affirmative answer to this question seems to rest on the following considerations: Śiva as the name of a deity is unknown to the ancient Vedic hymns, though they mention a tribe of Śivas.[5] The characteristics of Śiva are those of a fearful deity worshipped with propitiatory rites by primitive folk. Worshippers of the *liṅga* (phallus), the chief emblem of Śaivism, are condemned in the *Ṛg-Veda,* and Indra's intercession is sought against them (VII.21.5 ; X.99.3). Lastly, the discovery of several prehistoric relics of a phallic character from various parts of India, including the chalcolithic sites of Mohenjo-daro and Harappā, shows that the phallic cult with which Śaivism is closely connected was a widespread cult in pre-Vedic India. In the warrior clans of the *Ṛg-Veda,* the Bharatas, Purus, Yadus, and others, R. P. Chanda recognizes 'the representatives of the ruling class of the indigenous chalcolithic population' in whose service the Aryan *ṛṣi* (seer) clans came to seek their fortune, more or less as missionaries of the cults of Indra, Varuṇa, Agni, and other nature gods.[6]

But we can hardly proceed yet to reconstruct the history of the Ṛg-Vedic age in the manner suggested by Chanda. Though Śiva as a deity is unknown to the *Ṛg-Veda,* there can be no manner of doubt that the Vedic Rudra has furnished the foundation for Śaivism as we know it. That Rudra does not occupy in the hymns the high position which Śiva does later cannot make different deities of them ; for the fortunes of gods have varied in time no less than those of their worshippers. That some traits of non-Aryan aboriginal religion have gone into the make-up of the Śiva of Paurāṇic Hinduism can hardly be gainsaid ; but that is true of Viṣṇu as well, and, in fact, the absorption of pagan traits is the price that any proselytizing religion has to pay for its being accepted by fresh tribes or classes. It is not to be forgotten also that the expression '*śiśnadevāḥ*' may not signify

[5] *Archaeological Survey of India Memoirs,* 41. p. 3.
[6] *Ibid.,* 41. p. 25.

'men who had the phallus (*śiśna*) for deity', but rather, as Roth suggests, some 'tailed (or Priapic) demons', from whose unwelcome intrusion the Aryans sought the protection of Indra.[7] Further, even if the expression has reference to human worshippers of the phallus, it is impossible, in the absence of definite criteria about what is Aryan and what is non-Aryan,[8] to assert that these worshippers were not Aryans themselves.[9]

The interpretation offered by Sir John Marshall of the evidence from Mohenjo-daro rests on unproven, and to me improbable, assumptions on the chronology of Vedic literature. The interpretation of these data can hardly become final until the inscriptions on the seals are satisfactorily explained. While Marshall's explanations appear conclusive in regard to the Mother Goddess cult, the phallic cult, and the tree and animal cults, his speculations on the male god, who, he thinks, was the prototype of the historical Śiva, are rather forced, and certainly not so convincing as the rest of the chapter.[10] It is difficult to believe on the strength of a single 'roughly carved seal' that all the specific attributes of Śiva, as Maheśa, Mahāyogin, Paśupati, and Dakṣiṇāmūrti, were anticipated in the remote age to which the seal belongs. In his eagerness to discover the origin of Śaivism in this seal, the learned archaeologist suggests so many hypotheses that the less imaginative reader begins to feel rather sceptical about the whole attempt. 'The lower limbs are bare, and the phallus (*ūrdhva-meḍhra*) seemingly exposed, but it is possible that what appears to be the phallus is in reality the end of the waistband.'[11] Again, the three faces of this god may be 'a syncretic form of three deities rolled into one', because 'the conception of the triad or trinity is a very old one in India' and 'it was equally old in Mesopotamia; it is more likely, however, that in the first instance the god was provided with a plurality of faces in token of his all-seeing nature; that these images afterwards suggested the *trimūrtis* of Śiva, Brahmā, and Viṣṇu; and that the latter in their turn subsequently inspired such images as those of Devangana, Melcheri, and other places'. The elephant and tiger on the proper right of the god, and the rhinoceros and buffalo on his left, may be taken to imply that the god was the lord of the beasts (*paśupati*), or it may only be that the four quarters are represented, as on the capitals of Aśoka columns, by the four animals. The pair of horns, which makes a *triśūla* (trident) on the head of the god, with the head-dress proper, is admitted to be a pre-Aryan symbol of divinity that

[7] Muir, *Original Sanskrit Texts,* IV. p. 411.

[8] Keith, *The Religion and Philosophy of the Veda and Upanishads,* pp. 629-30.

[9] *Contra* R. G. Bhandarkar, *Vaiṣṇavism, Śaivism, and Minor Religious Systems,* p. 115.

[10] *Mohenjo-daro and the Indus Civilization,* I. 5; *Contra* O. Schrader in *Z. D. M. G.,* 1934, p. 191.

[11] *Ibid.,* p. 55, f.n. 5 shows clearly how eager Marshall is to accept the first explanation,

survived in later times in the *triśūla* of Śiva, and the *triratna*[12] of Buddhism. 'This emblem . . . while of itself proving nothing definite, nevertheless, provides another link in the chain which connects Śiva with the pre-Aryan religion, and to this extent supports his identification with the deity of the seal.' The deer throne of the god and his yogic posture are the two most unequivocal features left, and these prove nothing more than the antiquity of *yoga,* a system of physical discipline and mental magic. It should be observed that the yogic posture of our god is not unique in the Mohenjo-daro finds ; it occurs also in a statue of a male figure, and in a small faience seal, where a deity in the same attitude is apparently worshipped by a kneeling *nāga*.

Marshall's conclusions regarding Śaivism in pre-Aryan India are therefore open to doubt on two grounds. While the high antiquity of the Indus valley culture is very well established, it is not definitely proved that this culture was pre-Vedic, that is, pre-Aryan. Again, most of the data from which he draws his conclusions are, as he is himself aware, open to other interpretations which have nothing to do with Śaivism.

IS ŚIVALIṄGA A PHALLIC SYMBOL ?

Is the *śivaliṅga* a phallus? The discovery of phallic cult objects here and there, bearing evidence of the worship of the phallus among prehistoric tribes, has led to the easy assumption that the *śivaliṅga* was phallic in its origin. And the preponderance, real or supposed, of orgiastic rites in some forms of Śāktism has doubtless sometimes influenced modern students of Śaivism into accepting an exclusively phallic interpretation of the *śivaliṅga*. But the *liṅga* may have been in origin no more than just a symbol of Śiva, as the *śālagrāma* is of Viṣṇu. The worship of the *liṅga* as a symbol once started, there was little to prevent a confusion in the popular mind between this and the cult of the phallus, and legends came to be invented of the origin of the worship of the *liṅga* as the phallus of Śiva. In some such way we can explain the passages—not many after all, and rather late in the *Mahābhārata* and other works—, which lend colour to the phallic interpretation of the *śivaliṅga.*[13] 'Of all the representations of the deity which India has imagined,' observes Barth,[14] 'these (*liṅgas*) are perhaps the least offensive to look at. Anyhow, they are the least materialistic ; and if the common people make fetishes of them, it is nevertheless true that the choice of these symbols by themselves to the exclusion

[12] The Three Jewels: Buddha, Dharma, and Saṅgha.

[13] Bhandarkar (*op. cit.,* pp. 114-15) thinks that the cult of the *liṅga* was borrowed from aboriginal tribes, the Śiśnadevas of the *Ṛg-Veda*.

[14] *Religions of India,* p. 262.

of every other image was, on the part of certain founders of sects, such as Basava, a sort of protest against idolatry.'[15] The Pallava Mahendravarman, who set up a *liṅga* in Tiruchirappalli (Trichinopoly), centuries before Basava's time, gave unmistakable expression to the very same idea.

ŚIVA IN THE VEDAS AND THE ĀGAMAS

One of the numerous descriptions of Śiva in the *Śatarudrīya* is '*paśūnāṁ patiḥ*' (the lord of creatures), and this, with the texts cited by Abhinava Śaṅkara in his *Rudra-bhāṣya,* lays the foundation for the tenets of Śaivism concerning *pati, paśu,* and *pāśa* (bondage). The *Atharvaśiras Upaniṣad* raised the wearing of the holy ashes (*bhasma*) into a *pāśupata-vrata* (vow), calculated to release the *paśu* from the *pāśa*. Likewise the *Kaivalya Upaniṣad* has a famous passage prescribing Śiva-yoga as the means of release. A life of asceticism, leading to the development of powers that raise a man to equality with Rudra, is already hinted at in a late hymn of the *Ṛg-Veda,*[16] which extols the life of the *keśin* or *muni,* and the 'odour of sanctity' attaching to it.

Śaivism agrees closely with the Sāṁkhya in its dogmatics, and with the Yoga school in its practical discipline. Even the founder of the Vaiśeṣika is reputed to have entered on his work after securing the grace of Maheśvara by his excellent *yoga.*[17] Haribhadra, an early Jaina writer, states that the followers of Gautama and Kaṇāda were Śaivas.[18] But the affiliation of Śaivism with these systems of thought and discipline was apparently no more than a passing phase, for the tendency of Śaivism, in its later history, was to develop along peculiar lines of its own.

The *Mahābhārata* contains several passages attesting the spread of Śaivism and its increasing hold on society. Kṛṣṇa himself figures as the chief devotee of Śiva, and true to the injunction that 'Illumination comes through the teaching of the *guru*', he is initiated into Śiva-yoga by Upamanyu. 'Equipped with a staff, shaved, clothed with rags, anointed with ghee, and provided with a girdle, living for one month on fruits, for four months on water, standing on one foot, with his arms aloft, he, at length, obtained a glorious vision of Mahādeva and his wife, whom all the gods were worshipping, and among them Indra, Viṣṇu (the delight of his mother, Aditi), and Brahmā, all uttering the *rathantara sāman*.'[19]

By contact with many local cults, and possibly also by the influence

[15] This is no doubt the ground for the Paurāṇic exaltation of *liṅga*-worship over image-(*arcā*) worship, the former leading to release, and the latter only to some variety of prosperity. The *Liṅga Purāṇa* version of the origin of the *liṅga* as due to Śiva becoming a pillar of fire whose top and bottom could not be seen by Brahmā and Viṣṇu is also noteworthy.

[16] *R.V.*, X. 136 ; Muir, *op. cit.*, IV. p. 318.

[17] Praśastapāda at the close of his *bhāṣya*.

[18] Bhandarkar, *op. cit.*, p. 117.

[19] Muir, *op. cit.*, IV. p. 194.

of individual *gurus,* of whom Upamanyu is the type (Śiva himself in the aspect of *guru* came to be known as Dakṣiṇāmūrti), the practices of Śaivism began to develop variations, and this led to the growth of sub-sects at a very early stage. There also grew up a separate literature, highly esoteric in character, the literature of the Āgamas. The history of this growth is lost in obscurity; only the theories of a later age regarding it have come down to us. In a well-known passage of his *bhāṣya,*[20] Śrīkaṇṭha declares that, in his view, there is no difference between the Vedas and Śiva Āgamas; that the Vedas can also be with propriety called Śiva Āgamas, because Śiva is their author; and that consequently Śiva Āgamas are twofold: those meant for 'the three *varṇas* (castes)', and those for general acceptance (*sarva-viṣaya*). In his commentary on this text, and on the next succeeding section of the *Brahma-Sūtra* on the Pāñcarātra, Appaya Dīkṣita has brought together many texts from the Purāṇas and the *Mahābhārata,* which do not always support the syncretic position of Śrīkaṇṭha. They are inclined to treat the Śiva Āgamas as non-Vedic pseudo-scriptures (*moha-śāstra*).[21] These *moha-śāstras* were started by Śiva and Viṣṇu themselves engaging in a conspiracy of grace, so to say, by which they sought to lead back the stray sheep by easy stages to the higher Vedic path.[22] And in dealing with the legend in the *Kūrma Purāṇa* on the origin of these Śāstras, Appaya Dīkṣita makes a significant observation. This Purāṇa says that those who, on account of *govadha* (cow-killing), were declared by Gautama to be great sinners and outside the pale of orthodox society went up to Śaṅkara and Viṣṇu and humbly praised them by means of *laukika stotras.* This phrase is interpreted by Appaya to mean not merely non-Vedic, but vernacular hymns; and this is quite intelligible in a sixteenth century writer of South India with the whole history of Tamil Śaivism and Vaiṣṇavism present in his mind. Equally significant is the distinction made by the *Kūrma Purāṇa* itself between the pure Pāśupata-yoga, the essence of the Vedas, and the degenerate counterfeits thereof.

The *Vāyu Purāṇa* makes the same distinction, and expressly states that the *Kāmika* and other Āgamas belong to the heterodox variety. The *Varāha Purāṇa* is even more trenchant in its condemnation of the non-Vedic Pāśupata schools. In the *Mahābhārata,* on the other hand, there seems to be no evidence of hostility to the Āgamas, and what is more, they, like the Yoga, Pāñcarātra, and the Vedas, seem to be frankly recognized as one of the many modes of approach to God; at any rate, there is no evidence of sectarian exclusiveness or hostility. Kullūka Bhaṭṭa quotes a statement of

[20] On *Brahma-Sūtra,* II. 2. 38.
[21] Scriptures calculated to delude people.
[22] Abhinava Śaṅkara in his commentary on the *Śatarudrīya,* '*patīnāṁ pataye namaḥ*'.

Hārīta that Śruti is twofold: Vaidika and Tāntrika.[23] The attitude of the South Indian saint Appar on this question is no less remarkable. He says, for instance, in the most matter-of-fact way that just as the Vedas and their six *aṅgas* (branches) were the precious jewel to the Brāhmaṇas, so was '*Namaḥ Śivāya*' to himself and his followers.[24]

There was in progress an increasing differentiation among the schools of Śaivism; some of them adopted practices which met with disapproval from others, and tended to lower the tone of Śaivism as a whole. The attitude of the other sections of Hindus towards Śaivism became more and more critical.

HISTORICAL EVIDENCES OF ŚAIVISM

The earliest mention of Śiva worship that can be dated definitely is that of Megasthenes.[25] The prevalence of austere ascetic practices among the Śaivas is attested by Patañjali in the second century B.C. He mentions the Śiva-bhāgavatas, ascetics going about, iron trident in hand.[26] He also mentions images of Śiva, Skanda, and Viśākha made of precious metals, and apparently used in domestic worship.[27] The earliest coins bearing Śaiva emblems, an image of Śiva with trident in hand on the obverse and his bull on the reverse, are those of the Kuṣāṇas in the early centuries of the Christian era.[28] About the same time, there arose in the west of India a preacher who became famous as Lakulīśa, the last incarnation of Maheśvara and the founder of a sect of Pāśupatas, whose tenets are summed up by Mādhava in his *Sarva-darśana-saṅgraha* under the name Nakulīśa-Pāśupata.[29] Lakulīśa is generally represented conjointly with a *liṅga,* and the iconography of his figure is very clearly established from literary sources and the examples of his sculpture found practically all over India.

The flourishing condition of Śaivism under the Guptas is attested by the Mathura pillar inscription of Candragupta II Vikramāditya, which records that, in A.D. 380, Uditācārya installed the images of his *guru* and *guru's guru,* Upamita and Kapila respectively, in the *gurvāyatana.*[30] Uditācārya is said to have been the tenth *guru* after Kuśika, the direct disciple of Lakulīśa. This inscription furnishes therefore valuable testimony to the continuity of the *gurusantāna* (chain of teachers) from the

[23] On *Manu Saṁhitā,* II. 1. [24] Appar, II. 5. [25] Eliot, *op. cit.,* II. pp. 137-38.

[26] Bhandarkar, *op. cit.,* p. 116. Weber (*Indische Studien,* XIII. p. 347) and Barth seem to mistake the import of the *Mahābhāṣya* here.

[27] Weber, *Ibid.,* p. 344.

[28] Whitehead, *Catalogue of Coins in the Punjab Museum,* pp. 183-85, 187.

[29] D. R. Bhandarkar has done most to elucidate the history of Lakulīśa and his sect: *Journal of the Bombay Branch of the Royal Asiatic Society,* XXII. p. 151; *Archaeological Survey of India Annual Report,* 1906-7, p. 179. A Gupta inscription confirms the early date suggested for Lakulīśa: *Epigraphia Indica,* XXI. p. 7.

[30] *Epigraphia Indica,* XXI. pp. 1-9.

founder of the Lakulīśa-Pāśupata, and to the practice of conserving images, possibly portraits, of the successive *gurus* in a gallery set apart for the purpose. Udita prays all Māheśvaras and the succeeding Ācāryas to respect his gift and worship and honour the images, as if they were their own property.

The celebrated description of Bhairavācārya in Bāṇa's *Harṣacarita* furnishes another landmark in the history of Śaiva asceticism. The influence wielded by the ascetics of the Mattamayūra sect in the Haihaya kingdom of Tripurī marks yet another stage in the same line.[31]

In South India, Śaivism is traceable from very early times and its influence grew, like that of Vaiṣṇavism, by its conflict with Buddhism and Jainism in the age of the great Pallavas. The Saṅgam literature knows of Śiva and his exploits, and *Śilappadikāram* even mentions the *pañcākṣara* (the five letters of the '*Namaḥ Śivāya*' *mantra*).[32] The *Maṇimekalai* mentions the Śaivavādin[33] who expounds the doctrine of the eight forms of Īśvara, and His absolute lordship over creation and dissolution. Some at least of the sixty-three Nāyanmārs (Nāyanārs) or Aḍiyārs of legend may have lived in the centuries before the great period of South Indian Śaivism under the Pallavas. The *Mattavilāsa* of Mahendravarman, who was devoted to Śiva, contains, in some of its incidents, a shrewd criticism of the excesses of Śaiva ascetics. The pure love and ecstatic devotion that suffuse the outpourings of the four great Samayācāryas of South India,[34] are seldom surpassed in the history of religious experience. But by the side of this pure stream of *bhakti* (devotion), the somewhat gruesome manifestations of some of the Śaiva cults are amply attested by literature and inscriptions. Kāñcī, Tiruvorriyūr, Melpāḍi, and Koḍumbāḷūr were some of the strongest centres of the Kāpālikas and Kālāmukhas. A good collection can be made of the names of ascetics and *gurus* mentioned in the inscriptions of South India. These names end usually in *-rāśi, -śiva,* or *-paṇḍita.*

Buddhism and Jainism did not die out so completely in the age of the Pallavas, as we are sometimes apt to think. They long survived their conflicts with Hinduism, though only as minority creeds. It is interesting to note that the early Tamil lexicon, *Divākaram,* mentions the names of Kāmar-Kāyndon (destroyer of Cupid) and Tiriyambakan (three-eyed) among those of Arugan (Jina). And the Tamil Buddhists developed the belief that Agastya learned his Tamil from Avalokiteśvara.[35] Even in the midst of their conflicts, the different creeds did not fail to influence one another.

[31] *Archaeological Survey of India Memoirs,* 23. p. 110.
[32] XI. lines 128-30. [33] XXVII. lines 86-95.
[34] They are Appar, Tiru-jñāna-sambandar, Sundaramūrti, and Māṇikkavācagar.
[35] *Vīraśoḷiyam-pāyiram.*

THE EXPANSION OF ŚAIVISM

The great Coḷas were without exception Śaivas, and some were even prepared to suppress the rival creed of Vaiṣṇavism. Under them, the beginnings made under the Pallavas in the construction of temples and establishment of *maṭhas,* part monasteries and part schools and colleges, reached a more elaborate and systematic development. The canon of Tamil Śaivism became fixed, and this was followed by the growth of doctrinal literature. Some account of this literature will be given presently.

The Coḷas are said in later-day legends to have brought Śaivas from northern India to the Tamil country.[36] The Coḷa country must have had no lack of Śaivas of all sorts in the age of the great Coḷas, and there is evidence of their active connection with the centres of Śaivism elsewhere in India. An inscription of Rājendra I makes a sumptuous endowment as *ācāryabhoga* to Uḍaiyār Śarva Śiva Paṇḍita, the *arcaka* (priest) of the Tanjore temple, and his pupils, and their pupils, whether they lived in the Āryadeśa, Madhyadeśa, or Gauḍadeśa.[37] An inscription of the thirteenth century from the Telugu country mentions ten village guards, called Vīrabhadras, who came from the Coḷa country, wore matted hair, belonged to one of the four castes, and were ever ready, in safeguarding the interests of the village, to perform such violent acts as cutting off their own heads, or ripping their bowels open.

Śaivism spread to the islands of the Eastern Archipelago and to the Hinduized states of Greater India at a very early date. Fa-Hien found the Pāśupatas already established in the island of Java early in the fifth century,[38] and the prominence of Śaivism in the later religious life of Java is well known from the celebrated Śiva temples of Prambanam and Panataran. The early Hindu kingdom of Campā, on the east coast of the Indo-Chinese peninsula, was ruled by a line of kings who were clearly of Śaiva persuasion ; witness the construction of the shrine of Bhadreśvara, about A.D. 400, called after Bhadravarman, an early ruler of Campā. There was also a Bhagavatī temple at Po Nagar which took the place of a more ancient Mukhaliṅga shrine ; this Mukhaliṅga was believed in the eighth century to have been founded by the legendary Vicitrasāgara in the *dvāpara-* or even in the *tretā-yuga.* It is a remarkable coincidence that Bhagavatī shrines should be found flourishing at the western and eastern extremes of this area of Hindu culture.

In Fu-nan, the predecessor of Kambuja, were worshipped, in the fifth century, images of gods 'with two faces and four arms, four faces and eight

[36] Anantaśambhu's gloss on *Siddhāntasārāvalī* of Trilocanaśiva.
[37] *South Indian Inscriptions,* II. No. 20.
[38] Krom, *Hindoe Javansche Geschiedenis,* p. 82.

arms, each arm holding something or other—a child, a bird, beast, sun, or moon',[39] a description which recalls Skanda in the Soma-Skanda group, the parrot of Durgā, and the antelope of Śiva, as well as his moon. The dominant cult in Kambuja was Śaivism, though early examples of Hari-Hara are also found. In later times, in Kambuja, Śaivism and Buddhism, flourishing side by side, developed so many common traits that it is sometimes difficult to distinguish the images of one cult from those of the other without a minute examination. The cult of the *liṅga* and the custom of setting up images of dead kings associated with the *liṅga*, and sometimes the worship of similar images of living celebrities, are other noteworthy aspects of the Śaivism of these Hindu kingdoms.

ŚAKTI IN ŚAIVISM

The Soma-siddhānta, an obscure branch of Śaivism, regarding the nature of which several contradictory explanations are vouchsafed to us,[40] may be taken to be the bridge between the Pāśupata and Śākta cults. Barth has truly observed that, though the personification of Śakti is not peculiar to Śaivism, it is in Śaivism that the ideas centring round Śakti have found a soil most favourable for their expansion, and that they have been distorted into the most monstrous developments.[41] 'As in Śiva,' says Weber, 'first of all two gods, Agni and Rudra, are combined, so too his wife is to be regarded as a compound of several divine forms, and this becomes quite evident if we look over the mass of her epithets. While one set of these, as Umā, Ambikā, Pārvatī, Haimavatī, belongs to the wife of Rudra, others, as Kālī, Karālī, carry us back to the wife of Agni, while Gaurī and others perhaps refer to Nirṛti, the goddess of all evil.'[42]

Professor Vogel has drawn pointed attention to the prevalence of the practice of self-immolation by a head-offering to *devī* (goddess), a practice attested by the sculpture of South India, and by literature.[43] It is needless to enter here into the mysteries of *śrīcakra* and *pūrṇābhiṣeka*, so often described by students of these cults.[44] Perhaps the most sympathetic view of these rites is that of Barth: 'There is something else than licentiousness in these aberrations. The books which prescribe these practices are, like the rest, filled with lofty speculative and moral reflections, nay, even with ascetic theories ; here, as well as elsewhere, there is a profession of horror at sin, and a religiosity full of scruples ; it is with pious feelings,

[39] *Bulletin de l' École Française d' Extrême Orient*, III. p. 269.
[40] *Prabodha-candrodaya*, Act III and comments thereon, cited by Tucci, *Journal of the Asiatic Society of Bengal*, XXVI. pp. 130-32.
[41] *Religions of India*, pp. 199-200. [42] Muir, *op. cit.*, IV. p. 425.
[43] *Bulletin of the London School of Oriental Studies*, VI. pp. 539-43.
[44] *The Dabistan* (Shea and Troyer), II. p. 153.

the thoughts absorbedly engaged in prayer, that the believer is to participate in these mysteries, and it would be to profane them to resort to them for the gratifications of sense.'[45]

These developments exercised a powerful influence on later Buddhism, as it is found in Nepal and Tibet.

LITERARY HISTORY OF TAMIL ŚAIVISM

We may now turn to an examination of the nature and content of the literature of Tamil Śaivism. This literature is extensive, and its philosophy is complex. Our endeavour will be just to review the literary history of Tamil Śaivism. This has necessarily to start with a discussion of Tirumūlar and his work. The place of Tirumūlar in the history of Tamil Śaivism is indeterminate. He is believed to have been among the earliest exponents of Śaivism in the Tamil land. Of his life, we have only the weird legend of the *Periya Purāṇam*,—that he came to the South from Kailāsa, the home of the Pratyabhijñā school, animated the dead body of a cowherd,[46] and took three thousand years to compose his *Tirumandiram*. For this highly abstruse work, various dates have been assigned, ranging from the first to the ninth century A.D. As Tirumūlar is mentioned by Sundaramūrti, we may be sure that he must have lived earlier than the ninth century. Some statements in the *pāyiram* (preface) of the work imply that Tirumūlar was the first to interpret Śaivism to the Tamil world. But the highly intricate theology and dogmatics expounded in the work, and its pronounced sectarian character, may raise a doubt whether this curious work is really very early. It declares that to feed a Śiva-jñānin once is more meritorious than the gift of a thousand temples, or the feeding of a crore of Brāhmaṇas versed in the Vedas.[47] Yet it does not omit to manifest a more tolerant attitude towards the Vedic lore: 'The Āgama, as much as the Veda, is truly the word of God; one is general, and the other is special; though, on examination, some hold these words of the Lord, the two *antas*, to be different, yet are they not different (in the eyes of the wise).' This is, as we have seen, exactly the attitude of Śrīkaṇṭha on the question.

The canonical literature of Tamil Śaivism owes its present arrangement to Nambi Āṇḍār Nambi, who may certainly be assigned to the eleventh century, if not to the close of the tenth. Umāpati Śivācārya, who was the last of the Santānācāryas[48] and belongs to the early fourteenth

[45] *Op. cit.*, p. 205.

[46] It is remarkable that a similar story occurs in the accounts of Lakulīśa's life.

[47] *Tirumandiram*, 1860-61.

[48] The three earlier systematic expositors are Meykaṇḍār, Aruṇandi Śivācārya, and Maraijñāna-sambandar.

century, describes in a short work, *Tiru-muraikaṇḍa Purāṇam,* the redaction of the Śaiva canon by Nambi Āṇḍār Nambi. He states that Nambi, in the first instance, arranged the canon in the form of ten books: the first three comprising 384 *padigams* (hymns) of Tiru-jñāna-sambandar, books four to six made up of 307 *padigams* of Tiru-nāvuk-karaśu, 100 *padigams* of Sundaramūrti forming the seventh book, the *Tiruvācakam* of Māṇikkavācagar being the eighth, and a number of *tiruviśaippās*[49] by nine different authors and the *Tirumandiram* of Tirumūlar forming the last two books. We learn that subsequently, when the king requested Nambi to put together one more book from the *padigams* left over, including the *pāśuram* uttered by Śiva himself and calculated to procure *siddhi* (perfection), Nambi arranged the eleventh book of the canon. The *Periya Purāṇam* (this is its popular name, the true name being *Tiruttoṇḍar Purāṇam*) is counted by modern Śaivas as the twelfth book. Certainly the arrangement of the books is not chronological; for, to give the most striking instance, Tirumūlar was earlier than Sundaramūrti and is mentioned in the *Tiruttoṇḍattogai*; but the *Tirumandiram* is only the tenth book, whereas Sundaramūrti's hymns form the seventh.

The *Śiva-jñāna-bodham* of Meykaṇḍār (discoverer of Truth), written in the first half of the thirteenth century,[50] is the first attempt at a systematic statement of the tenets of Tamil Śaivism. This is a short treatise of a dozen aphorisms (*sūtras*) which seem to have been translated from a Sanskrit original;[51] the author has added *vārttikas* of his own, which explain and illustrate the argument of each of the *sūtras* and fix their meanings. The name *Śiva-jñāna-bodham* is explained thus: '*Śivam* is One; *jñānam* is the knowledge of Its true nature; *bodham* is the realization of such knowledge.' The scheme of the twelve *sūtras* is simple; the first three assert the existence of the three entities—God (*pati*), bondage (*pāśa*), and soul (*paśu*); the next three define and explain their nature and inter-relation; the next triad

[49] These contain hymns on the Tanjore temple and its copy, the temple of Gaṅgaikoṇḍa-Colapuram; this may be taken to give an indication of the date of Nambi Āṇḍār Nambi, if we may be certain that we have this ninth book as Nambi left it.

[50] *Sen Tamil,* III. pp. 189-90.

[51] Śiva-jñāna-munivar, the commentator on the *sūtras,* says that they form part of the *Raurava Āgama.* The view has often been expressed that the Tamil work is the original and the Sanskrit is the translation. See T. I. Tambyah, *Psalms of a Śaiva Saint,* p. xix. The arguments adduced in support of this position are inconclusive. The Sanskrit work is in *anuṣṭubh* verse, and like all Āgamas corresponds to the Tamil *sūtra* and does not contain anything corresponding to the Tamil *vārttikas.* Both Umāpati of the *Pauṣkara-bhāṣya* and Śivāgrayogi hold the view that the Sanskrit work is the original. See V. P. Kantimatinatha Pillai, *Tamilcciva-ñānabodac-cirappu* (1926), p. 54. Vidyāraṇya is said to have written an exposition of the Sanskrit work in a monistic sense (*Ibid.,* pp. 30, 47). Śiva as *guru* told Māṇikkavācagar that he held the *Śiva-jñāna-bodham* in his hand; this may be not so much a daring anachronism, antedating the work of Meykaṇḍār, as Pope thought (*Tiruvācakam,* xxii), as the expression of a belief in the antiquity of the Sanskrit work of that name. For Umāpati's references to the Sanskrit *sūtras,* see *Pauṣkara-bhāṣya,* pp. 14, 29, 256, 447.

deals with the means (*sādhanā*) of release; and the last is devoted to the nature of release. The key-position held by the work of Meykaṇḍār in the literature of Tamil Śaivism is brought out by a verse which says: 'The Veda is the cow; its milk is the true Āgama; the Tamil sung by the Four (see f.n. 34) is the ghee extracted from it; and the virtue of the Tamil work, full of wisdom (*bodham*), of Meykaṇḍār of the celebrated (city of) Veṇṇai, is the fine taste of the ghee.'

The systematic treatment of the doctrine by Meykaṇḍār was preceded by two short works which may be said to stand almost in the relation of text and commentary.[52] These are the *Tiruvundiyār* and *Tirukkaḷirruppaḍiyār* by two authors, teacher and disciple according to tradition, and both known by the name, or rather title, Uyya-vanda-devar. Both these are works meant to present in an easy style the main aspects of Śaiva doctrine and practice.

After the *Śiva-jñāna-bodham,* the next work of importance on the doctrine is the *Śiva-jñāna-śittiyār* of Aruṇandi, reputed in tradition to have been first the *guru* of Meykaṇḍār's father and then the disciple of Meykaṇḍār himself. Though written in verse, it is a terse statement of the true doctrine, introduced by a critical discussion of rival systems of which no fewer than fourteen, including four schools of Buddhism and two of Jainism, are passed under review. This great work, which is, in fact, the classic treatise on Tamil Śaivism—for the work of Meykaṇḍār is too cryptic and fails to explain the position of Śaivism *vis-à-vis* other systems—, has been the subject of many commentaries, and, to this day, is the most widely read manual of Śaivism among the Tamils. The *Iurpāvirupadu,* by the same writer, owes its name to the alternate use of the two metres in its twenty verses which expound the doctrine in the form of a dialogue between teacher and pupil. This work is said to have been composed by Aruṇandi to enshrine the memory of his beloved teacher in each of its verses; and so it does.

Another catechism, much the simplest of all the manuals of Śaivism, is the *Uṇmai-viḷakkam* by Manavāśagaṅgaḍandār of Tiruvadigai, who claims that his work makes not the slightest departure from the essence of the Āgamas. Umāpati Śivācārya, who lived at the close of the thirteenth and the early years of the fourteenth century,[53] was the author of eight works on the doctrine which complete the tale of Śaiva Siddhānta Śāstras in Tamil. Of these, *Śivappirakāśam,* an ambitious treatise of one hundred verses, is only less important than the *Śiva-jñāna-śittiyār.* Another work, *Saṅkarpa-nirākaraṇam,* is devoted, like the '*parapakṣa*' of the *Śittiyār,* to

[52] S. Anavaratavinayagam Pillai, *Śaiva Sittānta Varalāru.*
[53] He gives the Śaka date 1235 in his *Saṅkarpa-nirākaraṇam.*

a critique of other creeds. Unlike the earlier work, this is much exercised with the minute differences within the very fold of Śaivism. A third work, *Uṇmai-neri-viḷakkam*,[54] devoted to the path of realization, is also ascribed to him and deals with 'the ten *kāryas*'.[55]

The later religious experience of the Tamil Śaivas, apart from its dialectic and philosophy, is interpreted in the songs of the Siddhas, in which the spirit of the old *bhakti* (devotional) literature of the *Devāram* and the *Tiruvācakam* is captured again and reinterpreted. These songs are intensely theistic, and sometimes anti-Brāhmaṇical in tone, and resemble, even more than the hymns of the *Devāram* and the *Tiruvācakam*, the devotional literature of Christianity. But the hypothesis of Christian influence on Bhakti cults, that has been so often put forward, appears plausible only if we ignore the striking differences of the tenor of the Indian songs from that of Christian literature, and omit to notice the presence of other influences which might have acted, at least indirectly, on the growth of religion in South India. It is possible that there were Christians present in South India, especially on the west coast, in the early centuries of the Christian era. But so were the Romans, Persians, and Arabs. To none of these can we ascribe an influence of any significance on Hindu religious life, which is sufficiently accounted for by reference to its own sources. It is not impossible that merely by their presence these foreign creeds stimulated Hinduism to a greater effort in the direction of building up a sort of ecclesiastical organization in the *maṭhas* (monasteries) and their presiding *gurus*, but even this becomes doubtful if we recollect that there were models in the Buddhist organizations, and that *maṭhas* were known in North India as much as in the South.

TWO IMPORTANT ŚAIVA CULTS

Mention must be made finally of two developments which seem to stand outside the general line followed by Śaivism, but still in more or less close connection with it. First among these is the growth of the Liṅgāyata sect, which was founded in the twelfth century by Basava, the minister of Bijjaḷa, and is influential to this day in Karṇāṭaka. It started as a protest against Brāhmaṇism and caste, but has not been able to maintain its reformist features. The Liṅgāyatas are easily recognized, as they all carry a *liṅga* worn in some manner round the neck.

A more important and a much earlier development was a school of

[54] Both the authorship of this work and its place here among the classics of the doctrine have of late been called in question. *Tugaḷ-aru-bodham* of Śirrambalanāḍigaḷ of Sīkāḷi is included instead among the classics.

[55] These are: *tattva-rūpa*, *tattva-darśana*, and *tattva-śuddhi*; *ātma-rūpa*, *ātma-darśana*, and *ātma-śuddhi*; *Śiva-rūpa*, *Śiva-darśana*, *Śiva-yoga*, and *Śiva-bhoga*.

monistic Śaivism in Kashmir, of which the literature dating from about the ninth century has come down to us. How much older it may have been in its origin, it is not easy to determine. There are elements in common between the dogmatics of Kashmir Śaivism and those of South Indian Śaivism.[56] Yet, in their philosophy they differ perceptibly, the Kashmir school being idealist and the South Indian pluralist in its metaphysic. The historical relation between the two forms is not easy to decide, though the mention of Brāhmaṇas from Kashmir in South Indian inscriptions[57] may lead one to infer that South Indian Śaivism is also ultimately derived from Kashmir. Literary and epigraphic evidence, from South India and Java and other Indian colonies of the East, also connects the origin and spread of Śaivism with the march of Agastya from the North to the South, and his further progress towards the Eastern Lands.[58]

[56] Frazer, on 'Śaivism' in *Encyclopaedia of Religion and Ethics.*
[57] *Epigraphia Carnatica,* VII. Sk. 114. 19, 20.
[58] Poerbatjaraka: *Agastya in den Archipel,* pp. 35-36. Also 'Agastya' by the present writer in *J. B. G.*, 1936, pp. 471-545.

4

KASHMIR ŚAIVISM

DIFFERENT NAMES OF THE SYSTEM

IN this article we shall essay a brief exposition of the vision of Reality, the destiny of man, and the way and discipline leading to that destiny, as formulated in the system of spiritual philosophy known as Trika-śāsana or Trika-śāstra or simply Trika, and, more rarely, also as Rahasya-sampradāya and Tryambaka-sampradāya. It must have been an important system at the time of Mādhavācārya to merit an inclusion as Pratyabhijñā-darśana in his compendium *Sarva-darśana-saṅgraha*. The Trika is a virgin field of research, and will repay the most conscientious labour of philosophers for many years to come.

The Trika is so called either because it accepts as most important the triad, *Siddha, Nāmaka,* and *Mālinī,* out of the ninety-two Āgamas recognized by it ; or because the triad consisting of Śiva, Śakti, and Aṇu, or, again, of Śiva, Śakti, and Nara, or, lastly, of the goddesses Parā, Aparā, and Parātparā is recognized ; or because it explains three modes of knowledge of Reality, viz. non-dual (*abheda*), non-dual-cum-dual (*bhedābheda*), and dual (*bheda*).

The system has two main branches, Spanda and Pratyabhijñā. Many classics of the school include the word Spanda or Pratyabhijñā in their very titles. The Trika is also known as Svātantryavāda, Svātantrya and Spanda expressing the same concepts. Ābhāsavāda is another name of the system. It is called Kashmir Śaivism, because the writers who enriched its literature belonged to and flourished in this area.

A SPIRITUAL PHILOSOPHY

The Trika is a spiritual philosophy, because its doctrines regarding Reality, the world, and man are derived from a wealth of spiritual experiences, and are not constructions based upon an analysis of the ordinary experiences of man. Its concepts are, to borrow a phrase from Sri Aurobindo, experience-concepts. Its greatest exponents were *yogins* of high stature who showed wonderful insight into abstruse points of philosophy.[1] The substance of their teaching is not arrived at by an analysis of the ordinary cognitive, affective, and conative experiences of man, but embodies the findings of yogic ways of apprehension, enjoyment, and action. Means of apprehension and action, other than sensory and intellectual, have always

[1] *Pratyabhijñā-kārikā,* I. 38.

been recognized in India and other countries as being perfectly possible, indeed as within the reach of man. Various kinds of discipline, which may be generally called *yoga*, give the science of the inner being and nature of man, and the art of using the powers of knowledge and action hidden at present in unknown regions of our being and nature. The Trika, in short, is a rational exposition of a view of Reality obtained primarily through more-than-normal experiences.

LITERATURE

The system being both a statement about the nature of Reality and a way of life, the orthodox classification of its literature is into *parā, aparā,* and *parātparā,* according as the works set forth, respectively, the metaphysics, the rituals, and both the philosophy and the practical discipline enjoined by the system. We shall, however, for the sake of convenience, divide it into (i) Āgama-śāstra, (ii) Spanda-śāstra, and (iii) Pratyabhijñā-śāstra. Of these the first, the Śaiva Āgamas or Śāstras, is said to have eternal existence and to have been revealed to the sage Durvāsas by Śiva as Śrīkaṇṭha. Durvāsas is said to have ordered his three 'mind-born' sons, Tryambaka, Āmardaka, and Śrīkaṇṭha, to teach the eternal Śaiva philosophy (and faith), respectively, in its three aspects of *abheda, bheda,* and *bhedābheda.*

ĀGAMA-ŚĀSTRA

Among the Āgamas the chief ones are *Mālinīvijaya, Svacchanda, Vijñāna-bhairava, Ucchuṣma-bhairava, Ānanda-bhairava, Mṛgendra, Mataṅga, Netra, Naiśvāsa, Svāyambhuva,* and *Rudra Yāmala.* These were interpreted mostly as teaching a dualistic doctrine, to stop the propagation of which the *Śiva-Sūtra,* expounding a purely Advaitic metaphysic, was revealed to a sage called Vasugupta (*c.* ninth century). This work is also called *Śivopaniṣad-saṅgraha* and *Śivarahasyāgamaśāstra-saṅgraha.* On the *sūtras* of this work there are (i) the *Vṛtti* (the authorship of which is doubtful), (ii) the *Vārttika* by Bhāskara, and (iii) the commentary called *Vimarśinī* by Kṣemarāja.

Some of the Āgamas had commentaries written on them, the chief among which are the *Uddyota* on *Svacchanda, Netra,* and *Vijñāna-bhairava,* and the *Vṛtti* on *Mataṅga.* These commentaries are attempts to show that Āgamas, even prior to the *Śiva-Sūtra,* taught an Advaitic doctrine.

SPANDA-ŚĀSTRA

Of the Spanda-śāstra, which only elaborated the principles of the *Śiva-Sūtra,* without, however, giving much logical reason in support of them, the first and foremost is the *Spanda-Sūtra* or the *Spanda-kārikā,* attributed to Vasugupta himself ; and it is called a *saṅgraha-grantha* or a compendium. His pupil Kallaṭa wrote a *Vṛtti* on this *Sūtra,* and the two together are called *Spanda-sarvasva.* On the *Spanda-Sūtra* we have also the *Spanda-nirṇaya* and the *Spanda-sandoha* by Kṣemarāja (who also wrote *Śiva-Sūtra-vimarśinī*), the *Vivṛti* by Rāmakaṇṭha, and the *Pradīpikā* by Utpala Vaiṣṇava.

PRATYABHIJÑĀ-ŚĀSTRA

The Pratyabhijñā-śāstra is really the philosophical branch of the Trika. Siddha Somānanda, probably a pupil of Vasugupta, is credited with adopting the method of giving an elaborate treatment of his own views and refuting his opponents' doctrines, and is also praised as the founder of the logic of the system. On his work *Śiva-dṛṣṭi,* which is the foundation of this branch, the author wrote a *Vṛtti,* now lost, quotations from which are found in other works. The *Īśvara-pratyabhijñā* or the *Pratyabhijñā-Sūtra* by Utpala, a pupil of Somānanda, is a summary of the philosophy of his master. This shorter work became so important that the entire system came to be known by its name even outside Kashmir. Commentaries on it, still available, are the *Vṛtti* by Utpala himself, and the *Pratyabhijñā-vimarśinī* (*Laghvī Vṛtti*) and the *Pratyabhijñā-vivṛti-vimarśinī* (*Bṛhatī Vṛtti*) by Abhinavagupta. *Bhāskarī* is a lucid and very helpful *ṭīkā* on Abhinavagupta's commentary. *Paramārthasāra* and *Tantrasāra,* both by Abhinavagupta, and *Pratyabhijñāhṛdaya* by Kṣemarāja are three small but important works of the school. *Tantrāloka* by Abhinavagupta with Jayaratha's commentary on it is a veritable encyclopaedia of the system.

WHAT IS ŚĀSTRA?

According to the Trika, the Śāstras have eternal existence. The first thing to remember is that Śāstra does not originally mean a book, it means wisdom, self-existent and impersonal. It is also known as *śabda* and *vāc. Śabda* in the Āgamic philosophies indicates a slight stir, throb, or vibration in Reality, and the eternal self-revelation of Reality is this primal and original vibration. *Vāc* or word expresses something, and the self-expression of Reality is called *parā vāc* or the supreme Word. This self-expression of Reality is wisdom, Reality's awareness of Itself.[2] This is, from one point of view, the knowledge which descends through various levels to the intelligence of man ; from another, it is the universe as the self-manifestation of Reality, not as we know it, but as it is in its original condition in Reality. This is what is meant by saying that *śabda* creates or manifests everything.

[2] '*Śāstraṁ ca parameśvarabhāṣitameva pramāṇam*'—Śāstra is authority told or revealed by the supreme Lord. *Tantrasāra* (Kashmir Ed.), p. 4.

It follows that there is the most intimate connection between *śabda* and *artha,* word and the object. Indeed in the original condition, the subtlest speech, the *parā vāc,* is the universe. It is there existent as Reality's knowledge of Itself as the universe, it is there *vāṅmaya,* constituted of words. But the *parā vāc* reveals itself as the *paśyantī vāc,* the seeing word ; from the side of the universe, it may be described as the universe to be, still existing in an undifferentiated condition. Further objectification reveals it as the *madhyamā vāc,* the middle word, which may be said to be *cittavṛttis,* which are expressed through words as we speak them, and on the cosmic side, as inarticulate differentiation that waits to develop into particularization of objects. *Madhyamā vāc* is the link between the *paśyantī* and the *vaikharī vāc,* that is, word or speech as uttered by the human vocal organ and referring to differentiated objects of the world. It will be noted that the more the objectification of *vāc,* the less intimate is the relation between the word and the object. In the *parā* or transcendent stage they are identical, and it is not possible to say much about their relation. But while in the *paśyantī,* the name and the object are undifferentiated (which is not the same as identical, because the universe to be has now at least ideally emerged, though it has not as yet been alienated from the vision), the relation between them in the *madhymā* is notional, involving ideal separation only ; and in the *vaikharī,* or the human level of speech, the relation between the word and the object is only conventional, i.e. we just give a name to a thing without any reason inherent in it.

The Āgamas or Śāstras exist originally and eternally as the *parā vāc* and then as *paśyantī.* Human sages and seers only receive them from the *madhyamā* level. The Śāstras come to them from the *madhyamā vāc,* flowing out from the five faces (*pañcānana*) of the Deity (representing the five aspects of His power and glory, viz. *cit, ānanda, icchā, jñāna,* and *kriyā*) called Īśāna, Tatpuruṣa, Sadyojāta, Aghora, and Vāma. Thus the wisdom set forth in the Trika philosophy is originally the self-knowledge of Reality expressing itself, though distorted and deformed, as the Śāstras as we know them. Reality must be aware of Itself or Himself, which is the same as saying that the true knowledge of Reality exists in Reality and is not built up by the human brain. And this basic or original knowledge is obtainable by men only through revelation, which means that it is self-manifest (*svayamprakāśa*). That which exists can alone be revealed, and the revelation takes place only when some spiritual genius makes himself fit to receive it, as the result of the development of the proper faculty or faculties.[3]

[3] 'Veda' also originally means not a book, but knowledge, impersonal and unconstructed. Veda is referred to as *nitya-vāc,* the eternal Word. See, for instance, *Ṛ.V.,* VIII. 64. 6, where

METAPHYSICAL BACKGROUND

The ultimate Reality is variously designated as Anuttara, Cit, Caitanya, Pūrṇa or Parā Saṁvid, Śiva, Paramaśiva, Parameśvara, and Ātman ; that is, it is the Supreme, higher than which there is nothing, ineffable and indescribable as this or that or as not this or not that,[4] pure Consciousness, Self-consciousness, integral or supreme Experience, the benign One, the highest Good and Bliss, the supreme Lord, the Self of everything,[5] formless and, yet, informed with all forms, and free from all limitations in space and time.[6]

Reality is ineffable and beyond any descriptions, yet the Trika tries to formulate a philosophy about Its nature. It is to be understood that this formulation is regarding Reality as the creator or manifestor of the universe and not as It is in Itself. Thus Reality is conceived both as transcendent and immanent. As transcendent, it is described as Śiva, as immanent as Śakti. Śiva and Śakti are not two separate realities, but two phases or (conceptual) aspects of the same Reality. Śakti is always in the state of perfect identity with Śiva, but for the purpose of clear understanding the two are distinguished in thought only. Like fire and its burning power, Śiva and Śakti are the same identical fact, though they are spoken of as distinct.[7] Considered as purely transcendent, Śiva is *śava,* dead as it were ; but in truth there is perfect equilibrium, *sāmarasya,* between Śiva and Śakti, and, as such, the integrality is designated Paramaśiva. It is due to the limitation of language that we have to use phrases like '*between* Śiva *and* Śakti' and 'Śiva is the supreme Lord *of* Śakti'. But it must be understood that the Lord and His lordliness, the Īśvara and His *aiśvarya,* which is another name of Śakti, are one and the same. Śakti is described as the *hṛdaya* (heart), the *sāra* (essence) of Śiva.[8]

Cit, pure Consciousness, Illumination, cannot be without self-consciousness, without self-illumination. Cit is also Caitanya. Caitanya is the Śakti aspect of Reality and is compared to a clear mirror in which Reality

this phrase occurs—'*nityayā vācā codasva*'. The two *ṛcs,* I. 164. 39 and 46, plainly make out that there are four steps, *padāni,* of the word from which the speech issues ; the fourth step is ordinary human speech, the other steps or planes are hidden in secrecy. The parallel between the four levels of *śabda* or Śāstra as given in the Āgamas and the Vedic doctrine is striking. Even the Buddha, rather hastily judged by theologians as anti-Vedic, did not claim to invent the Dhamma ; he only discovered it. 'That which the Buddha preached . . . was the order of the law of the universe, immanent, eternal, uncreated, not as interpreted by him only, much less invented or decreed by him'—*Pali Dictionary* (Pali Text Society, London), *sub voce* 'Dhamma'.

[4] Abhinavagupta, *Parātriṁśikā-vivaraṇa.*

[5] *Śiva-Sūtra,* I. 1, with Kṣemarāja's commentary.

[6] *Tantrasāra,* p. 6. It is clear that Śiva in the Trika is the name of Reality, just as Kṛṣṇa is in the school of Bengal Vaiṣṇavism. As Bhāskara says: Śiva is the Reality inherent in all, and is not one among many deities, or a decorated image which is only a help to the uninitiated'—*Bhāskarī,* I. p. 395.

[7] *Śiva-dṛṣṭi,* III. 7.

[8] *Īśvara-pratyabhijñā,* I. 5. 14.

sees Itself. Caitanya is regarded as feminine, though Reality in Itself is neither masculine nor feminine.[9] Thus Consciousness is self-consciousness. Śakti is Śiva's power of turning upon Himself. We say 'Himself', because, at this stage of consideration, we are not regarding Reality as It is in Itself, but as the Lord of the universe-to-be. This is called *cit-śakti,* the power of Cit to reveal Itself and to know Itself. The Trika makes a fivefold distinction of the fundamental modes of Śakti. These aspects of Śakti are *cit, ānanda, icchā, jñāna,* and *kriyā. Cit* is the power of self-awareness; *ānanda* is the power of absolute bliss, or self-enjoying, without having to depend on anything extraneous; *icchā* is Śiva's power of absolute will to manifest the universe out of Himself; *jñāna* is the power of knowing the inherent relations of all manifested or manifestable things among themselves and with His own self; and *kriyā* is the power to assume any form. It must not for a moment be forgotten that these five are only aspects of the selfsame Śakti and not five different entities.

Śakti is also known as *svātantrya,* independence or freedom, because Her existence does not depend on anything extraneous to Herself. She is also *vimarśa,* which means various things at the same time. *Vimarśa* is vibration; it is Śiva's awareness of Himself as the integral and all-comprehensive ego. When there is the reflection of Śiva in Śakti, there emerges in the heart of Reality the sense of 'I' which is described as *ahaṁ-vimarśa.* This is the original *bimba* or reflection, of which everything in the universe is *pratibimba* or *ābhāsa,* a secondary reflection or shadow.[10] It is at this stage that we can first speak of the universe. For the universe in the Trika conception is a system of subjects and objects, *grāhakas* and *grāhyas.* All subjects or knowers are reflections of the original subject, the integral 'I', which Śiva is by virtue of *vimarśa.* Now the emergence of the 'I', *aham,* is not intelligible without the corresponding emergence of the 'it', *idam*; the *grāhaka,* the apprehender, must have *grāhya,* the apprehensible. That is why *vimarśa* is also described as the throb of the 'I' holding within itself and visioning within itself the world of objects.[11] Thus the 'I' or supreme *aham* is the whole universe, not, however, as we understand it in common parlance, but in its ideal state as a 'vision' in Śiva.

Once the conceptual distinction between Śiva and Śakti is made, the latter is regarded as a *dharma,* an attribute, of the former. The relation between the two is one of *tādātmya* (identity). Sometimes it is said to be *sāmarasya* (perfect equilibrium) also, and while they are regarded as two in one, or rather one in, or one as, two, the relation of substance and attribute

[9] *Kāmakalāvilāsa,* 2, with Puṇyānanda's commentary.
[10] This is why the system is known as Pratibimbavāda and Ābhāsavāda.
[11] *Īśvara-pratyabhijñā,* I. 5. 10.

holds between them. Only we should understand that the implication is that the substance, by virtue of its own inherent power, becomes the attributes. Now Śakti, in Her turn, is also regarded as a substance, because all manifestable objects are taken to be inherent and latent in Her womb. They have no existence apart from Śakti, and as such are like attributes of this substance.

Śakti is *prakāśa-vimarśamaya.* At the background is *prakāśa* or illumination, in the foreground is *vimarśa* or vibration of *prakāśa* as the sense of 'I'. *Prakāśa* can be taken to be Śiva, placid and transcendent, *vimarśa* or Śakti as dynamic and immanent. Keeping in mind the concept of *vimarśa* as not only Śakti in general, but also specifically as the sense of 'I', we can say that things are the same as *prakāśa,* their difference being due to having or lacking in *vimarśa.* The more of self-consciousness one has, the more of *vimarśa* also one has, and is thus the nearer to Śiva or pure Consciousness. Thus, while *vimarśa* is taken to be the cause of the manifestation and dissolution of the universe, it is so only in the wider sense of being Śakti and not as the reflection as 'I'. Or, in other words, while everything is a manifestation out of *vimarśa,* everything does not have *vimarśa.* A jar or a pot has no *vimarśa,* no sense of 'I', no self-awareness ; that is why it is material.[12] *Vimarśa* is defined as the *camatkṛti,* wonderment of the integral 'I', and that is why the practical discipline of the system enjoins the development of the sense of the 'I' as being the whole, as identical with the universe. The individual self is also said to be *prakāśa-vimarśamaya.* That is to say, the individual self is also of the nature of consciousness and has self-consciousness also. Analogically speaking, we can say *prakāśa,* in the case of the individual, is the shining intelligence and also the ideas, desires, memories, etc. which are its manifestations ; and *vimarśa* is the individual's awareness that 'those are mine'.

ŚAKTI AS THE PRINCIPLE OF UNIVERSAL MANIFESTATION

Śakti in its fivefold aspect therefore is the principle of the universal manifestation. *Cit-śakti,* the power of self-consciousness, entails *ānanda,* enjoyment and wonderment, on the part of Śiva ; bliss gives rise to *icchā,* desire, to create ; desire to create cannot be fulfilled unless there is *jñāna,* knowledge, of what is to be created and how it is to be created ; this knowledge is followed by the actual creation or manifestation, the power of which is *kriyā-śakti.* Sometimes, however, *cit-* and *ānanda-śaktis* are kept in the background, and *icchā, jñāna,* and *kriyā* are taken to be the principal powers.[13]

The universe originally exists in identity with Reality, which is

[12] *Īśvara-pratyabhijñā-vimarśinī,* I. 5. 13.

[13] *Tantrasāra,* p. 6.

simultaneously static and dynamic, being and becoming at the same time. The dynamic aspect or Śakti, when slightly 'swollen' as it were,[14] manifests the universe out of Herself, as the seed does the banyan tree (*vaṭadhānikāvat*).[15] Thus Śakti or Śiva considered not as transcendent identity, but as immanent unity, is both the material and the instrumental cause of the universe. When there is the self-reflection of Śiva, Śakti serving as a mirror, there emerges the 'ego' or the 'I' in Śiva. From here starts the universal manifestation, as has been said above. Since there is nothing apart from, or independent of, Śiva, the elements of the universe can be nothing but Śiva Himself. These constituent elements of the universe, which are 'constants' through *sṛṣṭi* and *pralaya*, are called *tattvas* or categories. *Sṛṣṭi*, which is nothing but self-manifestation, is described as opening out (*unmeṣa*), and *pralaya* as closing down (*nimeṣa*),[16] like a bud opening out as a flower, and the petals of the blooming flower closing down as the bud. *Sṛṣṭi* and *pralaya* follow each other in a never-ending process, each successive universe being determined in its character by its predecessor by a kind of causal necessity.

ŚIVA'S AṆUTVA THROUGH SELF-LIMITATION

This *unmeṣa* or opening out is in one sense a limitation of Śiva, His disappearance (*tirodhāna*). Śiva is said to have five eternal functions. They are *tirodhāna, sṛṣṭi, sthiti, saṁhāra* or *pralaya,* and *anugraha,* that is, limitation or disappearance, creation, preservation, dissolution, and compassion or grace. The universe, which is the collective name of the system of limited subjects and objects, cannot come into manifestation unless Śiva assumes limitation. It is only by coercing His infinitude and transcendent character that Śiva can manifest the universe out of Himself. This power of obscuration or self-limitation is called *tirodhāna,* and the limitation takes the form of *aṇutva* or atomicity. It is also called *saṅkoca,* contraction. Because of this contraction, there is effected a dichotomy in Śiva, who is consciousness-power. The dichotomy is that of *bodha* or consciousness on the one side, and *svātantrya* or power or independence on the other. *Bodha* tends to become devoid of *svātantrya,* and *svātantrya* of *bodha.* Though neither of them is completely devoid or empty of the other, still, for all practical purposes, we can say that there is a separation between consciousness and power. The aspect of consciousness loses the integral self-consciousness. Śiva does not see the universe to be identical with Himself. And since the universe is Śakti originally, we can say conscious-

[14] Maheśvarānanda, *Mahārthamañjarī*, 14, with commentary.
[15] *Pratyabhijñāhṛdaya*, 4, with commentary.
[16] *Spanda-nirṇaya*, I. 1, with commentary.

ness becomes static and sterile of His creative power, and power becomes blind without awareness of Her being truly consciousness. The situation is well described as 'an inert soul and a somnambulist force'.[17] Atomicity therefore is the condition of powerless awareness and senseless power.

After the primary limitation of *aṇutva* or atomicity, Śiva undergoes a secondary limitation with the help of Māyā, and then is described as Puruṣa. Though Śiva in His own nature is eternal, all-pervasive, omnipotent, omniscient, and all-enjoying consciousness, as Puruṣa He is limited in time and space, and has limited knowledge, authorship, and interest or enjoyment. This fivefold limitation is derived from Māyā which also provides both location and object to the Puruṣa by evolving the physical universe. We have said above that along with the emergence of the 'ego' or the 'I', that of the object or the 'it' has also to be conceived. In Śiva this dichotomy is absent, because He is the integral Reality and beyond the distinction of subject and object. But because of self-limitation of Śiva, there emerges, against the background of the distinctionless pure consciousness of Śiva, a polarity of 'subject' and 'object', *aham* and *idam*. At the outset, the dichotomy is only ideal. But as the process of opening out or manifestation of Śakti proceeds, the distance between the two increases till they are sundered apart.

THE FIVE KAÑCUKAS AND THREE MALAS

It is in *aśuddha-māyā* that the atomic Śiva is shrouded by the five *kañcukas* or covers of Māyā, viz. *kalā, vidyā, rāga, kāla*, and *niyati*.[18] This Māyā is *vedyaprathā*, the knowledge of difference, the creatrix of the divorce between the subject and the object, while Prakṛti, which comes simultaneously into existence with Puruṣa, is the power that actually manifests the universe down to material things. Māyā (which is itself sometimes regarded as a *kañcuka*) and the five *kañcukas*, together with the twenty-five *tattvas* (including Puruṣa) of the Sāṁkhya, make up the thirty-one categories that constitute the empirical world of finites. The recognition by the Puruṣa or the *paśu* as being in truth Śiva Himself presupposes not only the transcendence of the sense of difference, but also the realization of identity with everything. It implies not only the piercing of Māyā, but the progressive unification of the self with the whole universe. The five higher categories of *śuddha-māyā* represent the stages of this progressive unification

[17] Sri Aurobindo, *Sāvitrī*, 'The Vision and the Boon'.

[18] In most of the texts this *kañcuka* is called *vidyā*, though Abhinavagupta in his *Paramārthasāra*, 16, uses the word *avidyā*. Yogamuni, the commentator, however, reverts to the more usual term, viz. *vidyā*. See the list of categories in any text, for instance, *Ṣaṭtriṁśat-tattvasandoha* and *Parāpraveśikā* by Kṣemarāja. In this connection, it is noteworthy that the ordinary empirical knowledge of the world is designated as *jñāna* and not *ajñāna*. See next note.

and make up the total of thirty-six categories of the system. The atomic limitation or impurity of the bound self, *aṇutva* or *āṇavamala,* is responsible for the non-intuition, *akhyāti,* of the true nature of the self, and is twofold. First, there is the rise of the non-self, or rather that of the idea of non-self in the self, leading to the false sense of the self in the non-self.[19] Once Śiva has become self-limited, He is the *paśu* who is not the Lord of everything. As limited, *paśu* is not everything, and yet, because of non-intuition, the *paśu* falsely identifies himself with what he is not. The basic limitation, *āṇavamala,* is reinforced by two other impurities, viz. *māyīyamala* and *kārmamala. Māyīyamala* represents the whole series of categories, beginning from the covers or *kañcukas,* that create the physical organism on the subjective side, and evolves the physical world down to earth, the last of the *mahābhūtas,* on the objective side. *Kārmamala* is responsible for continuing the fetters of embodiment, and it is due to this impurity or *mala* that the Puruṣa becomes subject to good and bad acts,[20] and becomes entangled in repeated births and deaths.

All souls suffer from one or more of these three kinds of impurities. Three types of soul in bondage are recognized in the Trika: when a soul has only the *āṇavamala,* it is called *vijñānākala* ; when it has both the *āṇava-* and *kārma-malas,* it is known as *pralayākala* ; and when it has all the three *malas,* it is designated *sakala.* The *sakala* souls are embodied, and include both gods and men. All of them have bodies differing according to their planes of existence within the sphere of Māyā, technically called *māyāṇḍa,* the 'Māyā egg'.[21] The Trika accepts *mahāpralaya* or great dissolution, during which all the *tattvas* or categories lower than Māyā are absorbed into Māyā, their cause. In this state all bound souls become disembodied and without organs, and are known as *pralayākalas* or 'become disembodied during *pralaya*', but because of the persistence of the *kārmamala* they may become embodied again. Souls free from both *kārma-* and *māyīya-malas* transcend *aśuddha-māyā,* but do not, because of that, realize their identity with Śiva. Though they have ascended to the realm of *śuddha-māyā* and are known as *vijñānākalas,* they still have the *āṇavamala* to get rid of to lose their finitude. They are free from the sense of duality, but they do not achieve the perfect integration of consciousness and power, which is the nature of Śiva. This is why, it is said, the *vijñānākala* does not realize his identity with the universe, does not experience the fact that 'I am all this'. It is not possible for these souls to attain to Śivahood unless and until their impurity of atomicity is removed.

[19] *Śiva-Sūtra,* I. 2: '*Jñānaṁ bandhaḥ*' (knowledge is bondage), with commentary.
[20] *Īśvara-pratyabhijñā,* III. 2. 4-6. [21] *Paramārthasāra,* 4, with commentary.

REMOVAL OF THE AṆUTVA—ITS FIVE STAGES

Since atomicity is due to the self-contraction, *ātma-sañkoca,* of Śiva Himself, it can be removed not by the soul's own effort, but by some function of Him who imposed the limitation. This function of Śiva is *anugraha,* compassion or grace. As a result of grace, the soul, already delivered from Māyā, that is, from the false sense of duality between itself and the object, progresses towards the perfect integration of the object into itself. The *'idam'* must be absorbed into the *'aham'*, for, so long as they are separate, there is no attainment of the complete 'I'ness, the *pūrṇāhantā,* by the soul, and without that there is no bliss. Thus, the soul remains limited in various ways, until the atomic impurity is removed.

The stages of the removal of atomicity are the five *tattvas* or categories belonging to *śuddha-māyā* which, counted from below, are *sad-* or *śuddha-vidyā, īśvara, sādākhya* or *sadāśiva, śakti,* and *śiva.* From another point of view they represent, as said above, the progressive union of consciousness and power, of *bodha* and *svātantrya.*

In these *tattvas,* the 'I' and the 'it' have a common substratum, *samānādhikaraṇa,* while in Māyā and below that they have different *adhikaraṇas* or substrata. In other words, when the soul is in any of these *tattvas,* it regards the 'it' or the object to be within itself. There is the 'idea' or the sense of the object, but it is not regarded as separate in actuality. The bound soul, however, cannot regard the 'object' to be within itself. Since Śiva has the inherent awareness of the universe being within His own being, the liberated soul, who attains identity with Śiva, must have the same awareness. It is by the power of Māyā that Śiva shows whatever is within Himself as being external and separate. That is why souls, even when subject to *śuddha-māyā,* cannot have the sense of identity with everything. When Śiva, as a result of self-limitation, regards the object as not His own manifestation, but as separate and independent, He becomes a bound soul subject to Māyā. But before this actual separation is effected, there is an ideal emergence of the 'it' or the object, though it is regarded as being within oneself as the subject or *'aham'*.

In *sad-vidyā* or *śuddha-vidyā,* though the 'I' and the 'it' are not separate, still the 'it' is more prominent. In other words, in this category there is greater ideal separation between the subject and object than in the other four higher categories. *Śuddha-vidyā* represents a greater emergence of the 'it' or the object. The experience in this stage, expressed as 'I am I and this is this', is like the pointing by the finger at the head of a newly born baby. Truly speaking, the head is an integral part of the body, but still it is distinguished from the body. Here the diversity and difference of objective consciousness are not annulled, though they are now recognized as an experience of the subject and therefore in some way identical with it. In the *īśvara-tattva,* there is perfect balance between the two, neither being more prominent than the other. The experience that the soul has in this stage is 'I am this', while that in the former may be expressed in the form 'I am I and this is this'. *Sadāśiva* represents the stage where there is the sense of 'being' in the subject. But 'being' means 'being something'. Thus it is in this stage that the idea of the *idam* or 'it' first emerges. The experience of the soul in the *sadāśiva* stage may be formulated as 'I am this'. Its difference from the experience in the *īśvara* stage may be described as follows. In *sadāśiva, pūrṇāhantā* or the attainment of perfect subjecthood takes the form of a complete identification of the subject and the object, while in the *īśvara* stage they are not identified but held in equipoise.

The emergence of the object in the *sadāśiva* stage is only nominal, it is like the faint outline of a picture, or even like the initial desire in the mind of the artist to paint a picture.[22] Applying this analogy to the *īśvara-tattva,* it may be said that there the faint outline becomes somewhat clear. In the *śakti-tattva,* again, there is merely the idea or experience of being what may be expressed as 'I am'. We cannot say that in this stage the object or the *idam* has made an appearance. *Śakti-tattva* is described as the seed of the universe, the *bīja-bhūmi* of all ideas or *bhāvas* in the consciousness of Śiva. It is also described as void (*śūnya*) or great void (*mahāśūnya*), because nothing has manifested itself in this stage,[23] or because it negates the 'ideal' universe in Śiva ; whence its name *niṣedha-vyāpārarūpā* (process of negating).[24] Or, it might be said that it negates or suppresses the unitary character of the *śiva-tattva,* without which process the universe of manifoldness cannot be manifested.

In the five higher or pure (*śuddha*) *tattvas* just described, *cit-*, *ānanda-*, *icchā-*, *jñāna-*, and *kriyā-śaktis* are respectively predominant. The first throb or stir (*spanda*) of Śiva is *śiva-tattva,* which is only Śiva's awareness of Himself as 'I'. That is why *cit-śakti* is said to be predominant in the *śiva-tattva.* When the 'I' has the sense of being, when there is the experience of 'I am', there is bliss ; in other words, *ānanda-śakti* predominates in the *śakti-tattva.* In *sadāśiva* there is the predominance of *icchā-śakti,* because there is a will in Śiva to create in order to fill the void due to the *śakti-tattva.* *Jñāna-śakti* is said to be predominant in the *īśvara-tattva,* because there is in this stage the clear identification of the subject and the object, the experience being 'I am this'. In the *śuddha-vidyā,*

[22] *Īśvara-pratyabhijñā-vimarśinī,* II. pp. 192-93.
[23] *Paramārthasāra,* 14, with commentary.
[24] *Ibid.,* 13, 14, with commentary.

kriyā-śakti is predominant. Here the object or the *idam* has clearly emerged, and there is separation between subject and object, between *bodha* and *svātantrya*. The stage in which the objective element, the power aspect, becomes predominant as distinct from the self or consciousness is justifiably said to have *kriyā-śakti* prominent in it.

Beginning from *śuddha-* or *sad-vidyā* upto *śiva-tattva,* the endeavour of the aspirant soul is to absorb and integrate the object progressively into itself. The complete identification results in the realization of *pūrṇāhantā* or complete subjecthood, which means nothing but the experience of identity between the self and the universe. Subjecthood eats up objecthood, that is, it destroys the sense of separation. This, however, does not imply that the manifold variety of the universe is abrogated, but only that the sense of separation between 'I' and the 'it', the self and the universe, is completely overcome. This has been described as 'selfing' or the process of *ātmasāt,*[25] that is, making the other one's own. But even in *śiva-tattva* there is the taint of atomicity, at least its *saṁskāra* or trace remains.

The souls in the different *tattvas* are given different names as knowers or *pramātṛs*. Apart from *sakala, pralayākala,* and *vijñānākala* mentioned above, the *pramātṛs* or experiencers in the five higher *tattvas,* counting from below, are respectively called *mantra, mantreśvara, mantramaheśvara, śāktya,* and *śāmbhava.* But there is some difference of opinion on the subject.

UNIVERSE AS ŚIVA'S KRĪḌĀ OR PLAY

Thus, the universe is manifested with Śiva Himself as the basis or foundation.[26] And it is manifested on the basis of identity.[27] The manifestation is compared to the sleeping of Śiva. And when some spiritual aspirant recognizes himself as Śiva, it is symbolically expressed as the awakening of Śiva. When Śiva is awake, there is no sense of a separate universe. The emergence of the universe is also called descent of Śiva, and the spiritual self's journey towards Śiva is called ascent. If it is asked why Śiva should manifest Himself, the answer is that it is natural for consciousness to assume many forms. It is also said that Śiva's self-imposition of limitation upon Himself and also His breaking the fetters and returning to His own native glory are both *krīḍā* or play.[28]

[25] *Pratyabhijñāhṛdaya,* 15. [26] *Ibid.*, 4, with commentary.
[27] *Paramārthasāra,* 13, 14, with commentary.
[28] *Spanda-nirṇaya,* I. 1 ; cf. Abhinavagupta's phrase '*nityakrīḍā-rasotsukaḥ*' in *Bodhapañcadaśikā,* 6.

BONDAGE AND LIBERATION

Śiva as Śakti manifests Himself as a correlated order of knowers, knowables, and means of knowledge.[29] This threefold self-division of Śiva appears on the background provided by Śiva Himself. It presupposes, however, a limitation imposed by Śiva upon Himself. The self-limited Śiva is designated the *paśu* or the 'animal', Jīva, *saṁsārin,* etc. The signs of the *paśu* are false identification of the self with the not-self, ascribing the not-self to the self, having limited authorship, knowledge, interest, pervasion, and duration, and being subject to causality. To realize the unfettered condition, to recognize oneself as that which has become, or even is, everything, to have unlimited power to know, enjoy, and manifest self-bliss, to be infinite and eternal, to be completely free from and independent of *niyati,* that is, regulation or causality,—this is the destiny of the *paśu.* To be, or rather to recognize oneself as, Śiva is the goal of the Jīva.

Obviously, the limited individual is subject to ignorance (*ajñāna*), which, according to our system, is twofold, viz. *pauruṣa* and *bauddha. Pauruṣa ajñāna* is the innate ignorance in the very soul of man. It is the primal limitation, the original impurity or *āṇavamala.* It signifies the sense of the self in the not-self and vice versa and the separation of *prakāśa* and *vimarśa,* of *bodha* and *svātantrya.* This is the consequence of the limitation taken willingly and playfully by Śiva upon Himself, and is not removable by the bound soul's own efforts. Śiva alone can liquidate it. *Anugraha* or dispensation of grace, technically called *śaktipāta,* or the descent of Śiva's force, breaks this limitation. How and why and when this force will descend cannot be indicated, because His nature is freedom and spontaneity.

The descent of the force of grace achieves two purposes: first, *pāśa-kṣaya,* the destruction of fetters, and secondly, *Śivatva-yojana,* the restoration of Śivahood, which in effect means the removal of the atomic impurity. But, in spite of this great spiritual gain coming to the soul, the Jīva may not know it. For he is not only a soul or spiritual substance, but has his ordinary Māyic nature attached to him. He has to know things through the instrument of his *buddhi,* his intelligence, which is gross and impure. Thus, in spite of obtaining *Śivatva,* he cannot enjoy it, for his normal consciousness is not affected by what happens to his inner soul. In those on whom the *śakti* or grace descends in great

[29] The main idea is that *saṁvid* or consciousness is the one true source of knowledge. Siddha Somānanda, in *Śiva-dṛṣṭi,* argues against the other normally accepted *pramāṇas,* like perception and inference. Later writers, including Abhinavagupta, accept these *pramāṇas* as means of ordinary empirical knowledge, but insist that *saṁvid* is the real instrument not only in the field of true spiritual knowledge, but also in that of normal empirical cognition.

force (*dṛḍha-śaktipāta-viddha*), the purification of *buddhi* may also occur immediately. But it is a rare phenomenon ; so, actually speaking, the Jīva has to adopt other means to know and enjoy his newly won spiritual gain.

Thus, in spite of the restoration of *Śivatva,* the soul has still a lot to accomplish. *Śivatva-yojana* only means that the soul is given by its own higher self, i.e. Śiva, its lost or hidden essence of divinity. But to have the essence of divinity is not to be the supreme and integral Divine. It remains for the soul to develop in himself all the aspects of Śakti which really make Śiva all that He is. The becoming of Śiva in essence is accomplished by the removal of the atomic impurity, which alone can achieve full Śivahood. Here the soul achieves likeness to Śiva and becomes qualified to know Reality fully and completely.

Now let us recall for a moment that the fall of the soul from the *parārdha,* the higher region of the five pure (*śuddha*) *tattvas,* where the separation of the subject and the object is ideal, into the sphere of *aśuddha-māyā,* in which the separation is actual, is due to the fact that the soul loses its integral subjecthood, *pūrṇāhantā.* The Jīva has a sense of 'I' or subjecthood even in the sphere of Māyā, and that distinguishes him from material things. Indeed the Trika says that even in the condition of bondage, the Jīva fulfils the five eternal functions of concealment or disappearance, creation, preservation, dissolution, and grace, though in a very small and restricted measure.[30] Unless it were so, the identity of the limited bound soul and the infinite free Śiva could not be asserted. But in the sphere of Māyā, which may be described as the region of the *idantā* or objecthood, any sense of *ahantā* or subjecthood is derived from the object or the *idam* which has separated itself from the true subject. The true subject has not the sense of distinction from anybody or anything, but the subject of the Jīvas in Māyā is an instrument of perpetuating distinctions and not resolving them. It is *ahaṅkāra* and not *ahantā,* egoism and not real subjecthood, that is a product of Māyā which is the great *idam* in relation to the real and genuine *aham.* To attain integral Śivahood, the Jīva must recapture the all-inclusive pure 'I', which has no idea of the object, by adopting appropriate means.

The most important of these is *dīkṣā* or initiation. The Trika says that as a result of *śaktipāta* one is brought to a real *guru.*[31] *Dīkṣā* awakens the *kriyā-śakti* in the limited soul which is devoid of *svātantrya.* The development of *kriyā-śakti* ultimately means the soul's ability to absorb and integrate the 'it' or the object, seemingly separate from itself, within its own self. The consummation of this development is the soul's

[30] *Pratyabhijñāhṛdaya,* 10.

[31] *Paramārthasāra,* 96, with commentary.

recognition and realization of itself as the integral 'I', the enjoyment of the rapture and bliss of *pūrṇāhantā.* This is the dawning of *pauruṣa-jñāna,* the true knowledge about the real and ultimate nature of the Puruṣa. To be able to enjoy in life this inherent, reawakened Śivahood, which was so long veiled, *bauddha-jñāna,* or knowledge of this internal liberated condition through *buddhi,* must be attained also. This depends on the purification of *buddhi,* the means of which are the study of the Śāstra, *vicāra,* etc. *Bauddha-jñāna* does not mean scholarship or intellectual understanding of the scriptures or philosophy. It is a deeper discipline than a mere mental understanding. When with the rise of *bauddha-jñāna, bauddha-ajñāna* is removed, there dawns knowledge, even in *buddhi,* of the state of liberation. This is *jīvanmukti* (liberation during lifetime). Even without *jīvanmukti* the soul's liberation is accomplished with the liquidation of the innate ignorance of the atomic impurity. Only so long as *buddhi* is not purified and does not reflect the inner condition of freedom, the embodied being is not able to know and enjoy it.

The removal of *pauruṣa-ajñāna* is followed by the rise of spiritual knowledge, *pauruṣa-jñāna.* It is spiritual knowledge for two reasons: it is the knowledge of the spirit in all its aspects and integrality, it is also a knowledge obtained by the spiritual element in the Jīva. Though it is described in terms of knowledge, it is, to be precise, the realization of perfect and supreme *Śivatva,* that is, the state of Paramaśiva, which is the condition of equilibrium, also called *yāmala,* of Śiva and Śakti. It is the state in which neither *prakāśa* nor *vimarśa* is predominant over the other, and it is timeless eternity holding in itself endless succession. *Krama* and *akrama,* sequence and simultaneity, are both one and the same, according to the Trika; they are only two phases of the same perfect Reality. The attainment of the state of Paramaśiva is also to become the Lord of *śakti-cakra,* the circle of powers.[32] Between the initial rise of spiritual knowledge and its fullest development, when all the modes of Śakti are perfectly developed, there is such a thing as progress towards the consummation. One reason of this is that the *saṁskāra* of the atomic impurity persists, though the taint itself is liquidated.

THE FOUR UPĀYAS

There are four *upāyas* or means of attaining the supreme goal. They are *anupāya, śāmbhava, śākta,* and *āṇava-upāya.* Of these the first *anupāya* (no-means) or *ānandopāya* (blissful means) does not really involve any process. Due to *śaktipāta,* or descent of grace in a very intense degree, everything needed for the realization, beginning from the liquida-

[32] *Spanda-nirṇaya,* I. 1.

tion of the atomic impurity down to the recognition of the state of Paramaśiva, may be achieved by the aspirant immediately and without going through any *sādhanā* or discipline. Here the direct means is Śakti Herself, and a word from the *guru*, the spiritual teacher, regarding the identity of the individual with the ultimate Reality is sufficient to reveal the truth.[33] The soul immediately realizes its own transcendent nature along with the realization of the whole universe as its own glory reflected in its own integral 'I'.

Before taking up the exposition of the other means, a word about the Trika conception of *vikalpa* and *nirvikalpa* will be helpful. Our system conceives Śiva as *nirvikalpa*, free from *vikalpa* or determination consisting of conceptual unification of the 'many' into the 'one', distinguishing between one object of cognition and another, and between 'this' and 'not-this', and accepting one among many stimuli received from outside. But since Paramaśiva is the perfect inalienable identity, there is nothing from which it can be distinguished. Hence there is no *vikalpa* in Paramaśiva who is *nirvikalpa*. In the *śāmbhava-upāya,* the *nirvikalpa* knowledge is awakened in the aspirant through *dīkṣā* itself, and all *vikalpas* are immediately destroyed. Through *nirvikalpa* knowledge, the limited 'I' of the individual is united with the unlimited 'I' of its own higher self, as a result of which the 'this' or the object, so long apprehended separately from the soul, is absorbed into and unified with the 'I', which was so long limited and exclusive. This means is also called *icchopāya,* because the element of will plays a great part in it.

In the *śāktopāya,* conceptual determinations or *vikalpas* have to be purified before the soul can attain to the *nirvikalpa* illumination. For this purification are needed pure intuition (*sattarka*), knowledge of the right scriptures (*sadāgama*), and a genuine *guru* (*sadguru*). Getting instruction in the Āgamas from a true *guru* gives rise to a succession of *vikalpas* of the same nature (*sajātīya-vikalpa*). This is *sattarka* and is the gateway to *nirvikalpa-parāmarśa* (apprehension devoid of determination), because determinations of the same nature form a step towards unity or oneness. It is asserted that meditation, concentration, etc. do not help the rousing of *saṁvid* or consciousness. The purpose of these practices or disciplines is to wrest the *saṁvid,* which is involved and diffused, from the body, vital airs, and *buddhi*. But since *saṁvid* is the only Reality, knowledge of duality is nothing in itself, and it is removed through the rise of *śuddha vikalpa* or *nirvikalpa*. Through its own spontaneous freedom, *saṁvid* becomes its own *akhyāti,* non-intuition, resulting in the denial of its own

[33] Cf. *'Gurumukhādeva vidyā vīryavatī bhavati'*.

self-nature, and then, of its own accord, it blooms out as the true knowledge. The process is natural and due to *svātantrya*, and, as such, the practice of *yoga* is not a direct means towards its blooming. The right means therefore is *sattarka*, pure intuition, which can be attained through *yāga* (sacrifice), *homa* (oblation in fire), *vrata* (solemn vow), *japa* (repetition of holy word), and *yoga* (spiritual discipline).[34]

The main point about *āṇava-upāya* is that personal effort, *puruṣakāra*, is needed for the purification of *vikalpa*. Personal effort takes the form of certain definite disciplines. They are *dhyāna, uccāra, varṇa,* and observance of *bāhya-vidhi* or external injunctions. *Buddhi, prāṇa* (vital force), and the body are the means of these disciplines.

Dhyāna means meditation in the heart-space (*hṛdayākāśa*) on the supreme Reality inherent in all the *tattvas*, and also on the unification, in the supreme Consciousness, of the knower, means of knowledge, and the knowables, technically called *vahni, arka,* and *soma* respectively.[35] By this process of meditation the whole field of knowables is swallowed up and absorbed into the knower. Once the universe has been absorbed into one's own conscious self, it has to be manifested and externalized again, and one has to feel one's identity with the very highest, the *anuttara*; this will mean his control and mastery of the powers involved in the function of manifestation. With that achieved and without losing it, he has to have the experience of manifesting the universe, a world of objects, just as Śiva does. The re-manifestation of the universe, along with the realization of one's identity with it and with its ground, viz. Śiva, destroys all sense of duality. *Uccāra* essentially means the directing of *prāṇa*, the vital force, upwards. Here also the goal is the swallowing up or the destruction of the discrete knowable and also of the universe as a whole, and thus, ultimately, the destruction of the sense of duality. The recognition of the inherent identity with the Highest, *samāveśa* in *saṁvid*, is the ultimate aim. *Varṇa* is a discipline in which the *sūkṣma* or subtle *prāṇa* is the means of *sādhanā*. In the practice of *uccāra*, a kind of undifferentiated sound or *dhvani* spontaneously emerges and is called *varṇa*. Its form is the *bīja* or seed-word of creation and destruction. Constant repetition of the *bīja* results in the attainment of supreme *saṁvid*.

Through any of these means, the limited individual, poor in powers (*śakti-daridraḥ*), attains to the rich treasure of his own true Self. In point of fact, the individual all the time experiences nothing but Śiva, but being limited, does not give any attention to his constant apprehension of Śiva. When the much desired attention falls on the apprehension of the

[34] *Tantrasāra*, pp. 25-28.

[35] *Ibid.*, p. 36.

Self, which is no other than Śiva, there is *pratyabhijñā* or recognition of the fact that 'I am everything and simultaneously transcendent of everything, that is, nothing in particular and yet all things together'. In the state of Paramaśiva, there is no emergence, nor any absorption of the universe. To recognize oneself as the *sthiti-sāmya,* the perfect harmony of being and becoming, is what the soul should seek after and realize

HARMONY IS THE WATCHWORD OF TRIKA

The Trika does not stop with the deliverance of the soul from Māyā, from the delusion of duality; it goes further to the concept of divinization of the soul, which means the recognition of its own identity with Paramaśiva, with Parameśvara. This recognition is the same as realizing identity with everything and also freedom from everything. Thus, in a sense, harmony is the watchword of the practical spiritual discipline of the Trika.

The Trika philosophy promises to satisfy almost all sides of human nature, of knowledge, love, and will. Śiva being unitary consciousness as such, the realization of Śiva gives knowledge of everything by identity with everything; and Śiva being at constant play with His own Śakti, there is ample scope for *bhakti,* devotion or love; also to recognize oneself as Paramaśiva means mastery and lordship of *śakti* and thus implies sovereign and unrestricted will.

Two points remain to be noticed. The Trika does not give an independent reality to Prakṛti as the Sāṁkhya does, for according to it, Prakṛti represents a stage in the evolution of the universe out of Paramaśiva. At the same time, it does not reduce the universe to a mere illusion out of Māyā, as the Advaita Vedānta seems to do. In its Ābhāsavāda, it reduces the universe to an experience of Paramaśiva appearing to Him, not in the form in which it appears to a bound soul, but as if it were distinct like an object seen in a mirror. The theistic element, again, is brought out by the rejection of the Yoga view that release is attained by the unaided effort of the spiritual aspirant, and by the admission that the final step of liberation is provided by the grace of Śiva.

5

VĪRAŚAIVISM

HISTORICITY OF VĪRAŚAIVISM

THE inscriptions of Mohenjo-daro and Harappā have revealed that the cult of Śiva was probably current as far back as 3000 B.C. To quote Sir John Marshall, 'Among the many revelations that Mohenjo-daro and Harappā have had in store for us, none perhaps is more remarkable than the discovery that Śaivism has a history going back to the Chalcolithic age or perhaps even further still, and that it takes its place as the most ancient living faith in the world.'[1] Some are of opinion that Śiva is the God of the Dravidians, or Proto-Indians. The prominent characteristic of Śaivism from its very inception was the worship and meditation of the creative cosmic Principle. The image of Śiva (*śivaliṅga*), found in all the Śaiva temples throughout India, is only a plastic representation of self-existent Truth.[2] This *śivaliṅga* form of worship, as we have it in temples, is the characteristic feature of Śaivism.

It is rather difficult to determine the time when Śaivism was reduced to definite shape. However, the basic philosophy and practice of Śaivism have been set forth in the Āgamas. The two streams of thought, the Āgamic and the Vedic, gradually gravitated towards each other. In course of time, they acted and reacted upon each other and modified each other's contents and practices in religion. The Vedic fire-cult languished and decayed and was replaced by the Āgamic worship of the images in temples and houses. The Vedic *varṇāśrama* was accepted and incorporated in the Āgamic lore. Hence we find the influence of *varṇāśrama* running either subtly or grossly throughout all the schools of Śaivism. Thus Śaivism flourished, with minor differentiations, from pre-Vedic times to the end of the eleventh century, and its exponents hailed from the North as well as from the South. The beginning of the twelfth century saw the ascendency of Jainism and Vaiṣṇavism, and the decadence of Śaivism. By the middle of the twelfth century there appeared in Karṇāṭaka a great hero, named Basava, who arrested this deterioration of Śaivism, freed it from the shackles of the *varṇāśrama*, and infused a new life into it.[3] It is this revived, regenerated, and revolutionary Śaivism that goes by the name of Vīraśaivism or Liṅgāyata religion.

One of the monumental deeds of Basava, the founder of Vīraśaivism,

[1] *Mohenjo-daro and the Indus Civilization*, Preface, p. vii.
[2] Heras, *Mystic Teachings of the Haridāsas of Karṇāṭaka*, Historical Introduction, p. xlii.
[3] Prof. Sakhare, *History and Philosophy of Liṅgāyata Religion*, pp. 415-16.

was the founding of an institution called Śivānubhava-maṇṭapa (the religious house of experience).[4] We may fittingly call it the birth-place and cradle of Vīraśaivism. It was a spiritual as well as a social institution, organized by Basava and presided over by Allama Prabhu, a great saint. That this institution, so important in the religious history of India, was founded by Basava about A.D. 1160 is corroborated by the sayings of his contemporaries. Śivānubhava-maṇṭapa stands pre-eminent in the history of Vīraśaivism, since it was through this institution that the Liṅgāyata religion came into shape. It was a nucleus round which gathered persons of all ranks and professions, from prince to peasant, to take part in the discussions of religious, social, and spiritual matters. Among these learned persons, numbering about three hundred, there were about sixty women saints, of whom Akka Mahādevī was the greatest. To this institution we owe the *vacana* literature in Kannada, which is unique in the cultural history of Karṇāṭaka. From it emerged the Ṣaṭ-sthala philosophy, the most remarkable and essential feature of the faith. The institution, moreover, is responsible for introducing important religious practices, such as *pañcācāra* and *aṣṭāvaraṇa,* for undertaking activities of social amelioration, such as the elevation of the status of women, the abolition of caste distinctions, and the removal of untouchability, and for inculcating the dignity of manual labour and simplicity of life in the community.

ITS PRINCIPAL DOGMAS

There are two dogmas traditionally handed down in Vīraśaivism: (1) that Vīraśaivism was founded very long ago by the five great prophets, namely, Revaṇārādhya, Maruḷārādhya, Ekorāmārādhya, Paṇḍitārādhya, and Viśvārādhya ; and (2) that these prophets rose out of five great *sthāvara-liṅgas* of Balehalli in Mysore State, of Ujjani in Bellary District, of Kedāra in the Himalayas, of Śrīśaila Mallikārjuna in Madras State, and of Kāśī or Banaras, under different names in different ages. Prof. Sakhare has arrived at the conclusion that the *ācāryas* are not the originators of the Vīraśaiva faith, since some of them are found to be contemporaries of Basava, and others even later than he.[5] Dr. Ramana Sastri, in *Siddhānta-dīpikā,*[6] says that such opinions as the five great prophets founding the faith in each successive age should be taken only in a figurative sense and not in a literal sense. Labouring under the notion that high antiquity is a mark of soundness and adds to the greatness of its principles, some persons have enthusiastically attempted to push back the origin of Vīraśaivism to very ancient times. Such a view clearly lacks historical perspective. With the advance of

[4] *Ibid.*, pp. 416-18. [5] *Ibid.*, pp. 361-416. [6] Vol. XI.

historical research, it is becoming clear that Basava is the founder of the Vīraśaiva faith, that it is a religion with a *liṅga* as its guiding and central theme, that the Liṅgāyata religion has its own individuality and independent status, and that it has a path, practice, and philosophy all its own. Some information about the Liṅgāyata religion has already been supplied by learned scholars, among whom are Fleet, Rice, and Enthoven;[7] but on the whole, the information is scanty and even misleading in many places, because they were not in possession of the right material, which is only now becoming available.

We have already seen that the characteristic feature of Śaivism is the *śivaliṅga* form of worship, *śivaliṅga* being a plastic representation of self-existent Truth. But the distinctive mark of Vīraśaivism is the *iṣṭaliṅga* form of worship; that is to say, it advocates the wearing of a *liṅga* upon the body by each person, so that the body shall be a temple fit for God to dwell in. The *liṅga* thus worn becomes symbolic of the presence of God in the body, galvanizing and purifying every cell in it. Thus Vīraśaivism enjoins the habit of constantly living in actual contact with God. This cult has adherents, numbering about six millions, scattered all over India, but concentrated mainly in Karṇāṭaka.

PRACTICE OF RELIGION

The individual soul is covered with *mala* or impurity, but for which it would be all-knowing. One who is not so covered is not limited in knowledge, as for example, Śiva. It is this impurity of limitation that goes by the name of *āṇavamala*. Being thus covered or concealed, the individual soul begins to have experience of objects as distinct from the Self, and this perception of different objects constitutes *māyāmala*. From this *māyāmala* springs the whole material and mental world. The soul, being thus limited in knowledge and deluded in the perception of external objects, begins to act meritoriously or otherwise, and as a consequence undergoes transmigration. This is *karmamala* or impurity of action. And this action gives rise to *jāti* (nature of species), *āyus* (length of life), and *bhoga* (type of enjoyment). Tied by these three bonds, the individual soul is called *paśu*. The supreme Soul is called *pati*. The word '*pati*' means one who protects or controls *paśu* by the fivefold activity of creation, preservation, destruction, dispensation, and emancipation. But the human soul has to be reborn and reshaped and re-tempered, until it has learnt to be attuned to the Infinite.

How can this be brought about? Vīraśaivism says: by *dīkṣā*. *Dīkṣā* or

[7] For references see Dr. S. C. Nandimath, *A Handbook of Vīraśaivism*, pp. 231-32.

initiation is a very important ceremony in almost all the recognized religions of the world. It is a recurrent and dominant note in religion in one form or another. But the Vīraśaiva *dīkṣā* synchronizes with *liṅga-dhāraṇa* (wearing of the *liṅga*). It is a simple ritual with which are combined ethical preachings and the occultism of *yoga*. The gist of the initiation is that the *guru* transmits his spiritual power to his disciple, which pierces through the veil of nescience and liberates the soul from the three bonds. Thus the liberated soul, that is to say the soul which is freed from *malatraya*, the three kinds of impurity, by virtue of the triple *dīkṣā*,[8] is called *aṅga*, the Godward soul, the soul that aspires to ascend towards God. But this ascent can only be achieved by undergoing a course of strict spiritual discipline and by living a life of devotion to the Godhead or *liṅga*. Such a life of devotion and spiritual discipline forms the practice of this religion as it does of other religions.

The practice of Liṅgāyata religion comprises within itself (1) *pañcācāra* and (2) *aṣṭāvaraṇa*. *Pañcācāra* are the five codes of conduct which lay down the rules of behaviour for the individual members of the Liṅgāyata community as social beings. They are *liṅgācāra, sadācāra, śivācāra, bhṛtyācāra,* and *gaṇācāra*. *Liṅgācāra* enjoins upon a Vīraśaiva that he should daily worship *liṅga,* the representation of the Divine, and that he should be strictly monotheistic. *Sadācāra* requires that a Liṅgāyata should follow a profession and strictly lead a moral and virtuous life. He should earn money by honest work and utilize his savings and surplus for others in need. He should feed and clothe the *jaṅgamas,* the itinerant preachers of the Liṅgāyata religion. By *śivācāra* the members are required to make no difference between one Liṅgāyata and another, as they are all devotees of Śiva. *Śivācāra* therefore demands that a Liṅgāyata should dine and marry freely with other members of the same community, even if they follow different vocations. *Bhṛtyācāra* is the devotee's attitude of complete humility towards Śiva and His devotees. It enjoins upon the devotee to behave humbly and modestly towards men and women, and kindly to all animals. Lastly, *gaṇācāra* represents the spirit of vindication. The Liṅgāyata should not tolerate adverse remarks against the Godhead and ill-treatment of men and animals by others. As a member of the community, he has to strive for its upliftment and development.

Aṣṭāvaraṇa means the eightfold shields that protect the devotee from the onslaughts of nescience, and guide him safely to final beatitude. They shield him from the evils attaching to the worldly life by putting him in

[8] *Kriyā, mantra,* and *vedhā* are the three forms of *dīkṣā*. *Kriyā-dīkṣā* is attended with a proper ceremonial form when the *guru* invests the novice with *liṅga*. *Mantra-dīkṣā* makes the filthy body of flesh a holy one by the *mantra* being whispered in the ears of the novice by the *guru*. *Vedhā-dīkṣā* infuses knowledge into the disciple by direct contact.

tune with the Infinite. They are *guru, liṅga, jaṅgama* (ascetic), *pādodaka* (water sanctified by the touch of the feet of the *guru* or *jaṅgama*), *prasāda* (food so sanctified), *bhasma* (sacred ashes), *rudrākṣa* (rosary), and *mantra* (mystic words).

The *guru* is the spiritual and religious guide who initiates the novice into the Vīraśaiva faith with due forms. It is the *guru* who, by initiation, ushers the devotee into the second or spiritual birth, as it were. It is he who gives the devotee real insight into the principles of the Liṅgāyata religion, explains the inner meaning of the practices, and guides him on the path of righteousness. Since the *guru* has gained the first-hand knowledge of God and the world by experience, the devotee finds great delight in serving and imitating him, and in acquiring knowledge from him. Hence the *guru* has been given the first place among the *aṣṭāvaraṇas*.

The *liṅga* is the centre and basis of all religious practices and observances, because it is the Divinity concretely represented. The custom is that it is given by the *guru* to the body at the very birth. It should always be borne on the body by a person from the time of his birth to that of his death. A Vīraśaiva must not miss his daily worship of the *liṅga*, as it makes the wearer and worshipper conscious of his duty to the Godhead.

The *jaṅgama* is the third *āvaraṇa* and is peculiar to this religion. Its etymological meaning is dynamic knowledge, having the same root *gam* as in Āgama, Nigama, etc. in the sense of knowledge. When it is applied to a person, it means one who has dynamic knowledge of God. He is called a *cara*, because he travels from place to place, preaching religion and morality to all. He is therefore the itinerant *jīvanmukta* (a man emancipated even while living), moving about in the country for the sake of guiding the devotees in their religious and spiritual exercises. A Vīraśaiva is enjoined not to make any distinction between the *guru, liṅga*, and *jaṅgama*, as all of them are believed to be equal and to command the same reverence.

The *pādodaka* is literally the water from the feet of the *guru* or *jaṅgama*. Hence it means holy water. *Prasāda* means consecrated food. *Pādodaka* and *prasāda* are water and food made holy and spiritually magnetized by the touch, sight, or wish (*saṅkalpa*) of the *guru* or *jaṅgama*, which (food and water) in turn create *cidrasa* (divine aura) in the devotee. Apart from this occult meaning, the *pādodaka* and *prasāda* have a simple social significance. In the presence of the *guru* or *jaṅgama*, all devotees, irrespective of caste, colour, creed, age, and sex, are considered equal ; and all partake of the same food and water, thus suggesting a fraternal bond which is a very vital factor in communal solidarity.

The inner intuition which reveals the Self and burns up the illusion is called *bhasma*. As an outer symbol of this, the Liṅgāyata religion enjoins *bhasma-dhāraṇa*, i.e. besmearing the body with the holy ashes. The devotee has to change his angle of vision and try to perceive the Divine in all events and movements. This is the internal *rudrākṣa*. As an outward symbol of this, he has to wear the *rudrākṣamālā* (a rosary of *rudrākṣa* beads). *Mantra* really means meditation, whose vocal expression is embodied in the words '*Namaḥ Śivāya*' (Obeisance to Śiva).

These are the eight *āvaraṇas* which distinguish Vīraśaivism from other sects. These eight shields keep a Liṅgāyata pure in body and mind by protecting him from the onslaughts of Māyā. Thus, a Liṅgāyata is looked upon as a *śivayogin* or *śivaśaraṇa*, who, when he dies, is not burnt but buried, on account of his body and mind having been already burnt by the fire of knowledge. Absence of cremation by fire in Vīraśaivism is noteworthy. The Vīraśaiva believes that the *liṅga* is a great mass of light and fire which, when it is worn on the body, burns all the impurities of an individual by its constant contact. It is on the strength of this belief that the abolition of *pañcasūtaka*,[9] i.e. five pollutions, and the burial of the dead are upheld in Vīraśaivism.

ŚAKTIVIŚIṢṬĀDVAITA

In Vīraśaivism, *sthala* has a philosophical connotation, for the teachers of Vīraśaiva faith address the Divine or the ultimate Reality as *sthala*. The letter '*stha*' denotes the source form which the phenomenal world emerges and draws its sustenance ; and the letter '*la*' denotes the goal to which it tends and in which it ultimately loses itself.[10] Hence *sthala* represents the Divine, termed Parabrahman or Paraśiva, as the source and support of all phenomenal existence, as the ground and goal of all evolution. The *svarūpa* of Parabrahman, according to the Vedānta, is Saccidānanda ; and this nature of Paraśiva is well expressed in terms of His self-consciousness as *asmi, prakāśe, nandāmi*, that it to say, Paraśiva is conscious of His infinite presence, consciousness, and bliss. Hence He is free and unlimited, and *śakti* forms

[9] *Sūtaka* comes from the word *su* (to be born). *Sūta* is one that is born or begotten. Hence *sūtaka* comes to mean birth or production. As the process of birth is always attended with filth, *sūtaka* or birth is looked upon as impurity by *varṇāśrama-dharma*. In course of time, the word lost its original meaning 'birth', and came to be looked upon merely as impurity or pollution. *Sūtaka* is then any impurity or pollution. *Varṇāśrama-dharma* looks upon the act of dying as inauspicious as it visualizes the process of birth as impure. Thus death also is regarded as impurity or *sūtaka*. The idea of *sūtaka* does not restrict itself to the birth or death of an individual in a family. It is stretched still further so as to cover the whole genealogy of a tribe or *kula*. So *jāti-sūtaka* is impurity contracted through the death of a relative belonging to one's own pedigree. *Rajas-sūtaka* is menstrual pollution or impurity, *Ucchiṣṭa* means the food left in the dish after eating. Hence *ucchiṣṭa-sūtaka* means pollution contracted through the touching of food left after being eaten either by oneself or by others.

Hence *jāti-sūtaka, janma-sūtaka, maraṇa-sūtaka, rajas-sūtaka*, and *ucchiṣṭa-sūtaka* may be rendered into English respectively as pedigree pollution, birth pollution, death pollution, menstrual pollution, and leavings (touch of remnants of partaken food) pollution.

[10] Māyideva in his *Anubhava-Sūtra*.

part and parcel of His Self. *Vimarśa-śakti* is the power of self-consciousness of the Lord. It is the conscious nature of Śiva with all the contents still unalienated and unmanifested. The Divine is self-luminous, so is a jewel; but the jewel is not conscious of its capacity, while the Divine is both self-luminous and conscious of His self-luminosity. It is this self-consciousness of the Lord that goes by the name of *vimarśa, ātmavimarśa,* or *parāmarśa,* whose characteristic is that in it consciousness and energy, knowledge and force, are one.

Vimarśa, then, exists in the Divine by the relation of *sāmarasya* (identity), just as heat and light exist by the relation of identity in fire and the sun. It may be objected here that this kind of relation involves a difference between *śakti* (power) and *śakta* (possessor of power). To this the only reply is that the attribute is not different in nature from the substance, yet there is such an expression as the heat of fire, the light of the sun, etc. So it cannot be said that *bheda,* in being the attribute of a thing, and *abheda,* in being the nature of a thing, are always opposite. In other words, between the substance and the attribute there is an inseparable union, or essential identity, which points to a reality that continues to remain in the character of an undivided organic whole. It is for this reason that *Siddhānta-śikhāmaṇi* speaks of *śakti* as *Brahmaniṣṭhā sanātanī.*[11] It is clear from this that *śakti* is intrinsic and ever abiding in Śiva; hence He is characterized and distinguished by His self-conscious power to work wonders. This is Śaktiviśiṣṭādvaita. It is true that Śaiva philosophers of Kashmir imply *śakti-viśiṣṭatva* of Śiva,[12] but they do not express it in so many words. The Liṅgāyata philosophers, on the other hand, are bold enough to express it as Śaktiviśiṣṭādvaita. Here *viśiṣṭatva* does not suggest any inseparable union of two or more entities like soul, world, and God of the Rāmānuja system, or of South Indian Śaivism. *Viśiṣṭatva* simply connotes the nature of *vimarśa,* viz. self-conscious power, i.e. self-consciousness which is power, and, as such, has the fullest power of doing or undoing anything or doing it otherwise.

ṢAṬ-STHALA

We have already seen that the Liṅgāyata teachers address the Divine as *sthala.* The Divine is really unlimited, but the inherent, inalienable power in the Divine in its sheer plenitude brings about limitation in the unlimited. Thus the Supreme or Śiva bifurcates Himself into *liṅga* and *aṅga*; and the divine power into *śakti* and *bhakti.* Here we must mark the meaning of *bhakti. Bhakti* generally means the feeling of devotion

[11] *Siddhānta-śikhāmaṇi,* V. 39.
[12] *Pratyabhijñāhṛdaya* (Adyar Library Ed.), Introduction, p. 12.

or attachment to the Godhead. But here *bhakti* means *upāsanā* or worship, which represents a spirit of self-surrender. This is not to say that worship can be performed without devotional feelings, for these are at the root of all worship. *Liṅga* is *upāsya,* the worshipped; *aṅga* is *upāsaka,* the worshipper; and *bhakti* is *upāsanā,* the worship. *Ṣaṭ-sthala* is a hierarchy where *upāsanā* grows step by step, gaining in content till the apparent duality between *aṅga* and *liṅga* vanishes and *sāmarasya* or at-one-ment is achieved.

The one *sthala* becomes divided into *aṅga* and *liṅga,* each of which again undergoes a threefold modification. Thus we have three forms of *aṅga,* namely, *tyāgāṅga, bhogāṅga,* and *yogāṅga,* corresponding to the three forms of *liṅga,* termed *iṣṭa, prāṇa,* and *bhāva.* The soul in the waking condition is known as *viśvajīva,* that in the dreaming condition as *taijasajīva,* and that in the condition of deep sleep as *prājñajīva. Tyāgāṅga* means the transformed *viśvajīva.* He gives up attachment to worldly objects and so is called *tyāgāṅga,* because *tyāga* or detachment becomes the means through which he realizes his divine nature. *Iṣṭaliṅga* becomes the object of worship to a *tyāgāṅgin. Bhogāṅga* means the transformed *taijasajīva.* The subtle body is the means through which the *taijasajīva* experiences pleasure and pain by means of sensuous objects. The devotee, having given up carnal objects and taken to the realization of the Self, takes delight only in what is conducive to spiritual growth. Hence he is called *bhogāṅgin* to whom *prāṇaliṅga* becomes the object of worship. *Yogāṅga* means the transformed *prājñajīva.* He, being entangled in the causal body, the matrix of ignorance and *vāsanās* (desires), remains separate from Śiva. But the mind and the senses having changed their natural course, the devotee realizes in everything the divine peace and presence. So the old causal body is destroyed, and a new state of consciousness is formed. Hence it is called *yogāṅga,* as it leads to union of *aṅga* with *liṅga. Bhāvaliṅga* becomes the object of worship to a *yogāṅgin. Iṣṭaliṅga, prāṇaliṅga,* and *bhāvaliṅga* are therefore the three aspects of the Divine. *Iṣṭaliṅga* is the *individual* Divine extending itself in the realm of events or actualities. It fulfils what is contained in the truth, what works out the possibilities reflected by the mind, and what appears to us as the fact objectively realized. *Prāṇaliṅga* is the *universal* Divine which takes its stand on the possibilities. It has behind it the freedom of the infinite which it brings in us as a background for the determination of the finite. Therefore every action in the world seems to emerge from a balancing and clashing of various possibilities. *Bhāvaliṅga* is the *infinite* Divine which sees the truth in itself, as the truth in its becoming as well as in its essence. It contains comprehensively and not separately all that emerges as ideas.

Then the three modifications further become twofold each. Thus *iṣṭaliṅga* becomes *ācāraliṅga,* the practical, and *guruliṅga,* the preceptive; *prāṇaliṅga* becomes *śivaliṅga,* the auspicious, and *caraliṅga,* the dynamic; and *bhāvaliṅga* becomes *prasādaliṅga,* the gracious, and *mahāliṅga,* the great. Likewise, when *tyāgāṅga* becomes *bhakta,* who is characterized by a state of faith (*śraddhā-bhakti*) in *ācāraliṅga,* it is *bhakta-sthala*; and when it becomes *maheśa* characterized by firm faith (*niṣṭhā-bhakti*) in *guruliṅga,* it is *maheśa-sthala. Bhogāṅga* becomes *prasādin,* who is characterized by a state of undivided attention (*avadhāna-bhakti*) to *śivaliṅga,* and this is *prasādi-sthala*; and when it becomes *prāṇaliṅga* characterized by a state of experience (*anubhava-bhakti*) of *caraliṅga,* it is *prāṇaliṅga-sthala. Yogāṅga* becomes *śaraṇa,* who is characterized by a mode of pure delight (*ānanda-bhakti*) derived from the contemplation of *prasādaliṅga,* and this is *śaraṇa-sthala*; and it becomes *aikya* characterized by a state of identity (*samarasa-bhakti*) with *mahāliṅga,* the great, and this is *aikya-sthala.* This, in a nutshell, is the kernel of *ṣaṭ-sthala.*

THIRTY-SIX PRINCIPLES

The philosophy of the Liṅgāyatas being idealistic, the explanation of its thirty-six principles is bound to be psychological. The evolution of the principles is psychological rather than cosmological. These thirty-six principles are divided into three groups which go by the name of *cit, cid-acit,* and *acit.* The first group includes the first five principles of the 'pure road'; the second group contains the next seven principles from Māyā to Puruṣa; and the third group comprises all the remaining twenty-four principles from Prakṛti to the solid earth. The first five principles are *śiva, śakti, sadāśiva, īśvara,* and *vidyā* or *sadvidyā. Śiva-tattva* being the first manifestation, the power of being predominates in it. It is purely subjective and has no objective or predicative reference. This is *prasādaliṅga* of the Liṅgāyatas with *parā-śakti,* the transcendent power. The next category is *śakti,* the manifestation of which takes place almost simultaneously with the first. It is arbitrarily spoken as second, because consciousness presupposes being, as the rays do the flame. This is *caraliṅga* with *ādi-śakti,* originative or dynamic power. The third category is *sadāśiva*; this is so called because the power of will predominates in it. This is *śivaliṅga* with *icchā-śakti,* the power of will. The fourth category is *īśvara* in which the power of knowledge is dominant. It is perhaps to imply the idea of predominance of the objective element that this category is called *īśvara-tattva.* This is *guruliṅga* with *jñāna-śakti,* the power of knowledge. *Vidyā* or *sadvidyā* is the fifth category, which is marked by the predominance of the power of action. This is *ācāraliṅga* with *kriyā-śakti,* the power of action.[13]

The second group includes these seven categories, namely, *māyā, kāla, niyati, rāga, vidyā, kalā,* and *puruṣa.* Māyā, the sixth principle in order, works as a principle of obscuration which is both necessary and logical. Māyā means the power of voluntary self-limitation, and this gives rise to the five limitations which are but the five unlimited prominent characteristics of Śiva in limited forms.[14] The Divine's *nityatva* or eternity becomes *kāla* or time of limited duration ; *vyāpakatva* or all-pervasiveness becomes *niyati* or limited space ; *pūrṇatva* or perfection (hence desirelessness) becomes *rāga* or attachment to things ; *sarvajñatva* or omniscience becomes *vidyā* or *aśuddha-vidyā* or limited knowledge ; and *sarvakartṛtva* or all-creativeness becomes *kalā* or limited creation. Śiva takes upon Himself these five limitations (*kañcuka*), forgets His real nature, and appears as a Puruṣa or finite soul.

The last group contains the remaining twenty-four categories from Prakṛti to the solid earth.[15] Here Prakṛti needs an explanation. Prakṛti, according to the Sāmkhya, has three qualities or *guṇas* which are none other than three modes of matter. But according to the Liṅgāyatas, the three are psychological variations ; thus the qualitative Prakṛti becomes a subjective entity. On the strength of this subjectivity, the Liṅgāyata school maintains that the universe, when unmanifested, lies hidden in Paraśiva, as the waves, foam, and bubbles are hidden in the sea, and appear on the surface when it is agitated.[16] So there is nothing new in the manifestation of the universe. It is only the replica of the unmanifest already within the Divine.

[13] Sakhare, *History and Philosophy of Liṅgāyata Religion,* pp. 472-77.
[14] *Pratyabhijñāhṛdaya,* p. 49.
[15] The 24 categories are: *prakṛti, mahat* or *buddhi, ahaṅkāra,* five *tanmātras* (or five vital breaths according to the Vedānta), *manas,* five organs of knowledge, five organs of action, and five elements.
[16] *Siddhānta-śikhāmaṇi,* I. 3.

6

EARLY HISTORY OF VAIṢṆAVISM

VIṢṆU IN THE VEDIC LITERATURE

THE age covered by the composition of the Ṛg-Vedic hymns, not to speak of the various works of the entire Vedic literature, is considerably wide—between *c.* 1400 and 1000 B.C. according to some writers. It can be shown that, possibly owing to the wide prevalence of the union of Aryan males with non-Aryan females, the speech as well as the social and religious life of the Aryan people began to be modified very early on Indian soil. Attention may be drawn in this connection to the borrowing of the cerebral consonantal sounds from non-Aryan speech, to the gradual amalgamation of the Ṛg-Vedic god Rudra and the pre-Aryan Father-god Śiva-Paśupati, and to the germ of theism, a non-Aryan institution later completely absorbed in Indian (i.e. mixed Aryo-aboriginal) religious life, possibly to be traced in the reference in the *Ṛg-Veda* (I. 22. 20) itself to the *sūris* (meaning 'sectarian devotees of the god Viṣṇu' according to later works) as a class favoured by Viṣṇu.[1]

Viṣṇu is represented as one of the great gods even in some sections of the *Ṛg-Veda*; but he was not regarded as the greatest god in early Vedic times. The *Ṛg-Veda* (I. 155. 6) conceives Viṣṇu as one of the manifestations of the sun.[2] He is called *śipiviṣṭa,* i.e. 'clothed with rays of light' ('bald' according to some writers) and his greatness is said to be inconceivable (VII. 99. 1 ; 100. 5-6). Viṣṇu is described as enveloping the earth on all sides with his *mayūkhas,* i.e. rays of light. He is believed by scholars to represent the sun in its daily and yearly courses. According to a legend in the *Śatapatha Brāhmaṇa* (XIV. 1. 1), Viṣṇu's head was, by a trick of the gods, severed from his body and became *āditya,* i.e. the sun.[3] The later conception of him as *udyat-koṭi-divākarābha*[4] and *savitṛ-maṇḍala-madhyavartin* as well as his association with the *cakra* or disc resembling the disc of the sun and with the bird Garuḍa, adapted from the Ṛg-Vedic

[1] Cf. 'The Śākta Pīṭhas' in *Journal of the Royal Asiatic Society of Bengal,* Letters, XIV. pp. 100 ff.

[2] Viṣṇu is described as setting in motion, like a revolving wheel, his 90 steeds (days) with their four names (seasons), which apparently refers to the solar year of 360 days. Przyluski's attempt to trace the name of Viṣṇu to a Dravidian root is fantastic. Cf. *Quarterly Journal of the Mythic Society,* XXV. pp. 301-2. According to some writers, the word means 'a bird'. Macdonell (*Vedic Mythology,* p. 39) interprets the name as 'the active one' representing solar motion (from the root *viṣ*).

[3] The word *āditya* is derived from the name of the female divinity Aditi, the personification of the boundless sky. *Āditya* indicates the sun as well as a group of divinities associated with the sun and the sky.

[4] *Indian Culture,* II. pp. 131 f.

conception of the sun as a winged celestial bird, also point to his solar character. In many passages of the *Ṛg-Veda,* Viṣṇu is mentioned along with the Ādityas, while later works represent him as one of them.

The three strides of Viṣṇu, which no doubt formed the background of the Paurāṇic legend of Vāmana (an epithet of Viṣṇu in the *Śatapatha Brāhmaṇa,* I. 2. 5. 5) and Bali, as well as his highest place, are quite famous in the *Ṛg-Veda* (I. 22. 18 etc.). Viṣṇu, the unconquerable preserver, strode the three steps over this universe, thereby maintaining fixed ordinances (*dharmāṇi*). He is said to have three spaces associated with the three steps. Two of these spaces are called earthly, while the 'highest' of them is described as known to himself and visible only to the *sūris* 'like an eye fixed in the sky' (I. 22. 20). This *parama pada* of Viṣṇu, where there was a well of honey (I. 154. 5), is said to be a land (*pāthas* or *vāstu*) beyond ordinary mortal ken which 'man apprehends not, nor can the soaring winged birds pursue' (I. 155. 5) and in which 'gods rejoice' (VIII. 29. 7) and 'god-seeking men delight' (I. 154. 5). The Ṛg-Vedic poets pray (I. 154. 6) that people may go to this blessed abode of Viṣṇu, 'where he himself dwells, inscrutable', to enjoy felicity. Hopkins[5] thinks that the later popularity of the god lies in the importance of his *parama pada* which is said to have been the home of departed spirits (I. 154. 5-6). In later times, *Viṣṇu-pada* became a synonym of the sky and the abode of Viṣṇu became the goal of the spiritual aspirations of the devotees of that god and several places (usually on the top of hills) came to be styled *Viṣṇu-pada.*

According to Aurṇavābha, as indicated by Durgācārya in his commentary on Yāska's *Nirukta* (XII. 19), the three steps of Viṣṇu are the three periods of the sun's course, i.e. his rise, culmination, and setting.[6] But Keith[7] points out that this interpretation is not in keeping with the 'highest' place of Viṣṇu. Another ancient commentator, named Śākapūṇi,[8] believed that the three *padas* refer to the threefold manifestation of light in the three divisions of the universe, viz. fire on earth, lightning in the atmosphere, and the sun in the sky. According to the *Taittirīya Saṁhitā* and the *Śatapatha Brāhmaṇa* (I. 9. 3. 9) also, the three places of Viṣṇu are the earth, air, and sky. Viṣṇu's three imperishable steps or places, mentioned in the *Ṛg-Veda,* were endowed in later times with a spiritual meaning. The Besnagar inscription[9] of the second-first century B.C. inter-

[5] *Religions of India*, p. 56.

[6] Cf. *Samārohaṇe Viṣṇu-pade Gaya-śirasīti Aurṇavābhaḥ. Samārohaṇa, Viṣṇu-pada,* and *Gaya-śiras* have been explained as accession, meridian sky, and hill of setting respectively. This tradition seems to have had something to do with the recognition of the Viṣṇupada hill at Gaya as a holy place (*Journal of Indian History*, XXXII. p. 288). It should be noticed that the word *pada* is of ambiguous import, meaning 'foot', 'step', 'station', etc.

[7] *Religion and Philosophy of the Veda and Upanishads*, I. p. 108.

[8] Cf. Macdonell, *Vedic Mythology*, p. 38.

[9] Dines Chandra Sircar, *Select Inscriptions*, I. pp. 90 f

prets the 'immortal' *padas* as denoting 'self-control, renunciation, and vigilance which lead one to heaven', apparently pointing to the dwelling of Viṣṇu as the God of gods.

The *Ṛg-Veda* (I. 155. 6) also regards Viṣṇu as a youth who is no longer a child, and as a leader in battle who is said to have defeated Śambara. In the capacity of a warrior Viṣṇu is often associated with Indra and the two gods are supposed to be masters of the world (VI. 69 ; VII. 99). Viṣṇu is described as the worthy friend of Indra and is said to have walked the three strides with Indra's energy (I. 22. 19 ; VIII. 12. 27). Indra is sometimes represented as deserted by all the gods excepting Viṣṇu whom he asked to exert his greatest prowess in the slaying of Vṛtra (IV. 18. 11). According to a legend in the *Aitareya Brāhmaṇa* (III. 50), Varuṇa, Bṛhaspati, and Viṣṇu successively helped Indra in turning out the *asuras*. The Vedic legends no doubt contributed largely to the development of the Viṣṇu mythology in later times. Barnett[10] suggests that, according to the lay imagination, a transfusion took place of some of the live blood of Indra, the most truly popular god of action among the Ṛg-Vedic deities, into the veins of Viṣṇu, as a result of the close relation between the two gods in early Vedic conception.

A passage of the *Ṛg-Veda* (I. 156. 3) calls Viṣṇu the germ (*garbha*) of *ṛta* which may mean sacrifice or moral order. According to the *Śatapatha Brāhmaṇa* (I. 9. 3. 9), 'Viṣṇu truly is the sacrifice ; by striding, he obtained for the gods that all-pervading power which now belongs to them'. The equation of Viṣṇu with the spirit of sacrifice[11] was possibly suggested by the fact that both were considered to be helping or strengthening Indra and other gods. In later literature, Viṣṇu is essentially connected with sacrifice and is endowed with such names as Yajña, Yajñāvayava, Yajñeśvara, Yajñapuruṣa, Yajñabhāvana, Yajñavarāha, Yajñakṛt, Yajñatrātṛ, Yajñabhoktṛ, Yajñakratu, Yajñavāhana, Yajñavīrya, etc. According to the *Aitareya Brāhmaṇa* (III. 38), he averts the evil consequences of the defects in sacrifice, while Varuṇa protects the fruits of its successful performance. This work (I.4) regards Agni and Viṣṇu as the two *dīkṣāpālas* or guardians of initiation.

The *Śatapatha Brāhmaṇa* (XIV. 1. 1.) contains a legend which, with some variations, recurs in the *Taittirīya Āraṇyaka* (V. 1) and *Pañcaviṁśa Brāhmaṇa* (VII. 5. 6). According to this legend, there was a contention among the gods as to which of them was the greatest. It was proposed that he who by his deeds reached the end of sacrifice should attain the highest place among them. In this contest, Viṣṇu was victorious and hence it was said, 'Viṣṇu is the most excellent of the gods'. That Viṣṇu had already become the greatest god in the later Vedic period, at least with a section of

[10] *Hindu Gods and Heroes*, p. 41.

[11] *Ibid.*, pp. 39 f.

the people, is also indicated by the *Aitareya Brāhmaṇa* (I. 1) which calls him the *parama* (highest) and Agni the *avama* (lowest) among the gods, unless we mean by these two terms a 'heavenly' and an 'earthly' god respectively. But the same work also regards Viṣṇu as the *dvārapa* or door-keeper of the gods (I. 30). This is no doubt an uncomplimentary epithet, although the idea is probably that Viṣṇu regulated entrance into the heavenly world.

In the *Maitri Upaniṣad* (VI. 13), food that sustains the universe is called Bhagavat Viṣṇu, while, in the *Kaṭha Upaniṣad* (III. 9), the progress of human soul is compared to a journey, the goal of which is said to be Viṣṇu's *parama pada*, the abode of eternal bliss (cf. *Ṛ. V.*, I. 22. 20). This shows that Viṣṇu was often regarded as the greatest god in later Vedic times. According to the *Āpastamba, Hiraṇyakeśin,* and *Pāraskara Gṛhya-Sūtras,* the bridegroom is required to say to the bride at the time of taking the seven steps, 'May Viṣṇu be with you!' This is a development of the Ṛg-Vedic idea of the god as protector of embryos and promoter of conception (cf. VII. 36. 9; X. 184. 1).

Viṣṇu's association with cows is probably indicated by the epithet *gopā,* meaning 'protector of cows' or 'herdsman', found in the *Ṛg-Veda* (I. 22. 18 ; X. 19. 4). The same work (I. 154. 6) also describes the highest place of Viṣṇu as the dwelling of 'many horned swiftly moving cows'. The *Baudhāyana Dharma-Sūtra* (II. 5. 24) calls him *govinda* (cow-keeper or chief herdsman) and *dāmodara,* 'one with the cord round one's belly', i.e. a herdsman. This last name is usually believed to be derived from wheat-sheaf ; but herdsmen, in some parts of India, are known to tie a rope round their waist, from which coils of rope hang.[12] In later times, spiritual interpretations were offered for both the names (cf. *Mbh.*, V.70.8).

In the *Ṛg-Veda,* Viṣṇu is sometimes (I. 154. 2) compared to an animal causing depredations (*kucara*),* and is represented as stealing cooked mess (I. 61. 7 ; VIII. 77. 10). In later Vedic literature, he is often found to have recourse to cunning devices to help Indra and other friends and to defeat the *asuras.* These legends, some of which may be of non-Aryan origin, were no doubt responsible for some aspects of the Viṣṇu mythology in the epic and Paurāṇic literature.

THE IDEA OF BHAKTI OR DEVOTION

The Vedic Aryans tried to please Viṣṇu and other gods by means of sacrifice ; but this sacrificial religion was fundamentally different from the later religion characterized by *bhakti* (devotion of the faithful to God) and

[12] Cf. D. C. Sen, *Vaṅga-sāhitya-paricaya,* I. p. 721: *Kathokṣaṇe Sahadeva goālā-veśete, Go-puccha-lomer daḍī veḍiyā kaṭite.*

* Sāyaṇa and others interpret *kucara,* when referring to the deity, to mean 'pervading all quarters'—Ed.

prasāda (God's grace to the faithful). We have reason to believe that the conception of devotion and grace was borrowed from non-Aryan religious thought. According to Śāṇḍilya, *bhakti* is *parānuraktirīśvare*, 'supreme attachment to God'. Some resemblance to *bhakti* is noticeable in the Ṛg-Vedic hymns addressed to Varuṇa (with whom Viṣṇu was associated as a benefactor of the sacrificer in later Vedic literature), but not in those addressed to Viṣṇu. In the Vedic texts, Viṣṇu is associated more with sacrifice than with devotion and grace. Bhandarkar[13] thinks that the origin of the *bhakti* doctrine may be traced to the Upaniṣadic idea of *upāsanā* or fervent meditation, which magnifies what is meditated upon and represents it in a glorious form in order to excite admiration and love. He also draws our attention to the *Bṛhadāraṇyaka Upaniṣad* (I. 4. 8), which conceives the internal Ātman (soul) as dearer than the son, wealth, and everything else.

Some scholars find an early reference to the *bhakti* doctrine in the rule in the *Aṣṭādhyāyī* (IV.3.98) of Pāṇini (fifth century B.C.) for the formation of the words *Vāsudevaka* and *Arjunaka* in the senses of 'a person whose object of *bhakti* is Vāsudeva' and 'a person whose object of *bhakti* is Arjuna' respectively. As Vāsudeva seems to have been held in esteem by the people of Mathurā in the days of Megasthenes in the fourth century B.C. and was undoubtedly regarded as the highest god in the days of the *Gītā* (third century B.C.) and the Besnagar inscription (second century B.C.), Raychaudhuri[14] may be right in his contention that the word *bhakti*, in regard to Vāsudeva, is used in the above *sūtra* by Pāṇini in the sense of religious adoration. But the word is also used in the *Aṣṭādhyāyī* with reference to cakes, and the possibility of the meaning 'fondness' is not altogether precluded. The reference to two groups of persons as Vāsudeva-bhakta and Kaṁsa-bhakta in Patañjali's *Mahābhāṣya*[15] also is not quite clear. We do not know if Vāsudeva's deification by his own people at Mathurā was recognized, at such an early date, in Gandhāra where Pāṇini flourished. More important is therefore the *Śvetāśvatara Upaniṣad*[16] (a work nearly of the same age as the *Aṣṭādhyāyī*) which teaches *parā bhakti* (supreme devotion to God). That the idea of religious adoration for a leader of thought was not unknown in the days of Aśoka (272-232 B.C.) is indicated by the Rummindeī inscription,[17] according to which the Buddhist king went in

[13] *Vaiṣṇavism, Śaivism, and Minor Religious Systems*, p. 28.
[14] *Materials for the Study of the Early History of the Vaishnava Sect*, 2nd ed., pp. 30 f.
[15] Patañjali was a contemporary of Puṣyamitra Śuṅga (*c.* 185-149 B.C.); but the *Mahābhāṣya* appears to contain interpolations of about the beginning of the Christian era. Cf. *Indian Historical Quarterly*, XV. pp. 633 ff.
[16] Cf. V. 14. This Upaniṣad inculcating devotion to Śiva, originally a non-Aryan god, points to the non-Aryan contribution to the development of the Bhakti doctrine.
[17] *Select Inscriptions*, I. p. 70.

person to, and offered worship at, the birth-place of Śākyamuni Buddha, styled the Bhagavat (the holiest or most worshipful one).[18] Reference may also be made in this connection to the enshrinement of Buddha's relics for worship, referred to in early Buddhist literature as well as in records dating from the time of the Indo-Greek king Menander,[19] to the implication of *bhakti,* in the sense of religious adoration, in the stanzas of the *Therīgāthā,* and to the representation of some cult-deities of the Brāhmaṇical pantheon, on the pre-Christian coins of India.

The elaborate and mechanical system of sacrifice offered to the gods by the Vedic Aryans did not satisfy the religious spirit of all sections of the people, especially after they had inter-married with the pre-Aryan population and become familiar with the religious and philosophical beliefs of the latter. This led to religious speculations of a different type, and thinkers like the author of the *Muṇḍaka Upaniṣad* (cf. I.2.7) began to question the value and efficacy of sacrifice. The philosophical speculations of this age gave rise, among others, to religious sects like those of Vardhamāna of the Jñātṛkas, Siddhārtha of the Śākyas, and Vāsudeva of the Vṛṣṇis (all three favouring the doctrine of *ahiṁsā*) as well as to the philosophical ideas clothed in the words of the Upaniṣads.[20] We have to note that, even though the Jñātṛkas, Śākyas, and Vṛṣṇis all claimed the status of the Kṣatriya, the first and second clans were possibly Aryanized Mongoloids, like their kinsmen the Licchavis, while the third, if not originally non-Aryan, at least absorbed enough non-Aryan blood.[21] At the beginning, the

[18] Cf. *Journal of the Royal Asiatic Society of Bengal,* XIV. pp. 7-8.

[19] *Ibid.,* pp. 102 ff.

[20] A comparative study of the Upaniṣadic philosophy and the religious and philosophical ideas of the Polynesians has led some writers to think that the common conceptions were of Austric origin. The history of creation is described in different parts of the Polynesian world in hymns that echo the Ṛg-Vedic hymn of creation. E. S. Craighill, who has studied the Polynesian religion, says: 'The ancient esoteric teaching in cosmology postulated the pre-existence of a self-created world-soul which evolved the world and the universe out of itself, and called manifest existence out of nothingness by the power of the Word. Many of the creational accounts make no mention of this Being; the evolutionary process by which the universe evolved from nothingness is stated merely as a succession of stages, the first of which is characterized as Void or Night. But other records describing the course of evolution in terms similar to these definitely attribute it to a supreme Being as the cause of the emergence of tangible and visible reality out of or in the empty and lightless Void in which this Being existed alone.' Cf. '*Bhārata Kaumudī,* I. pp. 204 ff. The word *tābuva* used in the *Atharva-Veda* is believed to be an old form of the well-known *tabu* (taboo) of the Polynesians. There are also other coincidences.

[21] The tradition of the Ikṣvāku origin of the Śākyas proves nothing as the non-Aryans often claimed to have belonged to the maternal grandfather's family and as the Aryan origin of the Ikṣvākus themselves is as yet unproved. The Licchavis and Mauryas appear to have been two other Himalayan tribes of Mongolian origin claiming the status of the Kṣatriya. Some of these tribes are known to have been regarded by the orthodox Brāhmaṇas as Śūdra, Vṛṣala, or degraded Kṣatriya and were often classed with non-Aryan peoples and foreigners. Compare the case of the Dravidian Sātavāhanas (Andhras) who claimed the status of the Brāhmaṇa (probably as a result of matrimonial relations with a Brāhmaṇa family), but were called Vṛṣala in the Purāṇas. The Greek and Scythian foreigners were sometimes regarded as clean Śūdras, but sometimes as degraded Kṣatriyas (cf. *The Age of Imperial Unity,* ed. Majumdar, p. 103).

following of Vardhamāna, Siddhārtha, and Vāsudeva (religious leaders of whose type are known to have flourished in India in all ages in numbers) was meagre, but their systems gradually became prominent. The later success of Vāsudevism was principally due to the identification of Vāsudeva with the Vedic god Viṣṇu, with an ancient deified sage named Nārāyaṇa, with a number of tribal deities, as well as with Parabrahman (the supreme Spirit or All-Soul), conceived by the Upaniṣads.

VĀSUDEVA-KṚṢṆA OF THE VṚṢṆI FAMILY

In the epics and the Purāṇas, the ruling clan of Mathurā is called Yadu or Yādava, which was divided into numerous septs. Vṛṣṇi and Andhaka were the sons of the Yādava prince Sātvata. The names Sātvata and Vṛṣṇi are therefore both used often to indicate the same family in ancient Indian literature, as the names Raghu and Ikṣvāku are applied to the solar dynasty, and Bharata, Kuru, and Puru to the lunar. The Vṛṣṇi sept of the Yādava people was famous in later Vedic times as is proved by its mention in the *Taittirīya Saṁhitā* (III. 11. 9. 3) and *Brāhmaṇa* (III. 10. 9. 15), the *Śatapatha Brāhmaṇa* (III. 1. 1. 4), and the *Jaiminīya Upaniṣad Brāhmaṇa* (I. 6. 1). The Vṛṣṇis and the Andhakas are mentioned in Pāṇini's *Aṣṭādhyāyī* (IV. 1. 114). The *Kauṭilīya Arthaśāstra*[22] refers to the *saṅgha* or republican corporation of the Vṛṣṇi people. A coin of the Vṛṣṇi-rājanya-gaṇa (republic of the Vṛṣṇi Kṣatriyas), assignable to the first century B.C., with a *cakra* on the reverse and a pillar surmounted by an animal (believed to be half-lion and half-elephant, but may be really a crude representation of Garuḍa) on the obverse, was discovered probably in the North Punjab.[23] The Satvats, mentioned in the *Śatapatha* and *Aitareya Brāhmaṇas,* are apparently the same as the Sātvatas of the epic and Paurāṇic literature. Yadu, possibly a non-Aryan chief, is mentioned in the *Ṛg-Veda* occasionally with Turvasu. In later literature, Yadu and Turvasu are two of the four disobedient sons of Yayāti, who were cursed by their father and became the progenitors of the Yādavas, Yavanas, Bhojas, and Mlecchas respectively. We have to note in this connection the irreverent attitude of the Vṛṣṇis towards the Brāhmaṇas, which is attested by a number of authorities, and the fact that the most distinguished Vṛṣṇi hero was dark-complexioned (*atasī-kusuma-śyāma*). Thus, even if the Yādava-Sātvata-Vṛṣṇi people were not actually of non-Aryan origin, at least they must have absorbed a good deal of non-Aryan blood.

The *Bhagavad-Gītā,* which seems to contain the earliest dogmatic

[22] Shama Sastri's Translation, p. 13.

[23] See Allan, *Catalogue of Indian Coins: Ancient India,* pp. clv ff.; Banerjea, *Development of Hindu Iconography,* p. 145 and f.n. 1.

exposition of the religion characterized by *bhakti*, which may be called Vaiṣṇavism, represents Vāsudeva, otherwise called Kṛṣṇa and identified with the god Viṣṇu as well as with the supreme Spirit (but not yet with Nārāyaṇa), as a scion of the Vṛṣṇi (i.e. the Yādava-Sātvata-Vṛṣṇi) family. The *Mahābhāṣya* (under Pāṇini, IV. 1. 114) and the *Kāśikā* give the forms *vāsudeva, bāladeva,* and *āniruddha*, as derivatives of Vṛṣṇi names, meaning the sons of Vāsudeva, Baladeva, and Aniruddha respectively. The names of the five Vṛṣṇi heroes, referred to in the Mora (near Mathurā) inscription of the first century A.D., are given in the *Vāyu Purāṇa* as Saṅkarṣaṇa (son of Vasudeva by Rohiṇī), Vāsudeva (son of Vasudeva by Devakī), Pradyumna (son of Vāsudeva by Rukmiṇī), Sāmba (son of Vāsudeva by Jāmbavatī of non-Aryan origin), and Aniruddha (son of Pradyumna), all of whom are known to have been apotheosized and worshipped.[24] The *Mahābhāṣya* also speaks of the Vāsudeva-vargya or Vāsudeva-vargin to signify a follower of Vāsudeva. Curtius says that an image of Herakles (i.e. Vāsudeva-Kṛṣṇa) was being carried in front of the Paurava army, as it advanced against the Greeks led by Alexander the Great. The *Mahābhārata* (which sometimes mentions Vāsudeva as the Saṅghamukhya or Elder of the Republican Confederacy of the Vṛṣṇi, Andhaka, and other associate peoples) and the Purāṇas usually identify Vāsudeva-Kṛṣṇa of the Sātvata (i.e. Yādava-Sātvata-Vṛṣṇi) family with the highest god, and represent him as the founder of the religion characterized by *bhakti* and called the Bhāgavata, Sātvata, or Vaiṣṇava Dharma. In the *Bhāgavata Purāṇa*, the highest Brahman is stated to have been called Bhagavat and Vāsudeva by the Sātvata people, while the *Śāntiparvan* of the *Mahābhārata* states, apparently in reference to the *Gītā*, that the Sātvata or Bhāgavata Dharma was taught first by Vāsudeva-Kṛṣṇa to Arjuna. It has to be noted that the word *sātvata* has been used together with *sūri* and *bhāgavata* in the sense of a devotee of Vāsudeva-Viṣṇu in a canonical work of the Vaiṣṇavas.[25] The *Gītā* speaks of the Bhāgavata religion as *yoga*. The Tuśām (Hissar District, Punjab) inscription,[26] of about the fourth century A.D., also mentions a *bhagavad-bhakta* (i.e. Bhāgavata) as *Ārya-Sātvata-yogācārya*, 'teacher of the noble Sātvata *yoga*'.

Megasthenes (fourth century B.C.), the Greek envoy at the Maurya court, speaks of the Sourasenoi (Śūrasena people), whose country contained the two cities Methora (Mathurā) and Kleisobora (probably, Kṛṣṇapura),

[24] Cf. *Proceedings of the Indian History Congress*, 1944, pp. 82 ff.

[25] Cf. *Sūris-suhṛd-bhāgavatas-sātvataḥ pañcakālavit, Ekāntikas-tanmayaś-ca pañcarātrika ityapi* ; quoted from the *Padma Tantra*, one of the 108 Tantras or Saṁhitās, in *Journal of the Royal Asiatic Society*, 1911, p. 935. The names Ekāntika and Tanmaya appear to refer to the *yoga* aspect of the Bhāgavata religion.

[26] *Corpus Inscriptionum Indicarum*, III. p. 270.

and was watered by the great river Jobares (Yamunā), as holding Herakles (apparently the Greek substitute of Vāsudeva-Kṛṣṇa) in special veneration. The Śūrasenas were a branch of the Yādava-Sātvata-Vṛṣṇi people. This is indicated by the fact that the *Ghaṭa Jātaka*[27] speaks of the ruling clan of Mathurā in the North—as distinguished from Mathurā (Madurai) in the South in the Pāṇḍya country—, of which Vāsudeva-Kṛṣṇa was a member, as having perished owing to the irreverent conduct of its members towards the Brāhmaṇa Kṛṣṇa-Dvaipāyana, while the *Kauṭilīya Arthaśāstra* refers to the destruction of the republican corporation of the Vṛṣṇi people as a result of their attempt against Dvaipāyana (i.e. Vyāsa). The epic and Paurāṇic traditions that associate the Yādavas, especially Vāsudeva-Kṛṣṇa, with Mathurā and its neighbourhood have already been referred to above. The worship of Vāsudeva in that locality is further proved by a Mathurā inscription[28] of the time of the Śaka Satrap Śoḍāsa (first quarter of the first century A.D.). This inscription records the erection of a gateway, a terrace, and a *devakula* at the *mahāsthāna* of Vāsudeva.

The Buddhist canonical work *Aṅguttara Nikāya* (III. pp. 276 f.) mentions a number of religious sects such as Ājīvika, Nirgrantha (Jaina), Muṇḍaśrāvaka, Jaṭilaka, Parivrājaka, Magaṇḍika, Traidaṇḍika, Aviruddhaka, Gautamaka (Buddhist), and Devadharmika; but it does not speak of Vāsudevaka or Bhāgavata. The inscriptions of Aśoka, which mention the Śramaṇas, Brāhmaṇas, Ājīvikas, and Nirgranthas, do not speak of the followers of Vāsudeva. But in a passage occurring in the Buddhist canonical commentaries (first century B.C.) called the *Mahāniddesa* and the *Cullaniddesa*,[29] mention is made of the Ājīvika, Nirgrantha, Jaṭila, Parivrājaka, and Avaruddhaka side by side with the worshippers of the elephant, horse, cow, dog, crow, Vāsudeva, Baladeva (Saṅkarṣaṇa), Pūrṇabhadra, Maṇibhadra, Agni (Fire), the *nāgas, suparṇas, yakṣas, asuras, gandharvas, mahārājas* (the four *lokapālas*),[30] Candra, Sūrya, Indra, Brahmā, *deva,* and *dik*. The Bhāgavata sect worshipping Vāsudeva may not have been so prominent outside the Mathurā region (especially in the eastern part of India) about the third century B.C. The Bhāgavata religion probably originated with the Yādava-Sātvata-Vṛṣṇi people of the said area, and spread to western India and the northern Deccan with the migration of Yādava tribes to those regions. Vāsudeva appears to have been deified

[27] Cowell's Translation, IV. pp. 55 f.

[28] *Journal of the Bihar Research Society*, XXXIX. 1-2. pp. 45-48.

[29] Cf. R. G. Bhandarkar, *Vaiṣṇavism, Śaivism, and Minor Religious Systems*, p. 3.

[30] This is the generally accepted meaning and accords best with the context. Divinity was claimed by kings as, for instance, by Samudragupta (see *infra*). Reference may also be made to the Kuṣāṇa title *devaputra* and the representation on coins of some early Kuṣāṇa monarchs as flying above clouds and as having flames springing from the shoulder.

and worshipped by his own people as early as the age of Pāṇini or even earlier ; but he may or may not have been regarded as the supreme God. We have to note that the identification of Vāsudeva with the highest God is not recognized in the earlier sections of the *Mahābhārata*. A well-known scene of the *Sabhāparvan* proves that Vāsudeva-Kṛṣṇa's claim to divine honours was sometimes openly denied. Sometimes Vāsudeva is described as a pious hypocrite. Even the *Gītā* (VII. 19, 24 ; XVIII. 67) represents Vāsudeva-Kṛṣṇa as lamenting that the person of great soul who says 'Vāsudeva is All' is rare and that people scorn him when he dwells in human form. It is only some late passages of the *Mahābhārata* that represent him as a friend of the Brāhmaṇas and the origin of the Vedas, and also as perfectly identical with Viṣṇu. The *Mahābhāṣya* refers to the antagonism between the Kaṁsa-bhaktas who were *kāla-mukha* (dark-faced) and the Vāsudeva-bhaktas who were *rakta-mukha* (red-faced), although the reference may be to a dramatic representation of the slaying of Kaṁsa.

The Besnagar (old Gwalior State in Madhya Bharat) inscription of the last quarter of the second century B.C. refers to the setting up of a *garuḍa-dhvaja* (column surmounted by the figure of Garuḍa, the emblem or *vāhana* of Viṣṇu) at Vidiśā in honour of Vāsudeva, the *deva-deva* (the greatest God), by his Yavana (Greek) devotee Heliodoros of Takṣaśilā in Gandhāra, who called himself a Bhāgavata, i.e. a worshipper of the Bhagavat (Vāsudeva-Viṣṇu). Another inscription from Besnagar refers to the erection of a Garuḍa column for a temple of the Bhagavat. The Ghosundi (Chitorgarh District, Rajasthan) inscription[31] of the first century B.C. records the construction of a *pūjā-śilā-prākāra* (stone-enclosure for a place of worship, or an enclosure for the sacred stone called *śālagrāma*, the symbol of Viṣṇu as the *liṅga* is of Śiva), styled Nārāyaṇa-vāṭaka or -vāṭikā, by a Bhāgavata who had performed the Aśvamedha sacrifice in honour of Saṅkarṣaṇa and Vāsudeva. They are both called here *bhagavat* as well as *anihata* (unconquered or respected) and *sarveśvara* (supreme lord). The Nanaghat (Bombay State) inscription[32] of about the same age, belonging to the queen of a Sātavāhana performer of Vedic sacrifices including the Aśvamedha, begins with an adoration to the gods Dharma, Indra, Saṅkarṣaṇa, and Vāsudeva, the moon and the sun, and the four *lokapālas*, viz. Yama (differentiated from Dharma), Varuṇa, Kubera, and Vāsava (differentiated from Indra). The epigraphs cited above support what we already know from literary sources as regards Vāsudeva's association with Garuḍa and therefore with Viṣṇu, with the Vṛṣṇi hero Saṅkarṣaṇa, and with Nārāyaṇa, considerably before the birth of Christ. He is not called Kṛṣṇa in the early Indian inscriptions ; but the use of Kṛṣṇa, as another name of

[31] *Select Inscriptions*, I. pp. 91 f. [32] *Ibid.*, pp. 186 ff.

Vāsudeva, in works like the *Mahābhārata,* especially in the *Gītā* belonging to its early stratum, Patañjali's *Mahābhāṣya,* and the *Ghaṭa Jātaka* is probably pre-Christian. The spread of the Bhāgavata religion outside the Mathurā region and Vāsudeva's own clan (i.e. the Yādava-Sātvata-Vṛṣṇis), especially amongst the performers of Vedic sacrifices, has therefore the support of epigraphic evidence. But some people did not regard Vāsudeva, as late as the first century B.C., as the greatest of all gods, but only as an equal of deities like Dharma, Indra, and others. Even in the second century A.D. the Sātavāhana king Gautamīputra Śātakarṇi is described as an equal of Rāma (Balarāma), Keśava (Kṛṣṇa), Arjuna, and Bhīmasena, referring to Keśava as a hero merely.[33] But the Chinna (Krishna District, Andhra) inscription of Yajña-Śātakarṇi (last quarter of the second century) begins with an adoration to Vāsudeva alone and indicates the progress of Bhāgavatism in the South.

There is no iconic representation of the god Viṣṇu-Vāsudeva assignable to a date very much earlier than the beginning of the Christian era.[34] A four-armed figure of the deity with *cakra* in the upper left hand is found on the coins of a Pañcāla king named Viṣṇumitra in evident allusion to the name of the issuer. A similar representation of the four-armed Viṣṇu, with *śaṅkha, cakra, gadā,* and an indefinite object in the hands, is found on a Kuṣāṇa seal-matrix[35] attributed by Cunningham to Huviṣka. The Kuṣāṇa king is represented here as facing the deity in a reverential attitude with his hands in the *añjali* pose. Possibly he became for some time a worshipper of Vāsudeva. Some of Huviṣka's coins[36] bear the figure of the four-armed god named Ooshna in Greek characters (probably Viṣṇu and not Śiva as usually believed). The fact that Huviṣka's successor assumed the name Vāsudeva also indicates the Bhāgavata leanings of the later Kuṣāṇas who had an important gubernatorial centre at Mathurā.

Patañjali (under Pāṇini, IV. 3. 98-99) seems to make a distinction between Vāsudeva the *tatrabhavat* (i.e. the most worshipful Vāsudeva) and the Kṣatriya Vāsudeva. The *Padma Tantra,* a canonical work of the Bhāgavatas, similarly makes a distinction between the two Vāsudevas. It is said in a *Mahābhārata* story that, besides Kṛṣṇa of the Yādava-Sātvata-Vṛṣṇi family, there was another claimant for the status of Vāsudeva in

[33] *Ibid.*, p. 198.

[34] One of the earliest Vaiṣṇava images so far discovered in India is that of an attendant of Viṣṇu (having his appearance and attributes), now worshipped as Caturbhujī Bhagavān at Burhikhar near Malhar in the Bilaspur District of Madhya Pradesh. The image has four hands, the upper left and right hands holding respectively the *cakra* and the *gadā* and the lower two having the palms joined in the *añjali* pose. It bears an inscription in Brāhmī characters of about the first century B.C.

[35] Banerjea, *Development of Hindu Iconography,* pp. 143-44.

[36] Cf. *Select Inscriptions,* I. pp. 155-56, f.n. 5.

Pauṇḍraka-Vāsudeva, i.e. Vāsudeva, ruler of the Pauṇḍraka people, probably of North Bengal. Pauṇḍraka-Vāsudeva may have been really the leader of a rival religious sect.

The age of Vāsudeva-Kṛṣṇa cannot be determined with certainty. The evidence of the *Chāndogya Upaniṣad* would suggest a date in the sixth or seventh century B.C., to which the work is usually attributed. The story of his association with the legend of the Kuru-Pāṇḍava war, the authenticity, date, and original form of which are uncertain, appears to be less reliable, although some scholars are inclined to accept tenth century B.C. as the date of the event.[37] Jaina tradition makes Vāsudeva-Kṛṣṇa a contemporary of the legendary twenty-second Tīrthaṅkara Ariṣṭanemi who preceded Pārśvanātha, predecessor of Mahāvīra (sixth century B.C.), and seems to support the date suggested by the *Chāndogya Upaniṣad*.

NĀRĀYAṆA

There is reference in the *Śatapatha Brāhmaṇa* (XII. 3. 4) to a *puruṣa* (a word used often in the sense of the supreme Spirit) named Nārāyaṇa who is stated to have thrice offered sacrifice at the instance of Prajāpati. Nārāyaṇa is, however, not identified here with Viṣṇu or any of the Ādityas. Elsewhere the same work (XIII. 6. 1) mentions Puruṣa-Nārāyaṇa as the performer of a *pañcarātra-sattra* (sacrifice continued for five days) who obtained, as a result, superiority over all beings and 'became all-beings'. Some scholars trace the name Pāñcarātra or Pāñcarātrika applied to the Bhāgavatas (or to one of their important branches) to this five-day *sattra* attributed to Nārāyaṇa. The earliest evidence in favour of the identification of Nārāyaṇa with Viṣṇu is probably to be traced in the *Baudhāyana Dharma-Sūtra* (about the fifth century B.C.). The *Taittirīya Āraṇyaka* (X. 11) contains the passage: *Nārāyaṇāya vidmahe Vāsudevāya dhīmahi, tan no Viṣṇuḥ pracodayāt*, in which Nārāyaṇa, Vāsudeva, and Viṣṇu are regarded as one and the same deity. Here Nārāyaṇa is also called Hari and 'the eternal Deity, the Supreme, and Lord'. But this part of the *Taittirīya Āraṇyaka* is a later addition, and appears to be considerably later than the *Baudhāyana Dharma-Sūtra*. Several passages of the *Mahābhārata* support the identification of Vāsudeva, Viṣṇu, and Nārāyaṇa as found in the above passage.

According to certain passages of the *Mahābhārata*, Nārāyaṇa was an ancient *ṛṣi* who was the son of Dharma and was associated with another *ṛṣi* called Nara. They both went from the world of men to the world of Brahman and, being worshipped by the gods and the *gandharvas*, existed only for the destruction of the demons. Indra was helped by Nara and

[37] Cf. *Journal of the Royal Asiatic Society of Bengal*, Letters, XVI. p. 77.

Nārāyaṇa in his struggle with the *asuras*. In a passage, which was apparently retouched by a Śaiva, Nārāyaṇa, son of Dharma, is stated to have practised austerities in the Himalayas (the exact place is sometimes specified as Badarī) and thus become Brahman (the All-Soul). He is said to have become invincible by propitiating Śiva. According to one story, the sage Nara, equal to Nārāyaṇa himself, was born from Nārāyaṇa's austerities. Nara is identified with Arjuna and Nārāyaṇa with Vāsudeva-Kṛṣṇa.[38] The late Nārāyaṇīya section of the *Śāntiparvan* states how Nārāyaṇa, the eternal and universal Soul, was born as the son of Dharma in the quadruple form of Nara, Nārāyaṇa, Hari, and Kṛṣṇa. It also speaks of the white people of the White Island (Śveta-dvīpa), on the northern shores of the Milk Ocean, engrossed in the worship of Nārāyaṇa, a thousand-rayed deity, who, in consequence of his sun-like brightness, could not be seen by persons not devoting themselves exclusively to him. According to some scholars, the Nārāyaṇīya section of the *Mahābhārata* suggests a journey really undertaken by some Indian Vaiṣṇavas to the Christian countries, and points to an attempt, in the Indian eclectic fashion, to include Christ among the incarnations of the supreme spirit Nārāyaṇa. Others, however, take the story to be a mere flight of imagination. Raychaudhuri[39] seems to be right in emphasizing Nārāyaṇa's solar associations and in comparing Nārāyaṇa in the Śveta-dvīpa of the white islanders with the Ṛg-Vedic Viṣṇu in his highest station observed only by the *sūris*. According to Bhandarkar,[40] Nārāyaṇa has a cosmic character and is not an historical or mythological individual. He takes the word *Nārāyaṇa* in the sense of the resting place or goal of *nāra,* i.e. the multitude of *naras* (men). But it seems more reasonable to think that Nārāyaṇa (cf. Kāṇvāyana, Kātyāyana, etc.) was an ancient leader of thought, born in the family of another sage called Nara, that both of them probably advocated solar worship, and this ultimately led to the identification, especially of the former, with the solar deity Viṣṇu. It is difficult to determine whether the family of Nārāyaṇa had anything to do with the Yādavas. It is, however, not impossible that the followers of Nārāyaṇa were originally called Pāñcarātrika and were later merged into the worshippers of Vāsudeva-Kṛṣṇa.

We have referred to the Nārāyaṇa-vāṭaka mentioned in the Ghosundi inscription (first century B.C.). A fourth century record from the Guntur District speaks of a *devakula* of Bhagavat Nārāyaṇa.[41]

[38] There is some evidence in favour of the deification of Arjuna and the existence of a sect that worshipped him. It is possible that the conception of Nara as a companion of Nārāyaṇa was based on the interpretation of the word *puruṣa* in the expression *Puruṣa-Nārāyaṇa* in the sense of *nara,* as well as on the tradition regarding the association of Arjuna with Vāsudeva-Kṛṣṇa.

[39] *Op. cit.*, pp. 135, 157. [40] *Op. cit.*, p. 30. [41] Cf. *Select Inscriptions,* I. pp. 443 ff.

THE KṚṢṆA SAGA

The *Mahābhārata* and the Purāṇas usually explain the name Vāsudeva as 'the son of Vasudeva', although sometimes philosophical interpretations are also offered (cf. *Mbh.,* V. 70. 3 ; XII. 341. 41). Bhandarkar[42] draws our attention to the commentaries on the *Aṣṭādhyāyī* and the *Ghaṭa Jātaka* and suggests that Vāsudeva is not a patronymic, but the proper name of the person, whose name Kṛṣṇa shows that he belonged to the Kārṣṇāyaṇa *gotra*. In his opinion, the Brāhmaṇical *gotra* called Kārṣṇāyaṇa sprang from an ancient sage named Kṛṣṇa with whom Vāsudeva of a Kṣatriya family of the Kārṣṇāyaṇa *gotra* was identified at a later date. Although Kṛṣṇa may be a *gotra* name as suggested by the commentator on the *Ghaṭa Jātaka,* later traditions, according to which a son of Vasudeva was called Kṛṣṇa owing to the darkness of his complexion (cf. the names of Kṛṣṇa-Dvaipāyana and Kṛṣṇā-Draupadī), appear to be more reasonable. Patronymics like Vāsudeva as well as metronymics like Gautamīputra (as in the Vākāṭaka family) were often used in ancient India exactly as proper names. Other names like Janārdana, Keśava, etc., later applied to Vāsudeva-Kṛṣṇa, were derived in some cases from his identification with Viṣṇu and Nārāyaṇa, and in others, probably, also from his equation with certain local and tribal gods.

The *Chāndogya Upaniṣad,* supposed to be a pre-Buddhistic work, mentions the sage Kṛṣṇa-Devakīputra (i.e. Kṛṣṇa son of Devakī) who was a disciple of the *ṛṣi* Ghora of the Āṅgirasa family (III. 17. 6). Kṛṣṇa is not called Vāsudeva in this work, probably because the patronymic and metronymic of a person were not generally used together. His identification with Kṛṣṇa who lived on the river Aṁśumatī and is mentioned in the *Ṛg-Veda* is doubtful ; but it cannot be regarded as impossible in view of the facts that the Aṁśumatī, which flowed through the Kuru country, may be the same as the Yamunā,[43] on the bank of which both the Kuru city Indraprastha and the Śūrasena city Mathurā stood, and that the said section of the *Ṛg-Veda* may belong to the latest stratum of the work. Some scholars are doubtful as regards the identity of Kṛṣṇa-Devakīputra of the *Chāndogya Upaniṣad* with Kṛṣṇa, son of Vasudeva by Devakī of the Yādava-Sātvata-Vṛṣṇi clan of the Mathurā region, as suggested by the *Mahābhārata* (especially its early stratum ; cf. the *Gītā,* I. 41 etc.) and the Purāṇas as well as by works like the *Ghaṭa Jātaka* and Patañjali's *Mahābhāṣya.* Vāsudeva's association with Saṅkarṣaṇa (Baladeva, son of Vasudeva by Rohiṇī)

[42] *Op. cit.,* pp. 10 f.

[43] The name may have association with the solar rays. In later mythology, Yamunā appears as the daughter of Vivasvat (Sūrya) and sister of Yama to whom is ascribed, from the earliest times, the same father in both Indian and Iranian traditions.

in pre-Christian epigraphs, as well as in such passages of the *Mahābhāṣya* as *Saṅkarṣaṇa-dvitīyasya balaṁ Kṛṣṇasya vardhatām,* seems to support the epic and Paurāṇic tradition. The *Mahābhāṣya* also speaks of popular dramatical representation of the life-story of Vāsudeva-Kṛṣṇa with special reference to the *Bali-bandha* and *Kaṁsa-vadha* episodes, and actually quotes passages like *asādhur-mātule Kṛṣṇaḥ* and *jaghāna Kaṁsaṁ kila Vāsudevaḥ* from a poem on a similar subject. Kṛṣṇa's association with the Yādava-Sātvata-Vṛṣṇis of the Mathurā area seems also to be indicated by the name Kṛṣṇapura (Kleisobora), 'city of Kṛṣṇa', applied to a town in the neighbourhood of Mathurā by Megasthenes in the fourth century B.C. The story of Herakles and Pandaia, known to Megasthenes, points to the antiquity of the tradition regarding Kṛṣṇa's connection with the Pāṇḍavas. It has also to be noted that both the *Chāndogya Upaniṣad* and the *Mahābhārata* mention Kṛṣṇa's mother as Devakī which was rather an uncommon name.[44] The Āṅgirasa family, to which the Upaniṣadic Kṛṣṇa's teacher Ghora belonged, was again intimately related to the Bhojas, who were, like the Vṛṣṇis, a sept of the Yādava clan. In this connection Raychaudhuri's attempt[45] to trace some of the doctrines enunciated in the *Bhagavad-Gītā,* sung by Vāsudeva-Kṛṣṇa to Arjuna, in the lessons received by Kṛṣṇa-Devakīputra from Ghora-Āṅgirasa, according to the *Chāndogya Upaniṣad,* is very interesting. There is, of course, palpable difference between the character of the Upaniṣadic Kṛṣṇa and that of the epic Kṛṣṇa-Vāsudeva ; but this may be due to the latter representing a later stage in the development of the Vāsudeva saga. In spite of the difference, the same person can probably be discerned in the two figures. In the *Chāndogya Upaniṣad,* Kṛṣṇa appears in a passage where *tapas, dāna, ārjava, ahiṁsā,* and *satya-vacana* are extolled (III. 17. 4) ; the same virtues are inculcated by the epic Kṛṣṇa in the *Gītā* (cf. *dāna, dama, yajña, svādhyāya, tapas, ārjava, ahiṁsā, satya,* etc., in XVI. 1-2) as well as in several other passages of the *Mahābhārata.* Just as Ghora deprecates *vidhi-yajña,* in the same way the *Gītā* (IV. 33) belittles *dravyamaya-yajña* or material sacrifice. Ghora says that all the actions of the virtuous life of a man constitute a kind of sacrifice to the deities and help him to attain to the God of gods. This seems to be essentially identical with the theory of absolute resignation (i.e. dedication of the results of all actions to God) inculcated in the *Gītā.* While the Upaniṣadic Kṛṣṇa and his teacher were worshippers of the sun, the *Gītā* (VIII. 9-11), attributed to Kṛṣṇa, emphasizes the importance of meditation 'at the last hour' on the 'word which knowers of the Veda call

[44] The occurrence of the word *Acyuta* in the *Chāndogya Upaniṣad* (III. 17. 6) is rather significant, as this appears as an epithet of Kṛṣṇa in the *Mahābhārata.*

[45] *Op. cit.,* pp. 57 ff.

Imperishable' and on 'the sun-coloured being beyond the darkness' as the best means of attaining to the supreme Being. As both the *Chāndogya Upaniṣad* and the *Gītā* associate essentially the same doctrines with one and the same person called Kṛṣṇa, son of Devakī, it is quite probable that they were originally learnt by Kṛṣṇa from Ghora, and were later taught by the former to his disciples. But although the teachings of Ghora-Āṅgirasa to Kṛṣṇa appear to be the kernel of the *Gītā*, this work of the later followers of Vāsudevism shows considerable development of the original doctrine.

The Bhāgavata religion, propounded by Vāsudeva, which incorporated the earlier cult of Nārāyaṇa and was the source of later Vaiṣṇavism, was therefore the development of an original sun-cult. In the *Śāntiparvan* of the *Mahābhārata*, the *sātvata-vidhi* is stated to have been declared in old times by the sun. The *Gītā* (IV. 1) also says that the Bhāgavata doctrine was first taught by the Lord to the sun, then by the sun to Manu, and ultimately by Manu to Ikṣvāku.

At a later date a pastoral character was attributed to Kṛṣṇa. In the *Harivaṁśa* (a supplement to the *Mahābhārata*) and the Purāṇas (e.g. *Vāyu*, *Bhāgavata*, etc.) are to be found stories about his tender babyhood and wanton childhood as well as—conspicuously in some later works—about the dalliances of his youth. The popularity of the cowherd god can be gathered from the name of the Pallava king Viṣṇugopa (fourth century A.D.) and literary evidence from the third or fourth century A.D. Hopkins[46] believes that it was not till Kṛṣṇa became a very great, if not the greatest, god and condescended to be born in low life that such tales about his youthful performances began to grow. The stories regarding the early life of pastoral Kṛṣṇa probably developed partly out of the Vedic legends about Viṣṇu, called *gopā* in the *Ṛg-Veda* and *govinda* and *dāmodara* in the *Baudhāyana Dharma-Sūtra*. But there appear to be other factors that also contributed to the development of the mythology of the cowherd Kṛṣṇa. The Yamunā region was possibly conspicuous for its cows as early as the age of the *Ṛg-Veda*, and a Vārṣṇa (i.e. a member of the Vṛṣṇi clan) named Gobala (literally, 'one strong in the wealth of cows') is known from the *Taittirīya Saṁhitā* (III. 11. 9. 3) and the *Jaiminīya Upaniṣad Brāhmaṇa* (I. 6. 1). It is thus probable that the Yādava-Sātvata-Vṛṣṇis of Mathurā possessed large herds of cattle as did their western neighbours, the Matsyas (cf. the epic reference to Virāṭa's *gogṛhas*). Most of the stories about Kṛṣṇa's early life, especially the late tales about his questionable relation with the cowherd women,[47] appear, however, to have been principally due

[46] *Op. cit.*, p. 467.
[47] A Pabhosa inscription (*Epigraphia Indica*, II. p. 482) of the seventh or eighth century refers to a maker of images of Śrī-Kṛṣṇa and the milkmaids. One of the earliest extant

to his identification with certain gods worshipped by the Ābhīras and other allied peoples. It may be noted in this connection that the God Śiva was similarly brought into relation with Koc girls in some late mediaeval works (especially Tantras) of Bengal, apparently as a result of his identification with a tribal god of the Hinduized Koc people.[48]

According to Barth[49] and Hopkins,[50] Kṛṣṇa was not a human being, but a popular divinity whose identification with Viṣṇu resulted in the growth of sectarian Vaiṣṇavism. Both the scholars admit the possibility of his solar association ; but the latter considers Kṛṣṇa to be the tribal god of the Pāṇḍavas, supposed to be an aboriginal people, while the former regards him to be the *kuladevatā* or the ethnic god of some powerful confederation of Rajput clans.[51] But the theory of Kṛṣṇa's solar character has been rightly dismissed by Keith[52] with the remark that 'the "dark sun" requires more explanation than it seems likely to receive'. Macnicol[53] and Keith[54] think that the conception of Kṛṣṇa who is believed to appear, in the *Mahābhāṣya*, in a 'vegetation masque', contending with Kaṁsa for the possession of the sun, developed out of one of the vegetation deities extensively worshipped in all parts of the world. But the evidence discussed above seems to bear testimony to the human character of Kṛṣṇa, who was gradually associated with certain popular cults and festivals. The suggestion that Kṛṣṇa is a myth is unconvincing. It reminds us of similar attempts to prove that Buddha and Christ are imaginary figures.

SOME ESSENTIAL TEACHINGS OF THE GĪTĀ

The method of salvation taught in the *Gītā* is that a man should live a life of actions without hankering after their results, which should be dedicated to God. This is referred to as the Ekāntika Dharma in the Nārāyaṇīya section in the *Śāntiparvan* of the *Mahābhārata*. Chapter I of the work is introductory, while in the following five chapters the process of Karma-yoga (i.e. to do action without regard to fruit, having surrendered oneself to God), which leads to the attainment of freedom from passions, is

poetical compositions (cf. quotations in the *Mahābhāṣya* from a work on the *Kaṁsa-vadha* episode) on Kṛṣṇa's early life is the *Bālacarita* attributed to Bhāsa who was a predecessor of Kālidāsa (*c.* A.D. 400). This work speaks of Dāmodara and Saṅkarṣaṇa as *Vṛṣṇikumāras*, of Kaṁsa, king of Mathurā, as *Śaurasenī-māta*, 'one whose mother is a Śūrasena girl', and of Vasudeva as *Yādavī-māta*. It also refers to Dāmodara's foster-parents, Nanda-gopa and Yaśodā or Nanda-gopī, and to his relations with the cowherds, but not to his amorous ecstasies. A Mathurā sculpture representing Vasudeva as crossing the Yamunā with baby Kṛṣṇa in a basket has been assigned to the age of the Kuṣāṇas (*Archaeological Survey of India, Annual Report*, 1925-26, pp. 283-84, plate LXVII. fig. c).

[48] Cf. *Journal of the Royal Asiatic Society of Bengal*, Letters, XIV. p. 105.

[49] *Religions of India*, pp. 166 ff.

[50] *Op. cit.*, pp. 466 ff., 488.

[51] Barth, *op. cit.*, p. 168.

[52] *Journal of the Royal Asiatic Society*, 1908, p. 171.

[53] *Indian Theism*, pp. 37-38.

[54] *Journal of the Royal Asiatic Society*, 1915, p. 841.

described. In the next six chapters Bhakti-yoga (i.e. loving adoration of God) is delineated, while the remaining chapters sum up the discussion. Some of the teachings of the *Gītā* are paraphrased below.

By devoted performance of acts without attachment to other objects, man gets his desires uprooted, and finally attains inflexibility of will and complete serenity of soul. He obtains quiescence in Brahman (supreme Spirit) at the time of death (II. 71-72).

By knowing God man is purified, has his passions destroyed, and attains to the condition of God. The highest knowledge, by means of which man sees all things in himself and in God, makes man free from all sins and destroys the polluting effect of his actions. It makes man a totally free spirit (IV. 35-38).

Both *sannyāsa* (renunciation of work when Self is realized) and Karma-yoga (performance of work, dedicated to God, before the dawn of Self-knowledge) lead men to the same goal (V. 2). By means of *yoga,* man obtains *jñāna* when all things are seen in the same light and Brahman is realized (VI. 29). The best *yogin* regards all as himself in matters of happiness and misery. He becomes absorbed in God in peace (VI. 31-32).

God is the source and the resting place of the world and there is nothing higher than He (VII. 6, 7). When man takes refuge in Him, he gets rid of God's Māyā consisting of the three *guṇas* or qualities and conditions resulting from them (VII. 14).

God is easily attained by a man who meditates on Him with concentration of mind and absolute devotion, especially at the time of death. A man who reaches God is freed from subjection to transmigration (VIII. 10, 15).

Men worshipping various deities are also worshippers of God; but they do not get freedom from rebirth (IX. 23-24). A person who resorts to God attains the highest place and obtains perfect peace (IX. 31-32).

God is the soul dwelling in the heart of man. He is the beginning, the middle, and the end of all beings (X. 20). Persons with their souls centred on God enlighten one another about Him and become happy (X. 9).

The universe is only a fractional aspect of God (X. 42).

A man should fix his mind on God and concentrate his will on Him; if this is not possible, he should obtain God by constant remembrance; if this also is not possible, he should perform deeds for God's sake; if even this is not possible, he should give up desire for the fruits of his deeds (XII. 8-11).

The virtues especially dear to God are absence of hatred, friendship for all, kindness, humility, indifference to praise and censure, etc. (XII. 13-19).

The thing to be known is Parabrahman that has no beginning or end, is neither existent nor non-existent, that has hands and feet, head and face, and eyes and ears everywhere, and that pervades all. The supreme Spirit dwelling in the body is devoid of qualities and is unchangeable. It does not do any deed and is not contaminated (XIII. 12-14, 31).

The man who resorts to God by Bhakti-yoga becomes immortal by being free from the three qualities (*guṇa*) that cause bondage (XIV. 26); he comes to possess a serene mood in which pleasure and pain are alike and agreeable and disagreeable things have no difference (XIV. 24).

There are two categories of beings in the world, of which one (viz. the body-mind complex) changes, but the other (viz. the soul) is unchangeable. There is also the highest Soul which is Paramātman, i.e. God, the support of the three worlds (XV. 16-17).

There are two classes of men, viz. good and bad. The second class includes men who do not care for God or morality and follow doctrines other than the one preached in the *Gītā* (XVI. 6 ff.). Desire, anger, and greed constitute the three roads to hell and lead to spiritual death (XVI. 21).

Men may be divided into three classes, according to the three elements (*guṇa*), as good, active, and ignorant. Of these three classes, the first worships gods, the second evil spirits, and the third ghosts and spectres (XVII. 2, 4). This third class performs activities leading to attenuation (or mortification) of the elements of the body wherein God dwells (XVII. 6).

True renunciation is attained not by complete inactivity, but by giving up actions arising from desires and by abandoning the fruits of actions. Worship, charity, and austerity lead to purity of the soul and should not therefore be given up. Duty must be done without thinking of the result (XVIII. 1, 5, 6). A person should surrender himself absolutely to God, who will then free him from all sins (XVIII. 66).

THE DOCTRINE OF THE FOUR VYŪHAS

The *vyūha* doctrine is one of the principal tenets of the old Pāñcarātra system, which was absorbed in the Bhāgavata religion, as well as of the later Śrī-Vaiṣṇava philosophy. According to this doctrine, Lord Vāsudeva in his *para* aspect is the highest object of *bhakti*. He created from himself the *vyūha* (phase of conditioned spirit) Saṅkarṣaṇa and also Prakṛti (the indiscrete primal matter of the Sāṁkhyas). From the association of Saṅkarṣaṇa and Prakṛti arose the *vyūha* Pradyumna and also *manas* (*buddhi* or intelligence of the Sāṁkhyas). From the combination of Pradyumna and *manas* sprang the *vyūha* Aniruddha as also *ahaṅkāra* (consciousness), and from the association of Aniruddha and *ahaṅkāra* arose the *mahābhūtas* (elements with their qualities) and Brahmā who made out of those elements the earth and all that it contains. While Vāsudeva alone possesses the six ideal *guṇas* or qualities, viz. *jñāna, bala, vīrya, aiśvarya, śakti,* and *tejas,* each one of his three emanations possesses only two of the said *guṇas* in turn.[55] This philosophical interpretation of the relation of Vāsudeva with the other deified heroes of the Vṛṣṇi clan is apparently a later development. The *Gītā,* the earliest religious text of the Bhāgavatas, does not refer to the *vyūhas,* although they are referred to in several other (presumably late) sections of the *Mahābhārata* (e.g. a section of the *Bhīṣmaparvan,* the Nārāyaṇīya section of the *Śāntiparvan,* etc.). But these references do not give a consistent account of the *vyūhas.* Bhandarkar[56] thinks that, out of the five *prakṛtis* of Vāsudeva (viz. the five elements, mind, *buddhi,* egoism, and Jīva) as mentioned in the *Gītā,* Jīva, mind, and egoism were later on personfied into the *vyūhas* Saṅkarṣaṇa, Pradyumna, and Aniruddha. The *vyūha* doctrine may be alluded to in the *Mahābhāṣya* passage *janārdanastvātma-caturtha eva,* quoted apparently from an unknown poem on the life of Vāsudeva-Kṛṣṇa.

The Mora (seven miles west of Mathurā) inscription of the first century A.D. speaks of *bhagavatāṁ Vṛṣṇīnāṁ pañcavīrāṇāṁ pratimāḥ,* 'the images of the group of five divine heroes of the Vṛṣṇi family'.[57] The *Vāyu Purāṇa* (XCVII. 1-2) mentions the five *vaṁśavīras* of the Vṛṣṇis, and they were Saṅkarṣaṇa, Vāsudeva, Pradyumna, Sāmba, and Aniruddha. There can hardly be any doubt that the five Vṛṣṇi heroes were apotheosized and worshipped with the title *bhagavat* in the Mathurā region about the beginning of the Christian era, probably by people associated with the old Yādava-Sātvata-Vṛṣṇi clan. In the *Viṣṇudharmottara,* a work mentioned by Alberuni (A.D. 1030) and probably used by Brahmagupta (A.D. 628), there are rules for the construction of images of various divinities related to the Bhāgavata cult. These include the five Vṛṣṇi heroes mentioned above. Varāhamihira's *Bṛhatsaṁhitā* (sixth century) also contains details for the making of the images of Viṣṇu (Vāsudeva), Baladeva (Saṅkarṣaṇa), Sāmba, and Pradyumna ; but it does not mention Aniruddha (LVII. 31-40). The preference of Sāmba to Aniruddha exhibited in this work may point to the fact that its author Varāhamihira belonged to the community of the sun-worshipping Maga-Brāhmaṇas (hailing originally from Persia) who appear to have held Sāmba in special esteem. Sāmba, however, soon fell in the estimation of the Bhāgavatas. This was probably because he was represented as the champion of solar worship in India and was sometimes

[55] Schrader, *Introduction to the Pāñcarātra and the Ahirbudhnya Saṁhitā*; pp. 32-35. For the sub-*vyūhas,* see *ibid.*, p. 41.
[56] *Op. cit.*, pp. 12 f.
[57] *Proceedings of the Indian History Congress,* Madras, 1944, pp. 82-90 ; Banerjea, *Development of Hindu Iconography,* pp. 114-15.

identified with the Sun-god himself. Banerjea suggests that all the Vṛṣṇi heroes (i.e. the four *vyūhas* together with Sāmba) were independently worshipped. He is inclined to identify Sāmba with certain sculptured figures hailing from the Mathurā area. The custom of erecting *dhvajas* or votive columns in honour of different sectarian deities, especially near their temples, was popular in ancient India ; and Banerjea thinks that the fragmentary capitals with figures of Garuḍa, Tāla (fan-palm), and Makara (crocodile), found at Besnagar and Pawaya, point to the existence of the *dhvajas* and shrines respectively of the deities Vāsudeva, Saṅkarṣaṇa, and Pradyumna.[58] Certain early coins, including a few from Taxila, are supposed by the same scholar to bear the representation of columns with fan-palm capitals.[59] The earliest sculpture representing Balarāma comes from Mathurā and is now preserved in the Lucknow Museum. On stylistic grounds it has been assigned to the second century B.C., although it may actually belong to the early Kuṣāṇa age.

The *catur-vyūha* doctrine was undoubtedly an outcome of the deification of several Vṛṣṇi *vīras* besides Vāsudeva. But the non-mention of Pradyumna and Aniruddha along with Saṅkarṣaṇa and Vāsudeva in the Ghosundi and Nanaghat inscriptions, both belonging to the first century B.C., appears to suggest that the independent worship of the third and fourth *vyūhas*, who are not known to have been great religious teachers, was perhaps limited to the Vṛṣṇi circle. Their apotheosis may have been influenced partly by the practice, prevalent in the Mathurā region, of the installation of images of deceased ancestors in *devakulas*, as is indicated by an inscription[60] of Huviṣka (cf. the *Pratimā-nāṭaka*, III, attributed to Bhāsa). Saṅkarṣaṇa, also called Baladeva, Balarāma, and Rāma, however, appears to have been a more important figure and his independent worship spread over a wide area before the birth of Christ. The Ghosundi inscription calls him *bhagavat* and *sarveśvara* jointly with Vāsudeva. It is also interesting to note that, both in the Ghosundi and Nanaghat records, Vāsudeva is mentioned after Saṅkarṣaṇa, apparently because he was the younger of the two brothers, and that these records do not give more prominence to Vāsudeva, as is done in the works on the *vyūha* doctrine. In the *Mahābhārata*, Saṅkarṣaṇa is represented as specially honoured by the Kuru king Duryodhana. The *Kauṭilīya Arthaśāstra* speaks of a class of ascetics who had shaven heads or braided hair and adored Saṅkarṣaṇa as their *devatā*. The votaries of Baladeva are also mentioned side by side with those of Vāsudeva in the Buddhist Niddesa works. In the Jaina *Aupapātika-*

[58] Cf. *Proceedings of the Indian History Congress, loc. cit.*
[59] Banerjea, *op. cit.*, p. 144.
[60] *Journal of the Royal Asiatic Society*, 1924, p. 402. For some references to the images of later kings, cf. Raychaudhuri, *Political History of Ancient India*, 1938, p. 432 n.

Sūtra,[61] mention is made not only of the votaries of Baladeva and Vāsudeva, but also of Balarāma who is referred to as one of the eight renowned Kṣatriya teachers. Independent worship of Saṅkarṣaṇa, before the birth of Christ, seems also to be suggested by his image in the Lucknow Museum referred to above. In epic and Paurāṇic traditions, Saṅkarṣaṇa is sometimes represented as the incarnation of Śeṣa or Ananta Nāga.[62] This seems to point to his identification with some tribal god of the Nāgas. The *Kāliya Nāga* episode in the Kṛṣṇa saga probably suggests the victory of Bhāgavatism over the tribal cult of the Nāgas, who are known to have ruled in the Mathurā area about the third century A.D. In these traditions, Saṅkarṣaṇa figures as a great helper in the deeds of valour of his younger step-brother Kṛṣṇa, especially in the latter's struggle with Kaṁsa. The pastoral association of Saṅkarṣaṇa may have come partly from his relations with Kṛṣṇa and partly also from his identification with some tribal god or gods. In the *Bhīṣmaparvan* of the *Mahābhārata* and the *Ahirbudhnya Saṁhitā*, he is represented as an exponent of the Sātvata or Pāñcarātra system. The Nārāyaṇīya section of the *Śāntiparvan* regards Vāsudeva as identical with the Paramātman (supreme Soul) and Saṅkarṣaṇa with the Jīvātman (individual soul). In later times the devotees of Saṅkarṣaṇa appear to have merged themselves in those of Vāsudeva. The independent worship of the last two *vyūhas*, viz. Pradyumna and Aniruddha, gradually declined. Even the worship of Saṅkarṣaṇa lost its popularity owing to the increasing enthusiasm for the worship of some of the *avatāras* of Viṣṇu since the age of the Imperial Guptas.

BHĀGAVATISM AND OTHER CREEDS

The Ājīvikas were the followers of a great champion of fatalism named Maskarīputra Gośāla who flourished, like Buddha and Mahāvīra, in the sixth century B.C. Utpala (tenth century), while commenting on Varāhamihira's *Bṛhajjātaka*, seems to include the Ājīvikas amongst the Nārāyaṇāśritas (i.e. devotees of Nārāyaṇa or Viṣṇu),[63] although this has been doubted by some scholars. In later days the Ājīvikas appear to have mostly merged into the followers of Vāsudeva.

Jainism shares the doctrine of *ahiṁsā* with Bhāgavatism and Buddhism, and is permeated with the influence of Hinduism, especially of the Kṛṣṇa cult. The Jains regard Vāsudeva and Baladeva as two of their sixty-three *śalākā-puruṣas* who are believed to be directors of the course of the world. The legends of Mahāvīra's birth as known from Jaina mythology, again,

[61] Ed. Leumann, pp. 61, 69-70.
[62] Śeṣa and Ananta are often distinguished in literature.
[63] Cf. *Indian Antiquary*, 1912, pp. 286 f. in this connection.

appear to be modelled on those of Kṛṣṇa's birth. The later conception of the twenty-four forms of Viṣṇu, on the other hand, was very probably imitated from that of the twenty-four Jaina Tīrthaṅkaras. It may be noted that the Jaina Tīrthaṅkara Ṛṣabha was regarded by some Bhāgavatas[64] as an *avatāra* of Viṣṇu.

Senart and Poussin suggest[65] that the worshippers of Nārayaṇa exerted considerable influence on the making of the Buddhist doctrine from its very inception. The theory can hardly be accepted in its entirety, because the early centres of influence of the two creeds were different. It must be admitted, however, that the importance of *ahiṁsā* is recognized by both the Bhāgavatas and the Buddhists as by the Jains. There is also an obvious resemblance between the Dharma-cakra of the Buddhists and Viṣṇu's Sudarśana-cakra. The adoration of Buddha's footprints may have been borrowed from the conception of Viṣṇu's *pada,* a term, as already shown above, of equivocal import. The full development of the Avatāra-vāda, on the other hand, was probably influenced by the Buddhist conception of the former Buddhas who are known to have been worshipped in their own *stūpas* as early as the age of Aśoka (third century B.C.). The absorption of a large number of Buddhists into the fold of the Vaiṣṇavas in the Gupta and post-Gupta periods seems to be suggested by the recognition of Buddha as one of Viṣṇu's *avatāras* before the mediaeval age.

According to some scholars, much of Bhāgavatism, including the idea of *bhakti,* was borrowed from Christianity. It has been suggested that Kṛṣṇa himself was an adaptation of Christ.[66] We should, however, remember that the origin of *bhakti* in India, the deification and worship of Vāsudeva, and his identification with Kṛṣṇa are all pre-Christian conceptions. Much has been made of the resemblance between the stories about the child Kṛṣṇa and the child Christ. Hopkins[67] thinks that the coincidences are direct importations from Christian lands to India and points to the late date of the development of the Kṛṣṇa legends. But the fact that the *Mahābhāṣya* quotes passages from a *kāvya* on the *Kaṁsa-vadha* episode seems to suggest a pre-Christian origin of the Kṛṣṇa saga. Kṛṣṇa's cowherd association was widely known before the rise of the Imperial Guptas in the fourth century A.D. It has been shown, on the other hand, that the adoration of Virgin Mary is not much earlier than the fifth century. Kennedy[68] rightly points out, 'there is no Christian representation of the

[64] Cf. the section on the *avatāras* below.
[65] Cf. Macnicol, *Indian Theism*, pp. 65, 241-48.
[66] Cf. Seal, *Comparative Studies in Vaishnavism and Christianity*, pp. 30 ff. ; also *Asiatic Researches*, I. pp. 274 ff. ; *Indian Antiquary*, 1873, pp. 285 ff. ; 1874, pp. 21 ff. ; Bhandarkar, *op. cit.*, IX.
[67] *Op. cit.*, p. 430.
[68] *Journal of the Royal Asiatic Society*, 1907, p. 484.

suckling mother before the twelfth century, (but) there is a much earlier Hindu one'. The influence of Christianity on Vaiṣṇavism cannot be proved satisfactorily with the evidence at our disposal. Bhandarkar's theory[69] that the Ābhīras were responsible for bringing Christian legends to India and introducing them into the Kṛṣṇa saga is not supported by any evidence.

BHĀGAVATISM AND THE GUPTA EMPERORS

In the fourth century A.D. the Guptas established an empire comprising the major part of northern India and extended their influence over the peninsula of the Deccan. They were devotees of Viṣṇu as is suggested by their adoption of Garuḍa as the distinguishing emblem of the family. The coins of the Gupta emperors bear the representation of their Garuḍa standard. The Allahabad pillar inscription[70] refers to the *garutmad-aṅka* (Garuḍa seal) of Samudragupta and represents him actually as the god Viṣṇu in human form. Samudragupta is described as equal to the four *lokapālas,* viz. Kubera, Varuṇa, Indra, and Yama, and also as 'one who is a mortal only in celebrating the observances of mankind, but is otherwise a god dwelling on the earth'. This no doubt refers to the conception of a divine king similar to that found in the *Manu Smṛti* (VII. 4-8). But more important is another passage of the same record in which Samudragupta is represented as identical with the *acintya-puruṣa* or inscrutable Being, i.e. Viṣṇu, who is 'the cause of the prosperity of the pious and destruction of the wicked'. It is quite clear that this passage is an echo of a verse of the *Gītā* (IV. 8) which refers to the descent of God on the earth, in physical form, for protecting the pious and destroying the sinners.

Though Samudragupta was a Vaiṣṇava, he was apparently not a Bhāgavata. This is indicated by the fact that his successors apply the epithet *paramabhāgavata* only to themselves and not to that king.[71] Although in some cases the word *bhāgavata* no doubt implies Viṣṇu-worshippers in general (cf. *Bṛhatsaṁhitā,* LX. 19), it was sometimes also used in the sense of a particular sect of the Vaiṣṇavas. Bāṇa (seventh century) in his *Harṣacarita*[72] mentions the Bhāgavata and the Pāñcarātrika separately in a list of different religious sects. A late commentator explains these two expressions as Viṣṇu-bhakta and Vaiṣṇava-bheda respectively. If Bāṇa and the commentator are believed to have taken Bhāgavata in the sense of Viṣṇu-worshippers in general and Pāñcarātrika as one of their sects, we have to assume the existence of sects among the Vaiṣṇavas at least from the seventh century. A study of the early history of Vaiṣṇavism makes

[69] *Indian Antiquary,* 1912, p. 15.
[70] *Select Inscriptions,* I. pp. 254 ff.
[71] Cf. 'Sectarian Difference among the Early Vaiṣṇavas', *Bhāratīya Vidyā,* VIII. pp. 109-11.
[72] Ed. Fürer, p. 316.

it clear that the growth of sectarian or doctrinal difference among the early worshippers of Viṣṇu was inevitable. We have to remember that the Vaiṣṇavas effected a synthesis of different elements, among which prominent mention should be made of the worshippers of various divinities such as the Vedic Viṣṇu, the deified ancient sage Nārāyaṇa, and the deified Vṛṣṇi heroes Vāsudeva and Baladeva-Saṅkarṣaṇa. The followers of Arjuna, of the Vṛṣṇi heroes Pradyumna, Aniruddha, and Sāmba, of the *avatāras* including Buddha before their identification with Viṣṇu, and of such tribal gods as those of the Ābhīras may be included in the above list. The fact that the early Vaiṣṇavas were a combination of different religious sects no doubt points to the existence of some sort of original sectarian difference among them. But it is impossible to determine the nature of such difference in the present state of insufficient information. In a narrow sense Bhāgavatism may have indicated the worship of Vāsudeva as Viṣṇu, originally advocated by the Vṛṣṇi people or a section of them. Samudragupta therefore probably followed some other form of early Vaiṣṇavism like the original worshippers of the Vedic Viṣṇu and of the deified sage Nārāyaṇa who was first identified with Viṣṇu and later with Vāsudeva.

From the days of Samudragupta's son Candragupta II (A.D. 376-414), the Gupta emperors were the most influential advocates of the Bhāgavata form of Vaiṣṇavism. Their patronage seems to have been one of the causes of the great popularity of this creed all over the country from the fifth century A.D. The title *paramabhāgavata* (in some cases *paramavaiṣṇava* or *paramadaivata*) is noticed from this time in various royal families in different parts of India. On the obverse of the Cakravikrama type of the coins of Candragupta II, the king is represented as receiving a gift from the god Viṣṇu.[73]

THE AVATĀRAS OF VIṢṆU

An important aspect of the Bhāgavata religion of the Gupta age was the popularity of the worship of the *avatāras*, i.e. descents or incarnations of Viṣṇu. The origin of the *avatāra* conception may be traced in the later Vedic literature. Even in the *Ṛg-Veda* (VI. 49. 13) we have reference to Viṣṇu's three steps taken for (Manu or) 'man in distress'. The conception of the Dwarf (Vāmana), Fish (Matsya), and Tortoise (Kūrma) *avatāras*, not yet associated with that god, are found in the *Śatapatha* and other Brāhmaṇas. There is a story in the *Śatapatha Brāhmaṇa* (I. 2. 5) which speaks of the contention between the gods and demons for a place of sacrifice. The latter are stated to have agreed to concede as much land as

[73] *Journal of the Numismatic Society of India*, X. p. 104.

was equal to the size of a dwarf. Viṣṇu, the dwarf, was then made to lie down. But he grew so big as to encompass the whole earth which consequently passed on to the gods. The same Brāhmaṇa also says how, 'having assumed the form of a tortoise, Prajāpati created offspring', and 'in the form of a boar, he (Prajāpati) raised the earth from the bottom of the ocean' (XIV. 1. 2; cf. *Taittirīya Saṁhitā*, VII. 1. 5; *Taittirīya Brāhmaṇa*. I. 1. 3). According to the *Taittirīya Āraṇyaka*, the earth was raised from the waters by a black boar with a hundred arms. The same work also alludes to Nṛ-siṁha or Man-lion. The story of the Great Deluge in the *Śatapatha Brāhmaṇa* represents the fish that towed Manu's vessel into safety as a form of Prajāpati Brahmā and this is sometimes supported by epic and Paurāṇic tradition. In later mythology, however, the function of the Boar, Fish, and Tortoise forms of Prajāpati Brahmā is attributed to Viṣṇu, the most benevolent of the gods. In the *Gītā* and some other sections of the *Mahābhārata*, Viṣṇu is represented as an ideal divinity and an almighty saviour of mankind, as delighting in both moral goodness and ritualistic purity, and as incarnating himself from time to time in human or animal form for the maintenance of the standard of righteousness in the world.[74] The theory of *avatāra*, however, presents only a stage of development in the *Mahābhārata*, as the earlier sections of the epic contain no list of the incarnations.

Traditions as to the number of *avatāras* varied and the later lists of the *avatāras*, though the usual number ten is generally adhered to, very often offer different names. But the Paurāṇic verse enumerating Matsya, Kūrma, Varāha, Narasiṁha, Vāmana, the three Rāmas, Buddha, and Kalki as the ten *avatāras*, almost universally recognized since the mediaeval period, is found in a Māmallapuram inscription of about the eighth century A.D.[75] The *avatāra* theory, which must have undergone several stages of evolution, appears to be based on old tales about strange animals exhibiting mysterious powers of helpfulness.[76] Some of them, however, had originally little to do with Viṣṇu. As already stated, the Buddhist conception of the former Buddhas may have influenced the development of the conception.

A passage of the late Nārāyaṇīya section of the *Mahābhārata* (XII. 349. 37) mentions only four *avatāras*, viz. Boar, Dwarf, Man-lion, and Man (i.e. Vāsudeva-Kṛṣṇa). Another passage of the same section

[74] The idea of the *Gītā* (IV. 7-8) that God manifests Himself in all ages for the protection of the pious, for the destruction of the wicked, and for the establishment of religious order seems to have a universal appeal. The attempt appears to be to regard all religious teachers of the world as manifestations of God Himself.

[75] *Memoirs of the Archaeological Survey of India*, XXVI. p. 5.

[76] Cf. the conception of Dakṣiṇarāya, the tiger-divinity of the Sundarbans. Stories of mysterious helpers living in the waters of certain *bils* (lakes) are still current in rural Bengal. Cf. *Journal of the Royal Asiatic Society of Bengal*, XV. p. 106.

(339. 77-99) adds the deified heroes Rāma-Bhārgava and Rāma-Dāśarathi to the list making a total of six *avatāras*, while in a third passage (*loc. cit.*, 104), a list of ten incarnations is offered, by adding to the above six Haṁsa, Kūrma, Matsya, and Kalki (or Kalkin). The *Matsya Purāṇa* (XLVII. 237-48), which also gives a list of ten incarnations, states that there were three divine *avatāras*, viz. Nārāyaṇa, Narasiṁha, and Vāmana, besides seven human *avatāras*, viz. Dattātreya, Māndhātṛ, Rāma-Jāmadagnya, Rāma-Dāśarathi, Veda-Vyāsa, Buddha, and Kalki. The above section also occurs in the *Vāyu Purāṇa* (XCVIII. 71-104) ; but there the name of Kṛṣṇa replaces that of Buddha. The *Harivaṁśa* (I. 41) quotes another list of ten incarnations which omits Matsya, Kūrma, one of the Rāmas, and Buddha to make room for Lotus, Datta (Dattātreya), Keśava (Kṛṣṇa), and Vyāsa[77] (cf. also the *Brahma Purāṇa*, CCXIII). There are no less than four lists of the *avatāras* in the *Bhāgavata Purāṇa* (I. 3 ; II. 7 ; VI. 8 ; XI. 4) ; but they are different from one another. One of these lists (I. 3) admits that the incarnations are really innumerable (cf. the *avatāra* theory of the *Gītā*), but mentions Brahmā, Varāha, Nārada, Nara and Nārāyaṇa, the philosopher Kapila, Dattātreya, Yajña, the Jaina Tīrthaṅkara Ṛṣabha, the ancient king Pṛthu, Matsya, Kūrma, the physician Dhanvantari, Mohinī, Narasiṁha, Vāmana, Rāma-Jāmadagnya, Veda-Vyāsa, Rāma-Dāśarathi, Rāma Haladhara, Kṛṣṇa, Buddha, and Kalki. The *Agni Purāṇa* (II-XVI ; see also the *Varāha Purāṇa*, XXXIX-XLVIII) states that the incarnations including the past and future ones are really innumerable, but describes only ten *avatāras* including Buddha and Kalki, while the *Garuḍa Purāṇa* (I. 202) mentions no less than nineteen *avatāras* (called *mūrtis*), viz. Matsya, Trivikrama, Vāmana, Narasiṁha, Rāma, Varāha, Nārāyaṇa, Kapila, Datta, Hayagrīva, Makaradhvaja, Nārada, Kūrma, Dhanvantari, Śeṣa, Yajña, Vyāsa, Buddha, and Kalki. The Pāñcarātra work *Ahirbudhnya Saṁhitā*,[78] which may be assigned to a date earlier than the eighth century, mentions thirty-nine *vibhavas* or manifestations of the supreme Being, which include almost all the well-known *avatāras*, viz. Ekaśṛṅga-tanu (i.e. Matsya), Vihaṅgama (i.e. Haṁsa), Kamaṭheśvara (i.e. Kūrma), Varāha, Narasiṁha, Vāmanadeha, Paraśurāma (i.e. Rāma-Jāmadagnya), Rāma Dhanurdhara (i.e. Rāma-Dāśarathi), Ananta (i.e. Rāma Haladhara), Kalki, and Kṛṣṇa. In other early Pāñcarātra works like the *Viṣvaksena Saṁhitā*,

[77] Rāma and Buddha are represented as *avatāras* in a Vaiṣṇava temple of about the seventh century at Sirpur in the Raipur District. Figures of Narasiṁha, Vāmana, Varāha, and Kṛṣṇa (holding the Govardhana over the cow-settlement) are found in the Daśāvatāra temple at Ellora attributed to the eighth century. Some of the *avatāras* are also represented in the Pallava temple at Māmallapuram.

[78] Schrader, *Introduction to the Pāñcarātra and the Ahirbudhnya Saṁhitā*, p. 42. For the origin of the *avatāras* out of the *vyūhas*, as in *Viṣvaksena Saṁhitā* and *Padma Tantra*, see *ibid.*, p. 48.

Buddha, Arjuna, and others are included in the list of secondary *avatāras*. Buddha is mentioned as one of the ten *avatāras* in the *Daśāvatāra-carita* of Kṣemendra (*c.* A.D. 1050) of Kashmir and in the *Gīta-Govinda* of Jayadeva (*c.* A.D. 1200) of eastern India, and also, as we have seen above, he is mentioned as an *avatāra* in a Paurāṇic verse quoted in an eighth century inscription of the Tamil country. Jayadeva eulogizes Kṛṣṇa as Viṣṇu himself and sings in praise of his ten *avatāras*, viz. Fish, Tortoise, Boar, Man-lion, Dwarf, Rāma-Bhārgava, Rāma-Dāśarathi, Rāma Haladhara, Buddha, and Kalki. This list came to be regarded as the most authentic since the early mediaeval period, though there was still some difference of opinion in regard to the position of Kṛṣṇa. The Belava (Dacca District, East Bengal) inscription of *c.* A.D. 1125, which belongs to a *paramavaiṣṇava* ruler of East Bengal, mentions Kṛṣṇa as *gopī-śata-kelikāra* and *Mahābhārata-sūtradhāra* and also as *aṁśakṛtāvatāra*, i.e. a partial incarnation.[79] But an Ajmer inscription[80] of about the same age seems to include Kṛṣṇa among the ten *avatāras* of Viṣṇu.

The popularity of the worship of several *avatāras* is attested by the Indian epigraphic records of the period between the fourth and the eighth century A.D. The name Matsyagupta (literally, 'protected by the Fish') occurring in an inscription[81] of A.D. 101 seems to indicate the popularity of the Fish-god before the rise of the Guptas, although he may or may not have been identified with Viṣṇu at that date. The worship of Paraśurāma in western India is indicated by another early record of the second century A.D.; but his being conceived as an *avatāra* of Viṣṇu does not seem to be so early. An inscription[82] of Śaka Ṛṣabhadatta at Nasik mentions Rāmatīrtha which is known from the *Mahābhārata* (III. 85. 42) to have been the holy abode of Rāma-Jāmadagnya situated in the suburbs of Sūrpāraka (modern Sopara in the Thana District), not far to the north of Bombay. It is usually believed that the worship of Rāma-Dāśarathi was not popular in the Gupta age. But the idea seems to be wrong. As regards the *avatāra* theory it has to be remembered that the apotheosis and worship of an incarnation are earlier than his identification with Viṣṇu. Kālidāsa's *Raghuvaṁśa* (*c.* A.D. 400) speaks of Rāma, son of Daśaratha, as an incarnation of Hari (Viṣṇu). The Vākāṭaka queen Prabhāvatī (fifth century), daughter of Candragupta II, was devoted to Bhagavat Rāmagirisvāmin (lord of Rāmagiri, i.e. modern Ramtek near Nagpur), who appears to be identical with

[79] Later Vaiṣṇava literature recognized three kinds of *avatāras*, viz. (1) complete incarnation (*pūrṇāvatāra*), (2) incarnation of a portion of the power of a divine being called *aṁśāvatāra*, and (3) partial incarnation of a more or less temporary character called *āveśa*. Rāma-Dāśarathi and Kṛṣṇa are often regarded as complete *avatāras*. But there seems to have been difference of opinion on these points.

[80] *Epigraphia Indica*, XXIX. 1. Appendix, p. 5.

[81] *Ibid.*, XXVIII. p. 43.

[82] *Select Inscriptions*, I. p. 161.

Rāma-Dāśarathi.[83] The worship of the Ikṣvāku king in the sixth century is indicated by Varāhamihira's *Bṛhatsaṁhitā* (LVIII. 30) containing rules for the construction of Rāma's image. Saint Kulaśekhara, king of Keraḷa in the Malabar coast, was a votary of Rāma. The worship of Balarāma-Saṅkarṣaṇa, however, does not find mention in the inscriptions of the Gupta age. The Dwarf (Vāmana) is implied by the epithets *Indrānuja* and *Upendra* (both meaning Indra's younger brother) applied to Viṣṇu in records like the Bihar pillar inscription[84] of the fifth century. The Junagadh inscription[85] of Skandagupta also refers to Viṣṇu 'who, for the sake of the happiness of the lord of the gods, seized back from Bali the goddess of wealth and splendour'. The identification of Kṛṣṇa and Viṣṇu is alluded to in the name Viṣṇugopa (cf. Kālidāsa's *Meghadūta,* 15), popular among the early Pallavas from the fourth century, and in epigraphic passages mentioning the god Viṣṇu as 'a mighty bee on the water-lily which is the face of Jāmbavatī'[86] or as 'Mādhava, whose feet are graced by the attentions of Śrī (Lakṣmī) and who is born from Vasudeva'.[87] The Maukhari chief Anantavarman installed an image of Kṛṣṇa in a cave in the Pravaragiri (Barabar hills) in the fifth century.[88] The Narasiṁha incarnation is alluded to in such epigraphs as the Alina grant.[89] But the most popular *avatāra* appears to have been the Boar, who was widely worshipped in different parts of India in the Gupta age. The legend of this *avatāra* of Viṣṇu seems to have been originally associated with that of the Great Deluge. A stone image of Varāha bearing an inscription[90] of the reign of King Toramāṇa (*c.* A.D. 500) records the construction of a stone temple of 'Nārāyaṇa who has the form of a boar' at Eran in the Saugor District of Madhya Pradesh. A Damodarpur (North Bengal) inscription[91] of the time of Budhagupta (A.D. 477-95) speaks of the gods Śvetavarāhasvāmin and Kokāmukhasvāmin, both representing the Varāha *avatāra.* The temples of these gods stood on the Himavacchikhara (peak of the Himalayas) apparently at Varāhachatra (Varāha-kṣetra) at the junction of the rivers Kauśikī and Kokā in Nepal.[92] In the fifth century, an inhabitant of North Bengal seems to have visited the Varāha-kṣetra or Kokāmukha-tīrtha on pilgrimage and constructed temples for the installation of two deities of the same names near Damodarpur in the Dinajpur

[83] *Ibid.,* p. 415. Cf. the *Meghadūta* reference to the footprints of Raghupati on the Rāmagiri and the worship of Rāma, Sītā, and Lakṣmaṇa in the temples of Ramtek at the present time.

[84] *Select Inscriptions,* I. p. 316. See also the Alina plates of A.D. 766 (*Corpus Inscriptionum Indicarum,* III. p. 174).

[85] *Select Inscriptions,* I. p. 300.

[86] *Corpus Inscriptionum Indicarum,* III. p. 270.

[87] *Ibid.,* p. 206.

[88] *Ibid.,* pp. 222 ff.

[89] *Ibid.,* p. 188.

[90] *Select Inscriptions,* I. pp. 396 f.

[91] *Ibid.,* pp. 328 ff.

[92] Cf. *Indian Historical Quarterly,* XXI. pp. 56-60.

District of North Bengal. A Kadamba record[93] from Tagare belonging to the sixth century points to the popularity of the Varāha *avatāra* in the far south of India. The early Cālukyas of Badami had the boar as their family emblem which they are said to have obtained through the grace of Nārāyaṇa. Most of the inscriptions of these monarchs and their subordinates begin with a stanza in praise of the Boar form of Viṣṇu.

There is no reference to the independent worship of the *vyūha*—Saṅkarṣaṇa, Pradyumna, and Aniruddha—in the inscriptions of the Gupta age. The *vyūha* doctrine, however, finds a prominent place in the Pāñcarātra literature, some of the Saṁhitās being composed, according to Schrader, in Kashmir between the fourth and the eighth century. The *Amarakoṣa* (*c.* sixth century) also refers to all the *vyūhas*. It seems that the doctrine was not quite popular with the ordinary Viṣṇu-worshippers of the Gupta period. A modified form of Vyūhavāda can, however, be traced in the joint worship of Baladeva, Kṛṣṇa, and Subhadrā or Ekānaṁśā (sometimes identified with Subhadrā, but sometimes with the Devī born as the daughter of Nanda-gopa). Varāhamihira's *Bṛhatsaṁhitā* (LVIII. 37-39) gives rules for the construction of the composite image of Baladeva and Kṛṣṇa with Ekānaṁśā standing between them. An inscription[94] of the thirteenth century from Bhubaneswar, referring to the adoration of Baladeva, Kṛṣṇa, and Subhadrā, points to the popularity of their worship in mediaeval Orissa.

Some scholars believe that Bhāgavatism and Pāñcarātra had possibly been related at the beginning, but became completely different in the Gupta period.[95] They further suggest that the Vyūhavāda was exclusively associated with Pāñcarātra, but that it was completely different from the Avatāravāda in its ideological basis. The first of the two suggestions cannot be proved in the present state of our knowledge. The second also seems to go against the evidence of Pāñcarātra works like the *Ahirbudhnya Saṁhitā* and *Viṣvaksena Saṁhitā,* discussed above. It is clear that, while the Vyūhavādins were very much influenced by the *avatāra* theory as early as the days of the early Pāñcarātra Saṁhitās, Kṛṣṇa and Balarāma were recognized as *avatāras* in the Vaiṣṇava literature from practically the same age. We have, however, to note that there are indications regarding the existence of doctrinal differences amongst the Viṣṇu-worshippers of the Gupta age, to which reference has already been made above. This difference, the nature of which cannot be determined with certainty, appears to be illustrated, as indicated above, by the *Harṣacarita* and its commentary which make a

[93] *The Successors of the Sātavāhanas,* p. 304.
[94] *Epigraphia Indica,* XIII. p. 155.
[95] *History of Bengal* (Dacca University), I. p. 402.

distinction between the Bhāgavatas and the Pāñcarātrikas. Even in the Gupta age the Pāñcarātrikas, who may have favoured some of the doctrines inculcated by the ancient sage Nārāyaṇa, were probably sometimes regarded as a sect of the Bhāgavatas, the term *bhāgavata* (essentially a worshipper of Vāsudeva-Viṣṇu according to the *vidhi* or rules of the Sātvatas) being occasionally used, together with the term *vaiṣṇava*, in the sense of Viṣṇu-worshippers in general. The age of the Guptas witnessed the evolution of neo-Vaiṣṇavism from the tribal form of Bhāgavatism which was originally practised by the members of the Yādava-Sātvata-Vṛṣṇi clan.

ŚRĪ OR LAKṢMĪ, CONSORT OF VIṢṆU

Another interesting feature of Vaiṣṇavism in the Gupta age is the conception of Lakṣmī or Śrī as the consort of Viṣṇu. This goddess is called Sirimā Devatā in a Barhut inscription of the Śuṅga age[96] and her temple is referred to in the *Kauṭilīya Arthaśāstra* (II. 4). Her popularity is indicated by her appearance on early Indian coins such as the inscribed coins of Kauśāmbī and Ujjayinī, the issues of some early kings of Ayodhyā and Mathurā, and those of the Satraps of Mathurā and of Pantaleon, Agatholes, Maues, and Azilises.[97] The representation of Lakṣmī is conspicuous on the coins of the Imperial Guptas and some of their successors. Śrī-Lakṣmī is a Vedic goddess and, according to the Brāhmaṇa literature, she is full of riches, of which the gods despoil her. Her conception as the wife of Viṣṇu is, however, considerably late. The Junagadh inscription of Skandagupta mentions Viṣṇu as a perpetual resort of Lakṣmī, who is represented as Vāsudeva's wife in the Sarnath inscription of Prakaṭāditya.[98] In the Aphsad inscription of Ādityasena, Dāmodara is spoken of as the slayer of demons, and the feet of Mādhava, son of Vasudeva, as graced by the attentions of Śrī. The kings of Śarabhapura and some other royal families adopted the Gaja-Lakṣmī device, found on the Barhut sculptures and some early coins, as their emblem. A Kadamba record of *c.* A.D. 500 begins with a stanza in adoration of Bhagavat with Śrī on his breast and Brahmā on the lotus sprung from his navel.[99] The Earth (Bhū), called Vaiṣṇavī in such epigraphs as those of the Śarabhapura kings, was conceived as a second wife of Viṣṇu. Viṣṇu's *dhyāna* describes the god as

[96] Barua and Sinha, *Barhut Inscriptions*, pp. 73-74. Barua distinguishes Siri and Sirimā Devatā. Prakrit *Sirimā* actually stands for Sanskrit *Śrīmatī*. Another early representation of the goddess has been traced in a sculpture from Besnagar of about the second century B.C. Cf. Banerjea, *op. cit.*, pp. 370-71.

[97] Cf. Allan, *op. cit.*, pp. 131, 149, 173 ff., 252; Whitehead, *Catalogue of Coins in the Punjab Museum*, I. pp. 16, 135; Banerjea, *op. cit.*, p. 151.

[98] *Corpus Inscriptionum Indicarum*, III. p. 286.

[99] *The Successors of the Sātavāhanas*, p. 292, f.n. 1.

Indirā-Vasumatī-saṁśobhi-pārśvadvaya. The early Cālukya emperors claiming to be *Śrī-Pṛthivī-vallabha* (lord of Śrī and Pṛthivī) apparently claimed to be incarnations of Viṣṇu.[100] Sarasvatī is not referred to in the inscriptions of the Gupta age as Viṣṇu's wife. Indeed it is a late conception popular only in certain parts of the country, especially eastern India.

The Śrī-Lakṣmī cult may have something to do with the worship of Greek goddesses, especially Pallas Athene, which was introduced in India by the Indo-Greek kings as suggested by their coins from the beginning of the second century B.C. The Sāṁkhya doctrine of Puruṣa and Prakṛti also appears to have considerably influenced the conception of Lakṣmī as the consort of Viṣṇu, as well as of Devī as the consort of Śiva.

VAIṢṆAVISM AND VIṢṆU MYTHOLOGY IN THE RECORDS OF THE GUPTA AGE

In the Gadhwa inscription[101] of Kumāragupta I and many other records, Viṣṇu is mentioned, without reference to his name, only as the Bhagavat. The Eran inscription[102] of A.D. 484 describes the god Janārdana as 'the four-armed lord whose couch is the broad waters of the four oceans, who is the cause of the continuance, production, destruction, etc. of the universe, and whose ensign is Garuḍa'. A Kadamba inscription of the sixth century[103] refers to the god Hari as *jagat-pravṛtti-saṁhāra-sṛṣṭi-māyādhara.* The god Cāṅgu-Nārāyaṇa, i.e. Nārāyaṇa on Cāṅgu or Garuḍa, seems to have been in worship in a temple on the Dolaparvatá in Nepal before King Mānadeva's inscription of A.D. 464.[104] The god is described in various epigraphs as the troubler of the demons called Puṇyajana, as the supporting pillar of the three worlds (in the form of the boar), as the slayer of the demons Madhu and Mura, and as the bearer of the disc, the club, the bow of horn, the sword called Nandaka, the jewel called Kaustubha, and the garland of lotuses. The slumber of Madhusūdana during the four months of the rainy season is alluded to in the Gangdhar inscription of A.D. 423.[105] The Alina grant (A.D. 766) appears to refer to the *Pārijātaharaṇa* episode. The Mandasor inscription[106] of A.D. 404 probably refers to the *Śakra* festival as dear to Kṛṣṇa. The same record describes Vāsudeva as the lord (*vibhu*) who is *śaraṇya, jagadvāsa, aprameya,* and *aja* (cf. *ātmabhū* of the Jaunpur inscription of the Maukharis) and as a great tree with the gods as its fruits, the heavenly damsels as its fine shoots, the celestial palaces as its many branches, and the rains as its flow of honey. In this there seems to be an imperfect

[100] Cf. *Indian Culture,* II. pp. 131-33.
[101] *Corpus Inscriptionum Indicarum,* III. p. 41. [102] *Select Inscriptions,* I. pp. 326 ff.
[103] *The Successors of the Sātavāhanas,* p. 297, f.n. 1.
[104] *Select Inscriptions,* I. pp. 366 ff. [105] *Ibid.,* pp. 379 ff. [106] *Ibid.,* pp. 377 ff.

allusion to the Viśvarūpa conception of Viṣṇu, the germ of which is probably to be traced to a Ṛg-Vedic idea (X. 90 ; cf. I. 155. 6 ; VII. 100. 6) and to the Upaniṣadic concept of Brahman.

The influence of Vaiṣṇava mythology is also noticed in the archaeological remains in different parts of the country. The bas-reliefs at Badami, which belong to the age of the early rulers of the Cālukya family, some of whom were *paramabhāgavatas,* depict Viṣṇu lying on the serpent Ananta with Lakṣmī rubbing his feet, the Boar, Dwarf, and Man-lion incarnations, and also Hari-Hara. They also depict many legends of the Kṛṣṇa saga.[107] A temple at Deoghar (Jhansi District, U.P.), probably assignable to the sixth century, has the representation of Viṣṇu reclining on Ananta Nāga, while a sculpture at Pathari in Central India, probably belonging to the sixth century, is believed to represent the new born Kṛṣṇa lying by his mother's side. There are representations of the *avatāras* and other deities of the Viṣṇu pantheon also in the Daśāvatāra and Kailāsanātha temples at Ellora, attributed to the eighth century, as well as in the works of art at Māmallapuram near Madras, assignable to approximately the same age. A sculpture from Paharpur (North Bengal), attributed to the sixth or seventh century, represents Kṛṣṇa and his consort (probably Rukmiṇī). Her identification with Rādhā is rendered improbable by the fact that we have no undoubted reference to Rādhā in genuine epigraphic or literary records of an early date.

Some scholars believe that the Khoh copperplate inscription of the fifth or sixth century[108] records a grant of land in favour of Bhagavat and Ādityabhaṭṭāraka, pointing to the solar association of Vaiṣṇavism. But the suggestion is unjustifiable as the language of the record seems to suggest that a person named Viṣṇunandin constructed a temple of Bhagavat and obtained from the king half of a village on behalf of the god, while three merchants named Śaktināga, Kumāranāga, and Skandanāga, who had built a temple of the Sun-god, secured for that deity the other half of the same village. The inscription therefore does not prove that the same person worshipped both Viṣṇu and the Sun-god. That the Sun-god was not adored by the Vaiṣṇavas in the fifth century is indicated by the degradation of Sāmba, a champion of the solar cult and sometimes identified with the Sun-god, in the estimation of the Vaiṣṇavas. This seems to be also supported by verses 21-22 of the Gangdhar inscription of A.D. 423. This epigraph, however, speaks of the building of a temple, full of *ḍākinīs,* by a devotee of Viṣṇu, in honour of the divine Mothers 'who utter loud and

[107] See R. D. Banerji, *Bas-reliefs of Badami,* pp. 24 ff.
[108] *Select Inscriptions,* I. p. 370.

tremendous shouts in joy and stir up the oceans with the mighty wind rising from the magic rites of their religion (*tantra*)'. It evidently points to the influence of the Tantra cult on the Vaiṣṇavas of the fifth century A.D. It may be pointed out in this connection that the Maukhari chief Anantavarman installed in the same century an image of Kṛṣṇa in one of the caves in the Nāgārjuni hills and also the images of Bhūtapati (Śiva) and the Devī, i.e. Durgā (or probably a joint image styled Ardhanārīśvara), in another cave in the same hill. This apparently points to an early approach between Vaiṣṇavism, on the one hand, and the worshippers of Śiva and Śakti, on the other.[109] The early Cālukyas of Badami, who had Viṣṇu as their family god, similarly proclaimed their devotion to the god Kārttikeya and the Seven Mothers. In this connection we may also mention the cult of Hari-Hara (a combination of Viṣṇu and Śiva), Devī's rôle as the daughter of Kṛṣṇa's foster-father Nanda-gopa (cf. the *Harivaṁśa* and the *Bālacarita*), and the Trimūrti conception of the gods Brahmā, Viṣṇu, and Śiva. The attempt to identify different gods and to conciliate rival religious sects is old.[110] But, although one god, viz. Agni, is represented as the same as Varuṇa, Mitra, Indra, and Aryaman, in such an early work as the *Ṛg-Veda*, both sectarianism and attempt at conciliation were probably due mainly to non-Aryan inspiration. A gold coin of Huviṣka is believed to represent a composite image of Viṣṇu and Śiva, while a Gandhāra relief has been supposed to be the representation of a three-headed and six-armed Trimūrti.[111] These cases are, however, not entirely free from doubt. Adoration to Hari-Hara-Hiraṇyagarbha or to Hara-Nārāyaṇa-Brahmā are found in several early Kadamba inscriptions of the fifth and sixth centuries. As already noted above, the representation of Hari-Hara is found in a cave temple of the sixth century at Badami.

VIṢṆU WORSHIP IN THE FAR SOUTH

We have already referred to the adoration of Vāsudeva in the Chinna (Krishna District) inscription of the close of the second century A.D. and to the name of Pallava Viṣṇugopa in records dating from the fourth century. Reference has also been made to an inscription from the Guntur District, which may be assigned to the first half of the fourth century, as speaking of a temple of Nārāyaṇa.[112] The inscriptions of the Gupta age occasionally refer to temples or flagstaffs of the god Viṣṇu-Nārāyaṇa-Vāsudeva in all

[109] Cf. *Journal of the Royal Asiatic Society of Bengal*, Letters, XIV. pp. 104 ff.

[110] The same attempt is noticed in the enumeration of the 108 or 1,000 names of gods and goddesses. Cf. *Journal of the Royal Asiatic Society of Bengal*, Letters, XIV. p. 24 and note.

[111] Banerjea, *op. cit.*, p. 137 ; *Archaeological Survey of India, Annual Report*, 1913-14, pp. 276 ff., plate LXXII, fig. a.

[112] *Select Inscriptions*, I. pp. 443 ff.

parts of India—in Nepal and the upper reaches of the Beas in the north, in Bengal in the east, in Kathiawad in the west, and in the trans-Krishna region in the south. In the southernmost parts of India some of the early Pallava and early Western Gaṅga kings were devout Bhāgavatas. The worship of Viṣṇu was also prevalent in the kingdom of the early Kadambas ; but the popular religion appears to have been Jainism in that area. Some of the early Kadamba rulers, who called themselves *paramabrahmaṇya,* were probably Vaiṣṇavas. Several southern rulers claim to have been *kaliyuga-doṣāvasanna-dharmoddharaṇa-nitya-sannaddha.* Probably they tried to suppress heretical doctrines like Buddhism and Jainism, to revive the Brāhmaṇical religion, and possibly also to represent themselves, like King Samudragupta of the North, as incarnations of the god Viṣṇu, emulating his doings in the Boar form. There is another indication of the influence of Vaiṣṇava Brāhmaṇism in the far south of India. This is the importance attached to *go-brāhmaṇa* (i.e. the cow and Brāhmaṇa) in some Pallava and Kadamba records, exactly as in the Vaiṣṇava records from Eran. Certain later sections of the *Mahābhārata* represent Viṣṇu as the benefactor of the cow and the Brāhmaṇa (*go-brāhmaṇa-hita*). This indicates the association of the Brāhmaṇas with Viṣṇu-worship, and also the important position they attained in social estimation.

There is some evidence to show that the association of Vāsudevism with the Pāṇḍya country is old. In the fourth century B.C. the grammarian Kātyāyana explains the word *Pāṇḍya* as 'one sprung from an individual of the clan of the Pāṇḍus or the king of their country'. Kātyāyana therefore associates the Pāṇḍya country with the Pāṇḍus or Pāṇḍavas whom epic traditions intimately connect with Vāsudeva. Greek tradition, attributed to Megasthenes, derives the name of the Pāṇḍya country from its queen named Pandaia who is said to have been the daughter of Herakles (Vāsudeva-Kṛṣṇa). It is possible to think that there was a section of the Vṛṣṇi people among the colonizers of the Pāṇḍya country. At least this seems to be suggested by the name of its capital Madurā which is the same as Mathurā and is often specifically called the Mathurā of the South. This probably explains how the Tamil country soon became the greatest stronghold of the Bhāgavata religion and gave birth to the Āḷvārs and their compositions in Tamil on *bhakti* and the Kṛṣṇa cult. Ancient Tamil works prove the popularity of the worship of Kṛṣṇa and Baladeva in the Tamil land about the age of the Guptas. In the *Śilappadikāram* (*c.* sixth century A.D.) there are references to temples of the two gods at Madurā, Kāveripaṭṭinam, and other cities. They are described by the poet Kari-Kannan of Kāveripaṭṭinam as the dark-complexioned god bearing the wheel and the white-complexioned one having the flag of the palmyra.

THE ĀḶVĀRS OR VAIṢṆAVA SAINTS OF THE TAMIL COUNTRY

The best evidence of the great influence exercised by the Bhāgavata religion over the Tamil country is furnished by the devotional songs of the Āḷvārs constituting the Vaiṣṇava *Prabandham* of four thousand verses in classical Tamil. The Āḷvārs sang in praise of Nārāyaṇa and Kṛṣṇa as well as the *avatāras* Dāśarathi-Rāma, Balarāma, and Vāmana. Kṛṣṇa's dalliance with the *gopīs* or cowherd girls was also well known to them. A female Āḷvār is known to have regarded herself as a *gopī* and the god (in the form of Śrī Raṅganātha of the Śrīraṅgam temple) as her lover. The Āḷvārs knew the principal Purāṇas and revered the Vedic literature. The recitation of God's names, meditation on His different forms, and their worship in temples like those at Śrīraṅgam, Tirupati, and Alagarkoil were inculcated by them. The activities of the Āḷvārs, representing the emotional side of Tamilian Vaiṣṇavism, and their successors, the Ācāryas, representing its intellectual side, must have given rise to the tradition recorded in the *Bhāgavata Purāṇa* (XI. 5. 38-40), a work referred to by Alberuni about A.D. 1030, that large numbers of the worshippers of Vāsudeva-Viṣṇu flourished in the Dravida or Tamil country in the Kali age when they were rare elsewhere in India.

The date of the Āḷvārs is a disputed question ; but they may be roughly placed between the sixth and ninth centuries A.D. All of them appear to have flourished before the early Vaiṣṇava Ācāryas—Nāthamuni (tenth-eleventh century) and his disciple Puṇḍarīkākṣa (eleventh century) and grandson Yāmunācārya (eleventh century). The Vaiṣṇava tradition of the Tamil country speaks of twelve Āḷvārs, viz. (1) Poygai Āḷvār or Saroyogin, (2) Bhūtattāḷvār or Bhūtayogin, (3) Pey Āḷvār or Mahadyogin or Bhrāntayogin, (4) Tirumaḷiśai Āḷvār or Bhaktisāra, (5) Nammāḷvār or Śaṭakopa, (6) Madhurakavi, (7) Kulaśekhara, (8) Periyāḷvār or Viṣṇucitta, (9) Āṇḍāḷ or Godā, (10) Toṇḍaraḍippoḍi or Bhaktāṅghhrireṇu, (11) Tiruppāṇ Āḷvār or Yogivāhana, and (12) Tirumaṅgai Āḷvār or Parakāla. The first four Āḷvārs are believed to have flourished in the land of the Pallavas and the last three in that of the Coḷas. The seventh hailed from Keraḷa and the rest from the Pāṇḍya country. They came from different strata of the society. Only the eighth of the above list is stated to have been a Brāhmaṇa, although some regard him as a pariah. The fifth was a Veḷḷāḷa by caste and, while the seventh was a king, the twelfth came from a Kaḷḷa family, i.e. a family of robbers.

The three earliest Āḷvārs, who are supposed to be mythical in origin, are said to have composed a hundred stanzas each. They often refer to the *avatāras* of Viṣṇu, especially Trivikrama and Kṛṣṇa, and cannot be assigned to a date earlier than the Gupta age, as has sometimes been suggested. The fourth Āḷvār Tirumaḷiśai is regarded by some to have been a contemporary of Pallava Mahendravarman I (*c.* A.D. 600-30). The fifth Āḷvār, named Nammāḷvār or Śaṭakopa, composed nearly one thousand three hundred stanzas in four works of which *Tiruvāymoḷi* ('the holy word of the mouth'), with 1102 stanzas, forms the fourth and the last part of the *Nālāyira Prabandham*. The sixth Āḷvār Madhurakavi was a worshipper of his *guru* Nammāḷvār. The seventh Āḷvār Kulaśekhara was a king of Travancore. The *Mukundamālā*, attributed to him, quotes a verse from the *Bhāgavata Purāṇa* (XI. 2. 36). Bhandarkar[113] is inclined to assign him to the first half of the twelfth century; but there are no sufficient grounds for the date. The eighth Āḷvār Viṣṇucitta composed numerous songs. The ninth Āḷvār Āṇḍāḷ was Viṣṇucitta's daughter. She has 173 stanzas to her credit, which are highly mystical. The tenth Āḷvār Toṇḍaraḍippoḍi composed two small works, and the eleventh Āḷvār Tiruppāṇ composed only ten stanzas. The twelfth and last Āḷvār Tirumaṅgai composed 1361 verses (in six works) out of the 4000 constituting the celebrated *Nālāyira Prabandham* attributed to the Āḷvārs. There is a story that Tirumaṅgai was a contemporary of the Śaiva saint Tirujñāna Sambandar who was himself a contemporary of the Pallava king Narasiṁhavarman I (A.D. 630-68) of Kāñcī. If this tradition be true, Tirumaṅgai Āḷvār has to be assigned to the seventh century A.D., although he is placed by some scholars in the eighth century.

VAIṢṆAVISM IN GREATER INDIA

There is evidence to show that with the spread of Indian culture outside the limits of India the Viṣṇu cult also spread abroad, at least from the early centuries of the Christian era. In Java a king named Pūrṇavarman, probably belonging to the fifth century A.D., is compared to Viṣṇu in the Ci-arutön rock inscription.[114] He was deified probably as an incarnation of Viṣṇu and his footprints are known to have been worshipped.

The earliest inscription of the ancient kingdom of Campā in Annam, referring to Viṣṇu together with Maheśvara, Umā, Brahmā, and other deities, is on the My-son stelae belonging to about the fifth-sixth century.[115] Lakṣmī, Śrī, or Padmā, wife of Viṣṇu, was also a well-known goddess in Campā. In a later period the kings of Campā, like some of the Indian rulers, often claimed to have been incarnations of Viṣṇu.

The earliest inscriptions referring to the spread of Vaiṣṇavism in Cambodia (earlier Fu-nan and later Kambuja) are to be assigned to the beginning of the sixth century.[116] The Neak Ta Dambang Dek (province of Treang in South Cambodia) inscription begins with an invocation to

[113] *Op. cit.*, pp. 49 f.
[114] *Select Inscriptions*, I. p. 468, f.n. 4.
[115] *Ibid.*, p. 474.
[116] Cf. Majumdar, *Kambujadeśa*, pp. 33, 40-42.

Viṣṇu and refers to Śrī as the wife of that god, while the Thap Musi inscription of Guṇavarman records a donation to the image of Viṣṇu called Cakratīrthasvāmin, which is said to have been consecrated by Brāhmaṇas versed in the Vedas, Upavedas, and Vedāṅgas as well as sages versed in the Śruti. This record also speaks of the Bhāgavatas and refers to the cult of *bhakti* and to the theory of Karma. Although, as in India itself, the most popular god in early Cambodia, as also in other parts of Greater India, seems to have been Śiva, the composite form of Śiva and Viṣṇu, styled Śaṅkara-Nārāyaṇa, Śambhu-Viṣṇu (name applied to a *liṅga*), Hara-Acyuta, Hari-Śaṅkara, etc., was also in great favour.

7

BHĀGAVATA RELIGION : THE CULT OF BHAKTI

THE Bhāgavata Dharma is the religion of devotional love for God. It is a monotheistic religion of loving communion with God, the supreme Person. It is also called Nārāyaṇīya, Sātvata, Ekāntika, or Pāñcarātra religion. Its main sources are the Nārāyaṇīya section of the *Mahābhārata, Bhagavad-Gītā, Bhāgavata Purāṇa, Nārada-Sūtra,* and *Śāṇḍilya-Sūtra.* We shall not attempt here an historical treatment of the subject, but only expound the main tenets of the Bhāgavata religion based on these sources.

The origin of the cult of *bhakti* in Hinduism is shrouded in mystery. Some find in it the influence of Islam. Others trace it to Christianity. But to us, it seems to be an indigenous growth. The germs of this cult are found in the Vedic hymns and the Upaniṣads. The Vedic hymns to Varuṇa, Savitṛ, and Uṣas are replete with sentiments of piety and devotion. The doctrine of *bhakti,* or single-minded devotion to God, is clearly evident in the later Upaniṣads. 'The Self cannot be realized by the study of the Vedas, nor by intelligence, nor by deep learining ; It can be realized by him only whom It chooses or favours ; to him the Self reveals Its own nature' (*Ka. U.,* II. 23 ; *Mu. U.,* III. 2. 3). This is the doctrine of grace. The word *bhakti* occurs, for the first time, in the Upaniṣads. In the *Śvetāśvatara Upaniṣad* the doctrine of grace is emphasized, and the doctrine of *prapatti* or self-surrender also is suggested in it (VI. 23). The *Taittirīya Upaniṣad* (II. 7) and the *Bṛhadāraṇyaka Upaniṣad* (IV. 3. 32) describe Brahman as being of the nature of bliss and the source of all human joys. Thus the cult of *bhakti* is adumbrated in the Vedic hymns, and partly developed in the Upaniṣads. It blossoms forth in the epics and later devotional literature ; it is not satisfied with the impersonal Brahman of the Upaniṣads, but converts Brahman into the personal God or Īśvara.

THE CULT OF BHAKTI

God cannot be apprehended by the senses. He is beyond the ken of logic or argument, and is attained only through whole-hearted devotion. Penances and religious observances lacking in devotion cannot lead to the attainment of God. The revelation of God to man is the highest boon granted by Him to man (*Mbh.,* XII. 340. 16, 17). The devotees should meditate upon God with minds wholly concentrated upon Him (*Ibid.,* XII. 340. 19). Those who are conversant with the Pāñcarātra scriptures, who observe the religious duties enjoined by them, and who have whole-hearted devotion to God succeed in entering into Him (*Ibid.*, XII. 350. 71). One who is devoted to God with the whole mind and intellect attains to Him, and lives, moves, and has his being in Him. Śrī Kṛṣṇa says, 'Fix thy mind on me alone, concentrate thy intellect on me; hereafter thou shalt undoubtedly dwell in me alone' (*B. G.*, XII. 8).

God is always fond of those who are devoted to Him (*Mbh.*, XII. 343. 54, 55). No one is dearer to Him in the three worlds than those who are enlightened with wisdom (*pratibuddha*) and possessed of high souls. More dear even than these persons is one who is entirely devoted to Him (*Ibid.*, XII. 343. 65).

PRAPATTI (ŚARAṆĀGATI) OR COMPLETE RESIGNATION TO GOD

The gist of the teachings of the *Gītā* is summed up in the following verse: 'Relinquishing all religious rites and actions (yielding merits and demerits), take refuge in me alone. I shall deliver thee from all sins. Sorrow not' (XVIII. 66).

All persons are subject to the influence of Māyā (the Lord's inscrutable power). One can attain *mokṣa* (liberation) when one transcends *sattva* (illumination), *rajas* (activity), and *tamas* (inertia) which constitute Māyā. 'They alone can cross it (Māyā) who take refuge in me' (*B. G.*, VII. 14). The *Bhāgavata* also teaches the same thing. If the persons to whom God shows His grace shake off all hypocrisy and take refuge in Him with all their hearts, they transcend His Māyā, and are purged of egoism (II. 7. 42). Taking refuge in God is the highest good of men (IV. 29. 50). This brings us to the doctrine of grace.

THE GRACE OF GOD

In the Bhāgavata religion much stress is laid on the grace of God. Religion is the elevation of man to God, and the descent of God to man. Man can never acquire fitness for communion with God by his self-exertion. He can have a vision of God only when He chooses to reveal Himself to him. God can be attained only by His grace. He cannot be bought for any price or gift. No human attainments, physical, intellectual, moral, or spiritual, are adequate for the attainment of God.

The *Mahābhārata* teaches the doctrine of grace. He alone can see Nārāyaṇa to whom He becomes gracious (XII. 337. 20). It is God who awakens in us the desire to undergo penances. We cannot achieve wisdom by our own efforts. It is God who grants us wisdom. That person upon whom Nārāyaṇa looks with compassion succeeds in becoming enlightened (*buddha*). No one can become enlightened through his own wishes

(XII. 349. 75). Liberation depends entirely upon the grace of God (XII. 349. 73).

THE NATURE OF BHAKTI

Nārada defines *bhakti* as of the nature of intense love for God. It is of the nature of love (*preman*) which reaches its acme of perfection (*parama*). The word *parama* indicates three things: (1) Devotion is undivided love for God, free from attachment for worldly objects. (2) It is not overshadowed by knowledge and action. It is the highest end. It is not a means to any other higher end. (3) It is manifested in thought, word, and deed. Love for God is akin to love for near and dear ones. But there is a world of difference between the two. The object of all worldly attachment is perishable and finite, while the object of devotion is imperishable and infinite.

Śāṇḍilya defines *parā bhakti* or primary devotion as the most perfect attachment to God (*parā anurakti*). This definition is the same as that of Nārada. *Bhakti* or devotion is not attachment to earthly objects; it is attachment to God. Love for God, however, is not entirely different from love for earthly objects. There is attachment in both. Prahlāda therefore offers the following prayer: 'May not that uninterrupted attachment, as is entertained by undiscriminating men towards earthly objects, desert my heart, while I am constantly meditating upon Thee.'[1]

Bhakti is of the nature of attachment (*rāga*). But, as Śāṇḍilya says, *bhakti*, though of the nature of attachment, has for its object the highest and the best, and so ought not to be avoided.[2] Svapneśvara explains it thus: Devotion to God should not be avoided, as it does not bind one to the world, nor does it lead one astray from the path of *mokṣa* or liberation.

Bhakti is of the nature of *amṛta* (nectar or immortality).[3] Śāṇḍilya says, 'It has been taught by the *Chāndogya Upaniṣad* that he who has devotion (*saṁsthā*) to God becomes immortal. Or he who lives, moves, and has his being in God (*tatsaṁstha*) becomes immortal.'[4]

The *Bhāgavata* preaches the cult of unmotived devotion (*ahaitukī bhakti*) to God. That is the highest religion of man from which arises unmotived and uninterrupted devotion to God, which fills the soul with bliss (I. 2. 6). The *Nārada Pañcarātra* defines *bhakti* as realization of God alone as 'mine', accompanied by deep love (*preman*), and without attachment for any other object in the world. In later devotional literature a distinction is drawn between *bhakti* and *preman*. *Bhakti* is the spontaneous attachment for the desired object, God, being entirely possessed by

[1] *Viṣṇu Purāṇa*, I. 20. 17.
[2] *Śāṇḍilya-Sūtra*, 21.
[3] *Nārada-Sūtra*, 3.
[4] *Śāṇḍilya-Sūtra*, 3.

and absorbed in Him. *Preman* is the most concentrated love for God which is full of the most intense attachment, and which purifies the heart completely. Divine love (*preman*) is the completion and perfection of devotion (*bhakti*).

IS BHAKTI OF THE NATURE OF KNOWLEDGE OR OF WILL?

Śāṇḍilya thinks that mere knowledge does not constitute devotion, for it is present also in hate. Again, as we approach liberation, knowledge is gradually eclipsed by devotion. Further, if hatred is an emotion, the opposite of hate, i.e. love, must also be an emotion, and cannot be of the nature of knowledge. Besides, devotion is spoken of as *rasa,* which means attachment (*rāga*), and as *anurāga,* which clearly means attachment to the Lord. Lastly, persons having no knowledge, e.g. the milkmaids of Vṛndāvana, attained liberation simply through devotion to the Lord.[5]

Nor is devotion of the nature of desire or will, because desire is directed towards objects not yet attained, whereas attachment or devotion is directed towards objects already attained, as well as those not yet attained. Devotion, which is not the outcome of volition, is not of the nature of action, which is always the expression of volition. Unlike action which leads to a limited result, devotion leads to the attainment of the infinite and the highest good (*niḥśreyasa*).[6]

Devotion is not identical with faith (*śraddhā*) which forms a part of all actions. First there must be belief in God; then this is deepened into faith; at last, faith is deepened into devotion.[7] *Bhakti* is the burning faith in God.

BHAKTI AND DESIRE

Bhakti is free from desire, and is of the nature of inhibition of all desires (*nirodha*) by which, however, is meant not the extinction of all desires, but the consecration of all desires and actions to God. Inhibition also means undivided or whole-hearted devotion to God, indifference to all that is antagonistic to Him, and the giving up of all other supports.[8] We should take refuge in God alone.

It is almost impossible to suppress all desires and passions. We can only divert their course. Naturally they are directed towards earthly objects. But they should be directed towards God. We should dedicate all our actions to Him, and cherish all our passions, desire, anger, egoism, and the like only for Him.[9]

The *Bhāgavata* beautifully illustrates this truth (X. 29. 15). The

[5] *Ibid.*, 4-6.
[6] Svapneśvara on *Śāṇḍilya-Sūtra,* 8.
[7] *Nārada-Sūtra,* 84.
[8] *Ibid.*, 7-10.
[9] *Ibid.*, 65.

mind of the devotee of Śrī Kṛṣṇa is engaged in meditating upon His lotus feet; his words are engaged in describing the glories of the abode of Viṣṇu; his hands are engaged in cleaning the temple of Hari; his ears are engaged in hearing the pleasant talks about the Lord; his eyes are engaged in seeing the image of Kṛṣṇa; his body is engaged in coming in contact with His devotees; his nose is engaged in smelling the sweet scent of *tulasī* (sacred basil) leaves placed at the lotus feet of the Lord; his palate is engaged in tasting the offerings made to Him; his feet are engaged in going on pilgrimage; his head is engaged in bowing to the feet of the Lord; his desires are engaged in serving the Lord. Thus the whole being of the devotee is entirely dedicated to God.

BHAKTI AND KNOWLEDGE

Nārada discusses the different views as to the relation of devotion to knowledge. Some think that knowledge alone is the means of devotion. Others hold that knowledge and devotion are interdependent. But Nārada thinks that devotion is the fruit of itself.[10] Devotion is the means as well as the end of devotion.

But Śāṇḍilya feels the necessity of *yoga* or concentration of mind and cultivation of the intellect for the culture of devotion. The cultivation of the intellect for acquiring certain knowledge of Brahman should be continued till devotion is completely purified. Valid knowledge of Brahman (*Brahmapramiti*) is the end of the intellect. It cannot be brought about by any voluntary action. Still listening to the scriptures (*śravaṇa*), reflection (*manana*), and intellectual conviction (*nididhyāsana*) lead to the true knowledge of God. Knowledge is absolutely necessary for firmness and purity of devotion (*bhakti-dārḍhya, bhakti-pariśuddhi*). Following the preceptor's instructions, arguments in harmony with the Vedas, control of passions, and the like are necessary aids to the knowledge of God. Thus the life of devotion to God need not necessarily be a purely emotional one. Śāṇḍilya upholds the cult of devotion enlightened by reason.

The *Gītā* also preaches the cult of devotion enlightened by knowledge. Four classes of persons are said to be devoted to God: Distressed persons pray to Him for deliverance from misery; some persons adore God with the object of knowing Him; some pray to Him for the attainment of objects of desire; others who are wise are also devoted to God. Śrī Kṛṣṇa says, 'Of them the wise devotee (*jñānin*) is ever united with me in thought and is attached to me with single-minded devotion. I am excessively dear to him and he also is dear to me' (*B. G.*, VII. 17). We have an echo of this verse in the *Kūrma Purāṇa* also: 'Of all the devotees,

[10] *Ibid.*, 28-30.

he who ever worships me with knowledge is most dear to me, and no other' (II. 4. 24). The *Bhāgavata* also says that the sages who have faith in God have a vision of Him in their own selves by means of devotion combined with wisdom and renunciation (I. 2. 12). But it also emphasizes that devotion to the Lord gives rise to knowledge (IV. 29. 37). Again, 'That is real wisdom which generates attachment (*mati*) to God' (IV. 29. 49).

BHAKTI AND ACTION

A life of devotion is not necessarily a life of inaction. The *Gītā* calls upon us to give up weakness of the heart, shake off lethargy and impotency, and do our duty in the world (II. 3). We should not give up action. We cannot even maintain our life without action. But we should do our duty without any attachment. We should not care for success or failure. We should surrender the fruits of action to God. Whatever we do, whatever we eat, whatever we give in charity, whatever sacrifices we perform, and whatever penances we undergo, we should dedicate all these to God (IX. 29). We should live an active life completely dedicated to God.

The *Bhāgavata* also gives us the same message. That is real action which pleases God (IV. 29. 49). The actions that are done for the pleasure of God give rise to devotion, and devotion gives rise to knowledge (I. 5. 35). We should surrender all our actions to God without any desire for their fruits (XI. 2. 22). The complete surrender of the soul to God is the highest truth (VII. 6. 24).

The *Nārada-Sūtra* elaborates the teachings of the *Gītā* and the *Bhāgavata*. We cannot give up all action. Actions for the preservation of life, such as eating, drinking, and dressing, must be carried on so long as we live.[11] The body is the temple of God. Instead of making it an enemy and a source of distraction, we should make it an ally and a means of devotion. We should take care of our bodies so long as we live, in order to live in and love God.

We should purge ourselves of egoism, and dedicate all our actions to God.[12] He who renounces the fruits of action, and dedicates all action to God, rises above pleasure and pain, desire and aversion, and attains lasting peace.[13] We should observe our social and moral obligations, and perform our religious duties. But we should dedicate them all to God. In fact, we should dedicate our very self to God.[14]

BHAKTI AND SOCIAL AND RELIGIOUS OBSERVANCES

The Bhāgavata religion does not preach the cult of inactivism and quietism. It does not want us to give up all social and religious

[11] *Ibid.*, 14. [12] *Ibid.*, 65. [13] *Ibid.*, 48. [14] *Ibid.*, 61.

observances. The injunctions of the scriptures should be observed till faith in God is deepened ; otherwise there may be a fall. Social laws also should be observed till we acquire devotion to God.[15] We should not unnecessarily revolt against society. But we should have the courage to swim against the tide of public opinion and rise above all fear of the crowd.[16] Not only that, we should have also the courage to lay aside the scriptures, if they stand in the way of our culture of devotion, and develop an undivided and uninterrupted flow of love towards God.[17]

MARKS OF DEVOTION

The *Bhāgavata* says, 'Devotion has nine marks: listening to the name of God, chanting His name, recollection of Him, serving Him, worshipping Him, saluting Him, servitude, friendship, and self-dedication to Him' (VII. 5. 22, 23). These are aspects of secondary devotion. Primary devotion is disinterested and unobstructed devotion to God. This devotion alone leads to the realization of God (I. 2. 6). The disciples of Parāśara hold that attachment to the worship of God and the like are the marks of devotion. Garga thinks that attachment to talks of His glory is the sign of devotion. Śāṇḍilya holds that ardour in His worship and in talks of His glory is the mark of devotion. If, however, they draw the mind away from God and disturb the bliss of the soul, which it finds in communion with God, they are of no avail. Nārada thinks that dedication of all our actions to God and the feeling of extreme uneasiness on forgetting Him are the marks of devotion. The milkmaids of Vṛndāvana dedicated their whole life to Śrī Kṛṣṇa, and felt extreme uneasiness when he went out of their sight even for a short time.[18]

Śāṇḍilya observes that honouring Him, honouring any thing or creature that evokes His remembrance, thrill of joy in meeting Him, pangs of separation, aversion to all things that are not associated with Him, constant singing of the glory of God, preservation of life for His sake, the consciousness that 'I and everything that is mine are Thine', the consciousness that He is immanent in all things, and absence of hostility towards Him (i.e. not only not going against Him in thought and deed, but accepting everything that He does even if that costs one's life), are the marks of devotion.[19]

KINDS OF DEVOTION

The *Bhāgavata* describes three kinds of devotion, *tāmasa*, *rājasa*, and *sāttvika*. If a person's devotion towards God is motivated by malevolence,

[15] *Ibid.*, 12-14. [16] *Ibid.*, 83. [17] *Ibid.*, 49.
[18] *Ibid.*, 19, 21. [19] *Śāṇḍilya-Sūtra*, 44.

arrogance, jealousy, or anger, his devotion is *tāmasa,* i.e. dominated by the principle of darkness. If, actuated by the desire for fame, wealth, or any other object of enjoyment, he worships God, his devotion is *rājasa,* i.e. prompted by the principle of activity. If, in showing devotion towards God, he is actuated by the desire to do duty for the sake of duty, or to burn up the roots of *karma* (latent desires), or to please God, his devotion is *sāttvika,* since *sattva* (the principle of illumination) predominates in his character (III. 29. 8-10). These three kinds of devotion are secondary. The primary or the highest kind of devotion is absolutely unmotived, and is immediate devotion to the supreme Person (III. 29. 12). Primary devotion is devoid of the qualities of *sattva, rajas,* and *tamas.* It is the spontaneous uninterrupted inclination of the mind towards God. A person who has this kind of devotion does not care for anything but service of God. He does not care to accept the gifts of living in the same world with God (*sālokya*), exercising supernatural powers of God (*sārṣṭi*), being near God (*sāmīpya*), similarity of form with God (*sārūpya*), and union with God (*sāyujya*), even if they are offered to him (III. 29. 13). The devotee who clings to God with his whole soul does not crave even for absolute independence of the soul (*kaivalya*), not to speak of other things (XI. 20. 34).

Reference has already been made to the four types of devotees enumerated by the *Gītā* (VII. 16). Of these, the devotion of the distressed, the inquisitive, and the selfish is secondary ; it has ulterior objects in view.[20] But the devotion of the wise devotee is unmotived, selfless, and primary.

Śāṇḍilya also speaks of primary and secondary devotions. Primary devotion is single-minded, whole-hearted devotion to God (*ekāntatā*). It is the supreme devotion which directly leads to liberation. All the other processes constituting secondary devotion are indirect causes of liberation, inasmuch as they only lead to primary devotion.[21] The *Gītā* also teaches that the devotee undoubtedly enters into God by means of the supreme devotion (*parā bhakti*) to Him (XVIII. 68). Chanting the name of God, reciting it repeatedly, salutation to the deity, and worship of God constitute secondary devotion. They lead to the knowledge of the deity, through which attachment to Him (*rāga*) is engendered,[22] which ripens into love (*preman*) of God.

Nārada also divides devotion into two kinds, secondary and primary. Secondary devotion is born of desire, and is threefold according as *sattva, rajas,* or *tamas* is predominant in the character of the devotee. Or, it is threefold according as the devotees are distressed, inquisitive, or selfish.

[20] *Śāṇḍilya-Sūtra,* 72 ; *Nārada-Sūtra,* 56.
[21] *Śāṇḍilya-Sūtra,* 83, 84.
[22] *Ibid.,* 56, 57, with commentary.

Each preceding kind of devotion is superior to each succeeding one. The primary devotees are those who have only one end in view, namely, God.[23]

Nārada describes eleven forms of devotion. Though devotion is one in kind, still it appears in eleven forms. It assumes the forms of love for the attributes and greatness of God, for His beauty, for His worship, and for His recollection ; love for Him of a servant, a friend, a parent, and a beloved wife ; love of self-consecration to Him ; love of absorption in Him ; and love of the pang of separation from Him.[24] This aphorism beautifully describes the different grades of religious consciousness. At first we are overwhelmed with the consciousness of our own finitude, and of the infinitude and majesty of God ; and we adore Him as a superhuman Power. Then we come into more intimate touch with Him as the supreme Person (Puruṣottama), and cultivate personal relationship with Him. We love the sweetness of His transcendent beauty ; we adore Him with all our heart ; and we love His sweet memories. Then our love of God matures into personal love. First of all, the devotee serves the Lord as a servant serves his master. Then he approaches Him nearer, and loves Him as a friend. Then he rises higher, and manifests parental affection for the loved One, as a father for his son. And, at last, even the vestige of remoteness between them vanishes altogether. The two become one in spirit, and the devotee develops all the marks of a devoted wife's love for her beloved husband. Then the devotee consecrates his whole being to the beloved Lord, loses himself in Him, and feels His living presence everywhere.[25] And, finally, he feels the pang of separation from his Beloved, which is the highest consummation of love. Union is tinged with selfishness. Separation is selfless. Even in separation higher union is felt. The devotee is eternally united with Him in his separation from Him.

Nārada lays stress on constant servitude and unswerving wifely love to God. We should cultivate love and love alone for God, rising above the three forms of secondary devotion.[26] The *Nārada Pañcarātra* mentions the servitude to the Lord as the chief means of liberation. It does not mention friendship, parental affection, and wifely love. In later devotional literature, five kinds of personal relationship with the Lord are clearly mentioned: quietness (*śānta*), servitude (*dāsya*), friendship (*sakhya*), parental affection (*vātsalya*), and sweet wifely love (*mādhurya*). The inherent qualities of the preceding sentiment are included in the succeeding one.[27]

[23] *Nārada-Sūtra*, 67.
[24] *Ibid.*, 82.
[25] *Ibid.*, 70.
[26] *Ibid.*, 66.
[27] *Caitanya Caritāmṛta*, II. 8 ; dialogue between Caitanya and Rāya Rāmānanda.

MEANS FOR THE CULTURE OF DEVOTION

Nārada enjoins the following practices for the attainment of devotion:

Evil company should be shunned by all means, because it excites lust, anger, infatuation, lapse of memory, and loss of intelligence, and finally leads to utter ruin. These passions are natural to man. But when they are fanned by evil company, they assume huge proportions.[28] Conversation with those who are not devotees, touching their bodies, sleeping and eating with them, all pollute our souls with sins, and we should fly away from them as we do from poisonous snakes.[29]

Wealth and sex are the two rocks on which many souls are shipwrecked. Atheists disturb our faith in God. So we should not listen to talks about women, wealth, and the character of atheists.[30]

We should give up egoism, pride, and other passions.[31] We should not set up our finite will against the divine will. God hates the egotists, and is fond of meekness.[32]

We should not indulge in vain discussion about God. It is absolutely useless, as it can never lead us to certainty.[33]

Devotion to God arises from the renunciation of all objects of enjoyment and of every attachment for them.[34] He who uproots all earthly attachments gives up acquiring and preserving objects of enjoyment.[35]

These are the negative methods which prepare the mind for the attainment of devotion. Besides these, Nārada prescribes the following positive methods for the culture of devotion:

We should study the treatises on devotion, and constantly think of their teachings. We should perform those duties which are enjoined by them. We should observe non-injury to living beings, truthfulness, purity of body and mind, kindness, and cultivate faith in God and other excellences of character.[36] We should also develop the nine marks of devotion mentioned above.

We should incessantly pray to God.[37] The attraction for the objects of enjoyment can be overcome not by directing our attention to them, but by constant prayer to God. We have very little time left at our disposal for prayer after what is spent in the pursuit of pleasure, pain, desire, gain, and the like.[38] But how is the desire for prayer awakened?

Devotion is obtained, principally, by the grace of the great souls who are devoted to God, or from the least touch of divine compassion. The company of the great is difficult of attainment. But once we have an access

[28] *Nārada-Sūtra*, 43-45.
[29] *Nārada Pañcarātra*, II. 2. 6.
[30] *Nārada-Sūtra*, 63.
[31] *Ibid.*, 64.
[32] *Ibid.*, 27.
[33] *Ibid.*, 74, 75.
[34] *Ibid.*, 35.
[35] *Ibid.*, 47.
[36] *Ibid.*, 76, 78.
[37] *Ibid.*, 36.
[38] *Ibid.*, 77.

to their company, it is bound to awaken devotion in us.[39] The companionship of devotees is attained by the grace of God alone. The grace of God is followed by the response of the devotees, since there is no distinction between God and His men.[40] The *Gītā* says, 'I dwell in them, and they dwell in me' (IX. 29).

We should strive after love of God alone.[41] Being invoked, He will quickly reveal Himself to us and fill us with His influence.[42] He will give us a taste of His infinite sweetness.

RESULTS OF THE CULTURE OF DEVOTION

Nārada describes the results of the culture of devotion in glowing language:

By attaining devotional love a person becomes fulfilled, immortal, and contented.[43] He becomes free from the wheel of births and deaths, as they are due to desire. He does not crave for anything, since all his desires are fulfilled in God; he does not lament for the loss of anything, for in God he gains everything; he does not hate anybody, since his consuming love of God burns up the very roots of hatred; he does not delight in any earthly object of enjoyment, because his heart is soaked in divine love; he does not become zealous for worldly achievements, since by attaining love of God he has attained everything. He becomes intoxicated with joy, absolutely quiet, and completely self-satisfied.[44] The devotee becomes God-intoxicated. The clamour of his passions and cravings being drowned, he becomes absolutely quiet. Communing with the Lord of his heart, he delights in himself (*ātmārāma*), sees Him alone, hears Him alone, and thinks of Him alone.[45] His sense-organs, mind, and intellect are all directed towards God. He realizes Him through his whole being. He is filled with the presence of God. He feels His presence everywhere.[46] He offers his whole being to God. He belongs to Him, and not even to himself.[47]

Śrī Kṛṣṇa says, 'I am like one who is not free (*asvatantra iva*). I am entirely dependent on my devotees (*bhakta-parādhīna*). My heart is given over to my saintly devotees. I am their beloved. I have no liking either for myself or for my immortal consort, Lakṣmī, without the association of my saintly devotees whose sole refuge I am. How can I leave them who have renounced their wives, home, children, relations, wealth, and this world and the next, and completely surrendered themselves to me? They do not know anything other than me, nor do I know anything else but them' (*Bhā.*, IX. 4. 66-68).

[39] *Ibid.*, 38, 39. [40] *Ibid.*, 40, 41. [41] *Ibid.*, 42.
[42] *Ibid.*, 79, 80. [43] *Ibid.*, 4. [44] *Ibid.*, 5, 6.
[45] *Ibid.*, 55. [46] *Ibid.*, 70. [47] *Ibid.*, 73.

SIN AND ATONEMENT

Sins are not destroyed by penances, since they cannot root out *avidyā* (nescience), which is the root of all sins. The potencies of sins remain intact, and they give rise to other sins. What, then, is the chief form of atonement? A person can destroy all kinds of sins, physical, mental, and verbal, by means of penances, chastity, restraint of the senses and the mind, charity, truthfulness, and the like, only if they are performed with faith. But the best form of atonement is devotion to God. All sins are washed away by the flood of devotion. Even the subtle potencies of sins are uprooted by it.

Svapneśvara points out that singing the names of the Lord, salutation, meditation, constant recollection, worship, and dedication of all actions to God destroy all sins arising out of the impurities of mind, and give rise to purity. Devotion is the soul of purity.[48] Śāṇḍilya thinks that for heinous sins this mode of expiation should be continued till death. Repentance is an element in all kinds of atonement. When man begins to repent of his sins, the best form of atonement for him is the constant remembrance of the Lord. In the cult of devotion, all other atonements are done away with.[49] Thus devotion is the best kind of atonement for all sins.

BONDAGE AND LIBERATION

The *Bhāgavata* (I. 29. 36) teaches that supreme devotion to God can liberate us from bondage (*saṁsāra*). Śāṇḍilya thinks that the cause of births and deaths is not want of knowledge, but want of devotion. So long as devotion does not arise in the soul, it will be subject to births and deaths; but these cease for ever on the dawn of devotion.[50] Want of devotion is the cause of egoism which brings about *saṁsāra*. The fire of devotion burns up the sense of 'me' and 'mine', purges the soul of egoism by destroying the intellect completely, and brings about liberation (*mukti*).[51] We are liberated from the bondage of all actions, good and bad, by dedicating their fruits to God.[52] And by complete self-surrender to God, which is the mark of supreme devotion, we can attain the blissful state of Brahman, which is the highest end of life.[53]

THE PATH OF BHAKTI IS THE HIGHEST OF ALL

Nārada holds that devotion is higher than action, higher than knowledge, and higher than concentration of mind (*yoga*). It is higher than the other means of salvation, because it is its own reward.[54] It is not a

[48] *Śāṇḍilya-Sūtra*, 58, 59, with commentary. [49] *Ibid.*, 75, 76, with commentary.
[50] *Ibid.*, 98. [51] *Ibid.*, 96, with commentary. [52] *Ibid.*, 64.
[53] *Ibid.*, 96. [54] *Nārada-Sūtra*, 25, 26.

means to any other end; it is the highest end, the *summum bonum* of life. Knowledge and action are motivated by egoism and pride. So knowledge and action cannot excite God's compassion. But devotion is meek and humble. Those who are humble in spirit throw themselves entirely at the mercy of God, and bring down the grace of God on them. Therefore those who seek liberation should adopt the path of devotion alone, to the exclusion of others.[55]

The path of devotion is the easiest of all and superior to all.[56] It does not require any other proof; it is self-evident. The path of *bhakti* is easy, because it fills the soul with peace and ecstasy of joy.[57]

The cult of devotion is the best of all cults. Śrī Kṛṣṇa says, 'The *yogin* is greater than the ascetic; he is greater even than the man of wisdom. He is greater than the man of action.... And among the *yogins*, the most completely united with me, I consider, is he who adores me with full faith, and his inner self abiding in me' (*B. G.*, VI. 46-47). 'Neither *yoga*, nor knowledge, or performance of duties, neither study of the Vedas, nor austerities, or charities propitiates me so well as unswerving devotion to me' (*Bhā.*, XI. 14. 20). Thus, those who follow the path of devotion are superior to those who follow the path of action, knowledge, or *yoga*.[58]

THE CULT OF BHAKTI IS OPEN TO ALL

God is the God of love. He has no caste, or sex, or nationality. The *Gītā*, in preaching the cult of devotion, throws open the portals of devotional love and, through it, of salvation to all irrespective of caste, character, or sex. No one can deny anybody the right to love God.

Śrī Kṛṣṇa says, 'Even if a person of the vilest conduct worships me with undivided devotion, he should be regarded as a saint, for he has made the choice that is as irrevocable as it is righteous. He quickly becomes a virtuous soul and attains lasting peace. O Arjuna, this is my word of promise that he who loves me with all his heart never perishes. Even persons of sinful origin attain the supreme goal by taking refuge in me alone' (*B. G.*, IX. 30-32).

The *Bhāgavata* also throws open the path of devotion to all. Even a Caṇḍāla is purged of the impurity of his caste by firm devotion to God (IX. 14. 21). Sincere faith and devotion alone can uplift the soul to eternal communion with God. Even a Caṇḍāla, possessed of sincere faith and devotion, is dearer to God than a Brāhmaṇa, sadly lacking in faith (III. 33. 7). Even a person of low birth is liberated from bondage, if he utters the name of God only once (V. 1. 35).

[55] *Ibid.*, 33.
[56] *Ibid.*, 81.
[57] *Ibid.*, 58-60.
[58] *Śāṇḍilya-Sūtra*, 22, 23, with commentary.

Nārada and Śāṇḍilya also preach the universality of the cult of devotion. Nārada says, 'Among the devotees of God, there is no distinction of birth, learning, appearance, family, wealth, religious observances, and the like, since they all belong to Him'.[59] They are suffused with the spirit of God. They realize the presence of God everywhere in and around them. They are filled with the presence of God.[60] Śāṇḍilya says, 'All persons, even down to the lowest-born, have equal right to follow the path of devotion; it has been taught by generations of authorities'.[61] Svapneśvara, in commenting on it, remarks that just as non-violence or non-injury to living beings (*ahiṁsā*) is the common duty of all, so is devotion to God.

Jñāna or knowledge of the Self, and *karma* or religious observances such as sacrifices, are not meant for all. For example, Śūdras and women are excluded from the study of the Vedas. But there is no such restriction in the case of devotion. The desire for liberation is the starting point of devotion—the minimum qualification which entitles one to this path. The cult of *bhakti* is open to all. It is catholic and universal. Thus the Bhāgavata religion of devotion and love is the religion for all. It is a perfectly democratic religion.

[59] *Nārada-Sūtra*, 72, 73. [60] *Ibid.*, 70. [61] *Śāṇḍilya-Sūtra*, 78.

8

THE VAIKHĀNASAS

EARLY HISTORY AND LITERATURE

THE Vaikhānasas, though now a small minority, constitute an important sect among the Vaiṣṇavas of South India. There are different legends concerning the sage Vikhanas, the founder of the sect. One is that Brahmā incarnated himself as Vikhanas in the Naimiṣāraṇya, where the god Viṣṇu initiated him into the mysteries of worship, and another that at Viṣṇu's command, Vikhanas came down to the earth to organize the worship of the Lord in His *arcā* (image or idol) form.

The *Vaikhānasa-Sūtra,* into which the precepts of Vikhanas expanded in the course of centuries, is the latest of the Sūtras of the *Taittirīya-śākhā.* According to W. Caland, the *Smārta-Sūtra* section, comprising both *gṛhya* and *dharma* precepts, preceded the compilation of the other section, the *Śrauta-Sūtra,* which includes an elaborate *mantra-saṁhitā,* and is also called *Aukheya-Sūtra,* because the Vaikhānasas (Aukheyas) constituted a *śākhā* (branch) with the full complement of Saṁhitā, Brāhmaṇa, and Sūtras.

Baudhāyana, who flourished before the Christian era, mentions the *Vaikhānasa Śāstra,* which he describes as a guide to *vānaprasthas* (anchorites). Manu exhibits points of close resemblance to the *Vaikhānasa-Sūtra,* as Caland has shown. Barth's conclusion, which Caland approves, seems to be the best in the light of our present knowledge that, at the time of Baudhāyana, there were known 'prescripts' relating to the Vaikhānasa hermits, which later found their final redaction in the extant *Vaikhānasa-Sūtra.* Basing his thesis on philological and linguistic grounds also, Caland assigns the *Vaikhānasa-Sūtra* to the close of the third century A.D.

Haradatta, in his gloss on Gautama (III. 2), calls a *vānaprastha* (anchorite) a Vaikhānasa, because 'he lives according to the rule promulgated by Vikhanas', and adds 'that the sage chiefly taught that order'. There is a short résumé of the *Vaikhānasa Śāstra* in Baudhāyana (III. 3. 3). That the *Vaikhānasa Śāstra* set great store by purity of conduct is evident from Kālidāsa's *Śakuntalā* (I. 22), where King Duṣyanta inquires whether Śakuntalā was enjoined to observe *vaikhānasa-vrata.*

Vikhanas, the *sūtrakāra,* founded also the Āgamic school, named after him, which was later explained and enlarged by others. The Vaikhānasas figure prominently in Coḷa inscriptions, from the time of Rājarāja I. They were entrusted with the management of temples and their landed property, when they abandoned the forest-life and started living in villages and towns. They received endowments from the king or the local assembly, and entered into agreements with the revenue officers and the assemblies in matters relating to the cultivation of assigned and sometimes also of unassigned lands. They were the hereditary trustees of Viṣṇu temples, managed their properties, and conducted the divine service. An inscription from Chidambaram, dated A.D. 1539, records an edict of Acyuta Rāya, emperor of Vijayanagara, for the re-consecration of the image of Govindarāja, which had not been in worship for some centuries, according to the rituals of Vaikhānasa Āgama, and for the annual grant to the Vaikhānasa priests of five hundred *pon* (a gold coin of uncertain value) representing the revenue of four villages. The rise of the Rāmānuja school of Vaiṣṇavism to prominence, after the twelfth century, due to royal patronage liberally bestowed by the Hoysaḷas and the Vijayanagara emperors and their vassals, could not dislodge the Vaikhānasas from their age-long rights to temple worship. In the famous temple of Tirupati (Bālājī), Rāmānuja's influence was strongly established. Shrines to Rāmānuja and the Āḷvārs were added, and in the associated temples in Tirupati town and Tiruchanur, the Pāñcarātra form of worship was introduced. *Jīyars* (monks) of the Rāmānuja school took charge of the Bālājī temple, where the services were filled by Vaiṣṇavas of that school. Yet *pūjā* to Bālājī (Veṅkaṭeśa) in the sanctum continues to be done by the Vaikhānasas according to the *Vaikhānasa Śāstra,* which is purely in Sanskrit. There are more temples in South India today under the Vaikhānasa Āgama than under the Pāñcarātra.

The Vaikhānasas differ from the Pāñcarātras both in the description and disposition of the *parivāra devatās.* Then, again, the Pāñcarātras consecrate images of Āṇḍāḷ and other women devotees who, through the practice of the *nāyakī-nāyaka bhāva* of *bhakti,* have attained the status of the Lord's consort (*nācchiyār* in Tamil), on a par with Lakṣmī. The Pāñcarātras have rules regarding the location of the shrines of Rāmānuja and the Āḷvārs, who often receive all the honours that are paid to the principal deity. The Vaikhānasas do not subscribe to these changes in the tradition.

IMPORTANT TENETS

To the Vaikhānasa, Viṣṇu is the supreme Being, the highest Principle. The performer of the Vaikhānasa *śrauta* rituals is required to fix his thoughts on Nārāyaṇa alone (*Nārāyaṇa-parāyaṇa*). Nārāyaṇa is both *niṣkala* and *sakala.* The two aspects being inseparable, He manifests Himself everywhere in both the aspects. Śrī or Lakṣmī is His *vibhūti* or *aiśvarya.* She is *nityānanda-mūla-prakṛti śakti* (ever-blissful grand Potential) and, assuming different forms to suit the different *līlā saṅkalpas* (sportful volition) of Viṣṇu, She projects the universe of spirit (*cetana*) and matter (*acetana*), the latter being eightfold—the five elements, *manas, buddhi,* and *ahaṅkāra.* She is ever associated with Viṣṇu in His fivefold states as *para, vyūha, vibhava, antaryāmin,* and *arcā* ; and according to Vikhanas, the supreme Principle is Nārāyaṇa *with* Śrī (Puruṣa and Prakṛti in one).

The *para* form is realized through *jñāna.* Even as by constant churning of the *śamī* wood (*araṇi*) fire is created, the unmanifest is made manifest by constant meditation helped by devotion. Through *prāṇāyāma* and meditation, He is realized as the *antaryāmin* (the indweller). But devotion (*bhakti*) and self-surrender (*prapatti*) to His will are together the masterkeys to open the gates of divine grace. Vikhanas's chief contribution to spiritual life is his emphasis on the worship, service, and adoration of the Lord in the *arcā* (image) form, on which He 'descends with a non-material body', and in which He is present ever since, as the surest means of liberation. Though the conception of the five forms of Viṣṇu, viz. *para, vyūha,* etc. is common to many Vaiṣṇava schools, the Vaikhānasas place greater emphasis on *arcā* worship. The hymns of the three early Āḷvārs contain verses which say: Why visit different shrines, when the Lord who is worshipped in them dwells within the heart? Such an attitude the Vaikhānasas would never countenance: to them serving the *arcā,* the form the Lord Himself has assumed, is the primary duty, and the other modes of worship are supplementary. The later elaborations of Vikhanas's Āgamic precepts are attributed to Bhṛgu, Marīci, Atri, and Kaśyapa.

In common with other Vaiṣṇava schools, the Vaikhānasas accept as ultimate the three entities (*tattvatraya*) of Prakṛti (*acit,* matter), Jīva (*cit*), and Īśvara. They differ from some of the other Vaiṣṇava schools in the prominence they give to Śrī, who is not a glorified Jīva, but the power of the Supreme. The Vaikhānasas do not worship the Āḷvārs, Ācāryas, and *maṭhādhipatis* (pontiffs or monastic heads), though, owing to the influence of the Rāmānuja school, images of Āḷvārs and Ācāryas were set up in some temples under Vaikhānasa Āgamic worship ; nor do they brand their bodies with the Vaiṣṇava emblems of *cakra, śaṅkha,* etc. as the other schools do ; nor, again, do they recite the Tamil *Prabandham* during worship. A small endogamous sect, practically separatist in their social outlook, and confined to the Tamil and Telugu districts and the outlying parts of the Kannada country, the Vaikhānasas have been an important element in the spiritual life of South India, and no study of the Sūtra literature, or of the technique and significance of temple architecture and of iconography (*mūrti-lakṣaṇa*), will be complete without a knowledge of the Śrauta, Āgamic, and Smārta literature associated with the name of Vikhanas.

9

HISTORICAL EVOLUTION OF ŚRĪ-VAIṢṆAVISM IN SOUTH INDIA

BROADLY speaking, we can divide the thinkers whose views are found in the Upaniṣads into two great divisions. The first of these were the originators of what later on developed into the philosophic school of Advaita. They hold that Īśvara is identical with the universe consisting of the Jīvas (souls) and material products ; that Brahman alone exists and nothing else. From the first, this school seems to have believed that salvation means the identity of the Jīva with Brahman, and that this can be realized by meditative discipline, by a path of *jñāna,* which would enable one to understand the illusive character of the phenomenal world and the sole reality of Brahman.

There seems to have been from the beginning a different school which held that all objects were bodies of Īśvara ; that He was their Ātman ; that 'matter served the Jīvas by undergoing transformation and appearing as objects of enjoyment, as bodies in which the Jīvas dwell, and as senses and organs of action, which they use as instruments of enjoyment' ; and that Īśvara gives the Jīvas the fruits of their past *karmas,* and makes matter undergo such transformations as are needed for this purpose. In short, it was the school of *bhakti* or devotion.

THE THEISTIC CULT OF BHAKTI FOUNDED BY VĀSUDEVA

This cult of *bhakti* was, to a certain extent, not new. It had already progressed in connection with the worship of the sun in the capacity of Viṣṇu. But it was elaborated and given a distinct and permanent place in the religious development of this period by a member of the Sātvata-Yādava clan, who had the patronymic name of Vāsudeva, the matronymic title of Devakīputra, and the proper name of Kṛṣṇa. We may presume that the offering of worship was made in this school to God in the name of Bhagavat, the Adorable. The followers came, in consequence, we may presume, to be called the Bhāgavatas. When, in subsequent centuries, the devotional religion spread to different parts of India, the terms 'Sātvata' and 'Bhāgavata' became identical, though originally one term referred to the community to which the founder belonged, and the other denoted the cult of which he was the founder. The reputation of Vāsudeva-Kṛṣṇa spread fast,

Note: See *ante* article on 'Early History of Vaiṣṇavism' for the Vedic references to Viṣṇu and his emergence to prominence as a separate deity.

and his followers came to regard him, in course of time, as the Bhagavat Himself.

His teaching was based on the monotheistic doctrine that the goal of the Jīvas is to get rid of *saṁsāra* or cycles of births and deaths, and to obtain bliss of an eternal character by the grace of Īśvara, who is conceived as the highest Ātman, free from all imperfections, and as the seat of all infinitely high and noble qualities. Though primarily a religion of faith and devotion, it allied itself with the Sāṁkhya-Yoga system and came to adopt meditation on God as a fundamental part of it. Secondly, it allied itself with the pantheistic school of the Upaniṣads and so came to incorporate its essentials.

THE PĀÑCARĀTRA ĀGAMA

By the second century A.D., Bhāgavatism came to be generally known by the name of the Pāñcarātra Āgama.[1] The meaning of the term *pañcarātra* is uncertain. It is perhaps derived from the fact that the original adherents of the cult probably sacrificed five times a year, or observed some vows according to five *rātras* or seasons. The Brāhmaṇas, in fact, say that the *pañcarātra* was a sacrifice performed by Puruṣa or Nārāyaṇa over a period of five *rātris.* But, however distorted the etymology of the term *pañcarātra* was, it came to be regarded by the Bhāgavatas as superior to the Vedas—in fact, as their root, while the latter were only the trunk and branches. It came to be called a *mūla-Veda,* the holy teaching from Nārāyaṇa Himself to Nara and a succession of teachers like Śāṇḍilya, Prahlāda, Sugrīva, and others, till it was taught to mankind in order to save it.

The cult of Bhāgavatism was eminently a religion based upon God's grace to humanity. It emphasized, and developed for this purpose, the doctrine of *avatāra* or the divine incarnation. The *arcāvatāra* (the theory of the presence of God in images) was also elaborated in order to illustrate His easy accessibility. The science of iconography was consequently perfected in connection with the temple worship, and the popular mind was captured by the Āgamas and Tantras. Again, the more prominent among the Purāṇas assumed, to some extent, their present form by the beginning of the Gupta period, and the stories enshrined in the *Viṣṇu Purāṇa* and the *Bhāgavata* became current. The Tāntric observances of Śāktism were also fully utilized.

[1] The term *āgama* is the counterpart of *mantra* or Veda, and denotes a popular cult wherein practical religious formularies and offerings, in the form of fruits, flowers, food and drinks, etc., made with devotion, take the place of incantations and sacrifices in fire. For the term *pañcarātra,* see Schrader, *Introduction to the Pāñcarātra and the Ahirbudhnya Saṁhitā,* p. 25.

Calling themselves Bhāgavatas, the Gupta emperors devoted themselves to the popularization of the new Hinduism at the expense of Buddhism and Jainism. The example of the Guptas was followed by the numerous dynasties of Hindustan, the Deccan, and South India. The royal houses of Mālava, Magadha, Kanauj, Gauḍa, and Gurjara established the triumph of Paurāṇic Hinduism in the North. The Vākāṭakas, Śarabhas, Ikṣvākus, Sālaṅkāyanas, and Viṣṇukuṇḍins did the same in the Deccan. The Karṇāṭaka country was brought under the new influence by the Kadambas and Gaṅgas. All these dynasties encouraged the study of the Vedas and the *darśanas* and the principles and practices of the *varṇāśrama-dharma* (duties according to one's class and life-stage). They encouraged Brāhmaṇical supremacy once again in religious matters. They established *agrahāras*[2] for the Brāhmaṇas, and made endowments for the Vedic institutions. But they also fostered popular Hinduism, of which Bhāgavatism was the main element, by encouraging the compilation of new Purāṇas, the construction of temples dedicated to Viṣṇu, Śiva, and other major deities, the organization of temple festivals, and in other ways.

GROWTH OF PĀÑCARĀTRA LITERATURE

There was an ever-increasing output of devotional literature, general and technical. In the former branch, the Purāṇas and the Upapurāṇas, not to speak of the Sthalapurāṇas, came to be compiled on a large scale. The *Viṣṇu Purāṇa* and the *Bhāgavata* were perhaps the most celebrated in this collection, and they carried the teachings of the *Gītā* and the Nārāyaṇīya section of the *Mahābhārata* to their logical extremes. Even more so was the case with the technical literature of the Pāñcarātrikas. Known also occasionally as Tantras and Kāṇḍas, these Pāñcarātra Saṁhitās came to comprise, according to tradition, a set of 108 works, but as a matter of fact they number at least 215 works.[3] The earliest of the series were probably the *Pauṣkara, Vārāha,* and *Brāhma.* These were followed by the *Sātvata, Jaya,* and *Ahirbudhnya Saṁhitās.* Then came in succession the Saṁhitās known as *Pārameśvara, Sanatkumāra, Parama, Padmodbhava, Māhendra, Kāṇva, Pādma,* and *Īśvara Saṁhitās.* The last of these treatises

[2] Royal gift of lands or houses to Brāhmaṇas, especially for those returning from the *gurukula.*

[3] Dr. Otto Schrader refers, in his valuable introduction to his edition of the *Ahirbudhnya Saṁhitā,* to as many as 224 works. He points out that the *Nāradīya Pañcarātra,* which was first published by the Asiatic Society of Bengal, and which was taken by its scholars to be the only genuine work available on the subject, was, unfortunately, a spurious one. Dr. Schrader believes that there may be even more works. Pāñcarātra literature refers traditionally to one and a half crores of verses, and Dr. Schrader himself calculates the possibility of a million and a half. See his *Introduction to the Pāñcarātra and the Ahirbudhnya Saṁhitā.* See also *Journal of the Royal Asiatic Society,* October, 1911, where Sri Govindacharya gives references to the *Padma Tantra,* the *Bharadvāja Saṁhitā,* the *Śāṇḍilya Smṛti,* the *Vṛddha Hārīta Smṛti,* and other works.

is referred to by Yāmunācārya, the founder of the Viśiṣṭādvaita philosophy in the South, who belonged to the tenth and eleventh centuries. It mentions the Tamil Veda, or the work of the Āḷvārs, as well as the temple at Melkote in Mysore. By A.D. 850, the Āḷvār movement was over and the Ācārya movement had its beginnings.

THE ĀḶVĀR MOVEMENT: ITS GENERAL FEATURES

The Āḷvārs are traditionally twelve in number. They belonged to the Pallava times in the main and to all parts of the Tamil area. They included a woman too, as one of the most popular of them is the celebrated Godā or Āṇḍāḷ, to whom a magnificent temple was built and dedicated in later times at Śrīvilliputtur, her birth-place. The Āḷvārs included a saint of the depressed classes, the famous Tiruppāṇ Āḷvār, and of the others, Nammāḷvār, the greatest of the Āḷvārs, was a Veḷḷāḷa, and Tirumaṅgai Āḷvār, the second greatest, was a Kaḷḷa by caste. Another Āḷvār, Tirumaḷiśai, was a person of dubious parentage, and of the Brāhmaṇical Āḷvārs, one at least was a repentant sinner.

THE FIRST FOUR ĀḶVĀRS

The first three Āḷvārs are technically known by the names of Poygai, Pūdam (Bhūta), and Pey. These very names indicate the great feature of their life. They are called spirits and mad beings, because, in their self-forgetfulness and divine vision, they laughed, wept, danced, and sang like people who had lost their senses. God-absorbed and God-enamoured, they wandered from place to place, addressing psalms to the manifestations (*arcāvatāras*) of Viṣṇu in the different villages of the Tamil land. The three *Tiruvandādis*[4] they sang are, for this reason, regarded as the earliest sections of the *Nālāyira Prabandham,*[5] by which name the hymns of the Āḷvārs came later on to be collectively called. Saint Tirumaḷiśai, the fourth Āḷvār, was not only a great devotee, on which account he is known as Bhaktisāra, but a *yogin* as well. His *Nānmukham Tiruvandādi* and *Tiruccandaviruttam*[6] are illustrative of his singular devotion to Viṣṇu as an Ekāntika or true Bhāgavata.

NAMMĀḶVĀR AND MADHURAKAVI

The next Āḷvār, who is known by the different designations of Nammāḷvār, Māran, Parāṅkuśar, Śaṭakopar, Vakulābharaṇar, etc., is regarded

[4] The *tiruvandādi* is a type of Tamil verse, where the last portion of a previous line is the commencement of the next. The *Tiruvandādi* of the first three Āḷvārs is one of the earliest works in this style, and gives a clue to their chronology.

[5] Literally, the *Prabandham* of 4000 songs. Notice that the Tamil work is given the Sanskrit name *Prabandha*.

[6] The title indicates composition in a new kind of metre, and is therefore of great literary interest.

as the greatest of the Vaiṣṇava saints. Through a fond and worshipping disciple, Madhurakavi by name, who also has been raised by Vaiṣṇava tradition to the rank of the Āḷvārs, Nammāḷvār gave to the world the four poems known as the *Tiruviruttam*, the *Tiruvāśiriyam*, the *Periya Tiruvandādi*, and the *Tiruvāimoḷi*. These form the most important part of the *Nālāyira Prabandham*. The Śrī-Vaiṣṇavas call them the four Vedas in the Tamil garb ; and the great Vedānta Deśika calls the *Tiruvāimoḷi* the *Dramiḍopaniṣad*. More than the works of any other saints, Nammāḷvār's hymns have shaped the conduct and faith of the southern Vaiṣṇavas. Possessing a matchless cadence and simple grandeur, they are characterized equally by their literary charm and by their ethical and spiritual values. To the emotionally inclined, the psalms are simple and appealing prayers to the different local *arcāvatāras* of Viṣṇu. To the less emotional and more philosophical, they seem to be the outcome of great learning in the Vedas, the Upaniṣads, the Vedānta, the *Gītā*, and the *Bhāgavata* literature. To the practical spiritualist, they are of value as the achievement of one who was in holy communion with God. Nammāḷvār is called the *kūṭastha* by the later Ācāryas of the Viśiṣṭādvaita system, because the fundamental doctrines[7] of the Śrī-Vaiṣṇava faith, as current today, were taught by him. His disciple, Madhurakavi, who apotheosized him, taught the Śrī-Vaiṣṇava world that devotion to a teacher and devotion to God were equal.

KULAŚEKHARA, PERIYĀḶVĀR, AND GODĀ

The next Āḷvār, Kulaśekhara, was a king of Malabar whose contribution to the *Four Thousand* (*Nālāyira Prabandham*) is found in the exquisite poem *Perumāḷ Tirumoḷi*.[8] Retiring to Śrīraṅgam, he spent his life in pious poverty ; and it is believed that in addition to his *Tirumoḷi*, the celebrated lyric *Mukundamālā*, which, in its harmony and beauty, has been compared to the *Gīta-Govinda*, was his work. The next Āḷvār, Viṣṇucitta or Periyāḷvār, was a Brāhmaṇa of Śrīvilliputtūr, who is said to have miraculously conquered spiritual controversialists in the Pāṇḍyan court and brought the Pāṇḍya king within the pale of Vaiṣṇavism. The poem called *Tiruppallāṇḍu* gives the picture of the saint's vision of the Lord in all His glories, while He was going in procession organized by the king. Viṣṇucitta's adopted daughter was the celebrated Godā or Āṇḍāḷ, the only woman amongst the Āḷvārs. Tradition has made her the *avatāra* of Lakṣmī or

[7] These doctrines, termed *rahasyas,* form a set of three tenets based on (i) the *mūlamantra* or *aṣṭākṣarī,* (ii) the *dvaya,* and (iii) *caramaśloka* ; the first is *Om Namo Nārāyaṇāya* ; the second adds the term 'Śrī' in order to indicate the importance of the grace and the effort of the spiritual aspirant. The third is verse 66 of chapter XVIII of the *Gītā*. These are the bases of the *śaraṇāgati* theory, and a copious literature of commentaries has risen thereon.

[8] Literally, the holy word of Perumāḷ. Perumāḷ was the title of the Cera kings in this period.

Bhūdevī herself. Refusing to wed any man, Godā led the life of a lover of the Lord, like the ancient *gopīs,* and devoted herself to divine service in the local temple. In memory of these services, she has left two poems known as *Tiruppāvai* and the *Nācchiyār Tirumoḷi,* which are exceedingly popular with the Śrī-Vaiṣṇavas. Choosing the Lord of Śrīraṅgam as her bridegroom, she imagined herself to be his bride and behaved as such. Sometimes she would imagine herself to be Kṛṣṇa and address the *gopīs* as such. Her *Tirumoḷi* contains the outpourings of this maddening love to God. Traditions record that Godā was eventually absorbed in the image of Raṅganātha at Śrīraṅgam.

TOṆḌARAḌIPPOḌI AND TIRUPPĀṆAR

If the story of Godā shows that sex was no obstacle to liberation, that of Vipraṇārāyaṇa or Toṇḍaraḍippoḍi (he who purified himself with the dust of the feet of devotees) illustrates how an abandoned sinner could obtain, through the Lord's grace, the highest salvation. Two exquisite poems known as the *Tirumālai* and the *Tirup-paḷḷie-eḻucci,* which he composed in praise of the Lord, are even now favourite subjects of study among women, and serve as standing memorials of the readiness of the Lord to forgive temporary human weaknesses.

The story of Tiruppāṇar is more interesting as it shows how one brought up as a pariah could attain the honour of Āḻvārhood. It is said that the Lord of Śrīraṅgam commanded him to be carried by the chief priest of the shrine to the innermost part of it to be absorbed into His own personality. A decade of verses known as the *Amalan-ādip-pirān* is his contribution to the *Prabandham,* and he is regarded by the orthodox as an *avatāra* of Viṣṇu's *śrīvatsa.*

TIRUMAṄGAI ĀḺVĀR

The last of the Āḻvārs, the celebrated Tirumaṅgai Mannan, was a Veḷḷāḷa in the service of the Coḷa king, and a local military chief. He developed into a devotee of the Lord through his wife who belonged to a Vaiṣṇava family, and then devoted himself to the construction of the Śrīraṅgam temple, even by robbing the Buddhist temple of Nāgapaṭṭinam. He even resorted to highway robbery in order to carry out his holy works and charities. Tirumaṅgai's career is thus the story of a religious enthusiast who aimed at commendable ends even by foul means. The *Prabandham* includes six poems composed by him. These are: the *Periya Tirumoḷi, Tirukkurundāṇḍakam, Tirunedundāṇḍakam, Tiruveḻukūrirukai, Śiriya Tirumaḍal,* and *Periya Tirumaḍal.* In the *Maḍal* the Lord is represented as the lover, and the individual soul is compared to a lady deeply lost in love for Him. It is the view of the Śrī-Vaiṣṇavas that the six poems of Tirumaṅgai Āḷvār form a logical supplement to the four poems of Nammāḷvār. In fact, the works of Nammāḷvār are conventionally regarded as the four Vedas, while those of Tirumaṅgai as the six Vedāṅgas. The works of these two saints constitute the major portion of the Tamil Veda, by which name the *Prabandham* is known to the Śrī-Vaiṣṇavas.

THE MAIN TEACHINGS OF THE ĀḶVĀRS

The great feature of the Āḷvār movement is that it was emotional and not metaphysical. The Āḷvārs were devotees who believed in the impermanence of worldly enjoyment and in the acquisition of freedom from births and deaths by union with Viṣṇu, through loving surrender to His will. A corollary of this doctrine of *bhakti* was monotheism. The Āḷvārs were Ekāntikas, who worshipped Viṣṇu alone. Though there are occasional passages in the *Prabandham* showing toleration, the Āḷvārs were fanatical lovers of Viṣṇu. They call the latter by the various names of Bhagavat, Puruṣa, Vāsudeva, and Nārāyaṇa. The Lord is eternal, endless, and imperishable, and creates even Brahmā and Rudra. He is the seed of the universe, its soul. The animate and inanimate existences are only modes of His—limbs (*śeṣa*) constituting His body as it were. He is omnipresent, infinite, and immeasurable. The Vedas cannot reach Him. He is knowledge and bliss, a mass of intelligence and love. His grace to humanity makes Him an *avatāra* without losing His infinite nature. Though supreme Brahman, He limits Himself in images. Though the creator of Brahmā and the universe, He stands, in His love of every human being, like the father, mother, self, and so on. This easy accessibility enables man to cross the ocean of transmigratory existence without any difficulty, and is noticeable in every *avatāra*, but particularly in Kṛṣṇa, the companion of cowherds.

The individual soul is only a mode of the Supreme. It is the property of the Lord, who is its ruler and possessor. The soul is different from matter ; the latter changes, but the former is eternal. The Lord is its very life. When pure, it recognizes God and nothing else. Its dependence on God is as characteristic as its eternality. It struggles against the earthly illusions to obtain the privilege of His company and service. It is this service which is the eternal happiness of the soul and prevents its return to the world. The Āḷvārs aimed at the service in Vaikuṇṭha by performing it in this world in relation to the *arcāvatāras*. Service to the Lord includes service to His lovers ; the Lord's devotees should be loved as much as the Lord. God's gracious love to man prompts Him to create things and to animate them to attain Him ; man's love to God is his spiritual inspiration.

The obstacles to be overcome are the contact with matter, the desire for worldly things, and the love of self which confounds the body with the soul. The idea of 'me' and 'mine' must be given up ; one should surrender oneself completely to God. It is not obligatory to renounce the world ; it is enough if duty is performed for God's sake without an eye to the fruits thereof. Service to the Lord is not for the benefit of the devotee, but for the sake of the Lord. The body, though an obstacle to the union with God, is not useless, for it reveals the Lord's grace to man. Angels worship Him in the midst of happiness ; but it is the privilege of man to experience various ills in this body and seek the Lord in the midst of them. It is for the sake of the sinner that the Lord has His *avatāras* and His limitations in images.

Another great feature of the doctrine is that it extends the consolation of religion to all sorts of people. The path of devotion, in which meditation is a constant factor, is possible only to people of high attainments ; but the path of self-surrender (*prapatti*), which the Āḷvārs advocate, is characterized by no restriction in regard to knowledge, social status, observance, etc. It affords consolation to the most depressed and fallen among mankind ; and the gratitude of the latter led to the theory that the Āḷvārs were the *avatāras* of the Lord's servants, weapons, or ornaments.

THE RISE OF THE ĀCĀRYAS

We now come to a new epoch in the history of Śrī-Vaiṣṇavism—the age of the Ācāryas as distinguished from that of the Āḷvārs. The Ācāryas differed from the latter in the fact that they based their teachings on both the Sanskrit and Tamil scriptures. Further, they did not solely rely on *bhakti* as the Āḷvārs had done, but united *jñāna* and *karma* with it for realizing God. Their object was to reconcile the Vedas, the Upaniṣads, and the *Gītā* with the Tamil *Prabandham*. They, in fact, aimed at interpreting the latter in terms of the former. In consequence of this, posterity has given them the significant title of Ubhaya-Vedāntins. The Ācāryas regarded the Āḷvārs as objects of worship—in fact, as the incarnations of Viṣṇu's weapons, carriers, or immediate followers in Vaikuṇṭha. They regarded the *Prabandham* as the equal of the Vedas, and introduced it in public and private worship. They thus broadened the curriculum of holy studies so as to include Tamil scriptures, and were the promoters of the Āḷvār cult. Further, they elaborated and perfected the Viśiṣṭādvaita school of thought with the aid of the doctrines, particularly that of self-surrender, which they derived from the Āḷvārs. The Ācāryas were very orthodox Brāhmaṇas, versed equally in Sanskrit and Tamil, who passed through the different stages of orthodox life, and discharged their duties so as to serve as patterns for their followers. All the Śrī-Vaiṣṇava festivals, observances, fasts, vows, and customs can be traced to the rules laid down by the Ācāryas. They were thus the makers of modern Śrī-Vaiṣṇavism—its society, rituals, practices, and ideals. It is not surprising therefore that they, in their turn, have become objects of worship, and have been raised to equality with the Āḷvārs whom they themselves apotheosized.

NĀTHA MUNI (A.D. 824-924)

The first of the Ācāryas was the famous Nātha Muni, that is, Raṅganātha Muni. His father Īśvara Muni was a Pāñcarātrika who was the progenitor of the celebrated family of the Tātācāryas, which has played a very important part in the religious history of South India. Nātha Muni was an erudite scholar in the Vedas, Smṛtis, and other scriptures, a *yogin*, and a devotee. Once he heard some pilgrims address the local deity Rājagopāla in a Tamil song which contained the beautiful expression *ārāvamuda* (inexhaustible nectar). It seemed to him that to contemplate God with the psalms which contained such a word was sweeter than the realization of God by *yoga* itself. He therefore devoted himself to the task of discovering and popularizing those hymns, and succeeded in rescuing the *Prabandham* from oblivion.

He divided it into four parts of one thousand stanzas each, added introductory verses to each section, classified the verses according to different metres, and then introduced it to be sung in the temple of Rājagopāla in his village. The adoption of the *Prabandham* as a sacred text by the Śrīraṅgam temple, together with the celebration of it in the great *ekādaśī* festival in the month of Mārgaśīrṣa, lasting for three weeks and devoted to the chanting of the *Prabandham*, was followed, thanks to Nātha Muni's efforts, by a similar custom in the prominent Vaiṣṇava temples of South India. The establishment of the images of the Āḷvārs and the conduct of the recitation-festival soon spread throughout the Śrī-Vaiṣṇava world.

By giving the *Prabandham* the status of the Vedas in the temple festival, Nātha Muni proved that the holiness of the works written in Tamil was not in any way inferior to that of the works written in Sanskrit. One immediate and momentous result of the great reform was the rise of a new and extensive type of religious literature in South India, half Sanskrit and half Tamil, the object of which was to expound the Tamil Veda and reconcile its teachings with those of the *prasthāna-traya*. The *Prabandham*, again, came to be, like the Vedas, an essential part of a Śrī-Vaiṣṇava's education.

THE CREATION OF ĀCĀRYASHIP

Once made a holy authority, the *Prabandham* had to be intensively studied, obscure passages had to be explained, and commentaries had to be written. The words of the Āḻvārs had to be interpreted in the light of the Śrutis and Smṛtis. All this required the formal recognition of an authoritative pontiff. This necessity, together with that of expounding and defending the Pāñcarātra doctrine against rivals, led to the establishment of the post of a universal Ācārya, whose authority was law in religious worship and whose advice was a guide to temples and householders.

In connection with the establishment of an apostolic head of Vaiṣṇavism, one very important fact to be remembered is that the office was combined with the management of the Śrīraṅgam temple. The Ācāryas succeeded in their great task because of the power they had over the most important of the South Indian Vaiṣṇava shrines. When once they introduced the reform there, it was followed elsewhere. This is the secret of the success which attended the first Ācāryas, Nātha Muni, Yāmuna, and Rāmānuja. A time came when this combination of offices ceased, and then Śrī-Vaiṣṇavism began to be divided into sects.

It was natural that when the dignity of pontiff was established, the choice should fall on Nātha Muni. He was formally anointed in the Śrīraṅgam temple, and the whole Vaiṣṇava world paid him allegiance. With him Śrī-Vaiṣṇavism commenced a new era of activity and expansion. Scholar and thinker, he composed two well-known works—the *Yogarahasya*, which has been lost except in regard to stray passages quoted by the later Vedānta Deśika, and the *Nyāyatattva*, which was the first Viśiṣṭādvaita work in the Ācāryic age. Probably the doctrine of self-surrender, the most important dogma of Śrī-Vaiṣṇavism, was first authoritatively enunciated by him.

FUNDAMENTALS OF THE ĀCĀRYA CULT

According to the tenets of Bhāgavatism, a true Vaiṣṇava has to be a *pañcakāla-parāyaṇa* (devoted to fivefold daily duty) and to depend for this on the depth of faith in a *guru* (teacher). This faith in the teacher was raised to an equality of position with the worship of God Himself. The teacher imparts the mysteries of the creed to the novice in five ways which are known as the *pañca-saṁskāra*. These include the *tapas* or the Ācārya's initiating the student into the sacred fire by branding the latter's shoulders with the symbols of Viṣṇu; the *puṇḍra* or initiating into wearing the sect-mark, the symbol of the Lord's foot; giving a spiritual name like Nārāyaṇadāsa, Govindadāsa, etc. to the disciple; imparting the *mantra-traya* consisting of the *aṣṭākṣara*, the *dvaya*, and the *caramaśloka*; and handing over a *śālagrāma* or other concrete objects for daily worship. This *pañca-saṁskāra* ritual came to be regarded as absolutely necessary for one's being considered a true Śrī-Vaiṣṇava.

BHĀRANYĀSA AND ŚARAṆĀGATI

The *pañca-saṁskāra* initiation and the *pañcakāla* life are, in theory, sufficient to secure the devotee's entry into the blissful world of Viṣṇu ; but as a matter of fact, the suppliant of heaven realizes that, in spite of the regularity of his life and the purity of his conduct, he is not much nearer the goal. He finds that his past *karma* and present weaknesses are serious obstacles, that his *jñāna, bhakti,* and *karma* do not give him the spiritual advance he yearns for. He realizes that his efforts are futile without the Lord's grace, and therefore surrenders himself to the Lord to save him. This complete self-surrender, which is due to the individual's feeling of utter helplessness and complete belief in Lord's grace, is called *prapatti* or *śaraṇāgati* (self-surrender), and the devotee who does it is called the *prapanna.* The *prapanna,* again, is not able to ingratiate himself directly with the Lord ; he is in need of a mediator. He therefore has to go to a teacher and beg him to intercede for him and place his soul at the Lord's feet. This vicarious employment of the teacher is called *bhāranyāsa* (depositing the burden). The doctrine of self-surrender with its corollary, the laying down of the burden, is a unique development in Śrī-Vaiṣṇavism ever since.

YĀMUNĀCĀRYA'S ACCESSION AND LITERARY ACTIVITIES

Nātha Muni was succeeded, after two short periods of spiritual headships by Puṇḍarīkākṣa and Rāma Miśra, by his grandson Yāmunācārya or Āḷavandār. Yāmunācārya clearly laid down the lines on which Rāmānuja later on elaborated the system of Viśiṣṭādvaita. He left four works which are popular with the Śrī-Vaiṣṇavas. One of these, the *Śrī-catuḥślokī,* is a little poem of four stanzas on the position of Lakṣmī as the consort of Viṣṇu and the part played by her in the soul's salvation. His *Stotraratna* is a poem of seventy stanzas in praise of the Lord, but really an ardent praise of the doctrine of self-surrender. His *Siddhitraya* is a treatise in three sections, *Ātmasiddhi, Īśvarasiddhi,* and *Saṁvitsiddhi,* demonstrating the nature of the individual soul, the supreme Lord, and the relation between the soul and the objects of perception. In the last of these, he refutes the doctrines of *avidyā* and absolute identity which play such a conspicuous part in the philosophy of Śaṅkara. In his fourth work, the *Āgama-prāmāṇya,* Yāmuna establishes the orthodoxy of the Pāñcarātra school. He argues that the author of the *Vedānta-Sūtra* does not include this school among those to be rejected, but posits it as the only one to be accepted by mentioning it last. In his *Mahāpuruṣa-nirṇaya,* Yāmuna proves the supremacy of Viṣṇu, who, he holds, is the Mahāpuruṣa of the *Puruṣa-sūkta,* 'the essence of the Vedas'. He wrote in addition the *Gītārtha-saṅgraha.*

RĀMĀNUJA

It was given to Yāmunācārya to lay down only the fundamentals of the Viśiṣṭādvaita philosophy and not to compose a *bhāṣya* on the *Vedānta-Sūtra,* as Śaṅkara had done for Advaita. That task was achieved by Rāmānuja. Rāmānuja's father was a disciple of his brother-in-law, Śrīśailapūrṇa, Yāmuna's grandson and disciple, who is said to have obtained from the Lord Himself the title of *tātācārya.*[9] Rāmānuja is said to have been named as such by his maternal uncle who expected him to equal the great Lakṣmaṇa in his devotion to the Lord. The traditional date of Rāmānuja's birth is A.D. 1017, and he is said to have lived 120 years. Yāmuna died before Rāmānuja became Ācārya, and the interval was filled up by two scholars, Mahāpūrṇa and Śrīśailapūrṇa.

HIS THREE TASKS AND EARLY WORKS

Rāmānuja inherited three great tasks or missions from Yāmuna, viz. the perpetuation of the memory of Parāśara (the author of the *Viṣṇu Purāṇa*), the immortalization of the glory of Nammāḷvār, and the interpretation of Vyāsa's *Brahma-Sūtra* according to the Viśiṣṭādvaita system. One thing which facilitated Rāmānuja's advent to, and Ācāryaship at, Śrīraṅgam was his embracing the monastic life. He spent two years in studying the teachings of Yāmuna from the specialists who had been trained by him. He studied the *Prabandham,* the esoteric lessons of the *Rāmāyaṇa,* and other works from experts in the traditional interpretation of them. He is further said to have gone as far as Kashmir in order to copy the *vṛtti* or commentary of Bodhāyana which interpreted the *Brahma-Sūtra* in the Viśiṣṭādvaita mode. These preparations being over, Rāmānuja gave to the world, in succession, the several works which have made him the first amongst the Śrī-Vaiṣṇava philosophers. One of his early works was the *Vedārtha-saṅgraha,* an elaborate essay on the teachings of the principal Upaniṣads, in which he attacks the Advaitic meaning of '*Tattvamasi*' as well as the doctrine of Māyā laid down by Śaṅkara, and the Bhedābheda doctrines of the Yādava and Bhāskara schools. He then reconciles the Vedic passages with each other and formulates Viśiṣṭādvaita. He proves

[9] The story is that Śrīśailapūrṇa used to bring the water for the *abhiṣeka* (bathing) of Śrīnivāsa's image from the Pāpanāśatīrtha in the midst of the hills, and that the Lord Himself relieved him once from the arduous task in the guise of a youth, calling him *tātā* or grandfather

that the supreme Deity is to be called Nārāyaṇa and not by any other name known to the Upaniṣads. The *Vedārtha-saṅgraha* was followed by the *Vedāntasāra,* a lucid and short commentary on the *Brahma-Sūtra,* and the *Vedāntadīpa,* which explains the main lessons taught in the *Brahma-Sūtra* in a fuller and more discursive form than in the previous treatise. Other works of Rāmānuja in this period were the *Gadyatraya,* a devotional prose lyric embodying the principle of self-surrender, and the commentary on the *Gītā,* which has been in its turn expounded by Vedānta Deśika in his *Tātparyacandrikā.* His *magnum opus,* however, was the *Śrībhāṣya* on the *Vedānta-Sūtra.*

ŚRĪBHĀṢYA AND ADVAITA OF ŚAṄKARA

The Viśiṣṭādvaita philosophy as expounded by Rāmānuja in his *Śrībhāṣya* is less intellectual and more emotional than the philosophy of Śaṅkara. Again, while Śaṅkara taught idealism, Rāmānuja was an advocate of realism. A further point of contrast is that one is for a pantheistic neuter Brahman, while the other advocates a personal deity possessed of all auspicious attributes and capable of giving salvation to devotees in reward for their devotion. Lastly, the individuality of the Jīva is preserved in Rāmānuja's system even after *mokṣa,* while it is lost in Brahman according to Advaita. It is true that, so far as practical life is concerned, Śaṅkara's Saguṇa Brahman theory provides for a life of devotion; but Rāmānuja advocates this for the realization of *mokṣa* itself, while Śaṅkara regards it as secondary to the intellectual method of meditation, which brings complete identity with Brahman. Rāmānuja's doctrine regarding the soul's innate dependence on God's grace and its getting salvation through devotion, and his insistence on the reality of existence, in contrast to Śaṅkara's advocacy of the phenomenal (*vyāvahārika*) existence through Māyā, appealed to minds which were not satisfied with the teachings of Advaita.

After completing the *Śrībhāṣya,* Rāmānuja went on tour throughout the country to popularize his teachings. He defeated controversialists in various places and established local monasteries to keep his teachings alive. He made Tirupati a permanent centre of Vaiṣṇavism.

BHAṬṬA AND KURUKEŚA

Rāmānuja is said to have fulfilled his second vow of perpetuating Parāśara's name by calling on Bhaṭṭa, a son of his friend and follower, Kureśa, who was also named Parāśara, to compose a commentary on the *Viṣṇu-sahasranāma.* Besides *Bhagavad-guṇadarpaṇa,* the commentary on the *Sahasranāma,* Bhaṭṭa wrote a number of minor works such as the *Aṣṭaślokī.*

Rāmānuja fulfilled his third vow, viz. the perpetuation of Nammāḷvār's name, by authorizing Kurukeśa, the son of his uncle Śrīśailapūrṇa, and his own spiritual son, to compose an authoritative commentary on the *Tiruvāimoḷi* as taught and expounded by him. This is known amongst the Vaiṣṇavas as the *Six Thousand* (so called from the number of *granthas*, stanzas of 32 syllables), and it is the earliest and, in some respects, the best commentary on the hymns of Nammāḷvār. It was the model upon which many compositions were later written, particularly in the *maṇipravāla* or mixed Sanskrit-Tamil style.

THE ORGANIZING WORK OF RĀMĀNUJA

The steps which Rāmānuja took in order to popularize his teachings indicate that he was as great a practical organizer as he was a thinker. He divided the Vaiṣṇava world into a number of Ācāryic dioceses, over each of which he appointed a pious householder as the head, or *siṁhāsanādhipati* as he was called. A set of seventy-four spiritual leaders took up the work of teaching Viśiṣṭādvaita in the villages and homes throughout the land.

The Prabandhic biographers of Rāmānuja are particular in dilating on the excellence of his heart and the sympathy he displayed towards fellow-men. He is depicted as a friend of the lower classes, trying to uplift them in social and religious life. He is said to have risen above caste and status, and had non-Brāhmaṇa disciples like Piḷḷai Uraṅgāvillidāsa. He gave them a place in Vaiṣṇavism by allowing them to wear sect-marks, to dress themselves like Vaiṣṇavas, to imitate their customs and habits, and to study the *Prabandham*. It is true that the *Śrībhāṣya* and other writings of Rāmānuja indicate a thoroughly Brāhmaṇical exclusiveness which is not consistent with the catholicity attributed to him by the legends ; but the *Prabandham*, the temple festivals, the sect-marks, and the methods of life afforded ample opportunities for the democratization of Vaiṣṇavism without violating or infringing the sacred institutions of Vedic puritanism.

The *Guruparamparā* refers at this stage to the persecution of Vaiṣṇavism by Kulottuṅga I, one of the Coḷa emperors, and the consequent necessity on the part of Rāmānuja to flee to Mysore. He converted the great Hoysaḷa ruler, Biṭṭi Viṣṇuvardhana, from Jainism to Viśiṣṭādvaita, and persuaded a large number of local people to give up their belief in Advaita and to join his school. The Bhaṭṭas, the Hebbārs, the Hemmigeyars, the Kaḍāmbiyas, the Kandāḍais, the Nallān Cakravartis, the Tātācāryas, and other Tamil families of piety and learning, who came to settle in the land, as well as some of the non-Brāhmaṇical classes, testify to the proselytizing work of Rāmānuja.

RĀMĀNUJA'S LAST YEARS

When, on account of the cessation of Coḷa persecution, he returned to Śrīraṅgam, Rāmānuja arranged not only for an organization of local Ācāryas who could carry Viśiṣṭādvaita to the homes and public places of worship in every corner of South India, but also for a succession to the central apostleship at Śrīraṅgam. He authorized the expounding of the *bhāṣyas* by four of his most learned adherents—Kurukeśa, Praṇatārtihara, Varadaviṣṇu, and Dāśarathi, the first of whom he made the Prabandhic pontiff as well. Besides thus providing for an apostolic succession of teachers, Rāmānuja acceded to the unanimous request of his admirers and worshippers to have his own image dedicated in a shrine within the temple precincts.[10] What he was in life, he has been after death—a prince of devotees, ever standing in the presence of his Lord and contemplating him. No Vaiṣṇava temple is considered perfect without his image, no festival proper without the celebration of his greatness, and no ceremonial occasion adequately solemn without the invocation of his blessing and favour.

THE EPOCH OF SECTARIANISM

The death of Rāmānuja was followed by a period of sectarian split among the Śrī-Vaiṣṇavas which ended, by the close of the fourteenth century, in the permanent division of their ranks into the two sects of Vaḍagalais and Teṅgalais, that is, the followers of the northern and the southern learning, with two conflicting sets of works, two *Guruparamparās*, which give two different accounts of Rāmānuja's successors and their achievements.

It is necessary to glance at the causes which gave rise to this schism. One of these concerned the language of the holy works to be studied. It came to be disputed whether salvation could be obtained more easily through the Sanskrit holy works like the Vedas, the Upaniṣads, and the *Gītā*, or through the Tamil *Prabandham*. So long as Rāmānuja lived, both occupied a co-ordinate position ; the highest philosophy of the Vedānta was the same as the highest philosophy of the *Prabandham*. But, in course of time, two linguistic schools came into existence. The Sanskritists came, in course of time, to be called the Vaḍagalais and the Tamilists the Teṅgalais. There arose doctrinal differences too. It has been shown that the cult of *bhakti* was developed into the more extreme doctrine of *śaraṇāgati* or self-surrender in the time of the Āḷvārs and early Ācāryas. Both parties agreed

[10] Rāmānuja is said to have similarly authorized his images (which he himself embraced to give them life) to be consecrated at Śrīperumbudūr and Tirunārāyaṇapuram.

as to the necessity of self-surrender, but the Vaḍagalais say that before resorting to self-surrender there must be self-effort. It is only when this self-effort is unable to obtain the realization of God, and in consequence a feeling of complete helplessness and unalloyed faith in God's grace is firmly entertained, that one can resort to *prapatti*. According to the other school, no such self-effort is necessary, as God's love is spontaneous and will, of itself, bring salvation to mankind. One party asserts that the soul must exert itself to get saved, as the young monkey actively seizes its mother when she jumps from tree to tree ; this is the well-known *markaṭa-nyāya* (analogy of the monkey). The other party asserts that God's grace is like the care of the mother-cat for its young, which is independent of all efforts on the part of the latter. This is known as *mārjāra-nyāya* (analogy of the cat).

This divergence of views leads to a difference in the doctrine of sin and forgiveness. The belief that God's grace is spontaneous and no self-effort of man is necessary, gives rise, among the Teṅgalais, to the dogma that God condones sin, inasmuch as it gives Him a larger scope for the display of His grace. Another doctrinal disagreement concerns the position of Lakṣmī. One view is that she is indistinguishable from the Lord, equally infinite and illimitable, without whom the conception of the Lord is impossible ; in other words, she too can give final emancipation. The other view holds her to be a finite being, though divine, and just a superior servant of God. She can only be a mediator between the sinning folk and the Lord, but cannot exercise independent or co-ordinate power in granting salvation.

Another point of difference is in connection with the caste system. Can the Śūdra and others use the *mūlamantra* and the *praṇava*? Can a teacher be chosen from the lower castes? On the whole, the Prabandhic party has been more tolerant in these matters. Differences of views also came to exist in regard to many other points of practical importance, such as the extent to which pilgrimages could conduce to salvation, the duties of a *prapanna* if he was a *sannyāsin*, the details of ceremonials to be observed on certain special occasions, the extent of the purifying influence of contact with the Bhāgavatas, the shape of the sect-mark, etiquette, certain restrictions regarding food and its service, the relation between *sannyāsins* and householders, the tonsure of widows, and so on. Between the death of Vedānta Deśika and that of Varavara Muni, the two schools became so distinct as to form almost two sub-castes. There never has been a check to intermessing, intermarriage, and free social harmony at home or temple ; but the allegiance to different teachers, difference in philosophy, and the scramble for control over temples have perpetuated the division.

THE VAḌAGALAI VERSION OF APOSTOLIC SUCCESSION

According to the *Guruparamparā* of the northern school, Rāmānuja was succeeded by Kurukeśa, the head of the Tātācārya clan, already referred to. The period of his headship was characterized by the setting up of Rāmānuja's images in many temples of the South. Besides the *Six Thousand,* Kurukeśa has left a treatise on the *mantra* and the *rahasya.* His successor, Viṣṇucitta or Eṅgal Āḻvār, has immortalized himself by two works. In his *Sārārtha-catuṣṭaya,* he dwells upon the four topics of the nature of man, his chief objects of life, the ways of realizing these objects, and the obstacles to be overcome in realizing them. The second is the famous commentary on the *Viṣṇu Purāṇa* called the *Viṣṇucittīyam.*

Viṣṇucitta was succeeded by his disciple Varadācārya or Naḍādūr Ammāl. A native of Kāñcīpuram, Varadācārya preferred that place to Śrīraṅgam for his residence and activities, and the celebrated shrine of Devarāja came to be a great centre for the studies and arguments of Vaiṣṇava scholars. This change in the scene of Ācāryic activity had an unlooked-for effect in the rise and expansion of Teṅgalaism at Śrīraṅgam. As an author, Varadācārya is remembered for his *Tattvasāra,* an essay in verse on the essence of the teachings of the Upaniṣads. A substance of his lectures and interpretations of the *Śrībhāṣya* was committed to writing under the title *Śrutaprakāśikā* by a talented disciple of his named Sudarśanācārya. It is believed by both the schools of the Vaiṣṇavas that, but for the *Śrutaprakāśikā,* the clue to the actual interpretations of the *bhāṣya* from Rāmānuja onwards would have been lost. It is therefore regarded as second only to the *Śrībhāṣya.* Sudarśanācārya has left certain other treatises which the orthodox biographies ignore. These are the *Śrutapradīpikā,* a less extensive treatise than the *Śrutaprakāśikā,* and commentaries on the Upaniṣads, the *Vedārtha-saṅgraha* of Rāmānuja, and the *Bhāgavata,* the last being known as the *Śukapakṣīya.*

On the death of Varadācārya, the Ācāryaship devolved on Ātreya Rāmānuja, otherwise known as Kaḍāmbi Appiḷḷār. He was succeeded by his nephew, Vedānta Deśika or Veṅkaṭanātha, as the Ācārya.

THE LIFE AND WORKS OF VEDĀNTA DEŚIKA

In the history of Śrī-Vaiṣṇavism, the name of Vedānta Deśika is second only to that of Rāmānuja. Tradition regards him as the incarnation of the bell of the Lord of Tirupati. For more than three quarters of a century, Vedānta Deśika enriched the Vaiṣṇava world with his teachings and writings, and he obtained a reputation which led to his own apotheosis in course of time. His works number more than a hundred. They are characterized by versatility, beauty of style and thought, ethical fervour, and deep spiritual insight. As a poet, philosopher, and thinker, as a controversialist and popularizer, he was equally great. His writings include original works in Tamil, like those of the Āḻvārs, and a large number of commentaries, and may be divided into nine varieties or classes: (1) Panegyrics of a devotional character on different deities or Ācāryas, (2) Treatises in elaboration of the Viśiṣṭādvaita system, (3) Works in Tamil and Sanskrit reconciling the teachings of the Āḻvārs with those of the *prasthāna-traya*, (4) Secret doctrines of Vaiṣṇavism, (5) Original Tamil poems on various subjects, (6) Epic poems in Sanskrit, (7) Dialectical works directed against rival schools, (8) Treatises on practical daily life, and (9) Miscellaneous treatises. The first set includes the *Garuḍa-daṇḍaka, Garuḍa-pañcāśat, Hayagrīva-stotra, Devanāyaka-pañcāśat, Gopāla-viṁśati, Śrī-stuti, Varadarāja-pañcāśat, Raghuvīra-gadya, Yatirāja-saptati* (on Rāmānuja), *Abhītistava,* and fifteen other works. Amongst the philosophic treatises on Ubhaya-Vedānta[11] may be mentioned the following: *Adhikaraṇa-tarpaṇa, Gītābhāṣya-tātparya-candrikā, Vedārtha-saṅgraha-vyākhyāna, bhāṣya* on *Īśāvāsya Upaniṣad, Nigama-parimaḷam, Dramiḍopaniṣad-tātparya-ratnāvalī, Tattvaṭīkā* (an extensive gloss on the *Śrībhāṣya*), *Adhikaraṇa-sārāvalī* (a series of Sanskrit verses summarizing the discussions on the various topics of the *Vedānta-Sūtra*), *Nyāya-siddhāñjana* (a text-book of Viśiṣṭādvaita logic), *Seśvara-Mīmāṁsā* (a commentary on Jaimini's work, tracing the relationship between the Pūrva- and Uttara-Mīmāṁsās and refuting the common theory that the former is atheistic), and *Tattvamuktā-kalāpa* (an elaborate and critical discussion of the nature of the universe in the light of the Viśiṣṭādvaita philosophy, together with an explanatory gloss on it called *Sarvārthasiddhi*). Deśika's lectures on the ideals and daily practices of Śrī-Vaiṣṇavism were embodied in the allied treatises of *Saccaritra-rakṣā, Rahasya-rakṣā, Pañcarātra-rakṣā, Nikṣepa-rakṣā,* etc., which remain even today the most classical and authoritative works on the subject.

In explanation of the *mantras,* which together with the *bhāṣyas* and the *Prabandham* form the triple basis of Śrī-Vaiṣṇavism, he wrote, in the *maṇi-pravāla* style, the *Tattva-padavī, Rahasya-padavī, Tattva-navanīta, Rahasya-navanīta, Tattva-ratnāvalī, Paramapada-sopāna, Rahasyatraya-sāra,* and twenty-five other works, thereby clearly analysing, elaborating, and strengthening the views of Rāmānuja. For the sake of the lay people, he wrote the series known as *Mummaṇikkovai, Panduppā, Kalalpā, Ammāṇaippā Ūśalpā, Eśalpā, Aḍaikkalappattu,* etc. In his *Śatadūṣaṇī* he refutes Advaita from many standpoints. Vedānta Deśika arbitrated in a disputation between

[11] The Vedānta which harmonizes the teachings of both the traditional Vedānta and the teachings of the Āḻvārs.

Vidyāraṇya and Akṣobhya Tīrtha, the disciple of Madhvācārya, who became the pontiff of the Dvaitins, and pronounced a decision in favour of the latter. He also composed the Vedāntic drama *Saṅkalpa-sūryodaya* in criticism of Kṛṣṇa Miśra's *Prabodha-candrodaya.* It consists of ten acts, and is unrivalled in allegorical literature for dignity, grandeur, and intellectuality. Deśika further composed the epics of *Rāmābhyudaya, Haṁsa-sandeśa,* and *Yādavābhyudaya.* In the name of the second of these works there is a significance. The *haṁsa* (swan) was the form in which Viṣṇu taught the Pāñcarātra doctrine. The last named work is a fine and elegant poem which won the admiration of the renowned Appaya Dīkṣita in the sixteenth century, and made him compose a valuable commentary on it. The *Pādukāsahasra* is a poem of one thousand verses on the Lord's lotus feet, or rather His wooden sandals. Deśika also composed, in addition to his original *prabandhas* in Tamil, an elaborate commentary called the *Seventy-four Thousand,* which is lost. Amongst the miscellaneous works of the great saint, mention may be made of the *Subhāṣitanīvi* and other ethical treatises, written for a chief of the Andhra country, the *Śilpārtha-sāra,* and the *Vairāgya-pancaka* which he addressed to Vidyāraṇya in praise of resignation, when he was pressed to come under the sunshine of royal patronage. It is not surprising that Vedānta Deśika was called in his own age *kavitārkika-siṁha,* the lion of poets and philosophers, and *sarvatantra-svatantra,* the master of all science and knowledge. Many incidents can be cited to show the innate beauty of character of this ideal saint, scholar, and man. Not the least of his services was his saving the *Śrutaprakāśikā* from the chaos which followed the sack of Śrīraṅgaṁ in A.D. 1327. This is the reason why his name as Vedāntācārya is invoked by all Śrī-Vaiṣṇavas, without sectarian bias, in beginning the study of the *Śrībhāṣya.*

THE LATER HISTORY OF VAḌAGALAISM: THE AHOBILA MAṬHA

After the death of Vedānta Deśika the mantle of the Ācārya fell on the shoulders of his son, Varadācārya or Naināra; but after the latter there was no pontiff to hold the flock together. One of the leaders, Brahma-tantra-svatantra, withdrew to Tirupati and lost touch with the generality of people. Another, Prativādi-bhayaṅkara Aṇṇā, seems to have formally joined the Prabandhic party which made Śrīraṅgam its stronghold. The immediate result of this disorganization was that the Vaiṣṇavas of the Vaḍagalai school had to seek their own separate teachers. The division into local congregations and the inefficiency of householders as teachers soon gave rise to a movement for organized lead once again on the old model. This movement was headed by a celebrated saint named Ādi Vaṇa Śaṭhakopa Svāmin, the founder of the Ahobila Maṭha, whose original name was Śrīnivāsācārya. Śaṭhakopa tried to find a way to reconcile the two sects; but he failed in it, and became eventually the head of the largest number of Vaḍagalais alone. Śrīnivāsācārya embraced the life of a *jīyar* (monk), and then devoted his life to the popularization of the Deśika cult throughout South India by organizing its followers into a congregation under his own monastery in the name of Nṛsiṁha. Everywhere he acted as the servant of Śrī Lakṣmī-Nṛsiṁha, whose image he carried with him. A chain of local monasteries was established by him, and in these the works of Rāmānuja and Deśika came to be studied intensively. Śaṭhakopa, it is said, gave some privileges to the lower classes in the temples he built at Kadiri and elsewhere, and also instituted a class of missionaries called Ahobila Dāsaris for uplifting the hill-tribes. He arranged for their dances before the Ahobila deity and rewarded them with holy offerings.

A disciple of Śaṭhakopa, the celebrated Toḷappa (or Veṅkaṭanātha, to use his original name), composed a number of treatises on Vaiṣṇava observances, which gained him the title of *vaidika-sārvabhauma.* The most important of these were the *Smṛti-ratnākara* or *Sadācāra-saṅgraha,* a general treatise on the practical life of an orthodox Brāhmaṇa and a digest of all Smṛtis then known; the *Gṛhyaratna,* a work in twenty-one sections on the subject dealt with by Āpastamba in his *Gṛhya-Sūtra*; the *Khaṇḍabhūṣaṇa,* a commentary on the above; the *Pitṛmedhasāra* and the *Sudhīvilocana* on the funeral ceremonials to be observed by the Vaiṣṇavas; and the *Daśanirṇaya.*

There have been nearly forty apostolic successors after Ādi Vaṇa Śaṭhakopa to the present day. The *jīyar* undertakes tours throughout his jurisdiction, and ministers in all ways to the religious needs of his followers. The second *jīyar* has left as many as sixty works in every type of literature, and is therefore known as Abhinava (new) Vedānta Deśika. The sixth *jīyar,* Parāṅkuśa, was highly respected by the Vijayanagara emperor, and it was in his time that the Tātācāryas came to occupy a prominent place in the temples of the Vijayanagara empire. The next one wrote the dramatic work of *Vāsantikāpariṇaya.* In the time of the fourteenth apostle lived Kaḍāmbi Veṅkaṭādri whose *Viśvaguṇādarśa* is well known to Sanskrit scholars. The twenty-first *svāmin* has also left several works.

While a large number of Vaḍagaḷais are the followers of the Ahobila Maṭha, others have their own household *gurus.* They are technically called *svayamācāryas,* but they call themselves the followers of the *munitraya sampradāya.* This school is so called because it was promulgated by three *munis* or sages, Śrīnivāsa, Raṅganātha, and Vedānta Rāmānuja, who lived in the eighteenth century. The real founder of the cult was their preceptor, Gopāla Deśika, who contributed to the intensive study of Vedānta

Deśika's works by several well-known commentaries and original treatises. The *munitrayas* are decidedly more puritanic and exclusive. Their traditions have been carried on during the last hundred and fifty years by several lines of *sannyāsins*. It was a follower of theirs, Raṅga Rāmānuja, who has filled a gap in Śrī-Vaiṣṇava holy literature by composing commentaries on the Upaniṣads.

THE RISE AND PROGRESS OF THE PRABANDHIC SCHOOL

The Prabandhic school, or the Teṅgalai sect, traces the apostleship in succession to Rāmānuja in this way. They regard Embār, the cousin of Rāmānuja, as his immediate successor, though he died earlier. Embār's disciple was Parāśara Bhaṭṭa, the son of Kureśa, and the author of the *Sahasranāma-bhāṣya*. Bhaṭṭa's successor Nañjīyar, a convert from Advaita, rendered great service to the *Prabandham* by composing an extensive commentary called, from the number of its stanzas, the *Nine Thousand*. Nañjīyar's disciple Nampiḷḷai was a man of dynamic energy and founded a definite school out of his disciples. One of these, Periya Āccān Piḷḷai, put the Prabandhic lectures of his master into a single treatise called the *Twenty-four Thousand*. This eminent scholar also wrote the *Paranda-rahasyamālai, Māṇikkamālai, Navaratnamālai, Sakala-pramāṇa-tātparyam, Upakāra-ratnam, Gadyatraya-vyākhyānam, Caramarahasyam, Niyamanap-paḍi*, etc., which are favourite studies of the Teṅgalai sect even today. He also wrote several works in the *maṇipravāla* style to popularize the teachings of his school, besides minor treatises on the greatness of Yāmunācārya and the eight names of the Lord. Another disciple, Pinbaḷagiya Perumāḷ Jīyar, carried the doctrine of Ācārya-worship to its logical extreme and, besides composing the *Twelve Thousand* on the *Tiruvāimoḷi*, constructed, for the first time, a biography of the succession of the Ācāryas of the school. This treatise known as the *Guruparamparā* has served as the model for similar works.

On the death of Nampiḷḷai, the Prabandhic school was headed by Kṛṣṇapāda (or Vaḍakkutiruvīdi Piḷḷai). He composed a grand commentary called *Thirty-six Thousand* on the Tamil Veda. This work is generally known to the orthodox people under the name of *Īḍu*, literally 'the equal', for it was held by its talented author to be equal to the grandeur of Nammāḷvār's work, and, according to another view, to the highly learned commentary on the *Śrībhāṣya*, which his great contemporary Sudarśanācārya had composed on the basis of Varadācārya's lectures. The *Īḍu* was later on made a subject of compulsory study for the Prabandhic school by the great saint Varavara Muni (or Maṇavāḷa Mahāmuni).

Kṛṣṇapāda's son and successor, the famous Piḷḷai Lokācārya, the elder contemporary of Vedānta Deśika, is generally regarded as the founder of Teṅgalaism as a distinct sect. An intellectually brilliant man, he composed several treatises in order to uphold the teachings of his school. In his *Vacana-bhūṣaṇa* and in his brother's *Ācārya-hṛdaya* we have got, in a difficult and aphoristic style, the essentials of the doctrine of *prapatti* in all its bearings. For the benefit of women and the common people, Piḷḷai Lokācārya composed sixteen treatises on the *rahasyas* and the philosophy of Vaiṣṇavism, such as the *Nigamanappaḍi, Mumukṣuppaḍi, Tattvatraya, Arthapañcaka,* and *Navaratnamālai.* Most of these works are small in size; but they came to be regarded by the Prabandhic school as the only correct interpretation of the cults of Rāmānuja and the Āḷvārs.

His position as the leader of the Prabandhic school was taken by Śrīśaileśa. Making Āḷvārtirunagari (Tirunelveli District) the scene of his preaching activities, he carried on the traditions of the school throughout the period when worship at Śrīraṅgam was disorganized. His great work was to train the celebrated Aḷagiya-Maṇavāḷa or Varavara Muni, the acknowledged prophet of Teṅgalaism. Aḷagiya-Maṇavāḷa became a master of the Tamil Veda and other lore, and, on the death of his teacher, became the leader of the party. After a few years' stay at Āḷvārtirunagari, he removed to Śrīraṅgam and made it his headquarters, and this was facilitated by the resort of Nainār Ācārya, the son and successor of Vedānta Deśika, to Kāñcīpuram. Though he equipped himself in the lore of commentaries under teachers of the other party, he openly laid down the principle that the *Thirty-six Thousand* was the *Īḍu* or equal of the *Śrībhāṣya.* He introduced the *Īḍu* formally as a subject of holy studies. Varavara Muni wrote several treatises explaining the *rahasya* and writings of Piḷḷai Lokācārya. His works included a commentary on the *Tirumoḷi* of Periyāḷvār, a short poetic biography of the Āḷvārs and Ācāryas, a poem of one hundred stanzas summarizing the hymns of Nammāḷvār, two little pieces in praise of Rāmānuja, and a small treatise on methods of daily worship at home. Maṇavāḷa's works were limited in range and diction; but he gave a definite form to Teṅgalaism by his practical life and teachings. His magnetic personality elevated him, in the eyes of his followers, to the position of an *avatāra* of Rāmānuja. By the time of his death in 1443, he laid the fortunes of his school on a permanent basis by appointing authorized teachers in different parts of the Śrī-Vaiṣṇava world from Mysore to Kanyā-Kumārī. These leaders, or *aṣṭa diggajas* as they were called, made the Prabandhic creed, in a short time, highly prosperous throughout the land. Their descendants have carried on the torch of learning and teaching. The celebrated monasteries of Vanamāmalai, Tirupati, and other places have produced men of great attainments and character, who saw that the cult of Varavara Muni was popular in courts as well as in ordinary households. It is unnecessary to pursue the history of the Prabandhic school any further. It is enough to state that, in the centuries that followed the death of Varavara Muni, it captured the majority of the temples of the South, and its followers are perhaps greater in number than the Vaḍagalais, on account of its use of the vernaculars. The temple festivals in honour of the Prabandhic saints are therefore participated in with very great enthusiasm by the common people. A large number of non-Brāhmaṇa communities have professed Teṅgalaism and have lavished endowments on its temples and monasteries.

10

A SURVEY OF THE CAITANYA MOVEMENT

THE religious condition of Bengal was far from satisfactory at the time (A.D. 1485) when Śrī Caitanya (or Śrī Gaurāṅga) was born. Keeping awake at night, singing songs in praise of Maṅgala-Caṇḍī (a legendary goddess of secular good), and worship of Manasā (also a legendary goddess of serpents) were what the masses generally practised in the name of religion. Even the Brāhmaṇas cared very little for religious devotion; formally observant of religious prescriptions, they used to take greater delight in the pursuit of worldly affairs. No wonder therefore that they should be described in the Caitanya literature as *pāṣaṇḍins* (godless or unholy men), who cannot tolerate true devotion to God. The scholars explained religious texts, but got no inspiration therefrom. Scarcely could any vigorous sign of life be traced in the religious pursuits of even the ascetics who had renounced the world ostensibly for divine purposes. In short, the atmosphere of Navadvīpa, the birth-place of Śrī Caitanya and the greatest seat of learning in Bengal at the time, was, as it were, surcharged with worldliness.[1]

Only a few persons, however, followed the process of *jñāna*, a process practised by those who aim at merging themselves in Brahman. The Bhakti cult was at its lowest ebb; its followers could be counted on the fingers, viz. Śrīvāsa, Murāri Gupta, Śrīdhara, Advaitācārya, Haridāsa, and a few others.

ŚRĪ CAITANYA

Such was the state of religion at Navadvīpa till Śrī Caitanya passed the first twenty-two years of his life. Though his reputation as a scholar and a successful teacher had spread far and wide in the meantime, he too had not given any indication that he was above the ordinary level, before he went to Gayā to offer *piṇḍa* (cooked rice-ball) for the satisfaction of the departed soul of his father.

At Gayā he met a Vaiṣṇava savant, Īśvara Purī, who initiated him into the Bhakti cult. This initiation had a marvellous effect on him; it revealed a new phase of life, and brought home to his heart the most fascinating charms of Śrī Kṛṣṇa, so much so that he forgot, for the time being, his pupils, his country-wide reputation, his old and helpless mother, and his

[1] *Śrī Caitanya-Bhāgavata*, I. 2.

young and charming wife ; and it was with great difficulty that his companions induced him to come back.

He came back, but quite a new man—sometimes shedding tears in pensive mood, as if in deep pangs of separation from Kṛṣṇa, the Lord of his heart ; at other times, singing the names of God or talking about His charms, attributes, and pastimes (*līlās*) with tearful eyes. His mother and wife grew apprehensive. The few Vaiṣṇavas of Navadvīpa, however, were overjoyed at his change and began to encourage him in the new phase of life that had dawned upon him.

He realized God and His sweetness. He realized his own self and its relation to God. He realized that it was a misfortune to be deprived of the ecstatic joy of communion with God, and that it was a sheer waste of life to be engrossed in the pursuit of worldly enjoyment.

He abolished his *ṭol* (Sanskrit school), organized *saṅkīrtana*, i.e. singing the names of God in chorus, with the accompaniment of musical instruments, and plunged himself into it. He felt a strong desire for giving to all the heavenly bliss of loving God. Henceforth, it was the mission of his life to induce people to turn their mind to God.

This novel way, introduced by Śrī Caitanya, of uttering the names of Hari (God is so called as He fascinates one's mind by His sweet charms) caught the fancy of people, who shook off their indifference to spiritual matters and began to flock under his banner in hundreds and thousands. And before long, in almost every quarter of the town, people began to gather in small batches for *saṅkīrtana*.

Still there were some scoffers, some pundits and their pupils ; to win them over to the path of God, he left behind his old mother and beloved young wife, embraced asceticism at the age of twenty-four, and went to Purī to live there.

He spent the first six years of his asceticism in proselytizing tours through some parts of India. In the south he went up to Rāmeśvara ; in the west up to Vṛndāvana, through Kāśī and Prayāga (Allahabad) ; and in Bengal up to Rāmakeli near Gauḍa, the then capital of Bengal. The most important event that furthered the cause of his mission during his tours was the conversion to his creed of the two great Śāṅkara Vedāntins of the time, with their disciples. One of them was Prakāśānanda Sarasvatī, the most influential ascetic of the time in India, with ten thousand disciples in Banaras alone ; and the other, Vāsudeva Sārvabhauma, the greatest scholar of the time at Purī, at whose feet hundreds of ascetics used to take lessons in Śāṅkara Vedānta, though he was a householder himself. The two brothers Rūpa and Sanātana, high officials under Hussain Shāh, the then ruler of Bengal, renounced their homes at this time for living a religious life, met Śrī Caitanya at Prayāga and Kāśī respectively, and took lessons from him in the Bhakti cult. Under his directions, these two brothers and their nephew Jīva settled at Vṛndāvana in the district of Mathurā, and wrote a large number of books in Sanskrit on the tenets of his creed, on the philosophy and theology of his school, and on the *līlās* of Śrī Kṛṣṇa. Another Vaiṣṇava savant, Kṛṣṇadāsa Kavirāja, who flourished a few years later, wrote several books in Sanskrit, but only one in Bengali, viz. *Śrī Caitanya Caritāmṛta,* of undying popularity, which contains the essence of all the previous works of the school. These works constitute the foundation of the Śrī Caitanya school, and are still greatly revered by the Vaiṣṇava devotees and used as authoritative books of reference by the students of Vaiṣṇava literature.

During the last eighteen years of his life, Śrī Caitanya remained at Purī. He passed the last twelve years of his life almost incessantly in spiritual trances—sometimes in rapturous joy of union with Śrī Kṛṣṇa, but often in excruciating pangs of separation from Him—always identifying himself with Śrī Rādhā, the most beloved of Śrī Kṛṣṇa.

The secret of the success of Śrī Caitanya's mission seems to have been this, that he approached people through their heart. People generally have a hankering after beauty and sweetness, love and pleasure. Śrī Caitanya held before them the most relishable aspect of God.

THE ORIGIN OF BENGAL VAIṢṆAVISM

The Bengal Vaiṣṇavas are worshippers, mainly, of Rādhā-Kṛṣṇa. According to this school, the Rādhā-Kṛṣṇa cult seems to have originated with Mādhavendra Purī Gosvāmin, from whom his disciple Īśvara Purī Gosvāmin inherited it. He transmitted it to his disciple Śrī Caitanya, whose followers developed it into a full-grown system with a philosophy and theology of its own. Thus Mādhavendra is described as the seed, Īśvara Purī as the sprout, Śrī Caitanya as the trunk, Advaita and Nityānanda, his most prominent lieutenants, as the two main branches, and their followers as minor branches, etc. of the great tree of loving devotion.[2]

From the historical point of view, it appears that Caitanya took the detailed idea of the Rādhā-Kṛṣṇa cult, as current in the Bengal school, from Rāya Rāmānanda and transmitted it to Rūpa Gosvāmin at Prayāga and to Sanātana Gosvāmin at Kāśī. These two Gosvāmins and their nephew Jīva Gosvāmin elaborated this idea and placed it on a philosophical basis in their numerous works. These three lived at Vṛndāvana, reclaimed the village and many other places in the district connected with the sacred

[2] *Caitanya Caritāmṛta,* I. 9.

memory of Kṛṣṇa, transformed them into places of pilgrimage, and established a number of temples dedicated to Him. Since then, Vṛndāvana has become the great centre of Bengal Vaiṣṇavism in North India. Purī was the centre in the South, where Śrī Caitanya lived after embracing monasticism.

Śrī Caitanya, however, departed from this world in A.D. 1533. In or about A.D. 1591 both Sanātana and Rūpa, the main pillars of Bengal Vaiṣṇavism, departed, leaving behind them their nephew Jīva, Lokanātha, Gopāla Bhaṭṭa, Kṛṣṇadāsa Kavirāja, Raghunātha Dāsa, and others at Vṛndāvana and the whole Vaiṣṇava sect in India to mourn their loss. The surviving Vaiṣṇava teachers of Vṛndāvana kept up their tradition.

LITERATURE OF THE CAITANYA MOVEMENT

The only books besides the *Bhāgavata* that the Vaiṣṇavas seem to have valued during the lifetime of Śrī Caitanya were *Śrī-Kṛṣṇa-karṇāmṛta* and a part of *Brahma Saṁhitā,* both in Sanskrit.

Of the manuscripts sent from Vṛndāvana, with Śrīnivāsa and afterwards, the following deserve special mention as forming the foundation of the sect and helping the Vaiṣṇava exponents of the time in furthering the cause of the sect, viz. (1) *Bhaktirasāmṛta-sindhu* and (2) *Ujjvala-nīlamaṇi,* both by Rūpa Gosvāmin, with annotations by his nephew and disciple, Jīva Gosvāmin, (3) *Gopāla-campū* and (4) *Ṣaṭ-sandarbha,* both by Jīva Gosvāmin, (5) Annotations on the tenth *skandha* of the *Bhāgavata* by Sanātana Gosvāmin, and annotations on the whole of the same work by Jīva, (6) *Śrī Śrī Haribhakti-vilāsa* by Gopāla Bhaṭṭa Gosvāmin, with commentaries by Sanātana Gosvāmin, and (7) *Śrī Śrī Govinda-līlāmṛta* and (8) *Śrī Caitanya Caritāmṛta,* both by Kṛṣṇadāsa Kavirāja Gosvāmin. These books placed the Caitanya cult for the first time on a philosophical basis, with a systematized process of *sādhanā* and well-defined goal.

In the first quarter of the eighteenth century, another illustrious scholar and devotee, Baladeva Vidyābhūṣaṇa, wrote a large number of books, the most important of which is the *Govinda-bhāṣya,* a commentary on the *Brahma-Sūtra,* which placed the Caitanya cult on the basis of the Vedānta.

BRAHMAN OR ŚRĪ KṚṢṆA AND HIS LĪLĀS

According to the Śrī Caitanya school, Brahman is eternal, without a beginning and without an end. He is infinite and all-pervading. He possesses supernatural powers and attributes which also are infinite in number and infinite in magnitude. All these powers and attributes are eternally developed in Him in the highest degree, as implied by the word

'Brahman' which means absolute greatness. He is called Kṛṣṇa. Vāsudeva, Viṣṇu, Nārāyaṇa, Śiva, and other deities, whose names and attributes appear in the religious scriptures, are only so many manifestations of Kṛṣṇa. Every one of them is eternal, infinite, and all-pervading like Kṛṣṇa, but less perfect in respect of powers and attributes.[3] Hence they are said to be *svāṁśa,* or subjective of Kṛṣṇa.

However, Kṛṣṇa has a human form[4] which, though apparently limited like an ordinary human body, is really infinite and all-pervading;[5] it is perfect, eternal, non-material, perpetually in the prime of youth, and enchantingly beautiful.[6] He is Sat (absolute Existence), Cit (absolute Intelligence and Non-materiality), and Ānanda (absolute Bliss).[7] Of Sat, Cit, and Ānanda, the last seems to be the substance of Brahman or Kṛṣṇa, and the other two His attributes. Ānanda being the substance of Brahman, He comprises in Him all the possible varieties of bliss with all the shades of sweetness. He is therefore relishable; the Upaniṣads call Him Rasa, the most relishable thing (*Tai. U.,* II. 7). He relishes the sweetness of His *līlās* (blissful sports or pastimes) with His eternal associates, both as Śrī Kṛṣṇa and as His manifestations such as Nārāyaṇa and Viṣṇu, who also have their associates. He is called Kṛṣṇa (i.e. one who attracts), as He attracts every individual soul, human or otherwise—everyone of His manifestations—, by his charms.

Śrī Kṛṣṇa and His manifestations have all their heavens or abodes too, wherein they perform their *līlās.* The abode of Śrī Kṛṣṇa is called Vṛndāvana, Vraja, or Gokula; and that of Nārāyaṇa, Vaikuṇṭha. These abodes are all infinite, all-pervading, supra-material, and blissful.[8] His associates represent the different stages in the development of the love divine.

According to the degree of intensity of their love, His Vṛndāvana associates are divided into four classes. (1) *Dāsya-bhaktas* or loving servants, with the consciousness of the superiority of His position as their master. (2) *Sakhya-bhaktas* or comrades, who consider themselves equal to Him in every respect. (3) *Vātsalya-bhaktas* or parents. Being the ultimate Reality, Kṛṣṇa cannot have any parents; yet mother Yaśodā and father Nanda regard themselves as His parents, and they always consider Him absolutely dependent on their care and protection. (4) *Kāntā-bhaktas* or beloved youthful maids, known as *gopīs,* the chief of whom is Rādhā, others being her companions and attendants. In the *gopīs,* the divine love is developed in its

[3] *Laghubhāgavatāmṛtam,* I. 3. 86-90.
[4] *Viṣṇu Purāṇa,* IV. 11. 2; *Gopālatāpanī U.,* I. 10.
[5] *Caitanya Caritāmṛta,* I. 5. 15.
[6] *Ibid.,* II. 21. 83.
[7] *Ibid.,* II. 20. 132; *Bhakti-sandarbha,* V. 1.
[8] *Caitanya Caritāmṛta,* I. 5. 12-15.

fullest degree to the state technically known as *mahābhāva* or supreme love. Their loving services for Kṛṣṇa's pleasure know no restrictions whatsoever, as they are actuated by love alone which cares for nothing but His pleasure.

THE UNIQUE RELATION OF LOVE IN VṚNDĀVANA

It should be distinctly understood that in the union of the *gopīs* with Śrī Kṛṣṇa, there is no desire for (or action relating to) carnal pleasure in either.[9] Such a desire is actuated by Māyā which has no access to Vṛndāvana or any other abode of Kṛṣṇa (*Bhā.*, II. 5. 13). If it be permissible to study the infinite through the help of the finite, it may be inferred that the innate desire for love, which is found to lurk in all beings, may find its meaning in the eternal love between Śrī Kṛṣṇa and his associates. The relation between Him and the *gopīs* is the very ideal of a relation of unrestricted love between a lover and his beloved, which is contracted only for love and subsists on it alone.

However, the Vṛndāvana *līlā* of Śrī Kṛṣṇa has two aspects, manifest and unmanifest. Usually His *līlā* is not, and cannot be, visible to the worldly-minded, and as such it is known as unmanifest *līlā*. But if He pleases, He and His associates come down among those people as human beings and appear to pass through almost all the stages of human life. In such cases the *līlā* is said to be manifest.

In unmanifest *līlā,* the *gopīs* have an eternal belief that they are the wives of Śrī Kṛṣṇa. But in manifest *līlā,* they are believed to be the wives of other persons, though there have been neither any actual marriages nor any marital relations. In it neither Kṛṣṇa nor His associates have any consciousness of their real nature, or of their eternal relationships. The conventions of human society, however, force them to clandestine meeting.[10]

The conception of such an extra-conjugal relation in manifest *līlā* between Śrī Kṛnṣa and the *gopīs,* who are actually His own *śaktis* or energies, His own eternal consorts, seems to aim at representing the fact

[9] *Ujjvala-nīlamaṇi, Sambhoga,* 4.

[10] The *rāsalīlā* consists in dancing in a circle in a particular way, accompanied by singing. It is thus described in the *Bhāgavata*: On an autumnal full moon night, the *gopīs,* attracted by the flute of Kṛṣṇa, went out of their homes and met Him in the groves of Vṛndāvana. He first tried to send them back, but He failed. Then the *rāsa* began on the beach of the Yamunā, and when the *gopīs* were beside themselves with ecstasy, Kṛṣṇa suddenly disappeared from the scene. When they came to know of this, their sorrow knew no bounds. They searched for Him in every grove, bewailing all the while. They could not find Him out, though they marked His footprints here and there. In a dejected mood they all came back to the beach expecting His arrival, and began to mourn His disappearance loudly, when He suddenly reappeared in their midst. The dance was resumed, at the end of which they bathed in the Yamunā and played there for some time. Then they roamed about along the bank, enjoying the pleasant breeze, laden with the fragrance of flowers, after which they went home. This took place when Kṛṣṇa was in His eighth year.

that the love between Kṛṣṇa and His dearest associates is too powerful to brook any obstacle, however strong.

ŚRĪ RĀDHĀ AS THE EMBODIMENT OF MAHĀBHĀVA

Now to turn once more to *mahābhāva* (supreme love) and Śrī Rādhā. The highest aspect of *mahābhāva*, known as *mādana* or maddening delight, is possessed only by Rādhā and nobody else, not even by Kṛṣṇa Himself.[11] The unique feature of *mādana* relating to its subject Rādhā is that when it is awake, even a touch or a sight of Kṛṣṇa is attended with the thrilling delight of being simultaneously kissed, embraced, etc. by Him ; along with this delight of union is blended an acute feeling of separation from Kṛṣṇa, in spite of His proximity, which further intensifies her desire for union with Him.[12]

ŚRĪ GAURĀṄGA AS A COMBINATION OF RĀDHĀ AND KṚṢṆA

The delight Rādhā derives thereby is so immensely superior to what Kṛṣṇa enjoys as the object of her love and is so irresistibly tempting to Him that He cannot suppress His eagerness to taste His own charms and sweetness like Rādhā herself.[13] Accordingly, there is an aspect of Kṛṣṇa in which all the attributes of the Kṛṣṇa of Vṛndāvana as well as those of Rādhā coexist ;[14] so that, in this aspect, He, as the subject of *mādana*, relishes His own charms and sweetness ; and this is known as Śrī Gaurāṅga, who is thus Kṛṣṇa and Rādhā combined.

It is the custom with the Caitanya school to worship Gaurāṅga with his companions before worshipping Kṛṣṇa, and to think of the *līlās* of Gaurāṅga before thinking of those of Kṛṣṇa, because the devotees of this school believe that Gaurāṅga, as already said, is Kṛṣṇa Himself in a double aspect. He is thus an apt representation of self-delightedness (*ātmārāmatā*).

THE ŚAKTIS OF KṚṢṆA

Kṛṣṇa (or Brahman) has an infinite number of powers (*śaktis*). Of these, the three principal ones are: *svarūpa-śakti*, *māyā-śakti*, and *jīva-śakti*.

(i) The *līlās* of Kṛṣṇa are possible only through the agency of *svarūpa-śakti*. The realm of *cit* being its only sphere of action, it is also known as *cit-śakti* (sentient power). The aspect of *svarūpa-śakti* that helps the performance of His *līlās* is called *līlā-śakti*, and the aspect that makes Kṛṣṇa and His associates forget their true nature at manifest Vṛndāvana *līlā* is called *yoga-māyā*. His *svarūpa-śakti* has also three other aspects, viz.

[11] *Ujjvala-nīlamaṇi, Sthāyibhāva*, 155.
[12] *Ibid.*, 160.
[13] *Caitanya Caritāmṛta*, I. 4. 109, 115-16.
[14] *Ibid.*, II. 8. 239.

sandhinī, saṁvit, and *hlādinī,* corresponding respectively to *sat, cit,* and *ānanda,* the three aspects of Kṛṣṇa. A combination of these three is technically called *śuddha-sattva.*

(ii) *Māyā-śakti,* or that aspect of the power of Kṛṣṇa which is insentient, is constituted of three *guṇas—sattva, rajas,* and *tamas*—and has two aspects, *pradhāna* and *prakṛti.* As *pradhāna,* it is transformed through the creative energy of God into the inanimate material substance of the created universe and becomes its secondary material cause, and as *prakṛti,* it makes the worldly-minded souls assume material bodies in the created universe by suppressing the knowledge of their true nature and thus becomes the secondary efficient cause of the universe—the principal cause, both material and efficient, being God Himself.

(iii) All the Jīvas or living beings, human or otherwise, are in essence His *jīva-śakti,* i.e. *taṭastha-śakti* or marginal power. There are two classes of Jīvas, viz. those who are eternally free and those who are under the bondage of Māyā from eternity, though their bondage is terminable. This bondage is due to one's assumption of the *guṇas* (attributes) of Māyā, and one's liberation practically consists in its removal.

Śrī Kṛṣṇa with His *śaktis* manifests Himself as His *svāṁśa* (own part) and *vibhinnāṁśa* (separated part). Nārāyaṇa, Rāma, and the like are the *svāṁśa,* and the Jīvas are the *vibhinnāṁśa* of Kṛṣṇa.

THE GOAL OF HUMAN LIFE

We have many desires covering a wide range of objects, positive or negative. Throughout our life we search for love and pleasure or happiness, and however much we may attain them, our hankering after them never decreases. This desire seems to be linked with our inner self, the true essence of individual beings; its insatiable nature implies that it aims not at the fleeting love and pleasures of this world, but at eternal love and eternal bliss, unlimited in extent, intensity, and variety. But unlimited results cannot be expected of limited things. The only thing that can satisfy the cravings of the soul in its true essence is Śrī Kṛṣṇa, the ultimate Reality, who is bliss and love and infinite in all His aspects.

The innate and lifelong desire for love and bliss also implies that even on the realization of Śrī Kṛṣṇa, i.e. on attaining salvation too, the individual soul will retain its separate entity, without which love and the enjoyment of bliss are impossible, and the desire for them meaningless. In his separate entity, an individual being will love God and serve Him in His *līlās* on the lines of the associates. And it is on these grounds that Śrī Caitanya held that an individual being in his true essence is an eternal attendant or servant of Kṛṣṇa.

SĀDHANĀ

But circumstanced as we are, eagerness for sense pleasures has made us lose sight of God and our inner self. Identifying ourselves with the body, we are giving all our attention to things external. To retard the outgoing urge and to give it an inward direction requires some spiritual practices known as *sādhanā*.

The principal object of *sādhanā* is to remove our externalism, which is due to our forgetfulness of God, the only source of the bliss we hanker after. For this, we must get rid of our forgetfulness, which may be done only by remembering Him always. Hence to remember God always is the essence of *sādhanā*.

The goal of a Vaiṣṇava of the Caitanya school is to serve Kṛṣṇa at Vṛndāvana on attaining salvation, in collaboration with any of the four groups of His associates, maintaining his own separate entity, and to please Him through such loving services. If he desires to serve Him in collaboration with the *gopīs*, he will be there as a young *gopī* and an attendant of Rādhā ; and his work there will be to help in the love-pastimes of Kṛṣṇa with Rādhā and her confidants. If a Vaiṣṇava likes to serve Kṛṣṇa along with His *sakhās* (comrades), he will assume the spiritual form of a *sakhā*, and so on. But how to attain such a form suitable for one's desired services? By thought, meditation, or remembrance of Kṛṣṇa in His *līlā* with the associates of one's desired group, and by keeping oneself, in imagination, engaged in suitable services in their midst.

The Caitanya school enjoins that if a person wishes to serve Kṛṣṇa at Vṛndāvana with *madhura rati*, he should always think that he is a young *gopī*, beautifully dressed, attending on Rādhā in her love-pastimes with Kṛṣṇa, being principally subordinate to Rūpamañjarī, the chief of Rādhā's attendants known as *mañjarīs*. Similar is the mode of meditation for devotees with other *ratis*.[15]

But it is not an easy task, especially for a beginner, to concentrate one's mind on such ethereal objects. To help it, some external practices also are prescribed. Of these some are preliminary, some precautionary, and others directly promotive of devotion to, and love for, Kṛṣṇa. Under the last category, the following nine principal items have been enumerated in the *Bhāgavata*: (1) Hearing the names of God chanted or sung by others, or songs in praise of, or the narration of, Kṛṣṇa's charms, pastimes, attributes, etc. (2) Chanting or singing His names, narrating or singing His charms, etc. (3) Remembering or thinking of His names, charms, etc. (4) Showing respect to Kṛṣṇa by visiting the sacred places associated with His pastimes,

[15] *Ibid.*, II. 22. 91.

looking at His images or pictures depicting His pastimes, serving and keep ing company with His devotees, showing respect to things connected with His memory, etc. (5) Worship of Kṛṣṇa in images by offering flowers, sandal paste, food, etc. (6) Bowing down before Kṛṣṇa or His images at the place of worship. (7) Serving Kṛṣṇa in the attitude of a devoted servant. (8) Comradeship—to think that one is His loving and intimate friend and He too is such, and to behave towards Him accordingly, generally through His images. (9) Resignation to Kṛṣṇa—devoting oneself entirely to His services.

Śrī Caitanya attaches greater importance to the following five items: (1) To keep company with the devotees of Kṛṣṇa. In a devotee's company one may always hear talks about Kṛṣṇa and His *līlās* ; he creates around him an inspiring atmosphere of devotion that sets one to religious practices. (2) To chant the name of Kṛṣṇa. (3) To hear the narration of Kṛṣṇa's pastimes etc. (4) To reside at Vṛndāvana, the place of Kṛṣṇa's manifest *līlās,* mentally, if not physically. (5) To worship His image, firmly believing that it is He Himself. While observing any of these practices, one should always think that one is going through it in the presence of Kṛṣṇa and for His pleasure only. Mere mechanical processes cannot produce any salutary effect on the mind—can scarcely even purify it, not to speak of giving it a turn towards God ; even a single item properly practised may produce the desired effect, love and devotion to Kṛnṣa.[16] He attaches the greatest importance to the chanting of the Lord's name, which alone may take one to the highest goal,[17] and it is perhaps for this reason that the scriptures of the Bhakti cult admit no difference between Him and His name.[18]

Humility, tolerance, and respectfulness to others are the things necessary for the efficacy of chanting Hari's name. In order that he may attain love for Kṛṣṇa, a devotee must feel that he is humbler than even a piece of straw ; he must be as tolerant as a tree that gives shelter, fruits, etc. even to those who cut it off ; and, without expecting any return, he must respect every person, believing that Kṛṣṇa lives in him.[19]

He must not speak ill of any person, must not hanker after gain, respect, rank, or esteem, and must refrain from self-aggrandizement, self-indulgence, and jealousy. He must try to live a life of restraint. Honesty and simplicity, sincerity and straightforwardness, contentment and reliance on God should be the mottos of his life. He should always try to increase his devotion and resign himself to the will of God.

An orthodox Vaiṣṇava is a strict vegetarian. He does not take anything

[16] *Ibid.*, II. 22. 76, 77. *Bhaktirasāmṛta-sindhu*, I. 2. 128.
[17] *Caitanya Caritāmṛta*, III. 4. 65-66. [18] *Bhaktirasāmṛta-sindhu*, I. 2. 108.
[19] *Caitanya Caritāmṛta*, III. 20. 17-20.

without offering it to the Lord, and he will not offer Him anything cooked by a person who is not an initiated Vaiṣṇava. Suffering, austerity, or abstinence for its own sake is not recognized by this school,[20] as it hardens the heart, instead of softening it, and makes it unfit for loving devotion.

STEPS TO SUCCESS IN SĀDHANĀ

The successive steps to the success of spiritual practice are enumerated below:[21] (1) *Śraddhā* or faith in God and the scriptures, which is evidently the basis of *sādhanā.* (2) Keeping company with holy men or devotees, preferably those who have realized. (3) Religious practices which gradually purify one's mind. (4) Purging away of all sins and evil desires from the mind. (5) Steadiness in religious practices and having firm faith in their efficacy. (6) Great liking for religious practices. (7) Attachment to religious practices. At this last stage one can scarcely dissociate oneself from these practices, and, finally, one's heart becomes fit for the advent of *śuddha-sattva* (divine attributes), with a preponderance of *hlādinī-śakti* (bliss-giving power). This *śuddha-sattva,* received in a completely purified heart, is first transformed into what is known as *rati* or *premāṅkura,* i.e. the first stage of divine love.

The goodness arising out of *sattva-guṇa* concerns this world only, for it is a quality of Māyā; when the mind will be completely free from the influence of the *guṇas* of Māyā, *śuddha-sattva* will be transformed into *rati.*

A person having *rati* has nothing to gain or lose in this world; his mind is content entirely with matters concerning Kṛṣṇa. Its outward indications are as follows:[22] (1) Forbearance or perfect indifference to even irreparable loss or unexpected gain in worldly affairs. (2) The utilization of every second of time in religious practices and considering every moment spent otherwise as wasted. (3) Freedom from worldly attachment. (4) Want of desire for public esteem, and feeling oneself as the worst of all, though perhaps the best. (5) Firm belief that Kṛṣṇa will be merciful. (6) Ardent longing for union with God. (7) Great taste for always chanting the name of Hari. (8) Hankering for narrating the attributes of God. (9) Great liking for His abode or temples, or for the places of His manifest *līlā.*

Rati, however, ripens into what is technically called *preman,* which completely softens the heart and is marked with an attitude of 'mineness', i.e. with a feeling that Kṛṣṇa belongs to the devotee, and to no one else. Chanting the favourite names of the beloved Lord, with a completely

[20] *Ibid.,* II. 22. 82; *Bhaktirasāmṛta-sindhu,* I. 2. 121, 122.
[21] *Caitanya Caritāmṛta,* II. 23. 5-9; *Bhaktirasāmṛta-sindhu,* I. 4. 11.
[22] *Caitanya Caritāmṛta,* II. 23. 11-19; *Bhaktirasāmṛta-sindhu,* I. 3. 11.

softened heart, one laughs, cries, sings, and dances, just like a mad man, quite indifferent to the presence of other persons (*Bhā.*, XI. 2. 40). One possessing it will, after death, be born in a place where the manifest *līlā* of Kṛṣṇa is going on.[23]

There *preman* ripens into *sneha*. At the advent of *sneha*, so intense becomes the idea of 'mineness' that the devotee is not satisfied with mere sight, voice, etc. of Kṛṣṇa.[24] *Sneha* ripens into *māna* in which, by the peculiar nature of intense love, the subject, on account of a real or fancied grievance, conceals his or her own feelings and shows jealous anger or petulance to the object, Kṛṣṇa. *Māna* deepens into *praṇaya* which inspires confidence in, and dispels all sense of fear or reverence in respect of, the object of love, and thus produces a sense of equality of the subject with the object.[25] *Praṇaya* ripens into *rāga*, which indicates excessive eagerness for union with Kṛṣṇa. *Rāga* develops into *anurāga* in which the object of love, even though realized and relished always, appears to be clothed in fresh charms and attractiveness every moment.[26] This indicates insatiable eagerness for relishing the charms of Kṛṣṇa. *Anurāga* culminates in *mahābhāva* which has already been described.

The love of the servants (*dāsya-rati*) develops up to *rāga* ; that of the friends (*sakhya-rati*) upto *anurāga* ; that of the parents (*vātsalya-rati*) up to the last limit of *anurāga* ; and the love of the *gopīs* (*madhura-rati*) up to *mahābhāva*.[27]

The minimum stage in the attachment to God that may enable one to realize Him is called *śānta-rati* which develops up to *preman* only, and that too with an idea of Kṛṣṇa as Godhead, with His infinite superiority in powers and perfection. This inspires awe and thus bars the way to every thought of equality with, and the loving service of, Kṛṣṇa.[28] A *śānta-bhakta* therefore has no place in Vṛndāvana where Kṛṣṇa is looked upon not as God, but as the dearest and nearest friend and relative. The abode of a devotee of this class is Vaikuṇṭha where Kṛṣṇa is Nārāyaṇa.

BHAKTI-RASA

There are five principal *rasas*, viz. *śānta*, *dāsya*, *sakhya*, *vātsalya*, and *madhura*, corresponding to the five *ratis*. Etymologically *rasa* means anything that may be tasted or enjoyed. But technically it means a thing the taste of which is attended with delicious astonishment on account of its heightened sweetness. This realization practically consists in the relish of

[23] The Vaiṣṇavas believe that there are an infinite number of *Brahmāṇḍas* (worlds), and that Śrī Kṛṣṇa manifests His Vṛndāvana *līlā* in each of them successively (*Caitanya Caritāmṛta*, II. 20. 216, 316).

[24] *Ujjvala-nīlamaṇi*, *Sthāyibhāva*, 57.

[25] *Ibid.*, 78.

[26] *Ibid.*, 102.

[27] *Caitanya Caritāmṛta*, II. 23. 34 f.

[28] *Ibid.*, II. 19. 177.

bhakti or love, when it comes in contact with its object, Kṛṣṇa, and is associated with the emotions and sentiments consequent on such contact. At this stage the love is said to have been transformed into *bhakti-rasa*. As Rasika, Śrī Kṛṣṇa relishes *bhakti-rasa* when manifested through the loving services of His associates in *līlās*.

According to the *Bhāgavata*, Śrī Kṛṣṇa incarnated Himself for the destruction of the *asuras* or demons who proved themselves too heavy a burden for the Earth. But Kṛṣṇadāsa Kavirāja says that this was only a secondary reason ; the true reason was His own strong desire for relishing the sweetness of His associates' love for Him, and making them relish His own sweetness—which, for peculiar reasons, could not be tasted in all its aspects in the unmanifest *līlā*—, as well as for incidentally disclosing to the people of this world the best way to the realization of His sweetness and beauty.

MĀDHURYA AND AIŚVARYA

There is no doubt that the pre-Caitanya literature of India abounds in statements regarding the mercy of God, which may be said to be the connecting link between God and His creatures ; but Kṛṣṇadāsa Kavirāja is probably the first to announce, in his *Śrī Caitanya Caritāmṛta*, that His mercy goes so far as to make Him eager for the salvation of the distressed, and that such an eagerness is part of His nature.[29] Again, though the religious scriptures from the Vedas to the Purāṇas are illuminated with passages about His *aiśvarya* (almightiness) and *mādhurya* (sweetness), yet references to His *aiśvarya* are so frequent and so impressive as to make us believe that it is the essence of Godhead. The result is that we can scarcely think of God without a fear of being punished by Him for our misdeeds ; even those who have committed no misdeeds can scarcely dare to entertain any idea of loving Him and looking upon Him as their dearest and nearest friend ; so overawed are they at the thought of His almightiness. But Kavirāja Gosvāmin comes to our rescue by boldly announcing, in the words of Śrī Caitanya—based on the Śrutis that call Brahmaṇ Ānanda (the Bliss), Rasa (the fascinating Relish), Śiva (the Good), and Sundara (the Beautiful)—, that it is *mādhurya* and not *aiśvarya* that constitutes the essence of Godhead.[30] This disclosure, together with that about His mercy, leads us to a belief that God is here not simply to punish us, but, like an affectionate mother, to reclaim us and to guide us to the eternal bliss of His *līlās*.

According to the degree of predominance, the Caitanya school distinguishes three main aspects of Kṛṣṇa and three corresponding abodes too, viz. Vṛndāvana, Dvārakā, and Vaikuṇṭha. At Vṛndāvana, the *mādhurya*

[29] *Ibid.*, III. 2. 5.

[30] *Ibid.*, II. 21. 92.

is overwhelmingly predominant, completely subjugating and drowning the *aiśvarya*. At Dvārakā, the *mādhurya* is not so predominant as at Vṛndāvana. Here Kṛṣṇa and His associates are sometimes conscious of His Godhead; hence, though there are *dāsya, sakhya, vātsalya,* and *madhura ratis* at Dvārakā too, they are not so intense and so relishable as at Vṛndāvana. At Vaikuṇṭha, however, *aiśvarya* predominates overwhelmingly. Here Kṛṣṇa is known as Nārāyaṇa and overawes everyone by His *aiśvarya.*

PHASES OF SALVATION

The Gosvāmins make us acquainted also with an attractive phase of salvation corresponding to their conception of the *mādhurya* of Vṛndāvana. Hitherto, people heard of only five aspects of salvation, viz. *sārṣṭi* (having *aiśvaryas* similar to those of Nārāyaṇa), *sārūpya* (having a figure similar to His), *sālokya* (having residence in the same abode), *sāmīpya* (being allowed to live near Nārāyaṇa), and *sāyujya* (being merged in His body or in unqualified Brahman). Of these, the devotees may accept any of the first four, provided it affords an opportunity for serving God; but the last, *sāyujya,* they never like, as it obliterates their separate existence. The Vaiṣṇavas of the Bengal school, however, are not satisfied with any of these aspects of salvation. They are worshippers of the *mādhurya* of Vṛndāvana, and aim at attaining the loving and disinterested service of Śrī Kṛṣṇa. This aspect of salvation they call *prāpti.*

THE SAHAJIYĀ SECT

The Sahajiyā sect that came into prominence, perhaps after the time of Viśvanātha Cakravartin, who flourished during the last quarter of the seventeenth century, seems to be an open defiance of the Gosvāmins. In theology, the Sahajiyās do not differ much from the Gosvāmins; but in religious practices they discard their teachings which, they say, relate to *vidhi-mārga* (the path of injunctions and prohibitions, or the path of duties), as opposed to *rāga-mārga* (the path of spontaneous love), which they profess to follow. Their ways are rather diametrically opposite to those of the followers of the Gosvāmins. A Sahajiyā requires a woman other than his married wife as a companion of his *sādhanā,* looks upon his companion as Rādhā and himself as Kṛṣṇa, and imitates the love-pastimes of Kṛṣṇa with the *gopīs.* He worships Rādhā-Kṛṣṇa not in images, nor in his heart, but in his *guru* and the *guru's* female companion. On the other hand, to approach a person other than one's wife or husband, as the case may be, to look upon himself or herself or any mortal as Kṛṣṇa or Rādhā, and to imitate His *līlās* are strictly forbidden by the scriptures of the orthodox sect.

A Sahajiyā is not a vegetarian, nor does he observe the austerities prescribed by the Gosvāmins. In short, he does not bother himself much with any course of self-discipline. Naturally therefore the Sahajiyā cult became more popular than the Gosvāmin cult, and, in course of time, practically swallowed a considerable portion of the Caitanya sect, and gave rise to the Vairāgi-Vairāgiṇī sect, which has thrown the Caitanya sect into some disrepute and probably brought it down to its lowest ebb.

Since the dawn of the present century, however, the Caitanya sect may justly be said to be on a fair way to regaining its original glory and to have captured the imagination of the seriously minded people by its message of universal love, its *rasa* cult, and the most attractive aspect of the ultimate Reality.

Like many other sects, the Vaiṣṇavas of the Caitanya school believe in the conception of a personal God ; they also believe in the conception of *avatāras* (incarnations) and of the manifest *līlā*, which is only an amplification of the conception of *avatāra*.

If He is all-merciful and all-good, there is no bar to His coming down to us as *avatāra* for our good. If He be all-loving and all-lovable, there must be some to enjoy His sweetness, beauty, and love, and some to be loved and enjoyed by Him. He may therefore have His associates with whom He may perform His *līlās*.

11

ŚAṄKARA DEVA AND THE VAIṢṆAVA MOVEMENT IN ASSAM

FROM the beginning of the fourth century A.D. to the middle of the twelfth century, the ancient empire of Kāmarūpa, which comprised the present region of Assam and a portion of eastern Bengal, was ruled over by kings of the Varman, the Śālastambha, and the Bhauma Pāla dynasties. These kings were all Hindus, and the gods and goddesses of the Hindu pantheon were installed in gorgeously built temples and worshipped according to Śāstric rites. But, in about A.D. 1126, Tiṅgya Deva, the last ruler of the Bhauma Pāla dynasty, was killed in open battle by Vaidya Deva, the general of Kumāra Pāla, the king of Bengal. After this event, Buddhist Tāntrics, Sahajiyās, and Nāthas, who were representatives of powerful sects in Bengal, gradually penetrated into western Assam; and Mahāyāna Buddhists of northern India, being harassed by the Turks, found safe shelter in upper Assam, where tribal chiefs received them cordially. Assam became a stronghold of the Tāntric cult including its debased forms, and Kāmākhyā near Gauhati formed its chief centre.

ŚAṄKARA DEVA AND HIS FOREFATHERS

About A.D. 1326 Laṇḍa Deva, a Kāyastha chief of Kanauj, migrated with his kith and kin, and settled in the present Rangpur District in a village which was named Kanaujpur. Laṇḍa Deva was a Śākta and a worshipper of Durgā and Śiva. His son Caṇḍīvara alias Devīdāsa settled at Leṅgā-Māguri to the east of the present Gauhati Subdivision. Caṇḍīvara, being harassed by the Bhutias at Leṅgā-Māguri, settled in a village called Āli-Pukhuri in the present Nowgong District. His great-grandson was Kusumbara, of whom was born Śaṅkara Deva by his first wife, Satyasandhā.

None of the authentic biographies of Śaṅkara Deva mention the year of his birth, and even with regard to the month and the day they are not unanimous. Śaṅkara Deva died in A.D. 1568. Tradition ascribes to him a long life, but whether his date of birth can be pushed back to A.D. 1463 or 1461 or even 1449 is doubtful; contemporary historical events suggest A.D. 1486 as probably nearer the mark.

Śaṅkara Deva lost his mother on the fifteenth day after his birth, and his father in his seventh year. He was brought up by his grandparents, and well educated in a Sanskrit school. He developed considerable aesthetic abilities also. He became a poet, a musician, a singer, and a painter of repute.

At the age of nineteen, Śaṅkara Deva shifted with his family to Bardowa, a village nine miles to the north of the present Nowgong town ; at the age of twenty-one he married, and at twenty-five was favoured with a daughter. His wife, however, died immediately afterwards.

HIS PILGRIMAGE AND INFLUENCE OF VAIṢṆAVISM

Śaṅkara Deva went out on a pilgrimage at the age of thirty-three, and travelled for twelve full years. During his itinerancy, he went, amongst other places, to Gayā, Kāśī, Purī, Vṛndāvana, Mathurā, Kurukṣetra, Upa-Badarikāśrama, Varāhakṣetra, Puṣkara, Dvārakā, and Rāmeśvara. He noticed that Vaiṣṇavism was the ruling religion that had achieved, with a new outlook and movement, the unification of the people on a common basis through the medium of congregational prayer, accompanied with music. Vṛndāvana was agog with the songs of Vidyāpati and lyrics of Jayadeva. The Rāmāyat sect of the Vaiṣṇavas was powerfully organized in northern India. While at Purī, on the occasion of the *rathayātrā* festival, Śaṅkara Deva met Śrī Caitanya, who was in a state of divine ecstasy. Both gazed at each other, but there was no discourse between them. Śaṅkara Deva, however, knew all about the praise that all Orissa had been showering upon Caitanya.

Thus impressed and imbued with new ideas, Śaṅkara Deva returned to his native home.

Much against his wish, Śaṅkara Deva married again due to the pressure of his relatives. He became perturbed and restive in his mind. Luckily at this time, Jagadīśa Miśra, a learned pundit and travelling mendicant, came to Bardowa on his preaching tour, to explain the holy *Bhāgavata Purāṇa,* and stayed with Śaṅkara Deva.

Śaṅkara Deva regarded the pundit's stay with him as a divine grace showered on him. He cast off the ancestral Śākta moorings and started translating into Kāmarūpī the Tenth Book of the *Bhāgavata* on the *līlā* of Śrī Kṛṣṇa in simple verses adapted to music and singing them with his friends. This was *Kīrtana,* and its sweet melody, pathos, and love began to attract people to him.

But the political troubles in the east became menacing. His life became unsafe. Śaṅkara Deva migrated with his kith and kin to the north bank of the Brahmaputra in the Āhom territory, and settled first in the Darrang District, then in the North Lakhimpur Subdivision, and lastly in the Majuli area at Belguri on the bank of the Dhoa-lor or Dhoa-suti stream.

NEW ORIENTATION OF HIS CULT

The religion of the common people had been Hinduism, influenced greatly by Buddhist Tāntric observances and ceremonies. To adapt himself to the local environment, Śaṅkara Deva carved a wooden image of Śrī Kṛṣṇa, named it Madana Gopāla, and installed it in his prayer house with elaborate ceremonies. To fall in line with the prevailing Buddhist influence, he designated his form of initiation as *śaraṇa,* and divided it into three categories, as *nāma-śaraṇa, guru-śaraṇa,* and *bhakta-śaraṇa,* corresponding to the Buddhist *dharma-śaraṇa, Buddha-śaraṇa,* and *saṅgha-śaraṇa.* The congregational prayer house was called *nāma-ghar.* This worked well, and people began to gather round Śaṅkara Deva. Gayāpāṇi alias Rāmadāsa, a Kāyastha, became the interpreter of his mission ; and Śatānanda Kāyastha, a staunch Śākta, became a faithful Vaiṣṇava. Mādhava Deva, a young trader, the brother-in-law of Rāmadāsa, dedicated himself to the person of Śaṅkara Deva and to the propagation of his mission.

All went well for some time, but an unexpected calamity marred the whole atmosphere. For alleged neglect of duty in the elephant-catching arranged in the open forest by the Āhom king, the people who had gone to help in the catching were ordered to be arrested. Śaṅkara Deva escaped, but Mādhava Deva and Hari (Śaṅkara's son-in-law) were taken prisoners along with others. Mādhava Deva was, however, set free, being considered a mendicant ; but Hari and others were beheaded. Śaṅkara Deva sailed in boats with his family and followers down the Brahmaputra till he reached Barpeta and settled there.

Śaṅkara Deva continued his work of translating the *Bhāgavata,* composing songs, and writing dramas and short epics. The people, attracted by the simple composition, sweet melody, and easily intelligible high philosophic ideas, joined his mission in large numbers. Mohammedans, Garos, Bhutias, Mikirs, and the so-called low-caste Hindus also found equal position with others in his prayer house ; and some of them were appointed high priests of his mission.

In this area, Śaṅkara Deva adopted a simpler method. Instead of installing an image of Viṣṇu or Kṛṣṇa, which, as a matter of ancient tradition, required the services of the Brāhmaṇas, he introduced the system of placing a holy book on a wooden pedestal in the prayer house, or in the place where the prayer or *kīrtana* was held. For services before this emblem, any devoted man of any caste was eligible. This was a bold deviation from the time-honoured custom prevalent in the country, and the conservative Brāhmaṇas, who were already hard hit in their profession, in a body complained against him to the Koc king, Naranārāyaṇa, describing him as an iconoclast. At last a meeting of Śaṅkara Deva with the complainant Brāhmaṇas was arranged in the royal court. In the polemical discussion that ensued, Śaṅkara Deva conducted himself so well that Naranārāyaṇa was fully convinced of the extraordinarily high qualities of head and heart of the preacher of the new mission. He dismissed the Brāhmaṇas' complaint as futile, and offered Śaṅkara Deva a position of honour in his court. Śaṅkara Deva opened his permanent second headquarters at Cooch-Behar.

Śaṅkara Deva went out on a pilgrimage for the second time. On returning home, he went to Cooch-Behar again, where he wrote a drama on Sītā's marriage with Rāma, and himself took part in the play that was arranged in the palace. While still engaged in translating the holy *Bhāgavata*, he breathed his last in A.D. 1568.

WORKS OF ŚAṄKARA DEVA

Unlike many of the Vaiṣṇava preachers of other parts of India, Śaṅkara Deva did not write any commentary on the *Brahma-Sūtra* or on any classical book, nor did he write any book exclusively to propound his theory or principle. His views are expressed in his original compositions in the form of songs, sonnets, dramas, and also in translations of some of the classical books.

Śaṅkara Deva translated a chapter of the *Mārkaṇḍeya Purāṇa*, bearing on the life-story of Hariścandra. He translated in simple verse the whole of the First, Second, Eleventh, and Twelfth Books, and portions of the Third, Sixth, Eighth, and Tenth Books, of the *Bhāgavata* into Kāmarūpī, the spoken dialect of the local people. He composed *Bhakti-pradīpa*, bearing on the Bhakti cult as propounded in the *Garuḍa Purāṇa*, also in verse, in the Kāmarūpī language. He wrote *Bhakti-ratnākara* in Sanskrit, collecting the theory of Bhakti cult from different Śāstras. He was greatly influenced by *Bhakti-ratnāvalī* of Viṣṇu Purī of the Madhvācārya sect, and had it translated in verse by his disciple Mādhava Deva into the Kāmarūpī language. He composed *Kīrtana* in simple verse suited to music, dealing with the whole life-story of Śrī Kṛṣṇa as depicted in the *Bhāgavata*. His *Guṇamālā* is a synopsis of the whole of the *Bhāgavata*, so far as the life-story of Śrī Kṛṣṇa is concerned, in a very concise and simple form in verse.

Śaṅkara Deva wrote six one-act dramas known as *Aṅkiā-nāṭ*. Five are based on the life-story of Śrī Kṛṣṇa, bearing on the Bhakti cult, and the sixth is on the marriage of Sītā with Rāma. Apart from these, he composed several songs of deep philosophical import, and some others on the life-stories of Śrī Kṛṣṇa and Rāmacandra. These songs are highly classical so far as musical technique is concerned, and they are known as the *Bar-gīts* (great songs).

Under the instruction of his master, Mādhava Deva composed *Nāma-ghoṣā,* a book on the main tenets of the Bhakti cult, in simple Kāmarūpī verse. It contains the essence of the cult as inculcated in various Śāstras, and in many cases the originals have been translated verbatim. The book contains one thousand stanzas or psalms, and is commonly known as *Hājāri-ghoṣā* (*hājār,* thousand).

HIS PHILOSOPHY

Throughout all his writings on *bhakti,* Śaṅkara Deva is mainly influenced by the *Bhāgavata* and the *Bhagavad-Gītā.* The Bhakti cult consists in the cultivation of an intimate relationship between the worshipper and the eternal, omniscient, all-powerful God, who is a Person. It is opposed to Karma-mārga, the path of prescribed duty or sacrificial works, and to Jñāna-mārga, the path of knowledge (reasoning on impersonal Reality). It is a kind of revolt against the monism of the Advaita Vedānta and the agnosticism of the Sāṁkhya.

Śaṅkara Deva in his *Bhakti-ratnākara* admits that Jīva (the individual soul) and *jagat* (the world) are by no means different from Brahman, the supreme Divinity ; it is only *ajñāna* or nescience that gives rise to a feeling of difference. In his *Kīrtana* also he reiterates the same view ; who, he asks, can ascribe *dvaita* or duality to God when, on transcending the Māyā or nescience, it becomes clear that the same Nirañjana, or the supreme Divinity, exists in every item of His creation? The apparent difference, he asserts, is only in *nāma* (name) and *rūpa* (form), as between gold and the various ornaments made out of it. But at the same time, he asks, do I require the cultivation of such knowledge? And he replies that it is not necessary for one who seeks the pleasure of implicit devotion to the one God who pervades the whole universe.

Śaṅkara Deva explains the position more elaborately in his *Bar-gīts* (4, 7, Nath's Edition). He teaches that it is only the action of Māyā that deflects us from the realization that the whole universe, comprising the moving and the non-moving, the static and the dynamic, . . . is pervaded by one God, in the form of Īśvara, and all these are His parts. 'We are, Oh Lord!', says he, 'Thy parts (*teri aṁśā*).'

This clearly conforms to the teaching of the *Gītā* that the Jīvas are His parts (XV. 7). When Māyā is transcended, the cosmos does not disappear totally as a hallucination, but only changes its meaning and significance.

Śaṅkara Deva begins his *Kīrtana* with obeisance to Sanātana Brahman, who assumes a form (*rūpī*) and is the cause (*kāraṇa*) of all the incarnations (*avatāra*). He is Vāsudeva, the supreme Lord, Parameśvara, who dwells in the heart of every creature, and is the origin of the self and the cosmos. He is Puruṣa.

The question of creation leads to the popular Sāṁkhya philosophy of Puruṣa and Prakṛti, the dual cause of creation; but Śaṅkara Deva, true to the *Gītā*, solves it by saying that quite apart from Puruṣa and Prakṛti, and yet the cause and upholder of the two, is Parameśvara, Nārāyaṇa (*Nāma-ghoṣā*, 173). 'In this world the "inhabiter" or the "indweller" (Puruṣa) has two forms: the *kṣara* or the perishable individual soul, and the *akṣara* or the immutable Brahman. The Supreme (Uttama-puruṣa), who is otherwise called Paramātman, the Immutable, and the Lord, upholds the three worlds, having interpenetrated them. As I am beyond the *kṣara* and the *akṣara*, I am known, in the universe as well as in the Vedas, as the Puruṣottama' (*B.G.*, XV. 16-18). Śaṅkara Deva's Kṛṣṇa is this supreme Brahman, Paramātman, who is beyond the individuals and the immutable Brahman, and is, at the same time, the upholding and the interpenetrating spirit of them both.

Mādhava Deva explains this intricate discourse in his *Nāma-ghoṣā* (171) in the simple manner that '*kṣara* refers to this visible body or form (*deha*), and *akṣara* refers to Brahman (the unmanifest out of which all manifestations come), but greater and better (*uttama*) than the two is Hari who is known as Puruṣottama'.

Śaṅkara Deva accepts this Puruṣottama, Parameśvara, and Nārāyaṇa as identical with Vāsudeva Śrī Kṛṣṇa, the son of Nanda and Yaśodā, who is all-perfect and is Bhagavat (supreme Divinity) Himself. The *Bhāgavata* prescribes the method of worshipping this supreme Lord in the *kaliyuga* with *kīrtana*, by identifying Him with Śrī Kṛṣṇa and Rāmacandra, and addressing Him as Mahāpuruṣa (XI. 5. 32-34). Thus the Puruṣottama of the *Gītā* is the Mahāpuruṣa of the *Bhāgavata*. Śaṅkara Deva's religion is known as the Mahāpuruṣiā Dharma; and, as the main method of worship is *kīrtana* or singing the praise of the name of the Lord, it is also called the Nāma Dharma. The *mantra* for initiation is '*Hare Kṛṣṇa, Hare Rāma*'.

It is very probable that the term 'Mahāpuruṣiā' has been derived from the *Bhāgavata* passage referred to above; but it is popularly believed in Assam by a certain section of people that the term 'Mahāpuruṣiā', as applied to the cult of Śaṅkara Deva, has been derived from the sobriquet 'Mahāpuruṣa' (great soul), attributed to both Śaṅkara Deva and Mādhava Deva by their followers (who latterly began to treat them, in fact, as *avatāras* of Viṣṇu). This explanation is further supported by the fact that other cults of Assam are similarly called after the founders' names or sobriquets. For example, the cult of Dāmodara Deva is known as Dāmodariā, of Hari

Deva as Hari Deviā, and of Puruṣottama Thākura (Śaṅkara Deva's grandson) as Ṭhākuriā.

The *mantra*, or the *nāma* as it is called, is only a means to an end, for it is stated in the *Nāma-ghoṣā* (4) that this *nāma* is to be recited only to purify the mind, to help one to realize the supreme Deity, who is otherwise indescribable (*avyakta*) and formless (*mūrti-śūnya*).

As the *Gītā* strictly enjoins giving up all other practices and ceremonies, and instructs only implicit resignation to one God (*māmekaṁ śaraṇaṁ vraja*), Śaṅkara Deva also lays great stress on *eka-śaraṇa*. His religion is therefore known as Eka-śaraṇiā Dharma (religion of refuge in one Lord).

In support of his theory, Śaṅkara Deva quotes an expression from the *Bhāgavata*: 'As the trunk, branches, and twigs of a tree are nourished by pouring water only at the root of the tree, as the organs of the body are nourished by supplying food to the vital principle (taking food in the stomach) only, so all gods are propitiated only by the worship of Acyuta Kṛṣṇa' (IV. 31: 14).

Vaiṣṇavism enjoins that the devotee should establish a loving relationship with the object of his worship. This relationship can be of five types, viz. *śānta* (of a serene devotee), *dāsya* (of a servant), *sakhya* (of a friend), *vātsalya* (of a parent), and *madhura* (of a consort). Of all these, Śaṅkara Deva laid great stress on the *dāsya-bhāva*, teaching implicit sense of service to God, like a faithful servant, without hoping or asking for any reward in return. Mādhava Deva begins his *Nāma-ghoṣā* with obeisance to the devotee who is indifferent even to salvation. The *madhura-bhāva* with the Rādhā cult, which gathered a great impetus in Bengal thanks to the preaching of Śrī Caitanya, had no attraction for Śaṅkara Deva.

SPREADING OF THE MOVEMENT

After the death of Śaṅkara Deva, his Brāhmaṇa disciple, Dāmodara Deva, remodelled his institution, at Pātbāusi near Barpeta, with the help of his own Brāhmaṇa disciple, Vaikuṇṭhanātha Bhaṭṭa Deva, introducing many Brāhmaṇical rites and ceremonies. In the place of a holy book as the object of worship or obeisance, he installed the image of Viṣṇu with other paraphernalia of worship. Mādhava Deva established another institution, with a gorgeously constructed *kīrtana-ghar* (house for performing *kīrtana*), at Barpeta, where he strictly followed the system of his master.

Vaṁśī Gopāla Deva, a young Brāhmaṇa of North Lakhimpur in Upper Assam, who had once met Śaṅkara Deva at Belguri during his childhood, came to Barpeta in search of a master. He was initiated by Dāmodara Deva and trained up by Mādhava Deva ; and then he was sent to Upper

Assam to preach Vaiṣṇavism. In the face of great odds, and of opposition from the Buddhist Tāntric *gurus* of Upper Assam, Vaṁśī Gopāla Deva succeeded in establishing a large Vaiṣṇava institution first at Kalābāri and then at Kuruā Bānhi, where he installed a stone image of Govinda, brought from Orissa. Many Vaiṣṇava emissaries gradually went forth to the Upper Assam side where Vaṁśī Gopāla Deva had already prepared the way, and they started separate institutions in different parts of the country. Within a short time, the common people became attracted to the new cult. Officials of the Āhom king also became attracted to the religion and started patronizing the institution. After the death of Vaṁśī Gopāla Deva, the Āhom king Jayadhvaja Siṁha was initiated into Vaiṣṇavism in A.D. 1648 under the teaching of Nirañjana Bāpu, a learned pundit of the Kuruā Bānhi *satra* (centre of religious instruction). The king made extensive grants to his preceptor, and a separate *satra* was established for him at Auniāti. Other *satras* also received royal favours from time to time, and ultimately Vaiṣṇavism became the royal faith in the country.

FORMATION OF DIFFERENT GROUPS

Śaṅkara Deva's system was very simple and could be easily followed by everybody. Later on, when modifications were gradually introduced in rites and ceremonies, different schools of thought came into being. Śaṅkara Deva's school was known as Puruṣa Saṁhati (*saṁhati*, association, group).

Mādhava Deva, though a strict follower of his master, was very puritanical in his ideas and equally rigorous in practices. Over a slight difference in practices, there was started a new school known as Nikā Saṁhati (*nikā*, puritan). The Brāhmaṇical school, started by Dāmodara Deva (who was latterly regarded as an incarnation of Kṛṣṇa, and sometimes of Rāma, in his school), and expanded by Vaṁśī Gopāla Deva, Nirañjana Bāpu, and Vanamālī Deva, was known as Brahma Saṁhati or Bāmuniā school. Caste was more recognized in this school than in that of Mādhava Deva. Gopāla Deva of Bhowanipur, near Barpeta, a devout follower of Mādhava Deva, at last disagreed with his master on ideological principles and started at Kāljār, near Barpeta, a different school known as Kāla Saṁhati.

Aniruddha Deva, a Kāyastha youth of North Lakhimpur, was the disciple of Gopāla Deva ; he also parted with his master, as he developed a strong inclination towards the adoption of occult practices as a part of Vaiṣṇava rites. He started his own organization at Dinjoy (Dinjan) and initiated a large number of Morāns (a tribal race) and the people of the fisherman class. His school is known as Moā Moriā (or Māriā) or Māyā Morā (literally, the killer of nescience) Sampradāya (sect). Śaṅkara Deva's grandson, Puruṣottama Ṭhākura, introduced certain modifications in the rites and observances, and seceded from the followers of Mādhava Deva. His followers are known as Ṭhākuriās.

By the adoption of some of the practices of the Buddhist Tāntric observances in the Vaiṣṇava rites and ceremonies, various minor groups, though in principle they owed allegiance to one or other of the six groups, emerged as separate entities. They are Rāti-khovā (eaters at night), Pūrṇa-bhogiā (enjoyers to the full), Tāmul-no-khovā (non-eaters of betel-nut), etc.

Followers of all these groups or schools, however, accept the same philosophical principle of Śaṅkara Deva ; and the *Kīrtana* of Śaṅkara Deva and the *Nāma-ghoṣā* of Mādhava Deva are their main scriptures. The main difference consists in the observance of rites and ceremonies.

THE SATRA INSTITUTION

The building in which the holy book is placed on the pedestal, or the image is installed, for the purpose of worship is known as the *maṇi-kūṭa*, and the big house in front of it, where *kīrtana* is held, or drama is performed, is known as the *kīrtana-ghar* ; and the combination of the two is known by the general term *nāma-ghar*. In a permanent institution, a large number of devotees stay within or near the precincts of the *nāma-ghar* in separate huts, constructed in lanes on all the four sides. These lanes are known as the *hāṭis*. The whole institution is known by the term *satra* (literally, the refuge of devotees).

Śaṅkara Deva lived a family life with wife and children. In spite of his protests, his disciple Mādhava Deva led a celibate life, though he never encouraged others to follow this course. 'A celibate devotee', said Mādhava Deva, 'is like a soldier within a well-guarded fort, whereas a devotee leading a family life is like a soldier fighting in the open field.' Dāmodara Deva was a widower ; Vaṁśī Gopāla Deva remained a bachelor, but he handed over the charge of his Kuruā Bānhi *satra* to a married man in preference to a celibate. But later it became the custom in several of the Bāmuniā *satras* and some of the Mahāpuruṣiā *satras* that the chief *guru* of the *satra* or the *satrādhikāra*, as he is called, should be a celibate. The devotees living within the *satra* precincts also lead a celibate life, and they are called Udāsīn Bhakats or Kevaliās (or Keuliās). In some of the *satras*, these Bhakats are maintained by the *satras*, and in others they live independently on their own earnings. The Udāsīn Bhakats work as officers of the *satra* estate and perform other daily routine duties. They spend their whole time in cultural activities, including the pursuit of arts and crafts.

The system of succession is different in different *satras*:

(i) *Putrānukrama* or the hereditary claim of the eldest son.

(ii) *Jyeṣṭhānukrama* or the eldest male member of the family succeeding.

(iii) *Yogyānukrama* or the ablest and the most qualified male member succeeding.

The first two systems are followed in the *satras* where the *satrādhikāras* lead a married life, and the last is followed in the *satras* of celibate heads. In the last, the *satrādhikāra* selects any suitable young man, not necessarily from amongst his disciples or the Bhakats who had been living in the *satra*, but from any family he likes, and trains him under his care, giving him all the requisite education. This selection has to be approved by the elder Bhakats. At the demise of the *satrādhikāra*, this young man, known as *dekā-adhikāra* (*dekā*, young), is installed as chief with the approval of the Bhakats of the *satra*.

(iv) The Barpeta *satra* has recently adopted the method of votes for the selection of the *satrādhikāra*.

The position of women is not clearly defined. Śaṅkara Deva is said to have denied the privilege of formal initiation to women ; they were to be benefited only by hearing religious discourses and singing *kīrtana* songs. But Kanakalatā, the wife of Śaṅkara Deva's grandson Caturbhuja Ṭhākura, assumed the charge of the *satra* after her husband's death and initiated disciples. She was a highly educated lady, and was respected by all for her great proficiency in philosophical discourses. Padmapriyā, the daughter of Gopāla Deva, composed several songs of high philosophical value. The present position is that even the formal *śaraṇa* is denied to a woman. She can neither become a Keuliā or a Udāsīn Bhakat, nor become a *satrādhikāra* by the *jyeṣṭhānukrama* or *yogyānukrama*. Women are not allowed entrance into the *kīrtana-ghar* of any of the prominent *satras* of either the Udāsīn or the non-Udāsīn sects at the time of any ceremony ; they sit outside on the verandahs or in the yard and listen to what goes on inside. In ordinary village *nāma-ghars*, not belonging to any *satra*, women, however, are allowed to go inside while there are no male members, and perform *kīrtana* and sing prayerful songs by themselves.

12

EVOLUTION OF THE TANTRAS

PLACE OF THE TANTRAS IN INDIAN SPIRITUAL LORE

THE Tantras have remained a neglected branch of study, in spite of the fact that they include a very considerable number of texts, most of them still in manuscript, varying in date from the fifth century to the nineteenth. Some relegate them to the class of black magic, whereas others consider them full of obscenities and unfit for the study of a man of good taste. These contentions, however, do not represent the whole truth. It cannot be denied that in some texts there is what may be called black magic, and there are also a few texts full of obscenities; but these do not form the main bulk of the Tāntric literature. They also do not represent the Tāntric *sādhanā* at its best. The Tāntric literature essentially represents a very important part of Indian spiritual lore, so far as its practical aspect is concerned. A failure to appreciate its real significance renders our understanding of the ancient spiritual knowledge shallow and superficial.

The word *'tantra'* is derived in the *Kāśikāvṛtti* from the root *'tan'*, to spread, but some later writers have professed to derive it from the root *'tatri'* or *'tantri'*, meaning origination or knowledge. In a special sense it means 'the scripture by which knowledge is spread' (*tanyate vistāryate jñānam anena iti tantram*). But any branch of knowledge is not called Tantra now, though at one time this term seems to have borne diverse meanings. It is a cultural discipline in a wide sense, and, when used in a more limited sense, it is spiritual knowledge of a technical nature. When Śaṅkara calls Sāṁkhya a Tantra (as *Sāṁkhya-kārikā* itself does in *kārikā,* 70), he looks upon it as a technical branch of spiritual knowledge. In one standard Tāntric text, the *Kāmikāgama,* Tantra is defined as a class of texts 'which promulgates profound matters concerning *tattva* and *mantra*' (*tanoti vipulānarthān tattvamantra-samanvitān*).[1] The two words *tattva* and *mantra* have a technical sense: *tattva* means the science of the cosmic principles, while *mantra* means the science of the mystic sound. Tantra therefore concerns the application of those sciences with a view to the attainment of spiritual ascendancy.

The Tantra is regarded as a Śruti or Āgama, 'revelation', as opposed to a Smṛti or Nigama, 'tradition'. It is thus classed with the Vedas. It is

[1] Woodroffe, *Shakti and Shakta* (Second Ed.), pp. 18-19. I have differed from Woodroffe's interpretation of the verses.

usually defined as '*Śrutiśākhāviśeṣaḥ*', a particular branch of the Vedas. This claim is strongly maintained not only by the later Tantras, but also by the earlier ones. One of the oldest Tantras available in manuscript, *Niśvāsa-tattva Saṁhitā,* holds that the Tantra is the culmination of the esoteric science of the Vedānta and the Sāṁkhya. In fact, it combines with the ultimate reality of Brahman or Śiva the validity of the world as an expression of His Śakti. The consort of Śiva therefore is first taught the Vedānta, then the twenty-five Sāṁkhyas,[2] and after that the *Śiva Tantra. Piṅgalā-mata,* which is an equally old Tāntric text, says, 'The Tantra, first communicated by Śiva, came down through tradition. It is Āgama with the characteristics of *chandas* (Vedas)'.[3]

The later Tantras reiterate the same claim. The *Kularṇava Tantra* says (II. 140-41) that *kuladharma* is based on, and inspired by, the truth of the Vedas. In the same place, Śiva cites passages from the Śruti in support of His doctrine. *Prapañcasāra* and other Tantras cite *vaidika mahāvākyas* and *mantras* ; and as *mantras* are a part of the Vedas, the *Meru Tantra* says that the Tantra is a part of the Vedas.[4] The *Niruttara Tantra* calls the Tantra the fifth Veda, and *kulācāra* the fifth *āśrama,*[5] which follows all others. The *Matsyasūkta-mahātantra* says that the disciple must be pure of soul and a knower of the Vedas (XIII). He who is devoid of *vaidika-kriyā* is disqualified.[6] The *Gandharva Tantra* says that the Tāntric *sādhaka* must be a believer in the Vedas, ever attached to Brahman, living in Brahman, and taking shelter with Brahman.[7] The *Kulārṇava Tantra* says that there is no knowledge higher than that of the Vedas and no doctrine equal to the *kaula* (III. 113).[8]

This claim of the Tantras to be regarded as the Śruti, however preposterous it might appear, is perfectly logical. Our knowledge of the Śiva Tantras being limited, our judgement in this matter has often been guided by the later heterodox Tantras. In fact, a good deal of the heterodox element has been introduced into the Tantras from time to time, on account of the general community of purpose in the esoteric practices of all grades.

THE VEDAS AND THE TANTRAS

The essence of the Vedic religion is ritualistic. Whatever might have been the nature of the Vedic sacrifice in the early Vedic period, it developed into a highly mystical ritual in course of time. It assumed the character of a sort of magical operation, independent of the gods, efficacious by its

[2] The Sāṁkhya categories.
[3] P. C. Bagchi, *Studies in the Tantras*, p. 106.
[4] *Prāṇatoṣiṇī*, 70.
[5] *Ibid.*
[6] *Mahārudra Yāmala*, I. 15 ; II. 2. *Prāṇatoṣiṇī*, 108.
[7] *Prāṇatoṣiṇī*, 6.
[8] Woodroffe, *op. cit.*, p. 45.

own force, and capable of producing good as well as bad effects. The chief aim was ascendancy over the forces of nature, in order to guide them in the interests of the sacrificer. Correct recitation of the *mantras* was the most important means of producing the desired effect. The *mantras* invoke the gods, the embodiments of natural forces, to the ificial altar. The gods are imagined to come down to the altar by the force of the ritual and the recitation of the *mantras*. The ritual centres round the idea of bringing about the union of two principles, one male and the other female. The accomplishment of this union leads to the success of the ritual.[9]

The religious attitude in the Tantras is fundamentally the same as in the Vedic ritual. The Tāntric *sādhanā* also concerns the attainment of ascendancy over the forces of nature by the exoteric ritual of the Vedic type, as well as by the esoteric ritual involving the yogic practice, its aim being the union of the two principles, the Śiva and the Śakti. The Tantras not only use new symbols, and simplify the Vedic rituals to some extent, but introduce a greater complexity in the esoteric portion. The beginning of this esoteric turn of the ritual may also be found in the Brāhmaṇas and the Upaniṣads. To give one example, it is said in the *Śatapatha Brāhmaṇa*: 'The head is the chariot of Soma; the mouth, the *āhavanīya* fire; the crown of the head, the sacrificial post; the belly, the cart-shed; the feet, the two fires; the sacrificial implements, corresponding to limbs...' (I. 3. 2-3).[10] A similar esotericism is to be found in the opening verses of the *Bṛhadāraṇyaka Upaniṣad,* which repeat a *Śatapatha Brāhmaṇa* account. The Tantras place greater emphasis on this esoteric sacrifice.

From this point of view, it may be argued that the Tantras emerged out of the Vedic religion and were then developed as a distinct type of esoteric knowledge. The Vedic ritual continued to be practised even after the Tantra had been well established. It is practised to some extent even now, but it has survived more in form than in spirit. The more vigorous aspect of the Vedic religion was continued and developed in the Tantras.

The Vedic sacrifice was a technical operation capable of producing effects desired by the sacrificer. It could thus be used for both good and bad purposes, for both higher and lower ends. Thus one of its aspects could easily be developed into what is usually called black magic, and in the Vedic texts we already have traces of this. The *Sāmavidhāna Brāhmaṇa* and the *Adbhutādhyāya Brāhmaṇa,* which is a part of the *Ṣaḍviṁśa Brāhmaṇa,* are full of references to such practices. The *Atharva-Veda* is

[9] For this interpretation of the Vedic ritual, see Bergaigne, *La Religion Vedique.*
[10] Lévi, *La Doctrine du sacrifice dans les Brāhmaṇas,* p. 78.

commonly believed to be a code of such magical rites. In one place, the *Ṣaḍviṁśa Brāhmaṇa* says: 'If one wants to assure victory to one's army, one should go away from the camp, cut some herbs at both ends, and throw them in the direction of the enemy uttering the *mantra* "*Prāsahe kas tvā paśyati* (Prāsahā, who sees you?)...". Thus the army of the enemy disappears and is dissipated...'[11] This will serve to explain the occurrence of the magic practices frequently referred to in the Tāntric literature of later times. It is not impossible that in many cases they are derived from the religious practices of a primitive society assimilated into the Vedic society; but, logically speaking, they also represent a phase of the Vedic ritual, not practised for higher spiritual purposes, but for certain lower ends in which a group of people had always some interest.

ORIGIN AND DEVELOPMENT OF THE TANTRAS

The origin and development of the Tantras as a special class of literature, and Tantra as a special mode of *sādhanā,* were intimately connected with the rise of Śaivism and the Pāñcarātra, the Sāṁkhya-Yoga supplying them with a philosophical background. Both Śaivism, under the name of Pāśupata, and Pāñcarātra, which seems to be very old, are referred to for the first time in the Nārāyaṇīya section of the *Mahābhārata.*

The early canonical literature of the Pāñcarātra is lost. But whatever literature of this sect as well as of other contemporary ones has come down to us shows that it has always been regarded as a Tantra. One such text, the *Sātvata Saṁhitā,* studied by R. G. Bhandarkar, describes the system as *rahasyāmnāya*—'a secret method of *sādhanā*'. It further says: 'This Śāstra, along with *rahasya,* is fruitful to those who have gone through *yoga* with its eight parts, and whose soul is devoted to mental sacrifice. The *yogins,* who are Brāhmaṇas guided by the Vedas and who have given up the mixed worship, are competent for the worship of the single one, dwelling in the heart. The three orders, the Kṣatriya and others, and those who are *prapanna* or have resorted to self-surrender, are competent for the worship of the four *vyūhas* accompanied by *mantras.*'[12] The text also gives a mystic arrangement of letters and formulae and the meditations on them. It deals with the mystic modes of worship by means of *mantras* in various dispositions.

The Pāñcarātra, however, remained restrained in its development. It is Śaivism which supplied a more propitious ground for the development of the Tantras. The *Mahābhārata* says that the Pāśupata doctrines were first preached by Śiva-Śrīkaṇṭha. It has been suggested that this Śrīkaṇṭha

[11] Lévi, *op. cit.,* p. 130.
[12] R. G. Bhandarkar, *Vaiṣṇavism, Śaivism, and Minor Religious Systems,* p. 40.

was probably a human teacher. *Piṅgalāmata,* a Tāntric work preserved in Nepal in an old manuscript of A.D. 1174, speaks of Bhagavat Śrīkaṇṭhanātha as its author. Lakulīśa was probably his disciple. Lakulīśa and his disciples are mentioned in an inscription of Candragupta II of the Gupta dynasty. According to this inscription, Lakulīśa had four disciples: Kuśika, Garga, Mitra, and Kauruṣya. Variants of the last three names are found in the Purāṇas. They lived about ten generations before the time of Candragupta II. This would place Lakulīśa almost in the time of Patañjali who first speaks of Śiva-bhāgavatas in his *Mahābhāṣya.* Patañjali is mentioned in the inscriptions of Java along with the four disciples of Lakulīśa as 'five *devatās*'.[13]

Thus, Pāśupata was the oldest form of Śaivism prevalent in North India. This is what may be called Āgamānta Śaivism. The school possessed a considerable literature called Āgamas, a number of which are preserved in old manuscripts in the North Indian script of the eighth and ninth centuries. The literature must have come into existence at least in the Gupta period. The Āgamas were eighteen in number according to one tradition and twenty-eight according to another.[14]

THE ŚIVA TANTRAS

The eighteen Āgamas, which are also called Śiva Tantras, are the following: (1) *Vijaya,* (2) *Niśvāsa,* (3) *Svāyambhuva,* (4) *Vātula,* (5) *Vīrabhadra,* (6) *Raurava,* (7) *Mākuṭa,* (8) *Vīreśa,* (9) *Candrahāsa,* (10) *Jñāna,* (11) *Mukhabimba,* (12) *Prodgīta,* (13) *Lalita,* (14) *Siddha,* (15) *Santāna,* (16) *Sarvodgīta,* (17) *Kiraṇa,* and (18) *Pārameśvara.* Of these *Niśvāsa, Kiraṇa,* and *Pārameśvara* are still preserved in Nepal in manuscripts of the eighth and ninth centuries. There is also a copy of *Pārameśvara* in the Cambridge collection, the manuscript being dated A.D. 859. *Niśvāsa Tantra* itself mentions these eighteen Āgamas as constituting the Śiva-śāstra transmitted by Rudra. It also mentions ten more Śiva Tantras transmitted by Sadāśiva:[15] (1) *Kāmika,* (2) *Yogada* (?), (3) *Divya,* (4) *Karaṇa* (*Kiraṇa*?), (5) *Ajita,* (6) *Dīpta,* (7) *Sūkṣma,* (8) *Sahasra,* (9) *Asta* (?), (10) *Aṁśubheda.* The two lists might be two different ways of computing the same literature. Variations in the titles of some of these Āgamas are known, and some names are obviously corrupt.

The Āgamas or Śiva Tantras have ritualistic character.[16] They deal with the main elements of the Vedic ritual, such as *homa, abhiṣeka, dīkṣā,*

[13] P. C. Bagchi, 'Religion of Bengal' in *History of Bengal,* I. pp. 405-6.
[14] P. C. Bagchi, *Studies in the Tantras,* pp. 4, 95.
[15] The difference in number and names of books is due to different sources.
[16] P. C. Bagchi, *Studies in the Tantras,* p. 94.

yajñaprakaraṇa, and, in addition to these, the method of erecting a Śiva temple (instead of a sacrificial altar), the mode of worshipping Śiva, *yoga*, *mukti* (salvation), etc. These texts therefore hold that for *sādhanā* there is need of exoteric ritual of the Vedic type, as well as of esoteric practice like *yoga*. The purpose is the attainment of salvation (*mukti*). It maintains that the highest caste, the Brāhmaṇa, is alone eligible for the *sādhanā*. The god invoked is not any of the old gods of the Vedic pantheon, but Śiva. The texts further profess that they represent the culmination of a spiritual knowledge, the beginning of which is found in the Vedānta and the Sāṁkhya. Although a chronological scheme is not possible in the present state of our knowledge of the Tantras, it appears to me that the Tantras of the Āgama type were prevalent during the first five or six centuries of the Christian era, from the Kuṣāṇa period down to the end of the Gupta period.

THE YĀMALAS

The next phase in the development of the Tantras is probably represented by a class of literature called Yāmala.[17] The principal Yāmalas are eight in number: *Rudra, Kanda* (*Skanda*), *Brahma, Viṣṇu, Yama, Vāyu, Kubera,* and *Indra.* One of the principal Yāmala texts, the *Brahma Yāmala,* is preserved in Nepal in a manuscript of A.D. 1052. It gives a list of the eight Yāmalas and says that they were communicated by the eight Bhairavas—Svacchanda, Krodha, Unmatta, Ugra, Kapālin, Jhaṅkāra, Śekhara, and Vijaya. Whereas the original Śiva Tantras or Āgamas represent the Rudra or Sadāśiva tradition, the Yāmalas represent the Bhairava tradition. Bhairavas seem to have been human teachers who had attained complete spiritual emancipation and had almost become Śiva. Two other old texts belong to the Yāmala group. They are *Piṅgalāmata* and *Jayadratha Yāmala. Piṅgalāmata* explicitly states that *Jayadratha Yāmala,* an extensive work of about 24,000 *ślokas* (*caturviṁśati-sāhasra*), is a supplement to *Brahma Yāmala,* and that *Piṅgalāmata* itself is a supplement to *Jayadratha.* The *Jayadratha Yāmala* also exists in a manuscript of about the same period; but as the special mode of *sādhanā* called *śiraścheda* which it advocates was introduced in the Hindu colony of Kambuja (Cambodia) in the early ninth century, it must have existed in India much earlier. The Yāmala literature with its supplements may therefore be reasonably supposed to have come into existence at least between the sixth and ninth centuries. Additions might have been made to the supplementary texts down to the tenth century. The existence of the principal

[17] *Ibid.*, p. 6.

Yāmalas, excepting the *Brahma Yāmala,* is not known to us. There are fragments of the *Rudra Yāmala* published in Bengal, but it is difficult to say how far they have preserved the old text.

The Yāmalas indicate a great development in the Tāntric *sādhanā,* not only by trying to define for the first time the various Tāntric traditions, but also by introducing a great variety of cults of new gods and goddesses. They give us for the first time a well-developed Tāntric pantheon and apparently affiliate in many cases a large number of local cults, and open up the field of Tāntric *sādhanā* to people of other castes. While preserving the orthodox tradition of the earlier period, they thus assume a heterodox character.

In regard to the transmission of the Tāntric lore, the *Brahma Yāmala* gives an interesting account,[18] according to which Īśvara communicated the secret knowledge to Śrīkaṇṭha ; the latter incarnated himself in a village called Kaṇavīra near Prayāga. He communicated the Tantras in one hundred and twenty-five thousand *anuṣṭubh ślokas* to various disciples. One of the recipients was a Bhairava. That Bhairava communicated it to various other Bhairavas, to wit, Krodha, Kapāla, Padma. Padma Bhairava transmitted it to Devadatta, a Brāhmaṇa of the Oḍra country. Devadatta had fourteen disciples: Rakta Bhairava, Jvālā, Hela, Vāma, Vijaya of Madhyadeśa, Sīśaṁsa of Saurāṣṭra, Gajakarṇa, Caṇḍa of Sindhu, and others. It is interesting to note that many of them are said to have been Atharvan Brāhmaṇas, while Sīśaṁsa is said to have been a Śūdra.

THREE CURRENTS OF TĀNTRIC TRADITIONS

The same text further determines the Tāntric traditions according to *srotas* (current). There are three currents according to it, *dakṣiṇa, vāma,* and *madhyama.* They represent the three *śaktis* of Śiva and are characterized respectively by the predominance of each of the three *guṇas, sattva, rajas,* and *tamas.* The Tantras of each class follow a particular line of *sādhanā.* Hence there are three classes of Tantras: *dakṣiṇa,* which is characterized by *sattva,* is pure (*śuddha*) ; *vāma,* which is characterized by *rajas,* is mixed (*vimiśra*) ; and *madhyama,* characterized by *tamas,* is impure (*aśuddha*). The *dakṣiṇa* current issued from the right mouth of Śiva. It is classified according to the four *pīṭhas* (modes of *sādhanā*) and also according to the degree of purity. The four *pīṭhas* are *vidyā, mantra, mudrā,* and *maṇḍala.* The eight Bhairavas, givers of the eight Yāmalas mentioned before, belong to the *vidyāpīṭha.* The Tantras belonging to this *pīṭha* are *Yoginījāla, Yoginīhṛdaya, Mantramālinī, Aghoreśī,*

[18] *Ibid.,* pp. 102-5.

Aghoreśvarī, Krīḍāghoreśvarī, Lākinīkalpa, Mārīcī, Mahāmārīcī, and *Ugra-vidyāgaṇa.* The text also mentions the Bhairavas belonging to the *mantrapīṭha* and says that the two *pīṭhas, mantra* and *mudrā,* are closely connected with each other. The *maṇḍalas,* according to the text, are determined by gods like Rudra or Śiva, who are derived from the *mudrāpīṭha.* The *madhyama* current issues from the upper mouth of Śiva. The Tantras belonging to this class are *Vijaya, Niśvāsa, Svāyambhuva, Vātula, Vīrabhadra, Raurava, Mākuṭa,* and *Vīreśa.* The text then says that 'the Tantras of a higher class' are *Candrajñāna, Bimba, Prodgīta, Lalita, Siddha, Santāna, Sarvodgīta, Kiraṇa,* and *Pārameśvara.* Amongst those who promulgated these Tantras, there are the names of human teachers, such as Uśanas, Bṛhaspati, Dadhīci, Kaca, Lakulīśa, Sanatkumāra, and a few others. We have not found any explicit mention of the Tantras of the *vāma* current. Probably they are included in the list of Āgamas mentioned as 'the Tantras of a higher class'.

SOME OTHER TĀNTRIC SĀDHANĀS

The *Brahma Yāmala* also speaks of the worship of the local deities. It says in one place that one of the disciples of Krodha Bhairava worshipped the goddess Bṛhodarī on the outskirts of a village called Bṛhodarī and thus attained spiritual knowledge. This obviously indicates the process of assimilation of the local cults by the Tantras.

The two supplements of *Brahma Yāmala, Jayadratha Yāmala* and *Piṅgalāmata,* mention a much greater variety of Tantras and *sādhanās. Piṅgalāmata* mentions two classes of Tantras belonging to it: Kāmarūpī and Uḍḍiyānī.[19] These two are place-names, Uḍḍiyāna being in the north-west (Swat valley) and Kāmarūpa being in Assam. It gives a new list of seven supplements to *Brahma Yāmala,* namely, *Daurvāsya, Paicika, Sāra-svatamata, Jayadratha, Phetkāra, Raktādya* (?), and *Lampaṭādya* (?). *Jaya-dratha,* again, is said to have consisted of seven Sūtras: *Sūtra, Uttarasūtra, Śaktisūtra, Kriyāsūtra, Vimalajñāna,* and *Sarvasandoha.*[20] *Piṅgalāmata* belongs to the *Kriyāsūtra* of *Jayadratha.*

Jayadratha Yāmala is divided into four sections called *ṣaṭka,* each containing six thousand *ślokas.*[21] The text gives detailed information on the various modes of Tāntric *sādhanā,* together with a description of the various branches of the Tāntric literature. Besides the eight Yāmalas, there are three other classes of supplementary Tantras called *maṅgalāṣṭaka,*

[19] *Ibid.,* pp. 105 ff.
[20] The manuscript from Nepal on which this list is based does not mention the name of the seventh.
[21] P. C. Bagchi, *Studies in the Tantras,* pp. 109 ff.

cakrāṣṭaka, and *śikhāṣṭaka*. The eight *maṅgalas* are *Bhairavamaṅgala, Candragarbha, Śanimaṅgala* (?), *Sumaṅgala, Sarvamaṅgala, Vijayamaṅgala, Ugramaṅgala*, and *Sadbhāvamaṅgala*. The eight *cakras* are *Svaracakra, Varṇanāḍi, Guhyakākhya, Kālacakra, Saura, Haya* (?), and *Soma*.[22] The eight *śikhās* are *Śaukrī, Mandā, Mahoçchuṣmā, Bhairavī, Saṁvarā, Prapañcakī, Mātṛbhedī*, and *Rudrakālī*. The text also mentions the names of the sages who had promulgated each class of *aṣṭakas*.

The *Jayadratha Yāmala* mentions the cults of a large number of divinities, mostly Śaktis, such as Kālikā, Saṅkarṣaṇī, Kālasaṅkarṣaṇī, Carcikā, Ḍambarakālī, Gahaneśvarī, Ekatārā, Śavaśabarī, Vajravatī, Rakṣākālī, Indīvarakālikā, Dhanadakālikā, Ramaṇīkālikā, Īśānakālikā, Mantramātā, Jīvakālī, Saptākṣarā, Ṛkṣakarṇī, Bhairavaḍākinī, Kālāntakī, Vīryakālī, Prajñākālī, Saptārṇakālī, and Siddhilakṣmī. The text further mentions twenty-five kinds of *dīkṣā*, which clearly imply various modes of *sādhanā*: *tattva-dīkṣā, bhūvana-, pāda-, varṇa-, mantra-, śakti-, nāda-, prāṇa-, jīva-, cora-, sparśa-, vedha-, vastra-, ghaṭa-, sadyonirvāṇa-, nirvāṇa-, āloka-, jñāna-dīkṣā*, etc.

The supplementary literature of the Yāmala group indicates a new orientation of the Tāntric culture. The *sādhanās* of the Āgamas assume in them a more pronounced character of Śāktism. The religion of the Āgamas apparently developed through two channels, one exoteric and the other esoteric. The former was continued as pure Śaivism with greater emphasis on the devotional aspect of the worship of Śiva-Paśupati, with a view to attaining salvation. The latter was continued as Śāktism with greater emphasis on the various Śakti cults, not so much to attain salvation as to gain ascendancy over the forces of nature, and to carry on experiments with them in order to gain a detailed knowledge of their working. Salvation was too small a goal for the latter. The later literature of pure Śaivism ceases to be called Tantra. Tantra proper became more Śāktic in character. This character of Tantra became definitely established by the tenth century.

THE BUDDHIST TANTRAS

Buddhism also had developed a Tāntric aspect by this period. The Buddhist Tantras came into existence, according to the Tibetan evidence, after the time of Dharmakīrti. Their origin as a distinct class of literature and a mode of *sādhanā* may be placed in the seventh century, and they underwent great development during the three succeeding centuries. A large number of texts was compiled in this period, and an imposing

[22] The manuscript from Nepal does not mention the name of the eighth.

pantheon grew up. There are common elements as well as common bases in the Brāhmaṇical and Buddhist Tantras ; but it would be wrong to suppose that the Buddhist Tantra is nothing but a borrowed religion. Even when the elements and bases are common, the Buddhists use different symbols in explaining their intricate esoteric systems.

Buddhist mysticism assumed three different forms in this period, viz. Vajrayāna, Sahajayāna, and Kālacakrayāna, and had the general designation of Mantranaya. The philosophical background of these sects is supplied by the Mādhyamika and Yogācāra systems of philosophy. Vajrayāna and Sahajayāna represented two aspects of the same mysticism, the first dealing with mystic ritualism of a more exoteric nature, and the second laying more stress on the esoteric aspect. The first attaches importance to *mantra, mudrā,* and *maṇḍala,* and maintains that their practice is necessary for the awakening of psychic energy (*śakti*). The word for Śakti in these schools is Prajñā, which is the female principle, the male being Vajra. The Sahajayāna is said to have been developed by a set of mystics called Siddhas, who are traditionally believed to have been eighty-four in number. They seem to have flourished in the tenth and eleventh centuries. They discard every kind of formalism and place emphasis on the cultivation of the state of *sahaja.* It is by discarding all sorts of knowledge derived from outward sources, and by giving up formalism of all kinds, that this state can be brought about. The Tibetan texts say that Kālacakrayāna was developed outside India in a country called Sambhala, and was introduced into Bengal in the Pāla period. One of the great teachers of the school, Abhayākaragupta, was a contemporary of King Rāmapāla and wrote a number of books. The school attaches importance, in the matter of *sādhanā,* to the time factor, viz. *muhūrta, tithi, nakṣatra, rāśi,* etc. Thus astronomy and astrology came to be associated with the practice of *yoga.*

From about the tenth and eleventh centuries, there began a very complicated period of development of the Tāntric culture. The Brāhmaṇical and Buddhist sects (and sometimes the Jaina also) became mixed up, mainly on account of the decadence of Buddhism as a powerful religion in India. All that remained of it was a mystic form, very similar to Śāktism in its essence. The fusion of the two Tantras gave birth to new forms of esoteric religion.

THE BRĀHMAṆICAL TANTRAS

So far as the Brāhmaṇical Tantras of this period are concerned, we get a detailed picture of the new synthetic outlook in *Sammoha* (also called

Sammohana) *Tantra.*[23] In the general classification of the *pīṭhas* or modes of *sādhanā*, the principal ones according to it are: *vidyāpīṭha, śaktipīṭha, śaivapīṭha, gaṇeśapīṭha, candrapīṭha, svāyambhuvapīṭha, cīnapīṭha, bauddhapīṭha,* and *vaidikapīṭha.*

The *Sammoha Tantra* first deals with the various traditions and *mantras* of the Kālikāmata. The Kālikās are of nine kinds, Saṅkarṣaṇī, Siddhakālī, Kubjikā, Sundarī, Mahākhiladeveśī, Śrīmat-siddhakarālikā, Pratyaṅgirā, Śeṣikā, and Śeṣamantrā. A number of special cults are then enumerated: one cult of Jayā, three cults of Sundarī, two of Tārā, three of Kālī, one of Chinnā, two of Dhūmrā and Mātaṅgī, and two of Siddhavidyā. It further mentions twenty-four cults of the Vaiṣṇavas, two of the Sauras, and five of the Gāṇapatyas.

The text then speaks of *āmnāya* and the geographical classification of the Tantras. From the geographical point of view, the Tantras are divided into four classes, viz. Kerala, Kāśmīra, Gauḍa, and Vilāsa (?). The Kerala class is said to prevail in all countries from Aṅga to Mālava, the Kāśmīra class from Madra to Nepāla, the Gauḍa class from Śilahaṭṭa to Sindhu, while the Vilāsa class is found in all countries. There are six *āmnāyas*: *pūrva* (eastern), *dakṣiṇa* (southern), *paścima* (western), *uttara* (northern), *ūrdhva* (upper), and *pātāla* (nether). Another and a more important classification, made according to the nature of the *sādhanā,* is into *divya, kaula,* and *vāma.* Each of these again has two sects, *hārda* (inner) and *bāhya* (outer).

The text then mentions the number of Tantras belonging to each class. These numbers may in some cases be fictitious, but they show that the writer had a vague idea that each class contained a large literature. It says that the country of Cīna possesses one hundred principal Tantras and seven subsidiary ones, Draviḍa twenty principal and twenty subsidiary, the Jaina eighteen principal and twenty subsidiary, Kāśmīra one hundred principal and ten subsidiary, and Gauḍa twenty-seven principal and sixteen subsidiary ones.

About the number of Tantras belonging to the principal Brāhmaṇical sects, it gives the following:

(i) Śaiva Tantras: 32 Tantras, 325 Upatantras, 10 Saṁhitās, 5 Arṇavas, 2 Yāmalas, 3 Ḍāmaras, 1 Uddāla, 2 Uḍḍīśas, 8 Kalpas, 8 Upasaṅkhyās, 2 Cūḍāmaṇis, 2 Cintāmaṇis, and 2 Vimarṣiṇīs.

(ii) Vaiṣṇava Tantras: 75 Tantras, 205 Upatantras, 20 Kalpas, 8 Saṁhitās, 1 Arṇavaka, 5 Kakṣapuṭīs, 8 Cūḍāmaṇis, 2 Cintāmaṇis,

[23] P. C. Bagchi, *Studies in the Tantras,* pp. 96 ff. This discussion on the *Sammoha Tantra* is based on an old manuscript of the text in the Nepal State Library, and not on the later version of the text available in print.

2 Uḍḍīśas, 2 Ḍāmaras, 1 Yāmala, 5 Purāṇas, 3 Tattvabodha-vimarṣiṇīs, and 2 Amṛtatarpaṇas (?).

(iii) Saura Tantras: 30 Tantras, 96 Upatantras, 4 Saṁhitās, 2 Upasaṁhitās, 5 Purāṇas, 10 Kalpas, 2 Kakṣapuṭīs, 3 Tattvas, 3 Vimarṣiṇīs, 3 Cūḍāmaṇis, 2 Ḍāmaras, 2 Yāmalas, 5 Uddālas, 2 Avatāras, 2 Uḍḍīśas, 3 Amṛtas, 3 Darpaṇas, and 3 Kalpas.

(iv) Gāṇapatya Tantras: 50 Tantras, 25 Upatantras, 2 Purāṇas, 3 Sāgaras, 3 Darpaṇas, 5 Amṛtas, 9 Kalpakas, 3 Kakṣapuṭīs, 2 Vimarṣiṇīs, 2 Tattvas, 2 Uḍḍīśas, 3 Cūḍāmaṇis, 3 Cintāmaṇis, 1 Ḍāmara, 1 Candrayāmala, and 8 Pāñcarātras.

(v) Bauddha Tantras (not quite clear in the text): 5 Avatarṇakas, 5 Sūktas, 2 Cintāmaṇis, 9 Purāṇas, 3 Upasaṁjñās, 2 Kakṣapuṭīs, 3 Kalpadrumas, 2 Kāmadhenus, 3 Svabhāvas, and 5 Tattvas.

The text further gives a detailed description of the Vidyās or cults, according to the various schools. The objects of worship in these cults were the following goddesses: Aindrī, Gāyatrī, Brahmavidyā, Ardhanārīśvarī, Śrutidharī, Mātṛkā, Sarasvatī, Śāmbhavī, Śrīparāparā, Kāmarājeśvarī, Tripurā-bhairavī, Caitanya-bhairavī, Rudra-śakti, Kāmeśvarī, Mahā-tripurā-bhairavī, Aghora-bhairavī, Tripurā-nikṛnta-bhairavī, Annapūrṇā, Kukkuṭā, Śivā, Bhogavatī, Kubjikā, Saṅkarṣaṇī, Kriyāsaṅkarṣaṇī, Kālasaṅkarṣaṇī, Mahāvidyā, Śūlinī, Mādhavī, Caṇḍayogeśvarī, Cāmuṇḍā, Ratnavidyā, Siddhavidyā, Māyā, Māyāvatī, Ramā, Dhanadā, Śabarī, Durgā, Reṇukā, Sāmrājyasundarī, Rājarājeśvarī, Mahā-sāmrājyavidyā, Yakṣiṇī, Kinnarī, Siddhi, Pūtanā, Kavacā, Kuṣmāṇḍinī, Agastyavidyā, Vāgvādinī, Cāṇḍālī, Susukhī, Mātaṅginī, Māheśvarī, Rājamātaṅginī, Laghuvārāhī, Sutiraskāriṇī, Svapnavārāhī, Pādukā, Vārāhīpādukā, Jambukikkikā, Śukā, Vāgeśī, Śukatuṇḍā, Mohinī, Kirādinī (i.e. Kirātinī), Kṣemaṅkarī, Sumūrti, Śrī-mahātimiravatī, Kālamāyā, Ṣoḍaśī, Śrī-parāvidyā, Caraṇarūpiṇī, Śrīvidyā, Bālatripurā, Vagalā, Mahiṣaghnā, Mahālakṣmī, Mahāsarasvatī, Pratyaṅgirā, Bhavānī, Kālikā, Tārā, Chinnamastā, Dhūmāvatī, etc.

The *Sammoha Tantra* therefore presents a state of things far different from that of the Śiva Tantras of the Āgamic period. It shows that the Tantras had assumed a complete Śāktic character, assimilated a very large number of cults of various origins, regional, tribal, and sectarian, and thus established a well-developed and complicated pantheon of goddesses (all representing various aspects of Śakti). This state of things must have been attained by the fourteenth century, when the *Sammoha Tantra* seems to have assumed its final form. Later Tantras, either original or compiled, add to the number of *vidyās, mantras,* and *maṇḍalas.* Many of the old cults are either forgotten or dropped as obsolete.

THE KAULA SCHOOLS AND OTHER VAIṢṆAVA SECTS

The *Sammoha Tantra,* we have seen, mentions three classes of Tantras or rather Tāntric *ṣādhanās*: *divya, kaula,* and *vāma.* We know something definite about the origin of the Kaula classes. According to a very old text, *Kaulajñānanirṇaya,* the manuscript of which goes back to the eleventh century, the Kaula class of Tantras was introduced by Matsyendra Nātha. But, strictly speaking, he was the founder of one of the Kaula schools called Yoginī-kaula of Kāmarūpa. A number of other Kaula schools are also mentioned in the text: Vṛṣaṇottha-kaula, Vahni-kaula, Kaula-sadbhāva, Padottiṣṭha-kaula, Mahā-kaula, Siddha-kaula, Jñānanirṇiti-kaula, Siddhāmṛta-kaula, Sṛṣṭi-kaula, Candra-kaula, Śaktibheda-kaula, Ūrmi-kaula, and Jñāna-kaula. It is difficult at present to determine the nature of these sects, but it is clear that in the eleventh century the Kaula schools were quite developed, comprising a number of sects. *Kula* stands for Śakti, and so the Kaula schools were Śāktic in character.

The Yoginī-kaula of Matsyendra Nātha had a syncretic character. The doctrines of this school, as may be gathered from *Kaulajñānanirṇaya,*[24] have something in common with the Buddhist Tantras of the Sahaja class. Matsyendra, we know, is honoured by the Buddhist mystics as the first of the Siddhas under the name Lui-pāda. The fundamental doctrine of the Buddhist Sahaja school is the doctrine of Sahaja: 'The ideal state of the *yogin,* a state in which the mind enters the vacuity, becomes free from duality, and rejects the illusory character of the world.' The Yoginī-kaula also advocates the doctrine of Sahaja. It defines Sahaja almost in the terms of the Buddhist mystics as 'a state in which the mind attains immobility, becomes free from duality and illusion'. The Yoginī-kaula agrees with Buddhist Sahajiyā in many other respects too ; it disregards the traditional lore, discredits the outward purificatory rites, and denounces the attempt to attain salvation by the study of the Śāstras and by exoteric practices, such as sacrifices, fasting, bathing, visiting holy places, etc.

This syncretism, which began before the eleventh century, was responsible for the growth of two important esoteric sects during the succeeding centuries. They were the Nātha sect, which had a tinge of Śaivism, and the Sahajiyā, which had a tinge of Vaiṣṇavism.

The Nātha sect originated from the teachings of the Siddhācāryas, as its reputed founder Matsyendra Nātha was in all likelihood the same as the first Siddha Lui-pāda. The great teachers of this mystic sect were all called Nāthas, and the most famous among them were Mīna Nātha, Gorakṣa Nātha, and Cauraṅgī Nātha. Their teachings had a great influence

[24] P. C. Bagchi, *Kaulajñānanirṇaya and Minor Texts of the School of Matsyendra Nātha,* Introduction, p. 33.

in Bengal, and miraculous tales about them became the subject of popular songs in Bengali. The followers of Nāthism at first formed a monastic group, but later on constituted a caste in Hindu society.

The Vaiṣṇava Sahajiyā as a distinct sect was established in Bengal before the time of Caitanya.[25] The oldest reference to Sahajiyā is in an inscription of the thirteenth century (the Maināmatī plate). It speaks of the practice of Sahajadharma in Paṭṭikeraka in Tippera. Caṇḍīdāsa was the earliest Vaiṣṇava Sahajiyā, and lived, most probably, in the fourteenth century. In his songs, which have come down in a very much altered form, and in his *Śrī-Kṛṣṇa-kīrtana* we can trace some of the fundamental doctrines of the sect. Rādhā is the Śakti and Kṛṣṇa the supreme Reality. The Haṭha-yoga is the only *yoga* approved of by the sect. Every *sādhaka* has to make full use of his psychic energy in bringing about the union of the two principles. The various *nāḍīs* and *cakras* within the body are recognized. The topmost station within the body is the thousand-petalled lotus. The terminology used in these cases is borrowed from the Buddhist Sahajayāna and the Hindu Tantras. The Buddhist Sahaja texts speak of five kinds of psychic energy (*kula*): *ḍombī, naṭī, rājakī, caṇḍālī,* and *brāhmaṇī*. In the case of Caṇḍīdāsa it is *rajakī*. The names of the *nāḍīs* and the *cakras* are taken sometimes from the same source, but in other cases also from the Hindu Tantras.

Two other mystic sects seem to have originated in this period: they are the sects of the Avadhūta and the Bāul. The Avadhūta sect has great affinities with the Nātha sect, whereas the Bāul derives inspiration from the Vaiṣṇava Sahajiyā.

FOREIGN INFLUENCE ON THE TANTRAS

A few words should be said about the alleged foreign influence on the Tantras.[26] Mysticism by its very nature transcends sectarianism and regionalism in the highest stages of its development. Mystics of various countries thus easily discover the common elements in their respective modes of *sādhanā*. They also borrow from each other techniques of a complementary nature, which might help them in enriching their own religious experiences. This must have happened in every age. The historians of Alexander the Great spoke of the existence of a class of mystics called Gymnosophists in all countries from Egypt to India. Indian mystics were found in Alexandria as late as the fourth century A.D., and they are said to have been in close contact with their fellow-mystics in the Christian world.

[25] P. C. Bagchi, 'Religion of Bengal' in *History of Bengal*, I. p. 421.
[26] P. C. Bagchi, *Studies in the Tantras*, pp. 45 ff.

The *Sammoha Tantra,* to which we have already referred, speaks of the Tāntric culture of foreign countries like Bāhlīka, Kirāta, Bhoṭa, Cīna, Mahācīna, Pārasika, Airāka, Kamboja, Hūṇa, Yavana, Gandhāra, and Nepāla. This does not mean that the Indian Tantras were prevalent in all these countries, though we know they were prevalent in some of them. It means, if anything at all, that these foreign countries also possessed modes of esoteric culture, and that some of them were known in India and recognized as being similar to the Indian Tantras.

It is therefore very difficult to find out the borrowed elements, if any, in the Tantras. They are so well fitted into the system that they have lost their exotic character. Yet some stray references may be discovered in the Tantras to the borrowing of foreign modes of *sādhanā.* A particular mode of Tāntric *sādhanā* called Cīnācāra is found in the Tantras. The *Tārā Tantra,* adopted both by Hinduism and Buddhism, says that the cult of Cīnācāra came from Mahācīna. A well-known Brāhmaṇa sage, Vasiṣṭha, is said to have gone to the country of Mahācīna to learn this mode of *sādhanā* from Buddha. It was not to be found either in India or in Tibet. So Vasiṣṭha had to go to Mahācīna, where he was initiated by Buddha into the secret doctrines of Cīnācāra. He subsequently came back to India and propagated them. Some scholars were inclined to discover in this Cīnācāra a distant echo of the secret societies of China. It is the cult of Mahācīna-Tārā which is introduced by the Cīnācāra.

Mahācīna-Tārā, as can be ascertained from the Buddhist *sādhanās,* was the same goddess as Ekajaṭā, whose cult is said to have been discovered by Siddha Nāgārjuna in Tibet (*Ārya-Nāgārjunapādaiḥ Bhoṭeṣu uddhṛtam*). The description of Ekajaṭā is found in six different Buddhist *sādhanās.* It closely agrees with that of Mahācīna-Tārā, as found in some of the *sādhanās.* A comparison of the two goddesses shows that they are essentially identical, the only difference being found in the *bīja-mantra* which, in the case of Mahācīna-Tārā, is composed of three letters and, in the case of Ekajaṭā, is sometimes composed of four, sometimes of five. Corresponding to these goddesses, we find in the Hindu pantheon Tārā, Ugra-Tārā, Ekajaṭā, and Mahā-Nīla-Sarasvatī. The *dhyānas* of these goddesses, as found in the Hindu Tantras, literally correspond to those found in the Buddhist *sādhanā.* According to a legend recorded in the *Sammoha Tantra,* Nīla-Sarasvatī or Ugra-Tārā was born in a lake called Cola, on the western side of Mount Meru. This name Cola is probably to be connected with *kul, kol,* the common word for lake to the west and north of the T'ien-shan in the pure Mongolian zone. Besides, in the enumeration of the various female energies (Yoginī) in the Brāhmaṇical Tantras, we find a type called Lāmā (Rūpikā Cumbikā Lāmā). The corresponding god is called Lāmeśvara. The word Lāmā, like a few others, such as Ḍākinī, Śākinī, Lākinī, and Hākinī, in spite of their later explanations, seems to be exotic. Lāmā is certainly the Tibetan word 'Lha-mo', which means Devī (Śakti).

These evidences show that a number of foreign elements were introduced in the Tantras, most probably, between the eighth and the twelfth century, when communication with Tibet, China, and Mongolia became brisk. But these cults lost their exotic character, as they fitted well, in logical sequence, into a completely integrated system. In the same way, the practices of the Buddhist Siddhācāryas, and those of the early Vaiṣṇava Sahajiyās, seem to have received certain influences from Taoism, but at present, it is difficult to determine to what extent this borrowing was made. A thorough study of the Buddhist Sahajiyā and Taoist literature can alone solve the problem.

TANTRA AS A WAY OF REALIZATION

VAIDIKA AND TĀNTRIKA CULTURE

THANKS chiefly to the enlightened and fruitful labours of the Āgama Anusandhāna Samiti, of which both Sir John Woodroffe and Atal Behari Ghosh were the leading lights, the investigation of the philosophy, religion, and practice of the Tantra Śāstra is no longer under a ban. Only a few decades ago it was grudgingly admitted that the Tantra contained some sense in its 'high' metaphysics; but this was merely an oasis in an endless desert of nonsense—or worse, of 'lust, mummery, and superstition'. Investigation into the Tantra or Āgama Śāstra can now be reduced to a method. And what kind of method is this mainly to be?

The truth about the Śāstra cannot, for example, be attained on the basis of an assumption that it is only a burial ground of forms and ideas long dead and obsolete. The assumption is palpably wrong. Hinduism in its present form involves, no doubt, 'a double framework', Vaidika and Tāntrika, but Tāntrika wings have not simply been added from time to time to the ancient Vaidika mansion. The process has been in the nature of a remodelling of the old structure in which its ground-plan has subsisted, but the edifice has been permitted to wear a new form and expression suited to new times and conditions. Whatever be the origins or sources of the Tāntrika ideas and forms, for ages these have been assimilated into the organism of the Vaidika culture, and all apparent contradictions and conflicts have long resolved themselves into the cohesive components and coefficients of a comprehensive organic synthesis. This being so, it will not do to look upon the Tantra simply as a graft from a foreign plant which has since withered and decayed. The host tree has not simply cast off a dead limb; it lives in that limb as much as it lives in others. Some would even say that it lives in that limb more than it lives in any other. Others would go so far as to maintain that it is the foreign graft that has lived and thrived, leaving the host stock slowly to wither and decay. But whether the Tantra was or was not in the nature of a foreign graft, the relation of the Tāntrika to the Vaidika culture has long ceased to be the relation between a graft and a host. The graft theory by itself, for instance, will operate as a perpetual bar to the coming of that dawn of sense which will make one see the whole as a living and growing reality. The deeper affirmities, presumably pre-existing when the so-called engrafting was effected, which compose and evolve the whole living tissue of the resultant organism, will, in that case, remain unobserved and unrecognized.

The Tantra is not simply a graft or a formation, morbid or otherwise, on Hinduism. It is of the living kernel, and not of the sheathing, or sometimes rotting, husk. The common obsession of many educated people, both foreign and Indian, still is that the worth of the Tantra, whatever that may be, should be appraised substantially apart from a general scheme of values to which Hinduism in its essence and in its 'pristine purity' must be subjected. Secondly, this graft or backwater theory has, on the one hand, found itself in natural alliance with the view so commonly held that the graft has been in the nature of a parasite or 'pathological excrescence', so naturally suggestive of the surgeon's knife or the doctor's recipe, and that the backwater has been in the nature of a stagnant pool of black, foul water full of noxious weeds and giving off a stench, and having no outflow into the mighty current of general Hindu cultural life.

'LEFT-HANDED' PATH

Certain ill-understood 'left-handed' practices (*vāmācāra*), for instance, have been commonly supposed to exhaust nearly the whole content of Tāntricism. Whilst, as we shall see, *vāmācāra* is based on the profound knowledge of the 'return current' or *nivṛtti,* which seeks to reverse the process of creating and maintaining the bonds of propensities and conventions in which the Jīva or soul has been held as a *paśu* or animal, it must be clearly perceived that this path, as laid out in the Śākta Tantra with its special and esoteric ritualism (e.g. *pañcatattva*), is not the only one prescribed in the Tantra. The *Kulārṇava Tantra,* for instance, lays down as many as seven paths or *ācāras,* starting with *vedācāra* and ending with *kaula.* Some other Tantras have added two more to the list, viz. *aghora* and *yoga.* Here the important thing to note is that the denotation of the word *'tantra'* is as wide as it is varied, embracing not only the Śākta, but the Śaiva, Vaiṣṇava, Saura, and Gāṇapatya forms (with their numerous sub-species) within the fold of orthodox Hinduism itself. And we have well-developed Buddhist and other Tantras also outside this fold. All these various types, Hindu or Buddhistic, present, no doubt, many striking points of diversity, both as regards ideas and notations. As practical sciences of realization (*sādhana-śāstra*) bearing applicability to differing human competencies and constitutions, and different stages of the progress made by the 'healing' soul, the lines of treatment by the Śāstra and its prescriptions are bound to be of a varied nature. Aspirant souls in their spiritual endeavour have to carve out their own suitable paths or lines of approach, which will be found to diverge more or less at first from one another, but converge and tend to coalesce, as closer and closer approach is made to the final goal which is the same for all. So the wise will say: 'As many paths as persuasions (*mata*).'

The general body of Hindu ideas, beliefs, and practices will, on examination, be found to be permeated through and through by the cult of the Tantra, indeed so much so that the whole now bears a definitely Tāntrika character. The 'double framework' of Vaidika and Tāntrika has ceased in course of time to be 'double'. To take the case of the *vāmācāra* (which means the 'left'—*viparīta*—and not the 'left-handed' path) again: In this the *sādhaka* (aspirant) has to make use of a certain kind of ritual (technically called the *pañcatattva*) which, whilst leading admittedly to some abuse in unsuitable cases and conditions, has made, in the judgement of those who do not understand and discriminate, the whole cult of the Tantra suspect. Those who understand nothing of the 'return current' or 'reversing process', involved in the theory and practice of the so-called 'left' path, naturally fail to perceive that there may be any points of contact between this and the theory and practice of the Advaita Vedānta. Apart from the fact that a full-blooded counterpart of the essentials of the *pañcatattva* worship, in their 'gross', 'proxy', and 'esoteric' forms, can be traced down to all the Vedic strata, and also apart from the probability of a modified shape being given to, and a special emphasis being laid on, the ancient, immemorial Vedic worship, by influences coming from outside the limits of India proper (e.g. Tibet or Mahācīna), it ought to be recognized by all thinking people that the *pañcatattva* worship, in its principle and in its tendency, is a legitimate form of the Advaita worship.

The end of the *sādhaka* is, of course, to attain pure and perfect Cit—an untranslatable word—or Consciousness. This perfect Consciousness is also perfect Being and perfect Bliss. In the Vedānta as also in the Tantra, the word for this perfect state is Saccidānanda. Now, this perfect state is unattainable so long as that which limits or restricts it operates. The limiting power of Reality by which its unmeasured Being-Consciousness-Bliss is measured, and its alogical nature is made thinkable in terms of 'forms and categories', has been called Māyā in both. The Tantra, in particular, analyses the fundamental limiting power into certain special aspects called *kañcukas* or 'contractors'. But the essential thing is this that the *pūrṇa* or perfect state is not to be attained so long as Māyā and her *kañcukas* operate.

THE 'POLARITY' OF REALITY

By its self-limiting power, Reality 'polarizes' itself into that which is conscious and that which is not, that which is existent and that which is not, and that which is 'pleasant' and that which is not. The fundamental polarity of subject and object, *aham* and *idam,* is also evolved by it. By the process of polarization, that which is unmeasured becomes measured (*prameya*), the infinite is made finite, and the undifferentiated differentiated. By it, Reality which is absolute in itself becomes resolved, so to say, into a multiplicity of correlated centres of diverse natures, acting and reacting in diverse ways. It thus evolves into a universe of being and becoming. Some of the member centres of this universe evolve the power of feeling, cognition, and will, while others apparently lack this power. Some know, while some others are only known. Some enjoy, while others are only enjoyed. Some appear to act from within, while the rest are merely acted upon from outside. This power and the lack of it admit of all kinds of measures and degrees. But whatever these may be, all finite, correlated centres have their being and becoming determined by the conditions of the polarizing, finitizing, and limiting power by which they are created and evolved. The determining conditions which constitute, maintain, and evolve the centres necessarily limit or restrict them also. By them they are constrained to become or remain such and such centres. What they were, what they are, and what they will be are thus determined. They are distinguished and differentiated from one another. Their respective behaviours, their actions and reactions, become such and such, that is, determinate. The determinants are therefore 'bonds' or *pāśa,* as they have been called in the Tantra Śāstra. The Jīva or the self finds himself in *pāśa* or fetters. By these, however, the whole fabric of a centre's common life and behaviour is woven into being, and it is by them that it is maintained and differentiated. The *pāśa* is the basis of behaviour (*vyavahāra*); it is of pragmatic value.

THE REALITY AS A 'CENTRE'

Yet the Reality has never ceased to be itself, that is, perfect Consciousness, Being, and Bliss, in thus evolving by its own inscrutable power into a multiplicity of conditioned centres. The *pāśa,* the determinant, the conditioning factor, must therefore be not something inherent in, or intrinsic to, the Reality of which a given centre is a function, evolute, and manifestation; it must be a kind of veil by which the Reality is 'hidden' without being effaced or suppressed. That which has ever been and never ceased to be has been ignored and practically 'negatived'. This is implied in, and incidental to, the very process by which a manifold of heterogeneous correlated centres can evolve out of perfect Being-Consciousness-Bliss which, however, never ceases to be itself at any stage of the evolving act.

THE 'CENTRE' AS THE 'POINT'

Even a finite centre, in any position in the curve of evolution, must never cease to be a 'point' of pure and perfect Reality. By 'point' is here meant that at and through which the *pūrṇa* or whole 'opens' itself and through which it can be reached or realized. But what is thus a point of co-essentiality and 'flow' from the side of Reality becomes a veil and a restrictor from the side of the universe of behaviour and convention. Point-facing, the Jīva-centre is none other than the Reality. Veil-facing, it is finite, conditioned, and in bondage or *pāśa*. If the direction of the process, by which the veiling and all that is incidental to it have been produced, be called outgoing, then, surely, to face the 'point' (at and through which perfect Being-Consciousness-Bliss is 'opened up'), that direction must be reversed. The 'sign' of the function has to be changed. We must have the 'return current' in the place of the outgoing. *Rādhā* in the place of *dhārā, so'ham* for *haṁsaḥ*. What now operate as bonds, determinants, or *pāśa* must be so transformed and so directed that they may act as releasers or 'liberators', working out release from bondage. This is beautifully expressed by the saying: 'By that one must rise by which one has fallen.' It has been said also: 'The very poison that kills becomes the elixir of life when used by the wise.' The principle involved is a sound one ; and the whole theory and practice of the so-called 'left' *ācāra* is based on this principle. Every finite and determined centre is *ipso facto* a reversible apparatus. In ordinary life and behaviour, the apparatus works with a certain sign and with a certain result—which is a complex of bondage in *vāsanā* and *saṁskāra* (propensities and conventions, roughly speaking). Of the varied complex of *vāsanās,* some appear to be cardinal or primary. These are the prime movers of the Jīva in his ordinary activity ; these constitute, so to say, the key-knots of the net of 'wandering' in which he is caught and held. Now, the question is how to use these cardinal Jīva-impulses of *bhoga* or enjoyment so that their sign may be changed and their very nature transformed and 'sublimated'. If that can be done, the apparatus that now binds and grinds will then be 'reversed' in its working, and the 'centre' will turn round and face and become the 'point' of perfect Being-Consciousness-Bliss.

OUTGOING CURRENT

The outgoing process has made a *paśu* (animal) of the Jīva by creating duality (*dvaita*) where, in fact, there is none. Thus certain things are sought, while others are shunned ; some produce pleasure, others pain ; some are true, some false ; and so on. All such distinctions must be relative and pragmatic, if all be Brahman and there be nothing but Brahman. The cardinal desire of man and woman for each other, for example, and the fact of their physical union become 'carnal' on the relative and pragmatic plane, where the body is 'material' and the soul 'spiritual', and there is assumed a perennial conflict between the flesh and the spirit. The distinction is a valid one and may be of value so long as the Jīva remains on the plane of common conventions. But he is a *paśu* in *pāśa* or bonds on that plane. Moral or social conventions, however desirable or suitable on that plane, do not make him other than a *paśu*. To be free from *pāśa,* that is, to be Śiva, he must be able to resolve that and every kind of duality. He must be able to realize in fact that nothing exists and functions but Śiva-Śakti. The so-called body is that ; so is mind ; so is the soul or spirit. And all action is play or *līlā* of Śiva-Śakti. In this realization nothing remains 'carnal' or 'gross'; everything becomes an expression and attitude of perfect Being-Consciousness-Bliss.

The essential thing therefore is the recognition of a veiled and 'lost' identity. In Vedānta, the commonest act of perception implies the restoration of a lost identity (as *caitanya* or consciousness) between the perceiver and the perceived, *pramātṛ* and his *viṣaya.* This essential identity must be worked out consistently and thoroughly, without leaving any precipitate of difference whatever, if the aspirant is to go beyond the plane of duality which has made a Jīva of Śiva. *Aham* and *idam,* the knower and the known, the enjoyer and the enjoyed, action and reaction must all be equated fundamentally to each other, and all resolved into the identity of Śiva-Śakti or God as Power. The outgoing process is one of differentiation and diversification ; the return current must be one of increasing assimilation, integration, and identification. In the first, everything is ejected into separateness, exclusiveness, polarity, or even opposition. In the latter, it is drawn back and gathered into unity, harmony, and peace. The *laya* or *kuṇḍalinī yoga* is a practical demonstration of how the outwardly-directed evolving process is reversed, until the whole *prapañca* or universe is resolved into unitary Consciousness and perfect Bliss.

The projecting or outgoing process which is *haṁsaḥ* (represented particularly by the 'sun' and the 'vital breath') is reversed in that *yoga* as *so'ham.* The first evolves polarities and a manifold of diversities. It affirms *dvaita, bheda* or non-identity. But the two currents never operate singly, one absolutely exclusive of the other. They are concurrent, though the emphasis is laid now on this and now on that. The emphasis again oscillates ; it traces a curve. Hence in all affirmations of *dvaita* and *bheda,* the affirmation of *advaita* and *abheda* (that is, identity) is immanent. It is because of this that, even during the prevalence of the outgoing or *haṁsaḥ* aspect of the dual process, a universe or cosmos involving unities, equalities, and similarities arises, and not a mere chaos of jarring and colliding 'atoms'. Now, if we may call a conditional identity an equation (which holds true under certain assigned conditions, but not under others), then it appears that in the realm of ordinary experience involving the *haṁsaḥ* process we are given equations and not identities.

Take for example man and woman. One can be equated to the other subject to certain limits, measures, and conditions. The polarity, antithesis, or difference is patent. We should be able to resolve and get beyond *bheda.* Failing this, man and woman will be the *pāśa* of each other, as they often are in common experience. But if identity, as distinguished from mere conditional, tentative equality, can be affirmed and realized, then the two poles or opposites will resolve into unity and will form one integral whole. The *pāśa,* the noose, then disappears.

TWO WAYS OF REAFFIRMATION

Generally speaking, there are two ways of reaffirming the lost identity. One is elimination or negation till negation is dead or is no longer possible. This is the well-known *'neti neti'* method of Māyāvāda Vedānta. It is to negate as *asat* or unreal the crust, sheath, or husk (*upādhi*) of a given object. If the *upādhi* of any other object be similarly eliminated, it will be seen that in the kernel the one is the same as the other, and each is Ātman or Brahman. Every kind of *bheda* or duality must be rigorously reduced to zero.

But an approach may be made to identity from another standpoint. It is the way of sublimation. Man and woman, for example, may thus be sublimated into cosmic principles, polar to each other in the outgoing or *haṁsaḥ* aspect of the cosmic process, but identified and unified Śiva-Śakti in reality, which is experienced in the reversing of the outgoing current. In reversing the process, we have to bring the two complements or poles 'together' so as to reaffirm and realize the identical whole. Using for one moment the so-called 'erotic symbolism' of Tantra Śāstra, the physical union of man and woman is sublimated as the creative union of Śiva-Śakti (that is, perfect Consciousness at rest becoming dynamic as creative activity) ; the thrill of the act of union being *nāda* (a term later explained) ; and the 'seed' that issues from the union is *bindu.* In the *vāmācāra* or 'left' path, which under certain very stringent conditions prescribes to the *vīra* or 'hero' *sādhanā* or ritual readjustment with woman, such sublimation of the so-called 'carnal' act has to be effected till the supreme *advaita* Śiva-Śakti experience with its perfect *ānanda* or Bliss is attained. It is this 'carnal' desire that constitutes one of the strongest *pāśas* of the *paśu* Jīva. The object is to make even this the 'opening' to the perfect whole of experience.

THE STEPS IN THE PROCESS

The method of sublimation consists of the steps *śodhana, śuddhi* or purification, *uddhāra* (lifting) or elevation, and *caitanya* or reaffirmation of identity in consciousness. By the first, a thing or an act is purged of its usual dross of grossness. This is done by reversing the direction of the ordinary worldly process or *pravṛtti*. In the evolution of the cosmic principles (the thirty-six *tattvas* as they are called), a certain stage is reached where pure or *śuddha tattvas* 'cross the line' and pass into the impure or *aśuddha tattvas*. These latter constitute the realm of Nature (the region of Prakṛti and her evolutes), which is like a closed curve in which the Jīva is held a prisoner, and in which he wanders tracing his own curve of path in accordance with the equation of *karma*. Though essentially a centre of Śiva-Śakti, he is caught in the net of natural determinism from which there is no escape, unless the 'coiled' curve which encloses him can be made to uncoil itself and 'open' for his release and ascent in the realm of the *śuddha tattvas*. His hope lies in uncoiling the coil of Nature, technically called the 'awakening of the serpent-power or *kuṇḍalinī*'. Only thus can the impure elements or principles be purified and elevated from the *aśuddha* or *prākṛta* plane to the *śuddha* or *aprākṛta*. The face of the coiled serpent-power is ordinarily downwards ; it must be turned upwards. The next step is *uddhāra* or elevation. The order in which the principles are evolved in the outgoing activity must be reversed with the starting of the return current ; ascent must be made in the order opposite to that in which descent was made. From the grosser and more limited elements, we must rise to what are subtler and more general, until ascent is finally made to the level of perfect experience, which is Śiva-Śakti in one called *parā saṁvit*. The last step is the reaffirmation and realization in consciousness of the supreme identity.

Such is the general framework of the method to be followed. The Vaiṣṇava, the Śaiva-Śākta, and other Āgamas have their methods of sublimation that can be readily fitted into this framework. The *parā saṁvit* or the supreme experience may, however, be differently viewed. The Vaiṣṇava has, for example, his *śuddha* (pure), *aprākṛta* (supernal), and *cinmaya* (spiritual) *tattvas,* contradistinguished from others that are *aśuddha* (impure), *prākṛta* (common), and *jaḍa* (inert). The Jīva in his essence is of the former. But he is not to be identified with the supreme *tattva* who is Bhagavat Puruṣottama. He is of the same pure essence and is a manifestation of God-power in a certain aspect. He is a 'point' (*cit-kaṇa*) at and through which contact is established with the essence of divinity.

The Śiva-Śakti school of Tantra is a presentation of Advaita Vedānta from the point of view of a science of practical application and realization,

It is a Śāstra of *sādhanā* and *siddhi*. Pure and undifferentiated Consciousness (*nirviśeṣa cinmātra*) is, of course, affirmed as the basic aspect of Reality. But this pure *cit* is, in another aspect, the power to be and become, that is, to evolve as a universe of names and forms, and involve it again within itself as a seed. *Cit* as this power of self-evolution and self-involution is *cit-śakti*. *Cit* as the pure 'ether' or basis, and *cit* as the power to evolve and involve upon that basis, are not two, but one, viewed from the standpoint of being as such and from that of becoming. Perfect experience is experience of the whole—that is, of Consciousness as Being and Consciousness as power to become. The position has been fully discussed by Sir John Woodroffe and myself in our joint work, *The World as Power*.[1]

THE ACTUAL MODUS OPERANDI OF THE PROCESS

The Jīva as a centre represents a certain phase and position in the evolution-involution process of perfect *cit-śakti* by which a universe arises and is withdrawn. Broadly speaking, evolution means the patent, kinetic aspect, while involution means the latent, static, or potential. Every form of being or centre is thus a kinetic-static composite. An atom of matter is so; a unit of organic matter or a cell of protoplasm is so; mind or *antaḥkaraṇa* is so. The polarity of static-kinetic is everywhere. In the complex apparatus of 'the gross, subtle, and causal' forces, which is the 'body' or vehicle of the Jīva, the static or potential pole of creating, sustaining, and resolving *śakti* is represented by the *kuṇḍalinī* or the coiled serpent-power. It is the body's (including the gross, subtle, and causal) supporting base and magazine of power. It is the central pivot upon which the whole complex apparatus of the physical body, vital economy, and mental activity (conscious and subconscious) moves and turns. The Jīva apparatus is a closed machine of a specific, determinate character, with its bodily, vital, and mental powers and functions limited and defined, because of the specific ratio in which *kuṇḍalinī* or static power in the apparatus stands with respect to the kinetic power actually working in and as that given apparatus. To change the working efficiency of that apparatus, physically, vitally, or mentally, is to change that ratio. A transformation, dynamization, and sublimation of the physical, vital, and mental apparatus is possible only by what is called the 'rousing of *kuṇḍalinī*' and her reorientation from 'downward facing' to 'upward facing'. By the former, the apparatus has become a 'closed curve', limited in character, restricted in

[1] In six parts. I may refer especially to the last part called *Mahāmāyā* dealing with *cit-śakti*; the philosophically minded reader is also referred to my *Introduction to Vedānta Philosophy* delivered as a course of lectures in the University of Calcutta.

functions and possibilities. It is a 'little knower, doer, and enjoyer'. By the latter, it breaks the *pāśa* and transcends its 'littleness'.

The actual *modus operandi* of the rousing process and of the 'piercing' of the *cakras,* or spheres or planes as we may call them, is a very vital mode of Tāntrika and, we may add, of every form of *sādhanā.* The essential thing is to make an ascent, from spheres or planes that are more and more veiled, closed, and limited, to others that are more and more 'conscious' (*cinmaya*), 'open', and unrestricted—that is, from the *aśuddha* to the *śuddha tattvas.* Three 'Gordian knots' (*granthis*) which bind the soul to the *prākṛta* or natural order have to be cut in making a successful ascent. They are the ties of the three *guṇas* famous in the literature of Indian philosophy. They are the three components of Nature's *élan* or impetus—what presents, what moves, and what veils—PMV as I have called them in Sir John Woodroffe's *Serpent Power.* Perfect experience is unconditioned by the stress of PMV and, in this sense, is *guṇātīta* or beyond the natural *guṇas.* During its upward journey, the Jīva is not quite released from the natural frame till it reaches the sixth plane. Till then, it continues to possess, in a more and more refined, extended, and dynamized form, no doubt, the character of a centre in a certain type of *cakra* or sphere or universe. It has not yet reached *brahma-randhra* or the 'opening' for pure and perfect experience. In other words, the centre has not yet become the *bindu* or 'point', which the Śāstra mystically calls the 'perfect universe'. 'Point' is that at which the perfect experience is 'opened' to the centre, and the 'flow' is established. It is like making the limitless ocean flow into a 'little pond'. The little pond ceases to exist as such thereby ; it becomes one with the limitless ocean. If we should call the limitless aspect 'continuum', then a centre or Jīva, after transcending the natural order of the component *guṇas,* becomes transformed into a new being (*pūrṇābhiṣikta*), which then presents a double phase, a point phase and a continuum phase. This is one meaning of the two-petalled sixth lotus where he then finds himself. From the *mantra* point of view, the phases are *bindu* and *nāda.* Below that he was still piercing the *a, u, m* components of the *praṇava* or *Om.* A psychological sublimation goes on *pari passu* with it. The sixth plane represents the coalesced ('like the two halves in a grain of gram') duality of *prakāśa* (illumination) and *vimarśa* (thought) which evolves into the the relation of subject-object.

The end to be achieved is the realization of both pure and perfect Consciousness-Being-Bliss. In the highest plane, the pure *cit* of Advaita Vedānta is realized as the 'resplendent void' ; nay, Śiva-Śakti 'in close embrace' in the abode of the 'thousand-petalled lotus' is also realized. That abode is the abode of wholeness and perfection. The Vaiṣṇava will realize his *yugala* Rādhā-Kṛṣṇa in this abode of wholeness and perfection. And there can be perfect Bliss or *ānanda* only in such wholeness.

In the sixth plane the Jīva-centre, always under stress and strain, now expanding, now contracting (*sphurat-saṅkucat*), as nearly as possible approximates to the character of a perfect point or *bindu*, which means the state of infinite condensation and concentration and therefore of potency. Only by such an infinitely condensed potency can it pierce and gain access into the abode of perfection said to be made of 'the purest *maṇi* or *vajra*'. Only the like will pierce the like. The infinitely great will open itself only to the infinitesimally great which is *bindu*. *Nāda*, in one aspect, is the continuum aspect of the 'point'. In physics, by the way, *bindu* may be represented by the quantum, and *nāda* by the wave-system.

The abode of perfection made of *maṇi* or *vajra* (that is, of imperishable, impenetrable essence) appears to open even to the point through a kind of 'sluice gate'. In course of the ascent, we have to reach and pass successively through certain 'critical' positions. Generally, whenever one *tattva* passes into another, critical values and positions have to be taken into account. Now, in the ascent we are describing, we have to pass successively from one kind of *tattva* to another. To pass a *tattva* is to become it, for each represents a stage of actual realization.

Now, at every crisis or critical position the aspirant or *sādhaka* requires and often gets what we may call ultra-ego-centric 'help', or 'extra-scheduled' power. He gets it from Mother *kuṇḍalinī* herself, in that vital and supremely important aspect of hers which is called *guruśakti*. But really critical positions must be reached so as to make this power available, responsive, and operative for the aspirant. In one sense, it is the aspect of divine grace ; it is *kṛpā*. Grace descends whenever a real crisis comes or is coming. It then becomes patent and indispensable. Now, the sixth plane, or *ājñācakra* as it is called, is *par excellence* the place of *gurutattva*, which is to find the key of the last 'sluice gate' and open it for communion with perfect experience. It is the critical position *par excellence*, because here, more than anywhere before, the ego-centre must finally shed his 'ego', his very 'self'. The seed of *dvaita* must be burnt here. *Gurutattva* is thus the 'key' by which the power, which is as the limitless ocean, is switched on into the little reservoir which is the Jīva, filling the latter, making it overflow and cease to be the little reservoir. It is also the 'commutator' which reverses the ego-centric current, the current that imprisons. The place of *guru* and *dīkṣā* (initiation) is thus of vital importance. *Gurutattva* may, and often does, operate through a human body. But the Śāstra, seizing upon the kernel of the thing, forbids the *sādhaka* to look upon his *guru* as human. He is a form and embodiment of God-power.

CIT-ŚAKTI AND CID-VILĀSA

The *mantra* also must not be regarded as mere letter, and the image through which communion is established with God—who is the creator, sustainer, and destroyer of the world, is infinitely manifested, and is also beyond name, thought, and speech—must not be regarded as stock and stone. If the worship is intelligently done, that is, with an understanding and appreciation of the principles, then *mantra, yantra* (symbolic diagram), the offerings, the procedure, and the paraphernalia of worship are all transformed into forms and expressions of *cit-śakti* and *cid-vilāsa*. The object involved is to effect the transformation of the articles and acts of ordinary experience which are the material, limited, and limiting factors, operative in certain narrow spheres of usage and convention, into forms of *cit-sattā* (being), *cit-śakti* (power), and *cid-vilāsa* (*ānanda* and play). The *nyāsa, bhūtaśuddhi, prāṇāyāma, dhyāna, prāṇapratiṣṭhā,* and *mānasa* and *bāhya pūjā* are all calculated to effect this transformation of the worshipper, the worshipped, and the means and acts of worship into *cit* or *caitanya,* which they all are in their kernel ; and thus, they culminate in realizing the essential identification in perfect experience of the principle of 'thou' (*tvam*) and the principle of 'that' (*tat*). The final result achieved is the same as in *kuṇḍalinī yoga*. In fact, the final result cannot be attained through *mantra, yantra,* and *pūjā* unless thereby *kuṇḍalinī* is roused, the ego-centric, blinding, and binding current is reversed, ascent is made from the plane of *aśuddha* to that of the *śuddha tattvas,* and, finally, to pure and perfect experience itself. The *mantra yoga* or *japa* is a means of rousing *kuṇḍalinī* ; so are *nyāsa, pūjā,* etc. with external or internal *yantras,* images, and symbols. The *bhakta* or the *jñānin,* sometimes, may not have consciously and deliberately to set himself about the business of rousing *kuṇḍalinī* and making her pierce the six *cakras*. But this does not mean that *kuṇḍalinī* can be 'let alone' by him. She *is,* and *must be,* roused by the power of *bhakti* or *jñāna*.

From the principles we have broadly explained, it will appear that *kuṇḍalinī yoga* is not a 'mystery' or esoteric doctrine and ritual peculiar to the Tantras. It is the basis of every *sādhanā* in every form. But there are different forms of effort or *sādhanā* by which this magazine of latent power can be acted upon, and power 'laid up' can be lifted as by a lever. *Viśvāsa* (faith) and *preman* (love) do act as the most powerful lever. The Tantra fully recognizes this and uses it. It recognizes *yoga* and *jñāna* also. It recommends even music as *sura* or *nāda* Brahman. For the common aspirant, however, it serves out a mixed prescription of *karma, jñāna, yoga,* and *bhakti,* all 'scientifically' combined, graded and graduated, and regulated, according to varying conditions and needs.

TANTRA COMPARED WITH THE OBJECTIVE SCIENCES

In fact, Tantra may be aptly described as *sādhanā* reduced to a science, and *siddhi* or realization attained as an experimentally verified fact. For this, it is required that one should follow the lead of a guide who has tried the experiment before and 'seen' for himself.

The Tantras, though aiming at the realization of the supreme end, have also provided courses of discipline by which the so-called 'lower' ends of *artha* (wealth), *kāma* (desire), and *dharma* (virtue) are achieved. The spirit and attitude in which the subject, whether in the higher or in the lower phases, should be approached is precisely that in which one should investigate the problems of physical, biological, and psychological sciences, without prejudice, and with a settled resolve to experiment and see for oneself. There is no more sense in being frightened by *mantra, yantra,* etc. of the Tantra—the endless variety of the apparatus of ritualism suited to every sort of condition of time, place, and individual competence, than in being dismayed by the similarly complicated and elaborate 'ritualism' of modern experimental science. The 'proofs' are the essential thing. The Tantras claim to 'prove' that *mantra* is efficacious, that *yantra* is potent, that *devatās* and higher powers do exist, that *siddhis,* if and to the extent sought, do come, and that the aspirant rises through the *sādhanā* prescribed to higher and higher levels of perfection, till he becomes perfect Being-Consciousness-Bliss.

It has been said that the Tantras are a system of 'magic' and an elaborate process of 'auto-suggestion'. Such statements are true ; and they are false. They are true if 'magic' and 'auto-suggestion' are deeply understood. The first is not opposed to religion, but is the science of religion, by which power in the higher planes is opened and made available for use to the finite centre, including the power to believe and love and worship. The latter is to 'turn round' the self, so that it may be *en rapport* with the process of divine imagination (*kalpanā*) from which the universe arises and in which it subsists. If things come to exist and live by God's 'suggestion', they will come to exist and live by the suggestion of a *siddha* who 'lives, moves, and has his being' in divine Consciousness. The aspirant by self-purification, meditation, surrender, devotion, and intense, passionate seeking places himself *en rapport* with the grantor of all boons including the highest. Since the whole is involved at every 'point', contact and communion can be established with the whole at any point of the universe.

We began with *vāmācāra* which, owing partly to ignorance of the principles and partly to the prevalence of abuse, has made the whole science suspect. Such a method cannot be suited to every kind of competency.

It is not for the *paśu* who moves with the outgoing current and earns merit or demerit while moving with it. He has not yet subdued desire and cut the three knots of 'hate, fear, and shame'. The *sādhaka* competent for the 'left' path is the *vīra* who has assailed *kuṇḍalinī* at her repose at the base root and made her turn and rise. He is competent to 'play with fire' and burn his bonds with it. But there is a final *divya-* and *mahā-bhāva* state in which bonds do not exist in substance, and so they do not require to be burnt, but the semblance or mere form of them is dissolved in the 'ocean of nectar' of *divyabhāva*.

The word '*tantra*' which is sometimes derived from the root *tan*, to spread, means a system, a method, a discipline. It is a system of acts on the physical, vital, and mental planes by which a centre of being can render itself an apparatus efficient for the purpose of encompassing the twofold end of *abhyudaya* (progress or uplift) and *niḥśreyasa* (the supreme Good).

We have already referred to the fact how Tantra has effected a mutually helpful and perfecting co-ordination of *karma, yoga, jñāna,* and *bhakti*. It has emphasized will and effort, yet self-surrender, mercy, and grace have their vital place and function ; and it combines the systematized ritualism of *karma* with the inner purifying process of *yoga* ; the purest Advaita *jñāna* with the purest *bhakti* and the most passionate yearning and love.

14

THE SPIRIT AND CULTURE OF THE TANTRAS

CLASSES AND NUMBER OF THE TANTRAS

DR. Winternitz says, 'When we speak of Tantra, we think primarily of the sacred books of the Śāktas'. This shows how little attention is paid to the wide variety of meanings of the word *'tantra'*. We are here concerned with that class of Tantras which deals with worship or *sādhanā*. The Tantras lay down different forms of practice for the attainment of the highest aim of human existence by one living the ordinary life of a householder. In this respect they correspond to the *upāsanā-kāṇḍa* of the Śruti. The Tantras fall under five heads, viz. Śaiva, Śākta, Vaiṣṇava, Saura, and Gāṇapatya. These five classes of worshippers are collectively called *pañcopāsaka.* Each of these classes of worshippers has its own Tantras.

Scholars of the present day are much concerned to ascertain the age of the Tantras. In the Purāṇas we find that both the Vaidika and Tāntrika forms of worship are mentioned. Hence the Tāntrika forms must have existed during, if not before, the Purāṇas. The theory that the Tāntrika age followed the Paurāṇic age therefore falls to the ground. There are some who theorize that the Tantras are post-Buddhistic. This also cannot be accepted, if the authority of the *Lalitavistara* is of any value. In the seventeenth chapter of that book, it is said that Lord Buddha condemned the worship of Brahmā, Indra, Viṣṇu, Kātyāyanī, Gaṇapati, and so forth, many of which were well-known Tāntrika forms of worship. The Buddhists also have their own Tantras, which mention names of deities, such as Ādibuddha, Prajñāpāramitā, Mañjuśrī, Tārā, and Ārya-Tārā. If the texts of the Brāhmaṇic and Buddhistic Tantras are compared, considerable similarity will be found in the methods of the two classes.

The *Nārāyaṇīya Tantra* says that the Vedas have originated from the Yāmalas, which form a class of Tantras of considerable magnitude. The passage in question states that the teachings of the *Sāma-Veda* find expression in the *Brahma Yāmala,* those of the *Ṛg-Veda* in the *Rudra Yāmala,* those of the *Yajur-Veda* in the *Viṣṇu Yāmala,* and those of the *Atharva-Veda* in the *Śakti Yāmala.* These verses, which have been quoted by the great Siddha Sarvānanda in his compendium called the *Sarvollāsa Tantra,* may also mean that the Yāmalas preceded the Tantras.

There is a difference of opinion as to how many Tantras there are. According to the *Mahāsiddhasāra Tantra,* Bhāratavarṣa is divided into three *krāntās* or divisions, viz. *viṣṇu-krāntā, ratha-krāntā,* and *aśva-krāntā,* and each of these *krāntās,* it is said, has sixty-four Tantras. The *Śakti-maṅgala Tantra* says that the land east of the Vindhya Hills extending right up to Java is *viṣṇu-krāntā.* The country north of the Vindhya Hills including Mahācīna is *ratha-krāntā.* The rest of the country westward is *aśva-krāntā.*

The *Ṣaṭ-sambhava-rahasya* says that in Bhārata there are four *sampra-dāyas* (schools), viz. Gauḍa in the east, Kerala in the middle, Kāśmīra in the west, and Vilāsa, which is a sort of eclectic school, not confined to any particular region, but found everywhere.

TYPES OF SĀDHANĀS AND SĀDHAKAS

The different Brāhmaṇic or, as it is miscalled, Hindu forms of worship lead the worshipper to the supreme Brahman. The singular distinction of Brāhmaṇism is to have recognized that men vary in temperament and in various other ways. The Tantra classifies mankind primarily under three heads, viz. the man with a *divya* or divine disposition, the man with a *vīra* or heroic disposition, and the man with a *paśu* or animal disposition. The *Bhāvacūḍāmaṇi Tantra* gives a detailed description of not merely these classes of men, but also of the innumerable subsections under these heads. *Bhāva* (disposition) forms a very important factor in the process of *sādhanā.*

Padmapādācārya, the disciple of Śaṅkarācārya, in his commentary on the *Prapañcasāra,* says that there are five different ways in which the teachings of the Śāstra have to be considered. These five ways are: (1) *sthūla* (gross), (2) *sūkṣma* (subtle), (3) *kāraṇa* (causal), (4) *sāmānya* (cosmic), and (5) *sākṣin* (witness-like). Now every one is not competent to consider things from these five different view-points. The *paśu* man can hardly be expected to see beyond the *sthūla* or material aspect of things. In the *vīra* man there is an urge to reach the plane beyond matter, and the true *vīra* is he who is fighting the six enemies—the passions—which obstruct the path of spiritual advancement. The man of *divya* disposition is, as a result of his practice in previous births, endowed with qualities which make him almost divine. The *Kāmākhyā Tantra* says that the man of *divya* disposition is the beloved of all and is sparing in his words, quiet, steady, sagacious, and attentive to all. He is always contented and is devoted to the feet of his *guru* (teacher). He fears no one, is consistent in what he says, and is experienced in all matters. He never swerves from the path of truth and avoids all that is evil. He is good in every way and is Śiva's very self. The *vīra* is a man of fearless disposition, inspires fear in the man of *paśu* disposition, and is pure in his motive. He is gentle in his speech and is always mindful of the five *tattvas* (principles). He is physically strong, courageous, intelligent, and enterprising. He is humble in his ways and is ever ready to cherish the good. The *paśu* is a man whose inclinations are like those of an animal. He is a slave to his six enemies—lust, anger, greed, pride, illusion, and envy.[1]

THE SEVEN ĀCĀRAS AND THE SAPTA-BHŪMIKĀS

Closely connected with the three *bhāvas* are the seven *ācāras* or rules of conduct, which are given in the *Kulārṇava Tantra* as follows: *veda, vaiṣṇava, śaiva, dakṣiṇa, vāma, siddhānta,* and *kaula*. The aspirant rises step by step through these different *ācāras* till he reaches the seventh and highest stage, when Brahman becomes an experiential reality to him. In the first stage, cleanliness of the body and mind is cultivated. The second stage is that of devotion (*bhakti*). The third is that of *jñāna* (knowledge). *Dakṣiṇa,* which is the fourth stage, is that in which the gains acquired in the preceding three stages are consolidated. This is followed by *vāma* which is the stage of renunciation. This does not mean, as has been said by the detractors of the Tantra, the practice of rites with a woman (*vāmā*). *Vāma* is the reverse of *dakṣiṇa*; it means the path of renunciation. If a woman is at all associated in this practice, she is there to help in the path of renunciation, and not for animal gratification. A woman as such is an object of great veneration to all schools of Tāntrika *sādhakas* (seekers). She is considered to be the embodiment on earth of the supreme Śakti who pervades the universe. She should therefore be revered as such and, even if guilty of a hundred wrongs, she is not to be hurt even with a flower. It is a sin to speak disparagingly of any woman. The sixth stage, viz. *siddhānta,* is that in which the aspirant comes to the definitive conclusion after deliberate consideration as to the relative merits of the path of enjoyment and that of renunciation. By pursuing the latter path, he reaches the final stage of *kaula*. This is the stage in which Kula or Brahman becomes a reality to him. The first three of these seven stages, viz. *veda, vaiṣṇava,* and *śaiva* belong to *paśubhāva*; *dakṣiṇa* and *vāma* belong to *vīrabhāva*; and the last two belong to *divyabhāva*. According to some, the last alone is *divyabhāva*. And the *Paraśurāma Kalpa-Sūtra* says that during the first five stages the aspirant must be guided by the teacher, and it is only after he has passed the fifth stage that he is allowed to have freedom of action in every way. The *Viśvasāra Tantra,* alluding to the importance of the *bhāvas* and *ācāras,* says, 'He truly is liberated in this life who knows the seven *ācāras* comprised within the three *bhāvas*'. It may be noted here that the seven *ācāras* correspond, with very slight difference, to the seven

[1] The *Sarvollāsa Tantra* as also the *Kaulāvalī-nirṇaya* will help inquirers who cannot get the *Bhāvacūḍāmaṇi*. This latter book and the *Sarvollāsa* have not been published.

jñāna-bhūmikās (knowledge-planes) described in the *Yogavāsiṣṭha,* which are: *vividiṣā* or *śubhecchā, vicāraṇā, tanumānasā, sattvāpatti, asaṁsakti, padārthabhāvinī,* and *turīyā.* The difference between the *ācāras* of the Tantra and the *jñāna-bhūmikās* of the *Yogavāsiṣṭha* is that in the former the aspirant reaches *jñāna* through the path of *bhakti* (*vaiṣṇava ācāra*), whereas in the latter path of dry ratiocination, the stage of *tanumānasā* (*bhakti*) comes to him when, after passing through a number of insurmountable difficulties, he finds that without *bhakti* he can make no further progress..

THE TEACHER AND THE DISCIPLE

Like the Śruti, the Tantra lays great emphasis on the necessity of initiation. A good teacher is defined as a man of pure birth and pure disposition, who has his senses under control. He should know the true meaning of the Āgamas (Tantras) and other Śāstras (scriptures), always be doing good to others, and be engaged in repetition of God's name, worship, meditation, and offering oblations in the fire. He should have a peaceful mind and must possess the power of granting favours. He should know the Vedic teachings, be competent in *yoga,* and be charming like a god. The characteristics of a good disciple are as follows: He should be of good parentage and guileless disposition, and be a seeker of the fourfold aim of human existence.[2] He should be well read in the Vedas and be intelligent. He should have his animal desires under complete control, always be kind towards all animals, and have faith in the next world. He should not associate with non-believers (*nāstikas*), but should be assiduous in his duties in general, alert in the discharge of his duties towards his parents in particular, and free from the pride of birth, wealth, and learning in the presence of his teacher. He should always be willing to sacrifice his own interests in the discharge of his duties to the teacher, and be ever ready to serve him in all humility.

The disciple should always bear in mind that his teacher is immortal. This does not mean that the human teacher is so; he is the channel through which the spirit of God descends. The true teacher is the supreme Brahman or Śiva, or, as some say, the primordial Śakti. The position of the human teacher is one of very great responsibility, which does not end with initiation. He has to look after his disciple's welfare in every respect and guide him. He is called the physician of the soul, and a healthy soul can abide only in a healthy body. He has to see that even in matters of health the disciple goes the right way. The teacher

[2] Attainment of moral (*dharma*), economic (*artha*), and aesthetic (*kāma*) perfections, as well as of liberation (*mokṣa*).

who is conscious of his responsibility does not initiate in a hurry, and the Śāstra enjoins that the disciple should not accept a teacher to whom he is not attracted. The mode of initiation is not in every case the same and varies according to the disposition and the competency of the disciple. The ordinary mode of initiation is called *kriyā-dīkṣā*. This may be an elaborate process consisting of many rituals. Men of higher competency are initiated by other methods. The initiation which is the quickest and most effective is called *vedha-dīkṣā*. A person initiated according to this method realizes at once the oneness of his own self with that of the teacher, the *mantra* (sacred formula), and the deity. He becomes, as the Tantras say, the very self of Śiva. The disciples who are initiated according to other forms of *dīkṣā* arrive at this realization by slow degrees, each according to his competency.

DIFFERENT MODES OF WORSHIP

Our scriptures say that it is beyond the average man's intelligence to apprehend the supreme Being who is the ultimate Reality, *para-tattva*. It is said in the Tantras that Brahman, who is mere *jñāna,* impartite, and without a body, cannot be worshipped by the average man ; so a form is adopted by the aspirant for the purpose of his practice. The Tantra again says: 'The deity of the *vipra* (ritualist) is in the fire into which he offers oblations ; that of the man of contemplation is in his heart ; the man who is not awakened sees him in the image ; but the man who knows the Ātman sees him everywhere.'

It has already been said that there are five aspects in all Tāntrika teachings. Here four aspects of worship are given. The fifth aspect of the deity is beyond all description and all worship ; for that is the stage where the worshipper and the worshipped become one. In the *Prapañcasāra* by Śaṅkarācārya and the *Śāradātilaka* by Lakṣmaṇa Deśikendra are given accounts of all the five methods of worship and their subdivisions. The *Tantrasāra* describes the rituals.

INITIATION OR DĪKṢĀ

Initiation or *dīkṣā* means 'that which gives a knowledge of things divine and destroys all that leads to a fall'. The teacher, for example, explains how the three letters *a, u,* and *m,* constituting the Praṇava or *Aum* (*Om*), represent the three *guṇas—sattva, rajas,* and *tamas* ; how these are embodied in Viṣṇu, Brahmā, and Śiva ; and how these three deities, again, can function only with the help of their respective Śaktis. The *guru* also teaches how the *Om* is but a subtle form of the sacred formula '*haṁsaḥ*', also called the *ajapā-mantra,* which is the carrier (*vāhana*) of Brahmā, the

Creator, inasmuch as *haṁsaḥ* means 'the breath of life'. *Haṁ* is inspired breath and *saḥ* is that which is expired. Everything movable and immovable breathes, and therefore Brahmā, who is nothing but the creative aspect of the supreme Substance manifest in the world, is represented as seated thereon. To the ordinary man *haṁsaḥ* is a water-fowl. The aspirant has also to learn that the *praṇava* contains within itself, besides the aforesaid three letters, *bindu, nāda* (sound), *śakti* (power), and *śānta* (quiescence). When he has learned this, he is to know that which is beyond *śānta* (*śāntātīta*). These remarks apply to every *mantra.*

CREATION OF THE UNIVERSE

The universe, some say, has been created by Sadāśiva, others again say that it has been created by Viṣṇu, and so on. There are some who say that the universe has no creator, while others say that it has many. There are some who hold that it, being the product of nature (*svabhāvottha*), is eternally existing; there are others who say that it is the great Śakti that created it. There is another class of people who maintain that the Virāṭ Puruṣa (universal Being) has created it. According to the Tantra, Śiva or Brahman has two aspects, *nirguṇa* (attributeless) and *saguṇa* (with attributes). As the former, He is transcendent and therefore dissociated from Prakṛti or Śakti; and, as the latter, He is associated with Śakti. It is out of this that *śakti* emanates; from that, *nāda* (sound); and out of *nāda, bindu.* This conception is put in another way. At the time of *pralaya* or final dissolution everything is withdrawn into the supreme Śakti. Thereafter, when Śakti, which is the *tattva* (substance), approaches the Light, which is *cit* or knowledge, there arises in the former the desire to create (*vicikīrṣā*), and the *bindu* is formed. This bursts and divides itself, and out of that division there arise *bindu, nāda,* and *bīja. Bindu* partakes of the nature of Śiva or *jñāna, bīja* is Śakti, and *nāda* is the relation between the two as the stimulator and the stimulated (*kṣobhya*). When the *bindu* bursts, there arises an inchoate volume of sound. This sound is called Śabda Brahman, which is the *caitanya* (stress towards manifestation in all beings) pervading all creation, and is the source of the letters of the alphabet, of words, and of other sounds by which thoughts are exchanged. All sounds (*śabda*) have meaning; sound and meaning are inseparable.

MANTRA

From *śabda* there arises the ethereal region; from touch, air; from colour, fire; from taste, water; and from smell, earth. It will be seen that the gross comes out of the subtle in the process of unfolding, and when it is reversed the gross disappears in the subtle. In this way, the aspirant begins with a gross material accessory, viz. the image, and rises step by step to that which is beyond word and speech. The image that is used in worship is the form of the *mantra* that is chosen for the worshipper by his *guru*, and represents his conception of Brahman (*svakīya Brahmamūrtiḥ*). One's *deva* is the form of Brahman evolved out of one's *mantra*. The Tantra claims that a man who worships his *iṣṭadevatā* (chosen deity), which is another name for his image of Brahman, in the prescribed manner, lives a happy and contented life, enjoys the objects of his desire, and, at the same time, uplifts himself spiritually. The worship of the *deva* of one's adoption means the worshipper's uplifting himself to the level of that *deva*, and when once this is secured, he arrives at a stage when he becomes competent to apprehend the supreme *deva*, Brahman.

The Tantra holds that the highest stage is Kula. The man becomes a *kaulika* only after he has passed through the six *ācāras* previously mentioned. It is further necessary for him to know the other modes of worship. It has been said that it is only to that man whose mind is purified by the *mantras* of Śiva, Viṣṇu, Durgā, Sūrya, Gaṇeśa, and others that *kula-jñāna* manifests itself.

THE PAÑCA-MAKĀRAS

It is a favourite pastime of some uninformed minds to indulge in invectives against the Tantra for the use in worship of the five *tattvas* (principles), commonly called the five 'M's (*pañca-makāra*). By these are meant wine, meat, fish, cereals, and sexual union. These five articles have different meanings for different classes of worshippers. It is to be noted that what one is required to offer is the *tattva* (principle, essence) and not the article itself. The object of using these five *tattvas* in worship is that by the repeated practice of the ritualistic observances one acquires a nature whereby everything one does in ordinary life becomes an act of worship. Śaṅkarācārya in his magnificent hymn to the primordial Śakti concludes by saying, 'O Lady Supreme, may all the functions of my mind be Thy remembrance; may all my words be Thy praise; may all my acts be an obeisance unto Thee'. It is to induce a state of mind like this that the five things are used in worship.

The aspirant who partakes of the five *tattvas* to please the deity within him incurs no demerit. Such a man looks upon wine and meat as Śakti and Śiva, and is fully alive to the fact that the wine of which he is about to partake will make manifest the bliss that is Brahman within him. Every cup of wine is drunk with appropriate rites, and with the recitation of an appropriate *mantra*. Before drinking the first cup he says, 'I adore this, the first cup of nectar held in my hand. It is suffused with the nectar of the moon shining in the forehead of holy Bhairava. All the gods, goddesses, and holy men adore it. It is the ocean of bliss. It uplifts the Ātman'. An aspirant who is allowed to have ten cups meditates, while drinking, on his *guru* in the *sahasrāra,* the thousand-petalled lotus in the head, and on the goddess in the heart. He has his *iṣṭa mantra* at the tip of his tongue and thinks of his oneness with Śiva. The man who drinks the eleventh cup repeats the following *mantra*: 'I am not the doer, nor do I make any one else do, nor am I the thing done. I am not the enjoyer, nor do I make any one else enjoy, nor am I the object of enjoyment. I do not suffer pain, nor do I cause pain to others, nor am I pain itself. I am He (*so'ham*). I am Cit, I am Ātman.' These *mantras* have a threefold meaning: The gross one is the actual drinking of wine ; the subtle one is the drinking of the nectar which flows from the union of the *kuṇḍalinī* (the coiled-up power) with Śiva in the *sahasrāra* ; the third or the transcendent one is the nectar of happiness arising from the realization of the union of the supreme Śiva and the supreme Śakti.

The *Kulārṇava Tantra* says that the wine which gladdens is the nectar which flows from the union of the *kuṇḍalinī śakti* with Śiva at the *sahasrāra* in the head. And he who drinks this drinks nectar, and others are mere wine-bibbers. That man who kills by the sword of *jñāna* the animals of merit and demerit and leads his mind to the supreme Śiva is said to be a true eater of flesh. That man truly takes fish who controls all his senses and places them in his Ātman ; others are mere killers of animals. The *śakti* of the *paśu* (the lowest class of aspirant) is not awakened, but that of the *kaulika* is. The man who enjoys this *śakti* is said to be a true enjoyer of *śakti.* He is permeated by the bliss which arises out of the union of the supreme Śakti and Ātman, which is the true union ; others are no better than fornicators.

It should be noted that the term for the fifth *tattva* is derived from the word *mithuna,* which means a couple. Since nothing in the world of experience happens without the combination of two things—even consciousness is impossible without it—, *maithuna* symbolizes the unity which is behind all this duality, which is beyond ordinary human comprehension, and which the *jīvanmuktas* (liberated in life) alone can apprehend. By the offering of this *tattva* to the chosen deity is meant the offering of the sense of duality, so that the underlying oneness may be realized. This is the true significance of the fifth item.

THE FOUR STAGES OF SPEECH

Something ought to be said here about the four stages of speech, in three of which sound is inaudible ; it is only at the fourth stage that men give utterance to it. The first of these stages is *parā* located in the *mūlādhāra*, the lowest of the six centres in the spinal column, commonly called *cakras*. This is but a mere stress towards articulation. As this stress takes definite shape, it becomes *paśyantī*, which means 'seeing'. The next stage is reached when it arrives at the *anāhatacakra* opposite the heart; it then becomes *madhyamā*, which means 'middling'. These are the three names given in the Tantra to the three silent stages of vocal sound, and the last stage is *vaikharī*. There are some, the foremost among whom is Padmapādācārya, the chief disciple of Śaṅkarācārya, who hold that there are three other stages of sound prior to *parā*. Padmapāda, in commenting on the forty-third verse of the second chapter of the *Prapañcasāra*, says that the stages preceding *parā* are *śūnyā*, *saṁvit*, and *sūkṣmā*. The first is the vibrational stage, the next is that when the sound is about to form, and the third is that when it is forming. An adequate knowledge of sound is of vital importance in the Tantra.

THE SIX CAKRAS AND THE SIX ADHVANS

This leads us to the six centres, which are: (1) *mūlādhāra*, which is situated above the organ of generation and is the region of earth; (2) *svādhiṣṭhāna*, which is just above the previous one and is the region of water; (3) *maṇipura*, in the spinal cord opposite the navel, of fire; (4) *anāhata*, opposite the heart, of air; (5) *viśuddha*, opposite the base of the throat, of ether; and (6) *ājñā*, opposite the junction of the eyebrows, of psychic vision. There are other centres beyond the *ājñā*. Opinion is divided as to the number of these *cakras*; some say that there are sixteen, and others that there are more. The piercing (*bheda*) of the six *cakras* is a process whereby the elements of which the body is composed are purified.[3] It is laid down that the attempt to pierce the six *cakras* should be made under the immediate guidance of the teacher, for the least mistake may lead to disastrous results. By this process the six paths (*adhvans*) that lead to a realization of the Supreme are mastered.[4] They are *kalā* (attribute), *tattva* (category), *bhuvana* (region), *varṇa* (letters), *pada* (words), and *mantra* (mystic symbols or words). The *kalās* are *nivṛtti*, *pratiṣṭhā*, *vidyā*, *śānti*, and *śāntyatītā*. The *tattvas*, according to the Śaivas, are thirty-six, and according to the Vaiṣṇavas, thirty-two. The Sāṁkhyas recognize twenty-four *tattvas*. The *tattvas* of Prakṛti are ten in number and those of Tripura are seven. The *bhuvanas*, according to some, are the ethereal, the aerial, the

[3] It is described in detail in *The Serpent Power* by Arthur Avalon (Sir John Woodroffe). Dr. Hereward Carrington has attempted to put it in a popular form.

[4] In an article like this we cannot possibly enter into details. So in what follows we should content ourselves with a bare outline.

igneous, the aquatic, and the terrene regions. The *Vāyavīya Saṁhitā*, however, says that the lowest of these *bhuvanas* is *mūlādhāra* and the highest *unmanī*. It will be seen that whichever view is accepted, the different *bhuvanas* are the different stages of the mind of the aspirant. The *varṇas* are the letters of the alphabet with the nasal *bindu* superposed; and the *padas* are the words formed by the combination of letters. The way of *mantras* means the whole mass of *mantras* with their secret. At the time of initiation, the teacher shows how every letter of the alphabet, every word that is spoken, every *mantra* that was discovered by any sage, in fact, everything in existence points towards Brahman. By reason of our own limitations we are unable to see Him, though He is in and around us and is our very being.

Of very great importance are the letters of the alphabet. They are called *mātṛkā* (mother). They are collectively the source from which every word and every *mantra* is evolved. Out of the *mantra*, again, is produced its deity. Śaṅkarācārya, in the opening verse of the *Prapañcasāra*, which is an adoration of Śāradā, says, 'May Śāradā purify your mind'. The body of the goddess is composed of the seven groups (*varga*) into which the (Sanskrit) alphabet is divided. She is eternal and is the cause of the creation and of the dissolution of the universe.

ŚIVA AND ŚAKTI

The Tantras say that Śiva without Śakti is a lifeless corpse, because wisdom cannot move without power. It is at the same time said that the relation between Śiva, who is the possessor of Śakti, and Śakti Herself is one of identity; the one cannot be without the other. The attempt to identify Śakti with woman is an error. Śiva is commonly said to be the male principle, and Śakti the female principle. As a matter of fact, they are neither male nor female, nor are they neuter. The man who worships the wisdom aspect of Reality, commonly called the male principle, is a Śaiva; and he who worships the power aspect, or the female principle, is called a Śākta. Śiva as the ruler of the universe rides a bull, i.e. he rules according to *dharma*.[5] When Śiva is worshipped, His consort is also worshipped; for the two are inseparable. For the same reason, when Śakti is worshipped, Śiva is also worshipped. To some minds the Viṣṇu or pervasive aspect of Reality appeals as the proper way to realize the supreme Brahman. The rituals in Śaiva and Vaiṣṇava worship differ. Śakti is worshipped as Sarasvatī, the queen of speech. As such, in the enumeration of Śaktis, she is given the first place, and is the source from which all *mantras*

[5] *Satya* (truth), *śauca* (purity), *dayā* (kindness), and *dāna* (charity) constitute the four feet of *dharma* conceived as a bull.

emanate ; she has different aspects with different *mantras*. Other aspects of Śakti are Śrī or Lakṣmī, Bhuvaneśvarī, Durgā, and Kālī.

The Tantras declare that, by following the rules laid down by them, the aspirant, though living the life of a householder, may yet achieve high attainments. The mere study of the Śāstras may give us some idea of the Śabda Brahman, but it is only by a discriminative knowledge of the essentials (*viveka*) that the supreme Brahman can be experienced. The illumination comes to him alone who, through practice in the manner enjoined by his own Tantra, has acquired *jñāna*, which teaches him that Brahmā the Creator, Viṣṇu the Protector, and even Śiva the Destroyer (i.e. one who withdraws everything at the time of the final dissolution) are all perishable, and it is the supreme Truth alone which endures for all times. The man who has realized that Truth has no necessity to know any scriptures, just as a man who has tasted nectar to his heart's content has no necessity for food.

15

ŚAKTI CULT IN SOUTH INDIA

KORRAVAI-DURGĀ-BHAGAVATĪ

KORRAVAI and Aiyai are the names by which the Mother Goddess was known to early Tamil writers. The Eyinar and the Maravar, two ancient Tamil warrior classes, propitiated Her as the Goddess of victory by bloody sacrifices, human and animal, accompanied by ritual, music, and dancing. Her priestesses danced a weird dance, called the *veṭṭuvavari*, and, in the course of the performance, predicted what evils might befall the community and how they could be averted. She was also adored as the 'Goddess round whom the *tunaṅgai* (another old folk-dance) was danced'—She whose great womb gave birth to Śeyon, the Red-god (later identified with Skanda), resplendent with yellow ornaments, who killed the cruel demon on the expanse of the white waves of the sea. Heroes returning from battle placed their swords at Her feet as a thanks-offering.

The earliest Tamil literary works depict a society the culture of which is a composite one—a blend of the pre-Aryan with the Aryan. Vedic and Āgamic ideas altered the old forms of worship in the Tamil country during the early centuries of the Christian era ; and Korravai, the Tamil Goddess of war and victory, was easily identified with Durgā. The *Śilappadikāram*, a Tamil epic of about the sixth century, describes Her as the 'three-eyed Goddess whose crown is adorned with the crescent moon, whose lips, red as the coral, are parted in a beatific smile, whose waist is encircled by a serpent, whose arm wields the trident, and whose feet, bedecked with anklets, rest upon the severed head of Mahiṣāsura'. 'Praised by the gods and sages, She of the dark colour is the embodiment of victory, *dharma,* and wisdom.' 'Dwelling in the forest, She, who cleft asunder the hard bosom of Dāruka, witnesses the dance of Her spouse, the lord of Kailāsa.' According to the *Maṇimekalai,* another Tamil epic of the same period, priests, garbed as Bhairavas, officiated in Her worship, chanting Tāntric *mantras.* Hailed as the Magna Mater, She is also the eternal Virgin, enshrined in Kanyākumārī, one of the oldest shrines in the Tamil country dedicated to Durgā, mentioned by Pliny and the author of *The Periplus of the Erythraean Sea.*

Among the numerous sculptures that stand as monuments to the cultural greatness of the Pallava and Pāṇḍya rule, from the seventh to the ninth century, are the panels, representing Mahiṣamardinī, carved in the monolithic and cave temples of South India.[1] The Goddess is generally represented with a benign countenance, eight-armed, astride Her lion, and aiming a spear at the demon. In the Śiva temples of the early Coḷa period, a separate sub-shrine was assigned to Durgā, and in the later epochs, a shrine or niche to the north of the sanctum, where She is generally represented with four arms and standing on the head of Mahiṣa.

The Ṛg-Vedic Goddess Vāc was addressed in early Tamil literature as Cintā Devī. She was later called Kalaimagal, the Goddess of learning and arts. There are also references to Śrī or Lakṣmī, the Goddess who manifested Herself from the depths of the ocean, and who, seated on the breast of Viṣṇu, blesses those pure men who are free from the evil passions of lust and avarice. The conception of Durgā as the primordial Śakti and of Lakṣmī and Sarasvatī as Her aspects became familiar; and thus in Durgā the devotee visualized the triple aspect of power, beneficence, and wisdom. Here is the power that not only subdues and controls evil, but also elevates and emancipates.

The members of the famous mediaeval trading corporation, known as the *nānādeśīyatiśai-āyirattu-aiñ-ñūrruvar* ('the "five hundred" from different countries and the thousand quarters'), were worshippers of Bhagavatī Durgā, in whose honour they erected temples in different parts of the Deccan and South India. In one such temple in the Tamil country,[2] She is called Aiyāpolil Parameśvarī—the Parameśvarī of Aihole, where a famous Durgā temple was built by the early Cālukyas. To the Tamil members of this corporation, Durgā was *kandaḷi,* a Tamil word meaning the divine Principle, beyond form and name and transcending all manifestations.

While the common folk propitiate Durgā under different local names, too numerous to mention, and install Her as the guardian deity of villages, the initiated pray to Her for liberation.[3] She is invoked in one or other of Her nine forms (Navadurgā), or as Bhadrakālī, the auspicious Mother who transcends time and causation, in the lustrous flame, or in a *yantra* (mystic diagram), or in figures drawn with rice-flour, turmeric powder, and saffron; and the worship includes all the Tāntric rituals beginning with self-purification (*bhūtaśuddhi* and *ātmaśuddhi*) and ending with oblations (*bali* and *homa*). Along with *bīja mantras,* the *ṛcas* (hymns) of the *Durgā-sūkta* are often chanted.

[1] At Madattukkovil in the former Pudukkottai State and at Namakkal. There is a famous Mahiṣamardinī panel at Mamallapuram.

[2] At Kallampatti, about twenty miles to the south-west of Pudukkottai.

[3] 'Afraid of the pangs of worldly life, I bow unto Thee, who helpeth me to cross the ocean of earthly existence' (*namāmi bhavabhīto'haṁ saṁsārārṇavatāriṇīm*).

MINOR ŚAKTIS

There are reminiscences in South Indian temples of minor Śakti cults. The larger temples of the Pallava and early Coḷa periods had shrines dedicated to the Saptamātṛkās (Seven Mothers) and to Jyeṣṭhā. The Saptamātṛkā group comprised seven Devī idols—Brāhmī, Māheśvarī, Kaumārī, Vaiṣṇavī, Vārāhī, Māhendrī, and Cāmuṇḍā, with Gaṇeśa and Vīrabhadra on either side of the group. Jyeṣṭhā was represented as two-armed with a male attendant. Her banner bore the crow. These two cults disappeared by about the eleventh century, and all that remain of them are the neglected, and often mutilated, statues in the corridors of old temples.

To the common folk, who can scarcely comprehend the conception of a primordial Śakti, the hosts of village and old totem gods and goddesses are the objects of reverence, and the higher classes also occasionally participate in their worship. These divinities are much dreaded, and are propitiated to ward off calamities. Māriamman, the southern counterpart of Śītalā, is perhaps the most popular and is held in great dread as the goddess of smallpox.

The memory of chaste women was held in great respect. Arundhatī was praised in old Tamil songs. Draupadī is a common deity in South Indian villages, where an annual festival, lasting for eighteen days, is held in her honour, when the *Mahābhārata* is read. On the last day of the festival, votaries, with their heads adorned with flowers and their bodies decked with sandal and saffron, walk over a very hot fire extending many feet in length. A whole canto of the *Śilappadikāram* has for its theme the deification of Kannagi, the virtuous wife of the hero, Kovalan. This cult of the *paṭṭinī* (virtuous wife) spread from the Tamil land to Ceylon. Similar honours were paid to women who performed *satī*, and places where this rite was performed were called *mālaiyīḍu* (*mālai,* garland), because garlands were offered to their souls. To this day, Tamil homes cherish, at least once a year, the memory of *sumaṅgalīs* (those who predeceased their husbands) with worship and feasting.

Religious rites in the Tamil country were a mixture of sacrifice, music, and dancing. There are numerous references in Tamil inscriptions to *kūttus* or dance-plays enacted in connection with temple festivals ; perhaps the most important among them was the *śāntikūttu.* Folk-dance and drama are even today associated with temple worship in South Indian villages.

ŚRĪVIDYĀ-LALITĀ

South Indian Śaiva philosophy is a complex of many factors, three of which are of outstanding importance—first, the simple religion of the hymnists, known as the Nāyanārs, proclaiming the doctrine of pure love and self-surrender to the Lord's grace; secondly, the Tamil Āgamas, largely influenced by the Pratyabhijñā school of Kashmir, though with certain marked metaphysical differences; and thirdly, the doctrines of the Pāśupatas and Kālāmukhas, the followers of Lakulīśa. The *Pratyabhijñā-Sūtra* was freely drawn upon by both the Śaiva and Śākta devotees. While the Śaiva aspect was elaborated in the *Śivadṛṣṭi* and the later works based on it, the Śākta aspect was developed in such works as the *Cidghana-candrikā* and *Tantrāloka*. A much later Śākta treatise, based on the *Pratyabhijñā-Sūtra*, is the *Kāmakalā-vilāsa*.

The Śākta philosophy and rituals, expounded in Kashmir Tāntric treatises, in such works as *Candrakāla-vidyāṣṭaka* and *Śubhāgamapañcaka* and in Gauḍapāda's *Subhagodaya*,[4] relate to what is compendiously known as *śrīvidyā* or *Brahmavidyā*, which is rather the practical course or *sādhana-śāstra* not only of the monism of the Upaniṣads, but also to a large extent of the final liberation expounded in the Siddhānta (Tamil Śaiva philosophy). According to the Śaivas and Śāktas, Śakti is not different from Śiva, and they together constitute the ultimate Reality. Śiva or Kāmeśvara is *prakāśa* or subjective illumination, while Śakti, known as Kāmeśvarī, Śivakāmā, Kāmakoṭī, Lalitā, and Tripurasundarī, is *vimarśa* or Śiva's objective experience of Himself. This experience, in which 'I' or *aham* (subjective) and 'this' or *idam* (objective) are yet held in a unity, i.e. in which there is just a glimmer of a universe in idea, but no actual emergence of an objective world, is the first emanation of consciousness, known as *sadāśiva-* or *sādākhya-tattva*, Sadāśiva functioning with and through His Śakti, Manonmanī. The next emanation is *īśvara-tattva* with *māyā-śakti*, in which objectivity begins to prevail and from which ultimately, through different stages of evolution, emerge the *tattvas* or the different categories of mind, senses, and matter, leading down finally to the *pṛthvī-tattva* as in the Sāṁkhya system. In iconographic symbolism, the *liṅga* stands for *sādākhya* or *sadāśiva*, and the other forms (i.e. full-fledged images) of Śiva for the *īśvara-tattva*. Since *sadāśiva-tattva* comprises both Sadāśiva and Manonmanī, the need was felt for the representation of the latter in places of worship, and this accounts for the erection of a separate shrine to Devī, commonly known in the Tamil country as the Amman (Mother) shrine. These Amman shrines, which in the old Tamil inscriptions are mentioned as the *kāmakoṭṭam* (Kāmakoṭī's shrine), came into vogue from about the eleventh century. Before this time there were temples dedicated to Devī, independent of and

[4] The *Lalitopākhyāna*, which, together with the two exquisite *stotras*, *Lalitā-sahasranāma* and *Lalitā-triśatī*, is said to form the *Rahasyakāṇḍa* or 'the Book of Secret Doctrines' of the *Brahmāṇḍa Purāṇa*, contains the teachings of Hayagrīva to Agastya, which are said to have been imparted in Kāñcī. Obviously the author of the work is a South Indian. The work must have been written after the eighth century.

not related to Śiva shrines, but from about this time the twin shrines of Śiva and Amman came to represent the dual aspect of Śiva-Śakti.

The six forms of *saguṇa* worship, approved and propagated by Śaṅkara,[5] included the worship of Devī. In the *Saundaryalaharī* and some of his *prakaraṇas,* he expounded Her greatness and Her identity with the Ātman or Brahman. In all the Advaitic monasteries, founded by Śaṅkara and his successors, among whom Vidyāraṇya is perhaps the most outstanding, the mystic secrets of *śrīvidyā* and the worship of the *śrīcakra* are kept alive to this day. At Sringeri, one of the four oldest seats of the monastic order founded by Śaṅkara, the presiding deity Śāradā, who is enthroned on a *śrīcakra,* symbolizes the highest knowledge, 'the knowledge of the Self' (*Sarvavedāntārtha-prakāśinī Brahmavidyā Śāradā*).

Tradition ascribes to Śaṅkara and other seers the installation of the *śrīcakra* in important temples. The most celebrated is that in the Kāmākṣī temple at Kāñcī, known as the *kāmakoṭipīṭha,* a replica of which is worshipped by the *gurus* of the Kāñcī Advaita monastery, later transferred to Kumbakonam. In the *cid-ākāśa-rahasya* in Chidambaram, there is a *sammelanacakra,* a combination of *śivacakra* and *śrīcakra.* There is a *śrīcakrapīṭha* at Courtallam, and at Avadaiyarkovil (Tanjore District) worship is offered to the *pādukā* or sandals of Devī installed on a *śrīcakra.* In Jambukesvaram, near Tiruchirapalli, the Devī's ear-ornaments are of the shape of *śrīcakras.* This list may easily be multiplied.

About two centuries after Vidyāraṇya, Appaya Dīkṣita (sixteenth century) attempted to harmonize the monistic schools of the Vedānta and the Siddhānta or Āgama schools. His synthetic doctrine, known as the Ratnatrayaparīkṣā, explains how the attributeless Brahman, through the play of His inherent Māyā, assumed two forms—*dharma* and *dharmin.*[6] While *dharmin* is static, *dharma* manifests itself both as male and female (as Viṣṇu and Devī); and this manifestation is the material cause of the universe. Through this doctrine he emphasized the identity of the Śaṅkara-Pārvatī (Ardhanārīśvara) and Śaṅkara-Nārāyaṇa concepts, which many centuries earlier had found expression in the hymns of the early Nāyanārs and Āḷvārs and in the iconography of the seventh century. Nīlakaṇṭha, the grand-nephew of Appaya, was another great exponent of the *śrīvidyā* cult. Among later adepts was Bhāskararāya (seventeenth-eighteenth century) whose three works, *Lalitā-sahasranāma-bhāṣya, Varivasyā-rahasya,*

[5] One of the epithets of Śrī Śaṅkara is *ṣaṇmatasthāpanācārya,* i.e. the *ācārya* who has established the six cults, viz. Śaiva, Śākta, Vaiṣṇava, Saura, Gāṇapatya, and Kaumāra. In South India the Kumāra or Skanda cult, being very popular, could not be ignored; the Smārtas, however, admit the other five only and therefore practise *pañcopāsanā* or *pañcāyatana-pūjā* (the worship of five deities).

[6] *'Nityaṁ nirdoṣagandhaṁ niratiśaya-sukhaṁ Brahma-caitanyamekam, dharmo dharmīti bheda-dvitayamiti pṛthagbhūya māyāvaśena.'*

and *Setubandha,* are aptly described as the *prasthāna-traya* of *śrīvidyā,* and among his disciples Umānandanātha, who wrote *Nityotsava-paddhati,* based on the *Paraśurāma Kalpa-Sūtra,* deserves special mention. Lakṣmīdhara's commentary on *Saundaryalaharī* is another important treatise on *śrīvidyā.* The five hundred verses in praise of Śrī Kāmākṣī of Kāñcī, sung by Mūkakavi, are a source of inspiration to the devotees of the Mother. Muttusvāmī Dīkṣita and Śyāmā Śāstrin, two eminent composers, who rank among those who evolved and perfected Karṇāṭic music, were adepts in *śrīvidyā.*

MEDITATION ON LALITĀ

Lalitā Mahātripurasundarī, the presiding deity of *śrīvidyā,* is meditated upon as red in complexion with the brilliance of countless suns and the coolness of innumerable moons. She holds, in Her four hands, a sugarcane-bow symbolizing the mind (*manorūpekṣukodaṇḍā*), flowery arrows symbolizing the five primordial bases of the world of sense (*pañcatanmātra-sāyakā*), noose denoting attraction (*rāgasvarūpapāśāḍhyā*), and goad suggesting repulsion (*krodhākārāṅkuśojjvalā*). She sits on the lap of Śiva-Kāmeśvara, whose colour is white, because He is *prakāśa* (consciousness and illumination). The couch on which Kāmeśvara and Kāmeśvarī (Lalitā) sit is of the form of an inert corpse-like Śiva, dark in colour to represent colourlessness. He is *niṣkala* Śiva, the Absolute before He 'willed to manifest'. There is profundity in this conception of a *niṣkala* (static) Śiva and, above Him, the divine couple Kāmeśvara and Kāmeśvarī, the Being and the Power-to-Become, in close embrace.

Her subtle form is the *pañcadaśākṣarī,* the *mantra* with fifteen letters to which is sometimes added a sixteenth letter to make it *ṣoḍaśākṣarī.* This *mantra* is traced to the *Ṛg-Veda,*[7] and is elucidated in the *Tripurā* and *Devī Upaniṣads.* It is said to be the esoteric form of the *Gāyatrī mantra,* which is the quintessence of the Vedas and is identified with the *mahāvākyas* of the Upaniṣads. The votary of this *mantra* rouses the power (*cit-śakti*) latent in him, which represents the Jīva and is known as the *kuṇḍalinī,*

[7] *Ṛ.V.,* V. 47. 4 reads as *'catvāra īṁ bibhrati kṣemayantaḥ',* which means 'the four (priests), wishing benefit for themselves, worship this (god)'. But according to the orally transmitted tradition of some religious sects, the *mantra* is held to mean 'that which contains the four *īṁs* and confers benefit' and to refer to the *śrīvidyā mantra* which fulfils this condition. The *pañcadaśākṣarī mantra* has three *kūṭas* or groups of letters. The first five letters *'ka, e, ī, la, hrīṁ'* form the first *kūṭa,* the next six *'ha, sa, ka, ha, la, hrīṁ'* the second *kūṭa,* and the last four *'sa, ka, la, hrīṁ'* the third *kūṭa.* The final letter of each of these three *kūṭas,* and the sixteenth letter *śrīṁ,* which is added, end in *īṁ.* These are the four *īṁs.* *Īṁ,* which represents *kāmakalā,* is in itself an important *mantra.* Reference may be made in this connection to Naṭanānandanātha's commentary *Cidvallī* on the seventeenth verse of Puṇyānanda's *Kāmakalā-vilāsa,* where this alternative interpretation of this Vedic *mantra* is cited.

lying coiled at the base of the spinal column (*mūlādhāra*). When aroused, *kuṇḍalinī* penetrates the next four *cakras*, which are the centres of energy of the gross *tattvas* manifesting sensible matter, passes the sixth *cakra* or centre of the subtle mental *tattva*, and finally, reaching the *sahasrāra* in the head, unites with Śiva, where Jīva becomes one with Śiva.

Some of the holy shrines in the Tamil country symbolically represent these *cakras*. To mention a few at random: Tiruvarur represents the *mūlādhāracakra*; Kāñcī the *nābhi* (navel); Chidambaram the *anāhatacakra* (in the region of the heart); and Jambukesvaram, where Mother Akhilāṇḍeśvarī presides, the *ājñācakra* (in the region between the eyebrows). Madura (Madurai) is *dvādaśānta*, where Śrī Mīnākṣī manifests Herself in different forms as Bālā, Bhuvaneśvarī, Gaurī, Mātaṅgī, Śyāmā, Pañcadaśākṣarī, and Mahāṣoḍaśī, while Avadaiyarkovil represents *mahā-ṣoḍaśānta*, where Ātmanātha Śiva and Devī Yogāmbā are meditated upon as residing in the thousand-petalled lotus of the *sahasrāra*.[8]

SYMBOLISM OF ŚRĪCAKRA

Śrīcakra is a symbol of the universe (both macrocosm and microcosm) and its divine cause. There are in it two sets of triangles, one set composed of four male or Śiva triangles, and the other of five female or Śakti triangles.[9] In the centre, which is a point (*bindu*), reside Kāmeśvara and Lalitā in *abheda* (undifferentiated) union. Enclosing the *bindu* is an inverted triangle representing the *icchā* (will), *kriyā* (action), and *jñāna* (knowledge) aspects of Śakti, the three *guṇas*, and the deities presiding over them. The other *cakras* are the *aṣṭakoṇa* (eight triangles), *daśāra-yugma* (two *cakras*, each of ten triangles), *manvaśra* (fourteen triangles), *aṣṭadala* (eight lotus petals), *ṣoḍaśadala* (sixteen lotus petals), *vṛttatraya* (three circles), and three squares. These nine *cakras* are ruled over by Yoginīs or divinities, presiding over forms of mind, sense, and matter, and their special functions, who are also called *āvaraṇa* (veiling) *devatās*, because they veil pure consciousness (*cit*) and create the appearance of the world of mind, sense, and matter,

[8] *Dvādaśānta* and (*mahā-*) *ṣoḍaśānta* are two subtle centres in very close proximity to (or, according to some, within) the pericarp of the *sahasrāra-kamala* (thousand-petalled lotus in the brain). *Dvādaśānta*, as the term implies, is above twelve centres—the three higher centres, namely, *anāhata*, *viśuddha*, *ājñā*, and the nine subtle centres beginning from the middle of the forehead and going up to the *brahmarandhra*. The *dvādaśānta* represents *jñāna*, *sahaja-samādhi*, and transition from *turīya* to *turīyātīta* state, while *ṣoḍaśānta* represents the *nirviśeṣa Brahmavṛtti* or the *turīyātīta* state.

[9] According to the *Kāmikāgama*, from the view-point of the microcosm, the Śakti triangles denote the five *dhātus*, namely, *tvac* (skin), *asṛj* (blood), *māṁsa* (flesh), *medas* (fat), and *asthi* (bone), and the Śiva triangles *majjā* (marrow), *śukra* (vital fluid), *prāṇa*, and Jīva; and from the view-point of the macrocosm, the Śakti triangles stand for the five vital functions, the five senses of knowledge, the five senses of action, the five subtle and the five gross forms of matter, and the mind, while the Śiva triangles represent the four higher *tattvas*, viz. *māyā*, *śuddhavidyā*, *maheśvara*, and *sadāśiva*. For the thirty-six Śaiva-Śākta *tattvas*, see Sir John Woodroffe, *The Garland of Letters* (*Varṇamālā*), X (*Tattvas*) and XXVII (*Ṣaḍadhvās*).

and make what is *pūrṇa* (whole and undifferentiated) appear as *apūrṇa* (limited and differentiated).

The prescribed *upāsanā* is according to the *saṁhāra* or *laya krama* (method of absorption). The divinities of the eight *cakras* from the outermost squares to the innermost triangle, who are the Śaktis of the universe of sound and form, of the objects of experience by the Jīva, of the means of such experience,[10] of the bodily *vṛttis* or functions,[11] and of the mental *vṛttis* or the cognitive modifications of the mind,[12] are worshipped as but rays emanating from the central luminary, Śrī Lalitā, and are conceived of as being absorbed in Her.

Whether the worship is external, attended with rituals, or internal, based upon meditation, emphasis is laid on *bhāva* or the mental certitude that the Mother withdraws unto Herself all the categories that She has projected to create the appearance of the phenomenal world. Now that the *sādhaka* has transcended all *vṛttis,* he realizes, in the *binducakra,* the Mother Lalitā Tripurasundarī as the supreme Essence in whom the static or absolute and dynamic or manifesting aspects coalesce (*prakāśa-vimarśa-parabrahma-svarūpiṇī*) and as the highest Bliss (*parāmṛtaśakti*).

In the *upāsanā* of *śrīcakra* are harmonized the personal and impersonal aspects of Brahman. Ritual and meditation lead to the knowledge of oneness, having gained which one attains to supreme Peace.

[10] From the view-point of the macrocosm.
[11] From the view-point of the microcosm.
[12] From the view-point of the Dṛṣṭi-sṛṣṭi-vādin, who posits that the world is the creation of the mind as against the view held by the Sṛṣṭi-dṛṣṭi-vādin, who says that the universe of embodied matter was created by the *jaḍa-śakti* of Īśvara.

16

TĀNTRIKA CULTURE AMONG THE BUDDHISTS

THE history of Tāntricism is highly interesting. We shall here make an attempt to trace this history, with special reference to Buddhism, from early times, and examine the circumstances which proved favourable to the development of this unique system of psychic culture in India.

Professor Chintaharan Chakravarti, in an admirable article in the *Indian Historical Quarterly,*[1] has traced the references to Tāntrika practices in their earlier stages amongst the Hindus, Buddhists, and Jains. These references in ancient literature show that some of the rudimentary Tāntrika practices are as old as the time of the *Ṛg-Veda,* and the *Atharva-Veda* is full of them. In Buddhism such practices were found in abundance, and from references in early Buddhist literature it can be seen that many varieties of Tāntrika practices were then in vogue. The attitude of Buddhism seems to have been hostile to such practices ; but there are many references to show that some of the mystic practices of the harmless sort were definitely tolerated, nay, encouraged. References to Tāntrika practices are also available in the earliest Jaina literature. Thus, it is clear that the ground was well prepared for the development of a mystic science like Tāntricism.

ORIGIN OF BUDDHIST TĀNTRICISM

It appears very probable that Tāntricism received a great impetus from Buddhism. Buddha recognized the *ṛddhis* or supernatural powers and mentioned four *iddhipādas*[2] conducive to the attainment of supernatural powers. He himself practised the *āsphānaka-yoga*[3] (*yoga* of psychic expansion) when he was in search of the eternal Truth. In the *Vinaya Piṭaka,*[4] we hear stories of Buddha's own disciple Bharadvāja rising up into the air miraculously and bringing down the begging bowl which was held high above by a Seṭṭhi. Buddha is said to have expressed his great disapprobation of this wanton display of supernatural power on the part of his disciple. The question arises how the disciple acquired this miraculous power, unless it was from his own teacher.

While investigating the circumstances which made the Tāntrika practices popular, we should take into consideration the part played by

[1] 'Antiquity of Tāntrikism', VI. pp. 114 ff.

[2] They are: *chando* (will), *viriyam* (effort), *cittam* (thought), and *vīmaṁsā* (investigation). See R. C. Childers, *Dictionary of the Pali Language*, p. 157.

[3] *Lalitavistara,* edited by Rajendralal Mitra, p. 315.

[4] *Sacred Books of the East,* XX. pp. 78 f.

monasticism (*sannyāsa*) as developed in Buddhism. In early Hinduism, the life of renunciation, as we know, was open only to the Brāhmaṇas, and this must have been greatly resented by the masses. In Buddhism, *sannyāsa* was open to all, and in this respect, as indeed in many others, Buddhism was a challenge to Hinduism. In early Hinduism, *sannyāsa* was generally recommended for those who had already passed through the stages of *brahmacarya* (student's life), *gārhasthya* (householder's life), and *vānaprastha* (forest life).[5] But there were a few dissentients among the Hindus also, who advocated that the monastic vow could be taken by a Brāhmaṇa belonging to any of the above three stages, provided he had a keen sense of dispassion. The *Jābāla Upaniṣad* is particularly interested in this new doctrine. We do not know to what extent Jābāla's words may be taken as authority in the matter of taking *sannyāsa*, and how far his doctrines were respected in ancient times. But it is certain that Buddhism went a step further and promulgated that *sannyāsa* could be taken by any one, whether a Brāhmaṇa or not, belonging to any order of life, provided his mind was bent on obtaining *nirvāṇa*.

The preaching of Buddhism slackened many restrictions prevalent in Hinduism regarding the caste system and the four orders of life, and there is no doubt that the system introduced by Buddha became very popular. But he was very strict about the rules of morality to be followed by his disciples, especially those living in monasteries; and any violation of them was severely dealt with. He did not permit the use of fish, meat, wine, association with the opposite sex, etc. on the part of the monks. The latter, however, were not disciplined enough to be able to follow his strict injunctions with regard to these matters, because many of them embraced the monastic life without adequate preparation for it. The result was that, even during the lifetime of Buddha, many monks revolted against his injunctions, and he, being sorely perturbed by their unruly conduct, drove them out of the order.[6]

There were many others who were not bold enough to proclaim a war against the rules imposed on them, but violated them in secret. It is thus very natural to expect that there arose secret conclaves of Buddhists who, though professing to be monks, violated all rules of morality and secretly practised things that were considered by others to be revolting. After the death of Buddha, such secret conclaves must have grown in number in every province, until they formed into a big organization. If we add

[5] *Sannyāsa Upaniṣad*, II. 13.

[6] For details and references, see Bhattacharyya, *An Introduction to Buddhist Esoterism*, pp. 22 f.

to this the *yoga* practices and the practice of *mantras,* we get a picture of the Tāntrika cult at its early stage.

From what has been said above, it is easy to conceive that Tāntricism was a natural growth among the Buddhists, because the circumstances were most favourable for this. Hinduism also had a primitive kind of magic in the form of rituals and ceremonies, but there was no need to practise them in secret. The Brāhmaṇa could take to the monastic life in the usual course, and if he so desired, he could practise *yoga* and *haṭha-yoga.* And as he could enter the fourth stage of life after completing his experiences in the three previous stages, he had no more longing for objects of enjoyment. Endowed with a great control over his senses and thoughts, he was fully qualified for the monastic life, and no harm could be expected from people of his type when in the monastic order. The risk was much greater in Buddhism, because the opening up of the monastic life to all and sundry was not safe for those who had not gone through all the experiences of life.

THE GUHYASAMĀJAS OR SECRET CONCLAVES

The secret conclaves that grew on the ruins of the monastic order, as conceived and established by Buddha, developed in course of time into big organizations known as Guhyasamājas. Their teachings and practices, however, were not sanctioned in Buddhism ; so they had to practise their rituals in secret (*guhya*). But they were not slow to find out means of obtaining this sanction, without which they were in an unenviable position. As Buddhists they were outcastes, and they could not enter into the Hindu fold ; their secret practices would have served as a deterrent to their being incorporated in the Hindu fold, if such an attempt had been made.

The other alternative for the followers of the Guhyasamāja was to introduce their doctrines into Buddhism by the composition of a new *Saṅgīti* or collection of verses, all of which were to be taken to have been delivered by Buddha in an assembly of the faithful. Thus the *Guhyasamāja Tantra* was composed in the *Saṅgīti* form, and in it reasons were given why the teachings of this book were kept secret so long, and why there could not be any objection for practising, by a devout Buddhist, all that was enjoined in the Tantra, together with details of theories and practices, dogmas and rituals. Before we give an account of the innovations introduced by this Tantra, it is necessary to give some idea of the age in which it was written.[7]

Tāranātha is inclined to believe that the Tantras and Tāntrika ideas

[7] For a detailed discussion on the subject, see *Guhyasamāja Tantra* (Gaekwad's Oriental Series, No. 53), Introduction, pp. xxxii f.

of a secret nature were as old as the time of the great Buddhist teacher Nāgārjuna, who is to be distinguished from the Tāntrika teacher of the same name who flourished much later in the seventh century. Tāranātha also says that when the Tantras were handed down from *gurus* to disciples secretly for nearly three hundred years, they got publicity through the mystic teachings, songs, and miracles of the Siddhas, Nāthas, and Yogīs. It has been found out by subsequent research that the testimony of Tāranātha is materially correct. The doctrines of the *Guhyasamāja Tantra* are substantially the same as those found in the *sādhanā* (practice) of the *Prajñāpāramitā* composed by Asaṅga, the elder brother of Vasubandhu, who flourished in the third or, according to some, in the fourth century A.D. Moreover, the *Guhyasamāja Tantra* seems to have exploited the materials supplied by an earlier work, the *Mañjuśrī-mūlakalpa,* and thus it is dependent on the doctrines of the latter, which it subsequently developed and modified. The *Mūlakalpa,* again, is a difficult work to understand, because to a careful observer it presents a mass of subsequent additions in the same way as some of the Purāṇas do. The work, it appears, originally consisted of twenty-eight chapters or even less, and later on had fifty-five chapters, and in this form it is published by the Trivandrum Sanskrit Series. It had twenty-eight chapters when it was translated into Chinese in the beginning of the eleventh century. All the subsequent chapters were added after that date, but before the time when the present manuscript was written. Amongst these additions, there is a portion which gives the history of India with the names of kings and other famous personages in enigmatical language. The names of kings and others are generally mentioned with the initial letters, which make the understanding and identification extremely difficult.

The *Mañjuśrī-mūlakalpa* in its earliest part is a Mantrayāna work, which gives descriptions of deities, *mudrās* (poses), and *maṇḍalas* (diagrams), and of the processes by which the worshipper should proceed to offer prayers and perform the rituals. It therefore appears to be a compendium of earlier literature on the subject, which is now lost, because the worship is fairly elaborate and worked out with scientific regularity. This development is scarcely possible without a previous literature behind it. The *Mūlakalpa,* being the source on which the *Guhyasamāja Tantra* is based, should be earlier than the Tantra itself, which, being similar to the doctrines of Asaṅga, must belong to the third or the fourth century.

The *Guhyasamāja Tantra,* under the circumstances, appears to be clearly a product of the third century, and the *Mūlakalpa* of the second or the first century A.D. We can now proceed to state what it introduced into Buddhism, and how it may be considered a landmark in the system of Buddhist thought as well as in the history of the evolution of the Tāntrika culture.

INNOVATIONS BY THE GUHYASAMĀJA TANTRA

Amongst the innovations introduced by the book, the most important seems to be the declaration that emancipation does not depend on bodily sufferings and abstinence from all worldly enjoyments. In fact, the work definitely lays down that perfection cannot be obtained through processes which are difficult and painful, but only through the satisfaction of all desires.[8] Its teaching in this respect is direct and unequivocal.

In earlier days, the rules and regulations prescribed for a follower of Hīnayāna and of Mahāyāna were unduly severe, involving as they did much hardship and great bodily sufferings. Even then, the attainment of Buddhahood meant an inordinately long time or even many births. It was thus a great relief to learn from the *Guhyasamāja Tantra* that it had a new process by which Buddhahood could be attained within the shortest time possible, and even in one birth by indulging in all objects of enjoyment.

Another element which the book introduced into Buddhism is that of Śakti (woman, considered as a manifestation of divine energy), particularly for obtaining emancipation through *yoga* and *samādhi* (highest concentration). In the very opening chapter of the *Guhyasamāja Tantra,* the Lord transforms Himself in the form of five Dhyānī Buddhas (Buddhas in meditative pose) and associates each of them with a Śakti. Moreover, in the eighteenth chapter,[9] while describing the different ceremonies in connection with initiation, mention is made of *prajñābhiṣeka* or the initiation of the disciple with *prajñā* or a Śakti. There it is said that the preceptor should take the hand of the Śakti, who is beautiful, agreeable to the disciple, and an adept in the practice of *yoga,* and place it on the hand of the disciple after citing the Tathāgatas as witnesses. Then, after placing his own hand on the head of the disciple, he should say that, as Buddhahood is impossible of attainment by any other means, this *vidyā* (Śakti) should be accepted. The worldly phenomena, though non-dual in essence, appear to be dual outwardly. Therefore he should never abandon her in life. This is what is known as the *vidyāvrata* or the vow of *vidyā,* and any one who disregards this cannot obtain perfection of the *uttama* (highest) kind.

This introduction of Śakti in Tāntrika worship, made for the first time in the *Guhyasamāja Tantra,* is one of the most important events in the history of Tāntricism. In fact, the Tantras have to be divided into two broad divisions on the basis of Śakti, namely, those that are free from

[8] *Ibid.,* p. 27.

[9] *Ibid.,* p. 161.

the element of Śakti and those that advocate her worship. In the course of my studies, I have not met with a single reliable reference to the element of Śakti in works that are supposed to be anterior to the *Guhyasamāja Tantra*. In this connection, it should be remembered that the Buddhist Tantras were divided into four classes for four different types of disciples, as it were, namely, (1) the Caryā Tantra, (2) the Kriyā Tantra, (3) the Yoga Tantra, and (4) the Anuttarayoga Tantra. Out of these four, the first two are preparatory and are not given the element of Śakti, which is prescribed for the last two classes, regarded as higher in the scale of perfection.[10]

DHYĀNĪ BUDDHAS

Another new idea that was introduced by the *Guhyasamāja Tantra* is the theory of the five Dhyānī Buddhas presiding over the five *skandhas* or elements of which the universe is composed.[11] The five *skandhas*, as promulgated by Buddha, are *rūpa* (form), *vedanā* (feeling), *saṁjñā* (perception), *saṁskāra* (impression), and *vijñāna* (ego-consciousness) ; and these five, according to the *Guhyasamāja Tantra*, were presided over by the five Dhyānī Buddhas, viz. Vairocana, Ratnasambhava, Amitābha, Amoghasiddhi, and Akṣobhya, respectively. The Dhyānī Buddhas, like the *skandhas*, were considered eternal, and they manifested themselves without passing through the intermediate stage of a Bodhisattva, or in other words, without depending on others for their origin. The *Guhyasamāja Tantra*, to make the scheme perfect, gave each of the Dhyānī Buddhas a Śakti and mentioned their *sādhanā* (method of worship) in a magic circle.

This introduction of the Dhyānī Buddhas may be considered to be a landmark in the evolution of the Tāntrika culture among the Buddhists. Reference to them is not found in any work that is written before the third century ; but as this was one of the most important theories in Tantra, frequent mention of it is made in all later Tantra works. From this arose the various cults associated with the Vajrayāna ; and Buddhists were divided according to the relative importance given to one or other of the Dhyānī Buddhas, who were known as the progenitors of so many families, as it were. From the Dhyānī Buddhas and their Śaktis arose their families of Bodhisattvas and Buddhaśaktis, and these, when represented in art, are required to show their origin by holding on their heads a miniature figure of the Dhyānī Buddha to whose family they belong.

When we investigate the origin of the Dhyānī Buddhas, according to the conceptions of the Guhyasamāja school, we find in the *Saṅgīti* that a

[10] For the discipline enjoined on the disciples belonging to these schools, see *Sādhanamālā* (Gaekwad's Oriental Series, No. 41), II. Introduction, pp. lxiv f.
[11] *Guhyasamāja Tantra* (Gaekwad's Oriental Series), p. 137.

single power called Kāya-vāk-citta-vajradhara, that is, the holder of the *vajra* consisting of the three elements *kāya* (body), *vāc* (speech), and *citta* (mind)—the embodiment of Buddha—manifests itself in the form of the five Dhyānī Buddhas, their Śaktis, and so on. That is to say, the five Dhyānī Buddhas are nothing but the manifestations of one single power. This power, at other places in the same work, is described as the embodiment of *śūnya* or *vajra,* from which the name of the school Vajrayāna is derived. The power of *śūnya,* according to the *Guhyasamāja Tantra,* is expressed by the three eternal things, namely, body, speech, and consciousness, which are the three attributes of all human beings. It is said in the opening chapter that Kāya-vāk-citta-vajradhara, at the request of the members of the assembly, sat in different *samādhis* and uttered certain syllables, and the Dhyāṇī Buddhas were accordingly brought forth into existence. The order of creation, under the circumstances, seems to be first the eternal *śūnya,* from which evolved the three elements, *kāya, vāc,* and *citta,* and from them again the five Dhyānī Buddhas or the five *skandhas.* This is a curious mixture of philosophy, mysticism, and materialism; and thus, as a logical system of philosophy, the *Guhyasamāja Tantra* appears to be crude.

ATTITUDE TOWARDS SOCIAL RESTRICTIONS

The description of this *Guhyasamāja Tantra* will not be complete, if we omit to mention its preaching against the disciplinary methods enjoined by Buddha. Fish, flesh, wine, etc. were rarely permitted in the original Buddhism. But this book sanctions everything. Not only flesh of the most harmless kind, but all kinds of it, including human flesh, are permitted. Blood of all animals and wine of any quality could be taken by a follower of the *Guhyasamāja Tantra.*[12]

Moreover, the work has no respect for such objects of reverence, advocated in the earlier stages of Buddhism, as were useless. In one place, it definitely forbids its followers to erect *caityas* (temples), to repeat the sacred works of Buddhism, to draw magic circles, or to offer articles of worship to the Three Jewels.[13] For a *yogin* such things have no real existence, and are therefore considered redundant. Further, the *Guhyasamāja Tantra* asks its followers to disregard all social laws. It lays down: 'You should freely immolate animals, utter any number of falsehoods, take things which do not belong to you, and even commit adultery.'[14]

The above will appear to be revolting to any one who is not initiated

[12] *Ibid.,* Introduction, p. xii.
[13] Buddha, Dharma (the religion), and Saṅgha (the order); *ibid.,* p. 142.
[14] *Ibid.,* p. 120.

in the doctrine of the *Guhyasamāja Tantra.* Whether many of the terms used in the Tantra itself have any symbolic meaning, which is quite different from what appears on the surface, remains yet to be seen. Apart from this, it should be remembered that the book talks of mystic matters on the strength of experiences gained from actual practice, and these cannot be the same as those of ordinary human beings who are bound down by all kinds of conventional laws. To the *yogin* who has grasped the real truth, who has realized the *śūny* , the whole world appears as a drama without a substance behind. Before him the duality of the world disappears, and all things are as appearances. He cannot therefore have any respect for objects of general reverence, or feel hatred towards any object treated with disdain by ordinary mortals. He does not feel himself bound by any laws, social or other, which are mostly the creations of imperfect beings, because he is one with the ultimate Reality that creates, maintains, and destroys everything, and views the imperfect world from the standpoint of the *śūnya,* or the ultimate creative energy.

THE VAJRAYĀNA

It is also noteworthy that the *Guhyasamāja Tantra* not only gave instructions for attaining salvation, but also satisfied the popular needs by prescribing a number of *mantras* (charms), *mudrās* (mystic signs), *maṇḍalas* (circles of deities), and so forth, and by showing the way of attaining success in all normal human activities, including victory over rivals by miraculous means. Thus, it showed how to conquer armies of invading kings, obtain wealth, and attain various kinds of *siddhis* (supernatural powers). The lay followers were more interested in these matters than in emancipation, even though it was declared to be easily accessible.[15] The book thus combined in one sweep all forms of mysticism in its system, such as *yoga* and *haṭha-yoga,* mystic poses, diagrams and formulae, Dhyānī Buddhas, deities, the six cruel rites,[16] and a host of other rituals. This system thus developed into a form of Tāntricism, which was named Vajrayāna or the Vajra path to salvation. It was called Vajrayāna, because *śūnya* came to be designated by the term *vajra* on account of its indestructibility. The *śūnya* of the Vajrayāna is something different from the *śūnya* of the Mādhyamikas (nihilists) or the Vijñānavādins (idealists), because it includes the three elements *śūnya* (reality), *vijñāna* (consciousness), and *mahāsukha* (great bliss).

[15] *Ibid.,* p. 144.

[16] The six cruel rites mentioned in the Tantras are generally enumerated as *śānti* (propitiation), *vaśīkaraṇa* (controlling), *stambhana* (transfixion), *vidveṣaṇa* (separation), *māraṇa* (killing), and *uccāṭana* (destruction).

OPPOSITION TO VAJRAYĀNA PRACTICES

Whether the novel teachings of the Guhyasamāja school met with general approval remains to be seen. It says that when Buddha came to the world as Dīpaṅkara and Kāśyapa, he did not preach these secret doctrines, because people in those days were not found fit to receive the instructions.[17] Now that they have become fit to receive initiation into the mystic cult as set forth in the *Guhyasamāja Tantra,* the teachings are made public. But if this book is examined carefully, it will be seen that the teachings were opposed even when the work was first revealed. In the fifth chapter, the Lord declares in the assembly that emancipation through the Vajrayāna is possible of attainment for all men, howsoever vicious, cruel, or immoral they may be. Nay, even incestuous persons are not ill-fitted for emancipation in this branch of the Mahāyāna. When he had just finished his speech, there was a great consternation in the assembly, and volleys of protests came from the Bodhisattvas. They said, 'Why, O Lord, the master of the Tathāgatas, are you having recourse to these sinful utterances in a respectable assembly full of the Tathāgatas?'[18] The Lord expressed great surprise at this and said, 'O Kulaputras, do not speak thus. The conduct I have just mentioned is known as the *bodhi* conduct, which is immutable and pure, and is considered as such by the Buddhas who have realized the true essence, and which springs from the interpretation of the essential truth'. The moment these words were uttered, all the Bodhisattvas in the assembly became frightened and confused, and fell down senseless. The Tathāgatas, who could realize the truth of the assertions of the Lord, remained unaffected and requested the Lord to revive the Bodhisattvas, who could not realize the truth owing to their ignorance. The Lord thereupon sat in a special meditation, and when the rays issuing out of his person touched the unconscious Bodhisattvas, they all revived, sat in their respective places, and recited several *gāthās* (verses) in praise of the Lord. This shows that there was a considerable opposition to the teachings of the book, which people were not prepared to accept in their entirety ; and this may be another reason why this Tantra had to be kept in secret for several centuries before its teachings could be extensively made known.

CONTRIBUTIONS OF THE VAJRAYĀNA

The Vajrayāna made many contributions to Buddhism and Buddhist culture in general, and thus became very attractive. The Hindus were also impressed by its grandeur, and were induced to accept some of the Tāntrika doctrines, deities, *mantras, sādhanās,* etc. Not only did the

[17] *Guhyasamāja Tantra* (Gaekwad's Oriental Series), p. 144.
[18] *Ibid.,* Introduction, pp. xxii f. where this incident is described more fully.

Vajrayāna introduce elements of *yoga* into ordinary worship, but it also gave a regular system of *mantras*, which could be used for all possible purposes even by a householder. The exquisite art that the Vajrayāna developed did not fail to create a good impression, and the Buddhist art of that period may be considered to be its great contribution to Indian culture. There is no doubt that the Tantras assumed importance in the Pāla period, when even the universities like those of Nālandā and Vikramaśīla had to introduce them into their curriculum, and keep regular professors to hold classes for those who wanted to have a higher education in the Tantras, in their four subdivisions mentioned before.

It will not be an exaggeration to say that Nāthism derived its inspiration from the Vajrayāna ; or, in other words, the progenitors of the Nātha school Hinduized the teachings of the Buddhist Tantras. From the existing literature of the Hindus, no reference to Tāntricism can be found which may be placed before the third century when the *Guhyasamāja Tantra* was composed. The Nāthas were originally nine in number, and they are sometimes included in the list of the eighty-four Siddhas of the Buddhists. The Nāthas and their descendants are known in Bengal as the Yogīs or Yugīs. Regarding their origin and their present low status in Hindu society, many stories are current ; but it appears that they were the first to follow the Tāntrika practices amongst the Hindus, and were mainly the disciples of the Buddhists, who were not looked upon with great favour by the Hindus. The affinity of the Nāthas with the Buddhist Tāntrikas and their practice of the Tantras were probably the reasons why the Yogīs were regarded, in subsequent times, as 'untouchables'.

It will, however, be a mistake to think that the Nātha school was substantially the same as the Tāntrika school of the Buddhists. The Nāthas introduced many new theories in the sphere of *haṭhayoga* and *yoga*. In details of yogic practices, these theories were different from those advocated in the Tantras.[19] Very little is known about the Nāthas and their practices, because of scanty literature on the subject. Some Sanskrit works such as the *Gorakṣa Saṁhitā, Gorakṣa-śataka, Haṭhayoga-pradīpikā, Śiva Saṁhitā, Gheraṇḍa Saṁhitā*, and *Siddha-siddhānta-saṅgraha* are at present our only authentic materials to construct the history and practice of Nāthism. The Nāthas believed that the microcosm is a reflex of the macrocosm, and that everything that is found in creation has a parallel in the body. In this respect, Nāthism has a curious resemblance to the Sahajayāna as well as to the Kālacakrayāna.

[19] See Gopinath Kaviraj, *Siddha-siddhānta-saṅgraha* (Prince of Wales Saraswati Bhavana Texts, No. 13), Introduction.

THE SPREAD OF THE VAJRAYĀNA

The Vajrayāna, as we have already pointed out, is a product of the third century A.D. But its teachings did not get sufficient publicity in the first three hundred years of its inception. It was during the middle of the seventh century that, through the teachings and mystic songs of the eighty-four Siddhas, the Vajrayāna became popular, and its doctrines got wide publicity. The Vajrayāna travelled to Nepal and Tibet, and Tāntrika works were translated into Tibetan. Some of the works also travelled to China, as we know from their translations now found in the Chinese Tripiṭaka. Thousands of works were written on a variety of subjects connected with the Vajrayāna, such as *yoga, mantras,* Tantras, practices, and hymns ; and before the Mohammedans came, it was a great living religion. The Hindus took materials from the Buddhist Tantras and incorporated many of the practices in their religion and, thus, the Tāntrika culture reached its highest point.

The Vajrayāna also gave rise to several later Yānas (paths), such as the Sahajayāna, Kālacakrayāna, and Mantrayāna. We shall briefly notice here the most important teachings of these. All these later Yānas, however, may be considered to be mere offshoots of the Vajrayāna school, without differing materially from the original Yāna of the Guhyasamāja.

THE SAHAJAYĀNA

The Sahajayāna is believed to start with Lakṣmīṅkarā Devī (A.D. 729),[20] the sister of King Indrabhūti who styles himself the king of Uḍḍiyāna. The newness of Lakṣmīṅkarā's teachings consists in her declaration that no suffering, fasting, rites, bathing, purification, or obedience to the rules of society are necessary for the purpose of obtaining emancipation. According to her, it is not necessary to bow down before the images of gods which are made of wood, stone, or mud, but the worshipper should, with concentration, offer worship only to his own body where all gods reside. Lakṣmīṅkarā preached that when truth is known, there is no restriction of any kind for the worshipper. Like her brother Indrabhūti, she did not believe in restrictions regarding food or drink, and advocated Śakti-worship. The Sahajayāna thus belonged to the Yoga Tantra class.

THE KĀLACAKRAYĀNA

The Kālacakrayāna seems to be a later development of the Vajrayāna. This concerns itself with the Yoga Tantra and Anuttarayoga Tantra, and incorporates the doctrines of the Sahajayāna also. Waddell does not seem

[20] For authorities, quotations, and references, see Bhattacharyya, *op. cit.*, pp. 76 f.

to have a true conception of the grand system of the Kālacakrayāna, as will appear from his naive statement about this system in his *Lamaism*:[21] 'In the tenth century A.D., the Tāntric phase developed in northern India, Kashmir, and Nepal into the monstrous and polydemonist doctrine, the Kālacakra, with its demoniacal Buddhas, which incorporated the Mantrayāna practices and called itself the Vajrayāna or "the Thunderbolt Vehicle", and its followers were named Vajrācāryas or "Followers of the Thunderbolt" '

But the *Kālacakra Tantra* and its commentary, *Vimalaprabhā,* tell a different tale. According to the latter, Kālacakra is a deity and an embodiment of *śūnyatā* and *karuṇā* (compassion), is embraced by the goddess Prajñā, and represents the philosophical conception of *advaya* or nonduality. He is regarded as the Ādibuddha or the progenitor even of the Buddhas, that is to say, the Dhyānī Buddhas. The passage, 'one's own body, in which the whole world is manifest', has a curious resemblance to the doctrines of the Sahajayāna and Nāthism,[22] and this makes it probable that the Kālacakrayāna embodied in it the teachings of the Vajrayāna, Nāthism, and Sahajayāna and, thus, in historical evolution, seems to be later than all the three. As a school, it started in the tenth century.

The deity Kālacakra, like many other Vajrayāna deities, is fierce in appearance and is embraced by the Śakti, which shows that the Yāna is merely a branch of the Vajrayāna in its higher forms of Yoga and Anuttarayoga Tantras. The *maṇḍala* (circle) of the deity, as we understand from the *Kālacakra Tantra,* consists of all the planets and stars, and the book itself deals with many topics connected with astronomy and astrology, on which it lays great stress. The central deity, as the name Kālacakra indicates, represents the circle of time and is surrounded by such minor deities as would indicate time. The introduction of the *Kālacakra Tantra* is attributed to Mañjuśrī, and the commentary, *Vimalaprabhā,* was written in 12,000 *granthas* by one Puṇḍarīka.[23]

THE MANTRAYĀNA

The school called Mantrayāna or the 'Spell Vehicle', as styled by Waddell, originated, according to Tibetan traditions, with Nāgārjuna, who is alleged to have received it from the celestial Buddha Vairocana, through the divine Bodhisattva Vajrasattva, at the iron tower in southern India.[24] The Mantrayāna, strictly speaking, concerns itself with *mantras* and *yantras*

[21] *The Buddhism of Tibet or Lamaism,* p. 15.

[22] See the description of the *Laghu-kālacakra-tantra-rāja-ṭīkā* given by Mm. Haraprasad Shastri in *A Descriptive Catalogue of the Government Collection* (Asiatic Society of Bengal), I. pp. 73 f.

[23] *Ibid.,* p. 76.

[24] Waddell, *op. cit.,* p. 15.

or magic circles, and, incidentally, it includes such things as *dhāraṇīs* (memorized prayers), *mālā mantras* (garland of charms), *hṛdaya mantras* (short charms), etc. It believes that certain special mystic forces are generated by reciting words of a certain combination, pronounced in a certain manner, and that, with the help of these mystic forces, the worshipper can obtain whatever he desires, such as wealth, victory, *siddhis*, and even emancipation. The *yantras* are included in the same system, because the magic circles are not supposed to bestow any power unless the letters of the appropriate *mantra* are placed in their appropriate places in the magic circle.

It is very difficult to say when the system originated. *Mantras* and *dhāraṇīs* existed from very early times in Buddhism ; but they were elevated to a system very probably at the time mentioned in the Tibetan tradition. The *Mañjuśrī-mūlakalpa* is full of *mantras, maṇḍalas,* and *dhāraṇīs.* Similarly, the *Guhyasamāja Tantra* and the *Saddharma-puṇḍarīka* are also full of them, and since, as we have shown above, these are products of the second or third century, there is no wonder that the Mantrayāna, as a school, should be as old as the time of Nāgārjuna who flourished in the second century A.D.

17

THE CULT OF THE BUDDHIST SIDDHĀCĀRYAS

THE idea of *siddhi,* psychic and supernatural power, is universal in Indian religious systems. Almost all sects attach great importance to *yoga* in some form or other, and it is believed that the practice of *yoga* yields these powers. The Buddhist texts speak of ten kinds of powers (*iddhi, ṛddhi,* or *abhijñā*), such as 'to project mind-made image of oneself, to become invisible, to pass through solid things, such as wall, to penetrate solid ground as if it were water, to walk on water, to fly through the air, to touch sun and moon, to ascend into the highest heavens', etc.[1] The Brāhmaṇical texts speak of eight *siddhis,* such as *aṇiman, laghiman, mahiman* (powers of becoming minute, light, and vast at will), *prākāmya, prāpti* (powers of possessing irresistible will and obtaining anything desired), *vaśitva, īśitva* (subjugating all and establishing one's own superiority over others), and *kāmāvasāyitva* (having perfect control over or suppression of all desires). They signify more or less the same powers as mentioned in the Buddhist texts in more general terms. The texts sometimes mention the same powers under the term *siddhi,* which is also explained as *ṛddhi.* A *siddha* is one who possesses these powers.

As the attainment of *siddhi* was a difficult task, there were special mystic schools which were concerned with such practices. There is mention of such schools as Siddhakaula, Siddhāmṛta, etc. as well as of Siddhas who were responsible for building up those schools.[2] One of the standard Brāhmaṇical Tantras, the *Lalitā-sahasranāma,* speaks of three traditions of spiritual lore—*divya, mānava,* and *siddha.* Although there is much about *siddhi* and Siddha in the Brāhmaṇical Tantras, we do not find in them any coherent theory on the Siddhas or any attempt at synthesis of the various doctrines attributed to them.

THE EIGHTY-FOUR BUDDHIST SIDDHAS

The Buddhist mystic schools which flourished between the eighth and twelfth centuries developed a very systematic theory on the Siddhas. This theory was also accepted, in later times, by the mediaeval religious sects, such as the Kabīr Pantha, Nātha Pantha, etc. According to this theory, there were eighty-four Siddhas, all human teachers, who had attained

[1] Rhys Davids and Stede, *Pali Dictionary,* under *'Iddhi'.*
[2] P. C. Bagchi, *Kaulajñāna-nirṇaya* (Calcutta Sanskrit Series, No. III), Introduction, pp. 33-34.

powers through the practice of *yoga*. The *Varṇaratnākara* of Jyotirīśvara (fourteenth century) mentions the eighty-four Siddhas. The Tibetan sources also mention them and give a systematic biographical sketch of all the Siddhas. The sources must have derived their information from Indian texts which are now lost. The names of the Siddhas in the *Varṇaratnākara* and in the Tibetan texts are not always the same, but as the agreement between them is very large, it may be said that the differences are due to copyists' mistakes. Eighty-four Siddhas are also referred to by Kabīr in one of his songs.[3] The names of the eighty-four Siddhas, according to the Tibetan tradition, are the following:

(1) Lūhi-pā, (2) Līlā-pā, (3) Virū-pā, (4) Ḍombi-pā, (5) Śābara (Śabari-pā), (6) Saraha (Rāhulabhadra), (7) Kaṅkāli, (8) Mīna, (9) Gorakṣa, (10) Cauraṅgī, (11) Vīṇā, (12) Śānti, (13) Tanti, (14) Carmari, (15) Khaḍga, (16) Nāgārjuna, (17) Kāṇha-pā, (18) Kāṇarī (Āryadeva), (19) Thagana, (20) Nāḍa-pāda, (21) Śāli-pā (Śṛgāla-pāda), (22) Tilo-pā (Tailika-pāda), (23) Chatra, (24) Bhadra, (25) Dvikhaṇḍī, (26) Ajogi, (27) Kaḍa-pāda, (28) Dhovī, (29) Kaṅkaṇa, (30) Kambala, (31) Teṅki, (32) Bhāde, (33) Tandhī, (34) Kukkuri, (35) Cujbi (Kusūli), (36) Dharma, (37) Mahī, (38) Acintya, (39) Babhahi, (40) Nalina, (41) Bhusuku, (42) Indrabhūti, (43) Megha-pāda, (44) Kuṭharī, (45) Karmāra, (46) Jālandhari, (47) Rāhula, (48) Garbharī, (49) Dhakari, (50) Meḍinī, (51) Paṅkaja, (52) Ghaṇṭā, (53) Yogī, (54) Celuka, (55) Vāguri (Guṇḍarī?), (56) Luñcaka, (57) Nirguṇa, (58) Jayānanda, (59) Carṣaṭī, (60) Campaka, (61) Viṣaṇa, (62) Bhali (Telī, Tailī), (63) Kumari, (64) Cārpaṭi, (65) Maṇibhadrā, (66) Mekhalā, (67) Maṅkhalā, (68) Kalạkala, (69) Kanthaḍi, (70) Dauḍī, (71) Udhali, (72) Kapāla, (73) Kila, (74) Puṣkara, (75) Sarvabhakṣa, (76) Nāgabodhi, (77) Dārika, (78) Puttalī, (79) Panaha, (80) Kokilā, (81) Anaṅga, (82) Lakṣmīṅkarā, (83) Sāmudra, (84) Bhali-pā.

HISTORICITY OF THE SIDDHAS

It has been argued by some scholars that this list of eighty-four Siddhas has no historical value. It has been suggested that, on account of the mystic implication of the number eighty-four, it has been taken as the basis of a theory of enumeration. The names, whether fictitious or historical, have been put together to make up a list of eighty-four. In support of this explanation, it has been pointed out that in the Buddhist texts there is mention of eighty-four lacs of *yonis,* eighty-four thousand *dhammakhandas,* eighty-four thousand *stūpas,* etc. But, then, nowhere in these is there mention of simply eighty-four. It is therefore a far-fetched explanation to

[3] *Kabīr-granthamālā* (Nagari Pracharini Sabha Edition), p. 54.

establish the mystic value of the number eighty-four. The list of the Siddhas, as it is, contains some names which seem to be wrong, or merely repetitions of other names under different forms (for example, Tanti and Taṅdhī seem to be the same name ; Tilo or Tailika and Telī or Tailī are the same ; Bhadra and Bhāde are the same ; some names such as Babhahi, Nalina, Kalakala, etc. are not known from any other source). But, as it has already been said, the list is not perfect ; there are mistakes either due to the copyists or to a bad state of preservation of the source-books. If we had various independent lists, it would have been easy to establish a correct one. It is not therefore proper to dismiss the number as of mystic implication. We simply do not know why the number is eighty-four and not anything else.

WORKS OF THE SIDDHAS

On the contrary, we know that most of the teachers mentioned in the list were historical personages, known in the Buddhist Church of those days either for their learning or for their spiritual attainments. They had composed texts or written mystic songs which have been preserved partially in original and mostly in Tibetan translations. The songs of the following are preserved in the collection called *Caryācarya-viniścaya* (correct name being *Caryāścarya-viniścaya* or *Caryāgītikośa*:[4] Āryadeva (Kāṇarī), Bhāde, Bhusuku, Dārika, Dharma, Ḍombi, Guṇḍarī, Jayānanda, Jālandhara (Jālandhari), Kambala, Kukkuri, Kaṅkaṇa, Luyī (Lūhi), Mahī(dhara), Śānti, Śābara, Tanti, Teṇṭana, and Vīṇā. Two others, Kṛṣṇa (Kāṇhu or Kāṇha) and Saraha, are known not only from the *caryā* songs, but also from their *Dohākośas*.[5] Tilo-pā is known from one of his *Dohākośas* and Nāḍa-pāda from his commentary on the *Sekoddeśa*.[6]

Besides these original works, there are Tibetan translations of works, now lost, but originally written by a host of other Siddhas mentioned in the list. The translations are preserved in the *Bstan-hgyur* (Tanjur), Volumes XLVII and XLVIII. Volume XLVII contains the works of Indrabhūti, Keralī-pāda, Aja Mahāsukha, Saraha, Mahāśabara, Nāro-pā (Nāḍa-pāda), Āryadeva, Kṛṣṇa-pāda, Virū-pā, Karma-pāda, and Tilo-pā. Volume XLVIII contains the works of Śāntideva, Luyī-pāda, Thagana, Bhāde (Bhaṅde), Dhamma, Mahī-pā, Śabarī-pā, Kambala, Cāte-pā, Kaṅkāli, Mīna-pā, Acinda (Acintya), Gorakṣa, Coraṅghi, Vīṇā, Tanti, Śiali (Śṛgālī), Ajoki, Paṅkaja, Ḍombi-pā, Kukkuri, Karmarī, Cārpaṭi, Jālandhari, Kantharī, Luñcaka, Garbha-pāda (Garbharī), and others.

[4] P. C. Bagchi, 'Materials for a Critical Edition of the Old Bengali Caryāpadas', *Journal of the Department of Letters* (Calcutta University), XXX.
[5] P. C. Bagchi, *Dohākośa*, I.
[6] Carelli, *Sekoddeśa-ṭīkā* (Gaekwad's Oriental Series).

It is therefore clear that most of the Siddhas are historical personages and are authors of works on their special modes of *sādhanā* (spiritual practice), which are preserved either in the original or in Tibetan translations.

THE DATE OF THE SIDDHAS

We also know something definite about the age in which they lived. The first Siddha in the list, Luyī-pāda (Lūhi-pā), was, in all likelihood, the same as Matsyendra Nātha of other traditions. An attempt has been made elsewhere[7] to show that Matsyendra lived about the beginning of the tenth century A.D. Siddha Nāgārjuna lived in the tenth century, and Cārpaṭi also lived about the same time.[8] Tilo-pā was a contemporary of King Mahīpāla I of Bengal (*c.* 988-1038), and Nāro-pā was his disciple. Jālandhari and Kāṇhu-pā (Kāṇha-pā) lived also about the middle of the eleventh century.[9] The first Siddha lived in the tenth century and the most famous Siddhācāryas in the tenth and eleventh centuries. It thus appears that the period when the Siddhas, more familiarly known as Siddhācāryas, flourished was between the tenth and the twelfth century. It is almost certain that many of them were contemporaries, and were developing, in collaboration with each other, the mystic doctrines of the new school to which they belonged. The great majority of them, to all appearances, lived in the eleventh century.

PLACE OF THE GURU IN THE SIDDHA TRADITION

What was the special form of mysticism they adhered to? As the main part of the literature is still unknown to us, it is difficult to answer the question. A thorough study of the Tibetan translations can alone throw light on the problem. So far as can be gathered from the few texts discovered till now, it seems that the general trend of the teachings of the Siddhācāryas was esoteric. Nobody, except a qualified *guru* or preceptor, was allowed to initiate the disciple in the mysteries. This is why even in modern times the few followers of this school in Nepal call themselves *gubhāju* or *gurubhāju,* i.e. the followers or worshippers of the *guru.* They distinguish themselves from the followers of the Brāhmaṇical faith, who are called *devabhāju,* i.e. the worshippers of the god. The literature of the school is full of such statements as 'the truth that is free from duality is taught by the *guru*', 'there is nothing unattainable for the man whom

[7] *Kaulajñāna-nirṇaya,* Introduction, p. 27.

[8] Tucci, *Journal of the Asiatic Society of Bengal,* 1930, p. 137 ; Vogel, *Antiquities of Chamba State,* I. p. 81.

[9] *Kaulajñāna-nirṇaya,* Introduction, pp. 26-27 ; *History of Bengal* (Dacca University), I. pp. 326 ff.

the *guru* favours', 'the truth is clearly revealed through the instruction of the *guru*', and so forth. The texts clearly testify to the exalted position the *guru* enjoys in this school. But there is also a warning to the *guru* too. Siddha Saraha-pāda says: 'You should not initiate a disciple so long as you do not know yourself. If you do that, you will do like the blind man who, while trying to lead another blind man, drove him into a well and himself also fell into it.'

Though the *guru* was given that exalted position, it was no easy task for him to lead the disciple to this goal. He had to find out the special spiritual aptitude of the disciple and suggest to him the mode of *sādhanā* most suitable for him. In the analysis of the spiritual aptitudes of various types of disciples, the Siddhas seem to have arrived at a novel classification called *kula. Kula* symbolizes the special spiritual leaning of a disciple, and is the same as 'psychic energy'. There are five such *kulas,* technically called *ḍombī, naṭī, rajakī, caṇḍālī,* and *brāhmaṇī.* The nature of these *kulas* is determined by the five *skandhas* or the essences of the five basic elements (*mahābhūtas*) constituting the material existence of the being. The five *kulas* are the five aspects of the *prajñā,* which is the same as the *śakti* of the Brāhmaṇical Tantras. The *śakti* assumes five different forms according to the predominance of each of the five *skandhas* or constituents, and the best course for the *sādhaka* is to follow up his special *kula* or *śakti* during his spiritual march. In the technical language of the school, it is said that the five classes of *sādhakas* should carry on their mystic practice 'in the company of the five *prajñās,* called *ḍombī, naṭī, rajakī, caṇḍālī,* and *brāhmaṇī*'. They have been represented as female associates in the matters of *sādhanā,* and this has often led to many misleading interpretations of the mystic lore.

THE SPIRITUAL PRACTICE OF THE SIDDHAS

The question now arises, What was the *sādhanā* in which the *guru* had to initiate his disciple? This *sādhanā* involved the practice of a new form of *yoga* which seems to have evolved in the hands of the Siddhācāryas. According to it, there are thirty-two *nāḍīs* or nerve-channels within the body. It is believed that the psychic energy, which has its seat below the navel, flows up into the topmost station within the head through these channels. The topmost station is called *mahāsukha-sthāna* (the place of great bliss). Various names are given to the nerve-channels, such as *lalanā, rasanā, avadhūtī, pravaṇā, kṛṣṇarūpiṇī, sāmānyā, pāvakī, sumanā, kāminī,* etc. Of these the first three, *lalanā, rasanā,* and *avadhūtī,* are the most important and combine in themselves, at particular stations, the currents supplied by the rest. The *avadhūtī* is the middlemost channel and corresponds to the *suṣumṇā* of the Brāhmaṇical Tantras. The other two correspond to the *iḍā* and *piṅgalā*.

According to this system, there are also a number of stations, compared either to lotuses or wheels, within the body, and the psychic energy in its upward march has to pass through them. The topmost station is imagined to be a lotus having either sixty-four or a thousand petals. These stations are sometimes compared to places of pilgrimage like Uḍḍiyāna, Jālandhara, Pūrṇagiri, and Kāmarūpa. The intention probably is to discourage travel to distant lands to acquire religious merit as also to acquire a sense of the sanctity of the body with its different centres standing for different places of pilgrimage.

The ultimate goal is the creation of the state of *sahaja* which is one of great blissfulness. It is a state which is without beginning and without end, and a state which is free from duality. When this state is attained, the objective world disappears from view and all the aggregates, elements, and senses merge in it. The *sādhaka* then finds himself to be the sole reality, identical with the universe, identical with the Buddha—a being who is ever free. Everything else dwindles into nonentity.

METHODS OF TRANSUBSTANTIATION OF THE BODY

These are some of the main characteristics of the mysticism professed by the Siddhācāryas. It should, however, be remembered that mysticism is something which is highly personal. So in matters of practice every mystic has his own way of approach, and this gives rise to varieties in the method of *sādhanā*. In the system of the Siddhācāryas, the attainment of the highest goal meant also certain perfections of the physical apparatus, and hence a good deal of emphasis was placed on the *kāya-sādhanā*. The *kāya-sādhanā* involved attempts to bring about the transubstantiation of the body. Later followers of the Siddhācāryas carried this theory and practice to an extreme, and were thus concerned only with the means of attaining a perfect, changeless, and imperishable body which would help them to live long. But it is clear from the writings of the Siddhācāryas that they themselves never put so great an emphasis on this aspect of the *sādhanā*.

The Siddhācāryas believed that the perfection of the body could be attained in various ways. The most important of them was an upward movement of the *bodhicitta* (semen virile). When the psychic force moves upwards, a sort of introversion of the faculties (*parāvṛtti*) takes place. In that state the *bodhicitta* also can be made to move upwards to the topmost station within the head. This practice, which aims at saving every drop of the *bodhicitta*, the very essence of physical and spiritual existence, leads to the attainment of a perfectly calm mind and an imperishable body.

This practice led to the discovery of a number of ancillary methods, which have been described in the writings of the Siddhācāryas in a symbolic language.

The cultivation of the *bodhicitta* was not wholly unconnected with certain alchemical practices. One of the Siddhas, Nāgārjuna, was reputed for introducing alchemy in matters of *sādhanā*. Within the body, it is the *bodhicitta* which is the most important and, at the same time, the most restless *rasa*, and the attempt to carry it upward to the topmost station lies in converting it into a hard element (*vajra*), and thus destroying its restless character. Outside, it is mercury (*pārada*) which symbolizes the *bodhicitta*, and the alchemist tries to find out means of converting it into a hard metal (for example, gold) and using it for the transubstantiation of the body. The two methods, the esoteric and the exoteric, were complementary.

Besides these, the Siddhācāryas seem to have introduced other novelties in their system of spiritual exercises, but it is at present difficult to follow them, on account of the symbolical character of the language in which they are described.

18

THE NĀTHA CULT

THE esoteric cult, professed by the Split-ear (*kān-phaṭ* or *kān-phāṭā*) Yogī mendicants (practising *haṭhayoga* and wearing huge *mudrās* or ear-rings, either flat, called *darśana*, or cylindrical, called *kuṇḍala*) throughout northern, central, and western India, is now known as the Nātha cult, inasmuch as the names of all the masters of this faith end with the word *nātha*, meaning 'master, lord'. The original home of the cult, so far as one can deduce from the material available, was North and North-East Bengal. From this region, it spread out to the other parts of the country sometime after the twelfth or the thirteenth century. The earliest and most authentic records and traditions of the cult are found in Old and Middle Bengali literature only. The stories concerned with the faith, which are now current in other parts of India, viz. Bihar, Uttar Pradesh, Punjab, Sind, Gujarat, Maharashtra, and Rajasthan, indicate that the main characters belonged to Bengal. The traditional didactic and mystic verses that are held sacred by the non-Bengali Gorakh-panthī Yogīs bear unmistakable traces of Bengali origin for most of them.

In Bengal, the Nātha cult is practically dead. The followers of this cult have been steadily absorbed into allied yogic cults that later attached themselves, however superficially, to a kind of Vaiṣṇavism. The Bāul cult of Bengal is indeed a transformed form of the Nātha cult. The Bāuls have adopted the yogic practices of the Nāthas and have inherited their mystic poetry and talking in riddles. But they outwardly admit God and call Him Kṛṣṇa and Caitanya, as the Vaiṣṇavas do. The Nātha Yogīs had no concern with God ; each of them was God in the universe of his own body. As a distinct class of mendicants, the Nātha Yogīs, now nicknamed in Bengal 'Jugī', often a term of contempt, have survived in North Bengal, which had always been most hospitable to the cult. In other parts of India, there are different sub-sects attached to different monasteries ruled by elected *mahantas*. The lay followers of the cult in Bengal were formed into a distinct 'Jugī' caste, which is by no means confined to North Bengal. It has subcastes with different secular and religious practices ; greater divisions are found, however, elsewhere in India, each constituting a separate *pantha*. The main occupation of the caste was, till very recently, weaving coarse cloth, whence it was coupled with the Jolā (Muslim weavers). But other less reputable professions, like selling charms and amulets and practising magical rites and exorcisms, were also embraced by the itinerant fraternity. The distinctive surname of the caste is 'Nātha'. The lay Yogīs have retained some of their peculiar customs. The customary disposal of their dead—not invariably observed now—is by burial in a seated posture with the legs crossed as in meditation. This custom has been adopted by the Bāul Vaiṣṇavas also. The heterodox rite for the dead, their lowly occupation, their non-belief in (rather non-acceptance of) Godhead, and their non-observance of the Brāhmaṇic social order put the members of the Yogī caste outside the domain of the orthodox Hindu society. This made the caste at one time an easy prey to the aggressive Mohammedan faith. At the present day, however, the Yogīs are, for all practical purposes, incorporated within the Hindu community.

TRADITIONS OF THE CULT

It is generally believed that the Nātha cult is a Śaiva faith, and the use of *rudrākṣa* (berries of *elaeocarpus ganitrus*) rosaries and the triple mark (*tripuṇdra*) of ash on the forehead by the Yogīs may be cited in support of this view. In the Nātha cult there is no doubt a Śaiva strain, including association with the snake cult, and even looking upon Gorakṣa Nātha as a form of Śiva (Bhairava), in whose temples Nāthas sometimes officiate as priests. The use of the trident (*triśūla*) and the celebration of the yearly festival in Caitra (March-April) in honour of Śiva, when lay followers turn ascetics, as also of *Śivarātri,* complete the later picture of Śaiva affiliation. *Śivarātri* is, in fact, the major festival of the cult. Among non-Bengali Gorakh-panthī Yogīs, however, Śiva had probably less to do, and the Śaiva element of the religion may have come from Matsyendra Nātha, alleged to be the *guru* of Gorakṣa Nātha. In fact, strong Vaiṣṇava association in western India, Buddhistic affiliation in Nepal and eastern India, and even Jaina and Islamic touches in isolated places make up the complicated texture of the widely spread Nātha cult. Śākta elements are naturally widely and strongly represented, as the list of places of pilgrimage shows. The cult had, however, never been seriously theistic. The elusive and intangible supreme Being, who is manifested in the universe created out of Him, is called by the epithets Nirañjana (speckless), Śūnya (void), Anādi (beginningless), Ādi Nātha (primal Lord), etc. The story of the beginning of creation, according to the traditions of the Nātha cult, shows remarkable affinity with the Ṛg-Vedic hymn of creation (*R. V.*, X. 129) and the opening lines of the *Manu Saṁhitā.* Before the beginning of creation there was all-encompassing Darkness and Void. The impulse of creation made a ripple in the Void resulting in a bubble, an egg. The egg was hatched, and out of it emerged the primal God. The egg-shells formed the upper and lower limits of the universe. From the sweat of Ādi Nātha, the primal God (with whom, by the way, Ādi Nātha, the first of the nine Nātha *gurus*, was sometimes identified), was born his spouse Ketakā (also called Manasā). Impregnated without personal contact from Ādi Nātha, she gave birth to Brahmā, Viṣṇu, and Śiva. Brahmā came out of her mouth ; Viṣṇu appeared from the forehead ; and Śiva was born in the usual way. Before the birth of his sons, Ādi Nātha had left home to practise penance by the waters of the sacred river Ballukā. Instead of taking up the work of creation, which their father wanted them to do, the sons too went away to the Ballukā to practise austerities. After a time, Ādi Nātha wanted to test his sons. He approached them in the form of a decomposed cadaver floating down the Ballukā. Getting the putrid smell of the body from a distance, Brahmā made himself scarce. Viṣṇu waved it away. But Śiva at once knew it to be their father's body. The three brothers then cremated the corpse. From the ashes were born the five cardinal saints (Ādi Siddhas) of the Nātha faith. Mīna Nātha sprang from the navel ; Gorakṣa Nātha came out of the skull (according to other versions, from *ghor* or filth, whether sweat or dung) ; Hāḍi-pā originated from the bones ; Kānu-pā was born from the ears ; and Cauraṅgī Nātha came out of the feet.

THE FIVE ĀDI SIDDHAS

As Śiva appeared to be the shrewdest of the three, and as he was born as a mother's son in the natural way, he was chosen by Ādi Nātha to marry Ketakā. After her marriage with Śiva, she became known as Gaurī (or Caṇḍī). The five Siddhas became the followers of Śiva. The supreme knowledge (*mahājñāna*) was known to Śiva only. A knowledge of this secret would make a man unageing and undying. Gaurī coveted this secret. Śiva was not willing to divulge it to anybody. But he could not resist his wife for long. To ensure perfect privacy, Śiva took his wife to a platform on the deep sea. Mīna Nātha was aware that something tremendous was about to happen. He followed the couple at a distance and, turning himself into a fish (whence his name), took his station in water under the platform. When Śiva began to reveal the supreme knowledge, Mīna Nātha made Gaurī fall asleep, so that she might not listen to Śiva. Śiva was not aware that Gaurī was dozing. Mīna Nātha, imitating the voice of Gaurī, uttered short monosyllables at judicious moments, so that Śiva was led to believe that his wife was listening attentively. As soon as the talk was over, Gaurī's spell of sleep was broken. She demanded the supreme knowledge from her husband. Śiva then came to know that he had been deceived by Mīna Nātha. He made the imprecation on Mīna Nātha that a day would come when he would forget the supreme knowledge. In Nepalese and Tibetan traditions Matsyendra Nātha, who is the guardian deity of Nepal, is identified with Avalokiteśvara who, according to one account, came to be known as Matsyendra Nātha after he had overheard the teaching of Śiva as a fish. Tradition is strong on the point of his migration from East India to Nepal. Gorakṣa himself became an object of worship in Nepal, but he too plays a part in many local traditions of different parts of North and West India with dates between the eighth and the fourteenth century assigned to him. To return to the story:

Gaurī felt that it did not look well that the Siddhas should live as bachelors, while their elder brother Śiva led a family life. She requested them to marry and settle down. They would not do so. Then she put forth all her personal charms to force them to notice the attractiveness of women. The Siddhas were moved, but in varying degrees. Mīna Nātha was by far the easiest victim, and he was directed to go over to the country of Kadalī (literally, plantain, a synonym of *rambhā*, which is also the name of a celestial nymph) women and to rule over them. Hāḍi-pā, according to the desire aroused in his heart, was directed to go to the kingdom of Pāṭikā and serve as a stable-sweep to Queen Mayanāmatī. Kānu-pā was dispatched to Ḍāhukā ; his career there is not recorded. The young Siddha Śiśu-pā or Gābhur (probably Cauraṅgī Nātha is indicated) was compelled to consort with his step-mother. Gorakṣa Nātha remained unmoved. He admired Gaurī only as his might-have-been mother. This failure to ensnare him by her looks made Gaurī take desperate steps. To seduce Gorakṣa she stooped to despicable tricks ; but the Siddha could not be tripped. From him Gaurī received a thorough chastisement. Śiva came to her rescue, and to heal his wife's wounded pride, he arranged Gorakṣa's marriage with an ascetic princess. After the marriage ceremony, Gorakṣa was taken to his father-in-law's place. When the princess approached the bridal bed at night, she found her husband turned into an infant crying for the mother's breast. The girl was mortified. Gorakṣa said that he was neither a man nor a woman ; like a piece of dry wood, he was without sensibilities and physical reactions. She had only to thank Śiva for the fiasco. Gorakṣa did not like to leave her in blank despair. He gave her a drink of water in which was soaked a piece from his loin cloth. This she took and in a few hours she gave birth to a son. Gorakṣa named him Karpaṭi Nātha, as he was born from his loin cloth, and gave him initiation in the yogic path. Then he returned to his usual haunt, the shade of the *bakula* tree at Vijayānagara. It may be noted here that in different versions a similar miraculous birth has been ascribed to Gorakṣa Nātha himself, and even to Matsyendra Nātha, his *guru*.

A rivalry between two sub-sects of Nātha Yogīs, owing allegiance to Matsyendra Nātha and Jālandhari-pā (Hāḍi-pā), respectively, is perhaps indicated in the following story. One day Gorakṣa was seated under a tree. He suddenly felt a flying shadow fall on his person. He looked up and saw Kānu-pā soaring over his seat. He threw up a shoe and brought the other Siddha down. A quarrel and mutual recrimination followed, which revealed the whereabouts of their *gurus.* From Kānu-pā, Gorakṣa learnt that his *guru,* Mīna Nātha, ruling over Kadalī women, was at the end of his span of life. Gorakṣa told Kānu that the latter's *guru,* Hāḍi-pā, had been buried alive by the order of King Gopīcandra of Pāṭikā. The quarrel was soon made up. The two Siddhas hastened on their respective ways to rescue their *gurus.*

The first destination of Gorakṣa was the office of Yama, the god of death. There he looked up the ledger and saw that the account of his *guru's* span of life was about to be closed. He then cancelled the whole account and with a lighter heart went to the territory of the Kadalīs. But he could not get in, as the Kadalīs, anticipating such a move, had forbidden the entrance of a Yogī into their country. Gorakṣa then dressed himself as a Brāhmaṇa. This secured him entrance into the country, but not to the king's presence. On learning that of outsiders only a songstress or a danseuse could expect Mīna Nātha's audience, he put on the guise of a woman dancer. Even then he was kept waiting at the outer door of the audience hall. Then Gorakṣa began to play on his drum (*mṛdaṅga*). Mīna Nātha's interest was awakened ; he ordered the dancer to be brought before him. The disciple saw that his *guru* had forgotten the supreme knowledge and had almost lost his body and soul in living a family life in luxury. Even a son had been born to him. Gorakṣa was intensely moved and waited for a sign of recognition by the *guru,* but nothing happened. Mīna Nātha had lost all recollection of his previous life. Gorakṣa could not speak out, as it would bring about his instant expulsion. He was at last compelled to spell out the supreme knowledge in the code of his dancing steps and the beating of his drum. When the message was completed, Mīna Nātha's stupor of ignorance fell away, and all at once the lamp of the supreme knowledge was re-lit in his heart. Led by the disciple, the *guru,* accompanied by his son Bindu Nātha, left the place at once. The Kadalīs were turned into bats. One version of the story here concludes the activities of Mīna Nātha. According to another version, which was current in West Bengal till the eighteenth century, Mīna Nātha came to Mahānāda and established there a ruling house of the Yogīs, which was destroyed by the Mohammedans sometime in the fourteenth century.

To pursue the other Siddha. Hāḍi-pā (whose other name was Jālandhari) was serving as a stable-sweep at the palace of Queen Mayanāmatī of Pāṭikā. The latter was a Siddha Ḍākinī, i.e. a female Yoginī possessing occult powers. In early youth, she once met a Yogī Siddha on the way to her father's place. The Siddha asked her to cook for him a dish of arum leaves. She did so and satisfied the Siddha, who imparted to her the supreme knowledge. In spite of this occult power, which staved off decay and death, she could not make her headstrong husband, King Māṇikacandra, believe in the efficacy of the yogic lore. The king died when Gopīcandra, son of Mayanāmatī, had not yet been born. Before the birth of Gopīcandra, Mayanāmatī seems to have come in contact with Jālandhari, who was playing the humble rôle of a 'Hāḍi' (sweeper). When Gopīcandra came of age, he was married to two good-looking girls, Adunā and Padunā. When the story opens, the girls were aged seventeen, and the dowager queen Mayanāmatī had given up all hopes of any child being born to them. Fearing that her son would be short-lived like her husband, she repeatedly asked Gopīcandra to take initiation in the yogic path from Hāḍi-pā. The boy-king had to submit to his mother's ruling. He half-heartedly took initiation from Hāḍi-pā. After some time, Hāḍi-pā came to know that the young king was abusing his yogic power, and the *guru* withdrew it from the disciple. At this Gopīcandra was exasperated. He ordered the Siddha to be buried alive. Learning this from Gorakṣa, Kānu-pā, the chief disciple of Hāḍi-pā, hurried to Pāṭikā, and by a show of his occult powers got his *guru* dug up. Hāḍi-pā's wrath against Gopīcandra was removed by the intercession of Kānu. Hāḍi-pā was made to look at three golden statues of the king, which were instantly destroyed. Gopīcandra thus died three deaths by inanimate proxies. Then he willingly submitted to the will of the Siddha and left home as a Yogī mendicant in the company of Hāḍi-pā.

The versions of the Gopīcandra legend that are current outside Bengal differ but little from the above outline. Two new characters are introduced, Bharathari (i.e. Bhartṛhari) and Campādeī. The former was Mayanāmatī's brother and a devoted follower of Jālandhari ; he takes the place of Kānu-pā of the Bengali version. Campādeī was the sister of Gopīcandra and the wife of the king of Bengal. As destined, she died on recognizing her Yogī brother. Entreated by Gopīcandra, Jālandhari brought her back to life. In a later version, Gorakṣa is credited with this achievement and, in fact, with many other magical feats. The legends about Gorakṣa's miraculous powers increased in North India, including Nepal, more than in East India, especially in later literature connected with Gūgā and Pūran Bhagat, and were responsible for the establishment of important centres of the cult at Sialkot, Tilla, and other places situated north of the Vindhyas.

THE NĀTHA SIDDHAS AND THEIR WORKS

Historicity can be safely postulated for almost all the early Nātha Siddhas except Gorakṣa Nātha, the most important figure of them all, whose date and provenance are variously given in different accounts. These Siddhas are claimed by more than one contemporary esoteric cult. The Vajrayāna school of Tāntric Mahāyāna Buddhism accepts the early Nātha Siddhas other than Gorakṣa as its own masters. This is not as remarkable as it looks. Both the Nātha cult and the Vajrayāna had fundamental unity in their esoteric or yogic aspects. Munidatta (*c.* 1400) in his commentary on *Caryāgītikośa* quotes four lines from an Old Bengali mystic song by Mīna Nātha. The lines, in English translation, are as follows:

> The *guru* directs the path to the supreme goal;
> That is the trap-door to the fence of the stag *karma*.
> The lotus, when full blown, is not reported to a snail;
> But a bee forgets not to drink the honey.

Mīna Nātha was known also as Matsyendra Nātha or Macchaghna Nātha. Matsyendra is apparently a synonym of Mīna Nātha, and the addition of 'Nātha' is a tautology. Macchaghna (Matsyaghna, fish-killer) was probably based on the supposed caste of the Siddha. In non-Bengali tradition, Gorakṣa Nātha too is called a fisherman (Keoṭiya, i.e. Kaivarta). The derivative meaning of the name Jālandhari (or Jālandhara), namely, net-holder, is to be remembered in this connection.

In Nepal and in Tibet Matsyendra Nātha was assimilated to the Buddhist deity, Bodhisattva Avalokiteśvara. His annual car festival in Nepal is as notable an event as that of Jagannātha in Orissa. Among the lower classes of Bengali Muslims, Matsyendra turned into a Pīr called Machandali or Mocharā (perhaps derived from Mocandara, in which form the name occurs in *Gorakṣa-vijaya*), and Gorakṣa Nātha became the protecting diety of the milch cow, from the etymological meaning of the name and his identity with Śiva, whose cattle association, e.g. the bull vehicle, is well known.

Jālandhari (better known as Hāḍi-pā in Middle Bengali literature), according to Cordier's *Catalogue of Tibetan MSS.*, wrote in Sanskrit some treatises on Tāntric Buddhism or on the yogic cult, such as *Vajrayoginī-sādhana*, *Śuddhivajra-pradīpa* (a gloss on *Hevajra-sādhana*), *Śrīcakra-sambara-garbha-tattva-vidhi*, and *Huṅkāra-citta-bindu-bhāvana-krama.* But there is no reason to believe that one person was the author of all these works. None of the works, except the last, could have been written by a Nātha Yogī. Then again, there is nothing to show that the historical Jālandhari was a Nātha Yogī. His connection with Mayanāmatī indicates that originally Jālandhari was a Tāntric Yogī, for whom company of women was not strictly forbidden. On the other hand, there is positive proof that Kānu-pā, the chief disciple of Jālandhari, was a Kāpālika (i.e. Tāntric) Yogī. In one of his mystic songs in Old Bengali, Kāṇha (older form of the name of Kānu) appeals to his *guru*, Jālandhari, 'I shall make the reverend Jālandhari my referee' (*'Sākhi kariba Jālandhari-pāe'*).

Kṛṣṇa-pāda (Kāṇha in Old Bengali, Kāna-pā or Kānu-pā in Middle Bengali) can be called a major poet of Old Bengali literature, inasmuch as not less than twelve mystic songs written by him have come down to us. Didactic couplets (*dohā*) in Apabhraṁśa, written by him, are also extant. Several Sanskrit treatises on Tāntric ritualistic and mystic practices are ascribed to him. It is too much to suppose that all these emanated from the pen of a single person. But there is no justifiable reason for doubting that the Old Bengali songs and the Apabhraṁśa couplets were composed by one person, who was a Tāntric Yogī, if not a strict follower of the Nātha cult. It is quite possible that Kāṇha began his religious career as a Nātha Yogī, but later on he took to the Tāntric path. In one of his songs, partly translated below, Kāṇha says allegorically that his fascination for a Ḍom girl compelled him, who was a naked skull-bearing Yogī mendicant, to give up the outfit of a Yogī dancer:

> O Ḍombī, you sell gut string and wicker ware;
> For your sake I have discarded the wardrobe of a dancer.
> O! you are a Ḍom girl and I am a Kāpālika;
> For your sake I am wearing a chaplet of bones.

Cordier records a Sanskrit work *Vāyutattvopadeśa* by one Ācārya Cauraṅgī. From the title it appears to be a yogic treatise. So the author may well be the Nātha Siddha of the same name.

In non-Bengali tradition, there was a Nātha Siddha named Kaṇerī (Kāṇarī) Nātha. This name too is historical. Tāntric or yogic works of Kaṇerī exist in Tibetan translation.

The name of Gorakṣa Nātha does not appear as the author of any early yogic or Tāntric works, existing either in original or in Tibetan translation. What has been published as the *Gorakṣa Saṁhitā* is a rather late compilation, which has little to do with the Nātha Siddha. Although the historicity of the name of the Nātha Siddha cannot be vouched for now, it should not be concluded that Gorakṣa Nātha also is mythical. The teachings ascribed to Gorakṣa in Middle vernacular literature contain the essence of the Nātha cult. Gorakṣa was the true 'Ādi Siddha' of that strictly celibate and rigidly austere yogic cult, which may be called the cult of Gorakṣa (Gorakh Pantha of Hindi-Rajasthani). This cult, in later times, came to be mixed up with similar yogic and Tāntric cults which did not strictly forbid contact with women. The combined cult is the Nātha cult of Bengal. The Gorakh Pantha outside Bengal presents a much purer form of the celibate yogic faith, but even there rules of celibacy or continence are occasionally transgressed. It can be safely guessed that Mīna Nātha, Jālandhari, and Kāṇha originally belonged to an esoteric cult or cults, which allowed Yogīs to have the companionship of Yoginīs. The story of the spiritual awakening of Mīna Nātha by Gorakṣa (*Mīnacaitanya*, as it is sometimes called in Middle Bengali literature; the other name of the story, *Gorakṣa-vijaya*, lays emphasis on the achievement of Gorakṣa) indicates the conflict as well as the *rapprochement* of the cults of Gorakṣa and Mīna Nātha.

The liaison between Jālandhari and Mayanāmatī is hinted at in more than one version of the story of Gopīcandra. Jālandhari was called Hāḍi-pā not only because he did the work of a Hāḍi (the sweeper caste in Bengal), but also because he belonged to the same caste. The real cause of Gopīcandra's distaste for the Siddha was perhaps his mother's intimacy with such a low-born person. Hāḍi-pā's origin from the bones of Ādi Nātha is based on folk etymology, as in the case of Kānu-pā and Cauraṅgī. 'Kānu' comes from 'Kṛṣṇa', through the Old Bengali form 'Kāṇha', and not from '*karṇa*', as the story implies. Similarly, 'Cauraṅgī' does not come from '*caraṇa*', but from '*caturaṅga*' (from the particoloured robe taken up by him, as is done even now by the Bāul mendicants).

Gorakṣa's attitude to his infatuated *guru* is reflected in, and probably based on, the teachings of Saraha, as appearing in his Old Bengali songs and Apabhraṁśa couplets. Saraha's instructions and admonitions, intended possibly for the erring disciplehood, form the basis on which the story of Mīna Nātha's rescue by Gorakṣa Nātha was subsequently built up. To quote in translation some relevant sayings of Saraha:

> You took a wife in lower Bengal, and then your *vijñāna* was lost.
> On left and right, there are canals and trenches;
> Saraha says, my son (or father), the way lies straight ahead.
> She devours the husband; she is entertained in the Sahaja; she loves and she hates.
> Seated by her lover, she is corrupt at heart. So does the Yoginī appear to me.

THE FUNDAMENTALS OF THE NĀTHA CULT

The aim of the esoteric practices of the cult was the attainment of the state of 'nativity', i.e. neutrality (*sahaja*), where there is no birth and death as such. According to the philosophy of the cult, existence and extinction are the resultants of man's desire and cogitation ; his fetters and his release are, as it were, his own creation. A true Yogī moves beyond the world of thought ; to him activity (*karma*) has no appeal, and salvation (*nirvāṇa*) is meaningless. So says Saraha in one of his songs:

We, the Yogīs beyond the world of thought, know not
How birth and death and emancipation happen.
As birth is, so is death.
There is no distinction between the living and the dead.
If one has fear of death here,
Let him then hanker after the water of life and magic potions.

The attitude of a Yogī to the phenomenon of physical death is thus revealed in a song of Kāṇha:

The real Self in the state of neutrality is fulfilled in the Void ;
At the removal of the physical reflexes and mental attributes be
not depressed.
Say how Kāṇha would not exist,
When he is ever moving about, measuring the three worlds.
A fool is sorry to see the end of a show ;
Do the breakers ever dry up the sea?
Men, being ignorant, know not:
They perceive not the fat existing in milk.
In this existence one neither goes nor comes ;
With this outlook Kāṇha the Yogī fellow disports.

For the attainment of the state of neutrality, a Yogī, following his *guru's* instructions, has to check the downward flow of the semen, hold up the breath, and stabilize the mind. These processes are technically known as *bindu-dhāraṇa, pavana-niścāñcalya,* and *citta-nirodha.*

WAYS OF THE YOGĪS

An early and faithful portrait of a Yogī is painted in an Old Bengali song of Kāṇha. It is an idealistic self-portraiture:

Kāṇha, a skull-bearing Yogī, is on his round.
He walks through the township of the body in the same guise.
The vowels and the consonants are the bell anklets at his feet ;
The sun and the moon are made the ear-rings.
He covers himself with the ashes of love, hate, and infatuation ;
Supreme emancipation is worn as a string of beads.

In the Middle vernacular literature, Yogī mendicants often appear as professional dancers and tellers of tales. In late Sanskrit and early vernacular romantic tales, a male Yogī or a female Yoginī often features as the lovers' messenger or mediator. The sinister side of a Tāntric Yogī is painted grimly in the opening tale of *Vetāla-pañcaviṁśati*. It is the Yogī singers and dancers that have taken the epic tale of Gopīcandra from Bengal to the farthest corners of Aryan-speaking India.

Good living was shunned as poison by the Yogī ascetics. Their way of life was held in utter contempt by the orthodox society. But the people apparently feared the Yogīs much for their supposed occult power and for their mystic mummeries and mystifying trickeries. There is an illuminating story in *Sekaśubhodayā*. A Nātha Yogī, Candra Nātha, who in his early life was a cowherd named Sudhākara, came to the court of Lakṣmaṇasena. The king requested the Yogī to accept some food. The Yogī would accept the offer if only the sweetest dish (*amṛtānna*) were served to him. The royal kitchen made its best efforts. But the Yogī rejected the dishes. Seeing the king nonplussed, the Yogī asked him to consult a learned man. He consulted Govardhana Ācārya, who asked the king to serve to the Yogī a dish of coarse rice and boiled leaves of black arum. The Yogī ate it with the greatest relish. On being asked by the king, he said that good food was poison to the Yogīs and bad food acted as ambrosia to them.

Riddle (*rahasya*) poetry has always been a favourite device of Indian mysticism from the days of the Upaniṣads. It was specially cultivated by the Nātha Yogīs. The stock of such *prahelikā* (riddle) poetry, however, was a common heritage of the mediaeval esoteric cults in Aryan-speaking India. The mystic verses and couplets of the Nātha cult are mostly of Bengali origin. Even in some Hindi and Rajasthani couplets the Bengali original is not completely obscured.

19

SOME LATER YOGIC SCHOOLS

THE later yogic schools of India are fundamentally based on some esoteric yogic practices, which have been current in the country for a very long time. Without entering into the complicated controversy as to whether these were Vedic or non-Vedic in origin, we may say that in some form or other they served as a common heritage for many of the great and small religious sects and sub-sects of India. In later times, these practices were associated with different metaphysical and theological speculations of different schools—Hindu, Buddhist, and Islamic—in consequence of which they underwent various transformations, ultimately giving rise to some later esoteric schools.

It is customary to speak of these later esoteric schools as offshoots of Tāntricism. To be precise in our estimate, we must guard ourselves against the vagueness that hangs round the word Tāntricism as used in common parlance. Without going into the etymology of the word '*tantra*', we may say that, in spite of the heterogeneous elements incorporated in it, the Tantra, as a religious literature, is concerned primarily with *sādhanā* or religious endeavour, and not with any system of abstract speculation. The different metaphysical systems deal with the nature of Reality and the philosophic method for its apprehension; but the Tantra lays stress on the practical methods for realizing that Reality. This practical aspect of the *sādhanā* is the essential part of the Tantra.

THE PHILOSOPHY OF TĀNTRIC SĀDHANĀ

Now in this practical aspect the whole of Tāntric *sādhanā* was based on a cardinal belief that the truth is to be realized in and through the body. On analysis the statement resolves itself into two fundamental principles: firstly, the truth to be realized resides within the body of man; and secondly, the truth that resides in the body of man is to be realized through the medium of the body.

As for the first principle, the belief of the Tāntrikas is that the ultimate Truth is not an abstract principle transcending the universe, but is immanent in it, and that the human body is not merely a thing in the universe, but is an epitome of the universe—a microcosm in relation to the macrocosm. There is therefore nothing in the universe which is not there in the body of man. There is a perfect parallelism between the physical processes of the universe and the biological processes in the body of man.

With this idea in view, the Tantras try to locate the sun, the moon, the stars, the important mountains, islands, and rivers of the exterior world within the human body; the time-element of the universe in all its phases of day and night, fortnight, month, and year have often been explained with reference to the course of the vital wind (*prāṇa* and *apāna*). The implication seems to be that the human body, with its physical structure and biological processes, represents the manifestation of the same energy which is at play in the structure and processes of the vast cosmos. The human form is therefore the abode of truth of which the universe is a manifestation in infinite space and eternal time. Instead of being lost in the vastness of the incomprehensible universe and groping in its unfathomable mystery, the *sādhaka* should concentrate his attention on himself and realize the truth within, with the clear conviction that the truth that is realized within is the truth that pervades the universe without. The second principle points out that the body, according to the Tāntric *yogins*, is not only the abode of truth, but is also the best medium for realizing the truth. This, in a nutshell, is the *yantra-tattva* of the Tantras.

Predominance of *haṭhayoga* is a remarkable factor in Tāntric practices; and these Haṭha-yogic practices are not, as commonly believed, so many physical feats, adopted only with a view to gaining some occult power; they are practices through which the body is transformed into the best medium or instrument for realizing the truth. According to the Tāntric *yogins*, different plexuses (or lotuses, as they are called), nerves, and nerve-centres represent different *tattvas* (realities or essential principles); but the *tattvas* represented by them lie latent, until they are made patent through proper yogic culture and control. This subtle analysis of the physical (including the biological) system of man and the formulation of processes, through which this physical system may be transformed into a perfect instrument for reflecting the truth, constitute the best contribution of the Tantras.

To make a general survey of the later yogic cults, we may start with different Sahajiyā schools. The Sahajiyās, whether Buddhists, Vaiṣṇavas, or others, were all in a sense Tāntrikas; for the *raison d'être* of these schools is to be found in a particular 'sexo-yogic' Tāntric practice. Vedic or non-Vedic in origin, this 'sexo-yogic' practice, as a part of the religious *sādhanā*, captured, at different times, the mind of a set of *sādhakas* professing different faiths, and thus gave rise to different esoteric schools.

According to the Hindu Tantras, where we find it best explained, the absolute Reality, which is neutral by nature, has two aspects within it, *nivṛtti* and *pravṛtti*, which may be rendered as static and dynamic, or as negative and positive. In the Tantras these are generally conceived of as

Śiva and Śakti. Śiva is pure consciousness, qualityless, and, as such, the static or the negative principle, while Śakti is the cosmic energy, the world-force, and, as such, the dynamic or the positive aspect of Reality. But neither Śiva by himself nor Śakti by herself is the ultimate Truth ; they are not even separable ; the highest Truth is the state of neutrality produced through the union of Śiva and Śakti. The point to note here is that the union of Śiva and Śakti, which, under one condition, produces the highest state of neutrality in infinite bliss, produces, under different conditions, the world of manifestation, or the phenomenal process as a whole. When Śakti, associated with all her principles of illusion and defilement, dominates, the union of Śiva-Śakti, which takes place in the realm of *pravṛtti*, becomes responsible for the creation of the visible world ; but when Śakti rises to Śiva in a process of introversion, their union results in a state of neutrality in infinite bliss and tranquillity. So the union that binds may also liberate.

According to the *sādhakas,* or the practical *yogins,* this *tattva* of Śiva-Śakti lies within the body of man. Without entering into the details of the Tāntric *sādhanā,* we may state that Śiva is conceived of by the *yogins* as residing in the highest plexus (*sahasrāra*) in the cerebral region, and Śakti is conceived of as residing in the lowest plexus (*mūlādhāra,* the sacro-coccygeal plexus) ; the *sādhanā* consists in raising Śakti from the lowest plexus and making her proceed in an upward movement till she becomes united with Śiva. Again, the right side of the body is believed to be the region of Śiva, and the left that of Śakti ; this will explain the Tāntric and Paurāṇic conception of Ardhanārīśvara, i.e. the Lord as half woman and half man. The important nerve on the right side, well known as *piṅgalā,* through which flows the *apāna* air or current, is said to represent the principle of Śiva, while the left nerve, known as *iḍā,* through which flows the *prāṇa* air, is said to represent the principle of Śakti. The *sādhanā* consists mainly in uniting Śiva-Śakti by a perfect commingling of the right and left in various ways and neutralizing their functions in a middle course, called *suṣumṇā,* which is the way to neutrality or perfect equilibrium of opposing currents. Again, man represents Śiva and woman represents Śakti ; the perfect bliss that results from a strict discipline and yogic control of their union leads one to perfect tranquillity, which is the state of the Absolute.

SAHAJIYĀ BUDDHISM AND ITS SĀDHANĀ

Let us now see how this Tāntric *sādhanā* was adopted by a school of later Buddhists. Several centuries after the demise of Lord Buddha, the spirit of revolution, which served as the very kernel of all Buddhistic thought and religion, instead of accelerating with the course of time, was being retarded as a result of slow but continual friction with the current Hindu thoughts and practices. As a result, there seems to have developed a spirit of compromise. This spirit of compromise, combined with the Mahāyānic spirit of catholicity in throwing the portals of Buddhism wide open to people of various tastes, temperaments, and capacities, was responsible for the absorption of many of the important Hindu practices into Buddhism itself. This indicates the process by which Tāntricism made its way into Buddhism, giving rise to a composite religion, popularly known as Tāntric Buddhism. About the tenth century A.D., an offshoot of this composite religion developed some tendencies of its own, with exclusive stress on a system of *yoga,* and this school is popularly known as Sahajiyā Buddhism.

These Sahajiyā Buddhists (or the Tāntric Buddhists in general) developed a theology of their own, which is substantially different from the philosophy and religion of canonical Buddhism. It would be wrong to believe that the theology developed first and the yogic practices were adopted later on as required by the theology; on the other hand, we are tempted to believe that the practices were adopted first by a band of *sādhakas,* to whom the spirit of orthodox Buddhism was long lost and yet who were professed Buddhists; and a theology crystallized round these practices gradually with the materials supplied from popular Buddhist thoughts and ideas.

According to these esoteric Buddhists, *bodhicitta* is the highest Truth, it is the Absolute. It is the *sahaja,* the innate nature of the self and the world. This *bodhicitta* is explained as a unified state of *śūnyatā* (void) and *karuṇā* (universal compassion). What is *śūnyatā?* It is a perfect knowledge of the essencelessness of all that is and is not—it is perfect wisdom or *prajñā.* This *prajñā* is the static or the passive aspect of Reality. *Karuṇā,* as a strong emotion of compassion, is the dynamic principle that leads one to an active life for the liberation not only of the self, but also of others; it is therefore the active principle and is called the *upāya* (the means).[1] *Prajñā,* as pure consciousness (*vijñapti-mātratā*) or pure wisdom, represents the domain of *nivṛtti,* while *upāya,* as the active principle, represents the domain of *pravṛtti.* Thus *prajñā* and *upāya* stand in esoteric Buddhism for the same principles as Śiva and Śakti in the Hindu Tantras, the only difference being that, unlike Hinduism, the passive principle is taken here to be the Lady or the Goddess, while the active principle is the Lord.

In practice, this esoteric yogic school of Buddhism holds, as is consist-

[1] For a detailed study of *prajñā* and *upāya,* see S. B. Das Gupta, *Obscure Religious Cults as Background of Bengali Literature,* I.

ent with the spirit of the Tantras, that the body is the abode of truth and, at the same time, the best instrument or medium for realizing the truth. With this belief, it located four plexuses or lotuses in different parts of the body along the spinal column.[2] The first is the *maṇipūracakra* or the *nirmāṇacakra* situated in the navel region, representing the *nirmāṇakāya*, or the principle of material transformation ; the second is the *anāhatacakra* or the *dharmacakra* situated in the cardiac region, representing the *dharmakāya*, or the principle of non-dual cosmic existence ; and the third is the *sambhogacakra* situated near the neck, representing the *sambhogakāya*, or the principle of the body of bliss. Above all these and transcending all these is the lotus (or plexus) in the head (*uṣṇīṣakamala*), which is the seat of the absolute Truth. The cosmic energy (conceived as a feminine principle) remains as a fierce fire-force (*caṇḍālī*) in the *nirmāṇacakra*, and here, associated with all gross principles of defilement, she acts as the principle of phenomenalism. She must be roused and dissociated from all principles of defilement and given an upward motion, so as to reach the *uṣṇīṣakamala*, which is the region of perfect rest and purity. Again, the important nerve on the left side of the body, called the moon or the river Gaṅgā, represents *prajñā*, the Lady, and the nerve on the right side, called the sun or the river Yamunā, represents the *upāya*, the Lord. The left and the right should be controlled and commingled in such a way that all their functions (including the flow of the vital currents *prāṇa* and *apāna* in the two nerves) may be completely unified in the middle path, called the *avadhūtī*,[3] such perfect unification resulting, ultimately, in the realization of infinite bliss (*mahāsukha*), which is the quintessence of the *bodhicitta*. Again, *prajñā*, or the Goddess, manifests herself in every woman, and every man is the embodiment of *upāya*, the Lord (the ovum being the symbol for the Goddess and the seed for the Lord). In actual *sādhanā*, the man and the woman must first of all transcend their corporeal existence and realize their true self as *upāya* and *prajñā* respectively ; with such a realization they should unite and control the sex-act in such a way that the downward motion of the seed may be arrested and an upward motion[4] given to it till it reaches the highest plexus and remains there motionless. This motionless state of the seed in the highest plexus conduces to infinite bliss and tranquillity, and the realization of the highest bliss is the realization of the highest Truth, for bliss is the ultimate nature of Truth. *Prajñopāya* is therefore equivalent to *mahāsukha* (supreme bliss) and *samantabhadra* (entirely auspicious).

[2] *Ibid.*, IV.
[3] *Avadhūtī* has been explained in the Tāntric Buddhist texts as that which, through its effulgent nature, destroys all sin.
[4] See *Sekoddeśa-ṭīkā* (Gaekwad's Oriental Series).

VAIṢṆAVA SAHAJIYĀ SCHOOL AND ITS SĀDHANĀ

We find a new transformation of this 'sexo-yogic' practice in the Vaiṣṇava Sahajiyā school. Here the *yoga* is more psychological than physical or physiological. Let us first see how the yogic practice could be associated with the theology of Vaiṣṇavism, which is predominantly a school of devotion. As *bodhicitta* was conceived of in Sahajiyā Buddhism as the *sahaja* or the innate nature of the self and the world around, so in Sahajiyā Vaiṣṇavism love was conceived of as the *sahaja.* This *sahaja* or the Absolute playfully divides itself into two, as the lover and the beloved, as the enjoyer and the enjoyed, as Kṛṣṇa and Rādhā ; this playful division of the one into two is for nothing but self-realization. In terms of the Sahajiyās, the *sahaja* manifests itself in two currents: *rasa* (love) and *rati* (the exciting cause of love and the support of love), and these two currents of *rasa* and *rati* are represented by Kṛṣṇa and Rādhā. Again, it is held that man and woman on earth are but physical representations of Kṛṣṇa and Rādhā, or *rasa* and *rati* of Goloka ; in the corporeal forms, man and woman represent the *rūpa* or external manifestation of Kṛṣṇa and Rādhā, who reside, so to speak, in every man and woman as the *svarūpa* or the true spiritual self. The *sādhanā* consists first in the realization of the *svarūpa* in *rūpa,* and after this realization, the pair should unite in love ; the realization of infinite bliss that follows from such a union is the highest spiritual gain. The yogic *sādhanā* practised by the Vaiṣṇava Sahajiyās is substantially the same as practised by the Tāntrikas, with the modification that the former do not stop with the yogic practices, but resort to them mainly as preparatory to the union in love.

THE INFLUENCE OF PĀTAÑJALA YOGA ON THE SAHAJIYĀ PRACTICES

If we examine the doctrines and practices of the Sahajiyās from the point of view of Pātañjala Yoga philosophy, we shall find that the final aim in all such cases was the attainment of an infinitely blissful state of arrest (*samādhi*), either purely through a psycho-physiological process of *yoga* or through the absorbing emotion of love, strictly disciplined and intensified through practices of *yoga.* Intense human love, or sex pleasure, transformed beyond recognition, through strict physical and psychological discipline according to yogic practices, has the capacity to produce a supreme state of arrest.[5] In a unique flow of intensely blissful realization, uninterrupted by the notions of subjectivity and objectivity, there dawns an infinite oneness in the mind, which is said to be the state of *samarasa* (unity

[5] In this connection, see *Spanda-kārikā* (Vizianagram Sanskrit Series) and *Vijñāna-bhairava* (Kashmir Series of Texts and Studies)—two important texts of the Kashmir school of Śaivism.

of emotion). As it is said in Yoga philosophy that, when the states and processes of the mind are arrested, the *yogin* remains in his *svarūpa* (own true nature), so the Sahajiyās also say that, when all the subjective and objective disturbances of the mind are absolutely lost in a supreme realization of bliss, we attain our true self, which is *sahaja*. To judge this state of *samarasa* or *sahaja* as a pure state of *yoga*-arrest (*samādhi*), we should first of all examine the plane of mind (*citta-bhūmi*) in which people practise *yoga*. If it be a mere state of sleep of the senses, or a state of swoon of a temporary nature, it cannot be recognized as a state of *yoga* proper. The Sahajiyās were conscious of this possible confusion and the consequent aberrations, and it is because of this that they laid down elaborate and stringent preparatory conditions, before one was allowed to be initiated into these esoteric cults.

THE NĀTHA CULT AND ITS SĀDHANĀ

The Nātha cult, another esoteric yogic cult of much importance, seems to be synchronous with the Buddhist Sahajiyā cult, though, however, the origin of the cult may be traced to a much earlier date. It was essentially a Śaiva yogic school and developed, most probably, from the early Siddha cult of India. This school also is fundamentally based on the belief of the two aspects of the absolute Reality, represented by the sun and the moon, where the sun stands for the principle of destruction (*kālāgni*), through the process of death and decay, and the moon stands for the principle of immutability. The final aim of the Nātha Siddhas is the attainment of a non-dual state, through the attainment of immortality, in a perfect and divine body. This non-dual state of immortality, which is the state of the great Lord (Maheśvara), can be attained only through the union, or rather the commingling, of the sun and the moon. In its speculations on the attainment of an immutable and divine body, through the process of *haṭhayoga,* involving the theory of the sun and the moon, the Nātha cult seems to be akin to the Rasāyana school of Indian thought,[6] the main difference being that the medical and chemical science of Rasāyana became transformed into a science of *yoga* with the Nātha Siddhas.

The main *sādhanā* of the Nātha Siddhas is well known as the culture of the body (*kāya-sādhanā*). This culture of the body implies its transubstantiation first into a subtle ethereal body and that again, finally, into an immutable divine body having an eternal existence. According to these *yogins,* the moon, which is the depository of *soma* or *amṛta* (nectar), is situated just below the *sahasrāra,* the lotus of thousand petals. The quintessence

[6] S. B. Das Gupta, *op. cit.*, IX.

of the visible body is distilled in the form of *soma* in the moon; this *soma* rejuvenates the body and makes it immortal. In the ordinary course, this *soma* trickles down from the moon above and is dried up by the sun, the fire of destruction, situated in the navel plexus; this drying up of the *soma* by the sun leads ordinary beings to decay and death. This *soma* (also called *mahārasa*, the great juice) must be protected from the sun. How is that to be done? There is a curved duct (*baṅka nāla*, as described in the vernacular texts) from the moon to the hollow in the palatal region; it is like a serpent with mouths at both ends, and is well known in *yoga* physiology as *śaṅkhinī*. The mouth of this duct, through which *soma* pours down from the moon, is called the tenth door of the body (*daśama-dvāra*), as distinguished from the other nine ordinary doors. This tenth door must be shut up or well guarded, otherwise the best wealth of man will be stolen by the sun or *kāla* (time, death). How is the *soma* or *amṛta* to be saved from the sun? There are various yogic processes described in Haṭha-yogic and Tāntric texts. The main thing is a process of turning the tongue backwards into the hollow above, so as to reach the tenth door, and of fixing the sight between the eyebrows. The tongue, thus extended backwards, shuts up the tenth door, and the nectar, thus saved, is drunk by the *yogin* himself. In some of the texts, this secretion of nectar from the moon is associated with the rousing of *kula-kuṇḍalinī śakti* (the serpent power, lying dormant in the lowest plexus), and it is held that the rousing of this *śakti* and her march to the *sahasrāra* are instrumental in the trickling down of the nectar.

INFLUENCE OF YOGA ON BENGAL MUSLIMS

It is very interesting to note how the *yoga* ideals and practices greatly influenced a section of the Muslims of India. The influence of *yoga* on the practices of the Sufis is undeniable; but apart from this general influence of *yoga* on Sufism, there grew a school of Bengal Muslims, mostly hailing from the rural areas, who adopted fragments of *yoga* ideals and practices and synthesized them with the popular Islamic faith and ideas. The body has often been described by the village poets as the 'palace of the king'; the various plexuses have been described as the various lotus-ponds, and the six lotus-ponds (i.e. the six plexuses, excluding the highest one, the *sahasrāra*) are again associated with the six seasons. The idea is that as the king dallies in different seasons in different ponds, specially suited to the different seasons, so the one ultimate Truth resides and functions differently in the different plexuses. Again, in some of the texts we find that the ultimate Reality has two aspects, one aspect is symbolized by *vasanta* (spring) and the other by *hemanta* (the season of harvest, comprising the months of Kārttika and Agrahāyaṇa). *Hemanta* is the principle of phenomenalism, while *vasanta* is the path of introversion, the path for a return to the noumenon. *Vasanta* is *yoga,* union with the all-pervading One ; *hemanta* is the whirl of the world process. The former is the principle of immutability ; the latter is the principle of death and decay. The path of *yoga* is the path to *amṛta* (nectar, immortality), and the path of phenomenalism is the path of *kāla* (time, death). We have therefore to proceed in an introverted process from the world of becoming to the ultimate truth of Being.[7]

Another point to note is that many of the minor religious sects of later times spoke of *anāhata-yoga* among various other things, and this idea and practice of *anāhata-yoga* exerted strong influence on the Muslim *yogins* of Bengal also. What is this *anāhata-yoga*? The word '*anāhata*' generally stands for *anāhata-dhvani,* which means the uncreated and unobstructed sound, which is all-pervading and eternal. In the process of *becoming* of the Being, the first stage is the *śakti* (power) and the next stage is the sound, the cosmic vibration from which evolves the visible world. It is the first music, the cosmic music, the divine music. The plexus in the heart is the seat of this *anāhata.* To listen to it, the *yogin* must withdraw his senses from outward objects, turn them inwards, and then concentrate the mind on the centre in the heart ; through such concentration and some accessory yogic practices, the mystery of *anāhata* becomes unfolded to the *sādhaka,* and he comes to be in tune with the cosmic rhythm, which arrests all the states and processes of the mind and draws the *sādhaka* near to God.[8] The mediaeval devotional lyricists took this *anāhata* as the divine music and spoke frequently of it. The Muslim *yogins* of Bengal held that over the material body is the subtler principle of mind, above mind is the higher principle of divine lustre, and above this divine lustre, again, is the *anāhata,* which leads one to God.

[7] See Ali Raja, *Jñāna-sāgara* (in Bengali).
[8] Many other Haṭha-yogic practices are prescribed in the various yogic texts for the realization of this *nāda* (sound).

20

THE DOCTRINAL CULTURE AND TRADITION OF THE SIDDHAS

DEATH is rightly styled *debitum naturae* ; for when a man dies, his life but pays its debt to nature, a debt which it contracts through its coming into manifestation by natural laws set in motion by the haphazard connection of his perishable parents, and through his body being systematically fashioned and nourished thereafter in the lap of nature, till his body is claimed back by nature as the final repayment of a cumulated debt. A contemplation of the pain and desolation inseparable from death, and of the sudden standstill it occasions in the flow of life, brings with it the imperious question, 'Can this ugly death be avoided, if not wiped out?' Only the Siddha reassuringly answers the question in the affirmative, saying that death may either be put off *ad libitum* by a special course of restrengthening and revitalizing the body, so as to put it permanently *en rapport* with the world of sense,[1] or be finally ended by dematerializing and spiritualizing the body, according to prescription, so that it disappears in time in a celestial form from the world of sense and finds its permanent abode in the transcendental glory of God.[2] Of these two modes of deathlessness he would, for obvious reasons, set the latter above the former, unless he intended to keep indefinitely in long touch with the land of the living to serve a purpose of his own. The Siddha, who is both an Āgamic and Upaniṣadic, in a manner *sui generis*, and hence a metempsychosist, says further that either of these two modes of deathlessness will be the lot of only that person who has been rendered absolutely perfect not only by way of transmigration of his soul, but also by way of transubstantiation of his corporeal substance and of the concurrent transfiguration of his form, and that, in consequence, it is out of the question to think of freeing every one that sees the light from his due *debitum naturae*. Even if we be inclined to discount the doctrine of the transmigration of souls, the net result of the Siddha's doctrine comes to this, that instances are not wanting in India of saints and sages for whom the question of *debitum naturae* simply could not exist. To that extent, it would be wrong to lay down as a universal proposition that every birth must result in death. It will not be difficult to see in this connection that the

[1] The view of the Raseśvara Siddha and the Nātha Siddha.
[2] The view of the Māheśvara Siddha.

Ascension of Jesus, legitimatized by the half-truth of Docetism, bears the signature of a true Siddha.

The non-Siddhas aver that it is impossible to free from death a person who is born, but adroitly argue at the same time that, since there is no death without birth, the only way to avert death must be by ceasing to come into being by the portal of birth. The non-Siddha actually parts company with the Siddha in teaching virtually that once birth or embodiment has come about (be it the last in the transmigratory cycle), death is bound to follow as an inexpugnable consequence, and that the attainment of deathlessness or 'corpselessness' begins only indirectly, that is to say, *post mortem* and through the deletion of next rebirth or re-embodiment, and not directly, that is to say, *ante mortem*.

JIVANMUKTI AND PARAMUKTI

This belief takes the form that even the man who, whilst alive, has attained spiritual release, though he will not have a next rebirth, is sure to have his next death, as the inexorable concomitant of his present birth ; and that he attains final release only on the other side of the grave, what he has attained on this side of it being only the step penultimate to that final release. The above description clearly indicates that such a person cannot be a *mukta,* as judged by the standard set by the Siddha of the *śuddhāmnāya*. According to that standard, every one that attains spiritual release from the thraldom of matter, whether it be preliminary (*jīvanmukti*) or final (*paramukti*), can only do so whilst in the flesh, and the hall-mark of the person possessed of such release is to be proof not only against a further liability to be habited in the flesh, but emphatically also against death (*dehapāta*) ; for the *mukta* is a deathless monad into which both his body and his life have been inextricably integrated. He has a preternatural ethereal body during the brief period of his stay in this world, pending his final disappearance in space in his ineffable spiritual body.

The Siddha is emphatic that when a man dies, he is already habited in a new body, for the old body can fall off only in the presence of a new one, and that the subtle body clothes itself with a fresh gross body when the existing one tends to collapse from transmigrational stress. The natural body of man is formed of impure matter (*aśuddha-māyā*). But the riddance of impurity, induced by transmigrational cleansing, is but artificial, and cannot therefore compare favourably with the supernal grade of natural purity characteristic of pure matter (*śuddha-māyā*), out of which impure matter has evolved. Impure matter is always corruptible, just as pure matter is always incorruptible. A special method must consequently be resorted to for bringing the purified corruptible matter of *aśuddha-māyā* completely into line with the incorruptible and naturally pure matter of *śuddha-māyā* and transubstantiating the former into the latter. Till the body of *aśuddha-māyā* is thus transmuted into one of *śuddha-māyā*, bodily death, and hence transmigration, cannot cease, even in the absence of any karmic liability, as the *aśuddha-māyā*, however cleansed, cannot be rid of its native corruptible quality. But the transmigrator's spiritual urge may unexpectedly bring him in contact with a real *mukta* of the Siddha-mārga, ready to help him further forward along the correct track for eschewing bodily death. When the transmutation of the *aśuddha-māyā* into the *śuddha-māyā* has become an accomplished fact under the gracious guidance of the *mukta* in question, the body becomes incorruptible and freed from the thraldom of impure matter, that is to say, from animal limitations and disabilities, including mortal agony. The body incorruptible is named *praṇava-tanu* (body consisting of *Om*). The man with the *praṇava-tanu* is known as a *jīvanmukta,* being in touch with both the world of impure matter and the realm of pure spirit. But his touch with the world of impure matter is bound to be only of short duration, as he is on his way to permanent spiritual freedom (*paramukti*), a state in which he will find himself in the realm of pure spirit, in a transfigured body of glory and power, rid of every point of contact with the world of matter, pure and impure. This transfiguration of the *jīvanmukta's* body of *śuddha-māyā* into the *paramukta's* body of *mahā-māyā,* that is to say, into the body of glory and power, called the *jñāna-tanu* or 'spiritual body', of the finally redeemed, occurs when, at the end of his stay in this world in his *praṇava-tanu* for the sole purpose of guiding the spiritually qualified, the *jīvanmukta* permanently takes leave of the realm of matter, sensible and insensible, pure and impure, and suddenly disappears with his body into space in broad daylight.

PROCESSES OF OVERCOMING DEATH

Now, the key to the methods and disciplines wherewith to end death is only to be had in the elaborate processes indicated below. These processes begin with a purifying cure of the cells, tissues, and organs of the body by rigidly ordered general living based chiefly on restricted alimentation, as also by a concurrent practice of 'interior prayer'. They aim at setting up such unique molecular vibrations in the body as ought, in the long run, to change its composition and quality, and proceed, in due course, to alter, through a mastery of the nature of physiogeny by means of aptly directed spiritual exercises, the usual bodily functions called into play by the demands of workaday animal economy. Then they tend to bring about, in view of the changing orientation of the spiritual objective, the appearance of new organs, tissues, and functions in place of the old, allowed to pass away through disuse, inanition, and marasmus. The processes further make the new organs, tissues, and functions hold their own in relation to a new, simplified order of animal economy, till the processes, natural and preternatural, are ultimately directed to the dematerializing transmutation of the refined, albeit perishable, physical basis of life into a transphysical, incorruptible, and everlasting one. The changes in bodily structure and function, pending the transmutation of the corruptible physical into the incorruptible superphysical basis of life, reach their completion some time before the transmigrator is able to get out of the transmigratory whirlpool. The completion of those changes is an indication of his freedom from the lure of temporal interests.

The transmutation, when complete, does not outwardly interfere with the relative disposition of the bodily parts ; only their vitality is manifestly maintained on a ceaseless supply of unseen extra-physical nourishment. Though seemingly opaque, the transubstantiated body neither casts a shadow nor leaves a footprint. A slashing sword plunging through it can no more make an impression upon it than upon the air. It cannot be felt by touch or handling. The effect of the transmutation of the body into the *mantra-tanu* (body consisting of the sacred formula) empties the refined body, made up of impure *māyā*, of the remnants of its ponderous, corruptible material, and charges it instead with imponderable, incorruptible, deathless, ethereal substance, and thus makes of it a fitting tabernacle of purity and incorruption for the indwelling life. But when the Siddha changes from *jīvanmukta* into a *paramukta*, a veritable transformation supervenes, the transubstantiated body known as the *praṇava-tanu* or *baindava-śarīra* (body composed of the *bindu*) is transfigured, in the twinkling of an eye, into the eternal 'spiritual body' called the *divya-tanu* which is outside the range of human gaze. This transfigured body and the glorified life enter into an intimate, inseparable comradeship, which puts out of court even the possibility of death.

The Siddha is positive that the final release is not in sight so long as the power to lead a deathless life is not in evidence, and no final release from the whirligig of transmigration can come to any one *post mortem*, unless it be through the new animal body assumed some time before the actual death. Though the spiritually freed man has the capacity to lead an indefinitely long life of perpetual youth in his preternatural, death-proof, ethereal body, he does not generally choose to do so. He lives, on the other hand, the necessary span of his earthly life without exciting public notice, but directly his hour is struck, he disappears openly in the transparency of space, in his transfigured subtle body of incorruption, with no indication as to his future whereabouts. But, under exceptional circumstances, he can make himself visible to the denizens of this earth, if he so pleases, the length of stay in his ethereal body being solely determined by the spiritual needs of the 'converted' souls who have planted their feet on the 'pure path'.

Life cannot exist without form, and form implies possession of a body, which again is of substance, material or celestial. As the soul can never subsist without a body, it follows—and this is the law of transmigration as taught by the Siddha—that so long as there is need for renewal of form, life must continue to wander through the realm of matter, ever putting on a new form, sufficiently in advance of the rejection of the old. If advantage is to be taken of the law of final liberation, the need for renewing the form should be made away with by eternizing it. Final release can become an accomplished fact only through the annulment of bodily death. Spirit and matter, life and form, or soul and body are, at bottom, no more than phases of the one eternal substance.

THE NĀTHA SIDDHAS

A short account of some classes of Siddhas who have played a part in one way or another in shaping the religious beliefs of the Indian people may not here be out of place. The Nātha Siddhas of sub-Himalayan provenance, among whom Matsyendra and Gorakṣa are perhaps the best known, are nine in number, named rather differently in different parts of India, and are accorded special recognition in the South for their thaumaturgic attainments. They aim at rendering, by varied physio-chemical processes, the human body deathless, perpetually alive to the light and shade of the sense-world, and capable of wielding the eight supernatural powers (*siddhis*)[3] of a perfected thaumaturge. In this, the Nātha Siddhas are closely allied to the more ancient Raseśvara Siddhas of the Doab or Antarvedi, who achieve the same result by 'reverberating', 'cleansing', and 'projecting' the body with the help of a special *elixir vitae* prepared out of the blended *ens* of mica and *ens* of mercury. According to a Vīramāheśvara classic in Sanskrit, Gorakṣa, the said Nātha Siddha, lived about the middle of the twelfth century A.D. in the hilly Srisadam woods, south of the Tuṅgabhadrā. There he had the good fortune to come in contact with a remarkable Māheśvara Siddha of the Śuddha-mārga, habited in the preternatural ethereal body of a *jīvanmukta*, and to receive from him saving initiation into the highest mysteries of genuine *jīvanmukti* and *paramukti*.

[3] The eight superhuman powers are: powers of becoming minute, light, and great; irresistible will; absolute control over passions; possession or creation of anything at will; supremacy over all; and the subjugation of all at will.

Each of the nine Nātha Siddhas is generally held to stand at the head of a supra-longeval community of ten million expert alchemists, past masters in the preparation of unfailing antidotes against old age, diseases, and poisons. There are thus nine communities, ninety million strong *in toto,* corresponding to the nine Nātha Siddhas, and these ninety million antidotal alchemists bear the collective name 'Navakoṭi Siddhas'. In the view of some, however, these Navakoṭi Siddhas bear no relation to the Navanātha Siddhas, but merely constitute a most numerous fraternity of nine distinct orders, each of them more or less akin, in its outlook and tradition, to a definite disciplinary phase or experimental rule of the Raseśvara Siddhas. A third view, which is perhaps the most popular, holds these same ninety million Siddhas to be a band of death-defying theriacal and therapeutic alchemists indebted in all respects to Bhoga, a pre-Christian Taoist immigrant from China. Bhoga, in his methods of keying up the body of impure matter through 'reverberation' and 'projection' to the pitch of practically cancelling demise, merely sought to promulgate the lesser athanasic precepts of Lao-tze, since the vital objective of the *Tao-Teh-King* is the transfiguration of the immortalized ethereal body into a permanent garment of celestial virtue, in order to fit it to associate eternally with the Tao. There is, again, a further tradition that Bhoga taught the Śuddha-mārga of the Siddhas to both Śaivāgamics and Śāktāgamics in South India, ninety million in number, and was for that reason responsible for the founding of two Śuddha-mārga orders of Āgamic Siddhas, tinctured with the higher esoteric of Taoism. To this tradition of Bhoga's apostolate a further reference will presently be made.

THE MĀHEŚVARA SIDDHAS

But the time-honoured assemblage designated the Aṣṭādaśa Siddhas, comprising eighteen Māheśvara Siddhas of the Śuddha-mārga, is made up for the most part of people of South Indian origin, though it has also been customary loosely to envisage under the same designation any eighteen individuals, as suits one's fancy or interest, from out of a mixed congeries of about sixty influential Siddhas of diverse vogue, discipline, and domicile. The four classical South Indian apostles of Āgamic Śaivism, forming a class by themselves by reason of their outstanding spiritual powers and graces, to wit, Māṇikkavācaka, Vāgīśa (Appar), Jñānasambandha, and Sundara, as well as the bulk of the reputed Śaivāgamic saints, canonized or otherwise, in the Tamil districts and their environs, like Auvai, Mūlar, Ahappey, Pambāṭṭi, Kaḍuvāḷi, Iḍaikkāḍar, Karuvīrār, Śīralan, Kumāradevar, Muttuttāṇḍavar, Veṇkāḍar, Aruṇagiri, Bhadragiriyār, Śivavākyar, and Tirumāḷigaittevar, belong to the glorious tradition of the Śuddha-mārga of the Jñāna Siddhas and are known to have passed over by simple translation, untouched by corporeal death. The poet Tāyumānavar is not tired of singing the praises of these Jñāna Siddhas and their spiritual worth.

MŪLAR AND BHOGA

The Sanskrit form of Mūlar is Śrīmūlanātha, or simply, Mūla. He is eulogized, in what is presumably a self-complimentary verse, as one of the eight Siddhas who received their training direct from heaven, the others being Sanaka, Sanandana, Sanātana, Sanatkumāra, Patañjali, Vyāghrapada, and Tirumāḷigaittevar. It is further given out that himself, Kālāṅga, Aghora, Mālikadeva (identical with Tirumāḷigaittevar), Nādānta, Paramānanda, and Bhoga (the Taoist) are the Siddhas that founded the seven Śuddha-mārga monacal orders of athanasic discipline. Mūla says in his exordium, the genuineness of which is a moot point, that he had as his disciples seven Siddhas, to wit, Mālāṅka, Indra, Soma, Brahmā, Rudra, Kālāgni, and Kaṁsācala. From the indications scattered through his book, it can be easily made out that he had his propaedeutics in the culture of the soul under one of the Nātha Siddhas, or in one of the schools of their persuasion, on the Himalayas, which he perfected, in course of time, with the aid of the discipline of the Śuddha-mārga, as taught by the Āgamics of the same region. The Chinese Taoist, Bhoga, was apparently a contemporary of Mūla, if the recorded tradition is true. He is also said to have brought with him into this country a fellow-countryman of his, by name Pulippāri (as written and pronounced in Tamil), whom he turned into an expert in medicine, alchemy, and lower thaumaturgy. By one tradition, Bhoga was a junior contemporary of Agastya, the prince of Śuddha-mārga Siddhas, who is said to have come to South India from the trans-Himalayan North on a self-imposed mission and, without caring to pass away by translation, after the conquest of corporeal death, to have worked in full vigour in the flesh for hundreds of years both before and after the Christian era, making the Siddhakūṭa-parvata of the present Tirunelveli District in South India his permanent home. Among the Śaivāgamic disciples, Mālikadeva, who founded a monastic order of his own, was the foremost, and among those of Śāktāgamic persuasion, the celebrated Garbhapurīṣa (noticed already under the Tamil form of his name Karuvīrār) became in turn the head of a mendicant school of athanasic spiritual discipline, worked diverse miracles including those of raising men, women, and animals from the dead, and finally disappeared in the sight of all.

THE LEGEND OF THE NIGAMAVANA

While dwelling on this subject, the following legendary particulars may not be without historical or doctrinal value, as they seem to be redolent of an old-time clash of true and false teachings on the nature and character of *mukti*. The Vedas were so offended at the way their teachings were travestied by their custodians that they retired to a nook near Point Calimin to do penance in the guise of a forest, since called Nigamavana or Vedāraṇya, 'the forest of the Nigamas or Vedas', so that God might take compassion on them and restore their teachings to their native purity and also change their custodianship. The ancient name, Nigamavana, is preserved in its shortened form, Nigama, both in the *Periplus* (first century A.D.) and in Ptolemy's *Geography* (second century A.D.). The Vedas are supposed to be still occupied with the service of God in the Nigamavana (which is identified sometimes with the modern Vedaraniam, and sometimes with its outlier-forest, the Koṭivana), with the sacred host of the Navakoṭi Siddhas in close propinquity, inhabiting the sea-washed sands known as the Navakoṭi Siddhāśrama, and overshadowed by the white banyan, not seen of the ungodly. The great Agastya, the prince of the Siddhas of the Śuddha-mārga, is credited by tradition with abiding in a shrine near by (Agastya-grāma), watching with the fond care of a patron-saint the spiritual activities of the Nigamavana and the Navakoṭi Siddhāśrama. The allegory behind the legend imports that the Nigamavana planted itself beside the Navakoṭi Siddhāśrama, in order to be in contact with the vivifying influence of the teaching of the Śuddha-mārga of the Siddhas, as exemplified in the lives of the Navakoṭi Siddhas and ratified and expounded under the hierophantic sanction of Agastya. How the Vedas once gave ocular proof of their willingness to deliver up their inmost eschatological secrets, when faced by the right *adhikārin* (warantee), is common tradition, if not knowledge, to those familiar with the sacred narrative of the miracles worked by the two apostolic Siddhas, Vāgīśa and Jñānasambandha, on getting into the temple at Vedaraniam. These two Śaivāgamics, as true Siddhas of the Śuddha-mārga, had with them the keys of the kingdom of heaven, and were therefore fully conversant with the mysteries of godliness, that is to say, of the spiritual transformation of the material human vesture. This is the goal of every Siddha—the *siddhānta*. It is a secret, a mystery (*rahasya*), and is called the goal of the Āgamas, as the Paurāṇikas of the *śuddhāmnāya* aver. The selfsame Paurāṇikas also proclaim that Sanaka, Sanandana, Sanātana, and Sanatkumāra were the earliest sages to be initiated into the Śuddha-mārga by God in human guise. The Siddhas of Śuddha-mārga, who therefore form the lineal spiritual descendants of those earliest God-taught sages, constitute, in reality, the spiritual vanguard of the Āgamics and the Upaniṣadics.

LITERATURE OF THE SIDDHAS

The whole of the disciplinal, sacramental, mystical, and dogmatic sections of the theology, developed in the *Kāladahana Tantra* of the *Kāmikāgama* and the *Mṛtyunāśaka Tantra* of the *Vijayāgama*, is said to be taken up with a full-dress exposition of the diverse Śuddha-mārga disciplines for the attainment of the *siddhi* of *siddhis*, viz. the spiritual liberation of man by his monadic transfiguration and translation in broad daylight. A *résumé* of the Śuddha-mārga doctrine is available in Kumāradeva's *Śuddha-sādhaka*, to which perhaps may be linked, as a useful supplement, Rāvaṇārādhya's *Śivajñānadīpa*, the former treatise indicating, however, in the most summary and general way, the Āgamic and the Upaniṣadic sources for the doctrine.

In the opinion of the students of the Śuddha-mārga, there exists a hidden posterior half of an Upaniṣad, named *Brahma-jābāla* and affiliated to the *Sāma-Veda*, that contains a full and clear account of the *mukti* which is able to replace death of the body by its athanasic transfiguration and translation, and this *Brahma-jābāla* is but one among a collection of thirty-two Upaniṣads much valued by the Siddhas of the Śuddha-mārga for their emphatic enunciation of the true doctrine. Each of these Upaniṣads is divisible into an anterior and posterior half, the posterior half being the more practical, and for that reason kept back from the gaze of all but the true disciples. The collection of thirty-two may now be set out, according to their scheme of an ogdoad for each Veda. Thus the *Ṛg-Veda* has *Śrīrudra*, *Bṛhadāraṇyaka*, *Śvetāśvatara*, *Kaivalya*, *Kālāgni*, *Kaṭhavallī*, *Kātyāyana*, and *Brahma*; the *Sāma-Veda*—*Brahma-jābāla*, *Tejobindu*, *Vārjyāyanīya*, *Bodhāyanīya*, *Āśvalāyanīya*, *Śāṅkhāyanīya*, *Vājīrāyanīya*, and *Śaunakīya*; the *Yajur-Veda*—*Nārāyaṇa*, *Haṁsa*, *Paramahaṁsa*, *Bhāskara*, *Brahmabindu*, *Āruṇīya*, *Amṛtabindu*, and *Bahvapañca*; and the *Atharva-Veda*—*Śivasaṅkalpa*, *Śravaṇa*, *Pāraga*, *Kimpuruṣīya*, *Muṇḍaka*, *Māṇḍūkya*, *Muṇḍīra*, and *Mauṇḍīra*. It will not do totally to identify any item in this list with any other in the common corpus of the one hundred and eight merely by reason of their homonymy. Mention must also be made, as germane to the Śuddha-mārga of the Siddhas, of the soteriological parts enshrined in the inmost recesses of the *Siddhāgama*, the *Sūkṣmāgama*, the *Vīrāgama*, and the *Vātulāgama*. There is, as a matter of fact, hardly a Mūlāgama which does not contain, within the ample range of its corpus, an Upāgama or two, specializing in the disciplines of somatic athanasy, transfiguration, and ascension, associated with the eschatology of the order of Māheśvara Siddhas.

21

SKANDA CULT IN SOUTH INDIA

MURUGAN AND SKANDA

THE worship of Murugan, as Skanda is popularly called in the Tamil country, is very old in South India. No account of South Indian Śaivism, in fact, of no South Indian religious cult, will be complete without an exposition of the Murugan cult, as no deity in the Tamil country claims so many votaries as Murugan.

One of the oldest of the totem-groups in the South was that of the Nāgas (the Serpent tribe), which must have later coalesced with that of the Murugan, for the appearance of a serpent is even today considered by the common folk as betokening the presence of Murugan.

An old name of Murugan, perhaps the oldest, is Śeyon (the God with a red complexion). The oldest Tamil hymns refer to Him as the deity of the hilly regions, the God of the tribes of hunters—Velan (He who carries a *vel* or spear). He was believed to induce violent passions of love in the minds of girls, and was propitiated by magic rites. His priests and priestesses, wearing clusters of *veṅgai* flowers (*pterocarpus marsupium*) dripping with honey, sang and danced the *veriyāṭṭam*[1] or the *kuravai*.[2] His shrines adorned the villages on the banks of rivers and on hill slopes. The great town of Kaveripattinam, near the mouth of the Kāverī, witnessed numerous festivals in His honour, when women danced to the accompaniment of the flute, harp, and drum.

The foregoing description does not constitute the whole picture of the cult. Old Tamil works of the Saṅgam age picture Him as the victorious 'Red-god' who bears the 'gem-like' peacock flag and rides a peacock or an elephant. He is the commander of the hosts of heaven. The *Tirumurugārrup-paḍai* praises Him as a child of the daughter of Himavat, borne down to the earth by Agni and nursed by the six *kṛttikā-devīs* in the grassy pool on the Himalayas. Here the identification of Murugan with Skanda of the Aryans is complete. Nakkīrar, the poet who sang the *Tirumurugārruppaḍai,* tells us how Kurava girls on the hill-side planted a cock banner[3] smeared with ghee and mustard, offered to the God garlands of red oleander and green leaves, burnt incense, made oblations of balls of cooked rice mixed with

[1] A weird dance marked by the expression of frenzy.

[2] A dance in a ring.

[3] The finds in the old urn-burial sites at Adiccanallur include iron tridents (*vel*), banner bases, and representations of fowls in bronze. See K. A. N. Sastri, *Aryanisation of South India.*

goat's blood, and danced to the tune of sweet melodies. Elsewhere, the poet tells us that Brāhmaṇas, who strictly followed the six duties[4] and the codes of *dharma* and tended the sacred fires, worshipped Skanda with flowers chanting holy *mantras*. The mystic is not forgotten in the poem, and we are told that in his heart Guha (Skanda) was enshrined. The poet sees a significance in each one of the God's six faces. One removes the darkness and ignorance of the world and bathes it in light; the second grants boons to His devotees; the third protects the *yajña*; the fourth discourses upon the 'knowledge of the Self'; the fifth destroys evil demons; and the sixth glances lovingly at the face of Vallī, His bride from the hills. Nakkīrar mentions Tiruchendur, Tiruparankunram, Tiruvavinankudi (Palni), Tiruveragam (identified with Swamimalai), and Palamutirsolai (identified with Alagarkoil) as the places of Murugan's principal shrines; but, generally, all hilly tracts are sacred to Him. Murugan, the divine child of perennial beauty, is alike the God of the pre-Aryan Veḍḍa and Kurava, the Brāhmaṇa, and the mystic.

In the *Tirumurugārruppaḍai* and in the earlier poems that sing of Murugan's glory, there are clear references to Murugan vanquishing the demons. This theme has been expatiated upon at great length in the later Sanskrit and Tamil poems. As in Kālidāsa's *Kumārasambhava,* the Tamil Prabandhas considered His victory over the *asuras* and liberation of the *devas* from captivity as the prime purpose of His manifestation. The demoniac hosts were led by the three brothers, Śūrapadma, Siṁhamukha, and Tāraka, who represented respectively the three basic factors of *avidyā* or nescience, *ahaṅkāra* (self-centred ego governed by likes and dislikes), *krodha* (wrath), and *moha* (illusion). Skanda with His spear, representing illumination, destroyed the forces of *avidyā*.[5]

SKANDA-SUBRAHMAṆYA-ŚIVA

There is an unbroken continuity in the evolution of the Skanda cult in the Tamil land, as evidenced by the presence of the statues of this God dating from the seventh century. The Śiva temples of the early Coḷa period (ninth to tenth century) had a number of sub-shrines, ranging from seven to thirty-five in some cases, and Subrahmaṇya was installed in one of them. At Kannanur, there is a *svayampradhāna*[6] temple of Bāla-Subrahmaṇya, solely dedicated to this God, which was constructed in

[4] *Ṣaṭkarma*, viz. reciting the Vedas and teaching them, performing sacrifices and helping others to perform them, and giving alms and receiving them.

[5] A sculpture at Aihole, representing Skanda destroying Tāraka, and another at Tiruchendur, depicting His combat with Śūrapadma, exhibit considerable vitality and power combined with divine grace.

[6] A temple in the sanctum of which Subrahmaṇya is installed.

the reign of one Rājakesarī, identified with Āditya Coḷa I (A.D. 871-907). It is perhaps the earliest dated *karraḷi* or temple built with stone from the base to the finial. At each of the four corners of the roof over the sanctum of this temple is an elephant.[7] In this temple, and in those of later periods dedicated to Skanda, the niches on the walls of the sanctum have idols that are usually installed in the niches of Śiva temples. In the niche on the southern wall is Dakṣiṇāmūrti. The mutilated idol of Bāla-Subrahmaṇya in the Kannaṇur temple is represented with one of the hands in *cinmudrā* (the gesture of communicating divine wisdom), another holding a rosary, and a third bearing His weapon, the *śakti* (*vel*). At Tiruvengaivasal, there is a rare sculpture of Subrahmaṇya (eleventh century) in bas-relief, in the *vīrāsana* pose, represented as holding a rosary and the *śakti*. There are sculptures of Subrahmaṇya depicting Him as holding a jar of nectar (*amṛta kalaśa*) in addition to the rosary. The rosary, jar, and *cinmudrā* are associated with Dakṣiṇāmūrti—Śiva in His aspect as All-wisdom and the great *guru*. They are also associated with several forms of Devī, such as Śāradā and Bālā-Tripurasundarī, who are the wisdom aspects of Devī. Subrahmaṇya is also *jñāna-paṇḍita* and *guru*.[8]

By about the sixth century, the Skanda cult had shed its association with the earliest indigenous forms of worship practised by the hill-tribes, the Veḍḍas and the Kuravas, and had been incorporated in the Śaiva Āgamas. The *Kumāra Tantra* was looked upon as a branch of the Śaiva Tantras, and Skanda was invested with some of the attributes usually associated with Śiva, for instance, Mahāyogin, the great Teacher, the great Healer,[9] and the Lord of the Bhūtas. Śiva, though sharing His form with Umā, is still the ideal of asceticism.[10] Subrahmaṇya, the Lord of Vallī and Devasenā, is likewise the great Ascetic.[11] The five elements are the different bodies of Śiva. The sparks of effulgence that emanated from

[7] The elephant is one of the vehicles of this God. Sometimes He is sculptured as riding a goat, which represents the blending of the Agni and Skanda cults. Skanda is Vahnigarbha or Agnibhū (born of Agni). Agni is also identified with Rudra.

[8] In Swamimalai, Skanda is worshipped as Śivaguru or Svāminātha. There is a Tamil tradition that Skanda came to be called Svāminātha, the 'great Lord', because He expounded to Śiva the significance of the Praṇava. It will be of interest to compare this image of Svāminātha, represented in Swamimalai as an elderly sage with a beard and two arms, with the peculiar iconographic Javanese concept of Bhaṭṭāraguru, sometimes called Śivaguru, identified by some scholars as Agastya. Could it be that this concept combines the Murugan and Agastya cults which are two distinct Tamil contributions to Javanese art and religion? Such a synthesis is not unknown in Java, e.g. the Śiva-Buddha and Śiva-Sūrya combinations. The Javanese Bhaṭṭāraguru is represented either as two-armed or as four-armed, and the emblems and *mudrās* of either form are suggestive of some forms of Skanda in the Tamil country, e.g. the rosary, water jar, and trident. This suggestion was made by Sri K. R. Srinivasan of the Archaeological Survey of India, who recently visited Java ; it deserves further investigation.

[9] '*Gurave sarvalokānāṁ, bhiṣaje bhavarogiṇām*'—*Dakṣiṇāmūrti-stotra*.

[10] '*Kāntāsammiśradeho'pi . . . yaḥ purastād yatīnām*.'

[11] He is worshipped as such in the famous shrines at Palni and Swamimalai.

Śiva's eye manifested themselves first in *ākāśa* (ether), then in *vāyu* (air), then in *agni* (fire), then in *ap* (water), and finally in *pṛthvī* (earth), before they assumed the form of Kumāra Skanda.

SKANDA IMAGES

The earliest plastic representations that we know of this synthesis of Skanda with Śiva and Umā were expressed in the Somāskanda sculptures of the Pallava period from the seventh-eighth century. Somāskanda bronzes are among the finest examples of Coḷa art. In them are represented on the same pedestal Śiva and Umā with baby Skanda in between. The Somāskanda images mark an advance over the Umā-Maheśvara bronzes and sculptures of the Pallava and Coḷa periods, which had their counterpart in North India in the Hara-Pārvatī images of the Gupta and Pāla periods. Śiva is Sat (Existence) ; Umā is Cit (Knowledge) ; and Skanda is Ānanda (Bliss). The three together constitute Brahman who is Existence-Knowledge-Bliss Absolute. The *mantra* of Skanda consists of six letters, the first two are Śakti *bījas,* the second two Kumāra *bījas,* and the last two Śiva *bījas.* Skanda who is the form of Ānanda is an aspect of the Supreme.[12] Ānanda is the resultant of Sat and Cit. In the form of Ṣaṇmukha are both Śiva and Śakti. Five of His faces are those of Śiva,[13] and the sixth is that of Umā.[14] The weapons and *mudrās* in eleven out of His twelve hands are the emblems of the eleven Rudras, while the *śakti* that He holds in the twelfth hand represents Devī.

This synthesis is again emphasized in the following esoteric interpretation of *Skanda-tattva*: His vehicle, the peacock, represents the Vedas ; and He is the Praṇava (the syllable *Om*), the essence of the Vedas. His weapon, the *śakti,* is *Brahmavidyā,*[15] *jñāna-śakti* (power of knowledge). Vallī, His consort to the right, is *icchā-śakti* (power of will), and Devasenā, His consort to the left, is *kriyā-śakti* (power of action). The Vedas being the *śabda* or sound form of the universe, the peacock symbolizes the universe or the evolutionary trend of Māyā. The cock on Skanda's banner stands for *nivṛtti* or the path of wisdom leading to the knowledge of the Self. Śrī Śaṅkara, in his *Bhujaṅgaprayāta-stotra,* praises Skanda as Mahāvedabhāva (the essence of the Vedas) and Mahāvākyagūḍha (the Truth enshrined in the great Vedāntic maxims)

[12] *'Ānando Brahmeti vyajānāt'—Taittirīya Upaniṣad,* III.6.

[13] The five faces are Sadyojāta, Aghora, Vāmadeva, Tatpurusa, and Īśāna.

[14] *Skanda Purāṇa, Śaṅkara Saṁhitā, Sambhava-kāṇḍa.*

[15] *'Veda eva mayūrassyāt praṇavaṣṣaṇmukhastathā ; Brahmavidyāpi śaktissyāt mokṣastaddarśanāt smṛtaḥ'—Skanda Purāṇa.*

POPULARITY OF SKANDA IN SOUTH INDIA

The Skanda legends in the *Rāmāyaṇa,* the *Mahābhārata,* and the Purāṇas are popular in the South, but the most authoritative scripture of the cult is the story of His manifestation and *līlās* as narrated in the *Śaṅkara Saṁhitā* of the *Skanda Purāṇa,* which was rendered into Tamil in the epic *Kanda Purāṇam* in about the tenth century. Hymns in praise of Skanda are numerous in Tamil. Aruṇagiri (fifteenth century) and Kumāra Guru Para (seventeenth century) are the foremost among the hymnists who have sung of Skanda's glory. For sublimity of thought and depth of mystic feelings, Aruṇagiri's hymns have few rivals in the entire range of devotional literature. His songs transport the devotee from the adoration of Sakala Murugan to the contemplation of Niṣkala Paramānanda-veḷi (the formless expanse of infinite Bliss), which is the *svarūpa lakṣaṇa* or inherent attribute of Skanda.

The procession of devotees—men, women, and children of every rank and station in life, trudging their way to Murugan's shrines, invoking His holy names and bearing *kāvaḍis*[16] or ornamented bamboo poles, to which are hung small pots containing milk, sugar, honey, flower, and fruits—is a common but inspiring spectacle in the South. Murugan destroys the ills that flesh is heir to. He destroys likewise the ills of *saṁsāra,* the cycle of birth and death. Many a *siddha* in the Tamil land has invoked Him as Guru Guha (the divine Teacher who dwells in the cave of the heart).

[16] The *kāvaḍi* pole has an esoteric significance: to the initiate in Kuṇḍalinī-yoga, it stands for the spinal column, on one end of which is the pericarp of the lotus called *kulasahasra-kamala,* and on the other that of another lotus called *akulasahasra-kamala.*

22

THE RELIGION OF THE SIKH GURUS

GURU Nānak (A.D. 1469-1538), the founder of Sikhism and its first Guru, was born at Talwandi (Nānkānā Sāhib) in the Punjab and passed away after an eventful career. He travelled widely in India and is said to have visited Persia, Turkestan, Iraq, and even Mecca. Nānak preached liberal doctrines, religious as well as social, and tried to harmonize Hinduism and Islam by his life and teachings. He composed many religious hymns which formed the nucleus of the *Granth Sāhib,* the sacred scripture of the Sikhs. He was followed by nine other Gurus, in succession, under whom Sikhism gradually developed and received its final shape.

Aṅgad, the second Guru (1538-52), invented the Gurmukhi alphabet, the sacred script of the Sikhs. Amar Dās, the third Guru (1552-74), tried to organize the new sect and develop its teachings. He started the institution of *laṅgar* (common kitchen) to abolish caste-distinctions. Rām Dās, the fourth Guru (1574-81), son-in-law of Guru Amar Dās, founded the city of Rāmdāspur, which later came to be known as Amritsar, and started the construction of Harmandir Sāhib (the Golden Temple) there. He established friendly contacts with the Moguls.

Arjan, the fifth Guru (1581-1606), the youngest son of Guru Rām Dās, compiled the *Ādi Granth* (the nucleus of the *Granth Sāhib*) in 1604 and spread Sikhism. Under him the Sikhs began to acquire wealth and power and increased their trade and political contacts with other States, both within and outside India. He was the first Guru to introduce the new dress befitting the status of the Guru, who was now the secular head of the Sikhs in addition to being the spiritual. His fame and growing power roused the envy and fear of Emperor Jahāngīr who began to harass the Sikhs and their Guru. Har Gobind, the sixth Guru (1606-45), the only son of Guru Arjan, completed the process of change in dress and wore two swords, one denoting the spiritual (*faquīrī*) authority and the other secular (*amīrī*). He built the first Sikh stronghold for the protection of the Sikhs and the Hindus, and to his standard flocked the Sikhs. He was the first Guru to take up arms against the Moguls. Har Rāi, the seventh Guru (1645-61), grandson of Guru Har Gobind, entered into relations with Dārā Shukoh, elder brother of Aurangzeb, and came into conflict with the latter, who held the Guru's son, Rām Rāi, who had gone to negotiate peace, as a hostage. Therefore, on the death of Har Rāi, his second son, Har Kṛṣan, became the eighth Guru (1661-64) at the age of five. He too was summoned to Delhi by the Mogul emperor, and died there at the age of eight. Teg Bahādur succeeded him as the ninth Guru (1664-75). In his time there were schisms among the Sikhs. Nevertheless he was able to spread Sikhism. But the intolerance of Aurangzeb led to his seizure and execution at Delhi in 1675.

Guru Gobind Siṅgh, the tenth and the last Guru (1675-1708), son of Guru Teg Bahādur, was the most famous of all the Gurus after Nānak. Born at Patna in 1666 he became the Guru at the age of nine. He founded the Khālsā, the militant Sikh theocracy, to fight the intolerant Moguls and infused new life and vigour into the Sikhs by introducing the baptism of the sword and adding the suffix 'Siṅgh' (lion) to their names. He organized them into a well-knit religious and social body, abolished the succession of Gurus, and placed the *Granth Sāhib* in the place of the Guru. Two sons of his became martyrs to the Sikh cause, and he himself suffered untold hardships, fighting for the cause all his life, until, in the end, he was treacherously assasinated by a Pathan at Nanded in Hyderabad. His has been a wonderful life of noble character, valour, and self-sacrifice, and his unique personality has a great inspiration, secular as well as spiritual, to all Indians in general and to the Sikhs in particular.

Almost all the Gurus composed religious songs and hymns, which have been collected in the *Granth Sāhib*. The *Granth* also includes the compositions of other saints, several Hindu and some Muslim. The songs and hymns are set to music and are in different Rāgs (tunes), as they are called. The teachings of the Gurus are embodied in their different works, which are incorporated in the *Granth Sāhib*.

GOD AND HIS NAME

The aim of life, according to the Sikh Gurus, is not to get salvation or a heavenly abode called paradise, but to develop the best in us, which is God: 'If a man loves to see God, what cares he for salvation or paradise?' (Nānak's *Āsā*). 'All men hanker after salvation, paradise, or Elysium, setting their hopes on them every day of their lives. But those who live to see God do not ask for salvation: the sight itself satisfies their minds completely' (Rām Dās in *Kalyān*).

How to see God and to love Him? The question is taken up by Guru Nānak in his *Japjī*:

> What shall we offer Him that we may behold His council-chamber?
> What shall we utter with our lips, which may move Him to give us
> His love?

> In the ambrosial hours of the morn, meditate on the grace of the true Name;
> For your good actions may procure for you a better birth, but emancipation is from grace alone.

'We should worship the Name, believe in the Name, which is ever and ever the same and true' (*Śrī Rāg* of Nānak). The practice of the Name is prescribed again and again in the Sikh scriptures, and requires a little explanation.

God is described both as *nirgun* (*nirguṇa*) or absolute, i.e. without attributes and *sargun* (*saguṇa*) or personal, i.e. with attributes. Before there was any creation, God lived absolutely in Himself; but when He thought of making Himself manifest in creation, He entered into the realm of relation. In the former case, 'when God was Himself self-created, there was none else; He took counsel and advice with Himself; what He did came to pass. Then there was no heaven, or hell, or the three-regioned world. There was only the formless One Himself; creation was not then' (*Gujri-kī-Vār* of Amar Dās). 'There was then no sin, no virtue, no Veda or any other religious book, no caste, no sex' (Nānak's *Mārū Sohle,* XV, and Arjan's *Sukhmaṇī,* XXI). When God became *sargun* or manifest, He became what is called the Name; and in order to realize Himself, He made nature, wherein He has His seat and 'is diffused everywhere and in all directions in the form of love' (Gobind Siṅgh's *Jāp,* 80).

In presenting this double phase of the supreme Being, the Gurus have avoided the pitfalls into which some people have fallen. With them, God is not an abstract idea or a moral force, but a personal Being capable of being loved and honoured, and yet He is conceived of as a Being whose presence is diffused all over His creation. He is the common Father of all, fashioning worlds and supporting them from inside. But He is never born, He has no incarnation. He Himself stands for the creative agencies, like Māyā, the Word, and Brahmā; He Himself is Truth, Beauty, and the eternal yearning of the heart after Goodness (*Japjī*). In a word, the Gurus have combined the Aryan idea of immanence with the Semitic idea of transcendence, without taking away anything from the unity and the personal character of God.

> O! give me, give some intelligence of my Beloved.
> I am bewildered at the different accounts I have of Him.
> O happy wives, my companions, say something of Him.
> Some say that He is altogether outside the world;
> Others that He is altogether contained in it.
> His colour is not seen; His features cannot be made out,
> O happy wives, tell me truly—

He lives in everything ; He dwells in every heart ;
Yet He is not blended with anything ; He is separate.

—Arjan's *Jaitśrī*

Why dost thou go to the forest in search of God?
He lives in all, is yet ever distinct ; He abides with thee too.
As fragrance dwells in a flower, or reflection in a mirror,
So does God dwell inside everything ; seek Him therefore in the heart.

—Teg Bahādur's *Dhanāśrī*

Guru Nānak's *Āsā-dī-Vār,* in its preliminary stanzas, lays down the fundamentals of Sikh belief about God. It is a trenchant clear-cut monotheism. God is called 'the indweller of nature', and is described as filling all things 'by an art that is artless' (XII. 1-2). He is not an impotent mechanic fashioning pre-existing matter into the universe. He does not exclude matter, but includes and transcends it. The universe too is not an illusion. Being rooted in God who is real, it is a reality ; not a reality final and abiding, but a reality on account of God's presence in it (II. 1). His will is above nature as well as working within it, and, in spite of its immanence, it acts not as an arbitrary force, but as a personal presence working 'most intelligently' (XXX. 2). The first thing about God is that He is indivisibly one, above every other being, however highly conceived, such as Viṣṇu, Brahmā, or Śiva (I), or as Rāma and Kṛṣṇa (IV. 2). The second thing is that He is the highest moral Being (II. 2), who has inscribed all men with His Name or moral presence (II). He is not a God belonging to any particular people, Muslim or Hindu, but is 'the dispenser of life universal' (VI). The ways to realize Him are not many, but only one (XII. 3), and that way is not knowledge, formalism (XIV. 2 ; XV. 1-4), or what are conceived of as meritorious actions which establish a claim to reward (VIII. 2), but love (XIII. 2) and faith (XIV. 2), the aim being to obtain the grace of God (IV. 2 ; V. 2 ; VIII. 2 ; XIII. 1). The only way of worshipping Him is to sing His praises (VI. 1 ; VII ; IX ; XII. 2 ; XIX. 2 ; XXII. 3) and to meditate on His Name (II ; VIII 1 ; IX. 2 ; XVI. 1).[1]

UPLIFT OF MAN BASED ON CHARACTER

This life of praise is not to be of idle mysticism, but of active service done in the midst of worldly relations. 'There can be no worship without

[1] 'Name' is a term, like logos in Greek, bearing various meanings. Sometimes it is used for God Himself, as in *Sukhmanī,* 'The Name sustains the animal life ; the Name supports the parts and the whole of the universe' (XVI. 5). It is described as being 'immortal', 'immaculate', and 'indweller of all creation', and is to be sung, uttered, thought upon, served, and worshipped. In most cases it means the revelation of God as found in the sacred Word.

good actions' (*Japjī*). These actions, however, are not to be formal deeds of so-called merit, but should be inspired by an intense desire to please God and to serve fellow-men:

> Without pleasing God all actions are worthless.
> Repetition of *mantras,* austerities, set ways of living, or deeds of merit leave us destitute even before our journey ends.
> You won't get even half a copper for your fasts and special programmes of life.
> These things, O brother, won't do there ; for the requirements of that way are quite different.
> You won't get a place there for all your bathing and wandering in different places.
> These means are useless ; they cannot satisfy the conditions of that world.
> Are you a reciter of all the four Vedas? There is no room for you there.
> With all your correct reading, if you don't understand one thing that matters, you only bother yourself.
> I say, Nānak, if you exert yourself in action, you will be saved.
> Serve your God and remember Him, leaving all your pride of self.
>
> —Arjan's *Gaurī Mālā*

The Gurus laid the foundation of man's uplift, not on such short cuts as *mantras,* miracles, or mysteries, but on man's own humanity, his own character, as it is character alone—the character already formed—which helps us in moral crises. When we are face to face with an evil, we have to decide quickly. Temptations allow us no time to think. We cannot then consult a religious book or a moral guide. We must decide on the spot and at once. And this can be done only if virtue has so entered into our disposition that we are habitually drawn towards it, and anything evil, though pleasant for the time being, has no attraction for us. It was for this reason that the Gurus did not think it sufficient to lay down rules of conduct in a book for the formation of character ; they also thought it necessary to take in hand a whole people for a continuous course of schooling in wisdom and experience. This is the reason why in Sikhism there have been ten founders, instead of only one.[2]

Before the Sikh Gurus, the leaders of thought had fixed certain grades of salvation for men, attainable according to their different capacities,

[2] Sikhism is sometimes considered to have been founded by all the ten Gurus, since it was gradually evolved over a period of about two centuries, each Guru, from Guru Nānak to Guru Gobind Singh, contributing his share to its development.

whom they divided into high and low castes. Some people belonging to the favoured classes developed in them a few good qualities to a very high degree, while others, left to themselves, degenerated. The Gurus did not want to have such a lop-sided growth. They wanted to give opportunities of highest development to all classes of people.

> There are lowest men among the low castes.
> Nānak, I shall go with them. What have I got to do with the great?
> God's eye of mercy falls on those who take care of the lowly.
> It is mere nonsense to observe caste and to feel proud over grand names.[3]

Some work had already been done in this line. The *bhagats* (*bhaktas*) or reformers in the middle ages tried to abolish the distinction between the high-class Hindus and the so-called untouchables, by taking into their fold such men as barbers, weavers, shoemakers, etc. But the privilege of equality was not extended to men as men, but to those individuals only who had washed off their untouchability with the love of God. Kabīr, a weaver, and Ravidāsa, a shoemaker, were honoured by kings and high-caste men, but the same privilege was not extended to other weavers and shoemakers, who were still held as untouchables. Ravidāsa took pride in the fact that even 'the superior sort of Brāhmaṇas came to bow before him' (Ravidāsa in *Rāg Malār*) ; but the other members of his caste were not so honoured.

The Sikh Gurus made an improvement on the prevalent idea by declaring that the whole humanity was one and that a man was to be honoured, not because he belonged to this or that caste or creed, but because he was a man, an emanation from God, who had given him the same senses and the same soul as to other men.

> Recognize all human nature as one.
> All men are the same, although they appear different under different influences.
> The bright and the dark, the ugly and the beautiful, the Hindus and the Muslims, have developed themselves according to the fashions of different countries.
> All have the same eyes, the same ears, the same body, and the same build—a compound of the same four elements.
>
> —Gobind Singh's *Akāl Ustat*

Such a teaching could not tolerate any idea of caste or untouchability. Man rose in the estimation of man. Even the grovelling slaves of the

[3] *Śrī Rāg* of Nānak. See also Arjan's *Jaitśrī-kī-Vār*, VII ; Amar Dās's *Bhairoñ*.

so-called higher classes came to be fired with a new hope and courage to lift themselves as equals to the best of humanity.

Women too received their due. 'How can they be called inferior', says Guru Nānak, 'when they give birth to kings and prophets?' Women as well as men share in the grace of God and are equally responsible for their actions to Him (*Āsā-dī-Vār,* XIX). Guru Har Gobind called woman 'the conscience of man. *Satī* was condemned by the Sikh Gurus long before any notice was taken of it by Akbar (Amar Dās's *Vār Sūhī,* VI).

The spirit of man rose with the belief that he was not a helpless creature in the hands of a being with an arbitrary will, but was a responsible being endowed with a will of his own, with which he could do much to mould his destiny. He has already existed before he is born here. He inherits his own past as well as that of his family and race. But he is given a will with which he can modify the inherited and acquired tendencies of his past and determine his present conduct. If this were not so, he would not be responsible for his actions. This will, again, is not left helpless or isolated, for if, through the Guru's word, it be attuned to the supreme will, it acquires a force with which he can transcend all his past and acquire a new character.

This question of human will as related to the divine will is an intricate one and requires a little elucidation.

According to Sikhism, the ultimate source of all that is in us is God alone. Without Him, there is no strength in us. Nobody, not even the evil man, can say that he can do anything independent of God. Everything moves within the providential domain.

> Thou art a river in which all beings move:
> There is none but Thee around them.
> All living things are playing within Thee.
>
> —Rām Dās in *Āsā*

The fish may run against the current of the river or along with it, just as it likes, but it cannot escape the river itself. Similarly, man may run counter to what is considered good or moral, but he can never escape from the pale of God's will (*Japjī,* II).

Then who is responsible for his actions? Man himself. We learn from the first *śloka* of *Āsā-dī-Vār's* seventh *pauri* (stanza) that man is given free will, which leads him to do good or evil actions, to think good or evil thoughts, and to go in consequence to heaven or hell:

> Governed by his free will he laughs or weeps:
> Of his free will he begrimes or washes himself;

Of his free will he degrades himself from the order of human beings ;
Of his free will he befools himself or becomes wise.

In the next *śloka* we read:

Self-assertion gives man his individuality and leads him to action:
It also ties him down to the world and sends him on a round of births and deaths.
Wherefrom comes this assertion of self? How shall it leave us?
It comes to man from the will of God and determines his conduct according to his antecedents.
It is a great disease ; but its remedy also lies within itself
Then God sends grace to man, and he begins to obey the call of the Guru.
Nānak says: Hear ye all, this is the way to cure the disease.

The source of evil is not Satan, Ahriman, or any other external agency. It is our own sense of ego placed by God in us. It is the overweening sense of self that grows as a barrier between God and man, and keeps him wandering from sin to sin. 'The bride and the bridegroom live together, with a partition of ego between them' (Rām Dās in *Malār*).

The infinite is within us, 'engraved in our being'. It is like the light of the sun ever present, but shut out of our sight by the cloud of ignorance and selfishness. We sin as long as this light remains hidden from us, and we believe our own self to be everything to us. Regeneration comes when, at the call of grace, we begin to subject our tiny self to the highest Self, that is, God, and our own will is gradually attuned to His supreme will, until we feel and move just as He wishes us to feel and move.

Really the problem of good and evil is the problem of union and disunion with God (*Japjī*, XXIX). It is, however, so designed in the case of man that whenever he wishes he can come back to the bosom of his Father, God, and resume his position there. Guru Nānak says in *Mārū*:

By the force of union we meet God and enjoy Him even with this body ;
And by the force of disunion we break away from Him ;
But, Nānak, it is possible to be united again.

When we come into this world, there are in us divine things, which serve as forces of union, and also evil tendencies, inherited from our past lives, which serve as forces of disunion and draw us away from God towards moral death. Says Guru Nānak in *Mārū*:

Man earns his body from the union of his mother and father ;
And the Creator inscribes his being with the gift of the spirit and progressive tendencies.
But led away by delusion he forgets himself.

This teaching about the freedom of will and 'progressive tendencies' raises the spirit of man, and gives him a new hope and courage. But the temptation of evil is so strong and the human powers for resisting it are so weak that man stumbles at each step, and yet it is expected of him that 'He should always speak the truth, and never tell lies' (Farīd) ; 'He should beware even of an unconscious sin' (Teg Bahādur) ; and 'He should not step on the bed of another's wife even in a dream' (Gobind Siṅgh).

These commands cannot be fulfilled simply with the strength of knowledge and inherited tendencies. Then what is to be done?

The prophets of the world have given many solutions of this problem. Some get round the difficulty by supposing that there is no evil. It is only a whim or a false scare produced by our ignorance. Some believe in the efficacy of austerities ; still others in alms given in profusion to overwhelm the enormity of sin. There is, again, a higher sort of teachers who inculcate the love of some great man as a Saviour. What was the solution offered by the Sikh Gurus? They saw that, although it was difficult for a man to resist evil and to do good with his own powers, yet if he were primed with another personality possessing dynamic powers, he could acquire a transcendental capacity for the purpose. This personality was to be the Guru's.

THE GURU IN SIKHISM

The way of religion, as shown by Sikhism, is not a set of views or doctrines, but a way of life to be lived according to a definite model. It is based not on rules or laws, but upon discipleship. In the career of the disciple, the personality of the Guru is all along operative, commanding his whole being and shaping his life to its divine issues. Without such a personality there would be no direction in the moral forces of society and, in spite of a thousand kinds of knowledge, 'there would still be utter darkness' (*Āsā-dī-Vār*, I). There would be no force to connect men with men, and them with God. Everybody would exist for himself in moral isolation, 'like spurious sesames left desolate in the field' with a hundred masters to own them (*ibid.*). It is the Guru who removes the barriers of caste and position set up by men among themselves and, gathering them all unto himself, unites them with God.[4]

Such a creative personality must be perfect, because 'men take after him whom they serve' (Amar Dās in *Vār Bihāgrā*). If the ideal person is imperfect, the society and its individuals following him will also get imperfect development. But 'those who serve the saved ones will be saved' (*Mājh,* III).

[4] 'Nānak, the true Guru must be such as to unite all men' (*Śrī Rāg,* I)

The Sikh Gurus were perfect, and are described as such in the Sikh scriptures. Guru Nānak himself says in *Śrī Rāg*, 'Everybody else is subject to error, only the Guru and God are without error'. And Guru Arjan says in *Bhairoñ*, 'Whoever is seen is defective; without any defect is my true Guru, the Yogī'. The state of perfection attained by the Gurus is lucidly described in the eighth and eighteenth octaves of Guru Arjan's *Sukhmaṇī*. The same Guru says in *Āsā*:

> God does not die, nor do I fear death.
> He does not perish, nor do I grieve.
> He is not poor, nor do I have hunger.
> He has no pain, nor have I any trouble.
> There is no destroyer except God,
> Who is my life and who gives me life.
> He has no bond, nor have I got any.
> He has no entanglement, nor have I any care.
> As He is stainless, so am I free from stain.
> As He is happy, so am I always rejoicing.
> He has no anxiety, nor have I any concern.
> As He is not defiled, so am I not polluted.
> As He has no craving, so do I covet nothing.
> He is pure, and I too suit Him in this.
> I am nothing: He alone is everything.
> All around is the same He.
> Nānak, the Guru has destroyed all my
> superstitions and defects,
> And I have become uniformly one with Him.

In order, however, to be really effective in saving man, the Guru must not be above man's capacity to imitate, which would be the case if he were a supernatural being. He should have a nature subject to the same laws as operate in ordinary human nature and should have attained perfection through the same divine grace that is available to all men by implicit obedience to God's will. The Sikh Gurus fought with sin and overcame it. Some of them lived for a long time in error, until grace touched them, and they were perfected through a constant discipline in knowledge and love, and by experience in the association of their Gurus. When they had been completely attuned to the divine will and had been sanctified as Gurus, there remained no defect in them, and they became perfect and holy. Thereafter, sins did come to tempt them, but they never gave way, and were always able to overcome them. It is only thus that they became perfect exemplars of men, and transformed those who came under their influence into veritable angelic beings.

THE GURU IN THE SIKH AND IN THE PANTH

This transformation comes not only through a close association with the Guru, which is advocated in many other religions, but through the belief that the Sikh (*śiṣya,* the disciple) incorporates the Guru. He fills himself with the Guru and feels linked up with an inexhaustible source of power. 'The Khālsā', says Guru Gobind Siṅgh, 'is my other self; in him I live and have my being.' A single Sikh, a mere believer, is only one; but when he takes Guru Gobind Siṅgh into his embrace, he becomes, in the Sikh parlance, equal to 'one lakh and a quarter' (*savā lākh*). His nature is so reinforced in every way that, although hundreds may fall round him, he will stand as 'a garrison of the Lord of hosts', a host in himself—a host of 'one lakh and a quarter'. He will keep the Guru's flag always flying. Whenever tempted, he will ask himself, 'Can I lower the flag of Guru Gobind Siṅgh? Can I desert it? I, as Budh Siṅgh or Kahan Siṅgh, can fall; but can Guru Gobind Siṅgh in me fall?', and will declare, 'No, never'. This feeling of incorporation with the Guru makes the Sikh strong beyond his ordinary powers and, in times of emergency, brings him new hope and courage.

So far, we have considered what the Guru does for the Sikhs as individuals. We have seen how he strengthens their character and increases their power a thousandfold by filling their personalities with his own. In order to increase this power immensely more, the Guru made another arrangement. He organized them into *saṅgats,* holy assemblies, and put his personality again into them. This led to a very remarkable development in the institution of Guruship, and no description of Guruship will be complete without an account of this development.

The Sikh idea of religion, as we have seen, is something more practical than being merely mystic. It consists of *nām* and *sevā.* To practise *nām* (Name) means to practise the presence of God, by keeping Him ever in our minds by singing His praises or dwelling on His excellence. This is to be done not only in solitude and alone, but also in public, where worship of the Name is made more impressive by being organized in the form of congregational recitations or singing. The other element is *sevā* or service. The idea of service is that it should be not only liberal, but also efficient and economical, that is, it should do greatest good with the least possible means. It should not be wasteful. For this purpose, we have to organize our means. In every work of practical nature, in which more than one person is engaged, it is necessary to resort to organization. As religion too—especially a religion like Sikhism whose aim is to serve mankind—belongs to the same category, it requires organization of its followers as an essential condition of its success. It may not be necessary in the case of an individualistic religion, wherein the highest aim is to empty the mind of all desires, or to dream away the whole life in jungles or mountains; but where religion consists in realizing God mainly through service done within the world, where men have constantly to deal with men to promote each other's good, it is impossible to do without organization.

Guru Nānak had therefore begun with two things in his religious work: the holy Word and the organized fellowship. This organized fellowship is called *saṅgat*. The idea of *saṅgat* or holy fellowship led to the establishment of local assemblies headed by authorized leaders, called Masands. Every Sikh was expected to be a member of one or other of such organizations. The Guru was the central unifying personality and, in spite of changes in succession, was held to be identical with his predecessors.[5] The love existing between the Guru and the Sikhs was more intense than has ever existed between the most romantic lovers of the world. But the homage paid to the Guru was made impersonal by creating a mystic unity between the Sikh and the Guru on the one hand, and the Guru and the Word on the other.[6] Greatest respect began to be paid to the incorporated Word (scripture), even the Guru choosing for himself a seat lower than that of the scripture. The only form of worship was the meditation on, and the singing of, the Word.[7]

The Sikh assemblies also acquired great sanctity, owing to the belief that the spirit of the Guru lived and moved among them. They began to assume higher and higher authority, until collectively the whole body, called the Panth, came to be regarded as an embodiment of the Guru. Guru

[5] In the Coronation Ode of Satta and Balwand the following verses occur:

'Guru Nānak proclaimed the accession of Lehnā as a reward for service. He had the same light, the same method; the Master merely changed his body.'

'The wise being, Guru Nānak, descended into the form of Amar Dās.'

'Thou, Rām Dās, art Nānak, thou art Lehnā, thou art Amar Dās.'

'The human race comes and goes, but thou, O Arjan, art ever new and whole.'

Mohsin Fani, who wrote in the time of the sixth Guru, says about the Sikhs in the *Dabistān*: 'Their belief is that all the Gurus are identical with Nānak.'

Guru Gobind Siṅgh in his *Vicitra-nāṭak* says about the Gurus: 'All take them as different from one another; very few recognize them as one in spirit. But only those realize perfection who do recognize them as one.' See also the *Sadd* of Sundar, the *Svayyās* at the end of *Guru Granth Sāhib*, and Bhāi Gurdās's *Vārs*, I. 45-48; III. 12; XX. 1; XXVI. 34, 41.

The Gurus always signed themselves as *Nānak*.

[6] 'The Guru lives within his Sikhs, and is pleased with whatever they like' (*Gaurī-kī-Vār*, IV). 'The Guru is a Sikh, and the Sikh who practises the Guru's word is at one with the Guru' (*Āsā Chant*, IV). See also Bhāi Gurdās's *Vārs*, III.11; IX.16. 'The Guru is the Word and the Word is Guru' (*Kānarā*, IV).

[7] *Āsā-dī-Vār*, VI. 1. 'In this world the best practice is of the Word' (*Parbhātī*, I). 'My *yoga* is practised by singing Thy hymns' (*Āsā*, V). Sujan Rāi of Batala, writing about Sikhs in 1697, says in his *Khulāsā tut twārīkh*: 'The only way of worship with them is that they read hymns composed by their Gurus, and sing them sweetly in accompaniment with musical instruments.' In the Golden Temple, Amritsar, up to this time, nothing but continuous singing of hymns day and night by relays of singers is allowed.

Gobind Siṅgh himself received baptism from the Sikhs initiated by himself. After him, the Sikhs ceased to have any personal Guru. If we read the Sikh history aright, the Sikh community, as an organized unit, would appear to have undergone a course of discipline in the hands of the ten Gurus, until its character was fully developed and the Guru merged his personality in the body of the followers thus reared. The Guru, as mentioned above, worked with two things: the personal association and the Word. After the death of Guru Gobind Siṅgh, the personality and the Word were separated. The Panth was invested with the personality of the Guru, and the incorporated Word became the Gyān (Jñāna) Guru (diverse intelligence or the Guru as Knowledge). That is, in simple words, the Khālsā Panth was to be the Guru in future, not in supersession of the previous Gurus, but as the authorized agency to work in their name; and it was invariably to guide itself by the teachings of the Gurus as found in the holy *Granth*. It is because of this that the Sikhs came to regard Guru Nānak and the Guru Panth with equal respect.

Amṛt (*amṛta*, nectar) or baptism was made the basis of this organization. All those who wanted to serve humanity through Sikhism must join the Panth as regular members, and receive its baptism as the initial step. All must have the same creed, which should be well defined and should not be confused with the beliefs and practices of the neighbouring religions. The Guru ordered that 'the Khālsā should be distinct from the Hindu and the Muslim' (*Rahatnāmā* of Chaupa Siṅgh).

> He who keeps alight the unquenchable torch of truth, and never swerves from the thought of one God;
> He who has full love and confidence in God, and does not put his faith, even by mistake, in fasting or in the graves of Muslim saints, Hindu crematoriums, or Yogīs' places of sepulchre;
> He who only recognizes the one God and no pilgrimages, non-destruction of life, penances, or austerities;
> And in whose heart the light of the perfect One shines—he is to be recognized as a pure member of the Khālsā.
>
> —Gobind Siṅgh's *Svayyās*

Such a member of the Khālsā was to embody in himself the highest ideal of manhood, as described by Guru Gobind Siṅgh in his unpublished book, called *Sarb Loh*. Although the Khālsā was designed by the Guru himself, yet the Guru was so charmed by the look of his own creation that he saluted it, in the book, as his own ideal and master. The Khālsā was thought fit enough to administer baptism of the new order even to the

Guru, and was consecrated as the Guru incarnate. As a sign that the Guru had placed himself eternally in his Sikhs, it was declared by him, 'If anybody wishes to see me, let him go to an assembly of Sikhs, and approach them with faith and reverence ; he will surely see me amongst them' (*Prem Sumarag*).

In the ranks of the Khālsā, all were to be equal, the lowest with the highest, in race as in creed, in political rights as in religious hopes. Women were to be baptized in the same way as men and were to enjoy the same rights. The Sarbat Khālsā or 'the whole people' met once at the Akāl Takht, Amritsar, the highest seat of Panthic authority, on the occasion of *divāli* (*dīpāvali*) or Vaiśākhī, and felt that they were one. All questions affecting the welfare of the community were referred to the *saṅgats,* which would decide them in the form of resolutions called *gurmattas.* A *gurmatta* (*gurumata,* the verdict of the Guru) duly passed was supposed to have received the sanction of the Guru, and any attempt made afterwards to contravene it was taken as a sacrilegious act.

FORMS AND CEREMONIES

This institution of the Khālsā entails a certain additional disciplinary outfit in the shape of baptismal forms and vows. Religion, as taught by the Gurus, is a force that not only ennobles individuals, but also binds them together to work for a high purpose in the world. Organization is a means of enlarging the possibility, scope, and effectiveness of this work. In order that an organization itself may work effectively, it is necessary that the individuals concerned in it should be able to keep up their attachment to, and enthusiasm for, the cause. This is where discipline comes in, which keeps up the spirit of individuals against flagging in times of trial, and maintains their loyalty to the cause even in moments of distress. This discipline, or what is called *esprit de corps,* is secured by such devices as flags, drills, and uniforms in armies, and by certain forms and ceremonies in religion. Man would not need them, if he were only a bundle of intellectual and moral faculties ; but as he has also got sentiment and imagination, without which the former qualities would remain inoperative, he cannot do without articulating his ideas and beliefs in some forms appropriate to his sentiment. Forms should be related to his inner belief as words are to their meaning, tears to grief; smiles to happiness, and a tune to a song. It is true that sometimes words become meaningless, when we no longer heed their sense, or when the language to which they belong becomes dead. But there is no denying the fact that, when their inner meaning is real, and we are sincere about it, they do serve as very helpful interpreters.

Sometimes, however, when the forms are determined, not by the necessity of uniformity, which is so essential for discipline, but by local or racial causes, they narrow the applicability of the ideal and create division and exclusiveness, whereas they should have helped men to unite. When the spirit in which they had been originally conceived of dies out, they become mere handicaps to religion. It was such forms that Guru Nānak asked people to leave. 'Destroy that custom', he said, 'which makes you forget dear God' (*Vadhans-kī-Vār*). But the Sikh forms were neither conceived of in a spirit of exclusiveness, nor were they regarded as essential to the advancement of individual souls. They were prescribed merely to serve as aids to the preservation of the corporate life of the community, and any man who likes to serve humanity through the Sikh Panth can use them. The Sikhs, who are the soldiers of Guru Gobind Siṅgh and whose religion is surcharged with his personality, find the uniform worn and ordained by him as a real help in playing their part as units of the Panthic organization. This help comes from the appeal made to sentiment by the process of association with an ever-living personality that is itself a symbol of the highest personality. As is God, so is the Guru, and as is the Guru, so must be the follower. Wearing short drawers (*kach*) which ensures briskness of movement at times of action and serves as an easy underwear at times of rest, an iron ring (*karā*) on his right arm as a sign of sternness and constraint, and a sword (*kirpān*) by his side as an instrument of offence and defence and as an emblem of power and dignity,[8] the Guru presented an impressive picture of a simple but disciplined soldier. He, however, combined in him the saintliness of the old *ṛṣis* with the sternness and strength of a knight. Therefore, like his predecessors, he kept long hair (*keś*), which all the world over has always been associated with saintliness. A comb (*kaṅgh*) was a simple necessity for keeping the hair clean and tidy. These are the forms with which the Sikhs are invested at the time of their baptism, in order that they may look exactly like their master, as they are to behave exactly like him.

From the history of the Sikhs in the past as well as in the present, it is quite evident how effectively these baptismal forms, with the accompanying vows of purity, love, and service, have aided them in keeping themselves united and their ideals unsullied even in times of greatest trials. While keeping the Sikhs associated with their Guru and maintaining his spirit amongst them, they have not produced any narrowing effect on their beliefs or modes of worship.

[8] 'Charity and *kirpān* are the symbols of self-respect' (*Pākhiānō Caritra*, 322).

23

CULT-SYNCRETISM

THE evolution of different religious cults and sects in the post-Vedic period was a noticeable phenomenon in the religious and cultural history of India. This evolution was gradual, and the element that played a great part in it was that of *bhakti*. Primarily this denoted the loving adoration of some persons (or rarely, fondness for some objects) by others, but secondarily it meant the deep, affectionate, and mystic devotion for some personal deity who was the object of worship (in the developed sense of the term, i.e. *pūjā*) of a particular person or a group of persons. Belief in *one* personal god as a spiritual being, with whom was conceived a close bond or association of his devotee, was one of its most important constituents, and this mental attitude was the main guiding principle in the growth of the cults and the sects.

The gods round whom these cults developed were not primarily recruited from the orthodox Vedic pantheon, but from quite a different source, though for a few Vedic affiliations were later established. The originals of the sectarian gods were either actual human heroes like Vāsudeva-Kṛṣṇa, the son of Devakī,[1] Śākyamuni Gautama, and Mahāvīra, or mythological beings like Śiva or Rudra-Śiva, the *yakṣas* like Maṇibhadra and Pūrṇabhadra, the *nāgas* like Dadhikarṇa and others, and the goddess Umā-Durgā-Pārvatī-Vindhyavāsinī. With the exception of the semi-historical or historical figures in this assortment, the nucleus of an appreciable proportion of these god or goddess concepts may be traced to the pre-Vedic strata of Indian civilization, and a few like Śiva and Durgā-Pārvatī became very prominent as the central cult-pictures of some of the major cults of post-Vedic or Paurāṇic India. Cults also grew round the semi-historical or historical figures like Vāsudeva-Kṛṣṇa, Buddha, and Mahāvīra, which were adopted by large sections of ancient and mediaeval Indians.

The celestial luminary, Sūrya, so highly venerated in his various aspects by the Vedic and early post-Vedic Indo-Aryans, became a prominent cult-deity, especially in northern, western, and eastern India, when a particular form of his worship prevalent in eastern Iran was introduced into India by some of the foreign immigrants, in the beginning of the Christian era or perhaps even somewhat earlier. The primitive worship of the *yakṣas* and the *nāgas,* current among the lower section of the people from time immemorial,

[1] Kṛṣṇa Devakīputra of the *Chā. U.*, III. 17.

was canalized in the late Gupta period in the cult, among others, of the elephant-headed and pot-bellied Gaṇapati.

THE FIVE BRĀHMAṆICAL HINDU CULTS

Thus, in course of time, the five Brāhmaṇical Hindu cults of the Vaiṣṇava (Bhāgavata, Pāñcarātra, Sātvata, Ekāntika, etc., to mention some of its earlier designations), Śaiva, Śākta, Saura, and Gāṇapatya, and the non-Brāhmaṇical Bauddha and Jaina cults were developed. These Brāhmaṇical Hindu cults, along with the two other non-Brāhmaṇical ones, did not receive the sanction of orthodox Vedism in the beginning, for all of them at first found fault with Vedic sacrificialism in greater or lesser degree. But in the growing composite Hinduism of the epic and Paurāṇic times, orthodox Vedism made a compromise with some types of the former, the other two creeds, which were of too heterodox a character from the Vedic point of view, never receiving recognition, or rather, never caring to receive it.

The best exponents of the Brāhmaṇical cults from the literary point of view were the Purāṇas, many of the major and minor groups (Mahāpurāṇas and Upapurāṇas) of which espoused the cause of one or other of these religious systems. The two epics, especially the bigger one, were often redacted by the intellectuals belonging to one or other of these major cults in the interest of their own creeds. The general mass of the numerous followers, or the exclusive worshippers, of the cult-deities—Viṣṇu (or a composite god made up of Vāsudeva, Viṣṇu, and Nārāyaṇa), Śiva (also an amalgam of the Vedic Rudra, pre-Vedic proto-Śiva, and Paurāṇic Śiva), Śakti (having as constituent elements the pre-Vedic and Vedic Mother Goddess, the object of worship of the Vedic sage-clans like the Kātyas and the Kuśikas, and the epic and Paurāṇic Durgā-Pārvatī-Vindhyavāsinī), Sūrya, and Gaṇapati—formed the well-known sects (*dharma-sampradāya*), Vaiṣṇava, Śaiva, Śākta, Saura, and Gāṇapatya.

RIVALRY AMONG THE SECTS

There is no doubt about the fact that there existed among these different sects, especially among the major ones, a feeling of mutual rivalry and jealousy. But these feelings of animosity among the followers of different sects mainly found expression in the fabrication of mythological stories and the construction of interesting groups of images by way of illustrating them. Thus the story of the Śarabha incarnation of Śiva was illustrated by a weird type of Śaiva icon, which shows the god in the composite form of man, bird, and lion, killing Narasiṁha, the Man-lion incarnation of Viṣṇu. Śiva is said to have assumed this form, more hybrid than that of Narasiṁha, to punish the latter for his audacity in killing his devotee, the *daitya* king Hiraṇyakaśipu. There are many such Brāhmaṇical Hindu images which illustrate this sectarian ill-feeling, and some of the Vajrayāna icons of the mediaeval period, in which Buddhist deities are represented as oppressing Brāhmaṇical gods, are blatant examples of this mental attitude of a sectarian Buddhist towards Hindu sects. The Purāṇas are the great repositories of such mythological stories, which are narrated with naive unconcern to belittle or extol the character of these principal cult-deities in different contexts. Sculptural representation of the superiority of Śiva over Viṣṇu and Brahmā, for instance, might take the gross form of Brahmā in his swan-vehicle (*haṁsa-vāhana*) trying in vain to reach the top and Viṣṇu in the form of a boar to reach the bottom of a *śivaliṅga,* or the subtle form of Brahmā and Viṣṇu sprouting forth from the two sides of a central Śiva figure (Ekapāda-Trimūrti).

RECONCILIATION OF DIFFERENT SECTS

But this is only one side of the picture. Attempts at reconciliation and *rapprochement* between the rival creeds were being made even from a very early period, when many of them were getting systematized. The sentiment about different gods being ultimately forms of the one Being, so beautifully expressed in the famous couplet of the Dīrghatamas hymn[2] long before the evolution of the respective cults, never lost its force in subsequent times, and it exercised its deep influence on the exclusive worshippers of the different cult-deities. The attitude of the Vedāntin towards theism, in general, and the popular creeds based on it, and the liberal non-sectarian trend of guidance given in the Smṛti-śāstras for properly controlled and regulated living were also important factors in encouraging toleration among the Indian sects. Approved Smṛti works like some of the Dharma-śāstras of the pre-Christian and early post-Christian periods and the *Manu* and *Yājñavalkya Smṛtis* did not advocate the cause of any particular cult. Some epic passages like those in the *Gītā* (VII. 21 ; IX. 23 ; etc.), though extolling the greatness of Vāsudeva-Kṛṣṇa, in a way encouraged liberal and tolerant attitude among the sects.

PAÑCĀYATANA-PŪJĀ

Thus was developed among the followers of the injunctions laid down in the approved Smṛtis a liberal attitude towards religious matters, and these orthodox Brāhmaṇas, known usually as Smārtas, evolved a kind of worship described as *pañcāyatana-pūjā,* in which all the principal deities of the five approved Brāhmaṇical Hindu cults were the objects of veneration.

[2] *Ṛ.V.*, I. 164. 46.

The chief cult-object in it was aniconic in form, which contained the emblems, one each, of the respective cult-deities. It has not yet been possible to fix definitely the period when this custom came to be in vogue among the Smārtas, but there is distinct archaeological evidence to prove that this was introduced long before the mediaeval period, and possibly after Brahmā, who formed the classical trinity with Viṣṇu and Śiva, had lost his foothold in popular affection.

It will be useful to mention briefly the characterization of this form of religious ceremony, as given by a distinguished and keenly observant English Indologist and Sanskritist of the nineteenth century. Monier Williams describes the *pañcāyatana* ceremony, as he saw being practised by some of the believing Hindus of central and southern India and Mahārāṣṭra, in this manner: 'Five stones or symbols believed to be permeated by the essences of the five chief deities are (1) the black stone, representing Viṣṇu; (2) the white stone, representing Śiva's essence; (3) the red stone, representing Gaṇeśa; (4) the small piece of metallic ore, representing the wife of Śiva; (5) the piece of crystal, representing the Sun.... All five symbols are placed on a round open metal dish, called *pañcāyatana*, and are arranged in five different methods, according to the preference given to any one of the five deities at the time of worship.'[3] It should be noted that placing in the centre the symbol of any particular cult-deity like Viṣṇu, Śiva, Śakti, and others in the *pañcāyatana* arrangement (thus giving special importance to him or her), with the other four forming the four corners of a square, would indicate the particular cult-affiliation of the Smārta worshipper. Thus the tolerant attitude advocated by the Smārtas did not prevent many of them from affiliating themselves to particular cults.

CONTRIBUTION OF FOREIGN IMMIGRANTS—NUMISMATIC EVIDENCE

Another important contributory factor to the growth of cult-syncretism was the mental attitude of the early foreign immigrants into India—the Śakas, the Pahlavas, the Kuṣāṇas, and the Hūṇas. They were men of lesser culture compared with the people of India, and were very prone to be influenced by the latter. This proneness was very much pronounced in matters of religion, and they often paid equal homage to gods and goddesses of more than one creed. This tendency to some sort of eclecticism present among them can be proved with the help of coins which were issued by some of the rulers of India belonging to these alien races. The kings often used as devices on their coins (and sometimes on their seals) the figures

[3] *Religious Thought and Life in India*, pp. 411-12.

of the deities belonging to different religions, and there are reasons to believe that they had some feeling of respect and veneration for at least some of the originals of these devices. At first most of the deities were recruited from the Greek pantheon, and this was natural, for the Śakas and the Pahlavas really succeeded the Greeks in the sovereignty of parts of northern and north-western India.

P. Gardner, while commenting on the coin devices of these rulers, remarks: 'When we reach the issues of King Maues (a Scytho-Parthian ruler of the extreme north of India), we find a wealth of most remarkable and original barbaro-Hellenic figures; a figure resembling Tyche, holding in one hand a patera, in the other a wheel, who seems to be the original of the still more outlandish figure of Azes's coins.'[4] Another instance of syncretism is to be found on a coin device of Azes's successor, Azilises. R. B. Whitehead, while describing it, draws our attention to the 'syncretic panoply of the deity, a decidedly pantheistic type'.[5]

The syncretism, at first, lay no doubt in the fusion of Hellenic and non-Hellenic elements. Many of the latter were undoubtedly Indian, though very difficult in the early period to recognize and sort out. But from the time of Maues and Gondophares, in some of whose coins the Indian deity Śiva has been recognized (the present writer has conclusively proved that Śiva appears on the coins of the early foreign rulers of India for the first time on some square copper coins of Maues), the Indian element came to predominate by stages.

CONTRIBUTION OF THE KUṢĀṆAS

The great Kuṣāṇa king Wema Kadphises was undoubtedly a votary of Śiva, for it was this god and his emblems, the bull and the trident-battle-axe, that were invariably adopted by Wema as the reverse devices of his coins (in the Prākṛta coin-legends, he is almost always described as a Ma(ā)hi(ī)śvara, i.e. an exclusive worshipper of Maheśvara). His successors, Kaniṣka and Huviṣka, introduced the somewhat novel feature of the extremely 'varied reverse' of their coins, the deities being recruited from such widely divergent religious pantheons as Zoroastrian, Brāhmaṇical Hindu, Buddhist, and rarely Greek. Kaniṣka's affiliation with Buddhism is well known, but in this sort of medley of the devices on his coins, some scholars recognized long ago the evidence of the Kuṣāṇa king's eclectic belief in religious matters. It can be proved with the help of some of the little-known coins of Huviṣka, the second in succession from Kaniṣka, that

[4] *Catalogue of Coins of the Greek and Scythic Kings of India in the British Museum*, p. lviii.

[5] *Punjab Museum Catalogue of Coins*, I. p. 136, pl. XIII, fig. 336.

he paid his homage to more than one deity. Cunningham has reproduced some copper coins of Huviṣka,[6] on one side of which the king is made to appear before such deities as Nana and Umā (?) in a suppliant attitude. The present writer pointed out years ago the importance, from the cult point of view, of the reverse device of one of Huviṣka's unique gold coins in the collection of the British Museum. The figure usually identified as Śiva has been described by Gardner in this manner: 'Śiva facing, three-headed, nimbate; clad only in waist-band, ithyphallic; has four arms and hands, in which are goat, wheel, thunderbolt, and trident.'[7] It was remarked by the present writer, 'The *cakra* in one of the hands and the *ūrdhvaliṅga* feature, the latter so common in sculptural representations of Śiva from the late Kuṣāṇa period onwards, are noteworthy characteristics. Does the type show the beginning of the interesting composite icon of Hari-Hara of subsequent days?'[8] This is undoubtedly one of the earliest numismatic data about the beginnings of cult-syncretism.

NICOLO SEAL OF A HŪṆA CHIEF

This view is interestingly corroborated by the evidence of a nicolo seal device of a somewhat later date. This seal, originally attributed by Cunningham to Huviṣka, has rightly been assigned to some unknown Hephthalite Hūṇa chief of about the fifth century A.D. Its device shows the chief standing as a suppliant with his hands folded in the *namaskāra-mudrā* before a four-armed deity shown much bigger than him; the god wears a three-pointed ornamental head-gear, with a lower garment (*dhoti*) worn in Indian fashion, and many ornaments; his front right and left hands are placed on a peculiarly shaped mace and a wheel respectively, while the back ones hold two indistinct objects, possibly a ring and a flower. There is a two-line inscription in Tocharian script on the right margin of the elliptical seal, which Cunningham could not read, but which was correctly read by R. Ghirshman as *Miarka Yasnu Oezo,* which means Mihira, Viṣṇu, Īśa or Śiva, and this reading shows that the deity is of a composite character, being a combined form of Mihira (the Iranian Sun-god), Viṣṇu, and Śiva.

Reference has already been made to the introduction of the east Iranian Sun cult in India at a comparatively early period, and here is a syncretistic representation of the principal icons of that cult and two of the major Indian cults. The period to which this intaglio belongs marks an age during which the well-known Brāhmaṇical Hindu cults (Vaiṣṇava,

[6] *Coins of the Indo-Scythians and Kushans,* pl. XXII, figs. 21, 22.
[7] *Op. cit.*, p. 148, pl. XXVIII, fig. 16.
[8] Banerjea, *The Development of Hindu Iconography,* First Edition, p. 137.

Śaiva, and Saura) had developed to a great extent along their own lines. As has already been stated, even during the growth of these separatist tendencies, a spirit of *rapprochement* and reconciliation was discernible among the religious-minded Hindus.

SYNCRETISM THROUGH COMPOSITE ICONS

The combination of the cult figures of Śaivism and Śāktism can be traced to a very early period from an ancient foreign notice about India. The Greek author Stobaeus, flourishing *c.* A.D. 500, quotes a passage from Bardasanes who reports the account of an Indian visitor to Syria in the time of Antoninus of Edessa (A.D. 138-61). There is a striking reference in this report to an image of Ardhanārīśvara, the androgynous Śiva with Durgā forming the left half of his body. One of the earliest representations of a similar cult-emblem was traced by the present writer to a device on an early Gupta seal unearthed from Bhita by Spooner.[9]

V. S. Agrawala draws our attention to a miniature relief which depicts the same composite cult-emblem and belongs to the Kuṣāṇa period. But the close association of the cults of the primeval Father God and the Mother Goddess is not unexpected. There are many early and late mediaeval images hailing from different, specially central and eastern, parts of India, which demonstrate, in a very striking manner, clear ideas of cult syncretism which underlie them. In many of them the Sun-god forms one of the chief elements in the composition, as he does in the nicolo intaglio seal noticed above. Some of them can be described as Sūrya-Nārāyaṇa, Mārtāṇḍa-Bhairava, and Sūrya-Brahmā-Viṣṇu-Śiva; they thus illustrate a *rapprochement* between Saura and Vaiṣṇava, Saura and Śaiva, and Saura, Vaiṣṇava, and Śaiva cults, in the last combination of which Brahmā is included, thus emphasizing the concept of the Brāhmaṇical triad.

Images of Hari-Hara (half Viṣṇu and half Śiva) hailing from all parts of India, and belonging to different periods, from the late Gupta times onwards, illustrate, in a very striking manner, the reconciliation between the Vaiṣṇava and Śaiva creeds. But a curious mediaeval sculpture from Bihar, now in the collection of the Indian Museum, Calcutta, is one of the most typical examples of such syncretistic icons. The amalgam of the Vaiṣṇava and Śaiva cults is not only demonstrated here by the central figure of Hari-Hara, but the Buddha and Saura creeds are also represented in this composition, in a way, by the attending figures of Buddha and Sūrya on its two sides.

Reference has already been made to the *pañcāyatana-pūjā* of the Smārtas and the emblem they used in this form of worship. Early and late

[9] *Ibid.*, p. 199.

mediaeval composite icons, found in parts of northern and eastern India, may now be cited in support of the suggestion that this form of worship was well in vogue from a very early period. Persons frequenting the *ghāṭs* (bathing places), on the bank of the Gaṅgā, and temples at Banaras must have noticed the now uncared-for miniature shrines, really cult objects, showing on their four outer faces small niches with figures of Hara-Pārvatī in one, Viṣṇu in the second, Sūrya in the third, and Gaṇapati in the fourth. These objects thus characterize, in a very interesting way, the Smārta ideology of the *pañcāyatana* worship. Another group of sculptures, mostly hailing from Bihar, and now in the collection of the Indian Museum, also illustrate in a very curious way this concept. These have been wrongly described in the Museum records as *caturmukha śivaliṅgas,* which they really are not. The central block of stone, no doubt, stands for a conventional *śivaliṅga,* but on its four outer faces are carved the figures of Viṣṇu, Durgā, Sūrya, and Gaṇapati.

PART II

THE SAINTS AND THEIR TEACHINGS

24

THE ŚAIVA SAINTS OF SOUTH INDIA

THOUGH proofs of the existence of Śaivism so far back as 3000 B.C. are now forthcoming, very little is known of the great saints of South India who shaped the life and culture of the early people in the millennia preceding the Christian era. A passing mention may be made, however, of the sage Agastya. Though some stories would give him a northern origin, all accounts agree as to his home being on the Podigai Hills in the extreme south of the Tamil land. He has always been revered as a Tamil sage, and is reputed to be the author of the first known Tamil grammar. Several stories are told in the Purāṇas about Agastya, which show that he was a devotee of God as Śiva and as Murugan (Subrahmaṇya).

Coming to the age of the third Saṅgam (some time about the first century A.D.), we find that among the forty-nine poets of the Tamil academy of the Pāṇḍya court, Nakkīrar was an ardent worshipper of Śiva and Murugan, and had tangible evidence of their abounding grace.

Kaṇṇappa belonged possibly to the first or second century A.D. He was a hunter-prince of the hilly region near Kalahasti and had an intense love for Śiva. He worshipped Him, out of the promptings of his heart, with meat and other things, which were sacrilegious in orthodox eyes. In the course of worship, he even plucked out, in the rapture of divine love, one of his eyes and was about to pluck out the other, when he was blessed with a beatific vision of the Lord. He is reckoned among the sixty-three canonized saints of Śaivism.

Tirumūlar, who flourished before the sixth century A.D., is counted as one of the great *siddhas* or persons of superhuman powers, who came to the Tamil land and, entering the body of a dead shepherd, composed 3000 verses covering all aspects of the religious and mystic life. He says that superhuman powers are within the reach of all who take the necessary pains to acquire them.

THE FOUR GREAT ĀCĀRYAS

We shall now proceed to deal with the lives of the four great *ācāryas* who represent the four main paths of Śaivism, viz. the paths of *caryā, kriyā, yoga,* and *jñāna;* otherwise known as the Dāsa-mārga, Satputra-mārga, Saha-mārga, and Ṣat-mārga, i.e. the path of the servant, the path of the good son, the path of the friend, and the good (or true) path. These paths are respectively represented by Tirunāvukkarasu (Appar), Jñānasambandha, Sundaramūrti, and Māṇikkavācaka. The first three names are in historical order too. According to tradition, Māṇikkavācaka, the *ācārya* of Sat-mārga, was the first to appear, although according to some he was the last. In the myriads of Śiva temples in South India, their images are found side by side, though slightly varying in their order, that of Māṇikkavācaka being invariably the fourth.

MĀṆIKKAVĀCAKA

Māṇikkavācaka stood for the worship of the one supreme Lord, and declared that scriptural texts, fasts and penances, rites and ceremonies, logic and metaphysics, and the utmost exertion of the human self could not by themselves take the soul to the feet of the Almighty; the most efficacious way of making the Infinite reach out its hand to the finite was the way of love—pure, unselfish love welling forth from the depths of one's being. He was born of Brāhmaṇa parents in the village of Vadavur near Madurai. While he was yet in his teens, his reputation as a scholar of the first rank and as a person of high character reached the ears of the Pāṇḍya monarch. The king sent for the young man, tested him, and appointed him forthwith his chief minister. But even in the height of his power and influence, he pined for the vision of God.

At this time, the king commanded him to proceed to Tirupperundurai to buy for the army a large contingent of horses. Here he chanced to meet his *guru*. Instead of buying horses, he spent the royal treasure in building a temple to his *guru*, for which he was punished by his master and deprived of his position. But he hailed this with delight, as his soul had been illumined through the grace of his teacher. When he was not wrapped up in meditation, he wandered from shrine to shrine, chanting exquisite hymns, composed offhand. This gift of composition won him his name which means 'one whose utterances are gems'. His immortal work *Tiruvācakam* has been the fountain-head of all later devotional poetry in the Tamil land. It sets forth in sublime poetry the various stages of the soul's progress from a life of ignorance and sin to the ultimate realization of God. At Chidambaram, the most sacred place of the Śaivas, he defeated a band of Buddhist preachers in argument. When requested to expound the meaning of his hymns, he merely pointed to the mystic figure of Śrī Naṭarāja, the eternal Dancer, in the Golden Hall of the temple, and is said to have disappeared in a blaze of light. Māṇikkavācaka's is an illustrious example of a life which in its maturity was filled with unflickering God-consciousness.

APPAR

Appar and his younger contemporary, Jñānasambandha, belonged to the seventh century, the former being definitely known to be a contemporary of the great Pallava king Mahendra I (A.D. 600-630), whose capital was Kāñcī. Appar was born about A.D. 600 in a rich Veḷḷāḷa family at a village in the South Arcot District. He made rapid progress in his studies and with it developed a passionate hankering after truth. He got into touch with Jaina scholars and became a zealous convert to their faith. To get rid of an acute colic pain, he went, at the instance of his devout sister, into a Śiva temple and broke forth into a song of prayer. The pain left him, and a voice from heaven gave him the title of 'Tirunāvukkarasu' (the blessed king of speech).[1] Henceforth he became an ardent devotee of Śiva and, taking his cue from his sister, rendered bodily service to Him, besides being engaged in religious contemplation and composing prayers couched in fine poetry. His Jaina friends took alarm at this reconversion and besought the Pallava king to bring him back to Jainism. The king tried to take away his life in a number of ways, but, like a second Prahlāda, he came out unscathed every time, remaining steadfast in his faith. The Pallava king was so struck with these marvels that he asked forgiveness of the saint and had himself initiated by him into the Śaiva faith.

The boy saint Sambandha affectionately called him 'Appar' (father). Since then this appellation has generally come into vogue. In spite of their disparity in age and caste, the two became intimate and lifelong friends. In his last decad of verses, Appar prayed to the Lord to take him into His bosom—a prayer which was granted. This happened about A.D. 655. He lived a very simple life. As a result of his steady communion with the Supreme, he had intense love for God and man, his denunciations being only against hypocrisy. He possessed an iron will and withal was gentle as a child. He is said to have composed 49,000 decads of hymns, of which 311 are extant.

SAMBANDHA

Sambandha, or Sambandar, is believed to have been born about A.D. 639, in answer to the fervent prayers of a Brāhmaṇa couple of Shiyali to have a son who would be able to stem the tide of prevalent atheism and hypocrisy. As a child of four, one day he accompanied his father to the tank in the village temple. While the latter was immersed in water for a little while, the child, not seeing him, fixed his gaze on the temple tower and cried out, 'Mother! Father!' It is said that Pārvatī and Śiva, the universal

[1] The Sanskrit equivalent is Vāgīśa, the lord of *vāc* or speech. The saint is thus known as Vāgīśa also.

Mother and Father, appeared before him, and out of a golden cup the Mother fed him with milk full of spiritual potency. The child was at once inspired. Abiding wisdom, power, and bliss entered into him. He became 'Jñānasambandha' (one associated with divine wisdom). Sambandha constantly toured from village to village singing hymns to God. In every one of these, he put in a verse condemning what he disliked in the life and teachings of the Jains and Buddhists of his age. Soon after his enlightenment, a devotee, who belonged to the so-called untouchable class, but who was a highly skilled musician, was granted his request that he with his wife might be allowed to accompany him in his tours and to play his hymns on the harp.

Several miracles are recorded of the saint, to the majority of which there are references in his own hymns. Only one of them will be noticed here. In one of their joint pilgrimages, Appar and Sambandha reached a place called Vedaraniam. In the shrine there, they found that the door in front of the inner sanctuary remained permanently closed, and worshippers entered the holy place only through a side door. Sambandha was informed that, according to a hoary tradition, the front door was closed in some bygone age by the four Vedas after they had worshipped the Śiva's image within, issuing the injunction that none but themselves should reopen the door. On hearing this, Sambandha requested Appar to pray to the Lord for the self-opening of the door. The latter did so in a decad comprising 44 lines. The door flung itself open. The two saints, followed by a huge congregation, entered through this ancient doorway for grateful worship.

The significance of this miracle seems to be that the Vedas in archaic Sanskrit tended to hide the knowledge of God from the many who could not read them. Hence, under inspiration, Sambandha requested a non-Brāhmaṇa compeer of his in the realm of the spirit to remove the barrier through the instrumentality of a hymn in Tamil. The injunction of the Vedas that they alone should open the door was fulfilled in the sense that the hymns of Appar in Tamil contained the quintessence of the Vedas and were thus in substance one with them. This miracle is symbolical of the great heart of the divine child, Sambandha, and his noble wish that the wisdom locked up in the Vedas should be thrown open to the multitude through the medium of their own mother tongue.

After re-establishing Śaivism in the Pāṇḍya kingdom, Sambandha returned to the Coḷa land; from where he started on a northern tour. He was now sixteen years old and was exhorted by the elders to marry, to which he consented. But it is narrated that, before the marriage ceremony was over, he and his wife, together with his devotees, were, on his prayer, carried away by a divine light. Sambandha is said to have sung in all 16,000 decads of hymns, of which only 384 decads are extant. His life and hymns show that he put great stress on worshipping God as Father. His hymns strike a happy and buoyant note throughout. Their idyllic poetry reveals him as revelling in the enjoyment of the beauties of nature and the grace of God. He denounces the latter-day degradation of Jainism in trenchant language. One of his special contributions to the thought and life of the age was his insistence on the recognition of the dignity and beauty of womanhood. There is no decad of his, except one, which fails, while describing Śiva in his personal aspect, to mention His divine consort Umā. In a sense, he is held foremost among all the four Śaiva *ācāryas*.

SUNDARAMŪRTI

Sundara was born towards the close of the eighth century A.D. in the same Tamil territory which produced Appar. Sundara came of a family of Śaiva temple priests, but was brought up by the king of the land in his own palace. On the eve of his marriage ceremony, an aged Brāhmaṇa appeared and claimed the bridegroom to be his servant, who should forthwith follow and serve him. Documentary evidence was produced, and the visitor won his case. Sundara followed his strange master, who revealed himself to be none other than Lord Śiva who came to direct his life in a different channel. Sundara longed for nothing more than a life of renunciation and utter dedication to the service of the Lord. In this mood, he travelled from place to place praising God in mellifluous hymns, until he reached Chidambaram. There he had a divine message to proceed to Tiruvarur, where he was married to one Paravai, a non-Brāhmaṇa maiden, who was a great devotee of Śiva. The two souls, knit together by a common bond of love to God, led a life of spiritual bliss. Not only his biography, but his hymns, too, record how all the needs of his family were often miraculously supplied through divine grace.

A few miles north of Madras, there lived, in a village, a rich non-Brāhmaṇa virgin, who had declined all proposals of marriage and had been serving God. Sundara chanced to see her and felt a desire to marry her. The marriage was celebrated after he had given his word that he would not leave the limits of that village. But he could not reconcile himself to this life of seclusion. Finally, he resolved to march forth and face the consequences. The moment he crossed the village limits, he lost his eyesight. He knew it was the punishment for his breach of promise. He marched on, totally blind and with a sense of dreadful pain in his body. On his way to Tiruvarur, he would halt at every shrine and pray for forgiveness. More than the physical pain and loss of sight was his spiritual agony that his former relationship with the Lord had been lost. But he kept on praying for forgiveness, and it was at Kāñcī that one of his eyes was restored. The pain in the body subsided later, and the other eye was restored when he had reached Tiruvarur. Having passed through this fire of physical and mental suffering, the saint attained a serene peace. He composed 38,000 decads of hymns, of which only a hundred are now available. Many of these hymns breathe a sense of freedom and intimacy in relation to God, and are often enlivened with humour. It is to this saint that the Śaivas owe the list of their sixty-three canonized saints.

Of the four Śaiva *ācāryas,* the collection of hymns of the last three is known as the *Devāram.* These hymns are at once great as devotional, philosophical, and literary productions. All the four saints discouraged the worship of minor deities and preached, both by example and precept, that there is but one God whom, in His personal aspect, they called Śiva, but who takes numerous forms and names in His work of redeeming souls. His impersonal and incomprehensible aspect is never left out of account. The *ācāryas* speak with the authority born of direct knowledge, and do not therefore quote scriptures to support their statements. They, however, make free use of the Vedic and Paurāṇic stories and often hint at their esoteric significance.

OTHER ŚAIVA SAINTS

Only a brief account of some other Śaiva saints may now be given. One of these was a king named Meypporul Nāyanār. An enemy, who was unable to defeat him in battle, put on the symbols of a Śaiva devotee, gained access to the inner chamber of the king, and stabbed him fatally, as the latter prostrated himself before the hypocrite, mistaking him to be a genuine devotee of Śiva. When an attendant rushed at the murderer to kill him, the dying monarch not only prevented it, but also ordered the assailant to be escorted to a place of safety and held on to his ebbing life till he got the news that his behest had been carried out.

Sakya Nāyanār is another of these saints. An earnest seeker after truth, he first became a Buddhist. Further study and thought, however, led him to embrace Śaivism, but he kept on the robe of a Buddhist, which made no difference in his love for Śiva. He resolved to take his noon meal only after worshipping a *śivaliṅga.* One day he caught sight of a *śivaliṅga* in an open space. Love welled up from his heart, and he instinctively picked up a piece of stone within his reach and offered it as a flower to the Lord. From that day he made it his daily practice. His fellow-Buddhists misinterpreted this as a mark of his hatred of Śiva. One day Sakya was very hungry and sat down to eat, when he recollected that his daily stone-offering to the Lord had not been made. He ran to the *śivaliṅga* and made his usual offering with intense love and devotion. Then Śiva and Pārvatī appeared before him.

Mention must be made of another famous saint, Nandanār, who belonged to the so-called untouchable class. Once he was seized with the idea of visiting the holy city of Chidambaram. After months of hesitation he reached the place. But suddenly recalling the great sanctity of the city, he considered himself unworthy to enter it. So he stayed outside its walls, but with an intense yearning at heart to see the Lord in the shrine. The Lord, it is said, instructed the Brāhmaṇa priests to take the devotee to His presence. At the sight of His image, Nandanār was so filled with bliss that he fell into an ecstatic state.

The story of another saint of low birth, Tirunīlakaṇḍa Yaḷpānār, is equally interesting. It was he who, along with his wife, accompanied Sambandha in all his tours. We read that on two occasions, when he was rapturously singing devotional hymns outside great temples, he was by divine command taken to the holy of holies.

WOMEN SAINTS

It will be of interest to note that honourable mention is made of the wives of several of the saints for the part they played as unwavering spiritual companions of their husbands even in times of severe trial. Three of them are included among the sixty-three Śaiva saints. One of these, Kāraikkāl Ammaiyār (Mother belonging to Kāraikkāl), deserves special mention. The daughter of a merchant-prince, she was a devotee of the Lord from her childhood, and a dutiful wife after her marriage. Her husband, realizing in an extraordinary way that she was the object of divine favour and was spiritually far superior to him, quietly left her, married again, and settled in a distant city. On learning his whereabouts after some years, Kāraikkāl Ammaiyār went out to meet him. The husband, with his new family, reverently saluted her, and proclaimed to spectators that he considered her a person worthy of his worship. As soon as Kāraikkāl Ammaiyār realized his changed attitude towards her, she renounced all attachment for him and to the world and spent her life in search of God. She has enshrined her experiences in verses, many of which are remarkable for their depth of thought and lucidity of expression.

Auvai is another famous woman Śaiva saint. She, however, is not recognized as one of the sixty-three canonized saints. Many stories are told about her literary talents and religious devotion. Her immortal didactic verses are still taught in the Tamil schools. A mystic treatise in Tamil is also ascribed to her.

MINOR SAINTS

Of the minor saints who kept up the tradition of Śaivism, Meykaṇḍār's name comes first. He was gifted from his birth, and at the age of three had his initiation from a sage who named him 'Meykaṇḍār' (a seer of Truth). The sage asked him to write in Tamil a work comprising the knowledge he had gained. Meykaṇḍār accordingly composed twelve *sūtras* (aphorisms) in Tamil containing the true wisdom, and added an exposition in verse. These constitute the well-known *Śiva-jñāna-bodham.*

Once his erudite family-preceptor, puffed up with vanity, asked him in the presence of his pupils, 'Do you indeed know the nature of ignorance?' To this the young Meykaṇḍār replied by a look at the proud questioner himself. The preceptor understood the meaning of the look that he himself was a fine specimen of it, and became a disciple of the saint under the name Aruṇandi Śivācāriār. He, in his turn, taught the faith and gave initiation to Marai-jñānasambandar, who was a writer of great merit and whose chief occupation was to meditate on Śiva. In response to his master's wish, Aruṇandi wrote *Śiva-jñāna-śittiyār,* which is an expansion of Meykaṇḍār's *sūtras.*

Umāpati Śivam was one of the three thousand Brāhmaṇa Dīkṣitas who alone were permitted to offer worship to Naṭarāja at Chidambaram. Once when he passed by Marai-jñānasambandar in a palanquin, preceded by torches carried even in the day-time as a mark of honour, the latter remarked that a creature blind at noon was passing along. Umāpati's attention was drawn to the saint and, casting off all pride of caste and position, he approached him to seek his help. The saint began to run. But so great was Umāpati's veneration for him that he followed him, and even drank the remnant of gruel that had been drunk by the saint. This led to his excommunication by the people of his caste, and he was not allowed to worship Naṭarāja. But the Lord made them understand that if this was not rectified, His holy presence would shift to where Umāpati was offering his mental worship. The saint's breadth of outlook as well as spiritual power are seen from the fact that once he readily initiated a so-called untouchable devotee and made him attain the highest realization.

These four minor saints, the Santānācāryas as they are called, have contributed their share to the stock of Śaiva philosophical literature. Umāpati Śivam's contribution is particularly noteworthy. Of the fourteen authoritative philosophical treatises in Tamil on the Śaiva Siddhānta, eight are by him. He has also written a short biography of the sixty-three Śaiva saints. The relation between the Vedas, the Āgamas, and the contributions of the different groups of *ācāryas* has been thus expressed by an unknown author of old: The Veda is the cow. The true Āgamas are its milk. The

Tamil hymns of the four great Śaiva *ācāryas* are the butter in the milk, and the taste of that butter is the *Śiva-jñāna-bodham* of Meykaṇḍār of Tiruvennainallur.

THE UNBROKEN LINE

Several other saints have appeared in an unbroken stream in the later centuries almost up to the present day. Many of them have left no writings. But some are authors of hymns or regular treatises on religious themes. A passing reference to only four of these is made here.

Paṭṭinathar lived some time before the tenth century. He was a very rich merchant who carried on a large trade by sea. When he returned home one day in a jubilant mood, on learning that one of his storm-tossed vessels laden with rich merchandise had safely reached its destination, a small packet, given for delivery to him by a strange lad, was placed in his hands. On opening it he found nothing but a broken needle. At the sight of this the truth flashed upon him that not even such a worthless thing as that needle will accompany him after death. He forthwith renounced his vast wealth and all the enjoyments it might bring, and became an austere ascetic. He was joined by a king named Bhadragiri. Both of them are the authors of a number of poems, many of which are popular to this day. The impermanence of things worldly, the need for realizing God and the way of doing it, condemnation of the ways of the worldly-minded, and exhortation to all to wake up to a spiritual life are the main themes of their songs. Paṭṭinathar's tomb is at Tiruvottiyur, near the northern limit of Madras

Some five centuries later appeared another famous saint, by name Aruṇagiri. According to tradition, he had an infamous birth and in his youth led a riotous life of sin and shame. One day, the heinousness of his life caused him intense remorse from a simple remark of his sister. He forthwith ascended the high tower of a temple close by and threw himself down with the intent to kill himself. But the Lord miraculously saved him and made him His own. Thenceforth he became a great poet and described in charming verses the evil deeds of his past days and the goodness and greatness of God as Murugan (Subrahmaṇya). His unique hymns, known as *Tiruppugal,* are very popular for their matchless rhythm. He was the author of some other treatises as well.

Tāyumānavar is another great Śaiva saint who belonged to the seventeenth century and is still a living force in the religious life of South India. He was the son of Veḷḷāḷa parents and was attached to the great Śiva temple at Vedaraniam. By virtue of his learning and character, he soon became a high official in the court of the Nāik ruler of Tiruchirappalli.

But he was not satisfied with the power and pelf of this world, and yearned for a spiritual teacher. He got one and engaged himself in spiritual exercises in his leisure hours. But soon the king died, and the widowed queen tempted him with her hand and kingdom. The saint gave her noble advice as became a seer of Truth, and left her service and her kingdom. His hymns, though simple in diction, are a mine of spiritual experience and are exceedingly elevating in their effect. By his message of unity in diversity, he tries to reconcile the Vedānta with the Śaiva Siddhānta, the differences between which were probably over-emphasized in his age by rival groups of active controversialists.

Another brilliant group of five saints, who belonged to the Vīraśaiva or Liṅgāyata branch of Śaivism, flourished in the seventeenth century. Śivaprakāśa I, Śāntaliṅga, Kumāradeva, Śivaprakāśa II, and Cidambara Svāmin, who composed this group, were men of high spiritual attainments, and they have recorded their realizations in hymns and treatises. Several of the works of Śivaprakāśa II are literary masterpieces as well.

Ramalinga was a contemporary of Sri Ramakrishna Paramahamsa. He was born in a village in the South Arcot District in the family of a village accountant. It is doubtful whether he had any regular schooling at all. From his childhood his heart and mind were set upon God, and poetry came to him as a natural gift. He spent his boyhood with his elder brother at Madras, and was at first a passionate devotee of God as Murugan. He married, but lived a celibate life. He was grieved at the sight of differences and iniquities in the world and condemned them in simple verses full of fire and force. He was an advocate of the path of harmony. At Vadalur, in the South Arcot District, he built a shrine in which the flame of an oil-lamp was the only object of worship. He exhorted all to transcend caste, creed, and scriptures, and to realize the oneness of God through love and compassion for all living beings. He expressed his strong disapproval of men killing birds or beasts either for their food or as sacrifice to deities. The popular belief is that he simply disappeared in A.D. 1892 and might come back. The voluminous collection of his hymns is known as *Tiru Aruṭpā*, and many of these sweet pieces still move the people throughout the Tamil land.

25

THE VAIṢṆAVA SAINTS OF KARṆĀṬAKA

LIKE other parts of India, Karṇāṭaka too has played its part in shaping the history of India and contributing to her development in the fields of religion and philosophy, art and literature. The distinction achieved by the Karṇāṭaka kingdoms of Kadamba, Rāṣṭrakūṭa, Cālukya, and Vijayanagara in the history of South India is well known. In the field of philosophy, it has given birth to some of the most distinguished builders of Indian thought like Madhvācārya (Ānanda Tīrtha), Vidyāraṇya, and Vyāsarāya.

The great movement of Vaiṣṇava religious devotionalism, which began to spread and regenerate the masses during the middle ages, had its origin in what is called the Dāsa Kūṭa or the order of Vaiṣṇava psalmists and saints, inaugurated in the Karṇāṭaka country as a result of the spread of the realistic philosophy of Vedānta propounded in South India in the thirteenth century by Madhvācārya. The philosophy of Vedāntic realism spread over upper and lower Karṇāṭaka in the next two centuries and, in the course of time, began to inspire kindred waves and movements of religious devotionalism beyond the confines of Karṇāṭaka.

THE CULT OF DEVOTION TO VIṬHṬHALA

This order of the Dāsas (servants of God) was built up by a regular band of saintly souls, who dedicated themselves to the service of the Lord and, singing the praises of Hari, wandered from one end of the country to the other. These saints of the Dāsa order centred their affections on Viṭhṭhala of Pandharpur as the patron deity of their order. There is evidence to show that Karṇāṭaka had cultural sway over Pandharpur and its neighbourhood, where the worship of Viṭhṭhala developed in ancient times, though, in later days, the region passed under the political and cultural hegemony of Mahārāṣṭra, and Pandharpur itself was looked upon as the holy city of Mahārāṣṭra mysticism. Even as late as the time of the great Mahārāṣṭra saint Jñāneśvara, Viṭhṭhala of Pandharpur was still spoken of as 'the deity beloved of the Karṇāṭakas, enshrined in Karṇāṭaka'.[1]

The saints of Karṇāṭaka were thus the first to develop the cult of devotion to Viṭhṭhala, and make it a living faith and a powerful instrument

[1] One of the *abhaṅgas* ascribed to Jñāneśvara. See S. N. Rajapurohit, 'Mahārāṣṭra va Karṇāṭaka', *Kesarī*, 1912-13, p. 25 ; also A. P. Karmarkar, *Mystic Teachings of the Haridāsas of Karṇāṭaka*, Dharwar, 1939.

of mass uplift through the aid of their soul-stirring music and *bhajana* in the language of their province. Their example was subsequently taken up and carried further by the saints of the neighbouring province of Mahārāṣṭra, like Rāmadāsa, Tukārāma, and others. But the essential features of this cult, viz. the emphasis laid on true devotion to Viṭhṭhala and the comparative unimportance of social and caste barriers in the spiritual realm, are to be found no less passionately voiced in the songs of the early Dāsas of Karṇāṭaka than in those of the Mahārāṣṭra saints. The Dāsa Kūṭa may therefore be regarded as the earliest movement of religious devotionalism in the Deccan, whence it spread to other parts of upper India and produced kindred movements.

THE CHARACTER OF THEIR TEACHINGS

These saints of Karṇāṭaka exercised a powerful religious influence on the mass consciousness, and for the average Kannaḍigas, for women, and for people of the lower strata of society, not acquainted with Sanskrit, they did what the great writers on the Vedānta had done for the intelligentzia. They composed their songs in easy colloquial language, which captured the heart and imagination of the people. In this respect they differed from the authors of the Tamil *Devāram* and *Prabandham* literature, whose style was highly literary. The Dāsas moved through the length and breadth of the country, singing praises of Kṛṣṇa and Viṭhṭhala, extolling the merits of *jñāna* and *bhakti,* giving wholesome advice to the people in ethics and religion, and rousing the indifferent and pusillanimous spirits by the irresistible attraction of their teachings conveyed through melodious songs in diverse *rāgas* (tunes). Many of them were highly proficient in Sanskrit and in philosophical lore, and the most learned doctrines have been simplified and put in easily intelligible verses in their works. They were ardent followers of Madhva, and, naturally, tried to show how much more satisfying their own philosophical system was, compared to other ways of thought. Although viewing the world as full of misery and pain, and hence counselling men and women to turn to God to be rid of transmigratory existence, they were zealous advocates of reform and condemned sham and cant in most scathing terms. They criticized pseudo-religiosity, and exhorted their followers to be truthful in thought, word, and deed. They directed their reforming eyes to the dark problems of society, and offered wholesome solutions by way of self-discipline based on a very high standard of ethics. Unlike the Vaiṣṇava lyricists of Bengal, they did not advocate the erotic forms of personal devotion to God. Their attitude in this respect was more impersonal and austere.

The literature of the Dāsas falls into three groups—general, special, and sectarian. The earliest and most distinguished Dāsas like Śrīpādarāja, Purandaradāsa, and Kanakadāsa produced a literature that was meant for all classes and communities. The second group is represented by Vyāsarāya, Gopāladāsa, and others, who wrote for the Brāhmaṇical world in particular. The third group is represented by the stirring songs of Vijayadāsa, Jagannāthadāsa, and others, which were meant for the followers of Madhva and which dwelt exclusively upon theological matters. The Haridāsa movement strove to place a complete scheme of religion and morality before the people. It condemned formalism and ritualism in religion and immoderate hedonism in life. It preached the philosophy of *naiṣkarmya,* as interpreted by Madhva, that is, enlightened action in a spirit of devotion and dedication to God.

The history of the Dāsa literature is generally traced from the days of Narahari Tīrtha, one of the direct disciples of Madhva. This literature is very voluminous, and many interpolations and corruptions have crept in, owing to its wide diffusion and the lack of proper historico-literary traditions. It is thus difficult to determine the authentic contributions of individual authors. But the songs of particular saints may be distinguished by their style and *mudrikās* (pen-names). The bulk of the literature has been published from Udipi, Belgaum, and Bangalore. Tradition has preserved the names of a hundred saints of this order. The songs of earlier saints like Śrīpādarāja, Purandaradāsa, and Kanakadāsa deserve to be translated into English and other languages.

The initial inspiration of the Dāsas was derived from Madhva himself, who has left us some stirring devotional lyrics in such Sanskrit works as *Dvādaśa-stotra* and *Kṛṣṇāmṛta-mahārṇava. Madhvavijaya* (XV. 84) alludes to the many *gāthās, subhāṣitas,* etc. composed by him, though we have no trace of any compositions in Kannada or Tuḷu by Madhva. His disciple Narahari is believed to have composed a few songs under the pen-name 'Raghukulatilaka'.

ŚRĪPĀDARĀJA

But the historical founder of the Dāsa Kūṭa was Śrīpādarāja, alias Lakṣmīnārāyaṇa Tīrtha, who was the head of the *maṭha* of Padmanābha Tīrtha at Mulbagal in Mysore State. He was at once an erudite scholar in Sanskrit and a passionate devotee, and has poured forth beautiful songs in praise of the Lord under the pen-name 'Raṅga-Viṭhṭhala'. The use of the names of the Lord as *mudrikā,* instead of their own names, as was the practice with the Mahārāṣṭra and other saints, is characteristic of the devotion and humility of the Haridāsas of Karṇāṭaka. Śrīpādarāja's songs are more sublime than those of any others, and possess a happy blending of rhythm and meaning. His sincerity and passionate devotion are alike transparent in his songs. His important pieces are *Bhramara-Gītā, Veṇu-Gītā,* and *Gopī-Gītā.* There are also many other individual songs of a very high order of musical excellence and literary grace.

VYĀSARĀYA

His disciple Vyāsarāya attained fame as the foremost philosopher and dialectician of the Dvaita Vedānta. His erudite Vedāntic classic, *Nyāyāmṛta,* caused a stir in the Vedāntic circles and paved the way for the birth of neo-Advaitism, heralded by the composition of Madhusūdana Sarasvatī's *Advaita-siddhi.* Vyāsarāya was not only an eminent philosophical writer, but also a profound mystic and passionate devotee of God. He succeeded Śrīpādarāja as the leader of the Dāsas, and has left us many exquisite songs of great mystic appeal and devotional fervour in Kannada. He is believed to have had a mystic vision of Śrī Kṛṣṇa dancing before him, in one of his supreme moments of ecstatic devotion.

More even than for his songs and for his greatness as a Dāsa and as a philosopher, Vyāsarāya's name has come to be cherished as the discoverer of the two lofty geniuses of the saintly order of Karṇāṭaka, viz. Purandaradāsa and Kanakadāsa, whose names are on the lips of the people and whose songs are sung to this day in almost every village and home of Karṇāṭaka. They flourished in the sixteenth century during the heyday of the great Karṇāṭaka empire of Vijayanagara.

PURANDARADĀSA AND KANAKADĀSA

It is now widely recognized that Purandaradāsa was the father of the Karṇātic or South Indian system of music, which was standardized a century or so later by another son of Karṇāṭaka, the celebrated Veṅkaṭamakhi, in his *Caturdaṇḍi-prakāśa.* He was a native of Purandaragada (now in Poona District) and spent his days mostly at Vijayanagara, where he had settled down after his initiation into the Dāsa order by Vyāsarāya. He seems to have been a familiar figure in Vijayanagara during the days of Kṛṣṇadevarāya and his brother Acyutarāya. Purandaradāsa is reputed to have composed a very large number of songs. His songs have topics ranging from the most homely to the most sublime and can often move one to tears.

Vyāsarāya's second disciple, Kanakadāsa, was not a Brāhmaṇa by birth like Purandaradāsa. He was a person of humble birth and is believed to have been a Kuruba (shepherd), or more probably a hunter-chieftain (Beḍa). He belonged to the village of Kaginele (Dharwar District) and adopted, as *mudrikā,* the name 'Kāginele Ādikeśava', the deity of his village. He was a zealous reformer in outlook. The acceptance of Kanakadāsa as a disciple and prominent member of the Dāsa Kūṭa by the great Vyāsarāya was itself a tribute to the essential humanism of the Dāsa order, in general, and the catholicity of outlook of the great Mādhva religious teacher, Vyāsarāya, in particular.

Kanaka's name is a beloved one in Karṇāṭaka. He was a liberal thinker. Caste and creed, in his opinion, were no barriers to *mokṣa. Bhakti* alone counted. He was persecuted for his extreme views by the orthodox followers of Vyāsarāya. This fact is alluded to in one of the songs of Purandaradāsa, which says that 'the disciples of Vyāsarāya found fault with him for the favour shown to Kanakadāsa'. But Vyāsarāya is said to have stood firm by his disciple and revealed the true worth and greatness of Kanaka to his other followers. Even to this day *Kanakana-khiḍki* (Kanaka's window) in the temple of Śrī Kṛṣṇa at Udipi bears witness to his fervent devotion to God. Besides many devotional songs, including allegorical ones (called *muṇḍagis*), Kanaka wrote the following pieces: *Mohanataraṅgiṇī, Haribhaktisāra, Rāmadhyāna-mantra,* and *Nalacarita.* His portrayal of feelings is extremely vivid and penetrating. He could be most homely as well as sublime as occasions demanded and rise to the same inimitable perfection of art in both.

VĀDIRĀJA AND VIJAYADĀSA

Contemporary with Purandara and Kanaka was another distinguished saint, Vādirāja, who was an erudite Sanskrit scholar and a writer of great eminence in Dvaita Vedānta. He belonged to the historic country of Tuḷuva in the Karṇāṭaka and was a Tuḷu-speaking Brāhmaṇa like Madhvācārya, whose faith he adopted. He reclaimed the Mattu Brāhmaṇas of South Kanara District to the Vaiṣṇava fold, and kept on very friendly terms with the community of the Vaiṣṇava Brāhmaṇas of the Gauḍa Sārasvata group, which began to spread in that district at the time. It is recorded in one of his biographical accounts that he had followers of his creed in Gujarat. *Yuktimallikā,* his *magnum opus,* is a learned metrical work on the Dvaita philosophy.

The next prominent figure among the Dāsa Kūṭa saints was Vijayadāsa of Chipgiri (Bellary District). He was an ardent admirer of Purandaradāsa, about whose life and works he gives us ample materials. It is from these that we learn the details of the story of the dramatic change in the life of the wealthy but miserly Purandaradāsa, who renounced all his worldly possessions and became a great devotee of Viṭhṭhala.

JAGANNĀTHADĀSA

After the creative period of Purandara and Kanaka, the Kannada-speaking districts of Hyderabad State seem to have become the most congenial soil for the spread of the principles of the Dāsa cult. Most of the Dāsas who came after Vijayadāsa seem to have hailed from the different parts of this territory, including the redoubtable Jagannāthadāsa (eighteenth century), whose *Harikathāmṛtasāra* in mixed Kannada has become the favourite scripture of the lay people of Karṇāṭaka. It was in his days that the schism between the Sanskritic Advaita Vedānta and the vernacular Vaiṣṇavism based on Dvaita Vedānta found its final expression. The story of Jagannātha's penitence, of his conversion to humility, and of his respect for the Haridāsa order is graphically recorded by his successors.

THE NATURE OF THE DĀSA MOVEMENT AND ITS LITERATURE

The Dāsa Kūṭa movement was essentially a democratic one, in the sphere of religious philosophy, within the Vedānta. It has many points of similarity with the movement of the Āḷvārs and the work done by them. But unlike the Vīraśaivism of Basava and the Vaiṣṇavism of the Āḷvārs, it did not become an organized faith of the people, though its influence was felt in all strata of society in Karṇāṭaka. It did much for the advancement of the true spirit of religion and ethics, at least among a section of the followers of Madhva. It made no converts, in the ordinary sense of the term, and remained as a movement for religious revival within the framework of the Mādhva system.

The literature of the Dāsas expounded the main principles of the Dvaita system in a popular and attractive form in the language of the people. Such an attempt is in itself a proof of the fact that the Mādhva thought was a living force in the country and had a permanent message to give for the betterment of humanity, and that that message was not so much a cold philosophical doctrine as a dynamic way of life. The Dāsa literature deals with the mystic and spiritual experiences of enlightened life. Its appeal is to the religious emotions, and, as such, there is very little of the subtle arguments of pure philosophy in it. There is, however, a robust faith of underlying theism in these songs. The central idea of their philosophy is the existence of an independent, transcendent principle called God. Behind the veil of Māyā, He is the redeemer of human souls struggling from time immemorial to free themselves from the meshes of Prakṛti. The grace of God is the means of such redemption from the flesh and the cycle of births and deaths. This is obtained by *bhakti* (devotion) which flows from love of God, to the exclusion of everything else, with a deep sense of the dependence of souls on Him. The songs draw frequently upon the teachings and legends of the epics and Purāṇas to inculcate the spirit of devotion.

There is, however, no reasoned exposition of the philosophy of Madhva, which is the basic philosophy of the Dāsas. The drift of the songs is lyrical and didactic rather than logical and definitive. Hence we cannot expect any reasoned exposition of philosophical doctrines here. Nevertheless, certain tenets of the system like the doctrines of *tāratamya* (gradation of souls), *pañcabheda* (reality of fivefold difference in the universe), the nature of souls, the attributes of God, and the nature of *mokṣa* (liberation) are elaborately dealt with. The songs try to rouse the spirit of man from a life of worldly attachment and turn it Godward. They deal with all aspects of spiritual discipline taught by the scriptures and take us along the path of self-realization. Their philosophical system is just the same as that presented by the great writers of the Dvaita Vedānta in their original works in Sanskrit.

There are no distinctive religious practices and rituals associated with the order of the Dāsas, except perhaps the congregational prayers at Pandharpur, the initiation ceremony and administering oath of allegiance, and the employment of music and dancing as part of the devotional discipline.

Like the other redoubtable order of the Vīraśaiva Vacanakāras in Karṇāṭaka, the Haridāsas have produced, in Kannada, a remarkable, racy religious and devotional literature, covering diverse aspects of the mystic life, ranging from the various stages of self-search like spiritual quest and yearning, the sense of sin, penitence, the dark night of the soul and the vigil, and initiation and discipline, to intuition and the state of beatitude. All these are depicted by these saints in their inimitable songs of realized wisdom. This fact makes the works of these saints part and parcel of the *genre* of literature relating to the religious mysticism of the Hindus ; they have the same claim to universal recognition as have the works of the famous saints in other parts of India, who have left their mark on the spiritual history of the country. The messages of Caitanya, Tukārāma, Mīrābāī, Kabīr, and Nānak are spread all over the country. It is a great pity that nothing is known, outside the school of Madhvācārya, of the value and importance of the contributions of the great order of the saints of Karṇāṭaka headed by Śrīpādarāja, Purandaradāsa, and others. It is to be hoped that, when a true and comprehensive history of India will be written, the Haridāsa saints of Karṇāṭaka will be given their meed of recognition for their great contribution to Hindu religious thought.

26

THE MAHĀRĀṢṬRA SAINTS AND THEIR TEACHINGS

SAINTS are the citizens of the 'City of God'. Their affections are not constrained by the considerations of provinces or nations. Though they speak different languages, the thoughts expressed by them are essentially the same, since the subject-matter of their thought and discourse is the same, namely, God. Hence follows the essential equality, and even identity, of the teachings of all saints in the world, past and present. There is no monopoly or privilege in the realm of spiritual wisdom. The saints are the ripest fruits of the intellectual and moral and social and cultural progress of the world; they are born for its enlightenment. It is only for their own moral development and spiritual progress that men find it necessary to study and describe the various qualities and characteristics that go to constitute the greatness of saints. Lives of saints written by most of the biographers are, however, full of miracles and superstitions. A rational account of their spiritual development is what is needed most in these modern times.

The dates of birth and of other important events in the lives of all Mahārāṣṭra saints except Rāmadāsa are only approximately known. It is, however, an undeniable historical fact that Nivṛttinātha and Jñānadeva are the founders of the mystical school in Mahārāṣṭra, which later developed and assumed different forms at the hands of Nāmadeva, Ekanātha, and Tukārāma. Rāmadāsa, with a galaxy of eminent followers, formed a school of mystic thought of his own. The first school of mystics is known as Vārakarīs, or the mild devotees of God Viṭhṭhala of Pandharpur, and the second as Dhārakarīs, or the heroic followers of the cult of Rāmadāsa, the devotee of God Rāma; the former are more emotional, theoretical, and abstract in their view-point, while the latter are more rational, practical, and concrete in their thoughts. The difference between the two schools is, however, only apparent and not real, realization of God as the highest end of human life being common to both.

JÑĀNADEVA OR JÑĀNEŚVARA

Jñānadeva's grandfather and great-grandfather—Govindarāo and Trimbakpant—were disciples of the Nātha school of mystics. His father, Viṭhṭhalapant, married Rakhumābāī, the daughter of Siddhopant of Alandi, where he lived for a few years; and then, being disgusted with worldly life, he went to Rāmānanda at Banaras and embraced the monastic life. After a few years, Rāmānanda in his pilgrimage happened to visit Alandi, and came to know that Viṭhṭhalapant had become a monk without the consent of his wife. When he returned to Banaras, he sent his disciple back to his native place, Alandi, asking him to lead the life of a householder. Viṭhṭhalapant got from Rakhumābāī three sons named Nivṛttinātha, Jñānadeva, and Sopānadeva, and one daughter named Muktābāī, who are rightly regarded as the pride and glory of Mahārāṣṭra. But as they were born of a monk, they were excommunicated by the Brāhmaṇas; and they had to suffer terrible persecution at the hands of society. Viṭhṭhala was asked to go round the holy mountain of Brahmagiri near Tryambakeśvara, with his children. While he was undergoing this penance, he was frightened by a tiger. Nivṛttinātha, the eldest son, entered the cave of Gahinīnātha for protection from the tiger, and he was blessed by the latter there. In due course, he rejoined his father and brothers in their penance.

The sons proved very holy and intelligent and were readmitted to the Brāhmaṇa fold. Jñāneśvara, who was initiated into the spiritual life by his elder brother, Nivṛtti, is reported to have worked many miracles to convince the people of Alandi and Apegaon of his great spiritual powers. One of these was his curing Saccidānanda Bābā, a native of Nevase, of his dangerous disease, when he was almost on his deathbed. This man later became a very devout disciple of Jñānadeva, and wrote down the whole of the *Jñāneśvarī* as dictated by him, resting against a stone pillar in a temple at Nevase. The *Jñāneśvarī,* written about A.D. 1290, is a very original commentary on the *Gītā,* which deserves to be reckoned among the world's best mystical compositions. He also wrote a number of lyrical poems, the *abhaṅgas,* giving expression to his high mystic experiences. Rarely do we find a mystic of such eminence and variety of experience. He was thoroughly rational in his point of view, and yet expounded his philosophy of life in the most poetic language, with a rare wealth of imagery. Other important works of Jñānadeva are *Amṛtānubhava* and *Cāṅgadeva-praśasti.* His brothers and his sister also had their own share in the development of the mystic life and literature of mediaeval Mahārāṣṭra.

NĀMADEVA

Nāmadeva was born in a tailor's family. We are told that as a child he was very wild, and in his youth he took to the life of a robber, and once killed eighty-four soldiers. He was suddenly converted to the spiritual life, when he heard the piteous cries and curses of the helpless wife of one of his victims. The sense of remorse was equally vehement and, in his contrition, he attempted to commit suicide, from which he was saved by the revelation of God. He passed the major part of his life at Pandharpur, and was mainly responsible for building up the glorious tradition of the school of thought known as Vārakarī-sampradāya. He was initiated into mystic life by Visobā Khecara, who convinced Nāmadeva of the all-pervading nature of God. He travelled with his younger contemporary, Jñānadeva. Some of his lyrical verses are included in the *Granth Sāhib* of the Sikhs. The dominant note of his thoughts is earnest and whole-hearted devotion to God. Purification of the heart is possible only through suffering, and God can be realized through pure love. He wrote a number of *abhaṅgas* to show people the path to God through repetition of His name.

EKANĀTHA

Ekanātha was born at Paithan. He was the great-grandson of a celebrated saint, Bhānudāsa. When he was only twelve, he had a vision in which he was asked to go to Janārdana Svāmin at Devagad to get himself initiated by him into the spiritual life, which he did accordingly. He lived with his master for six years and then returned to Paithan. His life was an object-lesson in the reconciliation of practical and spiritual life. He observed no distinction of caste and creed, and once gave to the pariahs the food prepared as an offering to his forefathers. His sympathies knew no limits; he poured the holy waters of the Godāvarī (brought from a long distance at the risk of life for the worship of the Lord) into the throat of an ass that was dying of thirst. He published for the first time a reliable edition of the *Jñāneśvarī*. He was a voluminous writer, and his commentary on four verses of the *Bhāgavata* is famous. It was his custom to sing *kīrtana* (devotional composition) every day, and he observed it to the last day of his life. His mystic experiences are expressed most explicitly in his *abhaṅgas*. He popularized the Vedānta philosophy and the mystic teachings of earlier saints. He passed away in A.D. 1598.

TUKĀRĀMA

Tukārāma was born in the family of a farmer. He had some cattle and landed property, but lost them all in a great famine, together with his parents, one of his two wives, and a son. He became a bankrupt and got disgusted with his life. His other wife was a shrew, who abused his companion-devotees. Troubled both at home and outside, Tukārāma took to the study of the works of Jñānadeva, Nāmadeva, and Ekanātha, and began to meditate on God in solitary places on the hills of Bhambanatha and Bhandara. He was initiated by the saint Bābājī in a dream.

He also saw Viṭhṭhala and Nāmadeva in a dream, and was ordered to complete the hundred crores of *abhaṅgas,* which the latter had left unfinished. His poems were thrown into the river Indrāyaṇī by an envious person, Rāmeśvara Bhaṭṭa. Tukārāma observed a fast of thirteen days and was blessed with the vision of God. His poems were miraculously restored to him by divine grace. The miscreant felt a burning sensation all over his body, of which he was cured only by submission to Tukārāma. Later Rāmeśvara Bhaṭṭa became one of his most loyal disciples. Tukārāma was also troubled and tested by people in various other ways. But he was unmoved. He refused the offers of rich presents made by King Śivājī, and when Śivājī, impressed by his renunciation and devotion, desired to become his spiritual disciple, Tukārāma advised him to become a disciple of Rāmadāsa. His inward life, his earnest efforts to realize God, and the sufferings he passed through in order to achieve the Highest—all these represent important phases of a mystic's life. In the range of his mystic experience, in the lucid and forceful expression of his ideas, in his lofty conception of the purpose of life, and in the vigorous exposition of it to the people at large, he undoubtedly occupies a high place. He rightly describes himself as a coping stone of the edifice of mystic experience, of which Jñānadeva was the foundation.

RĀMADĀSA

Rāmadāsa was born in A.D. 1608 and lost his father when he was only seven years old. At the age of twelve, he ran away from home in search of God, practised penance at Takli near Nasik for twelve years, and was rewarded with the realization of God. He wandered throughout India for another twelve years, and finally settled at Chaphal on the banks of the Kṛṣṇā where he built a temple. He is reported to have initiated Śivājī at this time into spiritual life. Historians differ as regards his influence on the political life of Śivājī. But the fact remains that the influence was mutual, and some of the later writings of Rāmadāsa show a distinct dominance of political thought. This does not, however, mean that politics played any important part in his life and writings. As Jolly points out, even saints are, to a certain extent, influenced by their physical and social environments, and as Rāmadāsa was born in a period of political upheaval, he could not but be partly affected by it. But he regarded the realization of God as of primary, and politics as only of secondary, importance in life. He was a saint of a practical temperament and systematically organized his order. He established his monasteries throughout Mahārāṣṭra to serve as centres of spiritual and practical activities. In his monumental work, the *Dāsabodha,* he combines his vast knowledge of various sciences and arts with the synthesizing principle of spiritual life. He also wrote many *abhaṅgas* and some minor works, all of which inspire a deep love for the life of God-realization.

RELIGIOUS MOVEMENTS

From these few life-sketches, it is clear that the saints of Mahārāṣṭra occupy a very high position among the great mystics of the world. Universal interest in mysticism was one of the prominent characteristics of mediaeval India. This mystic movement had its origin in the philosophy of the great Vedic and Upaniṣadic seers, and in that of the thinkers like Śaṅkara and Rāmānuja. Rāmānanda, who drew his inspiration from the teachings of Rāmānuja, is the fountain-head of most of the religious movements in North India. If this Rāmānanda be identical with the spiritual master of Viṭhṭhalapant, then the mystic movement in Mahārāṣṭra may be connected with that in North India.

The cult of Viṭhṭhala, though of Karṇāṭaka origin, was made popular by Jñānadeva, Nāmadeva, Ekanātha, and Tukārāma in Mahārāṣṭra, as it was done by Purandara, Kanaka, Vijayaviṭhṭhala, and Jagannātha in Karṇāṭaka. The cult claims among its votaries many prominent saints from the Andhra and Tamil provinces also. This fact argues for the unity of the religious movements of South India in the mediaeval age. The Nātha cult, with Matsyendra, Gorakṣa, and Gahinī as its prominent historical representatives, seems to have influenced the religious development of the whole nation, especially of Mahārāṣṭra. As already mentioned, Nivṛttinātha was the disciple of Gahinīnātha ; Jñānadeva, Sopānadeva, and Muktābāī were disciples of Nivṛttinātha. Visobā Khecara, the master of Nāmadeva, was the disciple of Sopānadeva, while Cāṅgadeva was initiated into spiritual life by Muktābāī. Saccidānanda Bābā, the disciple of Jñānadeva, is reported to be the master of Rāghava Caitanya, the great-grand-teacher of Tukārāma. Thus Jñānadeva is rightly regarded as the source of the religious movement in Mahārāṣṭra in the mediaeval age.

Just at this time, there came into vogue a great religious cult known as Mahānubhāva Pantha. The cult fell into disrepute and incurred unpopularity among the Mahārāṣṭrians, perhaps because of its alleged disbelief in the caste system, disregard of the teachings of the Vedas, and non-adherence to the *āśrama* system. The leaders and followers of the cult had to carry on their spiritual propaganda and activities under great restraints enforced by the State. All their holy works were therefore written in symbolic script, a key to decipher which was supplied for the first time by the late V. K. Rajavade. Bhave, Chandorkar, and Pangarkar studied the works of the cult critically. The efforts of these scholars, as also of Y. K. Deshpande of Yevale and Kolte of Nagpur, will go a long way towards removing the prejudice of the Mahārāṣṭra public against the cult. Govinda Prabhu, a great mystic, was the founder of this cult, and Cakradhara its first apostle. Nāgadeva organized the cult on a systematic basis. Bhāskara, Keśavarāja Sūri, Dāmodara Paṇḍita, Viśvanātha, and Nārāyaṇa Paṇḍita were, amongst others, the most learned and important followers of the cult. Of the women followers, Mahadambā was an advanced mystic and a poetess of no mean order. The Mahānubhāvas were, in reality, the followers of the Bhāgavata cult. They regarded the *Gītā*, the *Bhāgavata*, and the *Sūtrapāṭha* (a collection of aphorisms of Cakradhara) as the standard and classical religious works. Śrī Kṛṣṇa and Dattātreya were their prominent deities. Devotion to Kṛṣṇa is, in their opinion, the only way to the realization of God. This was therefore primarily a cult of Śrī Kṛṣṇa. But later they accepted Dattātreya —a trinity in unity of Brahmā, Viṣṇu, and Śiva, representing the principles of creation, sustenance, and dissolution of the universe, with emphasis on Viṣṇu, or Viṣṇu as Kṛṣṇa. Thus the Mahānubhāva cult seems to combine the cult of Kṛṣṇa, represented by the Nāthas of Mahārāṣṭra, with that of Dattātreya, represented by Narasiṁha Sarasvatī and Janārdana Svāmin.

Ekanātha, who was the disciple of Janārdana Svāmin, was asked to join and develop the Viṭhṭhala cult. All the other saints, like Janābāī, Gorā, Sāṁvata, and Cokhāmeḷā, contemporaneous with Nāmadeva, were staunch devotees of Viṭhṭhala. Rāmadāsa alone seems to stand apart and unrelated to all these saints of Pandharpur. He cut out a new path for himself and founded a separate school of mysticism.

PRESUPPOSITIONS OF MYSTICISM

There are certain presuppositions or axioms of mysticism that have been recognized, supported, and preached by all the saints of Mahārāṣṭra. Of these, the most important one is the reality of the other world and the possibility of spiritual experience for all. It is possible for every earnest aspirant, says Rāmadāsa, to realize God fully even in this life. That even the lowest and the most sinful man can become a saint and attain salvation by real, sincere, and intense love for God is the teaching of most of the Mahārāṣṭra saints.

This experience of God-realization can be tested by the same criteria of truth that are used for ascertaining the reality of sensuous experience, viz. objectivity, universality, and necessity. Spiritual experience is as objective as sensuous experience: it is as independent of subjective ideas, and as different from various subjective hallucinations, as the certain and objective knowledge of the world. A mystic sees God as really as we see the phenomenal world, only with this difference that his knowledge of God is direct and intuitive, while our knowledge of the world is sensuous and discursive. Unlike our knowledge of the phenomenal world, which involves a duality of subject and object, mystic experience is unitive, and transcends the subject-object relation. Intuition is not, however, a separate faculty. It is only a more evolved state of reason, reason working on a higher plane. God-realization is regarded by Rāmadāsa and Jñānadeva as the gift of God, and an art by itself, which can be mastered only by the grace of God and the *guru*.

From the objectivity of mystic experience follows its universality. The main experiences of the mystics of all ages and climes are essentially identical, though there is ample scope for richness and variety in mystic experience on account of the infinity and perfection of God, who cannot be exhaustively and completely comprehended by any single mystic at any time. Only progressive and asymptotic approximation towards complete realization is possible. Whatever is objectively and universally true must be necessarily true.

The possibility of the realization of God, again, presupposes the divine nature of man. Unless there is an element of identity between man and the ultimate Reality, first-hand knowledge of the latter would be impossible. Realization of God therefore means the realization of the identity of the individual soul with the supreme Soul. This identity is qualitative and not quantitative, and hence the recognition of the fact by Jñānadeva that the knower of Brahman remains slightly different from Brahman Itself, in spite of the identity between the two.

God, implicitly present in man, is realized explicitly only by acquiring the necessary moral virtues. So God-realization presupposes perfect holiness; it is only the holy that are admitted into the kingdom of God. Of all the innumerable ways and means that are followed by various aspirants, the surest is the whole-hearted and disinterested love for God. Only those that have renounced everything for the love of God are blessed with beatific vision.

A mystic, even after attaining the highest experience, is found to serve society and strive for its spiritual good. This tendency is found in the majority of great mystics, though it cannot be regarded as absolutely universal, for the mystics differ in their temperaments, and are influenced by the psychological, intellectual, and social conditions of their environment, and the differences in their temperament persist, in spite of the identity of their highest mystic experiences. Hence we find various types among the saints: some are dominated by reason, some by feeling, and others by activity. Dr. R. D. Ranade rightly distinguishes different types of mystics among Mahārāṣṭra saints, namely, intellectualistic (Jñānadeva), democratic (Nāmadeva), synthetic (Ekanātha), personalistic (Tukārāma), and activistic (Rāmadāsa). A complete and exhaustive classification of all mystics is impossible, as the infinite individual differences refuse to be digested in any scheme of classification.

ABSOLUTE AND THE WORLD

In the writings of the Mahārāṣṭra saints, metaphysics is subordinated to mysticism. The highest principles determined by pure reason are to be apprehended in mystic experience. All the saints in Mahārāṣṭra generally accept the metaphysical concepts of Māyā and Brahman, propounded by the great non-dualistic philosopher, Śaṅkarācārya. Brahman or the Absolute alone is regarded by them as real, and everything else as illusory. Brahman is again described in the Sāṁkhya fashion as Puruṣa, and Māyā is identified with Prakṛti. Though the creation of the manifold world is the work of Prakṛti or Māyā, there is no interaction between Prakṛti and Puruṣa, which are entirely different from each other. Both are declared by Jñānadeva to be eternal, though they appear to be contradictory in their nature. The dualism is avoided by tacitly assuming the reality of Brahman or Puruṣa, and reducing Prakṛti or Māyā to non-being. Puruṣa is the unmoved mover of the motions in the world. He is the spectator that excites Prakṛti to a variety of actions, and yet himself remains unaffected, just as a mountain reflected in a river is not swept away by its current ; or again, he is like the magnet that moves the iron filings without itself moving.

The phenomenal world is compared to an *aśvattha* tree that has its roots in God, and cannot be determined as either being or non-being. The world is created through illusion. Jñāneśvara tries to reconcile in a higher synthesis the contradictory principles of the world and Brahman. The world along with the individual selves is regarded as mutable, while Brahman is immutable and formless. But both the mutable and the immutable, though contradictory in nature, exist simultaneously in the same locus, and are therefore in a state of unity. The supreme Person, who is beyond the reach of discursive reason, subsumes and transcends the contradictory principles of both the mutable and the immutable, just as the fire, that burns the fuel, ultimately burns itself out, or as the knowledge, that drives away ignorance, transcends itself.

A more convenient method of reconciling the contradiction, however, is to regard both man and the world as identical with God. In his *Sphūrtivāda,* Jñānadeva tells us that the Absolute expands Itself as the world, and without any prejudice to Its immutable simplicity, It appears as the knowing subjects that vary with the variations of the objects that are known. The world is the sport of the Absolute. The Absolute plays with Itself by becoming the world, as the water plays with itself by assuming the form of waves. There is no difference between the Absolute and the world, as there is none between the fire and its flames, or the diamond and its lustre (*Amṛtānubhava,* VII). The problem of the relation between the soul and the body is only a special instance of the problem of the relation between the Absolute and the world, and it is explained also by assuming the fundamental identity between the soul and the body, and of both with the Absolute.

NATURE OF GOD

God, the ultimate Reality, is formless, and hence all anthropomorphism is condemned by Jñānadeva. Rāmadāsa distinguishes four modes of divine existence—the images, the incarnations, the self, and the Absolute. The last two are identified with each other, while images and incarnations are given only secondary importance. God's existence is proved from the design and perfect order and harmony that obtain in the world, and it is argued that God, the supreme Agent, who created the world and the individual selves, must be prior to His creation. The Omnipresent is like a thread running through the souls of all beings. Like Plato, Jñānadeva very poetically describes God as the sun of Reality. God, in truth, is beyond all qualities. He is immeasurable, indeterminate, immaculate, and indescribable. Monism can be expressed only through dualism, as one has to draw a circle in order to explain what a void is like. 'One should outwardly declare that God exists,' Tukārāma puts it in one of his *abhaṅgas,* 'but should be inwardly convinced of His non-existence.' That is, in talks or in preaching we speak of the existence of God, as if He is something existing in a manifest form outside of ourselves, but, in reality, He does not exist anywhere in the outside world. He is not an external reality, existing somewhere in space or time—He is our very self. This identity of the individual self with the Absolute is the ultimate truth.

THEORY OF KNOWLEDGE

There is a detailed logical discussion about the nature of real knowledge in the works of both Jñānadeva and Rāmadāsa. The theory of knowledge also is subordinated to mysticism, and it is the most fundamental assumption of their theory that the highest Reality, call it Brahman, Ātman, or God, must be intimately known, and actually realized. Knowledge of the speculative, moral, and practical sciences is not real knowledge, nor can excellence in practical or fine arts be so regarded. Experiential, intuitive, and direct knowledge of God alone deserves to be called real knowledge, which therefore is open only to spiritual insight. Blind faith, says Jñāneśvara in one of his *abhaṅgas,* is of no use in spiritual life ; for such a faith is nothing but ignorance, and by ignorance none can ever reach God. The importance of reason in spiritual life cannot be overestimated. Rāmadāsa rightly emphasizes the fact that our experience must stand the test of thought or reason. But empirical knowledge and ignorance are both relative, and hence equally unreal ; both these categories have to be subsumed, synthesized, and transcended in a higher category of mystical, intuitive knowledge of God. Real, intuitive knowledge consists in seeing the One in the many, the supreme oneness and eternal identity of the microcosm and the macrocosm—the vision of the Self by the self.

VIRTUE IDENTIFIED WITH KNOWLEDGE

The ethics of the Mahārāṣṭra saints is individualistic and practical. An acute analysis and a detailed and vivid description of the various virtues, the attainment of which is regarded as an essential condition of mystic life, form a special feature of the works of Jñānadeva, Tukārāma, Ekanātha, and Rāmadāsa. Ethics is thus only preparatory to mystic realization. Virtue is associated with knowledge and spiritual insight. Humility, non-injury, purity, devotion to God and the *guru,* and dispassion are supposed to prepare one for real knowledge, while the opposites of these make for ignorance. The same truth is expressed in other words when the divine and the demoniac heritage are distinguished from each other, and identified with knowledge and ignorance respectively. The divine heritage consists of virtues, while the demoniac consists of vices. The one is constituted by the knowledge of oneness with the Ātman, while the other is made up of hypocrisy, envy, pride, anger, harshness, and ignorance. Man's mind is swayed by the three qualities—*sattva* (purity), *rajas* (activity), and *tamas* (inertia). The first and the last are responsible for the divine and the demoniac heritage respectively. *Sattva* is the source of knowledge and joy, and leads us towards God ; *rajas* is the source of activity that keeps us engrossed in worldly ambitions ; and *tamas* is the source of infatuation and ignorance, and takes us to hell.

SUMMUM BONUM OF HUMAN LIFE

God-realization is regarded by all Mahārāṣṭra saints as the *summum bonum* of human life and human conduct. God is the only good ; one should therefore leave everything and follow God. There is no end higher than God-realization. So it should be the one business of the aspirant's life to devote himself whole-heartedly and unceasingly to God. And anything that comes in the way of God-realization should be summarily dispensed with, howsoever good or valuable it may appear to be. The most precious things, the most loving and intimate relations like parents or friends, nay, even the spiritual teacher, should be straightway abandoned, if one is likely to be separated from God by associating oneself with any of these. The time required for the attainment of the ideal depends on the intensity, fervour, and firmness of faith and love for it, and God can be realized even in an instant if the aspirant is ready for it. Rāmadāsa rightly warns us not to trust people who say that God will be realized some day during the long course of evolution of our lives. They know nothing about the real nature of the ideal. God should be seen immediately, and even while the body lasts.

MATERIAL AND SPIRITUAL LIFE

The relation of the material life to the spiritual is conceived differently by different Mahārāṣṭra saints. This difference is mainly due to the difference in their temperaments, formed by the personal tendencies and the influence of the physical and social environment on them. Tukārāma clearly states that it is impossible to achieve both worldly pleasures and spiritual bliss. One cannot run with the hare and hunt with the hounds. If it were possible for an aspirant to secure spiritual bliss while pursuing worldly pleasures, great saints like Sanaka would not have abandoned the latter and gone to the forest. Ekanātha and Rāmadāsa, however, stand for a reconciliation of both the worldly and spiritual life. The actual life and teachings of Ekanātha prove the fact of reconciliation beyond all doubt. Rāmadāsa contends that success in *saṁsāra* (the world) alone vouchsafes success in *paramārtha* (spiritual life) ; the former is regarded as a necessary qualification for the latter, which is far more difficult and strenuous than the ordinary life. Both groups of saints agree that one should have no attachment to worldly life ; that a true spiritual aspirant should maintain a dispassionate attitude towards all things worldly, and should never get entangled in the meshes of their pleasures. He should never think of devoting himself to God only when he is free from the worries of this life, for they know no end. The only way of escape is to remain unaffected in the midst of these worries, to devote oneself to God, and to live like a lotus in water.

MORAL VIRTUES NECESSARY FOR SPIRITUAL LIFE

Success in life, either worldly or spiritual, is impossible without great effort or heroism. This fact is recognized and emphasized by all the saints of Mahārāṣṭra. The first and foremost moral qualification for a true aspirant is infinite capacity for effort. He should be all patience and should remain undaunted by difficulties and disappointments. His zeal for spiritual life should only be sharpened by his physical sufferings. He should realize that the span of life allowed to him is very short, and that nobody will save him from the clutches of death. It is a blunder to suppose that the saints take only a negative or pessimistic view of life, emphasize only miseries and sufferings, and ignore the infinite joys of life. The human body is acknowledged by all saints to be of the utmost spiritual importance ; for through it alone men attain beatitude. Pessimism is not an end in itself, and bodily sufferings are not recommended as a necessary means to the realization of the ultimate end. Most of the saints maintain that it is not necessary for an aspirant to go to the forest, torture the body, and undergo all kinds of physical suffering, in order to attain God. But what is regarded as essential is the purity of heart.

Everything in this world is holy except the mind of a person not devoted to God. One should make one's mind pure and holy by purging it of various passions. Moral evil is regarded as a disease. This disease can be cured by detaching the mind from the objects of sense pleasure. Neither over-indulgence in, nor complete rejection of, it, but moderation is prescribed by Rāmadāsa as a rule of moral life. A spiritual aspirant must observe the golden mean in all his actions. He should not go after whatever his mind asks for, but should keep it under control. He should conquer sleep, should be moderate in his meals, should not talk too much, and should resort to solitude. He should bid adieu to all idleness and shyness, and sit up for meditation in time, without feeling any hesitation whether he is likely to be observed or criticized by others. Any solitary place is welcome to Tukārāma, while Jñānadeva gives a vivid description of an ideal place for meditation. It should be quiet, shady, and beautiful, and a place so charming that even the mind of a person tossed by passions should be instantly composed, when he goes there.

The importance of practice in spiritual life cannot be over-stressed. Nothing is impossible of attainment through practice. The realization of God is supremely aided by self-control and constant meditation, and these are attained through practice. Those who are given to sex and money are bound ; freedom from attachment to these is the first step towards God-realization. God, immanent in our body, will not be seen until our emotions are purified and transmuted. No wicked feeling should arise in our mind. There should be complete annihilation of egoistic feelings. A man should not let others know his spiritual progress, as it is likely to make him proud and arrest his progress. He should sacrifice his all to God, and should so expand his self that he may hope to see God everywhere. He should always crave for the company of saints. He should feel satisfied in whatever condition of life he is placed, should have firm faith in God, and completely resign himself to His will. Repentance is of great value in spiritual life, for it burns up all sins committed through ignorance and passion and thus enables even the most despised sinner to become a saint. In spite of the acquisition of the moral virtues that qualify a man for spiritual life, God can be realized only through His grace. It is only the fortunate few that attain the Highest: very few of the blossoms of the mango-tree develop into ripe fruits.

GRACE OF THE GURU

The aspirant must be initiated into the mysteries of spiritual life only by a master who has realized God. It is only a burning lamp that can light other lamps. Initiation forms the first step in spiritual life. In this respect, the parents or other relatives are of no use; nor is God to be realized merely by strenuous independent thinking, or by mastering various sciences. Enlightenment is impossible without a *guru* (master). Sciences, contemplation, devotion, and various practices are of no avail without his grace. Trees bear flowers and fruits only when the spring sets in: devotion bears fruit only when one is blessed by the *guru*. Hence the supreme importance of the master in spiritual life. In initiating, the master gives God *in posse* to his disciple, who has to realize Him *in esse* by following the course of life prescribed by him. The mystics are right in declaring the superiority of the master to God, as he can make a gift of God. The grace of the master neutralizes the poison of sense pleasures, and leads the disciple gradually to ecstatic bliss. The master gives his disciple the key to the spiritual treasure, and takes him to infinite happiness, which is beyond the reach of imagination and intellect. Nothing is impossible for the grace of the *guru*.

Though the supreme significance of the real master is recognized by all mystics, they mercilessly criticize the pseudo-saints. All persons who pose as masters only on the strength of their occult powers are pretenders, and deserve to be condemned. They ruin the lives of their disciples. Great discrimination has to be used in the choice of the master. One who can make us actually see God is alone a real master. He instils into the minds of his disciples the light of self-knowledge by enabling them to realize the identity between the individual self and the universal Self. He is dispassionate, and is ever engaged in spiritual discussions or meditation; he is free from doubts, as he lives in God. Initiation by such a master alone is fruitful, and leads the disciple Godward. God is, however, realized not suddenly, but only progressively.

PLACE OF CONVERSION IN SPIRITUAL LIFE

Any strong emotional attitude towards God is sure to prove fruitful in the effort of the aspirant to realize Him. Intense love, warm affection like that of an infant for its mother, great fear, and even bitter hatred of God are all known to have been effective means of mystic experience. The emotion should be all-absorbing, leaving no scope for any other emotion in the heart. There have been great devotees in Mahārāṣṭra who might be cited as illustrations of all these different methods of God-realization. Even the greatest sinners and enemies of God, the most confirmed atheists, have been suddenly turned into great saints. It merely illustrates the psychological principle that a strong emotion that invades the whole region of a person's consciousness drives away all other emotions. If such an emotion is deliberately developed, it has the inevitable welcome tendency of transmuting all other emotions, auxiliary or adverse. Though there are not many instances of conversion in the history of mysticism in Mahārāṣṭra, yet there are some typical ones. The later spiritual life of Nāmadeva, as already mentioned, was the result of such a conversion. The conversion of Janārdana Svāmin was of a milder kind. In his confessions, we are told that he was given to all sorts of sensual pleasure and was only saved by the grace of his master, Narasiṁha Sarasvatī. The conversion of Cāṅgadeva from occultism and philanthropic work for the sake of fame to the life of real mysticism and disinterested service of others forms a class by itself. Conversion is not, however, the normal method of attaining spiritual experience. The royal road to mystic union with God is intense love of, and devotion to, Him. Hence love is rightly called the true hierophant of mystic life.

NATURE AND IMPORTANCE OF DEVOTION

Jñānadeva describes the road to God through intense love as the best of the roads to unitive life. There are four minor roads—of knowledge, meditation, action, and devotion—that meet it. This road to God is of infinite length, which only the blessed can discover and traverse. They find glorious revelations along the vista at each step on this avenue, and ultimately there is an end to all their miseries. Here, there is an attempt made to synthesize knowledge, devotion, contemplation, and action into a harmonious whole, though some saints maintain the superiority of love and devotion to knowledge and reason. For instance, Ekanātha declares that knowledge without love is of no account. Tukārāma seems to corroborate this view when he says that God is more under the control of the simple and the faithful than of the learned. Devotion is again regarded as the root of the tree of mystic life, of which dispassion is the flower, and knowledge the fruit. The faculty of imagination is also to be transmuted to serve the purpose of God-realization ; when the mind is made to realize the unimaginable, it is led Godward and is lost in Him.

All the faculties of the mind are to be transformed and utilized for the attainment of God. Miseries and sufferings in the world are described for urging the people to resort to a life of whole-hearted devotion to God. There is no distinction of caste, creed, colour, or nationality in devotion ; and wherever there is devotion there is liberation. Real devotion should be concentrated, whole-hearted, and all-absorbing. Tukārāma tells us that one should run after God with all the force of will and earnestness, as the waters of a fountain rise up in one jet. As a moth falls on a lamp directly and unhesitatingly, so should we courageously strive for the mystic union with God ; nay, the numberless difficulties in the way of realization should fill the mind of the aspirant with joy. Janābāī rightly remarks that real devotion is not easy to acquire, for it is as fierce as fire, as terrible as poison, and as sharp as the edge of a sword. It consists in seeing God everywhere ; the love for Him should be so overflowing and absorbing that one should be merged in God.

The path of devotion values a personal God more than the impersonal Absolute. The devotees request God to present Himself before them in some form, so that they may enjoy all the pleasures of unceasing love, while He may satisfy the seekers of knowledge with His absolute formless Being. In reality, God is neither personal nor impersonal ; He is both, and transcends both ; His real nature is beyond discursive knowledge, and beyond all description.

KINDS OF DEVOTION

Following the *Bhāgavata* view, the Mahārāṣṭra saints conceive devotion as ninefold: *śravaṇa* comes first in the order of logical development. It consists in hearing the glories of God, and reading the Śāstras and meditating on their spiritual ideas. It leads to dispassion by resolving all doubts, and heightens the love for God. It endows one with spiritual insight, and hence it is as necessary to a religious aspirant as his daily food. Equally important is *kīrtana* or singing the praises of God. What is required for this is not excellence in the art of music, or a sweet voice, but sincere and earnest love for God. God and His greatness alone should form the subject-matter of *kīrtana*. Ekanātha and Rāmadāsa lay down rules for performing the *kīrtana* which is useful for spiritual progress. The performer should never be a burden to others ; he should sing with joy the holy lives of the saints, and of the incarnations of God ; he should never sing of anything except devotion and knowledge, and should sing the Lord's praise in such a way that His form may be indelibly impressed on the hearts of the audience. This kind of *kīrtana* is rightly regarded by Tukārāma as the holy confluence of God, the devotee, and His name. It is a sure means of liberating oneself and others from the bondage of worldly existence. The joy in *kīrtana* is perennial and ever new. It infuses miraculous powers into a person, lifts him above all fears, and brings for him the bliss of unitive life in God. The saints declare that, if a devotee sings lying in his bed, God hears him standing ; if he sings sitting, God begins to nod in joy ; and if he sings standing, God begins to dance. *Smaraṇa* or remembering God's name, which comes next, is so highly praised by all that it forms a class by itself, and hence deserves to be considered separately. *Pādasevana* or service of the feet of God, *arcana* or worship of Him, and *vandana* or obeisance to Him are other forms of devotion and means of mystic union, which are described in detail by Ekanātha and Rāmadāsa. More important than these is *dāsya bhakti*. Muktābāī rightly states that a devotee becomes himself God by the whole-hearted service of God. One should give one's all to God, and should be ready to lose everything in order to gain *sakhya* or His friendship, which is regarded as the eighth kind of devotion. One should behave in a way that will please God, so that friendship may easily arise, and one should never forgo His friendship for any worldly gain, howsoever great it may appear to be. *Ātma-nivedana* or self-surrender, entire committal of oneself to God, is the last kind of devotion. It consists in the realization of the unity and identity of one's self with God by service to and grace of the *guru*.

Ekanātha illustrates how all these nine kinds of devotion were exclusively followed and developed to their utmost limit with the same ultimate result by the following saints of old: King Parīkṣit followed *śravaṇa* ; Nārada, *kīrtana* ; Prahlāda, remembering God's name ; Lakṣmī, service of God's feet ; Akrūra, worship of, and prostration before, God and saints ; Hanumat, whole-hearted service of God in all ways conceivable ; Arjuna, friendship of God ; and King Bali, absolute self-surrender. One attains the highest aim of life by intensively following any one of these nine kinds of devotion ; for psychologically each is of equal importance in creating an attitude of mind conducive to the mystic realization of Reality or the Absolute.

GLORY OF GOD'S NAME

Repetition of God's name is the simplest of all spiritual practices. People take only a sackful of corn to the field to sow, but reap and bring back to their homes cart-loads thereof; similarly, the simple repetition of God's name brings in its train as great a profit as the love of God. While repeating God's name, one should turn a deaf ear to the vilification and censure of others. This is the only way to purify the mind. Remembering God's name without love is as fruitless as painting the sun and the moon without their light. He who has no conviction of spiritual experience regards the name of God rather lightly; but once he gets the experience, he is released from the circle of birth and death.

A true devotee continues remembering His name with joy even when he is being overcome by death. All difficulties are destroyed by remembering His name. It should therefore be uttered in all conditions of the body and mind, regularly and continuously. Its power is ineffable. Remembrance of God's name is indeed Brahman, while forgetting it is Māyā. If a man silently remembers God, sitting in a quiet solitary place, God is sure to present Himself before him. There is a regular competition among the senses for God-realization, when His name is uttered with love. Even God does not know the glory of His name, and it is natural, for a lotus does not know its own fragrance; the devotees alone know the significance of His name. Several physical and psychological effects follow from the repetition of God's name: the body becomes calm and quiet; its lustre is enhanced by love; the mind is thoroughly cleansed of its sordid elements; and the evil tendencies are finally suppressed. One comes to know the unknowable, see the invisible, and speak what baffles the power of speech.

INITIAL EXPERIENCES

During the long and strenuous process of purification and contemplation, the beginner is blessed by the grace of God with mystic experiences like visions and auditions, which refresh him and strengthen his faith in the spiritual life. But these visions are entirely different from dreams and hallucinations, as they are marked by the presence of full self-consciousness, and are objective experiences and not subjectively induced states of consciousness. Their objectivity is evidenced by the following remark of Rāmadāsa that when we try to realize God, He cannot be realized; but when we try to leave Him, He cannot be left. We see Him unexpectedly on various occasions; and His form is seen, as Jñānadeva puts it, even when we shut our eyes, nay, we see Him even when we try not to see Him. That such visions are supersensuous is proved from the fact that they can be seen even by the blind, and His words are heard even by the deaf. The elementary mystic experiences are meant to create and sustain the interest of the aspirant in his search after God. Jñānadeva tells us that he was delighted to see a panorama of an inconceivable variety of colours. He also mentions that he saw invaluable and beautifully shaped pearls of a bright colour, and that he became all eyes and saw eyes everywhere. Nivṛttinātha speaks of God's wonderful fragrance.

'THE CENTRE OF INDIFFERENCE'

The progress of the seeker on the path of spiritual life is not uninterrupted and smooth. Though he sees some forms, lights, and colours, and hears some mystic sounds at intervals, yet when a certain stage of development is reached, he finds his enthusiasm for mystic life slackened, his progress arrested, and his mind overcome by various doubts as regards the reality of the spiritual life itself. This stage in mystic life is marked by all sorts of disappointments, combined with a variety of calamities that are hurled on him by the jealous God, as if to test his love for and faith in Him. This stage in spiritual life is known in mystic literature as the dark night of the soul. Most aspirants have to pass through this stage, which Carlyle calls 'the centre of indifference', before they reach the stage of further illumination or the stage of eternal 'aye'. Rare indeed are the saints like Jñānadeva whose progress in spiritual life is absolutely continuous.

Of the Mahārāṣṭra saints, Nāmadeva, Tukārāma, and Rāmadāsa had to pass through this dark night of the soul, and one finds a very pathetic and vivid description of this condition of their mind in their works. Tukārāma was dissatisfied with the praises about his realization by others, because he was inwardly convinced that he had not realized God. He had his doubts as regards the possibility of God-realization. He tells us that his yearning for God-realization was greatly increased by hearing the mystic experiences of those who had advanced in spiritual life; and he implored the saints to plead for him before God. Driven to desperation, Tukārāma quarrels with God, uses cutting words, and even abuses Him. He tells Him that He is miserly, ungrateful, and cruel, as is natural with one devoid of all qualities, and that he is ashamed to call himself His devotee; that all his prayers fall flat on God, as if he were praying before a corpse! Overwhelmed with grief and anxiety, Nāmadeva awaits the arrival of the cloud of mercy in the heavens; in despair, he entreats God to run to his rescue as does the mother whose child has fallen into fire. Both Nāmadeva and Tukārāma tell us how they are dying for God, how their condition is like that of a girl who is leaving her home for that of her husband for the first time, or like that of a fish out of water, and both entreat God to hasten to them with help before they expire. In his utter despair Tukārāma declares that for him God is dead. He finds the situation so unbearable that he decides to commit suicide, when he is blessed with the beatific vision of God. In many works of Rāmadāsa also, particularly in all his poems known as *Karuṇāṣṭakas,* there is expressed similarly intense and earnest longing for God-realization, marked by doubts and disappointments and ultimately relieved by continuous progress and the bliss of the unitive life.

VISIONS AND ILLUMINATION

The dark night of the soul is ultimately transcended and the mystic reaches his destination. One's mind is absorbed in hearing the mystic sound that destroys all passions. The sound is like the loud beating of the cymbals (Gorā); it is sometimes so extensive that one feels as if the heavens were reverberating with it or were endowed with tongues (Jñānadeva). The sound proceeds, Cāṅgadeva tells us, as from a machine, but no form is seen. The sweet notes of a stringed musical instrument are heard, and the mind is lost in that bliss. Nāmadeva had a combined experience of both light and sound. He realized his identity with God in the supreme light beyond the sun and the moon, and in the midst of the loud beatings of drums. The sound heard further developed into automatic speech or writing. This is the common experience of both Nāmadeva and Tukārāma. Jñānadeva and Rāmadāsa had similar experiences.

The divine love that fills the mystic's heart overflows in the form of words, which are therefore not his words, but God's: God is speaking through him. Equally important is the experience of light and form. Ekanātha describes his mystic experience of the beautiful pearls and shining jewels set in huge circles, and of the light burning without oil. God seems to light His devotee by bearing a torch in His hand and there is light everywhere (Jñānadeva). One sees a shower of stars, the light of the crescent and full moon; there is an end to all darkness, and one experiences the light of the sun at night, and of the moon by day. One sees the bright light of the dawn that fills the earth and knows no setting. Tukārāma exultingly tells of his having seen the face of God, shining like billions of suns, appearing extremely beautiful like a bright diamond set in the midst of a number of jewels. He lost all consciousness of the body when he saw the face of God. Ekanātha saw God everywhere in a nude state, with no covering, as if He had no sense of shame. He again saw Him in the form of a white boar, and yet again, in the beautiful form of Viṣṇu, four-armed, dressed in silk, and bearing different weapons in His hands. Janābāī had the vision of God everywhere and in all conditions. She says that she felt as if she ate and drank God and slept on Him. The vision of the omnipresent God is the highest aim of contemplation,

Tukārāma tells us that God pursued him wherever he went. Such a vision of God banishes all fear and renders the mystic silent. Jñānadeva saw God in infinite forms and dresses, and had all his doubts resolved.

The next stage in spiritual development is the experience of close contact with God. Jñānadeva tells us that he touched God without his hands, and that he embraced God without his body. God began to move and nod and dance in joy and whisper to him His secrets. One enjoys all the eightfold *sāttvika* emotions in such mystic realization of God: all at once the hair stands up, the body perspires and trembles with joy, tears trickle down, excessive joy wells up in the heart, the throat is choked up, the tongue is tied tight, and the breathing is quickened. One feels as if one was suddenly made the master of a rich heritage, and however much the spiritual bliss may be enjoyed, one does not feel satisfied, for such bliss knows no satiety.

THE UNITIVE LIFE

The last stage in the mystic life is the experience of the unity of the self with God or Brahman. This is known as the unitive life in God, a thing experienced by the majority of great saints all over the world in all times. Tukārāma informs us of his having seen the death of his own body and of having offered it to its Lord. He and Jñānadeva both had the experience of the identity of the self and God ; for they tell us that they found the form they were seeing to be identical with their own self. Ekanātha felt that he had himself become Brahman or Ātman ; everything that he saw was Brahman, there being no place that was not filled by It. Jñānadeva also experienced the oneness of himself with his *guru*. He asks, 'God, His devotee, and the *guru* are united together, as three rivers merge in a confluence ; when everything becomes God, how is one to worship Him?' A devotee who is blessed with this experience has no duties to perform, except to remain absorbed in the bliss of the unity with God. Jñānadeva and Tukārāma speak of their being crowned as the kings of the realm of the unitive life in God to the beating of drums. Now they possess complete sovereignty over everything in the world, even over death. Tukārāma says that he has in his hands the keys of the rich treasury of spiritual experience, and offers anything that is asked for, never saying 'no' to anybody. When such a devotee is on his deathbed and cannot sit up for meditation, God comes to his help and serves him. Jñānadeva remarks that the devotee's lifelong service of God would be of no avail if this does not happen. He considers it no wonder that the devotees who have attained to real *svārājya* (the sovereignty of the Self or the state of the resplendent Ātman) in this very life, and are eternally united with God, become God after their bodily death.

CHARACTERISTICS OF A TRUE SAINT

We shall conclude this very short account of the mystic philosophy of the Mahārāṣṭra saints with a brief survey of the main characteristics of an ideal saint as mentioned by them. The saints are disinterestedly generous like clouds, and fulfil all the aspirations of those that commit themselves to their care. They are free from all sense of egoism and attachment to their body. They never beg anything of anybody except God. Their contemplation is absolutely free from doubt. They never fail to practise meditation even in the midst of direst calamities. They are above the dualities of worldly experience, are free from desires, hypocrisy, and other ignoble qualities, and have firm faith in God and His name. Ekanātha rightly regards unfailing peace of mind as a characteristic of true saints. They are softer than wax and yet harder than adamant. The whole world is a home to them, and they have no enemy. True saints can confer a vision of God on their disciples.

The ideal saint, though a man of perfect realization, is yet, according to Rāmadāsa, a practical man. He is all-sided, always works, and leads people to the service of God. He brings himself down to the level of the lowest ; he understands their hearts and sympathizes with them ; he forgives their faults, and helps them to develop their merits. The real saint moves all to activity, keeping himself in the background ; he always supports the right cause. He does not perform any miracles, God performs them for him. The ideal saint demands from his disciples nothing but the service of God. He fills people's minds with discrimination, and sets the example of the service of God and man. His greatness and power lie only in silent work ; activity alternates with meditation in his life.

The saints live in heaven and are reborn time after time only to teach people right conduct, to conquer death, and to establish the kingdom of God on earth. They are smaller than the smallest and greater than the greatest ; they live in this world only to oblige others. Tukārāma adds that he has relieved all men of sins and asks them only to remember God. The one purpose in the life of a saint is to protect real religion and suppress atheism, to cleanse the minds of the people in the holy Gaṅgā of self-knowledge, and to fill men with ecstatic joy of divine love.

27

THE MEDIAEVAL MYSTICS OF NORTH INDIA

THE spiritual soil of India, like a delta, is made up of layer upon layer of its religious endeavours from time immemorial. Every day we are discovering fresh historical materials, which demonstrate how varieties of sustained religious striving have contributed to its formation. Religious faiths all seem to have worked on the principle of 'live and let live'. Unfortunately, in the struggle for existence, this spirit of toleration was gradually vitiated by invidious distinctions in the social and spiritual life.

THE ANCIENT RELIGIOUS MILIEU

Our knowledge of the pre-Aryan religion of India, whether of the aborigines or of the Indus valley people, is still sketchy and uncertain. The religious and cultural history of India begins practically with the coming of the Aryans in the early Vedic period, and gradually develops in all its manifold richness through the interaction of its different contributory factors. Just as the early Vedic religion grew up and developed around sacrifices as its centre, so the different schools of Tairthikas (advocates of holy places), including those of Buddhism and Jainism, grew up in the opposite direction around their own *tīrthas* (holy places). The followers of the Vedas (the Mīmāṁsakas) held up the householder's life as the ideal, and heaven as the goal, while the Tairthikas advocated asceticism as the ideal of life, and *nirvāṇa* or final deliverance as the end of all human endeavours.

While the Vedic religion was generally exclusive, the later religions, characterized by the predominant influence of *jñāna* (knowledge), *yoga* (concentrated meditation), and *bhakti* (devotion), were more inclusive. Thus we find that from very early times foreign tribes such as Śakas and Hūṇas were easily assimilated into the Buddhist, Vaiṣṇava, and Śaiva sects. Gradually, both the Vedic and post-Vedic religions lost their power and influence over the people ; then followed an age of spiritual disintegration, when the religious life of India stagnated and her spiritual forces were dissipated in mere repetition of one or other of the older religious forms, whether of the Vedic sacrifices or of Śaivism and Vaiṣṇavism. Some concentrated their energies on the resuscitation of the Vedas and conservation of the old social order with the help of the Smṛtis ; a few, on the other hand, attempted to conquer the heart of India with the help of the Tāntrika modes of worship.

THE NEW CHALLENGE

At this juncture, there appeared on the horizon a powerful religion from the west, the religion of the Prophet Mohammed. The Mohammedan proselytization of India did not begin with coercion and bloodshed; the first conversions were effected by its saints and mystics. As the Mohammedan saints and preachers came to India, the presence of the rival faith drove them to a more intense life of religious austerities. This virtual challenge inspired the religious men of India also to seek more earnestly for the truths of their own faith. Thus the coming of the Mohammedans to India inaugurated a period of earnest spiritual consciousness among both the Hindus and the Mohammedans. Hinduism and Islam, strictly bound by the tenets of their own scriptures, had no points of contact with each other. They were like the two banks of a river ever separated by the stream that flows between them. Who was to build the connecting bridge? The orthodox Hindus as well as the orthodox Mohammedans were unfit for this task, and it was left to the free spirits and lovers of humanity from both these groups, the Hindu *bhaktas* and the Mohammedan Sufis, to devote their lives to the construction of this bridge.

RĀMĀNANDA AND HIS FOLLOWERS

The founder of this great movement in North India was Rāmānanda, a teacher who was fifth in descent from Rāmānuja. He was born at Prayāga in a Brāhmaṇa family. He was not a founder in the sense that he started the movement—the work had already begun before he was born. But from his time onward, we can trace an uninterrupted flow of this stream of thought throughout the Indian middle ages. His unique contribution to Indian spiritual life was the spirit of synthesis observed in his teaching: he accepted all that was true and of permanent value in our spiritual heritage—the philosophy of meditation (*yoga*) and knowledge from the North and the absolute surrender (*prapatti*) of the Bhakti cult from the South—and rejected all that was untrue, ephemeral, or rigidly sectarian. There is a popular verse to this effect: '*Bhakti* arose first in the Draviḍa land; Rāmānanda brought it to the North; and Kabīr spread it to the seven continents and nine divisions of the world.'

At this critical period of India's religious history, every thinking person was keenly aware of the difficulty of the problem before him, and each tried to solve it according to his own light: Kumārila, Sāyaṇa, and others tried to re-establish the Vedas and the Vedic way of life on a stronger foundation by a fresh interpretation of the text; the philosophers, Śaṅkara and Rāmānuja and others, went deeper into the philosophy of *jñāna* and *bhakti*; Hemādri, Raghunandana, and other writers of the Nibandhas (digests of conduct) devoted their lives to the regulation and conservation of the social order; Āgamavāgīsa, Sarvānanda, Pūrṇānanda, and other Tāntrikas of Bengal, the various sects of Vaiṣṇavism and Śaivism, the schools of Nirañjana, Nāthas, and Yogīs—all made earnest attempts to find out a way that would answer the need of the times.

Rāmānanda borrowed ideas from all these various religious schools, vitalized them with the love and devotion of his heart, and founded a new path of spiritual realization. We do not come across many of his sayings, but the radiant personality of his disciples—the men he created—constitutes his living message. We come across only one song of his, incorporated in the *Granth Sāhib,* but this single poem is a sufficient indication of his philosophy:

'Where shall I go? The music and the festivity are in my own house, my heart does not wish to move, my mind has folded its wings and is still. One day, my heart was filled to overflowing, and I had an inclination to go with sandal and other perfumes to offer my worship to Brahman. But the *guru* (teacher) revealed that Brahman was in my own heart. Wherever I go, I see only water and stones (worshipped); but it is Thou who hast filled them all with Thy presence. They all seek Thee in vain among the Vedas. If Thou art not to be found here, we must go and seek Thee there. My own true *guru,* Thou hast put an end to all my failures and illusions. Blessed art Thou! Rāmānanda is lost in his Master, Brahman; it is the word of the *guru* that destroys all the million bonds of action.'

Though Rāmānanda used the popular name of Rāma, his God was the one God of love and mercy, without any imperfection—not the unconditioned Brahman of the Vedānta, but the beloved, the friend, and the lord of one's heart.

When Rāmānanda perceived that there is only one God who is the origin of all, all the distinctions of caste and creed vanished for him, and he saw humanity as one large family, and all men as brothers. One man is higher than another, not through his birth, but only through his love and sympathy. So he started preaching to all without any reserve, and his fundamental teaching was the gospel of love and devotion. He also gave up the use of Sanskrit and started preaching in the language of the people, thus laying the foundation of modern vernacular literatures.

It is said that his first twelve followers were: Ravidāsa the cobbler, Kabīr the weaver, Dhannā the Jāṭ peasant, Senā the barber, Pīpā the Rājput, Bhāvānanda, Sukhānanda, Āśānanda, Surāsurānanda, Paramānanda, Mahānanda, and Śrī Ānanda. But some of them were not personally initiated by him; they were drawn to his ideas and ideals long after his demise. The last six are said to have belonged to the order of Rāmānuja and to have left it along with Rāmānanda. Besides these twelve, Rāmānanda had a number of other followers, most of whom came from the lower castes; we find a few women also among them. He held that when a devotee surrendered his life to the divine will, his former life was lost in God, and a new life began for him.

RAVIDĀSA AND MĪRĀBĀĪ

Ravidāsa (Raidās) was a cobbler by birth, but his religious life was as exalted and pure as it was deep. There are over thirty hymns of Ravidāsa collected in the *Granth Sāhib* of the Sikhs. Kabīr also has expressed more than once his deep reverence for him. Ravidāsa was the worshipper of the one infinite God, who is above and beyond all religious sects and without beginning or end. He preached that the Lord resides within the hearts of His devotees, and cannot be known through the performance of any rites and ceremonies. Only one who has felt the pangs of divine love will find Him, and the highest expression of religion in life is the service of man.

It is said that Jhālī, the queen of Chitore, received her initiation into religious life from him, and Mīrābāī also completed her spiritual discipleship under his guidance.

Mīrābāī was the daughter of Rājā Ratan Siṅgh and the daughter-in-law of Mahārāṇā Saṅga of Mewar. She was devoted to God from her infancy. Her nine or ten years of domestic life with her husband Rājā Bhojarāja were years of quiet and unperturbed happiness; but her troubles began when she became a widow. Driven by the unjust treatment of her brother-in-law, she first sought refuge in her father's home, but finally gave up the world altogether and adopted the life of an ascetic. The story goes that Mīrā, a worshipper of Giridharalāla at first, was later initiated by Ravidāsa into the worship of the One and the Infinite. But the details of her personal life are uncertain. She is one of the greatest women saints of India, and her numerous songs, full of divine fervour, are sung all over the country.

SENĀ, DHANNĀ, AND PĪPĀ

Senā, another disciple of Rāmānanda, was a barber by caste. The Rājā of Bandhogarh, moved by a deep reverence for his religious life, accepted him as his *guru*. His descendants continue to recognize the family of Senā as their preceptors to the present day.

Dhannā, a peasant and Jāṭ by caste, was born about A.D. 1415.

Pīpā, born about A.D. 1425, was the ruler of a small principality of Rajasthan. When he adopted the religious life, his youngest wife also left home with him. His monastery at Pipawat near Dwarka is famous even today, and still attracts devout people.

SUKHĀNANDA AND SURĀSURĀNANDA

Sukhānanda came of a family of Tāntrika worshippers. When he came under the influence of Rāmānanda, his spiritual life attained its fullness in *jñāna, karma,* and *bhakti.* His daily round of activities was an intrinsic part of his life of worship and meditation ; thus his actions formed, as it were, a rosary of beads for remembering the name of God, which won him the title of 'Karmajāpī'.

When Surāsurānanda left his home, his wife wished to accompany him in his religious quest. He did not permit her at first, but finally acquiesced at the request of his *guru.*

KABĪR

We come last to the greatest of Rāmānanda's disciples, Kabīr, the central personality in the religious history of mediaeval India. During the middle ages, there was in North India not a single movement for freedom, whether spiritual or intellectual, that did not bear the stamp of Kabīr's influence. There has been a great deal of controversy around the question of his date, but most probably he was born in A.D. 1398.

Kabīr was the son of a Mohammedan weaver. These weavers had formerly been Hindus, and their place was very low in the Hindu as well as in the Mohammedan society. Thus they were free from the burden of useless religious traditions and customs. In such a free and untrammelled family was this great soul born.

Kabīr received a new impetus from Rāmānanda and struck firmly at the root of caste-distinctions, idolatry, pilgrimages, vows, fasts, and all the external paraphernalia of religious life. His relation with the Hindus and Mohammedans was equally cordial. He preached to the members of all castes, both men and women, without any distinction.

Though he led a religious life, Kabīr married, and it is said that the name of his wife was Loī. His son Kamāl was both a thinker and a devotee. When, after his father's death, he was requested to organize a sect in his father's name, he answered, 'My father had striven throughout his life against all forms of sectarianism ; how can I, his son, destroy his ideal and thereby commit his spiritual murder?' This remark estranged many of Kabīr's disciples from Kamāl.

After Kabīr's death, his Mohammedan disciples organized themselves in Maghar, where they founded a monastery ; his Hindu disciples were organized into an order by Surat Gopāla, with their centre in Banaras.

The chief scripture of this sect is the well-known *Bījak*. In course of time, this centre leaned more and more towards Vedāntic doctrines.

Kabīr believed in a simple and natural life. He himself wove cloth and sold it in the market like any ordinary weaver. He did not interpret religious life as a life of idleness ; he held that all should toil and earn and help each other, but none should hoard money. There is no fear of corruption from wealth, if it is kept constantly in circulation in the service of humanity.

Kabīr tried to express the simple thoughts of a simple heart in the common language of the people. He said, 'O Kabīr, Sanskrit is the water in a well, the language of the people is the flowing stream'. His simple words had infinite power.

He exhorted: 'Be truthful, be natural. Truth alone is natural. Seek this truth within your own heart, for there is no truth in the external religious symbols and observances—neither in the sects nor in the holy vows, neither in religious garb nor in pilgrimages. Truth resides within the heart and is revealed in love, in strength, in compassion. Conquer hatred, and extend your love to all mankind, for God resides in all.

'The difference among faiths is only due to difference in names ; everywhere there is yearning for the same God. Why do the Hindus and Mohammedans quarrel for nothing? Keep at a distance all pride and vanity, insincerity and falsehood ; consider others the same as yourself ; let your heart be filled with love and devotion. Then alone will your struggle be successful. Life is transitory, do not waste your time, but take refuge in God. He is within your own heart ; so why do you fruitlessly search Him in holy places, in scriptures, in rites and ceremonials?'

Kabīr was not in favour of useless mortification of the flesh. He advised: 'Be pure, live a natural, simple life. The whole of creation is within your own self, behold the Lord of creation there. There is no distinction of the outer and the inner, for all distinctions have been harmonized in Him who is beyond all distinctions. In this harmony are truth and realization.'

Kabīr has left behind many poems and songs. The mystics of that age expressed themselves mostly through these channels. Kabīr was great both as a poet and as a singer.

SADNĀ AND NĀMADEVA

The devotee Sadan or Sadnā, a butcher by caste, did not belong to the group of Rāmānanda's disciples. It is stated in the *Bhaktamāla* that he conquered all passions and desires, and lived a life of strict religious discipline. Two songs composed by him are found in the *Granth Sāhib*.

There was a devotee named Nāmadeva in Mahārāṣṭra ; another Nāmadeva founded a sect and a monastery in the District of Gurdaspur in the Punjab. Ālam Shāh, the last of the Sayyids, built this monastery of Nāmadeva and made an endowment for it in A.D. 1446. There was another Nāmadeva in Bulandshahr, who was a calico-printer. The Nāmadeva of Marwar was a carder of cotton.

ANANTĀNANDA AND NĀBHĀDĀSA

Anantānanda, though a follower of Rāmānanda, was outside the group of his immediate disciples. His monastery at Galta near Jaipur is well known even now. His disciple Kṛṣṇadāsa Paihārī had Agradāsa and Kīlha as his disciples. Kīlha founded a sect called Khākī in the north-west of India, while Agradāsa is better known as the *guru* of the great Nābhā. Nābhā was an 'untouchable' by birth ; but his name has become immortal as the author of the *Bhaktamāla* or life-stories of devotees, a work he composed at the command of his *guru*. The commentary on this great work was written by Priyādāsa.

TULASĪDĀSA AND SŪRADĀSA

Tulasīdāsa was born in a Brāhmaṇa family, long after Kabīr, and was inspired by the spiritual life of Rāmānanda. He flourished in the sixteenth century ; but the date and place of his birth are uncertain. He composed the great *Rāmacaritamānasa* or the *Rāmāyaṇa* in Hindi verse, which was, and still is, a great spiritual support of a large number of devotees throughout North India, and even in some parts of the South. His other work, the *Vinayapatrikā,* is a book of prayers uttered from the depths of a heart filled with fervent devotion. He does not belong to the group of Kabīr, Dādū, and other free spirits of the middle ages, because he did not reject the caste system and the other social and religious conventions of the time ; but his high poetic vision and deep devotion won him many admirers from among the liberal-minded Mohammedans of his time.

Sūradāsa was a great poet of the literature dedicated to Kṛṣṇa, as Tulasīdāsa was of the literature of Rāma. He belongs to the first half of the sixteenth century ; his date is fixed by some as between A.D. 1483 and 1563. He is said to have been blind from his very birth. His songs are sung all over India.

DHARMADĀSA AND MALŪKDĀSA

Dharmadāsa, a disciple of Kabīr, was a Baniā or merchant by caste, and founded a monastery at Chhatisgarh in Madhya Pradesh. Followers of his faith can be found in several parts of India. Dharmadāsa was a married man, and the heads of his order were required to marry. The line of teachers of this order has now become extinct.

Malūkdāsa (A.D. 1574-1682), one of the many followers of Kabīr, was born towards the end of the sixteenth century in the District of Allahabad. He was kind and compassionate, and, though a religious man, he lived the life of a householder. The monasteries of his sect are found all over North India and even beyond, from Bihar to Kabul. He too preached against the worship of images and other external forms of religion, and his followers rely entirely on the grace of God for their salvation. He was against mortification of the flesh, and taught that the true path of spirituality lay in the simple devotion of the heart.

DĀDŪ AND HIS FOLLOWERS

The most famous of the followers of Kabīr's ideals was Dādū. He was born of Brāhmaṇa parents in Ahmedabad in A.D. 1544 and died in 1603 in the village of Narāṇā or Nārāyaṇa in Rajasthan, where his followers (Dādū-panthīs) have now their chief centre. The great dream of his life was to unite all the divergent faiths in one bond of love and comradeship, and he founded the 'Brahma-sampradāya' or 'Parabrahma-sampradāya' to give effect to this great ideal. His sayings possess great depth and liberality and show clear traces of the influence of Kabīr.

Dādū believed not in the authority of scriptures, but in the value of self-realization. To attain this realization, we must divest ourselves of all sense of the ego and surrender our lives entirely to God. All men and women are as brothers and sisters in the presence of God. He resides within the hearts of men, and it is there that we must meditate on Him. Union with God is possible only through love and devotion, and it is deepened not by prayers, but by joining our service to His service of the universe. We are united with God when, shedding all sins and impurities, we sincerely surrender ourselves to the divine will.

Dādū taught: 'Be humble and free from egotism ; be compassionate and devoted in service ; be a hero, fearless and energetic ; free your mind from sectarianism, and from all the meaningless forms and semblances of religion ; be forgiving by nature and firm in your faith. The path of realization becomes easier, if you can find a true teacher.'

He himself was very simple by nature and strong in his faith, and his prayers were full of depth and sweetness. He was a householder, and he believed that the natural life of a householder was best suited for spiritual realization.

His two sons, Garībdāsa and Maskīndāsa, were men of very high spiritual attainments ; and his two daughters, Nānībāī and Mātābāī, spent their lives in devotion and have left behind them sayings of exceptional beauty.

At the request of Dādū, his disciples made a collection of the devotional writings of all the different sects, calculated to help men in their striving towards God. Such an anthology of the religious literature of different sects was perhaps the first of its kind in the world, for the *Granth Sāhib* was first compiled in A.D. 1604, while this anthology was completed some years before A.D. 1600. This collection includes many sayings of Mohammedan saints like Kāzī Kadam, Shaikh Farid, Kāzī Mohammed, Shaikh Bāhawad, and Bakhnā.

SUNDARADĀSA AND RAJJAB

Among the many disciples of Dādū, Sundaradāsa (A.D. 1597-1689), Rajjab, and others were distinguished personalities. Dādū persuaded his disciples to render into simple Hindi from Sanskrit the abstruse philosophical truths. He also made it a practice among them to write in Hindi prose and verse. Dādū admitted both Hindus and Mohammedans to his discipleship, and there have been many *gurus* in his sect who came of Mohammedan families. Even today, in Rajjab's branch of Dādū's sect, any one who attains to the height of spiritual realization is accepted as the head of the order, whether he be a Hindu or a Mohammedan. The songs and prayers of Rajjab are universal in appeal and superb for their spirit of devotion.

Rajjab says: 'It is dark all round, the only light is within our own hearts. Of what avail are renunciation and mortification? Will they bring us any nearer to the Light? Let your worship find its fulfilment in the temple and mosque of life ; if the mind creates trouble there, turn the unbeliever out. Let your spiritual aspiration be fulfilled in the realization of the wholeness of life—compassion and strength and wisdom and devotion, you must not neglect any of these parts of life. Be heroes, for it is only the hero who will attain the new vision.'

He also taught: 'There are as many sects as there are men ; thus has come into being the diversity of spiritual endeavour. The sacred stream of the Gaṅgā rises from the blessed feet of Nārāyaṇa, but the feet of the Lord are in the hearts of the devotees. Thus from the heart of every devotee flows a Gaṅgā of thought. If I can unite all the streams of thought in this world, such a confluence would indeed be the holiest of places.'

He further said: 'This universe is the Veda, the creation is the *Qur'an.*

The *paṇḍitas* and the *kāzīs* are indeed deceived when they think that the whole world is encompassed within the leaves of their dry books. The heart of the worshipper is the page on which the story of the universal truth is being written in letters of life. When all these hearts unite in the vast universe of man, there you will find all the Vedas and the *Qur'an*. This is the living Veda, the living *Qur'an* ; study that. Why do you waste your time over the dead books?'

OTHER KABĪR-PANTHĪS

The sect of Kabīr was split into twelve different schools, when his religion was preached in Kathiawad and Gujarat. Of these twelve *panthas* or schools, the Udās-panthīs, though followers of Kabīr, have beaten all the orthodox schools in their insistence on formalism and meaningless ceremonial purity. They have none of the lofty ideals of Kabīr, but merely cling to external purity.

Bhān Sāheb was the leader of the only branch of Kabīr's school that worked in Kathiawad with a living spirit and broad-mindedness. He flourished about the first half of the eighteenth century. His son Kṣem was also famed for his spiritual attainment, but the most influential of Bhān Sāheb's disciples was the 'untouchable' Jīvanadāsa. Ravi Sāheb, another disciple of his, was also a religious man of celebrity. Bhān Sāheb cherished the desire of removing the spiritual darkness and degradation of his people with the help of his disciples, which earned them the nickname 'Bhān army'.

Dharaṇīdāsa was born in A.D. 1556 in a Kāyastha family of the Chapra District. His teachings are also very liberal. He says: 'The only value of action is in realizing the ideal in this workaday world. The Lord of our hearts is not far from us ; we realize Him only through the pangs of love. External observances like vows and pilgrimages are useless ; the only thing that counts is love and longing.'

GURU NĀNAK

Guru Nānak (A.D. 1469-1538) was born at Talwandi near Lahore. He preached *nām* (the Name of God) as a potent means of religious realization. In his time, the impact of Islam on the people of North India was very powerful. He founded Sikhism and sought to harmonize in it the tenets of both Hinduism and Islam. He also tried to do away with caste-distinctions and to liberalize other social practices. He was succeeded by nine other Gurus, of whom Guru Gobind Singh, who organized the Sikhs into a powerful religious and political body, is the most famous.

PURĀṆ BHAGAT AND CHAJJŪ BHAGAT

The Yogīs Purāṇ Bhagat and Chajjū Bhagat are well known throughout the Punjab. Bābālāl, too, though born (*c.* A.D. 1590) in Malwa, lived and taught in the Punjab. His views greatly resembled those of Kabīr and Dādū. He declared: 'Self-restraint, purity of heart, compassion, service, simplicity, right vision, and conquest of the ego constitute the path of love and devotion that leads to God. The bliss of this love through communion with God cannot be expressed in words.' The liberality and depth of his religious life brought him into close contact with Dārā Shukoh.

DĀRĀ SHUKOH AND CARAṆADĀSA

Indian tradition remembers Dārā Shukoh not so much as an emperor's son, but as a mystic philosopher. The great dream of his life—a dream shattered by his untimely death—was the brotherhood of all faiths and the unity of mankind. After him, this great vision of unity was lost in the atmosphere of hatred and rivalry created by the warring sects and religious schools. One of the admirers of Dārā Shukoh was the devotee Śarmād, who was executed during the reign of Aurangzeb for the liberality of his religious views. Śarmād fearlessly declared his convictions up to the last moment. Āzam Shāh, a son of Aurangzeb, was an admirer of the poetry and spiritual practices of the Vaiṣṇavas.

The Āzāds of this period, though Mohammedans, held very liberal views about religion. The Rasūlshāhīs of Agra also followed the *yoga* and Tāntrika practices. They were lovers of poetry as well as wine.

Caraṇadāsa, born in A.D. 1703 in the village Dehara in Alwar, was one of the many whose religious outlook was broadened under the influence of Dārā Shukoh. The sect founded by him is noted for its moral purity. His emphasis on purity of life did much to check the corruption prevailing in society at the time.

Caraṇadāsa forbids the following: false, indecent, or harsh words, disputation, theft, adultery, hatred, evil-wishing, animosity, and pride. He recommends the following virtues: piety befitting a true householder, good company, reverence for one's own *guru* and for holy men, and devotion to God. His sect includes both householders and ascetics. The followers of this sect dress simply and unostentatiously.

Caraṇadāsa taught: 'This universe is permeated by Brahman; so symbols like the *tulasī* plant and the *śālagrāma* are useless. A good and pure life is the first word in religious life; love and devotion are its soul. But these are futile unless they are expressed through service, for the emotions of the heart are substantiated by action.' Two women relatives of his,

Dayābāī and Sahajobāī, reached great heights of spiritual realization through contact with him.

ŚRĪ CAITANYA AND ŚAṄKARA DEVA

Śrī Caitanya (A.D. 1485-1533) was born in a Brāhmaṇa family in Navadvīpa. He founded a new school of Vaiṣṇavism and was instrumental in spreading the cult of devotion in Bengal. He had several illustrious disciples and followers, who kept the flame of devotion burning bright and carried his doctrines to the masses in several parts of North India. He had a Mohammedan disciple too. Caitanya emphasized on all-embracing love and service of living beings as a means of God-realization.

Śaṅkara Deva of Assam (A.D. 1486-1568), a Kāyastha by birth, was another religious reformer with equally liberal views. The sect he founded admits Mohammedans and Nagas into its fold, and does not believe in images or temples. There are instances in it of Brāhmaṇas accepting the discipleship of Śūdras.

SOME MINOR SECTS OF BENGAL AND ORISSA

The Yogī Pantha (Yogī sect) also inspired many of its members to compose songs and lyrics. The influence of the songs of Gopīcandra of Bengal can be observed all over India. It is chiefly the Mohammedans who compose and sing these songs, and they are known in the north-west of India as Bhartharis or Bhartṛharis. Though Mohammedans, they wear the ochre robe of Hindu ascetics, and their presence is indispensable in many Hindu ceremonies.

The Nātha Pantha and the Nirañjanī Pantha were prevalent in Bengal and Orissa before Kabīr preached his philosophy. Later, the schools known as Mahimā Pantha and Kumbhīpaṭiā Pantha were founded in Orissa. The latter school, founded by Mukundadeva, does not believe in the efficacy of temples and images or in the superiority of Brāhmaṇas.

The numerous religious schools of Bengal such as Khuśī Viśvāsī, Sāheb Dhanī, Rāmavallabhī, Jagamohinī, Balarāmī, Neḍā (the shaven), Āul-Bāul-Darbeś-Sāiñ, Saṁyogī, and Kartābhajā were all greatly influenced by the Sahajī, Nirañjanī, and Nātha cults, and to a certain extent by Islam. These schools do not believe in castes or sects, temples or images, and do not also differentiate between the Hindus and the Mohammedans.

THE SUFI MYSTICS OF SIND

Any account of the mystics of Sind must begin with Shāh Karīm, who lived about A.D. 1600. He received his first religious inspiration from a

Vaiṣṇava saint near Ahmedabad, who initiated him into the mysteries of *Om*. This symbol served as a beacon-light to him.

The next mystic worthy of mention is Shāh Ināyat, a universally respected figure. When the Hindus of Sind, under the oppression of the Kalhora kings, were fleeing in numbers to save their life and faith, it was he who sheltered many such fugitive families in his own hermitage. His faith that God is not the property of any particular sect finally led to his execution.

But it is Shāh Latīf who holds the highest place among the mystics of Sind. He was the greatest poet and singer of the province, and his songs are sung by people even at the present day. His shrine at Bhit was a weekly meeting-place for both Hindus and Mohammedans of either sex, for spiritual communion.

It was not unusual to find in Sind a Hindu as the *guru* of the Mohammedans, or a Mohammedan as the *guru* of the Hindus. The songs of the Sufi mystic poets Bedīl and Bekaś are still widely sung by Sindhi men and women. The real name of Bekaś was Mohammed Husain. He died at the age of twenty-two, but has left a deep impression on the religious life of Sind. The poets Rohal and Qutub also belonged to the same fraternity, and have left behind them songs that are as sweet as they are profound. At their shrines both Hindus and Mohammedans used to congregate and keep all-night vigils, singing religious songs.

THE NEO-SUFIS OF DELHI

After the Sufis of Sind we come to the neo-Sufis of Delhi. About A.D. 1600, there lived near Delhi a Sufi mystic by the name of Bāwrī Sāheb. He was the *guru* of Biru Sāheb, a Hindu, who again was the *guru* of the great mystic Yārī Sāheb.

Yārī Sāheb, who flourished about A.D. 1668-1725, was free from all sectarianism. He says that the eyes should be painted with the dust of the *guru's* feet as with collyrium. His poems, in which the name of Allah is mentioned along with that of Rāma and Hari, are full of abstruse metaphysical truths. He says, 'This creation is a painting of the Creator on the canvas of void with the brush of love. He who has not experienced this joy through love will never know it through reasoning. Men and women are as bubbles on the ocean of divine love'.

THE SATNĀMĪS

Gulāl Sāheb and Jagjīvan were the disciples of Bullā, a disciple of Yārī Sāheb. Jagjīvan was the founder of a sect known as Satnāmī (Satyanāmī) and was, according to Grierson, born in A.D. 1682. He taught that spiritual realization was possible only through the grace of God, and he insisted on purity as the essence of a religious life. His aspiration was to unite the two streams of Hindu and Muslim religious life through love.

Bhikhā, who lived about A.D. 1720, was the disciple of Gulāl Sāheb and the *guru* of Gobind Sāheb. The latter had as his disciple the great Paltū Sāheb, who is remembered with respect in the religious tradition of India, especially for his famous poems in *kuṇḍaliā* metre. We shall speak of him later.

There were some other sects known by the same name of Satnāmī, both before and after Jagjīvan's time. One of these was founded by Ghāsīdāsa of the cobbler caste. The followers of this faith do not touch animal food or wine, do not believe in image-worship, and, though considered 'untouchables', do not acknowledge the superiority of the Brāhmaṇa and other castes. According to them, superiority consists in purity of character and conduct and devotion to God.

THE ALAKHNĀMĪS AND LĀLDĀSĪS

Another religious man of the same caste was Lālgīr or Lālbeg, who founded a sect known as Alakhnāmī or Alakh-gīr, which has a great vogue in Bikaner. The followers of this sect do not worship images, but meditate upon the invisible One who cannot be perceived by the senses. The first steps of a religious life, according to them, are non-violence, catholicity, charity, and purity. 'Do not be anxious about the next world,' they say, 'you will attain the highest bliss in this. Heaven and hell are within you.' They greet each other with the words '*Alakh kaho*' (take the name of God who is invisible).

Like the Kumbhīpaṭiā sect, of a much later date, the Alakhnāmī sect also does not acknowledge the superiority of the higher castes. They are not sorry that they are debarred from entering the temples, for they regard these as low places, where one is diverted from truth. The monks of this sect are noted for their gentle and restrained behaviour. They do not mind if they are refused alms.

The Lāldāsī sect was founded by Lāldāsa, who was born in a robber tribe of Rajasthan called Meo, in the latter half of the sixteenth century. The followers of this sect mostly come from the same tribe. This school has been deeply influenced both by Kabīr and Dādū, and their devotion consists chiefly in remembering and singing the name of God.

DARIYĀ SĀHEB AND GARĪBDĀSA

The followers of Dariyā Sāheb, though they do not call themselves Satnāmī, worship God under the name of Satnām or Satyanām. Dariyā

Sāheb was the son of Pīran Shāh, a great devotee of God, who belonged to a well-known Kṣatriya family of Ujjain. His ancestors once ruled in Jagdishpur near Buxar, and Pīran Shāh is said to have become a Mohammedan under compulsion. Dariyā Sāheb was deeply influenced in his religious life by the teachings of Kabīr. His followers pray like the Mohammedans in a standing posture called *korniś*, while their prayers in the sitting posture are known as *sizdā*. They do not believe in scriptures, rites and observances, pilgrimages, vows, vestments, or *mantras*. The worship of images or incarnations, caste-distinctions, the partaking of meat or wine, and all forms of violence are all strictly forbidden in this sect.

There was another Dariyā Sāheb who was born in A.D. 1676 in Marwar, in a Mohammedan family of cotton-carders. On account of a strong similarity of teachings, he is believed by some to be an incarnation of Dādū. He has many followers in Rajasthan, where the monasteries of his sect are scattered in different places. He worshipped God under the name of Rāma and Parabrahman. The section entitled *Brahma-paricaya* in his collected poems deals with the mysteries of *yoga*. His sect includes both householders and ascetics among its members, and his songs are very popular with both Hindus and Mohammedans.

There were many mystics bearing the name Garībdāsa. The earliest one was the son of Dādū. The second Garībdāsa was born in a Jāṭ family in the village Chhurani in the Rohtak District in A.D. 1717 and died in 1778. It is said that he was given spiritual initiation by Kabīr in a dream. This Garībdāsa was a householder, and the heads of his religious organization are also householders. He worshipped God under the different names of Rāma, Hari, and Allah. He also preached that all external forms and observances of religion were unreal and that the only true path was the path of love and devotion. His prayers are extremely touching. There was a third Garībdāsa in the Punjab, who tried his best to bring about a synthesis of the Hindu and the Mohammedan religious practices.

ŚIVANĀRĀYAṆA

Śivanārāyaṇa was born in a Rajput family in the Ballia District about A.D. 1710. He was a pure monist, and was completely against image-worship. He believed God to be without form and attributes. Any use of animal food or intoxicants is strictly forbidden in his sect, and the path laid down is one of single-minded devotion, purity of life, self-restraint, and love for humanity. This sect was open to members of all creeds and castes, and the union of all forms of faith in one universal religion was the dream of Śivanārāyaṇa's life. Śivanārāyaṇa was inspired, though not directly, by the ideas of Dārā Shukoḥ, and his philosophy contains elements from both the

Hindu and the Mohammedan religious traditions. It is said that Emperor Mohammed Shāh (A.D. 1719-48) was converted to his faith, and the poets Walī Allāh, Ābrū, and Nāzī also had a deep reverence for his spiritual life and teachings.

BULLE SHĀH

Bulle Shāh was a different person from Bullā Sāheb, the disciple of Yārī Sāheb. Some say that he was born in A.D. 1703, in a Sayyid family in the city of Constantinople (Istanbul), and that at a very young age he walked all the way to the Punjab hungering for spiritual truth. In the Indian mode of religious practice he found precisely what he was seeking, and settled down to a life of meditation and worship at Kasur. He was a fierce critic of the *Qur'an* and all other scriptures, and neither the Hindu nor the Mohammedan theologians could cope with him in argument. He was buried also at Kasur, and the place attracts numerous pilgrims and holy men.

Bulle Shāh says: 'You will find God neither in the mosque nor in the *Ka'aba,* neither in the *Qur'an* and other holy books nor in formal prayers. What was easy to understand, the scholars have made more intricate. Bullā, you will not find salvation either in Mecca or in the Gaṅgā ; you will find it only when you lay down your ego.

'I found the highest peace and joy when I discovered Allah within my own heart ; through death I have reached the life eternal ; I am ever journeying forward.

'O Bullā, intoxicate thyself with the wine of divine love. Men will slander you and call you a hundred names ; when they abuse you with the name of *kāfir,* say, "Yes, friend, you are right".'

PRĀṆANĀTHA AND SANTARĀMA

Prāṇanātha was born in Kathiawad, but he lived and preached in Bundelkhand between the years A.D. 1700 and 1750. He mastered both the Hindu and the Mohammedan holy books, and he too dreamed of the Hindus and Mohammedans being united in one great brotherhood. King Chatrasāl was one of his devoted admirers. Prāṇanātha had both Hindu and Mohammedan followers. His sect is very liberal in its outlook and respects both the religions equally. This strictly monotheistic sect is called 'Dhāmī', because the members speak of God as the *dhāman* or home. Their religious life is founded on moral purity, compassion, service, and love of humanity. In their places of worship, both Hindus and Mohammedans pray and dine together.

Santarāma or Rāmacaraṇa was born in the village Surasen of Jaipur between A.D. 1715 and 1720. His disciples are known as Rāmsanehīs or lovers of Rāma. They also do not believe in image-worship, and they approach God through the path of love.

NARASIṀHA MEHTĀ AND SAHAJĀNANDA

Narasī or Narasiṁha Mehtā was a well-known saint of Gujarat, who flourished in the second half of the fifteenth century. He wrote songs in Gujarati depicting the love of Rādhā and Kṛṣṇa, which are included in the *Suratasaṅgrāma*. Some of his devotional songs and prayers are even now very popular among the Gujarati-speaking people.

Sahajānanda was born in A.D. 1780 in Gonda District, and founded the sect known as Svāmī Nārāyaṇī. He succeeded in purifying the religious atmosphere of his province. His sect admits Mohammedans as well as Hindus from the lower castes. Its religious centre in Gujarat is very rich.

PALṬŪ SĀHEB, TULASĪ SĀHEB, AND DEDHRĀJA

The last three religious reformers of the mediaeval period are Palṭū Sāheb, Tulasī Sāheb Hāthrasī, and Dedhrāja. They are all contemporaries of Raja Rammohun Roy, and belong to the transitional period between the mediaeval and the modern age.

Palṭū Sāheb, the disciple of the saint Gobind Sāheb, lived from A.D. 1757 to 1825, and is sometimes called Kabīr the Second. The following are some of his sayings: 'The upper castes have ruined the lower castes, and ruined themselves too. He who has seen the truth makes no distinction between his own country and foreign countries. The highest truth is not the objective truth, but that which is realized within one's heart. There is no higher spiritual discipline than self-restraint and strength. God is not the property of any particular sect. Rise above your petty denominations of caste and sect. Humility is a virtue. Serve others and be gentle. You cannot see the truth as it is, unless you are possessed of naturalness. The truth is within; in vain do you seek it outside. He who has not seen God in man has exiled Him also from the temple.'

It is said that Tulasī Sāheb was born about A.D. 1760 in the family of the Peshwas. He was called Hāthrasī because of his settling at Hathras. He was an adept in both the Hindu and the Mohammedan scriptures and spiritual practices. He too holds that external observances and actions count for nothing; the worship within the heart is the only true worship. It consists in the establishment of a true relationship between one's own self and the universe. He was a bitter critic of the anomalies of all scriptures. Once seeing a Brāhmaṇa, who was bathing in the Gaṅgā, tell a Śūdra to move away considering him impure, he remarked, 'How inconsistent are your scriptures! They ascribe great holiness to the Gaṅgā because of its issuing from the feet of Viṣṇu, while they condemn as unholy the Śūdras emanating from the same source!' He passed away in 1842 in the village of Jogia near Hathras.

This brief account of the mediaeval saints of North India may be concluded with the story of Dedhrāja. He was born in A.D. 1771 in a Brāhmaṇa family in the Narnaul District. Driven by extreme poverty, he left his home for Agra at the age of fourteen, during the rule of Mādhoji Rāo Sindhia. He found employment in the house of Dewān Dharmadāsa, and there came in touch with the religious men of all sects, both Hindu and Mohammedan. Having experienced the truth within his own heart, he started preaching his own independent, liberal views at the age of thirty-three, and underwent much suffering throughout his life for the sake of his spiritual convictions. He preached against caste-distinctions, and himself married a Baniā's daughter. Later he returned to his native place to preach his faith, and he was imprisoned by Najāwat Āli, the Nawab of Jhajhar, for his heretical beliefs. His long term of suffering within the prison-walls came to an end when, during a political rising in the State, the warders set all the prisoners free. He then went to a village called Chhurina, and lived there till his death at the age of eighty-one.

His followers hold: 'God is one, unique, eternal, omnipresent, and ineffable. All images or symbols which attempt to represent Him are untrue. Caste-distinctions are erroneous conceptions of the mind. Men and women have an equal claim to the spiritual life, and the seclusion of women is an insult to them.' Hence the women of this sect enjoy freedom and join in the singing during worship. Equal respect is paid by the followers of this sect to the spiritual practices of both Hindus and Mohammedans, and God is worshipped by them under different names. They do not regard books like the *Rāmāyaṇa* and the *Mahābhārata* as infallible, though they accept their moral teachings. Their compositions are in the vernacular. This sect is also known as Naṅgā (naked), because its women do not observe seclusion. It believes in the fraternity of all faiths and in the kinship of all men and women who are the children of one and the same God.

28

TULASĪDĀSA AND HIS TEACHINGS

KNOWLEDGE and devotion, *jñāna* and *bhakti,* are two paths laid down in the Hindu scriptures as means of attaining God ; and those who follow these two ways wield a power in the world that kings and statesmen might well envy. For, in the whole of creation, there is nothing of such abiding value for the generations to come as saintliness of character. Deep wisdom and boundless love are the characteristics of a saint. The *jñānin* sees only the unity in the diversity of the world and so feels himself one with the whole of creation, and the *bhakta* radiates a peace—active and exalted—which silently and gently communicates itself to others, transforming many lives and lightening hearts that are heavy-laden with the sorrows and cares of the world.

One such saint, who lived in the sixteenth century, was the poet Tulasīdāsa. Modern scholars dispute the claim of his biographer, Veṇī Mādhavadāsa (Beṇī Mādhodās), that he lived for 127 years (A.D. 1497-1623) and assign to him a smaller span of life (1532-1623). He was a prince among devotees, and his *Rāmacaritamānasa* is classed among the best of the devotional literature of India.

EARLY LIFE

Tulasīdāsa, born of Brāhmaṇa parents, was a little orphan boy, when he was picked up from the streets of an obscure village in Uttar Pradesh by a *sādhu* called Naraharidāsa, who had been commanded in a dream to look after the little boy and instruct him in the life-story of Rāma. In obedience to this command, he became Tulasī's benefactor and *guru,* and made himself responsible for his literary and religious education as well as for his general upbringing. Naraharidāsa was himself a disciple of the great Vaiṣṇava saint and teacher, Rāmānanda, who gave a new impetus to the *bhakti* movement of the middle ages and left behind a band of eminent disciples like Ravidāsa and Kabīr.

Naraharidāsa took Tulasī to Ayodhyā, where he performed his sacred thread ceremony, gave him the '*Rāma*' *mantra,* and started his education in earnest. After ten months, they left Ayodhyā together for Sūkara-kheta, a place of pilgrimage on the banks of the river Sarayū in the District of Gonda. Here the master and the disciple lived in close association for five years, and it was at this place, as we learn from his *Rāmacaritamānasa* (*Bāla-kāṇḍa*), that Tulasī first heard the fascinating story of his *iṣṭadeva,* Rāma, whose divinely human life he was destined to relate and interpret to the world:

> I heard this story from my *guru* in Sūkara-kheta.
> Being a child and without understanding, I was unable
> to grasp it....
> Still my *guru* repeated it over and over again,
> And I assimilated a little of it, according to my understanding.

These lines give us some idea of the patience and perseverance that Naraharidāsa must have practised to educate this little beggar boy. And now, perhaps, we understand why ardent homage has been paid to his holy feet in beautiful lines in the opening verse of the following passage, which contains a pun on the word 'Narahari':

> I salute the lotus feet of my *guru,*
> The ocean of compassion, and God (Hari) in the form of man (*nara*),
> Whose words like the rays of the sun
> Dispel the heavy darkness of overpowering delusion.

Tulasī remained with his *guru* for six years in all. In spite of his low assessment of himself, he proved to be an exceptionally intelligent pupil with a very good memory. During this period, he had a good grounding in the grammar of Pāṇini ; and, as he himself says, the story of Rāma's life and its significance and lesson to humanity were taught to him over and over again. Another *sādhu,* called Śeṣa Sanātana, was greatly attracted by the bright and winning ways of Tulasī, and he persuaded Naraharidāsa to leave the boy with him for further education. Tulasī stayed with Śeṣa Sanātana and studied the Vedas and the Vedānta for fifteen years.

Tulasīdāsa married and lived a householder's life, but some chance words of detachment spoken by his wife opened his eyes, and he left home and took up *sannyāsa.* After performing the four great pilgrimages, namely, to Rāmeśvara, Dvārakā, Purī, and Badarikāśrama, he settled down finally in the holy city of Banaras, to which he always returned after short visits to Ayodhyā, Citrakūṭa, and other places.

HIS WORKS AND THEIR CHARACTER

Tulasīdāsa is known to be the author of more than a dozen books. The most noteworthy among them are *Gītāvalī, Kavitta Rāmāyaṇa* or *Kavitāvalī, Vinayapatrikā,* and *Rāmacaritamānasa,* the last named being by far the most important, the best known, and the largest of his works. His other books are *Dohāvalī, Vairāgya-sandīpinī, Rāmājñā-praśnāvalī, Rāma-*

lalā-nahachū, Baravai Rāmāyaṇa, Pārvatī-maṅgala, Jānakī-maṅgala, Kṛṣṇa-gītāvalī, Hanumad-bāhuka, and *Rāma-satasaī.*

Gītāvalī and *Kavitāvalī* are both supplementary to the main narrative poem, *Rāmacaritamānasa. Gītāvalī,* as its name denotes, consists of songs set to music and written in Brajabhāṣā dialect. The poet depicts the tenderness of Rāma's character, and so the sentiment of sweetness called *madhura rasa* reigns supreme here. 'In this way he gives the whole history of Rāmacandra in a delightful style, quite different from that of his formal epic. There is no verse in the book which is not a complete little picture, and most attractive of all are those in the first book, in which he tells of the baby life of his hero and his brothers' (Grierson).

The language of *Kavitāvalī* is a mixture of Āvadhī and Brajabhāṣā. His vocabulary is extraordinarily large in this book. 'His subject is heroic and, without having needless recourse to Sanskrit, he writes in a heroic style. In the battle-scene the words themselves by their very sound echo the clash of arms and the cries of the combatants, and, in the description of the burning of Laṅkā, the crackling of the flames' (Grierson).

The story as to how *Vinayapatrikā* came to be written throws light on the central theme of Tulasī's ideology. It is said that a homicide once came to Banaras on a pilgrimage of repentance, crying, 'For the love of Rāma, give alms to me, a homicide'. Tulasī, hearing the beloved name, gave him sacred food and declared him purified. When the Brāhmaṇas questioned Tulasī's action, he rebuked them for their lack of faith in the name of God; but they were not satisfied and asked for proof. It was at last agreed that, if the image of the sacred bull of Śiva in the Viśvanātha temple ate from the homicide's hand, they would accept Tulasī's judgement. The man was taken to the temple, and the bull ate out of his hands. This miracle had the effect of prompting thousands of men to lead good and reformed lives. The spirit of the modern age, Kali, offended at this sudden increase of piety, threatened to kill Tulasī. Thereupon Tulasī prayed to Hanumat, who appeared to him in a dream and asked him to become a complainant in the court of the Lord. The idea behind the composition of *Vinayapatrikā* is therefore that of a petition being presented to royalty. As supplications have first to be made to the door-keeper and courtiers for leave of access to the king, so in sweet humility Tulasī first addresses his prayers to Gaṇeśa, the Sun, Śiva-Pārvaṭī, Gaṅgā-Yamunā, Hanumat, *kṣetrapāla* of Kāśī, Citrakūṭa and its *pālaka* (protector), the brothers of Rāma, Sītā, and last of all to his master, Rāma. In this book, the majestic (*aiśvarya*) aspect of the Lord's character is kept in view; and Tulasī, as the supplicant, delights in effacing himself, so that the glory and greatness of his master, Rāma, may shine in undiminished splendour.

Rāmacaritamānasa, or the life-story of Rāma, proved to be a great force in preventing the disintegration of the Sanātana Dharma, and helped in giving back to the people confidence in themselves and faith in their own culture, which had been shaken by the Muslim rule. This great work proved to be an immediate success, and has been enshrined in the heart of the common man for the last four centuries. In all the Hindi-speaking provinces, many of its lines have become well-known quotations, and the influence of this book on the life and thought of the people cannot be over-estimated.

It is not to be imagined that this book is in any sense a translation of the *Rāmāyaṇa* of Vālmīki. The treatment of the hero's life is original, and there is a departure on many points from the epic of Vālmīki. It seems to follow more closely the *Adhyātma Rāmāyaṇa,* in which Śiva relates Rāma's life-story to Pārvatī. Tulasīdāsa's explanation for naming the work is both poetic and devotional. The *Rāmacarita,* he says, is the beautiful lake *Mānasa,* conceived in the mind of Śiva. For a long time he kept the *Mānasa* to himself, just as the waters of a lake remain secluded in the mountain, until one day the opportunity came to relate the whole story to Pārvatī. Scattered throughout the book and delicately woven into the texture of the story, we find literal translations of verses from the *Gītā,* the Upaniṣads, the *Bhāgavata,* and various other scriptures and echoes of many other works. Thus the wisdom of the sages was brought to the masses at large in their own familiar language.

Tulasīdāsa endeared himself to his countrymen, because, like Rāmānanda, he gave up the use of Sanskrit and wrote in the common language of the people. Banaras was the seat of Sanskrit learning and the stronghold of orthodoxy, and the opposition he met with from the pundits there was intense. His very life was in danger. But befitting his rôle as a teacher, and in refreshing contrast to his contemporaries, are the great qualities of vision and imagination that he showed in this departure from the intellectual conventions of his time. In an article entitled 'Tulasīdāsa, Poet and Religious Reformer', published in the *Journal of the Royal Asiatic Society,* 1903, Grierson writes, 'If we take the influence exercised by him at the present time, he is one of the three or four great writers of Asia. . . . Over the whole of the Gangetic valley this work is better known than the Bible is in England'. Enthusiastic praise was showered on *Rāmacaritamānasa* by Tulasī's contemporaries. Of particular interest is the following verse, ascribed to Akbar's minister, Abdur Rahīm Khānkhāna:

> The pure *Rāmacaritamānasa* is like life's breath to the holy ones ;
> It is the Veda to the Hindu, and verily the *Qur'an* itself to the Muslim.

PERSONAL AND IMPERSONAL GOD

The loving personal God of Rāmānuja, so full of grace and compassion to the Jīvas or bound souls, had already gained greater popularity than the formless Brahman of the Advaita Vedānta. Tulasīdāsa captured the imagination of the people further by making that Godhead live and move on earth. In giving form to the formless, he brought within the orbit of conceptual thought that Brahman which the Vedas describe as *neti* (not this). We are unable to meditate on the Nirguṇa Brahman, nor have we the patience or faith to practise austerities in the cave or the forest; but the very idea that God lived like one of us and shared our joys and sorrows brings peace and solace to the human heart.

Since the beginning of philosophical thought in India, the persistent question of how the Nirguṇa Brahman became Saguṇa has baffled man's intellect. This important metaphysical problem is presented by Tulasī in the form of a dialogue between Śiva and Pārvatī in the first canto of *Rāmacaritamānasa*. The latter asks:

> O Lord, sages, who are the knowers of Truth,
> Say that Rāma is Brahman without origin;
> Is he the same Rāma, who is the son of the king of Ayodhyā,
> Or is he some other unborn, unqualified, and invisible Being?
> If he is the king's son, how can he be Brahman?
> For the prince is distracted by the loss of his wife.
> Seeing his conduct, and hearing of his greatness,
> My intellect is confused.
>
> —*Bālakāṇḍa*, 107. 3, 4; 108.

To this question Śiva replies as follows:

> There is no difference between the qualified and the unqualified Brahman,
> So say the sages, the Purāṇas, the learned, and the Vedas.
> He who is unqualified, formless, and invisible
> Takes form through the love of his devotees.
> How is the unqualified, the qualified also?
> As water is identical with ice and hail-stone.
>
> —*Bālakāṇḍa*, 115. 1, 2.

KARMA

Having described the nature of God with and without form, in the second canto Tulasīdāsa brings in a description of the world. He also discusses the basic principle of the theory of Karma that we ourselves are responsible for our joys and sorrows in life. This theme is woven into the story in the following manner: After his banishment from his father's kingdom, on the second day Rāma halted on the banks of the Gaṅgā outside a small fishing village. The chief of the fishermen and Lakṣmaṇa kept guard at night, while Rāma and Sītā slept beneath an *aśoka* tree. The chief was inclined to blame Kaikeyī, the third queen of Daśaratha, for having sent Rāma to the forest. Lakṣmaṇa pacified him by speaking these words of deep wisdom:

No one gives happiness or sorrow to another,
O brother, we reap the fruit of our own action.
The meeting (of dear ones) and their separation, the good and
    evil happenings of life,
Friend, foe, and casual acquaintances are all knots of illusion.
Birth and death, prosperity and adversity, time and action,
And the world with all its complexity,
Land, home and town, wealth and family,
Heaven and hell, and all the concepts of life:
Though seen, heard, and thought over in the mind,
They are based on ignorance and do not exist in reality.

—*Ayodhyākāṇḍa,* 91. 2, 3, 4.

MĀYĀ

In spite of the seemingly Advaita doctrine propounded in the above passage, it is not to be supposed that Tulasīdāsa was a follower of Śaṅkara. He did not look upon the world as pure illusion as some Māyāvādins do. The following verses make this point clear:

Knowing all conscious and unconscious beings in the world
To be full of (Sītā and) Rāma,
With folded hands I salute the lotus feet of all.

—*Bālakāṇḍa,* 7c.

He is my best devotee, O Hanumat,
Who firmly believes that all beings, both
    movable and immovable,
Are the forms of the Lord,
And he is the servant of them all.

—*Kiṣkindhākāṇḍa,* 3.

The world as seen through space, time, and causation is Māyā. Māyā is unreal in the sense that the only reality is God; and yet, if Māyā had no reality, how could it produce the phenomenal world? All differentiation and change, creation, life, and destruction are the result of Māyā. Tulasīdāsa gives us his idea of Māyā in the following verse:

I and thou, mine and thine, this is Māyā,
Which has all embodied beings under its control.
Wherever sense and sense objects go, and as far as the mind
can take you,
Know all that, O brother, to be Māyā.
Listen to the difference in Māyā:
One is known as *vidyā* (knowledge) and the other as *avidyā*
(ignorance).
One is wicked and is the giver of sorrow;
Under its influence the embodied soul has fallen in the pit
of the world.
The other creates the world under the impulse of the three
qualities (of *sattva, rajas,* and *tamas*).
It is inspired by the Lord and has no power by itself.

—*Araṇyakāṇḍa,* 1. 1, 2, 3.

JĪVA

In describing the Jīva or the embodied soul, Tulasīdāsa says:

The Jīva is a part of God and is indestructible;
It is consciousness, pure, and blissful by nature.
O Master, it has fallen under the control of Māyā,
And is tied down like a parrot or a monkey.

—*Uttarakāṇḍa,* 116. 1, 2.

Tulasī's idea of the relationship between God, Māyā, and the embodied soul becomes clear from the following verse:

The proud Jīva is under the control of Māyā
And Māyā, the repository of all qualities, is controlled by God.

—*Uttarakāṇḍa,* 77. 3.

In talking of the paths of knowledge and devotion, he says:

The path of knowledge is like the sharp edge of a scimitar,
O king of the birds, one can fall from this path in the twinkling
of an eye,

But ignorance, the root of the round of birth and death,
Is destroyed through *bhakti* without much effort.

—*Uttarakāṇḍa*, 118. 1, 4.

DEVOTION TO GOD

To say that the path of devotion is easier than the path of knowledge is not sufficient for Tulasīdāsa ; he even makes the former superior to the latter. In the third canto, Rāma says to Lakṣmaṇa:

That by which I am easily pleased, O brother,
Is *bhakti* to me, which gives happiness to my devotee.
It is free and not dependent on anything.
Jñāna and *vijñāna* are under its control.

—*Araṇyakāṇḍa*, 15. 1, 2.

All the writings of Tulasīdāsa are a reflection of his own saintly heart, which is filled to the brim with love for Rāma, 'on whom he depends, who is his source of strength and his one and only hope and faith' (*Dohāvalī*, 277). The various characters of *Rāmacaritamānasa*, though all of them have distinct personalities with varying emotions, conflicts, and reactions, have one quality in common—whether in friendship, enmity, or love, their hearts are given to Rāma. Bringing in the simile of the *cātaka* bird, which quenches its thirst only with the water that falls from a cloud, Bharata says, 'Though the clouds, ever forgetful of the *cātaka* crying for rain, throw hailstones and lightning on it instead, yet the greatness of the *cātaka* lies in its constant longing and cry for the raindrop. And as gold shines in fire, so the servant glories in his love for, and loyalty to, his master' (*Ayodhyākāṇḍa*, 204. 2, 3). Again, Tulasī prays to Rāma, 'May thou be ever dear to me as gold is to the miser' (*Uttarakāṇḍa*, 130b).

REPETITION OF THE NAME OF GOD

Tulasīdāsa lays the greatest stress on the constant repetition of the name of God for the cultivation of *bhakti*. He says, 'I salute the name of Rāma . . . which is like Brahmā, Viṣṇu, and Śiva, the soul of the Vedas, and is without parallel'. Name and form are two attributes of God which cannot be described. The form of God is dependent on His name, for no form can be known without a name ; but greater than Brahman with or without attributes is His name, because both can be known through constant remembrance of the name. A few quotations will further illustrate this point:

For him who, even in his dreams,
Unconsciously utters the word Rāma,
Tulasī will give his own skin
To make the shoes of his feet.

—*Vairāgya-sandīpinī*

When meditation on the personal God is distasteful,
And the impersonal too is far away from the mind,
Remember the life-giving name of Rāma.

—*Dohāvalī,* 8.

In the Kali age, knowledge, dispassion, *yoga,* and *samādhi* are of no avail.
Constantly repeat the name of Rāma, with unwavering faith ;
Greater than austerity, pilgrimage, oblation, charity, disciplines, and fasts
Is the repetition of the name of God, O Tulasīdāsa.

—*Baravai Rāmāyaṇa*

NINE KINDS OF BHAKTI

In his search for Sītā, Rāma meets Śabarī, a woman ascetic of the jungle tribes, who was greatly devoted to him. To her he describes nine kinds of *bhakti.* He says, 'The first variety of *bhakti* is association with *sādhus,* and a love for the stories of my life is the second ; the third is service in all humility to the *guru,* and the fourth is to sing my glories with a pure heart. Firm faith in me with the repetition of the *mantra* is a path well known to the Vedas and is the fifth category ; control of the senses, good conduct, aversion to too much activity, and treading in the path of the holy ones make up the sixth ; to see the world as pervaded by me, while looking upon *sādhus* as greater than me, is the seventh. To be satisfied with what one gets and never to see the faults of others make up the eighth ; and simplicity of heart, guileless behaviour towards all, trust in me, and to be neither elated nor depressed, whatever may occur, constitute the ninth. Whoever has one kind of devotion out of all these, whether man or woman, a movable or immovable being, know him or her, O *bhāminī* (lady), to be dearly loved by me' (*Araṇyakāṇḍa,* 34. 4 ; 35. 4).

In the *Uttarakāṇḍa,* Rāma compares devotion to the jewel *cintāmaṇi,* the wish-fulfilling gem, the brilliant light of which the gloom of delusion cannot approach and the wind of avarice cannot extinguish. Its light destroys the darkness of deep ignorance and overcomes all shades of pride and conceit. Desire, anger, and other wicked feelings cannot approach him whose heart is illumined by this lamp of *bhakti.*

DEVOTEE'S HEART IS THE ABODE OF GOD

Devotion is embedded in the poetry of Tulasīdāsa, even in his description of simple events. When Rāma meets Vālmīki in the forest, he asks him to suggest a suitable place where he can build a hut and live with Sītā and Lakṣmaṇa for some time. At this simple question, out of the fullness of heart, Vālmīki replies thus:

> Listen, O Rāma, now I shall tell you
> Where you should live with Sītā and Lakṣmaṇa:
> Those whose ears, like unto the sea,
> By the stories of your life, like unto various rivers,
> Are always being filled, but are never satisfied;
> Their hearts are your home.
> Those whose eyes, being like the *cātaka* bird,
> Are ever longing for the rain-cloud of the vision of God,
> O giver of joy, O lord of the Raghus,
> Live in their hearts with your brother and Sītā.
> Your good name, being like the Mānasa lake,
> Those whose tongues, like the swans,
> Pick up the pearls of your divine qualities,
> Live in their hearts, O Rāma.
> He who can smell only the fragrant offering to God,
> He who offers his food to you before eating it,
> He whose very clothes and jewels are consecrated
> to the Lord,
> He whose head bows down to Brāhmaṇas, gods, and *guru*,
> With love and great humility,
> Whose hands daily worship the feet of Rāma,
> Who depends in his heart on Rāma and looks
> to no one else,
> Whose feet ever walk to the holy places of pilgrimage,
> O Rāma, live in their hearts.
> Those who desire only devotion to God as the fruit of all their
> good deeds in the world,
> Live in the temple of their hearts, O Sītā, and you two
> sons of Raghu.
> Those who have neither desire nor anger, nor pride, nor
> conceit, nor delusion,
> Who neither covet nor lament, and are without attachment
> or aversion,

Who have neither hypocrisy, arrogance, nor deceit,
O Rāma, live in their hearts.
Those who are loved by all and are well-wishers of all,
Who are the same in sorrow and happiness, praise and blame,
Who speak sweet words of truth, having pondered well on them,
Who, sleeping or awake, seek refuge in thee,
Who look upon the wives of others as their own mothers,
And on the wealth of others as the worst poison,
Who rejoice to see the prosperity of others, and grieve greatly
in their adversity,
They who love you more than life,
Their hearts are auspicious places for you to live in.
Those who look upon you as master, friend, father,
Mother, and teacher, to whom you are all in all,
Dwell in the temple of their hearts,
Both ye brothers with Sītā.
Those who never wish for anything,
Who love you quite naturally,
Live in their hearts for ever,
There is your home.

—*Ayodhyākāṇḍa,* 127. 2-131.

In this extremely beautiful passage, Tulasīdāsa seems to say that the first step in the path of God-realization is the control of the senses by dedicating all activities to God. Thus he speaks first of the ears, eyes, etc. Then only does he bring in higher moral qualities such as desirelessness and the conquest of anger. Such perfection of character, as he describes, seems to be beyond human endeavour, and so indeed it is. It is only when the human soul is linked with the Divine, through total self-surrender, that the sleeping spark of divinity is kindled, which envelops and consumes the mere animal existence in man.

GRACE OF GOD

Of all the characters of *Rāmacaritamānasa,* the most thought-provoking is that of Rāvaṇa, the villain of this great epic. The one single instance where he showed appreciation of the higher values gives a glimpse into the working of his mind. On this occasion he said, 'If God . . . has been born, then I shall force His enmity on myself and will die with His arrow in my heart, thus crossing the ocean of birth and death. . . . If they (Rāma and Lakṣmaṇa) are the sons of a king and mere human beings, I shall defeat them in battle and carry away Rāma's wife' (*Araṇyakāṇḍa*). In his first meeting with Sītā, though 'her words angered Rāvaṇa, yet in his heart he saluted her feet and felt happy' (*Araṇyakāṇḍa*). Except for these passages, Tulasīdāsa always speaks of Rāvaṇa as the wicked one, full of anger, arrogance, and pride. Though he is looked upon as the very personification of evil in the Indian tradition, Rāvaṇa attained salvation by 'the grace of Rāma which (being inexhaustible) is never satiated by its own compassion' (*Bālakāṇḍa*).

The greatest liberality of thought is shown in the devotional scriptures regarding numerous paths which lead the human soul to God ; not only through dedicated activity or love, but even through anger, fear, or hatred one may progress towards Him. Once the search has begun, the divinity immanent in man will do the rest. In devotional language, this is called the working of divine grace. The compassion and mercy of God, which is epitomized so forcefully in the salvation of Rāvaṇa, is the main theme of the songs of *Vinayapatrikā*. To quote one of the popular ones: 'O Hari, if you had looked to the faults of your devotees, then why would you have forced the enmity of Indra, Duryodhana, and Vālin on yourself? If, indifferent to *japa*, oblations, *yoga*, and fasts, your heart was not won only by love, then why would you have abandoned the homes of the gods and the good sages and lived in Vraja in the house of cowherds? . . . If you did not destroy the innumerable sins of Ajāmila, who called on his son taking your name, then the messengers of Death would have searched for bulls like me and yoked them to the plough (of the world). If you had not taken upon yourself the courageous and world-famous rôle of purifying sinners, then the wicked like Tulasī would not even dream of attaining liberation for ages' (*Vinayapatrikā*, 97).

HOLY COMPANY

Again, in accordance with the Hindu scriptures, Tulasīdāsa attaches the greatest importance to the habit of associating with the good and the holy. It is one of the recognized ways prescribed for ordinary mortals to help them to progress on the Godward path. Tulasīdāsa also delights in praising *sannyāsins*—those whose lives are dedicated to the finding of God. He compares *sādhus* to cotton. Their lives are as pure as cotton is white ; they are as dry as the cotton-pod, meaning that they are unattached to the things of the world ; again, they help others and try to cover up their faults even at the cost of their own lives, just as the cotton in the form of thread loses itself in filling up the holes of an old cloth, or in weaving a new cloth, which will cover the body and protect it from cold, rain, and wind (*Bālakāṇḍa*). Again, Tulasīdāsa says that *sādhus* are like a moving place of pilgrimage, the holy Prayāga, where the confluence of the three rivers

Gaṅgā, Yamunā, and Sarasvatī takes place. Their love for Rāma is the main stream, the Gaṅgā, while their idea of the impersonal Brahman is like the Sarasvatī, which is not visible to the eye, that is, the idea of the impersonal Brahman, though not distinguishable from devotion, supplies it with a philosophical background. Their rules of conduct are like the waters of the Yamunā. This moving pilgrimage, he says, is available at all times and in all countries. Discrimination is impossible to attain without the company of *sādhus,* which, in its turn, is impossible to have without the grace of Rāma (*Bālakāṇḍa*).

Tulasīdāsa never tires of repeating that 'greater than Rāma himself is the servant of Rāma', and his best tribute to the devotees of Rāma occurs in his praise of Bharata at the end of the second canto:

> If Bharata had not been born,
> Overflowing with the nectar of love for Sītā and Rāma,
> Who could have performed *yama* (control of senses), *niyama* (discipline), *śama* (tranquillity), *dama* (desistance from evil), fasts, and austerities,
> Impossible even to the sages?
> Whose good name would have served as the means
> For the removal of spiritual poverty, misery, pride, envy, and other defects?
> And in this age of Kali, who would have perforce
> Brought wicked ones like Tulasī into the presence of Rāma?

In conclusion, we must say that, though Tulasīdāsa did not preach any new doctrine, nor found a new sect, yet his own pure life and the magic of his poetry have done more for the Bhakti-mārga than the eloquence of hundreds of teachers. His memory is so greatly revered that tradition looks upon him as Vālmīki veritably reborn.

29

ŚAKTI-WORSHIP AND THE ŚĀKTA SAINTS

THE followers of Śāktism have always claimed a hoary antiquity for their faith,[1] and they trace its origin to the Vedas and refer to a number of kings and sages of Paurāṇic fame, like Kṛṣṇa, Vasiṣṭha, and others, who are stated to have attained success in their spiritual endeavours through the practice of Tāntric rites, especially those of the Śāktas. Paraśurāma, to whom is attributed the *Paraśurāma Kalpa-Sūtra,* which deals with the details of the worship of Śrīvidyā, is incidentally referred to in the *Tripurā-rahasya* (I. 18-20) as a devotee of Tripurā, another name of Śrīvidyā. According to the *Brahmāṇḍa Purāṇa,* Agastya learnt the details of the worship of Śrīvidyā from Hayagrīva (Viṣṇu). Vasiṣṭha is stated to have been successful in his spiritual aspirations only after worshipping the goddess Tārā. Lopāmudrā, the wife of Agastya, became celebrated through her worship of Śrīvidyā, and the *mantra* with which she offered the worship still goes by her name. An entire work, the *Rādhā Tantra,* describes the life-story of Kṛṣṇa, who is represented here as an ardent worshipper of Śakti and as one who attained spiritual success through his union with Rādhā. Whatever be the value of these claims of the latter-day followers of the Śākta school, it cannot be doubted that Śāktism has a long history behind it.

ŚĀKTISM IN PRESENT-DAY INDIA

Śāktism is a very important cult among the Hindus of the present day all over India. Śakti or the Mother Goddess is worshipped in various forms, and numerous shrines and images are dedicated to her in different parts of the country. One or other form of the deity is recognized as the *iṣṭadevatā* or tutelary deity by the Śāktas or Śakti-worshippers, who, far from being exclusive in their devotion, pay their respect to and worship other deities on ceremonial occasions, as also in connection with the worship of their tutelary deities. Feasts and festivities pertaining to these Śākta deities abound in different parts of the country. Occasionally these include rituals consisting of apparently sensual and revolting practices, which are responsible for the disrepute in which Tāntricism in general and Śāktism in particular are usually held in the modern world. It must, however, be admitted that these practices are by no means the characteristic or the most important feature of the Śakti cult. In fact, it has lofty spiritual ideals, its

[1] For a discussion of the antiquity of Tāntricism, see the writer's paper in *Indian Historical Quarterly,* VI. pp. 114 ff.

rituals aiming at practical realization of the Vedāntic principle of the identity of the individual soul with the supreme Soul or Brahman, who is none but the Śakti that pervades the entire universe. The various Tāntric rites will be found, on a close study, to have been so conceived as to help this realization in a graduated scale. The very first principle of Tāntric worship is that a worshipper should identify himself with the deity he worships. And hence the Tantras give preference to what is called internal worship, as also to pure meditation.

TĀNTRIC LITERATURE AND ITS CHARACTER

The rites and practices of Śāktism as well as its ideals are expounded in the extensive literature that has grown up from quite an early period. A critical study of this literature, which is yet to be undertaken, will be helpful in distinguishing the genuine from the spurious, the extent of which is evidently not very small. As a matter of fact, the exact number and correct texts of what may be called the original Tantras are not known with any amount of definiteness. We have here the same confusion as in the case of the Purāṇa literature, if not more. Different versions of the same work as well as immense textual irregularities and variations are known. Under these circumstances, much that is trivial and unauthoritative has passed as Tantra, causing a good deal of misconception with regard to the end and nature of the Tāntric form of worship. The tradition and exposition of the orthodox followers of the system may be regarded as the only guide in this intricate labyrinth. We have therefore to turn to Tantra digests and treatises by later scholars, among whom might be counted a good number of saints and sages, and to the life-stories of saints, which throw much welcome light on the secret and real nature of the cult.

It is true that the personal histories of most of these authors, who are spread over the whole of India, are not known. But it seems that most of them, if not all, made considerable progress in their journey along the spiritual path. This is indicated by some of their names ending in '*-ānanda nātha*', such names being given to persons who have performed particular advanced Tāntric rites. In a sense therefore, they may also be regarded as saints. The works composed by them are mainly of a ritualistic character. There are comparatively few works which directly expound the philosophy proper of the Tantras. In this connection, the works of Śaṅkarācārya, Bhāskararāya, Pūrṇānanda, and a few others are highly useful in realizing the esoteric implications of Tāntric rites. A thorough study of their works is indispensable for an understanding of the lofty ideals underlying the Tāntric practices. Works of other writers generally deal with the details of the worship of different aspects of Śakti or the divine Mother,

Of the ten major manifestations of the divine Mother, again, Tripurā (Ṣoḍaśī), Kālī, Tārā, and Bhuvaneśvarī claim, in a descending order, the largest number of worshippers and, consequently, the largest amount of literature. Chinnamastā (also known as Pracaṇḍa-caṇḍikā or Sumukhī), Dhūmāvatī, and Vagalā are principally worshipped in connection with the performance of the six magic rites for averting evils (*śānti*), subduing a man or woman (*vaśīkaraṇa*), arresting any feeling or force (*stambhana*), creating enmity between affectionate friends (*vidveṣaṇa*), overthrowing an enemy (*uccāṭana*), and causing death to somebody (*māraṇa*). They have few regular worshippers who regard them as their tutelary deities, so that the literature on them is quite scanty. Śākta deities like Gāyatrī, Kubjikā, and Caṇḍikā have only a limited local interest, being known and worshipped in particular localities. Of the various Tāntric rites, only the more important and popular ones like *dīkṣā* and *puraścaraṇa* are dealt with in independent treatises. A critical survey of the Tāntric literature will reveal the extreme paucity of works concerning apparently obnoxious rites. In fact, a very small portion of the extensive literature of the Tantras is occupied by them. This is an important indication of the true position held by them among Tāntric worshippers.

It is rather strange that there is no work dealing with Tāntric festivals. Tantra digests and valuable handbooks for Tāntric worship, which describe in detail the procedure to be followed in the worship of various deities, do not provide for any festive worship on a particular occasion. Smṛti works, containing elaborate accounts of feasts and festivities held all round the year, generally do not refer to any Tāntric festivals, though they are by no means less popular or all of a comparatively recent origin. As for the Bengal festivals, most of them are not earlier than the fifteenth or the sixteenth century.[2]

THE TĀNTRIC AUTHORS AND THEIR WORKS

It is now proposed to refer to the more important of the authors and the works produced by them to elucidate the teachings of the Tantras. It is, however, not possible to give anything like a comprehensive account of the extensive literature produced by writers hailing from all parts of the country at different times over a long period. And, as has already been noted, we know very little about the personal history of, or the influence exerted by, most of these authors. They are all of Brāhmaṇa caste, with some exceptions. There are a few works by persons belonging to other castes. The author of the *Bhairavārcā-pārijāta*, presumably a Kṣatriya,

[2] For a detailed treatment of the Śākta festivals of Bengal and their antiquity, see the writer's paper in *Indian Historical Quarterly*, XXVII. pp. 255 ff.

refers to himself as a prince of the Vāghela dynasty. Kṛṣṇamohana, who compiled the *Āgama-candrikā,* was a Kāyastha. These writers, however, make no apology for going out of what may be supposed to be their own jurisdiction. Kṛṣṇadeva Gaṇa, author of the *Cidānanda-mandākinī,* on the other hand, refers to the taboo on the use of religious books written by non-Brāhmaṇas and justifies his own action in writing the book by suggesting that the taboo does not apply to serious literature.

We should first of all refer to authors of all-India fame. Of these three names are outstanding.

The great Śaṅkarācārya, who is famous for his philosophical works, is usually considered by the followers of Tāntric worship to have been a torchbearer in the field of Tāntricism as well. His influence may have been instrumental in giving a reorientation to the outlook of the Tantras, which came to be broad-based on monistic principles. He is supposed to have been the author of some famous Tantra works, such as the *Prapañcasāra* and the *Ānandalaharī.*

Lakṣmaṇa Deśikendra, of whom no details are available, is the author of the *Śāradātilaka,* one of the most important and respected Tāntric compilations. This work has an all-India fame. It has been commented on by various scholars from time to time. It deals with the details of the worship of a good many deities, and also discusses certain aspects of Śākta philosophy and doctrine. We have references to a number of other works attributed to this author. Of these, the *Tārāpradīpa,* which appears to have enjoyed some popularity in Bengal, is a metrical work dealing with the details of the worship of Tārā. It may have been planned to supplement the *Śāradātilaka.*

Bhāskararāya or Bhāsurānanda Nātha, who came from Tanjore in South India, was a worshipper of Śrīvidyā. He was the author of a number of highly learned works, in which he gave an exposition of the details as well as the secrets of the worship of Śrīvidyā. His commentaries on the *Nityā-ṣoḍaśikārṇava* and *Lalitā-sahasranāma-stotra* and his *Varivasyā-rahasya* cannot be too highly commended to the notice of people desirous of getting acquainted with the basic principles of the rituals of the Tantras.

Mahāmahopādhyāya Parivrājakācārya seems to have been the earliest Bengali writer of a Tantra digest. Unfortunately, the proper name of the writer is not known. His only work that has come down is the *Kāmya-yantroddhāra.* A manuscript of the work described by Mm. H. P. Shastri was copied in Śaka 1297 (A.D. 1375). The author of the work therefore must have flourished before this date.

The most important name in Bengal as a Tāntric author is that of Kṛṣṇānanda Āgamavāgīśa. He is usually supposed to have been a contemporary of Śrī Caitanya (A.D. 1485-1533), though scholars would assign him to a much later date. He is believed to have conceived and introduced, through divine inspiration, the image of Kālī, as she is now worshipped in Bengal. His *Tantrasāra* is the most comprehensive and popular of the numerous digests that are known in Bengal. It is regarded as highly authoritative, and all Tāntric worship is performed according to the injunctions contained in it. A few manuscripts of the work have been found in non-Bengali scripts, and outside Bengal, showing thereby the extent of its popularity. The book deals with all kinds of Tāntric rites, such as initiation, process of worship, *homa* (ceremonial offering to fire), and *kulācāra,* contains hymns of various gods and goddesses, and describes their *yantras* (mystic diagrams). Many of the gods and goddesses, the processes of whose worship have been given in the book, are now very little known. Nor are the images of many of them known to have been found. It quotes long extracts from a good many original Tantras and digests, many of which are now known only by name.

Brahmānanda Giri was the *guru* or spiritual guide of Pūrṇānanda, who flourished towards the third quarter of the sixteenth century. Brahmānanda therefore flourished in the second, if not the first, quarter of that century. He was himself the disciple of Tripurānanda. It is not known if the *Tantrasāra,* referred to in his *Śāktānanda-taraṅgiṇī,* is identical with the celebrated work of the same name by Kṛṣṇānanda. Of his works, the *Śāktānanda-taraṅgiṇī* is perhaps the best known and most popular. In eighteen chapters it deals with the various rites to be performed in connection with the worship of Śakti. His *Tārārahasya,* in four sections, deals with the rites connected with the worship of Tārā and her various forms. Incidentally, it deals with *prātaḥ-kṛtya* (rites to be performed every morning, such as bathing) and initiation, meant for the worshipper of Tārā.

Pūrṇānanda Paramahaṁsa Parivrājaka was a great saint and a well-known Tāntric compiler of the sixteenth century. His date is definitely known from two of his works, namely, *Śāktakrama* and *Śrītattva-cintāmaṇi,* the former of which was composed, as is recorded in its concluding verse, in Śaka 1493 (A.D. 1571), and the latter, in Śaka 1499 (A.D. 1577), as he himself says in the beginning of the work. He was a Brāhmaṇa of the Rāḍhīya section hailing from Katihali, a village in the Netrakona Subdivision of the District of Mymensingh in East Bengal. He became the *guru* of a good many people of East and North Bengal, which position his descendants still hold.

Pūrṇānanda compiled several Tantra works. Of these the *Śyāmā-rahasya* is the best known. It deals with various rites in connection with the worship of the goddess Śyāmā or Kālī, and consists of sixteen chapters

His *Śāktakrama* deals, in seven chapters, with the rites of the Śāktas. His *Śrītattva-cintāmaṇi* describes the Tantra rites in general, with special reference to the cult of Śrīvidyā. It begins with a discourse on *tattvajñāna* (the highest Truth), and has a section on *prāyaścitta* or expiatory rites towards the end. His other Tantra works are *Tattvānanda-taraṅgiṇī* and *Ṣaṭkarmollāsa.* The latter deals principally with the magic rites of the Tantras mentioned above.

We may next mention the name of one who is generally known as Śaṅkara of Gauḍa.[3] He must have flourished some time about the sixteenth century, as a manuscript of his *Tārārahasya-vṛttikā* in the Maithilī character dated La. Saṁ. 511 (A.D. 1630) is known. In the concluding verse of this work, he says that he was the son of Kamalākara and grandson of Lambodara. In the colophon of this work, he definitely calls himself a native of Gauḍa (North Bengal). A number of Tantra compilations are attributed to him. Of these, the *Tārārahasya-vṛttikā* deals, in fifteen sections, with Tantra rites in general, such as initiation, with special reference to the worship of Tārā. His *Śivārcana-mahāratna* and *Śaivaratna* pertain, as their names imply, to the rites to be performed by a Śaiva. Two more of his works *Kulamūlāvatāra* and *Kramastava* are also mentioned.

From Mahārāṣṭra hailed Nīlakaṇṭha, the Śaiva, who is different from his more famous namesake whose reputation rests on his commentary on the *Mahābhārata.* This Nīlakaṇṭha was the author of a number of Purāṇa and Tantra works, which are not so well known. We are told that his great-grandfather, Mayūreśvara, earned for the family the surname Śaiva. Nīlakaṇṭha does not mention his date; but on the basis of the references he makes to authors and works, it would appear that Nīlakaṇṭha flourished not earlier than the middle of the eighteenth century. About half a dozen works of Nīlakaṇṭha are known, or have been mentioned. Of these, the commentaries on the *Devī-Bhāgavata* and the *Kātyāyanī Tantra* and his *Śaktitattva-vimarśinī* and *Kāmakalā-rahasya* deal with Śāktism.

Of Nepal, we may mention Navamīsiṁha (alias Ādyānandana). He introduces himself in the beginning of his *Tantra-cintāmaṇi* as the minister of King Bhūpālendra, who is stated to have been a man of learning and piety. The king seems to be identical with Mahīndra Malla or Bhūpālendra Malla of Kathmandu who ruled for about five years (A.D. 1689-94). We know of two extensive Tāntric digests by Navamīsiṁha, the *Tantra-cintāmaṇi* and the *Kulamukti-kallolinī.*

[3] His full name seems to have been Śaṅkara Āgamācārya, as is indicated by the colophon of the *Tārārahasya-vṛttikā* in the MS. of the India Office Library. For fuller information about Śaṅkara, Nīlakaṇṭha, Navamīsiṁha, Śrīnivāsa, Kāśīnātha, and Sāhib Kaula, see *Descriptive Catalogue of Sanskrit Manuscripts, Royal Asiatic Society of Bengal,* VIII. Introduction.

From South India came Śrīnivāsa Bhaṭṭa Gosvāmin, who had migrated from his original home to Banaras, where he and his descendants occupied a position of some distinction. A fair account of the family may be gathered from the comprehensive Tāntric digests compiled by the members of the family. It is known from the introductory verses of the *Śivārcana-candrikā* of Śrīnivāsa that there was a large village to the south of Kāñcī, called Ananta, which was inhabited by pious and learned Brāhmaṇas who had received the village as a grant from a certain king. Here was the ancestral home of a learned family of scholars, of whom Śrīnivāsa was the most prominent. Śrīnivāsa, who was specially versed in the Tantras, went on a festive occasion to Jālandhara (Jullundur), a famous *pīṭha* of Śakti-worship, and was initiated by Sundarācārya or Saccidānanda Nātha, presumably the author of the *Lalitārcana-candrikā* and the *Laghu-candrikā,* which may be an abridgement of the former. His post-initiation name appears to have been Vidyānanda Nātha. As desired by his preceptor, Śrīnivāsa came down to and settled in Banaras. He was the author of several Tāntric compilations, four of which he has mentioned by name at the end of his *Śivārcana-candrikā.* The dignity of the family was maintained, if not enhanced, by the successors of Śrīnivāsa. His son, Jagannivāsa, who was also versed in the Tantra lore, counted among his disciples a number of ruling chiefs of the time, of whom Devīsiṁha of Bundel has been mentioned by Śivānanda Gosvāmin, the eldest son of Jagannivāsa, who wrote the *Siṁha-siddhāntasindhu* at the request of the above-mentioned chief. Janārdana, another son of Jagannivāsa, probably the youngest, was the author of the *Mantra-candrikā.*

Kāśīnātha Bhaṭṭa Bhaḍa, alias Śivānanda Nātha of Banaras, was the author of a large number of small treatises, principally on Paurāṇic and Tāntric topics. He flourished some time in the seventeenth or the eighteenth century. He was a worshipper of Śiva and Śakti and followed what is called *dakṣiṇācāra* or the 'Rightist' form of worship of the usual and orthodox type, which he claimed to have established on a firm footing, at a time when *vāmācāra* or the 'Leftist' form of worship, with its apparently revolting practices, was fast becoming the order of the day. He took pains in his works to refute the doctrines of the *vāmācāra,* and set forth the rites and practices of the *dakṣiṇācāra.*

A number of Tāntric works dealing with the Śakti cult are known to have been attributed to Sāhib Kaula, which seems to have been a Tāntric ecclesiastical designation in Kashmir. The nature and function of the dignitary are not known. But that it was a highly dignified position is clearly indicated by the way in which it has been referred to in more than one of these works. It may be pointed out in this connection that the epithets Mahāmāheśvarācārya and Sāhib Kaulānanda Nātha are used either jointly or singly to refer to the authors of some of these works pointing to their spiritual greatness.

Among a host of Śākta saints and authors of Kashmir, the most renowned name, however, is that of the polymath Abhinavagupta (tenth or eleventh century). His *magnum opus,* and the most voluminous of his works, is the *Tantrāloka,* which is 'primarily concerned with the systematic presentation of the teachings of the Kula and Trika systems'. He was a great *sādhaka* as well as a vastly learned scholar. It is from the Kula system that he seems to have attained perfect satisfaction and peace. Presumably, it is on account of this that he paid a more glowing tribute to his Kaulika teacher, Śambhu Nātha, than to anyone else. He had to go to Jullundur to learn Kaulika literature and practices from this teacher.[4]

THE ŚĀKTA LYRICS OF BENGAL AND THEIR AUTHORS

There was also a large number of writers who wrote in regional languages. They were immensely popular and were highly regarded by the people at large.

The Śākta lyrics of Bengal, though not as much known these days as the Vaiṣṇava lyrics, are in no way inferior in value and importance. They enjoy sufficient popularity among the unlettered village folk. Their depth of devotional fervour is no less than what we find in the Vaiṣṇava songs, though, abounding in homely expressions, they do not exhibit the characteristic features of high poetry.

The spirit of devotion is found to permeate the poetical literature of the Śāktas, though it did not predominate over the religious rites of the sect. As a matter of fact, it would often seem to be in conflict with them. Some of the hymns and songs go so far as openly to denounce these rites. Many of the saints also, of whom we shall presently speak, were reputed not for the strict observance of religious rites in all their details, but for their ardent devotion to the Mother Goddess.

The poems which describe the deity as the child of the worshipper, as in the *āgamanī* (welcome) and *vijayā* (farewell) songs of the goddess Durgā, have indeed a peculiar appeal of their own. Here the divinity is conceived of as a little girl who, according to the old custom of the land, has been married at an early age and taken away from her parents to the house of her husband, whence she visits her parental home only occasionally. They are full of pathos and delineate the familiar experiences of an ordinary householder.

[4] For a detailed account of Abhinavagupta and his works, see K. C. Pandey, *Abhinavagupta —An Historical and Philosophical Study*.

Another and a curious phase of the devotional attitude is represented by the apparently sceptic and pessimistic tone noticed in some of these songs, which complain of the heartlessness of the divine Mother in that the people at large, even those that are firmly devoted to her, often groan under untold sorrows and sufferings. A mock threat is held out that, if such a condition is allowed to persist, no worship will be offered. It is of the nature of a loving child's complaint to his mother. It is, however, fully recognized, as is clear from so many songs, that it is through these exacting trials that the divine Mother tests her devotees and leads them to final beatitude.

One more notable point to be recorded in connection with these lyrics is that many of them aim at elucidating in a very popular way the rather intricate teachings of the Tantras.

Rāmaprasāda Kavirañjana, a well-known saint and poet, flourished about two hundred years ago in the village of Kumarhatta (Halishahar), a few miles from Calcutta. He is said to have attained to high spiritual eminence. He is famous as the author of a large number of lyric poems which bespeak his deep devotion for the great Mother, whose omnipotence is occasionally referred to. These songs have a firm hold on the people of Bengal and have acquired a much greater popularity than hundreds of similar songs of other poets, of which a good many are known.[5]

Kamalākānta is another saint and author of Śākta lyrics in Bengali, who is next in importance to Rāmaprasāda. He was born at Ambika (Kalna) in the District of Burdwan about one hundred and fifty years ago. Besides stray songs, he also composed a work called *Sādhakarañjana,* which sought to elucidate in simple Bengali verses the basic principles of *yoga,* as elaborated in the Tantras.

THE ŚĀKTA SAINTS OF BENGAL

After dealing with the saintly authors and their learned writings, we should now refer to those numerous saints who devoted themselves to practising and demonstrating through their lives the teachings of the Tantras. In fact, a very large number of the spiritual aspirants preferred to be occupied with religious practices themselves, rather than with the elucidation of old authoritative texts or in delineating their own spiritual experiences. A large number of these spiritual adepts and saints had not even the literary qualification for this task. Still they live in the minds

[5] Several collections of these songs have been published. They have been introduced to the English-reading people through the efforts of Thompson and Spencer who translated and classified a select number of these songs under the caption *Bengali Religious Lyrics—Śākta* (Heritage of India Series).

of generations of their devout disciples, who give publicity and regular form to their teachings. Anniversaries and festivities are arranged in honour of these saints at the seats of their religious practices. These are sometimes very popular and attract devotees from far and near. In fact, this latter class of saints is often more remembered by the people at large than many others who have left literary works behind them.

Among saints of this class, mention may be made of Sarvānanda, Gosāiñ Bhaṭṭācārya, Ardhakālī, and Vāmā Kṣepā, names which are household words in Bengal or parts of it, and, above all, Sri Ramakrishna, who flourished during the last century and whose name has spread all over the world. Of similar saints in Mithilā, reference may be made to Gaṅgeśa Upādhyāya, the famous Nyāya scholar, as also to Devāditya, Vardhamāna, and others.[6] It is stated that some of Mithilā's greatest saints were associated with Śakti-worship. In fact, saints of this type possessing local celebrity, but not widely known throughout the land, flourished in different parts of the country.

Sarvānanda flourished about four hundred years ago at Mehar, a village in the District of Tippera. He is stated to have been totally illiterate.[7] His spiritual success is reported to have been attained through the repetition of a *mantra,* while practising a very difficult Tāntric ritual or *sādhanā* with the help of a dead body. Thereafter, he earned the epithet of Sarvavidyā, as all forms of the divine Mother were revealed to him. His name is held in high esteem, and his descendants have to this day a large number of disciples all over Bengal. The Kālī temple in the village of Mehar has become a place of pilgrimage to the people of Bengal, and a festival is held there in his honour about the middle of January.

Ratnagarbha or Gosāiñ Bhaṭṭācārya, as he was popularly known, is stated to have been the *guru* of Cānda Rāya and Kedāra Rāya, two famous Bengali chiefs who flourished towards the end of the sixteenth century. It is said that he attained *siddhi* (spiritual success) in the temple of Digambarī at Mayaisar in the District of Dacca. He followed the *vīra* form of worship requiring the use of wine, meat, and corpses ; and many are the stories told of the supernatural powers acquired by him. His descendants have in their possession two symbolic representations (*yantras*) of the deity drawn by him, which are still held in esteem by the people of the locality.

[6] *Journal of the Bihar and Orissa Research Society,* XXXIII. 51. The life-story of Gaṅgeśa was dramatized by the great Śākta, Pandit Siva Chandra Vidyarnava (Calcutta, 1305 B.S.).

[7] It is not known if Sarvānanda Nātha, the author of the Tāntric compilation *Sarvollāsa Tantra,* is identical with Sarvānanda. The following works deal with the life-story of Sarvānanda: *Sarvānanda-taraṅgiṇī* (in Sanskrit) attributed to Śivanātha, son of Sarvānanda ; *Sarvānanda* (in Bengali) by Atul Chandra Mukherji ; and *Ṭhākura Sarvānanda* (in Bengali) by Nisikanta Chakravarti.

Ardhakālī,[8] so called on account of half of her body being dark, is believed to have been an incarnation of the divine Mother. A daughter of Dvijadeva Ṭhākura of Panditbari, a great devotee of the Mother, she was born about three hundred years ago in the District of Mymensingh in East Bengal. Her real name was Jayadurgā. She was married to Rāghavarāma, a pupil of her father. It is stated that, at the time of her marriage, she furnished convincing proof of her divinity to the sceptics. Rāghavarāma also was highly advanced on the spiritual path, and possessed yogic powers. The descendants of Dvijadeva, particularly those of his renowned daughter, still command great respect in Bengal among the worshippers of Śakti.

Vāmācaraṇa,[9] popularly known as Vāmā Kṣepā (mad Vāmā), was born about a hundred years ago in a poor Brāhmaṇa family at a village in the District of Birbhum. He was from his childhood absent-minded and could do no household work satisfactorily. This trait of his character obtained him the sobriquet by which he is known all over Bengal. He was a devotee of the goddess Tārā, but seldom did he offer any formal worship. His meditative temperament urged him, at a comparatively young age, to leave his home and retire to Tārāpīṭha, a famous centre of Tāntric worship, not far from his own village. There he practised meditation. He died about forty years ago, leaving behind a large circle of disciples and admirers, who gather together at Tārāpīṭha once a year in honour of their *guru* and worship goddess Tārā with great festivity.

The lives, teachings, and literary works of the Śakti-worshippers, referred to above, will show that Śakti-worship as such is not an evil ; that the malpractices of the misguided few do not follow from, and cannot represent, the high ideals of the Śākta Tantras ;[10] and that the ennobling spirit of devotion and the high tone of spirituality imparted by Śāktism have attracted and are still attracting a very large number of people not only in Bengal, but all over India.

[8] Her life is treated in Bengali in *Ardhakālī* by Atul Chandra Mukherji. A Sanskrit work called the *Rāghava-dīpikā* is also stated to have been composed by Viśvadeva Ācārya, a contemporary of Rāghava, to commemorate the life of Rāghava and Ardhakālī.

[9] Two books have been published in Bengali describing the life-story of Vāmācaraṇa: Jatindranath Chatterji, *Vāmā Kṣepā,* and Haricharan Ganguli, *Śrī Vāmā-līlā.*

[10] Compare, in this connection, the author's paper 'Ideals of Tantra Rites' published in the *Indian Historical Quarterly,* X. pp. 486 ff.

PART III

RELIGION IN PRACTICE

30

RELIGIOUS BELIEFS OF THE INDIAN TRIBES

THE aborigines of India number about twenty-five millions. They occupy the most inhospitable regions of the country, where they lead a miserable existence. With their limited resources, both material and intellectual, they have been waging a ceaseless war against their unkind environment. In the struggle for existence, religion and magic are their two most important allies. We shall try to describe here some of these religious concepts, which uphold the aborigines in times of distress and instil hope into them.

NATURE OF THE SOUL

According to the animistic school of anthropology, the concept of the soul is the foundation of religion throughout primitive society. There is hardly any primitive group which does not possess this elementary idea. The soul is commonly believed to have an ethereal existence. But the idea of its size and shape differs in different parts of India. Among the Lakhers of Assam, the soul is held to resemble the body in appearance and size.[1] The Thadou Kukis of Manipur, on the other hand, conceive the 'soul as a minute replica of the individual'.[2] This idea is also common among their Naga neighbours of Manipur[3] and the Naga Hills.[4] The Sema Nagas believe it to be the shadow or reflection of the body.[5] In Chota Nagpur and Madhya Pradesh, the soul is often conceived of as a *chāin* or *chāyā*, i.e. shade or shadow. It is often spoken of in such terms in these regions. The Oraons believe the soul to resemble a shadow, only it is lighter and more intangible.[6] A similar idea also prevails among the nomadic Birhor hunters of Ranchi District.[7] The Baigas of Madhya Pradesh believe the soul to be like a *chāyā*, which is called back to the house on the tenth day after death and installed within it with affectionate care.[8] The Murias of Bastar also have a similar belief.[9] The Chenchus of Hyderabad think that the soul proceeds to Bhagavantaru, immediately after death or later on, in human shape.[10] The Todas of the Nilgiri Hills have a very clear

[1] N. E. Parry, *The Lakhers*, p. 351. [2] William Shaw, *The Thadou Kukis*, p. 155.
[3] Facts collected by the author, but not yet published. [4] *Ibid.*
[5] J. H. Hutton, *The Sema Nagas*, pp. 199 ff.
[6] S. C. Roy, *Oraon Religion and Customs*, p. 187.
[7] S. C. Roy, *The Birhors*, pp. 252-54. [8] Verrier Elwin, *The Baiga*, p. 294.
[9] Verrier Elwin, *The Muria and Their Ghotul*, p. 144.
[10] C. von Fürer-Haimendorf, *The Chenchus*, I. p. 195.

conception of the soul, which resembles the individual and proceeds to the other world on death, and leads there a life almost similar to this one.[11] The shape of the soul may also be deduced from a number of mortuary rites. Among the Mundas of Ranchi, after cremation of a corpse, a small human effigy is made with tender grass and placed on a figure drawn on the ground with parched rice.[12] This effigy represents the deceased. Among the Hos of Kolhan was found a small human effigy made of earth, about a foot in height, riding a horse, with drawn bow and arrow in the hand. This represented the soul of an old man, on whose grave it was placed. If the deceased had been a woman, the effigy would have consisted of a standing female figure with a straw-pad (*biḍā*) on the head.[13] Similar figures also occur among the Murias of Bastar.[14] The Garo *kimas* also fall in line with these figures.[15] Dr. Hutton found human effigies at Ukha in the unadministered territories east of the Naga Hills.[16] These also represented the human souls. The ceremony of calling back the soul of the deceased to the sacred tabernacle within the house, so common in Chota Nagpur and further south and west, shows in what light the soul is held by these simple peoples of the hills and forests. It maintains all the human characteristics, such as susceptibility to hunger and thirst, to heat and cold, and even to the bites of gnats and mosquitoes. Among the Hos, the soul is sadly and solemnly coaxed to come back to the house in the following words: 'O, so-and-so (name of the person), come back to the house, inside its doors. Do not remain under trees or creepers where gnats and mosquitoes abound. You are getting cold.' This chant shows that the susceptibilities of the human body remain associated with the soul even after the destruction of the former.

MULTIPLE SOULS

Though it is commonly believed that each individual possesses only one soul, yet there are areas where the concept of multiple souls occurs. The Ao Nagas believe that for every individual in this world, there is a spiritual counterpart in the sky called *tiya* (fate).[17] For every man, there are three souls here, and his *tiya* in the sky also has three souls. Of the three souls of man, one is a celestial *mithan* (*bos frontalis*) in possession of his *tiya*, the second accompanies the individual whenever he leaves his house, while the

[11] W. H. R. Rivers, *The Todas*, pp. 397-400.
[12] S. C. Roy, *The Mundas and Their Country*, p. 462.
[13] Facts collected by the author, but not yet published.
[14] Verrier Elwin, *The Muria and Their Ghotul*, p. 165.
[15] A. Playfair, *The Garos*, p. 113.
[16] J. H. Hutton, *Diaries of Two Tours in the Unadministered Area East of the Naga Hills*, p. 19.
[17] J. P. Hills, *The Ao Nagas*, p. 224.

third remains within the hut. The *tiya* and the souls are pre-existent. The belief in multiple souls is also found among the Purums, an Old Kuki tribe of Manipur, according to whom every individual has five souls.[18] It may also be traced among the tribes in Chota Nagpur and Madhya Pradesh. Among the Birhors, each individual is supposed to have a shadow, which is enshrined in the house after death.[19] Besides this, he has two other souls, one male and the other female, which remain within the body when the individual is alive, but depart from it at death. They, however, always remain together and are reborn together in a new baby. During dream, the male soul goes out of the body, while the female one remains inside and keeps it alive till the return of the male soul, just as a Birhor wife keeps her *kumba* (hut) in order, when her husband is out on hunting or gathering roots and fruits. The Baiga has likewise three souls.[20] His *jiv* (life-essence) goes to Bhagavān, led by the latter's messengers; his shadow or *chāyā* is brought back to the house, but his *bhūt* (ghost) remains in the burial ground. The last one is the remnant of all that was base in him, and is therefore conceived of as hostile and dangerous to man. The Murias also believe in three souls, but the Marias in two only.

LAND OF THE DEAD

We have already seen that in the primitive society of India, the individual does not go out of existence with the destruction of his body, whether on the funeral pyre or on the corpse-platform or in the grave. A part of him, the soul, survives, and we have had glimpses of the conceptions as to its shape, size, and number among various tribes. The next question which naturally arises is, What becomes of this indestructible part? The general belief on this point among the primitive tribes of India, with the exception of those of Chota Nagpur, is that this indestructible part, called the soul, goes to the Land of the Dead. There is, however, some difference of opinion regarding the location of this land. It is held by some tribes to be situated in the sky; by some others, on this earth; by still others, again, underneath the ground. Most of the Naga tribes place it under the ground in the Wokha Hills. The Angami Nagas send the souls of the good to the sky, and of the rest to the underworld.[21] Among the Kukis, the souls go to the Mi-thi-kho, the Land of the Dead, but its exact location is not stated; the Purums place it in the sky towards the west.[22] Among the Chota Nagpur tribes, the concept of the Land of the Dead is generally absent. Among most of the tribes of this region, the *chāin* is brought back to the house,

[18] T. C. Das, *The Purums*, pp. 255 ff.
[19] S. C. Roy, *The Birhors*, pp. 253-54.
[20] Verrier Elwin, *The Baiga*, p. 294.
[21] J. H. Hutton, *The Angami Nagas*, p. 181.
[22] T. C. Das, *The Purums*, p. 256.

where it resides and receives regular offerings. Among the Kharias, however, there is a belief that the *jiom* or the immaterial soul goes to the underworld and joins the fathers, while the *chāin* is enshrined at home.[23] Among the Baigas, one of the souls (*jīv*) goes to Bhagavān who lives 'on this earth, to the east of the Maikal Hills'.[24] The Murias believe that the soul (*jīva*) proceeds to Mahāpurub (probably Mahāprabhu) who lives in Porrobhum (upper world) with his seven maiden daughters.[25] The Toda Land of the Dead (Amnodr or probably Yamanodr, world of Yama) lies below this world, and the same sun lights both this world and Amnodr alternately.[26] The latter idea is also found in the Lakher concept of Athikhi (Land of the Dead).[27]

The nature of life in this Land of the Dead, in most of the cases, does not differ much from what it is here. Such is the belief of the Rengma Nagas[28] and the Sema Nagas.[29] 'The same men marry the same women, and the same children are born. Those who were poor here are poor there; and those who were rich remain so. Among the Lakhers, a chief in this world remains a chief in the next, and a slave here has to carry on the same miserable existence there.'[30] The Purum soul goes straight to Khamnung (other world) where it joins its parents and grandparents, i.e. those who predeceased it, and leads a life almost similar to the one it led here.[31] Similar beliefs are also held by the Baigas. The food that a Baiga gives away during his lifetime is stored in his house in the other world, and his soul subsists on it there till the viands are exhausted, when it has to come back to this world and be reborn. The Toda buffalo herdsmen have their buffaloes and their dairies in Amnodr, where the souls follow the same daily routine of work and pleasure.[32]

DOCTRINE OF KARMA

How far does life in this world affect life in the other according to these primitive people of India? In discussing this point, we should bear in mind the fact that for a long time the aborigines of India have been under the influence of the Hindus in different degrees in different areas, and that the doctrine of Karma considerably influences the Hindu mind. It is not therefore impossible to find traces of the idea of retribution in different stages of development among the tribal peoples of India,

[23] S. C. Roy, *The Kharias*, p. 283.
[24] Verrier Elwin, *The Baiga*, p. 294.
[25] Verrier Elwin, *The Muria and Their Ghotul*, pp. 145-46.
[26] W. H. R. Rivers, *The Todas*, p. 397.
[27] N. E. Parry, *The Lakhers*, pp. 395, 414, 487.
[28] J. P. Mills, *The Rengma Nagas*, pp. 169-70.
[29] J. H. Hutton, *The Sema Nagas*, pp. 211-12.
[30] N. E. Parry, *The Lakhers*, p. 396.
[31] T. C. Das, *The Purums*, p. 210.
[32] W. H. R. Rivers, *The Todas*, p. 398.

who might have borrowed it from the Hindus. But, at the same time, it is not also impossible that these ideas are natural developments from within. Materials are scanty to arrive at a definite conclusion on this point.

The Indian aborigines differ in their ideas about the relation between the individual's activities here and the fate of his soul in the Land of the Dead. Some of the tribes hold that life here does not influence in any way the life in the next world. Happiness or misery in the other world is often believed to depend not on the activities of the individual here, i.e. his *karma,* but on the nature of his death or the nature of the disposal of his dead body. The Rengmas believe that the souls of men go to the happy Land of the Dead, with the exception of the souls of those who die by accident or murder, or in child-birth, or by any other unnatural means, which the Assamese call *apotia.* The latter go to a place which is not known to anybody. A similar idea is also found among the Oraons. Among the Khasis, entry into the garden of God, where betel-nut trees abound, and where the souls enjoy the supreme happiness of chewing these nuts uninterruptedly, depends on the proper performance of the funeral rites.[33] 'The spirits of those whose funeral ceremonies have not been duly performed are believed to take the forms of animals, birds, or insects and to roam on this earth.' The Kharias of Chota Nagpur do not make any distinction between the souls of good and bad men, nor do they have any conception of heaven or hell.[34] All the souls of the dead go to live with their ancestral spirits in the underworld, with the exception of those who die by unnatural means, or those who have sexual commerce with people of other castes and tribes. Reference to the last group of souls seems to be a later development, a feeble attempt to preserve tribal integrity by this defence mechanism. The Murias of Bastar (a branch of the Gonds) have no idea of heaven or hell ; there is even no word for 'sin' in Gondi (the language of the Gonds). 'Though the Murias believe in rebirth, they have no idea of *karma* and their picture of life after death is quite unmoralized.'[35] Again, in a large number of Assam tribes a better life in the other world depends on accidental factors, such as personal prowess in war and chase, success in love-affairs, and performance of sacrifices. This is the case among the Lusheis[36] and Lakhers.[37] Among the Angamis, the performers of *Zhatho genna* go to the abode of Kepenopfu, the Creator, where they consume unlimited quantities of food and drink, and enjoy hunting without its risks.[38] With

[33] P. R. T. Gurdon, *The Khasis,* pp. 105-6. [34] S. C. Roy, *The Kharias,* p. 282.
[35] Verrier Elwin, *The Muria and Their Ghotul,* p. 145.
[36] J. Shakespeare, *The Lushei-Kuki Clans,* pp. 62, 64.
[37] N. E. Parry, *The Lakhers,* p. 396.
[38] J. H. Hutton, *The Angami Nagas,* pp. 184-85. *Zhatho genna*: Among the Angami

the exception of unowned bastard children, who turn into wild animals after death, all others go to the Village of the Dead.

This state of complete dissociation, between the individual's activities in this world and the fate of his soul in the next, is replaced in another set of tribes by rudimentary ideas of association between them. Among the Baigas, charity in this world is rewarded with a longer stay in the happy island of Bhagavān.[39] This supernatural sanction for charity is not in keeping with the rest of their concept of the other world and seems to be a recent innovation. It may not be due to the Hindu influence, as only a single moral attribute is extolled leaving aside others which are usually associated with this virtue in the Hindu mind. In the Lhota Naga society, 'virtue in this world is vaguely believed to be rewarded with happiness in the next, but this belief weighs little with a Naga'.[40] In the Rengma World of the Dead, the thieves and wicked men of this world merely remember their wicked deeds and feel unhappy therefor, while the good pass their days in joy.[41] Among the Todas, every soul goes to Amnodr sooner or later, but the *karainol* (selfish people), the *kashtvainol* (jealous and grudging people), and the *kashpivainol* (those who have committed any offence against sacred or secular dairy) suffer from bites of leeches in the Puvurkin, the Toda Styx.[42] The offences mentioned here are connected with the two most important aspects of Toda life, namely, pastoralism and polyandry, which are the bases of their economic and social life respectively.

Nagas, those who aspire after social recognition perform a number of rites, one after another, which confer social status on the performers. The first three of these rites are of minor importance, and are really preliminary steps. But each of the next four raises an individual to higher and higher ranks. *Zhatho genna* is the second of the latter series. In this *genna*, the performer has to entertain his villagers with the meat of eight bulls and four pigs. He is also required to spend sixty maunds of paddy for brewing rice-beer and preparing boiled rice for the feast. In return, he is allowed to wear a particular type of dress and fence a part of the front porch of his house.

[39] Verrier Elwin, *The Baiga*, p. 294.

[40] J. P. Mills, *The Lhota Nagas*, pp. 119-20.

[41] J. P. Mills, *The Rengma Nagas*, p. 170.

[42] W. H. R. Rivers, *The Todas*, pp. 398-400.

Kashtvainol: The Todas practise polyandry. A woman, besides her husband, may have permanent sexual relation with certain other persons with the knowledge and permission of her husband. On certain occasions, again, she habitually entertains some other persons, and this is overlooked by society. Therefore the whole social order is based on a very loose sex life. Dr. Rivers suspects that 'according to Toda idea, immorality attaches rather to the man who grudges his wife to another' than to adultery. He further adds that the term '*kashtvainol* (grudging people) . . . includes those who would, in a more civilized community, be plaintiffs in a divorce court'. Therefore the supernatural sanction, referred to here, is for the maintenance of a more or less loose sexual relation which has grown up round polyandry.

Kashpivainol: The Todas are a pastoral people who keep buffaloes and live on their products. These animals are divided into two classes, viz. sacred and ordinary or secular, though they do not differ in breed in any way. The former are tended by a particular class of people, who also act as priests of the community in certain rites. The sacred buffaloes are kept in separate huts, which are regarded as sacred. Ordinary people may not enter into them. There are also other taboos surrounding these animals. The ordinary or secular buffaloes, on the other hand, live in sheds constructed inside the village, and are tended by common people.

But side by side with this idea, there is the belief that the souls of the two villages of Kavidi and Taradr proceed directly to Amnodr, however wicked they might have been in this life. Mythological evidences also show that Toda after-life is not dependent on ethical concepts. Influence of ethical qualities on the fate of the soul in the other world is clearer in some other tribes like Aos, Lakhers, Baigas, Chenchus, and Warlis.

CONCEPT OF GODS AND SPIRITS

Belief in gods and spirits is universal in the primitive society of India. In the whole of this country, there is not a single tribe among whom this belief is absent. It is found in all stages of social and economic development. From the most primitive Kadars and Birhors, who lead a miserable existence by hunting and gathering, to the civilized Gonds, Hos, and Khasis, belief in supernatural beings is common and constant. The core of primitive religion of India consists of these beliefs in the deities and spirits, and the practices to please or placate them. But there is considerable variation in the depth of this belief and in the nature, forms, and functions of these gods and spirits. Speaking in general terms, these supernatural beings of the aborigines of India may be classified into the following four groups: (1) the supreme Deity, (2) ancestor-spirits, (3) tutelary deities of the village, and (4) evil spirits of hills, forests, rivers, etc. who cause disease and death.

THE SUPREME DEITY

The concept of a supreme Deity is comparatively well developed among the Lushei-Kuki tribes. 'The Lakhers believe that the destinies of the universe are in the hands of one God who is known as Khazangpa.' He lives in the sky, and is a just and benevolent deity who punishes the evildoers and rewards the good.[43] Among the Thadou Kukis, He is known as Pathen, the all-powerful. He created heaven and earth, gave life to everything, rules the universe, and has the power to thwart the activities of all evil spirits, for which sacrifices are made to Him.[44] A similar, though not such an elaborate, idea is found among the Lusheis and the Old Kukis like Chirus, Anals, Koms, and Kolhens.[45] Among the Purums, He has been supplanted in recent years by Krishoa, i.e. Kṛṣṇa, the Hindu deity.[46]

Among the Naga tribes, the idea of a supreme God is far less prominent. We find a trace of it in the Angami Kepenopfu who created all living beings and spirits, but not the universe, and is always beneficent to

[43] N. E. Parry, *The Lakhers*, pp. 349-50. [44] William Shaw, *The Thadou Kukis*, p. 71.
[45] J. Shakespeare, *The Lushei-Kuki Clans*, pp. 61, 157, 159.
[46] T. C. Das, *The Purums*, pp. 206-7.

mankind. He lives in the sky where the good souls go.[47] The Sema Alhou is also regarded as the Creator who does not interfere with human affairs, but is usually beneficent.[48] The highest God of the Aos is Lungkijingba who lives in the sky, but as He does not cause any affliction to man's spirit, He is not worshipped communally.[49] Among the Rengmas and Lhotas, this concept of a supreme Deity or of a Creator is not at all found.

In Chota Nagpur, the hinterland of Orissa, Chattisgarh, and Madhya Pradesh, the idea of a supreme God is well developed. He is the Creator of men, animals, and plants, of gods and spirits, indeed of the whole universe. He is omnipotent and omniscient. He rules over the other gods, who act according to His will. The sun is sometimes regarded as His visible form, or as His abode, or, again, as His eyes with which He sees everything that is going on in the worlds of men and gods. The association of the supreme Deity with the sun is a characteristic feature of the religious beliefs of the tribes of this region ; it is not found among the tribes of Assam. Among a large number of tribes of this tract, the word for the sun is the same as that for the supreme Deity. This concept of the supreme Deity, with the aforesaid characteristics fully or partially belonging to Him, is found among the Oraons, Mundas, Hos, Asurs, Korwas, Kharias, Birhors, Malers, Malpaharias, Bhuiyas, Juangs, Khonds, Gonds, Santals, and others of Chota Nagpur region and adjacent territories. It is also met with in southern India among the Chenchus, Uralis, Kanikkers, and others. Among some of these tribes, there is a belief that the supreme Deity does not take much interest in men and their fate. Though a benevolent Deity, He does not always try to save men from the clutches of evil spirits who afflict them with disease, death, and scarcity. As a result, these tribes do not actually worship Him regularly, but pay more attention to the malevolent spirits. He is sometimes even characterized as a helpless being in the hands of His own creation.

ANCESTOR-SPIRITS

Worship of ancestors is the natural consequence of the concept of souls and belief in an after-life. Ancestor-worship is a very prominent feature of the tribal society of India. It has attained its maximum development on the plateau of Chota Nagpur. The spirits of the deceased ancestors of every family of the Mundas are its Ora-Bongakos (house-gods).[50] They are regularly worshipped by the head of the family in the sacred tabernacle

[47] J. H. Hutton, *The Angami Nagas,* pp. 180-81.
[48] J. H. Hutton, *The Sema Nagas,* p. 191.
[49] W. C. Smith, *The Ao Naga Tribe of Assam,* pp. 77-78.
[50] S. C. Roy, *The Mundas and Their Country,* p. 468.

within the house. The Ho house-father daily worships the Oa-Bongas (ancestral spirits) in the *ading* (sacred tabernacle) of his hut with offerings of a part of the food prepared for the day.[51] On festive occasions, elaborate preparations are made for this purpose.[52] The ancestor-spirits of the Birhor hunters are divided into two classes: those of the recently dead, called Burha-Burhi, and those whose names cannot be remembered, known as Chowrasi Haprom. The former reveal the breaches of sexual taboos of their descendants to the witch-doctor, in dreams, so that they may be stopped. Offerings are made to both the classes for success in hunting and prevention of diseases.[53]

Assam also provides numerous instances of ancestor-worship. It is found among the Lusheis and Lakhers. The Manipuris hold the tribal ancestors as one of the four orders of spiritual beings.[54] Among the Khasis and Syntengs, the ancestors receive periodic and occasional offerings. 'It is possible that the Khasi gods of today are merely the spirits of glorified ancestors.'[55] In the Naga group of tribes, ancestor-worship is not much in evidence. It reappears, however, in full vigour in the extreme south of India. In Travancore-Cochin most of the tribes practise this cult. Megalithic monuments like dolmens and menhirs are often connected with ancestor-worship in India.

TUTELARY DEITIES OF THE VILLAGE

The concept of a tutelary deity of the village is as old as Neolithic times, when settled habitation first came into being. It is one of the most ancient institutions of man, and is found both among the savage and the civilized. In India, it is a common feature of all the areas where primitive man is found. In Orissa, Madras State, and the extreme south of the Indian peninsula, it is a very prominent trait of rural Hindu life. In almost every village of Orissa, there is a *grām-deoti* (village goddess), who is often identified with one of the different forms of the Mother Goddess. Her altar is generally under a big tree, where one meets with heaps of terracotta figurines of horses and elephants which have been offered to the deity in fulfilment of vows, often taken for recovery from diseases. She is worshipped both periodically and occasionally by individuals as also by the entire village. On occasions of birth, marriage, first rice-eating, etc., the individuals concerned are sure to be taken to her place for her blessings. In case of an epidemic, in or near the village, her protection is eagerly sought after. These traits of the *grām-deoti* may also be traced in Bengal and

[51] D. N. Majumdar, *A Tribe in Transition*, p. 141.
[52] T. C. Das, *The Hos of Seraikella*, p. 58.
[53] S. C. Roy, *The Birhors*, pp. 305-7.
[54] T. C. Hodson, *The Meitheis*, p. 96.
[55] P. R. T. Gurdon, *The Khasis*, pp. 109-10.

other parts of northern India in one shape or another. But they become more prominent as we travel towards the south.

Among the aboriginal population of India, the tutelary deity appears in almost all the areas. In Chota Nagpur, this concept has made considerable progress. Among the Santals, Mundas, Hos, Oraons, Kharias, and others, every village has a sacred grove where the tutelary deities of the village reside, and where they are worshipped. This grove is generally a patch of the primeval *śāl* forest, left intact to serve as a sort of refuge for the local spirits, when the village was first established by clearing the surrounding area of its natural vegetation. It generally lies outside the village, at a little distance from it. The land of the grove belongs to the village community as a whole, and the trees in it are sacred and their cutting is tabooed. A few pieces of stone placed under some specified types of trees are the seats of the different gods and goddesses associated with the village. In many cases, agricultural activities are connected with the worship of these village deities. The concept may also be traced in Chattisgarh and Madhya Pradesh. Among the Murias of Bastar, Tallur Muttai or the Earth Mother is the most important village deity. She supplies food to the people, and causes crops to grow and the natural vegetation to flourish.[56] The Earth, the Clan-god, and the Village-mother are often conceived among the Hill Marias and Bison-horn Marias as different aspects or forms of the same deity.[57] In Hyderabad, owing to the individualistic tendencies of Chenchu life, economic, social, and religious, we do not meet with a village tutelary deity among them. Among the Reddis too of the same region, the 'conception of a village deity was originally foreign'. But they have imbibed it from the Hindus. As a result, the worship of Mutielamma is found in the bigger settlements, where organized village life exists. Their deity is not altogether malevolent, as amongst the low-caste Telugus of the area, nor fully benevolent, as among the Mundari tribes, but 'helps or harms man in proportion to his care or negligence of her cult'.[58]

In Assam, this concept has not made much progress. Among the Naga group of tribes, it does not occur at all. Most of the Kuki tribes also do not show any knowledge of its existence. But it is found among the Khasis and Kacharis. Traces of it are also visible among the Old Kukis, Lakhers, Sema Nagas, and Meitheis. Two facts may possibly account for the peculiar distribution of this trait-complex in Assam, viz. the influence of pre-Dravidian culture and the migratory nature of the people.

[56] Verrier Elwin, *The Muria and Their Ghotul*, pp. 181-82.
[57] W. V. Grigson, *The Maria Gonds of Bastar*, pp. 196-97.
[58] C. von Fürer-Haimendorf, *The Reddis of the Bison Hills*, pp. 225-27.

EVIL SPIRITS

In primitive belief, health of men and animals, welfare of crops, and supply of wild products depend on the whims of supernatural beings. Primitive man believes that by nature these beings are malevolent. They do not need an excuse to harm a man. They are extremely selfish, greedy, vicious, and devoid of all the higher qualities like mercy, justice, etc. Like thieves, they prowl about human habitations in the darkness of night and catch hold of the unwary villager who ventures to come out of the protection of his hut. In the forests, on the slopes of hills, they roam about freely, and the aborigines have to risk their lives every day, in the course of their occupational work in these tracts. The Naga 'shifting hill-cultivator' prepares his field in the densely forested slopes of hills. The Birhor hunter pursues his game deep into the jungles of Chota Nagpur. The Toda pastoral nomad leads his buffalo-herd through the grass-covered hills and dales of the Nilgiris. Thus, primitive man, in whatever stage of economic development he might be, cannot avoid the forest. He is therefore constantly confronted with the supernatural dangers which proceed from the uncanny and mysterious denizens of the jungles. The evil spirits not only reside in forests, they also occupy the hill-tops around the village. The rivers, streams, springs, pools, and lakes have also their indwelling spirits. They pounce upon the unfortunate villager when he goes to fish, draw water, or bathe in any one of them. Even the big trees and big boulders may serve as their residence. Primitive man is thus surrounded by these supernatural beings, who, though generally invisible, may appear before mortal eyes when necessary.

Disease and death emanate from these evil spirits. Their wrath may blight the crops. The fruit trees wither, the springs dry up, and the game disappears, if they will it. Man appears to be a helpless being in the hands of these powerful spirits, who control his life in this world. But this dependence is more apparent than real. Primitive man has found out means to fight with the supernatural beings. The Aos believe that, if the annual sacrifices are properly performed, they have nothing to fear from these enemies of mankind. Most of the tribes believe that by timely offerings of food and sacrifices these may not only be appeased, but may also be pleased to help man in his daily life. Besides prayers, offerings of food, and sacrifices to please these spirits, wherein man appears as a beggar, he has also evolved a technique to control these powerful beings. This is magic. The magician plays the part of the scientist in primitive society. He does not supplicate to powerful spirits for favour. Conscious of the efficacy of his means and methods, he proceeds to command as a master. The Purum *maipi* (female witch-doctor) orders the evil spirit responsible for death in child-birth to depart from the house in the following words: 'Kapar Santepa, rice is being scattered. Your eyes will be injured. Your teeth will be broken. The joints of your limbs will be shattered. Your bowels will go wrong. Go hence from today. Don't remain here. Your abode is far away. Your dwelling place is on the other side.'[59] There is no element of entreaty in this incantation. The magician harbours no doubt about the powers of his means and methods. He is sure of success, provided the procedure is correctly followed. With a powerful ally of this kind at his command, primitive man does not think himself to be a helpless victim of the vagaries of these supernatural beings. His life therefore is not a continuous round of cringing submissions, it has also its joys of subjugation.

Primitive man employs religion to solve the practical problems of his daily life, just as civilized man employs science. Both are concerned with the problems of this world, and not of the other. The aim is the same, though the means differ. Contact between the aborigines and the civilized has weakened the former's faith in their own means, and has led to changes in their outlook. The aborigines are now adopting more and more the ways of the civilized, being attracted by the glamour of the latter's material achievements. It lies with the future to show whether religion or science will win the race to secure real happiness for man.

[59] T. C. Das, *The Purums*, p. 232.

31

A GLIMPSE INTO HINDU RELIGIOUS SYMBOLISM

THROUGHOUT the history of the Hindu religion, symbols and forms and personalistic conceptions of the Divinity have played a great part in matters of worship.

Our vision is limited ; and all that we see is coloured by this limitation. What we see is not light as it is, but only a reflection, and that also within a certain range. Our understanding is also circumscribed. What we know, we know through the limiting adjuncts of our mind, through the medium of what Śaṅkarācārya calls *kāla, deśa,* and *nimitta*—time, space, and causation. In short, we are bound to the domain of the finite, of symbols, which point to the truth, but are not able to express it truly and fully.

But there are symbols and symbols, the real ones and the false ones. The mirage has got the appearance of water, but it is a delusive phenomenon which has nothing to do with water ; while the wave may be recognized as a true symbol of the ocean, because it rises out of it, is in touch with it, and also gets merged in it. Like the ocean, it is made of the same substance, water.

Further, there are lower and higher symbols. The alphabet or the image is a symbol of the sound or name ; the sound or name, a symbol of thought ; and even thought becomes a symbol of the reality which it tries to express, but can do so only inadequately.

In Hinduism, the domain of symbols and worship of divine personalities is a vast one, and therefore here we shall deal with only some of the symbols used, and divine personalities adored, in worship and meditation, from the Vedic times down to the present day, with a view to realizing God in some aspect or other.

But why should we care for the truth or for God? The answer is that there are many who cannot help it. As Śrī Kṛṣṇa says in the *Bhagavad-Gītā*: 'Four types of persons worship Me (God), . . . the distressed, the seeker for knowledge, the seeker after enjoyment, and the wise' (VII. 16). The man of spiritual illumination, to whom God is the only reality, spontaneously worships Him and speaks of His glory out of the fullness of his love and devotion. But, for others who seek divine protection in order to be saved from the miseries of life, or who want divine aid for the fulfilment of desires, God is a practical necessity. For, baffled in their search for succour from outside, those that are heavy-laden turn inward with a deep earnestness for a guide and friend who will never fail them.

DIFFERENT CONCEPTIONS OF THE GODHEAD

The conceptions about the nature of the divine Being whom men seek vary with the growth in knowledge of the seekers. Sri Ramakrishna observes: 'There are three classes of devotees. The lowest one says, "God is up there". That is, he points to heaven. The mediocre devotee says that God dwells in the heart as the inner controller. But the highest devotee says, "God alone has become everything. All the things that we perceive are so many forms of God".'[1]

'Think of Brahman, Existence-Knowledge-Bliss Absolute, as a shoreless ocean. Through the cooling influence, as it were, of the *bhakta's* love, the water has frozen at places into blocks of ice. In other words, God now and then assumes various forms for His lovers and reveals Himself to them as a person. But with the rising of the sun of knowledge, the blocks of ice melt. Then one does not feel any more that God is a person, nor does one see God's forms.'[2]

In our study of the Hindu scriptures, we come across various conceptions of the Godhead. Some devotees speak of Him as possessing both divine forms and attributes. They want to establish personal relationship with Him. Others speak of Him as being endowed with infinite power and knowledge and other qualities, and think that, though formless, He assumes various forms. While they take note of the personal aspect, they particularly stress the impersonal aspect, of which the former is a manifestation.

During the early stages of their spiritual life, most devotees cannot help associating human forms and sentiments with the Divine and thinking of Him as outside of themselves. Sometimes we find that, as the result of self-purification, brought about by sincere devotion, the devotee gets a vision within himself of the same divine Being he has been so long worshipping as an outside object. Then he realizes Him as the indwelling Spirit, as 'the Ear of ear, the Mind of mind, and the Life of life' (*Ke. U.*, I. 2). Next he finds Him to be the one Deity 'who is in the fire, who is in the water, who pervades the whole universe', 'who has become man and woman, youth and maiden, and is born in manifold form'.[3] God, to him, is now the principle immanent in all beings and things. He is not merely the God of gods, but is also the true Self of all, the Life universal. Proceeding further, the seer realizes Him as the transcendental Entity who is 'beyond speech and thought' (*Tai. U.*, II. 9), who is 'invisible, . . . devoid of all connotations, unthinkable, indefinable, essentially of the nature of Consciousness constituting the Self alone, . . . the Peaceful, supreme Bliss, and the Non-dual' (*Mā. U.*, 7).

[1] *The Gospel of Sri Ramakrishna* (Translated by Swami Nikhilananda, Second Ed.), p. 345.
[2] *Ibid.*, p. 77. [3] *Śvetāśvatara Upaniṣad*, II. 17 ; IV. 3.

The Vedic *ṛṣis* worshipped Indra, the thunderer and the giver of rains; Mitra, the god who regulated the course of the sun; Varuṇa, the god who dwelt in the bright blue sky and released the penitent from sin; and Agni, the god of fire, sometimes spoken of as father, and also as brother, kinsman, and friend (*Ṛ.V.*, I. 1. 9). Savitṛ, the solar deity who stimulated life and activity in the world, was invoked in order to guide the understanding of the devotee (*Ṛ.V.*, III. 62. 10). It was a very striking fact that, even at this early stage of spiritual consciousness, some of the Vedic seers could recognize the presence of an indwelling Spirit behind each and every natural phenomenon. And behind their apparently polytheistic conceptions, there lay an ingrained monotheism that was clearly expressed, as each god was invoked and worshipped in turn as omnipotent, omniscient, and even omnipresent. This is made clear in the well-known hymn that declares: 'To what is one, sages give many a name. They call Him Indra, Mitra, Varuṇa, and Agni' (*Ṛ.V.*, I. 164. 46).

Since the time of the *Ṛg-Veda*, a revolution has taken place in Hinduism, especially with regard to the symbols and names associated with worship and prayers. Names that were once of minor importance came to be prominent in later times, and vice versa, while new names were also added in later times. The worship, for instance, of incarnations and prophets like Rāma and Kṛṣṇa became popular in later times. But in the midst of these striking changes, the Hindu devotee's conception of the supreme Deity, his highest spiritual hopes and aspirations, his desire to seek divine aid and guidance, and his yearning for spiritual communion have remained unchanged. With the march of time, it has been recognized with greater clearness that the impersonal Principle forms the background of all the holy symbols and is the source of all divine personalities. Indeed, according to Advaita (non-dualistic) Vedānta, whatever be the symbol one may adopt or the personality one may adore, to begin with, the highest goal of spiritual life lies in the ultimate experience of the Impersonal, the One without a second, the Infinite, in which the worshipper—nay, God, souls, and the universe—is merged and becomes one with the Infinite.

IMPERSONAL AND PERSONAL ASPECTS OF THE DIVINE

In the Vedānta, we have monistic meditations that negate the non-Self and assert the Self. 'I am neither the mind nor the intellect, neither memory nor ego. I am not the sense of hearing or of taste, of smell or of sight. I am neither ether nor earth, nor fire nor air. I am Śiva (the auspicious), the Consciousness-Bliss Absolute. I am Śiva.'[4]

[4] Śaṅkarācārya, *Nirvāṇa-ṣaṭka*, 1.

'I am the indeterminate, changeless and formless, all-pervading and omnipresent. I am beyond the touch of all sense-organs. I am not even freedom, never having had any bondage ; I am beyond all relative knowledge. I am Śiva. . . .'[5]

This type of meditation is in line with the approach to the Reality followed by some of the boldest of the Upaniṣadic seers in their meditation on the Immutable: 'It is neither gross nor minute, neither short nor long, . . . without eyes or ears, without the vocal organ or mind, without interior or exterior . . .' (*Bṛ. U.*, III. 8. 8). 'This Immutable . . . is never seen, but is the Witness ; . . . It is never thought, but is the Thinker ; It is never known, but is the Knower' (*Bṛ. U.*, III. 7. 23).

Besides this lofty conception of the absolute, transcendent Reality, the One without a second, there are the ideas of the impersonal, immanent divine Principle, which manifests itself through finite forms and yet remains infinite and formless. Many aspirants prefer to worship such a divine Principle, as they feel no interest in the personal aspect of the Divine. They meditate: 'He is below, He is above, He is at the back, He is in front, He is in the south, He is in the north, He indeed is everywhere and in everything' (*Chā. U.*, VII. 25. 1). 'He is subtler than the subtlest, vaster than the vastest, the Self seated in the heart of all beings' (*Ka. U.*, II. 20). He exists in and through the earth, air, sun, moon, and stars ; He dwells in all beings ; He inhabits the eye, ear, mind, and intellect ; He controls everything and every being from within ; He is the internal Ruler, the immortal Self of the worshipper (*Bṛ. U.*, III. 7).

But as Śrī Kṛṣṇa has put it in the *Bhagavad-Gītā*: 'Greater is the difficulty of those whose minds are set on the Absolute. For the heights of the Absolute are very hard for embodied beings to reach' (XII. 5). Often it happens, however, that the symbol or the personal aspect of the Divine does not appeal to the philosophic sense of the devotee, while the Impersonal appears to be an abstraction. Hence the worship of, and the meditation on, the Impersonal, through the personal aspects and symbols, has been most popular in Hinduism in almost all forms of spiritual practice.

DIFFERENT TYPES OF WORSHIPPERS

Swami Brahmananda, a disciple of Sri Ramakrishna, tells us: 'Men incline to different ways of worship. To satisfy the various temperaments, the scriptures describe four distinct methods of reaching God.'[6] 'The highest spiritual discipline is the practice of Brahman-consciousness. The next is meditation. Chanting of hymns and repetition of the divine name

[5] *Ibid.*, 6.

[6] *The Eternal Companion*, p. 133.

form the third step. The lowest is external worship with the help of an image.'[7]

'The twice-born ritualists worship God in the fire. Men of meditation adore Him as the indwelling Spirit. The dull-witted worship Him with the help of the image. The same-sighted (non-discriminating) illumined souls find Him everywhere.'[8] Agni, as mentioned already, is the God of fire, or rather the God in fire. The Vedas speak of Him as immortal who has taken up His abode among the mortals. In this aspect, the Deity is called 'the mouth of the gods', through whom all other gods receive oblations and worship. Advanced souls do not mind the outside symbol; they meditate on the Deity as immanent, as dwelling in their own hearts. Persons of gross understanding can begin their spiritual life by worshipping the Deity with the help of the image, which is like a peg to hang their faith on. Enlightened souls, on the other hand, do not need any symbols, for they recognize the divine Spirit both inside and outside, as immanent and transcendent at the same time.

SOME SYMBOLS OF THE DIVINE

Śiva is worshipped in the image or in the form of a *liṅga,* which, whatever be its original significance, does not call up in the minds of the worshippers of Śiva any phallic association at all. To them, the *liṅga* is just a non-anthropomorphic, aniconic form or symbol of the supreme Spirit which, though manifest in forms, transcends them all. The Tāntric devotee takes the *liṅga* as a symbol of the divine male-female creative power. *Śālagrāma-śilā* is another non-anthropomorphic symbol associated with Viṣṇu, who is often worshipped in the four-handed image, holding conch, wheel, mace, and lotus, or in His divine incarnations as Rāma, Kṛṣṇa, etc. The followers of Tantra, and even others, sometimes worship the Deity in the *yantra* or geometrical diagrams representing the mystical body of the divine Being. Sometimes a *paṭa* or two-dimensional painting or picture, serves as the symbol, instead of the three-dimensional image in which the Deity is invoked. In many types of mystical worship, a *ghaṭa* (pot) full of water is used, either solely or in addition to other forms, to represent the formless, all-pervading Spirit. Agni or fire may also take the place of other forms. The lighted fire is regarded as the body of God and is worshipped by offering oblations into it.

At times, in refined types of worship, a *mantra* like *Om* or some divine

[7] *'Uttamo Brahmasadbhāvo dhyānabhāvastu madhyamaḥ,*
Stutirjapo'dhamobhāvo bahiḥpūjādhamādhamā.'

[8] *Uttara-Gītā,* III. 8.

name serves as the symbol. *Mantra* literally means 'a sound symbol which, when repeated and reflected on, frees the soul from bondage'.

As a sound symbol, *Om* represents the undifferentiated (*akhaṇḍa*) Brahman ; the other *mantras* or names represent the differentiated (*khaṇḍa*) aspects of the same Being. Different Tāntric divinities are assigned special *bīja* (seed) *mantras,* which are credited with the power of originating or evolving their corresponding divine forms or manifestations before the meditating devotee.

The holy names are the sound-manifestations of the divine power, which is awakened through *japa,* or the repetition of the word, and the meditation on its meaning. Says Śrī Caitanya: 'Various are Thy names, O Lord, and in each Thou hast infused Thy full power.'[9] The many names of the Deity represent His various aspects, which can be realized through *japa.* The practice of using multiplicity of names for the same God comes down from the Vedic times.

FORMS OF WORSHIP

To merge oneself in the Absolute, the One without a second, is the goal of the Advaitic spiritual practice. This state is reached through an uncompromising analysis of all experience in search of the ultimate Reality, the unchanging basis of the ever-changing phenomenal universe. The follower of this method, being established in perfect purity, negates all limiting adjuncts and reaches the ultimate Reality.

With a view to attaining this unity, a less qualified spiritual seeker may practise *ahaṁ-graha upāsanā,* a method of worship in which the worshipper is to identify himself with the object of his worship—God or Brahman or any particular deity. Meditation on the identity between the worshipper and the worshipped leads to the realization of the One without a second.

To those who find this process also difficult, *pratīkopāsanā,* worship with the help of some appropriate symbol, is prescribed. The Deity is worshipped not *as* the symbol, but *through* the symbol. The aim is to recognize in the limited the presence of the all-pervading Spirit which transcends all limitations of name and form. As Swami Vivekananda remarks: 'Where Brahman Himself is the object of worship, the *pratīka* stands only as a substitute or a suggestion thereof.'[10] The *pratīka* may be internal, like the mind, intellect, or the soul of the worshipper, or it may be external, like *Om,* the sun, *ākāśa* (space), *agni* (fire), etc. Through properly performed meditation, the same Spirit is ultimately recognized as

[9] *'Nāmnāmakāri bahudhā nijasarvaśaktistatrārpitā'* (*Śikṣāṣṭaka,* 2).
[10] *The Complete Works of Swami Vivekananda,* III. p. 60.

pervading and transcending both the internal and external planes of consciousness.

Those who find such forms of worship to be too subtle should begin with the use of the *pratimā* or image. 'If the image', says Swami Vivekananda, 'stands for a god or a saint, the worship does not lead to liberation, but if it stands for the one God, the worship thereof will bring *bhakti* (devotion) and *mukti* (liberation).'[11]

'Worship of the image, or the use of the image symbolizing the ideal, is the first step; then come repetition of the holy name and singing of divine glory. The next step is the mental worship, the last being to feel and realize "I am He".'[12]

USE OF SYMBOLS: LOWER AND HIGHER

God is one, but His aspects are many. As it is impossible for us to worship Him in all His fullness and glory, we take up some aspect or other of the Lord. But even in order to approach Him through any of His personal aspects, as Śiva or Viṣṇu or the divine Power, we need the help of different symbols—material, verbal, or mental—, which may be taken up either singly or jointly. The symbol is not the Reality. It is only a means of remembering the Lord, through the association of ideas.

The neophyte in spiritual life may take the help of material symbols in the form of the image, or *cakras,* or geometrical figures representing the ideal. As he advances, he may dispense with material help and make use of the sound symbols to call up the divine idea. Advancing further, he may do away with both the material and the sound symbols, and proceed with purely mental worship, on the plane of thought, silently and quietly. And even this he can give up, when, at the very thought of the Divine, he is able to lose his little self, like a salt doll, in the infinite ocean of Existence, in which all distinctions of the worshipper and the worshipped disappear completely.

FROM GODS TO THE GODHEAD

The true devotee sometimes looks upon the divine form he worships as an embodiment of the attributes that reveal the supreme Principle in some way or other. He means by the symbol or form a divine idea, and this idea, again, becomes a symbol of the Reality that is at the back of everything.

Śiva is one of the gods of popular Hinduism. The gross-minded

[11] *Ibid.,* III. p. 61.
[12] *'Prathamā pratimā-pūjā japa-stotrādi madhyamā,*
Uttamā mānasī-pūjā so'haṁ pūjottamottamā.'

worshipper may take Him to be the God of destruction, dwelling in the lonely mountains or the cremation ground. But to the evolved devotee, He is the embodiment of renunciation and the destroyer of all evil. He is, besides, the personification of contemplation and divine consciousness. The advanced worshipper sings His glory thus: 'O Lord, Thou art the universal Being without a second. Thou art everything.'[13]

The material-minded worshipper of Viṣṇu sees in Him the God of protection and preservation, who, out of His infinite mercy, incarnates Himself for the good of His devotees. But the devotee of the highest type sees in Him the embodiment of the divine Principle that permeates the entire universe, in whom is being enacted the world-play with its creation, preservation, and dissolution. And he prays: 'Lord, Thou abidest in all; Thou art all; Thou assumest all forms.'[14]

The Mother-Power, or the divine Energy, has many forms and symbols. Sometimes She is symbolized as the Goddess of death, playing the dance of destruction. In the form of Kālī, She is represented as the Power of creation, protection, and destruction, and as the Power in which all things rest after dissolution. She stands on the still, prostrate form of Śiva, the representation of the Absolute. This is symbolical of the entire cosmic process with the transcendental Reality as its basis. Reality is beyond both life and death, and, as such, the devotee should neither cling to life nor be afraid of death. He should rise, above both the pleasant and the terrible, to the transcendental plane from where he can say: 'The shade of death and immortality—both these, O Mother, are Thy grace supreme.'[15] And addressing Her, the devotee says: 'Thou hast neither name nor lineage, neither birth nor death, neither bondage nor freedom. Thou art the One without a second, known as the Being supreme.'[16]

Rāma is one of the incarnations of Viṣṇu, and is the embodiment of devotion to truth and duty. The ordinary worshipper stresses His lovely form and noble attributes. But the illumined devotee sees Him immanent in all, and prays: 'Thou art the embodiment of the highest virtues. Thou art the indweller, the supreme Being. Thou art the greatest refuge and saviour of mankind.'[17] 'Thou art the stainless, changeless, indestructible, pure, and eternal wisdom and truth.'[18]

The Kṛṣṇa ideal in its various forms is very wide-spread, but is also misunderstood by many. Crude-minded critics take His sport with the *gopīs* in Vṛndāvana in a vulgar sense. But devotees like Sri Ramakrishna saw in Him the highest ideal of divine love, which can be realized only by

[13] *Skanda Purāṇa*, IV. 1. 10. 126.
[14] *Viṣṇu Purāṇa*, I. 12. 71.
[15] Swami Vivekananda, *Ambā-stotra*, 5.
[16] *Mahākāla Saṁhitā*, *Mahākālī-stotra*, 6.
[17] *Vālmīki Rāmāyaṇa*, VI. 117. 14, 17.
[18] *Adhyātma Rāmāyaṇa*, I. 5. 56.

those who have become free from all traces of sensuality and crudeness. Realizing His 'universal form', manifest in every individual, Arjuna makes obeisance to Him, saying, 'Salutations to Thee before, and to Thee behind. Salutations to Thee on every side. O Lord, Thou art everything. Infinite in power and infinite in prowess, Thou pervadest all; Thou art all' (*B.G.*, XI. 40).

MAN'S RELATION TO GOD

As most of us are at present constituted, we have to take the help of images and imaginations. So long as we cannot rise to the transcendental plane of pure Consciousness, and cannot help making use of images and imaginations, let us have those that are pure and elevating, instead of those that are vile and degrading. Therefore does Swami Vivekananda say:

> . . . Be bold, and face
> The Truth! Be one with it! Let visions cease,
> Or, if you cannot, dream but truer dreams,
> Which are Eternal Love and Service Free.[19]

The beginner in spiritual life, very conscious of his embodied existence, looks upon God as separate from him, and worships Him as Master, Father, Mother, Child, Friend, or Beloved. As the result of dreaming such truer dreams, he evolves inwardly and comes to have a new attitude towards himself and the Divine. He comes to feel within himself an all-pervading divine presence, of which his own soul is a fragment or part. He may even look upon himself as atomic, and God as infinite. As he advances further in the course of his spiritual evolution, he realizes that it is the one infinite divine Principle that appears as the many—the divine personalities, souls, and universe—, and, finally, during the highest flights of his soul, he feels he is one with the Real, the Absolute.

'O Lord,' says a great devotee, addressing his Deity, Rāma, 'when I think that I am inseparable from body, I regard myself as Thy servant. When I take me as a Jīva, I think I am a part of Thee, and Thou art the Whole. When I look upon myself as the pure Spirit, beyond body and thought, I am no other than Thyself. This is my firm conviction.'[20]

God is like the infinite ocean. We, ordinary beings, who are preoccupied with the body-idea, are like bubbles. And divine personalities, great prophets, and seers are like waves, big or small. The bubble, in order to rise above its limited outlook, first attaches itself to a mighty wave

[19] 'To the Awakened India', *The Complete Works of Swami Vivekananda,* IV. p. 324.
[20] '*Dehabuddhyā tu dāso'smi jīvabuddhyā tvadaṁśakaḥ,*
Ātmabuddhyā tvamevāham iti me niścitā matiḥ.'

that is conscious of its unity with the ocean. As a result, it comes to know that it is the ocean that manifests itself as waves and bubbles, and, when the wave and the bubble forms subside, it is all one ocean. The final relation between God and the devotee is very aptly expressed by Śaṅkarācārya: 'Lord, it is the waves that get merged in the ocean, and not the ocean in the waves. So, when all limitations are removed from me, it is I who become merged in Thee, and not Thou in me.'[21]

THE BODY AS THE DIVINE ABODE

The Vedānta, in its all-comprehensive aspect, has got to find a place for the use of idols and symbols in worship, so long as most of us remain in a state of childhood in spiritual matters. 'This body of ours is a temple of the Divine', says one of the minor Upaniṣads.[22] The *Kaṭha Upaniṣad* expresses this idea by means of a charming simile: 'Know the Self within you to be the master of the chariot, and the body to be the chariot' (III. 3). Instead of worshipping God in the elements like fire and water, i.e. rivers etc., in plants and animals, or in images of clay, stone, and metal, we may worship Him in the image of the human body, regarding it as a temple, or a chariot, or a house of the Divine which dwells and shines in the hearts of us all. Through the worship of the all-pervading God in the microcosm, we come to realize Him also in the macrocosm, the microcosm being a miniature symbol of the macrocosm.

But if, instead of the divine Principle, the symbol, or form, or personality becomes more important, then the worship loses all its spiritual value. So it is necessary that, in order to profit by our worship and prayer, we cultivate the right mood and attitude, without which spiritual progress is not possible at all. But how is the right mood to be created? The later Yoga literature has laid down that this can be done by controlling lower planes of thinking, through a graded realization of the spiritual possibilities in us. The different planes of thinking, associated with the six yogic centres in the spinal cord and the seventh in the brain, may be likened to the different storeys of a building connected by a staircase. The centres are like points of contact between ourselves and the planes of thought. It is stated in *The Gospel of Sri Ramakrishna*: 'The mind of a worldly man generally moves among the three lower centres: those at the navel, at the sexual organ, and at the organ of evacuation. After great effort and spiritual practice, the *kuṇḍalinī* (the coiled up or sleeping soul-force) is awakened. . . . The *kuṇḍalinī*, when awakened, passes through the lower centres, and comes to *anāhata* which is at the heart. . . . At that time the mind of the

[21] Śaṅkarācārya, *Ṣaṭpadī-stotra*, 3.

[22] *Maitreyī Upaniṣad*, II. 1.

aspirant is withdrawn from the three lower centres. He feels the awakening of divine Consciousness and sees Light. . . . The centre known as *viśuddha* is the fifth plane. This centre is at the throat. When the *kuṇḍalinī* reaches this plane, the devotee longs to talk and hear only of God. . . . Then comes the sixth plane, corresponding to the centre known as *ājñā*. This centre is located between the eyebrows. . . . When the *kuṇḍalinī* reaches it, the aspirant sees the form of God. But still there remains a slight barrier between the devotee and God. . . . And last of all is the seventh plane, which, according to Tantra, is the centre of the thousand-petalled lotus. When the *kuṇḍalinī* reaches there, the aspirant goes into *samādhi* . . . loses all consciousness of the world.'[23]

This path of spiritual practice, in which the mind is made to rise from one centre to another up to the highest plane of spiritual consciousness, is a most difficult one. But every aspirant, who wants to follow the path of meditation, should try to raise the 'focus of will' or the centre of consciousness at least to the centre in the region of the heart. This centre may be likened also to an 'inner space'. Some find it easier to make the heart, and some the forehead, the centre of their consciousness.

Those who are not drawn towards any particular symbol or image may meditate, in some higher centre or plane of consciousness, on the divine Light that permeates not only one's own being, but the whole universe of men and things, while the aspirant who cannot do without a form may carry on meditation on the luminous form, which will ultimately lead to the meditation on the formless Luminosity, the light of the Spirit that illumines all things.

SOME NON-ANTHROPOMORPHIC SYMBOLS FOR MEDITATION

Besides the meditation on symbolic representations already mentioned, a few others may be briefly noticed.

The soul may look upon itself as a spark of the infinite, eternal, divine Fire, and meditate accordingly. Says the Upaniṣad: 'This is the truth. As from a blazing fire, there shoot out, by thousands, sparks of the same appearance, so do the various beings originate from the one imperishable Spirit ; and verily, into It they go back' (*Mu. U.*, II. 1. 1). The soul may also be likened to a river flowing towards the sea. The aspirant may think of himself as the river entering and uniting itself with the ocean, the symbol of the infinite Being (*Mu. U.*, III. 2. 8). The beginner in meditation, who does not care for anthropomorphic conceptions of God, may think of Him as the infinite ocean, in which he swims unobstructed like a fish, and

[23] *Op. cit.*, pp. 455-56.

realize, in course of time, His vast infinite nature. Or, he may liken himself to a pot immersed in the ocean of God. On all sides there lies the same infinite water of life, and he comes to know of its infinite glory by meditating on it. The aspirant may also consider himself to be an empty pot, immersed in the ocean of ether that permeates everything.[24] He wants to give up the false ego, the pot that separates him from the Infinite, and thus establish his union with It. The devotee may also look upon God as the infinite space in which, like a bird, he flies without any obstruction and realize His infinite nature and glory. He may even consider himself to be a ray of light reflected on a particle of sand, i.e. the body, with which, owing to ignorance, he identifies himself.[25] In truth, the ray is inseparable from the infinite Light that shines everywhere.

THE PATH AND THE GOAL

The course of our progress is this: With the help of the form, we have to reach the formless; with the aid of the holy names and attributes, we have to attain the Absolute which is beyond all names and attributes. To stimulate our souls, we may even visit holy places where the saintly and divine presence may be felt more than at others. But our goal is to attain to that which is beyond all bounds and limitations.

The following two prayers beautifully bring out this idea with a force and earnestness all their own.

'O Lord, in my meditations I have attributed forms to Thee who art formless. O Thou, Teacher of the world, by singing Thy glory, I have covered the idea that Thou art beyond all speech. By describing Thee as specially manifested at places of pilgrimage and the like, I have denied Thy omnipresence. O Lord of the universe, pray, forgive me for the threefold fault of mutilation committed by me.'[26]

'From the unreal lead me to the Real. From darkness lead me to Light. From death lead me to eternal Life.'[27]

[24] *Maitreyī Upaniṣad*, II. 27.
[25] Śaṅkarācārya, *Brahmanāmāvalimālā*, 22.
[26] *'Rūpaṁ rūpavivarjitasya bhavato dhyānena yat kalpitam,*
Stutyānirvacanīyatākhilaguro dūrīkṛtā yanmayā;
Vyāpitvañca nirākṛtaṁ bhagavato yattīrtha-yātrādinā,
Kṣantavyaṁ jagadīśa tadvikalatā doṣatrayaṁ matkṛtam.'
[27] *'Asato mā sadgamaya, tamaso mā jyotirgamaya, mṛtyormā amṛtaṁ gamaya'* (*Br. U.*, I. 3. 28).

32

RITUALS OF WORSHIP

RITUALS obtaining in Hinduism today may be classified into two groups, Vedic and Āgamic.[1] The word *'āgama'* means 'that which has come', and hence denotes a system or knowledge that has come from some other source. There are different opinions regarding the source from which Āgama has arisen; some trace it to the Veda itself, while others consider it to be of Dravidian or proto-Dravidian origin,[2] later on adopted by Indo-Aryans with modifications to suit Vedic practices. Perhaps, a proper deciphering of the script of the Mohenjo-daro people and a study of their religion may throw some light on this and allied problems; till then the theory of Dravidian origin cannot readily be accepted. Vedic and Āgamic forms of worship are apparently very different. A closer study will, however, reveal many points of similarity, and even identity, sufficient to warrant the probability of one being evolved from the other in the natural course of events.

PRESENT-DAY VEDIC AND ĀGAMIC RITUALS

There are two characteristics of Āgama *mantras* or ritualistic formulae: the presence of *bījākṣaras* (seed-letters)[3] as an essential element and the comparative modernness of their language. The latter factor signifies that Āgama and Āgamic formulae belong to a later period than that of the Vedas. It may also be noted that the later offshoots of Hinduism, such as Buddhism and Jainism, have ritualistic formulae indistinguishable from Āgamic ones.[4] Further, one cannot assert that Vedic ritualism did not use *bījākṣaras*. The *praṇava* or *Om* and terms such as *svāhā, svadhā*, etc. should really be classed with *bījākṣaras*; at any rate, the *praṇava* cannot but be such. The meanings given to the Vedic *praṇava* and the Āgamic *bījākṣaras* are both artificial and derived in the same manner. All *bījākṣaras* end in

[1] The terms Āgama and Tantra are often used to mean all the three: Saṁhitā, Āgama, and Tantra. In their specific sense Saṁhitā stands for Vaiṣṇava, Āgama for Śaiva, and Tantra for Śākta systems.

[2] The word 'Dravidian' is used to denote a culture-type and not a bio-type. A belt of ancient culture, with great similarity in script, is seen extending through Crete, Elam, Mohenjo-daro, Harappā, the Andamans, the Eastern Islands, etc. This culture is sometimes designated as Dravidian.

[3] *'Hrīṁ', 'kroṁ'*, etc. These terms or sounds have well-defined meanings and are rationally planned, though highly artificial and technical.

[4] Cf. *'Oṁ maṇipadme huṁ'* (*vidyāṣaḍakṣarī* of the Buddhists) or *'Oṁ hrīṁ hlīṁ vikṛtānana huṁ, sarva śatrūn nāśaya stambhaya phaṭ phaṭ svāhā'* (a Buddhist *śatrusaṁhāra* formula from *Āryamañjuśrī-mūlakalpa*. The text is corrupt in many places).

anusvāra (*ṁ*). It is probable that Āgamic *bījākṣaras* were fashioned after the *praṇava,* the most sacred and, as far as known, the earliest *bījākṣara.*

The term *Om* originally appears to have had only an affirmative sense ;[5] it is still used in that sense in certain *śrauta* or religious and *gṛhya* or social ceremonies.[6] *Om* as a *bījākṣara,* in one interpretation, connotes the triune functionaries, Brahmā, Viṣṇu, and Śiva, all three conceived together as one. According to *Manu Saṁhitā,* the three letters, *a, u, m,* constituting *Om,* were milked out of the three Vedas—*Ṛk, Yajus,* and *Sāman*—by Prajāpati, so that they represent the quintessence of the *trayī* (the three original Vedic canons). Buddhists and Jains freely use these *bījākṣaras* including *Om* in their ritualistic formulae.[7]

Vedic rites are almost non-existent today except for a few *gṛhya* (social) ones, such as marriage etc. ; and these are, strictly speaking, social rather than religious ceremonies. The *aupāsana* (tending of the sacred fire of the *gṛhastha* or householder), the *samidādhāna* (tending of the sacred fire of the *brahmacārin* or student), and the *sandhyā-vandana* (worship of the sun as Savitṛ or Creator of life[8] at dawn, noon, and evening) are considered to be the obligatory forms of Vedic worship for the first three *varṇas* or social classes. There are exceptions ; obligatory rites differ for the different *āśramas* or stages of life, and there is no ritualistic worship, Vedic or Āgamic, obligatory to the *sannyāsin.*

Sandhyā-vandana, as it is performed today in many parts of India, appears to be a composite form consisting of Vedic *mantras,* yogic measures, such as *prāṇāyāma* (a system of controlled breathing, wrongly called breathing 'exercise'), and Āgama rituals, such as *navagraha-tarpaṇa* or oblation of water to non-Vedic deities—the nine planets' etc. ;[9] certain classes also use non-Vedic *mantras* like '*Keśavāya namaḥ*', '*Anantāya namaḥ*', etc. for *ācamana* (ritualistic purification of mouth, eyes, ears, etc.).[10] Of the different rites (*saṁskāra*), all but *upanayana* (initiation into the study of the Vedas), marriage, and funeral rites have almost vanished from most parts of India ; even these three are today performed in an attenuated and perfunctory manner.[11] These social rites, however, are not to be classed as religious

[5] '*Om ityanumate proktam*' (*Viśvaḥ*).

[6] *Śrauta* ceremonies are Vedic forms of religious rites, while *gṛhya* ones are Vedic forms of social rites.

[7] See footnote 4.

[8] From the root *ṣūṅ, prāṇiprasave,* to bring forth.

[9] Keraḷīyas (Nampūtiris etc.) do not have *prāṇāyāma* with their *sandhyā-vandana* ; nor do they have *tarpaṇas* to non-Vedic *devatās* such as *navagrahas.*

[10] Most Nampūtiri Brāhmaṇas do not use any *mantra* for *ācamana.*

[11] The single important cause for such neglect appears to be the ignorance of the significance of the rites. In Keraḷa, among Nampūtiri Brāhmaṇas, one may still see all the *gṛhya* rites in a comparatively pure form. Even here, these are vanishing rapidly ; cine-records of the rites should be taken for their preservation and future study.

ceremonies, though in most of them there may be some form of 'worship' in the shape of oblations offered into the 'family fire' (*homa*) as concurrent rites

True forms of Vedic worship, such as *yāgas* and *sattras*, are very rare today. It is doubtful if even those can be called public or congregational worship, because the *yajamāna* or the householder, at whose expense and instance and with whose 'family fire' the *yāga* is conducted, is the sole beneficiary of the worship, even the officiating priests deriving no religious merit from the performance. Vedic religion does not appear to have had any form of public worship in the sense in which the word is generally understood; Āgamic forms, such as temple worship, too, may not be considered to be congregational worship, though temples are places for all to worship, and the deity is worshipped there by the priest for the benefit of the universe as a whole.[12] In fact, Hinduism cannot have congregational or public worship, as one of its important tenets is the individual's competency (*adhikāri-bheda*), which is based on many factors; all are not competent for all forms of worship.

Of the Vedic forms of worship, the *somayāga* and the *agniṣṭoma* appear to be the only surviving forms today;[13] even in the case of these, due to various influences, of which the *ahiṁsā* doctrine of Buddhism and Jainism is one, sacrifice of living animals has often given place to symbolic substitutes in the form of effigies of the animal in dough (*piṣṭa-paśu*).[14] The fact that the all-important *soma* plant itself cannot now be identified[15] points to the extent of time that must have elapsed since the rituals became rare. To all intents and purposes, Vedic ritualism, at any rate in its original form, is extinct today. In their original forms, a good many rituals will even seem revolting to modern Hindu notions.[16] The place of many of the Vedic forms is now taken up by Āgama substitutes. While using Vedic *mantras* or *ṛcas* (hymns), the participants also use Āgamic formulae, including *bījākṣaras,* press into service yogic measures, such as *prāṇāyāma,* and base the whole process on Upaniṣadic philosophy. Thus, what one gets in modern Hindu rituals is a composite form consisting of portions of Vedic

[12] The final benediction in every form of Hindu worship is '*Lokāḥ samastāḥ sukhino bhavāntu*' (May the whole universe be happy).

[13] At any rate it is so in Kerala.

[14] Common in South India, especially among Vaiṣṇavas.

[15] Some identify it as the climbing plant Sarcostema Viminalis. For several reasons this identification does not seem to be correct.

[16] Cf. rituals connected with cremation as contemplated in *Āśvalāyana Gṛhya-Sūtra* (IV. 3. 15 ff.): 'Take the omentum of the *anustaraṇī*—the cow killed for the cremation ceremony —and cover the head and face of the dead body with it reciting the *mantra* beginning with "Oh Fire, be this a shield . . .". Take out the kidneys and place them in the hands of the dead body, right in the right and left in the left, with the *mantra* beginning with "Run away dogs . . .". Place all the organs in their appropriate places on the dead body and then wrap the body in the skin of the *anustaraṇī* cow.'

ritualism, yogic measures, and Vedānta philosophy. Even the plan for the temple is derived from that of the *yāgaśālā* (hall for Vedic sacrifice), as will be evident from the comparison given below.

COMPARISON OF YĀGAŚĀLĀ AND TEMPLE

Yāgaśālā

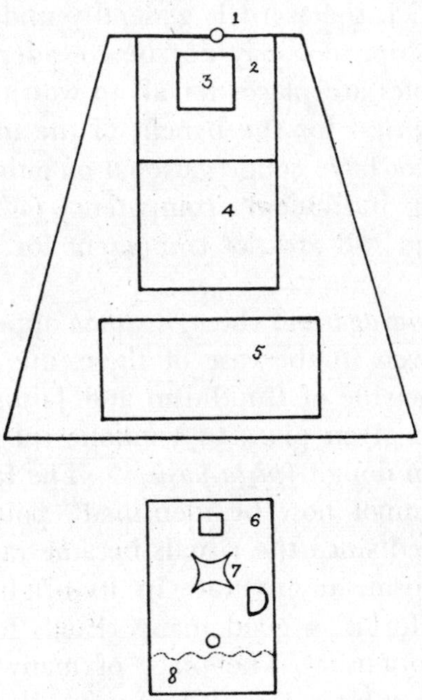

Temple

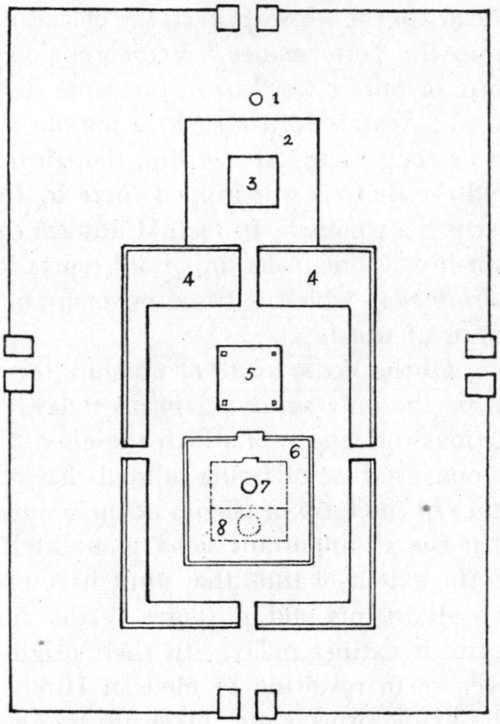

1	*Yūpa*	1	*Dhvaja* (flagstaff)
2	*Uttaravedi*	2	*Baligṛha*
3	*Daśapada*	3	*Balipīṭha*
4	*Havirdhāna*	4	Eastern portion of quadrangle Preparation of *havis* (food for offering) is done at the north-east or south-east corner only.
5	*Sadas*	5	*Maṇḍapa,* where Vedic recitations etc. are done.
6	*Agnihotraśālā*	6	*Garbhagṛha* (sanctum sanctorum)
7	Main *Vedi*	7	*Pratiṣṭha* (idol)
8	*Patnīśālā*	8	Where the Śakti of the main deity also has *pratiṣṭha,* it will be in this site.

Note: Same numbers denote equivalent factors.

Besides the similarities noted in the two plans given above, there is an *iṣṭakā-cayana* (paving with bricks) in the *garbhagṛha* or sanctum sanctorum of temples.[17] This strongly reminds one of the elaborate *iṣṭakā-cayana* in the Vedic *yāgas.* Again, Āgamic texts like *'Vitānāgninibhaṁ Viṣṇor-bimbaṁ . . .'* (the idol of Viṣṇu is equivalent to the *vitānāgni* or Vedic 'oblation fire') and *'Vaiṣṇave ca mahāyajñe sthāpayed-dhvajam-uttamam, yathaiva vaidike yūpaṁ śrutidṛṣṭaṁ vicakṣaṇaḥ'* (in Vaiṣṇava *mahāyajñas* the flagstaff should be raised, as the *yūpa* is raised for the Vedic *yāgas*) point to the relationship which their rites have with Vedic forms.[18] It may be remembered that pollutions to temples are reckoned on the basis of pollutions to the *vitānāgni* which is held sacred. In other words, the idol is fully identified with the Vedic oblation fire.

It is often said that there was no idol-worship in Vedic days. This does not appear to be the whole truth, at any rate in later Vedic days, as one meets with references to idols and temples in Brāhmaṇa literature,[19] the main authority on Vedic liturgy. As culture developed, the sense of *ahiṁsā* (humaneness) began to assume a dominant rôle. The story of Rantideva had a meaning of its own ; it pointed to the great destruction of life perpetrated in the name of religion in those days. This reacted on the minds of the thinking men of the times, and two results ensued: new religions like Buddhism and Jainsim that eschewed *hiṁsā* or hurt to living beings arose, and the mother religion itself soon began to substitute more humane and rational forms of worship in place of the cruel rituals enjoined in old liturgical texts. During the period that followed, there must have been a good deal of give and take between the mother religion and the daughter faiths. The net result was the slow but steady evolution of a form having the desirable features of both. This is the Āgama form or the form of Hinduism today.

BASIC SUPPORTS OF ĀGAMA

Towards the end of the Vedic period, whenever that might have been, rationalization began to supplant blind faith in matters of religion. Every doctrine and ritual appears to have been subjected to the severest criticism, which resulted in *darśanas* or systems of philosophy. Though all the *darśanas* have, in one way or other, helped in the development of Āgama, Yoga, which deals with measures that enable one to bring the

[17] *Tantrasamuccaya,* I. 80 ff.

[18] The first mentioned text refers to *Viṣṇu Saṁhitā,* XXV. 6 ; and the second is from *Puruṣottama Saṁhitā,* an unpublished work. This portion is quoted in the *Report of the Temple-entry Enquiry Committee* constituted under the authority of the former Government of Travancore.

[19] *'Devatāyatanāni kampante devatāpratimā hasanti'* (The houses of the deity shake, the idols of the deity laugh)—*Ṣaḍviṁśa Brāhmaṇa.*

involuntary functions of the body under fair volitional control, forms the bed-rock on which Āgama rests; its influence is seen and felt at every turn. There is no form of Āgama worship, from the simplest *japa*[20] to the most complicated forms of *saparivāra* worship,[21] without the yogic elements of *āsana, prāṇāyāma, nyāsa,* and *dhyāna.* In Āgama worship, only the simplest form of *āsana,* the *padmāsana* (common cross-legged posture), is used, as will be evident from the usual *āsana-mantra.*[22]

During worship, the *sādhaka*[23] or worshipper sits in the *padmāsana* posture on a plank, carpet, or other approved seat, generally facing east or west.[24] After *guru-vandana* and *Gaṇapati-vandana,* he purifies his hands and forearms by making 'passes' with the appropriate *mantras* and then proceeds to protect himself from malefic influences by *tālatraya, digbandha,* and *agniprākāra.* The first consists of three 'taps', with the fingers of the right hand on the left palm, in a vertical plane one above the other, as if an imaginary pillar is erected in front of the worshipper. *Digbandha* consists of ten 'snaps', with the thumb and index finger of the right hand, directed to the eight points of the compass and above and below. *Agniprākāra* or the 'wall of fire' is the erection of an imaginary fire-screen around the worshipper, and is done by drawing three circles in the air about him with the right index finger. These are done with *mantras,* usually with the *astra mantra* (formula of the weapon) of the *devatā* like '*sahasrāra huṁ phaṭ*'[25] etc. Thus protected, he does *prāṇāyāma,* when he will contemplate, using the prescribed *mantras,* that his spiritual body is being cleansed of all dross and converted into that of the Lord Himself.[26] This contemplation of the cleansing is known as *bhūtaśuddhi.* Today, these preliminaries

[20] Consisting of repeating the name of the deity or selected *mantras* while meditating on the *devatā.*

[21] Elaborate worship of the *devatā,* including *upacāras* to the servants of the deities. In temple worship the deity is treated as a king, and all royal honours are done to it.

[22] The *mantra* for consecrating the seat is '*Ādhāraśakti-Kamalāsanāya namaḥ*' (I bow to Kamalāsana, the supporting power). The complicated *āsanas* of *haṭhayoga* are later developments for special purposes, and are not used in Āgama worship.

[23] The word '*sādhaka*' does not mean worshipper. It means accomplisher. The idea is that he, with the help of certain measures, accomplishes or attains the object of his desire, viz. mental peace and beatitude.

[24] The commonest form of seat is a plank in the shape of a tortoise and is known by the name *kūrmāsana.* This alone is used in temple worship in Kerala. For purposes of *japa,* a woollen carpet (*ratnakambala*) or a *kuśa*-grass mat is occasionally used. The direction faced is north instead of west in some parts of North India.

[25] This particular *mantra* is Vaiṣṇava in form, '*sahasrāra*' denoting the *sudarśanacakra* or discus of Viṣṇu. '*Huṁ*' is the *bīja* of *kavaca* or protection (*kavacāya huṁ*), and '*phaṭ*', the *astra mantra* or offensive weapon (*astrāya phaṭ*). All together it means that he contemplates the discus of Viṣṇu to serve him as defensive and offensive weapon against enemies, viz. *kāma* (passion) etc.

[26] First, through *suṣumṇā,* one's own Jīva is transferred to the feet of the Lord in the *sahasrārapadma.* Then with the *vāyu-bīja, 'yaṁ',* the dross in the spiritual body is dried up (*śoṣaṇa*); then with the *agni-bīja,* '*raṁ*', the dross is burnt up; then with '*vaṁ*', the drossless body is bathed in ambrosia; and with '*laṁ*', a purified body is regenerated, now free from all dross and equal to the spirit of the Lord Himself.

are done as a mere formality. The original intention was different. These ought to be done in the strict yogic way and by trained *yogins,* who have acquired the requisite control over the body. To such a *yogin* the purificatory ritual is real and meaningful. Even to non-*yogins,* if done with faith, these preliminaries have great value as auto-suggestions, and a high degree of spiritual purity can thereby be achieved. After thus purifying the body, the worshipper does *ātmaprāṇa-pratiṣṭhā* with the *ajapā mantra,* the non-vocal formula, which every one repeats constantly with his inspiration and expiration, namely, *'so'ham'* (I am That), that is, he now conceives his spirit (Ātman) to be the Absolute (Paramātman) Itself. He now invests this Absolute with qualities and conceives It as his *iṣṭa-devatā* (chosen deity) seated in his *maṇipūracakra.*[27] This is *dhyāna* or meditation. To strengthen the meditation and to invest the figure contemplated with specific details, he does what is known as *nyāsa* or 'placing'. The mode of doing this is by touching the parts of the body with the hand showing particular *mudrās* or gestures and uttering particular *mantras.* There are many types of *nyāsas,* the commonest one being the *ṣaḍaṅga-nyāsa* or 'placing on six parts of the body'. The six *aṅgas* or parts of the body are the heart, the head, the tuft or protection of the head, the *kavaca* or the protection for the body, the three eyes representing the ability to envisage the past, the present, and the future, and the arrows or weapons of offence against enemies (passions), such as *kāma, krodha,* etc. More detailed are the *kara-nyāsa,* in which the different parts of the fingers are touched, and the *mātṛkā-nyāsa,* in which different parts of the entire body are touched. He now does *pañcopacāra* and then proceeds with his *japa.* If he is to do an open act of worship, which others also can see, he now 'transfers' the *devatā* from his *maṇipūra* to the idol (*vigraha*) or the lighted lamp that may be before him,[28] and proceeds with the *upacāras* due to the *devatā.* In the case of open worship on a *vigraha,* when the worship is over, the *devatā* is transferred back into the *maṇipūra* of the *sādhaka.* This is technically known as *udvāsana.* A final *pañcopacāra* is offered to the deity, and the worship is closed with a universal benedictory formula. The above-delineated yogic process is the substratum, the *sine qua non,* of every form of Āgama worship, from the pettiest to the most elaborate. Even the *pratiṣṭha-vigraha* (the fixed idol) in a temple is conceived to be in yogic posture, as is shown in the following illustration.

[27] The region of coeliac plexus of modern anatomy.

[28] This is known as *āvāhana* or 'bringing'. *Āvāhana* or *āhvāna* (invocation or welcome), *sthāpana* (fixing or placing), *sannidhikaraṇa* (bringing near or approaching), *pūjā* (worship or adoration), and *visarjana* (respectful dismissal after worship) are sometimes called the *pañcopacāras* of a deity.

CORONARY SECTION THROUGH A PRATIṢṬHA SHOWING
ṢAḌĀDHĀRA-PRATIṢṬHĀ

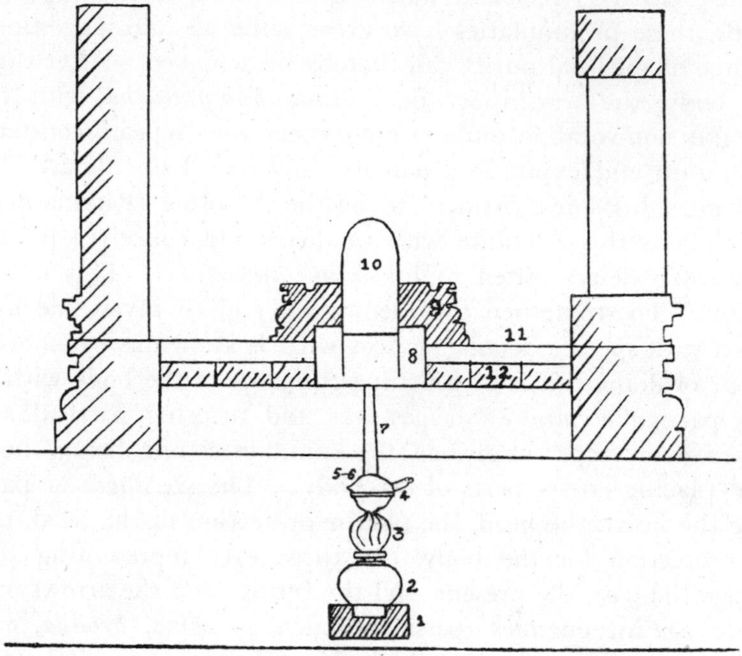

1 *Ādhāraśilā*
2 *Nidhikumbha*
3 *Padma*
4 *Kūrma*
5 Place for silver lotus and *kūrma*
6 Place for gold lotus and *kūrma*
7 *Yoganālī*
8 *Napuṁsakaśilā*
9 *Pīṭha*
10 *Vigraha*
11 Floor of *garbhagṛha*
12 *Iṣṭakā-cayana*

In the middle of the site for the *garbhagṛha* (sanctum sanctorum), where the idol will be placed, an excavation is made to a sufficient depth, and the following articles are ceremonially fixed therein, successively, with appropriate *mantras*. This is known as *ṣaḍādhāra-pratiṣṭhā* or the fixing up of the six *ādhāras* or supports.[29] It is an important ceremony and is done only by the chief priest or *tantrin*. The lowest is a square block of granite or other hard stone of definite dimensions. This is known as *ādhāraśilā* or 'support stone'. This represents the *mūlādhāra*, the lowest

[29] *Tantrasamuccaya*, I. 70 ff.

of the six *cakras* (plexuses) in the body. Over this comes a pot-like device in stone or copper, known as *nidhikumbha* (pot of deposit). This stands for the second or *svādhiṣṭhānacakra.* Above this comes a *padma* (lotus bud) made of stone; this represents the *maṇipūra.* Next comes a tortoise made in stone and known as *kūrma,* which stands for *anāhatacakra.* Above this comes an open lotus flower in silver with a tortoise of the same metal in it; this represents the *viśuddhacakra.* Over this comes a similar set of lotus and tortoise done in gold; this stands for the sixth or *ājñācakra.* Above this comes a hollow copper tube known as *yoganālī.* This represents the *suṣumṇā* or the spinal cord. The very names are sufficient to show the underlying yogic sense. This arrangement depicts the *kṣetra* (temple) itself as the *kṣetra* (body) of the *yogin.* The actual idol will be placed where the *sahasrārapadma* would be. Thus a perfect and complete yogic representation is given to the *pratiṣṭha-vigraha.*

VIGRAHAS AND THEIR SIGNIFICANCE

It is said that Hinduism, particularly the post-Vedic, is idolatrous; this is not the case, at least, in the sense that God has a form. The Hindu who does not conceive a form for God cannot have any idol of God; to him a *vigraha* is not the 'image' of God, but 'a symbolic representation' of the nameless, formless, qualityless Absolute, on whom qualities are superimposed (*adhyāropa*), in a well-defined and technical manner, to suit the natural qualities and leanings of the *sādhaka* (worshipper), in order to enable him to conceive and meditate upon the Absolute. Hinduism conceives only one God: *'Ekaṁ sad-viprā bahudhā vadanti'* (only One is; theologians call it by many names) is a well-known Vedic text. To the Hindu, God is without qualities and hence beyond any conception by the mind.[30] If that is the position, What are these idols and what do they represent? The Āgamas explicitly state that idols are a mere help, though a very necessary one, for the *sādhaka* to conceive and meditate upon the qualityless Absolute; further, they are intended for those whose capacity for abstract thinking is poor.[31] In other words, these idols represent a symbolic concretization of the abstract Absolute and that for a definite purpose. The Absolute is beyond comprehension by the mind; to render

[30] 'That which cannot be expressed by words, that which cannot even be conceived by the mind, that is Brahman' (*Ke. U.*, I. 4-8).

[31] 'Without a form how can God be meditated upon? If (He is) without any form, where will the mind fix itself? When there is nothing for the mind to attach itself to, it will slip away from meditation or will glide into a state of slumber. Therefore the wise will meditate on some form, remembering, however, that the form is a superimposition and not a reality' (*Viṣṇu Saṁhitā*, XXIX, 55-57). *'Pratimā svalpabuddhīnām'* (idols are for those of poor intellect)—*Viṣṇu Saṁhitā*.

It comprehensible, It has to be concretized, exactly as sound-waves are concretized and represented in the form of an undulatory line. A Hindu idol is a *vigraha,*[32] since it enables one to grasp the underlying abstract sense.

Brahman or the Absolute is beyond *guṇas* or qualities ; logically, It cannot even be stated as existent or non-existent.[33] Yet, It is the source from which everything originates, the plane on which everything manifests, and the goal to which everything returns.[34] As the Absolute is without qualities, It cannot convert Itself into the phenomenal universe ; the phenomenal universe can be conceived only as a 'projection' or, better still, a 'function' (in the mathematical sense) of the Absolute. This 'function' of Brahma-Prakṛti has two opposing phases, both operating continuously and simultaneously. The first one is additive or integrative in nature, whereby subtle *aṇus* (the finest material particles—something like the 'ions' of modern science), or imponderable homogeneous matter, become differentiated into ponderable matter by a sort of condensation, as it were. This is the *sṛṣṭi* or the creative phase and answers to the anabolic process of modern science. The second is the reverse process, *laya* or *saṁhāra* (dissolution), by which the manifested universe returns to its original unmanifested state. This is equivalent to the katabolic process of modern science. These two processes are ever going on in nature ; what our senses recognize as the phenomenal universe is simply the resultant of the above two processes. The quality underlying the integrating or creative process is known as *rajoguṇa* ;[35] the quality underlying the disintegrating or *laya* process is termed *tamoguṇa* ;[36] and the quality attached to the phenomenal phase of nature or the property subserving phenomenal existence is *sattvaguṇa.*[37] It should be remembered that these *guṇas* or properties do not belong to the Absolute, but only to Prakṛti. These *guṇa*s of Prakṛti will also be seen in man who is also a part of Prakṛti. In man, such of the qualities as help to preserve the universe as a whole are regarded as *sattvaguṇa* factors ; those that help to create affection, as *rajoguṇa* factors ; and those that tend to produce disintegration, as *tamoguṇa* factors.[38]

[32] *Vigraha* (*vi+gṛh*), to grasp firmly ; hence a representation which helps tne mind to grasp an abstract idea.

[33] *'Sad asad tat paraṁ yat'* (that which is beyond existence and non-existence)—*B. G.*, XI. 37.

[34] *'Janmādyasya yataḥ'*—*B. S.*, I. 1. 2.

[35] From *'rañj'*, to adhere, to stick on, etc.

[36] From *'tam'*, to faint.

[37] From *'sat'*, *bhāve*, existence, being.

[38] For the best and comprehensive classification of various factors under *guṇas* as they affect man, see *B. G.*, XVIII. 20 ff.

Nothing, however, will be met with, in the realm of Prakṛti, which is free from any of the three *guṇas* ; what one meets with will always be a complex of all the three *guṇas,* with one or other dominant. It may be noted that *guṇas* are also represented by colours, white for *sattva,* red or golden for *rajas,* black or blue for *tamas,* and mixtures for mixed *guṇas.*[39] This knowledge will enable one to understand the meaning of colours ascribed to deities, their dress, etc.

Prakṛti or nature is subdivided into two parts: the *parā* and the *aparā,* the former denoting the spiritual or life-factor (*jīvabhūtā*), and the latter, the material (*jaḍā*) universe with its eight elements.[40] Of the eight elements of *aparā* Prakṛti, the first five are the five states of existence of matter or the *pañcabhūtas,* and the last three are *manas* (mind, or the faculty of perception), *buddhi* (intellect or the faculty of reasoning), and *ahaṅkāra* (egoism or the I-sense). As none of the last three is possible without the material body, these are also included in the *aparā* group.

The conception of the *pañcabhūtas* is perhaps the most misunderstood of all *darśana* teachings. A knowledge of what they are and how they are represented in iconography is very desirable for a proper appreciation of various factors in *vigrahas. Bhūta* means the state of existence, the word being derived from the root *bhū,* to be. A careful study of the Vaiśeṣika *darśana* will show that the five states of existence or *pañcabhūtas, pṛthivī, ap, tejas, vāyu,* and *ākāśa,* stood for solidity, liquidity, radiation, gaseousness, and ethereality.[41] In iconography, *pṛthivī* or solidity is represented by a square or a cube ; *ap* or liquidity by a circle, water, or water-born plants and animals ; *tejas* or radiation by light, stellate figures as of interlacing triangles, bright objects, etc. ; *vāyu* or gaseousness by smoke, smoke colour, a globe, flying bodies, etc. ; and *ākāśa* or ether by emptiness (*śūnya*), heavenly bodies as the sun, moon, etc. The various shapes and forms of *vigrahas* and *yantras* (icons with forms and diagrammatic representations) are determined by conventions of the type noted above.

Āgamas are classed into three kinds according to their predominant *guṇa* factor: Vaiṣṇava Āgamas or Saṁhitās represent *sattva* ; Śākta Āgamas or Tantras, *rajas* ; and Śaiva Āgamas, the Āgamas proper, *tamas.* Within each of these types subdivisions occur according to the varying proportions of the *guṇas* which give different types of divinities. The following table will give the most prominent types according to sects.

[39] This colour representation appears to be almost universal.
[40] *B. G.,* VII. 4, 5.
[41] *'Yat kaṭhinaṁ sā pṛthivī, yad-dravaṁ tā āpaḥ, yaduṣṇaṁ tat tejaḥ, yat sañcarati sa vāyuḥ, yat suṣiraṁ tad-ākāśaṁ . . .*

Guṇa	Saṁhitās (Vaiṣṇava) *Sāttvika*	Tantras (Śākta) *Rājasika*	Āgamas (Śaiva) *Tāmasika*
Sattva	Anantaśayana	Śāntidurgā	Dakṣiṇāmūrti
Rajas	Rāma, Kṛṣṇa, etc.	Bhuvaneśvarī, Rājarājeśvarī, etc.	Śiva with Pārvatī, etc.
Tamas	Nṛsiṁha	Kālī	Aghoramūrti

A study of the *dhyānas* (forms in which the deities are to be conceived), as given in *Śilparatna* and such other works, will disclose the *guṇa* characteristics of the deities.

It has already been noted that *guṇas* are conceived both for the *devatā* (deity) and for the *sādhaka*. The most appropriate *devatā* will be one having *guṇas* identical with those of the *sādhaka*. There is one other factor also to be taken into account in determining the suitable *devatā* for a given worshipper. The type of emotional attachment to his fellowmen varies with each man ; one may be more attached to one's mother, another to father, a third to wife, a fourth to friends, and so on. Six important forms of natural attachment or emotional relationship or *bhāvas* are recognized by the Āgamas:

Name of *bhāva*	Type of emotional relation	Example
Śānta bhāva	man to his Creator	*Ṛṣis* to Viṣṇu
Dāsya bhāva	servant to his master	Hanumat to Rāma
Sakhya bhāva	friend to his friend	Arjuna to Kṛṣṇa
Vātsalya bhāva	parent to his or her child	Yaśodā to Kṛṣṇa
Āpatya bhāva	child to his or her parent	Mārkaṇḍeya to Devī
Kānta or *Madhura bhāva*	lover to his or her beloved	Rādhā to Kṛṣṇa

There are other forms, such as the *śatru* (enemy) *bhava*, which cannot ordinarily be used ; they are described to explain *mokṣa* (salvation) granted to such characters as Rāvaṇa.

Besides satisfying the *guṇa* factor, it is also necessary to meet the *bhāva* or emotional factor of the *sādhaka,* if he is to be benefited. Hence it becomes essential to find an *iṣṭadevatā* having *guṇas* and *bhāvas* corresponding to, or identical with, those of the *sādhaka*. This necessitates a large number of *devatās* for selection. This is the reason why Hinduism has apparently a plurality of gods. The large number of *vigrahas* one sees are conceived on a rational basis to meet specific needs as explained above. In former days, the selection of *iṣṭadevatā* was made by the *guru* (spiritual teacher and guide) under whom the *śiṣya* (disciple) served a long course of apprenticeship, during which the *guru* had ample opportunities of studying the *guṇa* and *bhāva* characteristics of the *śiṣya,* and was therefore in a position to select an *iṣṭadevatā* to suit the specific need of the disciple. Both the *guṇa* and the emotional bent are fully subconscious factors, and therefore the subject is not likely to recognize them himself; hence the specific need of a *guru* to make the selection.

Vigrahas used for worship may be *arūpa-vigrahas* (formless ones) or *sarūpa-vigrahas* (those with forms, having face, hands, etc.). The *sarūpa* ones may be anthropomorphic or otherwise. To denote that these *vigrahas* stand for something other than mere material objects, as they apparently seem, they are very often invested with one or more unnatural and impossible factors such as four hands, half animal body, and so on. The *arūpa liṅgas* or formless symbols are *śāligrāma* or *śālagrāma, śivaliṅga* or *bāṇaliṅga,* and *śrīyantra* or *śrīcakra,* and they represent Viṣṇu, Śiva, and Śakti, in whom *guṇas* are conceived as present in an undifferentiated form. Similar aniconic stone symbols for Śakti, Sūrya, and Ganeśa are also used in the *pañcāyatana* worship.

Śālagrāma represents the *saguṇa* form of the Absolute. It is a black, egg-shaped object, the remains of fossilized ammonite; it has a golden streak within its cavity and is obtained from rivers, notably, the Gaṇḍakī. This represents Hiraṇyagarbha or the primordial Golden Egg, the undifferentiated Totality that consolidated itself out of the *kāraṇajala,*[42] the inert material cause, often wrongly translated as the 'first waters'. It is out of this Egg that the whole universe becomes differentiated in course of time. This Egg corresponds to the primordial, homogeneous, luminous, nebulous mass of scientists, out of which the universe has evolved in due course.

Anantaśayana is the most sublime and complete *sarūpa* representation of Viṣṇu. He is here represented as lying on a three-coiled serpent, Ananta, in the middle of *kṣīrābdhi* (sea of milk). He is in *yoganidrā* (sleep of *yoga*). He has Śrī or Lakṣmī (goddess of wealth) and Bhūmi or Mahī (the earth) as his Śaktis (wives) by his side. He is represented as of dark colour.[43] From his navel arises the lotus in which the functionaries of creation, preservation, and disintegration (*sṛṣṭi, sthiti,* and *laya*) reside. His *āyudhas* (weapons) are the conch (*śaṅkha*), the flaming discuss (*cakra*),

[42] *Kāraṇajala* is not water. *Jal* means to be inert. *Kāraṇajala* is the inert homogeneous mass from which differentiated matter was formed.

[43] This description is on the basis of the *dhyāna* in use in the Padmanābhasvāmin temple at Trivandrum.

the mace (*gadā*), and the lotus (*padma*). His vehicle is the resplendent Garuḍa (the celestial bird). This symbolism is yogic in form and based on Vedāntic fundamentals. The term '*viṣṇu*' means all-pervading.[44] As an all-pervading factor can be conceived to rest only on a non-finite or limitless base, he is depicted as lying on Ananta (the endless).[45] To avoid the feeling that such a God may be extra-cosmic, Ananta is conceived as a three-coiled serpent to represent the *kuṇḍalinī-śakti* that is within us. His sleep represents the *nirvikārāvasthā* (the potential, undifferentiated, and non-kinetic state) of the Absolute. He is given a dark colour to show that he cannot be seen, i.e. known by the senses. In other words, our ignorance hides the Absolute, who is ever in us, from our ken. His two Śaktis, Bhūmi and Lakṣmī, represent *sattva-* and *rajo-guṇas,* while his *yoganidrā* represents *tamoguṇa* and stands for his third Śakti called Nītā by Pāñcarātras.[46] Thus it will be seen that the Anantaśayana form represents the Absolute with differentiated *guṇas* about It.

Śiva in *arūpa* aspect is represented by *śivaliṅga.*[47] This representation may be by a mere *liṅga* or phallus ; often it is in the form of a phallus placed in the *yoni* (female generative organ) of Prakṛti or nature,[48] conceived as female and the progenitress of species.[49] Here the *yoni* represents undifferentiated nature or Mūla-Prakṛti (root nature), and the *liṅga,* the impulse which initiates the differentiation. The *yoni* stands for the *upādānakāraṇa* or the material cause, and the *liṅga* for the *nimittakāraṇa,* efficient cause. Together they stand for the primordial cause as a whole. Thus again, as in the case of *śālagrāma,* the representation is that of the Absolute with *guṇas,* but without *guṇa* differentiation.

In the typical *sarūpa* aspect, Śiva represents *tamoguṇa.* He has many symbols of death on him ; the cremation ground where he dances, his garland of human skulls, ornaments of snakes, poison in his throat, etc., are some of them. The digit of the moon he wears on his head denotes Time, the great destroyer. His weapon, the battle-axe (*paraśu*), also shows the idea of destruction.

Śiva is the *iṣṭadevatā, par excellence,* of the *yogins* ; hence yogic symbolization is very pronounced in this form. The three eyes represent the sun, the moon, and the fire, or the *iḍā,* the *piṅgalā,* and the *suṣumnā,* according to the well-known and accepted yogic nomenclature. Gaṅgā

[44] From '*viṣlṛ*', *vyāptau,* to pervade.
[45] *An* (privative) + *anta* (end) ; hence endless.
[46] Bhūmi (*bhū,* to be) denotes existence ; hence stands for *sattvaguṇa.* Lakṣmī or wealth stands for the possessive factor ; hence *rajoguṇa. Yoganidrā* or sleep of *yoga* represents inaction ; hence *tamoguṇa.*
[47] The term '*liṅga*' means only 'representation' ; from '*liṅg*', *citrīkaraṇe,* to depict.
[48] *Vide B. G.,* XIV. 3.
[49] From '*stṛ*', *vistāre,* to spread.

represents the *amṛta* of the *sahasrārapadma,* and the small portion of it that oozes out through a strand of hair, the *citriṇī-nāḍi.* The moon on the head is the *candramaṇḍala* of the *yogins* ;[50] the *ḍamaru* (drum), the Nāda-brahman,[51] and the dark patch on the throat, the *khecarī-bandha.*[52]

In like manner, Brahma-Prakṛti or the Śakti of the Absolute, conceived in feminine form, is also represented in both *arūpa* and *sarūpa* aspects. The *arūpa* aspect is represented by a diagram and is known as the *śrīyantra* or *śrīcakra.* This *śrīyantra* or *śrīcakra* represents the undifferentiated Puruṣa-cum-Prakṛti aspect. It consists of nine *āvaraṇas* or enclosures: the outermost is square in form ; the next two are circular and contain sixteen and eight lotus petals respectively ; the fourth, fifth, sixth, and seventh are stellate figures formed by interlacing triangles ; the eighth is a single triangle ; and the ninth is a *bindu* or tiny sphere. This *yantra* is also known by the name *meru* (particularly if it is a three-dimensional solid one, as opposed to 'line' or *rekhā-yantra*), which means also the spinal column. This *yantra* has the yogic *cakras* or plexuses represented in it. The outermost square, known as *bhūpura,* stands for the *mūlādhāra*[53] and its *bhū-tattva.* The second and third, which are circular figures, together represent the *svādhiṣṭhāna* with its *ap-tattva.* The stellate form, made up of the fourth, fifth, sixth, and seventh *āvaraṇas,* stands for the *maṇipūra* and its *tattva, tejas.* The single triangle making the eighth *āvaraṇa* stands for the *anāhata* and its *tattva, vāyu.* The *bindu* or sphere in the centre stands for the *viśuddha* and its *tattva, ākāśa,* while the empty space within the sphere represents the *ājñācakra.* It is here that Mahāmāyā and Puruṣa are conceived together in *kāmakalā* posture (the mingling of *upādāna-* and *nimitta-kāraṇas* or the beginning of creation). This *yantra* also represents the *saptaprākāra* temple (temple with seven enclosures), when the eighth *āvaraṇa* or the innermost triangle represents the *garbhagṛha* (sanctum sanctorum), and the *bindu,* the *pratiṣṭha* therein.

Śakti in her typical form represents the *rajoguṇa* or the quality that affects the senses. And as nature in its phenomenal aspect is the only thing that can affect the senses, it represents Śakti. As the main characteristic of nature is its capacity to reproduce and spread (*stṛ,* to spread), nature is

[50] *Candramaṇḍala* is a white region conceived in the *sahasrārapadma.* Study of comparative anatomy leads one to surmise this to be the white roof (*corpus callosum*) of the triangular shaped (*yoni*-shaped) ventricles of the cerebrum. *Yoga,* of course, deals with the 'functions', while anatomy indicates the material basis for the functions.

[51] *Nāda* is a form of 'realization' for the *yogin,* wherein he 'feels' as if he is hearing a peculiar sound of a 'booming' character. This feeling is said to be generated when the *kuṇḍalinī* passes through the *anāhatacakra.* Hence, probably, the word '*anāhata-dhvani*'.

[52] A measure in *yoga,* in which the tongue is made to fall back and close the glottis at a certain stage in *prāṇāyāma.* This is to be done only by experts, or death is almost certain.

[53] '*Amuṣmin dharāyāścatuṣkoṇacakraṁ . . .*'—*Ṣaṭcakranirūpaṇa.*

depicted as feminine (*strī*). In the perfect *rajoguṇa* form, the commonest conception is that of Rājarājeśvarī. She is often represented as seated on the lap of Parameśvara, or as sitting on a *siṁhāsana* (throne), whose feet are Brahmā and other gods and whose seat is Sadāśiva himself.[54] She represents knowledge in its abstract sense and is often known as *śrīvidyā* (auspicious knowledge). She is the same as the 'Haimavatī Umā' of the *Kena Upaniṣad,* instructing Indra regarding the *yakṣa* or 'the worshipful'.[55] Her weapons are the sugarcane bow, arrows of flower, the noose, and the goad. *Kāmikāgama* explains the sense underlying these. The sugarcane bow stands for the mind (*manas*) or the faculty of perception (*manorūpekṣukodaṇḍā*) ; the five arrows of flower represent the five *tanmātras* or the *bhūta* (elemental) forms that can affect the five senses (*pañcatanmātrasāyakā*). Knowledge of any type can arise only as the result of action of the phenomenal universe on the mind through the senses. The knowledge that arises thus may be beneficial or dangerous ; it may be used for the good of the world or for its ill.[56] The noose stands for 'binding' or 'attaching' (*rāgasvarūpapāśāḍhyā*), and means that one should attach oneself to the beneficent form of knowledge. The *aṅkuśa* or the goad shows that dangerous knowledge should be kept under control as an unruly elephant (*krodhākārāṅkuśojjvalā*).

All the forms of deities one meets with in Hinduism are but the derivatives of the three above described types, designed to meet the needs of different *sādhakas.* There can also be composite forms such as Śaṅkara-Nārāyaṇa (combination of Śiva and Viṣṇu or *tamoguṇa* and *sattvaguṇa*).[57]

FORMS AND RITUALS OF WORSHIP

The forms of Āgama worship are three: *japa, homa,* and *tarpaṇa. Japa* consists of repeating the names (*nāma-japa*) or the *mūla mantras* (*mantra-japa*) of the deity. Mere repeating of the name of the deity is the simplest example of *nāma-japa. 'Oṁ namo Nārāyaṇāya'* for Viṣṇu, *'Oṁ namaḥ Śivāya'* for Śiva, and *'Ka e ī la hrīṁ, ha sa ka ha la hrīṁ, sa ka la hrīṁ'* for Śakti are typical *mūla mantras* (formulae) of different sectarian deities. When these are repeated after *prāṇāyāma* etc., as described earlier, it is known as *mantra-japa.* Though these *mūla mantras* are generally non-Vedic, there is one formula, known as the *'gāyatrī'*, for each and every *devatā,* which is fashioned on the lines of the Vedic Gāyatrī (*tat savitur vareṇyam . . .*). This formula always has this well-known form:

[54] *'Dhyāyet Kāmeśvarāṅkasthāṁ . . .'* (*dhyāna* as per *Kalpa-Sūtra*) ; *'Īśānādi padaṁ Śivaikaphalakaṁ . . .'*

[55] Śaṅkara annotates: *Tasyendrasya yakṣe bhaktiṁ buddhvā vidyā Umārūpiṇī prāḍurabhūt strīrūpā.'*

[56] Note the history of nuclear fission.

[57] *Śilparatna,* XXV. 79.

'*...vidmahe, ... dhīmahi, tannaḥ ... pracodayāt*' (the dotted ellipses being filled up by specific terms applicable to the deity concerned). This, however, is rarely used in place of the *mūla mantra*. *Homa* is the offering of oblations (ghee etc.) into consecrated fire, the consecration being done, in most cases, in the Vedic manner. *Tarpaṇa* is the worship of the deity with *upacāras* or offerings.

Japa is the best example of private worship ; no image is required here, not even a light is essential. *Homa* is, strictly speaking, Vedic ritualism adapted to Āgama requirements. Except in the case of Gaṇapati, the *homa* form of worship is comparatively rare.[58] The worship that is done in temples is mostly of the *tarpaṇa* form.

All *upacāras* and forms of worship, however complicated they be, are but the elaborations of the simple form known as the *pañcopacāra* (five offerings). Śaṅkara, in his *Saparyāhṛdaya*,[59] gives the true meanings of these *upacāras*. In the seventh and last verse of that monograph, he has put the whole thing in a nutshell:

'*Puruṣo bhagavān ihopahāraḥ prakṛtiḥ kālatanuḥ svayaṁ ca kartā havanādiṣu sādhyatā ca kartuḥ phalabhāktvena bhavatyupādhibhedāt.*' Puruṣa,[60] the all-pervading, Himself is Bhagavat[61] or the deity conceived as endowed with qualities. This means that the all-pervading Absolute is Itself the deity fit for worship, when qualities are ascribed to It. Prakṛti or manifested nature forms the materials with which It is to be worshipped. The worshipper himself is no other than the Absolute in the shape of time, that is, as limited by time. The esotericism of the *upacāras* is to conceive the return of the manifested universe to the unmanifested homogeneous unitary state, which is the Absolute, as a result of the effect of time, which itself is eternal and absolute. In its exoteric form, this truth assumes the shape of the offering of the five fundamental forms of existence and becomes the *pañcopacāra*.

Though called 'five' offerings, they are really six, including *naivedya* or the food-offering. The first five denote the material universe in the *bhūta*

[58] Common *homas* current in Kerala are: *Gaṇapati homa*, daily performed in the houses of means, and *Sudarśana homa* (Vaiṣṇava), *Mṛtyuñjaya homa* (Śaiva), etc. which are occasionally performed.

[59] *Saparyāhṛdaya* with its *vyākhyā*, *Upahāraprakāśikā*, and with a *vṛtti* by Mahāmahopādhyāya Goda Varma Bhaṭṭa, edited by A. Krishna Pisharoti.

[60] Puruṣa, from *pālana-pūraṇayoḥ*, that which pervades and fills up everything.

[61] The term '*bhagavat*' is defined as having the six *guṇas* (*ṣāḍguṇya paripūrito bhagavān*) ; hence the word is applicable only when the Absolute is endowed with qualities. The six qualities are: (1) absolute greatness (*māhātmya* or *aiśvarya*), (2) holiness (*dharma*) or power (*vīrya*), (3) renown (*yaśas*), (4) beauty (*śrī*), (5) knowledge (*jñāna*), and (6) detachment (*vairāgya*), or will or desire (*kāma*), or action or effort (*prayatna*). According to the *Viṣṇu Purāṇa*, 'He is to be termed Bhagavat who knows the birth and death, the coming (into this world) and going (out of it), and the knowledge and ignorance (regarding Ātman) of the Jīvas' (XI. 5. 78).

forms,[62] while the sixth or *naivedya,* with its *dhenu-mudrā* (sign of cow) and the *prāṇāhuti* or offering to the *prāṇas* or 'life-breaths' when material food is offered, denotes the offering of the life-principle or the Parā-Prakṛti. The *amṛta* (ambrosia, deathlessness) in the *naivedya mantra* (*Amṛte amṛtodbhave amṛtavarṣiṇi amṛtaṁ srāvaya srāvaya svāhā*) denotes the immortal factor or 'spirit' as the material offered. It is this offering of the Parā-Prakṛti or the life-factor that is represented by the animal sacrifice current in certain forms of Āgama worship. Vedic *yāgas,* too, may have influenced the creation and preservation of animal sacrifice that we find in Āgama worship.

These *upacāras* have a further esoteric sense ; *Upahāraprakāśikā* refers to the five offerings of water etc. as representing adherence, trust, adoration, love, and knowledge (*sneha-viśvāsa-sammāna-bhakti-jñāna-jalādinā*). *Upacāras* and their meanings may be tabulated to give a clearer understanding of their esotericism.

Upacāra	*Tattva*	*Bīja*	Material used	Implied emotional relation to the deity and its meaning
Pādya	*Ap*	*'Vaṁ'*	Water	*Sneha,* adherence, which denotes just an 'acquaintance relationship' to the deity.
Gandha	*Pṛthivī*	*'Laṁ'*	Sandal etc.	*Viśvāsa,* trust, that the worshipper will be protected by the worshipped. The deity is now a trusted friend.
Puṣpa	*Ākāśa*	*'Haṁ'*	Flowers	*Sammāna,* adoration, when the deity is the highest honoured Master.
Dhūpa	*Vāyu*	*'Yaṁ'*	Incense	*Bhakti,* intense love, where the worshipped is regarded as 'mine' by the worshipper.
Dīpa	*Tejas*	*'Raṁ'*	Light	*Jñāna,* knowledge, of the truth that the worshipper and the worshipped are one. This is still only a knowledge, and not yet a realization.
Naivedya	*Jīva*	*'Vaṁ'*	Food	*Tādātmyabodha,* realization of the identity of the worshipper with the worshipped.

[62] *Pañcopacāra mantras* are *'abātmanā jalaṁ kalpayāmi'* etc.

It should be remembered that in the *pañcopacāra* no materials are used; only when the *upacāras* are elaborated, materials such as water, flowers, etc. are used. The *pañcopacāra* is often elaborated into ten (*daśopacāra*), sixteen (*ṣoḍaśopacāra*), and at times even to sixty-four. In some texts, with *'vaṁ'* as the common *bīja, naivedya* replaces *pādya,* and the *pañcopacāra* begins with *gandha.*

Included in, and as part of, *upacāras* are *mudrās* or gestures with the hands. These are intended to strengthen the attention and mental concentration of the worshipper.

Men may be grouped into three classes: those in whom the faculty of intellect and reasoning is dominant; those in whom emotion plays the highest rôle; and those that are controlled by their impulses and instincts. To those who belong to the first group abstract thinking is easy, and they find satisfaction only in rational philosophy. This class is, naturally, a small group. For them ritualistic ceremonial religion is not suited; in other words, the members of this group are not *adhikārins* (competent) for ritualistic religion. The last group is composed of children and those with childish mentality. They cannot think; nor are their emotions developed. They can be trained to follow a routine which, in due course, may help them to enjoy a form of vegetative satisfaction, to borrow a term from biology. As children grow up and acquire emotional factors and capacity to think, the permanent members of this group are few and limited to those of low mental capacity. The bulk of humanity lies between these two, forming the second or intermediary group. In them emotion predominates; they are also capable of abstract thinking, but to a limited extent; and most of them would also require material and mechanical measures to stimulate their emotions to the desired strength. Bhakti-mārga or the emotional way of realization of God is for them, and Āgama ritualism is designed to satisfy the needs of this class. The most important thing to understand in Hinduism is that everything taught there is not intended for everybody; there is a definite question of suitability or *adhikāri-bhāva.* The greatness of Hinduism lies in this fact that it supplies forms, methods, and measures to suit all possible types of men.

33

INDIAN HYMNOLOGY

THE first literature of man is to be found in the hymns he sang spontaneously to his God, hymns that were motivated by the realization that, after all, man is but a toy (*krīḍanaka*) in the hands of his Maker. The ancient Indian looked to his revealed lore (*chandas*), in its formal and expressional aspect, as synonymous with everything that covers (*chādayati*) his sins, and took congenially to prayer as 'God's breath in man returning to his birth'. This is the logos (the Word);[1] all other utterances are mere waste of breath (*vāco viglāpanam*). The restriction of the expression of this deep religious sentiment primarily to its verse form and the throwing open of its use to one and all (*prapattiḥ sarvādhikārā*), without any distinction of caste, creed, or nationality, was a resourceful idea of fundamental importance. The attitude of regarding prayer and hymnology as 'the soul in paraphrase, the heart in pilgrimage' has become the dominant note in Indian thought since the middle ages, and memorable utterance was given to it by Śrī Caitanya.[2] Even the metaphysically minded Jain, in his *stotras* (hymns) to the Tīrthaṅkaras and in his prayers to the Vidyādevīs, vied with the devout Hindu in thus laying bare his heart. The Buddhist included in the cosmopolitan flights of his devotional self the Lord and His apostles and even the lesser and more malevolent manifestations, sometimes even the mound and the sepulchre as well as vague and abstract ideas.

BUDDHIST AND JAINA HYMNAL LITERATURE

Buddhānusmṛti, a hymn to Buddha in mixed Sanskrit, in the *Mahāvastu*, *Gaṇḍī-stotra*, in pure graceful Sanskrit, by Aśvaghoṣa, *Catuḥstava* by Nāgārjuna, *Catuḥśataka-* and *Śatapañcāśatikā-* and *Triratna-stotras* ascribed to Mātṛcetas, *Ekottarikā-* and *Miśraka-stotras* by Diṅnāga,

[1] *Śabdātmikā suvimalargyajuṣāṁ nidhānā-*
Mudgītharamyapadapāṭha-vatāñca sāmnām ;
Devi trayī bhagavatī bhavabhāvanāya
Vārtā ca sarvajagatāṁ paramārtihantrī.

'Being of the very essence of *śabda* (logos), thou art, O goddess, the holy *trayī* (Vedic trio), the repository of pure *ṛc* and *yajus* and of the *sāman* chanted sweetly through and along with the *udgītha* (the best part thereof). Thou art, withal, for the maintenance of mundane life, the abiding means of livelihood (agriculture, trade, etc.), and the great eradicator of the primary ills of all the worlds.' See '*Śakrādi kṛtā Devī-stuti*' in *Saptaśatī* (*Mārkaṇḍeya Purāṇa*).

[2] *Sarvātmasnapanaṁ paraṁ vijayate Śrī-Kṛṣṇa-saṅkīrtanam*—'There dominates verily the triumphant *kīrtana* (glorification in music) of Śrī Kṛṣṇa, which bathes and purifies the soul of all' (*Śikṣāṣṭaka,* 1).

Suprabhāta-stotra (like the *Prātaḥsmaraṇa-stotras*), in praise of Buddha, ascribed to Emperor Harṣavardhana, and *Paramārthanāma-saṅgīti* (like *Viṣṇu-sahasranāma* in the *Mahābhārata*, the hundred and one names of the Ahura-Mazdā in Zoroastrianism, and the ninety-nine names of Allah in Islam), among earlier works; the numerous Tārā hymns, of which a prominent one in *sragdharā* metre is ascribed to the Kashmiri poet Sarvajñamitra, *Lokeśvaraśataka*, in hundred *sragdharā* verses, in honour of the Bodhisattva Avalokiteśvara, and *Bhaktiśataka* by a Bengali Buddhist domiciled in Ceylon, amongst mediaeval works; and *Sapta-Buddha-stotras* and *Devatākalyāṇa-pañcaviṁśatikā*—the latter by a liberal Nepalese poet in honour of Buddha, the Bodhisattvas, the *tīrthas*, the *caityas*, and even Hindu deities—, among later works, are worth mentioning.

Similarly, the Jain, in his prayer in Sanskrit or in Ardha-Māgadhī, took recourse to meditations which enkindled the best and the tenderest feelings in man. *Uvāsaggahara-stotra*, a hymn to Pārśvanātha by Bhadrabāhu, *Praśna-vyākaraṇa*, in hymn-like *gāthās*, the far-famed *Bhaktāmāra-* and *Bhayahara-stotras*, in ornate Sanskrit, by Mānatuṅga, in honour of the saint Ṛṣabha, and *Pañcaparameṣṭhi-mantra*, often described as the Jaina Gāyatrī, among early compositions; *Kalyāṇamandira-stotra* by Siddhasena Divākara, *Vardhamāna-dvātriṁśikā*, in honour of Vardhamāna Mahāvīra, *Caturviṁśatijina-stava* and *Śobhana-stuti*, *Ajitaśānti-stava* and *Ṛṣabha-pañcāśikā*, the latter two in Ardha-Māgadhī, and *Vītarāga-stotra* of Ācārya Hemacandra, amongst mediaeval works; and *Jinastotra-ratnākara*, *Ṣaḍ-bhāṣā-vibhūṣita-śāntinātha-stavana*, the many *stotras* by the polymath Āśādhara, *Tribhuvana-vijayapatākā* by Merutuṅga, and *Mahāvīra-stava* by Yaśovijaya, among later hymns, deserve prominent mention.

It is thus a paradox that *stotras* in their scheduled forms were assiduously cultivated amongst these communities, and are earlier than similar hymns in Hinduism, if we leave out the *stotras* in the great epics, the *Rāmāyaṇa* and the *Mahābhārata*, which are regarded by some as of doubtful antiquity. In the latter epic, over and above the well-known *Viśvarūpa-darśana-stava*, we have the two popular *stotras* in the Nārāyaṇīya section of the *Mokṣadharma*, of which the prose one is a type by itself and is apparently quite old.

DIFFERENT APPROACHES AND ATTITUDES IN PRAYERS

The recognition of the *stūpas* and the religious buildings as 'towers of deliverance' and the frequent resort to them for prayers would go to indicate to what extent the Buddhist mind was permeated by a devotional approach, as in the case of other Indian creeds. In Jaina tradition, we read of the confession of Hemacandra, who is said to have offered his homage to Providence before the image of Somanātha in Gujarat, be He the accredited Lord of the Jinas, or Brahmā, Viṣṇu, or Śiva of the orthodox Hindus.[3] The efficacy of the diverse forms of hymnology such as the *nuti, stuti, smṛti, rakṣā, varman,* and *kavaca,* as preached and practised by the Paurāṇic Hindu and the Tāntric *sādhaka,* like that of the Psalms and Yashts in other spheres, lies in their appeal to our hearts.

So much about the *dṛṣṭa* (visible) aspect of prayers. But it is the *adṛṣṭa* (invisible) aspect of *karma,* which includes prayer as a necessary pendant, that has enriched the cultural history of the Indo-Aryans. In order to understand and interpret the spiritual aspect of the *stotras,* one has to place oneself in perpetual contact with, in the language of the Upaniṣadic *ṛṣis,* the 'origin, stay, and end' of one's being. In the context of such an inspiration, Arjuna seeks the help of the Lord, *'Namaḥ purastādatha pṛṣṭhataste namo'stu te sarvata eva sarva'*—Before, behind, and on every side, do I bow down to Thee, O pervasive Lord of my being (*B.G.,* XI. 40). This brings in its train an emphasis on the intimate relationship of the Lord with the devotee—a Thou-and-I (personal) relationship, as distinguished from a Thou-and-That (impersonal) relationship—, which has, in India, especially in Paurāṇic India, mainly centred round His *sākāra* (with form) manifestation. The Lord, in an oft-quoted passage, enjoins: 'Whatever thou doest, whatever thou eatest, whatever thou offerest as oblation, whatever thou givest, whatever austerity thou practisest, O son of Kuntī, do all that as an offering unto me' (*B.G.,* IX. 27). We read of a characteristic confession of his love for personal God by Madhusūdana Sarasvatī,[4] the great Advaitin, who had in him the make-up of a master-artist in the realm of hymnology, a fact testified by one of his oft-quoted verses in honour of Kṛṣṇa.[5]

[3] *Bhavabījāṅkurajananā rāgādyāḥ kṣayamupāgatā yasya,*
Brahmā vā Viṣṇurvā Haro Jino vā namastasmai.
Obeisance to Him, be He Brahmā, Viṣṇu, or Hara, or Jina, in whom have vanished the passions, attachment and the like, from which spring up the sprouts and seeds of worldly existence.'

[4] His candid and courageous confession is significant:
Kurvanti ke'pi kṛtinaḥ kvacidapyanante
Svāntaṁ nidhāya viṣayāntaraśāntimeva ;
Tvatpādapadmavigalan-makaranda-bindu-
Māsvādya mādyati muhur Madhubhin-mano me.
'Some few, worthy are they, entrust their hearts somewhere to an infinite Being and thus put an end to other objects of enjoyment. But as for me, O slayer of (the demon) Madhu, my mind, after it has got a hearty taste of the honey drops dripping from your lotus feet, revels in it over and over again.' His ambitious *stotra,* the *Ānandamandākinī,* is more conventional, though individual verses (e.g. 13, 26, 44, 47, 91) reach a high level.

[5] *Vaṁśīvibhūṣitakarānnavanīradābhāt,*
Pītāmbarādaruṇabimbaphalādharoṣṭhāt,
Pūrṇendu-sundaramukhādaravindanetrāt,
Kṛṣṇāt paraṁ kimapi tattvamahaṁ na jāne.
'I know no Reality higher than the lotus-eyed, yellow-robed Kṛṣṇa, blue as a new water-laden cloud, with his hands gracefully bedecked with the flute, with his upper and lower lips ruddy like a *bimba* fruit, and with his face as lovely as the full moon.'

There is a French proverb: 'Man is never greater than on his knees.' This emphasis on surrender relates to the personal aspect of the deity, and has been the central theme of many a hymn in which the attitude of humility (*śaraṇāpatti*) is the most dominant. This does not necessarily sever itself from its philosophical background, as is illustrated in the well-known *Śivamahimnaḥ-stava.*[6] It has throughout supported itself on the creed, 'Lord, Thy will be done'. *Śraddhā* (faith), as distinct from *vitta* (wealth) and *vidhi* (injunction), has the final determining voice in the assessment of our actions ; for whatever the *karmakāṇḍin,* blind in his formal servility to the letter of the law, may think, the Lord looks to the spirit (*bhāvagrāhī Janārdanaḥ*). In this mode of presentation, the Rāga-mārga (the way of attachment), as distinguished from the Vidhi-mārga (the way of injunction), becomes the way *par excellence.* The eternal feminine in man, as in the *madhura bhajana* or the *kāntā bhāva* of the Vaiṣṇavas, or as in the idealism of the divine Mother in the Śakti cult, has studiously kept aloof from the attitude of spiritual segregation and blatant self-assertion and offered itself wholly and completely to a sweet, gentle, and kindly Providence. The *aiśvarya* (majesty) of the Lord, judged from such a standpoint, begets awe ; the *mādhurya* (the fascinating element in Him) is what engenders confidence and endears Him to His devotees ; and this has been the striking note in Indian hymnology, best illustrated in the compositions of Līlāśuka Bilvamaṅgala[7] or in the prayer of the Maithilī poet Vidyāpati.[8]

It would, however, be perverse to infer from this any tendency to supineness and lack of stamina. The Vedic *ṛṣi,* in the celebrated Gāyatrī hymn, while praying to Savitṛ, the lord of light and activity, reflects on his pre-eminent lustre, energy, and prowess (*vareṇyaṁ bhargaḥ*). The Yajus priest, in a not so well-known prose formula, prays in terms of vigour and virility: '*Tejo'si tejo mayi dhehi, vīryamasi vīryaṁ mayi dhehi, balamasi balaṁ mayi dhehi, saho'si saho mayi dhehi*' (Energy Thou art, do instil into me that energy. Virility Thou art, grant unto me virility. Power Thou art, extend

[6] *Nṛṇāmeko gamyastvamasi payasāmarṇava iva*—'Thou art the only destination of men as the ocean is of the waters'.

[7] We read in his *Śrī-Kṛṣṇa-karṇāmṛta*:

He deva he dayita he jagadekabandho,
He Kṛṣṇa he capala he karuṇaikasindho,
He nātha he ramaṇa he nayanābhirāma,
Hā hā kadā nu bhavitāsi padaṁ dṛśor me.

'O Lord, O darling, O the one friend of the world, O Kṛṣṇa, O the fickle one, O the one ocean of compassion, O Nātha (spouse), O dallier, O the cynosure of my eyes, when, oh when, are you going to occupy the entire field of my vision?'

[8] Vidyāpati in his immortal *bhajana*-like *pada* sings:

Mādhava hāma pariṇāmanirāśā,
Tuṁhu jagatāraṇa dīnadayāmaya ataeo tuṁhāri viśoāśā.

'O Mādhava (Nārāyaṇa, the spouse of Lakṣmī), I entertain no hope of promising fulfilment. Thou art the deliverer of the world, compassionate to the wretched ; and that is why I have pinned my faith on thee.'

unto me power. Vigour Thou art, be pleased to give unto me vigour). The *Caṇḍī* or *Saptaśatī* (*Mārkaṇḍeya Purāṇa*) gives forth in a glorious vein the spirit of a happy synthesis of the will and the heart: '*Tvāmāśritānāṁ na vipannarāṇāṁ tvāmāśritā hyāśrayatāṁ prayānti*' (To them that resort to Thee, there comes no danger ; rather, they that resort to Thee become the refuge of others). Bankimchandra, one of the modern seers, in his immortal song *Vande Mātaram*, has reiterated his belief in the all-powerfulness of *deśamātṛkā* (the motherland): '*Tvaṁ hi prāṇāḥ śarīre*' (Thou art the vital breath in the body). She is *dharaṇī* (sustainer) and *bharaṇī* (nourisher) as well, and not an *abalā* (a weak one).

In the day to day application of hymns to the diverse necessities of life, we have this faith expressed in a thousand and one ways. The well-known *Madhumatī* hymn (*Ṛ.V.*, I. 90. 5-7) shows succinctly the yearnings of the devotee for an equipoise of the elemental forces and an abundance of amenities. God is not merely grace and tenderness ; He is law and order as well. And the Indian hymnologist is ever eager to give vent to the thought which finds a characteristic echo in the line of a modern poet: 'If He thunder by law, the thunder is yet His voice.' In a poetic formulation of his devotional creed, he declares of the divine Mother, the fountain-head of all activities, in the manner of the Vedic *ṛṣi*: 'Thou art the soft and tender light in the moon, the brilliant lustre in the sun, consciousness in man, power in the wind, sweetness in water, heat in fire ; anything minus Thee is an unsubstantial void.'

SCOPE, FORM, AND STYLE OF THE HYMNS

The distinguishing characteristics of the hymnal literature in India have been its monolatry, its henotheism or kathenotheism, in the phrase of Max Müller, and its comprehensive scope. This literature includes within its orbit hymns to Brahman or Ātman and God ; the different gods and goddesses ; the *navagrahas* (planetary bodies) ; the *bāṇaliṅga* and the *śālagrāma* (the sacred stone emblems of Śiva and Viṣṇu found in the Narmadā and the Gaṇḍakī) ; the seven *purīs* (cities) and the shrines associated with the twelve *jyotirliṅgas* (most sacred Śiva emblems) ; the Kumārī (the Virgin Mother) ; the *guru* and the *pitṛs* ; the sacred and sanctifying rivers, like the Gaṅgā, the Narmadā, and the Godāvarī ; the Paurāṇic *varṣas* or regions (e.g. the *Bhārata* hymn in *Bhā.*, V. 19) ; and trees and plants, like the *aśvattha, bilva,* and *tulasī.*

The hymnal literature generally did not lose touch with the life of the people. It is nonetheless significant that the eulogistic court-epics (e.g. *Sargabandha-mahākāvya*) were clad in sophisticated and artificial literary expressions, and consequently hymnody also gradually came to be readjusted largely to the taste of the classes for whom it had to cater. Thus there was generated a tendency to make the *stotra* literature more and more aristocratic, conventional, and formula-ridden. Conceit and classicism affected its substance and fervour, owing to the great constraint imposed by the canons of finished forms of poetic diction. However, being readily admitted to a place in classical poetry, *stotras* became the popular means of propagating religion and culture, though often they were highly polished and pedantic in their language and form and over-wrought in their syncretism as regards contents.

Vālmīki, in the *Rāmāyaṇa,* utilizes this *genre* in the *Āditya-hṛdaya* (the *Mahābhārata,* III. 2, dwells on the same topic) of twenty-three verses, which has swelled into the longer and more commonly used *stotra* of that name in the *Āditya Purāṇa.* This certainly forms a transition as regards manner and matter between the Vedic hymns and the later *stotras,* and was a pioneer effort in the field of *nāma-māhātmya* (glorification of God's name) and its connection with the mystery of institutional worship (*pūjā-rahasya*). Amongst court-epic writers, the Buddhist poet Aśvaghoṣa led the way in introducing the spirit and essence of form and finish as well as of thought and rapture in his *Gaṇḍī-stotra,* where religious message, musical execution, and fervent lyrical appeal are joined in a fine symphony. Kālidāsa, the prince of Sanskrit poets, has contributed to hymnology his spirit of toleration, sobriety, and assimilated scholarship, which are seen in his two well-known *stotras* in *Kumārasambhava* (II) and *Raghuvaṁśa* (X). Bhāravi, in spite of his innate impetuosity and strongly susceptible poetic fancy, charms us by his studied docility and sweet serenity, as in the concluding canto of his *Kirātārjunīya* (XX. 22-43), and has achieved great success in the face of the limitations of a *mahākāvya* craftsmanship. Māgha gives us a *via media* between rigid scholarship and feeling-saturation in *Śiśupālavadha* (XIV. 60-86). Ratnākara in his *Haravijaya* (XLVII) offers us a rather long and somewhat indifferent hymn to Caṇḍī in the true form and spirit of a Paurāṇic propagandist. Śivasvāmin, at the close of his *Kapphiṇābhyudaya,* treats us to an uninspiring prayer in a hymn of the sectarian type. Abhinanda in a *stotra* to the divine Mother in his *Rāmacarita* (XVI) shows his characteristic synthetic approach. Śrīharṣa in his *Naiṣadhacarita* (XXI. 54-118) evinces a rare combination of literary ingenuity, Paurāṇic faith and phraseology, and regional and dialectic tendencies. *Sūrya-śataka* of Mayūra, *Caṇḍī-śataka* of Bāṇabhaṭṭa, and *Viṣṇupādādikeśānta-varṇana-stotra* of Śaṅkarācārya are stock examples of hymns which are more literary than devotional, and remain isolated attempts. Lesser known poets in the line run in their narrow grooves, though each of them in his own way tries to efface the distinction between sacred and secular poetry (a distinction none too closely observed in practice in classical circles).

The style of the *stotras*, which is generally simple, has leaned, not infrequently, towards artificiality and long compounds, and towards pedantry, especially when there is a reference to Tāntric and philosophical topics. Notable examples of this type of hymns are *Kuṇḍalinī-stotra, Ānanda-stotra, Śrīsundarī-stotra, Dakṣiṇa-Kālikā-krama-stotra,* parts of *Sarasvatī-stotra (hrīṁ hrīṁ hṛdyeka bīje . . .), Saundarya-laharī, Pañca-stavī, Mahiṣamardinī-stava, Karpūrādi-stotra,* and *Laghu-stotra.*

HYMNS IN THE LIFE OF THE COMMON MAN

To the ordinary man, however, with the plan of life chalked out for him by sacred lore and time-honoured usage, this clash between tradition and innovation did not matter much. A ready acknowledgement of the divine spirit and a sincere observance of rites and ceremonies were his guiding principles in life. The *Mahābhārata* and the Purāṇas were his religious directory. In the earlier period, the Godhead in Its threefold manifestation of Brahmā, Viṣṇu, and Śiva, and later, owing to changes of time, place, and circumstances, the *pañcadevatā*, viz. Śiva, Śakti, Viṣṇu (with their *mūrtis, mahāvidyās,* and *avatāras* respectively), Sūrya, and Gaṇeśa (sometimes substituted by Skanda or Kārttikeya), were the major deities, with varying shades of importance. Side by side with an insistent demand for a simplification of life and purity in living, the old ideas about *yajñas* (sacrifices) and *ṛṇas* (obligations) yielded place to the cardinal principle of *pūjā* (worship), thus reintroducing the fading qualities of humility and self-abnegation into individual and social life and turning the year into a round of religious festivals. There was nothing higher than one's chosen deity (*nahi-iṣṭadevāt paramasti kiñcit*) and no better prescription for the ills and mishaps of life than the practice of obeisance (*vandana*), muttering of sacred formulae (*mantra-japa*), and prayerful attitude (*stuti*).

DIFFERENT TYPES OF HYMNS ILLUSTRATED

The old hymns, especially in their classical forms and emendations, formed the manual of religious worship; the theory of incarnations (Avatāravāda) gave a fillip to religious poetry. The *Mahābhārata* and the Purāṇas, especially the *Viṣṇu*, the *Bhāgavata*, the *Padma*, the *Skanda,* the *Mārkaṇḍeya,* and the *Garuḍa* (with the Upapurāṇas, the *Sāmba,* the *Gaṇeśa,* and the *Nāradīya*), as much as the Tantras, especially the Āmnāyas, the Yāmalas, the *Viśvasāra,* the *Yogasāra,* and the Pāñcarātra treatises, and the eclectic *Brahma Saṁhitā* have made a very liberal use of *stotras* for their cherished objective of inculcating a spirit of faith and fortitude. No wonder that some of the finest and most popular *namaskāras* and their accessories are accommodated in these treasure-houses of Indian lore, as, for example, in these lines addressed to different deities:

Tvameva mātā ca pitā tvameva . . . (to Viṣṇu),
Bāṇeśvarāya narakārṇavatāraṇāya . . . (to Śiva),
Bhavabhayaharamekaṁ bhānukoṭiprakāśam . . . (to Rāma),
Namo brahmaṇyadevāya go-brāhmaṇahitāya ca . . . (to Kṛṣṇa),
Namaḥ savitre jagadeka cakṣuṣe . . . (to Sūrya).

A valuable adjunct in the elaboration of this religious worship was a contemplation of the form of the deity (*dhyāna*). The epithets of gods in early literature, '*divo naraḥ*' (the men of heavens) and '*nṛpeśas*' (having the form of men), to mention only two prominent ones, betray the anthropomorphic tendencies of the early thinkers and worshippers. The Paurāṇic masters have built on this foundation a superstructure, solid, sublime, picturesque, and meticulously accurate in design, device, and details. The chanting of *stotras* individually or in unison and the practice of reading out sacred lore while circumambulating a shrine (*parikramā*) have helped in producing an almost unparalleled atmosphere of religious solemnity. The haunting sense of otherness, a prerequisite of devotional religion (*parā-pūjā*), is brought home even to the most materially-minded person, when he hears, in a place of worship (*pūjā-maṇḍapa*), the sonorous voice of the priest chanting a hymn on the divine Mother, such as the one given below, in a solemn attitude of meditation:

Jaṭājūṭasamāyuktām-ardhendukṛtaśekharām ;
Locanatrayasaṁyuktāṁ pūrṇendu-sadṛśānanām ; . . .
Aṣṭābhiḥ śaktibhistābhiḥ satataṁ pariveṣṭitām ;
Cintayet jagatāṁ dhātrīṁ dharmakāmārthamokṣadām.

'One should meditate on the Mother of the world, the bestower of *dharma, kāma, artha,* and *mokṣa,* as always surrounded by her eight Śaktis, the attendant goddesses of power, and as adorned with a mass of matted hair, with a half-moon as her crest, triple-eyed, and with a face lovely as the full moon.'

Similar is the case when one hears the devotee reciting the series of verses from *Āditya-hṛdaya-stotra* beginning with:

Yanmaṇḍalaṁ dīptikaraṁ viśālam,
Ratnaprabhaṁ tīvram-anādirūpam . . .
Punātu māṁ tat-saviturvareṇyam.

'May the pre-eminent lustre of Savitṛ purify me—Savitṛ of the primeval or eternal pattern, who is encircled with a spacious, intensely glowing halo, dazzling as a gem.'

Or, when one feels the sublimity of the metaphysical abstraction in the following *stotra*:

Tadekaṁ smarāmastadekaṁ bhajāmaḥ,
Tadekaṁ jagatsākṣirūpaṁ namāmaḥ ;
Sadekaṁ nidhānaṁ nirālambarūpam,
Bhavāmbhodhipotaṁ śaraṇyaṁ vrajāmaḥ.

'That One we remember ; to that One we dedicate ourselves ; to that One in the form of the perennial witness to all worldly events we bow down. We resort to that Refuge, the one Existence, the unsupported Support of all creatures, the Ship that takes one across the ocean of becoming.'

Again, one cannot but feel exhilarated when one presents to one's mind's eye the homely and appealing picture of the divine Mother as portrayed in the following lines of *Carcāstava* (V. 11):

Mūrdhni sphurat-tuhinadīdhiti-dīpti-dīptam,
Madhye lalāṭam-amarāyudha-raśmicitram ;
Hṛccakracumbi-hutabhukkaṇikāṇukāri,
Jyotiryadetadidamamba tava svarūpam.

'This refulgence, O Mother, is thy real form—the refulgence which, in the crest of your head, shines intensified by the sparkling rays of the cool-rayed (moon) ; which, in the middle of your forehead, shines variegated with the hues of the rainbow ; and which, again, radiates brilliance, like sparks of fire, reaching up to the circle of the heart.'

One may point to the *Durgāpradakṣiṇa-stuti* as the most effective of such hymns, especially when one sees the procession of the family going round the image and uttering all the while their heartfelt prayer in the well-known lines:

Durgāṁ śivāṁ śāntikarīṁ Brahmāṇīṁ Brahmaṇaḥ priyām ;
Sarvalokapraṇetrīñca praṇamāmi sadā-śivām.
Maṅgalāṁ śobhanāṁ śuddhāṁ niṣkalāṁ paramāṁ kalām ;
Viśveśvarīṁ viśvavandyāṁ Caṇḍikāṁ praṇamāmyaham.

'To Durgā, the gracious and the ever benign, to her as Brahmāṇī, the beloved spouse of Brahmā, to the ever-auspicious one, the manifestor of all the worlds, I offer my respectful obeisance. Devotedly do I bow down to Caṇḍikā, the majestic goddess ruling over all, the respected of all, to her who is auspicious, graceful, and pure, and who is the highest principle and, in her essential nature, is partless and without any manifestation.'

THE NON-PAURĀṆIC HYMNS

The non-Paurānic hymns, used in the daily practice of many a *sādhaka*, are a legion in themselves and include many which are anonymous and many more that are of doubtful authorship. Leaving out the shorter ones, like those attributed to the lesser Śaṅkarācāryas and to the teachers of different sub-schools of theological and philosophical thoughts, we come to the bigger ones like *Śivamahimnaḥ-stava, Pañcastavī, Harimīḍe, Ānanda-laharī,* and *Saundarya-laharī*, some of which are fairly old and have been widely read and commented upon in scholarly circles. The apocryphal Paurāṇic works contain fine hymns, such as the one in the *Adhyātma Rāmāyaṇa*, beginning with '*Aho kṛtārthāsmi jagannivāsa te padābja-saṁlagna*' (Ah, my Lord, the refuge of the world, at the touch of thy lotus-feet have I attained the object of my life), put in the mouth of Ahalyā when she was restored to her human form through the grace of Śrī Rāma-candra ; or the *stotra* '*Akṣaraṁ paramaṁ Brahma jyotīrūpaṁ sanātanam*' (the pre-eminent, undecaying, eternal deity in the form of light), put in the mouth of Indra, in the *Brahmavaivarta Purāṇa* (*Kṛṣṇajanma-khaṇḍa*). *Kumārī-stotra* in the *Rudra Yāmala, Ānanda-stotra* in the *Kulārṇava Tantra, Pādukāpañcaka* attributed to Lord Śiva, *Kṛṣṇa-karṇāmṛta* of Līlāśuka Bilvamaṅgala, exquisite and sustained in its effect, *Mukundamālā* of Kulaśekhara of Keraḷa, and the collected *stotras* of Rūpa and Jīva Gosvāmins, like *Stavāvali* and *Mukundamuktāvali*, as also the shorter hymns like *Sūryāryā-stotra* attributed to Yājñavalkya (though ascribed in an anthology to the poetess Vijjakā), are some specimens of hymns that moved millions of devotees in the past. Some of these are highly prized even now. They have thus, apart from their poetic excellence, an additional value in developing the Bhakti cult, which formed an integral part of the life and culture of the Paurāṇic and Tāntric India.

PURPOSE AND NATURE OF THE HYMNS

Spiritual emotion is roused to a high pitch by the recitation of these *stotras*, which are therefore regarded as the most tangible form of worship— a point nicely expressed in the well-known verse of the *Śiva-mānasapūjā-stotra*, itself inspired by an Upaniṣadic text:

Ātmā tvaṁ Girijā matiḥ sahacarāḥ prāṇāḥ śarīraṁ gṛham,
Pūjā te viṣayopabhogaracanā nidrā samādhisthitiḥ ;
Sañcāraḥ padayoḥ pradakṣiṇavidhiḥ stotrāṇi sarvā giro,
Yad yad karma karomi tattadakhilaṁ Śambho tavārādhanam.

'Thou art the Ātman ; Girijā, thy spouse, is the mind ; thine attendants are the vital breaths ; thy abode is the body ; thy worship lies in ministering to the enjoyment of sense objects or projection of the sensuous world of enjoyment ; the repose in sleep constitutes *samādhi* ; our locomotion is tantamount to the process of circumambulation with the feet ; all the words are hymns to thee. O Śambhu (Śiva), all that I perform is thy worship.'

The *Dakṣiṇāmūrti-stotra* of Śaṅkara has been justly regarded as one of the most famous devotional hymns.

Mythology is the very framework of the hymns and is an important aid to the literary and expositional art. A hymn not only mentions divine qualities, but also glorifies the divine exploits and acts of grace of divine heroes. In certain hymns, we have not merely a reference to legends, but also to the doctrines and creeds of several schools. Hymns in praise of *ṛṣis* and teachers, especially in the Hindu and Jaina mediaeval treatises, contain legends associated with them. The theme of some *stotras*, like *Sūryastava* which refers to curing Sāmba of leprosy, is palpably of this nature. In some other hymns, like *Ārtatrāṇa-Nārāyaṇa-stotra,* we have a series of such references intended to serve a common purpose. *Harimīḍe, Śiva-mahimnaḥ-stava,* and *Pañcastavī* combine philosophic expression and religious rapture.

The Hindu code of liturgical prayers (*sandhyā-vandana*), whether of the Vedic or Tāntric variety, is rigidly fixed, with its sequel of *nitya-naimittika-karma-paddhati* (the code of duties, obligatory and incidental), which is binding on the householder. The *stotras* offer scope for individual initiative and genius. From the view-points of logical argument and theological procedure, the skilful hymnographer follows an artistically sound plan, which often baffles imitation and hardly admits of any improvement. The celebrated *stotra* '*Namaste sate sarvalokāśrayāya*' (obeisance to the primal Being, the support of the whole universe), in the *Mahānirvāṇa Tantra,* is an example and a type by itself. It has attained universal recognition in India, in spite of its idea being more neo-Vedic and abstract than Paurāṇic and concrete. In the realm of the conception of Godhead, it touches the fringe of pure Existence (Sat or *parā sattā*), self-revealing Consciousness (Cit), and absolute Bliss (Ānanda). The Vedic *ṛṣi,* in a spirit of robust optimism, prays to the gods: 'May we hear with our ears pleasant and delectable sounds, may we see with our eyes comely and soothing sights . . .' This is the thing that the *bhakta* also values and aspires to achieve. His *bhakti* is its own reward, the greatest gain (*paramo lābhaḥ*), the *summum bonum* (*niḥśreyasa*). In several *stavas,* like those contained in the *Bhāgavata Purāṇa,* religious poetry has reached its climax.

It is profitable to remember that the several sects, into which religious devotion was canalized, have had each its own code of *stotras*. The monastic orders founded by Śaṅkara, Rāmānuja, and Caitanya, as also the Sikh community and the Ārya Samājists, to name only the prominent ones, have offered in this field much that is of abiding value. The Ramakrishna-Vivekananda movement, adjusting itself to the needs of modern life, but not severing itself from the ancient moorings, has followed suit in composing *stotra*. In our own times, we have the *Brahma-saṅgīta,* the song-offerings with a fine ethereal fragrance, from Rabindranath. The ephemeral element lay, in the case of older models, in extending the scope of adoration to the patron saints, apostles, and eminent ones in the sect ; the essential inner current of devotion to the Lord, however, is what has contributed to their abiding religious acceptability and literary grace.

LITERARY MERIT OF SANSKRIT HYMNS

It may be readily conceded as a general, though not as a universal, proposition that the later a *stotra* in Sanskrit is, the less is its literary value. It is not within the purview of this paper to make a critical estimate of individual *stotras* and to judge their merits and demerits. Be it sufficient to mention that their lapses, faults of omission and commission, certainly detract from their genuine worth. We leave aside the Tāntric *stotras,* which abound in out-of-the-norm forms and refractory derivatives, especially in the case of verbs (e.g. *hunet*). We have often in these hymns an excessive artificiality, beyond the limits of conventional liberty allowed in the field of *citrakāvyas* (literary curios) and *stotras.* Over and above such flaws, there are palpable blemishes in grammar and metre that jar on the ears of a devotee. For example, the two highly popular *Mahiṣamardinī-stotra* and *Annapūrṇāṣṭaka* bristle with anomalies and blunders in grammar and metre. In matter or content, as in the case of Sanskrit emotional literature in general, there is a palpable tendency towards standardization. Even some of the best hymnographers occasionally seem to lack the touch of individuality and to move in a circumscribed area.

There is one valuable quality in the *stotras,* their exquisite sense of rhythm, which raises them head and shoulders above all other literary achievements. The aim of the hymnographer is perfect unison with the object of his devotion. With tranquillity in thought he combines harmony in expression and symmetry in form. The relation between the evolution of the musical schools and the development of religious ecstasy in some of the sects is an interesting subject for research, though it concerns more the art critic than the general reader. In the mellifluous music of *mātrāvṛttas* (moric metre), including the *pajjhaṭikā* in its shorter form and the twenty-four *mātrā* and the thirty-two *mātrā* varieties in the longer ones, the hymns easily get the place of honour ; in the *akṣaravṛttas* (syllabic metre) they are decidedly superior, in their exploitation of the merits of the *toṭaka,* the *bhujaṅgaprayāta,* the *drutavilambita,* the *mattamayūra,* the *tūṇaka,* the *pṛthvī,* and the *pañcacāmara,* to their counterparts in secular poetry.

Besides the *śloka* and the *upajāti* metres, which rise to unusual heights of excellence, as in the *Saptaśatī,* the *Viṣṇu Purāṇa,* and the *Bhāgavata Purāṇa,* we have the *vasantatilaka,* the *śikhariṇī,* the *śārdūlavikrīḍita,* the *sragdharā,* and, though rarely, the *āryā* which are employed by the hymnologists in a very graceful way. A few characteristic stanzas taken at random from mediaeval and modern *stotras* are here cited to show this blending of music and feeling.

Avinayamapanaya Viṣṇo damaya manaḥ śamaya viṣayamṛgatṛṣṇām ;
Bhūtadayāṁ vistāraya tāraya saṁsārasāgarataḥ.

'Remove rudeness, O Viṣṇu, subdue the mind, quench the thirst of attachment to mirage-like objects of sense. Extend the scope of compassion to creatures and rescue us from the ocean of worldly life.'

Jayasi sarvataḥ Kāśi te rajaḥ,
Smṛtamaho'dhikaṁ sādhitasrajaḥ.
Tridaśasaṁsadi yābhinanditā,
Śritakṛtottarābandhisambhṛtā.
Śatanatārthināṁ gītinoditam
Mama nirāśrayaṁ mattamohitam ;
Luṭhati mandire svāntamantarā-
Vasathavandite lubdhamantarā.

'O Kāśī, you dominate over all. Behold, the dust clinging to you is declared better than a beautifully strung wreath of flowers. You are greeted in the assembly of the gods, being richly equipped with the prospects of transmitted, accomplished, and future destiny. There my helpless heart rolls, vainglorious and perplexed, but yearning within, propelled by the hymns (sung in thy praise) by hundreds of devoted petitioners in thy shrine, blessed by the Spirit in the inner sanctum.'

Namo devi Durge śive bhīmanāde
Sarasvatyarundhatyamoghasvarūpe ;
Vibhūtiḥ śacī kālarātriḥ satī tvam
Namaste jagattāriṇi trāhi Durge.

'Obeisance to thee, O divine Mother, Durgā, the benignant and yet terrific-roaring, the muse that never obstructs and is withal never fruitless in her own form. Thou art power, *śacī* (action), the dark night of destruction, the eternally existent. Obeisance to thee, the deliverer of the world. May thou protect me.'

Jaṭāṭavīgalajjalapravāhapāvitasthale
Gale'valambya lambitāṁ bhujaṅgatuṅgamālikām ;
Ḍamaḍḍamaḍḍamaḍḍamanninādavaḍḍamarvayam
Cakāra caṇḍatāṇḍavaṁ tanotu naḥ Śivaḥ śivam.

'On his neck, the entire tract of which is purified by the stream of waters flowing over the dense wilderness of his matted hair, supporting the long hanging necklace of serpents, and with his drum sounding the note *"ḍamaṭ, ḍamaṭ, ḍamaṭ, ḍamaṭ"* in harmonious vibrations—let Śiva, who is engaged in his impetuous *tāṇḍava* dance, grant us welfare.'

Gale kalitakālima prakaṭitendu bhālasthale,
Vināṭitajaṭotkaraṁ ruciraрāṇipāthoruhe,
Udañcitakapālakaṁ jaghanasīmni sandarśita-
Dvipājinamanukṣaṇaṁ kimapi dhāma vandāmahe.

'Ever and anon we bow down to that inscrutable effulgence, manifesting blueness in the throat, showing forth the moon on the tract of his forehead, with the mass of tangled locks dancing gracefully over the comely lotus-like hand, with a garland of skulls held aloft, and with the elephant-skin displayed over the bounds of his loins.'

Mathurāpuracirabhāsura saumyamadhuravigraha ;
Vṛndāvanavipināṭana kṛtadurjananigraha ;
Śrīvallabha śiśuballava sundara nava mādhava ;
Nārāyaṇa nalinanayana śamanaśamana māmava.

'Ever shining, in and around the city of Mathurā, of amiable and charming form, roaming the woods of Vṛndāvana, chastising the wicked, the young cowherd, handsome and vivacious, O lotus-eyed Nārāyaṇa, the spouse of Śrī (Lakṣmī), the extirpator of death, be gracious enough to extend to me thy protection.'

Padmadalāyatalocana he Raghuvaṁśavibhūṣaṇa deva dayālo,
Nirmalanīradanīlatano'khilalokahṛdambujabhāsaka bhāno ;
Komalagātra pavitrapadābja-rajaḥkaṇapāvita-Gautama-kāntam,
Tvāṁ bhajato Raghunandana dehi dayāghana me svapadāmbujadāsyam.

'With eyes wide as lotus petals, O kind Lord, ornament of Raghu's family, the sun that causes to bloom the lotus-like hearts of all beings, with a form blue like a stainless cloud, charge me, thy devotee, O kindness incarnate, with the service of thy lotus feet, which purified the delicate-limbed darling of sage Gautama with the dust particles thereof.'

Ayi girinandini nanditamedini viśvavinodini Nandasute,
Girivara-Vindhyaśirodhinivāsini Viṣṇuvilāsini Jiṣṇunute ;
Madhumadhure Madhu-Kaiṭabhagañjini kaitavabhañjini rāsayute,
Jaya jaya he Mahiṣāsuramardini ramyakapardini śailasute.

'O daughter of the Mountain, delighter of the earth, the enlivener of all ; O thou, the daughter of Nanda, that art wont to dwell on the top of the great Vindhya mountain, the delighter of Viṣṇu, the adored of Indra ; O thou that art flushed with wine, who scornest the demons Madhu and Kaiṭabha ; O daughter of the Hill, the dispeller of Māyā, the reveller in *rāsa*-dance, thou that art decked with beautifully braided hair, all glory to thee, the repressor of the Mahiṣa demon.'

In the more elaborate schemes, as in the case of *daṇḍaka* metre, it is the *stotra* literature again which carries off the palm. The well-known *Śyāmalā-daṇḍaka-stotra,* which tradition (perhaps without sufficient justification) ascribes to Kālidāsa, the popular *Devīstuti* in the *Devī Purāṇa* (XVII), and the nicely alliterated hymns to Śrī Kṛṣṇa in the *Ānanda-Vṛndāvana-campū* (XV) of Kavi Karṇapūra are instances in point.

VERNACULAR HYMNAL LITERATURE

This account of Indian hymnology would be incomplete without the mention of the outstanding contributions of the vernacular literature of India, covering a period of nearly a thousand years. The sweet and intensely sincere contributions of the Āḷvārs and other Vaiṣṇava and Śaiva saints of South India, which are unique in their poetic and devotional content, are universally acclaimed. We have in Rāmaprasāda, Vidyāpati, Tulasīdāsa, Sūradāsa, Mīrābāī, Kabīr, Nānak, Jñāneśvara, Tukārāma, Narasiṁhadāsa Mehtā, Purandaradāsa, Tyāgarāja, and others high class hymnologists who are the torch-bearers of the old thought and may be classed amongst the best representatives of Indian hymnology. Indeed, to the average Indian *sādhaka* and *bhakta* of the present day, hymnology has almost exclusive reference to hymns in vernacular literature. While circumstances of time and place and the personal factor have led to changes, the integrity and the continuity of the old devotional form have remained intact from the earliest hymns of the *Ṛg-Veda* down to the religious lyrics of the present day.

34

FESTIVALS AND SACRED DAYS

THE sanctity of certain moments and periods of time by association with memorable events, holy persons, and notable psychic experiences is the basic idea underlying the observance of sacred days and festivals, as well as the undertaking of pilgrimages to places considered specially sacred. Both are instruments of enrichment of the inner life and are so acknowledged by human nature, which is the same all the world over. But the distinction of the Hindu attitude in this respect is the thoroughness with which the principle is worked out in the programme of devotions and pious exercises for every month and almost every day. As a none-too-sympathetic European savant observes : 'There is not an object in heaven and earth which a Hindu is not prepared to worship—sun, moon, and stars ; rocks, stocks, and stones ; trees, shrubs, and grass ; seas, pools, and rivers ; his own implements of trade ; the animals he finds most useful ; the noxious reptiles he fears ; men remarkable for extraordinary qualities, viz. great valour, sanctity, virtue, or even vice ; good and evil demons, ghosts, and goblins ; the spirits of departed ancestors ; an infinite number of semi-human and semi-divine existences ; inhabitants of the seven upper and the seven lower worlds—each and all come in for a share of divine honour or a tribute of more or less adoration.'[1]

RECOGNITION OF THE ALL-PERVADING DIVINE

This worshipful attitude is due to the cardinal Hindu tenet that one divine Intelligence pervades all, and that links and filiations join all forms of life, past and present. The *Śvetāśvatara Upaniṣad* (VI. 11) speaks of 'the one God, hidden in all things, pervading all, the inner Spirit of all beings, the overseer of all actions, who dwells in all creatures, the witness, sentient, all alone, and devoid of attributes'. It is this idea which underlies the oblations to the *pitṛs* in which not merely the ancestors of the offerer, but all conceivable relations in this birth or any other, in whatever form of sentient being they may now be, are invoked in the *tarpaṇa* rite during the fortnight sacred to the manes. 'The gods, the *yakṣas,* as also the *nāgas* (serpents), the *gandharvas,* the *apsarasas* (celestial beauties), and the *asuras* (demons) ; the cruel ones (beasts of prey), the snakes, the creatures of fine plumage, trees and beings of crooked gait, birds, the *vidyādharas,* and the

[1] Monier-Williams, *Brāhmaṇism and Hinduism,* p. 350.

jalādhāras (aquatic beings) ; and those that move through the sky, the beings that have no food, those addicted to sin or practising virtue—for their satisfaction this water is offered by me'—so runs a *tarpaṇa mantra.* And the five great daily sacrifices incumbent on the householder are made in honour of the gods, the sages, the fathers, humanity, and all other creatures. And as regards the observance of festivals or sacred days, the racial memory of cherished experiences and handed-on associations of time, place, and persons went on accumulating as the ages passed, and as new groups of men were added to the original stock.

RELIGIOUS CHARACTER OF HINDU FESTIVALS

All Hindu festivals, whether magical or traceable to nature- or vegetation-myths in their origin, are now predominantly religious in character and significance. Like many of the deities of our pantheon, the rites and customs as well as the cults have undergone a process of evolution. The origins of many of them are lost in the gloom of a remote past. In many cases new ceremonies have been grafted on old occasions. There are many which, though traceable to archaic prototypes, have suffered a change which bars recognition of the old in the new. But all alike bear witness to the wide-spread popular faith and interest in the exercise of piety and devotion —in fasting, in vigils, in worship, in ablution, in offerings to the manes, in gifts to holy persons, and in the practice of austerities and physical hardships as benefiting the spirit within. They also show how festivities lent joy and zest and variety to life's monotonous routine.

FESTIVALS RELATING TO PERIODS OF TIME AND SEASONS

The new year of the Hindu calendar, which runs from about the middle of April, begins the business year in many parts of India with suitable auspicating rites. The husking beam is idle on this day and is adorned with rice-paste markings. The commencement of the four mythical archaic ages (*yugas*)—*satya, tretā, dvāpara,* and *kali*—is also commemorated, respectively, on the third day of the bright fortnight (*akṣaya-tṛtīyā*) in Vaiśākha, the ninth day of the bright fortnight in Kārttika, the dark thirteenth day of Bhādra, and the full moon day in Māgha. The Caitanya era begins on the full moon day in Phālguna, on which day the great Vaiṣṇava teacher was born. The Vikrama Saṁvat begins on the day following the *divāli* (*dīpāvali,* the festival of lights), that is, the new moon day in Kārttika. As the name of Agrahāyaṇa or Mārgaśīrṣa signifies, the year may have begun in the remote past in mid-November, as it did in Siam (Thailand) till recent times. The *navānna* (new rice), a ceremony of first fruits, is performed after the harvest has been gathered, and is accompanied with *śrāddha* and offerings to all creatures, birds of the air, and beasts of the field. It serves the purpose of a thanksgiving service on one of the appointed days in the calendar. In the Deccan it is named *poṅgal* (rice-cooking) ; for three days Indra, Agni, and Gaṇeśa are worshipped, and decorated cattle are taken in procession. And not only the first eating of the new rice, but the reaping of the harvest, the sowing and transplanting of paddy-stalks, the planting of trees, as also the digging of tanks are done on auspicious days.

Like the beginning of the year, the advent of the seasons also was marked by suitable celebrations. These had their origin in remote Vedic times, when three four-month celebrations were observed—the first at the close of winter or the beginning of spring (Phālguna), which was sacred to Viśvedevāḥ (All-gods) ; the second at the beginning of the rains in Āṣāḍha, which was sacred to Varuṇa ; and the third in autumn (Kārttika), when the first fruits were offered to the deity together with goat and ram as well as phallic emblems. This last is observed as a period of varied austerities. The *cāturmāsya* (four-months) begins from the waxing eleventh or the full moon in Āṣāḍha or at the *saṅkrānti* or solar transition to Śrāvaṇa and concludes after four months on corresponding days of Kārttika.

SOLAR TRANSITION AND OTHER AUSPICIOUS TIMES

In later times, the day of transition from one month to another, the *saṅkrānti* day, has been held sacred ; two of them are specially so, one being the day on which the sun passes to the sign of Aries (Meṣa), i.e. the end of the year, and the other being the day on which he enters Capricorn (Makara), when the month of Māgha begins. These are called respectively the *mahāviṣuva* and the *uttarāyaṇa saṅkrāntis*. On this latter day, pilgrims in hundreds and thousands gather at the mouth of the Bhāgīrathī—the Gaṅgāsāgara as it is called—to have a bath at the river's entrance into the sea. There they visit the *āśrama* (hermitage) of the sage Kapila, who, according to the Paurāṇic legend, had burnt to ashes the sixty thousand sons of Sagara, who were subsequently redeemed by the waters of the celestial Gaṅgā as it flowed over their ashes along the channel pointed out by Bhagīratha, in recognition of whose great efforts in bringing the river to the earth, it was named the Bhāgīrathī. This day, the day of *pauṣa-pārvaṇa*, is pre-eminently festive in Bengali homes. In Assam it is called *māgha-bihu* or *bhogālī-bihu,* the festival of feasts. Bonfires are lighted. The round of feasts and mirth continues for nearly a week. Formerly, pastries of different kinds were made and served to friends, neighbours, and relations. The *mahāviṣuva saṅkrānti,* which closes the year as well as the month of the layman's asceticism, saw in past times the gruesome practice of self-torture. Men with hooks in the muscles of their back whirled from a rotating bar at the top of a long pole, which was set up in the market place. This practice (*caḍaka-yātrā*) has now wholly disappeared due to legal ban. But during the month preceding, non-Brāhmaṇa householders, specially followers of the Gorakṣa Nātha cult, adopt an ascetic life in large numbers even in these days. They put on the sacred thread and the ochre robe and conclude the period by a pilgrimage on foot to some famous shrine of Śiva, such as of Tārakeśvara near Calcutta. These ascetic pilgrims on their way receive presents from householders, carry rice and green cocoanuts as votive offerings to the deity, and, as they trudge on in different groups, send up shouts of glory to their deity. The Assam celebration of the *saṅkrānti* is known as *naṅgālī-bihu,* the festival of amusements. It marks the close of the festive season which starts at *māgha-bihu.*

The last day of the month of Bhādra is the artisans' holiday, when all those who work with tools set them apart and offer worship to their patron deity Viśvakarman (the architect of the universe), the Indian Vulcan. Culinary operations are on this day suspended, and fried rice and confectionery are substituted.

Two fortnights are held in special esteem, the fortnight sacred to the fathers (*pitṛpakṣa*) and the fortnight following, which is sacred to the goddess Durgā (*devīpakṣa*).

Among the months some are reckoned specially sacred and suitable for acts of piety. These are Kārttika, Māgha, and Vaiśākha. All through these months the morning bath in some sacred stream is considered highly meritorious.

IMPORTANCE OF THE MOON IN TIMING RELIGIOUS OBSERVANCES

Of the two heavenly bodies (the sun and the moon) that apparently revolve round the earth, the moon, because of its many changes in form—the sixteen digits that it passes through—has everywhere afforded convenient periods for timing the religious observances. The *Viṣṇu Purāṇa* (I. 22) says : Brahmā appointed the moon to be the monarch of planets, plants, sacrifices, and penances. The moon-feasts, *darśa-paurṇamāsa,* comprised two days' sacrifice at the new moon and one day's at the full moon. It was the prototype of all sacrifices prevalent in ancient India. In Sanskrit plays, kings are represented as making an offering (*arghya*) to the full moon as it rises in the east. In the Hindu calendar, all the fifteen phases of the moon, lunar days or *tithis,* are distinguished as occasions for particular ceremonies. Every *tithi* has its special association and appropriateness for particular observances or worship of a certain deity. The first and eighth days as well as the end of the fortnight are days of rest from studies, especially the Vedic.

FESTIVALS OCCURRING ON DIFFERENT LUNAR DAYS

The first phase after the new moon in Kārttika is known as the gamblers' *pratipad.* On this day, in the streets of a city like Banaras, knots of people gather round the dice-box in a public place and try their luck. Success in the game is believed to be a happy augury for the coming year.

The bright second lunar day in Kārttika is known as *bhrātṛ-dvitīyā*, when sisters invite their brothers home, put sandal-paste marks on their foreheads, feast them, and present clothes to them. These marks of affection are also reciprocated by the other party.

The great festival of the second lunar day of the bright fortnight in Āṣāḍha is *ratha-yātrā,* when the car-journey of Jagannātha with Balarāma and Subhadrā is celebrated with great éclat in the towns of Orissa and Bengal. A hundred thousand or more pilgrims flock to the small town of Puri. Three cars, constructed anew every year and draped with cloth, blue, red, and white for Jagannātha, Subhadrā, and Balarāma respectively, and adorned with floral wreaths, flags, and festoons, are dragged over the broad path with thick ropes by pilgrims of both sexes and of all stations in life, with the Rājā of Puri sweeping the road before the car. The return journey takes place amidst like splendour eight days later. The car-festival in Puri is the most famous of its kind ; but there are like celebrations not merely in the case of Viṣṇu, but of other deities as well at their notable seats, such as Śiva's at Bhubaneswar and Rameswaram, Mīnākṣī's at Madurai, of both Śiva and Viṣṇu at Kancheepuram (Kāñcī). At certain places the image taken out in the car is different from that installed in the shrine and is known as the *yātrā-mūrti* or *utsava-mūrti* (the procession-image).

The *akṣaya-tṛtīyā* in Vaiśākha is considered a pre-eminently sacred day in the year. Many tradesmen start their year's business on this day. Gifts of pitchers filled with water, together with sweets and seasonal fruits, are held to be conducive to the benefit of departed ancestors.

The fourth day waxing in Māgha belongs to Gaṇeśa (*Gaṇeśa-caturthī*) as does the same in Bhādra.

On the fifth (*Śrī-pañcamī*), Sarasvatī, the goddess of learning, is invoked. This day waning in Āṣāḍha is also marked out for the worship of the serpent-goddess Manasā and the eight *nāgas.*

The bright sixth is sacred to Ṣaṣṭhī, the mother of Kārttika or Skanda, the divine warrior. As the protectress of children, she is adored with particular devotion by mothers wishing well of their progeny. There are, in her honour, special rites of worship with special designations in seven of the twelve months, that is, in all except the first, third, fourth, eighth, and tenth. The *pūjā* in Jyaiṣṭha is called *āraṇya-ṣaṣṭhī.* On this day matrons in parties go out of the village to a banyan tree in a neighbouring jungle, and hold a sort of picnic as a part of the function. This day sons-in-law are invited and entertained with food and clothes, whence it is also called the *jāmātṛ-ṣaṣṭhī*. *Chaṭ* is purely a folk-festival observed in Bihar and Uttar Pradesh, and also in other parts where the people of these provinces settle. It begins on the bright sixth of Kārttika. Observing fast on this day, women in gay clothes proceed to a sacred stream singing, attended by musicians with pipe and tabor ; and carts laden with plantains follow. The fruits are dipped in water and taken back home, and on the following day the fast is broken. The festival, held as it is in autumn, the 'season of mists and mellow fruitfulness', is observed by housewives having or desiring a home full of happy children.

The seventh lunar day of the bright fortnight is fixed for solar worship, and during its observance various kinds of restricted fare are prescribed in the twelve months of the year. Beginning with the *saṅkrānti* before Agrahāyaṇa to the end of the month, the deity is invoked every Sunday, under the name of Mitra in a small pitcher placed on a small earthen platform, wherein grains of barley and pulses and mustard sprout up and exhibit the power of the god who causes the growth of these *raviśasya* (*ravi*, sun ; *śasya*, corn).

The eighth is Śakti's own day, as also the ninth. The *aṣṭamī* day, both dark and bright, is of significance and value to the Hindus, presumably because it is the middle point of the lunar phases, and quite a number of religious observances pertain to it during the year. To Vaiṣṇavas it is a red-letter day in the calendar on account of the birth of Śrī Kṛṣṇa (*janmāṣṭamī*) which, according to the *Bhāgavata*, took place on a dark and stormy night in Bhādra, and immediately after, for safety, the divine babe was conveyed by Vasudeva across the Yamunā from Mathurā to Gokula. At the seats of Vaiṣṇavism, e.g. Vrindaban, Dwarka, Nathdwara, Puri, and Manipur, the day is celebrated with éclat. The *aṣṭamī* of the following bright fortnight is *Rādhāṣṭamī* or the day of the birth of Rādhā, Kṛṣṇa's consort. On the *aśokāṣṭamī* day in Caitra, tiny buds of the *aśoka* (sorrow-free) plant are taken by housewives to ensure immunity from sorrow. This is also the day for bathing in the Brahmaputra. In Āśvina, during the great *pūjās*, the *vīrāṣṭamī* is observed by women desiring heroic sons. The dark *aṣṭamī* is also appointed for the worship of Śītalā, the goddess who presides over smallpox. In the month of Kārttika or Agrahāyaṇa, there is the festival known as *goṣṭhāṣṭamī*. On this day cows are worshipped and sumptuously fed.

Like *janmāṣṭamī*, *Rāmanavamī* (the bright ninth in Caitra) celebrates the birth of Dāśaratha Rāma, and it is observed by Vaiṣṇavas of the Rāma cult with fasting and rites of worship. Although Hindus are characterized as worshippers of five deities, viz. Sūrya, Gaṇapati, Śiva, Viṣṇu, and Śakti, by far the largest number, in North India at least, worship one or other of the two human incarnations of Viṣṇu: Rāma, the ideal king and householder, and Kṛṣṇa, the embodiment of the ideal of harmony, detachment, and selfless activity. Corresponding to *Rādhāṣṭamī*, there is *Sītānavamī*—the bright ninth in Vaiśākha. Sītā is said to have risen from the furrowed soil, and was born of no human parents. To the ninth waxing also belong two Bengali variants of the Durgā worship, viz. that of Jagaddhātrī (protectress of the world) in Kārttika and of Annapūrṇā (goddess of plenty) in Caitra.

The day following *janmāṣṭamī* is celebrated as *Nandotsava*, or Nanda's great joy at his supreme luck in receiving the babe Kṛṣṇa and thus becoming his foster-father. On this day a magnificent procession used to be taken out at Dacca.

The tenth day of the bright fortnight in Āśvina, the *vijayā daśamī* (the *daśamī* of victory), concludes the *Durgā pūjā* celebration. Peace on earth and goodwill among men, reunion and reconciliation, obeisance to superiors, love and embrace to equals, and blessings to juniors distinguish the spirit and functions of the day. On the same *tithi* in Jyaiṣṭha, the river-goddess, Gaṅgā, is worshipped, and along the banks of the sacred river purificatory immersion is performed by masses of people.

The eleventh day of the dark fortnight as well as the new moon are suited to oblations to the manes. Both the eleventh and the twelfth days are sacred to Hari. On the eleventh waxing in Āṣāḍha begins Viṣṇu's sleep (*śayana-ekādaśī*); in Kārttika, his rise (*utthāna-ekādaśī*) is celebrated; and in Bhādra, it is the day on which he changes side (*pārśva-parivartana*). These days, as also the *ekādaśī* in Māgha called after Bhīma, the famous Pāṇḍava prince, are specially observed with fasts. Between the Āṣāḍha and the Kārttika eleventh waning lies the *cāturmāsya*, the four months' practice of austerities and privations.

The fourteenth day of the dark fortnight belongs to Śiva and to Śakti. The *mahālayā*, which closes the dark fortnight in Bhādra dedicated to the fathers, is the All Souls' Day.

The new moon in Kārttika, the darkest night of the year, is fixed for the worship of Kālī, the terrible, destructive form of Śakti. It is interesting to note that the Kṛṣṇa festivals, such as the swing festival in Śrāvaṇa, the *rāsa* or dance in a circle with the milkmaids of Vṛndāvana in Kārttika, the spring festival (*dolā-yātrā* or *holī*) in Phālguna or Caitra, and the bath festival (*snāna-yātrā*) at Puri in Jyaiṣṭha, mostly occur on full moon nights and suggest mirth, sport, and revelry. The full moon in Āṣāḍha is *guru-pūrṇimā*, the day of worship of the teacher or preceptor; and that in Āśvina called *kojāgara* is spent in vigil and is sacred to Lakṣmī.

SACRED FASTS AND PŪJĀS

Among fasts the most widely prevalent is that of *Śivarātri* or *Śiva-caturdaśī* in Phālguna. It is indeed declared an obligatory fast. The worship of Śiva goes on in the four watches of the sombre night in spring, with milk, curd, honey, and clarified butter. Worshippers gather at the Śiva shrines—particularly at Banaras, Tarakeshwar, Baidyanath, Walkeshwar (near Bombay), and Rameswaram. The notable shrines of Śiva—of Mahākāla at Ujjain, Candranātha at Sitakund (near Chittagong), Paśupatinātha in Nepal, Mallikārjuna at Sri Sailam in Kurnool District, the five-faced image at Ekaliṅga in Udaipur, and of the elemental images at Tiruchirapalli, Chidambaram, Tiruvannamalai, Tiruvallur, and Kalahasti—attract vast concourses of pilgrims.

By far the most popular of the festivals are connected with certain annual *pūjās*. Gaṇapati worship is performed with great splendour and gorgeous procession in Mahārāṣṭra. More extensive, however, is *Śrī-pañcamī* or *Vasanta-pañcamī* in Māgha. On this day Sarasvatī, the goddess of arts and letters, all white in colour and seated on a lotus and carrying a guitar (*vīṇā*) and books, is invoked in almost all parts of India. Educational institutions and academies of art naturally take a lively interest in this celebration.

HOLĪ, DURGĀ PŪJĀ, AND NAVARĀTRA

Western travellers visiting India are somewhat shocked at the noisy processions, the clash of cymbals, the beating of drums, the unsightly figures covered with red powder, and the jets of coloured water thrown at passers-by that characterize the *dolā* or *holī* festival. These features are, however, almost common to carnivals in all countries. In the higher ranks of society, the observance takes a more refined aspect—songs and music, floral decorations, and sprinkling of perfumed water.

But the festival which surpasses all others in its wide appeal, and reaches its acme of fervour and festal mirth in Bengal, is the *Durgā pūjā*. The *Devī-sūkta* shows its Vedic origin; and in the *Caṇḍī-saptaśatī* of the *Mārkaṇḍeya Purāṇa*, the worship of the earthen image of the goddess is described. The composite imagery of the supreme Śakti—the powers of all the gods centred in one, the Mother of the universe—with her offspring, the goddesses of learning and wealth and the gods of success and prowess; the lion in deadly grapple with the demon that centaur-like bursts from the fierce buffalo-form; the semi-circular tablet at the top showing the primal deities and the incarnations; the artistic grouping; and the harmonic idea are peculiarly Bengali. This imagery is subsequent to Buddhism in its later Mahāyānic phase of multifarious icons, and historic tradition traces its origin to Rājā Danujamardana. Sculptural relics of antiquity prove the all-India vogue of the Durgā cult, and even in the Deccan and North India, where this imagery is not set up for adoration, there prevails the *navarātra* or the autumnal nine-nights' worship with the consecrated pitcher of holy water and the bunch of nine kinds of herbs and roots (*navapatrikā*). The Jains also have their nine-nights' ritual. In North India and in Mysore, the Dusserah (*dasarā*) or the tenth day of the *pūjā* is a festive occasion. In ancient times Hindu princes used to set out on expeditions on this auspicious day. Its special feature is the pageant known as *Rāma-līlā*. This tableau exhibits the characters of the *Rāmāyaṇa* on platforms set up at cross-roads and market-places. Rāma is said to have vanquished his enemy through the grace of Durgā and shifted the worship from spring to autumn. The worship of Durgā in Caitra or spring (whence the name *Vāsantī pūjā*) is now becoming rare. The autumnal (*śāradīya*) function also, as performed by individual householders, is tending of late to be thrown into the shade by the *sarvajanīna* or communal type.

SACRED DAYS FOR HOLY BATHING

The living force of Hinduism is manifest even in these days at the venues of ceremonial bathing along the banks of the sacred rivers, such as Gaṅgā, Yamunā, Godāvarī, Narmadā, Sindhu, Brahmaputra, Kāverī (Vṛddha Gaṅgā), Gaṇḍakī, Kṛṣṇā, Sarayū, Tuṅgabhadrā (the Gaṅgā of the South), etc. The occasions of these baths shown in the almanac are numerous. The *saṅkrānti* or the day of solar transition from one sign of the zodiac to another is a day of bathing. So also is a solar or lunar eclipse. Every *pūjā* day is held sacred for the purpose. The months of Kārttika, Māgha, and Vaiśākha are especially regarded as purificatory. The *daśaharā*, the bright tenth in Jyaiṣṭha on which the Gaṅgā is worshipped, is said to purge ten kinds of sins, committed by the body, speech, and mind. For the whole month of Māgha, hundreds of thousands of pilgrims gather at the confluence of the Gaṅgā and the Yamunā at Prayāga (Allahabad). They put up in huts and thatched cottages and bathe thrice a day. *Sādhus* (holy men) and ascetics flock from all parts of the country. Austerities are practised and scriptures are read and explained. The *maunī amāvāsyā* (the new moon of silence) is specially observed by the sojourners at Prayāga. At *makara saṅkrānti* (winter solstice) a bath in the Gaṅgā with the offer of radishes prevails in Bengal. In the Deccan, bathing in the Kṛṣṇā, the Kāverī, and the Godāvarī is accompanied by the offering of cocoanuts. The dark thirteenth in Caitra is known as *vāruṇī*, and women bathe in the Gaṅgā and offer green mangoes on that day. Similarly, in the Karatoyā, the Mahānandā, and the Brahmaputra bathing is prescribed on special days.

THE KUMBHA-MELĀ

The most imposing bathing festivals are the *kumbha-melās* (*melā*, congregation), which are attended by millions of *sādhus* and *mahantas* (heads of religious organizations) of different sects from all parts of India. According to the Purāṇas, the *kumbha* or jar of nectar rose at the churning of the ocean in the beginning of creation. In the scramble between the gods in pursuit and the demons in flight, some of its contents splashed out of the jar held by Dhanvantari, the patron of the healing art, and fell on four spots, namely, at Haridvāra or Haradvāra (Hardwar), Prayāga (Allahabad), Ujjayinī (Ujjain), and Nāsika (Nasik). By rotation the *kumbha-melā* is held at these places, the function in the twelfth year at each place being called the *pūrṇa* (full) and the intermediate ones, six years after the full ones, being called the *ardha* (half). At Hardwar the fair continues for about a month and a half in Phālguna and Caitra, when the sun passes to Aries and Jupiter is in Aquarius. At Prayāga the period is Māgha, and the highest merit attaches to the bath on the new moon day. Jupiter is then in Aries and both the sun and the moon are in Capricorn. The bath at Ujjain on the bank of the Śiprā is fixed for the month of Kārttika, when these planets are in Libra. At Nasik on the Godāvarī, which is said to be the Gaṅgā of Gautama, the function is timed in Śrāvaṇa, when the three planets are in Cancer. The final bath is everywhere taken on the new moon day. At these festivals one visualizes the soul of India, the glory of the ascetic life, and the living faith that people still have in religion and religious observances. There are processions of *sādhus*, seated in decorated palanquins, on richly caparisoned elephants. Ascetics march in endless files, some naked and ash-covered, some with matted hair coiled into a high peak, blowing enormous copper-horns. Munificent gifts are made by kings and merchants, and food, cloth, and blankets are given away on a lavish scale.

THE FESTIVAL OF LIGHTS

Most picturesque by its contrast of light and darkness is the *divāli* (*dīpāvali*) or the festival of lights in Kārttika, about twenty days after the *Durgā pūjā*. It is held on the dark fourteenth and the following night on which Kālī (the Black One)—a form of Śakti—and Lakṣmī are worshipped. Against the background of the black night-sky, millions of lights shine on parapets, cornices, house-tops, at doors and windows, on temples, towers, and hill-sides. Lamps are hung in the sky in small baskets from pole-tops. They rise tier above tier along the banks of rivers with continuous flights of steps as may be seen at Banaras and Mathura. The custom is to keep these sky-lamps burning all through Kārttika to light the path of departed spirits across the sky. During *divāli* fireworks are displayed, and on tiny rafts of reeds earthen lamps are set afloat and are carried down the streams.

DAYS COMMEMORATING GREAT SPIRITUAL LEADERS

Besides the *pūjā* days, there are also days commemorating incidents in the lives of the great sons of India, her eminent spiritual figures. In modern India, the birthdays of Guru Nānak, the first Guru of the Sikhs, on the Kārttika full moon, and Guru Gobind Siṅgh, the tenth Guru, on the bright seventh of Pauṣa, are celebrated by the Sikhs and their admirers and friends. The bright fifth of Vaiśākha is the day of the birth of Śaṅkarācārya. The great Vaiṣṇava teachers Rāmānuja, Vallabha, and Madhva are commemorated by their followers at Kancheepuram and Srirangam, at Nathdwara (in Udaipur) and Bombay, and at Udipi and other Kannada-speaking areas. The commemorative functions that obtain amongst the Bengal and the Assam Vaiṣṇavas, the followers of Caitanya and Śaṅkara Deva, together with the special *pūjās* prescribed in their Smṛti works, make up a separate calendar. Rāmānanda, Kabīr, and Dādū, devotees and reformers who strove to break down exclusiveness and formalism, as well as Tulasīdāsa, Rāmadāsa, and Tukārāma have their places in the national calendar.

Recent additions to the hagiology are Raja Rammohun Roy, Swami Dayananda, Sri Ramakrishna, Swami Vivekananda, Tamil Śaiva saint Ramalinga, Swami Ramatirtha, Sri Aurobindo, Mahatma Gandhi, Sri Ramana Maharshi, and others. The sacred days of religious communities of recent origin like the Brāhmo Samāj and the Ārya Samāj are also finding place in the year's calendar. For it is thus in all ages that man's memory of the past and present experience jostle with and pass into each other, and between them weave the fabric of racial heritage.

The Hindu festivals and sacred days have their counterpart and complement, so to say, in those of the communities within India proper or outside in Greater India professing any of the religions that originated in this country—in those of the Jains and Buddhists and Sikhs, or of the peoples of Nepal and Siam, in which Hindu and Buddhist practices draw near and mingle. These observances of neighbouring countries and sister communities have certain kindred as well as distinctive features. In the Buddhist festivals the stress is laid on monachism or asceticism. The Jaina observances are largely those of a community of wealthy merchants, who value peace and amity and whose ceremonies are marked by pomp and pageantry. Compared with those of the Vedic times, later Hindu ceremonies, it has been remarked, are private rather than public functions. In the festivals of Nepal or Siam, the features of public and State ceremonies are more in evidence ; such features, in a larger measure, were the characteristics of the festive occasions of India in her days of past glory and regal power.

SACRED DAYS OF THE BUDDHISTS

The Buddhists celebrate the New Year's Day on the Phālguna or Caitra full moon day. They have four days of fasting in the month, called the *uposatha,* namely, the two quarter moon and the two terminal days. The latter two go back to the Vedic *darśa* and *paurṇamāsa* sacrifices, the other two being later additions. The *Dhammika-Sutta* enjoins the observance of the fourteenth day from the new moon in the short month and the fifteenth in the long month as fast-days. Business houses, schools, and courts of justice are then closed ; hunting and fishing are prohibited. The eight precepts are followed with special care. Confession of sins, absolution by the monks present, recital of the *Pātimokkha,* and abstention from creature comforts are some of the features of the day's routine. The *pātihārika-pakkha* is an extra fortnight of the three months of *vassā* (*varṣā*), particularly the first half of the 'robe-month' (*cīvaramāsa*), during which the practice of the eightfold path is inculcated. The *vassā* or the rain-retreat seems to be derived from the second four-month celebration of the Vedic society, the *Varuṇa-praghāsa* sacrifice. To avoid hurt to green herbs, vegetables, and minute creatures, *bhikkhus* used to stay in one place and look after the *vihāras.* It began either on the Āṣāḍha (June-July) full moon or a month later and had to be kept strictly for three months. This *vassupanāyika* had a solemn close, the *pavāraṇā,* when there was confession of sins followed by atonement. *Kaṭhina* or *kaṭhinatthara* succeeded immediately, and robes were given by believers to the *bhikkhus* of the Saṅgha. These robes were made of raw cotton and were hence designated *kaṭhina.* From the full moon days of Kārttika and Phālguna the two other four-month celebrations began, and monks were directed to stay, during the former, in *pannasālās* (*parṇaśālās*), for mutual instruction and to read the *bhāna* to the people, and, during the latter, under the trees, that is, in the open air, while out on peregrinations. The three most notable events in the life of Buddha, viz. his birth, enlightenment, and *mahāparinibbāna,* occurred at full moon in Vaiśākha, and his promulgation of the Wheel of Dharma (*dhammacakka-pavattana*) at full moon in Māgha. He renounced his home at the new moon in Kārttika. All these days are honoured by Hindus also, who too revere Buddha as the ninth incarnation of Viṣṇu.

HINDU AND BUDDHIST FESTIVALS OF NEPAL

Hindu and Buddhist rites show a curious mingling in the Nepalese observances. Under Gurkha rule the old national festivals of the Newars have declined in importance. These comprised the building of cars, making masks, painting, and dancing, and descended as a duty from sire to son. Beginning with the New Year's Day in Vaiśākha, the popular festivals of the present day bear the stamp of Hindu ceremonies, but they are joined by Buddhists also.

Śeorātri (*Śivarātri*) is a fast on the first day of Phālguna. *Biskati* or *Bhairab-jātrā* is in honour of Śiva, the guardian deity, who is also reckoned among Buddhist gods. It comprises dancing and buffalo sacrifice and is held at night, except every twelfth year when it is held in the day-time. *Gāi-jātrā* on the first day after full moon in Śrāvaṇa is observed by cow-worship and is akin to *goṣṭhāṣṭamī*. The Buddhists observe the festival for a fortnight, from the fifth day before the full moon to the tenth day after it. Temples and *vihāras* are visited, wax-trees representing the Bo-tree at Gaya are carried, and offerings are made to the many Buddhas. Images and pictures are exhibited in the *vihāras*. There are the four quarterly *banhrā-jātrās* in Vaiśākha, Śrāvaṇa, Kārttika, and Māgha, when alms are given to the *banhrās*. Amitābha's image, taken from the temple, is on view ; *Indra-jātrā* is held in the capital for four days before and after the full moon in Bhādra. A great Buddhist holiday is the birth of Svayambhū on the Āśvina full moon. The most important festival is the great *Macchendra-jātrā*, when the image of Macchendra Nāth (Matsyendra Nātha) is bathed and taken in a car in procession, and later, after unrobing, his shirt is exhibited. The small *Macchendra-jātrā* and the Neta Devi Rajatra take place in Caitra. The *Nārāyaṇa* festival is kept by Hindus and Buddhists alike.

RELIGIOUS OBSERVANCES AND SACRED DAYS OF THE JAINS

Among Jaina observances the *pajjusaṇa* is the most important. It is akin to the *cāturmāsya*, and is traceable, like the Buddhist *vassupanāyika*, to the Vedic *Varuṇa-praghāsa*. After one month and twenty nights of the rainy season have elapsed, the *pajjusaṇa* begins and is observed as a prolonged period of fast. The last three days of the dark half and the first five days of the bright half of Bhādra (with one day back in some Śvetāmbara groups or *gacchās*) are most sacred, and the period ends with *saṁvatsarī*, the closing day of the Jaina year. Taking whey or milk or hot water only, or fasting on alternate days, are variations of the fare for those observing partial fast (*dayā* or *saṁvara*). The fast is prolonged for a week more by Digambara (sky-clad) Jains. Readings from the *Kalpa-Sūtra* and the life of Mahāvīra are given in the *upāsarā* (monastery). Laymen practise *poṣaha* or the ascetic life temporarily and put on scarf and loin-cloth, like the Caitra *sannyāsins* among Hindus of the Goraksa Nātha sect.

On the eighth and fourteenth days of the fortnight, during the *pajjusaṇa, posaha* is regularly observed by some householders, just as some Hindus do, and is spent in fasting and meditation. On the *saṁvatsarī* day, men and women assemble separately in *upāsarās* adjoining temples, sit on the floor, and listen to expositions of the tenets of their faith and the twelve vows it enjoins; forgiveness for any wrongs done is asked for and quarrels are made up. Ascetics privately confess in the small rooms of the monasteries and do the yearly hair-plucking.

The event of the third day of the *pajjusaṇa* is the evening procession, organized by the Śvetāmbara sect, in which the manuscript of the *Kalpa-Sūtra* is taken in an elephant-trolley from the temple to the house of the person who makes the highest bid to have this honour. For the whole night his family and friends sit round the small table, on which the scripture lies, and sing and play music. The next morning the holy book is returned in procession to the temple. In the procession, a wooden elephant on a wooden trolley bears on its back row upon row of red and blue flags, a Brāhmaṇa holds a silver mace followed by boys with silver sticks, and a little girl on a horse carries the sacred book wrapped in brocade followed by boys carrying *ārati* lamps and groups of women singing. And on the book rests a cocoanut marked in red with the *svastika*. On the fourth day of *pajjusaṇa,* which, according to the Digambaras, is the birthday of Mahāvīra, a cradle covered with brocade is taken out in procession, instead of the scripture, by the Śvetāmbara sect, though, according to them, the birthday of Mahāvīra is on the bright thirteenth of Caitra.

The day of liberation of Mahāvīra is the *divāli,* which among Jains lasts for four days commencing at the end of Āśvina. The material lamp kindled is a remembrancer of the spiritual light that went out at Mahāvīra's *mokṣa.* In honour of Lakṣmī jewels and ornaments are polished on the first day; on the second, sweets specially prepared are left at the cross-roads to propitiate evil spirits; the third, *amāsā* (*amāvāsyā*), is the great day of Mahāvīra's *mokṣa.* On this evening is performed the worship of new account-books, *Śāradā pūjā,* as it is the last day of the business year, in the following manner: A Brāhmaṇa priest puts an auspicious mark on the forehead of the Jaina householder. '*Śrī*' is written many times in lengthening rows so as to form a pyramid. A very old gold coin or a rupee is placed on the new account-book by way of *Lakṣmī pūjā* along with rice, fruits, betel leaves, and nuts; and red powder is sprinkled over all, and the words '*lakṣa lābha*' (gain of a lac) are repeated. The first day of the bright fortnight of Kārttika begins the new year.

In Caitra and Āśvina the Saint-wheel (*siddha-cakra*), an eight-sided brass or silver disc, with figures of *triratna* (knowledge, faith, and conduct) and the five *parameṣṭhins* (*sādhu, upādhyāya, ācārya, arihanta,* and *siddha*) with *arihanta* at the centre, is carried from the temple to a lake or tank and ceremonially bathed once on each of the eight days of worship. A feast concludes this *jala-yātrā* (water-journey). At the full moon in Kārttika, Phālguna, Caitra, and Āṣāḍha, pilgrimages to the hills of Śatruñjaya (former Palitana State), Sametaśikhara (Pareshnath in Bihar), Girnar (Junagadh), and Mount Abu are held to confer great merit. From the full moon in Āṣāḍha to that in Kārttika, monks stay at one place and do not move about ; the nuns also do the same. This is analogous to the Buddhist *vassā* and the Hindu *cāturmāsya*.

The *jñāna-pañcamī,* the bright fifth of Kārttika, is a day on which all books are dusted and freed from insects, and then sandal-wood powder is sprinkled on them. The bright eleventh of Mārgaśīrṣa (Agrahāyaṇa) is generally chosen as a day of silence and of fasting (*maunagyārasa*). The fast is broken after the worship of eleven pieces of each of the eleven articles used in reading and writing, such as pen, book, ink-pot, etc. Eight days before the Caitra full moon, women, to obtain conjugal felicity, take vows, at the chief places of pilgrimage, to restrict their fare to one kind of grain and boiled water, or to one dish, or to eschew butter or molasses. *Molākata,* that is, abstaining from salted food, is also believed to gain a kind husband. *Aṭhama* (*aṣṭamī*), *amāsā* (*amāvāsyā*), *ponemā* (*pūrṇimā*), and the fourteenth of either fortnight are days of fasting to devout Jains, just as they are to the Buddhists. *Añjanaśalākā* or fixing of metal eyes on the forehead, followed by anointing with saffron, is the ceremony of consecration of an image. It is rare in these days for it is expensive. Still rarer, for the same reason, and occurring only once in twelve years on a large scale, is the lustration of Gomaṭeśvara at Shravanabelgola in Mysore State. The statue, carved out of a solid block, is about fifty-seven feet high. From a scaffolding on three sides a mixture of milk, curd, melted butter, saffron, etc. is poured on this immense figure. The privilege of first doing it is won by the highest bidder at an auction. *Rākhi* (*rakṣā*) *bandhana,* the binding of a friendly knot on the wrist, on the Śrāvaṇa full moon day, is a rite among Hindus as well. The Jains in their turn observe many Hindu fasts and festivals with modifications, such as the *holī,* Dusserah, and *makara-saṅkrānti*. On *Śītalāṣṭamī* day Jaina women offer drawings of eyes and money at Hindu shrines of the goddess ; they do not cook at the usual oven, but take a cold meal. Among Jains the Hindu *bhrātṛ-dvitīyā* takes on the form of two functions in Śrāvaṇa, the brother's and the sister's part being respectively known as *virapasalī* and *bhāibīj*.

PLACE OF FESTIVALS AND SACRED DAYS IN NATIONAL LIFE

A survey of the festivals and sacred days observed by the Hindus in all parts of the country from Kashmir to Cape Comorin, from Gujarat to Manipur, and across the border in outlying countries, in Nepal, in Tibet, and in distant Siam, even though executed on a modest scale, would require a considerable volume. To include those of all the peoples and tribes that profess any of the religions that had their origin in India and pre-eminently those of the Buddhists, Jains, and Sikhs would take up ampler space still. But there are affinities and points of contact which prove the kinship of the communities and a common ethos and mental atmosphere shared by them. For this reason a connected account of these festivals or sacred days is full of ethnological significance. The Hindu festivals furnished and still furnish points of contact and bonds of community among inhabitants of this extensive tract. When exploration for scientific ends was rare, these brought into prominence the beauty spots, the inaccessible extremities of the Indian subcontinent.

The shrines and confluences, forests, hermitages, and snow-clad mountain-tops, which pilgrims visit, serve to acquaint the masses with the features of this epitome of the world. They have an idea of the unity of the land, with its long distances, many races, various languages, and numberless customs.

These festivals enshrine and keep alive the men and the ideals that have left their impress on the history of the race. For three days, from the waxing first in Bhādra, *arghya* or honorific offering to Agastya, who Aryanized the South and whose statue has been found in distant Java, is still made. Bhīṣma, the selfless celibate hero, is still venerated as one of the great forefathers of the race, and on the eighth waxing of Māgha all posterity is bidden to do him the duty that his own offspring would have performed. The dark fourteenth in Jyaiṣṭha commemorates the Hindu ideal of wifely devotion in Sāvitrī, who revived her lifeless husband through a boon obtained from the god of death by her steadfast constancy to her husband. In the observance of the birth or death anniversaries of the spiritual leaders like Buddha, Śaṅkara, and Caitanya, the present pays its homage to the makers of the nation in the past and draws periodical inspiration from a recital of their achievements in the realm of the spirit.

35

PILGRIMAGE AND FAIRS: THEIR BEARING ON INDIAN LIFE

PILGRIMAGE to sacred places forms an important item of the spiritual discipline of the people of almost all religions in the world. The followers of every religion look upon certain places as especially holy, and it is the ambition of their life to visit those places at least once in their lifetime. What places are considered holy, and why, depend on the temperament of the people of different religions; but there is no religion whose followers do not regard certain places with particular associations as springs of inspiration in their religious life. What doubt is there that if a devoted Buddhist goes to Bodh-Gaya and sees the seat under the Bo-tree (*bodhi-vṛkṣa*), whereon Buddha attained *nirvāṇa*, his imagination will be stirred up and his thoughts will soar above all worldly things and give him an impetus to aspire after the highest goal of human life? A Christian devotee visiting Jerusalem will find his love for Christ greatly deepened, for all the incidents of the life of Jesus associated with that place will be strongly called to his mind.

There are persons who try to minimize the importance of the places of pilgrimage. But the spiritual genius of the Indians has never failed to utilize every place of fascinating beauty and grandeur as a perennial source of inspiration, affording supreme peace and consolation to the care-worn hearts of the people. Cape Comorin, the beauty-spot at the southernmost end of India, where the land merges in the vast, infinite ocean, has become the favourite seat of the divine Maiden (Kanyā Kumārī). Indeed, the beauty of a place is to the Indian mind a call to the soul from God. Sister Nivedita has rightly observed that the valuation of Niagara by humanity would have been quite different, if it had been situated on the Gaṅgā. Instead of fashionable picnics and railway pleasure-trips, there would have been an unceasing onrush of worshipping crowds from the different parts of India; magnificent sanctuaries would have adorned the place and commanded the homage of millions of pilgrims; and people would have rushed to the place to satisfy their spiritual hunger.

HINDU PLACES OF PILGRIMAGE—THEIR ORIGIN AND GROWTH

The Hindus have to their credit the largest number of holy places. From the Himalayas to Cape Comorin and from Dwarka to Assam, there are thousands of places which are considered sacred by the people all over India, without distinction of caste or creed. It would indeed be difficult to trace the cause of the importance of many holy places, round which have grown innumerable legends and traditions with the passing of ages. But this may be said, as a general rule, that every place now considered holy has had something associated with it, which was likely to have served as an incentive to religious feelings.

Of all places, the Himalayan region has been considered most suitable for spiritual practices through the ages; that may be one of the reasons why the Uttarākhaṇḍa has been covered with a network of prominent places of pilgrimage from time immemorial. We find a temple at Badrinarayan, another at Kedarnath, a cave at Amarnath, and so on, which draw crowds of pilgrims every year from all parts of India. Attracted by the inspiring grandeur of the Himalayas, the abode of Śiva, many people, from time immemorial, have been resorting to their caves and forest-retreats to solve the riddle of life. Verily has the great poet Kālidāsa described the Himalayas as '*devatātman*', divinity ensouled. And what of the Gaṅgā! She is the *suranadī*, the divine river. What a multitude of sacred associations there is with the names of the Himalayas and the Gaṅgā! Take away the Himalayas and the Gaṅgā, and the religious history of India dwindles into insignificance. Innumerable saints and sages have performed austerities on the banks of the Gaṅgā and attained realization, and this has made her holy in the eyes of the Hindus. Hence it is that the Gaṅgā has the largest number of *tīrthas* on her banks, compared with any other river in the whole of India.

In ancient India, there were many *āśramas* (hermitages) where *ṛṣis* used to live, far away from the haunts of men, in quiet solitude, devoting their time to spiritual culture. They would naturally draw persons of a religious frame of mind, who would, now and then, go to them for guidance and advice. Those *āśramas*, in the course of time, became places of pilgrimage to a wide circle of people. And as traditions began to grow round these places, they became more and more important.

Similarly, all the places associated with the life and activities of Rāma, Kṛṣṇa, and other such mighty souls became sacred in the eyes of the people. The case was similar with those places which had some connection with any incident narrated in the Purāṇas. As Hinduism began to spread through its cultural conquest or its assimilation of the aboriginal tribes, the number of sects in Hinduism began to increase. And every sect began to regard the places connected with the name of its founder as holy, and they became, in the course of time, places of pilgrimage. Gradually, these became objects of reverence to the people of other sects also, on account of the innate catholic spirit of Hinduism ; and thus, by losing their sectarian character, they received wide recognition. Some of the places were considered holy by the Hindus, the Buddhists, and the Jains alike. Besides, India, early in her history, attracted migrations, and became the home of many races, cults, and cultures, living in concord, for she did not seek the subjugation or extermination of others. She became the chosen home of diversity, and that is why she has been aptly called 'the epitome of the world'.

With the rise of the Mahāyāna school of Buddhism, image-worship came largely into vogue amongst the Hindus also. Thus arose the necessity of building temples for worship. Every place where a big sanctuary was built and worship was performed with gorgeous ceremonials began to attract crowds of people, and became a place of pilgrimage to following generations. Many rich persons considered it a great act of merit to build temples for the worship of their chosen deities, and they naturally wanted to build them in their own locality. This spirit accounts for the fact that almost every village in India has one or more temples or sacred spots of its own. Some of these temples receive wide attention, if they have any inspiring tradition, legend, or association connected with them.

All the above factors have contributed to the growth of so many places of pilgrimage throughout India, which in their turn have played an important part in the religious life of the nation.

Some are of opinion that Hinduism derived the idea of pilgrimage from the Buddhist *śramaṇas,* who used to roam the country, but the germ of the idea can be traced to a much earlier period. Even in the *Aitareya Brāhmaṇa* (VII. 33.3), there is a passage encouraging the idea of pilgrimage. It runs thus: 'There is no happiness for him who does not travel ; living in the society of men, the best man often becomes a sinner ; Indra is the friend of the traveller. Therefore wander.' In the *Mahābhārata* also there is a description of a large number of *tīrthas,* which Yudhiṣṭhira visited, and they cover an area extending from the Himalayas to the south beyond the Vindhyas. According to E. B. Havell, there existed in India temples dedicated to Brahmā, Viṣṇu, and Śiva, even before the Mahāyāna school of Buddhism gave an impetus to image-worship.[1]

INDIAN ATTITUDE TO PILGRIMAGE

Whatever might be the origin and history of the growth of pilgrimage in India, it speaks highly of the spiritual bent of the Indian mind that the places of pilgrimage existing on her soil have never ceased to draw

[1] *A Study of Indo-Aryan Civilization,* pp. 40 ff.

huge crowds of people. The number of pilgrims who visit Gaya is, according to one authority, about a lac per year. The number of those who visit Puri or Banaras is three times as great. At Pandharpur in Mahārāṣṭra, the temple of Viṭhobā or Viṭhṭhala draws about one and a half lac of pilgrims on special occasions. Neither idle curiosity nor blind faith can account for this unique phenomenon, for most of the pilgrims have to undertake long journeys involving much physical discomfort and heavy expenses.

Although the scriptures declare that mental discipline and internal purification have more or less the same effect as pilgrimage to holy places, the popular mind attaches special value to the latter and considers it an important part of one's religious life. Even famous saints are reported to have gone to sacred places for spiritual practices, in the belief that their efforts will be crowned with success with greater ease in such places. They looked upon the places of pilgrimage from a point of view quite different from that of the historians or the antiquarians. Thus Śaṅkara had some of his realizations at Banaras. Caitanya found the image of Jagannātha at Puri so very living that he was about to embrace the deity. Rāmadāsa saw the vision of Rāmacandra at the temple of Pandharpur. Tulasīdāsa had his realizations at Chitrakut. Sri Ramakrishna had many wonderful visions at Dakshineswar, Banaras, Vrindaban, and other holy places. The modern man may find it difficult to explain these phenomena ; but the fact is that, in all *tīrthas,* it is not what is seen with the naked eye, but the hoary association that counts. Where the sceptics see only stone and marble, the devotees feel the touch of divine life.

EFFECT OF PILGRIMAGE ON SOCIO-ECONOMIC LIFE

In any case, a monotonous life of routine often dulls the religious fervour in many. In such cases, a visit to holy places gives a fresh stimulus, especially as it brings them into contact with many devout minds and helps to awaken a sympathetic response in them. When pilgrimage is done on foot to Badrinarayan or Amarnath, one meets with countless pilgrims whose devotion and love for God cannot but make a deep impression even on a sceptical mind.

Pilgrimage is one of the causes that have contributed to the catholicity of Hinduism, for through it people of different religious persuasions get an opportunity to mix intimately with one another, and begin to appreciate the value and beauty of one another's creed. There are some sacred places in India where many sects of Hinduism are represented, and all the temples located there are visited by pilgrims without any distinction of creed or sect. Thus Banaras, with its two thousand sanctuaries and half a million images, is a standing parliament of religious sects of ancient and modern India. At Puri the rigour of orthodoxy is completely loosened, and Hindus dine together, forgetting all distinctions of caste.

Pilgrimage has been one of the important factors of education to the Hindus. It affords an opportunity to the people living even in distant villages to know India as a whole, and also her different manners and customs. Formerly, when pilgrimage was undertaken on foot, the opportunity was greater. Even those women who do not generally stir out of their homes observe freedom from conventions, when on a pilgrimage. This has a great educative influence upon their lives.

Many places of pilgrimage developed into great seats of learning. People, when in holy places, like to acquire an additional merit by acts of philanthropy, and some of their money is spent in encouraging learning. It is thus that Banaras, the spiritual capital of India, became the greatest seat of learning, and it has kept up the fame even now. In every important holy place, there are *sadāvratas* (free kitchens), *dharmaśālās* (free inns), and other institutions, where the poor are fed, the needy are helped, and indigent students are maintained.

It is but natural that in a place where there is a continuous stream of pilgrims throughout the year, there will be a great opportunity for commercial enterprise. It is thus that places like Banaras, Puri, and Amritsar have grown into centres of great commercial activity, specializing in particular industries like silk, shawl, brass ware, etc.

Architecture, sculpture, and painting received ample encouragement from pilgrimage. Even today, there may be seen a large number of temples throughout the length and breadth of the country, from the interior of the Himalayas to the remotest part of South India, which are commendable for their artistic beauty and admirable design and conception. Temples in India may rightly be said to represent philosophy in brick and stone, and temple worship was in a way responsible for the great development of sculpture and painting, and music and dancing.

NATIONAL UNITY THROUGH PILGRIMAGE

One of the greatest services the institution of pilgrimage has rendered to India as a whole is that it has impressed upon all people her fundamental unity in the midst of apparent diversity. It is through this institution that the country has been transformed into a vivid and visible reality. As a result, all parts of the country are deemed equally sacred and are objects of equal concern to the devotees. Again, there might be different castes in India, but they all follow the inspiration of the same scriptures ; there might be different dialects, but to all people Sanskrit is the sacred language.

Persons might be separated by long distances—some living far away in the Himalayas and some in the extreme south of the peninsula—, but their hearts pulsate with the same hopes and aspirations; they have the same gods to worship, the same goal to aspire after.

Even in the Vedic age, we find that a conscious and consolidated attempt was made to keep the people united through the bond of a common culture. When the Aryans were confined to the North, their river-hymns were limited to the rivers of the Punjab. But when, with the passing of time, the wave of Aryan culture reached the farthest end of India in the South, the rivers of that region were included in the hymns, as the following invocation testifies: 'Oh ye Gaṅgā, Yamunā, Godāvarī, Sarasvatī, Narmadā, Sindhu, and Kāverī, come and abide in this water (offered by me)' The important rivers of the North and the South were invoked on sacred occasions. The same thing was done with regard to the mountains also. In the *Mahābhārata* are named seven mountains which are held to be sacred, viz. Raivataka, Vindhya, Sahya, Kumāra, Malaya, Śrī-parvata, and Pāriyātra, and they are spread practically over the whole of India. Similarly, there are seven sacred places situated both in the North and the South—Ayodhyā, Mathurā, Māyā (Hardwar), Kāśī (Banaras), Kāñcī (Kancheepuram), Avantikā(Ujjain), and Dvārāvatī (Dwarka)—which are looked upon as possessing the power to grant salvation to one who visits them. Again, the twelve *jyotirliṅgas* and the fifty-one *śakti-pīṭhas* are located in different parts of the country. Naturally, the Hindus visiting those places would feel how the whole of India was one to them. Thus, through all these sacred associations, the vision of one united India was conjured up before the minds of the devotees.

A great service towards uniting all the Hindus by a common religious and cultural consciousness was done by Śaṅkarācārya, when he established the four sacred monasteries in the four extreme cardinal points of India, viz. at Badarīnārāyaṇa in the north, Śṛṅgerī in the south, Purī in the east, and Dvārakā in the west. Similarly, there were singled out four sacred lakes—Bindu, Pampā, Nārāyaṇa, and Mānasa, in the east, south, west, and north, respectively. And it would not be wrong to assume that the principle underlying the choice was mainly to lead the masses out of their homes, villages, cities, and provinces to undertake all-India tours of pilgrimage, so that they might know the different parts of their country, in all its variety, and get into touch with the people there. A spirit of nationalism naturally sprang from this geographical knowledge of the country as a whole. Under the peculiar religious system that obtains in India, the southerner will feel as much longing for Banaras (Kāśī) as a northerner for Setubandha (Rāmeśvara), and both will have a common longing for Dvārakā and Jagannātha or Purī. People from north, south, east, and west meet in the embrace of a religious life that transcends the narrow boundaries of place, sect, or creed. It is in this way that Hinduism, while deepening the spiritual consciousness of its followers, has always fostered a sense of solidarity among them through a lively sense of the mother country, which grasps the whole of it as a unit, despite its vastness and its continental variety.

From time to time, a great impetus was given to pilgrimage by the prophets and other towering religious personalities. Śaṅkara, Rāmānuja, Madhva, Caitanya, and other such spiritual giants of the land left a deep and permanent impression wherever they went. Thus Caitanya's influence can be traced even today in the South, and Śaṅkara is as much worshipped in the North as in his own place of birth.

THE RÔLE OF MELĀS IN NATIONAL LIFE

Melās or religious fairs are quite akin to pilgrimage in their purpose and utility. They are highly useful from the standpoint of religion, national solidarity, and economics. They constitute, in short, parliaments of religion, moving universities, and national exhibitions of arts and crafts. The origin of *melās* is veiled in obscurity, but their effect has been phenomenal and abiding. Some of the most important *melās,* like the *kumbha-melā,* have grown to be all-India institutions, but there are others which are regional or local in their character.

The *kumbha-melā,* though of hoary antiquity, has still preserved its glory as a great religious institution. It is mainly an institution of *sannyāsins* and wandering ascetics, and it is this large concourse of monks of diverse orders that draws millions of religious-minded people from all parts of the country. The four important places of pilgrimage, viz. Hardwar, Allahabad, Ujjain, and Nasik, where it is held at regular intervals by rotation, lend a special sanctity to the gathering. There is no definite organization behind it ; yet thousands of monks—some of whom have perhaps lived for years in solitude, far away from the haunts of people—assemble there. The *kumbha-melā* is held every three years, probably to keep up the religious enthusiasm of the people and to prevent them from falling into a life of stagnation.

Many villages also witness occasional sittings of *melās,* which create considerable interest amongst the people of the locality. Even in the interior of the Himalayas, one may see *melās* held round about some important local temple, which promote the religious feeling of the people and indirectly stimulate industry. Sometimes they are held on the banks of rivers which have got some sacred association. One of the biggest of such fairs is the Hariharachatra-*melā* of Sonepur on the Śoṇā in North Bihar, where elephants, horses, cattle, etc. are sold on a large scale. In many fairs, there can be seen wandering ascetics who give religious discourses to the people that assemble on the occasion.

Thus, the importance of pilgrimage and religious fairs in the cultural evolution of the Indian people can hardly be over-estimated. From time immemorial, they have been woven into the very texture of our national being, and have served to mould our destinies in some form or other at every stage of our corporate growth. These indigenous institutions, which have preserved the spiritual aspirations of the people and stimulated in the Indian mind a deep love for the country, in spite of her manifold diversities, should always receive due encouragement from the religious-minded people of India. In short, it is these religious institutions that constitute the very bed-rock of our synthetic outlook and lofty spiritual idealism.

36

METHODS OF POPULAR RELIGIOUS INSTRUCTION IN SOUTH INDIA

IN no country of such vast dimensions could the country-side be found to be so imbued with the teachings of the religion of the land as in India, and it is remarkable how, in the past, when the modern means of communication and the mechanical aids for the dissemination of information were lacking, the *ācāryas* could spread their teachings from one end of the country to the other. In this ancient land, the teeming millions were no doubt illiterate, but they were never uninformed or uncultured. The ancient teachers, concentrating on the direct communication of essential knowledge, helped people to be imbued with effective culture without scholastic education. It is significant that knowledge is called in Sanskrit *śruta* and in Tamil *keḷvi,* which mean 'that which is heard'. In fact, the high level of the moral and spiritual attainment of the unlettered, like the shopkeeper and the hunter, and the so-called repositories of learning, like the Brāhmaṇas, taking a lesson or two from them, is a recurring theme in the epics, e.g. the Tulādhāra and Dharmavyādha stories in the *Mahābhārata.* That our religious history has thrown up saints from among weavers, cobblers, potters, shepherds, and Harijans shows how widely the soil has been irrigated and fertilized by the country's spiritual engineers.[1]

RECITATION AND EXPOSITION OF ITIHĀSAS AND PURĀṆAS

The Himalayan waters of Vedic faith and Upaniṣadic philosophy were brought to the plains of the people through several projects, the biggest of which were the Itihāsas and the Purāṇas. Vyāsa says that the *Mahābhārata* was specially composed to broadcast the Vedic lore to the people at large, and that the four Vedas became complete with the fifth, namely, the *ākhyāna* or epic. Vālmīki composed his musical epic to reinforce the Vedic teachings. Illustrating the teachings of the Vedas through the stories of *rājarṣis* (sage-kings), who upheld truth and right, and those of the sports of God, who became incarnate to salvage the reign of *dharma,* and by giving, incidentally, an epitome of the knowledge of cosmogony, periods of time, and the like, the Itihāsas and the Purāṇas proved themselves to be the most efficient means of popular instruction in religion and philosophy. As the rhetoricians put it, the commands of the lord-like Vedas (*prabhu-*

[1] See V. Raghavan, 'Adult Education in Ancient India', *Memoirs of the Madras Library Association,* 1944, pp. 57-65.

sammita) were put to the people by the Itihāsa and Purāṇa in the persuasive manner of the friend (*suhṛt-sammita*). According to the preface of all the Itihāsas and the Purāṇas, they were recited to vast congregations of people gathered at sacrificial sessions (*sattras*) by a class of reciters called *sūta-paurāṇikas*. The evidence of numerous inscriptions establishes the fact of continuity of this practice of exposition all through the course of Indian history ; the wide provenance of these records shows that this machinery of popular religious education was active not only in every part of the mother country, but in Greater India too.

If, without flame and sword, Hinduism spread over the whole of the Far East, it was possible because the *Rāmāyaṇa* and the *Mahābhārata*, through the oral expounder, the sculptor, and the dancer, went forth in advance clearing the way and conquering the peoples' imagination. As early as A.D. 600, one Somaśarman is found to present to a temple in Cambodia the *Mahābhārata*, the *Rāmāyaṇa*, and the Purāṇas, and provide for their daily exposition ; a regular temple to Vālmīki was raised in Campā by King Prakāśadharman, and, in the tenth century, the kings of Cambodia had a *kavi-paṇḍita* attached to them to expound the *Rāmāyaṇa* and the *Mahābhārata*. In North India, we have epigraphic evidence to show that endowments were made for the popular recital of the epics and the Purāṇas.[2] From Bāṇa's *Kādambarī* we know that the *Mahābhārata* was recited in the Mahākāla temple, and, from his *Harṣacarita*, that *Vāyu Purāṇa* was recited in his own village-house.

The South Indian rulers, the Pallavas, the Coḷas, and the Pāṇḍyas, knew the value of the Itihāsa and Purāṇa, and epigraphs found all over the peninsula show how these kings helped these works to fulfil their mission of disseminating country-wide religious education. In the Kūram and Taṇḍantoṭṭam plates of the Pallavas, provisions are specified for the reading and exposition of the *Mahābhārata* (*Bhāratākhyāna*).[3] A portion of the endowment was specified for the *Bhārata*-expounder (*Bhāratappaṅgu*), and a stage (*ambalam*) was assigned for his discourse in the temple at Śendalai in Tanjore District (No. 63 of 1897).[4] In A.D. 1048, in the time of the Coḷa Rājādhirāja I, the college at Tribhuvani was required by the endowment to expound for the people the *Bhārata* and the *Rāmāyaṇa*. The *Mahābhārata-vṛtti* in the form of land was given to two brothers by Māravarman Sundara Pāṇḍya for the exposition of the *Mahābhārata*, the *Rāmāyaṇa*, and the Purāṇas (No. 546 of 1922 found at Tiruttāṅgal), and Māravarman Kulaśekhara (A.D. 1268) conferred a privilege on a Brāhmaṇa at Āḻvār-tirunagari (No. 467 of 1909), who expounded the Purāṇa and Itihāsa.

[2] See Bhandarkar, *Summary of Inscriptions of North India*, Nos. 623, 1639.
[3] *South Indian Inscriptions*, I. pp. 150-51.
[4] *Ibid.*, VI. p. 12.

Besides the epics and the Purāṇas, other religious books were also expounded under these endowments: the *Manu Saṁhitā* and *Vaikhānasa-Sūtra* at Tribhuvani ; the *Śivadharma* in the assembly hall in the Tirunāgeśvaram temple (A.D. 1054 ; No. 214 of 1911) and at Tiruvalīśvaram (No. 327 of 1916). Even the more difficult works of philosophy were studied: the *Rāmānuja-bhāṣya* at Kāñcī (No. 493 of 1919) and the Vedānta by a follower of Śaṅkara at the same place (A.D. 1293).[5] The Śaiva hagiological text, *Śrī Purāṇa* of Āḷuḍaiyanambi (Sundaramūrti), and the *Somasiddhānta* form the subjects of exposition provided for according to some other records (Nos. 241 of 1911, 321 of 1917, and 403 of 1896). In the times of the Vijayanagara empire, a grant of Acyutadevarāya does the same thing for the exposition of a Vaiṣṇava scripture called *Bhaktisañjīvinī* (A.D. 1534-35).

Thus the practice of popular exposition of the epics and the Purāṇas has been handed down to the present day in an unbroken tradition. Today such expositions, though to a lesser extent, constitute one of the leading forms of popular religious instruction all over South India, especially in the Tamil country. The Purāṇas are only rarely taken up ; even the *Bhārata,* which, as inscriptions prove, was originally more popular, is not so frequently handled ; the epic that holds the people enthralled is the *Rāmāyaṇa.* Whether it be Vālmīki's Sanskrit original, as is more often the case, or Kamban's Tamil version, hardly a day passes without some sweet-voiced, gifted expounder sitting in a temple, *maṭha* (centre of religious preaching), public hall, or house-front and expounding to hundreds and thousands the story of the *dharma* that Rāma upheld and the *adharma* by which Rāvaṇa fell. Sometimes the Paurāṇic accounts relating to particular shrines and holy waters, *kṣetra* and *tīrtha,* become themes of such popular expositions at certain pilgrim centres or during certain seasons, e.g. the *Tulākāverī-māhātmya* during the holy bathing season of Māgha. This *purāṇa-pravacana* (exposition of Purāṇa) is in vogue in Keraḷa also, where it is called *pāṭhakam.*

TRANSLATIONS AND COMPOSITIONS OF RELIGIOUS WORKS

If the Purāṇas and the Itihāsas were created to put the Vedic teachings in a popular form, it soon became obvious that to bring them still closer to the masses, it was necessary that, along with their oral exposition, the original Sanskrit texts themselves should be given to the people in their own languages. A more masterly epitome of the teachings of the Śrutis and Smṛtis than the *Tirukkuraḷ* of Tiruvaḷḷuvar, revered as a Tamil Veda, cannot be produced. A host of authors brought, through poems and didactic

[5] *Epigraphia Indica,* XIII. p. 196.

writings, the entire wisdom of the *ṛṣis* to the Tamils. Under royal patronage, the epics and the Purāṇas began to appear in Tamil, Telugu, Kannada, and Malayalam translations. The *Mahābhārata* was rendered into Tamil by the Pāṇḍya king Pūḷiyan himself,[6] and about A.D. 1210 a Śaiva named Aranilaivisākhan Trailokyamallan Vatsarājan composed the *Bhārata* again in elegant Tamil (Tiruvālaṅgāḍu, No. 482 of 1905). In the eleventh century, the Telugus also got their *Bhāraṭa* from Nannaya Bhaṭṭa ; in the next century, under the Coḷas, Kamban sang his famous Tamil *Rāmāyaṇa* ; two later Pāṇḍya kings, Ativīra and Varatuṅga, in the sixteenth century, rendered into Tamil the *Kūrma Purāṇa,* the *Liṅga Purāṇa,* the *Kāśī-khaṇḍa,* and the *Brahmottara-khaṇḍa* ; from two earlier records at Cuddalore (A.D. 1111-19), it appears that two persons, named Parasamaya Koḷari Mahāmuni and Kamalālaya Bhaṭṭa, had not only written in Tamil the local *Kannivana Purāṇa,* but also had rendered into it all the eighteen well-known Purāṇas.[7]

ROYAL PATRONAGE TO DEVOTIONAL SINGING

The Pallavas and the Coḷas extended munificent patronage to men of learning through educational institutions called *ghaṭikās,* temples, and foundations of *agrahāra*-settlements, from where they carried on their educational activities. If the Tamil country had been acclaimed in the *Bhāgavata-māhātmya* as the birth-place of *bhakti,* the credit of spreading that devotion all over the South belongs not only to the saints and teachers, but to the great Pallava and Coḷa monarchs themselves, who, besides giving encouragement to these teachers, were themselves great devotees ; Mahendra Vikrama and Rājasiṁha Pallavas are referred to as *paramamāheśvara, śivacūḍāmaṇi,* and *āgamapriya* ; and Kocceṅgaṇān and Gaṇḍarāditya Coḷas are counted among Śaiva saints and canonical hymnists. By far the most important of the religious activities inaugurated and carried forward in the Pallava times are those of the groups of Śaiva and Vaiṣṇava saints, the Nāyanārs and Āḷvārs. Patronized by the Pallava kings, these saints went from place to place, sang their devotional hymns to the deities at the several shrines they visited, disputed with and put down their religious opponents, and spread among the people the gospel of devotion to Śiva and Viṣṇu.

Moving in their appeal, by virtue of both their devotion and music, the Tamil hymns of these Śaiva and Vaiṣṇava saints, called *Devāram* and *Tiruvāimoḷi,* respectively, embodied the truths of the Vedas and the Vedānta, and came to be revered truly as the Tamil Veda. Although they were collected and codified only during the reign of Rājarāja Coḷa (tenth cen-

[6] Larger Śinnamanūr Plates, *South India Inscriptions,* III. p. 454.
[7] *South Indian Inscriptions,* VII. pp. 752-53.

tury), in the Later Pallava age itself attempts were made for popularizing these sacred hymns, *Tiruppadiyam,* by instituting special endowments for their recital in Śiva and Viṣṇu temples. In the time of Nandivarman III Pallava, an endowment was made for the recital of *Tiruppadiyam* at Tirumallam;[8] in Parāntaka Coḷa's time, their recital by Brāhmaṇas was arranged for at Lālguḍi and Āttūr (Nos. 373 of 1903 and 99 of 1929); in the times of Rājarāja I, Rājendra I, and Rājādhirāja, endowments were made for the singing of the *Tiruvāimoḷi* at Uttaramerūr, Śrīraṅgam, Eṇṇāyiram, and Tribhuvani (Nos. 181 of 1923, 61 of 1892, 176 of 1923, 194 of 1923, 333 of 1917, and 557 of 1919); a fifteenth-century record (No. 70 of 1909) in the former Pudukottai State makes a gift of a village to a reciter of the hymns of Śaṭhagopa.

A similar series of inscriptions recording the practice of singing the Śaiva canon, *Devāram,* is found throughout the Coḷa times (No. 349 of 1918, issued in Rājakesarī's time, and No. 99 of 1929, in Parāntaka's time); a large number of epigraphs show that in the great Rājarāja's time this arrangement was in full swing (Nos. 333 of 1906, 275 of 1917, 40 of 1918, 423 of 1908, and 624 of 1909), no less than 40 of the 212 servants at the big temple at Tanjore having been engaged in the recital of these hymns with musical accompaniments. Realizing the appeal of music and the power of that art to aid spiritual exaltation, the authors of the *Devāram* hymns sang them as musical compositions in different melodies; in a Tiruvorriyūr record of Vīrarājendra Coḷa (No. 128 of 1912), sixteen gifted songstresses of the temple-dancers' class (*devar-aḍiyār*) were commissioned to sing these hymns in classic style (*aha-mārga*). This institution is still alive in South Indian temples; a special class of temple-singers called *oduvārs* recite them every evening in a hall in the temple, and, during festivals, accompany the deity in procession, singing the *Devāram* in a party.

MAṬHAS AS CENTRES OF RELIGIOUS PREACHING

Corresponding to the *āśramas* and *tapovanas* of *ṛṣis* mentioned in ancient Sanskrit literature, there developed, in later historical periods, centres of spiritual endeavour and headquarters of different kinds of saints and their religious activities called *maṭhas,* which were originally natural habitations in the form of mountain caves, *guhais* (*guhās*), but were later enlarged into structural buildings. The rich epigraphic records of South India, again, reveal a continuous succession of these *maṭhas* and the part they played in the religious life of the people. In the Later Pallava times, we had at Tiruvorriyūr a *maṭha* presided over by Nirañjanaguru and

[8] *Ibid.,* III. p. 93.

Caturānana Paṇḍita, who were both looking after the temple affairs and services. Attached to the same shrine, there arose several other *mathas,* called after Tiru-jñāna-sambandar, Rājendra Coḷa, Nandikeśvara, and Aṅgarāya. It is from such beginnings that there developed the Tamil *maṭhas* now functioning at places like Dharmapuram, Tiruvāvaḍuturai, and Tiruppanandāl, which are centres of Śaiva teachers having the charge of temple management. The Liṅgāyata *maṭhas* of the Telugu and Kannada areas also had a similar course of evolution ; other religious sects of Advaitic, Viśiṣṭādvaitic, and Dvaitic persuasions developed their own *maṭha*-organizations for keeping up their religious propaganda among the people. Besides teaching texts of higher philosophy to select sets of qualified students, the heads of these *maṭhas,* who are constantly on the move, accompanied by disciples and scholars, come into close contact with the people, to whom they give popular discourses. That the imparting of such popular discourses forms a regular and time-honoured function of these *maṭhas* is attested by an inscription of Vijayagaṇḍa Gopāla (A.D. 1293), which records a grant to a Śaṅkara Maṭha at Kāñcī for the exposition of the Vedānta.

TEMPLES AS CENTRES OF RELIGIOUS AND CULTURAL EDUCATION

The temple, as seen above, was the place where the Itihāsa and Purāṇa were expounded, sacred hymns recited, and *maṭhas* developed. It is to the great work of the Pallavas and the Coḷas that South India owes the temple—its most glorious achievement, its primary and all-comprehensive religious institution, and, in fact, the very centre of all its cultural activity. Starting as excavations on mountain-sides in the Early Pallava times, and gradually becoming stone-structures, the South Indian temples grew in the golden age of the Coḷas into huge establishments, dominating the entire locality and co-ordinating all the aspects of local life, religious, social, and economic. Āditya I Coḷa is said to have covered the banks of the Kāverī with them ; king after king vied with his predecessor, and one dynasty excelled the other, till throughout South India no village or town was left without its visible symbol of the spread of *bhakti.* Not only through worship and daily service of the images of the deities, but through the grand celebrations of their annual festivals, when the deities were taken out in procession, these temples created religious fervour among huge crowds of people drawn from far and near. The car-festival, specially, drew together the entire population of the locality. That such festivals in temples served as suitable occasions for religious discourses is also known from a reference in the Tamil poem *Peruṅkathai* (*Bṛhatkathā*).

The temple was also an art gallery, even as it was a hall for concert, lecture, or transaction of local affairs. The masterpieces of sculpture in the temples taught the entire mythology and the deeds of gods to the mass of people gathering there. All temples had paintings of similar religious themes, and even now, once a year, during festival time, the walls of temples are painted over with divine pictures. In the Pallava Kailāsanātha temple at Kāñcī, in the Jaina cave-temple at Śittannavāśal, and in the Bṛhadīśvara temple at Tanjore, we have the exquisite paintings of olden times still preserved. All these show how the art of painting also was harnessed for religious teaching in ancient India.

A class of mendicants known as Maṅkhas went about exhibiting religious pictures.[9] We see from the *Mudrārākṣasa* that a class of mendicants went about showing scrolls painted with the horrors of hell (*yamapaṭa*) and exhorting people to observe *dharma*. In Saṅgam literature in Tamil, we find the *Paripāḍal* mentioning pilgrims edified by the religious paintings in the Tirupparankunram temple.

DANCE AND DRAMA

The appeal of the arts of dance and drama was not ignored by the ancient teachers. The educative, didactic, and religious usefulness of the play was emphasized by Bharata himself in his *Nāṭya-śāstra*; rhetoricians also said that drama and poetry taught the same lessons as the Vedas and the Purāṇas, but in the winning manner of the beloved (*kāntā-sammita*). All through its history, we find that the drama was, for the most part, enacted in temples during festivals. In the Tamil poems, *Jīvakacintāmaṇi* (2573) and *Peruṅkathai*, we find references to dramatic presentations in temples. Ample light on the systematic use of religious drama in temples, especially during festival times, is thrown by the Coḷa inscriptions. The greatness of the shrine of Rājarājeśvara at Tanjore was depicted in the form of a *nāṭaka* by one Śāntikkūttan at Tanjore (No. 55 of 1893, issued in Rājendra's time). At Cuddalore, the *māhātmya* of the shrine was presented by Kamalālaya Bhaṭṭa through his *Pūmpuliyūr-nāṭaka*.[10] *Śākkai* or *kūttaccākkayan* was a dancer, and an endowment made for his art in a temple was called *śākkakkaṇi* or *nṛtyabhoga*. One Alayūrccākkai was given a grant for enacting three scenes of *śākkaikkūttu* at Tiruvālandurainallūr (No. 250 of 1926). In Rājarāja's time, at Tiruvāvaḍuturai and Tiruviḍaimarudūr, two *śākkais*, named Kumāran Śrīkaṇṭan and Kittimaraikkāḍan, were engaged to do the seven acts of *āriyakkūttu* in the temple (Nos. 120 of 1925 and 154 of 1895). Similarly, in Rājendra's time, Śākkai Mārāyan Vikramacoḷan performed the *śākkaikkūttu* at Kāmarasavalli (No. 65 of 1914) thrice during the Mārgaśīrṣa or Vaiśākha festival. That the *śākkai*

[9] See V. Raghavan, 'Picture-Showmen: Maṅkha', *Indian Historical Quarterly*, XII. p. 524.
[10] *South Indian Inscriptions*, VII. pp. 752-53.

and the dance he performed on a mythological theme were old institutions is known from the Tamil epic, *Śilappadikāram* (XXV.III. 65-80), in which we find the king Śeran Śeṅkuṭṭuvan and his queen witnessing at the *nāṭaka-raṅga* (theatre) the *koṭṭiccheda* dance of Śiva (the *ḍima* of Tripuradāha) by a *śākkai* of Paraiyūr.

As a vehicle of popular religious instruction, this dramatic recital has persisted to this day in the *śākkaikkūttu* or *prabandhamkūttu* of Keraḷa, where it has exercised a wholesome influence on the life of the people. This dance recital, as it now obtains in Keraḷa, is done by a *cākyār* on a stage in the temple, *kūttambalam,* to the accompaniment of a drum played by a *nambiyār* and time kept with cymbals by a lady, *naṅgiyar.* The *cākyār* recites his theme, dances, gesticulates, and, with a gift of wit, brings under his review, during his exposition, the whole course of contemporary affairs, not excepting, in the freedom of speech sanctioned to his office, even the king from the scope of his criticism. Born out of this *cākyārkūttu* is the *tuḷḷal,* which Kunjan Nambiyar fashioned as a further popularized form. During festivals, one finds these performances taking place in the corridors of Keraḷa temples, and Koṭiliṅga Yuvarāja gives a fine picture of these in the description of the Bhagavatī temple at Cranganore in his *Rasasadanabhāṇa.*[11]

Besides these, plays in local languages on Paurāṇic themes were developed in all the linguistic regions of South India, their aim and inspiration being as much religious as literary or artistic. In Andhra arose the *yakṣagāna*[12] and the Kūcipūḍi *Bhāgavatamu* ; *yakṣagānas* are operatic plays on mythological themes, and cognate with them are the *bayal-āṭa* (open air play) of the Kannaḍa area and the *terukkūttu* (street play) of Tamilnāḍ. There is a manuscript in the *Mackenzie Collection* which informs us that Akkaṇṇa and Mādaṇṇa, the Hindu ministers of the Qutb Shāhi rulers of Golconda, maintained their own troupe of *yakṣagāna* players and made them tour the entire Qutb Shāhi dominion every year.

Kūcipūḍi is an *agrahāra* in the Krishna District where Bhāgavatas, the Brāhmaṇa devotees of the Lord, took to the art of dance for the propitiation of the Lord, and enacted, with music and gesticulation, dramas on the sports of Kṛṣṇa. From this tradition, the *Bhāgavata-melā-nāṭaka*[13] of some villages in the Tanjore District, like Meraṭṭūr, Ūttukkāḍu, Nallūr, Śūlamaṅgalam, etc., took its birth. Even today, Brāhmaṇas of these villages stage plays like *Prahlādavijaya, Uṣāpariṇaya, Rukmāṅgada,* and *Mārkaṇḍeya-*

---

[11] *Kāvyamālā*, XXXVII. pp. 56-57.
[12] See V. Raghavan, 'Yakṣagāna', *Triveni,* VII. 2.
[13] See V. Raghavan, 'Bhāgavata-melā-nāṭaka', *Journal of the Indian Society of Oriental Art,* V.

carita, before the temple deity, during the spring-time festivals. The plays are part of the worship, some of the actors playing the divine parts even observing fast; and the entire population for five miles around gather and sit through the night watching the devout Brāhmaṇa Bhāgavatas present their *nāṭakas* with song and gesticulation. Their ideal, best set forth in the text which they quote, is that it is the sacred duty of the Bhāgavatas to adore the Lord with song and dance, with as much devotion to it as they have to statutory rites prescribed by the Vedas (*Viṣṇorgānaṁ ca nṛttaṁ ca . . . kartavyaṁ nityakarmavat*).

Corresponding to this, the Malayalam country has its own religious plays. Taking its inspiration originally from the singing and gesticulation of the *Gīta-Govinda* of Jayadeva, the religious drama of Keraḷa developed into the Sanskrit *Kṛṣṇāṭṭam,* and from that evolved into the Malayalam *kathakaḷi,* the last having been fashioned by the chief of Koṭṭūrakkara in the latter half of the seventeenth century for the sake of a wider popular appeal. With elaborate make-up, song, and very detailed gesticulation, the *kathakaḷi* presented, through several nights, cycles of epic and Paurāṇic stories to large audiences, which sat all through the night in the open to watch them. All these forms of dance-drama, as well as the puppet-shows, *bommalāṭṭa,* and the shadow-plays, *tolpāvai,* prevalent all over the South, had the same religious setting and promoted the same religious purpose.

DEVOTIONAL MUSIC

If the greatest contribution of Tamilnāḍ to the sphere of devotional music is the body of hymns called *Devāram* and *Tiruvāimoḷi,* the outstanding contribution of the Kannada-speaking area to the same sphere is represented by the large body of musical compositions, *padas, devaranāṃas,* and *kīrtanas,* sung by the members of the Dāsa Kūṭa tradition. Couched in popular language, enlivened by homely wit, and glowing with the truths of spiritual realization, the compositions of the Dāsa Kūṭa saints, forming a triple heritage of literature, music, and philosophy, and sung by them in their pilgrimages from shrine to shrine, served to create among the masses a spiritual awakening and religious enthusiasm. The Dāsa Kūṭa, the origins of which are traced to a line of Smārta devotees beginning with Acalānandadāsa (ninth century) of the Rāṣṭrakūṭa times, was later represented by a line of Mādhva saints—Narahari Tīrtha (A.D. 1281), Śrīpādarāja who sang the whole of the Tenth Book of the *Bhāgavata,* Vyāsarāya (fifteenth century), Purandaradāsa (1480-1564), his shepherd contemporary Kanakadāsa, Vijayadāsa, Jagannāthadāsa, and others. The greatest of these is Purandaradāsa, and if ancient South Indian music is indebted to the *Devāram* and *Tiruvāimoḷi* of the saints of Pallava times, modern South Indian music (Karnatic) owes its evolution to this Karṇāṭaka saint-musician, Purandaradāsa. Side by side with these Haridāsas, who fostered the growth of *Viṣṇu-bhakti,* the Vīraśaiva saints, Basava and Allama of the twelfth century and the Śivaśaraṇas who followed them, spread *Śiva-bhakti* with their *vacanas* among the Kannaḍigas (Kannada-speaking people).

The mission of evoking devotion among the people through songs was then taken over by Telugu, which gave from Tirupati the large corpus of *saṅkīrtanas* composed by a family of devotees called the Tālappākkam poets, Annamācārya, Tiruveṅkaṭa, and others, who flourished in the fifteenth and sixteenth centuries; their numberless lyrics addressed to the 'Lord of the Seven Hills', preserved in heaps of copperplates at the hill-temple, form a substantial contribution to Telugu music and to the path of adoring the Lord through song, the *bhajana-paddhati.* Next in importance are the *kīrtanas* which Rāmadāsa of Bhadrācala (seventeenth century), a devotee of Rāma who was imprisoned by Tani Shāh of Golconda, sang from his prison and which are current all over the Telugu country. While, on the side of actual practice and literary propaganda, these devoted souls popularized this cult among the learned and the lay by writing hymns and treatises and by organizing congregational singing of divine praise and founding *bhajana-maṭhas* for this purpose, the renowned saint-musician, Tyāgarāja (1757-1847), made an outstanding contribution with his songs and provided a rich musical medium for this method of worship. This school infused a new life into the old path of devotion. *Bhajana* now developed on a large scale, and the visit, to Tanjore and other centres, of performers of *saṅkīrtana* from the north, especially from Mahārāṣṭra, perfected the *bhajana-paddhati* which came to be maintained by a chain of *maṭhas* in places both big and small.

The climax of this movement of singing the name and glory of the Lord was reached in the Kāverī delta, in the heart of Tamilnāḍ, where the cult of *nāma-siddhānta,* recital of God's name as the most potent means of salvation, was developed by saint-authors of the eighteenth century, like Śrīdhara Veṅkaṭeśa and Bodhendra.

From very ancient times, the month of Mārgaśīrṣa (November-December) was considered especially sacred and appropriate for adoring the Lord, and both the Śaivas and the Vaiṣṇavas had their own devotional recitals for this month, the *Tiruvempāvai* and the *Tiruppāvai*; and even special temple-endowments were made for the latter in Coḷa times (Nos. 12 of 1905, 421 of 1912, and 128 of 1912). This special adoration of the Lord through devotional singing in Mārgaśīrṣa has continued to the present day. Parties of devotees get up early in the Mārgaśīrṣa mornings, bathe despite the chill, and go round the local temple and the tank singing devotional songs. This practice, popularly called *bhajana,* is also referred to as *giripradakṣiṇa* (going round a sacred hill), pointing perhaps to its origin in the circumambulation of the early mountain-cave temples, which the Nāyanārs did with hymns on their lips. While a few gifted singers, who led these *bhajana* parties, stopped at particular places to sing elaborate songs, there were *nāmāvalis* or simple strings of God's names and epithets which they uttered as they moved on and which the accompanying congregation took up in chorus. As each song or *nāmāvali* was finished, the leader pronounced what is called a *puṇḍarīka,* an expression of devotion to God like *'Namaḥ Pārvatīpataye'* or *'Sītā-kāntasmaraṇam',* to which the whole party responded with formulas like *'Hara Hara Mahādeva'* and *'Jaya Jaya Rāma'.* This *bhajana* was conducted in a more organized manner, within the precincts of *bhajana-maṭhas,* every day or on special week-days or on holy days like the *ekādaśī* (the eleventh lunar day).

In a far more elaborate manner, a whole *bhajana*-session was conducted for several days once or twice a year, when the Bhāgavatas would celebrate festivals, *utsavas,* of the marriage of Sītā-Rāma or of Rādhā-Kṛṣṇa. In the manner of an *upākarman* (a ceremony performed to restart the reading of the Vedas after the break during the rains) during the *cāturmāsya,* the Bhāgavatas go through, during these days, their entire repertoire, *Gopikā-gītā,* Jayadeva's *aṣṭapadīs,* the *devaranāmas* of Purandara, the *kīrtanas* of Rāmadāsa, the *Kṛṣṇalīlā-taraṅgiṇī* of Nārāyaṇa Tīrtha, a Sanskrit operatic composition on the whole story of Kṛṣṇa, and similar devotional songs. Besides these, the Bhāgavatas sing, during these festivals, special series of songs called *utsava-sampradāya kīrtanas* and songs invoking the Lord with simple addresses and epithets called *divyanāma-saṅkīrtanas,* to both of which Tyāgarāja made his contribution. Some of these are sung with a simple dance movement around a brass lamp-stand or a *tulasī* pot, in imitation of the circular *rāsa*-dance. Some *utsava*-specialists among these execute more difficult dances, carrying the lamp-stand or circumambulating it with their prostrate bodies. Large numbers of devout people of either sex take part in these *bhajanas.*

HARIKATHĀ OR RELIGIOUS STORY RECITAL

An exposition of a mythological story with music and dance is defined by Bhoja in his work on *alaṅkāra* under the name *ākhyāna* ; Bhoja's remarks in another context show that this refers to the art of the *kathaka.* It is to this ancient form of the *kathaka's* art that we have to relate the *kathākālakṣepa* or *Harikathā,* as it evolved later in Tamilnāḍ, and is now widely prevalent in South India. The exposition of a religious story took the present *kālakṣepa* form at Tanjore, as a result of the impact of the *kīrtana* style of some Mahārāṣṭra *buvas* (religious preachers), chiefly Ramachandra Buva Morgaunkar (1864), who visited Tanjore. Before this time, *kālakṣepa,* which was an old way of spending time listening to a holy discourse, was not perfected as an art-form with the addition of music and dramatic touches. Krishna Bhagavatar (1847-1903), who refashioned it after listening to the Mahārāṣṭrian style, even introduced some dancing in his performances.

The main Bhāgavata (*Harikathā* reciter) stands in front, usually supported by a musician-assistant standing behind him, and the minimum instrumental accompaniment is a *mṛdaṅga* (a kind of drum). The Tamil Bhāgavatas who took this up handled the art with their emphasis shifting between music and exposition, according to their individual gifts.[14] The themes are from the *Rāmāyaṇa,* the *Mahābhārata,* the Purāṇas, lives of saints, not only of the Tamilnāḍ, but of the other parts of the country also, like Rāmadāsa, Kabīr, and the Mahārāṣṭra saints. After some preliminary invocatory singing on Gaṇeśa, Sarasvatī, Hanumat, and the *guru,* the Bhāgavata sings a song which is the text of his sermon. This song emphasizes that devotion to the Lord, or a particular mode of His worship, is the only means of salvation, or that the Lord is the only refuge of man. To illustrate this, the Bhāgavata takes up a story which forms the main part of the performance. It is called the *Harikathā.* In the end the story is wound up by harking back to the burden of the first song, to illustrate which the story was expounded. During the exposition of the story, the Bhāgavata's wide learning in sacred literature is to be brought into display. He has to elevate the listeners with his knowledge, drive home with wit moral and ethical principles, and move the hearts of his audience with his dramatic and devoted narration. In fact, as an art-form, the *Harikathā* is almost a mono-drama. Undoubtedly this, along with the *purāṇa-paṭhana,* forms the most effective vehicle of popular religious instruction in South India.

[14] For further details on this form, see V. Raghavan, *Commemoration Volume* in honour of the leading lady *kathā* artiste of Madras, Srimati C. Saraswati Bai, 1939, pp. 57-58.

37

DIFFUSION OF SOCIO-RELIGIOUS CULTURE IN NORTH INDIA

I

FROM the earliest times, religion has been the pivot round which social life in North India has revolved. Neither the invasion of the Muslims nor the advent of the British has, to any great extent, changed the course of that life, so far, at least, as the Hindus are concerned. Sometimes the Hindus and Muslims have been equal partners in some of the most popular social activities, enjoying the same music and art, drawing their inspiration from the same literature and philosophy as well as actively contributing to it, joining unreservedly in the same festivities and fairs, and, not infrequently, participating in the same *pūjās* and prayers. In spite of the diversities of race and religion and occasional conflicts, we generally get a pleasing picture of social amity and co-operation among the people.

MUSIC, DANCE, AND DRAMA IN SOCIO-RELIGIOUS LIFE

It is only against this background that the social life of the people can be understood. For, in the case of the Hindus, the social activities were almost invariably associated with religion. Singing, dancing, and enacting dramas were indulged in before gods in the temples, at the coronation ceremonies of kings, and on other auspicious occasions. The *Abhinaya-darpaṇa* (Mirror of Gestures) of Nandikeśvara says: '*Nāṭya* (drama) and *nṛtya* (dance) should be witnessed particularly at the time of religious festivals. Those who wish for good luck or well-being should cause *nṛtya* to be performed on occasions like the coronation celebrations of kings, a major festival, a procession with an image of a god, a marriage ceremony, union with a friend, entry into a new town or house, and the birth of a son, for it is auspicious.'[1]

A description of the learned audience is given in the same work: 'The audience shines forth like a *kalpataru* (wish-fulfilling tree), with the Vedas as its branches, the Śāstras as its flowers, and the scholars as the (humming) bees.'[2]

The *Abhinaya-darpaṇa* was written more than a thousand years ago, and is an authoritative work on Hindu histrionic art. After Bharata's

[1] *Abhinaya-darpaṇa*, edited by Dr. Monomohan Ghosh, p. 2.
[2] *Ibid.*, p. 3.

Nāṭya-śāstra, it has set the standard in the art of dancing and acting. This shows the antiquity of the practice of dancing, singing, and stage-playing as popular institutions in India. They were inspired mainly by religious considerations, and were guided and controlled by rules which afforded a scientific basis for the proper culture of those arts. Just as, in the case of poetry in India, various attempts were made to discover the laws of rhetoric and metre and to place the technique of literary composition on a universal basis, so also, in the cultivation of music and theatricals, great pains were taken to discover laws of taste and to standardize their technique.

The earliest source of the development of music in India may be traced to the Vedas. We see there a simultaneous growth of the intellectual and aesthetic side of human nature. That part of the Vedas which is called *sāman* was originally intended to be sung with proper intonation and appropriate gesture, meant to indicate *rāga* and *tāla.* This practice is not merely confined to the *Sāma-Veda,* but extends to the scriptural texts of various religious sects. The *Gītā* is often read with proper intonation as a religious book, and so also the *Bhāgavata.*

People are often in the habit of singing aloud the name of the Lord or reciting a string of divine names, so that not only men, but lower creatures as well may hear the divine name and attain spiritual uplift in this or the next life. Sometimes a large congregation, living merely on a dole or subsistence allowance, assembles together for chanting the name of the Lord.

The musical reading of scriptures found enthusiastic support during the Indian renaissance, when the sudden revival of literature in the vernaculars revitalized religious thought and practice. At times, this took the form of *kathakatā,* i.e. exposition, in the regional tongue, of difficult sacred texts in Sanskrit. With this new-found channel of expression, people turned to the translation of the Sanskrit texts, and a host of works came out in the vernaculars. In this way, many translations of the *Rāmāyaṇa* and the *Mahābhārata* appeared in the different vernacular languages. This was a potent means of diffusing knowledge, which was at one time the close preserve of the learned few. With the diffusion of knowledge through vernaculars, which undoubtedly marks the most important phase of social awakening, began a wide-spread socio-religious activity among the people, for the epics and the semi-religious literature created among the people an earnest longing for spiritual advancement. The Vaiṣṇavas made it a point to sing vernacular songs at the time of begging for alms. The practice of singing also came into vogue among women at the time of marriage and other socio-religious ceremonies and during the performance of *vratas* (religious vows) etc. This movement took various shapes and forms with the development of tunes (*sura*) and cadences (*tāla*) in North India. A complete treatise, *Saṅgīta-ratnākara,* came from the pen of Sāraṅga Deva in the twelfth or thirteenth century and, one or two centuries later, a learned commentary on it was produced by Catura Kallinātha.

Music is generally consecrated to the gods. The *rāgas* and *rāgiṇīs,* through which vocal and instrumental music finds its wealth of expression, are presided over by different divinities. The song literature of North India is immensely rich, and it has mostly Rāma and Kṛṣṇa, the two most popular figures in the Hindu pantheon, for its theme.

Dance, too, has a religious foundation, and is performed in the temples in celebration of certain festivals sacred to particular gods and goddesses, and also in connection with the observance of *vratas* by women. The god of dance is Naṭarāja, Śiva himself. In the country-side in Bengal, Śiva is still worshipped by his votaries in the month of Caitra, and dance forms an integral part of this worship.

Song and dance led gradually but inevitably to theatricals or *nāṭyas.* '*Nāṭya*', as the word indicates, is related to *naṭa* or *nāṭa,* which means to dance. The *āṅgika abhinaya,* which consists in graceful movements of the body required in dancing, is also a necessary factor in acting. Theatrical or histrionic art is very old in India. Along with the development of music and dancing, it made great progress, and rules were framed for the successful performance of the art. It is sometimes said that in ancient India *nāṭakas* were mainly danced and not acted, i.e. action was wanting. But the composition of the well-known dramas, like *Śakuntalā, Mṛcchakaṭikā* (Little Clay-cart), and *Veṇī-saṁhāra* (Braiding up the Hair), shows unmistakably that dramaturgy in India was developing along the same lines as in other countries.

POPULAR FESTIVITIES AND ENTERTAINMENTS

Of all the springs of action that move the masses, religion is the most potent. The social activities, which are calculated to influence the life and conduct of a whole mass of people, must have a spiritual background. And because in India the masses were reached through various festivities and entertainments, prescribed in religious books and characterized by religious fervour, the concentrated wisdom of ages could easily permeate through the various strata of society, from the highest to the lowest. Through mythological plays called *yātrās,* the teachings of the Purāṇas, the epics, and the Śāstras have found their way even to the illiterate section.

Yātrā, in the sense of an open air performance of *nāṭakas,* is not a very old institution, but it has done more than any other institution to popularize the virtues inculcated in the *Rāmāyana* and the *Mahābhārata,* the *Bhāgavata* and the other Purāṇas. The word '*yātrā*' means a festival in which sometimes dramatic performances are held. In this sense, it may be affiliated to the dance-festivals of some primitive tribes like the Oraons, the Santals, etc. and to the *nāṭa-gīta* (dance-song) mentioned in early Bengali literature. Literally, *yātrā* means setting out or going from one place to another ; hence, it also means a procession. Derivatively, it has come to mean a festival, as in *snāna-yātrā* (ablution-festival), *hindolā-yātrā* (swing-festival), *rāsa-yātrā* (festival of circular dance), *ratha-yātrā* (car-festival), and *dolā-yātrā* (*holī* festival, in which coloured water is thrown at each other by people for amusement). *Yātrā* also means a theatrical performance, as in *Kṛṣṇa-yātrā, Rāma-yātrā,* etc. There is no doubt that these theatricals have come from the representations of the *nāṭakas* of old.

The festivals in honour of the gods, such as *snāna-yātrā, rāsa-yātrā,* etc. in which large numbers of people take part, seem to have been known from the earliest times. It is probable that, from this, *yātrā,* in the sense of dramatic performance, came into vogue. Bhavabhūti refers to the *yātrā* of Kālapriyanātha, in which his *Uttara-Rāmacarita* was going to be presented. The points to be noticed are, firstly, *yātrās* usually formed part of festivities, mostly religious. Secondly, they were connected with the epics or Purāṇas. Thirdly, the musical parties were moving from place to place as travelling troupes, and had no fixed place for the performance, nor any curtains and scenes to represent landscapes and surroundings relating to the plot. Indian *yātrās* have still retained their primitive simplicity.

The earliest mention of such performance, perhaps, is found in the *Harivaṁśa,* an appendix (*khila*) of the *Mahābhārata.* It refers to the staging of the exploits of Rāma, in the presence of Vajranābha, the king of Vajrapura. It is also significant that it is nowhere mentioned that the performance was a novel phenomenon or an innovation. That it was a true dramatic representation can be judged from the following facts. First of all, female characters were introduced in the play. Secondly, there was a *prekṣāgṛha* (auditorium) where the audience was seated. Thirdly, there was a *śrutidhara* or prompter with the party. And, lastly, various musical instruments were used, such as drum, flute, lyre (*rudravīṇā*), etc. The story of this dramatic performance in *Harivaṁśa* was reproduced with embellishments by a Bengali poet, Guṇarāj Khān, who lived in the early part of the fifteenth century.

In this context, we may mention the performance in which Śrī Caitanya himself took part. At the house of Candraśekhara, a devout Vaiṣṇava, a performance was held at the direction of Caitanya. A canopy was hung up, and dresses, including those of female characters, were procured. The whole of Navadvīpa turned up, including Caitanya's mother and wife, to witness the play.

A few years later, Rūpa Gosvāmin produced two very remarkable plays *Vidagdha-Mādhava* and *Lalita-Mādhava,* and Rāya Rāmānanda wrote his well-known drama *Jagannātha-vallabha.* In *Lalita-Mādhava,* Rūpa Gosvāmin has introduced a dramatic performance as an episode in the drama. Śrī Kṛṣṇa, while at Dvārakā, grieved at the separation from Rādhā, and a dramatic performance was arranged to soothe his feelings. One very curious thing about it is that the play reproduced Śrī Kṛṣṇa himself and his sport at Vṛndāvana.

Reference has already been made to the dramatic performance instituted at the instance of Śrī Caitanya. It was yet very far from the open air representations of modern times, in which some episode in the life of Kṛṣṇa or Rāma or some other divine personage is enacted. For, in the performance at Candraśekhara's house, we do not find any unity of plot. In the elaborate description of it given in the *Caitanya-Bhāgavata,* written about the middle of the sixteenth century, one misses the theme on which a whole-night performance was organized. In fact, the dance of Caitanya forms the most important attraction, but it is not clear whether in the impersonation of the Śaktis of different deities or personages Caitanya changed dresses, or the characters were merely the different ways in which he was viewed by the audience.

In northern India, the corresponding institution is *Rāma-līlā,* and, though the stages of its evolution are by no means so marked as in the case of Bengal, *Rāma-līlā* performances have evoked great enthusiasm among the masses in northern India from very early times. Men and women are moved by the scenes of Śrī Rāmacandra's life. Rāma's going to the forest, on the eve of his coronation, to keep his father's promise to Kaikeyī, the voluntary exile of Sītā who wanted to share the sorrows and privations of her husband, the fraternal affection of Lakṣmaṇa which led him to accompany his brother in exile, the renunciation of Bharata, and lastly, the loyalty and devotion of Hanumat have been enshrined in the hearts of the people, and hundreds and thousands of spectators of all sects and creeds witness and enjoy the *Rāma-līlā* festivities which last for several days at a time. Sometimes the performers, placed on a high platform or pedestal, are dressed in gorgeous attire, and attempts are made to approximate their costumes and movements to the descriptions given in Tulasīdāsa's *Rāmacaritamānasa.*

The origin of *Rāma-līlā* can be traced to the singing of the *Rāmāyaṇa* by Kuśa and Lava, the two sons of Rāma, who sang melodiously the superhuman exploits of Rāma with masterly skill. Centuries have elapsed between Vālmīki and Tulasīdāsa, but today the great sage lives in Tulasīdāsa, who introduced a vein of piety and devotion on a scale hitherto unknown in any literature. Moreover, the *dohās* and *caupāīs* of

Tulasīdāsa yield more easily to their rendering into folk-music. In *Rāma-līlā* festivities, music plays a great part, as in the *yātrās* of Bengal.

In these naive dramatic representations, it is often the traditional tunes that are played, using traditional instruments, sometimes accompanied by vocal demonstrations of a high order. But the tendency is apparent now to march with the times and, as a result, the *yātrās* have lost much of their original simplicity, naive charm, and also the popularity they once enjoyed. They are being replaced by theatricals or performances on a fixed stage, embellished with artistically painted scenes, which lend a touch of reality to the plays. However, the moral motive is seldom absent from these popular representations. The epic and the mythological themes continue, and even from modern cinemas such themes have not been banished altogether. The popular appeal of these is not totally lost.

KATHAKATĀ

While *pāṭha* means the reading of a scripture, a Purāṇa, or an epic, *kathakatā* generally means discourse on the Purāṇas. Usually, *kathā* means speech; but it is also used in the sense of descriptive narration, especially in connection with discourse on God or religion. This derivative sense has its origin in the practice, prevalent in many places in North India, of reading (*pāṭha*) from the scriptures or mythologies. For example, the Vaiṣṇavas congregate together to listen to recitals from the *Gītā*, the *Bhāgavata*, and other Purāṇas by those who are well versed in them. The Sikhs also have their practice of reading from the *Granth Sāhib*.

Not merely are texts recited by the *kathaka* from the Purāṇas, but stories are told from the wide field of mythologies to make the lesson attractive, and interpretations are given so as to make the difficult texts intelligible to the people of very ordinary intelligence. Sometimes learned scholars take to this profession, and it is always ennobling to listen to their impressive discourses, based upon an extensive knowledge of the Śāstras, on life, death, life after death, the inevitable consequences of sin, and the invariable rewards of virtue. It is a frequent topic of *kathakatā*, both in Hindu and Sikh congregations, that this world or *saṁsāra* (relative existence) is vain; vain are its joys, and the ties that bind one to this life perish with this body. The wages of sin is death. Truth is to be taught; light is to be sought; and love is to be cultivated—this is the only way to attain salvation. These are illustrated with the help of the lives of the saints, which the people are exhorted to follow. In this way, the interests of religion are promoted and religious fervour is kept alive among the people.

The secret of the success of these discourses lies in the background of culture which has been inherited from the past. Unless we understand this background, it is not possible to assess the value of *kathakatā* as a method of popular religious instruction. It is not easy for a foreigner to understand how widely philosophy has permeated the popular literature in India. The most abstruse ideas of metaphysics and theology have found expression in the popular poetry, fiction, and drama. From one end of the country to the other, the teachings of the *Rāmāyaṇa*, the *Mahābhārata*, and the *Bhāgavata* have inspired the literature, and even the folklore. As a matter of fact, the invasion of western culture and its modern ideas has not been able to disturb the placid stream of India's spiritual life, so far, at least, as the masses are concerned. The eternal verities, which have found expression in our philosophical and religious literature, are held in undiminished reverence in the popular mind through the efforts of teachers and preachers, artistes and sculptors. The institution of pilgrimage has also helped to keep alive the mythological imageries and the traditional sanctity of spiritual ideals.

KIRTANA

Ordinarily, *kīrtana* means laudatory recital, verbal and literary, of the name and qualities of a person. But its technical meaning consists in the repeated utterance of the name and description of the qualities of the divine being or beings. Of the nine *lakṣaṇas* or modes of *bhakti*, *kīrtana* is the second. But in a still more technical sense, it means a variety of devotional music used in singing the name or praise of the Lord. The Āḷvārs and other saints of South India developed devotional poetry of a high order and used to sing their compositions in shrines and at other places of worship. In the sixteenth century, the Rajput princess Mīrābāī renounced her worldly relations and dedicated herself to Giridhara or Śrī Kṛṣṇa, before whom she sang and danced. Her songs, known as *bhajanas*, have come down to us as specimens of the loftiest feelings of devotion and piety. *Bhajana*, like *kīrtana*, has a twofold meaning: it is a praise of the Lord, and also music of a particular type. The *abhaṅgas* of Tukārāma, glorifying the god of his adoration, are regarded as among the best specimens of devotional poetry in western India. Tukārāma used to compare *kīrtana* to the river Gaṅgā: it is regarded as a counter-current of purification, inasmuch as the Gaṅgā, rising from the lotus-feet of Viṣṇu, comes downward on the earth for the purification of mortals, and the stream of *bhakti*, in *kīrtana*, rising from the heart of mortal men, goes upward and reaches the feet of Hari for His delectation.

Kīrtana songs were composed by hundreds of poets from one end of the country to the other. *Kīrtana* is regarded in two aspects, viz. *nāma-kīrtana* and *līlā-kīrtana*. *Nāma-kīrtana* consists in constantly uttering the name and singing the glory of the Lord, or expressing repentance for one's sins, both inherited and acquired. The Vaiṣṇavas emphasize that constant remembrance of the name of the Lord is the only means of salvation for weak mortals of the *kaliyuga* (the present age of vice).

This is pre-eminently due to the teaching of Śrī Caitanya who, along with his spiritual brother, Nityānanda, is considered to be the father of modern *saṅkīrtana*. *Saṅkīrtana* was not unknown before them; but what seems to be the unique contribution of this immortal pair is the emphasis which they placed on it, and the consequent enthusiasm with which the masses acclaimed it. Although it did not exactly conflict with the Brāhmaṇical religion, it is probable that the old orthodox church of Bengal looked askance at this invasion by the new congregational and revivalistic mode of worship, in which distinctions of caste, which thrive on rituals and other formal modes of worship, were almost done away with. The Brāhmaṇa and the cobbler, the rich and the poor, met on a common platform, so far as the celebration of God's name was concerned. Formerly, the Brāhmaṇas alone were entitled to enter the sanctum sanctorum and were regarded as intermediaries between the worshipper and the worshipped. Now, devotion to God became the only criterion of worth.

In the other form of *kīrtana*, which is known as *līlā-kīrtana*, songs describing the various sports, dalliances, and deeds of Kṛṣṇa are sung. Rādhā, who is intimately associated with Kṛṣṇa, is the embodiment of the highest emotion of love with which God can be loved. More technically, *līlā-kīrtana* passes through the exposition of *pūrva-rāga* (dawn of yearning), *anurāga* (love or attachment), *kalahāntaritā* (estrangement), and *rāsa* (merry group-dance) and other sports to the inevitable *viraha* (separation) in which the vision beatific enchants from a distance.

The fivefold or rather fourfold *rasa* or sentiment, through which the *līlā* or life-story of Kṛṣṇa is realized, consists mainly of loyalty (of the servant for the divine master), friendship (love of the cowherd boys for Kṛṣṇa, their divine playmate), filial affection (love, more of the parents for their divine son than of the son for the parents), and, lastly, love (of the cowherd girls for their divine sweetheart). The songs or *padāvalīs* distribute themselves among these *rasas*, and their object is to promote the corresponding feelings in the minds of the listeners. The religious significance is of the first importance in these songs, and those which cannot arouse a spiritual longing or interest may be held to have failed in their purpose.

Kīrtana in Bengal reached the acme of emotional expression through music, largely due to the influence of Caitanya and his followers. Tears, shivering, horripilation, perspiration, loss of colour or complexion, loss of vigour, loss of voice, and loss of consciousness constitute the eightfold pure signs of true devotion, and the object of both *nāma-kīrtana* and *līlā-kīrtana* is to induce these states in the singer and in the audience.

The musical instruments, such as *mṛdaṅga* (a kind of drum akin to *mādal* of the aborigines) and cymbals, are said to have been invented by, or at least associated with, Caitanya. He wanted to make *kīrtana* the expression of his religion of love ; and the *khola,* or drum with an earthen body, and the *karatāla,* or cymbals made of brass, are within the means of the poorest of the poor. So, by introducing *kīrtana* as adaptable to mass singing and making its musical accompaniments simple and available to all, Caitanya's object was fulfilled in a large measure, for a wave of enthusiasm passed over the country, and, in course of time, four different schools of *kīrtana* music grew up in different parts of Bengal. The extent of its popularity can be gathered from the fact that in Bengal, at any rate, it has been adapted in many other forms of popular musical entertainment, such as *yātrās,* theatres, Brāhmo community-singing, and even the congregational music of the Indian Christians. Even the modern songs of Rabindranath Tagore, Dwijendra Lal Roy, Atul Prasad Sen, and others have largely drawn upon *kīrtana* tunes.

It was undoubtedly Caitanya's preaching of the religion of love which was responsible for popularizing the earlier masters like Jayadeva, Vidyāpati, and Caṇḍīdāsa, and infusing inspiration among a host of other poets who threw open the floodgates of lyrical poetry, which had for its one theme the romance of Rādhā and Kṛṣṇa and the *sannyāsa* (renunciation) of Nimāi, i.e. Śrī Caitanya, himself.

It is customary not to begin *kīrtana* without due obeisance to Caitanya in the form of an appropriate *Gauracandrikā* or event in the life of Caitanya, which is intended to serve as an introduction to the particular *līlā* of Kṛṣṇa to be sung. The *Gauracandrikā* also helps to remind the singer, as well as the audience, that the mind must be purged of erotic associations likely to be roused by the *kīrtana padāvalīs,* which depict sensuously the love of Kṛṣṇa and Rādhā, when they remember the purity of the personal life of Caitanya.

Śrīnivāsa Ācārya, who converted the independent king Vīra Hambīra of Vishnupur (Bankura District), paved the way for the spread of Vaiṣṇavism over the whole of South-West Bengal. Another contemporary of Śrīnivāsa, namely, Śyāmānanda, spread it in Orissa, the culture of which is still largely influenced by his teachings and those of his famous disciples, Rasika and Murāri. It was through his influence that *kīrtana* was spread throughout the length and breadth of Orissa, for which the ground had already been prepared by the stay of Caitanya in Puri during the whole of the latter part of his life. In the north-eastern regions of India, a disciple of

Narottamadāsa Ṭhākura spread Vaiṣṇavism in the remote principality of Manipur, where one can still find the traces of living Vaiṣṇavism and hear *kīrtana* recited and the *padāvalīs* sung. Jayadeva of Kenduli (Kenduvilva) in Bengal was perhaps the first poet to call his exquisitely charming lyrical poetry by the name of *padāvalīs,* and his famous poem *Gīta-Govinda* is sung in many temples throughout India even to this day. Many of the later poets wrote in an artificial language, called Brajabulī, which lends itself easily to musical renderings. These Brajabulī poems, which grew into a considerable volume, derived their great influence and popularity from *kīrtana,* at least in Bengal. Their theme is either the divine love of Rādhā and Kṛṣṇa or the events in the life of Caitanya.

But it must not be thought that these *padāvalīs* were confined to Bengal. We find quite a vast *padāvalī* literature in other parts of northern India. Some of the best known among the *padāvalī* writers of this region are Sūradāsa, Raskhan, Nandadāsa, and others.

A word may be said about the devotional mysticism which underlies *kīrtana* and *padāvalīs.* The love of Rādhā and Kṛṣṇa may be interpreted allegorically as the relation between the individual and the universal (Ātman and Paramātman). The individual longs to be united with the universal, but he can do so only if he sheds his individuality, his finite aspect, his self and its antecedents. When one sings or listens to *kīrtana,* one rises above the pettinesses of this earthly existence, transcends the subject-object relation, and loses oneself in the sea of bliss.

In Bengal and elsewhere, the members of the musical party are garlanded and besmeared with sandal-paste on the forehead before the *kīrtana* starts, and, at the end, sugar-cakes are scattered on the ground for the audience to pick up and taste as *prasāda* or votive offering to God. It is technically called *lūṭ* (loot), as the members of the audience have to scramble to reach the small sugar-cakes which symbolize divine grace. The Caitanya school of Vaiṣṇavism, in its revivalistic *kīrtana* gatherings, supplied the elements of congregational worship and enlightened mass consciousness through emotional rapport, which the earlier individualistic and contemplative mode of approach to the Divine lacked. No wonder that it should prove one of the most potent methods of popular religious instruction in North India.

II

THE MAṄGALA LITERATURE

The picture of diffusion of religious knowledge given above would be incomplete without some reference to the contributions in vernaculars of writers of diverse castes, occupations, and grades of learning to the propagation of religious ideas in certain parts of North India, especially in the eastern side. While the learned depended for their religious exposition on Sanskrit texts, a large number of people were being introduced to a new kind of religious literature which drew its materials from non-Aryan sources and popular tales. This literature, which originated in the twelfth or the thirteenth century and reached its climax in the eighteenth, is known as the Maṅgala literature in Bengal. The word *'maṅgala'* (auspiciousness or welfare) has not been very satisfactorily derived. It may have had reference to the *rāga* or melody called *maṅgala* in the beginning ; but subsequently it came to signify the blessings of this or that popular deity and also the works and exploits of this or that prominent member of a religious group (e.g. Caitanya, Advaita, etc.).

Now, in Bengal, this Maṅgala literature is an extensive one, and has been associated with such major deities as Śiva, Viṣṇu (Kṛṣṇa), Sūrya, and Śakti (Caṇḍī, Durgā, Kālikā, Annadā, Gaurī, Bhavānī, etc.), and also with such minor deities as Manasā (the goddess of serpents), Śītalā (the goddess of small-pox), Ṣaṣṭhī (the protective deity of children), Śāradā (the goddess of learning), Lakṣmī (the goddess of fortune), Gaṅgā, and even the tiger and the crocodile, the lords (*rāya*) of the jungles and waters of the Sunderbans, respectively. Many of these deities have come down from Dravidian or aboriginal sources, but, in course of their absorption into the Aryan cult, most of them have been identified with this or that Brāhmaṇic deity, or related to him or her by some bond of family connection. In the process of absorption, the deities brought with them their priests (of non-Brāhmaṇa and even untouchable castes) and their cults also, with the effect that, when they were absorbed and widely worshipped in higher circles, literary justification, both vernacular and Sanskritic, had to be found for them. In this way was necessitated the composition not only of vernacular songs and narratives, but also of some of the later Upapurāṇas or the interpolation of narratives concerning these deities in the later semi-classical Paurāṇic literature. The Maṅgala literature became the *Rāmāyaṇa* of the masses in many areas in East and West Bengal.

THE CULT OF THE MAṄGALA DEITIES

The cult of these deities included not only private worship at home by men and the adoption of vows (*vrata*) by women, but also periodic or seasonal gatherings (*bāroyāri*) in public places and big private halls of worship (*Caṇḍīmaṇḍapa*) or halls of religious dance (*nāṭamandira*) attached to a temple to celebrate the exploits of the deities and also to offer them special worship on important occasions like marriage, wearing of the sacred thread, etc. The celebration took the form of musical performance, the main singer (*gāyen*) with his fly-whisk (*cāmara*) and tinkling anklets (*nūpura*) taking the help of repeaters (*dohār*) and instrumentalists. The dates fixed for worship generally have reference to the deity worshipped ; the general plan of such celebration is that a small period, say, of eight days, is devoted to an intense and continued remembrance of the deity daily in two sittings, one by day and another by night, through recital of different themes (*pālā*) extolling his power and beneficence. One of these days, generally towards the end of the celebration, practically the whole night is spent in religious singing. This vigil is known as *jāgaraṇa*. The last-day song (or the whole series) is called *aṣṭamaṅgala*. Perhaps because of the name, the celebration usually begins on a Tuesday (Maṅgala-vāra), and the history of the introduction of the worship among men is recounted with a direction that, if any one wished prosperity, he should worship the deity with proper respect.

From these tales, it appears that the method adopted by these deities to compel people to acknowledge them was by threatening them with dire calamity, if they were not accepted, and promising earthly prosperity, if accepted. Reference may be made, in this connection, to Manasā, who was apparently absorbed from Dravidian and other sources, but was not accepted as a deity till she had brought calamity to some leaders of the trading community who had refused to recognize her. The interest of the story lies in setting up certain standards of virtue like the chastity and devotion of Behulā, who brought her dead husband to life with the help of the appeased Manasā, whom her father-in-law had not accepted and thus offended.

Similarly, the worship of Caṇḍī, who is not to be identified with the Aryanized deity of the Purāṇas and is akin to the *mātṛkās* or *yoginīs* of the Śakti cult, was initiated only when she brought misfortune to a rich merchant and was finally accepted in the community. References to Caṇḍī are also found in Buddhist and aboriginal sources in addition to the Paurāṇic. In the *Durgā-maṅgala*, the character of the deity is considerably transformed from that of the fighting Durgā to that of a gentle daughter returning to her parents' home, during the autumnal (or vernal) festival in Bengal, with her two sons, Gaṇeśa and Kārttikeya, and her two daughters, Lakṣmī and Sarasvatī. The *āgamanī* (welcome) songs of joy and the *vijayā* (send-off) songs of sadness, connected with the worship, can still be heard in the country-side of Bengal along with the chanting of the *Caṇḍī-* or *Durgā-saptaśatī* of the *Mārkaṇḍeya Purāṇa*.

Another deity known as Dharma has been derived from diverse religious sources—Vaidika, Bauddha, and aboriginal. His worship is specially wide-spread in the western part of Bengal and is celebrated with solemnity with a stone, mostly tortoise-shaped, as his emblem. Identified probably with the Sun, he has his celebrations over twelve days (probably because the Ādityas were twelve, according to the months or signs of the zodiac), and the musical performance by night draws respectable gatherings. Latterly, he became identified with Śiva, and the musical recitals in his honour were transformed into the *gājana* of Śiva.

The pre-Aryan Śiva was very popular in western Bengal, where he was, and still is, celebrated in various forms, especially in the month of Caitra (March-April). Men and women, particularly the followers of the Nātha cult, which contains Śaiva and Buddhistic elements, celebrate the festival of Śiva by accepting a temporary monastic vow and singing his exploits (*Śivāyana* or *Śiva-maṅgala*), which is known as the *gambhīrā* in Malda District and *gājana* elsewhere. Fairs held on such occasions draw large gatherings in important centres of Śiva-worship, and the marriage of Śiva and Pārvatī is enacted.

In certain non-ascetic forms of celebration, *yātrā,* or a dramatic representation of the lives of the deities, is performed. Where an elaborate performance is not done, the celebration takes the form of *nāṭa-gīta,* in which the dialogue element is mostly absent and lyrical songs take its place.

PAINTINGS AND PUPPET-SHOWS

Coarser representations of religious themes, to excite popular devotion, take the form of exhibiting scrolls of paintings (*paṭa*) depicting the life and activity of the epic, Paurāṇic, and popular deities to the accompaniment of songs. There are isolated paintings (like the earlier *Yama-paṭa* mentioned in the *Mudrārākṣasa*) which have no musical accompaniment; these are known as *cauka-paṭas* or isolated framed drawings. But there are *dīghala-paṭas* or long scrolls of paintings, representing a complete legend, which are exhibited with suitable accompanying songs. According to seasons, these *paṭas* would be different; for instance, the theme of the *Manasā-maṅgala* would be exhibited during the rains when serpent-bite takes place on a large scale, whereas during the harvesting season, when the circular dance (*rāsa*) of Kṛṣṇa is celebrated, scrolls representing Vaiṣṇava themes are shown round the villages. In this way, a fillip is given to the enjoyment of the festival of the time. The horrors of different hells might be similarly presented through scrolls to induce people to keep to the moral path.

A still more crude but realistic representation of religious themes is done through puppet-shows, generally in fairs. This representation by means of solid figures draws very little upon imagination, which description and painting do, because here even children and illiterate people can enjoy the realistic form in which mythological characters of some events described in the Purāṇas or the epics are shown. In North India, the show is managed by men remaining invisible behind a curtain and holding aloft the figures and manipulating the locomotion and gestures by their own movement and by pulling the strings attached to the various parts of the images or dolls. Suitable dialogues are introduced by the puppet-manipulators, as if the puppets themselves were carrying on the conversation. Professional parties go round the country-side on festive occasions on hire to arrange exhibitions and regale the large gathering with their entertaining shows. The puppet-shows, however, are primarily intended for producing mirth, though those unable to read the tales are enlightened about ancient events and mythological themes through visual representation.

POPULAR RELIGIOUS EDUCATION

We shall now notice the last stages of the development of old popular religious education and its degeneration and virtual disappearance. The enjoyment of a religious theme depends upon a faith in its reality. Once that faith wanes, the instructions lose their efficacy and fall flat upon the audience, who come more for entertainment than for spiritual edification. Again, the presentation of a religious theme in the past often meant a fair amount of expense, as the function lasted for a number of days. Rich patrons were needed to run these religious functions and keep the tradition alive. In the unsettled times after the decline of the power of the emperors of Delhi, rich patrons were difficult to find. Matters became worse by the inroad of English upon vernacular education. As the educated classes began to lose touch with the country-side and its innocent enjoyments, they began to fancy other types of composition and representation which, though nominally based upon the old religious literature, were really mere feats of intellect and ready wit, which urban aristocracy enjoyed and patronized. Thus the old *pāñcālī,* which was at one time a synonym of the Maṅgala literature as discoursed peripatetically, was revived in urban areas with a new motif altogether. The themes were supposed to be Paurāṇic in many cases, but the urban people demanded excitement which the dull monotony of the old singers failed to produce. They therefore fastened upon certain aspects of the life of the gods of yore which were likely to yield more excitement.

The love theme of Rādhā and Kṛṣṇa had more of erotic than of devotional elements, and the presentation degenerated also into a contest for supremacy between two contending groups which began to take the place of a single party of narrators or singers. One of the parties would pose certain problems through songs, and the other would reply similarly thereto. Naturally, the musical element almost evaporated as excitement increased, and the ready composition and reply and rugged versification became the major part of the entertainment. While the ancient form survived in the performance called *tarjā,* where a singer, a drummer, and a musician sufficed to carry on the show, the *kavis* or *kavivālās* (extempore versifiers) formed two groups, each opposing and trying to excel the other by impromptu answers and witty sayings. Similarly, the old *pāñcālī* degenerated into a not very savoury representation of Rādhā and Kṛṣṇa, Rāma and Sītā, Śiva and Gaurī, and was, in course of time, practically secularized.

Further degeneration took place when the system of showing comparative musical talent was introduced. Different *ākhḍās* grew up to coach singers of mythological themes. But, as the name indicates, they were really 'wrestling grounds', of which the main objective was training for winning in a competitive test. Two musical parties would show their talents one after another to win the vote of the audience, but the urban atmosphere was not propitious for the retention of religious purity. An offshoot of this *ākhḍāi* (competitive) song was the half *ākhḍāi,* in which a single singer showed his ready wit by replying to questions of his critical and querying hearers through ready verses, often leaving the music behind. He often deviated considerably from orthodox descriptions of religious anecdotes and concocted stories of his own to meet the situation in hand. The last stage was reached when perverse moral taste and acrimonious tendency invaded what was primarily intended to be the narration of a religious theme. This last form, known as *kheuḍ,* is really nothing but indecent sallies of wit intended to floor the opposite party by ready repartee and scurrilous insinuation. No wonder that this system should die a natural death, when the moral sense of educated people reasserted itself and noble religious reformations improved the moral outlook and, at the same time, damped the Paurāṇic ardour of the then educated classes.

It is not to be concluded, however, that the social aspect of religious enthusiasm disappeared altogether. As education spread and people began to possess first-hand information of their own scriptures, and as hostile attacks upon indigenous religion by alien faiths began to be resented, even the reformed ways of religious life felt the need of a congregational mode of religious enjoyment. Today, religious music and religious processions have come back into the life of the community. Many well-informed teachers and preachers have taken upon themselves the responsibility of explaining the scriptures to a large educated public, through the press and the platform, and religious discourses in the form of *kathakatā* are given by men of faith, whose intimate knowledge of religious topics is responsible for diffusing both enlightenment and entertainment. Even dramatic representation of religious themes is coming back to its own not only through the stage, but also through the cinema. The temporary obscuration from which religious interest suffered is now lifting, and there is today a more wide-spread knowledge of the sublime religious beliefs of ancient India, for which the awakening of the national consciousness is partly responsible. With this turn of events, it is hoped that new methods of touching the hearts of the populace, in consonance with the spread of education, will be evolved, and the continuity of popular religious instruction will be maintained in the new democratic set-up.

PART IV

RELIGIONS FROM BEYOND THE BORDERS

38

ZOROASTRIANISM

THERE is a natural desire in everybody to know something about the lives of great men of other lands. And if that person is the founder and prophet of a great religion, it is specially desirable to know something about his life and his work. The founders of every faith have been men of very high spiritual stature, and therefore their position in the history of our world must be supreme.

BIRTH AND PARENTAGE OF ZARATHUSHTRA

Maharṣi[1] Zarathushtra was one of these great ones of the earth. At the time of his birth, the ancient faith of Iran, taught by earlier teachers, had fallen into the hands of evil people. Truth, gentleness, charity, and other virtues seemed to have disappeared, and Iran was lying crushed. There was none to lead the people aright. At this critical period in the world's history, so say the *Gāthās* of the Avesta, Mother Earth appeared before the throne of the Almighty in the shape of a cow (*Geush urvan*). She raised aloud her voice in complaint: 'I have been oppressed and outraged by tyrants, and I cannot bear this suffering any longer. Why hast Thou created me? I see no helper. Save me and send a hero to rescue me.' Hearing these words, the supreme Lord, the creator of Mother Earth, soothed her anguish and said: 'I shall send down Zarathushtra. He shall undertake thy succour, and shall become thy saviour.'

Soon after this, in the ancient city of Rae (Ragha), a son was born to Pourushaspa, a prince of the royal house of Iran. Pourushaspa was as virtuous as he was learned, and he was deeply devoted to the worship of God. His wife, Dugdhovā, was in every way his worthy partner. There existed deep love between these two, and they had both dedicated themselves to the service of the Lord.

Later tradition has enriched the life of the prophet with a number of miracles. Before the child was born, the tyrant chiefs and oppressors in Iran began to have evil dreams. They encountered ill omens, and soothsayers told them that the child of Pourushaspa would be their destroyer. They therefore began to plan measures to kill the child before he was born. Pourushaspa heard of this and so he sent away his dear wife to her father's home at Rae. So bright was the divine light radiating

[1] Zoroastrians prefix the epithet *asho* before his name. This word has about the same meaning as the Sanskrit word *ṛṣi*.

from the child that it could be seen emanating even through the body of the mother. As the time of birth drew near, the body of mother Dugdhovā became more and more radiant with the light that was within her.

Children always cry as they are born into this world, but the face of this child was wreathed in smiles: it seemed as if he had brought down with him the joy of heaven. He was given the name Spitama after a great and heroic ancestor. Even during the first few months of his life, the evil ones made several attempts to destroy him, but God had sent him specially to redeem suffering humanity and He protected His servan..

ZARATHUSHTRA'S EARLY LIFE AND SPIRITUAL ATTAINMENT

Pourushaspa could quite clearly see the signs that marked out the great teacher. So he himself undertook the teaching of this son of his.[2] It was the father who taught the future p: ›phet his first lessons in love and devotion to God. In those days in Iran, ɿ young man, when he attained his fifteenth year, sought out a wife, married her, and settled down to rear a family. But instead of entering the state of a householder (*gṛhastha*), Spitama retired into solitude at the age of fifteen. He renounced all worldly pleasures, possessions, and desire for a successful life in the world. In his solitary retirement, he strove to unite himself with his Maker, and in this supreme effort he spent fifteen strenuous years.

When a servant of the Lord undertakes the work of saving the world, the powers of darkness assemble all their forces to break up his preparations. To hinder Lord Buddha in his work the demon Māra and all his host came to him, as he sat under the Bodhi-tree in meditation. Jesus was tempted by Satan, who promised him the empire of the whole world. So also was Spitama attacked by the spirit of all evil, as he sat in meditation. The spirit of evil, Ahriman (Aṅgra-Mainyu), put before him all sorts of temptations, promised him the sovereignty of the world, told him that no good would come to him from God, and that he would come to grief in the end. But Spitama was neither afraid of the threats, nor was he tempted by honeyed words. His reply to Ahriman was, 'My life might be forfeit, the bones of my body might be scattered, but I will never give up my faith in, and devotion to, Mazdā'. On hearing this reply, the wicked Ahriman fled howling into the darkness impenetrable, which was his home. Spitama achieved his goal and stood forth in all grandeur as Zarathushtra (*zaratha*, 'golden', *ushtra*, 'light'), which means 'he of the golden light'. After achieving Illumination, he was refulgent with all the light of divine wisdom and heavenly love; hence this name.

[2] Pourushaspa had other sons and daughters. Spitama was the third of his five sons.

ZARATHUSHTṚA'S MESSAGE AND ITS PROPAGATION

Zarathushtra came back home to his own family, full of unshakable faith in God and in his own mission. As soon as he arrived home he began to preach. His message was no new one. He taught the same eternal Truth; he exhorted men to worship the same supreme Being, as all other great ones had done in other lands and in other ages. The eternal Truth (Sanātana Dharma) is forgotten time after time; hence in different ages and in different languages it has to be repeated again and again.

The first to accept the message of Zarathushtra was his cousin Maidyoimāoṅgha, the son of Pourushaspa's brother Ārāsti. For many years Maidyoimāoṅgha was his only disciple, for the prophet's divine mission and his teachings were not properly appreciated by the worldly-wise people of western Iran. Zarathushtra also wandered for years from one end of Iran to another, but in vain. It was Bākhdhi (Bactria), far to the east, that first welcomed the prophet. The ruler of that land, Vīshtāspa, accepted the new faith, and with him his two ministers, the brothers Jāmāspa and Frashaoshtra, also became the disciples of Zarathushtra.

After this the new religion of Zarathushtra progressed rapidly. Vīshtāspa had, indeed, to undertake several wars in defence of the new creed, but truth triumphed at last. The wicked princes of Iran were defeated, and peace and justice were re-established. Zarathushtra lived to an advanced age to see the complete triumph of his religion and became a martyr in its cause.

There are various opinions regarding the date of Zarathushtra. The ordinarily accepted opinion among western scholars puts it at about 1000 B.C. Other opinions assign him to sixth century B.C. We may safely assert that the great prophet of Iran was a contemporary of the *ṛṣis* who composed the earlier hymns of the *Ṛg-Veda,* for not only is the language closely similar, but the contents of his *Gāthās* show a marked similarity to those of the Veda. There is, besides, another Parsi tradition which says that the successors of Zarathushtra who held the highest pontifical seat at Ragha, of whom several were great reformers, also bore the name Zarathushtṛa or Zarathushtratema (most resembling Zarathushtra). In fact, the spiritual head of Iranian priesthood always bore the name of the founder. It is further stated that Zarathushtra, mentioned in the Sassanian tradition, was not the founder, but the last great reformer bearing that name. In any case, the Sassanian tradition, upon which western scholars rely, is very doubtful, and it may be merely asserted at present that he was a contemporary of the earlier Vedic *ṛṣis*.

RELIGIOUS BELIEFS OF THE ARYANS OF INDIA AND IRAN

Let us consider first the religion of the people of Iran before Zarathushtra's advent. In far-off ancient days, there lived somewhere about Central Asia a great people who called themselves *ārya.*[3] They were very proud of this name, and the epithet *anārya* was regarded as the worst form of insult. They lived for many centuries in the region of the Pamirs and observed the same set of social and religious customs and spoke one language. They worshipped the great powers created by God—the sun, the fire, the moon, the waters, the wind, etc. They composed hymns to these 'shining ones' (*devas*) and chanted them during ceremonials to the accompaniment of music. But they had full realization of the oneness of God, the one life-giver, the Father of us all, who is behind and beyond all the phenomenal manifestations. They called Him Ahura (Asura), the Lord of life, and they knew that He is the only Existence, whatever the name by which He may be invoked: 'Existence is one, sages call it differently, as Fire, Death, or Wind' (*Ṛ.V.*, I.164.46). The Upaniṣads have called Him 'the One without a second'—'*ekamevādvitīyam*' (*Chā. U.*, VI.2.1).

The ideals of the Aryans were very noble and lofty. Their greatest ideal in life was expressed by the Vedic word *ṛta.* This same word is found in the Avesta as *asha.*[4] The word has almost the same connotation as the later Hindu word *dharma,* which Buddha also adopted in his religion as *dhamma.*

These people recognized three main divisions of society, Brāhmaṇa (the teacher, Avesta: Āthravan); Kṣatriya (the ruler, Avesta: Rathaeshtār); and Vaiśya (the agriculturist, Avesta: Vāstryosh). Non-Aryans, who were the subject races, generally formed the fourth division called Śūdra (the servant, Avesta: Hutokhsha). The first three classes, i.e. all the Aryans, had to go through the *upanayana* ceremony at a certain age, when the child was invested with certain symbolical garments and received as a member of their faith. This was their 'second birth', and they were then named *dvijas* (twice-born). The Parsis have the same ceremony today, which they call the *navajota* (new birth). This marked the spiritual birth, admission into the *dharma-saṅgha* (the fraternity of the faithful). This sacrament was for boys as well as for girls, and though the Hindus have, at present, dropped it for girls, the Parsis have still kept it for both. From that time onwards, the Aryan *dvija* could be recognized by a special dress. We find the relics of this among the Hindus in the *yajñopavīta* (sacred thread), the *mekhalā*

[3] The term '*ārya*' is used here in the restricted sense of 'Indo-Iranian', as these were the only people who called themselves by that proud name.

[4] *Ṛta = areta = arta = arsha = asha,* these are the variants of the word found in the Avesta. The word '*ṛṣi*' originally meant 'one who possesses *ṛta*'; in Avesta we have the word '*ratu*' used in the sense of *ṛṣi*.

(sacred girdle), and the *śikhā* (tuft of hair on the top of the head), and among the Parsis in the *sudreh* (sacred shirt), the *kustī* (girdle), and the cap which always covers the head.

RELIGIOUS CRISIS IN IRAN BEFORE THE ADVENT OF ZARATHUSHTRA

This great race, following the same ideals and observing the same ancient faith (Sanātana Dharma), lived as one people for many centuries. Then there came a division. Very probably, it arose in some dispute over religious matters, for certain ancient words relating to worship came now to mean the exact opposite with one or the other of the two factions. The Hindus inverted the meaning of *asura* (*ahura*), and, in their turn, the Iranians took the word '*deva*' (*daeva*) in the sense of a 'power of evil', a demon. So also among the Iranians the ancient deities, like Indra,[5] the Nāsatyas, Vidhātṛ, and others, became 'demons'. Yet Haoma (Soma), Hvar (Svar, Sūrya), Māoṅgha (Mās, Candramas), Mithra (Mitra), Yima (Yama), and many others continued to be the 'adorable ones' for both the divisions. Both branches also retained most of their ancient ceremonies and sacraments, as well as their social divisions and customs.

In the course of ages, the worship of the one supreme Father and life-giver (*asuraḥ pitā naḥ*) was gradually forgotten, and the supreme position of Ahura came to be occupied by certain minor deities. Side by side with this, the noble Aryan path of *asha* (*ashahe pantāo = ṛtasya panthāḥ*) was also lost sight of. Old ways were given up ; tyrants obtained supreme power over Iran, and the good and the pious were oppressed. At such a crisis in the history of the Iranian race, the great teacher Zarathushtra was sent down upon our earth to teach again to the people the worship of Ahura-Mazdā and to point out anew the path of *asha*.

LITERATURE OF ZOROASTRIANISM

The teachings of Zarathushtra have been, fortunately, still preserved for us almost in his own words. In the course of the ages which followed, Iran had to suffer at least two catastrophic defeats, which have been recorded in history. The first was in 331 B.C. at the hands of Alexander of Macedon. The second was at the hands of the Arabs in A.D. 651. On both these occasions the scriptures were scattered and destroyed,[6] but

[5] Strangely enough, Indra as Vṛtrahan (Avesta: Verethraghna) is worshipped by the Iranians. In later days he is the 'angel' Behrām (Varharan), the giver of victory. He is the special *iṣṭadeva* of the Sassanians.

[6] Alexander himself destroyed the Zoroastrian scriptures, when he wantonly burnt down the palace at Persepolis. At the Arab conquest the scriptures were not destroyed immediately, but some centuries later. We find a Zoroastrian priest giving a detailed table of contents of all the twenty-one sacred volumes (the *nasks*) of Zoroastrian faith in the reign of the Khalif

a good portion of them was preserved, as the priests had most of the important texts by heart, and these were handed down from generation to generation. The most important texts were contained in the collection known as the *Yasna* (*yajña*), and this has been preserved almost intact, for it was used all through the year for the daily, monthly, and yearly (seasonal) ceremonies. It consists of 72 *hās* (sections), and among these are to be found the precious *Gāthās* of Zarathushtra. These are five in number: *Ahunavaiti* (*Yasna,* XXVIII-XXXIV), *Ushtavaiti* (*Yasna,* XLIII-XLVI), *Spentā-Mainyu* (*Yasna,* XLVII-L), *Vohu-Khshathra* (*Yasna,* LI), and *Vahishtā-Ishti* (*Yasna,* LIII). These five, especially the first, contain the whole of the prophet's teaching, and thus they form the very foundations of Zoroastrian religion.

Zarathushtra's message can be treated under three heads: (i) the acknowledgement of the supreme Creator, Ahura-Mazdā, (ii) the problem of good and evil, and (iii) the teaching about how to live our lives in the world.

AHURA-MAZDĀ AND HIS SIX GREAT EMANATIONS

Zarathushtra revived the ancient teaching that there is but one God who is the Creator of the whole universe. 'There is none beside the Creator Ahura-Mazdā; everything emanates from Him and merges back in Him at the end'—this, in short, is the teaching. Zarathushtra has strongly deprecated the worship of any other being, and he, as it were, removed at one stroke all other deities from the religion. Ahura-Mazdā is formless (like the Nirguṇa Brahman of the Hindus), and so there is only one way in which ordinary mortals may worship Him, or can even think of Him. That way is through His six great 'aspects', which are called Ameshā-Spentās (the holy immortals).[7] They are Asha-Vahishta (Ardibehesht), Vohu-Mano (Bahman), Khshathra-Vairya (Shahrivar), Spentā-Ārmaiti (Spendārmad), Haurvatāt (Khordād), and Ameretāt (Amardād).[8] These may also be called 'emanations' or 'rays' from the eternal Source of all light, and they are indeed spoken of as such in the *Gāthās*. They occupy the most important place in Zoroastrian theology. The aspirant has to develop along one of these at a time, and meditating on these successively, he integrates them, one by one, within himself.

The Asha-Vahishta or *asha* (*ṛta*) had been a well-known idea from very ancient times He represents the divine will. It is on account of

Al Ma'mūn (A.D. 813-33). Practically all, except two nearly complete books and fragments from three or four more out of the twenty-one, have been destroyed.

[7] Some writers compare them to the 'archangels'; but that is a later idea.

[8] The names in brackets are their modern forms.

asha that Ahura-Mazdā Himself is at the head of all evolution and progress. The best description of *asha* may be given in the words of Tennyson as:

> That God, which ever lives and loves,
> One God, one law, one element,
> And one far-off divine event,
> To which the whole creation moves.

Asha is the 'divine event' which, at the beginning of creation, was embodied in the divine will. In a secondary sense, *asha* means submission to this will—a virtue which we, as human beings, ought to develop. It means working in accord with the divine law, helping the work of evolution and progress. Submission (not blind, but with full understanding) to the will of God—what the Prophet of Arabia called '*islam*'—is *asha*. One of the finest passages in the Zoroastrian scriptures expresses the hope: 'Through the best *asha,* through the highest *asha,* may we see Thee (Ahura-Mazdā), may we come near unto Thee, may we be in perfect union with Thee' (*Yasna,* LX.12).

The idea of *asha* is deeply philosophical, and is well above the grasp of the average man. It is hard to meditate upon this abstraction, and the prophet therefore gave a symbol for *asha.* Fire represents this first of the holy immortals, and is the physical representative of the divine emanation. There seem to be two reasons why fire has been chosen. In the first place, fire changes everything it touches into itself; and secondly, the flame always leaps upwards. For this reason the Zoroastrians are 'Fire-worshippers', and Asha-Vahishta (the best *asha*) is the Lord of fire, both earthly and divine.

Vohu-Mano (good mind) is the second ray of God. The mind of the Lord must be good, and therefore everything He creates must also be good. Vohu-Mano is divine wisdom; and his other name is Love. He is the 'strong Son of God, immortal love'. He leads us into the path of *asha,* and in our greatest difficulties he sustains and supports us. This love embraces not only all humanity, but also our 'lesser brothers' of the animal kingdom. So Vohu-Mano is the 'guardian angel' of animals. By fostering cattle, by giving them fodder and drink, and by protecting them and being kind to them, we can best please him, and in return he sends us his blessings. Parsis, though usually meat-eaters, abstain from meat on the days consecrated to Vohu-Mano and his associate 'angels',[9] and the orthodox amongst them abstain from meat during the whole of the eleventh month, which bears the name of Bahman. The 'gift of Vohu-Mano' is the pure mind, which shows us clearly our upward path and brings us wisdom.

[9] These are the second, twelfth. fourteenth, and twenty-first days of each Parsi month.

Khshathra-Vairya (the power supreme) is divine activity and creation.[10] Western scholars often translate the name as 'the Kingdom of God', which, though happy, is not quite exact. God is the sole Creator of the universe, and Khshathra represents the creative power which creates and maintains all that exists. To human beings he teaches the path of action (Karma-yoga), and his followers become workers for the Lord. On the physical plane, he rules over the mineral kingdom, because the possession of this measures the strength and power of a race upon earth.

The remaining three holy immortals represent the Mother-aspect of God, while the first three represent the Father-aspect. This is a very important factor, which shows that Zarathushtra regarded man and woman as absolutely equal in all spiritual matters.

Spentā-Ārmaiti (holy piety) represents unswerving faith and single-minded devotion towards God. She rules over religion. At the time of the 'second birth', the child 'chooses' her as its friend and mother. All *dvijas* are under her special care. On the physical plane, she is our Mother Earth, who sustains us all upon her ample bosom. During life the Zoroastrian is in her charge, and after death he returns to her.[11]

Haurvatāt represents the wholeness, the perfection of the Supreme. God is perfect, and each soul has to be perfect 'as the Father, who is in Heaven, is perfect'. She rules over the waters, the element of purity and health. Both she and the next Ameshā-Spentā have been mentioned but rarely in the scriptures.

Ameretāt (immortality) is the constant companion of Haurvatāt. She represents immortal life and frees mankind from the fear of death. She rules over the vegetable kingdom, and is closely associated with the tree of life and the heavenly plant of immortality.

These six, together with Ahura-Mazdā as the seventh, make up the sevenfold Lord, held up by the prophet as worthy of our profoundest veneration and love. Fire was the outward symbol of the faith, and Zarathushtra taught the Iranians to worship *ātar* (fire) as the purest and holiest of God's creation.[12]

[10] Note that these first three Ameshā-Spentās represent the *icchā, jñāna,* and *kriyā* of the supreme Godhead.

[11] After the dead body is deposited in the Tower of Silence, all assembled chant an invocation saluting Ārmaiti.

[12] This is the reason why Parsis do not burn their dead, because contact with the dead and decaying flesh would pollute the holy fire. For the same reason they can neither bury the dead body, nor cast it into water. So they build walled-in platforms of masonry, open to the sky, and therein expose the dead body. It is soon devoured by birds, and the bones crumble to dust by the action of the sun, the rain, and the wind. This bone-dust is finally swept up into the large pit in the centre of the tower, where all, rich and poor, wise and foolish, good and bad, at last mingle together in the bosom of the mighty Mother, Spentā-Ārmaiti.

Besides these six and the fire, Zarathushtra has proclaimed the eminence of another divine power and has put him on a level just lower than that of the holy immortals. He is the *yazata* (the adorable) Sraosha. The name is derived from the root *śru* (to hear), and the meaning is almost the same as that of the Sanskrit word *śuśrūṣa*. Sraosha is the highest virtue for a man to cultivate ; so, as a divine being, he represents devotion to God, unquestioning faith in His laws, and obedience to His will. When we fully attain Sraosha, we see the path of salvation straight before us. In a prayer composed by Zarathushtra himself it is said:

'O Mazdā, may Sraosha go, together with Vohu-Mano, to the person whom Thou lovest.'

This means that, if God's grace descends upon a person, the desire to serve Him is kindled within him, and his mind becomes pure.

Besides those mentioned above, none of the other divinities of later Zoroastrian theology are named in the *Gāthās.* The obvious conclusion is that the prophet has emphasized the worship of the sevenfold Ahura-Mazdā ; and as the first and most important step towards salvation, he has pointed out the attainment of Sraosha, i.e. obedience to God's will. In the *Gāthās,* it is very necessary to be clear about the exact sense in which each of the names has been used. Sometimes these are used in their literal meaning, and at others they indicate a divine power, an aspect, or an emanation of God.

THE PROBLEM OF GOOD AND EVIL

The very first question tackled in the *Gāthā Ahunavaiti* is the problem of good and evil in the world. This constitutes the essential philosophy of Zarathushtra's message. This teaching has been given in a few but very clear words. We are taught that at first two Mainyus (spirits) were created by Ahura-Mazdā. These were opposed to each other and shall ever remain so. 'When first these twin spirits came together, one created life and the other not-life, so that creation's purpose might be fulfilled' (*Yasna,* XXX.4). These two Mainyus are called Spenta-Mainyu (the good spirit) and Aṅgra-Mainyu (Ahriman, the evil spirit). And manifestation is possible only when these two come together. If we look a little below the surface, we see clearly that the evil spirit, too, is a creation of God, and as such he aids us to realize the true meaning of 'good', and thus helps forward the march of evolution. But the evil spirit is ultimately destined to be defeated, because the only reason for his being is the realization of good in the end. The deeper we are enmeshed in the world of material objects, the stronger is the hold of evil upon us. But we are from God and are therefore, in essence, good. Spenta-Mainyu, too, has his share in our making, and our work in this world is to allow the light of good to shine forth more and more clearly from within us.

From another point of view, Aṅgra-Mainyu is merely an illusion, a negation. His 'creation' is 'not-life',[13] which is pure negation. So evil is merely a negation, an *abhāva*. Still it appears to us as very real, because we have the veil of ignorance before our eyes. When this veil is lifted, the effulgent light of Spenta-Mainyu shall shine forth undimmed. Just as light and shade are eternally found together, so must good and evil be always associated together. As long as we remain in the shade and cannot see the light, so long do we grope about thinking that darkness is something very real. But really it is mere negation, the mere absence of light.

This teaching about the twin spirits has led many western scholars to call Zoroastrianism a sort of 'dualism'. But the two have been categorically mentioned as being 'created by Mazdā' ; so the ultimate source of all is 'the One without a second', and the teaching of Zarathushtra is pure monotheism.

HOW TO LIVE IN THE WORLD

All this is pure philosophy dear to the heart of the learned scholar and thinker. But the average man understands only devotion to God as Father and Friend, and looks upon the Ameshā-Spentās as great archangels. He looks upon Aṅgra-Mainyu as some terrible demon and strives to keep him off. He is afraid of this arch-fiend, just as a child is afraid of the dark. If Zarathushtra had confined himself merely to these metaphysical speculations, his religion could never have had such extensive acceptance as it actually once had. There was something else in his great message which appealed directly to the average man. This was the teaching regarding the best use to be made of our lives in the world of men. It is this which has caused him to be remembered with love and reverence by millions of human beings during all these centuries.

The path to God taught in every religion is found, in the last analysis, to be threefold. A man can find his God by the *yoga* of *jñāna* (knowledge), of *bhakti* (love), or of *karma* (service). The great saviours of humanity, of course, realized within themselves all these three before they attained perfection. But the average man is attracted by one of the three according to his innate nature. As among individuals, so also among nations, some can follow one path more easily than others. But, whether it be an individual or a nation, it is only by following one's own particular bent

[13] Most students of the *Gāthās* have translated this word here as 'death'. But the original is *a-jyāiti* (not-life) ; by missing the negative prefix we lose the whole implication of the passage.

that one's destiny is best fulfilled. The path of Iran was that of Karma-yoga, and it was along that path that the Iranians reached the zenith of their power. Zarathushtra, in his religion, laid special emphasis on this method of 'attainment through service of humanity'. Parsis even now have remained true to this teaching, and their position in India today is the direct result of the life of service they are trying to lead.

THE AHUNA-VAIRYA MANTRA OF SERVICE

It is mentioned in one of the sections of the *Yasna* (*hā* 19) that at the time of creation Ahura-Mazdā chanted the *manthra* (Sanskrit, *mantra*) known as Ahuna-Vairya, and that this was the Word that brought forth all the universe. When Aṅgra-Mainyu, the spirit of negation, brought forth all his wiles to tempt Zarathushtra, the prophet chanted aloud the same *mantra*, and the arch-fiend with all his hosts fled. This *mantra* is regarded to be the holiest and the most powerful among the Avestan texts. Often it has been said that 'Ahuna-Vairya protects the body'. In another place, it has been asserted that, if this *mantra* is chanted but once by any person 'with proper intonation and rhythm' and with a correct realization of its meaning, the religious merit accruing therefrom is equivalent to that of reciting all the remaining holy texts. There can be only one rational explanation for this belief, viz. that it embodies the great truths of life, that it contains the very core and essence of Zarathushtra's message. Leaving aside the deeper spiritual implications, even from the ordinary point of view, this *mantra* teaches us some of the eternal verities, and from this one can easily understand why the Parsis have still clung to their ancient faith. A translation of this *mantra*, which consists of three lines, is given below:

> 'Just as an *ahu* (a king) (is) all-powerful (upon earth), so also (is) a *ratu* (a *ṛṣi*) (all-powerful everywhere) by reason of his Asha ;
> The gifts of Vohu-Mano are for (those who are) working for the Lord of life ;
> And the Khshathra of Ahura (is bestowed) upon him who constitutes himself the helper of the meek or lowly.'[14]

The first line compares the rank and power of the *ahu* and the *ratu*. By *ahu* is meant a chief upon earth, a ruler on the physical plane. A *ratu*, on the other hand, is a *ṛṣi*, a master of divine wisdom, a ruler in the spiritual

[14] The translation has been arranged in the order of the original. It must be mentioned here that there have been over two dozen different renderings of this famous *mantra*. Each scholar has done it according to his own particular bent of mind. Without claiming any finality or any authority in this matter, the present author gives here his own version for whatever it may be worth.

world. However great an *ahu* may be upon earth, the *ratu* is greater in his power and his position. The *ahu's* authority is confined to his own domain. But the *ratu* is revered not only in every country of the world, but also in the higher world of spirit. And this greatness is due to his *asha*. The great soul who has understood the secret of *asha* attains a very high rank among God's workers. As in Āryāvarta, so also in Iran, the Āthravan (spiritual teacher) was always regarded as higher than the king. In Avestan prayers, the 'Lord of religion' (Zarathushtra) ranks higher than the 'Lord of the land'. This is due to the divine light to which the former has attained.

Next we are told that a person who wishes to tread the path of *asha* should give a particular direction to all his actions. He should be continuously 'working for the Lord of life'. Treading the path of *asha* means doing the will of God ; in other words, helping in the advancement and evolution of the world. A man so desirous should dedicate every act he performs to God, he must do everything 'in His name'.[15]

The second line states that the reward for such deeds done for the Lord consists of the gifts of Vohu-Mano. Vohu-Mano is good mind or love, and his gifts mean the cleansing and purifying of the lower mind. The mud and the slime of selfishness settle down, and the mind becomes like a clear mountain lake ; the image of the Lord can then be clearly reflected from its crystal waters. The aspirant can now understand more and more clearly the will of God and can therefore follow it better. He becomes calm and is without passion, and understands the true difference between the real and the unreal, the substance and the shadow.

And the last line declares that he who makes himself a helper of the meek gets the Khshathra (strength) of the Lord.[16] By the word 'meek' here is meant anyone who lacks anything in life. If we possess anything which another lacks, it is our duty to share it with him. We have to supply our brothers' wants from our own God-given stores. Some are rich in money and material possessions, some in learning and wisdom, others in strength of the body, and yet others in spiritual wealth. But these riches bestowed by God are not meant to be kept selfishly for one's own use, but to be shared with our brothers. We are not to become stagnant pools, but flowing channels of God's mercy. Our wealth and knowledge and strength never diminish by sharing ; rather, they increase, inasmuch as they would then bring us greater satisfaction. And there is the promise of the Lord that those that give shall be given in greater measure. The greater the

[15] Cf. *B.G.*, IX. 27.

[16] It may be noted that the first three holy immortals—Asha, Vohu-Mano, and Khshathra —are mentioned by name in the three lines. There is a deeper esoteric meaning in this.

measure of these blessings poured upon us, the greater the opportunity offered us to serve His creatures. Thus the reward for serving our brother man is opportunity for greater service. In one word, service is the sum and substance of the Zoroastrian ideal of life. Service is the opposite of self-seeking, and the path of service is but one aspect of the path of *asha*.

Thus we see how sublime a *mantra* Ahuna-Vairya really is. One who chants it, 'fully understanding its meaning', would indeed defeat the 'demons of darkness'. The first *Gāthā* of Zarathushtra is named *Ahunavaiti*, because it is, in a sense, a commentary on the Ahuna-Vairya.

THE THREE GREAT COMMANDMENTS

The prophet of Iran gave three great commandments to enable mankind to lead the perfect life which he had taught. These are *humata* (good thought), *hūkhta* (good word), and *huvarshta* (good deed). These three contain within themselves all other commandments ever given to mankind. No activity of man, whether in thought or word or deed, should be such as would injure another being.

The first place is, of course, given to *humata* or good thought; for thought is the most important instrument for the use of man on the spiritual journey. A man who commits sin in thought is as much a sinner as one who does the deed. So the first thing needed is purity of thought, and as long as a man has not acquired that, he cannot advance a single step on the path of *asha*.

By *hūkhta* Zarathushtra means exactly what Manu has said in a similar connection: 'Speak the truth, but speak it pleasantly; do not speak an unpleasant truth, but never utter a pleasant untruth.'[17] The ancient Iranians were famed throughout the world for their adherence to truth. Even the Greeks, their national enemies, acknowledged this, and Greek States used to carry their disputes to the great king of Iran for settlement, because they had full faith in his truth and justice.

Huvarshta is the Karma-yoga we have already indicated above. This idea is summed up finely in the opening line of the *Ushtavaiti Gāthā*: 'Happiness comes to him, through whom happiness goes out to others.'

MIGRATION OF PARSIS TO INDIA

As long as the Iranians held on to these noble ideals of life, taught by their great master, they flourished in the world and carried their culture successfully into many countries around. In course of time, however, these ideals began to be forgotten, and the leaders of the nation became

[17] *Manu Smṛti*, IV. 138.

selfish and self-seeking. As a consequence, the great Aryan religion of Zarathushtra declined. Its true inner spirit departed, leaving only a skeleton of outward ceremonial. As a result, when Iran had to face the new and vigorous faith from Arabia, Zoroastrianism could not hold its own, and was very nearly wiped out from the land of its birth. A few of the faithful, however, still clung to the ancient fire of Ahura-Mazdā, and these left their ancient motherland and took refuge in the sisterland of Āryāvarta (A.D. 936).[18] These Parsi 'Pilgrim Fathers' brought with them the sacred fire of ancient Iran. They erected and consecrated a temple for it on Indian soil, and, after many vicissitudes, the sacred Irānshāh fire has now been established at Udwada, a small town about eighty miles north of Bombay. There the sacred flame is kept burning and helps to kindle anew the Inner Fire—the Son of Ahura-Mazdā—in the hearts of the faithful.

The Parsis are happy in the land of their adoption, now verily their motherland, for they arrived here quite a thousand years ago. They are now among the favoured children of Mother India, and they are friendly with all. There is but one reason why such a mere handful have survived among the millions of this great country; it is due to the fact that they have remained true to the religion of their great *guru,* Zarathushtra. A new awakening has also been stirring Iran of late. The true lovers of Iran are trying once again to understand the message of the greatest of the Iranians, Zarathushtra. The eternal truths which Zarathushtra proclaimed ages ago in Iran are still kept alive as living ideals amongst the Parsis in India.

[18] At present there are about 100,000 Zoroastrians in India and about 12,000 or so in Persia.

39

THE RISE AND GROWTH OF CHRISTIANITY IN INDIA

I. SOUTH INDIA

FROM historic times, that part of the Indian subcontinent known as Dakṣiṇa Bhārata, bounded on the north by the Vindhyas, on the west by the Arabian Sea, and on the east by the Bay of Bengal, has lived a life of its own, though linked in many respects with the rest of India socially, culturally, and politically. The storms of invasion that swept the North and the vicissitudes that befell its ruling dynasties have but occasionally affected the even tenor of life of the people in the southern peninsula. The result was that South India was able to develop certain features of life and civilization which welded its different parts into a cultural unity.

South India, in spite of Hinduism being the dominant religion, has offered hospitality to other faiths from very early times. Buddhist as well as Jain influence was at one time wide-spread in the South. From the beginning of the Christian era, if not earlier, the Jews found an asylum in Cochin. In the wake of the Jews came the first unknown missionaries of the gospel, who were in all probability either merchant-adventurers or immigrants from the region of the Red Sea and the Persian Gulf. Some centuries later came the followers of Mohammed, who have now established themselves as a well-knit social and cultural group, known as Moplas, in Malabar. Such was the environment in which the Christian Church took root in the soil of India, and contributed its share to the formation of the variegated religious and cultural pattern of South India.

The origins of Christianity in South India are connected with three seaports, which at one time carried on a flourishing trade with Western Asia and beyond. Of these, Cranganore and Goa lie on the west coast, and Tranquebar on the east. It is from these three spots that Christianity spread in various directions. Christianity in the South may be said to be a river formed by the confluence of three streams, each with a distinct character of its own, the Syrian, the Roman Catholic, and the Protestant. We shall consider each of these in brief compass.

THE SYRIAN CHURCH OF SOUTH INDIA

There is considerable obscurity about the spread of Christianity in the early centuries of the Christian era and the missionaries that took part in it. Even the identity of India in which early missionaries are supposed to have laboured is not certain, for Ethiopia, Arabia, and a wide tract beyond Mesopotamia shared this name with the India of later times. The Christians of South India, known as the Syrian Christians, claim an apostolic foundation for their Church. According to tradition, St. Thomas (Mar Thoma), one of the apostles of Jesus Christ, after being in Parthia and in the kingdom of Gondophares in north-western India for some time, landed near Cranganore in *c.* A.D. 52, preached the gospel, and established several churches on the Malabar coast. The Brāhmaṇas of Palur (modern Chowghat), whom he converted, provided later the sacerdotal classes of Malabar Christians till the advent of the Portuguese. He moved later on to the east coast, where he died as a martyr for the faith at a place near Madras, since known as San Thome, probably identical with the harbour Batumah (Beit Tumah, the house of Thomas) mentioned by the Arab merchant Suleiman in A.D. 851. Much controversy has raged round this claim of the Syrian Church for an apostolic origin, but scholars are less sceptical of it at present than they were fifty years ago. Dr. Mingana says, 'It may, or it may not, be true that Thomas evangelized the Indians'.[1] Dr. J. N. Farquhar's verdict may be taken as typical of the attitude of a number of scholars on the subject at the present time: 'Thirty years ago, the balance of probability stood absolutely against the story of the apostolate of St. Thomas in India; today the balance of possibility is distinctly on the side of historicity.'[2]

There is somewhat stronger evidence for the arrival in Malabar, in A.D. 345, of a body of Christian immigrants from Persia and Mesopotamia, who presumably fled from a severe persecution by Sapor II which began in A.D. 343 in Persia, and the welcome they received from the Hindu king who held sway in the coastal regions. They are supposed to have landed in Cranganore, not far from Cochin, known to ancient Greeks as Muziris, and to have built up a flourishing colony there in course of time. Their leader is generally known among Malabar Christians as Knae Thomman (Thomas Cananaus), that is, Thomas the Merchant. This was the earliest establishment of Christians on the Malabar coast known to historians today.[3]

[1] *Early Spread of Christianity,* p. 4.

[2] J. N. Farquhar, 'The Apostle Thomas in South India', *Bulletin of the John Rylands Library* (Manchester, 1927), pp. 32 ff.

A more recent historian makes the following comment on the St. Thomas tradition: 'The tradition of the Malabar Christians is so ancient and continuous as to deserve a reasonable share of probability.' D. Ferroli, *The Jesuits in Malabar* (Bangalore, 1939), I. p. 58.

[3] The king of the country around Cranganore (Cheraman Perumal?) is said to have conferred certain honours and privileges on the Christians, which included, according to Gouvea's *Jornada,* riding on elephants—a privilege granted only to the heirs of kings—, use of carpets, and wearing a golden flower on the hair at the time of marriage. See *Jornada,* fol. 4, col. 2, Coimbra, 1606. There is no unanimity of opinion about the date of migration under Thomas the Merchant, some placing it nearly four centuries, or slightly more, later.

The earliest historical evidence, however, regarding the existence of a Church in South India dates from the sixth century A.D. It is to be found in a book written by an Alexandrian merchant, Cosmas Indicopleustes (Cosmas the voyager to India), who visited India in the second quarter of the sixth century A.D. He says, in his *Christian Topography*, as follows: 'On the island of Taprobane (Ceylon) in Further India, where the Indian ocean is, there is to be found a community of Christians consisting of both clergy and the faithful. . . . Similarly in Male (Malabar, perhaps more particularly Quilon, which was later known as Kullam-male among the Arabs), where pepper grows, and in the place called Caliana (Kalyan, near Bombay), there is also a bishop, who receives imposition of hands from Persia.'[4]

From the sixth to the sixteenth century, little is known of the Syrian Church beyond what is contained in inscriptions or accounts of visitors from the West. Archaeological evidence points to the fact that there were different waves of migration from Western Asia to the Malabar coast and that the immigrants received a cordial reception at the hands of the ruling princes of Keraḷa. Certain copperplates, probably belonging to the ninth century, and containing charters of privileges granted by these princes, testify to the high position enjoyed by Christians among the people of the land. The Persian crosses (or the so-called 'Thomas' crosses) with inscriptions in Pahlavi, one found in St. Thomas Mount, Madras, and two in a church in Kottayam in Travancore, are evidence of the connection of the Malabar Church with the Church in Persia, which eventually came to be known as the East Syrian or Nestorian Church or the Church of the East. In the copperplates also Pahlavi is used, but sometimes mixed with other languages.

Among visitors to the Malabar Church in the middle ages may be mentioned the names of Marco Polo, the Venetian traveller (1293), John of Monte Corvino, a Franciscan friar (1292-93), Friar Jordan of Toulouse, a Dominican (1302), and John de Marignolli (1348). From all the evidence that is available, we may infer that, during this period, the Christians on the Malabar coast established themselves as good traders as well as patriotic soldiers and administrators.[5] It may be noted that 'Christians of St.

[4] Cosmas Indicopleustes, *Christiana Topographia,* III (Migne, *Patrologia Graeca,* LXXXVIII. cols. 169-70). See J. Richter, *A History of Missions in India* (Translated by S. H. Moore), pp. 31-32.

[5] J. de Marignolli, who stayed at Quilon for over a year, writes: 'On Palm Sunday (1348) we arrived at a very noble city of India called Quilon, where the whole world's pepper is produced. . . . Nor are the Saracens the proprietors, but the Christians of St. Thomas, and these latter are the masters of the public weighing office from which I derived, as a perquisite of my office as Pope's Legate, every month a hundred gold *fanams* and a thousand when I left. . . . (Quoted in D. Ferroli, *op. cit.*, p. 66).

Thomas' was the name usually applied to these people who in more modern times are known as Syrian Christians, on account of their connection with the Syriac-speaking Churches in the East, and the use of Syriac as their ecclesiastical language.

INFLUENCE OF THE ROMAN CATHOLIC AND OTHER CHURCHES

With the arrival of Vasco da Gama in Calicut, in 1498, the history of the Syrian Church enters a new phase. The influence of the Roman Catholic Church was brought to bear upon this ancient Church, and though the relations between the two were at first friendly, they became gradually strained to the breaking point. A crisis was reached during the visit of Alexio de Menezes, Archbishop of Goa, in the summer of 1599. At the Synod of Diamper (Udayamperoor), mostly through circumstances beyond its control, the Syrian Church was obliged to promise obedience to the Pope and merge itself in the Roman Church. But, thanks partly to the conquests of the Dutch, who were friendly to the Syrians and hostile to the Roman Catholics, the tide soon turned in favour of the Syrians, and in 1653, large numbers of them took a solemn oath to renounce the authority of the Pope and asserted the independence of the Malabar Church. This is known as the Coonen Cross Declaration, which reminds one of the Solemn League and Covenant in Scottish history. The Syrian Church organized itself under a bishop sent out by the Jacobite Patriarch of Antioch, and thus forged a new link with another of the historic Churches of the East. This change-over in ecclesiastical relations from the Nestorian to the Jacobite Church is one of the puzzles of Church history, but it may be explained by the simple fact that the Malabar Church had kept itself free from too close a connection with Churches outside, except in the matter of consecration of its bishops.

In the nineteenth century, the Syrian Church came into contact with some of the most virile sections of the Church from overseas, represented by the London Missionary Society in South Travancore, the Church Missionary Society in Central Travancore, and the Basel Mission in Malabar. As a result of this, new life was infused into this ancient Church, in its worship, organization, missionary outlook, education, and philanthropic activities. Another result of a less desirable nature was the splitting of the Church into different denominations, creating problems of various kinds for the future. The Syrian Christians of Travancore, Cochin, and Malabar, about two million in number, are now divided into the following main sections: (a) those who owe allegiance to the Pope of Rome and follow the Syrian rite (Romo-Syrians); (b) those who owe allegiance to the Jacobite Patriarch of Antioch, including those who stand for local autonomy under a Catholicos who is virtually independent of the Patriarch (Jacobite Orthodox Syrians) ; (c) those who have organized themselves into a Church entirely independent of foreign control (Mar Thoma Syrians) ; (d) those who are under the jurisdiction of the Nestorian 'Catholicos of the East', now residing in the U.S.A. (Chaldean Syrians) ; and (e) those who are members of the Church of South India, until lately closely connected with western Churches.

SERVICE TO THE COUNTRY

In promoting literacy, in raising the status of women, and in encouraging cottage industries, western missions, such as the Carmelites, the London Missionary Society, the Church Missionary Society, and the Basel Mission, have rendered magnificent service to the people of Malabar without distinction of caste or creed. Members of the Church in Malabar have contributed much to the development of Malayalam literature, the promotion of primary, secondary, and collegiate education, the adaptation of Christianity to Indian conditions, and the *rapprochement* between different communities in the field of political and philanthropic activities. By way of illustration, one may say that the names of George Mathan, K. I. Verghese Mapillay, C. Anthapai, and K. V. Simon will be gratefully remembered in the history of Malayalam literature. The Syrian Church has the distinction of being a Church accustomed to oriental ways of worship and of being manned and supported entirely by the children of the soil. Being thus truly indigenous, it is able to extend its hand of fellowship to Christians all over the world. One other fact that may be noted in this connection is that Christian women enjoy a large measure of freedom in Kerala, on account of their education and culture, and they occupy positions of responsibility in the service of the State.

THE ROMAN CATHOLIC CHURCH

The arrival of Vasco da Gama in Calicut, in 1498, may be taken as a landmark not only in the history of the Church, but also in the cultural contacts of India with the West. From this time European nations were attracted towards India, and several of them attempted to establish themselves in this land of pepper and spices, of silk and peacocks. As regards the beginnings of the Church in South India, it is true that the missionary followed the trader, and that for a time, at least, they were on friendly terms with each other. The Portuguese colonial empire in India was at the height of its power in the sixteenth century, and the same century saw also the heyday of prosperity for the Roman Catholic missions in the South. Goa, on the west coast, was the headquarters of the Portuguese viceroy as well as the seat of an archbishopric. With Goa, Cochin, and Tuticorin as their bases, Portuguese missionaries preached the gospel to the fisherfolk in the coastal regions, in the first instance, and later penetrated into the interior.

Francis Xavier (1506-52), known as the apostle of the Indies, was the first Jesuit missionary to arrive in India, and has rightly become celebrated as one of the greatest in the whole history of the Church. Another famous name is that of Robert de Nobili (1577-1656), an Italian nobleman, who was most original in his methods of presenting the Christian message to the intelligentzia of this country. He adopted the attire and ways of life of a *sannyāsin,* and attracted many by his habits and ideals as well as by his erudition. The Society of Jesus, to which both Xavier and de Nobili belonged, was in the vanguard of missionary work in South India in the sixteenth and seventeenth centuries. Although in its work in the South there was little that was as spectacular as its mission to the Great Mogul in North India, it was true to the ideals of service and suffering set forth by its pioneers. The seminaries established by the Jesuits at Goa, Vaipicotah (Cochin), and Cranganore, though primarily meant for purposes of Christian propaganda, encouraged liberal education within certain limits. The first printing presses were brought to India by the Jesuits about 1550, and the Spanish lay-brother John Gonsalves was the first to cast types with which a catechism in Malayalam was printed in 1577.

Jesuit missions declined in prestige and influence, when the Portuguese retreated from the political horizon of India. Soon other missions followed, sponsored by monastic orders, such as the Franciscans (*c.* 1517), the Dominicans (*c.* 1548), the Augustinians (*c.* 1572), and the Carmelites (*c.* 1656). The Franciscans were the first religieux to come to India (1517), and the first bishop of Goa, Dom John de Albuquerque (1537-53), was chosen from this order. In 1557, Goa was raised to the status of an archdiocese.

The contribution of Catholic missions in the field of education is a notable one. In a number of districts in the South, primary education as well as higher education was in the hands of Jesuit missionaries for several generations. This is still the case to a lesser extent. Although Roman Catholics are to be found in most of the important towns in South India, the following are especially associated with their work—Goa, Mangalore, Ernakulam, Changanacherry, Quilon, Negapatam (Nagapattinam), Pondicherry, Trichinopoly (Tiruchirapalli), and Bangalore. The Roman Catholic missions showed signs of a vigorous growth in the nineteenth century. The Roman Church has a genius for organization as well as administration, and this is much in evidence in the diocesan and missionary organization of the Church. To the credit of the Roman Church, it must be said that long before the Protestants thought of the idea, she made attempts at developing an indigenous leadership for the Church in India. Many of the dioceses of the Church are now therefore under Indian bishops. The total membership of the Roman Church in South India is larger than that of all other Churches put together.

THE PROTESTANT MISSIONS

Tranquebar near Trichinopoly has gained the honour of being 'the birth-place of Protestant Christianity in South India', as Serampore in Bengal is of the North. In this sea-coast town, which was once a flourishing seaport, landed, in 1706, the first Protestant missionaries to India, German Lutherans, sent out under the protection of the king of Denmark to his Indian possessions. They laboured there amid much opposition from their co-religionists who were concerned more with their pockets than with their souls. As Dr. Latourette says: 'Upon the morals of the majority of the Europeans, the inherited Christianity had but little effect. Of all nationalities it was true, as it was to be in the nineteenth century, that "east of Suez the Ten Commandments did not hold".'[6] Zeigenbalg's translation of the four Gospels (1714) is one of the earliest specimens of modern Tamil prose. The most illustrious name among the Tranquebar missionaries is that of C. F. Schwartz (1726-97). He lived and worked for nearly half a century in various parts of South India, especially in Tranquebar, Trichinopoly, and Tanjore. He had a broad outlook regarding the status and functions of a missionary and, in this respect, reminds one of C. F. Andrews of more recent times. Schwartz was the trusted friend and counsellor of the Raja of Tanjore and the mediator between Haider Ali and the British East India Company. He was also instrumental in saving a large number of people from famine during the Carnatic wars.

The Danish Tranquebar Mission flourished in the eighteenth century, and was succeeded in the nineteenth century by a number of other missions established in various parts of South India. This was made possible by the adoption of a more liberal attitude to missionary work by the Directors of the East India Company. Until 1812, no Christian missionary had been granted a licence by the Company to reside in its settlements. But pressure was brought to bear by the British Parliament and people upon the Company at the time of revision of its Charter in 1813. As a result of this, an ecclesiastical establishment, with an episcopal see at Calcutta,

[6] K. S. Latourette, *A History of the Expansion of Christianity* (Eyre and Spottiswoode, 1940), III. p. 283.

came into being (1814), which eventually paved the way for the organization of a branch of the Church of England in India. One of the provisions of the Charter was that a sum of £10,000 was to be set aside annually by the Company for 'native education, oriental and occidental'. The Charter of 1833 threw the way open for non-British missions to enter India. Some of the earliest missionaries were American Baptists and Lutherans who worked respectively at Nellore (1840) and Rajahmundry (1848). By 1850, there were to be found in South India not only missionary societies from Great Britain, but also from various parts of the continent of Europe and the United States of America.

The half century from about 1900 saw the growth of the Church in various parts of South India, especially among the unprivileged and the under-privileged in Madras and Andhra States. In this development the older Churches in South India have played a notable part, especially the Church in Tinnevelly. The mission of the Tinnevelly Church to Dornakal in Hyderabad is an instance in point. The Malas and Madigas of Hyderabad joined the Church in large numbers, because they found in the Church something which answered to their needs in various directions. Notwithstanding such local efforts, the credit for the expansion of the Christian Church in South India belongs to missionary societies from the West. In 1947, there were over 150 missionary societies at work in India, and a fair proportion of these was represented in the South. Among these may be mentioned a few which have a long record of varied service in different areas and towns in the South, such as the Christian Missionary Society in Tinnevelly and Central Travancore, the London Missionary Society in South Travancore and northern Tamil districts, the Methodist Missionary Society in Mysore and Hyderabad, the Basel Mission in South Kanara and North Malabar, the Church of Scotland Mission in and near Madras City, the American Baptist Mission in the region between Madras and Bezwada (Vijayavada), and the American Lutheran Mission in and around the Godāvarī area. Most of the societies, however, have merged themselves in the Church of South India which was formed in 1947.

REORIENTATION OF THE MISSIONARY WORK

An interesting fact in connection with the work of the Christian missions in South India is that with the passage of years they have interpreted the missionary task in terms of the varied needs of the country. While the early missionaries were content to preach the gospel of salvation to all and sundry, their modern counterparts believe that the gospel is a message of life and fuller life for all human beings. So we find the doctor, the specialist in agriculture, the teacher, the sanitary engineer, and other technical experts in the ranks of missionaries today. The missions have played a noble part in improving the rural economy of South India as well as in pioneering India's fight against ignorance, disease, and dirt. The Y.M.C.A. rural reconstruction centres at Martandam in South Travancore and Ramanathapuram in Coimbatore District, the American Arcot Mission agricultural farm at Katpadi, the medical college at Vellore, the mission hospital of the London Missionary Society at Neyyoor, as well as other institutions scattered in different parts of the country, bear testimony to the beneficent work of the Church in South India.

Another factor in the life of the Church in South India is the desire for unity manifested in various sections of the Church established by foreign missions. This desire found its consummation in the formation of the Church of South India in September 1947. Although this Church does not at present embrace Christians belonging even to all the non-Roman denominations in the South, it is likely to set the pace in future for unity and co-operation, and that not merely in its immediate neighbourhood. The Church of South India has a membership of over a million, more than half of the entire non-Roman Christian population of the South. Another symbol of unity as well as its instrument is the National Missionary Society (Bharat Christiya Sevak Samaj), an indigenous missionary society founded in 1905, dependent entirely on Indian resources in men and money. Educational and other institutions too are increasingly becoming, as a matter of policy, union institutions in which different missions and churches co-operate whole-heartedly. The Madras Christian College at Tambaram, the Women's Christian College at Madras, the Union Christian College at Alwaye, the Christian Medical College at Vellore, and the Tuberculosis Sanatorium at Madanapalle are significant instances of union efforts in the South.

ACTIVITIES OF THE CHURCH IN SOUTH INDIA

We shall now briefly review the life and activities of the Church in South India and indicate some of its salient features, especially in the realm of its service to our motherland.

One of the chief contributions of Christian missionaries has been the service they have rendered for over two centuries to the language and literature of the land. Though the beginnings of the Tamil language go further back than the Christian era, there was much to be done to vivify the language and enable it to take its place amongst the well-developed modern languages of India. This is equally true of the younger members of the Dravidian family of languages—Telugu, Kannada, and Malayalam. The translations of the Bible as well as the creation of a Christian literature in these languages gave an impetus to their development in various directions. The work in Tamil of Father Beschi (1680-1747) and of Dr. Caldwell is of outstanding significance. Other languages too are indebted in a similar manner to the devoted, if less well-known, labours of missionaries and Indian Christians in the field of poetry and drama, prose and fiction, as well as of grammar and lexicography. Take, for instance, the judgement of a historian of the Kannada literature: 'It deserves to be added that Kanarese is indebted to the missionaries probably for the introduction of printing, and certainly for improvement of its typography by the preparation of fresh founts of beautiful type for the printing of successive editions of the Bible. Missionaries have also led the way in the careful study of the language and literature. Witness the English-Carnataca and Carnataca-English dictionaries prepared by Rev. W. Reeve of Bellary; the scholarly Kannada-English dictionary and historical Kannada grammar by Rev. F. Kittel; the same scholar's editions of the *Chandombudhi* and *Śabdamaṇidarpaṇa*; and useful anthologies, grammars, etc. by Revs. Moegling, Weigle, Würth, and others.'[7] The names of Vedanayagam Sastriar and H. A. Krishna Pillay in Tamil, Gundert and Verghese Mapillay in Malayalam, and Choudary Purushottam and Garrum Joshua in Telugu are such as will not be easily forgotten by the people in the South.

Another aspect of the literary efforts of missionaries is the work they did as interpreters of Indian thought and culture to the West through translations of works from Sanskrit and other Indian languages. Dr. Pope's translation of *Tirukkuraḷ* and *Tiruvācakam*, some of the publications of the Y.M.C.A. in the series on the 'Religious Quest of India' and 'The Heritage of India', and other similar works show that the missionary has attempted not only to give, but also to receive of the best India had to offer him.

Still another line of activity in which the Church has consistently been interested is the service of the unprivileged, the neglected, and of all who are handicapped in the race of life. The Blind School at Palamcottah, the Leper Home in Chingleput, the numerous homes for orphans and waifs and strays, the work of rescue and rehabilitation of girls and women who have fallen victims to inhuman customs and conventions, as illustrated in the work of the Dhonavur Fellowship in the Tinnevelly District—these and similar institutions are not collateral growths in the missionary enterprise, but are embodiments of the very soul and spirit of the Christian gospel.

The school has been an adjunct of the Church all through its history,

[7] E. P. Rice, *Kanarese Literature* (Second Edition, Y.M.C.A. Press, Calcutta), pp. 101-2.

and this is true of South India as well. Missionaries have been pioneers in the field of education, especially after the creation of the western educational system about 1835. Roman Catholics and Protestants alike found in English education not only a valuable ally to missionary propaganda, but also a solution to some of the problems with which India was confronted in the nineteenth century. In course of time, educational institutions came to be regarded in a more liberal context. They became an expression of Christian service in combating ignorance on the one hand, and in setting up high ideals of training in character and citizenship on the other. This accounts for the popularity of institutions such as Madras Christian College, Tambaram, American College, Madurai, Sarah Tucker College, Palamcottah, St. Joseph's College, Trichinopoly, St. Aloysius College, Mangalore, Wilson College, Bombay, and the Andhra Christian College, Guntur. Educationists like William Miller, L. P. Larsen, and F. W. Kellet of Madras, and Father H. Heras of Bombay have left behind a record which is full of inspiration for coming generations. Amongst the ranks of Indian Christian teachers, too, there are well-known names, such as those of J. P. Cotelingam (Bellary), J. V. Challiah (Jaffna), Paul Daniel, and K. C. Chacko (Travancore).

HINDUISM AND CHRISTIANITY: THEIR MUTUAL INFLUENCE

India is a meeting place of various cultures and religions, and it would indeed be surprising if Christianity and Hinduism did not influence each other. Such influences are naturally more in evidence where Christianity has been established the longest. In some of the social customs of the Syrian Christians of Malabar, we find a tendency to approximate to the code of behaviour obtaining among the Nairs of Malabar. The caste system was at one time nearly as widely prevalent in sections of the Church in South India as among Hindus; and the Church had to wage a war against it, as relentless as that in which reformed Hinduism is engaged today, before some of its worst features could be suppressed. It is only true to say that even today the shadow of caste hangs over certain groups of the Christian community in the South. But there have been at work other and more beneficent influences of one religion over the other, though it is difficult to gauge the depth and extent of such influences, because they enter into the very warp and woof of the life of an individual and of the community. Reflections, however, of this may be caught in the literature, music, and other fine arts which attempt to express the soul of the people. The *Tirukkuraḷ*, an ancient Tamil poem, belonging to the eighth or ninth century, is generally known as the Bible of South India. No one reading this work can fail to be struck by the similarities in thought and expression with some of the passages in the New Testament. Dr. Pope, the translator of the *Kuraḷ* into English, gives it as his opinion that 'the Christian scriptures were among the sources from which the poet derived his inspiration'.[8]

Many parallels have been traced between the language of the *Bhagavad-Gītā* and that of the *Gospel of St. John*, and some scholars explain this phenomenon as due to the influence of Christian ideas. The Bhakti movement in Hinduism, which reached its height about the twelfth and thirteenth centuries, may also owe something to the Christian conception of love (*agape*) and faith (*pistis*) in a personal saviour from sin and death. On this last point, Dr. Grierson comments as follows: 'But it was in southern India that Christianity, as a doctrine, exercised the greatest influence on Hinduism generally. Although the conceptions of the fatherhood of God and of *bhakti* were indigenous to India, they received an immense impetus owing to the beliefs of Christian communities reacting upon the mediaeval Bhāgavata reformers of the South.'[9]

Professor Garbe, R. G. Bhandarkar, and Dr. N. Macnicol are in substantial agreement with Dr. Grierson's contention. Dr. Macnicol says: 'That the influence of Christian teaching on the ideas of later Vaiṣṇavite and Śaivite theism was considerable and increasing from about the thirteenth century onwards seems highly probable.'[10]

Nationalism has affected Christianity in a variety of ways. It has created or revived amongst Indian Christians the natural desire to become masters in their own house. It has also challenged the more serious minded amongst them to rethink Christianity in terms of Indian thought and life, and to express its genius in Indian modes and patterns. It is against such a background that one has to view the emergence of Christian *āśramas* in South India. The first Christian *āśrama* to be established in the South was the Christakula Ashram at Tirupattur, North Arcot District, founded in 1921. In the wake of this Ashram, a dozen others have come into being standing for the same ideals of communion with God and fellowship in the service of humanity. Evangelism is the motive power behind all these Ashrams. Christianity has found itself at home in

[8] G. U. Pope, *The 'Sacred' Kurraḷ of Tiruvaḷḷuva-Nāyanār* (London, 1886), Introduction, p. iv.

[9] *Encyclopaedia of Religion and Ethics* (First Edition, Edinburgh), II. p. 550.

[10] Dr. N. Macnicol, *Indian Theism* (Oxford University Press, 1915), p. 277. See Appendix C in this book on 'The Alleged Indebtedness of Indian Theism to Christianity', from which the following extract is taken: 'It seems highly probable, when we consider the region in which the revival of *bhakti* in the time of Rāmānuja took place, and its nearness to the Nestorian Christians of South India, that he had some acquaintance with the Christian truth. . . . R. G. Bhandarkar is probably on surer ground when he suggests that "some of the finer points in the theory of *prapatti* may be traced to the influence of Christianity". . . . This is in agreement with our view that the whole intensification of the spirit of *bhakti*, of which the doctrine of *prapatti* is an instance, may be due to Christian sentiment making itself felt in the South.'

the ancient institution of the *āśrama,* revived and redirected to the service of India. Simplicity, service of the poor and the needy, a fellowship which transcends the bounds of social custom and convention, and communion with the Source of all light and power—these *āśrama* ideals are true alike of the genius of Christianity as of higher Hinduism. The chapel at Tirupattur is built in the style of temple architecture in South India. Indian tunes and Indian musical instruments have come into their own in connection with Christian worship in the Ashrams. In fact, the change that has come over the face of the Church in the South, in certain aspects, in the last half century, is nothing short of a revolution.

Christianity has found a true home in the South and has now become a member of the family of religions in India. In so far as Christians are true to the life and spirit of their Master, Jesus Christ, they will be able to serve the best interests of the land they belong to, as well as of the world at large.

II. NORTH INDIA

In making a general survey of the rise and progress of Christianity in North India, we may, for the sake of convenience, divide the period to be covered into two main divisions, viz. (i) from the beginning up to the arrival of William Carey (A.D. 1793) and (ii) from A.D. 1793 to the present time. In the first period, we get but fugitive glimpses of the attempts of Christian missionaries to plant the gospel in India, while, in the second, we see the Christian Church as an integral part of the Indian religious landscape. The Church today has taken root in the soil of India, and it is interesting to look back upon the long and adventurous path she trod before she reached the present position.

Before we attempt to trace the beginning of Christianity in North India, it may be helpful to turn our attention to India's neighbours in Western Asia with whom she was in contact in the early centuries of the Christian era. From our knowledge of Church history in general, it is clear that it was from countries in the Euphrates-Tigris Valley, Persia, and southern Arabia that Christian influence travelled eastwards to India and Central Asia and beyond. Armenia, lying between the upper waters of the Euphrates and the Tigris, was the first country where Christianity became an established religion, and this was the result of missionary labours of Gregory the Illuminator (A.D. 257-331). Edessa, a small princedom lying between Armenia and Persia proper, became quite early a stronghold of Christianity and was responsible for introducing the new faith into many parts of Persia. Edessa was 'the home of Syriac Christianity and the place where the Peshito version of the Bible was produced'. The province of

Adiabene, situated east of the Tigris with Arbel as its capital, was another important centre. It is said that 'in A.D. 225 there were more than twenty bishoprics in Mesopotamia and in Persia, one of which was among the Dailams near the Caspian Sea'.[11] Bardaisan of Edessa writing in *c.* A.D. 196 refers to the existence of Christians in Parthia and Bactria, the region between the Hindukush and the Oxus. Persia itself became the home of a flourishing Church, because the Persian king, as a matter of policy, offered asylum to Christians who had been put under the ban of his traditional enemy, the emperor of Rome, on account of their departure from orthodoxy. The Persian Christians refused to accept the decisions of the Council of Chalcedon (A.D. 451), and declared themselves Nestorian in 484. That the Church in Persia was both large in numbers and staunch in faith is evident from the fact that in the reign of Sapor II (fourth century) the number of martyrs was no less than 16,000. It was this Church—the Church of the East or the Nestorian Church—, whose Catholicos resided at Seleucia on the Tigris, that became a great missionary Church in later centuries. In southern Persia in the region of the Persian Gulf, in southern Arabia, in the island of Socotra, and on the borders of the Red Sea, especially on the trade routes going south from Alexandria, there were to be found churches in the early centuries of the Christian era. When it is realized that western and northern India had contacts with other nations for purposes of trade and commerce, it will be seen how easy it was for the gospel to reach India through normal contacts with those who professed the faith and who lived not far from her borders.

THE PERIOD BEFORE A.D. 1793

The origins of Christianity in North India are a subject of speculation among students of history. The tradition that St. Thomas the Apostle visited North India is one that has been brought to the fore in recent years, on account of the fact that archaeological discoveries have lent support to the historicity of a king named Gondophares, mentioned in the *Acts of Judas Thomas,* a book written in the second century A.D. at or near Edessa and dealing with the martyrdom of St. Thomas. But, as one swallow does not make a summer, we can only endorse the cautious words of Dr. Farquhar when he says that 'it is probable that the story is true'.[12] Considering the facilities in communication by sea and land between India and the eastern Mediterranean region, including Persia and Mesopotamia, there is nothing inherently impossible in the view that St. Thomas preached the gospel in North-West India, now a part of West Pakistan, belonging in historical

[11] A. Mingana, *Early Spread of Christianity,* p. 4.

[12] J. N. Farquhar, *The Apostle Thomas in North India,* p. 29.

times to the Parthian kingdom of Gondophares. Dr. Mingana states that 'there are solid grounds for believing that a fairly large Christian community existed in India from very early times', and that there is 'every possibility that a stream of Christian missionaries and merchants had in the long past penetrated through the passes that connect India by land with its northern and north-western neighbours'.[13] Dr. Latourette believes that 'it is not improbable that before the end of the third century Christianity had arrived in India itself'.[14]

Whatever be the nature of the early connection that was established between North India and the regions beyond North-West India in the interests of the spread of Christianity—that is, whether through the apostolic labours of St. Thomas or through merchant adventurers from the region of the Persian Gulf and the Arabian Sea or through refugees fleeing from persecution in Persia in the reign of Sapor II—, we are on safer ground when we come to the seventh century, when India was the seat of a metropolitan who may have had some ten bishops under his jurisdiction.[15] The Christians in India were numerous in the Malabar coast and the north-western regions which were not far from a strong Christian centre in Persia named Riwardasire near modern Bushire, which is claimed by Dr. Mingana as the 'key to early Christianity in North-West India'. It is a well-known fact that from the seventh to the fourteenth century, the Church of the East carried its missionary conquests right across Asia as far as Peking, and the Nestorian monument at Si-ngan-fu, discovered in 1625 and belonging to the eighth century (779-83), bears silent testimony to the fact to this day. Dr. B. J. Kidd quotes a fourteenth-century source which says that there were 13 metropolitans in India, 12 in China, 18 in Samarkhand, 19 in Turkestan, and 23 in Khan Bhalik, and that each had from 6 to 12 suffragans under him.[16]

Patna is mentioned as the seat of a metropolitan in the year A.D. 1222, and Marco Polo, who visited India about the end of the thirteenth century, states that there were then in Middle (Central) India six great kings and kingdoms and that three of these were Christian and three Saracen'.[17] We have evidence to show that at Thana and Kalyan near Bombay there were Christian families and also in places as far apart as Gandispur (modern Shahabad) in the Punjab and Pegu in Burma. Four Franciscans, the first European monks in India who were martyred at the hands of Muslims

[13] A. Mingana, *op. cit.*, p. 6.
[14] K. S. Latourette, *op. cit.*, V. p. 107.
[15] A. Mingana, *op. cit.*, p. 10.
[16] B. J. Kidd, *Churches of Eastern Christendom*, p. 92.
[17] Codiers, *Marco Polo*, II. p. 437, quoted by J. S. Stewart in *Nestorian Missionary Enterprise*, p. 92.

at Thana in 1321, had been received by a small community of Nestorian Christians. It must be said to the credit of the Mohammedan emperor of Delhi, Ghiyas-ud-dīn, the founder of the Tughluq dynasty, that, when he heard of the crime, he punished the governor of Thana with death.

Christianity in North India, however, received a set back under Muhammad bin Tughluq, Timur, and other Muslim rulers. The blow was so shattering that the churches became extinct, and all traces of their existence were obliterated by the end of the fifteenth century.

MISSIONARIES TO NORTH INDIA FROM GOA

With the arrival of Vasco da Gama in Calicut, in 1498, Christianity enters upon a new phase of development. As Stephen Neill has said, 'for good and ill, Christian expansion in the last four centuries has been associated with the political and commercial expansion of Europe'.[18] This is true of India too. Albuquerque took Goa in 1510 and laid the foundation of the colonial empire of Portugal. And the next phase of the growth of the Church in North India followed the fortunes of the Portuguese power in India. The king of Portugal under the influence of a bull received from Pope Nicholas V, giving him a right to half of the world, felt an obligation to spread the faith, and this led to the advent of Franciscans and Dominicans and, later, Jesuits as missionaries of the gospel in India. The best known of the latter group was Francis Xavier, a companion of Ignatius Loyola who founded the Jesuit Order, who like a flaming torch moved from place to place starting from Goa and passing through the islands of the Malay Archipelago and Japan, till he died off the coast of China in 1552, at the age of 46, in his attempt to enter China. Some of the other religious orders have special connections with North India. The Augustinians, with the Portuguese factory at Hooghly, north of Calcutta, as the base of their operations in the early years of the seventeenth century, established a number of stations in Lower Bengal and along the sea coast from Pipli in Orissa to Chittagong, at present in East Pakistan. From 1707, the Italian Capuchins, similarly, pushed north into Nepal and Tibet from their bases in Chandernagore and Patna. The Carmelites, resident in India from 1616, were to be found in Surat, Bombay, and in Travancore and Cochin.

JESUIT MISSION TO THE MOGUL COURT

The story of the Jesuit mission to the Mogul court in the sixteenth century is a heroic chapter in the history of missionary work in India. At the invitation of Akbar (1556-1605), a mission, starting from Goa in

[18] *Christian Society*, p. 247.

November 1579, arrived at his court at Fatehpur Sikri in February 1580, after travelling through Surat, Mandu, Ujjain, Sarangpur, Suroj, Marwar, Gwalior, and Dholpur. The missioners explained the tenets of the Christian faith to the king and pointed out the evils of polygamy. The king was cordial in his relations with the missionaries and encouraged round-table conferences between them and the mullahs. They had been granted full liberty to preach Christianity and to make converts.[19] Yet they soon realized that Akbar had no intention of becoming a Christian. The mission returned to Goa in 1583. A second time, again, in response to the king's request, a mission was sent to his court at Lahore in 1591. A school was started by the mission which was attended by the sons of nobles and by members of the royal family. A third mission followed (1595-1605) which met with a slightly better reception. A church was built in Lahore and opened in 1597 by the governor of the city. The heir apparent, Prince Salim (later known as Jahāngīr), became a firm friend and protector of the mission. Christmas and Easter were celebrated with great pomp and publicity in Lahore, and churches were built in Agra and other places. Jahāngīr, even after succeeding his father in 1605, remained friendly to the missionaries, and some of his nephews were allowed to be publicly baptized. The chief feature of Jesuit activity in the later years of Jahāngīr's reign is the adventurous journey of Father Antony de Andrade to Tibet in 1624 via Badrinath. He reached the town of Tsaparang in the upper Sutlej valley, saw the king and queen of that region, and preached to them through a Hindu interpreter. A mission was maintained there for some years, a church was built, and some converts were made. Though the mission to the Mogul court was maintained in the time of Shāh Jahān (1627-58) and Aurangzeb, it became weaker as Portuguese prestige declined in the country. By the middle of the eighteenth century, the Jesuits had only five churches in Mogor proper—one each at Marwar, Jaipur, and Agra, and two at Delhi. In 1759, when the Jesuits were banished from the Portuguese dominions, the work of the mission was entrusted to Carmelites of Bombay and to Capuchins who established themselves in Patna and looked after the church in Agra. In the eighteenth century, there was also a fair number of European, Armenian, and Eastern Christians scattered about in various parts of India, particularly in the trading centres in western and north-eastern India.

[19] Dr. M. L. Roy Choudhury, in a paper on 'The Position of Christianity in the Moghul Empire', says, 'Akbar treated the Christians, more or less consistently, courteously and generously. He liked their intellect. He not only granted them permission to build churches and make conversions ; he went so far as to adopt the son of a Christian, Yaqub of Aleppo, also known as Mirza Sekandar'.

FROM 1793 TO THE PRESENT TIME

The arrival of William Carey in 1793 opens a new chapter in the history of Christianity in India. With him begins, according to Dr. Latourette, 'a new era in Protestant missions not only in India, but also in the entire world'. Though there were missionaries in India before his time, like those of the Danish-Halle Mission in Tranquebar and John Kiernander of Sweden (1758-86), who built the Old Mission Church in Calcutta with the help of Lord Clive, William Carey was the first missionary to be sent out by a missionary society from the West. Carey has a secure place in history as 'the father of the modern missionary enterprise'. His pioneering work in the field of Bible translation, primary education, and journalism, apart from his work as a preacher of the gospel, gives him a unique place in the history of modern Bengal as well as in that of the Christian Church in North India. Serampore College, which he founded in 1818 for the promotion of 'piety and learning', has one of the oldest university charters in Asia. Carey and his colleagues had to fight hard against heavy odds, for the East India Company, which held the reins of power at the time, was not friendly towards mission work, as the Directors feared it might affect their dividends. But the policy of the Company was gradually changed in a favourable direction by the force of public opinion in England, and the position was consolidated by the action of the British Parliament in 1813 and 1833.

The establishment of a bishopric of the Church of England in Calcutta, with chaplaincies in Bombay and Madras, was an important result of the revision of the Company's Charter in 1813. Bishop Middleton, the first Bishop of Calcutta (1815-22), founded the Bishop's College with a view to training Indian Christians as preachers and teachers, and for a long time the Bishop's College served the cause of general education too. It was in this institution that the illustrious son of Bengal, Krishna Mohun Banerji, served as a professor from 1851 to 1868. Christianity in North India owes much to the work of chaplains like David Brown, Henry Martyn, and Claudius Buchanan. Among the bishops who succeeded Middleton are such well-known leaders as Reginald Heber (1823-26), poet and hymn-writer, and Daniel Wilson (1832-58), the first Metropolitan of India and a great administrator, and, in more recent years, Foss Westcott (1919-45), a friend of C. F. Andrews and Mahatma Gandhi. The Church of England in India became a self-governing Indian Church in 1930, known as the Church of India, Burma, and Ceylon, and it has now ten diocesan bishops, with headquarters in various cities in northern and western India, and an Indian metropolitan with headquarters in Calcutta.

THE COMING OF DIFFERENT MISSIONS

The door was thrown wide open for the entry of missions by the Charter Acts of the British Parliament passed in 1813 and 1833. One of the earliest bodies (other than those connected with the Church of England such as the Christian Missionary Society) to take advantage of this was the Church of Scotland, whose first missionary, Alexander Duff, landed in Calcutta in 1830. He gave a new turn to missionary work by making education an evangelistic agency. With the help of Raja Rammohun Roy, he started a school which later developed into the present Scottish Church College. Following the success of the experiment, the Church of Scotland laid special emphasis on the formation of schools and colleges in its work in other provinces too. The educational programme of missions received an impetus from the policy adopted by the government, under Lord William Bentink, of imparting English education in schools and colleges in accordance with Lord Macaulay's *Minute* of 1835. The colleges founded by various missions, Roman Catholic as well as others, such as the Madras Christian College, Wilson College (Bombay), St. Xavier's College (Calcutta), St. John's College (Agra), Ewing Christian College (Allahabad), and American College (Madura), have borne a noble share in educating India's youth over several generations. In 1954, there were, under the auspices of the National Christian Council, 46 colleges, 448 high schools, 553 middle schools, and 103 teacher-training institutions in the whole of India. In 1951, the Roman Catholics had 42 colleges, 474 high schools, and 4,362 primary schools.

Missionaries from America, Canada, Australia, New Zealand, and from the continent of Europe, followed in the wake of those who hailed from Great Britain. In the number of missionaries sent out and in the area covered by its work, the Methodist Episcopal Church holds an important place. Some of its pioneers were William Taylor (1821-1902), J. M. Thoburn (1836-1902), and Dr. Clara Swain, the first woman medical missionary who came out to India in 1857. Gordon Hall (died 1826), one of the first representatives of the American Congregationalists, started work in Bombay in 1813, and the great Baptist, Adoniram Judson, in Rangoon, about the same time. Judson was later known as 'the Apostle of Burma'. The Rev. John Newton of the American Presbyterian Mission arrived in Ludhiana, Punjab, in 1835 and established a network of mission stations in North India. From the work of such pioneering efforts as these has grown the Christian Church in India as a whole, which, according to the *Directory of Churches and Missions in India and Pakistan, 1951,* showed a total of 24,494 congregations among non-Roman Churches. The services rendered to the country, through organizations auxiliary to the Church, too, cannot be forgotten, and among these may be mentioned the Bible

Society, the Christian Literature Society, the Sunday School Union, the Y.M.C.A., and the Y.W.C.A.

THE WORK OF THE MISSIONS

The methods of work employed by the missions were as varied as the needs of the people. The Christian missionary agencies carried on a relentless war against illiteracy, disease, and poverty, the three crying evils in society over a hundred years ago, as they are today. At present, there are over 500 hospitals and dispensaries scattered throughout India and Pakistan where the Christian ministry of healing is exercised. What the missions have done, and are still doing, for the defective and the handicapped, such as the blind and the deaf, and for lepers and the 'criminal' tribes, is something that puts India under an eternal debt of gratitude to the Churches in the West. Christian hospitals contain approximately 16,000 beds for the general treatment of disease. In the treatment of leprosy and tuberculosis, Christian missions have rendered outstanding service. The Mission to Lepers cares for 55 hospitals and homes for lepers, with a total of nearly 9,000 patients. Besides, there are other institutions maintained by the Salvation Army and other groups without aid from the mission. 'The names of such mission doctors as Muir, Lowe, Cochrane, and Brand rank high in the research and in progress in the treatment of leprosy in this country.'[20] There are at present 11 Christian sanatoria for tuberculosis patients with 1,300 beds, besides the provision in general hospitals for the treatment of this 'No. 1 scourge of India'. In the profession of nursing as well as in medical and health education, the work of Christian agencies is acknowledged to be a great boon to the country. The gradual expansion in the scope of missionary service is indicated by the way in which rural reconstruction and agricultural education have been taken care of by missions during the last fifty years. The Allahabad Agricultural Institute and the Village Service units in Uttar Pradesh organized by the American Presbyterian Mission are two outstanding examples in this direction.

WORK AMONG THE TRIBAL PEOPLES

Among the most successful types of work undertaken by the missions is that among tribal peoples and Harijans. In several tribal areas missionaries have reduced the spoken language to writing, introduced schools, hospitals, and social welfare schemes, and have thus effected a change for the better in the mode of life of these peoples. This is true of people like the Garos, the Khasis, and the Lusheis in Assam, the Oraons and the Mundas

[20] From a statement published by Dr. E. M. Wilder, Secretary of the Christian Medical Association of India, Nagpur (1952).

in Chota Nagpur, the Santals in Bihar, and the Khonds in Orissa. The work among the Harijans has been most marked in the Bhil country in western India, in certain parts of the Punjab, Uttar Pradesh, and East Bengal.

Before we pass on from this section dealing with the work of the missions, it may be pertinent to ask whether Churches in India or from the West engage in the manifold forms of service described above for the sake of luring the unwary into the Christian fold and thus swelling the numbers in the Christian population of the country. The Indian public generally appreciate Christian service in the social, economic, educational, and medical fields, but cannot understand why this should be linked with a desire to preach the gospel. The evangelistic purpose and the call to service in every form are inseparable parts of an obligation that is laid on the conscience of every faithful disciple of Jesus Christ. It is an inescapable duty on his part to share with others the spiritual gift he has received from his Lord and Master in humility and love and without any ulterior motive. Looked at from this point of view, it will be seen that Christian service and evangelistic work form an integrated whole in Christian witness.

We may now consider some aspects of present-day Christianity in North India as a whole.

THE CHURCH: ITS INDIANIZATION AND UNIFICATION

In the first place, the Church is seeking to shed its 'foreignness' and to become indigenous to the soil. The Churches in North India, until about 1914, hardly had a life and character of their own, apart from that of the missionary societies from the West, with which they were associated. The Church in each area was tied to the apron-string of the mission, and in many respects was but a pale imitation of the latter. In worship, rituals, music, architecture, no less than in its theology, it faithfully followed the lines laid down by the missionaries who first preached the gospel in a particular area. The result was that the Churches planted in India tended to reproduce the pattern of Churches in the West. But thanks to the influence of the national movement and the leadership of a few forward-looking Indian Christians and missionaries, this state of affairs is becoming a thing of the past. The Indian Church is coming into its own. In some areas and in connection with some denominations, the Church is fully independent, as for instance, the Gossner Evangelical Lutheran Church in Chota Nagpur. In other areas, while the direction and control is either fully in Indian hands or jointly in the hands of representatives of missions and Churches, the financial support comes mostly from the West. Only in the case of some congregations or Church bodies can it be said that the direction as well as the financial support is entirely the responsibility of the Church in the area.

Not only in the matter of organization, but in appreciating the spiritual background of India too, the Church in North India is turning a new leaf. This is seen in the work of Henry Martyn School of Islamics in Aligarh and of the Society for the Study of Hinduism and its organ *The Pilgrim*. The Christa Prema Seva Ashram at Poona and the Christian Ashrams at Sat Tal, Satna in Vindhya Pradesh, and Sihora in Madhya Pradesh are again attempts at adapting Indian institutions to Christian purposes. The writings of Pandit Nilkanto Shastri, also known as Nehemiah Goreh, and N. V. Tilak, the Christian poet of Mahārāṣṭra, are significant as interpretations of Christian truths through the medium of literature, while A. D. Thomas and Angelo da Fonesca are doing a similar service in the realm of art. Christianity has shown an amazing adaptability in relation to the cultures of different countries it has come into contact with, and there is no reason to doubt that in due course it will make itself perfectly at home in Indian soil and give expression to its genius in modes of thought and practice which are entirely Indian.

Another ideal that the Church in North India is striving to realize is that of unity. On account of various circumstances over which she had little control, the Church in North India has been cut up over the last 150 years into many units owing allegiance to their Mother-Churches overseas and caring little for other sections of the Church in India itself. The divisions in the Church in India, as elsewhere, are a scandal to the Christian name. Indian Christian leaders were among the first to realize this, and various attempts were made in the past by them, in co-operation with missionaries, to find a remedy for this evil. The National Christian Council, formed soon after the World Missionary Conference held in Edinburgh in 1910, has done much in bringing Christians belonging to various denominations together in common enterprises in evangelism, literature, education, and medical service. A desire has thus been kindled in the hearts of the Christians to seek unity by evolving one Church for the whole of India. Negotiations are now going on for bringing about organic unity among the five important branches of the Church in North India, viz. the Church of India (Anglican), the Methodist Church of Southern Asia (Episcopal), the Methodist Church (British and Australian Conferences), the United Church of Northern India (which is itself a union of Congregational and Presbyterian Churches in northern and western India), and the Churches associated with the Baptist Missionary Society in India and Pakistan.

CONTRIBUTION OF INDIAN CHRISTIANS TO NATIONAL RECONSTRUCTION

Further, it may be stated that service of humanity is given high priority by the Church, and, to society in general, several individual Christians have made a significant contribution. Michael Madhusudan Dutt, Toru Dutt, Pandita Ramabai (1858-1922), Kali Charan Banerji (1847-1907), Rajah Sir Harnam Singh (born 1851), Sushil Kumar Rudra (died 1925), Madhusudan Das, and Dr. S. K. Dutta are among those who deserve honourable mention in this connection. The country has benefited not only by the services of a few outstanding men, but from the faithful service of ordinary men and women who have been loyal to the spirit and teachings of their Master. B. L. Rallia Ram of Lahore has stated: 'All over India, Indian Christians are playing a silent and worthy part in national reconstruction. The work of Indian Christian women is particularly remarkable; so far they have been the main stay of educational services.' Another Indian Christian leader recently made the following claim: 'I do not think that any minority community has done so much for the welfare of our country as we have done.'[21]

INFLUENCE OF CHRISTIANITY ON NATIONAL LIFE

Before we close this review, we may ask: What influence has Christianity in North India exerted on the life and culture of the people as a whole? It is not easy to answer the question with any degree of satisfaction. For one thing, it must be borne in mind that Christianity entered North India effectively only about a century and a half ago, and that even now it remains the religion of a minority unevenly distributed over large areas stretching from Assam to Kashmir. Further, it suffered from the handicap of being considered the religion of the conqueror and an agent in the cultural conquest of India by the West. Notwithstanding these difficulties, it may be said that Christianity created a healthy ferment in Indian society, particularly in the nineteenth century. Dr. J. N. Farquhar claims that Christianity has exerted both a direct and an indirect influence on the development of the movements amongst Hindus, Muslims, and Parsis, which he describes in his book.[22] He says further that 'almost without exception, the methods of work used in the movements have been borrowed from the missions'.[23] 'The Christian doctrine of the love of God, which is a necessary element in the Fatherhood, passed into the teaching of the Brāhmo Samāj and the Prārthanā Samāj, and has deeply influenced most of the other movements.'[24]

Christian influence on the development of the Bhakti movement in Hinduism is a subject of fascinating interest to students of Indian history and culture. It is not claiming too much to say that Christian thought and

[21] Dr. P. V. Cherian, Chairman of the Legislative Council, Madras, made this claim in a public speech, which is quoted in the *National Christian Council Review*, January 1955, p. 47.
[22] J. N. Farquhar, *Modern Religious Movements in India* (Lahore, 1943), p. 433.
[23] *Ibid.*, p. 442.
[24] *Ibid.*, p. 436.

practice have had some influence on the development of Bhakti thought and ritual in Indian religions. In support of this the following observation may be quoted as typical of those who make the claim: 'Through Sufi mysticism . . . Vaiṣṇavism of Bengal has received indirect Christian influence. There may have been direct influence also. Regarding later Vaiṣṇavism in Bengal, and especially in the case of the followers of Kabīr, direct Christian influence is an indisputable fact.'[25]

Similarly, about Islam one writer observes: 'To a considerable extent, the modernization of Islam was, in form, a reaction to the stimulus of Christian assault. Almost without exception, reformers wrote their exposition of the new Islam as apologetic answers to their criticisms of the missionaries.'[26]

English education, in imparting which Christian missions played a notable part, has effected revolutionary changes in the social and political outlook of Indians of all classes. According to Jawaharlal Nehru, 'English education brought a widening of Indian horizons, an admiration for English literature and institutions, a revolt against some customs and aspects of Indian life, and a growing demand for political life'.[27] Referring to another aspect of the work of missions, Nehru observes: 'The desire of the Christian missionaries to translate the Bible into every possible language thus resulted in the development of many Indian languages.'[28]

It would be foolish to claim that the inspiration for some of the brightest ideals that characterize various movements in India at the present time is to be found altogether outside the noble elements of religious and ethical heritage of India. And yet, at the same time, no student of history could be so blind as to deny that, in the matter of humanitarian service, social reform, and the creation of a society based on the worth and dignity of the individual, Christian ideals have exerted a stimulating and beneficent influence on the thoughts and aspirations of the intelligentzia in Indian society for the last one century and a half, and, we may hope, will continue to inspire every section of the teeming millions of India in the years to come.

[25] S. Estborn, *The Religion of Tagore* (Christian Literature Society), p. 21.
[26] W. C. Smith, *Modern Islam in India* (Lahore, 1943), p. 44.
[27] *The Discovery of India* (Second Edition, Signet Press, Calcutta, 1946), p. 337.
[28] *Ibid.*, p. 376.

40

ISLAMIC CULTURE

NO one can deny that the Islamic religion has contributed considerably to the progress of the world, its civilization, its knowledge, and its culture, although, even in this enlightened age, the admission is made rather grudgingly and with some hesitation. Anatole France in *The Bloom of Life* said, 'The greatest tragedy in history was the battle of Poitiers, when the science, the art, and the civilization of Arabia fell before the barbarism of the Franks'.

Briffault in his *Making of Humanity* wrote as follows: 'Neither Roger Bacon nor his later namesake has any title to be credited with having introduced the experimental method. Roger Bacon was no more than one of the apostles of Muslim science and method to Christian Europe; and he never wearied of declaring that knowledge of Arabic and Arabic science was for his contemporaries the only way to true knowledge. Discussions as to who was the originator of the experimental method . . . are part of the colossal misrepresentation of the origin of European civilization. The experimental method of the Arabs was by Bacon's time wide-spread and eagerly cultivated throughout Europe. . . . It was not science only which brought Europe back to life. Other and manifold influences from the civilization of Islam communicated its first glow to European life.

'For although there is not a single aspect of European growth in which the decisive influence of Islamic culture is not traceable, nowhere is it so clear and momentous as in the genesis of that power which constitutes the permanent distinctive force of the modern world, and the supreme source of its victory—natural science and the scientific spirit.

'. . . The Greeks systematized, generalized, and theorized, but the patient ways of investigation, the accumulation of positive knowledge, the minute methods of science, detailed and prolonged observation, and experimental enquiry were altogether alien to the Greek temperament. Only in Hellenistic Alexandria was there any approach to scientific work conducted in the ancient classical world. What we call science arose in Europe as a result of a new spirit of enquiry, of new methods of investigation, of the method of experiment, observation, measurement, of the development of mathematics in a form unknown to the Greeks. That spirit and those methods were introduced into the European world by the Arabs.'[1]

[1] Quoted by Iqbal in his *Six Lectures*.

LOVE OF KNOWLEDGE IN ISLAM

Speaking of Ibn Khaldūn, Professor Meyerhof in *The Legacy of Islam* refers to him as the talented Arabian philosopher of history and the greatest intellect of his century. Professor Gibb, in the same book, speaking of Ibn Hazm, said that his name was honoured in the West as the founder of the science of comparative religion. It is not necessary to refer in detail to the contribution of Islam to science, art, literature, philosophy, architecture, music, or to the development of various kinds of industries.

Islam is a religion whose vitality depends on continual progress, and the decadence of Islamic kingdoms in modern times is due to the fall from this standard set in clear terms in the holy *Qur'ān* and the *Hadīs* of the holy Prophet. Let us set down here one quotation from the sayings of our revered Prophet: 'Acquire knowledge, it will enable you to distinguish between right and wrong, it will light the way to heaven, it will be your friend in the desert, your society in solitude, your companion in loneliness, your guide to happiness, the sustainer in your misery, the ornament among your friends, and the armour against your enemies.'

The knowledge essential in a Muslim is that there is only one God. The holy Book says that man was made to worship this one God, and that this is his only function in life (LI. 56). As a matter of fact, the Arabic word used, *iabadun*, implies that man's sole duty is to transform himself into a perfect slave of God. To attain to this state, that is to say, to concentrate his whole soul on God throughout life, man has first to understand God to the best of his capacity, and it is quite clear that man's progress, according to Islam, must depend on how far he has approximated his knowledge of God to the absolute truth about God.

THE NATURE OF GOD AND HIS REMEMBRANCE

We meet with a paradox in the holy *Qur'ān* where we find this description of God: 'The Originator of the heavens and the earth, He made mates for you from among yourselves and mates of the cattle too, multiplying you thereby; nothing is like a likeness of Him; and He is the hearing, the seeing' (XLII.11). So transcendent is God that man cannot conceive even a likeness of Him. The *Qur'ān* further describes Allah as the first and the last, the hidden and the manifest, and says that whichever way we turn, we see His face and that He is with us wherever we be. And in VI.104, it declares: 'Vision comprehends Him not, but He comprehends all vision; and He is the knower of all subtleties, the aware.'

In spite of this clear declaration in the holy Book that God is incomprehensible, Muslims are enjoined to keep Him always in mind: 'Oh you who believe, let not your wealth or your children divert you from the remembrance of Allah; and whoever does that is a loser (LXIII.9). 'Remember Me and I will remember you' (II.152). 'Ask of Me and I will respond to you' (XL.60). This continuous remembrance of God is insisted upon in every line of the *Qur'ān*. In XX. 124-26, we find the following: 'But he who turneth away from remembrance of Me, his will be a narrow life, and I shall bring him blind to the assembly on the Day of Resurrection. He will say, "My Lord, wherefore hast Thou gathered me (hither) blind when I was wont to see?" He (Allah) will say, "So (it must be). Our revelations came unto thee, but thou didst forget them. In like manner thou art forgotten this day".'

It is obvious that the word *dhikr* or remembrance covers a very wide range, varying from a mere passing thought to actual vision in the case of a *majdoob* or a person who is God-intoxicated. Even the repetition of one of God's names is a method of remembrance: 'And Allah's are the best names, therefore call on Him thereby, and leave alone those who violate the sanctity of His names; they shall be requited for what they did' (VII.180). In the *Hadīs-i-Qudsī* we find the following: 'When My servant practises My *dhikr* and his lips move for My sake, I am with him at the time; and I am the companion of one who remembers Me.' 'To one who remains engaged in My *dhikr*, without troubling Me with requests, I give more than to the man who asks of Me.' There is a familiar saying that between man and his *rabb* (Lord) there are 70,000 curtains. The holy *Qur'ān* has, in clear terms, indicated how these thousands of curtains can be removed, so as to get an immediate, though imperfect, vision of Allah. The way indicated is through the acquisition of knowledge. And this explains how the *Qur'ān* inspired the Muslims to adopt the empirical method of inductive reasoning, which led to the rise of modern science.

UNDERSTANDING GOD'S SOVEREIGNTY THROUGH KNOWLEDGE

Some passages may be quoted from the holy Book to illustrate the point: 'Lo! in the creation of the heavens and the earth, and (in) the difference of night and day, are tokens (of His sovereignty) for *men of understanding*, such as remember Allah, standing, sitting, and reclining, and consider the creation of the heavens and the earth, (and say): Our Lord! Thou createdst not this in vain. Glory be to Thee! Preserve us from the doom of Fire' (III.190-91).

'And He it is who hath set for you the stars that ye may guide your course by them amid the darkness of the land and the sea. We have detailed our revelations for a *people who have knowledge*.

'And He it is who hath produced you from a single being, and (hath given you) a habitation and a repository. We have detailed our revelations for a *people who have understanding*' (VI. 98-99).

'Lo! in the creation of the heavens and the earth, and the difference of night and day, and the ships which run upon the sea with that which is of use to men, and the water which Allah sendeth down from the sky, thereby reviving the earth after its death, and dispersing all kinds of beasts therein, and (in) the ordinance of the winds and the clouds obedient between heaven and earth, are signs (of Allah's sovereignty) for *people who have sense*.

'Yet of mankind are some who take unto themselves (objects of worship which they set as) rivals to Allah, loving them with a love like (that which is the due) of Allah (only)—those who believe they are staunchest in their love for Allah—Oh, that those who do evil had but known, (on the day) when they behold the doom, that power belongeth wholly to Allah, and that Allah is severe in punishment!' (II.164-65).

As one's knowledge of the actual phenomena of nature increases, one begins to get a glimmering of the might and power of Allah, and it is thus that man should endeavour to reach Allah and meet Him in this life itself.

MAN'S PLACE IN THE UNIVERSE AND HIS DUTY IN THE WORLD

Thus it will be seen that although God's essence is unknowable, yet man is to concentrate his whole soul into an attempt to understand Him through His attributes with the aid of knowledge. The acquisition of knowledge, which is essential to transmute man into a complete slave of Allah, is also necessary to enable him to come into His kingdom on this earth. As the *Qur'ān* says, 'Surely we offered the trust to the heavens and the earth and the mountains, but they refused the burden and feared to receive it. Man alone undertook to bear it, but proved unjust, senseless' (XXXIII. 72).

There are many passages in the holy Book which show that man was destined to have complete command of all the forces of nature, of the sun, the stars, the wind, all the animals, the trees, the sea, the tides, the mountains, and the moon; and that man will be exalted in proportion to his knowledge. 'Allah will exalt those of you who believe and those who are given knowledge in high degrees, and Allah is aware of what you do' (LVIII.11).

Islam holds out to its followers a life of activity with a continuous remembrance of, and reliance on, God as its ideal, whereby a man's powers for good will fully mature and all his potentialities in the direction of virtue will be completely developed. This double insistence on believing and doing good is to be found in almost every line of the *Qur'ān*. A life spent in meditation or contemplation is insufficient; life has to be lived in strenuous endeavour and toil by man amidst men.

MAN'S ATTITUDE TOWARDS GOD

The chapter known as 'The Kingdom' in the *Qur'ān* begins with this verse: 'Blessed is He in whose hand is the kingdom, and He has power over all things. Who created death and life that He may try you—which of you is best in deeds; and He is the Mighty, the Forgiving' (LXVII.1-2). In his attitude towards God, in his journey through life, man has to balance himself on two wings, namely, the fear of God and the love of God. Mere love of Allah alone may lead man, in his first blinding vision of mystic consciousness, to lose that respect for the power, the might, and the omnipotence of Allah, which is due to Allah. That is why the highest title or honour in which the Prophet delighted was that he was the *abd* or slave of Allah.

It is for the purpose of infusing this feeling of awe in man towards Allah that acquisition of knowledge is necessary for man (XXXV.28). It was really a defect in that great Muslim mystic Mansūr Al-Hallāj when, in moments of ecstasy, he muttered '*Ana'l Haqq*' (I am the Truth). As knowledge and science advance, man begins to realize the omnipotence and power of God and his own helplessness. Says the *Qur'ān*, 'And with Him are the keys of the invisible. None but He knoweth them. And He knoweth what is in the land and the sea. Not a leaf falleth but He knoweth it, not a grain amid the darkness of the earth, naught of wet or dry, but (it is noted) in a clear record' (VI.59).

Although acquisition of knowledge is necessary for man to set him on the path of getting a glimpse of the eternal vision in life, man can never comprehend Allah through the intellect alone. But man can, according to the *Qur'ān*, come into contact with reality, if he will follow the rules set forth therein.

There is a minimum requirement fixed in the Islamic religion before a man can be regarded as a true Muslim. He must make the declaration that there is no God but Allah, and that Mohammed is His apostle; pray at five fixed intervals of time during the day and night; fast during the month of Ramadhān every year from sunrise to sunset; contribute one-fortieth of his income for the benefit of the poor; and make the *haj* pilgrimage at least once in his lifetime. Besides these five obligations, the holy *Qur'ān* contains throughout its pages instructions for those who wish to come into contact with Allah. All the compulsory prayers are fixed and are the same as those performed by the holy Prophet. These prayers were taught to the Prophet by Allah Himself through the angel Gabriel, the

Ruhul Ameen of the *Qur'ān* (XXVI. 192-96). The prayers have to be uttered in Arabic in the same form and with the same accent as Allah Himself taught. There is a mystic significance in this rigid and inflexible discipline.

THE POWER OF THE WORD IN ISLAM

Words have always been mysterious, so much so that the holy Bible refers to them in equally mysterious language. The eastern people have always realized the hidden significance of the power of words, for example, in charms, in sorcery, in invocations to the unseen powers. If we keep this fact in mind, we shall be able to understand the compelling power that the original Arabic words of prayer have on the minds of Muslims in inducing mystic consciousness. The word 'Allah' is frequently used by Muslim Sufis to induce mystic consciousness. Muslims further believe that the heart beats this word 'Allah', and that the wind in the brain mutters the word '*hu*', as one can hear for oneself, if one closes one's ears with the hands.

Another example of the importance of the original Arabic in the Muslim prayer is to be found in the opening chapter of the holy *Qur'ān*, which is always repeated at the beginning of each prayer. The verse begins with the Arabic equivalent of 'ALHMD'—A standing for Allah, L for Gabriel, H for Hauwa or Eve, M for Mohammed, and D for Adam. There is only one Q in this chapter, and that occurs in the word 'straight' in the line 'Guide us into the straight path' ; and here Q stands for the *Qur'ān*.

ISLAMIC FORMULA ABOUT GOD AND HIS MESSENGER

The Islamic formula 'There is no God but Allah, and Mohammed is the messenger of Allah' gives the key to the whole religion. The first portion contains a negation and an affirmation, the denial being that the attributes of Allah can never be ascribed to a created being, and the affirmation that the attributes of Allah belong to and are appropriate only to Allah. An idolater who worships an idol is a sinner, if he regards the idol as the possessor of certain attributes, but he commits no sin, if he is conscious of the fact that certain attributes represented by the features and pose of the idol are the attributes of God.

In the holy *Qur'ān*, Allah asked the Prophet to say that he was himself no more than a man, and was like any other man, but that it had been revealed unto him that God whom man worshipped, however diverse the creed and race of man might be, was one in His essence. The diversity and difference in the conception of God in the heart of man is thus due not to there being different gods, but because the *nafs* or ego of man is obscured by his own desires and sins ; hence the distorted and varying conceptions of God in the mind of man. The remedy suggested by the *Qur'ān* for man is to turn to God and kill his desires.[2]

The whole Islamic formula *'Lā ilāha ilallāh Mohammed-urrasūlallāh'* is of vast importance in Islamic mysticism. When one talks of the love of God, it means very little, for God is intangible and cannot be sensed. That is why there must be some representative of God, who will appear as man and who will evoke from man this feeling of love, by the noble life he will lead, and such were Moses, Jesus Christ, and Mohammed. The holy *Qur'ān* says, 'Say: If you love Allah, then follow me ; Allah will love you and forgive you your faults ; and Allah is forgiving, merciful' (III. 30). The condition laid down is that to love Allah and to get His love in return the only way in Islam is to follow the holy Prophet's rules and his example. The holy *Qur'ān* speaks of prayers in the stillness and silence of night, when the heart whispers its trust and love to its Creator and a ready response is heard. The holy Book commands the Muslims to call upon Allah by any one of His hundred names indicated to man by Allah Himself. 'And when My servants ask you concerning Me, then surely I am very near ; I answer the prayer of the suppliant when he calls on Me, so they should answer My call and believe in Me that they may walk in the right way' (II. 186).

CONDITIONS OF MYSTIC ATTAINMENT

The holy *Qur'ān* has laid down rules which must necessarily be strictly observed before the seeker after truth can set forth on this journey. The compulsory ordinances relating to prayers, fasting, almsgiving, and the *haj* pilgrimage must be observed before a Muslim can realize the truth. Assuming that he observes these simple rules, if he practises the *dhikr* or remembrance of Allah, he can easily get the mystic experience which his soul yearns for. But in practising *mushāhida* (realization) and *murāqaba* (meditation), as the Sufi calls the effort to get this experience, the slow, quiet recital of a name of Allah is necessary to strip the aspirant's mind of all mental images and to induce that love for Allah which will suddenly transport him from worldly consciousness to mystic experience.

It is always the heart, the inner intuition, to which God whispers, and if it is properly attuned, not only can one hear the 'still sad music of humanity', but one can even acquire knowledge, wisdom, solace, comfort, guidance in troubles, and protection from harm. This is the *ilm ladunni* referred to in the chapter called 'The Cave', and the *Qur'ān* is full of examples of this

[2] See the commentary of Muhayadin El Arabi on the *Qur'ān*, II. 54.

kind of knowledge and guidance acquired by the prophets of old. The aim and object of every Muslim Sufi is to get not only a vision of the next world in this life itself, but actually to hear Allah's mysterious messages and voice every minute of his life. This kind of prayer is well described in the following extract from the great Muslim mystic Ghazālī's lecture on 'Absorption in God':

'Prayers have three veils, whereof the first is prayers uttered only by the tongue; the second is when the mind, by hard endeavour and by firmest resolve, reaches a point at which, being untroubled by evil suggestions, it is able to concentrate itself on divine matters; the third veil is when the mind can, with difficulty, be diverted from dwelling on divine matters. But the marrow of prayer is seen when He who is invoked by prayer takes possession of the mind of him who prays, and the mind of the latter is absorbed in God whom he addresses, his prayers ceasing and no self-consciousness abiding in him, even to this extent that a mere thought about his prayers appears to him a veil and a hindrance. This state is called 'absorption' by the doctors of mystical lore, when a man is so utterly absorbed that he perceives nothing of his bodily members, nothing of what is passing without, nothing of what occurs to his mind—yea, when he is, as it were, absent from all these things whatsoever, journeying first *to* his Lord, then *in* his Lord. But if the thought occurs to him that he is totally absorbed, that is a blot; for only that absorption is worthy of the name which is unconscious of absorption.'[3]

An endeavour has been made in this short article to explain the principal points in the religion of Islam and why it is (as Iqbal has pointed out in his *Six Lectures*) that Goethe, while making a general review of Islam as an educational force, said to Eckermann: 'You see this teaching never fails; with all our systems, we cannot go, and generally speaking no man can go, further than that.'

[3] See Sirdar Ikbal Ali Shah, *Oriental Caravan* (Denis Archer, London, 1933), p. 77.

41

ISLAM IN INDIA

THE Muslims form one of the most important constituents of the national economy of India. For at least a thousand years, they have, particularly in the North, supplied one of the major forces in the shaping of India's economic, political, and social history. Small groups may have trickled into the country at even earlier periods, but about the end of the first millennium, the trickle deepened into a steady stream, which flowed into the land without any sign of sagging for almost eight hundred years. Woven into the intricate pattern of Indian life, the Muslims have yet maintained their individuality. They have contributed to the symphony of Indian life and yet retained a distinct timbre that can be clearly recognized. An essential part of Indian life, but with a distinctiveness of their own, they present a phenomenon which has few parallels elsewhere. India has assimilated almost all foreign races and cultures that entered the land at different times by broadening her faith and her social structure. In most other countries, Muslims have also assimilated the land into the main stream of Islamic culture. India is the one exception where neither has Islam been overpowered by India, nor has India been absorbed into the Islamic world.

TWO INFLUENCES IN THEIR MENTAL MAKE-UP

In order to understand the Indian Muslim and his place in Indian history, one must remember that two factors have contributed to his mental evolution and make-up. On the one hand, there has been the influence of Islam and the philosophy of life represented by it. On the other, there has been the pervasive influence of Indian culture and civilization. These two forces have acted steadily throughout the centuries and shaped his life and character. If the Indian Muslim is distinct from his counterpart in other parts of the world, this is due to the interaction of these two forces at many levels. The fact that the Muslims came to India not in one solid and compact block, but in driblets that were spread through centuries has further helped this process of assimilation.

The main contributions of Islam to the mental make-up of Indian Muslims have been the insistence on a militant democracy, liberal rationalism in practical conduct, and an uncompromising monotheism that, at times, verged on iconoclasm and intolerance. It is generally recognized that Islam's democratic urge is perhaps its greatest contribution to world culture. True, there are both Semitic and Aryan parallels, but no other religion has insisted on it so strongly, nor succeeded in instilling into its adherents an equal sense of democratic spirit among the faithful. In theory, every religion recognizes the principles of fatherhood of God and brotherhood of man. In practice, however, the fatherhood of God often remains an article of faith divorced from the realities of life. Clash of colour and inequalities of birth, station, and wealth make the brotherhood of man a mere ideal unrelated to the daily activities of life. Even its worst enemies have, however, admitted that Islam broke down the barriers of colour and birth absolutely in the formal act of worship and with negligible restrictions in daily social intercourse.

The liberalism of Islam is seen in its comparative freedom from geographic limitations. This is a corollary as much to its emphasis upon equality of men as to its missionary character. A democratic attitude is, in a sense, a direct consequence of rationalism. The human intellect is the same whatever be one's colour or nationality. Islam's attempt to break away from the domination of priestcraft and its comparative freedom from mystical speculation and superstition are other manifestations of its rationalism. It is well known that the Prophet of Islam himself never claimed any superhuman quality or virtue. He was never tired of insisting that he was a man among men. His precedence over others came not so much from any authority based on revelation, as from the quality of intelligence applied to the solution of the problems of life.

Reason is the same for all, and insistence upon the universality of spiritual laws was only the obverse of the insistence on the unity of reason. Faith in an ultimate revelation through Mohammed for the spiritual uplift of the whole human race tended to intensify missionary zeal. Islam thus recognized no limitation whatsoever to the application of its laws of spiritual life. The new faith in unitary reason would therefore allow of neither exception nor qualification. Truth was one and unique, and anything which differed from the true must therefore be false. Consciousness of the value of Truth was therefore matched with the repudiation of whatever differed from it. It was inevitable that, in such circumstances, the religious zeal of Islam should, in the application of its relentless logic, develop into iconoclasm and beget, at times, especially in some of its earlier phases, narrowness and intolerance.

The Indian Muslims were, however, equally subject to the influence of the traditions of India. In some ways, these represented an entirely different outlook on life. If Islam insisted on the unity of Truth, it was the diversity and manifoldness of its manifestations which had their greatest appeal to the Indian intellect. India looked at Reality as a substance with infinite attributes, all of which had equal validity. In its perception of the importance of the gradations of Truth, India, at times, went to the other extreme, where even evil was looked upon as a lesser good and tolerated as a necessary adjunct of the Real. The Indian genius for synthesis has rightly evoked the admiration of the entire world, but the weakness inherent in its acceptance or tolerance of everything, without discrimination, has not always been noticed.

Many of the institutions, which are peculiarly Indian, can be derived from this synthetic outlook on life. Caste, which is a division of human beings into different grades, is repugnant to the non-Hindu mind. When one interprets it as an attempt to find a function for different stages of evolution of the human personality, it, however, attains a new significance. So long as caste was functional and not hereditary, it served as a principle of democracy, rather than otherwise. It was only when its fluidity was lost and, instead of being the expression of co-operation between different elements of one organism, it became the embodiment of sharply differentiated social strata, that caste became the national and social problem that it is today. In any case, caste attempted to find a place, however inferior, for those who had been conquered, as opposed to certain other types of colonization or conquest, where the conquered are entirely segregated or even annihilated.

The Indian Muslims were therefore subject, on the one hand, to Islam's insistence upon social homogeneity and, on the other, to the Indian tradition of rigid stratification according to caste. They thus acquired some of the habits and prejudices which characterized the later rigid form of the caste system, but, because of the Islamic insistence on equality of man, retained something of its original flexibility. This is clearly seen in the manner in which caste expressed itself in Indian Muslim society. Early Islam insisted on equality of man and repudiated even family names, as these tended to perpetuate distinctions. The Indian Muslims could not therefore accept a system of caste based on the fact of birth alone. In its place, Muslim society in India evolved a type of caste based on wealth and station.

The Muslim variation of caste is seen most clearly in the institution of feudalism. Inconsistent with the spirit of Islam, in India it became associated especially with the Muslims. Military conquest always tends to produce a feudal society, and in India it became a necessary element in the Muslim system of land administration. Absence of modern means of communication made the control of so vast a country as India, from one common centre, impossible. It was inevitable that a good deal of authority should be delegated to the local representatives of the king. In time, they grew into petty chieftains or kinglings rather than administrators serving a central authority. Social life was disfigured by the existence of a large number of slaves, both male and female, in the household of kings and nobles. Indigenous converts often failed to attain the social status of those who had foreign blood in their veins and, in a plutocratic regime, the poor tended to form a separate class. Converts tended to carry over their caste prejudices to their new faith. Difference in social esteem among converts from different castes could not thus be altogether avoided.

Indian philosophy has always emphasized the wholeness of life and brought with it an attitude of toleration and forbearance. Indian Muslims were influenced by this spirit of catholicity of the traditions of ancient India. It is significant that the attempts at *rapprochement* between Islam and Hinduism were as strong from the Muslim side as from that of the Hindus. Just as the teachings of Rāmānanda, Nānak, and Caitanya tended to narrow the distinction between Hinduism and Islam, there were also Kabīr, Chishti, and Dārā Shukoh who attempted an understanding and unification of the two faiths from the side of the Muslims. Nor must it be forgotten that, though orthodoxy looked askance, one of the supreme architects of this movement for synthesis was Akbar the Great.

THE ADVENT OF ISLAM IN INDIA

The fact that Muslim penetration into India was not a case of wholesale colonization, but of successive waves of military attack ensured that each invading group would, in its turn, be subject to the pervasive influence of Hinduism when it settled down. Small groups of men who came as military conquerors were themselves largely conquered culturally. We have also to remember that, except the original invaders of Sind, the Muslim conquerors were not Arabs, but mainly Turks or Turko-Afghans who had themselves acquired Islamic civilization and culture comparatively recently. Rightly or wrongly, the Arabs were convinced of the superiority of their own culture. Where, however, Islam came to a country through other races, no such cultural supremacy could be established, as the conquerors were, in many cases, inferior in civilization to the people whom they conquered. It is a matter of history that, where Islam came to a country through the Arabs, there was a process of virtual cultural conquest. This was achieved sometimes by partial absorption of some ingredients of local culture, sometimes by the imposition of Arab culture on the conquered.

If the conquest of India had been undertaken by the Arabs, it is probable that they would have taken over some of the elements of Indian culture. While drawing on India's past, the Arab conquest was, at the same time, likely to have attempted the imposition of Arab culture on the Indian masses. This has been the pattern of Arab cultural conquest in other regions. It must be remembered that even the highly developed civilizations of Iran and Egypt could not withstand the onslaught of the Arab wave. Like the remnants of Greco-Roman civilization in Constantinople, the ancient cultures of Egypt and Iran were lost in the Arab wave. Characteristically enough, the Arabs accepted, in course of time, some of the ancient traditions, heroes, and legends of these countries as part of their own national heritage. The fact that a new race was reared by fusion with local converts, male and female, helped the process, for they transmitted their national stories as nursery tales. Thus Alexander is as much an Arab hero as a Greek. The exploits of Rustum have been taken up into the common currency of Muslim tradition. The queen of Sheba and the diverse manifestations of Egyptian civilization were equally absorbed in the general current of Arab history.

The Arabs thus tried to impose a composite Arab culture, based on their own language and script, on the local peoples, after absorbing some elements of value in the indigenous civilizations. The Turko-Afghans, who in successive waves conquered India, followed a different policy. They were at first content to preserve for themselves fragments of the Arab culture they had inherited: they sought neither to impose it on India nor enrich it by drawing upon the rich heritage of the land. One reason for this may be that they were perhaps not in a position to attempt a cultural synthesis. The Iranian-Arab culture which they flaunted was for them a comparatively new acquisition, and had not entered into the texture of their life and being. They had, however, all the zeal of a new convert. Therefore, for a long period after their advent on the Indian scene, they sought to remain aloof. In course of time, however, the processes of geography and economy proved stronger than such racial exclusiveness. They were slowly woven into the Indian pattern, drawn by the tolerance and responsiveness of the Indian mind and their own capacity for absorption and imitation.

It is not necessary to describe in detail the consequences which followed from centuries of common life. Throughout India, an initial clash was followed by fusion and synthesis. These contacts had a profound influence on the way of life of the peoples inhabiting this land. There were far-reaching changes in their dress, food, language, literature, art, painting, architecture, music, and philosophy. In a way, a *rapprochement* was inevitable from the very nature of the case. Administration cannot be carried on for long by mere force or with the help of imported functionaries. The needs of administration led to innovations which were, in almost every case, compromises. As a result of living in the land, the Muslim invaders were gradually absorbed into its economy. They developed an attitude at first of toleration and then of appreciation and love for the culture of the land.

There was hardly any racial distinction between the earlier rulers of the different so-called Pathan dynasties and the Moguls who came later. The difference in their approach and outlook is, however, fundamental and is the inevitable consequence of common life through centuries.

FACTORS LEADING TO THE SPREAD OF ISLAM

One reason which made a fusion of Hindu and Muslim outlooks not only easy, but in a sense inevitable was the fact that large masses of the native people entered the fold of the new faith. History tells us that there was no large-scale colonization by the Muslims. It was a case of infiltration of small groups who came in successive waves. In some cases, those who were conquered had the faith and outlook of their conquerors imposed on them. In many cases, there was no question of any imposition. There was a willing acceptance of the new faith by large numbers, on whom the existing social order pressed heavily. It also attracted those who had developed a sense of dissatisfaction with the prevailing religion of the country. It was therefore not only the oppressed and unprivileged, but also a section of the intelligentzia who were drawn by the simplicity and vigour of the new faith. There were, no doubt, many who were influenced by the worldly advantages offered by the new faith. Equally strong must have been its appeal to those whose innate sense of social justice and human dignity rebelled against the rigidity of caste.

By the time of the advent of the Muslims, Hindu society had become ossified with its rigid strata of castes. Earlier attempts to rebel against the authority of the Brāhmaṇas had reached their culmination in the great movements of Buddhism and Jainism. For a time, it seemed as if Buddhism, with its emphasis on equality and common humanity, would permanently change the structure of Indian life. By the end of the seventh century, Buddhism had, however, spent itself. Neo-Brāhmaṇism began to dominate India about the time of Śaṅkara, but the triumph of neo-Brāhmanism was not swift or easy. The Buddhist tradition continued longest in areas like Bihar and Bengal. Even after the triumph of Brāhmaṇism, the defeated Buddhists did not give up the fight. They seized opportunities to express their resentment against the unwelcome domination, and actually helped Mohammed ibn-Qāsīm in defeating the Brāhmaṇa king Dāhir of Sind near Raor in A.D. 712.

In the greater part of India, the Brāhmaṇical supremacy had been re-established by the seventh or the eighth century. In Bengal, however, this process was not completed till about the end of the ninth century. When Muslims appeared in Bengal, they found everywhere large, disgruntled groups who had been in opposition to, if not more powerful than, the dominating religious group of the day. When one looks at the record of the struggles of this period, one is repeatedly struck by the fact that small groups of Muslims triumphed over very much larger indigenous armies. This cannot be explained in terms of personal valour. The records are clear that in sheer bravery there was nothing to choose between the protagonists. It may be true that better strategy and military tactics often gave the invaders an advantage. It is, however, obvious that a small group of military conquerors could not for long withstand the resistance of a vast mass of local people, especially in a country like India, unless there were elements within the country itself which, for some reason or other, deserted the local rulers and lent their support to the invaders. This is corroborated by the record of events. In many cases, the conquerors from outside had local allies, who played an equally important rôle in the outcome. Local morale may, at times, have been affected by fear, based on the military reputation and the alleged relentlessness of the invaders. The defections were, however, too wide-spread to be explained by mere prudence or love of gain.

Popular interpretation of events in Bengal assumes this theory of internal support for the Muslim conquerors. For reasons mentioned above, a large number of the people did not accept neo-Brāhmaṇism except under duress. In Bengal, the embers of departed Buddhism were still hot when the Muslims came. This is recorded in the ballads and legends of the period. Ballads, incorporated among the vernacular religious literature of the land, announce that the Muslim conquerors came as the champions of *dharma,* in order to rescue from oppression the masses of the people. There is also a legend that eighteen horsemen, who came in the guise of horse-sellers, sufficed to conquer the capital of Lakṣmaṇasena, the last king of the neo-Brāhmaṇical tradition. In the light of later research, this legend may be regarded as a crystallization of the fear-motive of the people who had already heard of Bakhtiyār Khaljī's success in Bihar. Similarly, the ballad about *dharma* coming in the guise of Muslims may be explained as an expression of resentment against the prevailing social structure among those who had been obliged to forsake Buddhism and assigned a lower status in Hindu society. Even if we question their factual content, these ballads and legends prove that a large section of the people were ready to acquiesce in, if not welcome, the Pathan conquest of Bengal.

This fact also helps to explain the large proportion of Muslims in the population of Bengal, even though it was so far removed from the centre of Pathan or Mogul power. Some Buddhists preferred Hinduism to Islam and found some sort of a place within the Hindu social system, but there are indications that large numbers accepted the new faith, from whatsoever motive, in the new political regime. The fact, however, that large masses joined the new faith ensured that the faith itself would be modified by the new converts. Men can change their religion, but it is not so easy to change their ways of life. These neo-Muslims gave to Indian Islam an indigenous temper which made *rapprochement* between the two religions easy and natural.

SYNTHESIS OF HINDU AND MUSLIM THOUGHT AND CULTURE

The process of integration which followed profoundly changed the character of pristine Islam. We have already referred to the growth of feudalism and of a kind of modified caste. Islam has always condemned a separate priesthood, but there are unmistakable signs of such a growth among Indian Muslims. They also show a marked fondness for ritual and elaborate ceremony. Islam was iconoclastic, but Indian Muslims often display a veneration for saints and their tombs that reminds one of the worship of relics. Mohammed stressed the uniformity of natural law and laid hardly any store by miracles, but the Indian Muslim felt unhappy till he had built up a halo of sanctity, if not divinity, round his religious heroes. Muslim practice in India thus tended to conform to Hindu religious customs. Members of the two communities also participated in one another's religious festivals. The Wahhābī movement, which sought to develop among Indian Muslims a puritanic outlook, challenged such practices. The estrangement was carried further by the growing political rivalry between the two communities.

Such influences were not, perhaps cannot be, one-sided. There are reasons for suspecting Muslim influence in some of the citadels of Hindu orthodoxy. Śaṅkara is perhaps the greatest architect of modern Hinduism, and yet there are in his thought elements which betoken a spirit of revolt against all pluralism. His extreme monism, his repudiation of the semblance of duality, his attempt to establish this monism on the authority of revealed scripture, and his tendency to regard his own activity as mere restoration of the purity of an original truth are all elements which, barring the doctrine of Māyā, have strange parallels in Islam. Perhaps every one of these items can by itself be derived from old Upaniṣadic sources. But do their synthesis into one body of compact thought and the nature and temper of the synthesis achieved suggest the operation of some new catalytic agent? Was Christianity or Islam a factor in his monistic interpretation, or did he derive his inspiration solely from the line of indigenous teachers mentioned by him?

Historical factors do not exclude the possibility of Śaṅkara's acquaintance with the elements of Islamic thought. The first Arab fleet appeared in Indian waters in A.D. 636, but was beaten off. But, according to Rawlinson, the first Muslim Arabs settled in the Malabar coast about the end of the seventh century. Francis Day, in his *The Land of the Perumals,* and Sturrock, in his *South Kanara, Madras District Manuals,* make similar statements. Elliot's accounts of the causes of the Arab invasion of Sind also indicate that Arab settlements had already been established on the west coast. Innes, in his *Malabar and Anjangode District Gazetteer,* quotes an inscription of a tomb from Kollam of one Ali who died there in A.H. 166, i.e. A.D. 788. Further circumstantial evidence is offered by the revolt in A.D. 758 of a colony of Muslims established at Canton in China. It is obvious that this colony could not have been founded without intermediate stations, of which the Malabar coast was likely to be one. Caldwell picked up near Kayalapattam in Tinnevelly, near the mouth of the Tāmraparṇī, a number of Arab coins bearing dates from A.H. 71, i.e. A.D. 693. Since definite first-hand information is not available, only guesses and inferences can be made. Some of the facts stated above do, however, indicate that Arabs had regular trade connection with South India, and their religious beliefs and habits may have been known to the local population.

Fawcett, in his notes on the people of Malabar (*Anthropology,* III. 1), draws attention to the growth of the Bhakti cult in the South. He suggests that this was due mainly to the influence of Islam. Grierson, Logan, and Bhandarkar had expressed the opinion that this was due to the influence of Christian communities in the South where, according to Grierson, Islamic mysticism or Sufism, which influenced Bhāgavatism in North India later, was little known, while Carpenter and Barnett regarded this as due to internal causes. Barth, in his *Religions of India,* also suggests a similar explanation for the advent of new religious movements in the South. Fawcett points out that Christianity was not then sufficiently important to influence Hindu thought. He quotes the tradition that the king of Kaladi, where Śaṅkara was born, had been converted to Islam at the time of Śaṅkara's birth. If this can be substantiated by means of reliable data, it would go to show that in that region, at least, Islam was a force. Śaṅkara's excommunication by the Brāhmaṇas and his performance of the last rites of his mother with the help of the Nairs also suggest that Śaṅkara was not afraid of daring innovation in practice. The evidence may not be conclusive, but is yet sufficiently strong to demand a revision of some of our preconceived ideas about the sources of Śaṅkara's philosophy and a fresh inquiry into the religious movements of the period which influenced his thought.

Some of the results which followed from Muslim settlement in India may now be briefly indicated. The first was a reopening of the doors to the West. Ancient India had its contacts with Rome, Greece, and Egypt. In the political vacuum which followed the collapse of the Gupta power, these were largely lost. Another reason for the loss of these contacts was the gradual decay in Indian naval power. Arab contacts with India had, however, continued on a small scale even during this period. After the conversion of the Arabs to Islam, there was an efflorescence of the Arab spirit, which expressed itself in almost every sphere of life. One immediate consequence was a great expansion in Arab mercantile and naval fleets. There is evidence to show that, before the end of the seventh century, Arab groups had settled near about Calicut and built up flourishing establishments. This resulted not only in commercial contacts, but also in an exchange of ideas, customs, and traditions and perhaps led to a quickening of contemporary local thought.

Another consequence of the establishment of Muslim rule was the restoration of internal peace throughout northern India under one uniform administration. The break-up of the Gupta power had led to the rise of small States which were continually fighting one another. This must have prevented a smooth or uniform development of social life. The unity of India was thus often lost sight of behind local manifestations which were divergent. The unitary form of administration—first of the Delhi Sultanate and later of the Mogul Empire—helped to repromote the unity of Indian outlook. This was reinforced by a uniformity in social manners introduced by the Muslims. Whether in the North or in the South, the Muslims had a uniformity in dress, food, customs, and beliefs which could not escape the notice of their non-Muslim neighbours. The result was a growth of uniformity in social manners throughout the country, particularly in urban areas. Court etiquette largely influenced the conduct, irrespective of community or creed, of all who desired worldly advancement. As early as the time of Bābur, this was becoming perceptible, so that he described it in his autobiography as the growth of the Hindustani way of life. This process towards uniformity was further strengthened by the introduction of a common revenue system and the gradual spread of common methods in war and peace.

The consequences of co-operative living are most manifest in the realm of art and letters. The achievements of Indo-Saracenic art were made possible by a combination of the Indian instinct for ornamentation with the Saracenic sense of form. This is exemplified not only in the wonderful architecture of the period, but also in painting, weaving, metallurgy, and garden craft. The miniatures which evoke our admiration, the shawls of inimitable workmanship, the swords with their delicate inlaid work, the muslins of incomparable quality, and the wonderful gardens which the Moguls built—all reveal a balance between form and content that is as perfect as it is rare.

Even more significant was the co-operation of the communities in the evolution of a common language, wherever Muslims settled among Hindus. Urdu, Hindi, or Hindustani—whatever be the name given to it—was evolved out of material derived from ancient Indian sources as well as the innovations brought in by the new settlers. Along with this growth of a common language, there was the remarkable phenomenon of the growth of literature in the different Indian languages. Before the advent of the Muslims, Sanskrit held the pride of place among all learned men. It was *deva-bhāṣā,* the language of the gods, and demanded all the devotion and energy of the people who had any pretensions to the culture of India as a whole. The mother tongue was hardly more than a dialect restricted to local interchange of thought ; in any case, it was a vernacular fit only for people of inferior social and intellectual status. The great religious teachers had, no doubt, often preached in Prakrit or mixed Sanskrit, but, in course of time, chaste Sanskrit reasserted its supremacy.

This domination of Sanskrit retarded the growth of literature in any of the dialects. The advent of Muslim power created a new situation in which Sanskrit was gradually dethroned from its position of privilege. Religious reformers, mostly non-Brāhmaṇa and some even non-Hindu, made their appeal in local dialects. This was followed by an outburst of literary activity in all the local languages. This efflorescence of literature was most marked where the affinity between Muslims and Hindus was greatest. The result was the achievement of a common outlook, which softened the sharp formalism of Islam and simplified the elaborate rituals of Hinduism. Large-scale intermixture which followed conversion led not only to the establishment of a more or less homogeneous racial type, but also to the development of a common political and cultural pattern. The Pathan rulers of Bengal identified themselves completely with the people of the land. As a result, a fairly homogeneous cultural group supported them in their fight against attempts at domination from Delhi. This also explains why they were great patrons of Bengali literature and provided in their courts the incentive and opportunity for the development of indigenous poetry. With local variations, a similar process was at work in Gujarat, Malabar, and the present Uttar Pradesh. These are also the areas where modern literature in regional languages grew up.

The synthesis in the field of religion has often been noticed and does not require elaborate description. It is enough to say that, both from the Muslim and from the Hindu point of view, there was an attempt at *rapprochement*. The lives of men like Rāmānanda, Kabīr, Nānak, Dādū, and others offer unmistakable testimony of this fact. The similarities between Vaiṣṇavism and Sufism have often been noticed and need not be stressed. Their affinity must have contributed to the popularity of Sufi saints in India. Both Vaiṣṇavism and Sufism lay great emphasis on the rediscovery of man. Both seek to find for him self-realization outside the limitations imposed by convention and rigid dogma.

By the end of the sixteenth century, a *modus vivendi* between the different Indian communities had already been achieved in the North. At the top, the aristocracy had attained a uniformity in behaviour, mode of life, and general outlook, regardless of differences in faith. Here, the dominant note was that of the courts with their almost complete acceptance of the culture of Iran. At the other end of the scale, the masses also had established a kind of mutual toleration, which enabled them to face their common problems and share common festive delights.

EFFECT OF BRITISH RULE ON THE SYNTHESIZING PROCESS

With the advent of the West, an entirely new situation developed. The two communities reacted in entirely different ways to this new force. Large elements among the Hindus accepted western education without any qualms. To large sections of Muslims, the very existence of European power in India was a constant reminder of their own defeat. It is not therefore surprising that, even after British power had been consolidated, the Muslims, for a long time, maintained an attitude of utter non-co-operation with everything British. This meant not only a denial of opportunities in services and commerce, but, what in the end proved even more disastrous to them, it meant a failure to imbibe the science and knowledge of the West. Deprived of their own traditional modes of learning and unable to benefit by the new knowledge brought to India by the British, the Muslims, as a community, went through a period of intellectual sterility, the effects of which are perceptible even to this day.

The British attitude towards the Muslims was also a factor which kept the Muslims away from this new source of knowledge and strength. For a long time, the British did everything in their power to curb the Muslim intelligentzia and undermine their influence in every sphere of life. Indian history was rewritten in a manner which laid one-sided emphasis on the oppressive character of Muslim rule, from which the British had liberated the people of the land. An attitude of hostility towards Muslims was thus encouraged among the other communities. Simultaneously, administrative and political policy was so shaped as to undermine their economic and cultural position. It is not necessary to go into details. Let us take the example of the province of Bengal, where the British first established their power. We can trace the gradual elimination of Muslims from every position of vantage through State action in the successive instruments of of Permanent Settlement, Resumption Proceedings, and the Education Circulars. The Permanent Settlement resulted in many families, mainly Muslim, losing their lands, and they were substituted by a new class of landlords, who owed their origin to, and depended for their survival on, the British power. The Resumption Proceedings impoverished the few Muslim families which had survived the Permanent Settlement and tended to destroy the economic basis of all Muslim institutions of knowledge and learning. The substitution of English for Persian in educational institutions and government business contributed still further to the discomfiture of the Muslims in almost every field.

The British hostility towards Indian Muslims was further enhanced by the abortive struggle of 1857. Hindus and Muslims had alike taken part in the rising. Some of the most distinguished protagonists were from Mahārāṣṭra. Nevertheless, the fact that the Mogul emperor was the figurehead of the revolt and that the Muslim landed classes in Bihar, Uttar Pradesh, and Delhi had largely sided with the insurgents deepened the British antipathy to the Muslim community. After the rising had been quelled, the British hand was heavier on Muslim participants than on those belonging to other communities. In a word, from the beginning of the eighteenth to almost the end of the nineteenth century, the British looked upon the Muslims as their chief enemies or potential sources of danger. It was only in the last two decades of the nineteenth century that there started a shift in British policy. The rise of the Indian middle classes—mainly Hindu in their composition—led to the establishment of the Indian National Congress as the instrument for achievement of power. This evoked in the British administrators of the day an uneasy feeling that, while the danger from the Muslim community had perhaps disappeared, a new threat had arisen from an entirely unexpected quarter.

From 1886 to 1909, British policy was hesitant, divided, and uncertain. The old fear of the Muslims continued, even though the basis of the Muslim threat had been destroyed. The old habit of utilizing the new Hindu middle classes could not be totally given up, even though, from 1886, the more discerning among the British began to sense that the main challenge to their power was bound to come from these classes. After almost twenty years' hesitation, the British decided to transfer their patronage from the Hindu middle classes to their counterparts among the Muslims. The Muslim League was thus born under British patronage, and devoted itself to a re-establishment of the position of the community by a dual policy of courting the favour of the rulers and challenging the position of the non-Muslims. We need not go into the troubled and sorry history of the conflicts and intrigues of the recent decades. It is enough to say that these ultimately led to the partition of the country, in 1947, and the emergence of the two separate States of India and Pakistan.

The process of growth, both among the Hindus and the Muslims, for almost nine centuries was one of contact, assimilation, and synthesis. The intrusion of the new element of western influence started a process of dissociation between the two communities, and was an inroad upon the common culture built up through a millennium. Among both Hindus and Muslims, there was an attempt to resuscitate the original form and pattern of their respective cultures. This was in many cases impossible, as the process of time made a reversion to original types impossible. Even in such cases, there was often an attempt to overlook the period of common life and to reorientate the old forms in the light of new factors introduced by the western impact. History cannot, however, be re-lived. The re-creation of the past is itself subject to the influence of all that has happened in between. India's determination to establish herself as a secular, democratic State is a recognition of this fact. It is an acceptance of her history without seeking to deny or repudiate any element that has once entered the national life. The rôle of Indian Muslims in the new set-up is to help in this process by bringing to the common heritage the power of synthesis and assimilation, which their forefathers—whether native to India or settlers from outside—exhibited throughout the days of their supremacy.

42

SUFISM

I

THE origin of the term 'Sufi' is from the word '*ṣūf*' (wool), i.e. a Sufi is one who wears garments of wool. It is not derived from *ṣaff* (rank) or *ṣafā* (purity). As woollen raiment used to be regarded as an emblem of simplicity and a silent protest against the growing luxuries of the world, those who lived a simple life and were intoxicated with Truth, in any form, were termed Sufis.

The theories connected with the genesis of Sufism are varied and even contradictory. Four of them are important and are delineated below:

(1) It represents the esoteric doctrine of Prophet Mohammed. There exist some stray references in the *Qur'ān* and the *Hadīs* (Traditions) to the Prophet saying, 'I was a hidden treasure and I desired to be known; therefore I created Creation that I might be known', and 'Whosoever knoweth himself, knoweth his God'. But it is not possible to evolve a system of thought out of these stray and rare utterances. Although many Muslim saints, even at a very late date, tried to idealize the physical form and beauty of Prophet Mohammed, they were not dubbed heterodox, for the guise of Sufi terminology fits in with the established faith of Islam.

(2) It must be regarded as the reaction of the Aryan mind against a Semitic religion imposed upon it by force. There are, no doubt, some resemblances between Sufi doctrines, in their more advanced forms, and the Vedānta, which can be referred to their common origin in India. It is an established fact that, as early as Naushirwan's time, cultural contacts were established between India and Iran by exchange of scholars and envoys. Even earlier than that, Buddhism extended its sway over Iran and Afghanistan, through the efforts and missionary zeal of the Indian emperor, Aśoka. The pacifism, contentment, and non-violence which gained ground in Sufism can claim their origin in Buddhism.

(3) It was due to neo-Platonist influence. Plotinus himself is stated to have visited Iran with seven neo-Platonist philosophers, who were driven out from their home and compelled to flee to Iran in the times of Naushirwan.

(4) It has an independent origin. Because Sufism meets the requirements, and satisfies the cravings, of a certain class of minds, existing in all ages and in most of the civilized communities, the evolution of this

system of thought should be regarded as a phenomenon of spontaneous, independent, and indigenous growth, recurring in many similar and unconnected forms, wherever the human mind continues to concern itself with the problems of the wherefore, the whence, and the whither of the Spirit.

SUFISM AND VEDĀNTA

Sufism is a catholic development of a system of thought in Islam, which found special favour in the fertile land of Iran. It is decidedly a case of eclecticism against dogmatism, and great Sufis, like Jalālud-Dīn Rūmī and Mansūr Al-Hallāj, were, in reality, the exponents of various heretical doctrines and were persecuted on account of their religious opinions, though the same opinions were subsequently canonized by later Sufis. They all believed in the essential unity of all religions, transmigration and eternality of the soul, and the immanence of God. Rūmī, the great and celebrated founder of the Vedāntic type of Sufism in Islam, introduced *samā'*, a particular kind of devotional dance akin to *kīrtana*. Mansūr Hallāj, the greatest monist in Islam, was accused of blasphemy when he said '*Ana'l Haqq*' (I am the Truth), and was executed on account of this heretic declaration. Bāyazīd Bistāmī announced: 'I am the unfathomable ocean, without beginning and without end. I am the throne of God, the preserved tablet, the pen or creative word of God. Praise be to me, I am the Truth, I am the true God, I must be celebrated by divine praises.' Farīdud-Dīn 'Aṭṭār, the famous author of the allegorical poem 'Logic of Birds', declared, 'Verily I am God ; there is no God but me'. Junayd said: 'God spoke with mankind by the tongue of Junayd, though Junayd was no longer there, and men knew it not.' These Sufis and their utterances were not looked upon with favour by devout and orthodox Muslims.

THE QUEST OF SUFISM

In Sufism, importance is attached more to the activities of the inner self than to the observance of outward religious practices and rituals. Sufism is an expression of dissatisfaction with the Islamic idea of a transcendent God. The *Qur'ān* and the *Sunnat* (Reason) do not give complete satisfaction to a searching mind in its quest for finality ; it begins to believe in 'illumination' or 'intuition'. The quest, which is another name of 'knowledge', is of three kinds: (1) Knowledge received *from* God, based on the law revealed by God ; (2) Knowledge obtained *with* God, which is of the mystic path ; and (3) Knowledge acquired *of* God, possessed by prophets, saints, and teachers who are in direct communion with God and work under His guidance and illumination.

The hostile or apathetic attitude of the Umayyad Caliphs encouraged the pious Muslims to have recourse to meditation and contemplation, and the conviction grew upon them that this world was but an illusion and that they should pay more attention to the achievement of paradise in the next world. Constant war was an additional reason, and the idea of the preservation of culture and beauty, against the vandalism wrought by belligerents, was uppermost in the minds of those who were catholic in outlook. Poverty was not one of the prerequisites of Sufism, but it was certainly considered to be a meritorious condition for advancement in it.

Ibrāhīm and Rābi a (a woman from Basra) were amongst the earliest Sufis. They, at times, disregarded even the prophets and wanted to be in direct contact with God. Both lived in the second century of the Hijra, i.e. the eighth century A.D. In the second phase, Zu'lnūn, Bāyazīd Bistāmī, and Al-Ghazālī presented different views. Zu'lnūn declared, 'The man who knows God best is the one completely lost in Him'. Bāyazīd exclaimed, 'Glory to me! How great is my glory! O God, how long will there be "I" and "Thou" between me and Thee. Take this away that my "I" may become "Thou", and "I" be nothing'. Al-Ghazālī pointed out that scholasticism was an excellent corrective against heresy, but could not cure the disease of lack of religious certainty. His three principles are recognized universally in Islam: *naql* or tradition, i.e. authority of the *Qur'ān* and the *Sunnat*; *'aql* or reason, the basis of analogical reasoning and philosophical theology; and *kashf* or illumination, the direct revelation made to the mind of the Sufi.

The whole system of Sufism centres round two questions: 'How is man to realize God in himself?' and 'What is God in relation to the individual and the creation?' Sufism shows *tarīqat* or path, in answer to the first, and imparts *ma'rifat* or knowledge which describes God, both pantheistically and monistically, in answer to the second.

To Sufis, God is pure Being and absolute Beauty. He is everywhere and in everything, 'closer to us than even our neck-vein'. It is generally believed that seventy thousand veils hide the absolute Being or Beauty, and a Sufi, in his journey along the inward path of self-realization, tears off these veils and identifies the self with God.

Purification, devotion, and deification are the three main stages for realization. Repentance, abstinence, renunciation, voluntary poverty, and trust in God are the methods of purification. Meditation, nearness to God, love, fear, hope, longing, intimacy, tranquillity, contemplation, and resignation are the means of devotion. Certainty, illumination, and realization are the other names for deification.

The 'path' is divided into seven stages: service, i.e. observance of the

Law and service to God ; love of God ; renunciation of all worldly desires ; knowledge, i.e. contemplation of the nature, attributes, and works of God ; ecstasy of contemplation of God ; union, i.e. seeing God face to face ; and, finally, absorption in the essence of the eternal Being.

The whole superstructure of Sufism in Islam is built upon two cornerstones: (1) teacher, *pīr* or *murshid* (*guru*), and (2) love. To be initiated into the Sufi cult, one is required to have an implicit faith in his teacher, who is considered in no way less than God Himself. His commands are divine, and the path shown by him, the straightest. He is the intercessor who gets divine powers delegated to his disciple from the Unseen. All actions done according to his instructions are necessarily good, even though apparently they may appear to be otherwise. Without his help, it is impossible to get on to the right path. Perfect devotion to the teacher ensures speedy realization of the Truth. As to *love*, a Sufi is expected to possess an abundant store of it, and all beings, coming into contact with him, must of necessity be charged with his love. His love should not only be pure and transparent, but voluntary and selfless also, not expecting any return. A Sufi's love should be able to attract not only the creation, but the Creator also. The lover and the beloved have to identify themselves with each other. The lover is to become the beloved, and the beloved the lover, thus forging a complete fusion of the two into one.

SUFISM IN INDIA

The Muslim conquests of India brought in their wake a large number of Sufis. Originally, the Sufis in northern India accompanied the Muslim raiders, and, after the political conquest of a particular region, they preached Islam and joined hands with the rulers to consolidate Muslim power and to convert Hindus to Islam. Their patience, tolerance, sympathy, and friendly spirit brought them Hindu followers, though mostly from the lower and depressed classes. Farīdud-Dīn Ganj-i-Shakar and Alī Hujwaịrī Dātā Ganj Bakhsh belonged to this class of Sufis. But, later on, many Sufis gave up their evangelistic zeal, and, instead, devoted themselves to a comparative study of the religions and philosophies of India. Mīān Mīr, Dārā Shukoh, Abul Fazl, and Fayzee come under this category.

Sufism in India underwent a considerable change towards the end of the seventeenth century. Some Sufis got disgusted with the ruthless methods that Aurangzeb employed for the propagation of Islam, and were driven towards a sympathetic study of Hinduism. The Vedānta philosophy captured their minds ; the Bhakti movement influenced their ideas ; and in the Punjab, the stronghold of Islam, Muslim mystics held the view that nothing was real except God, and everything else was illusion or Māyā.

The doctrine of transmigration and reincarnation was soon taken up and was later supplemented by the theory of Karma. Mohammed, who remained the perfect model of man for Sufis elsewhere, was not necessarily the ideal of the Indian Sufi. Intellectually advanced Sufis sometimes ignored him, or reduced him to the rank of the prophets of other religions. He became a hero and a beloved like Kṛṣṇa in the *Bhāgavata* lore. The condemnation of idols was given up, and Muslim Sufis accepted idolatry as another way of worshipping God. Some Sufis even abstained from eating meat, and preached the doctrine of *ahiṁsā,* of loving all life, animal and human. The *Qur'ān* was also treated on a par with other holy scriptures. Religious toleration was advocated by many Sufis, who denounced religious bigotry and fanaticism.

After these new developments, Sufism can be classed into the following three schools of thought:

(1) The orthodox school: The Sufis of this school believed in conversion from one religion to another. They held the *Qur'ān* to be the best among revealed books, and Mohammed as God's last and greatest prophet on earth.

(2) The philosophic school: The Sufis of this school were so much influenced by the Vedānta that to them differences of religion, country, and sect were immaterial. They thought the rituals and dogmas of all religions to be unnecessary. They attached no importance to conversion.

(3) The popular school: The Sufis of this school had little or no education. They collected the beliefs and superstitions of different faiths and preached and practised them. Mohammed continued to be their only prophet, and the *Qur'ān,* the best revelation ; but they accommodated other prophets also in the long list of their own accredited saints.

II

GOD, THE ONLY BEING

The most torturing pain from which human beings suffer is the pain due to the feeling of personal responsibility, the feeling that we have caused pain to others. From this worst form of human suffering, the Sufistic doctrine that God is the only Being and that He is the only real agent saves us by one stroke. Jalālud-Dīn Rūmī expresses this idea in his great *Masnavī* thus:

If He makes of me a cup, a cup am I ;
If He makes of me a dagger, a dagger I.
If He makes me a fountain, I pour forth water ;

If He makes me fire, I give forth heat. . . .
If He makes me a friend, I serve my friends.
I am as the pen in the fingers of the writer,
I am not in a position to obey or not, at will.

Sachal, one of the greatest Sufis of Sind, has expressed the same idea in a beautiful song well known in that province. The charm of the original is impossible to retain in the translation, which runs as follows:

Open your eyes; behold the show; all is a picture of the Lord.
Here, there, and everywhere is that heart-ravisher, all around.
In some places He is a nightingale; in some, a flower; in some, a garden and springtime verdure. . . .
In some, He wears the coarse cloth of a dervish; in some, He wears silk.
In some, He speaks all tongues; in some, He is dumb.
In some, He is a Sunni; in some, a Shia; in some, He has the true insight.
In some, He is a lover; in some, a beloved; in some, He is all blandishments and coquetry.
In some, He shows Himself in one way; in others, in some other; my beloved is a great deceiver.
He is like cloth of one name, with innumerable patterns on it.

Guru Arjan, whom the Sufis include in their fold, has the same ideas running practically throughout the *Sukhmaṇī*. *Aṣṭapadī* (II) is specially devoted to these:

The cause of cause is one God, there is none other. . . .
What pleaseth Him shall come to pass. . . .
Having created, He beholdeth His own greatness;
Nānak, God is contained in all things. . . .
The Searcher of hearts sporteth and is pleased;
He causeth men to do as He wisheth.
Nānak, there is nothing seen but Him.

The question, whether God is the only Being and other beings are mere appearances, whether He is the one single source of all the unceasing activity, simply does not arise. For the sake of the comfort the idea brings, if we wish to accept it as true, there is nothing to prevent us from doing so. Some rearrangement of our ideas is necessary, and it is easily accomplished.

The continuity of the self is only one of the many appearances in the world of continued existence of the same thing, when, in reality, everything about it is new, except the name or the appearance. In the case of a rainbow, it is always the freshly formed one that we see every moment, the drops of water and the light they refract into our eyes being subject to continuous change. So, after all, there may be nothing in the so-called self; it may be a mere appearance, with a very interrupted existence; and He alone may be existing, creating these appearances at all those spots where His action may not be immediate and complete, but is accompanied by some sort of hesitation and resistance.

ANNIHILATION OF THE SELF

Nobody, however, likes the uncomfortable process of the annihilation of the self that the Sufistic doctrine appears to suggest. But this annihilation consists merely in the progressive removal of the obstruction in the way of complete action, in killing the alleged considerations that produce hesitation before a move is made, and increases—it does not decrease—our cheerfulness and joy. This is known to those who, by experience, have had their sympathies enlarged, and who, entering into other people's lives, become quick and effective in their action. These have a larger share of the world's happiness, though they become less self-willed. Several of us, besides, do undergo many extinctions in our lifetime, when our outlook changes so totally that we become dead to our former selves, so to say. We give up old associations, old friends, old occupations; and even a temporary return to them appears like a return to a foreign element that is well-nigh choking. When one self dies, another is born. When the last disappears, who knows, we may find ourselves as God, present at all points and enjoying all states.

THE PROBLEM OF EVIL

The real difficulty in accepting the idea that God is the only real agent is the problem of the origin of evil. In accepting God as the only real agent, we have also to accept that He is the agent of evil actions; but as evil is evil, we find it impossible to attribute that to Him. The problem of evil is considered to be insoluble; every solution of it that is attempted is found to be absurd. When a problem leads to absurd solutions, it indicates that the terms in which the problem has been stated need revision; and it is invariably found that they already assume things that require to be proved. In asking for an explanation for the origin of evil, we have already assumed that evil exists. The absurd explanations indicate the necessity of revising that assumption.

The idea of evil begins its career thus. Because your action leads to consequences that I do not like, or the social group in which you live does not like, it is described as evil. The term evil is, at the start, a mere description of a feeling on the part of a single individual or a group of individuals. It merely indicates a feeling of dislike. Then the word suggests an idea, and the idea, a real thing. Finally, the thing needs an explanation for its existence.

One single action picked out by the intellect may, and does, appear ugly, exactly as does a single black thread in a pattern, if one's attention is fixed only on it, but which, as a part of the pattern that is being woven, is as important and beautifying as any other. Browning expressed this beautifully when he wrote:

> On earth, the broken arcs;
> In heaven, the perfect round.

That which in another strikes me as stupid and ugly, as long as he and I belong to different groups and are considered separate, becomes clever and beautiful as soon as we begin to associate. If, even for one instant, in a moment of exaltation, one realizes the oneness of all life, the so-called evil of others becomes one's own and wears another aspect. And this recognition enormously increases one's power of help.

Sufis give a beautiful illustration of how evil may become transformed. A pool of standing water becomes dirty when dirt is thrown into it, and remains so. It takes the colour of whatever it comes in contact with, and retains it. But if it can get connected with a perennially flowing stream, it becomes sooner or later purified. So long as an individual remains an individual and considers himself responsible for the activities that appear to flow from him, these activities leave their traces on him. But if, somehow, he is able to become one with the universal life, the activities become those of the universal life and cease to have a moral colouring.

Dalpat, a great Sufi who belonged to Sehwan, but who lived most of his life at Hyderabad (Sind), expresses the Sufistic attitude to good and evil thus:

> In everything, Thou alone art living;
> Why (then) hast Thou concealed Thyself?
> Vicious and virtuous acts Thou Thyself performest;
> Why (then) hast Thou built a heaven and a hell? . . .
> Dalpat (says), e'en for an instant, separate from Thee I do not become;
> Why (then) hast Thou union and separation affirmed?

CONSCIENCE AND MORAL INSTINCT

Another idea that obstructs the acceptance of this doctrine of God being the only agent is the idea of conscience and the moral instinct that have been attributed to us. But these are words to express our hesitation at the junction of two activities—one that we are about to give up, and the other that we are about to go in for. At the initial stages, the hesitation is in favour of the old activity, and at the later, it is against the new one being given up, the so-called conscience now working in favour of the new activity. So, conscience, like the self, is an expression of life's innate sluggishness; it resists the introduction of a new mode, but when once it has gained volume, it resists dropping it equally well.

So far as moral instinct and moral values are concerned, the truth appears to be like this. Life is infinite and infinitely restless; it is always moving of its own accord in one or another direction, always pushing forward in fresh ways, always changing. It follows that with every change in the direction of life's flow, there must occur a change in the order of merit, in the activities going on round about it. From the point of view of values, things, tendencies, and activities rearrange themselves in a new series every time there is a change in life's direction.

THE FACT OF PAIN

The last of the family of ideas we have created is the idea of pain. Why did He create this real thing, pain? As long as it lasts, it is certainly more real than anything else. But even this pain is not quite as real as it appears to be. The pain of children, when they make a great fuss, and actually shed tears, over a piece of stick that has been taken away from them by their playmates, or because a flimsy toy has got broken, appears foolish. So does our own pain after we have passed through it. It is not only not remembered, but when it is, we are ashamed of it. Even when we are in pain, it is possible for many of us to shift and ally ourselves with something deeper and be free from it. Even then the question remains, Why did He create pain at all? Could there not be a universe without it? No, certainly not, unless it be a universe without a relish. No risks, no struggles, no failures, and no pain—it is unbearable. We want all of it and more. God may be doing the same. All this occurs to any one without anything like an inclination towards God or anything associated with that name. But when He becomes the object of one's love, one may well cry, like Shāh Abdul Latīf:

> All is sweet (that comes) from the side of the beloved;
> There is no bitterness, if you but taste it with insight.

LOVE: HUMAN AND DIVINE

Acceptance of the above doctrine colours one's activities and, slowly but surely, leads to an inner realization of it. But if love for God visits an individual, all doubts depart and the realization becomes considerably quicker. Sufis therefore think very highly of love. Rūmī has the following on love in his *Masnavī*:

Through love bitter things seem sweet,
Through love bits of copper are made gold....
Through love stings are as honey,
Through love lions are harmless as mice.
Through love sickness is health,
Through love wrath is as mercy.
Through love the dead rise to life,
Through love the king becomes a slave.

Because the ordinary love for human beings removes fear of conventions and conquers prestige, personified into the Kazi in Sufistic poetry; because it enables one to discard the normal scale of values, even if it be for a short time, and 'reconciles, by mystic wiles, the evil and the good'; and because it secures freedom from the harassing considerations of duty, Sufis welcome even worldly love. Jāmī, one of the greatest poets of Persia, has said in his *Yūsuf Zulaikha*:

I heard, a seeker went to a *pīr*,
That he might receive aid in his company.
(The *pīr*) said, 'If your foot hasn't moved on the path of love,
Go, become a lover and then come to me'.

Elsewhere it is stated that God plays hide and seek with His lovers. He vivifies a form and makes it appear more beautiful than the rest; we are drawn to it; but, by the time we are there, He leaves it and goes to vivify another. And so the game goes on; form after form He makes us pursue in search of Himself, till by chance, in our desolation, we get a glimpse of the very spring of beauty.

Cases are known of those that love each other strongly and therefore are unable to look at each other; unable to speak to each other; unable even to mention each other's name; and keep themselves quietly engaged in what each thinks will make the other happy. Shāh Abdul Latīf asks us to learn the way of love from a kiln, that keeps burning inside and still never gives an indication of the fact.

Another form of love described is somewhat easier to appreciate. Tulasīdāsa appeals to his beloved God: 'Say but once, "Tulasīdāsa is Mine".' This implies a love so full and deep, and so thoroughly selfless, that the sole satisfaction it seeks is that it wants only to be accepted. It is not seldom that one meets with persons that are thirsting to be accepted—eyes looking about, hearts unsatisfied. These hearts are full of love, but the stream of love that starts from there has not found its normal direction, namely, that of God, and so, blindly it runs after every object in the world with a hope; and if any one accepts their love, they are grateful. These 'wanderers o'er eternity, whose bark anchored ne'er shall be' can be satisfied only if their love gets directed towards Him.

Sufis think that real love for God is too dangerous a thing to play with. It means death at every instant, a death severer than that of the body. The following is a translation of a fine Persian couplet on the point:

> The delicate ones must not practise love.
> The lion-hearted, calamity-bearing ones, alone place their foot
> in this dangerous valley.

Another point about love that the Sufis state, and is known to be true, is that love comes when it likes and goes when it likes. There is no knowing when and how it will come. No preparation can be prescribed for it, for love is God and is as free as He. It is said that a person asked Sādik, a well-known Sufi, to fill him with the love for God. Sādik sent for the potter of the place and asked him in the presence of that person if he himself chose the clay for the pots, or the clay insisted on being chosen for the purpose. The potter, of course, replied that he was the sole judge in the matter. Even so, Sādik said, has God the sole choice in this matter.

Therefore the blessing that a Sufi saint showers on you, if he be pleased, runs thus: 'May God grant you His love! May God make you His own!'

Shāh Latīf has said, 'The Beloved has caught hold of my heart, by habituating me to His love by degrees'. Otherwise, it is said, this frail vessel would give way. Love is that immortal fire that would burn up the ordinary body. When it comes in its full force, it lays waste everything before it. The intellect stops working and one may go mad. 'When the lion of love enters the forest (of ideas), other creatures (that is to say, ideas) depart.' When it goes back, they return. But they have known their smallness and lost their dignity. The lion may come again and again, each time staying for a longer period than before, with the result that each time the other creatures run away and return considerably altered. At last, when the lion of love decides to make a permanent stay, they owe allegiance to him and live in peace and amity. The intellect and the ideas it creates can be subservient to love. They are always at the disposal of love, whatever it likes to do:

> All thoughts, all passions, all delights, what'er stirs this mortal frame,
> All are but ministers of love, and feed his sacred flame.

SUFIS' ATTITUDE TO INTELLECT

Therefore the Sufis' attitude towards thinking is very peculiar. They hold that the intellect and the intellectual life in general are not only valueless, but that they are a positive hindrance. In the words of a great Sufi of Rohri (Sind), known as Bedil (without heart), 'He who got entangled in letters (ideas), climbed not at all the incline of love'. Another great Sufi is reported to have said to the intellectuals of the city who went to become his disciples, 'To be able to receive aid from me, you must go back to forget all that you have learnt'. Thought is believed to lead to action, to guide and illumine it. But the Sufis will not accept this view. The relationship of thought and action is not quite a simple affair. All is not said when it is stated that thought leads to action. More often thinking spoils action. Thoughtless action is the best. On the other hand, action is often used to stop thinking, as in cases of worry, when even running puts the mind right. Thinking does not help even judgement, which comes somehow directly, the reasons usually given for it being an after affair, and meant for social purposes.

In the case of development of moral qualities, if they are secured by the control and cultivation of thought, they become mechanical and their grace disappears. Humility adopted by thought becomes conscious and a subtler form of pride. But that humility which is unconscious, the fruit of an inner realization, which is known to Him alone who knows all hearts, is beautiful; it draws us all towards Him and makes our life fuller and sweeter.

THE PURPOSE OF CREATION

It appears that the intellect is concerned merely with the birth of ideas; their utility or otherwise, or their correspondence to reality, simply does not matter. But, then, if ideas need neither be real nor useful, why must they be continually created? That brings us to the Sufistic explanation of the creative process. The last question of every thinker is just this: What is after all the purpose of creation? Really none whatsoever, unless play be a purpose. The way that the Sufi poets of Persia think of creation is as follows: God, who is all-powerful and all-beautiful, cannot stay quiet, and so starts to play with Himself. He is all-beauty; but the beauty must be enjoyed and so must be manifested. Just as a mother having a beautiful child, in order to enjoy its existence, especially her own share in it, holds it afar to have a loving look at it and then brings it back closer to herself and goes on repeating the process, each time observing new beauties in the child, so He too pushes out a portion of Himself, looks at it, enjoys its beauty, and then sucks it in. This breathing-out and breathing-in process goes on without an end.

God must be, and is, all-powerful too. To enjoy His power, He must have some sort of difficult task to accomplish. So He must deceive Himself into believing that He is weak or sluggish or inert ; and then He must work up to raise Himself. We ourselves live at different levels of life at different times ; and these levels can be altered at will. We may pull up, arise ourselves by an effort, and be able to attend to everything before us. Or, we may let ourselves go, become sluggish like matter, be at the disposal of outside influences or external forces, and act only when absolutely necessary. By His own will, then, He lets Himself go, relaxes Himself, and then starts an up-hill task for Himself against this make-believe material part. This relaxed, sluggish portion of God forms the matter of the universe, against which He applies His push to lift it and, in the attempt to lift it, enjoys His power keenly. The chief characteristic of matter is to repeat itself, to keep doing what once it has been made to do. Repetition alone is the mark of sluggishness. The characteristic of life, on the other hand, is to be always moving of its own accord in one or another direction, always pressing forward in fresh ways, always changing. From our usual point of view, this sluggishness is good, because it makes for the stability of the world and society ; because it supplies the necessary fulcrum for our activity ; because it lies at the root of our hopes and expectations, and so makes the actual life bearable. But from the point of view of the general life itself, which has started the game of expressing its beauty and power, this sluggishness is good because it makes its stay at each beauty longer. Prevented from running through a beautiful landscape by some resistance that lets you take only one step at a time, you enjoy it all the better ; you notice every detail of it. On this creative process, Śamī of Shikarpur has a fine verse:

> The really non-existing error, the Lord has thrown into His mind.
> He has donned, of His own accord, the shirt of anxiety.

Who can remove this confusion without the Lord's self-awaking? It is a common saying among the Sufis that 'the world does not consist in family and possessions, but it consists in the forgetting of God ; your having a family and possessions does not make you worldly, that you become only when you forget Him. Having all these, if you constantly remember Him, the world does not exist for you. The world comes into being as soon as you begin to be unconscious of Him, and exists only as long as you remain so'.

In the creation of forms and the processes thereof, then, God is enjoying His own beauty and power. But the most beautiful power of His is this very power of creation ; and so He must create a creator. This creator is man with his intellect and intellectual processes. And that is why man has been described as having been made in the image of God.

THE MURSHIDS

Oneness of being, greatness of love, and inadequacy of thought, these three are the corner-stones of the Sufistic edifice, the fourth being the relationship of *murshid* (teacher) and *tālib* (disciple). *Tālib* literally means a seeker, and *murshid* is the person who is able to satisfy the seeking impulse. Of all the relationships known to the human mind, this is the best, happiest, and most perfect. Shāh Latīf has the following on this:

> Guru and Govind, both are standing (before me) ;
> To whose feet shall I attach myself?
> I am ready to be sacrificed for that Guru
> Who made known to me the name of Govind.

Kabir extols the position of the *murshid* thus:

> God entangled me in the world ;
> *Murshid* did the disentanglement.

About the saints that act as *murshids,* Guru Arjan says:

> 'Nānak, the glory of the saints is merged in that of God.'
> 'Nānak, there is an understanding between God and His saints.'
> 'The supreme Being dwelleth in the hearts of saints.'
> 'Saith Nānak, my brothers, there is no difference between God and His saints.'

The details of what happens to those who associate with saints are also given fully thus:

> By association with saints, the face becomes bright,
> By association with saints, all filth is removed,
> By association with saints, pride is effaced,
> By association with saints, divine knowledge is revealed,
> By association with saints, all enemies become friends,
> By association with saints, man feeleth not enmity for any one.

What happens to the slanderers of saints is also described at great length ; but then,

> Nānak, even a slanderer shall be saved in the company of saints,
> If the merciful saints but show him mercy.

Lastly, Rūmī has expressed a similar thought in his oft-quoted couplet thus:

One instant in the company of saints
Is better than a hundred years of prayers and piety.

You go to a Sufi saint in a proper receptive mood and stay there for some time; though nothing appears to have happened, you return somewhat changed, the change showing itself afterwards in your way of dealing with things as they arise; the circumstances develop the change and you are surprised. Something occurs between the two hearts behind the conscious part of yourself. And so we are advised when we visit a saint, or a place where saints have lived, that we pass a night there. Behind the veil, the alchemical process is gone through, without the *tālib* knowing how (and why) it is accomplished.

The *murshid* acts as a perfect administrator. He arranges circumstances for your growth, for the development of the seeds he throws into your soil. Your weaknesses are made to expose themselves to your view and then drop off; and this is done, not by a word of mouth, but by the circumstances arranged for that purpose.

The Sufi knows that 'The only good man is he who goes with every bad one' (Kahlil Gibrān), and so, if he wants you to realize it, he does not say that to you. But, in His name, there are sent to you persons of all sorts, good, bad, and indifferent with whom you must go, to do them service. And slowly but surely, without an effort and without a struggle, there is developed in you a feeling that all are alike.

He also knows, 'All service ranks the same with God', and so he may keep you occupied with work that you love to do in His name, but which otherwise you would consider unimportant, yielding no results, till at last unconsciously the idea of relative importance and of results leaves you and you find yourself, 'without haste, and without rest', moving about, as He wills it, with 'hands in work, and heart with God'.

The *murshids* say very little. Whatever they say implies always that you must place others above yourself. 'Become your enemy's friend', is a common advice. So is the following: 'They rebuke you; you must not speak in return' (Shāh Latīf).

And the one thing they insist on is that you do everything in His name. The only work that is really done, according to them, is the one done in His name. Even the silence they enjoin must be adopted to repeat His name, when it becomes a real silence that suggests solutions and brings comfort to others, and in the presence of which the very desire for undesirable conversations disappears.

The *murshids* never argue. No proof is ever advanced. But they give you wonderful illustrations and beautiful stories to fix in you what they wish to. The conviction comes to you direct from their heart; these stories and illustrations probably help in the rearrangement of the mind with which we are hampered. On the relationship of God and man, for instance, they would say: The hearts of men are like the boats on the ocean that is God; He moves them as He likes; He carries them with the rising tide and leaves them on the desert land, where they must wait till once more He comes and takes them to a beautiful island. On the question whether it is right for a Hindu to go to a Muslim saint, or vice versa, they would ask, 'Does the butterfly that loves the light inquire about the caste and the religion of the person in whose house it finds it?'

Regarding religious discussions, they would give you a pertinent story from the *Masnavī*. Four friends, a Persian, an Arab, a Turk, and a Greek, while on an excursion, found a coin and quarrelled over the fruit they must purchase with it. The Persian wanted *angūr,* the Arab, *'inab,* the Turk, *uzum,* and the Greek, *astafeel,* and each went into raptures over the qualities of the fruit. A wise man passing by and hearing the cause of the quarrel, asked for the coin and brought, from a neighbouring village, grapes, the one fruit they had all been wanting, only their terms for it being different, owing to the difference of language.

If a seeker adopts of his own accord a course of conduct involving more of control and sacrifice, there is always some feeling of hesitation and uncertainty about his actions. But if, after some time, a word on the point from the mouth of the *murshid* reaches the ears of the seeker, things appear to get settled. It is not merely a case of a sanction received or of faith, 'He says it; it must be so'. Some walls appear to have been broken, obstructions removed; and there is an access of power. Till the *murshid* speaks, it is a business of an individual; a case of control of his desires. After he speaks, it becomes God's affair, and the very seeds of desire seem to disappear.

The love of the *murshid* for the seeker is said to be greater than that of the seeker for his *murshid*. His love is the very essence of love, and so, tremendous in intensity. But he releases only as much as the seeker-son can bear. He attends to all the details of his life, outer as well as inner; sometimes he has to wait and watch from afar; but his irresistible love draws, and keeps drawing, till the seeker-son, whom he has chosen to make his own, accepts the *murshid* consciously.

GRACE IS SPONTANEOUS

It is never true that we have to knock at the door in order to have it opened unto us. It is the *murshids* that keep knocking at the doors of our consciousness till we listen, turn back, and open its doors. 'The hound from heaven' is always at our feet, once we have been chosen for grace. And until we learn to accept everything we want from His loving lap, our individual search after the fulfilment of our hearts' desires always fails and, at each failure, however much we may try to run away from the 'hound', the hound's barking becomes more and more insistent. Fortunate and happy are those that get attached to the *murshids* of the world. And happiest is that seeker that can say inwardly to his *murshid*, 'As thou wishest, so let it be. Only let me remember all the while that thou wishest so'; and, later on, 'But if for the fulfilment of thy purposes, thou wishest to induce in me the forgetting of thyself, let it be so too'.

It is sad sometimes to think that there is no such thing as individuals fighting for a prize; that 'God's puppets, best and worst, are we; there is no last nor first'; that even in the matter of remembering Him, we have no choice, for 'he uttereth God's name whom He causeth to utter; he singeth God's praises whom He causeth to sing'. The least selfish desire of getting love for Him, or even praying to Him for that grace, cannot be initiated by us, for 'the only prayers He listens to are those that He makes with your lips'. But, then, the consolation is that even this sadness belongs to Him, which He wants to enjoy; more than that, it is an indication that where this sadness occurs, He has got tired of the drama that has been unfolding and that He is about to absorb it back into Himself. For truly has Sachal said:

> Here Sachal remembers the beloved; (but that indicates that)
> There, there is the remembrance of Sachal (by the beloved).

SIND, THE LAND OF SUFISM

Sind seems to have been chosen as the place for Sufism. Geographically Sind is accessible from all sides, and on two sides the ocean opens it for the inroads of foreign culture. The Buddhistic influence had already broken the barriers, external and internal, that had been created by Brāhmaṇical thought, when the Muslim invasion took place and Mohammed ibn-Qāsīm brought great men of religion and culture to consolidate what he had expected the arms of his generals would secure. The Muslim faith in the oneness of God and the brotherhood of man, the only basis for true democracy, touched men's minds, which were prepared by the Buddhist monks, whose impersonal doctrine about the nature of God lacked the moving power that comes from the personal way of looking at Him. This helped the Muslim faith. The Sindhi mind appears to be 'open', like Sind itself, and every new way of looking at things, spiritual as well as temporal, is easily accepted. Guru Nānak's thought, in no way different from that of the Sufis, when the time came, spread like wild-fire. Lastly, the 'four friends', Muslim by birth, came from the north-west to spread Sufism, pure and simple, in Sind and elsewhere. First they reached the ancient place Sehwan, where, in memory of their coming, a flat platform with four pillars at four corners has been constructed on the top of a small hill with a cave inside having a single pillar in the centre, as if it were the support of the roof. Out of the four, Qalandar Lāl Shāhbāz Sarhandī alone stayed in Sehwan; the other three left for other parts of North-West India.

Several places in Sind acted as definite centres of Sufistic influence. There is the ancient village of Jhok near Tando Mahomed Khan, the place of Shāh Ināyet, also known as Shāh Shahīd, where an annual gathering takes place; there is the place of Sachal near Ranipur; that of Bedil and Bekaś at Rohri; of Dalpat and Kutub Shāh at Hyderabad; and of others at Tando Saneendad, Kumber, and other places. Great Sufis, men of spiritual realization, after they left their bodies, having attained union, *wisāl* as they call it, with God, had their work continued by their successors.

But, what is peculiar in this connection is that the heart of Sind is Sufistic. There is absence of caste and creed and of untouchability; and in the villages, where the influence of intellectual development has not broken the hearts into bits, one can see all over a desire to prefer others' comfort to one's own; there is the heart's hospitality and openness to receive any newcomer; and all social customs are observed with that geniality that makes them living and useful to all as one whole. All this is Sufistic in essence. The stories that are current are all Sufistic, illustrating Sufistic truths and experiences. Above all, the singing to which the Sindhi is most inclined is the *kāfī*, which is essentially a tune suited to the wailings of separation, to the expression of thoughts that rise with the memory of long-left home, which is best illustrated by the story of Umar, prince of Umarkot, and Maruī, the beautiful peasant girl of the neighbouring village of Malir. Shāh Latīf has given the story a fine spiritual meaning: the songs sung in the name of Maruī are the songs of the soul that, in the face of temptations, is constantly longing for its companions and its home.

PART V

SOME MODERN REFORM MOVEMENTS

43

THE BRĀHMO SAMĀJ

IN this age of exaggerated emphasis on the political and economic factors in the evolution of man, one risks a good deal by attempting to demonstrate that religion is no less, probably more, important a factor in the development of humanity. This is particularly true of the ancient and mediaeval periods, when religion served as the main channel through which flowed the creative energies of the nations, fertilizing the banks of history, from century to century, with the immortal contributions of man, such as literature, art, philosophy, ethics, rituals, etc., reflecting the poetry of social life. In fact, all that went to characterize, in the permanent sense, the real assets of a nation grew out of a pervasive religious experience. This experience may come by accident to an individual, to a special clan or group, or to a vaster concourse of humanity developing a mass movement. But in every case, religion, in its creative stage, has elevated individuals, clans, and groups above the limitations of the immediate present to build enduring structures of human civilization having reference to the Ultimate and the Eternal. This applies particularly to Indian history and the Indian people. We too have, recorded in our annals, the facts of political conquest and economic exploitation like those of any other country. But the real mass movements in India were the direct outcome of the promulgation of a new truth embodied in a new religion. This has been admitted so far as our ancient and mediaeval periods are concerned, which show a unique record of philosophical and spiritual research as well as of charity and philanthropy through Jainism and Buddhism, Vaiṣṇavism and Śaivism, down to the various Bhakti cults of mediaeval India, immortalized by Rāmānanda and Kabīr, Nānak and Caitanya.

In the case of modern India, however, it was supposed by many indigenous as well as foreign investigators that India was modernized by shedding many of her social and historical habits, which were summarily disposed of as antiquated traditions or noxious superstitions. In the sudden invasion of the 'modern', India was supposed to have surrendered at discretion, relinquishing her past and prostrating herself before the innumerable challenges of the present. A deeper study of the personalities and events of the dawn of modern India, however, convinces us of the fact that the break of the present with the past was more apparent than real. While the age of 'illumination' was inaugurated in Europe with a temporary negation of religion, in the case of India such an epoch was inaugurated by Raja Rammohun Roy, in the last quarter of the eighteenth century, following our traditional method of revitalizing decaying society through a new religion, by founding Brāhmo Dharma, based on our age-old principle of unity underlying the Vedāntic monism.

THE NATION AT THE BIRTH OF RAMMOHUN

In those early days of the foundation of British power in India, the Indian people, Hindu or Mohammedan, had very little to boast of in the domain of politics and economics, both being equally dominated by the aggressive and efficient occidental nations who came to dictate the pace of our modern history. But even in that age of abject degradation, the Indian people as a whole, not only the unlettered millions of our villages, but also the *élite,* clung tenaciously to their ancestral faith and traditions, and faced successfully the deadly onslaughts of outlandish modernism. The Hindus and the Muslims, chastened by common suffering, the great equalizer, came to forget the political disparity that existed between them as rulers or the ruled. Only the consolation of spirit, that never failed the nation, percolated the soul of the Hindus as well as of the Muslims through innumerable *ṭols* and *muktabs* (village seminaries), so wonderfully efficient and pervasive in character as to put to shame the record of our bureaucratic primary education a century later. Sanskrit and the various vernaculars derived from it were cultivated side by side with Persian and Arabic. The court of Maharaja Krishna Chandra was adorned by notable writers from both communities. Bharatchandra was an adept in composing gems of literature in Bengali, as well as in Persian; and when, during the last quarter of the eighteenth century, Christianity was slowly assuming a proselytizing character, Ramram Bose showed a remarkable adaptability by co-operating with the Christian missionaries and by composing the earliest hymnology in vernacular for the Christian churches, although he remained himself a Hindu till the last day of his life.

The first thirty years of the life of Rammohun Roy are more or less veiled in obscurity. The stories of his early life depicting his preoccupation with religious reform and consequent conflict with his family, a stronghold of orthodoxy, and of his wanderings in different parts of eastern India, and even as far as Tibet, may or may not be true. But this much is certain that in his intellectual and spiritual make-up Rammohun showed all the traces of indigenous influence which were found in his immediate predecessors. He had a liberal education, which then meant a mastery of Sanskrit, Persian, Arabic, as well as a critical study of Hindu and Islamic law, literature, and philosophy, which prepared him wonderfully well for the rôle of the first prophet of progressive reform in our religion and society, during the first quarter of the nineteenth century.

CONTRIBUTIONS OF RAMMOHUN AND HIS CONTEMPORARIES

Raja Rammohun Roy says in his *Autobiographical Sketch*: 'When about the age of sixteen, I composed a manuscript calling in question the validity of the idolatrous system of Hindus. This, together with my own sentiments on the subject, having produced a coolness between me and my immediate kindred, I proceeded on my travels and passed through different countries, chiefly within, but some beyond the bounds of Hindusthan.' The authenticity of the *Autobiographical Sketch*, however, is admitted by some and disputed by others, and, for that reason, we cannot affirm that Rammohun composed the manuscript above referred to. In any case, the manuscript was probably never printed, nor has it yet been traced. What has been traced up to now, which is in the form of court-records, relates to his ancestral property and to his own independent sources of income before the death of his father in 1803, when Rammohun was past thirty. But it is a significant fact that his earliest writing so far traced—*Tuhfat-ul-Muwahhidin* (A Gift to Deists)—introduces Rammohun to us in his well-known historical rôle of a free thinker in religion, if not as a religious reformer. This valuable treatise was composed in Persian with an Arabic introduction, which confirms the tradition attested by many of his contemporaries that Rammohun was deeply read in Persian and Arabic literature. Yet, not a single document has so far been traced to indicate the steps leading to his mastery in those languages. Nor has anything definite been found as yet to show how he managed to gain that mastery in handling Sanskrit and Bengali, his mother tongue, as we find him doing in his published works between 1815 and 1832. Let us hope that intensive research will bring out more positive facts relating to the formation of that wonderful personality. What we do not know as yet about the early life of Rammohun should not prejudice our appreciation of that illustrious pioneer, who left an indelible mark on the history of our national progress, during the early days of the nineteenth century. Very characteristically Rammohun inaugurates the new century with these significant lines in his *Tuhfat-ul-Muwahhidin*:

'I travelled in the remotest parts of the world, in plains as well as in hilly lands, and found the inhabitants thereof agreeing generally in the personality of one Being, who is the source of all that exists and its governor, and disagreeing in giving peculiar attributes to that Being and in holding different creeds consisting of the doctrines of religion and precepts of *harām* (forbidden) and *halāl* (lawful). From this induction it has been known to me that turning generally towards one eternal Being is like a natural tendency in human beings and is common to all individuals of mankind equally.'

This generalization surely was the result of years of study and intensive thinking, and Rammohun was to some extent anticipating many of his remarkable thoughts and activities when he expressed himself in the following lines of his first published work:

'The followers of different religions, sometimes seeing the paucity of the number of believers in one God in the world, boast that they are on the side of the majority. It is to be seen that the truth of a saying does not depend upon the multiplicity of the sayers, and the non-reliability of a narration cannot arise simply out of the paucity of the number of the narrators. For it is admitted by the seekers of truth that truth is to be followed, although it is against the majority of the people.

'It is strange to say that after the lapse of hundreds of years from the time of these religious leaders, with whom the prophetic mission is said to be closed, Nānak and others, in India and other countries, raised the flag of prophetic mission and induced a large number of people to become their followers and were successful.

'O God! Notwithstanding implicit faith in the orders of the *mujtahid* or the doctors of religion, there is always such an innate faculty existing in the nature of mankind that if any person of sound mind, before or after assuming the doctrines of any religion, makes an impartial and just inquiry into the nature of the principles of religious doctrines of different nations, there is a strong hope that he will be able to distinguish truth from untruth and true propositions from fallacious ones, and also that he, becoming free from the useless restraints of religion, which sometimes become sources of prejudice of one against another and causes of physical and mental troubles, will turn to the one Being, who is the fountain of the harmonious organization of the universe, and will pay attention to the good of society.'

Two fundamental principles or laws have been discovered and repeatedly emphasized by Rammohun: the basic unity of mankind as the goal of human research on the intellectual plane and the welfare of society as the dominant consideration and the ultimate goal of our moral endeavour. Thus the philosopher-theologian, as well as the great social reformer, who came to vindicate the honour of modern India amongst the progressive nations of the world, stands clearly before us, even while we read his earliest treatise. Perfect free lance and free-thinker that he was, Rammohun was not free from a legitimate pride in his Brāhmaṇa heredity which, amidst a thousand persecutions, held aloft the torch of

Brahmavidyā, the divine knowledge, which alone leads to immortality. There is a touching note of autobiography in the lines we quote below:

'The Brahmins have a tradition from God that they have strict orders from God to observe their ceremonies and hold their faith for ever. There are many injunctions about this from the divine authority in the Sanskrit language, and I, the humblest creature of God, having been born amongst them, have learnt the language and got those injunctions by heart, and this nation (the Brāhmaṇas) having confidence in such divine injunctions cannot give them up, although they have been subjected to many troubles and persecutions and were threatened to be put to death by the followers of Islam.'

Yet rarely could we find a greater admirer of Islam and of other historic religions than Rammohun, who formulated, at that early age, the profound truth that 'social laws depend on an understanding of each other's meaning'. That is why, even in the midst of heated controversies, religious, social, or political, Rammohun ever showed that phenomenal lack of personal bitterness, that enlightened tolerance, and that profound sympathy which lend an epic grandeur to his personality. He found 'contradictory precepts' clouding the cardinal truths of all religions, and he wanted to test them as to how far they were 'consistent with the wisdom and mercy of the great, generous, and disinterested creation'.

PUBLICATION OF THE UPANIṢADS AND VEDĀNTA

Twelve years after the publication of *Tuhfat-ul-Muwahhidin* from Murshidabad, we find Rammohun finally established in Calcutta and publishing, almost simultaneously in Sanskrit, Bengali, and English, his studies on the Upaniṣads and Vedānta (1815-19). His was the earliest published study on those valuable texts of Brāhmaṇical philosophy and religion. There were few good libraries in those days, excepting the libraries attached to the Asiatic Society of Bengal and to the Fort William College, where rare books and manuscripts were being collected, through the noble endeavours of Sir William Jones, Colebrooke, Carey, and others. Rammohun is now known to have possessed a house of his own in Calcutta as early as 1792 and, consequently, might have frequented some of those libraries; and we find him writing with deep appreciation whenever he referred to the works of pioneer orientalists like Jones and Colebrooke.[1]

DEBATES AND CONTROVERSIES

But before settling down in Calcutta, Rammohun came into intimate contact with the representatives of various sects, such as Vaiṣṇavas, Tāntrikas,

[1] *Vide* his Preface to *Essay on the Rights of Hindus over Ancestral Property* (1830).

Jains, Mohammedans, etc. He frequently arranged discussion-meetings among them, during his residence at Rangpur (1809-14), where he is said to have made a careful study of Tāntrika works with the help of a Bengali mendicant named Hariharananda Tirthaswami. Rammohun's appreciation of the *Mahānirvāṇa Tantra* is an important link in this chain of evidence. He is also reported to have entered into discussion with another great scholar, Utsavananda Saraswati. But the discussion soon developed into downright controversy, from 1817 onwards, when we find Rammohun publishing the tract *A Defence of Hindoo Theism in Reply to the Attack of an Advocate for Idolatry at Madras.* Side by side with the pundits of Madras appeared stalwarts from Bengal, the Bhattacharyas and the Goswamis, joining issues with Rammohun, who was showing a real flair for enlightened controversy on recondite topics. At the same time (1817-20), he was vindicating the moral conscience of his people by pleading for the abolition of the cruel rites of suttee (*satī*), making most touching appeal to his countrymen, reminding them of the glory of Indian womanhood, the real *śaktis* of our nation. Between 1820 and 1823, we find him engaged in the historic controversy with the missionaries on the fundamentals of Christian religion.

It is now generally admitted that Rammohun did not make serious study of English till the very end of the eighteenth century, when he was approaching thirty. But how quickly and efficiently he mastered that difficult tongue was clearly demonstrated through his remarkable English compositions. His capacity for mastering foreign languages was phenomenal, as has been attested by eminent foreigners like Abbé Gregoire, James Buckingham, and Victor Jacquemont. But through language, Rammohun always drew spiritual nourishment, strengthening his cosmopolitan personality, as has been clearly demonstrated by Brojendra Nath Seal in his remarkable study, *Rammohun, the Universal Man.*[2] So, when the Christian controversialists met this pagan Brāhmaṇa philosopher, they soon discovered that he deserved more than a mere patronizing attention. Rammohun was already pre-eminent in theological controversies with his own compatriots, ever attempting to disentangle the eternal foundations of Hindu faith and culture from the debris of later centuries ; and if he engaged now in a prolonged controversy with the Christian missionaries, it was because they totally misunderstood the inner significance and the abiding grandeur of Hindu spiritual idealism. India of the Upaniṣads and Vedānta need not feel the least humiliated before the champions of any other religion, so the Raja maintained, and he exposed the fallacies and weaknesses of the

[2] Rammohun Death Anniversary Address at Bangalore on the 27th September, 1924.

overbearing polemists of early Christian missions of India. His legitimate pride in the spiritual heritage of his ancestors was clearly expressed through the following memorable lines:

'By a reference to history, it may be proved that the world was indebted to our ancestors for the first dawn of knowledge, which sprang up in the East, and thanks to the goddess of wisdom, we have still a philosophical and copious language of our own, which distinguishes us from other nations who cannot express scientific or abstract ideas without borrowing the language of foreigners.'

CONSTRUCTIVE STATESMANSHIP

It would be doing, however, great injustice to this pioneer of our national progress, if by constant references to his controversies with his own countrymen, as well as with foreigners, we exaggerate the apparently destructive side of his genius; for Rammohun left a record of constructive statesmanship, rarely paralleled by any other in that epoch of our history, especially in the two vital departments of national education and national politics. In modernizing our antiquated and effete system of education, he shines as one of the founders of the Hindoo College, as the intimate friend and co-worker of David Hare and Rev. Alexander Duff, and, above all, as the most enlightened co-operator with every champion of science and modernism, official or non-official, who then came over from Europe to work in India. His letter on English education to Lord Amherst is a veritable landmark in the educational history of modern India; for he urged therein for the promotion of a more liberal and enlightened system of instruction, embracing mathematics, natural philosophy, chemistry, anatomy, and other useful sciences, and for the establishment of a college with necessary books, instruments, and other apparatus. This was in 1823, more than a decade before the foundation of the first medical college in India, and more than a quarter of a century before the foundation of the first university in India.

ORIENTALISM VERSUS OCCIDENTALISM

Rammohun has been frequently misunderstood, because of his zealous advocacy of occidental sciences and vigorous criticisms levelled against the mummified oriental systems of education. He yielded to no one in his admiration for the deathless treasures of ancient philosophy and religion, both of his own country as well as of other oriental nations, including even the Chinese, not to speak of the contribution of the Greeks and the Hebrews, the Persians and the Arabs. His rich mind has well been compared by Brojendra Nath Seal to a universal encyclopaedia, embracing all that is best and enduring in the culture of the major branches of the human family. He was a veritable pioneer in collecting and publishing the texts of the Upaniṣads and Vedānta at that early age, and, not satisfied with that scholastic achievement, Rammohun ever strove to convey to common men and women the significance of those texts by means of lucid translations in the vernaculars. Some of his translations in Hindi are unfortunately lost. The Bengalis will ever remember Rammohun as their first grammarian (of course, he had his missionary predecessors like Halhead and Carey), and as their first inspiring prose-writer. Thus Rammohun's contributions, as an orientalist, both in the department of language and literature as well as in Hindu law, were undisputed; and that is why, long before his visit to Europe, Rammohun had the honour of being nominated (July 1824) by the Asiatic Society of Paris as its first Hindu honorary member.

Why the orientalist Rammohun so vigorously championed the cause of the occidentalists in our educational history would be clear from his significant remarks that 'the natives of Europe have carried (the sciences) to a degree of perfection that has raised them above the inhabitants of other parts of the world'. He wanted 'to instruct the natives of India in mathematics, natural philosophy, chemistry, anatomy, and other useful sciences', because those sciences, as he was convinced, were responsible for the predominant position of the Europeans in the world. The conclusion is therefore inevitable that Rammohun was longing to see his countrymen in the same position of eminence and efficiency in the family of nations as the Europeans had achieved, following one and the same method—the conquest and control of nature through the sciences.

NATIONALISM AND INTERNATIONALISM

Another characteristic symptom is his instinctive *penchant* for politics and publicity. He was not satisfied with quiet meditation or mere metaphysical debates within his own self. He was ever bringing all his grievances and complaints, no less than his positive programmes and patriotic dreams, before the open forum of the public, challenging and being challenged, but always fighting a clean fight. The politics of Rammohun was but another aspect of his humanism, as we clearly find in his noble words, penned a few months before his death, protesting to the Ministry of Foreign Affairs of France against the restrictions imposed on foreigners desiring to visit France:

'It is now generally admitted that not religion only, but unbiased common sense as well as the accurate deductions of scientific research lead to the conclusion that all mankind are one great family, of which the numerous nations and tribes existing are only various branches. Hence enlightened men in all countries feel a wish to encourage and facilitate human intercourse in every manner by removing, as far as possible, all impediments to it, in order to promote the reciprocal advantage and enjoyment of the whole human race.'

The last phrase of this valuable document, dated December 1831, was nothing but an amplification of the same theme discussed in his earliest published treatise, *Tuhfat-ul-Muwahhidin,* of 1803. Everything that arrests and denaturalizes the healthy relations 'of the whole human race' must be opposed and fought to a finish. This was what politics meant to him, and his politics of perfect candour and constitutional rhythm was but another name for philanthropy. That was, probably, why Jeremy Bentham, the great English philosopher, greeted him as 'his intensely admired and dearly beloved collaborator in the service of mankind'. In his report submitted before the Judicial Committee of the British Parliament, Rammohun concluded by 'beseeching any and every authority to devise some method of alleviating the miseries of the agricultural peasantry of India and thus discharge their duty to their fellow creatures and fellow subjects'. This friend of the poor ryots of India also befriended, with rare courage and tact, the last unfortunate Mogul emperor of Delhi, Akbar II, whose cause he started championing as early as 1828. This led to his being sent out to England as the ambassador of the Mohammedan emperor, for whom Rammohun pleaded eloquently and secured the redress of his grievances.

In his bold agitation against the Press Regulations of 1823, we find the same grasp of general principles which elevates his 'Petitions' high above the level of occasional writing, so much so that those were supposed to have the dignity and conviction of an *Areopagitica.* 'The attachments of the natives of India', the Raja observed, 'to the British Government must be as permanent as their confidence in the honour and justice of the British nation. Resistance of a people advanced in knowledge has ever been not against the existence, but against the abuses of the governing power.'

His specific observations on the value of the freedom of the Press are equally remarkable:

'A Free Press has never yet caused a revolution in any part of the world, because, while men can easily represent the grievances arising from the conduct of the local authorities to the supreme Government and thus get them redressed, the grounds of discontent that excite revolution are removed; whereas, where no freedom of the Press existed, and grievances consequently remained unrepresented and unredressed, innumerable revolutions have taken place in all parts of the globe, or if prevented by the armed force of the Government, the people continued ready for insurrection.'

Freedom was restored to the Indian Press by Sir Charles Metcalf five years after the death of Rammohun, but in the Free Press Dinner given to Sir Charles Metcalf at the Calcutta Town Hall (February 1838), Mr. Leith, an Englishman, proposed a toast 'to the memory of Rammohun Roy', which was seconded by Prasanna Coomar Tagore, a friend and colleague of the Raja in the foundation of the Brāhmo Samāj.

RELIGIOUS REFORMS

As early as 1803, in his preface to *Tuhfat-ul-Muwahhidin,* Rammohun recorded in unmistakable terms his convictions about the unity of Godhead, and his life thereafter seemed to be but an improvisation on that theme. Almost simultaneously with his settling down in Calcutta, we find him establishing the Vedanta College, in 1816, for the 'propagation and defence of Hindu Unitarianism'. Shortly before, Rammohun founded the Ātmīya Sabhā with some of his illustrious contemporaries as members: Dwarka Nath Tagore, Prasanna Coomar Tagore, Nanda Kishore Bose (father of Rajnarain Bose), Brindaban Mitra (grandfather of Dr. Rajendra Lal Mitra), and others. Two renowned Sanskrit scholars, Pandit Sivaprasad Misra and Hariharananda Tirthaswami, joined the Sabhā. Pandit Sivaprasad signed some of the controversial writings actually composed by Rammohun. Hariharananda was the mendicant friend of the Raja from the days of his religious discussions with him at Rangpur. The Swami not only contributed substantially to the philosophical make-up of the Sabhā, but gave his own brother, Pandit Ramchandra Vidyavagish, who became the first minister of the Brāhmo Samāj founded by the Raja. For the first two years (1815-16), the Ātmīya Sabhā held its weekly meetings in the garden-house of Rammohun at Manicktolla. There were recitation and expounding of sacred texts and the singing of hymns composed by Rammohun and his friends. In 1819, a memorable debate took place between Subrahmanya Sastri of Madras and Rammohun, when the latter is reported to have completely vanquished the former in a discussion on idol-worship in the presence of the leading citizens of Calcutta including Radhakanta Dev, who was the leader of the orthodox Hindus and who later on, in 1830, promoted the foundation of the Dharma Sabhā, the rival organization of the Brāhmo Samāj. Between 1815 and 1819, most of the important texts and translations relating to the Vedānta and the Upaniṣads were published by the Raja, who simultaneously started his campaign of social reform with the anti-suttee agitation. These publications not only created a stir in his own country, but roused the attention of his European contemporaries; for we find that, in 1816-17, the *Monthly Repository of Theology and General Literature* published a lengthy and appreciative review of the Raja's *Abridgement of the Vedānta.* About the same time, Abbé Gregoire, Bishop of Blois, wrote a striking pamphlet in French in which we read: 'The moderation with which he repels the attacks on his writings, the force of his arguments, and his profound knowledge of the sacred books of the Hindoos are proofs of his fitness for the work he has undertaken; and the pecuniary sacrifices he has made show a disinterestedness which cannot be encouraged or admired too warmly.'

In 1817, Mr. John Digby arranged for the publication of the first volume of the Raja's work in London, and between 1823 and 1824, his *Precepts of Jesus* was published by the Unitarian Society of London and was reprinted in America in 1828. From far-off America, Rev. H. Ware of Cambridge (Mass.) corresponded with the learned Raja on the prospects of Christianity in India. The famous controversy with the Christian missionaries of Serampore, in 1821, was the result of the Raja's converting Mr. William Adam, the Baptist missionary, to his Unitarianism. The Trinitarian Christians made violent and often undignified attacks on the Raja through the pages of the *Friend of India* and the Bengali *Samācāra Darpaṇa.* The Raja published at this time his *Brāhmaṇical Magazine,* and when the Baptist Mission Press refused to print his *First Appeal to the Christian Public,* the Raja started his Unitarian Press (1823). The Ātmīya Sabhā meetings were discontinued after 1819, but the Calcutta Unitarian Committee was formed by the Raja in 1821, who raised a large sum to support Mr. William Adam, as well as to maintain the Anglo-Hindu School. Along with a few British barristers, attorneys, and merchants, we find, as members of the Unitarian Society, Dwarka Nath Tagore, Prasanna Coomar Tagore, and Radha Prasad Roy, the eldest son of the Raja, standing by his side. But occidental Unitarianism did not take root in Indian soil, and the Raja soon thought of establishing an indigenous institution based on the bed-rock of Upaniṣadic idealism. On the 20th August, 1828 (6th Bhādra, Śaka 1750), at 48 Chitpore Road, Jorasanko, Calcutta, was founded the Brāhmo Sabhā, with Tarachand Chakravarty as its Secretary. 'Two Telugu Brahmins used to recite the Vedas in a side-room, screened from the view of the congregation, where non-Brahmins would not be admitted; Utsavananda would read texts of the Upaniṣads, which were afterwards explained in Bengali by Pandit Ramchandra Vidyavagish, who would then preach or read the sermons, some of which were written by Rammohun Roy. Singing of hymns terminated the ceremony.'[3] The services of the Brāhmo

[3] Pandit Sivanath Sastri, *History of the Brāhmo Samāj,* I.

Sabhā (the popular name of the Brāhmo Samāj) began to attract a large number of sympathizers, so that within two years Rammohun was able to raise sufficient funds for the purchase of a house to serve as the permanent place of worship for the members. Mr. Montgomery Martin in his *History of the British Colonies* gives the following account of the opening ceremony of the Brāhmo Samāj at this new house at 55 Upper Chitpore Road (at present occupied by the Ādi Brāhmo Samāj of Maharshi Devendra Nath Tagore):

'The institution was opened by the late Raja Rammohun Roy accompanied by the writer (the only European present) in 1830. There were about 500 Hindus present and among them many Brahmins who, after the prayers and singing of hymns had been concluded, received gifts in money to a considerable extent.'

That Rammohun devoted a considerable part of his fortune to the propagation of the cause was attested by another European contemporary, James Silk Buckingham, the editor of the *Calcutta Journal*:

'He has done all this, to the great detriment of his private interests, being rewarded by the coldness and jealousy of all the great functionaries of Church and State in India, and supporting the Unitarian Chapel, the Unitarian Press, and the expense of his own publications . . . out of a private fortune, of which he devotes more than one-third to acts of the purest philanthropy and benevolence.'

Rammohun's religion was the crowning glory of his career as a scholar, a statesman, and a patriot. We can easily understand why he laid so much emphasis on unity in this land, where man and man, sect and sect, community and community were weakened and degraded through irrational and interminable wranglings resulting in disunion. The success of his pioneer activities in connection with the unification (cultural as well as spiritual) of India, inhabited by persons of so many races and religions, should not be judged by the numerical strength of the congregation which he founded. It is rather the fundamental truth of human fellowship and unity underlying the memorable trust deed of the Brāhmo Samāj (dated 8th January, 1830) that should be cherished as a priceless legacy of the Raja to posterity:

'And that in conducting the said worship or adoration no object, animate or inanimate, that has been, or is, or shall hereafter become, or be recognized, as an object of worship, by any man or set of men, shall be reviled or slightingly or contemptuously spoken of or alluded to either in preaching, praying, or in the hymns, or other mode of worship that may be delivered or used in the said messuage or building.

'And that no sermon, preaching, discourse, prayer, or hymn be delivered, made, or used in such worship but such as have a tendency to the promotion of the contemplation of the Author and Preserver of the Universe, to the promotion of charity, morality, piety, benevolence, virtue, and to the strengthening of the bonds of union between men of all religious persuasions and creeds.'

MAHARSHI DEVENDRA NATH TAGORE

The relation of Rammohun Roy with the personalities and movements of the subsequent epochs was so intimate that a learned Christian writer, Dr. H. C. E. Zacharias, in his famous book *Renascent India* observes:

'Of such personalities—good, bad, and indifferent—who have become prominent in this Indian renascence, the number is very great indeed and ever swelling; but, in the last instance, all really can be said to go back in their spiritual parentage to one man—Rammohun Roy.

'Rammohun Roy and his Brāhmo Samāj form the starting-point for all the various reform movements—whether in Hindu religion, society, or politics—which have agitated India during the past hundred years and which have led to her wonderful renascence in these our own days.'

When Rammohun passed away in distant Bristol, fighting till the last days of his life to vindicate the rights of his countrymen, his Brāhmo Samāj, here in India, was little more than an aspiration and a dream. For years after his death, Pandit Ramchandra Vidyavagish kept the lamp burning, and it was only in 1843 (7th Pauṣa, Śaka 1765) that Devendra Nath Tagore, son of Dwarka Nath Tagore, brought a new inspiration and strength to the Samāj. He underwent a formal ceremony of *dīkṣā* (initiation) at the hands of Vidyavagish, who lived to pass the torch, as it were, to this spiritual successor of the Raja. Born in 1817, Devendra Nath Tagore, endowed with an inborn hankering for things spiritual, as we read in his remarkable *Autobiography*, came across, accidentally, the opening verse of the *Īśa Upaniṣad*: 'God is immanent in all things, in whatsoever lives and moves in the universe: enjoy therefore without being attached; covet not the wealth belonging to others.'

This spark of ancient Indian wisdom would have had a poor chance of blazing forth into conviction, had it fallen on the damped religious spirit of early nineteenth-century Europe, convulsed with the stormy competition for material wealth engendered by the Industrial Revolution. But to Devendra Nath, the young mystic, it brought a different kind of revelation. Born and brought up, as he was, in the lap of luxury, he felt the imperious call of the Essential, drowning the clamour of gaudy unessentials. In October 1839, he established, with some of his friends and relatives, an association which grew into the Truth-teaching Society or

Tattva-bodhinī Sabhā, which marked an epoch in the literary and spiritual history of eastern India. Starting with only ten members, whose number later rose to five hundred, the Sabhā attracted some of the leading men of that period, including the Raja of Nadia, the Maharajadhiraja of Burdwan, and others.

Being an association formed by young men, it spontaneously took to the idealistic training up of our youth under that eminent scholar Akshoy Kumar Dutta, who is one of the rare writers of early Bengali prose and who gave us a famous study on the 'Religious Communities of India' (*Bhāratavarṣīya Upāsaka-sampradāya*). He was also the first editor of the monthly journal of the Society, *Tattva-bodhinī Patrikā,* which marked an epoch in the history of Bengali literature. Some of the outstanding *litterateurs* of that age, Pandit Iswar Chandra Vidyasagar, Dr. Rajendra Lal Mitra, and others, were amongst its contributors. It began to publish a translation of the *Ṛg-Veda* in 1847, when Max Müller was studying the same Veda in Paris under the great French Sanskritist, E. Burnouf. Starting the translation of the Upaniṣads, Devendra Nath found that a knowledge of the Vedas was indispensable, and therefore he sent a student from his Sabhā to Banaras in 1844. Before long, in 1845, a controversy on Vedic infallibility cropped up in the Sabhā, and three more students were sent to Banaras to bring authentic information on the Vedic texts. That was nearly twenty years before the initiation of Swami Dayananda Saraswati by his master Virajananda, who enjoined upon him the solemn task of propagating the truths of the Vedas. While, in 1845, the Brāhmo Samāj under Devendra Nath was publicly proclaiming the Vedas and Vedāntism as the basis of its faith, the very same year the rival faith from the occident claimed a respectable Hindu, Umesh Chandra Sarkar, as a convert to Christianity. This threw the public of Calcutta into convulsion. A meeting of the leading Hindu citizens was called by Devendra Nath, and a sum of rupees thirty thousand was raised, with a view to stemming the tide of conversion. The controversy between Dr. Alexander Duff and the members of the Sabhā, represented by Rajnarain Bose, would be read with interest by those who have followed similiar controversies between Rammohun Roy and the Baptist missionaries, a quarter of a century earlier. But there were perfect tolerance and openness to conviction amongst the members of the Sabhā, many of whom did not believe in Vedic infallibility, especially the rationalistic group headed by Akshoy Kumar Dutta. Devendra Nath paid a personal visit to Banaras in 1847, while the four Brāhmaṇa students returned with positive information on the Vedas. The inevitable rejection of the creed of Vedic infallibility led to the formulation of the fundamental principles of natural and universal theism through the *Brāhma Dharma,* a compilation from the Upaniṣads published by Devendra Nath.

Rationalism thus triumphed over creeds and cults and, quite in keeping with the tradition of Rammohun, it refused to remain as a mere intellectual pastime. On the contrary, it began attacking some of the fundamental iniquities and abuses of society. Intemperance, polygamy, etc. were denounced ; widow remarriage and female education were strongly advocated by the Brāhmo Samāj of Devendra Nath, expressed through his famous *Patrikā* (1850-55). A little tired with rationalistic debate, in the course of which some members proposed to settle their belief in God by counting votes, Devendra Nath retired to the Himalayas and for a couple of years (1856-58) remained absorbed in studies and meditation. When he returned from the hills, he rejoiced to find a new recruit in Keshub Chandra Sen, the grandson of Dewan Ramkamal Sen, the first Indian Secretary to the Asiatic Society of Bengal. Keshub, a talented young man, was born in 1838 and was then barely twenty. We turn a new leaf in the history of the Brāhmo Samāj with the Devendra Nath-Keshub episode.

DEMOCRATIZATION AND EXPANSION

Keshub was drawn to the Brāhmo Samāj by a chance study of *What is Brahmoism,* a tract of Rajnarain Bose who, along with Akshoy Kumar Dutta and Iswar Chandra Vidyasagar, continued to be a literary and intellectual exponent of Brāhmoism. The Brāhmo Samāj was managed by the Tattva-bodhinī Sabhā, and the Secretary of the Samāj was the illustrious Vidyasagar, who resigned the post in 1859, owing to some differences of opinion regarding administrative details, and Devendra Nath and Keshub Chandra became the Joint Secretaries of the Samāj, which took over the printing press, the library, and other properties of the Sabhā, then dying a natural death. To inaugurate, as it were, a new period of expansion, the two leaders, young and old, undertook a voyage to Ceylon in September 1859, which must have opened a new perspective to them. On his return, Keshub developed a youth movement, delivering addresses and publishing tracts such as *Young Bengal, This is for You* etc., which attracted a large number of young men and college students to the Samāj. Vidyasagar had retired, but his noble championing of the cause of the poor Hindu widows inspired this leader of the younger generation, for we find Keshub utilizing the stage to rouse public sympathy, through the performance of the sensational drama *Vidhavā-vivāha.* The enthusiasm was irresistible, especially after 1861, when Keshub gave up a lucrative government post in the Bank of Bengal and, with his young idealistic friends and colleagues, organized a spiritual fraternity, the Saṅgat Sabhā. Here, by the side of the Hindu scriptures, we find the works of Theodore Parker, Hamilton, Victor Cousin, and Prof. F. W. Newman studied with rare zeal. But it was not a group of book-worms or theologians indifferent to the conditions around them. For we find Keshub publishing *An Appeal to the British Nation,* for the promotion of mass education in India, which was circulated in England, through his learned correspondent Prof. F. W. Newman. Such a progressive programme was more remarkable, as it came within three years from the foundation of universities in India (1858). In 1861, Keshub also organized relief funds to mitigate the sufferings of millions in the then North-Western Provinces, ravaged by a terrible famine. Thus social service came to be a part of the work of the Samāj, and in the same year, which witnessed the birth of Rabindranath, Keshub started, with the financial backing of Devendra Nath, the influential journal, *Indian Mirror,* which, along with the *Hindoo Patriot,* edited by Harish Mookerjee and Kristo Das Pal, came to be the harbinger of social and political reform in our country. In 1862, Keshub delivered his memorable address 'The Destiny of Human Life' and was elevated by Devendra Nath to the post of the Ācārya or minister of the Brāhmo Samāj, when he was barely twenty-four. In 1863, just thirty years after the death of Rammohun, Keshub was driven to defend the Samāj against the attacks of the Christian missionaries led by Rev. Lal Behari Dey. His brochure, *The Brāhmo Samāj Vindicated,* proved what fibre Keshub was made of. The miserable condition of our womenfolk, imprisoned in our homes by age-long custom, did not fail to rouse the reforming zeal of Keshub and his associates, who started the first journal for women, *Vāmā-bodhinī,* in 1863. Courting persecution and social ostracism, these young reformers defied caste, celebrated intermarriages, and tried in many ways to remove the barrier between man and man and man and woman.

The apostolic zeal of the younger group carried the message of the Brāhmo Samāj to the remote villages of Bengal, and very soon to places beyond the limits of Bengal, as a result of Keshub's first preaching tour through Madras in 1864. The Prārthanā Samāj of Bombay was organized in 1867, on the lines of the Brāhmo Samāj, under the inspiration of eminent reformers of western India like Ranade and Bhandarkar. From an article in the *Indian Mirror* (January 1866), we find that there were then 54 Samājas: 50 in Bengal, 2 in North-Western Provinces, 1 in the Punjab, and 1 in Madras. Quite a large number of boys' and girls' schools were maintained by the Brāhmos, and there were 37 periodicals devoted to the propagation of Brāhmoism, most of them in Bengali and English, 1 in Urdu from North-Western Provinces, and 1 in Telugu published by the Veda Samāj of Madras. Thus it assumed the character of an all-India movement. But, unfortunately, in the course of the years 1865 and 1866, the differences between the old conservative party and the party of youthful reformers came to be so serious that a schism was inevitable. The old party shrank into the Ādi Brāhmo Samāj, and the new party formed the Brāhmo Samāj of India (1866). The attitude of Devendra Nath during this party struggle was as calm as it was dignified and, till his last days, he continued to welcome and support every earnest Brāhmo who cared to seek his advice. Laying the foundation of Santiniketan Ashram, which was later to be the principal seat of activity of Rabindranath, Devendra Nath Tagore, the venerable patriarch of the Samāj of Rammohun Roy and revered and loved by all sections of the community as Maharshi, passed away in 1905.

'He was without so long ; but now He revealed Himself to my spirit within ; I beheld Him in my soul.' Such profound lines from the pages of his *Autobiography* go to prove that modern India was not all mad for modernism, but that the eternal search of India for immortality, instead of material wealth, was still being expressed through the lives of our modern mystics.

THE BRĀHMO SAMĀJ OF INDIA

When, on the 24th January, 1868, Keshub laid the foundation of the Mandir of the Brāhmo Samāj of India (Bhāratavarṣīya Brāhṃa Samāj), a big *saṅkīrtana* party went round the city singing the memorable song:

'To grant salvation the merciful God has sent His new faith of Brāhmoism. Lo! the gates of salvation are wide open ; He calls one and all ; entrance through His gate is free ; no one ever returns disappointed ; the rich and the poor, the wise and the ignorant, all are equally welcome there.

'Men and women of all classes have an equal right ; whoever truly loves God, the same shall be saved, there is no caste distinction here.'

Henceforth, in most of the utterances and writings of Keshub, we find a great spirit of catholicity and earnest endeavour to harmonize the apparently conflicting creeds of all religions. But he was misunderstood, for his lecture 'Jesus Christ: Asia and Europe' (1866) encouraged a Christian preacher, Mr. Tinling, to hope for the conversion of the Brāhmos into Christianity. His introducing devotional exercise through *saṅkīrtana* branded him, in the eyes of radical Brāhmos, as a backslider to Vaiṣṇavism, as a result of the influence of his devoted friend Vijay Krishna Goswami. With the same curious logic, some may consider him to be a Śākta, because in a prayer included in his *Śikṣā-saṅgraha* (1866) Keshub cries out passionately, 'Oh Thou Mother Divine! bind me with Thy mercies'.

The fact is that the deep sentiments of *bhakti* surged in his soul, and he evolved a new mysticism of his own based on the reconciliation of all faiths, which found its culmination, in January 1881, in his announcement of the New Dispensation (Nava Vidhān). Eleven years earlier, when Keshub visited England, he had a phenomenal success as a spiritual ambassador of India, no less than as a great social reformer, who promoted inter-caste marriages in this caste-ridden country, who waged the early campaigns for temperance, and who, by his unrivalled eloquence, could make the heart of an Englishman as well as of an Indian pulsate with equal sympathy.

The East and the West spoke simultaneously their profound spiritual messages through the harmonious voice of Keshub, who was admired by his countrymen no less than by eminent foreigners, like the Very Rev. Dean of Westminster, Dr. Martineau, John Stuart Mill, Prof. Max Müller, Grant Duff, Louis Blanc, and others. He showed that there was no conflict between the Hindu instinct of spirituality and the deeper spiritual experiences of Christianity or Islam.[4] At the same time, Keshub commanded that penetrating vision which enabled him to discern and respect the revelation of truths in the orthodox Hindu religion, as manifested in the careers of Swami Dayananda Saraswati and Sri Ramakrishna Paramahamsa. The former met him in 1870, shortly after Keshub's return from England. The probable date of the meeting of Keshub with Ramakrishna was 15th March, 1875, and we read in the *Indian Mirror* (28th March, 1875) the following touching lines:

'We met one (a sincere Hindu devotee) not long ago and were charmed by the depth, penetration, and simplicity of his spirit. The never-ceasing metaphors and analogies, in which he indulged, are most of them as apt as they are beautiful. The characteristics of his mind are the very opposite to those of Pandit Dayananda Saraswati, the former being so gentle, tender, and contemplative, as the latter is sturdy, masculine, and polemical. Hinduism must have in it a deep sense of beauty, truth, and goodness to inspire such men as these.'

While sectional and denominational controversies would raise a thousand questions to cloud the main issues, no sane man will doubt that Keshub's contribution as a reconciler of apparently contradictory creeds was considerable, and that his communion with the unlettered sage of Dakshineswar forms one of the sweetest chapters of spiritual kinship. Towards the end of his short, yet brilliant, career, Keshub was getting more

[4] Under Keshub's inspiration and direction, Babu Giris Chandra Sen prepared and published the first complete translation of the *Qur'ān* (with commentaries) from the original Arabic into Bengali.

Indian and more Asiatic, as we feel from his prophetic lines in 'Asia's Message to Europe' (20th January, 1883):

'I am a child of Asia ; her sorrows are my sorrows, her joys are my joys. From one end of Asia to the other, I boast of a vast home, a wide nationality, and an extended kinship. Upon Asia's soil have flourished and prospered those at whose feet the world lies prostrate. The great religions which have given life and salvation to millions of men owe their origin to Asia.'

THE SĀDHĀRAṆ BRĀHMO SAMĀJ

Keshub died prematurely when he was about forty-six, only three years after his proclamation of the New Dispensation. A man of masterful personality, Keshub had many difficulties as regards the financial and administrative aspects of the Samāj. As early as 1871-72, we find that some of his junior contemporaries were becoming impatient, owing to the lack of a rational and constitutional procedure in the Samāj, which they thought was more or less dominated by one individual. This constitutional party, moreover, did not like certain conservative tendencies among the *entourage* of Keshub. The radical group organized itself, in 1874, as the Samadarśī party, counting among its leaders, A. M. Bose, a Cambridge wrangler and one of the earliest leaders of the Indian National Congress, D. M. Das, the uncle of C. R. Das, and D. N. Ganguli, who risked his life investigating the pitiable condition of the coolies of the tea-plantations in Assam. They were soon strengthened by the comradeship of Nagendra Nath Chatterjee, the biographer of Rammohuṇ Roy, and Pandit Sivanath Sastri, the life and soul of the Sādhāraṇ Brāhmo Samāj. A temporary reconciliation between this radical group and the conservative group of Keshub was effected through his granting a sort of a representative assembly composed of the members of both parties. But the unfortunate controversy growing out of the marriage of his eldest daughter with the prince of Cooch Behar, in contravention of Act 3 of 1872 which fixes the marriageable age for girls at fourteen, completed the rupture. On the 15th May, 1878, the new party held a public meeting in the Town Hall and formally organized the Sādhāraṇ Brāhmo Samāj. The venerable Maharshi Devendra Nath sent his message of blessing to the new Samāj. At the time of this second schism, there were 124 Samājas: 80 in Bengal, 8 in Assam, 6 in Bihar, 11 in North-Western Provinces, 5 in South India, 5 in Oudh, 7 in Bombay Presidency, and 2 in Sind. Altogether they conducted 21 periodicals in English, Bengali, Marathi, Urdu, and Hindi.

The foundation of the Sādhāraṇ Brāhmo Samāj Mandir was laid on the 11th Māgha, Śaka 1800 (A.D. 1878), the building fund of which received generous donations also from sympathizers in other parts of India, to mention among others, the Maharaja Scindia and Sirdar Dayal Sing of Amritsar. The anniversary celebration, in January 1879, was memorable for two other events: A meeting organized by the new Samāj in honour of Raja Rammohun Roy was held at the house of Devendra Nath, while another meeting was organized by Keshub's party. Secondly, the foundation was laid of the City School, which soon developed into the City College of Calcutta under the able guidance of Ananda Mohun Bose, who met the initial expenses, and of Surendranath Banerjea who, though not a member of the Samāj, offered to be one of its first teachers. Another noticeable institution was the Students' Weekly Service, arranging for the growing student community of Calcutta lectures on religious, social, moral, and political topics, preceded by a short divine service. In quick succession followed the establishment of a society for the progressive ladies, who used to meet to discuss and read papers. A library and printing press also gradually developed with the two organs of the new Samāj, *Tattvakaumudī,* in Bengali, and *Brāhmo Public Opinion,* in English. The year 1881 saw the completion and consecration of the Mandir and, through the renewed activities of the missionaries of the Samāj, 15 new Samājas were founded in different parts of the country in 1883. Maharshi Devendra Nath and Rajnarain Bose blessed the congregation by preaching from the pulpit, and the same year we find a lady occupying the Samāj pulpit.

In 1884, the famous Bengali weekly, *Sañjīvanī,* edited by Krishna Kumar Mitra, started its career, and a regular social service centre was organized to bring relief to the famine-stricken people of Birbhum. In 1888-89, the Brāhmo Girls' School was opened and missionary activities were carried into the Khasi Hills, Assam. In 1896, Rev. J. T. Sunderland visited the Samāj as the representative of the British and Foreign Unitarian Association and succeeded in bringing together the leading men of the three sections of the Samāj to form a committee for the purpose of selecting a candidate to receive theological training in the Manchester College, Oxford. A second representative, Rev. James Harwood, from the same Association visited the Samāj in 1897, presented a whole set of the Hibbert Lectures to the Samāj library, and strengthened further the ties of the Brāhmo Samāj with the Unitarian Societies abroad. By the end of the nineteenth century, the Samāj, unfortunately, lost many of its valiant workers: D. M. Das, Rajnarain Bose, D. M. Ganguli, Ramtanu Lahiri, Sib Chandra Dev, and others. But a new generation of workers, under the inspiring guidance of Pandit Sivanath Sastri, stepped into the breach and started their work in a spirit of service to the motherland.

Thus, from the very beginning of our national awakening, this numerically small family of social-radicals have ever tried through their best representatives, like J. C. Bose and P. C. Ray, Aurobindo Ghosh and Bepin Chandra Pal, Lord Sinha and C. R. Das, and Sarojini Naidu and Sarala Devi Chaudhurani, to further the cause of social, educational, and political advancement of India.

It is a matter of sincere congratulation that both during the celebration of the centenary of the Brāhmo Samāj in 1928, as well as during the death centenary of its illustrious founder, Raja Rammohun Roy, in 1933, representatives of Islam, Christianity, Buddhism, Sikhism, Ārya Samāj, the Ramakrishna-Vivekananda Movement, and various other denominations of Hinduism participated in a most laudable spirit of fraternal co-operation. In the Parliament of Religions in Chicago, Swami Vivekananda sat side by side with Pratap Chandra Mazumdar, and in the one held at the Senate Hall, Calcutta University, under the auspices of the Brāhmo Samāj Centenary, the spirit of fellowship through religion, which was the basic principle of Brāhmoism, came to be gloriously vindicated by the delegates and representatives of the various religious denominations of the East and the West. The incarnation of this spirit of tolerance and fellowship was our national poet Rabindranath Tagore, the son of Maharshi Devendra Nath and the spiritual grandson of Rammohun Roy. The deathless truths of the Upaniṣads, on which the Raja and his noble successors based the Brāhmo Samāj, found their universal expression through the creations of Rabindranath, the poet laureate of Asia, who was, during his lifetime, hailed by the republic of letters as a world-poet. His *Naivedya* and *Gītāñjali, Sādhanā* and *Creative Unity,* and *Personality* and *Religion of Man,* to mention only a few of his immortal creations, have won for India a permanent place in the world of beauty and truth. And in this age, when Mahatma Gandhi has opened a new chapter in the history of modern India, with the solemn declaration of rights of all individuals, high or low, Brāhmaṇa or pariah, we feel that the struggles of the Brāhmo Samāj in the vindication of the principles of equality and unity have not been in vain, and may have lessons of permanent value in our national history as well as in the general progress of humanity in the orient.

44

THE ĀRYA SAMĀJ

JUST as the impact of Islam gave a fillip to Bhakti systems in India in the middle ages, so has the inroad of western civilization given rise to a number of reform movements in Hinduism in modern times. All these are contributing in different ways to the furthering of Indian renaissance that is going on apace. Of these, the Ārya Samāj takes its stand on the bed-rock of the Vedas, which, it believes, hold the key to all our socio-religious problems. It challenges the good sense of humanity to subject to a crucial test the time-old wisdom revealed to the *ṛṣis* and see if their life-giving message can be replaced to advantage by the varied materialistic 'isms' of modern days.

DAYANANDA AND THE VEDAS

Swami Dayananda's interpretation of the Vedas, the 'primeval scripture of humanity', has given a new orientation to the Hindu faith. Scoffed at and ridiculed in the beginning, the view-point of the Swami has of late been hailed by savants both of the East and the West. Says Sri Aurobindo:

'There is then nothing fantastical in Dayananda's idea that the Veda contains truths of science as well as truths of religion. I will even add my own conviction that the Veda contains other truths of a science which the modern world does not at all possess, and, in that case, Dayananda has rather understated than overstated the depth and range of the Vedic wisdom.'[1]

'Immediately the character of the Veda is fixed in the sense Dayananda gave to it, the merely ritual, mythological, polytheistic interpretation of Sāyaṇācārya collapses, and the merely mateological and materialistic European interpretation collapses. We have, instead, a real scripture, one of the world's sacred books and the divine word of a lofty and noble religion.'[2]

To Pavagi, the Veda appears to contain truths of such widely different branches of learning as geology and modern political science. In the opinion of Rele, Vedic gods are figures of biology.

Maurice Philippe writes in his *Teachings of the Vedas*: 'We are justified therefore in concluding that the higher and purer conceptions of the Vedic hymns were the results of primitive revelation.'

[1] *Dayananda, the Man and His Work*, pp. 18-19.
[2] *Ibid.*, p. 16.

Says Edward Carpenter in his *Art of Creation*: 'The same germinal thoughts of the Vedic authors come all the way down history even to Schopenhauer and Whitman, inspiring philosophy after philosophy and religion after religion.'

DAYANANDA'S ATTITUDE TOWARDS OTHER RELIGIONS

Elements of truth are present in every system of divine faith. While prophets in every land have tried to unite humanity, it is the priests that have sown seeds of discord and disunion. Swami Dayananda raised his mighty voice against the confusing babble of the priests. He went so far as to invite a conference of the representatives of all religions on the occasion of the Delhi Durbar in 1877. Keshub Chandra Sen, Sir Syed Ahmad, and Munshi Alakhdhari were among those who responded to the invitation. Dayananda's proposal was premature, but his idea that the exponents of various faiths should put their heads together to evolve a formula of united activity was unique in those days, when ideas of jehads and crusades prevailed, and signified the true conception of religion that it was a unifying and not a dividing force. Though the conference led, at that time, to no practical result, yet it paved the way for the later religious parliaments and conferences, in which preachers of different faiths met on a common platform and offered to one another the olive branch of goodwill and peace. To Swami Dayananda, truth, wherever it is found, is of the Veda.

SOCIAL REFORM AND EDUCATION

Like every reform movement, the Ārya Samāj set itself first to purge the society, in which it had arisen, of its rampant evils. The Vedas enjoin worship of one formless God. Service of elders, literally 'fathers', of individual families and of the community at large, is repeatedly insisted on. *Varṇa-vyavasthā*, as taught in the Veda, is the fourfold division of society based on the character of individuals. The Vedic conception of marriage is that of a sacrament that binds a grown-up couple in matrimonial bonds, while the status of woman, recognized in that hoary scripture, is that of a divine helpmate of man in all the spheres, private and civic, of human life. The propaganda of the Ārya Samāj has, in the provinces in which it has had the opportunity of working, extirpated social abuses, which were a perversion of these divine behests. The Ārya Samāj regards untouchability as un-Vedic. It has invested lacs of 'untouchables' with the sacred thread and thus made them honourable members of the Hindu society, enjoying the same social rights as the so-called caste-Hindus. The portals of the Vedic Church have been thrown open even to non-Hindus. Historical researches have proved that Hinduism assumed its non-missionary character in the days of its decadence. All the foreign races and tribes, such as Greeks, Scythians, and Hūṇas, that made India their home in different ages, have been assimilated into the Hindu society. An inscription belonging to the second century B.C., found at Besnagar near Bhilsa, bears testimony to the adoption of the Vāsudeva cult by Heliodorus, a Greek ambassador. Even so late as the middle ages, the Hindu saints, beginning with Rāmānanda and his disciples, allowed the non-Hindus to join the ranks of their orthodox following as members of the same social organization. This practice has been revived by the Ārya Samāj. The last two reforms, namely, the reclamation of the depressed classes and proselytization of non-Hindus, have cost the Ārya Samāj a number of martyrs, who have preferred death to submission to the arrogant demands of unreasonable superstition and wilful fanaticism.

The uncompromising attitude of the Ārya Samāj against what it regards as 'false gods' and the gauntlet it has thrown in the name of the ancient *ṛṣis* have earned it the epithets 'Church militant' and 'aggressive Hinduism'. The Hindu, at the time of the advent of the Ārya Samāj, was very docile. One might ridicule the gods he worshipped and the faith he had idealized for centuries, yet, in the face of all this vilification, he would not be roused, making one doubt if he was alive with power to feel and act. With the advent of the Ārya Samāj, this attitude of undisturbed indifference was rudely shaken. The Hindu was infused with new faith and dynamism. He began to take pride in his religion and, if need be, was prepared to lay down his life for it. The weapon that the Ārya Samāj has been using, in its campaign against what, in its eyes, is untruth, is that of rational persuasion wedded to unflinching faith. In its self-evoked fight against heavy odds, it has had to offer on the altar of religion the lives of some of its most devoted workers and saints. To the immortal honour of the Church of Dayananda, it has always been the breast of the Ārya Samājist that has been stained with blood, never his hand. The noble example of the founder has been followed faithfully by the devoted adherents of his Church.

The leaders of the Ārya Samāj realized, from the very beginning, the vital importance of education in opening the eyes of the people to their true cultural heritage. In order to propagate knowledge among the people, the Ārya Samāj has spread widely a network of *gurukulas,* colleges, and schools, both for boys and girls, throughout the country as well as in some colonies overseas, where it has been carrying on its beneficent activities. The Gurukula at Kangri, near Hardwar, is the first Indian university to adopt an Indian vernacular, Hindi, as the medium of instruction, right up to the graduate, and even post-graduate, standard. It has resuscitated the Vedic and Sanskritic studies and assimilated to them modern art and science. By the revival of the ancient institution of *brahmacarya* and by giving morality the first place in its scheme, the Ārya Samāj has made it possible to make character the basis of juvenile education. In times of earthquakes, floods, and famine, the work of relief undertaken by the Ārya Samāj has meant a new lease of life for many a distressed individual, family, and community. By starting widows' homes and orphanages, it has made provision for the maintenance of the needy, who, otherwise, would have been the waifs and strays of humanity. Many of the important reform movements in the Hindu society have found the Ārya Samāj in the vanguard. This position has been won at the cost of continued sacrifices and privations. Being champions of the lowly and the lost, the Āryas have had to face the opposition of the orthodox and the calumny of the unscrupulous. But they clung to their post and won in the end, so that today, emulating the example set by the Ārya Samāj, other societies too have opened institutions for the education of the masses and relief of the distressed. In the matter of social reform, a common outlook is fast developing in the whole Hindu community. All this tremendous work has been accomplished by the Ārya Samāj on the basis of a constitution devised in accordance with the teachings of the Vedas, which in itself is a landmark in the history of the Hindu religion.

THE PRINCIPLES OF THE ĀRYA SAMĀJ

The Ārya Samāj was founded on the 10th April, 1875, at Bombay. As is evident from a perusal of the principles formulated then, the original plan of the founder was to establish a central Samāj in every country and append to it a network of subordinate Samājas, which might cover every town and village. In practice, however, this plan did not succeed. The world was not yet ready for concerted activity on such a large scale. In every large town, where Swami Dayananda went, he opened a Samāj, which was constitutionally independent of other Samājas.

With the opening of the Ārya Samāj at Lahore on the 24th June, 1877, the constitution of the Ārya Samāj underwent a formal change. Its *niyamas* or principles were precisely stated. The *upaniyamas* or rules and regulations were re-drafted and incorporated in a separate document. Their importance was recognized to be subordinate to that of the *niyamas*. In the *niyamas,* after stating the two principal items of the creed, namely, belief in God and faith in the Vedas, the universal objects of the Ārya Samāj were set forth in outline. The *niyamas,* formulated by Dayananda himself, run as follows:

The first (efficient) cause of all knowledge and all that is known through knowledge is Parameśvara (supreme Lord).

Īśvara (God) is existent, intelligent, and blissful. He is formless, omnipotent, just, merciful, unborn, endless, unchangeable, beginningless, unequalled, the support of all, the master of all, omnipresent, immanent, unaging, immortal, fearless, eternal and holy, and the maker of all.

Vedas are the scripture of true knowledge. It is the first duty of the Āryas to read them, teach them, recite them, and hear them being read.

One should always be ready to accept truth and give up untruth.

Everything should be done according to the dictates of *dharma,* i.e. after due reflection over right and wrong.

The primary object of this Society is to do good to the whole world, that is, to look to its physical, social, and spiritual welfare.

One's dealings with all should be regulated by love and justice, in accordance with the dictates of *dharma.*

One should promote *vidyā* (knowledge of subject and object) and dispel *avidyā* (illusion).

One should not be content with one's own welfare alone, but should look for one's own welfare in the welfare of all.

One should consider oneself under restriction to follow altruistic rulings of society, while in following rules of individual welfare one should be free.

A candidate, for enlistment as a member of the Ārya Samāj, has to put his signature to these principles.

Swami Dayananda's conception of his Church was that of a democratic body. He did not recognize the intervention of any intermediary between God and His worshippers. Every man or woman who was an Ārya *sabhāsad* (member of the Ārya Samāj) was given the right to vote. While principles were formulated by Dayananda himself, the *upaniyamas* were the result of the collaboration of all *sabhāsads,* of whom Dayananda considered himself one. The founder of a Church placing himself, in the matter of its administration, on the same footing as its ordinary members, and thus upholding the principle of equality, is a phenomenon which is rare in the history of religion.

The danger to the Church of Dayananda does not lie in that the priest or the pontiff will arrogate to himself powers greater than a person can honestly handle, but in that, in the midst of overwhelming odds comprising the laity, his wise counsels may go unheeded and prove to be a solitary cry in the wilderness. The mind of man has been emancipated from the shackles of a privileged priesthood. If the Church of Dayananda is to thrive, it is necessary that every one of its members should assume a part of the rôle of the priest himself.

What Swami Dayananda found impracticable in his own day has, with the passage of time, become practicable. The Ārya Samājas in the different provinces have organized themselves into compact bodies called Pratinidhi Sabhās, to which they return members in proportion to their own numerical strength. The followers of the Ārya Samāj in some of the British overseas colonies have also evolved their own Pratinidhi Sabhās. All these Sabhās, within India as well as overseas, send representatives to the International Aryan League or the Sārvadeśika Ārya Pratinidhi Sabhā, which has its headquarters in Delhi. In order to settle questions of creed, a Dharma Ārya Sabhā has been established under the auspices of this Sārvadeśika Sabhā.

The inspiration of Dayananda was derived from personal communion with the Divinity. Of this, we find ample glimpses in his autobiographical and devotional writings. He was a dynamic saint and has imparted his dynamism to the entire Ārya Samāj, which serves as a channel for the distribution of his inexhaustible spiritual resources. The Ārya Samāj is Dayananda writ large, and it reflects his versatile personality. It has in it saints, philosophers, organizers, scholars, thinkers, and the laity—all reflecting in their different prisms, in protean ways, the light of the brilliant sun of lofty moral and spiritual ideals that Dayananda embodied. There is no doubt that his personality will leave its impress on humanity, and will influence, in an increasing measure, the religious history of India and the world.

45

WHAT THEOSOPHISTS BELIEVE

THE name 'Theosophy' is an exact translation of the well-known Sanskrit term '*Brahmavidyā*', for it is made up of the two Greek words *theos,* God, and *sophia,* wisdom. Its first use was in the third century A.D. in Alexandria by the Greek philosopher Iamblichus. He used the term to mean the inner knowledge concerning the things of God, which were taught in Greek mysteries. The word 'Theosophy', today, has been popularized by the Theosophical Society, founded by Madame H. P. Blavatsky, Colonel H. S. Olcott, W. Q. Judge, and others.

Theosophy, then, is a word which signifies a knowledge of Brahman, or the Absolute. The knowledge as to Brahman is found, in the East, in the Upaniṣads and Hindu philosophies ; in the West, in the philosophies of Pythagoras, Plato, and other Greek philosophers ; in ancient Egypt ; and in certain mystic teachings which are found to have existed in the early days of Christianity.

THE BASIC TENETS OF THEOSOPHY

Today, however, Theosophy means a body of philosophical ideas sponsored by Theosophists. These ideas have been briefly summarized by Dr. Annie Besant, the late President of the Theosophical Society, in the following statement:

(1) There is one transcendent, self-existent Life, eternal, all-pervading, all-sustaining, whence all worlds derive their several lives, whereby and wherein all things which exist live and move and have their being.

(2) For our world, this Life is immanent, and is manifested as the logos, the Word, worshipped under different names, in different religions, but ever recognized as the one Creator, Preserver, and Regenerator.

(3) Under Him, our world is ruled and guided by a hierarchy of His elder children, variously called *ṛṣis,* sages, or saints, among whom are the world-teachers, who for each age re-proclaim the essential truths of religion and morality in a form suited to the age ; this hierarchy is aided in its work by the hosts of beings—again variously named *devas* (shining ones) or angels—discharging functions recognized in all religions.

(4) Human beings form one order of the creatures evolving on this earth, and each human being evolves by successive life-periods, gathering experiences and building them into character, reaping always as he sows, until he has learned the lessons taught in the three worlds, the earth,

the intermediate state, and the heavens, in which a complete life-period is passed, and until he has reached human perfection, when he enters the company of 'just men made perfect' that rules and guides the evolving lives in all stages of their growth.

GENERAL IDEAS OF THEOSOPHY

Closely analysing the above principles, we find that modern Theosophy can be described as follows:

(1) It is not an atheistic philosophy, but the reverse. It starts with the assertion of the existence of a divine, absolute Principle. This Principle reveals itself in a cosmic process, which is the universe, through a series of emanations.

(2) The universe is a process of the unfoldment of potentialities. These potentialities are both of the universe and of the individual soul. This unfoldment is not a mechanical process, but one planned from the beginning by the Creator, who is the first emanation, and through whom all successive emanations appear. Though each individual soul is rooted in the absolute Principle as a potentiality, it is Īśvara, the first emanation, that awakens all potentialities into active Jīvas, in the same way as the womb of the mother is necessary before the germ, which is the embryo, can grow.

(3) The cosmic process is accepted as real and not as Māyā or illusion, though the full and inmost nature of Reality cannot be grasped by the human brain.

(4) This process, called evolution, takes place not only in the visible parts of the universe, but also in those more extensive parts of it which are invisible. These invisible parts consist of planes or worlds (*lokas*) composed of finer matter.

(5) There is a cyclic nature in the development of the universe, since there are periods when activities begin, come to their maximum, and then diminish, to be followed by a period of quietude. During this period of *pralaya* or cessation, however, the results achieved by the work of the universe are not destroyed; they become germinal, so that at the next awakening of activity the work is carried on to greater heights from the point where it was suspended.

(6) The Absolute emanates souls from within Itself. Therefore every soul, called a monad, is fundamentally divine and of the nature of the Absolute, and partakes of Its triple nature of Sat, Cit, and Ānanda—absolute Being, pure Intelligence, and perfect Bliss. But when emanated, the monads are in a state of unawareness, and they may be thought of as dormant, as the germs in seeds are before they germinate; they become

awake and aware through a process which has been termed 'the descent into matter'.

(7) This descent into matter is a process in which the dormant monads are encased in various 'vehicles' or encasements of matter, so as to receive through them vibrations which slowly awaken them into awareness. For long ages, the descent takes place in invisible worlds of matter, in grades of life called by the Theosophist 'elemental kingdoms'. Then in the downward descent, the monad becomes encased in mineral matter, then later in vegetable forms, and later still in the forms of animals. The monad is still dormant ; the first signs of its awakening are seen when an animal responds to human affection, or when the animal's intelligence shows conscious adaptation under human guidance. Thereupon follows a great climax, which is a quickening into self-conscious evolution. This climax is termed by the Theosophist 'individualization'. Thenceforth, the monad is an individual soul separate from other souls, though sharing with them all a common divine nature and origin, and thus forming with all an indivisible universal brotherhood. After individualization, the soul becomes aware of the purpose of its existence as a monad, which is to reveal and realize its innate divinity and to further the plan of evolution.

(8) After individualization, the soul begins to identify itself consciously with the process of its unfoldment, which has already been taking place through long ages. The process is now hastened through rebirth, that is to say, by repeated incarnations in human bodies. There is no reversion to animal incarnations, as no experience useful for the growth of the soul can be obtained through the small and primitive brains of animals.

(9) From the moment of individualization, when conscious evolution begins, there comes into operation a law of evolution called the law of Karma. Briefly summarized, it means that when a soul does right, that is, acts in accordance with the divine will, the result of its action creates for it conditions which help its unfoldment ; whereas, when it does wrong, that is, acts contrary to the divine will, the result creates for it conditions which thwart its unfoldment.

(10) From this standpoint, good *karma* is what helps the divine plan of evolution, and evil *karma* is what puts obstacles in the way of that plan. Good *karma* adds to the harmony in the universe established by the divine will, and so produces for the doer both happiness and opportunities for further growth. Evil *karma* creates a discord in the harmony by opposing the working of the divine will ; the harmony must be restored by the evil-doer at the cost of pain. *Karma* has therefore been called the law of adjustment. There is no thought of punishment in *karma,* any more than there is when we burn ourselves ; the fire does not punish us ; we create pain

for ourselves by infringing the laws of nature through our ignorance of them.

(11) Rebirth, life after life, has as its purpose the gaining of experience, so that right action may become natural to man. Since the purpose of existence is to be a conscious co-worker with the Divinity, a life of righteousness becomes the highest mode both of fulfilling the divine plan and of unfolding the highest in oneself. But this perfect life is not achieved at once. Many experiments have to be made by a person before he knows for himself the fundamental laws of righteousness that exist in his own inmost nature, for every law of right conduct proclaimed to him by the great founders of the religions is only an exteriorization of the divine nature latent within him. But he must be sure that the law is his own and not another's. Through many a blunder, and at the cost of suffering due to his ignorance, he discovers at last his own true self.

(12) All the pains, which come as the result of blunders in testing the divine law, have as their purpose adjustment or rectification, in order to make the soul aware of the existence of that law. Misery and suffering have as their ultimate gain the illumination of the soul. Similarly, through co-operation with the law, and from the resultant joy and happiness, the soul grows in illumination.

REINCARNATION AND LIBERATION

These general ideas of the Theosophical philosophy are further developed by the following teachings. Rebirth takes place in the many races of the world. In fact, the many races which appear age after age are part of the divine plan, so that through incarnations in them the souls may gain the necessary experiences. Each race that appears in the course of the world's history has its own variations and differences not only in the structure of the physical body, colour of the skin, texture of hair, etc., but also in its neural and psychological responses to visible and invisible influences. Each race with its special characteristics is intended to awaken certain aptitudes which are latent in the soul. Again, each race has its habitat in a part of the globe with its own environmental characteristics; and these characteristics are intended to mould the forms of response on the part of the soul to the influences of the Divine, which surround it all the time and are striving to awaken it. Similarly, the varying traditions of the races in different countries of the world are all intended to awaken some attribute of knowledge, or power, or love, which is dormant in the soul.

In the process of reincarnation, the soul lives in bodies, both of man and of woman. The two sexes are expressions of two polarities of consciousness and of action in the soul; and the soul, which has within itself the attributes of both sexes, must awaken the highest characteristics of both by incarnation in each sex. There is therefore no superiority in man as man, nor inferiority in woman as woman. In the course of hundreds of incarnations, which are necessary for a soul before it attains to perfection, it will be reborn as often as a woman as a man. The soul will be by turns son, husband, and father ; or daughter, wife, and mother.

From what has been said, it will be obvious that the soul of man is in the midst of a process of 'becoming aware of its divine nature'. It is this process that has been termed as *mokṣa, nirvāṇa,* salvation, or liberation. But these terms do not signify escape from any danger or ending of existence as such. The terms signify the freeing of the soul from the ignorance which surrounds it and liberating and saving it from all limitations. Liberation means not the ending of activity, but rather the beginning of self-conscious and beneficent activities of far nobler types than those which are possible for a soul while embodied as a human being.

After liberation, the soul is a self-conscious worker in the divine plan. It is no longer bound by the process of reincarnation, and it need not appear any more in a human form. But wherever the liberated soul functions, stage by stage and aeon by aeon, it becomes a larger embodiment of the wonders of the Divinity. Its expanding consciousness and increasing capacities intensify in it the sense of bliss, which is its divine heritage, and it lives to shed that bliss on others on this earth as a *jīvanmukta,* 'liberated while embodied', or in other planets, solar systems, or stars, or in invisible worlds of being and action.

The ideal of the Theosophist is therefore not to be the soul which has freed itself to enter into some kind of a unity with the Divine to enjoy bliss, thus completely forgetting millions of other souls which are still struggling in darkness on their way to liberation. On the contrary, his ideal is that of the 'master of the wisdom', who renounces for a period the bliss of liberation to continue to be a worker for mankind. Freed from all limitations imposed on him by the process of evolution, his very freedom makes him rejoice all the more that he is free now to help his fellow-men.

THE GREAT HIERARCHY AND ITS FUNCTIONS

One of the very important ideas which dominate the Theosophical philosophy is the conception of great adepts, who are not merely *sannyāsins* or recluses meditating and thereby radiating peace and blessing, but are directors or agents of the evolutionary process, working under divine guidance, for the benefit of man. The Theosophist continually talks of 'the divine plan', meaning thereby a plan of the evolutionary process formulated by the Divinity, which is being steadily put into execution by Its agents, who are Its emanations. The perfected man is the adept who has linked his liberated consciousness with that of the logos, the ocean of divinity, and thenceforth is, in a sense, an *avatāra* who has descended from on high. He has still within him, however, all the attributes of humanity, with the memories of his past struggles, but is joined to the divine consciousness, which is now his. The adept is not merely an embodiment of divinity, but he is also perfect in human sympathy.

These perfected men, according to the Theosophist, work in graded ranks. They form an organization called the Great Hierarchy or the Great White Brotherhood. They are not all of equal capacity, because some achieved liberation ages ago and others but recently, and therefore the former have a longer record of work and experience. But all of them are united by one will, which is to serve the plan of God for men. They are the flowers of the evolutionary process, since their consciousness is all the time in intimate communion with that of the Divinity. The adepts are of seven types of temperament or action called the seven rays. They have three chiefs under whose orders they work, and these are: (1) the lord of the world, who is the head of the Great Hierarchy, (2) the Buddha, and (3) the Mahācohan.

The work of the adept brotherhood consists of the supervision of all the world's processes, visible and invisible. Associated with them are various types of orders of souls of other forms of evolution, who are called *devas* or angels. There are grades among them, some being the great *devas* and others lesser or minor *devas,* but all work under the direction of the head of the Great Hierarchy. The adepts and the *devas* working in unison do the following:

(1) They supervise all physical phenomena concerning nature. What we usually term natural laws are in reality forces which are controlled and directed by mighty *devas* and adepts.

(2) The diverse races are guided in their origin and in their migrations by the adepts. Various parts of the earth are peopled according to the needs of humanity. The clash of races and their expansion, the peopling of unoccupied territories, the colonization of foreign lands, etc. all take place under the guidance of the Great Hierarchy.

(3) All religious teaching, which appears either through great religious founders or through minor teachers, is directed by the adepts. The greatest religious teachers are the adepts themselves, who appear among mankind to give such type of religion as is best suited for the people to whom they come. Also, wherever there is any religious leader who, though not advanced sufficiently to be an adept, is nevertheless unselfish

in his devotion to mankind, he is inspired by the adepts. It is well known that even among the traditions of primitive and barbarous cults of worship among savages, now and then there appear traces of a higher cult of purity and dedication. This is usually attributed by the savages to some wonderful being who once appeared among them. Such a being was one of the adepts, or one of their disciples, who implanted among the savages the higher teaching.

(4) All the developments in science, art, philosophy, commerce, industrial expansion, etc. are under the supervision of the adepts and the angelic brotherhood. Indeed, everything that happens that is of any benefit to humanity is definitely the working out of God's plan for men, and that plan manifests itself through a powerful inner government of the world, which has its many departments, with their chiefs, all of whom are working under the direction of the lord of the world. Among all who inhabit this globe, he is supremely the one personality who enshrines in himself more of the fullness of God than any other. Indeed, he is the nearest to our conceptions of omnipotence, omniscience, omnipresence, and perfect love and beneficence. Every event on our globe takes place within the ken of his consciousness, for that consciousness envelops the entire earth.

ATTITUDE TOWARDS LOWER BEINGS

It has already been mentioned that the divine life in its descent into manifestation expresses itself in different forms, the mineral kingdom, the vegetable kingdom, and the animal kingdom. Every one of these forms of substance and life is also directed in its growth by the great plan. Even the animals, in their incalculable millions, are all a part of the divine plan and are guided in their work and growth. What Christ said once that 'not a sparrow falls but that your Father in Heaven knows' is utterly true. There is a special and intimate relation between humanity and its next lower order of creation, the animal kingdom. Animals are not intended to be exploited by man, nor to be used cruelly, nor for 'sport', as in hunting and racing. They are, indeed, the younger brethren of humanity; and association between them and men is intended to be of mutual benefit. If animals serve men, when they are domesticated, man in return owes to the animal kingdom not only kindness, but also great care, so that the animal consciousness may be developed in the right direction to the point where individualization can take place; and a monad from the bosom of God can consciously begin its great work as a soul for liberation or self-realization.

ATTITUDE TO LIBERATION

On all sides therefore, as the Theosophist looks at the myriad manifestations of life, he sees them all striving towards liberation or self-realization. But this liberation is not an escape from an inevitable Māyā, or from an evil process of undeserved suffering. The striving is like undergoing training in a laboratory, or in a gymnasium, or in a workshop, in order to become an expert. The aim of existence is to become a conscious co-operator in the divine plan and a channel for the expression of divine immanence. This wonderful heritage is not reserved only for a few, whom we call saviours, but is the heritage of every soul, however low he may seem to be at present.

In the process of self-unfoldment leading to liberation, a person is not left alone to work out his destiny. While the divine nature is resident in him in its fullness, and no one can add to it from outside, nevertheless he can be guided to achieve his liberation as speedily as possible. To aid people in this task, certain of the adepts or *ṛṣis,* called 'masters of the wisdom', accept candidates as their pupils, to train them in various forms of work for mankind, and through that work to help them achieve their perfection. The modern Theosophical movement has strongly emphasized the fact that adept teachers still exist, and that the way to find them is open as of old to those who prepare themselves to tread the path of holiness through purity of life and self-sacrificing service.

ATTITUDE TO HUMAN AFFAIRS

From these fundamental postulates of Theosophy, an attitude arises towards life which is characteristic of the true Theosophist, whether he is formally a member of the Theosophical Society or not. He holds that all religions are derived from one source, and that therefore no one single religion is the exclusive road to salvation. He recognizes various grades in religious thought, because the term 'religion' covers not only forms of loftiest worship, but also modes which are characteristic of the most ignorant savages with their crude beliefs. But each religion is considered by the Theosophist as having its rôle to fulfil in a great plan for all men, just as the seven rays in the solar spectrum have all their distinct functions in fostering the growth of living things.

Similar, too, is the Theosophist's attitude towards the races of the world. He does not ignore the distinctions among them, catalogued in works on ethnology and comparative religion. While some races may show characteristics of the highest civilization, and others of the most primitive, nevertheless, men and women born in all these races are recognized by the Theosophist as having within them one common divine nature. Since all men, the lowest and the highest, the most ignorant and backward as well as the most cultured and the perfect, enshrine within themselves the divine immanence, the universal brotherhood of humanity, without distinction of race, creed, sex, caste, colour, or social position, becomes a fact of nature, and, when rightly understood, it will be found to be the supreme fact in the life of all mankind.

In the development of civilization, there appear among men the distinctions just mentioned. Sometimes some of these distinctions have a fundamental basis, since, in the main, the souls in the lower classes or castes are the less evolved, and those in the higher the more evolved. This is a very general principle, but it has exceptions, for it does not always follow that because a man or a woman is born in a particular grade of life, high or low, he or she will necessarily manifest the typical characteristics of that grade. He or she may be there temporarily for reasons of his or her *karma.* In spite of racial and cultural differences, however, the supreme duty of all men and women, who understand the divine plan, is to minimize, in every possible way, the hardships and handicaps consequent upon class, caste, and race distinctions. Race, especially, is no true or valid indication of the grade in the evolution of a soul. No fact in nature is ever intended to thwart the growth of a soul, but, on the contrary, all facts are intended to help it. Therefore civilization is arranged in the divine plan with grades, so that the souls born into inferior grades may not have thrust upon them tasks too strenuous for them, or a morality too exacting for their capacities.

One branch of Theosophical studies, which is of the greatest consequence for mankind, deals with the gathering of information concerning life beyond the grave. Already many facts have been gathered in past ages and are found scattered in religious traditions. These facts have been correlated and systematized by Theosophists, and much important new material has been added by their researches into conditions beyond the grave. These researches are not the results of mediumship or of any phenomena of spiritualism, but are due to a few Theosophists who have trained themselves by methods of *yoga,* which permit them to leave their physical body at will and get into a state of trance, to enter and observe the invisible worlds in full consciousness, and to record their observations on their return. The same observations may be made by them while wide awake, and without entering into trance, with all the faculties of a trained observer. Through such processes of *yoga,* some of the invisible worlds have been scientifically examined, and the record of these researches forms one of the most important departments of modern Theosophical knowledge.

From all that has been said, it will be obvious that the Theosophist is characterized, first, by a profound belief in the existence of a divine wisdom which explains all the intricate processes of nature; and secondly, by a determination to be an agent in God's plan for men. The Theosophist therefore is essentially a reformer engaged in the most strenuous forms of social service. The Theosophist realizes that in any relation between human beings, whether within the family, the community, or among nations, if ever there is any infringement of the law of universal brotherhood, the result must inevitably be evil both for the individual and for all among whom the individual lives. Therefore a conscious attempt to understand what is best for the whole, and not only for the part, becomes the constant endeavour of the Theosophist. He thinks that he will find in the ideals of his philosophy a fuller guidance in the intricate affairs of life than in any other religion or philosophy.

THEOSOPHY AS A GOSPEL OF CONDUCT

Most religious people in India place before themselves the ideal of a personal liberation or *mokṣa,* to be attained in some life in the future, if not in this. This is the goal set before the individual in Hinduism, Buddhism, and Jainism. But we know that in both Hinduism and Buddhism there is also another ideal, though certainly it is not meant for all men and women at their present stage of spiritual unfoldment. While Hinduism proclaims as the ideal the *mukta,* the liberated soul, it also gives a record of certain great souls who did not pass away to enter into liberation, which they had earned, but remained with mankind to help it. These are the *jīvanmuktas,* 'the liberated while embodied'. Similarly, in Buddhism, too, there was once a strong advocacy of the ideal of the Bodhisattva who, when he becomes the *arhat,* and therefore completely free from the 'wheel of births and deaths', places before himself the ideal of becoming, in some future life, a Buddha, a saviour, in order to proclaim to mankind, once again, the ancient teachings.

Theosophy, today, revives these very high ideals of self-sacrifice for the sake of mankind. It proclaims that all men make one chain, the highest and the lowest, the wisest and the most ignorant forming its links. This is the principle of universal brotherhood. No man therefore can stand completely alone, even when he is on the threshold of *mokṣa* or *nirvāṇa.* Theosophy, in addition, proclaims that, as an essential part of the spiritual development of a person who seeks liberation, there should be a development of all his noble emotions, and not merely of the powers of his intellect. This emotional development is not to be directed solely as devotion or *bhakti* to God, but is also to be expressed through tender sympathy with the sufferings of mankind and dedication to its service. This is the ideal of the 'masters of the wisdom' who founded the Theosophical Society, and who are pledged to lead a life of sacrifice. One of the masters exhorts the Theosophists in the oft-quoted maxim in *Light on the Path*: 'Try to lift a little of the heavy *karma* of the world; give your aid to the few strong hands that hold back the powers of darkness from obtaining complete victory.'

Whenever therefore Theosophists meet, their fundamental purpose is to understand the working of God's mind, and the aim of this understanding is dual. First, it is to build up their character in such a way that their minds will work parallel to God's mind. Secondly, it is also to help others to adjust themselves in a similar fashion.

There is no need for any Theosophical society or movement, if the aim of a Theosophist's life is merely personal liberation. Such a liberation is so individual that each must achieve it by himself without external help, save perhaps the temporary assistance of a *guru*. The cause of personal liberation is not furthered by gathering together into groups and forming associations. But, on the other hand, if the ideal is not personal liberation, but to help bring all mankind to liberation, then it is necessary to plan and work together as a band of brothers dedicated to human and divine service. This is the reason why, if mankind is to be freed from its miseries of ignorance, poverty, and degradation, men and women must form an organization.

It is the aim of Theosophists, as they meet at federations and conventions, to keep before their minds the words quoted above: 'Try to lift a little of the heavy *karma* of the world.' Then, as they work in lodges, federations, and conventions, the elder brethren, the 'masters of the wisdom' who are *jīvanmuktas*, will infuse each true Theosophist with their strength and inspiration.

All that has been written about Theosophy, as a system of thought and as a gospel of conduct, is summarized in three truths stated by a 'master of the wisdom':

(1) The soul of man is immortal, and its future is the future of a thing whose growth and splendour have no limit.
(2) The Principle which gives life dwells in us, and without us, is undying and eternally beneficent, is not heard or seen or smelt, but is perceived by the man who desires perception.
(3) Each man is his own absolute lawgiver, the dispenser of glory or gloom to himself, the decreer of his life, his reward, his punishment.

PART VI

SRI RAMAKRISHNA AND SPIRITUAL RENAISSANCE

SRI RAMAKRISHNA

46

SRI RAMAKRISHNA AND SPIRITUAL RENAISSANCE

I. MARCH OF EVENTS

FROM the close of the eighteenth century right up to the middle of the nineteenth, India had been wading through a bewildering welter of cultural ideals. Politically overthrown by the British, she had been fast coming under the sway of an exotic civilization. Complete breakdown of her political power shook her faith in the potency of her age-old culture. A surging freshet of European ideas and ideals that rushed in the train of British supremacy was all that was necessary to sweep her off her old cultural moorings.

The process of disruption of her inner life was accelerated by the trend of education under the new regime, which tended to turn out men who were to be Indian in blood, but English in tastes and intellectual outlook. In this strange academic *milieu,* young minds began to swallow queer cultural shibboleths, such as that India had no culture worth the name, that her entire past was a foolish quest after false ideals, that if she wanted seriously to live, she would have to remould herself thoroughly in the lathe of European civilization. No wonder these incantations lulled the self-consciousness of the Indians to sleep.

An impartial observer of this period would therefore naturally find nothing but a complete cultural chaos, particularly within the zone of English education. The spiritual foundation of the Hindu social structure was terribly shaken, and perhaps it was going to be blown off altogether.

REFORM MOVEMENTS

But, towards the second quarter of the nineteenth century, the hypnotic spell of foreign civilization began to recede, slowly but steadily, before a rising wave of self-consciousness of the Hindus. Mighty movements of socio-religious reform sprang up, one after another, to resuscitate the ancient culture of India and lead her once more to evolve a glorious future.

The earliest of these movements was the Brāhmo Samāj founded in 1828 by Raja Rammohun Roy, who made an extensive study of both Islamic and Christian theology and developed a thoroughly modern as well as cosmopolitan outlook. With necessary materials gleaned from the Hindu scriptures, the Raja built up, on a central concept of the formless

God with attributes, a lofty monotheistic creed that could vie easily with the unitarian faiths of foreign origin. The gates of the Samāj were flung open to all men, irrespective of caste, community, or nationality, provided they agreed to leave behind all ideas of God with particular names and forms.

This primarily religious movement brought in its wake a wave of social reform. The Brāhmo Samāj went solidly for the emancipation of women from all sorts of social iniquities. Later on, it launched a crusade against the caste system and succeeded in banishing it altogether from the Brāhmo fold.

With such a social and religious credo, the Brāhmo Samāj took the field simultaneously against atheism, Christianity, and Hindu orthodoxy. Under the able guidance of its brilliant leaders like Raja Rammohun Roy, Maharshi Devendra Nath Tagore, and Brahmananda Keshub Chandra Sen, who came in close succession, the Samāj passed through several phases of a highly useful career.

In its conception of religious faith as well as social reform, the Brāhmo Samāj leaned, at times, to a considerable extent, on exotic ideals. From its very inception, it bore the stamp of western Christianity. Raja Rammohun borrowed freely from Protestant Unitarianism to gloss over his Upaniṣadic creed, and Keshub Chandra went so far as to soak the very core of the Brāhmo creed with Christian ideals. Social customs also came to be flavoured, rather too richly, with the spices of westernism.

Yet, considering the circumstances the Samāj was born to fight with, one must admit that it did exactly what was needed urgently to serve its purpose. Nothing less than a veneer of European civilization on the social and religious framework of the Hindus could stop the wild craze of the young intelligentzia for changing their skin. And this was precisely what the Samāj did.

The Prārthanā Samāj of Bombay, which was an offshoot of the Brāhmo Samāj, founded in the sixties of the nineteenth century, put in substantial service in the same direction through the efforts of eminent persons like R. G. Bhandarkar and M. G. Ranade.

In 1875, up rose another powerful religious movement, namely, the Ārya Samāj, launched by Swami Dayananda in Bombay. The sponsor of this movement was a thoroughbred Hindu *sannyāsin,* a vastly erudite Vedic scholar, and a thundering controversialist of the Indian type.

Swami Dayananda stood firmly by the Vedas and returned the malignant attacks of Christian missionaries on Hinduism by his sledge-hammer blows on Christianity. Of Islam also, he was a sworn adversary He could not shake hands even with Brāhmo leaders, because they could not be at one with him in acknowledging the divine origin and infallibility of the Vedas and in accepting the doctrine of rebirth. Besides, he had absolutely no sympathy for the post-Vedic developments of Hinduism. He translated and interpreted the Vedas according to his own lights. In his religion, there was no room for the absolute Brahman of the strict monist, nor for the dualist's object of worship with various names and various forms. His iconoclastic zeal, very naturally, compelled him to walk out and make a room for the Ārya Samāj outside the precincts of the Hindu society.

This religious movement also was accompanied by sweeping changes in social customs. The caste system, as a religious institution, was abolished ; the monopoly of the Brāhmaṇas over the Vedas was denied ; women were liberated from a number of social disabilities. Besides, enthusiasm for a wide range of philanthropic activities, including the spread of education, became a remarkable feature of the Ārya Samāj.

The replacement of image-worship by Vedic sacrifical rites with sacred fire and oblations lent something like a romantic charm to the Ārya faith. Moreover, the radical changes of social customs were perfectly in line with the spirit of the age. All these combined to crown the proselytizing efforts of the Ārya Samāj with phenomenal success all over northern India, especially in the Punjab.

Mention may be made here of another religious movement that put in a timely appearance in India from abroad and went to check, to a certain extent, the influence of the Christian as well as materialistic thoughts of the period. This was the Theosophical movement.

It was in the hands of Madame Blavatsky, a Russian lady, and Colonel Olcott, a former army officer of England, that Theosophy turned into a vigorous proselytizing creed, and the Theosophical Society got its start in New York, in 1875, to carry on a systematic and well-organized propaganda on behalf of the creed.

Drawing profusely from the occult and cabalistic elements of Tibetan Buddhism, and dressing up the creed in techniques borrowed from the Hindus as well as from the modern spiritualists, the protagonists of this movement imparted to Theosophy an oriental look and succeeded in making converts in the West by thousands.

Moreover, by its fairly extensive publication of Hindu scriptures with translations, the Theosophical Society has put in some amount of solid work for Hinduism and contributed substantially to revive the faith of the enlightened Hindus in their own sacred lore. Thus Theosophy, though ostensibly a new and eclectic creed, initiated in this country a movement that resembled, to a considerable extent, the reform movements of Hinduism, so far as its salutary effect upon the Hindu society was concerned.

In and through these movements the self-consciousness of the Hindus asserted itself, made its way up through the opposing forces, and endowed Hindu culture with a fresh lease of life. But, while proceeding with the best of motives to put the entire house of the Hindus in order, both the Brāhmo Samāj and the Ārya Samāj found themselves thrown out of the orthodox Hindu society, and were compelled to shift for themselves by creating independent folds.

The orthodox masses, however, under the traditional lead of Hindu saints and classical scholars (*paṇḍitas*), plodded on in their old socio-religious ruts. Rightly or wrongly, they chose to stand or fall with the entirety of Hindu traditions and refused to accept any type of sectional Hinduism from the reformers.

In the eyes of the reformers, however, this attitude of the orthodox masses appeared to be fanatic and hazardous to a degree. They believed that the stolid indifference of the masses to the time-forces and to the urgent need of overhauling their creed was bound to end in a disaster.

HINDU RENAISSANCE

But the orthodox society had not to wait long, when a phenomenon of paramount importance took place to infuse enormous strength into the entire range of Hindu convictions, and thus to bring about a complete renaissance of the Hindu religion. The life and message of Sri Ramakrishna constituted precisely such a phenomenon.

Sri Ramakrishna appeared before the Hindu society with a phenomenal life of intense spirituality, a remarkably broad and synthetic vision of Hinduism, and an extraordinarily simple and illuminating exposition of all the ideas and ideals of Hindu theology. Like the sages, seers, and prophets who had preceded him, he took a very firm stand on the bed-rock of realization and 'spake like one in authority'.

That real religion begins with such realization is the fundamental belief that has governed Hindu life for ages. It is clearly in deference to such a fundamental demand for realization that the Hindu mind has been able to accommodate any sectarian creed that has succeeded in demonstrating the efficacy of a practical method of realizing spiritual truths. This is how the highly metaphysical and discriminative processes of the Advaitins, the technical methods of concentration of the followers of the Rāja-yoga, the austere bodily disciplines of the *haṭha-yogins*, the ritualistic devotion and culture of divine love of the Śākta, Vaiṣṇava, and other followers of the Bhakti cult, and the dark rites of the occult schools of Śāktism and Vaiṣṇavism, including the ceremonial orgies of the dreaded Kāpālikas, came to form a bizarre conglomeration of spiritual disciplines that Hinduism, in its enthusiastic quest after the eternal and transcendent truths, had occasions to evolve. It was, moreover, the same inner urge for spiritual realization that ushered in innumerable orders of monks and ascetics with absolutely different schedules of religious life.

A practical demonstration of the truths behind all the various creeds incorporated in Hinduism, by the deep and extensive realizations of a majestic seer, was a desideratum that alone could stir up the Hindu masses to bring about a fresh and vigorous revival of their religion. Sri Ramakrishna came to fulfil such a need. In him the orthodox society found a pre-eminent seer who had the potency of bringing about a mighty awakening of the old religion of the Hindus with all that it stands for. As Mahatma Gandhi has put it, 'The story of Ramakrishna Paramahaṁsa's life is a story of religion in practice. His life enables us to see God face to face. . . . In this age of scepticism, Ramakrishna presents an example of a bright and living faith which gives solace to thousands of men and women who would otherwise have remained without spiritual light'.

The radicals, too, found in the realizations of Sri Ramakrishna a wonderful solution of their intellectual doubts. This is why a truculent advocate of modern thought like Narendranath (Swami Vivekananda), who had drunk deep from the dangerous fountains of rational atheism and also from the refined springs of Brāhmo theism, could surrender himself completely to this extraordinary man of phenomenal spiritual insight.

II. SRI RAMAKRISHNA'S LIFE: A WEB OF SPIRITUALITY

Ramakrishna's life lacks the wealth of events and striking achievements that are commonly associated with the lives of great men. The aristocratic dignity of Maharshi Devendra Nath Tagore, the reputed oratory and majestic personality of Keshub Chandra Sen, and the vast erudition and polemical zeal of Swami Dayananda were all in striking contrast with the humble and unostentatious life of Ramakrishna. Neither aristocracy of birth, nor wealth, nor academic distinction, nor power and prestige in the temporal sense had anything to do with his career.

Yet, this humble life had something of immense value and significance, something very subtle that eludes the grasp of the common historian. Like the lives of the general run of great men, his life did not draw all its materials from the sense-world. His entire being, from the centre right up to the circumference, was a marvellous web of spirituality. Spiritual ecstasy and realization were the yarn of which this wonderful texture was made.

THE WONDER-CHILD

In the early dawn of the 18th February, 1836, Ramakrishna was born in Kamarpukur, a quiet, out-of-the-way village in the District of Hooghly in West Bengal. In this village lived an orthodox Brāhmaṇa couple, Khudiram Chattopadhyaya and Chandra Devi, with a little group of children and near relatives, in a house consisting of a few cottages with mud walls and thatched roofs. In this house, Khudiram and his consort led their simple and pious lives centring round the daily worship of their family deity, Raghuvīra (Rāma).

Within the house, there was a tiny thatched shed set apart for extracting rice grains. It was in a corner of this blessed shed that Chandra Devi gave birth to her illustrious child, who came to be known, in later life, as Ramakrishna. In due time, the child was christened Gadadhar, after the name of the deity in the holy temple of Gaya ; it was a vision of this deity that had enlightened Khudiram about the coming child, while he had been on a pilgrimage to Gaya.

During the first few years of his life, there was nothing unusual about him. But, before long, somehow he stumbled into the region of ecstasy ; and with this incident his life stepped out of the ordinary rut. One summer day, Gadadhar, a child of six or seven, was out in the rice fields. As he was moving along a raised narrow and meandering path, dividing small plots of paddy land, a dark cloud suddenly appeared in the horizon and swiftly spread over the whole sky. The child's gaze was fixed on the gathering clouds, when a flight of snow-white cranes appeared in view and flew across the murky bosom of the thunder-cloud. The contrast of colours wove an enchanting sight that got a stranglehold on the boy's mind and steeped it into an overwhelming ecstasy of joy. Lost to outward sense, he fell down on the ground, from where he had to be picked up and carried home. The case of the unsophisticated mind of a boy of six or seven being plunged headlong into a trance by a charming sight of nature is perhaps a unique record of mystic experience.

His passionate and instinctive love for the beautiful marks him out as a born artist. For hours he would sit attentively by the potters and learn to mould and paint images of clay till he became quite an adept. He was an ardent lover of music and poetry, and took great delight in singing pastoral airs, reciting beautiful passages from the Hindu epics, and enacting, with a group of his village chums, interesting episodes out of the Purāṇas.

Once, when he was about nine years of age, he had to appear in the rôle of Śiva in a dramatic performance in his village. Suddenly his mind was swung up from the normal plane to the holy ideal he was going to represent. He was overpowered by a similar emotion on another occasion, when he was out with a party of women for paying homage to the goddess Viśālākṣī in a neighbouring village.

Meditation on a deity would call up the real form before his mind's eye, and immediately his outward consciousness would be sucked in a whirpool of surging emotions. As soon as a trance was over, no trace of abnormality could be found anywhere about Gadadhar, though, of course, there was something assuredly supernormal in his trances, which, he believed, brought him in touch with Divinity.

One of the interesting pastimes of the boy was to spend hours in the company of wandering monks and pilgrims who, on their way to the holy city of Puri, would halt at the village rest-house. Gadadhar loved to serve these holy men by fetching for them water and fuel, and delighted in listening with rapt attention to their songs, hymns, and religious discussions. He would pick up from their talks and store in his little brain stories about saints, pictures of holy places, and interesting details of exclusively religious lives. Thus, on the plastic mind of young Gadadhar were imprinted, clearly and indelibly, the time-honoured traditions of Hindu ascetics and devotees.

At the age of nine, he was duly invested with the holy thread of the Brāhmaṇa, and the privilege of worshipping the family deity was thrown open to him. Nothing delighted him so much as contemplating the divine glory of the Lord of the universe and pouring out his sincere love and devotion through the ceremonial worship of Raghuvīra. Moreover, every religious function in the neighbourhood, especially of a congregational nature, would attract Gadadhar irresistibly.

However, to everything else the boy was lukewarm. The school had very little attraction for him. It is curious that mathematics particularly repelled him. Perhaps the idea of calculation associated with it ran against the very grain of his inner life. The only irrepressible desire of his life was to hold communion with God, and, consequently, he held in scant regard anything that could not help him in realizing this object.

In his mature age, he used to say that just as vultures would fly high up in the air, but their gaze would invariably be fixed on the stinking carrion on earth, so impious scholars might soar very high on the wings of their intellect, but their minds would always remain chained to the sordid objects of the sense-world. But learning, combined with modesty, purity, selflessness, and devotion, he held in high esteem, and this is why Ramakrishna went to pay his compliments to the magnanimous scholar, Iswar Chandra Vidyasagar. Nevertheless, he laid more stress on spiritual practice for realizing God than on book-learning.

THE YOUNG PRIEST

In the year 1855, Ramakrishna's eldest brother, Ramkumar, accepted the charge of a newly erected temple near Calcutta as its chief priest. As the founder of the temple, Rani Rasmani, a rich lady of Calcutta, happened to belong to an inferior caste, Ramakrishna's orthodox mind revolted at the idea of having to live within the precincts of the temple. For a considerable length of time, Ramakrishna lived with his brother in Rani Rasmani's temple without partaking even of the food offered to the deity. The following year his eldest brother died, and he found himself installed as the head priest of the temple. From this time on, almost up to the end of his life, the temple continued to be his permanent residence and the prominent background of his spiritual career. By accepting the charge of the temple, Ramakrishna entered the second and the most momentous chapter of his life. The environment of the temple, together with his priestly functions, went to stir the depths of his soul.

The temple, to which Ramakrishna, at the age of twenty, became attached as the chief priest, is situated in Dakshineswar, a suburban village about four miles to the north of Calcutta. Within the compound, there are quite a number of temples meant for the worship of different deities; the biggest one, however, is reserved for the goddess Kālī, the divine Mother. Hence the temple is now commonly known as the Dakshineswar Kālī temple.

The temple stands directly on the Gaṅgā, on its eastern bank, and covers a fairly extensive area of land. The northern section of this land and a portion in the east contain an orchard, flower gardens, and a couple of tanks; the southern section is finished in brick and mortar. Exactly at the centre of the latter, a long flight of steps of an imposing bathing *ghāṭ* leads from the Gaṅgā to a roofed open terrace. On each side of this terrace stand in a row six temples dedicated to Śiva. Adjoining the terrace and the long line of Śiva temples lies a large paved court, rectangular in shape and running from north to south. In the centre of this court, there are two stately temples; the bigger one facing south belongs to Kālī, and the other facing the Gaṅgā is dedicated to Rādhākānta, the master of Rādhā's heart, that is, Kṛṣṇa. Immediately to the south of the Kālī temple, there is a spacious music hall supported by a number of pillars, and all around the paved courtyard, save on the west, there are rooms set apart for kitchen, stores, quarters for the temple-staff, and guests. In the northwest angle of the court, just beyond the last of the Śiva temples on that side, one can still find a humble room with a semi-circular portico facing the Gaṅgā. This was the room in which Ramakrishna spent a considerable portion of his life.

Within the main temple, there is a basalt figure of the goddess Kālī, dressed in a gorgeous apparel of gold brocade and decked lavishly with precious ornaments. She stands on the white breast of Śiva, who is lying stock-still on a thousand-petalled silver lotus. A garland of skulls hangs loosely from her neck, and a girdle of human arms runs round her waist. She has two pairs of arms, one on each side. With the lower left hand she holds a severed human head and with the upper she grips a blood-stained sabre, while with one of the right hands she offers boons and with the remaining one she allays fears. Seeing her holy consort Śiva beneath her feet, she blushes and expresses her delicate sentiment, like an Indian lady, by biting her protruded tongue. Her three eyes strike dismay into the hearts of the wicked, and yet pour out affection for the devotees. Thus stands, in her benignly cruel majesty, Kālī, the divine Mother, in the magnificent central temple of Dakshineswar, and is addressed every day by a large concourse of devotees and pilgrims as Bhavatāriṇī, Saviour of the world.

Besides Kālī, representing cosmic power, Ramakrishna had before him, in a separate temple within the same compound, Kṛṣṇa, symbolizing divine love and beauty, and in each of the twelve temples along the Gaṅgā, Śiva, suggesting the Absolute. The awful and yet lovely goddess of the Tāntrikas, the soul-enthralling divine flute-player of the Vaiṣṇavas, and the self-absorbed and all-renouncing Lord of the Śaivas lived together before his eyes, representing so many distinct ideals of Hindu devotees. Of the divine household, however, Bhavatāriṇī or Kālī captivated the supple mind of the young priest and brought it completely under her majestic sway.

From early dawn till nine o'clock in the evening, Ramakrishna remained engaged in the service of the divine Mother. Every day, he bathed her, dressed her, fed her, and led her to repose on a silver bed. With a devout heart and scrupulous care, he would go through the daily round of scheduled rituals and chant, in his melodious voice, sacred hymns and *mantras* (holy texts) in the prescribed order.

THE MAD QUEST ON UNCHARTED SEAS

Thus, Ramakrishna's thoughts were glued to the service of the divine Mother, and soon he became intoxicated with a great yearning for seeing the goddess in her glory. Nothing else could appease the 'great hunger' of his soul. He could not content himself, like an ordinary priest, with plodding punctiliously through a fixed routine of ritualistic observance. Neither could he work up the zest of the common worshipper in praying for wealth, honour, and worldly success. He craved to see God face to face. He believed, with the credulity of a child, that Rāmaprasāda and other devotees had actually been blessed with the beatific vision of the Mother. With absolute faith in the grace of the Mother, he would cry helplessly before her like a forlorn child and beseech her importunately to appear before him in her glory. For hours, he would sit before her absorbed in meditation and, at times, break out into passionate appeals to the Mother through soul-stirring songs, hymns, and prayers. At the end of each day, with bitter tears in his eyes, he would fling himself down on the ground and roll on it in despair, bemoaning piteously the loss of one day of his life without attaining his object.

Not conversant with *yoga*, the traditional Hindu science of disciplining one's mind, and led solely by the impetuous zeal of his ecstatic moods, Ramakrishna advanced fearlessly along the hazardous path pointed out to him by his own unsophisticated mind. One day, unable to stand the painful separation any longer, and seized by a grim determination, he rushed frantically to put an end to his life, when, all on a sudden, the Mother's grace descended upon him. The veil was off, the beatific vision was unfolded before his eyes, and he became immersed in an ocean of ecstasy.

Regarding this vision, let us hear from his own lips: 'One day, I was torn with intolerable anguish. My heart seemed to be wrung like a wet towel. I was racked with pain. A terrible frenzy seized me at the thought that I might never be granted the blessing of this divine vision. I thought, if that were so, then enough of this life. A sword was hanging in the sanctuary of Kālī. My eyes fell upon it, and an idea flashed through my brain: The sword! It will help me to end it. I rushed up to it, and seized it like a mad man. . . . And lo! the whole scene—doors, windows, the temple itself—vanished. It seemed as if nothing existed any more. Instead, I saw an ocean of Spirit, boundless, dazzling. In whatever direction I turned, great luminous waves were rising. They bore down upon me with a loud roar, as if to swallow me up. In an instant they were upon me. They broke over me, they engulfed me. I was suffocated. I lost consciousness and I fell. How I passed that day and the next I know not. Round me rolled an ocean of ineffable joy. And in the depths of my being, I was conscious of the presence of the divine Mother.'

After two days, Ramakrishna emerged out of the trance of ecstatic joy with the sweet and endearing word 'Mother' issuing passionately from his quivering lips. Though the immediate effect of the first vision of the divine Mother was to intensify the 'great hunger' of his soul and increase his feverish anguish of separation, it landed him gradually and unwittingly in an altogether new arena of spiritual consciousness. Whenever his paroxysm of pain became unbearably acute, he began to lose his outward consciousness and see before him, in his trance, the divine Mother in her matchless splendour granting boons to her devotees and bidding them to take courage.

The divine Mother commenced to appear before him in his hours of meditation and even to speak to him and give him instructions concerning his daily duties. During this period, while going in for meditation, he used to have a strange experience. He would distinctly hear rattling sounds proceeding in a certain order through the joints of his body, and feel as if somebody was locking them up and fixing up the body in an absolutely steady posture. Hours would pass by, his body remaining clamped to the earth like a piece of stone; until he heard similar sounds in a reverse order and felt that the joints were unlocked, it would be physically impossible for him to rise from his seat or even to shift an inch from his rigidly fixed posture.

Soon the scales fell completely from his eyes, and he required neither trance nor meditation to invoke the vision of the Mother. The stone image melted away for ever. It was thoroughly metamorphosed. In its place, he invariably found, with his eyes wide open, the divine Mother pulsating with life, radiating her smiles, and showering her blessings upon him. He would actually feel her breath upon his hand. At night, in the lighted room, he could not discern, even with peering eyes, any shadow cast by her radiant form. When, after his daily round of ritualistic duties, he would retire to his room, he would hear the tinkling of anklets and feel that the Mother, like a young girl, was tripping up to the first floor of the temple. With his heart hammering in his breast, he would immediately rush out of the room, and from the court outside he would clearly see the Mother on the balcony of the upper storey, with her dark tresses streaming loosely about her and her gaze fixed intently on the Gaṅgā.

These visions brought him closer to the Mother, and he clung to her with the earnestness of a babe. His familiarity with her stepped out of the limits of sacerdotal etiquette. He was no longer to be tied down by the codes and formulas of ritualistic worship. He would see his Mother actually partaking of the food even before it was offered ceremoniously to her. Sometimes, he would approach the throne of the goddess with a morsel of food in his hand and, putting it to her lips, entreat her to eat. At times, he would himself take a portion of the food and then, putting the remainder to the mouth of the goddess, say, in a perfectly familiar tone, 'Well, I have eaten, now it is your turn'. Often, with his eyes and chest flushed, he would approach her with tottering steps, touch her chin endearingly, and commence to sing, or talk, or joke, or laugh, or even dance. Every morning, while plucking flowers for the Mother's garland, he would be seen speaking to or caressing somebody, or laughing, or indulging in merriment. He would never close his eyes during the night, and would spend it always in an exalted mood, talking to some one, or singing, or sitting in meditation under the *āmalakī* tree.

Rani Rasmani, the proprietress of the temple, and her son-in-law and right-hand man, Mathur Babu, came like protecting angels to the rescue of the young priest, when his so-called sacrilegious behaviour had infuriated the fastidious officials of the temple. These two privileged souls felt instinctively that his strange method of worship proceeded from a genuine and extraordinarily profound love for the divine Mother.

Soon, however, Ramakrishna found it physically impossible to attend to the normal duties of the chief priest of the temple. His mind was on the wings of ecstasy ; his nerves were on the edge ; and he could not stand the worries involved in priestly duties. He required rest. Mathur Babu accepted his suggestion and permitted his nephew, Hriday, to act as his substitute for a while.

About this time, with the help of Hriday, he had the wild place about the *āmalakī* tree cleared up and got four other holy trees planted there, in order to prepare a suitable place for his spiritual practices. It was on a raised platform under this group of umbrageous trees that Ramakrishna practised most of his spiritual courses during the subsequent period of his life. This place is now known as the Panchavati or the grove of the five trees, and is held in great regard by the pilgrims visiting the Dakshineswar temple.

During this period, he wanted to see God in other forms also. The ravenous hunger of his soul was not to be appeased by realizing only one particular aspect of God. For a time, he was mad after seeing God as Rāma, the tutelary deity of his family. As soon as he was drawn towards this divine ideal, his plastic mind got itself moulded completely after Hanumat, the 'monkey' chieftain and the greatest devotee of Rāma. He began to eat, drink, and jump about on trees like him, with the name of Raghuvīra constantly on his lips. At the end of this strange spiritual practice, he was blessed with a vision of the peerless consort of Rāma, Sītā, who has been held by Hindu women as the ideal of chastity through thousands of years.

Severe strain due to continued spiritual exercise and ecstasy for about three years at a stretch told seriously upon his health. Mathur Babu very kindly placed him under the treatment of a reputed physician of Calcutta. But this failed to heal him. Trying all possible remedies and failing to bring him round, Rani Rasmani and Mathur Babu ultimately sent him down to his village home for a while, thinking that a change of environment might improve his health. Some time in the year 1859, he was back at his native village, Kamarpukur. Here he would retire at night to the neighbouring cremation ground and practise severe austerities. His relatives thought that he was mad. His mother even went the length of calling in an exorcist to see if her son was possessed

However, after a few months' stay in the village, he pulled himself together a little, and his mother surmised that marriage, perhaps, might bring a change upon his mind. Curiously enough, Ramakrishna, in his simplicity, readily agreed to the proposal of marriage. Finding his mother and elder brother exhausted in their search for a bride, Ramakrishna, in a mood of self-absorption, told them one day that his future mate was waiting for him in the house of Ram Chandra Mukhopadhyaya of Jayrambati. They made an inquiry, and were surprised when they discovered in the specified house Ram Chandra's daughter, Saradamani, a little girl of five years. Both parties agreed and, within a few days, Saradamani was wedded ceremoniously to Ramakrishna.

After the marriage was over, Ramakrishna stayed on in his village home for about a year and a half ; then he returned to Dakshineswar and again took charge of the worship of the divine Mother.

Again did start, with redoubled vigour, the mad career of his hungry soul. Piteous cries for the Mother began once more to rend the sky. Ecstatic fits began racking his nerves. Strange visions soothed and consoled him in the hours of meditation. During this period, he almost forgot the existence of his body.

By the light of his naive discrimination, he made a vigorous search of his mind and uprooted from it whatever appeared to stand between him and his divine Mother. And the process was strikingly original. In order to banish from his heart any possible attachment to wealth, he hit upon the following expedient: Taking a few silver coins in one hand and a handful of earth in the other, he would argue that money was no better than earth. Far from helping one towards spiritual realization, it gave rise to arrogance and desire for sense-enjoyment. Hence it was as useless as a handful of dust. Thus cogitating, he would mix up the coins and the earth and throw them both in the water of the Gaṅgā. He repeated this process several times, till he felt that his renunciation of wealth was complete. To root out caste-prejudice and all ideas of superiority, he washed, for a time, the latrines of pariahs with his own hand, wiping the floors with his long hair. To maintain the unsullied purity of his mind, he scrupulously avoided the company of women and also of impure and worldly-minded men. During the rest of his life, the lightest touch of a woman would generally cause him excruciating physical pain, contact with an impure man would shock his nerves terribly, and even the simple touch of a coin would immediately throw the muscles of his hand into agonizing cramps.

The burning sensation all over his body, oozing of blood through the pores of his skin, and violent spasms on his different limbs, together with complete sleeplessness and want of appetite, appeared once again with increased virulence. Medical treatment proved ineffective as before.

As his sufferings sprang out of his severe austerities and exalted spiritual moods, he required some one who could harness his impetuous mind, train and direct his ecstasies according to the recipes of yogic science, and thus, eventually, cure him also of his physical troubles. He had not to wait long, when such a spiritual guide came.

ON BEATEN TRACKS

Tāntrika Sādhanā: One day, in or about 1862, a fairly tall and handsome lady alighted from a country boat at the foot of the bathing *ghāṭ* and walked up to the terrace of the Dakshineswar temple. She was on the right side of forty; her long dishevelled hair and saffron robe indicated that she was a Bhairavi, a female ascetic of the Tāntrika school. She possessed extensive knowledge of the Tāntrika lore and *bhakti* scriptures, as well as considerable experience of practical religion.

She was out in search of a particular blessed soul to whom she had been commissioned by God, in a vision, to deliver a message. At the very first sight, she was thrilled to recognize in Ramakrishna the favoured child of God she had been looking for, and she engulfed him forthwith in her motherly affection.

Ramakrishna laid bare before her his aching heart and sought her care and counsel like a helpless child. He told her everything about the severe austerities he had gone through, directed solely by his own untutored mind, the various visions and ecstasies he had experienced, and the terrible sufferings that had been racking his body for a long time.

From Ramakrishna's narrative the Bhairavi realized, to her utter surprise, that it was *mahābhāva,* or the highest phase of ecstatic love for God, that he had been passing through, and that it was this exalted spiritual state that lay at the root of all his physical troubles. She consulted the holy texts, compared notes, and was bewildered with joy to discover that Ramakrishna's experiences coincided on all points with the ecstatic moods of Śrī Rādhā and Śrī Caitanya. Even his physical ailments tallied completely with the physical symptoms of *mahābhāva,* as described in the sacred books. All these convinced the Bhairavi of the fact that she had at last come upon a person who did really rank with the exceptionally rare souls figuring in the spiritual history of the Hindus as incarnations of Divinity.

She made it clear to him that his intense physical sufferings were the invariable consequences of the highest phase of love for God. She demonstrated the truth of her statement by healing almost miraculously some of the terrible symptoms of Ramakrishna's strange malady by very simple and curious methods according to the directions laid down in the holy texts.

Soon after, she had an assembly of devotees and scholars, well versed in Vaiṣṇava and Tāntrika literature, called at Dakshineswar. Before this assembly, she recounted the mental and physical states of Ramakrishna, compared these with relevant descriptions in the scriptures, and proved up to the hilt her finding that Ramakrishna was an incarnation of God. The assembly accepted her verdict without demur ; she carried the day.

The unanimous verdict of the assembled scholars and devotees created a profound impression upon all present. Ramakrishna had already received Tāntrika initiation from one Kenaram Bhattacharya, and now he wanted the Bhairavi to lead him through spiritual practices according to the directions of Tāntrika texts. She gladly accepted the charge.

According to the requirement of Tāntrika practices, two *āsanas,* or specially sacred seats, were prepared, one in the Panchavati and the other at the northern end of the temple garden under a *bilva* tree. The Bhairavi used to collect the various rare ingredients necessary for different Tāntrika rites and arrange them on either of the sacred seats, where Ramakrishna would retire at night and perform the rites according to her direction. In this way, she put him through all the spiritual exercises mentioned in the sixty-four principal Tantras.

These Tantras present practical methods of realizing the ultimate Truth preached by Vedānta, namely, the essential unity of the devotee's soul with God. But, unlike the path of knowledge prescribed by monistic Vedānta for realizing this fundamental oneness, the Tāntrika method, a marvellous combination of *yoga* and *karma,* is characterized by rituals. Through contemplation of God in concrete forms and performance of ceremonial worship, Tāntrika *sādhanā* provides a graded course of tuning up the naive mind of the devotee. He is enjoined to meditate on his oneness with the formless Absolute and then to think that out of the formless impersonal God emerge both his own self and the distinct and living form of a goddess whom he is to place before him, through imagination, and worship as the divine Mother.

The Tāntrika rites place before the devotee objects of sense-enjoyment and then require him to deify these by his thought and gradually to sublimate, by this process, his sense-attraction into love for God. For instance, certain rites require the presence of the opposite sex in poses of direct sense-appeal; but the devotee has to curb his carnal desires by looking upon them as sacred manifestations of the divine Mother. In this way, one is required to conquer one's flesh and prepare one's mind for spiritual realization, not by avoiding temptations, like the *jñāna-yogin*, the spiritual aspirant on the path of knowledge, but by boldly facing and overcoming them.

Ramakrishna passed through the entire course without flinching an iota from his ideal of motherhood in all women, and without even partaking of wine, so commonly associated with Tāntrika practices.

During this period, he had quite a multitude of wonderful visions that followed one another in quick succession. Of all the divine forms he witnessed, Ṣoḍaśī or Rājarājeśvarī appeared to him to be the loveliest. Moreover, he perceived the upward march of the *kuṇḍalinī-śakti*, described in the Yoga and Tāntrika scriptures as the coiled-up divine energy lying normally in every man at the lower end of the spinal canal. When it is made to rise farther up by spiritual practice, its progress through the different stages is marked by distinct phases of spiritual experience on the part of the devotee, culminating in mergence in the Absolute. Ramakrishna verified the scriptural statements by experiencing all the various spiritual moods and visions corresponding to the different stages of ascent of the coiled-up divine energy.

His unique success in Tāntrika practices, without any connection with wine or sex, has undoubtedly restored the purity of these ancient practices and stamped them afresh as a sure and distinct approach to the realization of God.

Vaiṣṇava Sādhanā: Immediately after he had come to the end of the path of the Tantras, his mind was drawn irresistibly to approach God through the avenue of Vaiṣṇavism. His spiritual guide, the Bhairavi, though well versed and firmly grounded in Tāntrika lore and practice, happened to be a Vaiṣṇava devotee at heart. Her chosen ideal was Raghuvīra, whose emblem she carried with her and worshipped every day with great devotion. Besides, her motherly attitude towards Ramakrishna, whom she treated as her Gopāla or child Kṛṣṇa, reflected much of genuine Vaiṣṇavism. All these, perhaps, combined to attract him towards a systematic practice of this cult.

The path of the Vaiṣṇavas is exclusively one of *bhakti* or love. The followers of this school do not want to step out of their individual ego and become merged in the impersonal God, which the travellers on the path of knowledge call *mukti*, or salvation, and consider to be the consummation of all forms of spiritual practice. The Vaiṣṇavas look upon *parā bhakti* or supreme love for God as an end in itself. The fountain of this love exists in every human heart; only one has to open it up by purifying one's mind and diverting it from the objects of the sense-world to God by creating an intense longing for God through regular and methodical worship, hymns, prayers, repetition of *mantras,* and constant meditation on the personal God. Kṛṣṇa and Rāmacandra are the favourite ideals of the two major sects of Vaiṣṇavism.

For developing one's love for God, Vaiṣṇavism prescribes a perfectly natural method consisting in humanizing God. The *iṣṭadevatā* or chosen ideal is to be looked upon as one's parent, master, friend, child, or sweetheart, and these *bhāvas* or attitudes are known respectively as *śānta, dāsya, sakhya, vātsalya,* and *madhura.* Each of these attitudes, followed up faithfully, can lead one to the goal of blessedness.

As we have seen, Ramakrishna's untutored mind had already scaled the heights of Vaiṣṇavism through the first two attitudes—by his devotion to Kālī as his mother and to Rāmacandra as his master. Subsequently, he also developed to perfection the *sakhya* attitude. So now he had only two modes of Vaiṣṇava discipline left, namely, *vātsalya* and *madhura.*

About this time, Jatadhari, an itinerant Vaiṣṇava monk and a master of the parental attitude towards God, made his appearance at Dakshineswar. He was a devotee of Rāma and looked upon him as his child. He had with him a metal image of Rāmalālā, or child Rāma, that he nursed, fed, played with, and even put to bed at night. With his beloved Rāmalālā throbbing with life and clinging to him like a pet child, he had been making a tour of pilgrimage through the sacred places of India, and it was in the course of this tour that he halted for a while at the Dakshineswar temple.

Though Jatadhari had told nobody about his mystic experience and cherished it, obviously, as the most precious secret of his life, Ramakrishna read his heart like an open book. He became a blessed spectator of the divine drama enacted before his eyes by Rāmalālā and his devotee-parent. Every day, he began to observe with keen interest how Rāmalālā talked, behaved, and played his childish tricks with Jatadhari. Gradually, Ramakrishna realized that the divine child was getting more and more attached to him and even preferring his company to that of Jatadhari.

At this, Ramakrishna's parental emotions surged up towards Rāmalālā, and he began right away to caress, bathe, feed, and sport with him. Thus getting Rāmacandra as his own son, Ramakrishna began to spend his days on one of the least accessible heights of Vaiṣṇava *sādhanā.* Rāmalālā became so dear to him that he could not bear his separation even for a moment. Meanwhile, Jatadhari had his cup of bliss filled to the brim, and perceived that he had no longer any need of ceremonial worship. So, on the eve of his exit from Dakshineswar, he cheerfully handed over to Ramakrishna the metal image of Rāmalālā, whose living form he henceforth carried in his bosom.

After a short period, however, the *madhura bhāva,* or the ecstatic emotions of a sweetheart, came upon Ramakrishna's mind with a terrific rush and swept it away. He looked upon himself as one of the legendary *gopīs* or milkmaids of Vṛndāvana, racked by the terrible pangs of separation from their supreme lover, Kṛṣṇa. He fixed himself up in the pose of a *gopī* and began to dress, talk, behave, and move about like a faithful young woman sorely distressed by her lover's indifference. He went almost mad in his passionate love for his divine sweetheart. His intense mental anguish and severe austerities brought back his old physical sufferings. The burning sensation all over his body, oozing of blood through the pores of his skin, and almost complete cessation of physiological functions during ecstatic fits visited him for the third time and brought him again to the limit of physical endurance. After he had passed a few months through this terrible ordeal of disappointed love for Kṛṣṇa, he, however, was blessed one day with a vision of Rādhā, the peerless exemplar of the *madhura bhāva.*

A few days after this, he came to the end of this heart-rending love episode. The curtain suddenly rose; Śrī Kṛṣṇa with his soul-enthralling grace appeared, walked up to him, and merged in his person. The thrill of the vision kept him spell-bound for a period of three months, during which he would always see Kṛṣṇa in himself and in everything about him, sentient or insentient.

One day, while he was listening to the reading of the *Bhāgavata,* in the hall of the temple of Rādhākānta, he had a significant vision. In an ecstatic mood, he saw Śrī Kṛṣṇa in his resplendent beauty standing before him, and observed that luminous rays emanating from his lotus-feet touched the *Bhāgavata* and then his own chest, thus linking up for a while the holy trinity—God, the scriptures, and His devotee.

Advaita Sādhanā: Thus did Ramakrishna cover the entire range of dualistic realizations, through which the blessed devotee is united with the personal God in a bond of ecstatic love. Since the beginning of his mad quest in 1856 up to the end of 1864, for a period of nearly nine years, he had been thinking of nothing but God in one or other of His divine aspects, and the bulk of this period he had spent in the living presence of the personal God with different names and different forms.

Yet his divine Mother spurred him on to proceed farther and appease for ever his ravenous hunger by realizing the identity of his own soul with the final cause of the universe, God impersonal. The divine Mother commanded him to follow the Vedāntic guide who appeared on the scene at this psychological moment, and to plunge like a salt-doll in the ocean of the impersonal God.

The new spiritual guide was Tota Puri, an itinerant monk of the Advaita Vedānta school, who, yet unaware of his mission, halted one day, towards the end of 1864, at the Dakshineswar temple, in the course of his long tour of pilgrimage. He hailed from the Punjab, and was an out-and-out monist, believing in the Nirguṇa Brahman or the Absolute as the only Truth, and looking upon everything within creation as nothing more than an illusory appearance.

According to the usage of this order, a novice has to be initiated into the all-renouncing life of *sannyāsa* or monasticism before he is permitted to step on to the road of knowledge He has to cut himself off from his relatives, brush aside his entire past as a vanished dream, tear off all worldly ties of obligation, and begin with *sannyāsa* an entirely new life of renunciation and spiritual freedom.

In a thatched hut close to the Panchavati, Ramakrishna sat before his *guru* (teacher) on an auspicious day and went scrupulously through all the details of the *sannyāsa* ceremony. In lieu of the insignia of his Brāhmaṇa-hood, his hair-tuft and sacred thread, which he had to burn in the sacred fire before him, he received from his preceptor a loin-cloth and an ochre robe as the holy badges of his new life.

Tota Puri communicated to Ramakrishna's pure, concentrated, and luminous mind the findings of the Advaita Vedānta that the entire phenomenal existence is only a fabric of illusion wrought by *avidyā* or primal ignorance. As soon as this *avidyā* is dispelled by right knowledge, the cosmic texture of time, space, and causation melts into nothingness; what remains is the undivided existence of impersonal God, and with Him the *jñāna-yogin,* at this stage, realizes his absolute oneness. This is the supersensuous and superconscious state, known technically as *nirvikalpa samādhi.*

Ramakrishna was asked by his *guru* to withdraw his mind from all sense-objects and meditate on the real and divine nature of his self. He detached his mind from the world in a trice, but the radiant and living form of his divine Mother remained glued to his mind, and he could not shake it off in spite of his best efforts. However, after another desperate attempt, he succeeded in cleaving into two the divine form of Kālī with the sword of discrimination. The last plank on which his mind had been resting was thus thrown off, and immediately it dived headlong into the fathomless depths of *nirvikalpa samādhi.*

For three days and three nights at a stretch, he remained in this state, when his *guru* brought back the throbs of his life. Indeed, Tota Puri was amazed to see that his disciple realized in one day what he himself had taken forty years to attain.

Some time in 1865, Ramakrishna's impetuous mind wanted to remain merged in the *nirvikalpa samādhi*. Soon his consciousness whisked past the realm of phenomena, which it scarcely revisited in the course of the next six months. During this entire period, not a sign of life could be discerned in his body except at long and rare intervals, and that too of very short duration. A monk who chanced to come to the Dakshineswar temple at that time realized from the serene glow of the face what was going on within the apparently dead physical frame of Ramakrishna. He appeared on the scene just at the right moment, almost like a divine messenger, and set about preserving Ramakrishna's inert body.

At the end of the period, he received one day the command of his divine Mother that he must remain on the threshold of relative consciousness for the sake of humanity. However, when Ramakrishna became rather settled on the normal plane, he could play alternately, at will, on both the strings of *bhakti* and *jñāna*. He could now say with a firm conviction: 'When I think of the supreme Being as inactive, neither creating nor preserving nor destroying, I call Him Brahman, or Puruṣa, the impersonal God. When I think of Him as active, creating, preserving, destroying, I call Him Śakti, or Māyā, or Prakṛti, the personal God. But the distinction between them does not mean a difference. The personal and the impersonal are the same Being, like milk and its whiteness, or the diamond and its lustre, or the serpent and its undulations. It is impossible to conceive of the one without the other. The divine Mother and Brahman are one.' Moreover, he could now play with equal mastery also on the twin chords of *yoga* and *karma*, in which he had become an adept in the course of his Tāntrika practice. Evidently Hinduism had nothing more to teach him.

ON ALIEN PATHS

Immediately after his survey of the entire sea of Hindu *sādhanā* had been over, Ramakrishna felt the urge of exploring the alien paths of Islam and Christianity, one after the other.

Islam: Towards the end of 1866, he observed in the temple garden a devout Muslim, whose earnest prayers, humility, and absorbed mood convinced Ramakrishna of the fact that he was a seer of God. Ramakrishna approached him and wanted to be initiated into Islam.

After formal initiation, his plastic mind was completely cast in the mould of Islam. He began to live outside the precincts of the temple, like any of the non-Hindu visitors, and started dressing, dining, praying, and behaving in every way like an orthodox Muslim. All his thoughts, visions, and ecstasies associated with Hindu gods and goddesses vanished for the time being, and he went on repeating the name of Allah and reciting the *namāz* regularly like a devout Mohammedan faquir.

His arrival at the goal was marked by a vision, probably of the Prophet: a personage with a white beard and grave countenance approached him in his effulgent glory. Immediately he realized the formless God with attributes as described in the Islamic scriptures, and then became merged in the impersonal God, Brahman without attributes. Thus the transcendental region of the Absolute, the One without a second, the supreme Brahman beyond the pale of any differentiation, appears from Ramakrishna's experience to be the last halting place to which both the paths of Hinduism and Islam equally lead.

Christianity: Nearly eight years after this, some time in November 1874, Ramakrishna was seized with a desire to see where the path of Christianity led to. Close by, a rich and enlightened Hindu, named Shambhu Charan Mullick, of Calcutta, came to live occasionally in his spacious garden-house. And at his request Shambhu Charan began to read out the Bible to him. Ramakrishna eagerly imbibed all that he heard about Christ.

Shortly afterwards, while sitting in the parlour of another neighbouring garden-house belonging to Jadu Nath Mullick, Ramakrishna discovered a picture representing the Madonna with the baby Christ in her arms. Instantly the holy figures appeared to be warmed into life; he observed that they were radiating rays of light that pierced his flesh and went straight to his heart. Immediately the Hindu child of the divine Mother became thoroughly metamorphosed into an orthodox devotee of the Son of Man. Christian thought and Christian love appeared for three successive days to be the sole contents of his mind.

On the fourth day, while strolling by the Panchavati in the afternoon, he caught sight of a strange personage who drew very near him, and a voice came up from the depths of Ramakrishna's heart: 'This is the Christ who poured out his heart's blood for the redemption of mankind and suffered agonies for its sake. It is none else but that master-*yogin* Jesus, the embodiment of love.' Immediately after that, Christ merged in Ramakrishna, who forthwith lost his outward consciousness and became completely absorbed in the *savikalpa samādhi,* in which he realized his union with Brahman with attributes.

Buddhism: One may reasonably point out that one of the great religions of the world, viz. Buddhism, is missing in the unparalleled itinerary of Ramakrishna's spiritual travel. A little scrutiny will make it clear, however, that he had really travelled along this road while carrying on his practice of the Advaita Vedānta. The latter practically comprehends Buddhism, so far as both the method of spiritual discipline and the goal are concerned. The two paths may be equally labelled as the path of knowledge. Both discard the personal God and all dualistic thoughts and forms of worship with equal emphasis. Both insist on moral perfection, contemplation of the unreality of the objective world, and withdrawal of the mind completely from the illusory existence as the cardinal points of spiritual practice. So far, they are identical regarding method. Only the Advaita Vedānta prescribes meditation on the reality of the human soul and its oneness with the Nirguṇa Brahman as an additional and very important feature of spiritual practice. Nevertheless, a *jñāna-yogin* has to cover all that Buddhism prescribes. Of course, by 'Buddhism' is meant here the purest form of this religion as preached by Lord Buddha. Then, regarding the goal, the *nirvāṇa* of the Buddhist is nothing but merging in the Absolute, and corresponds to the *nirvikalpa samādhi* of the Advaitin.

So Ramakrishna, after having gone through the entire course of the Advaita *sādhanā* and spent six months on the transcendental realm of the Absolute, had nothing more to attain through Buddhism. Regarding Buddhism and its mighty sponsor, he himself said, 'There is not the least doubt about Lord Buddha's being an incarnation. There is no difference between his doctrines and those of the Vedic *jñāna-kāṇḍa*'.

ON TERRA FIRMA

Ramakrishna's tireless and almost breathless journey on the various roads of religion had practically come to an end with his Advaita realization. The alien paths he tried only to see if they led to the same goal of Divinity that he had already realized in all its diverse aspects; and he was satisfied. After his six months' sojourn on the transcendental heights of the Absolute, he had practically cried halt and wanted to spend his remaining days in the company of men. From the depths of his heart had gone up the prayer: 'O Mother, let me remain in contact with men. Do not make me a dry ascetic.' And the prayer had been granted by his receiving the imperious command of his divine Mother: 'Stay on the threshold of relative consciousness for the love of humanity.'

The remaining days of his life he spent in the company of men and enjoyed to his satisfaction the thrilling play of the divine Mother on the human plane. The universe lay unmasked before his illumined eyes. He saw his own self in everybody and everybody's self in himself. At frequent intervals, his spirit would skip over the realm of differentiation and remain merged in the Absolute. But immediately after such a spell of *nirvikalpa samādhi,* he would find above, below, within, and all about him one undivided ocean of Divinity, of which the multifarious contents of nature would appear like foam, ripples, and billows. With his eyes fixed on this all-pervasive and beatific Oneness and his heart full of the nectar of divine love, Ramakrishna addressed himself to meet the demands of social life.

His genial countenance, artless manners, and inspiring talks, enlivened now and then with interesting and illuminating parables and sparkling wit; his jovial mood, alternating with the serene composure of divine ecstasy; and, above all, his endless sympathy for everybody cast a spell on all the good souls that chanced to meet him and stirred up in them an intense craving for spiritual realization.

It is delightful to picture how a little group of earnest men, sitting before Ramakrishna either in his small room or under the shady trees of the Panchavati, would listen with rapt attention to the inspired outpourings of his illumined heart. Ramakrishna's appearance, though not imposing, was comely and had a subtle charm about it. He was a man of medium height and brown complexion, and he wore a short beard. His large, dark eyes, sparkling with lustre, would always remain half-closed suggesting the introspective bent of his mind, and his lips would often part to release the flash of a bewitching smile. With a simple cloth about his loins and across his chest, he would sit cross-legged and with folded hands before the little group of earnest souls and keep them spell-bound for hours together by rapturous talks surging up from the depths of his heart. Without the least trace of any air of superiority about him, he would behave like a simple and innocent child and leave on the minds of his select audience the impress of a perfect picture of humility. He would lay no claim to originality and would ascribe the wisdom of his talks to his divine Mother, who, as he felt, was the moulder of his thoughts and expressions. He was blissfully ignorant of drawing-room manners, and his speech lacked the tone and polish of the cultured society, as also the rhetorical flash of a finished orator. He would use the homely language, with its characteristic accent, of the simple village folks belonging to the particular district of Bengal from which he came. Writes one who saw him: 'His spirit stood on a pedestal so high that those who approached him could only look up at it in incredulous astonishment. Men marvelled when they heard him, comprehending or mystified. His lucidity was as remarkable as his wisdom was unfathomable.'

WITH OLD-SCHOOL SCHOLARS AND DEVOTEES

The ideas of practical religion passed from his lips to many a seeker of truth and blessedness, and through each to his own group of disciples and followers. Thus, from the quiet retreat of the Dakshineswar temple, Ramakrishna, without beat of drums or flash of stump oratory, breathed life into Hinduism with all its kaleidoscopic phases and ushered in an era of Hindu renaissance.

Numerous were the spiritual aspirants—monks and ascetics of various denominations, householder devotees belonging to different sects, and classical scholars with genuine desire for God-realization—who came to be impressed by Ramakrishna's magnetic personality and benefited by his inspiring contact, since the conclusion of his Tāntrika practice. A cursory glance at a few members of this group may interest us.

Pandit Gauri Kanta Tarkabhushan came to Dakshineswar in 1870, obtained his spiritual guidance, and, with his permission, slipped away quietly from the place in order to plunge into his *sādhanā*. Pandit Narayan Sastri, an orthodox Brāhmaṇa scholar of Rajasthan, well versed in all the six systems of Hindu philosophy, obtained from him initiation into *sannyāsa* and stepped silently out of the scene. Pandit Padmalochan Tarkalankar, the chief scholar under the Maharaja of Burdwan, came to regard Ramakrishna as a divine incarnation, and benefited exceedingly by his soul-enthralling company. Krishna Kishore, an ardent devotee of Rāma, who lived within a couple of miles from Dakshineswar, as well as Chandra and Girija, two other disciples of the Bhairavi, received from him an impetus to proceed straight towards the goal of God-realization.

WITH GURUS

Tota Puri, his spiritual guide, was so attracted by his charming personality that he chose to stay at Dakshineswar for eleven months at a stretch. He had discarded the entire objective world, including even personal God, as a golden dream of childish fancy, and would often banter Ramakrishna for his unwarranted sallies into the illusory realm of the divine Mother.

But Ramakrishna's outlook was different. His realization of divine immanence had convinced him of the existence of two distinct phases of Māyā, which he termed *avidyā-māyā* and *vidyā-māyā*. The former is the grosser aspect of appearance that fixes human souls on the world of the senses and whirls them through the round of births and deaths; and it is this aspect of the illusion that the Advaita *sādhakas* are rightly taught to fight. But Ramakrishna realized that after one had perceived one's identity with the supreme Brahman, and come back to the world of appearance, Māyā would appear altogether in a new rôle. The transcendental appeared to be immanent in the realm of relative existence. It was this aspect of the appearance that Ramakrishna designated as *vidyā-māyā.*

His consciousness hovered, as it were, about the borderland of the transcendent and immanent aspects of the selfsame Brahman. Ecstatic devotion to the divine Mother and Her play alternated with complete absorption in the serene ocean of absolute Oneness. This made him lay equal emphasis on both the aspects of Brahman.

Jñāna-yogins fixed their attention almost exclusively on the transcendental aspect of Brahman as the only truth, looked askance at the other aspect as a mere illusion, and rather condescendingly approved of its relative merit by way of a necessary concession to the puerile faith of the *bhaktas.* The *bhaktas,* on the other hand, made capital out of the immanent aspect of God and shut their eyes to the transcendental phase, which, they apprehended, might dry up their hearts by evaporating their love for God, personal and immanent, that they wanted to enjoy through eternity. They wanted to taste sugar and refused to see any sense in becoming one with it. They craved the beatific company of God and not to be lost in Him. Even the monists among the *bhaktas,* who believed in essential Oneness, chose to qualify their monistic outlook by retaining a shade of dualism up to the above extent. Thus the *jñānins,* or the absolute monists, and the *bhaktas,* including the dualists and the qualified-monists, had parted ways, and for centuries the gulf between them had been widening. But it was given to Ramakrishna, a master of both the schools of spiritual practice, to know fully the strength as well as the limitations of them both. He poised himself in the middle and bridged the gulf between them by his epoch-making discovery of the truth behind both the transcendent and immanent aspects of Divinity.

With love, due reverence, and extreme humility would Ramakrishna put up with Tota Puri's innocent banter, and point out to him, at opportune moments, the error involved in his partial and one-sided view of Truth. Gradually, he succeeded in bending the obdurate mind of the stern ascetic and making him feel that it was the formless ocean of the Absolute that appeared to get congealed by the cold spell of devotion into the personal God with various names and various forms, and that this personal God again melted, as it were, into the formless impersonal under the blazing fire of *jñāna.* Step by step, Tota Puri was led to perceive the astounding truth behind the realization of his disciple and to revise his own opinion in its light.

Ramakrishna's relation with his Tāntrika *guru,* the Bhairavi, was no less perplexing. Since his acquaintance with her, he had been looking upon her as his mother, and she practically remained like a member of his household for six years at a stretch. When, in 1867, Ramakrishna went over to his native village, the Bhairavi also accompanied him and lived with him in his village home. Ramakrishna spent nearly seven months at this place, and his wife, Saradamani, then only a girl of fourteen, also came to stay with him.

The contact of his wife and the devotion of his neighbours to him became unbearable to the Bhairavi. Her motherly love for Ramakrishna proved to be almost a fetish, and she wanted to monopolize his heart. Moreover, she was obsessed with the pride of having such a worthy disciple as Ramakrishna.

Ramakrishna, however, did not change even by a shade his respectful attitude towards her. By Ramakrishna's patient, loving, and illuminating contact, soon the Bhairavi came to realize her folly, and she left the place abruptly to dive deep into her spiritual *sādhanā*.

WITH RELATIVES

Surely, Ramakrishna made a departure from the traditional life of *sannyāsa* by staying in his village home for seven long months and being in close touch with his relatives. Hindu *sannyāsins* have not been heard to acknowledge over again the family ties which they clipped with their own hands. Nevertheless, Ramakrishna did this without any hesitation or compunction. Obviously, he did not mean reform, because he never asked his monastic disciples to tread this path. It was peculiarly his own stand, and it was perfectly easy and natural with him.

To him the Absolute and the relative were equally divine. It was this position of his on the threshold of relative consciousness that enabled him to fuse the apparently contradictory schemes of monastic and householder's life into an undivided synthetic attitude. Through his mother, wife, nephews, and nieces, he saw Kālī appearing in so many garbs, and, very naturally, he accepted the relations in which they stood to him. His relatives got from him his genuine love, sincere attention, and earnest service, as much as they could possibly expect from him. But, certainly, even while playing the householder, he could do nothing that might touch vitally the *sannyāsin* behind. The facts that he could not even touch a coin, that his nature rebelled against the idea of hoarding money, that he refused to accept an offer of ten thousand rupees from a devotee for his personal comforts, that a lie could never slip through his lips even by way of a joke, that the contact of shrewd, worldly-minded men was exceedingly galling to him, that in every woman—even in a woman of the street—he invariably saw the divine Mother, and that he could never touch even with a pair of tongs the grosser objects of sense-enjoyment prove unmistakably that the heart beneath the householder's mask was pitched permanently on the lofty ideals of monasticism.

Ramakrishna's behaviour towards his wife, however, beats all records. Who has ever seen or even heard of a perfect *sannyāsin,* with a complete mastery over the senses, in the rôle of a husband? Ramakrishna's uncommon attitude towards his wife left no room for sex suggestions. Once, while massaging her husband's feet, Sarada Devi wanted to know what he thought about her. Prompt came the amazing reply from his lips: 'The divine Mother who is worshipped in the temple is verily the mother who has given birth to this body and who is now putting up in the music tower, and again it is she who is massaging my feet at the present moment ; verily, I look upon you as a representation of the blissful Mother in human flesh.' It takes one's breath away to comprehend how easily Ramakrishna saw the divine Mother in his wife and yet played out faithfully the rôle of husband by permitting her to massage his feet at dead of night. On one occasion, Ramakrishna made a solemn avowal of the fact that he saw the goddess Kālī under the veil of his wife. On the new moon night of May 1872, he made her sit before him ceremoniously as a goddess and worshipped her with all the ritualistic details of *ṣoḍaśī pūjā* prescribed by the Tantras.

Yet Ramakrishna, who regarded Sarada Devi as the divine Mother and actually worshipped her as such, looked upon her as his wife as well. With extreme care and earnestness, he used to instruct her in all matters, secular as well as spiritual, whenever she came to stay with him. And he received from his wife her unbounded and pure love, genuine devotion, and earnest service. Thus, after his sojourn at Kamarpukur in 1867, the holy couple met at Dakshineswar off and on from March 1872, and lived together in a unique bond of mutual love and devotion till the end of Ramakrishna's life in 1886.

It is a fact, however strange it may appear, that Sarada Devi also came to regard Ramakrishna as the divine Mother, and she maintained this attitude towards her husband up to the end of her life. Considering that she had been widowed at her husband's demise, she proceeded to put on the widow's garb, which, however, she could not do, as she came to feel the continued presence of Ramakrishna with her.

Who can imagine what a homogeneous synthesis of the divine Mother, a beloved wife, and a favourite disciple comes to? And again, can anybody conceive what a perfect blending of the divine Mother, a dear husband, and a spiritual guide looks like? These are obviously beyond the range of human comprehension, and language fails hopelessly to characterize them. The householder's ideal of self-control has been lifted to the standard of divine purity! The *sannyāsin's* ideal of conquest of the flesh has risen triumphantly above the ordeals of temptation to the heights of absolute sexlessness! And this has been done by both the members of the holy couple, so that individuals belonging to both sexes may get necessary light and inspiration for gaining mastery over the senses.

WITH SUFFERING HUMANITY

Ramakrishna's heart would break at the sight of misery. On one occasion, some time in 1868, when he had been out on a pilgrimage with Mathur Babu visiting many holy places, he made a halt at Deoghar or Baidyanath Dham. This town, with its neighbourhood, was at that time in the grip of a terrible famine. The Santal inhabitants of the place were going without food for days; their bodies were reduced to skeletons; they had hardly any stuff to cover themselves with; and they were dying of starvation. The sight was more than what Ramakrishna could bear. He took his seat by the side of the unfortunate victims of famine, wept bitterly with them like one of their fellow-sufferers, and was determined to fast unto death, unless something was done to redress their sufferings. Mathur Babu had to spend a lot of money for feeding and clothing the famine-stricken people, before he could get out of that impasse.

Another instance is to the point. Some time in 1870, Mathur Babu, while going out to visit one of his estates for the collection of rent, took Ramakrishna with him. For two consecutive years the harvests had failed, and this had brought the people of the locality to the verge of starvation. Ramakrishna's tender heart was shocked by the sight of appalling poverty around him, and he immediately asked Mathur Babu to feed the tenants and help them financially, instead of demanding his dues from them. He convinced Mathur Babu of the fact that the divine Mother was really the owner of the property, that he was only her steward, and, as such, he ought to spend Mother's money for allaying the miseries of her tenants. His realization of Divinity in the phenomenal world had thrown open to him a new vista, in which he saw his divine Mother, his relatives, and, in fact, all including suffering humanity on the same plane and in the same phase of Reality.

We know how Ramakrishna made it clear to his disciple, Narendranath, or Swami Vivekananda, in which name he appeared before the world in later life, that the Jīva was no other than Śiva, that every creature was God Himself in a particular garb of name and form. His attitude towards suffering humanity surpassed the ideal outlook of the *bhaktas*. Śrī Caitanya, the great prophet of Bhakti-yoga, preached the attitude of kindness towards all creatures as one of the cardinal requirements in the make-up of a genuine devotee's heart. Ramakrishna, however, could not content himself merely with this attitude. Addressing Narendranath and some other disciples, he said one day, 'They talk of mercy to the creatures! How audacious it is to think of showering mercy on the Jīva, who is none other than Śiva. One has to regard the creature as God Himself and proceed to serve it with a devout heart, instead of taking up the pose of doling out mercy'.

Narendranath, on that very day, said to one of his brother-disciples, 'I have heard today a saying of unparalleled significance. Time permitting, I shall communicate to the world the profound import of this marvellous utterance'. And Swami Vivekananda did live to redeem his promise by introducing in the world the novel method of divine worship through the service of suffering humanity as a veritable manifestation of God, and by inaugurating the Ramakrishna Mission to demonstrate the spiritual value of this method by practical experiments along the line.

There are people who are apt to confuse Ramakrishna's worship of God through the service of suffering man with the acts of kindness prescribed by Buddhism and Christianity. But Buddhism does not believe in worshipping God in any form ; and Christianity lays down: 'Love thy neighbour as thyself.' By 'self', of course, Christianity never means God, because it does not subscribe to the Advaitin's belief in the identity of self and supreme Brahman. The Christian injunction therefore simply emphasizes the intensity of love which one has to develop for fellow-beings by trying to look upon others' miseries as one's own. Any way, humanitarian service, according to either of these two religions, is a part of a complete programme of spiritual practice and is endowed only with a moral value.. But Ramakrishna presents altogether a different ideal. The service of suffering humanity with the subjective outlook and attitude of worshipping Divinity is by itself an entire programme of a new form of spiritual practice that can independently lead an aspirant up to the goal of God-realization. Surely, this is an innovation and a precious acquisition in the world's storehouse of religious *sādhanās*.

Ramakrishna's realization of the divinity of man was at the basis of this message. He was firm in his conviction that one could certainly realize God by serving Him through man as through an image. The common love of a relative and even that of a philanthropist, with their almost invariable tinge of selfishness, have to be distinguished from the worship of God through the service of humanity.

Ramakrishna also made this distinction between the two types of humanitarian service, the moral and the spiritual. One of his rich acquaintances, Shambhu Charan Mullick, informed him one day of his intention of spending a considerable amount of money on a number of charitable acts. The latter's enthusiasm for charity appeared to be much more intense than that for realizing God; and, without doubt, he had nothing more than the ordinary idea about charity. Hence very pertinently did Ramakrishna ask him not to think too highly of this kind of social service and to turn his eyes towards the supreme object of realizing God. This incident proves conclusively how Ramakrishna distinguished between the type of humanitarian service contemplated by Shambhu Charan and the worship of Divinity through man.

WITH MODERN INTELLECTUALS

Ramakrishna would be pained exceedingly to find how many among the modern intellectuals in their vanity would look down upon the idea of God and religion as a sham and mockery. Whenever he met any of these enlightened atheists and agnostics, he spared no pains to correct their flippant attitude towards things spiritual by his humble, yet piercing, remarks. However, if he learnt that any individual of the educated section was really serious about religious life, he would take delight in serving him with all humility by his inspired talks, in order to broaden his religious outlook and spur him on towards the goal of God-realization.

Among the noteworthy intellectuals of his day, Ramakrishna met Michael Madhusudan Dutt, the great Bengali poet, Bankim Chandra Chatterjee, the father of the Bengali novel, Pandit Iswar Chandra Vidyasagar, the reputed nineteenth-century savant of Bengal, and Maharshi Devendra Nath Tagore, the distinguished leader of the Ādi Brāhmo Samāj and father of the famous poet, Rabindranath Tagore. But the most interesting and significant contact he made with the enlightened section was through his voluntary meeting, in 1875, with Keshub Chandra Sen, the celebrated Brāhmo leader, in a villa not very far from the Kālī temple. This was followed by a growing intimacy between the highly cultured and renowned dignitary of the Brāhmo Samāj and the humble and barely literate saint of Dakshineswar. Ramakrishna would sometimes call on Keshub, either in his church or at his house, and Keshub would, on occasions, come to meet him at Dakshineswar.

Keshub was struck by the broad and catholic outlook of Ramakrishna towards all religions, by his original and illuminating utterances, and, above all, by his radiant life of spirituality. Keshub, with many Brāhmo devotees like Pratap Chandra Mazumdar, Vijay Krishna Goswami, Pandit Sivanath Sastri, and Trailokyanath Sanyal, would sit enthralled for hours listening to the rapturous utterances of Ramakrishna regarding his wonderfully liberal view about the different religions. Indeed, he did not merely tolerate the various faiths, but actually accepted all of them as so many paths leading to the realization of God. Firm in his conviction, he would say unequivocally: 'I have practised all religions, Hinduism, Islam, Christianity, and I have also followed the paths of the different Hindu sects. . . . I have found that it is the same God towards whom all are directing their steps, though along different paths. . . . Wherever I look, I see men quarrelling in the name of religion—the Hindus, Mohammedans, Brāhmos, Vaiṣṇavas, and the rest—, but they never reflect that He who is called Kṛṣṇa is also called Śiva, and bears the name of primitive Energy (Śakti), Jesus, and Allah as well, the same Rāma with a thousand names. The tank has several *ghāṭs.* At one Hindus draw water in pitchers and call it *jala*; at another Mohammedans draw water in leathern bottles and call it *pāni*; at a third Christians do the same and call it water. The substance is one under different names, and everyone is seeking the same substance; nothing but climate, temperament, and names vary. Let each man follow his own path. If he sincerely and ardently wishes to know God, peace be unto him! He will surely realize Him.'

Pratap Chandra Mazumdar, the accomplished Brāhmo preacher and right-hand man of Keshub, has left a faithful record of his own impression about Ramakrishna's influence over this group of modern intellectuals: 'What is there in common between him (Ramakrishna) and me? I, a Europeanized, civilized, self-centred, semi-sceptical, so-called educated reasoner, and he, a poor, illiterate, unpolished, half-idolatrous, friendless Hindu devotee? Why should I sit long hours to attend to him, I, who have listened to Disraeli and Fawcett, Stanley and Max Müller, and a whole host of European scholars and divines? . . . And it is not I only, but dozens like me who do the same.' And, after due deliberation, he comes to the conclusion that it is his religion that is his only recommendation. But his religion itself was a puzzle: 'He worships Śiva, he worships Kālī, he worships Rāma, he worships Kṛṣṇa, and is a confirmed advocate of Vedāntic doctrines. . . . He is an idolater, yet is a faithful and most devoted meditator on the perfections of the one formless, absolute, infinite Deity. . . . His religion is ecstasy, his worship means transcendental insight, his whole nature burns day and night with a permanent fire and fever of a strange faith and feeling.'

Another statement made by the same gentleman goes to show how Ramakrishna's ideas were absorbed by the group of Brāhmo devotees who had the occasion of coming in contact with him: 'He (Ramakrishna) by his childlike *bhakti,* by his strong conceptions of an ever-ready Motherhood, helped to unfold it (God as our Mother) in our minds wonderfully. . . . By associating with him, we learnt to realize better the divine attributes as scattered over the three hundred and thirty millions of deities of mythological India, the gods of the Purāṇas.

Such statements went to introduce Ramakrishna to the educated middle class of Calcutta, from which section came most of his disciples.

WITH DISCIPLES

Of the persons who came to light their torches from the blazing fire of Ramakrishna's spirituality, some, specially the elderly ones, remained householders up to the end of their lives, while most of the younger ones embraced the life of *sannyāsa*. Ramachandra Dutta, Girish Chandra Ghosh, Mahendranath Gupta, Balaram Bose, Durgacharan Nag, Purna Chandra Ghosh, Kalipada Ghosh, Devendranath Mazumdar, Surendra Nath Mitra, Manomohan Mitra, and many others, including a number of women devotees, belonged to the householders' group, and everyone of these blessed souls has left a brilliant record of spiritual achievement.

Ramakrishna asked this group of elders not to renounce the world, and he taught them how like *karma-yogins* they were to practise detachment in the midst of worldly concerns. They were to give up the idea of proprietorship and believe that all their earthly possessions as well as their near and dear ones really belonged to God. And, as humble servants of God, they were to take up seriously the worldly duties as so many sacred tasks imposed upon them by their divine Master. Thus the ideal of selfless work combined with devotion to God, the age-old message of the *Bhagavad-Gītā,* would be indelibly impressed on the minds of his lay disciples by Ramakrishna's blazing words: 'When you are at work, use only one of your hands and let the other touch the feet of the Lord. When your work is suspended, take His feet in both your hands and put them in your heart!'

He noticed that each individual had a distinct line of spiritual growth and guided each along his or her own path. Hence, there was a wide range of spiritual practices prescribed by him for different individuals.

On one occasion, the lay disciples witnessed a phenomenal descent of divine grace upon them at the galvanizing touch of their Master. It was the 1st January, 1886, and it has since been observed by some of them as the red-letter day of their spiritual life. About thirty of them met Ramakrishna in the garden-house at Cossipore, a northern suburb of Calcutta, where he had been removed for treatment during the last days of his life. Ramakrishna, in a mood of divine ecstasy, blessed and touched each of these persons individually, and instantly their minds were overwhelmed by a sudden rush of spiritual thoughts and emotions. A new realm, resplendent with spiritual light and beatitude, stood revealed before their eyes, and everyone, for the time being, utterly oblivious of the world about him, became thrilled with the vigorous pulsations of a new life and the intense joy and wonder of mystic experience.

The younger disciples, however, were required to tread a different path. Their search for spiritual truth was not to end merely in attaining their own blessedness and salvation, but also in transforming themselves into stupendous levers for the spiritual uplift of thousands of human souls. This was why, when Narendranath, the indomitable leader of this group of disciples, wanted to remain absorbed in the beatitude of *nirvikalpa samādhi,* Ramakrishna was quick to reprove him with the remark, 'Shame on you! I thought you were to be the great banian-tree giving shelter to thousands of weary souls. Instead, you are selfishly seeking your own well-being. Let these little things alone, my child'. With this group of disciples, Ramakrishna was building up, slowly and silently, a new order of monks to whom he was to bequeath the legacy of his spiritual attainment.

This was precisely the reason why Ramakrishna was particular about testing the physical as well as the moral stamina of every person, before admitting him into this select group. A fresh young mind, not yet tainted by worldly thoughts, and plastic enough to be cast in his spiritual mould, was what he valued most as entitling one to be a member of this holy band. Hence this batch came to be composed mostly of young ardent souls. And, with one exception, all of them came from the educated middle class of Bengal.

Latu (Swami Adbhutananda), a Bihari by birth and the young servant of a Bengali devotee, was the exceptional member, who was blissfully ignorant of the three R's. Gopal (Swami Advaitananda) was rather advanced in years, and Tarak (Swami Sivananda) was older than the rest. Hari (Swami Turiyananda) was scarcely fourteen ; Subodh (Swami Subodhananda), Gangadhar (Swami Akhandananda), and Kali (Swami Abhedananda) were very nearly of the same age. Sarada (Swami Trigunatitananda) was quite a boy when he met Ramakrishna for the first time in 1885. Hariprasanna (Swami Vijnanananda), destined to be a monk of this holy order in later life, came to Ramakrishna with the cousins Sarat (Swami Saradananda) and Sasi (Swami Ramakrishnananda), when all of them were going through college education. Narendra (Swami Vivekananda), Rakhal (Swami Brahmananda), Baburam (Swami Premananda), Jogin (Swami Yogananda), and Niranjan (Swami Niranjanananda) were almost of the same age, and were perhaps just crossing their teens when they came to the Master.

His way of training these young souls was unique. He did not rule them like the traditional *gurus* with the rod of iron, nor did he believe in thrusting doctrines or dogmas into their young minds. He was all love and compassion for these young pupils, and chose to meet them almost on an equal footing. *Suaviter in modo, fortiter in re,* he led each one of them by the hand along the path best suited to his taste, temperament, and capacity.

The melancholy air of the stoic was not to touch their tender minds. He would rather strive to keep up the lustre and buoyancy of these young souls by humouring them occasionally with endearing words, interesting parables, and witty remarks, and sometimes by making them roar with laughter by his marvellous mimicry of worldly men and women in a variety of funny poses. Even the consciousness of sin, which sits heavily on the hearts of devotees of particular schools, was not permitted to cast a gloom on their bright countenance. Ramakrishna told them with emphatic perspicuity: 'The miserable man who repeats tirelessly "I am a sinner" really becomes a sinner.'

Instead of burdening their minds with dogmas or fettering their feet with a fixed code of rituals, he urged them simply to verify the truths mentioned in the Śāstras by their own experiment and observation. He pointed out to each a particular path and asked him to proceed with the balanced attitude of an empiricist and discover for himself the sublime spiritual truths that lay at the end of the path. His method perfectly suited the trend of the modern mind and, very naturally, appealed to the rational understanding of his young disciples. Moreover, instead of allowing them to indulge in vain controversies about metaphysical and theological themes, he would stir up in their hearts, by his very presence as well as by his pointed and emphatic words, an intense yearning for realizing God.

And, for realizing God, he told them clearly that no half-hearted measure would be of any avail. They must withdraw their minds entirely from the sense-world and turn them inward, before they could expect to stand face to face with Truth eternal. Lust and greed for wealth had to be banned, if they wanted seriously to realize spiritual truth. Thus would he work up their zeal for embracing a life of renunciation, selflessness, and purity. One day, he actually made them beg their food like *sannyāsins*, and, on another occasion, distributed among them ochre cloth, the robe that distinguishes the Hindu monk from the householder. Thus did Ramakrishna breathe the spirit of *sannyāsa* into the supple, yet vigorous, minds of his picked group of young disciples, initiate them, in his simple and unceremonious way, into monastic life, and lay firmly and securely the foundation on which the Ramakrishna Order of monks was to be built up in the fullness of time.

It was during the last protracted illness of Ramakrishna that his young disciples really banded themselves together, under the leadership of

Narendranath, into a holy brotherhood. Ramakrishna's fatal throat trouble began in the middle of 1885 and lasted for about a year ; and of this period, he had to spend nearly four months in a Calcutta house and about eight months in a suburban villa at Cossipore. His lay devotees met the entire expenses of his treatment, while his young disciples, strengthened immensely by the presence and vigilant service of the Holy Mother (Sarada Devi), shouldered the responsibility of nursing him.

Ramakrishna saw the potential leader in Narendranath. He scanned him thoroughly and observed: 'Ordinary souls fear to assume the responsibility of instructing the world. A worthless piece of wood can only just manage to float, and if a bird settles on it, it sinks immediately. But Naren is different. He is like the great tree trunks, bearing men and beasts upon their bosom in the Gaṅgā.' Naturally, he entrusted to Narendranath the serious task of consolidating the holy brotherhood by looking after the spiritual growth of all the members of this group. Ramakrishna told him plainly one day, 'I leave these young people in your charge. Busy yourself in developing their spirituality'.

Three or four days before Ramakrishna passed away, he called Naren alone to his side, fixed his affectionate gaze upon him, and became absorbed in an ecstasy. Naren's mind remained spell-bound for a while, after which he heard the Master saying rather piteously, 'Today I have given you my all, and now I am only a poor faquir possessing nothing. By this power you will do infinite good to the world, and not until it is accomplished will you return'. On the last day of his life, August 15, 1886, Ramakrishna charged Narendranath repeatedly with the words, 'Take care of these boys', before he entered into *samādhi* for the last time and left the mortal frame behind.

THE BEACON LIGHT

The hurried survey of Ramakrishna's life made in the foregoing pages may appear to be rather bewildering to the modern mind. His father's dream about his divine origin, the ecstatic visions of his early age, his critical estimate of bread-winning education during a precocious adolescence, his frantic quest in youth after the supersensuous scriptural truths, his earnest and vigorous spiritual practices according to the directions of different schools of religion, his realization of God through every one of these diverse methods within an incredibly short period of time, the spiritual uplift and illumination of his disciples by his benign and potent will, and, lastly, his mysterious transmission of spiritual power into Narendranath on the eve of his passing away—all these, surely, lie beyond the range of normal experience. Even his almost unprecedented record of purity and love, his amazing syntheses of opposing phases of life, thoughts, and emotions, his edifying contacts with the old-school scholars and devotees, including his own *gurus*, and also with the modern intellectuals, broadening their religious outlook by his message of harmony of religions, dissemination of all the spiritual ideas and ideals upheld by some of the most important faiths of the world, inspiring his young disciples with the spirit of renunciation, and infusing into Narendranath the idea of worshipping God through the service of suffering humanity—even these contain elements that our sophisticated minds are not prepared to accept without demur.

Among the moderners, there are many who do not believe in anything outside the reach of the senses or the intellect, and look upon religion as an interesting pastime of puerile minds. To these bold free-thinkers, the supernormal elements of Ramakrishna's life may appear like the dreamy stuff of a fairy-tale, or perhaps like the unmistakable symptoms of a psycho-neurotic patient. But, before passing any such verdict, one should pause to consider, with a critical and unbiased mind, if through Ramakrishna's phenomenal life the world has encountered a fresh and convincing mass of evidence in favour of spiritual truths.

Ramakrishna, through his deep and extensive observations, discovered the fact, often ignored or misunderstood even by theologians, that it is to God as the primary underlying substratum, the final cause of the universe, that all religions, in spite of their distinct and apparent mythological and ritualistic crudities, aim at drawing our attention. If, according to his finding, God of the theologians be no other than the philosophers' 'logical ground of existence' and the final cause, then, surely, He lies beyond the scope of our category-ridden minds.

A modern man may recoil from Ramakrishna's apparently anthropomorphic visions of the final cause in different forms of the personal God, and may not hesitate to equate these with hallucination. But since the same visions, with all their minute details, have been witnessed by countless seers before him, and since identical visions are held by them all to be open to any one who will strive seriously to attain them, the spiritual visions cannot surely be classed with the wild fantasies of a particular deranged brain. By his own empiric observations with pure intelligence or spiritual intuition, Ramakrishna became convinced of the fact that any method of practical religion, if sincerely followed, was sure to develop this faculty that lies dormant in every person, and through it to lead him to visions of the personal God in various forms. This is a perfectly humanistic and universal fact, as good as law, bearing on the development of a particular aspect of human nature and consequent possibilities of extension of the range of human knowledge beyond the normal scope of the unedified mind.

Ramakrishna, like all other men of realization, found that it was not the physical conditions that determined his mystic visions, as in the case of hallucination ; rather, he observed with empiric accuracy how events occurred in the physical world according to the will of his divine Mother, as communicated to him through his visions.

He assessed the truth of his mystic visions by his own observation and found them capable of leading him up to the brink of a transcendental realization of the supreme Reality. Hence to him the spiritual visions appeared to be closer to Reality than the things of the world, and from the comparatively greater amount of joy, purity, strength, and illumination he derived from these visions, he gave them a greater value than the contents of sense-impressions.

But the mystic intuition of a pure heart cannot impart finality to knowledge, in so far as it reveals only a glimpse of the Reality, which lies beyond mind and beyond speech. It was only when he transcended both reason and intuition that his consciousness stepped out of all limits and realized its absolute identity with the eternal and unchangeable, nameless and formless substratum, Reality. Ramakrishna used to say: 'You have to draw out a thorn with another, and then reject them both.' With the visions wrought by *vidyā-māyā* or spiritual intuition, one has to free oneself from the tyranny of sense-impressions, and then one has to leave aside even the spiritual intuition and transcend the plane of mystic visions, before the individual soul is able to realize its identity with the eternal Spirit.

But certainly the Absolute beyond time, space, and causation cannot be objectified to our consciousness through reason, intuition, or imagination, and hence cannot be known in this sense ; yet the Absolute became 'more than known' to him, inasmuch as his own consciousness became one with it. With him the transcendental existence, instead of being merely a construction of philosophical speculation, mathematical abstraction, or poetic imagination, became a tangible and living fact of experience through his frequent plunges in the ocean of nameless and formless Reality.

Through his extensive observations of numerous and distinct God-visions, in the course of his search along the different paths of religion, he found that these visions differed only in colour and outline, name and form, but they coincided thoroughly so far as the substance was concerned. In and through them all he had the unerring perception of the transcendental Absolute. The formless appeared before his pure mind through divine forms. To his clear vision the difference between the personal and the impersonal God was no more than that between ice and water, and the difference between the various forms of the personal God appeared like that between the distinct forms of the same actor playing different rôles.

Moreover, his mystic experiences brought fresh data from planes beyond the reach of the senses, and left the intellect to study them and discover through them the truth of essential oneness behind all appearances. Thus did he comprehend that the entire diversity of appearances, which we call nature, was nothing but a manifestation of the selfsame Absolute—visions of the personal God forming its apex and those of the physical world its base. Before his spiritual vision was unfolded a majestic and magnificent oneness of the universe, towards which all sciences and all philosophies are surely and steadily converging. It is this realization of a living oneness that alone can furnish the world with the rationale behind the concept of equality and fraternity, and provide it with the basis on which it may build up the much-needed edifice of universal brotherhood.

Indeed, the world has been sorely in need of a seer like Ramakrishna with such a fresh, brilliant, perfect, and extensive record of spiritual experiences, in order to dispel the gathering clouds of doubt and reinstal the faith of humanity in the eternal Truth. It was a conspicuous feature of his life that he valued those very things which the modern world is trying to ignore and set aside. Religion was the breath of his life, morality his backbone. In his perspective, realization of God was the worthiest object of life, and devotion, purity, sincerity, selflessness, love, and humility constituted the real wealth of man, far superior in value and significance to anything of the external world. And he developed all these to a unique degree of perfection. In his life, one finds an unsurpassed record of God-intoxication, spotless purity, and surging love for humanity. And then, with his mind broad as the sky, strong as adamant, and pure as a crystal, he plumbed the depths of spirituality, collected the treasures of the entire wisdom of the past, tested their worth, and reinvested them all with a fresh hall-mark of truth. From his lips, the world hears the voice of the ancient prophets ; in his life, it discovers the meaning of the scriptures. Through his life and teachings, man has got an opportunity of learning the old lessons afresh.

By his deep and extensive spiritual experience of the entire range of Upaniṣadic truths, Ramakrishna has surely heralded an epoch-making Hindu renaissance. He discovered the wonderful spirit of catholicism within the sealed bosom of Hinduism, and released it through his own realizations to spread all over the globe and liberalize all communal and sectarian views.

By touching the entire gamut of spiritual experience, his life and message have their appeal to all men of all countries. This is why the late lamented French savant, Dr. Sylvain Lévi, rightly observed: 'As

Ramakrishna's heart and mind were for all countries, his name too is a common property of mankind.'

Through his superhuman power of transmitting spirituality by a mere glance, touch, or will, through his phenomenal syntheses of contradictory phases of life, thoughts, and emotions, of *bhakti* and *jñāna,* work and renunciation, *gārhasthya* (life of a householder) and *sannyāsa,* and through his almost unprecedented measure of selfless love and purity, Swami Vivekananda saw in him the highest expression of Divinity on the human plane, a combination of the intellect of Śaṅkarācārya and the heart of Buddha or Caitanya.

Through all the different readings about him taken by persons belonging really to the first rank of intellectuals, of the modern as well as of the old school, one thing has become very clear, namely, that when humanity, in the midst of a chaos and confusion of ideals, clashes and conflicts of interests, was about to lose its hold on religion, Ramakrishna's blazing life of realizations suddenly appeared like a new and very bright luminary in the spiritual firmament of the world. In the light of this resplendent life, the rationale behind all religions and the precious nuggets of truth embedded in all creeds have been revealed, and this revelation may be expected to convince the modern empiricists, as also the rationalists of all schools, about the values of religion.

It is encouraging to notice that a voice, though very feeble, has been raised in the modern world by a distinguished band of thinkers, poets, philosophers, and scientists, a voice that is tending to rationalize the wisdom of the seers and prophets, and thus to lift up the eyes of mankind towards spirituality. It is sure to grow in volume and intensity and get a wider hearing. The more this voice becomes audible, the more will humanity be in a position to understand correctly the import of Ramakrishna's life as a beacon light that has appeared at a critical moment in the history of man, in order to illumine the upward path of human civilization, and thus to help it out of the present welter of cultural ideals and direct it towards a great world-wide spiritual awakening. It was given to Swami Vivekananda, the illustrious leader of his young disciples, to realize this significance of Ramakrishna's phenomenal life and to announce to the world, in his trumpet voice, the thrilling tidings of such a glorious future.

Through the voice of the disciple, the world is really listening to the voice of the Master. The disciple is the dynamic counterpart of the Master. If the life of the Master be a book of revelations, that of his worthy apostle is its appropriate commentary and a compendious guide-book of its practical application.

III. SWAMI VIVEKANANDA AND SPIRITUAL FEDERATION

We have noticed how Ramakrishna recognized in Narendranath a potential leader of men, entrusted to him the serious responsibility of tending his brother-disciples, inspired him to dedicate himself entirely to the service of humanity, and finally, by transmitting his own spiritual power into him, became spiritually one with his disciple. We have also observed that it was Vivekananda who grasped the deeper imports of Ramakrishna's life and broadcasted the same practically all over the world.

He verified the truth of his Master's message by his own experiments and observations, and then, with a firm conviction born of his own realizations, he presented, amplified, and elucidated before the world the precious lessons he had learnt at the feet of Ramakrishna. He made, moreover, important practical deductions from the Master's message that might go to exalt both individual as well as collective life. He analysed the deeper aspirations of the human heart, and scanned its doubts and confusions. He studied the entire course of human progress through centuries, compared different epochs of cultural advance, and weighed the various ideals of human civilization ; and from all these data he discovered and pointed out to humanity the path that might lead it to a glorious future.

Indeed, like Bhagīratha of Hindu mythology, Vivekananda brought down the clear and vitalizing stream of spirituality from the celestial heights and seclusion of Ramakrishna's life, and made it break through the cliffs of doubt and scepticism and rush down hills and valleys in an ever-widening mighty current, inundating the unhealthy slimes and cesspools of sordid thoughts and enriching the soils of the earth with a fresh, charming, and vigorous life of spirituality.

THE ROCK OF ADAMANT

'Vivekananda' was the monastic name of Narendranath Datta, who was born on the 12th January, 1863, in an aristocratic Kṣatriya family of Calcutta, the then capital of India. His mother was a spirited and accomplished lady with an air of majesty in her demeanour, and his father an enlightened free-thinker with liberal views, a compassionate heart, and a leaning towards an ostentatious and rather extravagant mode of living. In all these details, Narendranath differed widely from his spiritual Master, whose home environment, as we have noticed, was marked by rustic simplicity.

The contrast was, perhaps, no less prominent in their physical constitution, temperament, and cultural training. As opposed to Ramakrishna's delicate physique and almost feminine grace, Narendranath, with his strong

SWAMI VIVEKANANDA

and athletic build, was Promethean in vigour and thoroughly masculine in deportment. Through systematic courses of physical culture, Narendranath became an adept in wrestling and boxing, as much as in racing, riding, and swimming. Among his companions, he made himself conspicuous by his bold and free movements, loving heart, and straight and unconventional manners. If Ramakrishna displayed the *sāttvika* (serene) trait of the true Brāhmaṇa, his disciple had all the *rājasika* (active) signs of a true-born Kṣatriya. Narendranath too, like his spiritual Master, was a lover of music. But unlike the inspired dreamer Ramakrishna, who only sang pieces gleaned from the strolling minstrels, in tunes picked up from the wayside, this enthusiastic realist underwent a prolonged course of regular training under able guides, till he qualified himself as a master of vocal and instrumental music. While Ramakrishna refused to engage himself seriously in picking up the bare essentials of the three R's in a primary school, Narendranath came to be a full-fledged university graduate. At college, he impressed his professors and compeers by the extraordinary versatility of his genius, and made his mark as a powerful controversialist. However, even from his childhood, he had a religious bent of mind, and in this, surely, he resembled his Master. In the immature age when boys find nothing more interesting than play, Narendranath delighted in spending long hours in a meditative pose before the images of God.

But in adolescence, he grew up to be a rationalist to the core of his being. He was at heart a seeker of truth. But his nature rebelled against the idea of accepting anything on faith. His reason had to be satisfied by convincing and incontrovertible evidence, before he could bend to recognize the validity of a statement, scriptural or scholastic. He pored over books, discussed with scholars and churchmen, overwhelmed amateur and professional lecturers on religious topics with sallies of penetrating questions, but nowhere did he find adequate light for solving his own sincere doubts about the ultimate verities of life and existence. Finding idealism as inefficient to fulfil his craving for truth as agnosticism or positivism, he surrendered himself for a time to the popular, refined, and considerably christianized tenets of the Brāhmo Samāj, propounded by the illustrious Keshub Chandra, who was then at the height of his glory. But the intense yearning of his searching soul could not compromise itself with all that this enlightened creed held out to him, and he literally smarted under the pressure of disappointment. In his restlessness, he went about the city to meet religious worthies, but from nobody did he receive anything that could convince him about the existence of God and the possibility of man attaining perfection.

When, baffled in his attempt, this precocious, rationalistic seeker of truth had reached almost the verge of scepticism, he met the great saint of Dakshineswar accidentally in the house of a Brāhmo devotee. This was in November 1881. Ramakrishna became highly impressed by Narendranath's religious songs, and perhaps his penetrating gaze discerned something behind the charmingly melodious voice, which convinced him of the immense potentialities that lay dormant in the heart of the meteoric youth. He attracted Narendranath forthwith within his own orbit by inviting him to visit the Dakshineswar temple. This chance meeting of the two souls really proved to be pregnant with all the possibilities of Narendranath's subsequent career.

The meeting of Ramakrishna with Narendranath, which ended eventually in their spiritual union, appears, moreover, to symbolize the meeting of the ancient culture with the modern, scriptural faith with imperious reason, mysticism with positivism. Behind their Indian skin and complexion were two souls representing two different types of cultural groups, one clinging credulously to the scriptural ideology of the old days and the other getting itself freed from all trammels of dogma.

Ramakrishna revealed through his life the spirit of Hinduism at its best and highest. Narendranath, on the other hand, when he met Ramakrishna for the first time, represented the searching, analytical, rationalistic, truth-seeking, and vigorous spirit of the modern West. He was a votary of reason, and had absolutely no faith in church dogmas, sentimental effusions, and apparently meaningless ceremonials. He could not regard ecstatic vision as anything more than hallucination. He had waded tirelessly through the path of intellect under the implicit guidance of European thinkers of great repute ; he had mastered different systems of western philosophy, which had scraped off the thin veneer of Brāhmo theism from his mind. Searching the archives of western thought for an idea or inspiration with which he might console himself, he had tried the impassioned pantheism of Shelley, the spiritual raptures of Wordsworth, and had for a time tested the worth of an adventitious medley of the pure monism of Vedānta, the objective idealism of Hegel together with the basic ideals of the French Revolution—liberty, equality, and fraternity. None of these could satisfy him for long. He had developed grave doubts about the existence of God. It was not a craving for God-vision like that of a Hindu spiritual aspirant, but a passionate urge for finding unbounded peace and unrestricted knowledge that tormented the soul of this precocious enthusiast. Such was Narendranath, a thoroughbred, up-to-date moderner, when he rushed by chance into the orbit of Ramakrishna.

Shortly afterwards, Narendranath visited the saint and, with all his critical faculties on the alert, observed Ramakrishna minutely, weighed his words and thoughts cautiously, and scrutinized his conduct as thoroughly as he could. He put before the sage his straight, earnest, and crucial query, tersely and pointedly: 'Sir, have you seen God?' He expected, perhaps, a negative, dubious, or devious reply, as he had so long received from all acclaimed seers whom he had approached with this challenge. This time, however, the young rationalist was stunned by a prompt, unexpected, and amazingly unambiguous reply in the affirmative: 'Yes, I see Him just as I see you here, only in a sense much more intense.' In a state of bewildering surprise he listened to what followed: 'God can be realized; one can see and talk to Him as I am doing with you. But who cares to do so? People shed torrents of tears for their wife and children, for wealth and property, but who does so for the sake of God? If one weeps sincerely for Him, He surely manifests Himself.' The simple, clear, and spontaneous outpourings of Ramakrishna's heart had the effect of impressing the sincerity of his conviction upon Narendranath, though, of course, he was not yet prepared for accepting all that he had said. Narendranath has left a record of this impression in the following words: 'For the first time, I found a man who dared to say that he had seen God, that religion was a reality to be felt, to be sensed in an infinitely more intense way than we can sense the world. As I heard these things from his lips, I could not but believe that he was saying them not like an ordinary preacher, but from the depths of his own realizations.'

Narendranath's realistic frame of mind got a rude shock on that very day, when Ramakrishna called him aside, showered upon him an unexpected measure of affection, and addressed him in the perfectly familiar tone of an old and very dear acquaintance, referring, all the while, to strange, unintelligible, and mysterious things purporting to be the antecedents of his own earthly career. These utterances appeared to him like the ravings of a maniac. He came away that day from the holy sage with a confused feeling of unstinted reverence for his unimpeachable sanctity mixed with lurking doubts about his absolute sanity.

Yet an unaccountable and tremendous attraction urged him to repeat his visit to the saint within a month. This time he had an occasion of witnessing, to his utter dismay, the wonderful potency of Ramakrishna's touch, which made everything about him swim and spin before his eyes and dissolve into empty space. He felt as if he was facing death and cried out in consternation, 'What are you doing? I have parents at home'. This drew a genial laugh from the saintly wizard of Dakshineswar and made him pass his hand over Narendranath's breast with the remark, 'All right. Let us leave it at that for the moment'. Immediately, to his infinite surprise and relief, Narendranath regained his normal vision. Considering the fact that he possessed a robust physique and a very strong and indomitable mind, he could not but marvel at the immensity of Ramakrishna's mesmeric power But, so far as the spiritual greatness of Ramakrishna was concerned, Narendranath was not yet in a position to come to any definite conclusion.

The next visit followed very quickly, and on this occasion Ramakrishna's powerful touch steeped Narendranath immediately in a trance. While he remained in that state, the Master elicited from his inner mind whatever he wanted to know about his antecedents and whereabouts, his mission in this world, and the duration of his earthly life. The information thus received tallied completely with Ramakrishna's foreknowledge about these things. Regarding this incident the Master afterwards said to his disciples: 'I asked him several questions while he was in that state. He dived deep into himself and gave fitting answers to my questions. They only confirmed what I had seen and inferred about him.'

Narendranath was very much impressed by Ramakrishna's inscrutable and overwhelming power, and he felt a great attraction towards the sage. But, while his heart swayed towards the Master, his intellect guarded its independence jealously and would not permit him to be befooled by any form of probable charlatanry. He would have nothing to do with Ramakrishna's panegyrics about the divine Mother, or other gods and goddesses, or even about the Nirguṇa Brahman of Advaita Vedānta, before he could satisfy his own reason by adequate evidence on behalf of their existence. He dared even to challenge Ramakrishna's sanity during his ecstatic visions and asked him with piercing frankness, 'How do you know that your realizations are not the creations of your sick brain, mere hallucinations?' Perhaps his intellect, by its excessive and audacious zeal, tried to put a brake on his heart, which had been pulling him with powerful and incomprehensible force towards the holy saint of Dakshineswar. During this period, Narendranath's inner life became a tumultuous scene of continued and implacable war between his domineering intellect and spiritually disposed heart. It was this heart that had resisted, by its disapprobation and dissatisfaction, his intellect's unrestricted march towards the cultural ideas of the modern West, and now it was his intellect that stood in the way of his heart's outgoing impulses for owning allegiance to the age-old spiritual ideals of India.

Narendranath's intellectual predilection for positivism did not, however, ruffle Ramakrishna's equanimity. He appreciated and even enjoyed Narendranath's pungent polemics issuing, as he knew, out of a bed of intellectual sincerity. He would even stimulate the young rationalist's critical spirit by such encouraging words addressed to his disciples as

'Do not accept anything because I say so. Test everything for yourselves'. Thus did the Master, in his almost infinite affection and patience, give Narendranath a very long rope to indulge in free and sincere expression of his own thoughts, no matter how impudently aspersive and iconoclastic these might appear to other people about him.

BORING THE ROCK

The sage was perfectly rational in his method of approach towards his spiritual pupils and in presenting before them his own knowledge. He appeared, in his unassuming and liberal pose, more like a fact-finding and liberty-giving modern savant than a dictatorial spiritual preceptor of the traditional stamp. His method was based on a deep and extensive knowledge of human psychology, and it never contradicted reason. Through all these as well as through the piercing logic of Ramakrishna's repartee, and the stupefying harmony of reason and creative imagination behind his illuminating analogies and parables, Narendranath saw the intellectual counterpart of Ramakrishna's ecstatic exterior, and wondered at this extraordinary combination of heart and intellect. In later days, he referred to this and juxtaposed it to his own temperamental outlook by the following epigram: 'Outwardly he was all *bhakta,* but inwardly all *jñānin.* . . . I am the exact opposite.'

Narendranath, with all the ardour of his impetuous soul, started an enthusiastic career of spiritual practice, in order to verify the worth of Ramakrishna's instructions by his own realization. He took up different modes of spiritual *sādhanā* prescribed by the Master, and put his heart and soul into them.

During this period, the change that came upon Narendranath amounted to nothing less than an astounding and unthinkable *volte-face.* Regarding this credal somersault, Brojendranath Seal, one of the leading rationalists of modern India, who happened for a time to be the 'friend, philosopher, and guide' of young Narendranath, records his own impression by the following scholarly exclamation: 'I watched with intense interest the transformation that went on under my eyes. The attitude of a young rampant Vedāntist-cum-Hegelian-cum-revolutionary like myself towards the cult of religious ecstasy and Kālī-worship may be easily imagined; and the spectacle of a born iconoclast and free-thinker like Vivekananda, a creative and dominating intelligence, a tamer of souls, himself caught in the meshes of what appeared to me an uncouth, supernatural mysticism, was a riddle which my philosophy of the pure reason could scarcely read at the time.'

In 1884, his father died leaving his family in debts and abject penury.

Narendranath, being the eldest brother, had to exert himself to his utmost to face the distressing situation boldly and squarely.

His faith in the existence of a just and merciful God, in a world where millions die of starvation, was shaken to the core. The sceptic in him jumped up from the deeper layers of his mind, where it had retired before the invasion of Ramakrishna's conquering spirituality, and it asserted itself in openly denying any good or gracious Existence beneath such an apparently diabolical world. Ramakrishna, however, had unshakable faith in him, and he waited patiently for the psychological moment when Narendranath would exhaust of himself the superficial atheistic contents of his mind.

After a fairly long period of continued suffering, Narendranath, when he had reached an extreme state of physical and mental exhaustion, perceived, to his utter surprise, the first and almost miraculous rush of spiritual current from within. By an intuitive flash, he found the rationale that could reconcile divine graciousness with the miseries of the world, and he felt relieved. He intuitively realized that the life of a householder was not meant for him.

He resolved to renounce the world ; and on the very day he wanted to slip away, he met Ramakrishna in a devotee's house in Calcutta. At the Master's express desire, Narendranath accompanied him to Dakshineswar and spent the night there. Ramakrishna read his mind like an open book, and he asked him not to renounce the world so long as he was alive. Narendranath went back to his family, but he could not secure any permanent and substantial office on which the members of his family might depend. One day, at Dakshineswar, at the suggestion of the Master, he attempted thrice to pray to the divine Mother to improve the financial condition of his family. But each time, in his ecstatic fervour of love and faith, he forgot all about his distressed family and prayed only for knowledge and devotion, discrimination and renunciation. After this, Ramakrishna, however, assured him that by the grace of God, his mother and brothers would find just enough means to make both ends meet.

From this day, he became a new man and practically started on a new career. His atheistic reactions were over, and his faith, coming from within the depth of his heart, coloured and controlled all his thoughts, words, and deeds.

This new outlook enabled him to surrender himself completely to the Master. Realizing the supreme efficacy of spiritual intuition and the perfect mastery of it by Ramakrishna, he slackened his stubborn hold on the proud intellect and engaged himself with persevering tenacity in opening wide the gate of spiritual knowledge under the benign guidance of his beloved Master.

His first-hand knowledge of abject poverty and also of the heartlessness of the people about him became sublimated into an intense feeling of sympathy for all the poor and downtrodden people on earth. It was this widening of his heart by the erosion of poverty, combined with the spiritualizing of it by his Master's inspiration, that led him afterwards to proclaim to the world his epoch-making faith in deified humanity: 'The only God in whom I believe is the sum total of all souls, and above all, I believe in my God the wicked, my God the miserable, my God the poor of all races.'

It was during the last days of the Master in the Cossipore villa, when Narendranath was about twenty-three years of age, that a glimpse of beatitude calmed his surging humanitarian instinct, dimmed, for a time, even his hallowed vision of deified humanity, and stirred up in him an inordinate passion for merging his soul completely in the absolute Reality through *nirvikalpa samādhi* and remaining absorbed in that state for ever. For this he prayed to the Master, and one day his consciousness stepped suddenly out of all limits and became one with the supreme Brahman; and after its descent, Ramakrishna charged him with the mission of his life. He pointed out to him that it was not for him to harbour individualism to the extent of remaining constantly absorbed in spiritual ecstasy, and that his mission consisted in serving mankind as a lever for its spiritual uplift. In the light of the Master's words, Narendranath resolved to sacrifice even the intense bliss of transcendental union with the supreme Self. His heart, standing midway between the Absolute and the relative, was swayed constantly by a surging love for deified humanity, and yet, at times, it would be stilled into a perfectly calm lake mirroring the transcendental glory of the formless Divinity and shutting out the world with all its contents. Thus selfless love for God in man and absorption in God impersonal came to be the two spiritual terminuses between which his consciousness plied. Convinced by his own realization of the spiritual value of his Master's injunction to him, he combined, in later days, the twin ideals of individual salvation and universal well-being, while framing the motto of the Ramakrishna Order of monks.

Thus, after working slowly, imperceptibly, and perseveringly for nearly six years on the adamantine rock of Narendranath's heart, Ramakrishna bored it completely by his unswerving love and benign grace.

HARNESSING THE STREAM

Ramakrishna commissioned Narendranath to look after the spiritual well-being of his brother-disciples, and under his able and loving guidance the young disciples banded themselves together into an incipient brotherhood of potential monks, while attending the sick-bed of their dear Master at the Cossipore villa.

Immediately after the Master had passed away, a tornado of renunciation and intense yearning for God-realization swept over their minds, wrenching them all, one group after another, from their family moorings. Tarak, Latu, and Gopal (senior), who had already renounced their homes, continued to live in the Cossipore garden-house. The other brothers of this band, with Narendranath at their head, came there every day to spend a considerable time in earnest spiritual exercise and contemplation on the life and teachings of their Master. The period of the lease expired in a month, when with extreme reluctance they had to leave the precincts of the house, sanctified and endeared by the holy association of their beloved Master and charged with the pathos of his separation.

A small, old, and dilapidated house was rented forthwith at Baranagore, almost half-way between Cossipore and Dakshineswar, and the little group shifted there from the garden-house with the Master's relics and eventually ushered into existence a monastery for the Ramakrishna Order of monks. The expenses were met by some of the lay disciples of Ramakrishna, such as Surendra Nath Mitra, Balaram Bose, Girish Chandra Ghosh, and Mahendranath Gupta. In the absence of the inspiring touch of their Master, these householder disciples felt very keenly the need of a pure atmosphere of unalloyed spirituality produced by the ardent devotion, renunciation, and consecration of the younger group.

Towards the end of the mournful year 1886, Narendranath, together with most of the young visionaries, went to spend a few days in the village home of Baburam. It was in the midst of the quiet and natural surroundings of this village that the young spiritual enthusiasts were fired with the ideals of absolute renunciation by the burning words of Narendranath and welded permanently into a brotherhood. One by one, the young disciples of Ramakrishna felt the urge of sacrificing everything for God and man, and proceeded to take the solemn vow of *sannyāsa,* that is, of absolute renunciation and consecration.

After they had come back from the village with a fresh and intensified ardour for renunciation, they severed themselves completely from their family ties, and, in course of a couple of years, all of them joined the Baranagore monastery. They stayed here till 1892, when they shifted to another house at Alambazar, a place immediately to the south of Dakshineswar. One auspicious day, the Baranagore monastery became sanctified by the traditional ceremony of *sannyāsa,* when all the inmates went through the rigid formalities according to the holy custom of the Śaṅkara school of Hindu monks. Clad in ochre robes and loin-cloths and invested with new monastic names, they started a fresh career, supplementing, by such necessary forms and externals, the spirit of monasticism that they had imbibed from their Master and nourished so long with earnest devotion.

Seized by a frenzy of spiritual fervour, these young monks imposed upon themselves with passionate zeal the austere discipline of the recluse and devoted themselves entirely to the quest of spiritual truth as the only immediate and worthy object of their lives. Allowing themselves only spare food and meagre rest for their physical sustenance, they strove, constantly and seriously, to remain absorbed in spiritual exercise. Meditation, contemplation, hymns, prayers, and religious songs and discourses came to be their only occupation.

One of the brothers, Ramakrishnananda, preserved all the relics of the Master in a separate room, placed a portrait of his on a pedestal, and served it with the entire devotion of his heart, just as he had done when Ramakrishna had been alive.

This new feature introduced by Ramakrishnananda lent a real charm to the monastery. Through this, all disciples, lay and monastic, found something with which they could solace their hearts aggrieved by the separation from their dear Master. But, unless proper safeguards were taken, this might develop into a mere cult and fix the brotherhood for ever within the narrow groove of a new sect. Vivekananda was thoroughly alive to this danger, and placed before them the lofty ideas and ideals that he had received from the Master ; and these appeared to his penetrating insight to be the essential and indispensable materials for building up the Ramakrishna Order of monks. He would call up before their imagination the vision of an entirely new type of monastic life characterized by a deep spiritual foundation combined with a broad, humanistic, and universal religious outlook. He made them conscious of the fact that the Master's life was the very negation of sectarianism: it was, in fact, a living embodiment of all faiths. Thus, Vivekananda charged all the brothers of the new Order of monks to become conscious of the tremendous responsibilities that had been laid imperceptibly on their shoulders by their beloved Master.

Ramakrishnananda alone remained glued to the service of the Master, and would not stir out of the monastery. The rest of the brotherhood felt the occasional urge to lead the severely lonely life of the wandering monk or that of the solitary recluse.

Some of the brothers like Abhedananda, Yogananda, and Adbhutananda had started the career of a *parivrājaka* or wandering monk immediately after the Master's departure. Vivekananda contented himself occasionally with short trips to Deoghar or Banaras, his sole attention being fixed on the solidarity of the Order. But, before long; even he could no longer hold himself within the bounds of the monastery. In 1888, a couple of years after the Master had passed away, he passed through Banaras, Ayodhya, Lucknow, Agra, Vrindaban, and the Himalayas. With his heart filled with ecstatic devotion to God, and yet remaining open to receive the aesthetic impress of monumental productions of art, he travelled with equal zeal through places of religious association as through those of historic interest.

In 1889, Vivekananda had to go over to Allahabad to nurse Yogananda, then suffering from an attack of smallpox. Here he heard about the great saint of Ghazipur, Pavhari Baba, whom he proceeded to meet early in the following year.

This saint impressed him very much, and for a time he felt tempted to receive from him lessons on *yoga*, so that, contrary to his Master's wish, he might remain absorbed in *samādhi*. For several consecutive days he resolved to surrender himself to the saint as his disciple, but every night he had a vision of his beloved Master standing before him with a mute appeal in his look for dissuading him from his strange resolution. Intuition got the upper hand, and by its revelation the desire was shaken off his mind.

From Ghazipur he hurried to Banaras to nurse ailing Abhedananda. Here he spent some time in the garden of Pramadadas Mitra, practising severe austerities, till the sad news of the death of Balaram Bose, one of the devoted lay disciples of Ramakrishna, called him back to the Baranagore monastery.

He stayed in the Baranagore monastery for about a couple of months. The recluse in him, however, made him restless, and he resolved to leave the monastery at once and never to return to it, unless he could develop his spiritual potentiality to such a degree as might enable him to transform a man by a mere touch. With this grim resolve he set out, with the blessings of the Holy Mother (Sarada Devi), in July 1890, on an indefinitely long journey.

Akhandananda had already made an extensive tour in the northern parts of India including Kashmir, the Himalayas, and even Tibet. Vivekananda took him as his companion and guide and passed through Deoghar, Bhagalpur, Banaras, Ayodhya, and Nainital to Almora in the Himalayas. It was in the last named place that, through a deep meditation under a banian-tree, he realized a momentous piece of spiritual truth, of which he made the following fragmentary note in his diary of that date: 'The microcosm and the macrocosm are built on the same plan. Just as the individual soul is encased in the living body, so is the universal

Soul in the living Prakṛti (Nature), the objective universe. Śivā (Kālī) is embracing Śiva; this is not a fancy. This covering of the one (Soul) by the other (Nature) is analogous to the relation between an idea and the word expressing it: they are one and the same, and it is only by a mental abstraction that one can distinguish them. Thought is impossible without words. Therefore, in the beginning was the Word etc. This dual aspect of the universal Soul is eternal. So what we perceive or feel is this combination of the eternally Formed and the eternally Formless.' His Master's words about the identity of the Jīva and Śiva, which had appealed so long only to his intellect, now became living in the flash-light of his own intuition. This was, perhaps, why immediately after rising from his seat of meditation he told his companion Akhandananda: 'Here, under this banian-tree, one of the greatest problems of my life has been solved.'

At Almora, Vivekananda received the heart-rending news of his sister's suicide. He started forthwith in search of a quiet region of the Himalayas. But soon his sudden illness as well as that of Akhandananda forced him to abandon his search for solitude and proceed to Srinagar in Garhwal, and eventually to Dehra Dun. Leaving his brother under the benign care of a chance acquaintance, Vivekananda moved on to Rishikesh with Saradananda and Turiyananda, who had meanwhile joined him. But, within a few days, he had a terrible attack of fever which brought him almost to the point of death. After recovery, his delicate health did not permit him to stay any longer in the extreme climate of the mountainous tract, and he was practically forced to retire to the plains. Thus, his search for a suitable spot on the Himalayas, where he might devote himself to a long course of meditation, was brought to an abrupt end by a combination of fortuitous circumstances.

However, the party, joined by Brahmananda at Hardwar, proceeded to Saharanpur and thence to Meerut, where they met Akhandananda and stayed for nearly five months. But his Master's injunction regarding the service of mankind as the mission of his life was constantly before Vivekananda's mind, and since his realization at Almora about the divine harmony in nature, nothing could possibly make any breach between the spiritual yearning of his soul and the service of deified humanity. Still his mind was not at rest. He had not yet discovered his precise line of action. For this he required concentration of thoughts, a closer study of the condition of the people of the land, of which he had nearly covered the northern half by his travel, and a more intimate and extensive knowledge of the Hindu scriptures as also of modern thought. For all these he resolved to travel to the southern extremity of India and visit the holy temple of Kanyā Kumārī, and thus complete his cultural and economic survey of

India from the Himalayas to Cape Comorin. Accordingly, towards the end of January 1891, he rent asunder the ties that bound him to his brother monks and slipped away without notice.

From Meerut he went to Delhi, and thence he proceeded, often on foot, through Rajasthan, Kathiawar, Bombay, Mysore, Travancore-Cochin, and Madras, till, by the end of 1892, he reached the holy temples of Rāmeśvara and Kanyā Kumārī at the extreme south of India. He passed through deserts and forests without any companion, had a narrow escape from the inhuman clutches of revellers in religious orgies, came within an ace of death through starvation, met with scorn and rebuff from many a heartless stranger, and yet he marched undaunted, trampling upon the dangers that beset the path of the adventurous *parivrājaka*. With his shaven head, ochre robes, wanderer's staff, and begging bowl, the Swami accepted the hospitality of a depressed pariah with as much grace and contentment as that of a feudatory chief, and with equal composure he would retrace his steps from an uncharitable door. In his poem 'The Song of the *Sannyāsin*', composed about three years later, perhaps he gave a glimpse of his own mental equipoise by the following words:

> Heed then no more how body lives or goes,
> Its task is done. Let *karma* float it down ;
> Let one put garlands on, another kick
> This frame ; say naught. No praise or blame can be
> Where praiser, praised, and blamer, blamed are one.
> Thus be thou calm, *sannyāsin* bold! Say—*Om tat sat, Om.*

He was verily the antithesis of weakness. As a free soul, he always held his head high, and would never bend his knees before anybody on earth. No prejudice, no tradition, and no considerations of caste or communal barriers could restrict the intrepid movements of this unleashed lion. Neither orthodoxy nor rank westernism could hold him within its bounds. Even regarding the scriptural statements, he had his own views, and he refused to depend solely on the writings of the great commentators. Yet, by his outstanding personality, he carried all before him. He impressed people by his genuine love and sympathy for all, his purity and firmness of character, his serene and peaceful composure, and, above all, by his radiating spirituality.

Besides his all-consuming love for God and deified humanity, his heart was swayed by a devouring passion for a ceaseless extension of knowledge. The dividing line between secular and spiritual knowledge had vanished for ever from his sight. Man was composed of different sheaths—physical, intellectual, and spiritual ; the different compartments of knowledge referred ultimately to one or other of these sheaths superimposed on the God-in-man. Through politics and economics, sociology and ethnology, psychology and biology, history and biography, through material science and rational philosophy, authors might present sectional views of man, but he was out to co-ordinate all these and hold before the world a comprehensive, accurate, and synthetic picture of the puzzling complex known as the human individual.

However, he did not shut himself up entirely within the cover-pages of books. He sought knowledge as much from the living men around him as from books. And his open and receptive mind made him feel the throb of the saint even beneath the breast of the worst of sinners.

Besides, he drew no less valuable lessons from his first-hand readings regarding the social, economic, and cultural life of the people. Men belonging to different castes, sects, and communities, with different regional shades in their widely varying thoughts and ways of life, proved to be a highly engrossing subject of his study. By the time he reached the end of his journey in the South, he had realized how myriads of kaleidoscopic patterns of social life, scattered all over the country, were all ultimately based on the same spiritual foundation laid by the seers of old, the *ṛṣis* of ancient India. Thus, his direct experience opened his eyes to the fact that a central unity could accommodate thousands of varieties on the surface—that unity in variety was a law which held good not only so far as religious creeds were concerned, as demonstrated by his Master's realizations, but also operated behind the entire panorama of nature and governed even the social customs of man.

But while his intellect busied itself in storing up facts and probing them, his heart smarted under a terrible sympathetic pain for suffering humanity on all sides through whatever place he passed. His direct experience of the appalling misery of the downtrodden masses, the helpless victims of a dreadful system of social iniquity, set his whole being on fire. With such a conflagration in his volcanic heart, he reached the southernmost limit of India, paid his homage to the goddess Kanyā Kumārī at Cape Comorin, and swam across to a neighbouring rock, cut off entirely from the mainland, now known as Vivekananda Rock. Seated in the absolute solitude of the rock and surrounded by the dashing waves of the ocean all about him, he looked at the mainland and visualized the whole of India before him—India filled with the agonies of millions of human hearts. A spasm of intense love, boundless sympathy, and infinite despair squeezed his mighty mind into a spell of utter silence, and in the midst of that breathless silence, spiritual intuition flooded his heart with light, in which he saw clearly and unmistakably the path that he was to tread.

The real self of India stood revealed before his eyes. The nation appeared to be a sleeping leviathan, and all that it required to stand on its feet was a spiritual awakening. And it became equally clear to him how he was to rouse it from its disgraceful lethargy. Rising from his seat, he proceeded, through Ramnad and Pondicherry, to Madras, in order to launch forthwith his plan of action. In this great city of the South, teeming with intellectual and energetic people, the Swami announced his resolution of carrying a mission to the West.

About four months earlier, he had heard of the Parliament of Religions to be held in 1893 at Chicago, U.S.A., in connection with the World's Fair. It was before this august assembly of the chosen representatives of different religions that he desired to unburden his soul. He was firm in his conviction that, if the Hindus were to rise to the heights of glory, Hinduism must become aggressive. He thought that he was duty-bound to place before the world the spiritual treasures of Hindu India, lying hidden in caves and forests, temples and religious seminaries since the heyday of Buddhist and Hindu evangelism. He was, moreover, convinced that a free and honourable exchange of ideas and ideals between the East and the West was a desideratum of the age. This would break both the spell of torpor of the conservative masses and the spell of cultural hypnotism of the modern intelligentzia, and inspire both the wings to work for a complete rejuvenation of the land.

Vivekananda's towering personality, vast and varied range of knowledge, great command over English and Sanskrit, unusual powers of repartee, sparkling wit, and, above all, his patriotic fervour and beaming spirituality made a deep and lasting impression in Madras and Hyderabad. His young and enthusiastic disciples went about the cities and collected the necessary money for his journey. He sought for and obtained, through correspondence, the benediction of the Holy Mother before he finally decided to sail for America.

En route to Bombay, he met two of his brother-disciples, Brahmananda and Turiyananda, at the Abu Road station, where he halted for a few days. The Swami's attitude and talks revealed to his brothers the tumultuous emotions that were about to break through the walls of Vivekananda's heart and sweep over the earth in a torrential rush. Addressing Turiyananda he said, 'Hari Bhai, I cannot understand your so-called religion! But my heart has grown very much, and I have learnt to feel (for others). Believe me, I feel it very keenly'. After releasing a fragment of his deep-seated feelings for suffering humanity through these few words, he sat silent for a while, and tears streamed down his cheeks. The brother whom he had addressed said long afterwards to a group of interested listeners, 'Are these not, I thought, the very words and feelings of the Buddha?'

TORRENTIAL RUSH

The Hindus had not been accustomed to sea-voyage for centuries. Their social laws would not permit them to stir out of their land. Vivekananda had to overstep this social barrier right at the start on his chosen path of action. He had also to suppress even the instinctive craving of a Hindu monk for seclusion and for holy places of pilgrimage. Was not the entire world a sacred manifestation of the Divine? Was not man behind all shades of complexion equally holy as an expression of the Lord? With such a universal and deified outlook, and defying the anachronistic and meaningless restrictions of the Hindu society, he left the shores of Bombay on the 31st May, 1893.

He proceeded to America along the Pacific route. What little he had occasion to see of China and Japan convinced him of the existence in both the countries of an undercurrent of spiritual thoughts that had flowed out of India in days long gone by. This made him visualize the glorious days of ancient India.

He landed in Vancouver and thence proceeded straight to Chicago by train. The World's Fair burst before his eyes like a dazzling epitome of western civilization. He felt, admired, and stood stupefied before the glorious grandeur of occidental culture.

The painful contrast of this picture with that of his motherland, filled with poverty and squalor, pierced his tender heart. With a gaping and hidden wound in his heart, he roamed about in the Fair and made necessary inquiries about the Parliament of Religions. He was surprised to hear that none but duly authorized delegates could think of addressing the august assembly, and he was utterly dismayed to learn that the time for enrolling new delegates had already expired. Cold waves of depression benumbed the disillusioned monk. However, he pulled himself up quickly, gave up the idea of speaking in the Parliament, and turned his mind to see as much of the country as he could afford to do.

Victimized by sharks almost at every step of his journey, he had come to the end of his resources. Moreover, he had not provided himself adequately against the severities of the approaching winter. Hearing that living was comparatively cheap in Boston, he started immediately for that city. In the railway train, luckily, he met an American lady, who, with overwhelming sympathy, invited him to her house in Boston and introduced him later to Professor Wright of the Harvard University. The professor was so much impressed by the Swami's talk that he furnished the Swami forthwith with a very strong letter of introduction to one of his friends, who happened to be the chairman of the committee for selecting delegates for the Parliament. The tone of the letter can be felt through the following sentence, 'Here is a man who is more learned than all our learned professors put together'. Armed with this letter and encouraged by a reviving hope, the Swami went back to Chicago. He went about the city in search of his destination. After a weary and fruitless endeavour, he sat down exhausted in the street, when a generous lady from the opposite house stepped out, almost like a godsend, and proceeded to help him out of his difficulty. With her help, he got himself enrolled, without delay, as a delegate for the Parliament of Religions and lodged with the other oriental delegates.

The Parliament of Religions commenced its first session on the 11th September, 1893. The Swami's majestic appearance, expressive of a virile manhood, combined with his strikingly attractive apparel, made him conspicuous among the oriental delegates. He waited till the end of the day to take the last turn of making a short speech by way of announcing himself before the great assembly. He opened his lips to accost the audience endearingly as 'sisters and brothers of America', and he was overwhelmed by deafening cheers from all corners of the hall. Silence followed, and Vivekananda poured out his heart. Bereft of cold formalities, rigid dogmas, and hollow, stilted, or illusive phraseology, his artless and spontaneous speech proceeded from the fullness of his heart, and verily 'he spake like one in authority'. The surging stream of spirituality, of endless love for God and deified humanity, of universal faith in all religions—the stream that had had its birth on the snow-capped heights of the heavenly life of Ramakrishna and had descended to the immaculate heart of his chosen disciple—suddenly broke through all barriers and gushed out in a torrential rush of apostolic love and wisdom. The house was flooded by waves of spirituality.

Before the final session of the Parliament on the 27th September, he delivered ten or twelve speeches, through which he acquainted the house with the lofty ideas and ideals connected with various aspects of Hinduism, and also with his central theme of universal Religion based on the findings of the Vedic seers. In the inspired utterance with which he concluded his address at the final session, one sees a revelation of the spirit of Ramakrishna, and gets the key-note of Vivekananda's message to the West. He declared with all the emphasis that he could command: 'The Christian is not to become a Hindu or a Buddhist, nor a Hindu or a Buddhist to become a Christian. But each must assimilate the spirit of the others and yet preserve his individuality and grow according to his own law of growth.

If the Parliament of Religions has shown anything to the world, it is this: It has proved to the world that holiness, purity, and charity are not the exclusive possessions of any Church in the world, and that every system has produced men and women of the most exalted character. In the face of this evidence, if anybody dreams of the exclusive survival of his own religion and the destruction of the others, I pity him from the bottom of my heart, and point out to him that upon the banner of every religion will soon be written, in spite of his resistance: "Help and not Fight", "Assimilation and not Destruction", "Harmony and Peace and not Dissension".'

His clear and impressive exposition, combined with his all-embracing love and prophetic vision, elicited from the American press a chorus of admiring and reverential applause. *The New York Herald* frankly announced him as 'undoubtedly the greatest figure in the Parliament of Religions', and added: 'After hearing him, we feel how foolish it is to send missionaries to this learned nation.'

The doors of the rich, the learned, and the religiously disposed were flung open to him, and he was overwhelmed by the reverential courtesy and luxurious hospitality of his admiring hosts. His days were spent in talks and discourses in parlours and public places, and in keeping hundreds of engagements with interested people who would flock to him from different quarters.

For a time, he placed himself under a Lecture Bureau and toured through a number of important cities including Chicago, St. Louis, Detroit, Boston, Washington, and New York. At Boston, he courted the displeasure of the audience by his scathing criticism of certain aspects of western life. Vivekananda's plain-speaking, instead of being an eye-opener, wounded the national vanity of his Boston audience, irritated for a while the press, and gave a handle to jealous partisans bent upon mischief. The Swami, however, remained unperturbed, paid no heed to the reactionary wave of indignation, and looked with compassion upon the agents of mischief.

At Detroit, he broke away from the Lecture Bureau and proceeded independently on his lecturing tour through a number of cities. Ultimately, he settled in New York with a band of earnest souls around him and held with them regular classes on Jñāna-yoga and Rāja-yoga, that is, a system of Hindu metaphysics and Hindu science of practical religion. Of the devoted American followers who remained faithful to him up to the end of their lives, mention may be made of the following Miss Greenstidel (afterwards Sister Christine), Miss S. E. Waldo (afterwards Sister Haridasi), Mr. and Mrs. Leggett, Mrs. Ole Bull, and Miss Josephine Macleod. In New York, his first course lasted from February to June 1895; and about this time, he had finished dictating to Miss S. E. Waldo his illuminating treatise *Rāja-yoga,* which was valued as much by scholars, like the American philosopher William James, as by spiritual aspirants, like Count Leo Tolstoy of Russia.

In the summer of 1895, the Swami retired, with nearly twelve devoted disciples, to a quiet hill-retreat, the Thousand Island Park, on the bank of the River St. Lawrence. It was here that he converted his philosophical seminar into a full-fledged hermitage and initiated his disciples into the discipline of *āśrama* life by way of a temporary experiment. Each day the Swami's 'inspired talks' opened a new vista of noble thoughts and sentiments, and his closer spiritual contact went to chasten and exalt the lives of the earnest group of spiritual aspirants. It was here that he released before his disciples his thoughts and sentiments about his Master, Ramakrishna.

In September 1895, he went over to England, via Paris, for a change on grounds of health ; but, instead of taking rest, he worked hard for his mission. During his short stay in England, the Swami's magnetic personality and illuminating discourses made a great impression upon many and won the esteem even of learned and aristocratic circles.

Towards the end of 1895, he returned to America for a brief sojourn of about three months. Besides conducting his regular classes in New York, he went through a whirlwind course of lectures before learned audiences, like the Metaphysical Society of Hartford, the Ethical Society of Brooklyn, and the Philosophical Seminar of Harvard, as well as before the general public in various places in New York, Boston, and Detroit. About this time, a young Englishman, J. J. Goodwin, dedicated his life entirely to the Swami's service. It was the devoted application of this idealistic stenographer that went to preserve the later lectures of Vivekananda. In February 1896, he introduced Ramakrishna to the New York public through his brilliant discourse on 'My Master'. The most important business of the Swami during this period was the consolidation of his American work by organizing the Vedanta Society of New York under Francis Leggett as its President.

Thus placing his mission in America on a permanent footing, and writing to one of his brother-disciples, Saradananda, to come and take charge of the New York centre, he left for London by the middle of April 1896. Saradananda, who had already arrived in London, took necessary instruction from the Swami and proceeded to New York by the end of June. The Swami again applied himself vigorously to do some solid work in England through public lectures as well as through regular classes on Vedānta philosophy. This time he became intimate with the old and venerable Indologist of Oxford, Max Müller, and attracted a band of staunch followers, like Miss Margaret E. Noble (later Sister Nivedita), Mr. and Mrs. Sevier, and Miss Henrietta F. Müller. With the Seviers he spent about a couple of months on the Continent. The Swami stayed for a while in the bracing climate of Switzerland, in order to refresh his tired nerves, went to Germany to meet, on invitation, Paul Deussen, the great Vedāntic philosopher of Europe, and then returned to England, visiting Holland on the way. The sublime Alpine scenery of Switzerland suggested to the Swami the idea of establishing on the heights of the Himalayas a monastery where his eastern and western disciples might find a suitable place for union. The Seviers took up the idea and made it their life-work to give it a practical shape. By the end of December 1896, the Swami left the shores of England, made a short stay in Italy, and then proceeded to India. The Seviers accompanied him to spend the rest of their lives in India, devoting themselves exclusively to spiritual practice as well as to work out the Swami's idea about the Himalayan monastery.

REVITALIZING THE RELIGIONS

Thus, Vivekananda spent more than three years of the best part of his life in America and Europe. He acquainted his western audience with the faith of the Hindus rooted in the oldest of scriptures, the Vedas; he told them about the impersonal character of its teachings, its universal message of unbounded catholicism, its presentation of various readings of Divinity, monistic, qualified-monistic, and dualistic, and also about various kinds of religious practice grouped under four fundamental types, namely, Jñāna-yoga, Rāja-yoga, Bhakti-yoga, and Karma-yoga, covering the entire range of human tastes, temperaments, and capacities. He explained to them the doctrine of Karma and rebirth, and enlightened them on the Hindu idea of salvation through the realization of one's identity with the Absolute. Then, by his rational exposition, he showed how the Hindu view of religion could stand the severest scrutiny of reason and exist in perfect amity with the findings of science. Above all, he laid special emphasis on the fact that the broad and liberal message of Vedānta contained the science of all religions that might enable the world to realize the essential unity underlying all religions and to stand united on the magnificent pedestal of universal Religion. He showed how the findings of the Upaniṣadic seers regarding the fundamental verities of life and existence were perfectly non-denominational in their character, and these could be assimilated by all sections of humanity, in order to secure their faith in their respective creeds against the aggressions of critical reason and also to liberalize their outlook on all other religions.

The Swami's definition of religion as 'the manifestation of the

Divinity that is already in man' went surely to clear a mass of prejudice against religion. According to him, religion is a growth from within till one reaches the last stage of human evolution, when the individual realizes within his own self all his dreams of perfection and absolute freedom, and discovers the kingdom of heaven that has been lying all the time within the heart. Since evolution presupposes involution, the evolving man must have within himself the potentiality of perfection, which he is trying to manifest, consciously or unconsciously, through all his thoughts and endeavours. When man conquers his inner nature, he becomes perfect and finds God, the ever-free Master of nature, the living ideal of perfection and absolute freedom, as the essence of his own being. When one attains such a state, he is said to be religious. Hence did the Swami say: 'Religion is neither in books, nor in intellectual consent, nor in reason. Reason, theories, documents, doctrines, books, religious ceremonies are all helps to religion; religion itself consists in realization.' Thus, instead of laying stress merely on authority, tradition, and dogmas, instead of clouding the issue with supernaturalism, instead of making any peremptory demand on the credulity of people regarding things and ideas unwarranted by scientific knowledge and positivistic common sense, the Swami presented religion as a perfectly 'natural and normal element of human life'.

Then the Swami pointed out that religion is not only a natural and normal element, but also a universal phenomenon of human life. He observed that the craving for perfection, for infinite life, bliss, and knowledge, is a deep-rooted instinct of man. This was why the Swami announced: 'It is my belief that religious thought is in man's very constitution, so much so that it is impossible for him to give up religion until he can give up his mind and body, until he can give up thought and life.'

Besides being a natural, universal, healthy, and ennobling function, religion was declared by the Swami to be the source of the highest kind of happiness. The lower types of humanity in all nations find pleasure in the senses, while the cultured and the educated find it in thought and philosophy, in the arts and the sciences. Spirituality is a still higher plane. The subject being infinite, that plane is the highest, and the pleasure there is the highest for those who can appreciate it.

Yet the Swami was not a believer in the valuation of religion on the grounds of utility; he taught that religion as a laudable quest for eternal truth was its own reward, and he challenged the utilitarian assessor: 'What right has a person to ask that truth should be judged by the standard of utility or money? Suppose there is no utility, will it be less true? Utility is not the test of truth.' He went farther to declare that it was not only the individual, but the entire society in its collective existence that was benefited by religion, because religion appeared to be the most potent and salutary force for sustaining the very life of a social group. The Swami declared emphatically: 'Of all the forces that have worked and are still working to mould the destinies of the human race, none certainly is more potent than that the manifestation of which we call religion. No other ideal can put into us the same mass of energy as the spiritual. I do not deny that men, on simply utilitarian grounds, can be very good and moral. . . . But the world-movers, men who bring, as it were, a mass of magnetism into the world, whose spirit works in hundreds and in thousands, whose life ignites others with a spiritual fire, such men, we always find, have that spiritual background. Their motive power came from religion. In building up character, in making for everything that is good and great, in bringing peace to others, and peace to one's own self, religion is the highest motive power, and therefore ought to be studied from that standpoint.'

The Swami was emphatic in his assertion that the value of the life of an individual or a society was to be assessed on its spiritual progress, and not merely on its material possessions or intellectual attainments. Hence culture of the cardinal virtues, namely, purity, devotion, humility, sincerity, selflessness, and love—all that contribute to spiritual progress—should claim our attention more than anything else on earth. He assured his western audience that this outlook, instead of standing in the way of material and intellectual advancement, would rather go to improve the condition of the world by eliminating all disruptive and disintegrating forces, all clashes and conflicts arising out of the present leaning towards the negation of the nobler traits of human nature.

While proclaiming the supreme necessity of religion for the progress of civilization, the Swami was not blind to the historical data regarding the untold sufferings that had been brought upon human society by fanatics in the name of religion. The Swami, however, pointed out that religion was not to blame for the misdeeds carried out in its name. Religious intolerance and fight proceeded, like all other conflicts, from ignorance, vanity, selfishness, and brutality ingrained in the baser nature of man.

The Swami made it clear that quarrels between different religions arose from over-emphasis on 'secondary details', and that there was unanimity regarding the fundamental aim and scope of religion, which he laid down briefly and pointedly in the following words: 'The aim is to get rid of nature's control over us. That is the goal of all religions. Each soul is potentially divine. The goal is to manifest this Divinity within, by controlling nature, external and internal. Do this either by work (Karma-yoga), or worship (Bhakti-yoga), or psychic control (Rāja-yoga), or philosophy (Jñāna-yoga), by one or more or all of these—and be free. This is the whole of religion. Doctrines, or dogmas, or rituals, or books, or temples, or forms are but secondary details.' He drew the attention of all to the fact that the great religions of the world were of one opinion, so far as belief in the existence of God, potential divinity of the soul, and possibility of salvation through transcendental experience of God were concerned. All great religions derive their origin and validity from the realizations of one or more seers of outstanding personality. All of them owe allegiance to certain books as their scriptures, and while urging mankind to attain freedom through the knowledge of God, all of them prescribe certain forms and symbols, glorification of names of God, and worship of holy personages as aids to spiritual growth. Said the Swami: 'The language of the soul is one, the languages of the nations are many; their customs and methods of life are wholly different. Religion is of the soul, and finds expressions through various nations, languages, and customs. Hence it follows that the difference between the religions of the world is one of expression and not of substance; and their points of similarity and unity are of the soul. intrinsic. The same sweet harmony is vibrant there also, as it is on many and diverse instruments.'

The Swami pointed out that, while philosophy was the substantial core, the central theme, the very soul of every religion, mythology and rituals were only its outer sheath, 'secondary details', mere expressions, and that there was no reason for claiming these secondary details to be invariable components of religion. The Swami pointed out that it was owing to this mistaken attitude towards the externals of religion that different sects and communities fought with one another.

The Swami, however, said: 'External helps and methods, forms, ceremonies, creeds, doctrines, all have their right place, and are meant to support and strengthen us until we become strong. Then they are no more necessary. They are our nurse and as such indispensable in youth.'

He explained, moreover, that religion had evolved a multitude of creeds on the same fundamentals, in order to suit the different temperaments of distinct groups of people. Variety of faiths has enriched the world and made religion accessible, comprehensible, and practicable to all men. The Swami said: 'You cannot make all conform to the same ideas; that is a fact, and I thank God that it is so. . . . It is the clash of thought, the differentiation of thought, that awakes thought. So I want sects to multiply in every country, that more people may have a chance to be spiritual.'

The fundamental elements of all religions, divested of all special names, forms, and local colour, were conceived by the Swami to be the universal Religion: 'It must be one which will have no location in place or time; which will be infinite, like the God it will preach, and whose sun will shine upon the followers of Kṛṣṇa and of Christ, on saints and sinners alike; which will not be Brāhmaṇic or Buddhistic, Christian or Mohammedan, but the sum total of all these, and still have infinite space for development; which in its catholicity will embrace in its infinite arms, and find a place for, every human being.'

Finally, in order to convince the world of the feasibility of conceiving and practising the universal Religion, the Swami, in a mood of apostolic fervour, proclaimed his own burning faith through the epoch-making utterance: 'I accept all religions that were in the past and worship them all. I worship God with everyone of them, in whatever form they worship Him. I shall go to the mosque of a Mohammedan; I shall enter the Christian's church and kneel before the Crucifix; I shall enter the Buddhistic temple, where I shall take refuge in Buddha and his Law. I shall go into the forest and sit down in meditation with the Hindu, who is trying to see the light which enlightens the heart of everyone. Not only shall I do all these, but I shall keep my heart open for all that may come in the future. . . . The Bible, the Vedas, the Koran, and all other sacred books are so many pages, and an infinite number of pages remain yet to be unfolded. I would leave it (my heart) open for all of them.'

Thus, through his rational exposition of the necessity and essentials of religion, and through his elucidation of the grand concept of universal Religion, the Swami applied the spiritual message of Vedic India, which had been reaffirmed by Ramakrishna's and his own realizations, for vitalizing all the different religions of the world and enabling them to hold their ground before the crusades of scientific findings and critical reason.

AWAKENING THE MOTHERLAND

Swami Vivekananda, with his devoted followers, Mr. and Mrs. Sevier and Mr. Goodwin, landed at Colombo on the 15th January, 1897; and after visiting a few places in Ceylon, the Swami proceeded through Rameswaram, Ramnad. Madura, and Madras to Calcutta. From the second week of May till the end of the year, he made an extensive tour in northern India through Uttar Pradesh, Punjab, Kashmir, and Rajasthan; and wherever he went, he broadcasted through his animating talks and discourses whatever he had to say about the much-needed salvation of his beloved motherland. Before sailing again for America in June 1899, he made another tour in the northern provinces and went on pilgrimage to the holy shrines of Amaranātha and Kṣīrabhavānī in Kashmir. He spent nearly two years and a half in India and, during this entire period, in spite of his failing health, he worked breathlessly for propagating his message and organizing the corps of his standard-bearers.

His spirit of universalism had appealed very strongly to the imagination of the western races, who had hailed him as the 'cyclonic monk of India' and discerned in him the likeness of Buddha and Christ. This unqualified appreciation of the Swami by the progressive people of the West certainly flattered the vanity of his countrymen. They saw in him a redeemer of India's honour. Very naturally, the 'cyclonic monk of India' was hailed by his countrymen as the 'patriot saint of India'. In him, they discovered not only the fulfilment of their human aspirations after perfection, but also a redoubtable champion of the sacred cause of their motherland, whose bright past had been totally eclipsed by the gloomy present.

The helpless condition of the unlettered, poverty-stricken, and down-trodden masses, unrelieved by the sympathy of the rich and the enlightened ; the travesty of the lofty ideals of the Vedic religion at the hands of the pharisaical leaders of orthodox society, forging reprehensible formulas of untouchability in the name of religion and dehumanizing the dumb millions by the obnoxious pressure of social iniquities ; the abominable self-forgetfulness of the enlightened liberals and their reckless and alarming strides towards westernism in thought and manners ; the rapid disintegration of the Hindu society into innumerable fighting sects of fundamentalists and an ever-swelling rank of educated heretics—all these had been oppressing the tender and patriotic heart of Vivekananda as long as he stayed with the methodical, progressive, organized, virile, and prosperous races of Europe and America. In order to stimulate the patriotic as well as religious sentiments of the Indians and to direct these on right lines, he had already worked up the enthusiasm of a group of followers to start an English journal and publish it regularly from Madras. Thus, in spite of all his preoccupations in the West, the Swami's keen solicitude for the well-being of India had been almost the central theme of his thoughts and feelings as long as he had been away from his country. And, as soon as he touched the soil of India, all the pent-up feelings of his heart for his beloved country surged up tumultuously. From one end of India to the other, from Colombo to Almora, Swami Vivekananda, like a veritable 'lion of Vedānta' roared to rouse the 'sleeping leviathan'.

Through his teachings, the Indians felt the thrilling touch of their mighty and glorious past ; they realized the potency of their age-old culture, the stupendous strength, the sublimity, as well as the utility of the spiritual lore handed down to them by their forefathers, the *ṛṣis* of old. Then, again, in the light of his teachings, his countrymen could measure accurately the depth of their present degradation ; they saw clearly how their physical deterioration, inertia, and lethargy, their lack of manliness, self-help, seriousness, spirit of obedience, practicality, and organizing capacity, and, above all, their awful dearth of love, generous feelings, and cultural integrity had reduced them to a very miserable sample of humanity. With the same breath, the Swami made them discover the infinite potentialities that still lay hidden in the depth of their hearts beneath the superficial film of filth and degradation, and they were made to visualize the bright and glorious days of a thoroughly rejuvenated future India.

He asked them to be bold enough to admit their own mistakes and try seriously to correct them. He asked his Hindu brethren to realize the fact that just as individuals reap the fruits of their own actions, so also does the entire society. Forgetting the broad and humanistic teachings of the Vedic seers, losing gradually the spark of spiritual life, and consequently setting a premium on the externals of religion and on a strange and unworthy class-consciousness for maintaining and asserting with vengeance their fictitious superiority, the mediaeval leaders of the Hindu society had stooped to fetter the people with rigid and invidious laws. During this period, the Vedic religion, the epitome of catholicism, came to be almost synonymous with a hot-bed of untouchability, sectarian hatred, and social tyranny. The foreigners came to be branded as *mlecchas* and *yavanas*; severe strictures were passed against sea-voyage; reprehensible excesses of caste-prejudices were encouraged in the name of religion; invidious barriers were raised within the Hindu fold; and acute sect-consciousness came to be the ruling idea of religious life, and divided the society into innumerable hostile camps. All these, surely, went to disintegrate the Hindus, and disabled them from thinking of uniting with the other religious communities within the land. Thus Hinduism, which could very well boast of furnishing the whole world with lofty ideas, ideals, and incentives for establishing universal brotherhood, came to be, by an irony of fate, an appalling zone of disintegrating forces.

The Swami emphasized the fact that, if the Hindus could again live up to the lofty ideals of their own original scriptures, the Vedānta, they might pull down all barriers that divided man from man, and, by this process, they might develop a gigantic power of cohesion that could integrate all the various Indian sects and communities into one mighty nation. The Swami, moreover, pointed out that the Vedāntic ideas about the divinity of the soul and the oneness of the universe, and of consequent 'fearlessness', would go not only to unite the people of India by harmonizing all differences, but they would also infuse enormous strength into the nation and raise it from the slough of lethargy and despair.

Addressing particularly his enlightened co-religionists, who, under the hypnotic spell of western culture, had become blind to the potency and efficacy of their own religious ideas, the Swami explained clearly why renaissance of Hinduism through the revival of the Vedāntic thoughts should be placed on the forefront of any programme for national reconstruction. The Swami said: 'I see that each nation, like each individual, has one theme in this life, which is its centre, the principal note round which every other note comes to form the harmony. In one nation, political power is its vitality, as in England. Artistic life in another, and so on. In India, religious life forms the centre, the key-note of the whole music of national life; and if any nation attempts to throw off its national vitality, the direction which has become its own through the transmission of centuries, that nation dies, if it succeeds in the attempt. And therefore, if you succeed in the attempt to throw off your religion and take up either politics or society, or any other thing as your centre, as the vitality of your national life, the result will be that you will be extinct. To prevent this, you must make all and everything work through that vitality of your religion.'

Thus, he pointed out that the choice of the Hindus of old in making spirituality the basis of their entire civilization, the mainspring of their social, economic, and political life, was the greatest achievement of the genius of their race. It was this choice that had enabled the Hindus to survive so many social and political cataclysms and, even after a lapse of thousands of years, to retain their racial individuality. The Swami tried to disillusion his westernized countrymen, who looked at the Indian problems and their solution through imported glasses of politics and radical social reform, by scanning the errors of the dominant races of the world and the jeopardized state of their society: 'The political systems that we are struggling for in India have been in Europe for ages, have been tried for centuries, and have been found wanting. One after another, the institutions, systems, and everything connected with political government have been condemned as useless, and Europe is restless, does not know where to turn. . . . Europe, the centre of the manifestation of material energy, will crumble into dust within fifty years, if she is not mindful to change her position, to shift her ground and make spirituality the basis of her life.' Almost like a prophet of the age, Vivekananda declared that even the latest movements of socialism or communism would never be able to achieve their goal until and unless they took their stand on spiritual ideals.

He laid before his countrymen practical formulas of social service deduced from the fundamental teachings of the Vedānta. 'God is here before you in various forms,' said the Swami, 'he who loves His creatures serves God.' He enjoined on the privileged classes to feel intensely for the misery of the teeming millions and to serve them with all the devotion, sacrifice, and reverence due to deified humanity. The Swami's piercing words are still ringing in one's ears: 'I consider that the great national sin is the neglect of the masses, and that is one of the causes of our downfall. No amount of politics would be of any avail until the masses in India are once more well educated, well fed, and well cared for. They pay for our education, they build our temples, but in return they get kicks. They are practically our slaves. If we want to regenerate India, we must work for them.' 'So long as the millions live in hunger and ignorance, I hold every man a traitor who, having been educated at their expense, pays not the least heed to them!' Thus did the Swami make the classes conscious of their duties towards the masses.

The sunken vitality of the helpless victims of social tyranny was to be restored by providing them with life-giving food, physical, intellectual, as well as spiritual. Once this was done, once the downtrodden section of the society could recover their lost vigour, physical as well as mental, they would become efficient enough to evolve new social laws, new institutions suited to the pressing requirements of the modern age. Thus, in the field of social reform, he preferred the process of evolution to that of revolution. He encouraged neither drastic reform from above nor fight from below; both were ruinous. The former would convulse the cultural ideals, and the latter would force the ebbing life out of the social body. The society was to be led gently to realize its own errors and made strong enough to eliminate by a healthy, natural, and evolutionary process all that would appear to it to be prejudicial to its progress. And he said to his people: 'Meddle not with so-called social reform, for there cannot be any reform without spiritual reform first.'

He believed that the untold sufferings of the weak, the miserable, the downtrodden of all races could be mitigated only by the application, on a world-wide scale, of the Vedāntic ideas, such as the divinity of the soul and oneness of the universe. But the world cannot possibly accept the Vedāntic findings for readjusting its affairs before it finds convincing proofs of their worth in Indian life. Hence, he was convinced that the path of the redemption of the world lay in the redemption of India through the potency of her Vedāntic culture. A practical demonstration of this potency by the Hindu society would automatically set the world moving towards a thorough overhauling of its modern civilization in the light of the Vedāntic teachings. He pointed out to his countrymen that this was precisely the mission, to fulfil which India had outlived centuries of oppression and vandalism. With her gospel of universal love for deified humanity, she would help the entire mankind to advance surely and steadily in a really progressive career. Such being his reading of the holy and lofty mission of his motherland, the Swami exhorted his countrymen to remember, even while they were engaged in building up their own nation, the central fact that they were required to stand for universal peace and harmony and to extend their unqualified love and service to all parts of the world for all time to come.

CONSOLIDATING HIS MISSION

Besides touring over the length and breadth of India and broadcasting his life-giving message everywhere, Swami Vivekananda thought it absolutely necessary to start a permanent organization that might establish real man-making institutions in India and abroad for turning out individuals who would live up to the lofty spiritual ideals and dedicate their lives for the uplift of humanity. Naturally, he conceived that this organization must be monastic in its basic structure, and that, instead of being exclusive and individualistic in its spiritual aspirations like the traditional monastic orders, it must work in co-operation with the high-souled and interested public for the much-needed service of mankind, without discriminating between creeds and colours.

At the earliest opportunity after his return from America, he approached his brother-disciples, who had meanwhile shifted the Baranagore monastery to a neighbouring place called Alambazar, and mooted his ideas before them. He convinced them, though with a little initial difficulty, that the ideas were not entirely his own, that these really came from the Master, Ramakrishna himself. Thus, he persuaded his brother-disciples, who had meanwhile developed into robust spiritual stalwarts, to see through his eyes the import and significance of Ramakrishna's life and teachings, and induced them in this way to incorporate the ideal of serving suffering humanity as a manifestation of Divinity within the scheme of their monastic organization. He made them conscious of the fact that they were required by the Master to evolve an altogether new order of monks combining all the spiritual methods of *jñāna, bhakti, yoga,* and *karma,* of which Ramakrishna's life was a perfect and glorious epitome. Through meditation they were to realize God in the depth of their own existence, and through service they were to realize the selfsame God, the Virāj, in the entire universe. Individual salvation and service of deified humanity were to be blended harmoniously to form the motto of the new order of monks (*Ātmano mokṣārthaṁ jagaddhitāya ca*).

With his spiritual brothers and all the lay disciples of Ramakrishna, the Swami laid the foundation of a corporate body, named the Ramakrishna Mission, on the 1st May, 1897. This Mission was to train monastic workers to live up to and propagate the Vedāntic religion in the light of Ramakrishna's life and teachings, establish fellowship among the followers of different religions, and serve suffering humanity without making any distinction of caste, creed, or community.

With money contributed by his devoted English admirer, Miss Henrietta F. Müller, and by his American follower, Mrs. Ole Bull, the Swami purchased lands at Belur on the opposite bank of the Gaṅgā about five miles up Calcutta, built up a monastery there, and endowed it with a permanent fund, thereby providing his organization with a home of its own. Thus, in January 1899, the Belur Math (monastery) was established, and it was to serve as the headquarters of the Ramakrishna Order of monks, its principal centre of monastic training, and the place from which were to be started, guided, and regulated branch Maths in different parts of India and foreign countries. And the Belur Math, naturally, came to be also the *de facto* headquarters of all missionary and philanthropic activities of the Ramakrishna Mission organization. After his return from his second tour in the West, in 1901, the Swami imparted to his monastic organization a legal status through a deed of trust, and made his brother-disciple Swami Brahmananda, pre-eminently the fittest of them all on account of his towering spiritual personality and outstanding organizing capacity, the first President of the Trustees. Swami Saradananda, the capable, cool-headed, and infinitely patient apostle, was replaced by the vastly erudite Swami Abhedananda in the New York centre, and the former was entrusted with the charge of helping Swami Brahmananda in the task of organizing all the different activities of the Order.

Swami Premananda, one of the prominent apostles conspicuous for his spotless purity and unbounded love, was entrusted with the task of managing the affairs of the Belur monastery. Meanwhile, a few ardent young souls had been admitted into the Order. In 1898, some of the western followers of the Swami, including Sister Nivedita, came over to India, and all these novices were placed under systematic and necessary spiritual training. Swami Ramakrishnananda, the peerlessly steadfast devotee of Ramakrishna who had stuck to the monastery from its very inception after the Master's departure, was sent to start a centre at Madras as early as March 1897. Towards the middle of the same year, another brother-disciple and highly advanced spiritual soul, Swami Sivananda, was despatched to preach the message of the Master in Ceylon. And in February 1899, two other brother-disciples were sent over to Gujarat. Besides sending out monks for missionary work, the Swami stirred up the enthusiasm of his spiritual brothers and disciples for carrying on relief work among people distressed by famines or epidemics at various places in Bengal and Bihar. Swami Akhandananda went over to relieve the famine-stricken people of Murshidabad and eventually opened there, in 1899, the first permanent home of service of the Ramakrishna Mission. In March of the same year, Vivekananda, with the help of Mr. and Mrs. Sevier's energy and resources, realized his desire for a cosmopolitan Himalayan monastery by establishing the Advaita Ashrama at Mayavati, in the District of Almora. A few months later, the monthly English journal *Prabuddha Bharata* (Awakened India) was transferred from Madras to Mayavati, and was placed under the management of Mr. Sevier and the editorship of one of the Swami's ablest Indian disciples, Swami Swarupananda. And, in the beginning of the same year, a monthly Bengali journal, *Udbodhan,* had been started and published from Calcutta under the able editorship of Swami Trigunatitananda.

Thus, through Sri Ramakrishna's inspiration and Swami Vivekananda's one-pointed devotion, a monastic organization, with an absolutely new spiritual outlook suited to the requirements of the age, was ushered into existence.

On the 20th June, 1899, the Swami set out on another journey to the West, where, this time, he spent nearly a year and a half. He induced one of his great brother-disciples, Swami Turiyananda, to accompany him, as he wanted to place before his American followers a living example of the well-disciplined life of a Vedāntic monk of India. Vivekananda proceeded through London and New York to the Pacific coast of the United States. Here also, as in the States of the east, centre, and middle west, where he had concentrated his activities during his previous visit to the country, the people became exceedingly interested in his teachings, and several Vedānta centres were started, the prominent among which was the one at San Francisco. Leaving this centre as also the neighbouring ones under the care of Swami Turiyananda, and finding his New York Vedanta Society safe in the able hands of Swami Abhedananda, he left America, in July 1900, to attend the Congress of the History of Religions in Paris.

He spent nearly three months in France and attended the Congress. Leaving Paris towards the end of October, he visited some of the prominent States of Central Europe and then proceeded through Egypt to India, reaching the Belur monastery on the 9th December, 1900.

A few days after his return, in January 1901, he paid a short visit to the Advaita Ashrama at Mayavati, and after a few months made a public tour in some of the districts of East Bengal and Assam. Towards the end of the year, Rev. Oda, a learned Buddhist abbot of a Japanese monastery, together with a companion, Mr. Okakura, came all the way from Japan to invite the Swami to attend a religious congress to be held in their country. With Mr. Okakura, he went on a pilgrimage to Bodh-Gaya, and thence he went to Banaras. This journey was undertaken, in spite of his bad health, in the earlier months of 1902. At Banaras, he inspired a band of enthusiastic young men to serve the diseased and the helpless, which led this group eventually to build up there the Home of Service (Sevashrama) under the auspices of the Ramakrishna Mission.

Thus, after spreading the message of his beloved Master in India, Europe, and America, and consolidating his mission by organizing the Ramakrishna Order of monks, inspiring it with his ideas and ideals, and placing it on a permanent and secure basis, Swami Vivekananda passed away on the 4th July, 1902, at the premature age of thirty-nine. Within such a brief span of life, the Indian Prometheus of our age, unlike the classical hero, did bring down the celestial fire at God's own command, and utilize it in bringing about a new order of things—in building up a new world where science was to shake hands with religion, different faiths were to stand united on the same pedestal of universal Religion, the down-trodden masses were to be released from age-old oppressions, human civilization was to be secured firmly on a spiritual basis, and the entire human race was to get a fresh lease of healthy and useful life and march triumphantly in a really progressive career under the banner of 'renunciation and service—universal love, peace, and harmony'.

IV. GLIMMERINGS OF A NEW DAWN

After the Swami passed away, the Ramakrishna Order of monks, under the benign spiritual aegis of the Holy Mother and the able steering of Swami Brahmananda, with the substantial co-operation of his brother-disciples, went on growing in bulk by admitting new members to the Order and extending its missionary and philanthropic activities on the lines chalked out by the departed leader.

THE RAMAKRISHNA MATH AND MISSION

In course of time, with the broadening of its scope of public work and consequent increase of its responsibilities, the organization had to split itself formally into two distinct bodies. For efficient management, as also for the unavoidable exigency of imparting a legal status to the service aspect of the organization, all philanthropic, educational, charitable, and missionary activities were placed under a corporate body and registered formally, in 1909, as 'The Ramakrishna Mission' under Act XXI of 1860 of the Governor-General of India in Council. According to the rules, the Trustees of the Belur Math formed the Governing Body of the Ramakrishna Mission, which also had its headquarters at the Belur Math. Swami

Brahmananda, who had continued to be the President of the Trustees of the Belur Math since 1901, became the first President of the formally registered Ramakrishna Mission. And the grave and onerous function of the first Secretary was carried on with great skill and precision by Swami Saradananda.

The Trustees of the Belur Math, among other things, look after the spiritual training, growth, and consolidation of the Ramakrishna Order of monks, and start, guide, and control branch monasteries as training grounds of the members of the Order at various suitable places; while the Ramakrishna Mission carries on different types of social service work, including temporary relief measures during floods, famines, earthquakes, epidemics, and other such occasional calamities, as well as regular and continuous charitable, missionary, and educational measures through permanent institutions in the shape of hospitals, dispensaries, maternity and child-welfare centres, preaching centres, orphanages, colleges, industrial schools, residential high schools and primary schools both for boys and girls, hostels for school and college students, as well as arrangements for part-time cultural training and peripatetic teaching for the masses. In the course of five decades after the passing away of Swami Vivekananda, the Ramakrishna Order has been able to count its monastic members by hundreds and spread almost a network of branch monasteries (Maths and Ashramas) all over India; while the Ramakrishna Mission has, within this period, carried on relief works on numerous occasions in different parts of the country and established its permanent humanitarian institutions at various places in India (including Pakistan), Burma, Ceylon, the Federated Malaya States, Fiji, and Mauritius; and quite a number of preaching centres have been opened in North America, South America, and Europe. Besides all these, the steadfast devotion of the monks of this Order to the ideal presented by the lives and teachings of Sri Ramakrishna and Swami Vivekananda, and their practice as well as preaching through talks and discourses and through a number of English monthlies, published in India and abroad, and several journals in different vernaculars of this country, have been gradually inspiring people with the spirit of the Master.

RESURGENCE OF HINDU CULTURE

India has passed through a number of successive phases of ebb and flow of her spiritual life, and with each epoch of religious upheaval, there has always been an all-embracing renaissance of her cultural life. It is encouraging to notice that with the resurgence of Hinduism in all its phases, in the wake of Sri Ramakrishna's life, has synchronized a steady cultural revival of the Hindus on all fronts. Sri Ramakrishna passed away in 1886 and Swami Vivekananda in 1902, and the very beginning of the twentieth century is marked unmistakably by a complete recovery of the cultural self-consciousness of the Hindu community, and this is expressing itself through the different activities of its social life.

With Swami Vivekananda's preaching of the universal doctrines of the Vedānta in the western countries, the ancient religion of the Hindus has been released from the stigma of a crude and superstitious creed, and it has positively stepped on to a new phase of evangelism that has been termed 'aggressive Hinduism' by Sister Nivedita. Hinduism has become aggressive not in the sense of seeking converts from any particular fold, but as confirming the faith of all people in their respective Churches by furnishing them with the underlying rationale of all creeds. The Hindus are no longer ashamed of any constituent of their religious faith and philosophy of life. On the other hand, they are found in the rôles of bold exponents of 'the Hindu view of life' even before the universities, scholars, and savants of Europe and America, and many among their western audience are found to be really interested in the hoary culture of the Hindus.

The Hindus are naturally becoming fired with a remarkable zeal for unearthing the buried past and arriving at correct findings regarding the ancient and mediaeval history of India. A band of brilliant historians and archaeologists has come up from Indian universities and set itself seriously to construct this important and necessary plank of nation-building. One remembers how Swami Vivekananda, while at Alwar in the early nineties of the last century, felt intensely the need of an Indian school of historical research, and one surely feels delighted to see how the Swami's wish is being fulfilled by the urge of the national mind.

Though the Indian National Congress was inaugurated in 1885 with the object of bringing about political advancement of the country, it is since the beginning of this century that a strong and genuine feeling for the social, political, and economic well-being of India has seized the nation with a pre-eminent vigour. Social service institutions for the uplift of the masses are being established in different parts of the country not only by the Ramakrishna Mission, but also by various other national organizations; relief works for serving distressed humanity during occasional calamities are also being conducted by different groups of social workers besides the Ramakrishna Mission. Educational institutions co-ordinating the Vedic ideals with modern academic requirements have sprung up under the auspices of several organizations and under the inspiration and guidance of great patriots like Rabindranath Tagore and Madan Mohan Malaviya. Indian patriotism, instead of developing on narrow and parochial lines, appears to become broad-based on a genuine feeling of universal brotherhood. The non-violent creed of Mahatma Gandhi, the universalism of Rabindranath Tagore, and the message of harmony of faiths and inter-racial concord of the followers of Ramakrishna and Vivekananda characterize Indian patriotism by a positively humanistic and spiritual outlook.

The school of oriental arts is a product of this period ; and it is interesting to observe that besides Abanindranath Tagore, the names of Mr. Havell and Sister Nivedita have also to be remembered in connection with the revival of this phase of the cultural life of India. India has discovered her old genius and tradition of the fine arts and taken a resolute stand to revive, develop, and expand them by assimilating the best and conformable elements from the western school.

In the field of letters, India has already made a mark in this century through the precious idealistic contributions of Tagore to the literary treasure-house of the world. Besides, it may be noticed that all the languages within the land, with Bengali as the vanguard, have commenced a progressive career within this period, inaugurating in this way an era of literary renaissance all over the country.

It is particularly within this period that the spirit of scientific research spread over India through the different universities, and some of the scientists of the country, like J. C. Bose and P. C. Ray, M. N. Saha and C. V. Raman, obtained distinctive honour from foreign institutes of science. It is worth noticing that, even in this academic field, the researches of J. C. Bose on the sensation in plant life bear the characteristic hallmark of the ancient Hindu mind. He himself confessed before his western audience that he was demonstrating with modern instruments, and elucidating through modern scientific ideology, a truth about plant life that had been discovered ages ago by the Hindu seers. P. C. Ray's *History of Hindu Chemistry* and B. N. Seal's *Positive Sciences of the Ancient Hindus* show unmistakably how the self-consciousness of the Hindu mind is expressing itself, even in the realm of science, by recovering and holding before the world all that ancient India thought and achieved.

THE OCCIDENT IN THE MELTING POT

Thus, in every branch of thought and activity of Indian life, there has been an appreciable resurgence with the beginning of this century, and through each the cultural self-consciousness of the people has been asserting itself. But, unfortunately, our western brothers and sisters have been, during this period, passing through an ordeal of fire. Forces for equalizing human interests and levelling the status of social and national units have been let loose from the hearts of the depressed and suppressed millions, and these are clashing sharply with the forces on behalf of vested interests and hitherto unhampered avarice and unchallenged superiority. The result has been a disastrous loss of balance within and outside the nations, giving rise to internecine revolutions and fratricidal wars. People, in their confusion, do not realize that it is the spiritually fittest who really survive others—that it is Buddha and Christ who live through centuries and not the merciless wielders of the forces of destruction. Who can say that the western world is not passing through a necessary and transitional phase of sad experience, in order to correct its old mistakes and confusions about human ideals and readjust its society on a broader, healthier, and more exalted basis? Who can assert that the gloomy and ominous present of the occident may not prove to be a prelude to a more glorious future?

PROMISE OF A GLORIOUS FUTURE

H. G. Wells, towards the close of his book, *The Outline of History,* raises one's hopes when he remarks: 'But, out of the trouble and tragedy of these times and the confusion before us, there may emerge a moral and intellectual revival, a religious revival, of a simplicity and scope to draw together men of alien races and now discrete traditions into one common and sustained way of living for the world's service. . . . Religious emotion, stripped of corruptions and freed from its last priestly entanglements, may presently blow through life again like a great wind, bursting the doors and flinging open the shutters of the individual life, and making many things possible and easy that in these present days of exhaustion seem almost too difficult to desire.' The keen intellect of the erudite author perhaps visualized the correct picture of a happy future. But Wells pointed out that such an epoch-making revival was likely to have a very humble beginning and not to come upon the world with the beat of drums. Said he: 'The beginnings of such things are never conspicuous. Great movements of the racial soul come at first "like a thief in the night", and then suddenly are discovered to be powerful and world-wide.'

Anyone, observing with critical eyes the world-wide celebrations in connection with the first birth centenary of Sri Ramakrishna, the prophet of religious federation, social liberty, and inter-racial amity, is apt to think that the benign forces of a really humanistic revival are already at work. In spite of the fact that the outside world knows very little about India, it is an undeniable fact that some of the towering intellectuals of modern Europe, together with hundreds of seekers of truth and peace hailing from almost all the big continents of the world, rallied enthusiastically round the birth centenary of a poor and barely literate Brāhmaṇa priest of the nineteenth century, belonging to an out-of-the-way village of Bengal.

Through this astounding event, one realizes the unmistakable, though humble, onset of the revivalist world-wide movement anticipated by Swami Vivekananda, when he said: 'Once more the wheel is turning up; once more vibrations have been set in motion in India which are destined at no distant date to reach the farthest limits of the earth. Once more the voice has spoken whose echoes are rolling on and gathering strength every day.' The Swami prophesied: 'Before the effulgence of this new awakening, the glory of all past revivals in her history will pale like stars before the rising sun, and compared with this mighty manifestation of renewed strength, all the many past epochs of such restoration will be as child's play. . . . Strong in the strength of this new spiritual renaissance, men, after reorganizing these scattered and disconnected spiritual ideals, will be able to comprehend and practise them in their own lives and also to recover from oblivion those that are lost. . . . So, at the very dawn of this momentous epoch, the reconciliation of all aspects and ideals of religious thought and worship is being proclaimed; this boundless, all-embracing idea had been lying inherent, but so long concealed, in the Religion Eternal (Sanātana Dharma) and its scriptures, and now rediscovered, it is being declared to humanity in a trumpet voice. This new dispensation of the age is the source of great good to the whole world, specially to India; and the inspirer of this dispensation, Sri Bhagavan Ramakrishna, is the reformed and remodelled manifestation of all the past great epoch-makers in religion. O man, have faith in this, and lay it to heart. . . . Of that power, which at the very first impulse has roused distant echoes from all the four quarters of the globe, conceive in your mind the manifestation in its fullness; and discarding all idle misgivings, weaknesses, and the jealousies characteristic of enslaved peoples, come and help in the turning of this mighty wheel of new dispensation.'*

* Abridged by the author from his original article which was published in the first edition (1937) of *The Cultural Heritage of India* and also reprinted in book form by the Ramakrishna Mission Institute of Culture.—Editor

BIBLIOGRAPHY AND INDEX

BIBLIOGRAPHY

GENERAL

ABHEDANANDA, SWAMI, *Attitude of Vedanta towards Religion.* Ramakrishna Vedanta Math, Calcutta, 1947

AIYANGAR, S. K., *Contribution of South India to Indian Culture.* Calcutta University, 1923

AUROBINDO, SRI, *Essays on the Gita.* The Sri Aurobindo Library, New York, 1950

BANERJEA, J. N., *Development of Hindu Iconography.* Calcutta University, 1956

BARNETT, L. D., *Hindu Gods and Heroes.* London, 1922

———, *The Heart of India.* John Murray, London, 1913

BARTH, A., *Religions of India.* Translated by J. Wood. Kegan Paul, Trench, Trubner & Co., London, 1921

BHANDARKAR, R. G., *Vaiṣṇavism, Śaivism, and Minor Religious Systems.* Trubner & Co., Strassburg, 1913

BRAHMA, N. K., *The Philosophy of Hindu Sādhanā.* Kegan Paul, London, 1932

BUHLER, G., *The Laws of Manu.* Sacred Books of the East, XXV. Clarendon Press, Oxford, 1886

CARPENTER, J. E., *Theism in Mediaeval India.* Constable & Co., London, 1926

CHATTERJEE, SATISH CHANDRA, *The Fundamentals of Hinduism : A Philosophical Study.* Das Gupta & Co., Calcutta, 1950

COOMARASWAMY, A. K., *Hinduism and Buddhism.* Philosophical Library, New York

DAS, BHAGAVAN, *Science of Social Organization or the Laws of Manu in the Light of Ātma Vidyā* (3 vols.). Theosophical Publishing House, Adyar, Madras

———, *The Essential Unity of All Religions.* Theosophical Publishing House, Adyar, Madras, 1940

DASGUPTA, SURENDRANATH, *A History of Indian Philosophy* (5 vols.). Cambridge University Press

DESMUKH, P. S., *The Origin and Development of Religion in Vedic Literature.* Oxford University Press, London, 1933

ELLIOT, SIR CHARLES, *Hinduism and Buddhism* (3 vols.). Routledge and Kegan Paul, London, 1954

FARQUHAR, J. N., *An Outline of the Religious Literature of India.* Oxford University Press, London, 1920

GANDHI, M. K., *Hindu Dharma.* Edited by Bharatan Kumarappa. Navajivan Publishing House, Ahmedabad, 1950

GOLDSTUCKER, THEODORE, *Inspired Writings of Hinduism.* Susil Gupta (India) Ltd., Calcutta, 1952

GRIFFITH, R. T. H., *Valmiki Ramayana.* Translation. Trubner & Co., London, 1870

HAIG, H., *Leading Ideals of Hinduism.* Susil Gupta (India) Ltd., Calcutta, 1952

HASTINGS, J. (Ed.), *Encyclopaedia of Religion and Ethics* (13 vols.). T. & T. Clark, Edinburgh

HOPKINS, E. W., *Epic Mythology,* Trubner & Co., Strassburg, 1915

———, *Religions of India.* Ginn, London, 1902

HUME, R. E., *The Thirteen Principal Upanishads.* Oxford University Press, Madras, 1951

JHA, GANGANATH, *Manu-Smṛti.* Translation and notes. Calcutta University, 1920-26

KANE, P. V., *History of Dharma-śāstra* (Vols. I-IV). Bhandarkar Oriental Research Institute, Poona

KARMARKAR, A. P., *Religions of India.* Mira Publishing House, Lonavla, 1950

KEITH, A. B., *The Religion and Philosophy of the Veda and Upanishads* (2 vols.). Harvard Oriental Series. Cambridge (Mass.), 1925

KRAMRISCH, STELLA, *The Hindu Temple.* Calcutta University, 1946

KUMARAPPA, B., *The Hindu Conception of the Deity as Culminating in Rāmānuja.* Luzac & Co., London, 1934

MACDONELL, A. A., *Vedic Mythology.* Trubner & Co., Strassburg, 1897

MACNICOL, N., *Indian Theism.* Oxford University Press, London, 1915

MADHAVANANDA, SWAMI, *Bṛhadāraṇyaka Upaniṣad.* Text with translation of Śaṅkara's commentary. Advaita Ashrama, Calcutta, 1950

MONIER-WILLIAMS, M., *Hinduism.* Susil Gupta (India) Ltd., Calcutta, 1951

———, *Religious Thought and Life in India.* London, 1891

MORGAN, K. W. (Ed.), *The Religion of the Hindus.* Roland Press, New York, 1953

NIKHILANANDA, SWAMI, *Essence of Hinduism.* Ramakrishna-Vivekananda Center, New York, 1946

———, *The Bhagavad-Gītā.* Translated with notes, comments, and introduction. Ramakrishna-Vivekananda Center, New York, 1944

———, *The Upanishads* (2 vols.). Harper & Brothers, New York

NIRVEDANANDA, SWAMI, *Hinduism at a Glance,* Vidyamandira, Dhakuria, 1946

NIVEDITA, SISTER, *Religion and Dharma.* Advaita Ashrama, Calcutta, 1952

RADHAKRISHNAN, S., *Bhagavad-Gītā.* Translation. George Allen & Unwin, London, 1948

———, *East and West in Religion.* George Allen & Unwin, London, 1933

——— (Ed.), *History of Philosophy : Eastern and Western.* Sponsored by the Ministry of Education, Government of India. George Allen & Unwin, London, 1952

———, *Indian Philosophy* (2 vols.). George Allen & Unwin, London, 1948

———, *Principal Upaniṣads.* Edited with introduction, text, translation, and notes. George Allen & Unwin, London, 1953

———, *Religion and Society.* George Allen & Unwin, London, 1947

RADHAKRISHNAN, S., *The Hindu View of Life.* George Allen & Unwin, London, 1936

RAO, T. A. GOPINATH, *Elements of Hindu Iconography.* Madras, 1916

RENOU, LOUIS, *Religions of Ancient India.* Translated by Sheila M. Fynn. London University, The Athlone Press, London, 1953

ROY, P. C., *The Mahabharata* (11 vols.). Translation. Oriental Publishing Co., Calcutta

SASTRI, H. KRISHNA, *South Indian Images of Gods and Goddesses.* Government Press, Madras, 1916

SEN, M. L., *The Ramayana* (3 vols.). Translation. Oriental Publishing Co., Calcutta

SHARVANANDA, SWAMI, *Īśa, Kena, Kaṭha, Praśna, Muṇḍaka, Māṇḍūkya, Taittirīya,* and *Aitareya Upaniṣads.* Text and translation with notes. Sri Ramakrishna Math, Madras

SWARUPANANDA, SWAMI, *Śrīmad Bhagavad-Gītā.* Advaita Ashrama, Calcutta, 1948

TILAK, B. G., *Śrīmad Bhagavadgītā Rahasya or Karma-yoga-śāstra* (2 vols.). Translated by B. S. Sukhthankar. Tilak Brothers, Poona, 1935-36

TYAGISANANDA, SWAMI, *Śvetāśvatara Upaniṣad.* Text and translation with notes. Sri Ramakrishna Math, Madras

VIRESWARANANDA, SWAMI, *Śrīmad Bhagavad-Gītā.* Text with translation of Śrīdhara's gloss. Sri Ramakrishna Math, Madras, 1948

WILKINS, W. J., *Modern Hinduism.* Thacker Spink & Co., Calcutta, 1900

WILSON, H. H., *Essays and Lectures on the Religions of the Hindus* (2 vols.). Edited by R. Rost. Trubner & Co., London, 1861

ŚAIVISM

BARNETT, L. D., *Paramārthasāra of Abhinavagupta.* With Yogarāja's commentary. Translated in *Journal of the Royal Asiatic Society of Great Britain,* 1910

CHATTERJI, J. C., *Kashmir Shaivaism.* The Research Department, Kashmir State, Srinagar, 1914

IYER, C. V. NARAYANA, *The Origin and Early History of Śaivism in South India.* Calcutta, 1923

KUMARASWAMIJI, SHREE, *The Vīraśaiva Philosophy and Mysticism.* V. R. Koppal, Dharwar, 1949

LEIDECKER, K. F., *Pratyabhijñāhṛdaya* (*The Secret of Recognition*). Translation with notes. The Adyar Library, Madras, 1938

MARSHALL, J., *Mohenjo-daro and the Indus Civilization.* Arthur Probsthain, London, 1931

NANDIMATH, S. C., *Handbook of Virashaivism.* Edited by Literary Committee. L. E. Association, Dharwar, 1942

PANDEY, KANTICHANDRA, *Abhinavagupta : An Historical and Philosophical Study.* Chowkhamba Sanskrit Series Office, Banaras, 1936

PAWATE, S. D., *Virashaiva Philosophy of the Shaivagamas.* W. B. Bile Angadi, Hubli, 1927

PILLAI, J. M. NALLASWAMI, *Śivajñāna-bodham.* Translated with notes and introduction. Dharmapuram Adhinam, 1945

———, *Śivajñāna-siddhiyār (Supakkam)* of Aruṇandi Śivam. Translated with notes. Dharmapuram Adhinam, 1948

———, *Studies in Śaiva Siddhānta.* Meykandan Press, Madras, 1911

PILLAI, TIRU G. S., *Introduction and History of Śaiva Siddhānta.* Annamalai University, 1948

SAKHARE, M. R., *History and Philosophy of Liṅgāyata Religion.* Belgaum, 1942

SASTRI, S. S. SURYANARAYANA, *Śivādvaitanirṇaya* of Appaya Dīkṣita. With introduction, translation, and notes. Madras

SIVAPADASUNDARAM, S., *The Śaiva School of Hinduism.* George Allen & Unwin, London, 1934

SUBRAMANIAN, K. R., *Origin of Śaivism and Its History in the Tamil Land.* Madras University, 1927

VENKATARAMANAYYA, N., *Rudra-Śiva.* Madras University, 1941

VAIṢṆAVISM

AIYANGAR, S. K., *Early History of Vaiṣṇavism in South India.* Oxford University Press, London, 1920

BARUA, K. L., *Early History of Kamarupa.* Shillong, 1933

CALAND, W., *Vaikhānasa Smārta-Sūtras.* Translation. Asiatic Society of Bengal, Calcutta, 1927

———, *Vaikhānasa Śrauta-Sūtras.* Translation. Asiatic Society of Bengal, Calcutta, 1929

COWELL, E. B., *Śāṇḍilya Sūtras.* With Svapneśvara's commentary. Text with translation of commentary in *Bibliotheca Indica.* Calcutta, 1878

DE, S. K., *Early History of the Vaiṣṇava Faith and Movement in Bengal from Sanskrit and Bengali Sources.* General Printers and Publishers, Calcutta, 1942

GOVINDACHARYA, ALKONDAVILLI, *The Divine Wisdom of the Drāviḍa Saints.* Madras, 1902

KENNEDY, M. T., *Chaitanya Movement : A Study of the Vaishnavism of Bengal.* Association Press, Calcutta, 1925

NATH, R. M., *The Background of Assamese Culture.* A. K. Nath, Shillong, 1948

RAJAGOPALACHARIAR, T., *The Vaishnavite Reformers of India.* G. A. Natesan & Co., Madras, 1909

RAO, T. A. GOPINATH, *History of Śrī Vaiṣṇavas.* Madras University, 1923

RAU, S. SUBBA, *Śrīmad Bhāgavata Purāṇam.* Translation. Tirupati, 1928

RAYCHAUDHURI, H. C., *Materials for the Study of the Early History of the Vaiṣṇava Sect.* Calcutta University, 1936

SANYAL, J. M., *Śrīmad Bhāgavatam* (5 vols.). Translation. Oriental Publishing Co., Calcutta

SARKAR, JADUNATH, *Chaitanya's Life and Teachings.* Translation of Kṛṣṇadāsa Kavirāja's *Caitanya Bhāgavata.* M. C. Sarkar & Sons, Calcutta, 1932

SCHRADER, F. O., *Introduction to the Pāñcarātra and the Ahirbudhnya Saṁhitā*. The Adyar Library, Madras, 1916

SEN, D. C., *Chaitanya and His Age*. Calcutta University, 1922

———, *The Vaiṣṇava Literature of Mediaeval Bengal*. Calcutta University, 1917

TIRTHA, BHAKTI PRADIP, *Chaitanya Mahaprabhu*. Gaudiya Mission, Calcutta, 1947

TYAGISANANDA, SWAMI, *Nārada Bhakti-Sūtras*. Text and translation with notes. Sri Ramakrishna Math, Madras, 1952

VASU, NAGENDRA NATH, *The Social History of Kāmarūpa*. Calcutta, 1926

WILSON, H. H., *The Viṣṇu Purāṇa*. Translation. Edited by F. Hall. Trubner & Co., London, 1864-77

ŚĀKTISM, TĀNTRICISM, YOGIC SCHOOLS, AND OTHER MINOR CULTS

AUROBINDO, SRI, *Bases of Yoga*. Arya Publishing House, Calcutta, 1949

———, *Lights on Yoga*. Arya Publishing House, Calcutta, 1948

———, *Synthesis of Yoga*. The Sri Aurobindo Library, New York, 1950

AVALON, ARTHUR (SIR JOHN WOODROFFE), *Kāmakalāvilāsa*. Translation. Ganesh & Co. Ltd., Madras, 1953

———, *Principles of Tantra*. Ganesh & Co. Ltd., Madras, 1952

———, *Shakti and Shakta*. Ganesh & Co. Ltd., Madras, 1951

———, *The Great Liberation (Mahānirvāṇa Tantra)*. Text and translation. Ganesh & Co., Ltd., Madras, 1953

———, *The Serpent Power (Ṣaṭcakra-nirūpaṇa and Pādukāpañcaka)*. Ganesh & Co. Ltd., Madras, 1953

BAGCHI, P. C., *Studies in the Tantras*. Calcutta University, 1939

BASU, MANINDRAMOHAN, *Post-Caitanya Sahajiyā Cult of Bengal*. Calcutta University, 1930

BHATTACHARYYA, BENOYTOSH, *Buddhist Esoterism*. Oxford University Press, London, 1932

BRIGGS, G. W., *Gorakhnāth and the Kānphaṭa Yogīs*. Oxford University Press, London, 1938

CHAKRAVARTI, P. C., *Doctrine of Śakti in Indian Literature*. General Printers and Publishers, Calcutta, 1940

CHAPMAN, J. A., *Religious Lyrics of Bengal*. Calcutta, 1926

DAS, SUDHENDUKUMAR, *Śakti or Divine Power*. Calcutta University, 1934

DAS GUPTA, S. B., *An Introduction to Tāntric Buddhism*. Calcutta University, 1950

———, *Obscure Religious Cults*. Calcutta University, 1946

DASGUPTA, SURENDRANATH, *Yoga as Philosophy and Religion*. Kegan Paul, London, 1924

———, *Yoga Philosophy in Relation to Other Systems of Indian Thought*. Calcutta University, 1930

DIKSITAR, RAMACHANDRA, *Lalitā-Cult*. Madras University, 1942

GHOSH, ATAL BEHARI, *Śiva and Śakti*. Rajshahi, 1935
JHAVERY, M. B., *Comparative and Critical Study of Mantraśāstra*. Sarabhai Manilal Nawal, Ahmedabad
NATH, RADHA GOVINDA, *The Yogis of Bengal*. Mani Bhusan Nath, Calcutta, 1909
PAL, D. N., *Śiva and Śakti : An Elaborate Discourse on Hindu Religion and Mythology* (2 vols.). Calcutta, 1910
SASTRI, R. ANANTAKRISHNA, *Lalitā Sahasranāma Stotra*. Translation. The Adyar Library, Madras, 1925
———, *Śakti-Sūtra*. With notes. The Adyar Library, Madras, 1896
SINGH, MOHAN, *Gorakhnāth and Mediaeval Hindu Mysticism*. Lahore, 1937
THOMPSON, E. J., AND SPENCER, A. M., *Bengali Religious Lyrics : Śākta*. Association Press, Calcutta, 1923
WADDELL, L. A., *The Buddhism of Tibet or Lamaism*. W. H. Allen & Co., London, 1895
VASU, SRISCHANDRA, *Haṭhayoga-pradīpikā*. Text and translation. Panini Office, Allahabad

SIKHISM

BANERJEE, I. B., *Evolution of the Khalsa*. Calcutta University, 1936
CUNNINGHAM, J. D., *History of the Sikhs*. John Murray, London, 1849
GREENLEES, DUNCAN, *The Gospel of the Guru-Granth Sahib*. The Theosophical Publishing House, Madras, 1952
MACAULIFFE, M. A., *The Sikh Religion : Its Gurus, Sacred Writings, and Their Authors*. Clarendon Press, Oxford, 1909
SINGH, BAWA CHHAJJU, *The Gurus and Their Teachings*. Lahore, 1903
SINGH, KARTAR, *Life of Guru Nanak Dev*. Amritsar, 1937
———, *Life of Guru Gobind Singh*. Lahore Book Shop, Ludhiana, 1951
SINGH, PURAN, *The Book of the Ten Masters*. Sikh University Press, Lahore, 1920
SINGH, TEJA, *Essays in Sikhism*. Sikh University Press, Lahore, 1944
———, *Sikhism : Its Ideals and Institutions*. Lahore Book Shop, Lahore, 1938
TRUMPP, EARNEST, *The Ādigranth or the Holy Scripture of the Sikhs*. Translation. W. H. Allen & Co., London, 1877

SAINTS OF INDIA

BAHIRAT, B. P., *The Philosophy of Jnanadeva*. Pandharpur Research Society
BARTHWAL, P. D., *The Nirguṇa School of Hindi Poetry*. Indian Book Shop, Banaras, 1936
BENGERI, H. G., *Main Outlines of Haridāsa Kūṭa*. Kollegal, 1931
DEMING, W. S., *Rāmdās and the Rāmdāsīs*. Calcutta, 1928
FRASER, J. N., AND EDWARDS, J. F., *Life and Teaching of Tukārām*. Madras
GRIERSON, G. A., 'Notes on Tulasī Dāsa'. Published in *Indian Antiquary*, 1893
HILL, W. D. P., *The Holy Lake of the Acts of Rāma*. An English translation of Tulasīdās's *Rāmacaritamānasa*. Oxford University Press, London, 1952
HOOPER, J. S. M., *Hymns of the Āḷvārs*. Association Press, Calcutta, 1929

KARMARKAR, A. P., AND KALAMDANI, N. B., *Mystic Teachings of the Haridāsas of Karṇāṭaka.* Karnataka Vidyavardhaka Sangha, Dharwar, 1939

KEAY, F. E., *Kabīr and His Followers.* Association Press, Calcutta, 1931

KINGSBURY, F., AND PHILLIPS, G. E., *Hymns of the Tamil Śaivite Saints.* Association Press, Calcutta, 1921

MACNICOL, N., *Psalms of Marāṭhā Saints.* Association Press, Calcutta, 1919

OMAN, J. C., *Mystics, Ascetics, and Saints of India.* London, 1903

RANADE, R. D., *Mysticism in Maharashtra.* Poona

SEN, KSHITIMOHAN, *Mediaeval Mysticism of India.* Translated by Manomohan Ghosh. Luzac & Co., London, 1929

SINGH, MOHAN, *Kabīr and Bhagti Movement.* Atma Ram & Sons, Lahore, 1934

SINGH, PRITAM, *Saints and Sages of India.* Oriental Publishing Co., Calcutta

TAGORE, RABINDRANATH, *One Hundred Poems of Kabir.* Macmillan & Co., Calcutta, 1943

WESTCOTT, G. H., *Kabīr and the Kabīr Panth.* Susil Gupta (India) Ltd., Calcutta, 1953

RELIGION IN PRACTICE

AIYAR, G. V. JAGADISHA, *South Indian Festivities.* Higginbothams Ltd., London, 1921

AVALON, ARTHUR, AND AVALON, ELLEN, *Hymns to the Goddess.* Translation. Ganesh & Co. Ltd., Madras, 1952

AVALON, ARTHUR, AND SAUBHAGYAVARDHANI, *Ānandalaharī or Wave of Bliss.* Translation. Ganesh & Co. Ltd., Madras, 1953

BUCK, C. H., *Faiths, Fairs, and Festivals of India.* Thacker Spink & Co., Calcutta, 1917

CROOKE, W., *Religion and Folk-lore of Northern India* (2 vols.). Oxford University Press, London, 1926

CULSHAW, W. J., *Tribal Heritage.* Lutterworth Press, London, 1949

DUBOIS, J. A., *Hindu Manners, Customs, and Ceremonies.* Clarendon Press, Oxford, 1906

GUPTE, B. A., *Hindu Holidays and Ceremonials.* Thacker Spink & Co., Calcutta, 1919

HUTTON, J. H., *Caste in India.* Cambridge University Press, 1952

——— (Ed.), *Census Report of India for 1931.* Government of India

LABY, R. L., *Holy Land of the Hindus.* Robert Scott, London, 1913

MACDONELL, A. A., *Hymns from the Rigveda.* Association Press, Calcutta, 1923

MAX MÜLLER, F., *Vedic Hymns.* Sacred Books of the East, XXXII. Clarendon Press, Oxford, 1891

MUKERJI, ABHAY CHARAN, *Hindu Fasts and Feasts.* The Indian Press, Allahabad, 1918

OMAN, J. C., *Indian Life : Religious and Social.* Fisher Unwin, London, 1879

RAYCHAUDHURI, G. K., *Hindu Customs and Manners.* M. M. Mazumdar, Calcutta, 1888

SARKAR, B. K., *Positive Background of Hindu Sociology.* Panini Office, Allahabad, 1937

SARKAR, B. K., AND RAKSHIT, H. K., *The Folk Elements in Hindu Culture.* Longmans, Green & Co., London, 1917

SASTRI, NATESA, *Hindu Feasts, Fasts, and Ceremonies.* Madras, 1903

UNDERHILL, M. M., *The Hindu Religious Year.* Association Press, Calcutta, 1921

YATISWARANANDA, SWAMI, *The Divine Life.* Sri Ramakrishna Math, Madras, 1951

———, *Universal Prayers.* Sri Ramakrishna Math, Madras, 1954

ZOROASTRIANISM, CHRISTIANITY, AND ISLAM

AKHILANANDA, SWAMI, *Hindu View of Christ.* Philosophical Library, New York, 1949

ANDREWS, C. F., *Renaissance in India : Its Missionary Aspect.* United Council for Missionary Education, London, 1912

ARBERRY, ARTHUR JOHN, *An Introduction to the Study of Sufism.* London, 1942

CHAKRAVARTI, ATULANANDA, *Hindus and Musalmans of India.* Calcutta, 1940

CHAUDHURI, R., *Sufism and Vedānta* (2 parts). J. B. Chaudhuri, Calcutta, 1945-48

FERROLI, D., *The Jesuits in Malabar.* Basal Mission Press, Bangalore, 1939

GANDHI, M. K., *Christian Missions : Their Place in India.* Navajivan Publishing House, Ahmedabad, 1941

GORWALA, D. M., *The Light of Iran or the Coming of Zarathushtra.* Bombay, 1935

GREENLEES, DUNCAN, *The Gospel of Zarathushtra.* The Theosophical Publishing House, Madras

HOUGH, JAMES, *History of Christianity in India.* Seeley & Burnside, London, 1839

HUNTER, W. W., *The Indian Musalmans.* Comrade Publishers, Calcutta, 1945

IQBAL, SHAIKH MUHAMMAD, *The Reconstruction of Religious Thought in Islam.* Oxford University Press, London, 1934

JACKSON, A. V. W., *Zoroaster, the Prophet of Ancient Iran.* Macmillan, New York, 1879

JHABWALA, SAWAK H., *Zoroastrianism.* Bombay, 1934

KASHYAP, R. R., *The Vedic Origins of Zoroastrianism.* Dayananda Anglo-Vedic College, Lahore, 1940

KHUDABUKHSH, S., *Essays : Indian and Islamic.* Kegan Paul, London, 1927

LATOURETTE, K. S., *A History of the Expansion of Christianity.* London, 1940

LOBLEY, J. A., *Church and the Churches in Southern India.* Beighton, Cambridge, 1870

NICHOLSON, R. A., *Studies in Islamic Mysticism.* Cambridge University Press, 1921

OTTO, R., *India's Religion of Grace and Christianity Compared and Contrasted.* Translated by F. H. Foster. Student Christian Movement, London, 1930

SHERRING, M. A., *History of Protestant Missions in India.* Trubner & Co., London, 1875

SHURREEF, JAFFUR, *Qanoon-e-Islam or the Customs of the Mussulmans of India.* Translated by G. A. Herklots. Madras, 1863

SMITH, W. C., *Modern Islam in India.* Lahore, 1943

SORLEY, H. T., *Shah Abdul Latif of Bhit (Sind).* Oxford University Press, London

TARACHAND, *Influence of Islam on Indian Culture.* The Indian Press, Allahabad, 1936

TARAPOREWALA, I. J. S., *Religion of Zarathushtra.* Theosophical Publishing House, Madras, 1926

———, *The Divine Songs of Zarathushtra.* Bombay, 1951

TREVOR, GEORGE, *India : Its Natives and Missions.* Religious Tract Society, London, 1799

BRĀHMO SAMĀJ, ĀRYA SAMĀJ, AND THEOSOPHICAL MOVEMENT

AUROBINDO, SRI, *Bankim-Tilak-Dayananda.* Arya Publishing House, Calcutta, 1947

BAL, UPENDRANATH, *Rammohun Roy.* U. Ray & Sons, Calcutta, 1935

BESANT, ANNIE, *Popular Lectures on Theosophy.* Theosophical Publishing Society, Banaras

———, *Theosophy and the New Psychology.* Theosophical Publishing Society, London, 1904

BLAVATSKY, H. P., *Key to Theosophy.* Theosophical Publishing Society, London, 1893

CHAKRAVARTI, SATISHCHANDRA (Ed.), *Rammohun Roy : The Father of Modern India.* Rammohun Roy Centenary Committee, Calcutta, 1935

DAYANANDA SARASWATI, SWAMI, *Light of Truth (Satyārtha Prakāśa).* Translated by G. P. Upadhyaya. Kal Press, Allahabad, 1947

FARQUHAR, J. N., *Modern Religious Movements in India.* New York, 1915

JINARAJADASA, C., *Theosophy and Modern Thought.* Theosophical Publishing House, Madras, 1915

LEADBEATER, C. W., *Outline of Theosophy.* Theosophical Publishing Society, London

———, *Spiritualism and Theosophy.* Theosophical Publishing House, Madras, 1928

LEONARD, G. S., *A History of the Brahma Samaj from Its Rise to 1878.* Calcutta, 1936

LILLINGSTON, F., *The Brahmo Samaj and Arya Samaj in Their Bearing upon Christianity.* London, 1901

MAJUMDAR, JATINDRAKUMAR, *Raja Rammohun Roy and Progressive Movements (1775-1845).* Calcutta, 1941

MAX MÜLLER, F., *Ram Mohan to Ramakrishna.* Susil Gupta (India) Ltd., Calcutta, 1952

MOZOOMDAR, P. C., *The Faith and Progress of the Brahmo Samaj.* Calcutta, 1934

———, *The Life and Teachings of Keshub Chunder Sen.* Nababidhan Trust, Calcutta, 1931

RAI, LAJPAT, *Arya Samaj.* Longmans, London, 1932

RANADE, M. G., *Religious and Social Reform.* Gopal Narayan & Co., Bombay, 1902

ROY, RAJA RAMMOHUN, *The English Works of Raja Rammohun Roy (Social and Educational).* Sadharan Brahmo Samaj, Calcutta, 1934

SASTRI, SIVANATH, *The New Dispensation and the Sadharan Brahma Samaj.* Madras, 1881

———, *History of the Brahmo Samaj* (2 vols.). R. Chatterjee, Calcutta, 1911-12

SINGH, KHARAK, AND CLARK, H. MARTYN, *The Principles and Teaching of the Arya Samaj.* 1887

SARMA, D. S., *Studies in the Renaissance of Hinduism.* Banaras, 1944

SEN, P. K., *Keshub Chander Sen.* Calcutta, 1938

TAGORE, DEVENDRANATH, *The Autobiography of Maharshi Devendranath Tagore.* Translated by Satyendra Nath Tagore and Indira Tagore. Macmillan, London, 1944

RAMAKRISHNA-VIVEKANANDA

EASTERN AND WESTERN DISCIPLES (OF SWAMI VIVEKANANDA), *The Life of Swami Vivekananda.* Advaita Ashrama, Calcutta, 1955

GAMBHIRANANDA, SWAMI, *Holy Mother, Shri Sarada Devi.* Sri Ramakrishna Math, Madras, 1955

'M' (MAHENDRANATH GUPTA), *The Gospel of Sri Ramakrishna.* Translated by Swami Nikhilananda from original Bengali. Sri Ramakrishna Math, Madras, 1947

MAX MÜLLER, F., *Ramakrishna : His Life and Sayings.* Advaita Ashrama, Calcutta, 1951

NIKHILANANDA, SWAMI, *Vivekananda : The Yogas and Other Works.* Ramakrishna-Vivekananda Center, New York, 1953

NIVEDITA, SISTER, *The Master as I Saw Him.* Udbodhan Office, Calcutta, 1953

ROLLAND, ROMAIN, *The Life of Ramakrishna.* Advaita Ashrama, Calcutta, 1954

———, *The Life of Vivekananda and the Universal Gospel.* Advaita Ashrama, Calcutta, 1953

SARADANANDA, SWAMI, *Sri Ramakrishna, the Great Master.* Translated by Swami Jagadananda from original Bengali. Sri Ramakrishna Math, Madras, 1952

VIVEKANANDA, SWAMI, *The Complete Works of Swami Vivekananda* (8 vols.). Advaita Ashrama, Calcutta

Disciples of Sri Ramakrishna. Advaita Ashrama, Calcutta, 1955

Life of Sri Ramakrishna. Advaita Ashrama, Calcutta, 1955

INDEX

Inscription(s)—*Continued*
Chidambaram, 161; Chinna, 118, 141; Ci-arutön rock, 144; a Damodarpur, 136; Eran, 139; Gadhwa, of Kumāragupta I, 139; Gangdhar, 140; Ghosundi, 117, 120, 128; Harappā, 98; Huviṣka, 128; Jaunpur, of Maukharis, 139; of Java, 215; Junagadh, of Skandagupta, 138; Kadamba, 139, 141; Khoh copperplate, 140; Kollam, of Ali, 587; larger Śinnamanūr plates, 506n.; Māmallapuram, 133; of King Mānadeva, 139; Mandasor, 139; Mathurā, of Śaka Satrap Śoḍāsa, 116; Mathurā pillar, of Candragupta II, 70; Mohenjo-daro, 98; Mora, 115, 127; Nanaghat, 117, 128; Nasik, of Śaka Ṛṣabhadatta, 135; Neak Ta Dambang Dek, 144; Pabhosa, 123n.; Rājendra I, 72; Thap Musi, of Guṇavarman, 145; Tusām, 115; of Vijayagaṇḍa Gopāla, 508; of Yajña-Śātakarṇi, 118
Inter-caste marriages, 628, 630
Internal enemies, six, 26, 242, 243
Intuition, 594, 689, 702, 703
Involution, 18, 712
Iqbal, Sir Mohammed, his *Six Lectures,* 571n., 578
Iran, 24, 27; civilization of, 583
Īśāna, 63, 64, 82
Islam, 25, 388, 465, 539, 580, 586, 617, 630, 633, 634, 654, 672, 673, 683; advent of, in India, 582-84; civilization of, 571; compulsory ordinances of, 577-78; factors leading to spread of, 584-86; holds out a life of activity and remembrance of God, 574; impact of, 386; influence of, on different religious schools of Bengal, 388; its influence in shaping religious doctrines of North India, 61; insistence on equality of man by, 581; a levelling and leavening influence, 11; liberalism of, 580; love of knowledge in, 572; main contributions of, to mental make-up of Indian Muslims, 579; man's place in the universe and his duty according to, 574-75; man's progress according to, 572; militant democracy of, 579; modernization of, 570; power of the word in, 576; prophet of, 580; a proselytizing religion, 58; rationalism of, 580; three principles universally recognized in, 595; uncompromising monotheism of, 11
Islamic, culture, 571-78; mysticism (see Sufism); races, 6
Iṣṭadevatā (chosen deity), 247, 408, 456, 669; selection of, 457
Iṣṭaliṅga, 105; form of worship, 100; twofold, 106
Īśvara, 21, 71, 83, 106, 205, 217, 638, 641
Īśvara, -praṇidhāna, 26; *-tattva,* 90, 106, 255
Īśvara Purī, 186, 188
Itihāsas and Purāṇas, recitation and exposition of, 503-5

Jagaddhātrī worship, 485
Jagamohinī sect, 388
Jagannātha(dāsa), 351, 360; his *Harikathāmṛtasāra,* 354
Jahāngīr, Emperor, 314, 563
Jain(s), 6, 8, 618; Digambara, 492; religious observances and sacred days of, 491-93; Śvetāmbara, 492
Jaina, cave-temple, 509; Nirgrantha sect, 37, 116
Jainism, 10, 12, 20, 23, 25, 36, 37, 38, 39, 129, 377, 584, 613, 649; ascendency of, 98; believes in law of Karma, 16; cause of its remaining outside the pale of orthodoxy, 44; decline of, 48-49; its emphasis on self-reliance in spiritual life, 27; multitudes of heavens and hells admitted in, 17; patrons of, 8, 44, 47; permeated with influence of Hinduism, 129; position of Vāsudeva and Baladeva in, 129; powerful centres of, 44; tenets of, 39; two sects of, 44
Jālandhara (Jullundur), a *pīṭha* of Śakti-worship, 414
Jālandhari (see Hāḍi-pā)
Jāmbavatī, 115
James, William, 710
Janābāī, 361, 374; on difficulty of acquiring real devotion, 370
Janārdana Svāmin, Ekanātha's *guru,* 358, 361; conversion of, 369
Jaṅgama(s), 101, 102
Janmāṣṭamī, a red-letter day to Vaiṣṇavas, 484
Japa, 96, 406, 438, 450, 451, 460, 461
Jatadhari, 669-70
Jātaka tales, 16
Jaṭilaka sect, 116
Jayadeva, 59, 202; his *Aṣṭapadīs,* 513; his *Gīta-Govinda,* 53, 56, 135, 511, 524
Jayrambati, birth-place of Sarada Devi, 665
Jerusalem, 495
Jesuit(s), 562; mission to Mogul court, 562-63; Order, 562
Jesus (see Christ), 6, 534; Ascension of, 301
Jews, 10; of Cochin, 57; colony of, 6
Jīva(s), 16, 18, 127, 185, 189, 205, 228, 232, 234, 235, 237, 257, 258, 259, 399, 401, 424, 441, 641, 680, 681; -centre, 237; their illusory character denied by theistic commentators of *Brahma-Sūtra,* 21; -impulses of *bhoga,* 231; *-śakti,* 192, 193; and Śiva, identity of, 232, 703; two classes of, 193
Jīva Gosvāmin, 189, 473; his *Gopāla-campū,* 189; his *Ṣaṭ-sandarbha,* 189
Jīvanmukta(s), 102, 302, 644, 649, 650
Jīvanmukti, 94, 301-2
Jñāna, 24, 25, 35, 82, 125, 127, 238, 240, 243, 244, 246, 251, 339, 377, 378, 381, 395, 402, 672, 677, 691, 720; *-bhūmikās,* 244; -mārga, 25, 205; *-pañcamī,* 493; *-paṇḍita,* 311; *-śakti,* 106; *-tanu,* 302; -yoga, 709, 711, 714; *-yogin,* 668, 671, 674, 677
Jñānadeva (Jñāneśvara), 349, 356, 357, 358, 360, 364, 365, 372, 373, 374, 375, 478; his *Amṛtānubhava,* 357, 364; his *Cāṅgadeva-praśasti,* 357; describes God as the sun of reality, 364; describes intense love as the best road to unitive life, 369; his experience of oneness with his *guru,* 375; intellectualistic outlook of, 363; his *Jñāneśvarī,* 357, 358; reconciles world and Brahman in a higher synthesis, 363;

Mystic(s)—*Continued*
387; Bāwrī Sāheb, 389; Bhān Sāheb, 386; Bhāvānanda, 379; Bhikhā, 390; Biru Sāheb, 389; Bullā Saheb, 389, 392; Bulle Shāh, 392; Caitanya, Śrī (see Caitanya); Caraṇadāsa, 387; Chajjū Bhagat, 387; Dādū (see Dādū); Dārā Shukoh, 314, 387, 582, 596; Dariyā Sāheb, 390-91; Dariyā Sāheb of Marwar, 391; Dayābāī, 388; Dedhrāja, 393, 394; Dhannā, 379, 380; Dharaṇīdāsa, 386; Dharmadāsa, 383, 384; Garībdāsa, 384, 390, 391; Ghāsīdāsa, 390; Gobind Sāheb, 390, 393; Gulāl Sāheb, 389, 390; Jagjīvan, 389-90; Jīvanadāsa, 386; Kabīr (see Kabīr); Kamāl, son of Kabīr, 381; Kīlha, 383; Lālbeg or Lālgīr, 390; Lāldāsa, 390; Mahānanda, 379; Malūkdāsa, 60, 383, 384; Maskīndāsa, 384; Mātābāī, 385; Mīrābāī (see Mīrābāī); Mukundadeva, 388; Nābhā(dāsa), 383; Nāmadeva, of Punjab, 383; Nānak, Guru (see Nānak); Nānībāī, 385; Narasiṁha Mehtā, 393; Palṭū Sāheb, 390, 393; Paramānanda, 379; Pīpā, 379, 380-81; Prāṇanātha, 392; Priyādāsa, 383; Pūraṇ Bhagat, 387; Qutub, 389; Raidās (see Ravidāsa); Rajjab, 385, 386; Rāmānanda (see Rāmānanda); Ravi Sāheb, 386; Rohal, 389; Sadan or Sadnā, 382; Sahajānanda, 393; Sahajobāī 388; Śaṅkara Deva (see Śaṅkara Deva); Santarāma (Rāmacaraṇa), 392-93; Śarmād, 387; Senā, 379, 380; Shāh Ināyat, 389, 610; Shāh Karīm, 388-89; Śivanārāyaṇa, 391-92; Sukhānanda, 379, 381; Sundaradāsa, 385; Sūradāsa, 383, 478; Surāsurānanda, 379, 381; Surat Gopāla, 381; Tulasīdāsa (see Tulasīdāsa); Tulasī Sāheb, 393; Yārī Sāheb, 389, 392
Mysticism, 19, 694, 697; erotic, 21; presuppositions of, 361-63

Nābhā(dāsa), his *Bhaktamāla*, 383
Nācchiyār, Lord's consort, 161
Nācchiyār Tirumoḻi, 168
Nāda, 233, 236, 246
Nāḍi(s), 52, 224, 277
Nag, Durgacharan, 684
Nāgārjuna, 263, 271, 272; introduced alchemy in *sādhanā*, 279; Siddha, 225, 276
Naidu, Sarojini, 633
Naimiṣāraṇya, 160
Naivedya, 461, 462
Nakkīrar, Śaiva saint, 310, 339
Nakulīśa (see Lakulīśa)
Nālāyira Prabandham (see *Prabandham*), 144, 167
Nām, 324, 386
Nāma, 205, 207; Dharma (see Mahāpuruṣiā Dharma), 206; *-ghar(s)*, 203, 210; *-karaṇa*, 21; *-kīrtana*, 521; *-māhātmya*, 469; *-śaraṇa*, 203; *-siddhānta*, cult of, 512
Nāmadeva, Mahārāṣṭra saint, 60, 356, 357-58, 359, 360, 361, 373, 374, 383; his later spiritual life, 369; was democratic, 363
Namaskāra(s), 471; *-mudrā*, 334
Name, and form, 402; of God (see *nām*), 315-17
Nammāḻvār, 143, 166-67, 174; four poems of, 167; is called *kūṭastha*, 167, 169; his *Tiruvāimoḻi*, 144, 167
Nampiḷḷai, of Prabandhic school, 183
Nana, deity, on Huviṣka's coins, 334
Nānak, Guru, 314, 315, 355, 478, 489, 582, 590, 598, 606, 610, 613, 616; his *Āsā*, 315; his *Āsā-dī-Vār*, 320, 322; on custom, 328; founder of Sikhism, 386; on fundamentals of Sikh belief about God, 317; his *Japjī*, 315, 316, 318, 320, 321; his *Mārū*, 321; his *Mārū Sohle*, 316; preached the potency of *nām*, 386; his reliance on faith and grace, 61; sought to harmonize tenets of Hinduism and Islam, 386; his *Śrī Rāg*, 316, 319n., 322; two things in the works of, 325
Nanda, father of Kṛṣṇa, 190, 206
Nandanār, Śaiva saint, 345
Nandikeśvara, 508; his *Abhinaya-darpaṇa*, 515
Nandotsava, 485
Naṅgālī-bihu, 482
Nañjīyar, his *Nine Thousand*, 183
Nannaya Bhaṭṭa, 506
Nara, identified with Arjuna, 120n.; a sage, 119, 120
Nārada, 150, 371; his conception of devotion, 150; his definition of *bhakti*, 148; describes eleven forms of devotion, 154; on marks of devotion, 152; practices enjoined by, for attainment of devotion, 155; preaches universality of the cult of devotion, 159; his twofold division of devotion, 153
Nārada Pañcarātra, 148, 154, 155n.
Nārada-Sūtra, 146, 148n., 150n., 151n., 152n., 154n., 155n., 156n., 157n., 158n., 159n.; on the importance of action, 151
Naraharidāsa, a disciple of Rāmānanda, 395; Tulasī's benefactor and *guru*, 395
Narahari Tīrtha, Dāsa literature traced to, 351
Naranārāyaṇa, Koc king, 203, 204
Narasī Mehtā (see Narasiṁha Mehtā)
Narasiṁha, 56, 331; the man-lion incarnation of Viṣṇu, 330
Narasiṁha(dāsa) Mehtā, saint of Gujarat, 393, 478
Nārāyaṇa (see Viṣṇu),, 42, 114, 115, 117, 119, 120, 190, 193, 197, 199, 206, 385, 477; abode of, 190; Bhagavat, 120; called Hari, 119; his cosmic character, 120; cult of, 123; festival, 491; *Mahābhārata* describes him as an ancient *ṛṣi*, 119; sense of the word, 120; solar association of, 120; son of Dharma, 120; Vāsudeva, and Viṣṇu are same deities, 119; -vāṭaka (-vāṭikā), 117, 120; worship, its influence on Buddhism, 130
Nārāyaṇāśritas, 129
Naren(dra)(nath) (see Vivekananda), 657, 680, 681, 685, 687, 688, 691, 694
Nāro-pā, 276
Nāsika (Nasik), 6, 7, 488, 501
Naṭarāja, Śrī, 340, 346; god of dance, 517